Human Sexuality in a World of Diversity

Human Sexuality in a World of Diversity

SIXTH EDITION

Spencer A. Rathus
New York University

Jeffrey S. Nevid
St. John's University

Lois Fichner-Rathus
The College of New Jersey

Boston • New York • San Francisco
Mexico City • Montreal • Toronto • London • Madrid • Munich • Paris
Hong Kong • Singapore • Tokyo • Cape Town • Sydney

Series Editor: Kelly May
Editorial Assistant: Adam Whitehurst
Marketing Manager: Karen Natale
Production Editor: Michelle Limoges/Paula Carroll
Compositor: Publishers' Design and Production Services, Inc.
Composition and Prepress Buyer: Linda Cox
Manufacturing Buyer: Megan Cochran
Interior Design: Joyce Weston
Photo Research: June Whitworth
Art Design: Maria Sas, NuGraphic Design
Cover Design: Linda Knowles

For related titles and support materials, visit our online catalog at www.ablongman.com.

Between the time Web site information is gathered and then published, it is not unusual for some sites to have closed. Also, the transcription of URLs can result in unintended typographical errors. The publisher would appreciate notification where those errors occur so that they may be corrected in subsequent editions.

Library of Congress Cataloging-in-Publication Data

Rathus, Spencer A.
    Human sexuality in a world of diversity / Spencer A. Rathus, Jeffrey S. Nevid, Lois Fichner-Rathus.-6th ed.
        p.   cm.
    Includes bibliographical references and index.
    ISBN 0-205-40615-7 (casebound : alk. paper) -ISBN 0-205-43931-4 (paper : alk. paper)
    1. Sex.   I. Nevid, Jeffrey S.   II. Fichner-Rathus, Lois, 1953–   III. Title

HQ21.R23 2005
306.7–dc22

                                                                2004050545

Printed in the United States of America

10 9 8 7 6 5 4 3 2   VHP   08 07 06 05

(Photo credits continue on page SI-18 which constitutes a continuation of the copyright page)

*Dedicated with love
to our children
Taylor Lane Rathus
and Michael Zev Nevid,
who were born at the
time the first edition
of this book was written.*

Brief Contents

Contents

2 Research Methods in Human Sexuality 32

3 Female Sexual Anatomy and Physiology 60

4 Male Sexual Anatomy and Physiology 106

5 Sexual Arousal and Response 136

6 Gender Identity and Gender Roles 168

13 Sexuality in Childhood and Adolescence 424

14 Sexuality in Adulthood 456

15 Sexual Dysfunctions 490

16 Sexually Transmitted Infections 526

17 Atypical Sexual Variations 570

18 Sexual Coercion 602

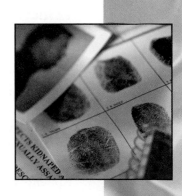

19 The World of Commercial Sex 638

Feature Boxes

A World of Diversity

A Closer Look

Human Sexuality in the New Millennium

Self-Assessment

Preface

There are more things in heaven and earth, Horatio,
Than are dreamt of in your philosophy.
                    Shakespeare, Hamlet

There are indeed more kinds of people in this world, and more ways in which people experience their sexuality, than most of us might imagine. Human sexuality may be intimately related to human biology, but it is embedded within the fabric of human cultures and societies. The approach that has separated *Human Sexuality in a World of Diversity* from other human sexuality textbooks is its full embrace of the richness of human diversity.

Let us first consider what has changed in the sixth edition, including the new pedagogical package that further enhances learning and retention. Then we will consider the themes of the text, which represent continuing concerns in the realm of human sexuality. We will also discuss the features that give the book its vitality and motivational force.

What's New in the Sixth Edition

Although previous editions of *Human Sexuality in a World of Diversity* have been well received, times change. We are also always aware of the instructor's perennial concern, which can be expressed as "What have you done for my students lately?" The answer is "Much." The sixth edition of *Human Sexuality in a World of Diversity* embodies many exciting changes—changes that reflect our entrance into the largely unknown universe of the new millennium. The key new elements in the sixth edition are outlined in the paragraphs that follow.

A General Updating

Because of the rapid developments in the behavioral and social sciences, and in biology and medicine, there are literally hundreds of new references throughout the text. No part of the text has been left untouched by change. Here are just a few examples of updating within chapters:

Chapter 1
Expanded coverage of values and sexual choices
Expanded coverage of critical thinking, as related, for instance, to self-help books about sex

Chapter 3
Complete update of research on breast cancer and cancer of the sex organs
Complete update of research on menstrual problems, particularly PMS and PMDD
New questionnaire on PMS

Chapter 4
Complete update of research on cancer of the reproductive organs
Expanded coverage of andropause

Chapter 5
New research on pheromones and the vomeronasal organ in humans
New research on drugs that may (and drugs that don't) act as aphrodisiacs
New coverage of the "date rape" drug

Chapter 6

Expanded coverage of conflicting theories of transsexualism, including the views of Ray Blanchard, J. Michael Bailey, and John Money

New coverage of evolutionary theory and the male's "roving eye"

Chapter 7

New coverage of attraction online

Chapter 8

New approaches to the coverage of jealousy, including the evolutionary and cognitive perspectives

New coverage of Gottman's research on satisfaction in relationships

New coverage of the active-listening controversy

Chapter 9

New coverage of beliefs about masturbation in Indian (Asian, that is) society and anxiety about masturbation among Indian men

Updated research on sex differences in beliefs about the acceptability of masturbation

New coverage of use of sexual fantasies as a measure of the strength of the sex drive

New information about fisting

Updated research on use of fantasy during sexual intercourse

Chapter 10

New coverage of sex differences in sexual orientation, including the relevancy of the two-dimensional model of sexual orientation for females and the one-dimensional model for males

Expanded coverage of history of cultural responses to sexual orientation, including homosexuality in fifteenth-century Florence

Expanded, updated coverage of biological/genetic contributions to sexual orientation

Expanded, updated coverage of civil unions and gay marriage

Chapter 11

New diversity feature on the use of sex selection methods to ensure having a male child in the country of India

New feature on preventing one's baby from being infected with HIV

Updated information on odor receptors in sperm cells

Updated information on the incidence of infertility and the incidence of birth defects with the method of intracytoplasmic sperm injection (ICSI)

Updated information on the use of episiotomy and cesarean section (C-section) during childbirth

Updated information on postpartum depression (PPD) and breast-feeding versus bottle-feeding

Chapter 12

New feature: "Where Is the Perfect Contraceptive? The Search Goes On"

New feature: "Abortion Views Contradictory"

Updated information on the effects of oral contraceptives

Updated information on the effects of vasectomy

Updated information on partial-birth abortion and related congressional action

Updated information on the effects of the "morning-after" pill

Chapter 13

New diversity feature: "U.S. Falls Behind in Sex Education"

New feature: "Keeping Teenagers in Line Online"

New information on the effects of bed-sharing with parents

New information on the (lack of) effects of parents' sexual orientation on children

Updated information on sex differences in masturbation among preadolescents and adolescents

Updated information about adolescents' sources of information about sexuality
Updated information about the effects of sex education
Updated information about ethnicity and age of menarche
Updated information on factors in premarital intercourse among adolescents
Updated information on the incidence of teenage pregnancy
Updated information on the effects of making condoms available to students

Chapter 14
New diversity feature: "Effects of Divorce on Chinese and African Children"
Updated information on the incidence of "singlehood," age of first marriage, and cohabitation
Updated information on ethnicity and marriage: intermarriage

Chapter 15
New feature: "Development of Biological Treatments of Sexual Dysfunction in Women"
New coverage of debate about when or whether lack of sexual desire in women is a sexual dysfunction
New research on the effects of cocaine on sexual performance
New discussion of the "medicalization" of sexual dysfunctions
Updated discussion of biological treatment of erectile disorder, including discussion of Levitra and Cialis

Chapter 16
New diversity feature on AIDS: "Killer of Dreams"
Updated figures on the incidence of STIs, including the resurgence of syphilis
New research on the effects of HAART on the resumption of "reckless" sexual activity in the United States
Updated research on current trends in the incidence of infection by HIV
Updated research on the effects of circumcision on transmission of HIV
Updated research on the treatment of HIV/AIDS, including the use of HAART and fusion inhibitors
Updated research on the effects of human papilloma virus (HPV)
Updated research on prevention; clarification of the distinction between exposure to HIV and infection by HIV

Chapter 17
New case study on topic of exhibitionism (Michael)
New coverage of autogynephilia as a motive in transvestism
Updated research on potential dangerousness of men with paraphilias
New research on biological factors in atypical sexual variations (research on level of sex drive, on evoked electrical potentials, and on connections between pain circuitry and reward circuitry in the brain)
New research on treatment of paraphilias, including outcomes of cognitive-behavioral therapy and the use of selective serotonin reuptake inhibitors (SSRIs)

Chapter 18
New Self-Assessment: "Cultural Myths That Create a Climate That Encourages Rape"
New feature: "The (Highly Controversial!) Evolutionary View of Rape"
New feature: "How Child Sexual Abuse May Set the Stage for Psychological Disorders in Adulthood"
New focus on contrasting views of the motivation of rapists—the view that rape (especially date rape) may be motivated by sexual desire versus the feminist view that rape involves desire to dominate women
Updated figures on the incidence of rape
New research (by Baumeister and colleagues) on how men and women may have different cognitive perspectives on sexual assault
New research on the effectiveness of rape prevention programs
Updated figures on the incidence of sexual abuse of children

Chapter 19

Updated research on the effects of poverty and child sexual abuse on women who become prostitutes

Reporting of parents in Thailand who sell their daughters into prostitution/slavery

Updated research on the sex differences that contribute to men's interest in prostitution and pornography

Updated research on sexual orientation and male prostitution

Expanded coverage of pornography on the Internet

Updated information on child pornography and the law

Updated research on how people use pornography

New coverage of evolutionary theory and the use of pornography

New research on the links between pornography and violence against women

Enhanced Emphasis on the Evolutionary Perspective

The behavioral and biological sciences today recognize the influence of evolution not only on physical traits but also on social behavior, including sexual behavior. The process of natural selection has led to some fascinating adaptations among species throughout the animal kingdom, including humans. As humans and their ancestors evolved over millions of years, their fitness for survival gained prominence in terms of physical and psychological traits that permitted them to reach sexual maturity and bear and rear children—not only their brawn, their sharpness of eye, and their fleetness of foot, but also their ability to acquire skills, their language ability, and their tendency to form bonds of attachment with their mates and their children.

The sixth edition of *Human Sexuality in a World of Diversity* demonstrates recognition of the importance of adaptation via natural selection in a section in Chapter 1 called "The Evolutionary Perspective." However, the interplay between evolution and sexuality is illustrated in nearly every chapter, as noted in the following examples:

Chapter 1: Discussion of evolution and "erotic plasticity" and of (the lack of) female monogamy throughout much of the animal kingdom

Chapter 4: Discussion of the evolution of the penis

Chapter 5: Discussion of the evolution of sexual attractants (for bees, if not for birds) in plants

Chapter 6: Discussion of (possible) evolutionary contributors to gender-typed behavior patterns

New coverage of evolutionary theory and the male's "roving eye"

Chapter 7: Discussion of (possible) evolutionary contributors to gender differences in preferences for mates

Chapter 8: Discussion of the evolution of, and (possible) gender differences in, jealousy

Chapter 10: Discussion of the possible evolution of differences in sexual orientation

Chapter 11: Discussion of the evolutionary advantages (we can't think of any others!) in "morning sickness"

Chapter 18: Discussion of the controversial issue of whether sexual aggression is "natural" in males (We show that even if it is, sexual aggression remains completely unacceptable.)

New feature: "The (Highly Controversial!) Evolutionary View of Rape"

Chapter 19: New coverage of evolutionary theory and the use of pornography

"Human Sexuality in the New Millennium"

A *new* boxed feature entitled "Human Sexuality in the New Millennium" highlights the ways in which human social and sexual experience is being transformed in response to scientific developments in biology, chemistry, and electronics. At times it seems that there are new discoveries about the causes and treatment of cancers of the reproductive organs every month or even every week. We now have an abundance of possible biological contributors to behavior patterns connected with gender-typing, sexual orientation, sexual dysfunctions, atypical patterns of sexual behavior, coercive sex, and even the consumption of pornography. We also find more chemical/medical treatments available not only for cancers of the reproductive organs and sexually transmitted infections, but also for sexual dysfunctions, atypical variations in sexual behavior, and sexual coercion.

We spend more and more time "cruising the information superhighway"—that is, going online. People today go online not only to plan travel to foreign countries but also to find mates and arrange for sexual liaisons around the world. People go online to obtain information not only about dieting and wills and pop stars but also about pregnancy, breast-feeding, and cancers of the sexual organs. People go online not only to view photos and films of Paris and Buenos Aires but also to interact with pornographic sites. A few years ago, American Express advertised its credit card with the slogan "Don't leave home without it." Today, many people in search of sexual experiences no longer leave home at all. Instead, they surf for sex on their computers. Yet the World Wide Web has done much more than bring titillation into the home; it has brought instant access to the great libraries and archives and research institutes of the world. And much of the information is free.

Sometimes the changes that are occurring are not social and cultural responses to developments in the hard sciences but, rather, changes in society and culture themselves. Witness, for example, the advent of civil unions and gay marriage and the appearance of reality TV shows such as *Queer Eye for the Straight Guy*.

Following are some examples of new "Human Sexuality in the New Millennium" features:

Chapter 2: "A Tale of Two Surveys"

Chapter 4: "Andropause and Chemistry: Must Testosterone Be Toxic?"

Chapter 5: "The Search for a 'Magic' Love Potion: On the Threshold?"
"The 'Date Rape' Drug: Decidedly *Not* an Aphrodisiac"

Chapter 7: "The (Electronic) Nearness of You?"

Chapter 10: "A First at *Bride's* Magazine: A Report on Same-Sex Unions"
"Queer Guy with a Slob's Eye"

Chapter 11: "Preventing Your Baby from Being Infected with HIV"

Chapter 12: "Where Is the Perfect Contraceptive? The Search Goes On"

Chapter 13: "Keeping Teenagers in Line Online"

Chapter 15: "Development of Biological Treatments of Sexual Dysfunction in Women"

PQ4R—An Enhanced Pedagogical Package

For the sixth edition, a new pedagogical package has been added. The PQ4R method stimulates students to engage the subject matter *actively*. Students are encouraged to become *proactive* rather than *reactive*.

PQ4R stands for Preview, Question, Read, Reflect, Review, and Recite—a method that is related to the work of educational psychologist Francis P. Robinson. PQ4R is more than the standard built-in study guide. It goes well beyond the isolated questions and exercises that are found in many textbooks. It is an integral part of every chapter. It flows throughout every chapter. It begins and ends every chapter, and it accompanies the student page by page.

Preview: Previewing the material helps shape students' expectations. It enables them to create mental templates or "advance organizers" into which they categorize the subject matter. Each chapter of the sixth edition of *Human Sexuality in a World of Diversity* previews the subject matter with a *Truth?Fiction?* section and a chapter *Preview*. The *Truth?Fiction?* items stimulate students to delve into the subject matter by challenging folklore and common sense (which is often common *non*sense). Then the *Preview* outlines the material in the chapter, creating mental categories that guide students' reading.

Chapter 7

Truth?Fiction?

T / F? Beauty is in the eye of the beholder.

T / F? College men would like women to be thinner than the women want to be.

T / F? People are regarded as more attractive when they are smiling.

T / F? Women who are randomly assigned names like Kathy and Jennifer are rated as more attractive than women assigned names like Harriet and Gertrude.

T / F? Physical appeal is the most important trait we seek in partners for long-term relationships.

T / F? "Opposites attract." We are more apt, that is, to be attracted to people who disagree with our views and tastes than to people who share them.

T / F? It is possible to be in love with someone who is not also a friend.

T / F? Committed couples can remain in love even after passion fades.

Question: Devising questions about the subject matter, before reading it in detail, is another feature of the PQ4R method. Writing questions gives students goals: They attend class or read the text *in order to answer the questions.* Questions are placed in all primary sections of the text to help students use the PQ4R method most effectively. They are printed in **bold italics.** When students see a question, they can read the following material in order to answer that question. If they wish, they can also write the questions and answers in their notebooks, as recommended by Robinson.

Read: The first R in the PQ4R method stands for "read." Although students will have to read for themselves, they are not alone. The text helps them by providing:

- **Truth?Fiction?** sections that stimulate students by challenging common knowledge and folklore.
- **Previews** that help them organize the material.
- Presentation of the subject matter in clear, stimulating prose.
- A **running glossary** that defines key terms in the margin of the text, near where the terms appear in the text.
- Development of **concepts** in an orderly fashion so that new concepts build on previously presented concepts.

Our writing style is "personal." It speaks directly to the student and employs humor and personal anecdotes designed to motivate and stimulate students. The style of *Human Sexuality in a World of Diversity* is as alive as the students it embraces, and it is intended to leave readers informed, interested, and refreshed.

Review: The second R in PQ4R stands for "review." Regular reviews of the subject matter help students learn. Therefore, Review opportunities follow all major sections in the text.

Reviews contain three types of items that foster active learning, retention, and critical thinking. The first of these, fill-in-the-blank items, ask students to *produce,* not simply *recognize,* the answer. For example, Review section on the external sex organs in the chapter entitled "Female Sexual Anatomy and Physiology" looks as shown at left.

Review sections also have *Reflect* items and questions for *Critical Thinking.*

Reflect: Students learn more effectively when they reflect (the third "R" in PQ4R stands for "reflect") on what they are learning. Psychologists who study learning and memory refer to reflection on subject matter as *elaborative rehearsal.* One way for students to reflect on a subject is to relate it to things they already know about, whether academic material or events in their own lives (Willoughby et al., 1994). Reflecting makes the material meaningful and easier to remember (Woloshyn et al., 1994). It also makes it more likely that students will be able to *apply* the information to their own lives (Kintsch, 1994). Through effective reflection, students can embed material firmly in their memory so that rote repetition is unnecessary.

Because reflecting on the material is intertwined with relating to it, the second kind of item in each Review section is termed *Reflect.*

Recite: The PQ4R method recommends that students regularly recite the answers to the questions aloud. (Hence the fourth R stands for "recite.") Reciting answers aloud helps students remem-

Review: External Sex Organs

Reflect

How do people from your own sociocultural background regard the external female sexual organs? Are they seen as something of beauty or something to keep hidden? Explain.

Critical Thinking

Do you believe that disapproval of female circumcision by Americans and other Westerners shows cultural condescension or cultural insensitivity? Why or why not?

1. The word _____, which refers to the external female genitals, derives from a Latin word meaning "something to be ashamed of."

2. At puberty the _____ becomes covered with pubic hair.

3. The labia _____ are large folds of skin that run downward from the mons along the sides of the vulva.

4. The _____ is the only sex organ whose only known function is the experiencing of pleasure.

5. The clitoral shaft contains spongy masses called corpora _____ that become engorged and erect in response to sexual stimulation.

6. The clitoris and penis develop from the same embryonic tissue, which makes them (*Homologous* or *Analogous?*).

7. Urine passes from the female's body through the _____ opening.

8. The _____ is a fold of tissue across the vaginal opening that may remain at least partly intact until a woman engages in coitus.

9. During sexual arousal the pressure from _____ forces out moisture from small blood vessels in the vaginal wall to create lubrication.

pressure from this engorgement causes moisture from the many small blood vessels that lie in the vaginal wall to be forced out and to pass through the vaginal lining, forming the basis of the lubrication. In less time than it takes to read this sentence (generally within 10 to 30 seconds), beads of vaginal lubrication or "sweat" appear along the inner lining of the vagina in response to sexual stimulation, in much the same way that rising temperatures cause water to pass through the skin as perspiration.

Pelvic floor muscles permit women to constrict the vaginal and anal openings. They contract automatically, or involuntarily, during orgasm, and their tone may contribute to coital sensations.

Question: Now that we have examined the external female sexual organs, what are the internal female sex organs?

Internal Sex Organs

The internal sex organs of the female include the innermost parts of the vagina, the cervix, the uterus, and two ovaries, each connected to the uterus by a fallopian tube (see Figures 3.3 and 3.6). These structures comprise the female reproductive system.

The Vagina

Vagina The tubular female sex organ that contains the penis during sexual intercourse and through which a baby is born. (Latin for "sheath.")

Question: What is the vagina? The **vagina** extends back and upward from the vaginal opening (see Figure 3.3). It is usually 3 to 5 inches long at rest. Menstrual flow and babies pass from the uterus to the outer world through the vagina. During coitus, the penis is contained within the vagina.

The vagina is commonly pictured as a canal or barrel; but, when at rest, it is like a collapsed muscular tube. Its walls touch like the fingers of an empty glove. The vagina expands in length and width during sexual arousal. The vagina can also

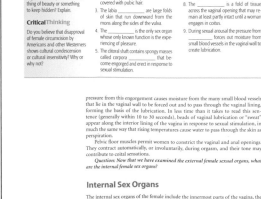

ber them by means of repetition, by stimulating students to produce concepts and ideas they have learned, and by associating them with spoken words and gestures (Dodson & Schacter, 2001).

Recite sections are found at the end of each chapter. They help students summarize the material, but these are active summaries. They are written in question-and-answer format. To provide a sense of closure, the summaries repeat the questions found within the chapters, and are again printed in **bold italics**. They include most of the key terms found in the text.

The Recite sections are designed in two columns so that students can cover the second column (the answers) as they read the questions. Students can recite the answers as they remember or reconstruct them and can then check what they have recited against the answers they had covered. Students are not necessarily incorrect just because their answers do not coincide exactly with the answer suggested in the second column. Their approach might be slightly different but even more inclusive. The answers provided in the second column are intended to guide students' learning. They are not carved in stone.

---

422   CONTRACEPTION AND ABORTION

will *not* say they are satisfied with their decision. Similarly, 310,000 women (31%) each year will *not* be able to say they would do it again, and 280,000 women each year will *not* be able to say that they found the effects of the abortion to be more beneficial than harmful.

Our conclusion is that both sides are correct. The great majority of women appear to be psychologically well adjusted a couple of years after having an abortion. It is also true that hundreds of thousand of women per year cannot say that they are satisfied with their decision to have an abortion. In other words, numbers alone do not tell the whole story. There is no simple answer to questions about the psychological effects of having an abortion.

What *is* clear is that neither side is entitled to make overgeneralized, extreme claims. Pro-choice advocates cannot claim that women who have abortions suffer no psychological ill effects. (Some women do.) Nor can pro-life advocates argue that having an abortion has devastating psychological effects on women. (Most women who have abortions are well adjusted.)

Recite

1. What is contraception?	Contraception is any technique that prevents a sperm cell and ovum from uniting.	
2. What happened during the legal battle over contraception in the United States?	In the United States, Anthony Comstock lobbied successfully for passage of a federal law in 1873 that prohibited the dissemination of birth-control information through the mail on the grounds that it was obscene and indecent. In 1918 the courts ruled that physicians must be allowed to disseminate information that might aid in the cure and prevention of diseases. Dismantling of the Comstock Law had begun.	
3. What is "the pill"?	Birth-control pills include combination pills and minipills. Combination pills contain estrogen and progestin and fool the brain into acting as though the woman is already pregnant, so that no additional ova mature or are released. Minipills contain progestin, thicken the cervical mucus to impede the passage of sperm through the cervix, and render the inner lining of the uterus less receptive to a fertilized egg. Oral contraception is nearly 100% effective. The main drawbacks are side effects and potential health risks. "Morning-after" pills prevent implantation of a fertilized ovum in the uterus.	
4. What is the morning-after pill?	This is a pill with high hormone content that prevents fertilization or implantation.	
5. What is Norplant?	Norplant consists of tubes containing progestin that are surgically embedded under the skin of the woman's upper arm. Norplant provides continuous contraceptive protection for as long as 5 years.	
6. What is the IUD?	The intrauterine device (IUD) apparently irritates the uterine lining, causing inflammation and the production of antibodies that may be toxic to sperm or fertilized ova and/or may prevent fertilized eggs from becoming implanted. The IUD is highly effective, but there are possible troublesome side effects and the potential for serious health complications.	
7. What is the diaphragm?	The diaphragm covers the cervix and should be used with a spermicidal cream or jelly. It must be fitted by a health professional.	
8. What are spermicides?	Spermicides block the passage of sperm and kill sperm. Their failure rate is high.	
9. What is the contraceptive sponge?	The contraceptive sponge absorbs sperm and also contains a spermicide.	
10. What is the cervical cap?	Like the diaphragm, the cap covers the cervix and is most effective when used with a spermicide.	

The Themes of *Human Sexuality in a World of Diversity*

The sixth edition of *Human Sexuality in a World of Diversity* builds upon the strong themes for which it has come to be known. Four themes are woven throughout the text:

- The rich diversity found in gender roles, sexual attitudes, and sexual behaviors and customs
- Critical thinking
- Making responsible sexual decisions
- Sexual health

Theme 1: Human Diversity

Colleges and universities are undertaking the mission of broadening students' perspectives so that they will appreciate and tolerate human diversity.

The United States is a nation of hundreds of different ethnic and religious groups, many of whom endorse culturally distinctive beliefs about appropriate gender roles for men and women and distinctive sexual practices and customs. Diversity is even greater within the global village of the world's nearly 200 nations and those nations' own subcultures. *Human Sexuality in a World of Diversity* incorporates a multicultural, multiethnic perspective that reflects the diversity of sexual experience in our society and around the world. Our book thereby broadens the student's understanding of the range of cultural differences in sexual attitudes and behavior around the world and within our own society. Discussion of diversity encourages respect for people who hold diverse beliefs and attitudes. We also encourage students to question what is appropriate for women and men in terms of social roles and sexual conduct in light of cultural traditions and standards.

Theme 2: Critical Thinking

Colleges and universities in the new millennium are also encouraging students to become critical thinkers. Today's students are so inundated with information about gender and sexuality that it can be difficult to sort out truth from fiction. Not only do politicians, theologians, and community leaders influence our gender- and sex-related attitudes and behaviors, but newspapers, TV programs, and other media also brim with features about gender roles and issues concerning human sexuality.

Critical thinking means being skeptical of information that is presented in print or uttered by authority figures or celebrities. Critical thinking requires thoughtful analysis and probing of the claims and arguments of others in light of evidence. Moreover, it requires a willingness to challenge conventional wisdom and common knowledge that many of us take for granted. It means scrutinizing definitions of terms, evaluating the premises or assumptions that underlie arguments, and examining the logic of arguments.

Throughout this book, we raise issues that demand critical thinking. These issues are intended to stimulate student interest in analyzing and evaluating their beliefs and attitudes toward gender roles and sexuality in light of the accumulated scientific evidence.

Moreover, the sixth edition fosters critical thinking through a section called "Thinking Critically about Human Sexuality," in Chapter 1, and by including questions for critical thinking in every Review section.

Theme 3: Responsible Sexual Decision Making

We also encourage students to make responsible sexual decisions. There are psychological and physical dangers in "going with the flow" or being passive about our sexuality. Of course, we do not encourage students to be sexually active (such a decision is personal). On the other hand, *we do encourage students to make their own sexual decisions actively, on the basis of accurate information.*

Decision making is deeply intertwined with our sexual experiences. For example, we need to decide

- Whom to date, and how and when to become sexually intimate
- Whether to practice contraception and which methods to use
- How we will protect ourselves against HIV/AIDS and other sexually transmitted infections (STIs)

Responsible sexual decision making is based not only on acquiring accurate information but also on carefully evaluating this information in the light of one's own moral values. We encourage students always to consider their own values, needs, and interests, rather than going along with the crowd or merely acceding to the wishes or demands of their partners.

Throughout the text we provide students with the information they need to make responsible decisions about their physical health, the gender roles they will enact, sexual practices, birth control, and prevention of sexually transmitted infections.

Theme 4: Sexual Health

Human Sexuality in a World of Diversity places a strong emphasis on issues relating to sexual health, including extensive coverage of such topics as HIV/AIDS and other STIs, innovations in contraception and reproductive technologies, breast cancer, menstrual distress, sex and disabilities, and diseases that affect the reproductive tract. The text encourages students to take an active—in fact, a *pro*active—role in health promotion. For example, it includes exercises and features that will help students examine their bodies for abnormalities, reduce the risk of HIV infection, and cope with menstrual discomfort.

Features

Like earlier editions, the sixth edition of *Human Sexuality in a World of Diversity* contains various features that stimulate student interest and enhance understanding.

"Human Sexuality in the New Millennium" Features

The Human Sexuality in the New Millennium features highlight the relationships between human sexuality and the technological and societal transformations that people are experiencing as they enter the new millennium. For example, developments in electronics not only gave birth to the "information superhighway," they also made surfing the Internet a way of finding dates, seeking sexual stimulation and gratification, and learning about biomedical developments, such as innovations that aid in the detection and treatment of diseases of the sex organs and STIs. Also, social changes have given birth to media offerings such as the television show *Queer Eye for the Straight Guy,* which is discussed in one New Millennium feature.

"A World of Diversity" Features

The World of Diversity features highlight the rich variety of human sexual customs and practices in our own society and around the world. Viewing human sexuality in a multicultural context helps students better understand how cultural beliefs, values, and attitudes can influence the expression of sexuality. Students may come to understand that their partners, who may not share the same ethnic or religious heritage as themselves, may feel differently than they do about sexual intimacy. Students will learn about cultural differences related to gender roles, sexual orientation, sexual jealousy, and premarital and extramarital sexual patterns.

"A Closer Look" Features

The Closer Look features provide in-depth discussions of scientific techniques (for example, "Physiological Measures of Sexual Arousal"), skill-building exercises ("Breast Self-Examination," "Self-Examination of the Testes," "What to Do If You Suspect You Have Contracted an STD," "How to Respond to an Exhibitionist"), and even humor ("Big" and "Sex and the Single Lizard").

Self-Assessments

Self-scoring questionnaires stimulate students' interest and provide self-insight by helping them satisfy their curiosity about themselves. These questionnaires also enhance the relevance of the text to students' lives. Examples include "Are You a Romantic or a Realist? The Love Attitudes Scale" and Sternberg's "Triangular Love Scale" (which may help you decide whether you are "in love" and, if so, just what *type* of love you are in).

Learning Aids

A textbook is more than a "good read." It is also a teaching tool—a device for presenting material in a way that stimulates learning and critical thinking. *Human Sexuality in a World of Diversity* was designed to maximize this goal by means of several pedagogical aids.

Use of the PQ4R Method The PQ4R method, described above, integrates a proven pedagogical package throughout the textbook.

"Truth?Fiction?" and "Truth?Fiction? Revisited" Sections Many students assume that they are experts on sexual matters. After all, they have seen the soap operas and the TV talk shows and have "been around" for a while.

Are they experts? "Truth?Fiction?" sections allow students to find out just how expert they are. These unique chapter-opening devices motivate students by challenging common sense (which is just as often common *non*sense), stereotypes, and folklore.

"Truth?Fiction? Revisited" sections are interspersed throughout each chapter and provide feedback to students regarding the accuracy of their assumptions in light of the evidence presented in the chapter.

Running Glossary   Research shows that most students do not make use of glossaries at the end of books. Searching for the meanings of terms is a difficult task and distracts them from the subject matter. *Human Sexuality in a World of Diversity* therefore has a running glossary. Key terms are **boldfaced** in the text and defined in the margins near where they appear. Students can readily find the meanings of key terms without breaking their concentration on the flow of the material.

The Package

Human Sexuality in a World of Diversity presents instructors with a wide range of ancillaries and teaching aids.

Instructor's Supplements

Instructor's Resource Manual
Martha Rosenthal—Florida Gulf Coast University

A wonderful tool for classroom preparation and management. Each chapter includes an At-A-Glance Grid, with detailed pedagogical information and links to other available supplements; a detailed chapter outline; teaching objectives covering major concepts within the chapter; a list of key terms; lecture material and student activities; a comprehensive list of videos; and an updated list of Web links. In addition, this manual includes a preface, a sample syllabus, and an appendix offering a comprehensive list of student handouts.

Test Bank
Kelly Wilson—Texas A&M University

This thoroughly revised and updated test bank helps students prepare for exams with challenging questions that target key concepts. Each chapter includes over 100 questions, including multiple-choice, true/false, short-answer, and essay questions, each with an answer, justification for the answer, page reference, difficulty rating, and type designation. In addition, the appendix includes a sample open-book quiz. This product is also available in a TestGen 5.0 computerized version, for ease in creating tests for the classroom.

PowerPoint® Presentation
Katherine Demitrakis—Albuquerque Technical-Vocational Institute

A completely revised, exciting interactive tool for use in the classroom. Each chapter includes key points covered in the textbook; images from the textbook, with demonstrations; and a link to the Companion Website for corresponding activities.

Transparencies for Human Sexuality

This fully revised set of 100 full-color acetates to enhance classroom lecture and discussion includes images from Allyn and Bacon's major human sexuality texts.

Human Sexuality Interviews Video; Interviews by Michael Bailey

A wonderful tool, with approximately 20 video clips covering the human sexuality syllabus. Clips include interviews with sex researcher Michael Bailey, an obstetrician, transsexuals, a sex therapist, an escort, and many others.

Human Sexuality VideoWorkshop, Instructor's Teaching Guide

A CD-ROM including 14 robust video modules, offering a multitude of ideas for integrating VideoWorkshop into your course. Includes correlation grids for individual human sexuality texts, summaries for each video clip, critical thinking questions, multiple-choice questions, Web links, and an answer key for the Student Learning Guide. For your review, the CD-ROM and Student Learning Guide are also included in the Teaching Guide, giving you the complete program in one easy reference!

CourseCompass

Powered by Blackboard, this course management system uses a powerful suite of tools with which instructors can create an online presence for any course.

Student Supplements

Companion Website
http://www.ablongman.com/rathus6e

A unique resource for connecting the textbook to the Internet. Each chapter includes learning objectives; chapter summaries; updated Web links for additional sources of information; flash card glossary terms; and online practice tests with multiple-choice, true/false, and essay questions. A great way for students to master the main concepts.

Grade Aid Workbook with Practice Tests
Tara Woolfolk—University of Delaware

A comprehensive and interactive study guide filled with in-depth activities. Each chapter includes "Before You Read," with a brief chapter summary and chapter learning objectives; "As You Read," a collection of demonstrations, activities, and exercises; "After You Read," containing three short practice quizzes and one comprehensive practice test; "When You Have Finished," with Web links for further information; and crossword puzzles using key terms from the text. An appendix includes answers to all practice tests and crossword puzzles.

Human Sexuality VideoWorkshop, Student Learning Guide

A CD-ROM including 14 robust video modules. Includes summaries for each video clip, critical thinking questions, multiple-choice questions, and Web links. A great way for students to learn human sexuality concepts through video!

Research Navigator Guide: Human Sexuality

Allyn and Bacon's new Research Navigator™ is the easiest way for students to start a research assignment or research paper. Complete with extensive help on the research process and three exclusive databases of credible and reliable source material (including EBSCO's ContentSelect Academic Journal Database, New York Times Search by Subject Archive, and "Best of the Web" Link Library), Research Navigator™ helps students quickly and efficiently make the most of their research time. The booklet contains a practical and to-the-point discussion of search engines; detailed information on evaluating online sources and citation guidelines for Web resources; Web activities for human sexuality; Web links for human sexuality; and a complete guide to Research Navigator.

Acknowledgments

The authors owe a great debt of gratitude to the many researchers and scholars whose contributions to the body of knowledge in the field of human sexuality is represented in these pages. Underscoring the interdisciplinary nature of the field, we have drawn on the work of scholars in such fields as psychology, sociology, medicine, anthropology, theology, and philosophy, to name a few. We are also indebted to the many researchers who have generously allowed us to quote from their work and reprint tabular material representing their findings. We also wish to thank our professional colleagues who reviewed this text at various stages in its development:

Michael Bailey, Northwestern University; Keith E. Davis, University of South Carolina; Randy D. Fisher, University of Central Florida; Kam Majer, Glendale Community College; Patricia A. Tackett, San Diego State University; Michael L. Vinson, College of Charleston; Mark A. Yarhouse, Regent University.

Spencer A. Rathus
New York University

Jeffrey S. Nevid
St. John's University

Lois Fichner-Rathus
The College of New Jersey

*Human Sexuality
in a World
of Diversity*

Chapter 1

Truth?Fiction?

T / F? Knowing enough about the biology of sex will enable you to make the right sexual decisions.

T / F? The books on sex that you find in bookstores are written by respected authorities.

T / F? In ancient Greece, a mature man would take a sexual interest in an adolescent boy, often with the blessing of the boy's parents.

T / F? Throughout most of human history, women were considered to be the property of their husbands.

T / F? The production of illustrated sex manuals originated in modern times.

T / F? The graham cracker came into being as a means for helping young men control their sexual appetites.

T / F? Female redback spiders eat their mates after they have been inseminated.

T / F? Trobrianders consider their children old enough to engage in sexual intercourse when they are . . . old enough.

T / F? In our dreams, airplanes, bullets, snakes, sticks, and similar objects symbolize the male genitals.

What Is Human Sexuality?

Preview

We are about to embark on the study of human sexuality. But why, you may wonder, do we need to *study* human sexuality? Isn't sex something to *do* rather than to *talk about*? Isn't sex a natural function? Don't we learn what we need to know from personal experience or from our parents or our friends?

Yes, we can learn how our bodies respond to sexual stimulation—what turns us on and what turns us off—through personal experience. But personal experience teaches us little about the biology of sexual response and orgasm. Nor does experience inform us about the variations in sexual behavior that exist around the world, or in the neighborhood. Experience does not prepare us to recognize the signs of sexually transmitted infections (STIs) or to evaluate the risks of pregnancy. What many of us learned about sex from our parents can probably be summarized in a single word: "Don't." The information we received from our friends was probably riddled with exaggeration and even lies. Many young people today do receive accurate information through sex education courses in the schools, but they are usually taught about STIs and contraception, not about sexual techniques.

You may know more about human sexuality than your parents or grandparents did at your age, or do today. But how much do you really know? What, for example, happens inside your body when you are sexually aroused? What causes erection or vaginal lubrication? Can people who are paralyzed from the neck down become erect or lubricated? What factors determine a person's sexual orientation? What are the causes of sexual dysfunctions? How do our sexual responsiveness and interests change as we age? Can you contract a sexually transmitted infection and not know that you have it until you wind up sterile? Can you infect others without having any symptoms yourself?

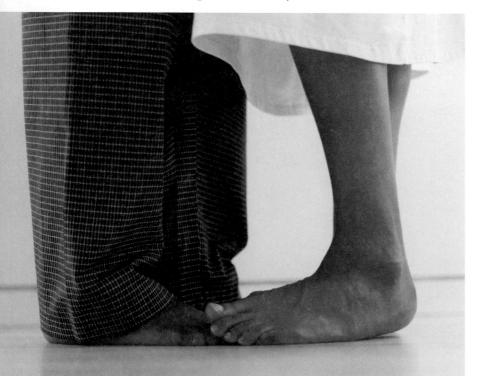

These are just a few of the issues we will explore in this book. Much of the information we present was discovered in recent years. It is almost as new to us as it may be to you. We also expect to debunk some common but erroneous ideas about sex that you may have picked up before you began this course. Before we proceed further, let us define our subject.

What Is Human Sexuality?

Question: What is human sexuality? This is not a trick question. Consider the meaning, or rather meanings, of the word *sex*. The word derives from Latin roots meaning "to cut or divide," signifying the division of organisms into male and female genders. One use of the term *sex*, then, refers to our **gender**, or state of being male or female. The word *sex* (or *sexual*) is also used to refer to anatomic structures, called sex (or sexual) organs, that play a role in reproduction or sexual pleasure. We may also speak of sex when referring to physical activities involving our sex organs for purposes of reproduction or pleasure: masturbation, hugging, kissing, sexual intercourse, and so on. Sex also relates to **erotic** feelings, experiences, or desires, such as sexual fantasies and thoughts, sexual urges, or feelings of sexual attraction to another person.

We usually make our usage of the term "sex" clear enough in our everyday speech. When we ask about the sex of a newborn, we are referring to anatomic sex. When we talk of "having sex" (a rather ugly phrase, because it implies that we engage in sexual activity as we "have" a ham sandwich), we generally mean the physical expression of erotic feelings. The term *gender* refers to the state of being male or female, as in **gender identity** and **gender roles**.

The term *sexual behavior* refers to physical activities that involve the body in the expression of erotic or affectionate feelings. Sexual behavior may or may not involve reproduction. *Masturbation,* for example, is sexual behavior that is performed for pleasure, not reproduction. Kissing, hugging, manual manipulation of the genitals, and oral–genital contact are all sexual behaviors that can provide sensual stimulation, even though they do not directly lead to reproduction. They may also be used as forms of **foreplay**, which leads to **coitus**, which can lead to reproduction.

We can now define **human sexuality** as the ways in which we experience and express ourselves as sexual beings. Our awareness of ourselves as females or males is part of our sexuality, as is the capacity we have for erotic experiences and responses. Our sexuality is an essential part of ourselves, whether or not we engage in sexual intercourse or sexual fantasy or even if we lose sensation in our genitals because of injury.

The Study of Human Sexuality

The study of human sexuality draws upon the scientific expertise of anthropologists, biologists, medical researchers, sociologists, and psychologists, to name but a few of the professional groups involved in the field. These disciplines all make contributions, because human sexuality reflects biological capabilities, psychological characteristics, and social and cultural influences. Biologists inform us about the physiological mechanisms of sexual arousal and response. Medical science teaches us about STIs and the biological bases of sexual dysfunctions. Psychologists examine how our sexual behavior and attitudes are shaped by perception, learning, thought, motivation and emotion, and personality. Sociocultural theorists examine relationships between sexual behavior and religion, race, and social class. Anthropologists focus on cross-cultural similarities and differences in sexual behavior. Scientists from many disciplines explore parallels between the sexual behavior of humans and other animals.

Science provides us with information, but it cannot make sexual decisions for us. In making sexual decisions, we also consider our **values**. *Question: How do our values come into play in determining our sexual choices and behavior?* The Declaration of Independence endorsed the fundamental values of "life, liberty, and the pursuit of happiness"—not a bad beginning. Our religious traditions also play a prominent role in shaping our values, as we see in the following section.

Gender The behavioral, cultural, or psychological traits typically associated with one sex.

Erotic Arousing sexual feelings or desires. (From the Greek word for love, *eros*.)

Gender identity One's personal experience of being male or female.

Gender roles Complex clusters of ways in which males and females are expected to behave within a given culture.

Foreplay Mutual sexual stimulation that precedes sexual intercourse.

Coitus (co-it-us or co-EET-us). Sexual intercourse.

Human sexuality The ways in which we experience and express ourselves as sexual beings.

Values The qualities in life that are deemed important or unimportant, right or wrong, desirable or undesirable.

Sexuality and Values

Our society is pluralistic. It embraces a wide range of sexual attitudes and values. Some readers may be liberal in their sexual views and behavior. Others may be conservative or traditional. Some will be staunchly pro-choice on abortion, others adamantly pro-life. Some will approve of premarital sex for couples who are dating casually. Others will hold the line at emotional commitment. Still others will believe that people should wait until marriage.

Because we encourage you through the course of this text to explore your own values about the issues we discuss, let us reveal two values that guided *our* writing:

1. *Sexual knowledge and critical thinking skills are of value because they allow us to make informed sexual decisions.* Your authors admit that they hold different values about a number of the issues we discuss. Therefore, we—your authors—do not try to persuade readers to adopt a particular stance concerning issues raised in the textbook. We present opposing points of view on controversial matters such as abortion and the distribution of condoms in schools. We hope that readers will critically consider their preconceptions and that the views they form will be their own.

2. *Students should take an active role in enhancing their health.* In this text we will urge you, for example, to examine your bodies for possible abnormalities, to see your physician when you have questions about painful menstruation or other physical complaints, to become sensitive to the signs of STIs, to get good prenatal care, and so forth.

People's sexual attitudes, experiences, and behaviors are shaped to a large extent by their cultural traditions and beliefs. Now let us consider the various value systems that people draw upon in making sexual decisions.

Value Systems for Making Responsible Sexual Decisions

Making choices is deeply intertwined with our sexual experience. Although sex is a natural function, the ways in which we express our sexuality are matters of personal choice. We choose how, where, and with whom to become sexually involved. We face a wide array of sexual decisions: Whom should I date? When should my partner and I become sexually intimate? Should I initiate sexual relations or wait for my partner to approach me? Should my partner and I practice contraception? If so, which method? Should I use a condom to protect against sexually transmitted infections (or insist that my partner does)? Should I be tested for HIV (the virus that causes AIDS)? Should I insist that my partner be tested for HIV before we engage in sexual relations?

Question: What kinds of value systems do people have? We all have unique sets of moral values—as Americans, as members of one of America's hundreds of subcultures, as individuals. No single value system defines us all. Indeed, the world of diversity in which we live is a mosaic of different moral codes and cultural traditions and beliefs.

Value systems provide a framework for judging the moral acceptability of sexual options. We often approach sexual decisions by determining whether the choices we face are compatible with our moral values. Our value systems—our sexual standards—have many sources: parents, peers, religious training, ethnic subcultures, the larger culture, and our appraisal of all these influences. Value systems that provide a guiding framework to determine the moral acceptability of sexual choices include legalism, situational ethics, hedonism, asceticism, utilitarianism, and rationalism.

Legalism The legalistic approach formulates ethical behavior on the basis of a code of moral laws derived from an external source, such as the creed of a religion. The Bible contains many examples of the moral code of the Jewish and Christian religions. In the Book of Leviticus (20:10–17) in the Hebrew Bible we find many of the prohibitions against adultery, incest, sexual activity with people of one's own gender, and bestiality:

> And the man that committeth adultery with another man's wife, even he that committeth adultery with his neighbor's wife, both the adulterer and the adulteress shall surely be put to death. . . . And if a man lie with mankind, as with womankind, both of them have committed abomination: they shall surely be put to death; . . . And if a man lie with a beast, he shall surely be put to death; and ye shall slay the beast. . . . And if a man shall take his sister, . . . and see her nakedness, and she sees his nakedness: it is a shameful thing; and they shall be cut off in the sight of the children of their people. . . .

Leviticus also proscribes intercourse during menstruation.

Many religious followers today accept the moral codes of their religions as a matter of faith and commitment, not necessarily because they can logically or rationally derive them from contemporary societal needs. Some people find it reassuring to be informed by religious authorities or scripture that a certain course of action is right or wrong. Others, however, take a more liberal view. They say that the Bible was inspired by God but that it was written or transcribed by fallible humans and is subject to various interpretations. They may also assert that the Bible reflects the social setting of the time in which it was written, not just divine inspiration. At a time of burgeoning population growth in many parts of the world, biblical injunctions to be fruitful and multiply may no longer be socially and environmentally sound. Prohibitions, such as that against coitus during menstruation, may have been based on prescientific perceptions of danger. Liberal people may thus view religious teachings as a general framework for decision making rather than as a set of absolute rules.

Situational Ethics Episcopal theologian Joseph Fletcher (1966, 1967) argued that ethical decision making should be guided by genuine love for others rather than by rigid moral rules. Fletcher advocated that sexual decision making should be based on the context of the particular situation that the person faces. For this reason, his view is termed *situational ethics.* According to Fletcher, a Roman Catholic woman will have been taught that abortion is the taking of a human life. Her situation, however—her love for her existing family and her recognition of her limited resources for providing for another child—might influence her to decide in favor of an abortion.

Fletcher argues that rules for conduct should be flexible guidelines. "The situationist is prepared in any concrete case to suspend, ignore, or violate any principle if by doing so he can effect more good than by following it" (1966, p. 34).

Ethical Relativism Ethical relativism assumes that diverse values are fundamental to human existence. Ethical relativists reject the idea that there is a single correct moral view. One person may believe that

What Role Is Played by Our Values in Making Responsible Sexual Decisions? *In making decisions about sexual behavior, people consider not only their knowledge of biology and sexuality but also their values. There are a variety of value systems, some of which are based on religion and some, like utilitarianism, which are not.*

premarital sex is unacceptable under any circumstances, whereas another may hold that "being in love" makes it acceptable. Still another person may believe that premarital sex is morally permissible without an emotional commitment between the partners. The ethical relativist believes that there is no objective way of justifying one set of moral values over another. In this view, the essence of human morality is to derive one's own principles and apply them according to one's own conscience. Opponents of ethical relativism argue that allowing people free rein to determine what is right or wrong may bring about social chaos and decay.

One form of ethical relativism is cultural relativism. From this perspective, what is right or wrong must be understood in terms of the cultural beliefs that affect sexual decision making. In some cultures, premarital sex is tolerated or even encouraged, whereas in others it is considered immoral. Cultural relativism, like ethical relativism, does not ascribe moral superiority to one cultural tradition over another.

Hedonism The hedonist is guided by the pursuit of pleasure, not by whether a particular behavior is morally or situationally justified. "If it feels good, do it" expresses the hedonistic ethic. The hedonist believes that sexual desires, like hunger or thirst, do not invoke moral considerations.

Asceticism Religious celibates, such as Roman Catholic priests and nuns, choose asceticism (self-denial of material and sexual desires) in order to devote themselves to spiritual pursuits. Many ascetics in Eastern and Western religions seek to transcend physical and worldly desires.

Utilitarianism Ethical guidelines can be based on principles other than religious ones. The English philosopher John Stuart Mill (1806–1873) proposed an ethical system based on utilitarianism—the view that moral conduct is based on that which will bring about "the greatest good for the greatest number" (Mill, 1863). The utilitarian characterizes behavior as ethical when it does the greatest good and causes the least harm. This is not license. Utilitarians may come down hard in opposition to premarital sex and bearing children out of wedlock, for example, if they believe that these behavior patterns jeopardize a nation's health and social fabric. Mill's ethics require that we treat one another justly and honestly, because it serves the greater good for people to be true to their word and just in their dealings with others.

Rationalism Rationalism is the use of reason to determine a course of action. The rationalist believes that decisions should be based on intellect and reasoning, rather than emotions or strict obedience to a particular faith. The rationalist assesses the facts in a sexual situation and then logically weighs the consequences of courses of action to make a decision. The rationalist shares with the utilitarian the belief that reasoning can lead to ethical behavior. The rationalist is not bound, however, to the utilitarian code that makes choices on the basis of the greatest good for the greatest number. The utilitarian may decide, for example, to prolong an unhappy marriage because of the belief that the greater good (of the family and the community) is better served by maintaining an unhappy marriage than by dissolving it. The rationalist might decide that the personal consequences of continuing an unhappy marriage outweigh the consequences to the family or the community at large.

These ethical systems represent general frameworks of moral reasoning or pathways for judging the moral acceptability of sexual and nonsexual behavior. Whereas some of us may adopt one or another of these systems in their purest forms, others adopt a system of moral reasoning that involves some combination or variation of these ethical systems. Some also shift from one ethical system to another from time to time, sometimes reasoning legalistically and sometimes adopting a more flexible situationist approach.

Review: What Is Human Sexuality?

Reflect

Which value system or systems guide your ethical decision making? Is it one of those discussed in the chapter, or is it another? How did you develop your system of values?

Critical Thinking

Is it possible to have a legalistic value system yet make decisions based on the situation?

1. We define human _____ as the ways in which we experience and express ourselves as sexual beings.

2. _____ inform us about the physiological mechanisms of sexual arousal and response.

3. _____ examine how our sexual behavior and attitudes are shaped by perception, learning, thought, motivation and emotion, and personality.

4. _____ theorists examine relationships between sexual behavior and religion, race, and social class.

5. _____ systems provide a framework for judging the moral acceptability of sexual options.

6. The _____ approach formulates ethical behavior on the basis of a code of moral laws derived from an ex-

ternal source, such as the creed of a religion.

7. Fletcher argued that sexual decision making should be based on the context of the _____ faced by the individual.

8. Ethical _____ reject the idea that there is a single correct moral view.

9. The _____ is guided by the pursuit of pleasure.

10. The self-denial of material and sexual desires is termed _____.

11. Mill's system is based on _____, or "the greatest good for the greatest number."

12. _____ teaches that sexual decisions should be based on intellect and reasoning, rather than emotions or religious obedience.

Many students will not only be making sexual decisions. They will also be deciding what kind of value system to use in making these decisions. One tool they can use in deciding is critical thinking. The following section describes what is meant by critical thinking and applies it to issues concerning human sexuality.

Thinking Critically about Human Sexuality

We are flooded with so much information about sex that it is difficult to separate truth from fiction. Newspapers, TV shows, and popular books and magazines contain one feature after another about sex. Many of them contradict one another, contain half-truths, or draw unsupported conclusions.

Most of us also tend to assume that authority figures like doctors and government officials provide us with factual information and are qualified to make decisions that affect our lives. But when two doctors disagree on the need for a hysterectomy, or two officials disagree as to whether condoms should be distributed in public schools, we wonder how both can be correct. Critical thinkers never say, "This is true because so-and-so says that it is true."

To help students evaluate claims, arguments, and widely held beliefs, most colleges encourage *critical thinking*. **Question: What is critical thinking?** The core of critical thinking is skepticism—not taking things for granted. Critical thinking means being skeptical of things that are presented in print, uttered by authority figures or celebrities, or passed along by friends. Another aspect of critical thinking is thoughtful analysis and probing of claims and arguments. Critical thinking requires willingness to challenge the conventional wisdom and common knowledge that many of us

Thinking Critically about Self-Help Books on Sex: Are There Any Quick Fixes?

Five Minutes to Orgasm Every Time You Make Love: Female Orgasm Made Simple; The New Sensual Massage: Learn to Give Pleasure with Your Hands; The New Joy of Sex; The Art of Seduction; Male Multiple Orgasm: Step by Step; The Complete Idiot's Guide to Amazing Sex; How to Have an Orgasm . . . As Often as You Want; The New Male Sexuality; The Art of Erotic Massage; How to Attract Anyone, Anytime, Anyplace: The Smart Guide to Flirting; Body Language Secrets: A Guide during Courtship & Dating; She's Gotta Have It: Euphoria, Sexuality, Orgasm; 302 Advanced Techniques for Driving a Man Wild in Bed . . .

These are just a few of books about sex that have flooded the marketplace in recent years. Every day, shy people, anxious people, confused people, and people with sexual problems scan bookstores and supermarket checkout racks in hope of finding the one book that will provide the answer. How can they evaluate the merits of these books? How can they separate the helpful wheat from the useless and sometimes harmful chaff?

Unfortunately, there are no easy answers. Many of us believe the things we see in print, and anecdotes about how Tyrone increased the size of his penis by 30% and how Maria learned to reach orgasm "every time" have a powerful allure, especially when we are needy.

Be on guard. A price we pay for freedom of speech is that nearly anything can wind up in print. Authors can make extravagant claims with little fear of punishment. They can lie about the effectiveness of a new sexual cure-all as easily as they can lie about sightings of the departed Elvis Presley or of UFOs.

How can you protect yourself? How could you know, for example, that *The New Male Sexuality* was authored by a respected psychologist? How could you know that ethical helping professionals would never promise that they could enable women to reach orgasm in five minutes, every time they make love?

Try some critical thinking:

1. **First, don't judge the book by its cover or its title.** Good books as well as bad books can have catchy titles

Are They Buying What Is Being Sold?
Critical thinkers carefully consider the premises of arguments, weigh all the evidence, and arrive at their own conclusions. Critical thinking is important in matters of human sexuality and is of value in all areas of life.

and interesting covers. Dozens, perhaps hundreds of books are competing for your attention. It is little wonder, then, that publishers try to do something sensational with the covers.

take for granted. It means scrutinizing definitions of terms and evaluating the premises of arguments and their logic. It also means finding *reasons* to support your beliefs, rather than relying on feelings. When people think critically, they maintain open minds. They suspend their beliefs until they have obtained and evaluated the evidence.

Principles of Critical Thinking

Critical thinkers maintain a healthy skepticism. They examine definitions of terms, weigh premises, consider evidence, and decide whether arguments are valid and logical. Here are some principles of critical thinking:

1. *Be skeptical.* Politicians, religious leaders, and other authority figures attempt to convince you of their points of view. Even researchers and authors may hold certain biases. Accept nothing as true until you have personally weighed the evidence.

2. *Examine definitions of terms.* Some statements are true when a term is defined in one way but not in another. Consider the maxim, "Love is blind." If love is

2. **Avoid books that make extravagant claims.** If it sounds too good to be true, it probably is. No method helps everyone who tries it. Very few methods work overnight. Yet people want the instant cure. The book that promises to enable you to reach orgasm in five minutes will probably outsell the book that says it can take up to half an hour or more and still remain within normal limits. The book that advertizes 302 sexual techniques may sound more useful than the book that advertizes 151 techniques. Responsible helping professionals do not make lavish claims.

3. **Check authors' educational credentials.** Be suspicious if the author's title is just "Dr." and is placed before the name. The degree could be a phony doctorate bought through the mail. It could be issued by a religious cult rather than a university or professional school. It is better if the "doctor" has an Ph.D., Psy.D., M.D., or Ed.D. after her or his name, rather than "Dr." in front of it.

4. **Check authors' affiliations.** There are no guarantees, but helping professionals who are affiliated with colleges, universities, clinics, and hospitals may have more to offer than those who are not. The Web site of the author of *The Complete Idiot's Guide to Amazing Sex* states that she holds a B.S. and an M.S. from Ivy League universities but says nothing about education and training in the area of human sexuality. (Having noted that, her book is not bad, but her "credentials" alone are irrelevant to expertise in human sexuality.)

5. **Consider authors' complaints about the conservatism of professional groups to be a warning.** Do the authors boast that they are ahead of their time? Do they berate professional organizations in the area of human sexuality as being pigheaded or narrow minded? If so, be suspicious. Most helping professionals and other scientists are open minded. They just ask to see evidence before they jump on the bandwagon. Enthusiasm is no substitute for research and evidence.

6. **Check the *evidence* reported in the book.** Bad books usually make extensive use of *anecdotes*. Anecdotes are unsupported stories or case studies about fantastic results with one or a few individuals. Responsible helping professionals check the effectiveness of techniques with large numbers of people. They carefully measure the outcomes. They use qualified language. For example, they say "It appears that . . ." or "It may be that . . ."

7. **Check the reference citations for the evidence.** Legitimate research is reported in the journals you will find in the reference section of this book. These journals mainly report research methods and outcomes that seem to be scientifically valid. If there are no reference citations in the book you are considering, or if the list of references seems suspicious, you should be suspicious, too.

8. **Ask your instructor for advice.** Ask for advice on what to do, whom to talk to, what to read.

9. **Read textbooks and professional books, like this book, rather than an off-the-shelf book.** Search the college bookstore for texts in fields that interest you.

10. **Stop by and chat with your professor.** Talk to someone in your college or university health center.

defined as head-over-heels infatuation, there may be substance to the statement. Infatuated people tend to idealize loved ones. But if love is defined as deep caring and commitment based on a more realistic (if still somewhat slanted) appraisal of the loved one, then love is not so much blind as a bit nearsighted.

3. *Examine the assumptions or premises of arguments.* Consider the statement, "Abortion is murder." *Webster's New World Dictionary* defines murder as "the unlawful and malicious or premeditated killing of one human being by another." The statement is true, according to this dictionary, only if the victim is a human being (and if the act is unlawful and malicious or premeditated). Most pro-life advocates argue that embryos and fetuses are human beings. Most pro-choice advocates claim that they are not. So the argument that abortion is murder rests in part on the premise that the embryo or fetus is a human being.

4. *Be cautious in drawing conclusions from evidence.* In Chapter 14 we shall discuss research findings that show that married people who cohabited before marriage are more likely to eventually get divorced than are those who didn't cohabit first. It may seem at first glance that cohabitation is a *cause* of divorce. However,

Truth?Fiction?
Revisited

You cannot trust everything that finds its way into print. It is true that some of the books you find in bookstores are written by respected authorities, but that "fact" does not make them accurate. You can only judge a book's accuracy by carefully weighing the evidence. In general, there are few if any quick fixes to problems concerning sex and relationships. Do your homework. Become a critical consumer of the books with the tantalizing covers and titles.

married couples who cohabit before marriage may differ from those who do not in ways other than choosing cohabitation—which brings us to our next suggestion for critical thinking.

5. *Consider alternative interpretations of research evidence.* For example, cohabitors who later get married may be more likely to eventually get divorced because they are more liberal and less traditional than married couples who did not cohabit before marriage. Eventual divorce would then be *connected* with cohabitation but would not be *caused* by cohabitation.

6. *Consider the kinds of evidence upon which conclusions are based.* Some conclusions, even seemingly "scientific" conclusions, are based on anecdotes and personal endorsements. They are not founded on sound research.

7. *Do not oversimplify.* Consider the statement, "Homosexuality is inborn." There is some evidence that sexual orientation may involve inborn predispositions, such as genetic influences. However, biology is not destiny in human sexuality. Gay male, lesbian, and heterosexual sexual orientations appear to develop as the result of a complex interaction of biological and environmental factors.

8. *Do not overgeneralize.* Consider the belief that gay males are effeminate and lesbians are masculine. Yes, some gay males and lesbians fit these stereotypes. However, many do not. Overgeneralizing makes us vulnerable to accepting stereotypes.

The nearby "Closer Look" applies critical thinking to the selection—and rejection!—of off-the-shelf books on human sexuality.

Review: Thinking Critically about Human Sexuality

Reflect

Who are the authority figures in your own life? Have others encouraged you to follow the demands of authority figures without examining them critically? How do you feel about this?

Critical Thinking

What kinds of intellectual and interpersonal conflicts are likely to be encountered by people who decide that they will become critical thinkers?

13. The core of critical thinking is _____; that is, not taking things for granted.
14. Critical thinkers do not accept arguments just because they are made by _____ figures.
15. Critical thinkers pay close attention to the definitions of _____ used in arguments.
16. Critical thinkers are cautious in drawing _____ from evidence.

Perspectives on Human Sexuality

Human sexuality is a complex topic. No single theory or perspective can capture all its nuances. In this book we explore human sexuality from many perspectives. In this section we introduce a number of them—historical, biological, evolutionary, cross-species, cross-cultural, psychological, and sociocultural. We draw on these perspectives in subsequent chapters.

The Historical Perspective

Question: What is the role of the historical perspective on human sexuality? History places sexual attitudes and behavior in context. It informs us as to whether sexual behavior reflects trends that have been with us through the millennia or the customs of a particular culture and era. History shows little evidence of universal sexual trends. Attitudes and behaviors vary extensively from one time and place to another. Contemporary American society may be permissive when compared to the Victorian and post–World War II eras. Yet it looks staid when compared to the sexual excesses of some ancient societies, most notably the ruling class of ancient Rome. History also shows how religion has been a major influence on sexual values and behavior. Let us trace some historical changes in attitudes toward sexuality. We begin by turning the clock back 20,000 or 30,000 years, to the days before written records were kept—that is, to *pre*history.

Prehistoric Sexuality: From Female Idols to Phallic Worship Information about life among our Stone Age ancestors is drawn largely from cave drawings, stone artifacts, and the customs of modern-day preliterate peoples whose existence changed little over the millennia. From such sources, historians and anthropologists infer a prehistoric division of labor. By and large, men hunted for game. Women tended to remain close to home. Women nurtured children and gathered edible plants and nuts, crabs and other marine life that wandered along the shore or swam in shallow waters.

Art produced in the Stone Age, some 20,000 years ago, suggests the worship of women's ability to bear children and perpetuate the species (Fichner-Rathus, 2004). Primitive statues and cave drawings portray women with large, pendulous breasts, rounded hips, and prominent sex organs. Most theorists regard the figurines as fertility symbols. Stone Age people may have been unaware of the male's contribution to reproduction.

As the ice sheets of the last Ice Age retreated (about 11,000 BCE) and the climate warmed, human societies turned agrarian. Hunters and gatherers became farmers and herders. Villages sprang up around fields. Men tended livestock. Women became farmers. As people grew aware of the male role in reproduction, **phallic worship** sprang into being. Knowledge of paternity is believed to have developed around 9000 BCE, as a side benefit of the herding of livestock. When people began to observe the same animals throughout the year, they also began to understand that a predictable period of time elapsed between copulation and the birth of new animals.

The penis became glorified in art as a plough, an ax, or a sword (Friedman, 2001). **Phallic symbols** played roles in religious ceremonies in ancient Egypt. The ancient Greeks sometimes rendered phalluses as rings and sometimes as necklaces. In ancient Rome, a large phallus was carried like a float in a parade honoring Venus, the goddess of love.

The **incest taboo** may have been the first human taboo. All human societies apparently have some form of incest taboo (Harris & Johnson, 2003; Whitten, 2001). Societies have varied in terms of its strictness, however. Brother–sister marriages

Phallic worship Worship of the penis as a symbol of generative power.

Phallic symbols Images of the penis.

Incest taboo The prohibition against intercourse and reproduction among close blood relatives.

were permitted among the presumably divine rulers of ancient Egypt and among the royal families of the Incas and of Hawaii, even though they were generally prohibited among commoners. Father–daughter marriages were also permitted among the aristocracy and royalty of ancient Egypt. Incestuous relationships in these royal blood lines may have kept wealth and power, as well as "divinity," in the family.

The Ancient Hebrews   The ancient Hebrews viewed sex, at least sex in marriage, as a fulfilling experience intended to fulfill the divine injunction to "be fruitful and multiply." The emphasis on the procreative function of sex led to some interesting social customs. For example, childlessness and the development of a repulsive abnormality, such as a boil, were grounds for divorce. Male–male and female–female sexual behavior were strongly condemned, as they threatened the perpetuation of the family. Adultery, too, was condemned—at least for a woman. Although the Hebrew Bible (called the Old Testament in the Christian faith) permitted **polygamy**, the vast majority of the Hebrews were **monogamous**.

The ancient Hebrews approved of sex within marriage not simply for procreation but also for mutual pleasure and fulfillment. They believed that sex helped strengthen marital bonds and solidify the family. Jewish law even legislated the minimum frequency of marital relations, which varied according to the man's profession and the amount of time he spent at home:

> Every day for those who have no occupation, twice a week for laborers, once a week for ass-drivers; once every thirty days for camel drivers; and once every six months for sailors. (Mishna Ketubot 5:6; Ketubot 62b–62b)

Among the ancient Hebrews, women were to be good wives and mothers. According to the Book of Proverbs, a good wife rises before dawn to tend to her family's needs, brings home food, instructs the servants, tends the vineyards, makes the clothes, keeps the ledger, helps the needy, and works well into the night. Despite all this, a wife was considered the property of her husband and could be divorced on whim. A wife could also be stoned to death for adultery, but she might have to share her husband with secondary wives and concubines. Men who consorted with the wives of other men were considered to have violated the property rights of those men and might have to pay for "damages."

In case the notion that a woman is a man's property sounds ancient to you, we must note that in many cultures it remains current enough. For example, in the year 2000, Zambian judge Alfred Shilibwa ordered a hotel employee, Obert Siyankalanga, to pay a woman's husband $300 in compensation after he slipped his hand into the woman's blouse and fondled her breasts ("Man pays victim's husband," 2000). The woman, a hotel employee named Bertha Kosamu, had been ironing at the time. She explained the scars on Obert's face and head: "I clobbered him on the head with the iron." There is one contemporary ring to the story: Because Obert was Bertha's supervisor, the judge also found him guilty of sexual harassment.

The Ancient Greeks   The classical or golden age of ancient Greece lasted about 200 years, from about 500 BCE to 300 BCE. Within this relatively short span lived the philosophers Socrates, Plato, and Aristotle; the playwrights Aristophanes, Aeschylus, and Sophocles; the natural scientist Archimedes; and the lawgiver Solon. Like the Hebrews, the Greeks valued family life. But Greek men also admired the well-developed male body and enjoyed nude wrestling in the arena. Erotic encounters and

Polygamy The practice of having two or more spouses at the same time. (From the Greek roots meaning "many" [*poly-*] and "marriage" [*gamos*].)

Monogamy The practice of having one spouse. (From the Greek *mono-,* meaning "single" or "alone.")

off-color jokes characterized the plays of Aristophanes and other playwrights. The Greeks held that the healthy mind must dwell in a healthy body. They cultivated muscle and movement along with mind.

The Greeks viewed their gods—Zeus, god of gods; Apollo, who inspired art and music; Aphrodite, the goddess of carnal love whose name is the basis of the word *aphrodisiac;* and others—as voracious seekers of sexual variety. Not only were they believed to have sexual adventures among themselves, but they were also thought to have seduced mortals.

Three aspects of Greek sexuality are of particular interest to our study of sexual practices in the ancient world: male–male sexual behavior, pederasty, and prostitution. The Greeks viewed men and women as **bisexual**. One of their heroes, Hercules, is said to have ravished 50 virgins in a night. Nevertheless, he also had affairs with men. Male–male *sex* was deemed normal and tolerated so long as it did not threaten the institution of the family.

Pederasty means love of boys. Sex between men and prepubescent boys was illegal, however. Families were generally pleased if their adolescent sons attracted socially prominent mentors. Pederasty did not impede the boy's future male–female functioning, because the pederast himself was usually married, and Greeks believed people equally capable of male–female and male–male sexual activity.

Prostitution flourished at every level of society. Prostitutes ranged from refined **courtesans** to **concubines**, who were usually slaves. Courtesans were similar to the geisha girls of Japan. They could play musical instruments, dance, engage in witty repartee, and discuss politics. They were also skilled in the arts of love. No social stigma was attached to visiting a courtesan. At the lower rungs of society were streetwalkers and brothel prostitutes. The latter were not hard to find. A wooden or painted penis invariably stood by the door.

As in many Middle Eastern countries even today, women held low social status. The women of Athens had no more rights than slaves. They were subject to the authority of their male next-of-kin before marriage and to their husbands afterwards. They received no formal education and were consigned mostly to women's quarters in their homes. They were chaperoned when they ventured out of doors. A husband could divorce his wife without cause and was obligated to do so if she committed adultery. The legal and social rights of women in ancient Athens were similar to those of their contemporaries in Babylonia and Egypt and among the ancient Hebrews.

The World of Ancient Rome Much is made of the sexual excesses of the Roman emperors and ruling families. Julius Caesar is reputed to have been bisexual—"a man to every woman and a woman to every man." Other emperors, like Caligula, sponsored orgies at which guests engaged in sexual practices including **bestiality** and **sadism**. Sexual excesses were found more often among the upper classes of palace society than among average Romans, however.

Romans disapproved of male–male sexual behavior as a threat to the integrity of the Roman family. The family was viewed as the source of strength of the Roman empire. Although Roman women were more likely than their Greek counterparts to share their husbands' social lives, they still were the property of their husbands.

Western society traces the roots of many of its sexual terms to Roman culture, as indicated by their Latin roots. **Fellatio**, for example, derives from the Latin *fellare,* meaning "to suck." **Cunnilingus** derives from *cunnus,* meaning "vulva," and *lingere,* "to lick." **Fornication** derives from *fornix,* an arch or vault. The term stems from Roman streetwalkers' practice of serving their customers in the shadows of archways near public buildings such as stadiums and theaters.

Bisexual Sexually responsive to either gender. (From the Latin *bi-,* meaning "two.")

Pederasty Sexual love of boys. (From the Greek *paidos,* meaning "boy.")

Courtesan A prostitute–especially the mistress of a noble or wealthy man. (From Italian roots meaning "court lady.")

Concubine A secondary wife, usually of inferior legal and social status. (From Latin roots meaning "lying with.")

Bestiality Sexual relations between a person and an animal.

Sadism The practice of achieving sexual gratification through hurting or humiliating others.

Fellatio A sexual activity involving oral contact with the penis.

Cunnilingus A sexual activity involving oral contact with the female genitals.

Fornication Sexual intercourse between people who are not married to one another. (If one of the partners is married, the act may be labeled *adultery.*)

The Early Christians Christianity emerged within the Roman Empire during the centuries following the death of Jesus. Early Christian views on sexuality were largely shaped by Saint Paul and the church fathers in the first century and by Saint Augustine in the latter part of the fourth century. Adultery and fornication were rampant among the upper classes of Rome at the time, and early Christian leaders began to associate sexuality with sin.

In replacing the pagan values of Rome, the early Christians, like the Hebrews, sought to restrict sex to marriage. They saw temptations of the flesh as distractions from spiritual devotion. Paul preached that celibacy was closer to the Christian ideal than marriage. He recognized that not everyone could achieve celibacy, however, so he said that it was "better to marry than to burn" (with passion, that is).

Christians, like Jews before them, demanded virginity of brides. Masturbation and prostitution were condemned (Allen, 2000; Laqueur, 2003). Early Christians taught that men should love their wives with restraint, not passion. The goal of procreation should govern sexual behavior—the spirit should rule the flesh. Divorce was outlawed. Unhappiness with one's spouse might reflect sexual, thus sinful, restlessness. Dissolving a marriage might also jeopardize the social structure that supported the church.

Saint Augustine (353–430 CE) associated sexual lust with the original sin of Adam and Eve in the Garden of Eden. According to Augustine, lust had transformed the innocent procreative instinct, instilled in humanity by God, into sin. Following their fall from grace, Adam and Eve cloaked their nakedness with fig leaves. Shame entered the picture. To Augustine, lust and shame were passed down from Adam and Eve through the generations. Lust made any sexual expression, even intercourse in marriage, inherently evil. Only through celibacy, according to Augustine, could men and women attain a state of grace.

Nonprocreative sexual activity was deemed most sinful. Masturbation, male–male sexual behavior, female–female sexual behavior, oral–genital contact, anal intercourse—all were viewed as abominations in the eyes of God (Laqueur, 2003; Stengers et al., 2001). To the Jews, sex within marriage was a natural and pleasurable function. To the early Christians, however, sexual pleasure, even within marriage, was stained by the original sin of Adam and Eve. But marital sex was deemed less sinful when practiced for procreation and without passion.

Sexuality and Eastern Religions Islam, the dominant religion in the Middle East, was founded by the Prophet Muhammad. Muhammad was born in Mecca, in what is now Saudi Arabia, in about 570 CE. The Islamic tradition treasures marriage and sexual fulfillment in marriage. Premarital intercourse invites shame and social condemnation—and, in some fundamentalist Islamic states, the death penalty.

The family is the backbone of Islamic society. Celibacy is frowned upon. Muhammad decreed that marriage represents the only road to virtue. Islamic tradition permits a sexual double standard, however. Men may take up to four wives, but women are permitted only one husband. Public social interactions between men and women are severely restricted in more conservative Islamic societies. Women are expected to keep their heads and faces veiled in public and to avoid all contact with men other than their husbands.

In the cultures of the Far East, by contrast, sexuality was akin to spirituality. To the Taoist masters of China, who influenced Chinese culture for millennia, sex was a sacred duty—a form of worship that led toward harmony with nature and immortality.

The Chinese culture was the first to produce a detailed sex manual, which came into use about 200 years before the birth of Jesus. The man was expected to extend intercourse as long as possible to absorb more of his wife's natural essence, or *yin*. Yin would enhance his own masculine essence, or *yang*. Moreover, he was to help bring his partner to orgasm so as to increase the flow of energy that he might absorb. (Her pleasure was incidental.)

Taoists believed that it was wasteful for a man to "spill his seed." Masturbation, acceptable for women, was ruled out for men. Sexual practices such as anal intercourse and oral–genital contact (fellatio and cunnilingus) were permissible, so long as the man did not squander *yang* through wasteful ejaculation. Another parallel to Western cultures was the role accorded women in traditional Chinese society. The "good wife," like her Western counterparts, was limited to domestic roles.

Perhaps no culture has cultivated sexual pleasure as a spiritual ideal to the extent of the ancient Hindus of India. From the fifth century CE onward, temples show sculptures of gods, heavenly nymphs, and ordinary people in erotic poses. Hindu sexual practices were codified in a sex manual, the *Kama Sutra*. The *Kama Sutra* illustrates sexual positions, some of which would challenge a contortionist. It also holds recipes for alleged aphrodisiacs. This manual is believed to have been written by the Hindu sage Vatsyayana sometime between the third and fifth centuries CE, at about the time that Christianity was ascending in the West.

In its graphic representations of sexual positions and practices, the *Kama Sutra* reflected the Hindu belief that sex was a religious duty, not a source of shame or guilt. In the Hindu doctrine of *karma* (the passage of souls from one place to another), sexual fulfillment was regarded as one way to become reincarnated at a higher level of existence. Indian society grew more restrictive toward sexuality after about 1000 CE, however.

The Middle Ages The Middle Ages, sometimes called medieval times, span the millennium of Western history from about 476 CE to 1450 CE. The attitudes of the Roman Catholic Church toward sexuality, largely unchanged since the time of Augustine, dominated medieval thought. Yet some currents of change crept across medieval Europe in the social standing of women. The Church had long regarded all women as being tainted by the sin of Eve. But in the Eastern church of Constantinople, the cult of the Virgin Mary flourished. The ideal of womanhood was in the image of Mary: good, gracious, loving, and saintly. Imported by the Crusaders and others who returned from the East, the cult of the Virgin Mary swept European Christendom and helped elevate the status of women.

Two conflicting concepts of women came to dominate medieval thought: one, *woman as Eve*, the temptress; the other, *woman as Mary*, virtuous and pure. Contemporary Western images of women still show the schism between the good girl and the bad girl—the Madonna and the whore. Part of the fascination of the rock star Madonna is that she combines the name of the Virgin Mary and crucifixes with an open display of undergarments and simulated lovemaking on the stage and in her videos.

The Protestant Reformation During the Reformation, Martin Luther (1483–1546) and other Christian reformers such as John Calvin (1509–1564) split off from the Roman Catholic Church and formed their own sects, which led to the development of

***An Illustration from the* Kama Sutra** *The* Kama Sutra, *an Indian sex manual believed to have been written sometime between the third and fifth centuries CE, contained graphic illustrations of sexual techniques and practices.*

the modern Protestant denominations of Western Europe (and later, the New World). Luther disputed many Roman Catholic doctrines on sexuality. He believed that priests should be allowed to marry and rear children. To Luther, marriage was as much a part of human nature as eating or drinking. Calvin rejected the Roman church's position that sex in marriage was permissible only for procreation. He believed that sexual expression in marriage also strengthened the marriage bond and helped relieve the stresses of everyday life.

The Victorian Era Early settlers brought to the New World the religious teachings that had dominated Western thought and culture for centuries. Whatever their differences, each religion stressed the ideal of family life and viewed sex outside of marriage as immoral or sinful. A woman's place, by and large, was in the home and in the fields. Not until 1833, when Oberlin opened its doors to women, were women permitted to attend college in the United States. (Not until the 20th century did women gain the right to vote.)

The middle and later parts of the 19th century are generally called the Victorian period, named after Queen Victoria of England. Victoria assumed the throne in 1837 and ruled until her death in 1901. Her name has become virtually synonymous with sexual repression. Victorian society in Europe and the United States, on the surface at least, was prim and proper (Horowitz, 2002). Sex was not discussed in polite society. Even the legs of pianos were draped with cloth for the sake of modesty. Many women viewed sex as a marital duty to be performed for procreation or to satisfy their husbands' cravings. Consider the following quotation:

> I am happy now that Charles calls on my bed chamber less frequently than of old. As it is, I now endure but two calls a week and when I hear his steps outside my door I lie down on my bed, close my eyes, open my legs and think of England. (Attributed to Alice, Lady Hillingdon, wife of the Second Baron Hillingdon)

Women were assumed not to experience sexual desires or pleasures. "I would say," observed William Acton (1814–1875), an influential English physician, in 1857, "that the majority of women (happily for society) are not much troubled with sexual feeling of any kind." Women, thought Acton, were born with a *sexual anesthesia*.

It was widely believed among medical authorities in England and the United States that sex drains the man of his natural vitality. Physicians thus recommended that intercourse be practiced infrequently, perhaps once a month or so. The Reverend Sylvester Graham (1794–1851) preached that ejaculation deprived men of the "vital fluids" they need to maintain health and vitality. Graham preached against "wasting the seed" by masturbation or frequent marital intercourse (Laqueur, 2003; Stengers et al., 2001). (How frequent was "frequent"? In Graham's view, intercourse more than once a month could dangerously deplete the man's vital energies.) Graham recommended that young men control their sexual appetites by a diet of simple foods based on whole-grain flours.

It appears, though, that the actual behavior of Victorians was not as repressed as advertised. Despite the belief in female sexual anesthesia, Victorian women did experience sexual pleasure and orgasm. Consider some findings from an early sex survey conducted in 1892 by a female physician, Clelia Duel Mosher. Though her sample was small and nonrandom, 35 of the 44 women who responded admitted to desiring sexual intercourse. And 34 of them reported experiencing orgasm. Women's diaries of the time also contained accounts of passionate love affairs.

Prostitution flourished during the Victorian era. Men apparently thought that they were doing their wives a favor by looking elsewhere. Accurate statistics are hard to come by, but there may have been as many as 1 prostitute for every 12 men in London during the 19th century; in Vienna, perhaps 1 for every 7 men.

The Foundations of the Scientific Study of Sexuality Against this backdrop of sexual repression, scientists and scholars began to approach sexuality as an area of legitimate scientific study. The English physician Havelock Ellis (1859–1939) published a veritable encyclopedia of sexuality between 1897 and 1910, *Studies in the Psychology of Sex*. Ellis drew information from case histories, anthropological findings, and medical knowledge. He argued that sexual desires in women were natural and healthy. He promoted the view that many sexual problems had psychological rather than physical causes. He also argued that a gay male or lesbian sexual orientation was a natural variation within the spectrum of normal sexuality and not an aberration. As do most health professionals today, Ellis treated gay male and lesbian sexual orientations as inborn dispositions, not as vices or character flaws.

Another influential **sexologist**, the German psychiatrist Richard von Krafft-Ebing (1840–1902) vividly described case histories of individuals with sexual deviations in his book *Psychopathia Sexualis* (1886). Cases included deviations such as sadomasochism (sexual gratification through inflicting or receiving pain), bestiality (sex with animals), and necrophilia (intercourse with dead people). Krafft-Ebing viewed deviations as mental diseases that could be studied and perhaps treated by medical science.

At about the same time, a Viennese physician, Sigmund Freud (1856–1939), was developing a theory of personality that has had an enormous influence on modern culture and science. Freud believed that the sex drive was our principal motivating force.

Alfred Kinsey (1894–1956), an Indiana University zoologist, conducted the first large-scale studies of sexual behavior in the 1930s and 1940s. Kinsey had been asked to teach a course on marriage. When researching the subject matter, Kinsey found that little was known about sexual practices in American society. He thus embarked upon an ambitious research project, conducting detailed interviews with nearly 12,000 people across the United States. The results of his surveys were published in two volumes, *Sexual Behavior in the Human Male* (Kinsey et al., 1948) and *Sexual Behavior in the Human Female* (Kinsey et al., 1953). These books represent the first scientific attempts to provide a comprehensive picture of sexual behavior in the United States.

The books made for dry reading. They were filled with statistical tables rather than racy pictures or vignettes. Nevertheless, they became best-sellers, exploding on a public that had not yet learned to discuss sex openly. Their publication—especially the book on female sexuality—unleashed the dogs of criticism. Kinsey's work had some methodological flaws—especially in its selection of participants—but much of the criticism branded it immoral and obscene. *The New York Times* refused to run advertisements for the 1948 volume on male sexuality. Many newspapers refused to report the results of his survey on female sexuality. A congressional committee in the 1950s claimed that Kinsey's work undermined the moral fiber of the nation, rendering it more vulnerable to a Communist takeover. Despite all the brouhaha, Kinsey and his colleagues made sex research a scientifically respectable field of study and helped lay the groundwork for discussing sexual behavior openly.

The Sexual Revolution The period of the mid-1960s to the mid-1970s is often referred to as the *sexual revolution* (Allyn, 2001; Kamen, 2002). Dramatic changes occurred in American sexual attitudes and practices during the "Swinging Sixties." When folksinger Bob Dylan sang "The Times They Are A-Changin'," our society was

Sexologist A person who engages in the scientific study of sexual behavior.

Are Today's Young People More or Less Liberal in the Expression of Their Sexuality than People in Earlier Generations? *Today the threat of HIV/AIDS hangs over every sexual encounter. While many young people today are selective in their choice of partners and take precautions to make sex safer, more teenagers are engaging in sexual activity, and at younger ages, than in previous generations.*

on the threshold of major social upheaval, not only in sexual behavior, but also in science, politics, fashion, music, art, and cinema. The so-called Woodstock generation, disheartened by commercialism and the Vietnam War, tuned in (to rock music on the radio), turned on (to drugs), and dropped out (of mainstream society). The heat was on between the hippies and the hardhats. Long hair became the mane of men. Bell-bottomed jeans flared out. Films became sexually explicit. Critics seriously contemplated whether the pornography "classic" *Deep Throat* had deep social implications. Hard rock music bellowed the message of rebellion and revolution.

No single event marked the onset of the sexual revolution. There was no charge up a sexual San Juan Hill. Social movements often gain momentum from a timely interplay of scientific, social, political, and economic forces. The war (in Vietnam), the bomb (fear of the nuclear bomb), the pill (the introduction of the birth control pill), and the mass media (especially television) were four such forces. The pill lessened the risk of unwanted pregnancy for young people. It permitted them to engage in recreational or casual sex, rather than procreative sex. Pop psychology movements, like the Human Potential Movement of the 1960s and 1970s (the "Me Decade"), spread the message that people should get in touch with and express their genuine feelings, including their sexual feelings. "Doing your own thing" became one catchphrase. "If it feels right, go with it" became another. The lamp was rubbed. Out popped the sexual genie.

The sexual revolution was tied to social permissiveness and political liberalism. In part reflecting the times, in part acting the catalyst, the media dealt openly with sex. Popular books encouraged people to explore their sexuality. Film scenes of lovemaking became so commonplace that the movie rating system was introduced to alert parents.

More teenagers are sexually active today, and at younger ages (Henshaw, 2003). In addition to premarital sex, two other features of the sexual revolution have become permanent parts of our social fabric: the liberation of female sexuality and a greater willingness to discuss sex openly. For example, in 1998 TV networks broadcast President Bill Clinton's grand jury testimony, with explicit references to oral sex with White House intern Monica Lewinsky, during daytime hours.

What, then, does history tell us about sex? Is there a universal standard for defining sexual values, or are there many standards? All societies have some form of an incest taboo. Most societies have placed a value on procreative sex within the context of an enduring relationship, usually in the form of marriage. Marriage provides security for children, maintains or increases the population, and ensures the orderly transfer of property from generation to generation.

Other sexual practices—masturbation, promiscuous sex, male–male sexual behavior, female–female sexual behavior, prostitution, polygamy, and so on—have been condemned in some societies, tolerated by others, and encouraged by still others.

Some historians argue that the pagan "degradations" of Rome led to its demise—a "purer" Rome might otherwise still bestride the earth. They warn that the "excesses" of our own sexual revolution may also bring us down. Rome, however, suffered from the administrative difficulties of tending to a far-flung empire. Rome was besieged by "barbarians" in the outposts and, eventually, at the city gates. In fact, the civilizations of ancient Greece and Rome maintained their prominence for hundreds of years. When we consider their contributions to Western art, philosophical thought, and the languages we speak, we may question whether they fell at all.

The Biological Perspective

Question: What is the role of the biological perspective? The biological perspective focuses on the roles of genes, hormones, the nervous system, and other biological factors in human sexuality. Sex, after all, serves the biological function of reproduction. We are biologically endowed with structures that make sexual behavior possible—and, for most people, pleasurable.

Study of the biology of sex informs us about the mechanisms of reproduction. It informs us of the mechanisms of sexual arousal and response. Biology teaches us that erection occurs when the penis becomes engorged in blood. We learn that vaginal lubrication is the result of a "sweating" action of the vaginal walls. We learn that orgasm is a spinal reflex as well as a psychological event.

Biological researchers have made major strides in assisting infertile couples to conceive, for example, through laboratory-based methods of fertilization. Knowledge of biology has furthered our understanding of sexuality and our ability to overcome sexual problems. To what extent does biology govern sexual behavior? Is sex controlled by biological instincts? Or are psychosocial factors, such as culture, experience, and decision-making ability more important? Although the sexuality of other species is largely governed by biological processes, culture and experience play vital roles   and in some cases, the more central roles-in human sexuality. *Human* sexuality involves a complex interaction of biological and psychosocial factors.

The Evolutionary Perspective

Species vary not only in their physical characteristics but also in their social behavior, including their mating behavior. Scientists look to the process of **evolution** to help explain such variability. *Questions: What is evolution? How might the sexual behavior of various species, including our own, be influenced by evolutionary forces?*

The English naturalist Charles Darwin (1809–1882) is considered the founder of the modern theory of evolution. He believed that animal and plant species were not created independently, but evolved from other life-forms through **natural selection**, or "survival of the fittest." In each species, some individuals are better adapted to their environments than others. Better-adapted members are more likely to survive to reproduce. Therefore, they are also more likely to transmit their traits to succeeding generations. The fittest members of a species produce the greatest number of surviving offspring. They are not necessarily the strongest or fleetest of foot, although these traits are adaptive for some species and enhance their reproductive success.

When environmental conditions change, natural selection favors members of a species who possess traits that help them adapt. These forms of the species proliferate, eventually replacing forms that fail to survive and reproduce. Species that lack forms that possess adaptive traits eventually become extinct.

Evolution The development of a species to its present state, which is believed to involve adaptations to its environment.

Natural selection The evolutionary process by which adaptive traits enable members of a species to survive to reproductive age and transmit these traits to future generations.

Darwin was too early—the technology of his day did not allow him to find the microscopic structures that transmit traits from generation to generation. We know now that traits are transmitted by units of heredity that we call **genes**. Traits are determined by the combinations of genes that offspring inherit from their parents.

Genes are segments of **chromosomes**, which are composed of **DNA** (Plomin & Crabbe, 2000). The chemical structure of genes provides genetic instructions. Each human cell normally contains a complement of 46 chromosomes, which are arranged in 23 pairs. Each human chromosome consists of more than 1,000 genes. A child normally inherits one member of each pair of chromosomes from each parent. So each offspring inherits 50% of his or her genes from each parent. The particular combinations of genes that one inherits from one's parents account for whether one has blue eyes or brown eyes, light or dark hair, and a wide range of other characteristics.

New variations in species are introduced through random genetic changes called **mutations**. Mutations occur randomly but are subject to natural selection. Some mutations are adaptive and enhance reproductive success. As more members of the species come to possess these traits, the species as a whole changes in form.

In recent years, some scientists—including **evolutionary psychologists**—have suggested that there is a genetic basis to social behavior, including sexual behavior, among humans and other animals (Bruene & Ribbert, 2002; Fisher, 2000; McAndrew, 2002). This theory proposes that dispositions toward *behavior patterns* that enhance reproductive success—as well as physical traits that do so—may be genetically transmitted (Cory, 2002). If so, we may carry traits that helped our prehistoric ancestors survive and reproduce successfully, even if these traits are no longer adaptive in modern culture (Plomin, 2002). "Modern culture"—dating, say, from classical Greece—is but a moment in the lifetime of our species.

The Evolutionary Perspective and Erotic Plasticity   Consider the concept of "erotic plasticity" (Baumeister, 2000), which addresses the fact that in response to various social and cultural forces, people show different levels of sex drive and express their sexual desires in a variety of ways. Roy Baumeister (2000) reports evidence that women show greater erotic plasticity than men do. For example, (a) individual women show greater variation than men in sexual behavior over time; (b) women seem to be more responsive than men to most specific cultural factors, such as cultural permissiveness or restraint; and (c) men's sexual behavior is more consistent with their sexual attitudes than women. Baumeister concludes that evolutionary, biological forces may be an important factor in the greater female erotic plasticity.

Are Adaptive Traits "Good"?   There is a tendency to think of adaptive traits as somehow more "worthy," "good," or "admirable" than less adaptive traits. Evolution is not a moralistic enterprise, however. A trait either does or does not enhance reproductive success. It is not in itself good or bad. It is apparently adaptive for the female of one species of insect eat the male after mating. "Dad" then literally nourishes his offspring during the period of gestation. In evolutionary terms, his personal sacrifice is adaptive if it increases the chances that the offspring will survive and carry his genes. In other species, it may be adaptive for fathers to "love them and leave them"—that is, to mate with as many females as possible and abruptly abandon them to "plant their seed" elsewhere.

Some evolutionary psychologists argue that men are naturally more promiscuous than women because they are the genetic heirs of ancestors whose reproductive success was related to the number of women they could impregnate (Bjorklund & Kipp, 1996; Buss, 1994). Women, by contrast, can produce only a few offspring in their lifetimes. Thus, the theory goes, they have to be more selective with respect to

Genes The basic units of heredity, which consist of chromosomal segments of DNA.

Chromosomes The rodlike structures that reside in the nuclei of every living cell and carry the genetic code in the form of genes.

DNA Deoxyribonucleic acid—the chemical substance whose molecules make up genes and chromosomes.

Mutations Random changes in the molecular structure of DNA.

Evolutionary psychologist Psychologist who studies the effects of evolution on behavior and mental processes.

their mating partners. Women's reproductive success is enhanced by mating with the fittest males—not with any Tom, Dick, or Harry who happens by. From this perspective, the male's "roving eye" and the female's selectivity are embedded in their genes (Townsend, 1995). Evolutionary psychology theory is also sometimes drawn upon to explain why the incidences of infanticide and sexual abuse of children are higher in stepfamilies than in families where everyone is genetically related (Daly & Wilson, 1998).

To some evolutionary psychologists, human beings are like marionettes on strings being tugged by invisible puppet masters—their genes. Genes govern the biological processes of sexual maturation and the production of sex hormones. Hormones, in turn, are largely responsible for regulating the sexual behavior of other animal species. Extending evolutionary psychology to human behavior sparks considerable controversy, however. Critics contend that learning, personal choice, and sociocultural factors may be more important determinants of human behavior than heredity (Hyde & Durik, 2000).

Truth?Fiction?
Revisited

It is true that Trobriander boys and girls were expected to engage in intercourse when they were biologically old enough. According to custom, they would pair off and exchange a coconut, a bit of betel nut, a few beads, or some fruit from the bush. Then they would go off and engage in intercourse. (Malinowski, 1929, p. 488.)

The Cross-Species Perspective

Question: What is the role of the cross-species perspective? The study of other animal species places human behavior in broader context. A surprising variety of sexual behaviors exists among nonhumans. There are animal examples, or **analogues**, of human male–male sexual behavior, female–female sexual behavior, oral–genital contact, and oral–oral behavior (i.e., kissing). Foreplay is also well known in the animal world. Turtles massage their mates' heads with their claws. Male mice nibble at their partner's necks. Most mammals use only a rear-entry position for **copulation**, but some animals, such as apes, use a variety of coital positions.

Cross-species research reveals an interesting pattern. Sexual behavior among "higher" mammals, such as primates, is less directly controlled by instinct than it is among the "lower" species, such as birds, fish, or lower mammals. Experience and learning play more important roles in sexuality as we travel up the evolutionary ladder.

The Cross-Cultural Perspective

Question: What is the role of the cross-cultural perspective? The cross-cultural perspective, like the historical perspective, provides insight into the ways in which cultural beliefs affect sexual behavior and people's sense of morality. Unlike historians, who are limited in their sources to the eyewitness accounts of others and the shards of information that can be gleaned from fading relics, anthropologists can observe other cultures firsthand. Interest in the cross-cultural perspective on sexuality was spurred by the early-twentieth-century work of the anthropologists Margaret Mead (1901–1978) and Bronislaw Malinowski (1884–1942).

In *Sex and Temperament in Three Primitive Societies* (1935), Mead laid the groundwork for recent psychological and sociological research challenging gender-role stereotypes. In most cultures characterized by a gender division of labor, men typically go to business or to the hunt, and—when necessary—to war. In such cultures, men are perceived as strong, active, independent, and logical. Women are viewed as passive, dependent, nurturant, and emotional. Mead concluded that these stereotypes are not inherent in our genetic heritage. Rather, they are acquired through

Analogue Something that is similar or comparable to something else.

Copulation Sexual intercourse. (From the Latin *copulare,* meaning "to unite" or "to couple.")

A
Closer
Look

Females throughout the Animal Kingdom Are Monogamous—*Not!*[1]

Many scientists and philosophers have looked to the behavior found throughout the animal kingdom in an effort to determine what kinds of behaviors are "natural" for people. Are there lessons about human behavior in the following examples? Perhaps, but read at your own risk . . .

Contrary to what biologists once thought, females of most species are promiscuous—which explains a lot of weird behavior. For example, in the ordinary course of events, a male dung fly copulates with a female for a full 40 minutes, and even when he is finished delivering what he came to deliver and disengages, he hangs onto her for an additional 20 minutes. Otherwise, she is likely to—how to put this?—collect sperm from another suitor.

When a male ghost crab mates, his first move is to shoot into his beloved a bit of fluid that hardens into an epoxylike plug. The plug blocks any rival sperm that may have arrived earlier from swimming out of the tract where the female stores the wiggly gifts that males deposit, and so keeps the other guys' sperm from reaching her eggs. Only then does the latest crab, optimistic about his paternal chances, introduce his own sperm.

More Bizarre than the *Kama Sutra*

From behavior to physiology to anatomy, sex throughout the animal kingdom has always been and will surely always be more bizarre than the *Kama Sutra* lets on. But at least it's becoming less mysterious. Such previously inexplicable facts of life as weird genitalia and ludicrous copulatory practices (such as the 79 straight days that stick insects remain *in flagrante delicto*), biologists are now realizing, are adaptations to something they managed to overlook for a few millenniums: female promiscuity. Says biologist Tim Birkhead (2000) of the University of Sheffield in his book *Promiscuity,* which recounts scores of recent studies. "It is now clear that . . . females of most species . . . routinely copulate with several different males."

How routinely? Once they started looking, biologists found promiscuous females in some 70% of the species they studied. A clutch of grasshopper eggs can have several fathers. Thirty-five percent of baby indigo buntings, a pretty little songbird, are sired by a male other than the guy Mom came in with. So are 76% of

Are Females throughout the Animal Kingdom Monogamous? Want a quick answer? It's no. Females in many species, including chimpanzees, are likely to have offspring who have been sired by more than one father.

Australian fairy wrens. In five hours, a female Scottish Soay sheep paired up with seven rams for a total of 163 encounters. Female chimps copulate a total of 500 to 1,000 times for each pregnancy: A study using DNA to run paternity tests found that 54% of baby chimps were fathered by males other than Mom's supposed partner. A single clutch of goshawk eggs is inseminated some 500 times.

The Exception Rather than the Rule

Female monogamy is the exception rather than the rule, contrary to the view that only men gain an evolutionary edge by

Truth?Fiction?
Revisited

The male redback spider, seconds after inseminating a female, does a somersault into her mouth so he becomes her post-coital meal; because matings followed by cannibalism last twice as long as those that don't, his sacrifice improves the chance that his own sperm will fertilize her eggs before someone else can have at her.

cultural expectations and socialization. That is, men and women learn to behave in ways that are expected of them in their particular culture.

Malinowski lived on the Trobriand island of Boyawa in the South Pacific during World War I. There he gathered data on two societies of the South Pacific, the Trobrianders and the Amphett islanders. The Amphett islanders maintained strict sexual prohibitions, whereas the Trobrianders enjoyed greater freedom. Trobrianders, for example, encouraged their children to masturbate. Adolescents were expected to have multiple sex partners until they married. Malinowski found Trobrianders to be less anxiety-ridden than Amphett islanders. He attributed the difference to their sexual freedom, thus making an early plea to relax prohibitions in Western societies.

Cross-Cultural Commonalities and Differences in Sexual Behavior In 1951, Clellan Ford, an anthropologist, and Frank Beach, a psychologist, reviewed sexual behavior in preliterate societies around the world, as well as in other animals. They found great variety in sexual

spreading their seed widely. Surveys find that human females'—that is, women's—"ideal number" of lifetime sexual partners is less than men's, and that they indeed have fewer partners than men. Based on that, "a lot of people want to simplify human mating and say that women are monogamous and men are promiscuous," says psychologist David Buss of the University of Texas. "But that's a gross over-simplification: Both sexes pursue both strategies."

Female promiscuity triggers a war between the sexes. If a male is to have a fighting chance of fathering offspring and getting his genes into the next generation in the face of faithless females, he needs both crafty mating habits and seemingly outlandish mating equipment. One favored adaptation is a penis decked out with features much more elaborate than your basic sperm-meets-ova job requires. Hence the tools of male damselflies and dragonflies: Both are covered with horns and hooks whose purpose, biologists have deduced, is to scoop out sperm that have arrived in the female's genital tract before theirs. The wild variety in testes size (relative to body size) throughout the animal kingdom suddenly makes sense in light of female promiscuity, too: The more promiscuous the females of a species, the larger the male's penis grows so his sperm have a swimming chance at

fatherhood. That's why gorillas' testes are small (faithful females) but chimps are . . . well, there's a reason circus chimps are usually clothed.

Scientists aren't sure what influences the females of a species (or the males, for that matter) to remain monogamous. But in humans, female promiscuity is a response to tough living conditions. In Bhutan, many women practice polyandry because in the poor valleys of the Himalayas a lone husband cannot support a family. Spouse exchange among the Inuit improves their chance of survival in the unforgiving Arctic because kin are morally obliged to provide for each other; the more in-laws, the more support.

Which brings us to the central question: What do females get out of promiscuity? (No, besides that.) One benefit of polyandry is increased resources and protection for a female and her brood. Most males are happy to trade food for sex; every male a female cricket copulates with brings her a protein-rich meal, good for her eggs. And female Adelie penguins collect a stone, to build a nest, every time they offer themselves to a male. Females also gain by sowing the seeds of confusion, paternity-wise. Each Galapagos hawk that mates with a female helps rear her chicks, even though some are not the sires. But by trading sex for paternal care,

the female increases the chance that her chicks will survive. Female red-winged blackbirds who copulate with multiple males are less likely to lose their chicks to predators: Each male attacks would-be predators. Male primates and lions commit infanticide against babies not their own; by confusing paternity, female chimps and lionesses keep more of their offspring out of harm's way.

Female promiscuity may bring not more offspring (as male promiscuity does) but better ones. Females of several species seem to have a mysterious detector built into their reproductive system that rejects "genetically incompatible" sperm but accepts sperm whose DNA complements their eggs', producing the most viable offspring. Several studies find that females produce better-quality offspring by mating with several males; scientists are only starting to figure out how females discriminate duds from winners.[2]

---

1. Reprinted from Sharon Begley with Erika Check (2000, August 5). Sex and the single fly. *Newsweek*, pp. 44–45.

2. The first and second authors of this text point out that it is not necessarily advantageous for females to have the ability to discriminate duds from winners. The third author confesses that she wishes she had had that capacity years ago.

customs and beliefs among the almost 200 societies they studied. They also found some fairly common threads. Ford and Beach reported that kissing was quite common across the cultures they studied, although not universal. The Thonga of Africa were one society that did not practice kissing. Upon witnessing two European visitors kissing each other, members of the tribe commented that they could not understand why Europeans "ate" each other's saliva and dirt. The frequency of sexual intercourse also varies from culture to culture, but intercourse is relatively more frequent among young people everywhere.

Societies differ in their attitudes toward childhood masturbation. Some societies, such as the Hopi Native Americans of the southwest United States, ignore it. Trobrianders encourage it. Other societies condemn it.

Eighty-four percent of Ford and Beach's (1951) preliterate cultures practiced polygamy. The researchers concluded that monogamy was relatively uncommon. More common is the form of polygamy called **polygyny**, in which men are permitted to have more than one wife. Similarly, Frayser (1985) found that polygyny was practiced by the great majority (82%) of societies in her cross-cultural sample. In

Polygyny A form of marriage in which a man has two or more wives. (From the Greek *gyne,* meaning "woman.")

Truth?Fiction?
Revisited

To a psychoanalyst, dreams of airplanes, bullets, snakes, sticks, and similar objects may indeed symbolize the male genitals. But this is the case according to psychoanalytic theory, and not necessarily supported by research evidence. Freud himself maintained a bit of skepticism about the import of dream symbols. He once remarked, "Sometimes a cigar is just a cigar."

Polyandry A form of marriage in which a woman has two or more husbands. (From the Greek *andros*, meaning "man" or "male.")

Psychoanalysis The theory of personality originated by Sigmund Freud, which proposes that human behavior represents the outcome of clashing inner forces.

Defense mechanisms In psychoanalytic theory, automatic processes that protect the ego from anxiety by disguising or ejecting unacceptable ideas and urges.

Repression The automatic ejection of anxiety-evoking ideas from consciousness.

Erogenous zones Parts of the body, including but not limited to the sex organs, that are responsive to sexual stimulation.

many cultures, a man's number of wives is an emblem of his wealth and status. Nevertheless, monogamy is more prevalent worldwide. Few societies have the oversupply of women that universal polygyny would entail (Harris & Johnson, 2003; Whitten, 2001). Rarer still is **polyandry**, a practice that permits women to have more than one husband. Frayser (1985) found polyandry in only 2% of societies she studied. In fraternal polyandry, the most common form of polyandry, two or more brothers share a wife, and all dwell in the same household (Harris & Johnson, 2003; Whitten, 2001).

Polygyny has a long tradition in Western culture. King Solomon was reputed to have 700 wives. Polygyny was practiced in the 19th-century United States by an early leader of the Mormon church, Brigham Young, and some of his followers.

The cross-cultural perspective illustrates the importance of learning in human sexual behavior. Societies differ widely in their sexual attitudes, customs, and practices. The members of all human societies share the same anatomic structures and physiological capacities for sexual pleasure, however. The same hormones flow through their arteries. Yet their sexual practices, and the pleasure they reap or fail to attain, may set them apart. If human sexuality were predominantly determined by biology, we might not find such diversity.

Psychological Perspectives

Question: What do psychological perspectives have to offer? Psychological perspectives focus on the many psychological influences—perception, learning, motivation, emotion, personality, and so on—that affect our sexual behavior and our experience of ourselves as female or male. Some psychological theorists, such as Sigmund Freud, focus on the motivational role of sex in human personality. Others focus on how our experiences and mental representations of the world affect our sexual behavior.

Sigmund Freud and Psychoanalytic Theory Sigmund Freud, a Viennese physician, formulated a grand theory of personality termed **psychoanalysis**. Freud believed that we are all born with biologically based sex drives that must be channeled through socially approved outlets if family and social life are to carry on without undue conflict.

Freud proposed that the mind operates on conscious and unconscious levels. The conscious level corresponds to our state of present awareness. The unconscious mind refers to the darker reaches of the mind that lie outside our direct awareness. The ego shields the conscious mind from awareness of our baser sexual and aggressive urges by means of **defense mechanisms** such as **repression**, or motivated forgetting of traumatic experiences.

Although many sexual ideas and impulses are banished to the unconscious, they continue to seek expression. One avenue of expression is the dream, through which sexual impulses may be perceived in disguised, or symbolic, form. The therapists and scholars who follow in the Freudian tradition are quite interested in analyzing dreams, and the dream objects listed in Table 1.1 are often considered sexual symbols.

Freud introduced us to new and controversial ideas about ourselves as sexual beings. For example, he originated the concept of **erogenous zones**-the idea that many parts of the body, not just the genitals, are responsive to sexual stimulation.

One of Freud's most controversial beliefs was that children normally harbor erotic interests. He believed that the suckling of the infant in the oral stage was an

TABLE 1.1
Dream Symbols in Psychoanalytic Theory*

Symbols for the Male Genital Organs

airplanes	fish	neckties	tools	weapons
bullets	hands	poles	trains	
feet	hoses	snakes	trees	
fire	knives	sticks	umbrellas	

Symbols for the Female Genital Organs

bottles	caves	doors	ovens	ships
boxes	chests	hats	pockets	tunnels
cases	closets	jars	pots	

Symbols for Sexual Intercourse

climbing a ladder	flying in an airplane
climbing a staircase	riding a horse
crossing a bridge	riding an elevator
driving an automobile	riding a roller coaster
entering a room	walking into a tunnel or down a hall

Symbols for the Breasts

apples	peaches

*Freud theorized that the content of dreams symbolized urges, wishes, and objects of fantasy that we would censor in the waking state.

Source: Adapted from Rathus, S. A. (2002). *Psychology in the new millennium,* 8th ed. Fort Worth, TX: Harcourt College Publishers.

erotic act. So too was anal bodily experimentation through which children learn to experience pleasure in the control of their sphincter muscles and the processes of elimination. He theorized that it was normal for children to progress through stages of development in which the erotic interest shifts from one erogenous zone to another, as, for example, from the mouth or oral cavity to the anal cavity. According to his theory of **psychosexual development**, children undergo five stages of development: oral, anal, phallic, latency, and genital, which are named according to the predominant erogenous zones of each stage. Each stage gives rise to certain kinds of conflicts. Moreover, inadequate or excessive gratification in any stage can lead to **fixation** in that stage and the development of traits and sexual preferences characteristic of that stage.

Freud believed that it was normal for children to develop erotic feelings toward the parent of the other gender during the phallic stage. These incestuous urges lead to conflict with the parent of the same sex. In later chapters we shall see that these developments, which Freud termed the **Oedipus complex**, have profound implications for the assumption of gender roles and sexual orientation.

Learning Theories To what extent does sexual behavior reflect experience? Would you hold the same sexual attitudes and do the same things if you had been reared in another culture? We think not. Even within the same society, family and personal experiences can shape unique sexual attitudes and behaviors. Whereas psychoanalytic theory plumbs the depths of the unconscious, learning theorists focus on environmental factors that shape behavior.

Behaviorists such as John B. Watson (1878–1958) and B. F. Skinner (1904–1990) emphasized the importance of rewards and punishments in the learning process. Skinner termed events that increase the frequency or likelihood of behavior *reinforcements.* Children left to explore their bodies without parental condemnation will learn what feels good and tend to repeat it. The Trobriand child who is rewarded

Psychosexual development In psychoanalytic theory, the process by which sexual feelings shift from one erogenous zone to another.

Fixation In psychoanalytic theory, arrested development, which includes attachment to objects of an earlier stage of psychosexual development.

Oedipus complex In psychoanalytic theory, a conflict of the phallic stage in which the boy wishes to possess his mother sexually and perceives his father as a rival in love. (The analogous conflict for girls is the *Electra complex.*)

Behaviorists Learning theorists who argue that a scientific approach to understanding behavior must refer only to observable and measurable behaviors.

Acquisition of Gender Roles *According to social-learning theory, children learn gender roles that are considered appropriate in their society by means of reinforcement of certain behavior patterns and by observing the gender-related behaviors of their parents, peers, and other role models in media such as TV, films, and books.*

for masturbation and premarital coitus through parental praise and encouragement will be more likely to repeat these behaviors than the child in a more sexually restrictive culture, who is punished for the same behavior. When sexual behavior (like masturbation) feels good, but parents connect it with feelings of guilt and shame, the child is placed in conflict and may vacillate between masturbating and swearing off it. If, as young children, we are severely punished for sexual exploration, we may come to associate sexual stimulation *in general* with feelings of guilt or anxiety. Such early learning experiences can set the stage for sexual problems or dysfunctions in adulthood.

Social–learning theorists also use the concepts of reward and punishment, but they emphasize the importance of cognitive activity (anticipations, thoughts, plans, and so on) and learning by observation. Observational learning, or **modeling**, refers to acquiring knowledge and skills through observing others. Observational learning involves more than direct observation of other people. It includes seeing models in films or on television, hearing about them, and reading about them. According to social–learning theory, children acquire the gender roles deemed appropriate in a society through reinforcement of gender-appropriate behavior and through observing the gender-role behavior of their parents, their peers, and other models on television, in films, in books, and so on.

Psychological theories shed light on the ways in which sexuality is influenced by rewards, punishments, and mental processes such as fantasy, thoughts, attitudes, and expectations. Sigmund Freud helped bring sexuality within the province of scientific investigation. He also helped make it possible for people to recognize and talk about the importance of sexuality in their lives. Critics contend, however, that he may have placed too much emphasis on sexual motivation in determining behavior and on the role of unconscious processes.

The Sociocultural Perspective: The World of Diversity

Sexual behavior is determined not only by biological and psychological factors, but also by social factors. Social factors contribute to the shaping of our sexual attitudes, beliefs, and behavior. Anthropologists contribute to our understanding of cross-cultural variance in sexuality. *Question: What is the role of sociocultural theorists?* Sociocultural theorists focus on differences in sexuality among the subgroups of a society, as defined, for example, by differences in religion, race/ethnicity, country of origin, socioeconomic status, marital status, age, educational level, and gender. Such a society is the United States.

Consider the issue of the numbers of sex partners people have. Table 1.2 reports the results of a national survey concerning the number of sex partners people report having since the age of 18. It considers the factors of sex, age, marital status, level of education, religion, and race/ethnicity (Laumann et al., 1994). For example, males report having greater numbers of sex partners than females do. One male in three (33%) reports having 11 or more sex partners since the age of 18, as compared with fewer than one woman in ten (9.2%). Throughout the text, we shall be focusing on gender differences and why men seem generally more likely than women to seek a wide range of sexual experience.

Consider age. The numbers of sex partners rises with age into the 40s. As people age, they have more opportunity to accumulate life experiences, including sexual

Social–learning theory A cognitively oriented learning theory in which observational learning, values, and expectations play key roles in determining behavior.

Modeling Acquiring knowledge and skills by observing others.

experiences. But then the numbers of partners fall off among respondents in their 50s. Older respondents entered adulthood prior to the sexual revolution and were thus exposed to more conservative sexual attitudes. We shall find this sort of age difference, or age gradient, throughout the text as well.

Level of education is also connected with sexual behavior. Generally speaking, education appears to be a liberalizing influence. Therefore, it is not surprising that people with some college education, or who have completed college, are likely to have more sex partners than those who attended only grade school or high school.

If education is a liberating influence on sexuality, conservative religious experience is apparently a restraining factor. In Table 1.2, those who report no religion and liberal Protestants (e.g., Methodists, Lutherans, Presbyterians, Episcopalians, and United Church of Christ) report higher numbers of sex partners than do Catholics and conservative Protestants (e.g., members of Baptist Churches, Pentecostal Churches, Churches of Christ, and Assemblies of God).

Ethnicity is also connected with sexual behavior. Throughout the text, our coverage of diversity will address differences between European Americans, African Americans, Latino and Latina Americans, Asian Americans, and Native Americans. The research findings listed in Table 1.2 suggest that European Americans and African Americans have the highest numbers of sex partners. Latino and Latina Americans are mostly Catholic, and Catholicism, as noted, tends to restrain sexual behavior. Asian Americans would appear to be the most sexually restrained ethnic group. However, as noted in the footnote to the table, the sample sizes of Asian Americans and Native Americans may be too small to draw accurate conclusions.

The sociocultural perspective informs us of the relationship between sexuality and one's social group within a society. Sociocultural theorists view sexual behavior as occurring within a sociocultural system. They study the ways in which the values, beliefs, and norms of a group influence the sexual behavior of its members. To a certain extent, we share attitudes and behavior patterns with people from similar backgrounds. Even so, not all Protestants or all members of a given ethnic group act or think alike.

Gender Roles Sociocultural theorists also study gender roles. In Western cultures, men have traditionally been expected to be the breadwinners, whereas women have been expected to remain in the home and rear the children. Traditional gender roles also define sexual relations. Men are expected to be assertive; women, compliant. Men are to initiate romantic overtures. Women are to perform a "gatekeeping" role and determine which advances they will accept. Today, many of these traditions have fallen by the wayside. Most women today are members of the workforce. Many are pursuing careers in traditionally male domains, such as law, medicine, and engineering. Some women command naval vessels. Others pilot military helicopters. Yet even women who become presidents and vice presidents of corporations are still burdened with the bulk of household chores. Sexual practices are also changing to some degree. More women today initiate dates and sexual interactions than was the case in past generations.

Multiple Perspectives on Human Sexuality

Given the complexity and range of human sexual behavior, we need to consider multiple perspectives to understand sexuality. Each perspective—historical, biological, cross-species, cross-cultural, psychological, and sociocultural—has something to teach us. Let us venture a few conclusions based on our overview of these perspectives. First, human sexuality appears to reflect a combination of biological, social, cultural, sociocultural, and psychological factors that interact in complex ways. Second, there

TABLE 1.2

Number of Sex Partners since Age 18 as Found in the NHSLS[†] Study

Social Characteristics	Number of Sex Partners (%)					
	0	1	2–4	5–10	11–20	21+
Gender						
Male	3.4	19.5	20.9	23.3	16.3	16.6
Female	2.5	31.5	36.4	20.4	6.0	3.2
Age						
18–24	7.8	32.1	34.1	15.4	7.8	2.8
25–29	2.2	25.3	31.3	22.2	9.9	9.0
30–34	3.1	21.3	29.3	25.2	10.8	10.3
35–39	1.7	18.9	29.7	24.9	14.0	10.8
40–44	0.7	21.9	27.6	24.2	13.7	12.0
45–49	2.0	25.7	23.8	25.1	9.6	13.9
50–54	2.4	33.9	27.8	18.0	9.0	9.0
55–59	1.3	40.0	28.3	15.2	8.3	7.0
Marital Status						
Never married (not cohabiting)	12.3	14.8	28.6	20.6	12.1	11.6
Never married (cohabiting)	0.0	24.6	37.3	15.7	9.7	12.7
Married	0.0	37.1	28.0	19.4	8.7	6.8
Education						
Less than high school	4.2	26.7	36.0	18.6	8.8	5.8
High school graduate	3.4	30.2	29.1	20.0	9.8	7.4
Some college	2.1	23.9	29.4	23.3	11.9	9.3
College graduate	2.1	24.1	25.8	23.9	11.1	13.0
Advanced degree	3.5	24.6	26.3	22.8	9.6	13.2
Religion						
None	2.6	16.2	29.0	20.3	15.9	15.9
Liberal, moderate Protestant	2.3	22.8	31.2	23.0	12.4	8.3
Conservative Protestant	2.9	29.8	30.4	20.4	9.5	7.0
Catholic	3.8	27.2	29.2	22.7	8.1	9.1
Jewish*	0.0	24.1	13.0	29.6	16.7	16.7
Race/Ethnicity						
European American	3.0	26.2	28.9	22.0	10.9	9.1
African American	2.2	18.0	34.2	24.1	11.0	10.5
Latino and Latina American	3.2	35.6	27.1	17.4	8.2	8.5
Asian American*	6.2	46.2	24.6	13.8	6.2	3.1
Native American*	5.0	27.5	35.0	22.5	5.0	5.0

Source: Adapted from Laumann, E. O., Gagnon, J. H., Michael, R. T., & Michaels, S. (1994). *The Social Organization of Sexuality: Sexual Practices in the United States.* Chicago: University of Chicago Press, Table 5.1C, p. 179.
[†]National Health and Social Life Survey, conducted by a research team centered at the University of Chicago.
*These sample sizes are quite small.

are few universal patterns of sexual behavior, and views on what is right and wrong show great diversity. Third, although our own cultural values and beliefs may be deeply meaningful to us, they may not indicate what is normal, natural, or moral in terms of sexual behavior. The complexity of human sexuality—complexity that causes it to remain somewhat baffling to scientists—adds to the wonder and richness of our sexual experience.

Review: Perspectives on Human Sexuality

Reflect

Throughout much of history, women were considered to be the property of their fathers and then their husbands. Are their "remnants" of this belief in people from your own ethnic background? Explain.

Critical Thinking

The biological, evolutionary, and cross-species perspectives may offer some insights into what kinds of sexual behavior are "natural." If a sexual behavior pattern is judged to be natural, does that mean that it is right or good? Explain.

17. _____ informs us as to whether sexual behavior reflects trends that have been with us through the millennia or the customs of a particular culture and era.

18. History shows (*A great deal of* or *Little*?) evidence of universal sexual trends.

19. The art of the _____ Age suggests that peopled worshiped women's ability to bear children and perpetuate the species.

20. In ancient Rome, a large _____ was carried like a float in a parade honoring Venus, the goddess of love.

21. Brother–sister marriages were permitted among the presumably divine rulers of ancient _____.

22. The ancient Hebrews (*Approved* or *Disapproved*?) of sex within marriage for the purpose of pleasure.

23. The ancient Hebrews, Greeks, and Romans, viewed a wife as the _____ of her husband.

24. The ancient Greeks viewed men and women as being (*Heterosexual, Homosexual,* or *Bisexual*?).

25. Early _____ began to associate sex with sin.

26. _____ culture first produced a detailed sex manual.

27. The ancient Hindus of India created the sex manual known as the *Kama _____*.

28. Although prostitution flourished, sexuality was generally repressed during the _____ era in the West, which was named after the Queen of England.

29. During the 19th century, the Viennese physician, Sigmund _____, wrote that the sex drive was our principal motivating force.

30. Alfred _____ conducted the first large-scale studies of sexual behavior in the United States.

31. The _____ perspective focuses on the roles of genes, hormones, and the nervous system in human sexuality.

32. According to the _____ perspective, the fittest members of a species produce the greatest number of surviving offspring.

33. Sexual behavior among "higher" mammals, such as primates, is (*More* or *Less*?) directly controlled by instinct than it is among the "lower" species, such as birds or fish.

34. Mead and Malinowski are major contributors to the _____ perspective.

35. According to _____ theory, dreams of airplanes, bullets, snakes, sticks, and similar objects may symbolize the male genitals.

36. _____ such as Watson and Skinner emphasized the importance of rewards and punishments in our learning about "proper" sexual behavior.

37. Social-_____ theorists emphasize the importance of acquiring sexual knowledge and skills through observing others.

38. _____ theorists focus on differences in sexuality among the subgroups of a society, as defined, for example, by differences in religion, race/ethnicity, income, age, education, and gender.

Recite

1. What *is* human sexuality?

The term *human sexuality* refers to matters of gender, sexual behavior, sexual feelings, and the biology of sex. Human sexuality concerns the ways in which we experience and express ourselves as sexual beings. The study of human sexuality draws upon the expertise of anthropologists, biologists, medical researchers, sociologists, psychologists, and other scientists.

2. How do our values come into play in determining our sexual choices and behavior?

Along with accurate knowledge about human sexuality, our values inform our sexual decisions.

3. What kinds of value systems do people have?

People tend to draw on value systems including legalism (as in deriving what is right and wrong from within a religious tradition), situational ethics, ethical relativism, hedonism, asceticism, utilitarianism ("the greatest good for the greatest number"), and rationalism.

4. What is critical thinking?

Critical thinking is a skeptical approach to evaluating claims, arguments, and widely held beliefs. Principles of critical thinking include examining definitions of terms, examining the assumptions or premises of arguments, being cautious in drawing conclusions from evidence, considering alternative interpretations of evidence, and avoiding oversimplification and overgeneralization.

5. What is the role of the historical perspective on human sexuality?

History places our sexual behavior in the context of time. History shows little evidence of universal sexual trends. There is evidence of prehistoric worship of generative power in women and men. Jews and Christians have emphasized the role of sex as a means of propagation and have generally restricted sex to the context of family life. The ancient Greeks and Romans dwelled in male-oriented societies that viewed women as chattel. Some Eastern civilizations equated sexual pleasure with religious experience and developed sex manuals. Repressive Victorian sexual attitudes gave way to the sexual revolution of the 1960s and 1970s in the West.

6. What is the role of the biological perspective?

The biological perspective focuses on the role of biological processes, such as genetic, hormonal, and neural factors, in explaining sexual behavior. Knowledge of biology helps us understand how our bodies respond to sexual stimulation and enables us to enhance our sexual health.

Recite

7. What is evolution? How might the sexual behavior of various species, including our own, be influenced by evolutionary forces?

Evolution is the development of species by means of the natural selection of adaptive traits. Organisms tend to inherit traits that allow their ancestors to reach the age of sexual maturity and reproduce. Evolutionary psychology proposes that dispositions toward social behavior (including sexual behavior) that enhance reproductive success—as well as physical traits—may be genetically transmitted.

8. What is the role of the cross-species perspective?

The study of other animal species reveals the variety of sexual behaviors among nonhumans. For example, there are animal analogues of male–male sexual behavior, female–female sexual behavior, oral sex, and foreplay. We find that experience and learning play more important roles in sexuality as we travel up the evolutionary ladder.

9. What is the role of the cross-cultural perspective?

This perspective, like the historical perspective, provides insight into the ways in which cultural beliefs affect sexual behavior and people's sense of morality. Anthropologists observe other cultures firsthand when possible. Cross-cultural evidence challenges the notion of the universality of gender-role stereotypes. All cultures apparently place some limits on sexual freedom, but some are more permissive than others.

10. What do psychological perspectives have to offer?

Psychological perspectives focus on the processes of perception, learning, motivation, emotion, and personality that affect gender and sexual behavior in the individual. Sigmund Freud formulated the theory of psychoanalysis, which proposes that biologically based sex drives come into conflict with social codes. Erogenous zones shift through the process of psychosexual development, and defense mechanisms keep threatening ideas and impulses out of conscious awareness. Learning theorists focus on the roles of rewards, punishments, and observational learning on sexual behavior.

11. What is the role of sociocultural theorists?

Sociocultural theorists focus on differences in sexuality among the groups within a society, as defined, for example, by differences in religion, race, country of origin, socioeconomic status, age, educational level, and gender. Education, for example, appears to be a sexually liberating experience.

Chapter 2

Truth?Fiction?

T / F? You could study the sexual behavior of millions of Americans and still not obtain an accurate picture of the sexual behavior of the general American population.

T / F? Case studies have been carried out on people who are dead.

T / F? Some sex researchers have engaged in "swinging" with the people they have studied.

T / F? Masters and Johnson created a transparent artificial penis containing photographic equipment to study female sexual response.

T / F? People who attend church regularly tend to be more satisfied with their relationships.

T / F? Viagra causes risky sexual behavior.

T / F? Women who suffer sexual problems and dysfunctions after having their clitorises cut out in fundamentalist societies are likely to continue the practice with their own daughters.

T / F? Researchers often publish the names of participants in sex research in professional journals.

Research Methods in Human Sexuality

Preview

Have you ever wondered about questions such as these: Are my sexual interests and behavior patterns unique or shared by many others? Does alcohol stimulate or dampen sexual response? Why do people engage in male–male or female–female sexual behavior? How do people contract AIDS? Does pornography cause rape?

You may have thought of such questions. You may even have expressed opinions on them. But scientists insist that opinions about behavior, including sexual behavior, be supported by evidence. Evidence, in turn, must be based upon careful observations in the laboratory or in the field. In this chapter we explore the methods that scientists use to study human sexuality. We then focus on ethical issues in research on sex.

A Scientific Approach to Human Sexuality

Scientists and researchers who study human sexuality take an **empirical** approach. They base their knowledge on research evidence, rather than on intuition, faith, or superstition. Scientists' and other people's intuitions or religious beliefs may suggest topics to be studied scientifically. Yet once the topics are selected, answers are sought on the basis of the scientific method. *Question: What is the scientific method?*

The Scientific Method

Critical thinking and the scientific approach share the hallmark of skepticism. As skeptics, scientists question prevailing assumptions and theories about sexual behavior. They are willing to dispute the assertions of authority figures such as political and religious leaders—even other scientists. Scientists also recognize that they cannot gain perfect knowledge. One era's "truths" may become another era's ancient myths and fallacies. Scientists are involved in the continuous quest for truth, but they do not see themselves as experiencing revelations or defining final truths.

The *scientific method* is a systematic way of gathering scientific evidence and testing assumptions through research. It has a number of elements:

1. *Formulating a research question.* Does alcohol inspire or impair sexual response? Scientists formulate research questions on the basis of their observations of, or theories about, events or behavior. They then seek answers to such questions by conducting empirical research.

2. *Framing the research question in the form of a hypothesis.* Experiments are usually undertaken with a **hypothesis** in mind—a precise prediction about behavior that is often derived from theory. A hypothesis is tested through research. For instance, a scientist might theorize that alcohol enhances sexual responsiveness either by directly stimulating sexual response or by reducing feelings of guilt associated with sex. He or she might then hypothesize that an intervention (called, in experimental terms, a "treatment"), such as drinking alcohol in a laboratory setting, will lead to heightened sexual arousal in the presence of erotic stimuli (such as sexually explicit films).

3. *Testing the hypothesis.* Scientists then test hypotheses through carefully controlled observation and experimentation. A specific hypothesis about alcohol and sexual arousal—that alcohol either increases or decreases sexual responsiveness— might be tested by administering a certain amount of alcohol to one group of people and then comparing their level of sexual arousal following specific types of sexual stimulation (such as exposure to sexually explicit films) to the level of sexual arousal of another group of people who were shown the films but not given any alcohol.

4. *Drawing conclusions.* Scientists then draw conclusions or inferences about the correctness of their hypotheses, based on their analyses of the results of their studies. If the results of well-designed research studies fail to bear out certain hypotheses, scientists can revise the theories that served as the frameworks for the hypotheses. Research findings often lead scientists to modify their theories, and in turn, generate new hypotheses that can be tested in further research.

Goals of the Science of Human Sexuality

Question: What are the goals of the science of human sexuality? The goals of the science of human sexuality are congruent with those of other sciences: to describe, explain, predict, and control the events (in this case, the sexual behaviors) that are of

Empirical Derived from or based on observation and experimentation.

Hypothesis A precise prediction about behavior that is tested through research.

Kissing Gouramis *These fish obtain their moniker from pressing their open mouths against one another. Yet if the word* kissing *is meant to imply affection, think again. Prolonged observations of the fish suggest "kissing" is more likely to be a test of strength. Describing the behavior of the fish as "kissing" confuses inference (that is, drawing conclusions) with description. One of the challenges to scientists is to separate description from inference.*

interest. Description is a basic goal of science. Before we can understand sexual behavior, we must be able to describe it. Scientists attempt to be clear, unbiased, and precise in their descriptions of events and behavior. The scientific approach to human sexuality describes sexual behavior through techniques as varied as the field study, the survey, the individual case study, and the laboratory experiment.

To underscore the importance of the need for unbiased description, consider the name of a tropical fish that will be familiar to many readers: the kissing gourami. These small, flat fish—particularly males—press their open mouths against one another. Yet the term *kissing gourami* may be a misnomer if it is meant to imply affection. Prolonged observations of the fish suggest that it is more likely that kissing in gouramis is a test of strength. The error in describing the behavior of gouramis as "kissing" involves confusing **inference** with description. It is, in fact, an **anthropomorphic** inference; it involves applying human standards to explain animal behavior. One of the great challenges to scientists is the separation of description from inference.

Inference, like description, is crucial to science. Inference allows us to move from observations or descriptions of particular events or behavior to general principles that can be woven into models and theories that help explain them, such as the psychoanalytic and learning theories or models.

Researchers attempt to relate their observations to other factors, or **variables**, that can help explain them. For example, researchers may attempt to explain variations in the frequency of coitus by relating—or *correlating*—coitus with **demographic** variables such as age, religious or social background, or cultural expectations. The variables that are commonly used to explain sexual behavior include biological (age, health), psychological (anxieties, skills), and sociological (educational level, socioeconomic status, ethnicity) ones. Explanations of behavior can involve reference to many variables.

Theories provide frameworks within which scientists can explain what they observe and make predictions. Theories must allow us to make predictions. One test of the soundness of psychoanalytic and learning theories is whether or not they allow us to predict behavior. Sex researchers study factors that may predict various types of sexual behavior. Some researchers, for example, have examined childhood interests and behavior patterns that may predict the development of a gay male or lesbian sexual orientation. Others have explored factors, such as the age at which dating begins and the quality of the relationships between teens and their parents, that may predict the likelihood of premarital intercourse during adolescence.

The concept of "controlling" human behavior does not mean coercing people to do the bidding of others. Rather, it means drawing upon scientific knowledge to help people create their own goals and marshal their resources to meet them. Reputable scientists are held to ethical and professional standards that safeguard the rights of participants in research.

The science of human sexuality does not tell people how they *ought* to behave. Rather, it furnishes information that people may use to help themselves or others make decisions. For instance, the science of human sexuality provides information that increases the chances that a couple who are having difficulty becoming pregnant will be able to conceive. At the same time, it develops and evaluates means of birth control that can be used to help couples regulate their reproductive choices. "Control" also takes the form of enabling couples to give and receive more sexual pleasure, of enhancing fetal health, and of preventing and curing sexually transmitted infections.

Inference Conclusion or opinion.

Anthropomorphism The attributing of human characteristics to an animal.

Variables Quantities or qualities that vary or may vary.

Demographic Concerning the vital statistics (race, gender, age, etc.) of human populations.

Review: A Scientific Approach to Human Sexuality

Reflect

Does it seem appropriate to you to study human sexual behavior scientifically? Why or why not?

Critical Thinking

Does the science of human sexuality aim to tell people how they *ought* to behave? Why or why not?

1. Scientists and researchers who study human sexuality base their knowledge on _____ rather than intuition, faith, or superstition.

2. The _____ method is a systematic way of gathering scientific evidence and testing assumptions.

3. The scientific method has four elements: formulating a research question, framing the question as a(n) _____,

testing the hypothesis, and drawing conclusions.

4. The goals of the science of human sexuality are to describe, explain, _____, and control the behaviors that are of interest.

5. _____ provide frameworks within which scientists can explain what they observe and make predictions.

Let us now examine the ways in which scientists study human sexuality. The first thing scientists do is to identify *whom* or *what* they will study, which brings us to the topic of sampling.

Populations and Samples: Representing the World of Diversity

Researchers undertake to learn about populations. *Question: What is a population?* **Populations** are complete groups of people or animals. Many researchers have attempted to learn about people in the United States, for example. Other researchers may identify American adults or American adolescents as their population. Still other researchers attempt to compare the sexual behavior of African Americans to that of Latino and Latina Americans and other Americans. These are termed the *populations of interest*, or *target populations*. These target populations are all sizable. It would be expensive, difficult, and, in fact, all but impossible to study every individual in them.

Because of the impossibility of studying all members of a population, scientists select individuals from the population and study them. *Question: What is a sample?* The individuals who participate in research are said to compose a **sample**. However, we cannot truly learn about the population of interest unless the sample *represents* that population. If we wished to study the sexual behavior of Asian Americans, our population would consist of *all* Asian Americans. If we used only Asian American college students as our sample, we could not **generalize** our findings to all Asian Americans.

Including everyone in the United States in a study of sexual behavior would be impossible. We cannot even find all people in the United States when we conduct the census each decade. Sex research would undoubtedly cause many more people to refuse to participate than would a simple counting of noses. Sampling a part of a target population makes research practical and possible. *Question: What sampling methods do researchers use to represent populations?*

Sampling Methods

Now and then magazine editors boast that they have surveyed samples of 20,000 or 30,000 readers, but size alone does not mean that a sample is representative.

Populations and Samples To what populations do you belong? College students? Returning students? What of your gender? What about your ethnic background? How do researchers obtain samples that represent populations such as these? What problems do they encounter in attempting to do so?

Population A complete group of organisms or events.

Sample Part of a population.

Generalize To go from the particular to the general.

Truth?Fiction?
Revisited

It is true that you could study the sexual behavior of millions of Americans and still not obtain an accurate picture of the sexual behavior of the general American population. Researchers need to obtain samples that represent the target population.

Random sample
A sample in which every member of a population has an equal chance of participating.

Stratified random sample A random sample in which known subgroups in a population are represented in proportion to their numbers in the population.

Volunteer bias A slanting of research data that is caused by the characteristics of individuals who volunteer to participate, such as willingness to discuss intimate behavior.

Psychology Today and *Playboy* regularly poll readers, but their readers do not represent the general population. Readers of *Psychology Today* are "biased" in that they tend to be better educated and more liberal than the population at large. Readers of *Playboy* are "biased" in that they are seeking sexual stimulation but not explicit pornography.

One way of acquiring a representative sample is through random sampling. A **random sample** is one in which every member of the target population has an equal chance of participating. In a **stratified random sample**, known subgroups of a population are represented in proportion to their numbers in the population. For instance, about 13% of the American population is African American. Researchers could therefore decide that 13% of their sample must be African American if they are to represent all people in the United States. The randomness of the sample would be preserved because the members of the subgroups would be selected randomly from their particular subgroups.

Random samples can be hard to come by, especially when it comes to asking people about their sexual attitudes or behavior. For instance, sexual research is almost invariably conducted with people who volunteer to participate. Volunteers tend to differ from people who refuse to participate (Quartaro & Spier, 2002; Zelenski et al., 2003). For example, volunteers tend to be more open about their sexuality than the general population. They may even tend to exaggerate behaviors that others might consider deviant or abnormal.

One study attempted to assess the incidence of male–male sexual behavior that placed Hong Kong men at risk for contracting HIV, the virus that causes AIDS (for example, anal intercourse without use of condoms), by means of random telephone numbers generated by a computer (Lau et al., 2002). Eighty-five men of 2,074 men contacted (4%) admitted to having sex with other men and described their sexual behavior. But how can we determine whether there were many others who had sex with men but denied doing so? How can we know whether the men who admitted to male–male sexual behavior accurately described their contacts? Another study assessed the usefulness of brief telephone interviews in a Boston neighborhood believed to have many lesbian residents (Meyer et al., 2002). There was a high (94%!) level of cooperation with the researchers, and 14% of respondents identified themselves as lesbians. But did every one of the 94% who cooperated tell the truth? And what can we conclude about the incidence of a lesbian sexual orientation in the general population from such a survey?

The problem of a **volunteer bias** is a thorny one for sex researchers, because the refusal of people who have been randomly selected to participate in the survey can ruin the representativeness of the sample. Because it would be unethical to coerce people to participate in a study on sexual behavior (or any other type of study), researchers must use samples of volunteers, rather than true random samples. A low response rate to a voluntary survey is an indication that the responses do not represent the people to whom the survey was distributed.

In some cases, samples are samples of convenience. They consist of individuals who happen to be available to the researcher and who share some characteristics with the target population, perhaps religious background or sexual orientation. Still, they do not truly represent the target group. Convenience samples often consist of European American, middle-class college students who volunteer for studies conducted at their schools. They may not be (and probably are not) representative of students in general.

Review: Populations and Samples: Representing the World of Diversity

Reflect

How would you define yourself? What population or populations would you represent if you were recruited for a study on human sexuality?

CriticalThinking

How would you define a "scientific sample" of people?

6. _____ are complete groups of people or animals.

7. A(n) _____ is a subgroup of a population that is used in research.

8. Samples should be drawn so that they _____ populations.

9. In a(n) _____ sample, every member of the target population has an equal chance of participating.

10. In a(n) _____ random sample, subgroups of a population are represented in proportion to their numbers in the population.

11. Samples of _____ consist of individuals who are available to the researcher.

Methods of Observation

Once scientists have chosen those they will study, they observe them. In this section, we consider several methods of observation: the case-study method, the survey method, naturalistic observation, ethnographic observation, participant observation, and laboratory observation.

The Case-Study Method

Question: What is a case study? A **case study** is a carefully drawn, in-depth biography of an individual or a small group. The focus is on understanding one or several individuals as fully as possible by unraveling the interplay of various factors in their backgrounds. In most case studies, the researcher comes to know the individual or group through interviews or other contacts conducted over a prolonged period of time. The interviewing pattern tends to build upon itself with a good deal of freedom, as opposed to the one-shot, standardized set of questions used in survey questionnaires.

Researchers may also conduct case studies by interviewing people who have known the individuals or by examining public records. Sigmund Freud, for example, drew upon historical records in his case study of the Renaissance inventor and painter Leonardo da Vinci. Freud concluded that Leonardo's artistic productions represented the sublimating, or channeling, of male–male sexual impulses.

Reports of innovative treatments for sexual dysfunctions often appear as detailed case studies. A clinician may report the background of the client in depth, describe the treatment, the apparent outcomes, and suggest factors that might have contributed to the treatment's success or failure. In writing a treatment case study, the therapist attempts to provide information that may be of help to therapists who treat clients with similar problems. Case studies or "multiple case studies" (reports concerning a few individuals) that hold promise may be subjected to controlled investigation—ideally, to experimental studies involving treatment and control groups.

Despite the richness of material that may be derived from case studies, they are not as rigorous a research design as an experiment. People often have gaps in memory, especially concerning childhood events. There is also the potential of observer

Truth?Fiction?
Revisited

It is true that case studies have been carried out on people who are dead. Such case studies rely on historic records rather than interviews with the individuals themselves or their contemporaries.

Case study A carefully drawn, in-depth biography of an individual or a small group of individuals that may be obtained through interviews, questionnaires, and historical records.

The Survey Method *What kinds of surveys are there? How do researchers attempt to encourage people to participate? How do gaps in memory, volunteer bias, and social desirability distort the results of surveys?*

Survey A detailed study of a sample obtained by means such as interviews and questionnaires.

bias; that is, clinicians and interviewers may unintentionally guide people into saying what they expect to hear. Researchers may even inadvertently color people's reports when they jot them down—shape them subtly in ways that reflect their own views.

The Survey Method

Wardell B. Pomeroy, one of Alfred Kinsey's associates in the 1940's, was interviewing a man about his first ejaculation. He asked, "When?" The man answered, "Fourteen." Pomeroy then asked, "How?" and was surprised to hear: "With a horse."

In his biography, *Sex the Measure of All Things: A Life of Alfred C. Kinsey,* Jonathan Gathorne-Hardy records what happened next. Pomeroy asked the man, "How often were you having intercourse with animals at 14?"

The man looked confused and said, "Well, yes, it is true I had intercourse with a pony at 14." Pomeroy, it turned out, had misheard the man's previous answer. It was "with whores," not "with a horse." So the man was stunned that Pomeroy had had the insight to ask him the horse question out of the blue. (Boxer, 2000)

The question was asked during the Kinsey surveys of sexual behavior in the United States—the best known surveys in the history of surveying sexual behavior. ***Question: What is the survey method?***

The **survey** method typically gathers information about behavior through questionnaires or interviews. Researchers may interview or administer questionnaires to thousands of people from particular population groups to learn about their sexual behavior and attitudes. Interviews such as those used by Kinsey and his colleagues (1948, 1953) have the advantages of face-to-face contact and of giving the interviewer the opportunity to *probe*—that is, to follow up on answers that seem to lead toward useful information. A skilled interviewer may be able to set a respondent at ease and establish a sense of trust or *rapport* that encourages self-disclosure. (Unskilled interviewing may cause respondents to conceal information.)

Questionnaires are less expensive than interviews. The major expenses in using questionnaires involve printing and distribution or posting them on a Web site. Questionnaires can be administered to many people simultaneously. Respondents can return them unsigned, so that they are anonymous. Anonymity may encourage the disclosure of intimate information. Questionnaires, of course, can be used only by people who can read and record their responses. Interviews can be used even with people who cannot read or write. But interviewers must be trained and paid for their time.

Some of the major surveys described in this book were conducted by Kinsey and his colleagues (1948, 1953), the University of Chicago group (Laumann et al., 1994), and the Kaiser Family Foundation (2003). The book also discusses surveys conducted by popular magazines such as *Elle.* By and large, these surveys have reported the incidence and frequency of sexual activities among men and women; both married and single; male–female, male–male, and female–female sexual activity; and the sexual behavior of adolescents, adults, and older people.

Many of these surveys have *something* to offer to our understanding of human sexuality, but none represents the American population at large. Most people consider their sexuality to be among the most intimate, *private* aspects of their lives. People who willingly agree to be polled on political matters may resist participation in surveys about their sexual behavior. It is thus difficult, if not impossible, for researchers to recruit a truly representative sample of the population. Even the best surveys provide, at best, an approximation of sexual attitudes, beliefs, and behaviors.

Let us review the methods of some surveys of human sexuality, beginning with those used by Kinsey and his colleagues.

The Kinsey Reports Kinsey and his colleagues (1948, 1953) interviewed 5,300 males and 5,940 females in the United States between 1938 and 1949. They asked questions on various sexual experiences, including masturbation, oral sex, and coitus that occurred before, during, and outside of marriage. Kinsey obviously could not use direct observational methods, such as sending his researchers to peer through bedroom windows. Kinsey chose not to try to obtain a random sample. He believed that a high refusal rate would wreck the chances of accurately representing the general population. Instead, he used *group sampling*. He recruited participants from the organizations and community groups to which they belonged, such as college fraternities and sororities. He contacted representatives of groups in diverse communities and tried to persuade them to secure the cooperation of fellow group members. If he showed these individuals that they would not be subjected to embarrassment or discomfort, Kinsey hoped that they would persuade other members to participate. In some cases he obtained the full participation of a group.

Still, Kinsey's samples did not represent the general population. People of color, people in rural areas, older people, the poor, and Catholics and Jews were all underrepresented in his samples. Statisticians who have reviewed Kinsey's methods have concluded that there were systematic biases in his sampling methods (Barth et al., 2002; Sharp, 2002). It is thus unlikely that Kinsey's results accurately mirrored the U.S. population at the time. In Chapter 10 we shall see that his estimate that 37% of the male population had reached orgasm at least once through male–male sexual activity was probably too high. But the *relationships* Kinsey uncovered, such as the positive link between level of education and participation in oral sex, may be more generalizable.

Kinsey took certain measures to obtain honest answers. Participants were assured of the confidentiality of their records. Kinsey's interviewers were trained to conduct the interviews in a matter-of-fact style and to reassure participants that they were not passing judgment on them. Interviewers were trained not to show emotional reactions that respondents could interpret as disapproval (they held a "calm and steady eye" and tone of voice). On the other hand, all of Kinsey's interviewers were men. Women respondents might have felt more free to open up to female interviewers.

Kinsey checked the **reliability** of his data by reexamining hundreds of interviewees after 18 months or more had passed. Their reports of the **incidence** of sexual activities (for example, whether or not they had ever engaged in premarital or extramarital coitus) were highly consistent, but reports of the **frequency** of sexual activities (such as the number of times one has masturbated to orgasm, or the frequency of coitus) were less consistent. People seem to find it more difficult to estimate the frequencies of their activities than to answer whether or not they have ever engaged in them.

Kinsey knew that consistency of responses across time did not guarantee **validity**. That is, repeat interviews did not show whether the reported behaviors actually took place as described. He could not validate self-reports directly, as one might validate reports that one is drug-free by urine analysis. He had to use indirect means to validate the data such as comparing the reports of husbands and wives. There was high consistency in the reports of 706 pairs of spouses, suggesting that their self-reports were accurate.

The NHSLS Study The National Health and Social Life Survey was intended to provide general information about sexual behavior in the United States and also specific information that might be used to predict and prevent the spread of AIDS. It was

Reliability The consistency or accuracy of a measure.

Incidence A measure of the occurrence or the degree of occurrence of an event.

Frequency The number of times an action is repeated within a given period.

Validity With respect to tests, the degree to which a particular test measures the constructs or traits it purports to measure.

conducted by Edward O. Laumann of the University of Chicago and three colleagues—John H. Gagnon, Robert T. Michael, and Stuart Michaels—in the 1990s and published as *The Social Organization of Sexuality: Sexual Practices in the United States* in 1994. A companion volume authored by Michael, Gagnon, Laumann, and Gina Kolata—a *New York Times* science reporter—was also published: *Sex in America: A Definitive Survey*. *Sex in America* is a bit less technical in presentation but offers some interesting data not found in the other version. The NHSLS study was to be originally supported by government funds, but Republican Senator Jesse Helms of North Carolina blocked federal financing on the grounds that it was inappropriate for the government to be supporting sex research (Bronner, 1998). The research team therefore obtained private funding but had to cut back the scope of the project.

The sample included 3,432 people. Of this number, 3,159 were drawn from English-speaking adults living in households (not dormitories, prisons, and so forth), ages 18 to 59. The other 273 were purposely obtained by oversampling African American and Latino and Latina American households, so that more information could be obtained about these ethnic groups. Although the sample probably represents the overall U.S. population quite well (or at least those of ages 18 to 59), there may be too few Asian Americans, Native Americans, and Jews to offer much information about these groups.

The researchers identified samples of households in geographic areas—by addresses, not names. They sent a letter to each household, describing the purpose and methods of the study, and an interviewer visited each household one week later. The people targeted were assured that the purposes of the study were important and that the identities of participants would be kept confidential. Incentives of up to $100 were offered for cooperating. A high completion rate of close to 80% was obtained in this way. All in all, the NHSLS study could be the only one since Kinsey's day that offers a reasonably accurate picture of the sexual practices of the general population of the United States.

Two of the NHSLS researchers and French colleagues (Gagnon et al., 2001) compared the results of the NHSLS study with a national survey of sexual behavior among adults aged 18 to 59 in France. They found that the sexual behavior of couples who were living together was quite similar in both countries. However, despite the French reputation of being sexually liberal, the French were more likely to be monogamous than Americans. On the other hand, gender differences were greater in the United States than in France, especially among older American women, who were more likely than their French counterparts to report no sexual partners.

The Playboy Foundation Survey The Playboy Foundation commissioned a survey of sexual practices in the 1970s, which was reported in Morton Hunt's 1974 book, *Sexual Behavior in the 1970's*. The Playboy or Hunt survey sought to examine the changes in American sexual behavior between Kinsey's day and the early 1970s.

The Playboy sample was drawn randomly from phone book listings in 24 American cities. People were asked to participate in small group discussions focusing on trends in sexual practices in the United States. Hunt argued that his final sample of 2,026 participants was stratified properly as to the ages and races of urban residents across a diverse sample of American cities, but many groups such as rural people and inmates of prisons and mental hospitals were grossly underrepresented. But the major flaw in the method is volunteer bias; 80% of the people contacted refused to participate. It is logical to assume that the 20% who did participate were more open and frank about sexual issues than the population at large.

The Magazine Surveys Major readership surveys have also been conducted by popular magazines, such as *Psychology Today*, *Redbook*, *Ladies' Home Journal*, and

Cosmopolitan. Although these surveys attain large samples (up to 100,000 people or more), their sampling techniques are unscientific and biased. Each sample represents, at best, the readers of the magazine in which the questionnaire appears. Moreover, we learn only about readers who volunteer to respond to these questionnaires, which is a small percentage of the overall readership. Finally, readers of these magazines are wealthier than the public at large, and readers of *Cosmopolitan, Psychology Today,* and even *Redbook* tend to be more liberal. The samples only represent readers who are willing to complete the surveys.

Surveys of Specific Populations The Kinsey and NHSLS studies were broad based. They queried men and women from different localities, socioeconomic strata, and age groups. Some researchers have focused their efforts on particular populations, such as adolescents, older people, people from particular racial/ethnic groups, and gay men and lesbians.

In recent years, large-scale studies in the United States and other countries have been conducted to acquire information concerning sexual practices that might prove useful in the fight against AIDS. In the United States, for example, researchers from the Battelle Memorial Institute of Seattle interviewed a nationally representative sample of 3,321 men between the ages of 20 and 39 in order to determine the prevalence of unsafe sexual practices among young adult men (Billy et al., 1993; Tanfer et al., 1993).

In 1978 and 1981 the Indiana University Institute for Sex Research, also called the Kinsey Institute, reported the results of a survey of 979 gay people from the San Francisco area and a reference group of 477 people matched for age, race, and educational and occupational achievements (Bell & Weinberg, 1978; Bell et al., 1981). In their book, *Homosexualities,* researchers Alan Bell and Martin Weinberg (1978) recognized that their findings could not necessarily be extended to gay people who lived in other cities or sections of the country. Indeed, they acknowledged that their sample might not even represent gay people in San Francisco. It consisted of people who had "come out of the closet" to join gay rights organizations, who attended gay bars and baths, and so forth. Nevertheless, these reports have provided wide-ranging information on parent–child relationships and sexual orientation and on the diversity of lifestyles among gay people (see Chapter 10).

Questions abound about the sexual behavior of Native Americans and African Americans. Kinsey did not survey Native Americans, and the number of Native Americans in the NHSLS study was too small to draw many conclusions. Kinsey obtained some data on the sexual behavior of African Americans but did not report it in his surveys because African Americans were underrepresented in his samples. However, more recent studies by Gail Wyatt and the NHSLS group have reported some useful information.

UCLA researcher Gail Wyatt and her colleagues (Wyatt, 1985, 1989; Wyatt et al., 1988a, 1988b) examined the sexual behavior of a sample of 122 European American and 126 African American women in Los Angeles County. The women ranged in age from 18 to 36 years. Women in the study were sampled randomly from telephone listings. People who agreed to participate were selected to balance the sample with respect to demographic characteristics such as age, education, number of children, and marital status. One in three prospective participants refused to cooperate. The participants were interviewed in Kinsey-style, face-to-face interviews that lasted three to eight hours.

One of the striking differences between Kinsey's data and Wyatt's was that women in her 1980s sample—African American and European American—engaged in intercourse for the first time at earlier ages than was the case in Kinsey's sample.

A Tale of Two Surveys

You might think that with everything we now know about the need for representative samples of populations and sampling techniques, surveys conducted in the new millennium would be flawless in their methodology. You would be wrong. What we find is a combination of carefully conducted studies reported in scientific journals, and a host of "pop" studies reported in magazines and on Web sites. Let us have a look at two studies reported in 2003—one that was designed to add to our scientific knowledge and one that was apparently intended to sell magazines.

THE NATIONAL SURVEY OF ADOLESCENTS AND YOUNG ADULTS

The Kaiser Family Foundation (2003) made every effort to obtain a sizeable nationally representative sample of adolescents and young adults, ages 13 to 24. They selected telephone numbers at random and conducted telephone interviews with 1,854 young people either in English or Spanish, depending on the preferences of the respondent. They purposefully oversampled people in ethnic minority groups—African Americans, Latino and Latina Americans, and Asian Americans—because most studies do not generate enough information about these groups. Parents provided permission to interview minors (adolescents under the age of 18). The response rate was 55%, which may not sound overwhelming, but compare it with the 20% response rate obtained by Morton Hunt for the Playboy Foundation.

We will be reporting results of this survey throughout the text, especially comparing the sexual attitudes and behaviors of young people from diverse ethnic groups. But let us note some of the major findings here:

- Four out of five respondents reported that they were concerned about how issues of sexual health might affect them.
- About one adolescent in three reports having been pressured to have sex—exceeded only by the number who report being pressured to drink alcohol.
- Sixty percent of the sample agreed with the statement that "Waiting to have sex is a nice idea but nobody really does."
- One adolescent in three has engaged in oral sex, sometimes to avoid intercourse. By and large adolescents and young adults underestimate the risk of contracting a sexually transmitted infection through oral sex.
- Although the rate of teenage pregnancy has been declining in recent years, 70% of sexually active young adults and 40% of sexually active adolescents report that they or their partner had a pregnancy test.
- Four out of five adolescents reported that adolescents tend to drink or use drugs before sex. Many adolescents and young adults reported doing more than they had planned to do under the influence of alcohol or drugs, including engaging in unprotected sex (that is, sex without using a condom).

Kinsey reported that by the age of 20, about one in five women had engaged in premarital coitus. By contrast, Wyatt reported that 98% of the people in her study (African American and European American) had experienced premarital intercourse by that age (Wyatt, 1989). When social class differences were taken into consideration, the ages of first intercourse for African American and European American women in Wyatt's sample were quite similar.

Wyatt's research, of course, was limited to Los Angeles and cannot be said to represent the general U.S. population. Kinsey's sample was also geographically skewed. Kinsey overrepresented the northeastern United States, although he included respondents from other regions.

Limitations of the Survey Method   One limitation of surveys involves the fact that they are self-reports of respondents' behaviors. But self-reports are subject to inaccuracies or biases because of factors such as faulty memory; tendencies to distort or conceal information because of embarrassment, shame, or guilt; or attempts to present a socially favorable image of oneself. People may not recall the age at which they first engaged in petting or masturbated to orgasm. People may have difficulty recall-

- Many adolescents do not know the details as to how many STIs are transmitted and the health problems caused by these STIs.

- About 70% of adolescents erroneously believe that other forms of contraception provide better protection against STIs than condoms do.

- Although 90% of adolescents say that using condoms is a sign of respect and caring for one's partner, about half are reluctant to discuss condoms with their partners, fearing, for example, that raising the subject would be embarrassing or suggest that one is suspicious of one's partner's sexual history.

- More than three adolescents and young adults out of four say they would like to have more information about STIs.

THE *ELLE*/MSNBC.COM SEX & BODY IMAGE SURVEY

In the same year, *Elle* magazine (2003) reported the results of a survey conducted on its Web site. The magazine boasted more than 30 times the number of respondents obtained in the National Survey of Adolescents and Young Adults—nearly 60,000 people. However, the National Survey of Adolescents and Young Adults contacted people pretty much at random across the country, and 55% of those contacted participated. *Elle,* which publishes in 35 countries, contacted mainly its readership, a group of perhaps millions of fashion-conscious young adults. Moreover, those who participated were computer-savvy enough to navigate their

way to the specified Web site. Sixty thousand is not a high percentage of one or two million or more.

What are some of the findings of the *Elle* survey? First of all, about 80% of the respondents said that their faces were "nice" or "very attractive." Even more telling, 41% of the women and 52% of the men characterized their bodies as "good" or "great"—this in a day and age in which most surveys tell us that the great majority of women in our culture believe that they are too heavy.

We could go on, but why bother? It is obvious that the *Elle* survey was completed by people who are not only fashion-conscious but also body-conscious. They do not represent the people in our culture at large (poor pun?), and they probably do not even represent the entire readership of *Elle.* There is that old bugaboo of volunteer bias: Given that the majority of the respondents also say that they prefer making love with the lights on, they probably also believe that they have (literally) less to hide than most of us.

Edward Laumann and his colleagues (1994), who labored so hard to obtain a nationally representative example for the NHSLS study, are particularly harsh in their judgment of such surveys. They write that "such studies, in sum, produce junk statistics of no value whatsoever in making valid and reliable population projections" (p. 45). What is there to add?

Magazine Surveys *Magazines like* Elle *have recruited many thousands of subjects to respond to their questionnaires. Whom do these individuals represent?*

ing or calculating the frequencies of certain behaviors, such as the weekly frequency of marital intercourse. Survey data may also be drawn from haphazard or nonrepresentative samples and thus not represent the target population.

Participants in surveys of sexual behavior may feel pressured to answer questions in the direction of **social desirability**. Some respondents, that is, try to ingratiate themselves with their interviewers by offering what they believe to be socially desirable answers. Some people may not divulge sensitive information for fear of disapproval by the interviewer. Others may fear criminal prosecution. Even though interviewers may insist that participants will remain anonymous, respondents may fear that their identities may be uncovered someday. You can assess your own tendency to provide socially desirable answers by taking the nearby questionnaire.

For some respondents, exaggeration is the "socially desirable" response. In our culture men may tend to exaggerate their sexual exploits. Women may tend to play them down (Ferraro, 2004; Nanda & Warms, 2004). Males and "liberated" females may fear that the interviewer will think less of them for reporting only infrequent sexual contacts or for sounding too "straight." Some respondents falsify their attitudes

Social desirability
A response bias to a questionnaire or interview in which the person provides a socially acceptable response.

Self-Assessment

Would You Tell an Interviewer the Truth on a Survey about Your Sexual Behavior? The Social-Desirability Scale

Researchers into human sexuality frequently encounter the problem of social desirability in their subjects. That is, many people being interviewed tell the researcher what they think he or she wants to hear, rather than divulge the truth about their sexual attitudes and behavior. The reason is often to earn the approval of the researcher. The tendency to respond in what people believe to be the socially desirable direction distorts the accuracy of the results in the case-study and survey methods.

What about you? Would you provide an interviewer with honest answers about your sexual attitudes and behaviors, or would you misrepresent your beliefs and behaviors to earn his or her approval?

You can complete the Social-Desirability Scale devised by Crowne and Marlowe to gain insight into whether you have a tendency to produce socially desirable responses.

Directions: Read each item and decide whether it is true (T) or false (F) for you. Try to work rapidly and answer each question by circling the T or the F. Then turn to the scoring key in the appendix to interpret your answers.

T F 1. Before voting I thoroughly investigate the qualifications of all the candidates.

T F 2. I never hesitate to go out of my way to help someone in trouble.

T F 3. It is sometimes hard for me to go on with my work if I am not encouraged.

T F 4. I have never intensely disliked anyone.

T F 5. On occasions I have had doubts about my ability to succeed in life.

T F 6. I sometimes feel resentful when I don't get my way.

T F 7. I am always careful about my manner of dress.

T F 8. My table manners at home are as good as when I eat out in a restaurant.

T F 9. If I could get into a movie without paying and be sure I was not seen, I would probably do it.

and exaggerate the bizarreness of their behavior, perhaps to draw attention to themselves, perhaps to foul up the results.

Because many people refuse to participate in surveys, samples are biased by large numbers of volunteers. Volunteers tend to be more sexually permissive and liberal-minded than nonvolunteers. The results of a survey based on a volunteer sample thus may not accurately reflect the population at large.

You might think that these problems would render the survey method useless as a means of learning about human sexuality. Actually, carefully conceived and executed surveys offer many insights into sexual attitudes and practices. In many cases they are the only available means. Before Kinsey we had little information about the sexual practices of people in our society.

The Naturalistic-Observation Method

Question: What is the naturalistic-observation method? In **naturalistic observation**, also called the *field study,* scientists directly observe the behavior of animals and humans where it happens. Anthropologists, for example, have lived among preliterate societies and reported on their social and sexual customs. Other disciplines, too, have adopted methods of naturalistic observation in their research on human sexuality. Sociologists have observed the street life of prostitutes. Psychologists have observed patterns of nonverbal communication and body language between couples in dating situations.

Naturalistic observation A method in which organisms are observed in their natural environments.

T F 10. On a few occasions, I have given up something because I thought too little of my ability.

T F 11. I like to gossip at times.

T F 12. There have been times when I felt like rebelling against people in authority even though I knew they were right.

T F 13. No matter who I'm talking to, I'm always a good listener.

T F 14. I can remember "playing sick" to get out of something.

T F 15. There have been occasions when I have taken advantage of someone.

T F 16. I'm always willing to admit it when I make a mistake.

T F 17. I always try to practice what I preach.

T F 18. I don't find it particularly difficult to get along with loudmouthed, obnoxious people.

T F 19. I sometimes try to get even rather than forgive and forget.

T F 20. When I don't know something I don't mind at all admitting it.

T F 21. I am always courteous, even to people who are disagreeable.

T F 22. At times I have really insisted on having things my own way.

T F 23. There have been occasions when I felt like smashing things.

T F 24. I would never think of letting someone else be punished for my wrong-doings.

T F 25. I never resent being asked to return a favor.

T F 26. I have never been irked when people expressed ideas very different from my own.

T F 27. I never make a long trip without checking the safety of my car.

T F 28. There have been times when I was quite jealous of the good fortune of others.

I F 29. I have almost never felt the urge to tell someone off.

T F 30. I am sometimes irritated by people who ask favors of me.

T F 31. I have never felt that I was punished without cause.

T F 32. I sometimes think when people have a misfortune they only got what they deserved.

T F 33. I have never deliberately said something that hurt someone's feelings.

Source: D. P. Crowne and D. A. Marlowe, A new scale of social desirability independent of pathology, *Journal of Consulting Psychology* 24 (1960): 351. Copyright 1960 by the American Psychological Association. Reprinted by permission.

Scientists take precautions to keep their naturalistic observations *unobtrusive.* They try not to influence the behavior of the individuals they study. Over the years, naturalistic observers have been placed in ethical dilemmas. They have allowed sick or injured animals to die, rather than intervene, when medical assistance could have saved them. They have allowed substance abuse and illicit sexual behavior to go unreported to authorities. The ethical trade-off is that unobtrusive observation may yield data that will benefit large numbers of people—the greatest good for the greatest number.

The Ethnographic-Observation Method

Question: What is the ethnographic-observation method? **Ethnographic** research provides us with data concerning sexual behaviors and customs that occur among various ethnic groups—those that vary widely across cultures and those that are limited to one or few cultures. Anthropologists are the specialists who typically engage in ethnographic research. They have lived among societies of people in the four corners of the earth in order to observe and study human diversity. Margaret Mead (1935) reported on the social and sexual customs of various peoples of New Guinea. Bronislaw Malinowski (1929) studied the Trobriand islanders, among other peoples. Ford and Beach's (1951) account of sexual practices around the world and in non-human species remains to this date a classic study of cross-cultural and cross-species comparisons. Ethnographers are trained to be keen observers, but direct observation

Ethnography The branch of anthropology that deals descriptively with specific cultures, especially preliterate societies.

Physiological Measures of Sexual Arousal

A Closer Look

Scientific studies depend on the ability to measure the events of interest. Sexual arousal may be measured by different means, such as self-report and physiological measures. Self-report measures of sexual arousal are considered *subjective*. They ask people to give their impressions of the level of their sexual arousal at a given time, such as by circling their response on a ten-point scale that ranges from zero, "not at all aroused," to ten, "extremely aroused." Physiological devices measure the degree of vasocongestion that builds up in the genitals during sexual arousal. (Vasocongestion—that is, congestion with blood—leads to erection in men

and vaginal lubrication in women.) In men, vasocongestion is frequently measured by a **penile strain gauge**. This device is worn under the man's clothing. It is fitted around the penis and measures his erectile response by recording changes in the circumference of the penis. The device is sensitive to small changes in circumference that may not be noticed (and thus not reported) by the man.

Physiological measurement of sexual arousal in women is most often accomplished by means of a **vaginal photoplethysmograph**. The vaginal photoplethysmograph is a tampon-shaped probe with a light and a photocell in its

tip. It is inserted in the vagina and indicates the level of blood congestion by means of measuring the amount of light reflected from the vaginal walls. The more light that is absorbed by the vaginal walls, the less that is reflected. Less reflected light indicates greater vasocongestion.

Sex researchers sometimes measure sexual arousal in response to stimuli such as erotic films or audiotaped dramatizations of erotic scenes. What happens when physiological devices give a different impression of sexual arousal than those offered by self-report? Objectively (physiologically) measured sexual arousal does not always agree with subjective

Truth?Fiction?
Revisited

It is true that some sex researchers have engaged in "swinging" with the people they studied.

It is true that Masters and Johnson created a transparent artificial penis ("coition machine") containing photographic equipment to study female sexual response. It was perhaps their most controversial device.

has its limits in the study of sexual behavior. Sexual activities are most commonly performed away from the watchful eyes of others, especially from those of visitors from other cultures. Ethnographers may thus have to rely on methods such as personal interviewing to learn more about sexual customs.

The ethnographer who studies a particular culture or subgroup within a culture tries not to alter the behavior of the members of the group by focusing attention on some facets of their behavior. Falling prey to social desirability, some people may "straighten out their act" while the ethnographer is present. Other people may try to impress the ethnographer by acting in ways that are more aggressive or sexually provocative than usual. In either case, people supply distorted or biased information.

The Participant-Observation Method

Question: What is participant observation? In **participant observation**, investigators learn about people's behavior by directly interacting with them. Participant observation has been used in studies of male–male sexual behavior and mate-swapping. In effect, participation has been the "price of admission" for observation. In some cases, researchers have engaged in coitus with participants during "swinging parties," which raises questions as to what is permissible "for the sake of science."

The Laboratory-Observation Method

Question: What is the laboratory-observation method? Rather than study individuals in their natural settings, the laboratory-observation method brings them into the laboratory, where their behavior can be more carefully monitored.

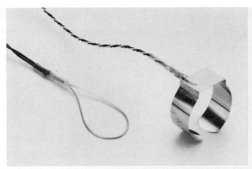 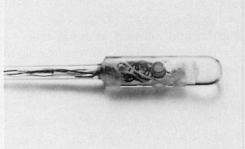

The Penile Strain Gauge and the Vaginal Photoplethysmograph *These devices measure vasocongestion in the genitals of men and women, providing an objective measure of their level of sexual arousal. Can you think of other aspects of sexual arousal?*

feelings of sexual arousal, as measured by self-report. For example, a person may say that he or she is relatively unaroused while the physiological measures suggest otherwise. Which is the *truer* measure of arousal, the person's subjective reports or the levels shown on the objective instruments?

Discrepancies across measures suggest that people may be sexually aroused (as measured by physiological indicators) but psychologically unprepared to recognize it or unwilling to admit it. In the real world of human relationships, sexual arousal has psychological as well as physiological aspects. The reflexes of erection and vaginal lubrication do not necessarily translate into "Yes."

In *Human Sexual Response* (1966), William Masters and Virginia Johnson were among the first to report direct laboratory observations of individuals and couples engaged in sexual acts. In all, 694 people (312 men and 382 women) participated in the research. The women ranged from 18 to 78 in age; the men, from 21 to 80. There were 276 married couples, 106 single women, and 36 single men. The married couples engaged in intercourse and other forms of mutual stimulation, such as manual and oral stimulation of the genitals. The unmarried people participated in studies that did not require intercourse, such as measurement of female sexual arousal in response to insertion of a penis-shaped probe and male ejaculation during masturbation. Masters and Johnson performed similar laboratory observations of sexual response among gay people for their 1979 book, *Homosexuality in Perspective.*

Direct laboratory observation of biological processes was not invented by Masters and Johnson. However, they were confronting a society that was still unprepared to speak openly of sex, let alone to observe people engaged in sexual activity in the laboratory. Masters and Johnson were accused of immorality, voyeurism, and an assortment of other evils. Nevertheless, their methods offered the first reliable set of data on what happens to the body during sexual response. Their instruments permitted them to directly measure **vasocongestion** (blood flow to the genitals), **myotonia** (muscle tension), and other physiological responses.

The artificial penis enabled Masters and Johnson to study changes in women's internal sexual organs as they became sexually aroused. From these studies, they observed that it is useful to divide sexual response into four stages (their "sexual response cycle"): excitement, plateau, orgasm, and resolution.

One confounding factor in Masters' and Johnson's research is that people who participate in laboratory observation know that they are being observed and that their responses are being measured. The problem of volunteer bias, troublesome for sex surveys, is even thornier in laboratory observation. How many of us would

Penile strain gauge A device for measuring sexual arousal in men in terms of changes in the circumference of the penis.

Vaginal plethysmograph A tampon-shaped probe that is inserted in the vagina and suggests the level of vasocongestion by measuring the light reflected from the vaginal walls.

Participant observation A method in which observers interact with the people they study as they collect data.

Vasocongestion Congestion from the flow of blood. (From the Latin *vas*, meaning "vessel.")

Myotonia Muscle tension.

assent to performing sexual activities in the laboratory while we were connected to monitoring equipment in full view of researchers? Some of the women observed by Masters and Johnson were patients of Dr. Masters who felt indebted to him and agreed to participate. Many were able to persuade their husbands to participate as well. Some were medical students and graduate students who may have been motivated to earn extra money (participants were paid for their time) as well as by scientific curiosity.

Observing people engaged in sexual activities may also alter their responses. People may not respond in public as they would in private. With these constraints in mind, it is perhaps remarkable that the people studied by Masters and Johnson were able to become sexually aroused and reach orgasm.

Review: Methods of Observation

Reflect

What are your own feelings about the methods of laboratory observation used by Masters and Johnson? Why?

CriticalThinking

Which strikes you as the *truer* measure of sexual arousal—the person's subjective reports of arousal or the levels shown on objective instruments such as the penile strain gauge or vaginal photoplethysmograph? Support your answer. (*Hint:* Critical thinkers pay attention to definitions of terms. What do you believe is meant by the word "truer"?)

12. A(n) _____ study is a carefully drawn, in-depth biography of an individual or a small group.

13. The _____ method typically studies large numbers of people through questionnaires or interviews.

14. The _____ reports interviewed 5,300 males and 5,940 females in the United States between 1938 and 1949.

15. Kinsey used a _____ sampling method.

16. Kinsey checked the _____ of his data by reexamining hundreds of interviewees after 18 months or more had passed.

17. The _____ of a survey is the degree to which verbal reports actually reflect the behavior of respondents.

18. The more recent _____ study interviewed 3,432 people, including an oversampling of African American and Latino and Latina American households.

19. Through payment and personal assurances, the NHSLS study obtained the cooperation of _____% of the people it contacted.

20. The Playboy sample, by contrast, obtained the cooperation of _____% of the people it contacted.

21. According to Edward Laumann and his colleagues (1994), magazine surveys tend to obtain "_____ statistics."

22. Gail Wyatt and her colleagues compared the sexual behavior of _____ American and European American women who lived in Los Angeles.

23. Surveys are subject to limitations imposed by gaps in memory, volunteer bias, and the tendency to answer questions in a socially _____ direction to earn the approval of the interviewer.

24. _____ research provides with data concerning sexual behaviors and customs of various ethnic groups.

25. In _____ observation, investigators learn about people's behavior by directly interacting with them.

26. Masters and Johnson used the _____-observation method.

27. Participants engaged in sexual behavior while laboratory equipment measured changes in _____ (blood flow to the genitals) and _____ (muscle tension).

Researchers have since developed more sophisticated physiological methods of measuring sexual arousal and response. Masters and Johnson's laboratory method is now used, with some variations but with less controversy, in research centers across the country.

The Correlational Method

What are the relationships between age and frequency of coitus among married couples? What is the connection between socioeconomic status and teenage pregnancy? In each case, two variables are being related to one another: age and frequency of coitus and socioeconomic status and rates of teenage pregnancy. *Question: What is the correlational method?* The correlational method describes the relationship between variables in numerical terms, and as positive or negative.

A **correlation** is a statistical measure of the relationship between two variables. In correlational studies, two or more variables are related, or linked to, one another by statistical means. The strength and direction (positive or negative) of the relationship between any two variables is expressed with a statistic called a **correlation coefficient**.

Research has shown relationships (correlations) between satisfaction with a relationship and a host of variables: communication skills, shared values, flexibility, frequency of social interactions with friends, and churchgoing, to name a few (Figure 2.1). Although such research may give us an idea of the factors associated with satisfaction in a relationship, the experimenters have not manipulated the variables of interest. For this reason we cannot say which, if any, of the factors is causally related to happiness in the relationship.

Research has also shown relationships between the use of sildenafil (Viagra) to enhance sexual response and risky sexual behavior among gay and bisexual men (Kim et al., 2002). Men who use Viagra also report a greater number of sex partners and higher levels of anal sex without using a condom. But there is no evidence that Viagra *causes* risky sexual behavior.

Correlation A statistical measure of the relationship between two variables.

Correlation coefficient A statistic that expresses the strength and direction (positive or negative) of the relationship between two variables.

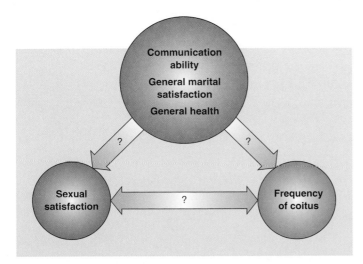

Figure 2.1. What Is the Relationship between Frequency of Intercourse and Sexual Satisfaction? *Couples in relationships who engage in more frequent sexual relations report higher levels of sexual satisfaction, but why? Because researchers have not manipulated the variables, we cannot conclude that sexual satisfaction causes high coital frequency. Nor can we say that frequent coitus causes greater sexual satisfaction. Perhaps both variables are affected by other factors, such as communication ability, health, and general satisfaction with the relationship.*

Correlations may be *positive* or *negative.* Two variables are positively correlated if one increases as the other increases. A Spanish study of 412 university students correlated sociodemographic, psychological, and interpersonal variables with sexual behavior and feelings of intimacy (Yela, 2000). It was found that commitment, feelings of intimacy, and frequency of sexual relations correlated positively with feelings of love and sexual satisfaction for both men and women. However, the researcher did not manipulate the variables. Therefore, we cannot conclude that sexual satisfaction *causes* high coital frequency. It could also be that frequent sexual activity contributes to greater sexual satisfaction. It is also possible that there is no causal relationship between the variables. Perhaps both coital frequency and sexual satisfaction are affected by other factors, such as communication ability, general marital satisfaction, general health, and so on (see Figure 2.1). Similarly, height and weight are positively correlated but do not cause each another. Other factors that we label the growth process contribute to both.

Dutch researchers found a negative correlation between anxiety disorders and the sexual functioning of 44 women with panic disorder or obsessive–compulsive disorder (Van Minnen & Kampman, 2000). Women with anxiety disorders reported less sexual desire and a lower frequency of sexual contact with their partners than women who lacked anxiety disorders but were otherwise similar. Women with anxiety disorders were also more likely to report sexual aversions—that is, a strong distaste for sexual contact.

Although correlations do not show cause and effect, they can be used to make predictions. For example, we can predict that women who have been circumcised

Review: The Correlational Method

Reflect

Would you expect that there would be a positive or negative correlation between satisfaction in a relationship and communication? Explain.

CriticalThinking

Couples who attend church more frequently report higher rates of marital satisfaction. Can researchers conclude that going to church enhances marital satisfaction? Why or why not?

28. The _____ method describes the relationship between variables in numerical terms, and as positive or negative.

29. A correlation _____ can be positive or negative.

30. Correlation (*Does* or *Does not*?) reveal cause and effect.

(had their clitorises cut out) in fundamentalist Islamic cultures will be prone to sexual problems and dysfunctions. Egyptian psychiatrist Mohammed El-Defrawi and his colleagues (2001) interviewed 250 women in Ismailia, Egypt, who had been circumcised during preadolescence. Female circumcision, discussed in Chapter 3, is carried out in some societies in the belief that it stems the expression of female sexuality, which these societies perceive as an abomination that threatens the social structure. Critics of the practice, including Dr. El-Defrawi, refer to female circumcision as *genital mutilation.* In any event, El-Defrawi and his colleagues found that women who had been circumcised were more likely to report painful menstruation, vaginal dryness during intercourse, lack of sexual desire, and difficulty reaching orgasm than uncircumcised women. The authors suggest that circumcision has a negative effect on women's sexual lives. It is also possible that the fundamentalist beliefs in the cultures to which these women belong lead both to female circumcision and to sexual problems and dysfunctions.

The Experimental Method

The best method for studying *cause-and-effect* relationships is the **experiment.** *Question: What is the experimental method?* Experiments permit scientists to draw conclusions about cause-and-effect relationships because the experimenter directly controls or manipulates the factors or variables of interest and carefully observes their effects.

In an experiment on the effects of alcohol on sexual arousal, for example, a group of participants would receive an intervention, called a **treatment**, such as a dose of alcohol. (In other experiments, the intervention or treatment might involve the administration of a drug, exposure to violent pornography, a program of sex education, etc.). They would then be carefully observed to learn whether this treatment made a difference in their behavior—in this case, their sexual arousal.

In an experiment, the variables (treatments) that are hypothesized to have a causal effect are manipulated or controlled by the researcher. Consider an experiment designed to determine whether or not alcohol stimulates sexual arousal. The design might involve giving one group of participants a certain dosage of alcohol, and then measuring its effects. In such an experimental arrangement, the dosage of alcohol is considered an **independent variable**, whose presence and quantity is manipulated by the researchers. The measured results are called **dependent variables** because changes in their values are believed to depend on the independent variable or variables. In this experiment, measures of sexual arousal would be the dependent variables. Dependent variables are outcomes; they are observed and measured by the researchers, but not manipulated. Sexual arousal might be measured by means such as physiological measurement (gauging the degree of penile erection in the male, for example) or self-report (asking participants to rate their sexual arousal on a rating scale).

In a study of the effects of sex education on teenage pregnancy, sex education would be the independent variable. The incidence of teenage pregnancy would be the dependent variable. Researchers would administer the experimental treatment (sex education) and track the participants for a period of time to determine their pregnancy rates. Ideally, as we see in the next section, the incidence of pregnancy among

Experiment A scientific method that seeks to confirm cause-and-effect relationships by manipulating independent variables and observing their effects on dependent variables.

Treatment In experiments, an intervention that is administered to participants (e.g., a test, a drug, or sex-education program) so that its effects may be observed.

Independent variable A condition in a scientific study that is manipulated so that its effects may be observed.

Dependent variables The measured results of an experiment, which are believed to be a function of the independent variables.

Web Sites for Use in Research on Human Sexuality

The following Web sites are not highly technical sites that explain the minute details of research methods. Rather, they are sources of information that you can use in your formal research (academically related) and informal research (checking into what's going on in the United States and the world from day to day). The government sites contain enormous data bases that you may be able to use in class projects. The newspaper and other public information sites often report the results of important research in lay language. You can follow up by going to the Web sites of the journals and other sources mentioned in those articles.

The Web site of SSSS–the "Four S's"–that is, the Society for the Scientific Study of Sexuality. SSSS was founded in 1957 as an international organization dedicated to the advancement of knowledge about sexuality. It includes an interdisciplinary group of professionals who believe in the importance of both research and the clinical, educational, and social applications of research in sexuality. The society supports the study of sexuality as a valid area for scientific research. Members include biologists, physicians, nurses, therapists, psychologists, sociologists, anthropologists, histo-

rians, educators, and theologians. SSSS publishes the *Journal of Sex Research* and the *Annual Review of Sex Research*.

http://www.ssc.wisc.edu/ssss/

The AASECT Web site: The American Association of Sex Educators, Counselors and Therapists. AASECT promotes sexual health through the development and advancement of the fields of sex therapy, counseling, and education. The Association provides for the education and certification of sex educators, counselors, and therapists, as well as individuals who supervise sex therapists in training. AASECT also encourages research in sex education, counseling and therapy. AASECT publishes the *The Journal of Sex Education and Therapy* and provides links that enable users to locate qualified sex therapists.

http://www.aasect.org/

The Web site of the Centers for Disease Control and Prevention (CDC). The CDC is located in Atlanta, Georgia, and is an agency of the Department of Health and Human Services. The mission of the CDC is to promote health and quality of life by preventing and controlling disease, injury, and disability. Many of the issues covered by the CDC are sexual, as in its list of topics from A–Z. The Web site is an encyclopedia of

these subjects would be compared to that among subjects who do not receive sex education but are similar to the subjects in all other respects.

Experimental and Control Groups

Experimental group A group of study participants who receive a treatment.

Control group A group of study participants who do not receive the experimental treatment. However, other conditions are held comparable to those of individuals in the experimental group.

Selection factor A bias that may operate in research when people are allowed to determine whether or not they will receive a treatment.

Well-designed experiments randomly assign people or animal study participants to experimental and control groups. Participants in **experimental groups** receive the treatment. Participants in **control groups** do not. Every effort is made to hold all other conditions constant for both groups. By using random assignment and holding other conditions constant, researchers can be reasonably confident that the independent variable (treatment), and not extraneous factors (such as the temperature of the room in which the treatment was administered or differences between the participants in the experimental and control groups), brought about the results.

Question: Why do experimenters assign individuals at random to experimental and control groups? Consider a study conducted to determine the effects of alcohol on sexual arousal in response to sexually explicit material, such as "adult" films. If we permitted participants to choose whether or not they would drink alcohol, we might not know if it was the alcohol itself that accounted for the results. Some other factor, called a **selection factor**, might discriminate between people who would or would not choose to drink alcohol. One difference might be that people who chose to drink

research information about sexual behavior and related health issues in the United States.
http://www.cdc.gov/

The Web site of the U.S. Census Bureau. The mission of the Bureau is to be "the preeminent collector and provider of timely, relevant, and quality data about the people and economy of the United States." The Bureau aims to provide timeliness, relevancy, quality, and cost for the research data it collects and disseminates. Exploration of this Web site will reveal that the Bureau does much more than simply tally numbers. It also analyzes data and projects trends, many of them related to issues such as family composition—a key topic in human sexuality.
http://www.census.gov/

The Web site of *The New York Times.* The Web sites of *The New York Times* and other important newspapers across the country (e.g., *The Washington Post, The Los Angeles Times*) and the world are found online. You can read the day's news, editorials, and so on without having to find (or purchase) the paper. You can also go to specialized parts of the paper that are most relevant to human sexuality. When you reach *The New York Times* Web site, for example, you can click on Science/Health in the left-hand column. You can also

search the archives of the various newspapers using key words that may be relevant to class projects, such as *AIDS* or *prostitution.*
http://www.nytimes.com/

The Web site of the Cable News Network (CNN), the original television provider of around-the-clock news. Other TV networks (e.g., ABC, MSNBC) also have Web sites with news. These Web sites, like the newspaper Web sites, include stories related to human sexuality, and you can usually click on Health to find them. The Web sites also typically have archives and search functions.
http://www.cnn.com/

The Web site of *Time* magazine. Like newspapers and TV network Web sites, the Web sites of the news magazines (*Newsweek, U.S. News & World Report,* etc.) have areas such as Health, archives, and search functions. Newspapers, TV network news services, and news magazines frequently report the result of surveys on issues relevant to human sexuality.
http://www.time.com/time/

The Web site of the Gallup Organization of Princeton, New Jersey, which conducts the Gallup polls. Click on "Gallup Poll" for current releases, or for survey results of topics A–Z.
http://www.gallup.com/

might also have more permissive attitudes toward sexually explicit material than the others. Their permissiveness rather than the alcohol could affect their sexual responsiveness to these stimuli. If this were the case, experimental outcomes might reflect the effects of the selection factor rather than the alcohol.

Although scientists agree that the experimental method provides the strongest evidence of cause-and-effect relationships, experimenters cannot manipulate many variables of interest directly. For example, we conduct experiments to determine the effects of cohabitation on college students. We cannot assign an experimental group to cohabitation and a control group to separate living quarters. We can only compare groups of students who have chosen to cohabit to groups who have not. Our research may thus inform us that cohabitors who get married are more likely to eventually get divorced than married couples who have never cohabited, but it cannot show that these problems are caused by cohabiting (see Chapter 14). Cohabitors and noncohabitors may differ on other factors—such as nontraditional versus traditional attitudes—that give rise to different outcomes of marriage.

Similarly, we cannot conduct experiments to determine the effects of pornography on children and adolescents. Societal prohibitions and ethical standards preclude experimenters from exposing children or adolescents to erotic materials. Researchers use other approaches, such as the correlational method, to study variables that cannot be manipulated.

Review: The Experimental Method

Reflect

Would it be possible to run an experiment to study the effects of rape on psychological health? Why or why not?

CriticalThinking

To run a true experiment on the effect of a new drug on people with HIV/AIDS, some people with AIDS would have to be assigned to a control group. To control for the effects of expectations, they might be told they are being given the real drug when they are really receiving "sugar pills" that look like the real thing. Can researchers justify withholding the real drug from people in the control group? What do you think?

31. The best method for studying *cause-and-effect* relationships is the _____.

32. In an experiment, one group of subjects receives a(n) _____ while a control group does not.

33. The measured results are termed _____ variables.

34. Experimenters assign subjects to experimental or control groups at _____.

Truth?Fiction?
Revisited

It is not true that researchers publish the names of participants in sex research in professional journals. Sex researchers must keep the identities and responses of participants confidential to protect them from possible harm or embarrassment.

Ethics in Sex Research

Sex researchers are required to protect the people being studied. This means that people will not be subjected to physical or psychological harm and will participate of their own free will. In colleges, universities, hospitals, and research institutions, ethics review committees help researchers weigh the potential harm of administering the independent variables and review proposed studies in light of ethical guidelines. If the committee finds fault with a proposal, it may advise the researcher how to modify the research design to comply with ethical standards and withhold approval until the proposal has been modified. *Question: What kinds of ethical issues are raised concerning sex research?* Let us consider a number of these issues:

- *Exposing participants to harm:* Individuals may be harmed if they are exposed to pain or placed in stressful situations. For this reason, researchers do not expose children to erotic materials in order to determine the effects. Nor do researchers expose human fetuses to male or female sex hormones to learn whether they create predispositions toward tomboyishness, gay male or lesbian sexual orientations, and other variables of interest.

- *Confidentiality:* Researchers can do many things to ensure the confidentiality of participants. They can make questionnaires anonymous. Interviewers may not be given the identities of interviewees. In reports of research, enough information about participants' backgrounds can be given to make the studies useful (size of city of origin, region of country, religion, age group, race, educational level, and so on) without divulging their identities. Once the need for follow-up has passed and the results have been fully analyzed, the names and addresses of participants and their records can be destroyed.

- *Informed consent:* The principle of **informed consent** requires that people freely agree to participate after being given enough information about the procedures and purposes of the research, and its risks and benefits, to make an informed decision. Once the study has begun, participants must be free to withdraw at any time without penalty.

- *The use of deception:* Ethical conflicts may emerge when experiments require that participants not know all about their purposes and methods. For example, in experiments on the effects of violent pornography on aggression against women, participants may be misled into believing that they are administering electric shocks to women (who are actually confederates of the experimenter), even though no shocks are actually delivered. The experimenter seeks to determine participants' willingness to hurt women following exposure to aggressive erotic films. Such studies could not be carried out if participants knew that no shocks would actually be delivered.

Research is the backbone of human sexuality as a science. This textbook focuses on scientific findings that can illuminate our understanding of sexuality, help enhance sexual experience, prevent and treat sexually transmitted diseases, and build more rewarding relationships.

Confidentiality *Ethics requires that sex researchers keep the identities and behaviors of participants in research confidential. Sometimes records are coded so that someone breaking into them would not be able to decipher the identity of participants. Records are also usually destroyed after all useful information has been gleaned from them.*

Informed consent The term used by researchers to indicate that people have agreed to participate in research after receiving information about the purposes and nature of the study, and its potential risks and benefits.

Review: Ethics in Sex Research

Reflect

What types of harm could occur if a researcher disclosed the identity of an individual in a sex survey and his or her sexual behavior?

Critical Thinking

In experiments on the effects of violent pornography on aggression, men are led to believe that they are shocking women by pressing a button when they actually are not. Do you believe that this deception is justified? Can you think of a more ethical way of measuring "aggression"?

35. _____ aim to prevent subjects in experiments from being exposed to harm.

36. Sex researchers keep the identities of participants _____ to protect them from harm.

37. The principle of _____ consent requires that people freely agree to participate after being given information about the research.

38. When knowledge of the purposes and methods of an experiment would make it useless, subjects may be _____ about these matters.

Recite

1. **What is the scientific method?**

The scientific method is a systematic way of gathering scientific evidence and testing assumptions through empirical research. It entails formulating a research question, framing a hypothesis, testing the hypothesis, and drawing conclusions about the hypothesis.

2. **What are the goals of the science of human sexuality?**

The goals of the science of human sexuality are to describe, explain, predict, and control sexual behaviors. People often confuse description with inference. Inferences are woven into theories, when possible.

3. **What is a population?**

A population is a complete group of people or animals that researcher targets for study.

4. **What is a sample?**

A sample is a subgroup of a population that a researcher selects in order to study the population.

5. **What sampling methods do researchers use to represent populations?**

Researchers use random sampling, when possible, to assure that every member of a population has an equal chance of being selected. In a stratified random sample, identified subgroups within a population are selected according to their numbers in the population.

6. **What is a case study?**

Case studies are carefully drawn biographies of individuals or small groups that focus on unraveling the interplay of various factors in individuals' backgrounds.

7. **What is the survey method?**

Surveys typically gather information about behavior through interviews or questionnaires administered to large samples of people. Gaps in memory, use of volunteers, and the tendency of respondents to offer socially desirable responses are sources of bias in surveys.

8. **What is the naturalistic-observation method?**

In naturalistic observation, scientists directly observe the behavior of animals and humans where it happens—in the "field." The scientists remain as unobtrusive as possible in an effort to avoid affecting the behavior they wish to study.

9. **What is the ethnographic-observation method?**

Ethnographic research provides us with data concerning sexual behaviors and customs that occur widely across cultures and those that are limited to one or few cultures. It is usually conducted by anthropologists.

Recite

10. What is participant observation?

In participant observation, investigators learn about people's behavior by interacting with them.

11. What is the laboratory-observation method?

In the laboratory-observation method, people engage in the behavior under study in the laboratory setting. When methods of observation influence the behavior under study, that behavior may be distorted. Masters and Johnson studied people involved in sexual activity in the laboratory to learn how their bodies respond to sexual stimulation.

12. What is the correlational method?

Correlational studies reveal the strength and direction of the relationships between variables, such as communication ability and satisfaction with a relationship. However, they do not show cause and effect.

13. What is the experimental method?

Experiments allow scientists to draw conclusions about cause-and-effect relationships because they directly control or manipulate the variables of interest and observe their effects. The variables manipulated are called independent variables; the outcome variables are termed dependent variables.

14. Why do experimenters assign individuals at random to experimental and control groups?

Well-designed experiments randomly assign individuals to experimental and control groups to avoid the selection factor. Thus it can be assumed that different outcomes between groups represent the manipulation of the independent variables and not differences between the individuals in the experimental and control groups.

15. What kinds of ethical issues are raised concerning sex research?

Ethical standards require that research may be conducted only when the expected benefits of the research outweigh the anticipated risks to participants and when the experimenter attempts to minimize expected risks. Sex researchers keep the identities and responses of participants confidential and obtain their informed consent to participate, but must occasionally deceive people as to the purposes and procedures of a study.

Chapter 3

Truth?Fiction?

T / F? A name for the external female genitals is derived from Latin roots that mean "something to be ashamed of."

T / F? Women, but not men, have a sex organ whose only known function is the experiencing of sexual pleasure.

T / F? Women urinate and engage in sexual intercourse through the same bodily opening.

T / F? One may determine whether or not a woman is a virgin by examining her hymen.

T / F? Women with larger breasts produce more milk while nursing.

T / F? Women who have had abortions are at greater risk of breast cancer.

T / F? The American Cancer Society recommends that women engage in a breast self-examination once a month.

T / F? The ancient Romans believed that menstrual blood soured wine and killed crops.

T / F? At menopause, women experience debilitating hot flashes.

T / F? Menopause signals an end to women's sexual appetite.

Female Sexual Anatomy and Physiology

Preview

The French have a saying, "*Vive la différence!*" ("Long live the difference!"). It celebrates in the differences between men and women. Their gender-differences, at least their anatomic differences, have often been met with prejudice and misunderstanding, however. Men have historically exalted their own genitals. Too often, the less visible genitals of women have been deemed inferior. The derivation of the word **pudendum**, which refers to the external female genitals, speaks volumes about sexism in the ancient Mediterranean world.

Even today, this cultural heritage may lead women to develop negative attitudes toward their genitals. Girls and boys are both sometimes reared to regard their genitals with shame or disgust. Both may be reprimanded for expressing normal curiosity about them. They may be reared with a "hands-off" attitude, to keep their "private parts" private, even from themselves. Touching them except for hygienic purposes may be discouraged. One woman recalls:

> When I was six years old I climbed up on the bathroom sink and looked at myself naked in the mirror. All of a sudden I realized I had three different holes. I was very excited about my discovery and ran down to the dinner table and announced it to everyone. "I have three holes!" Silence. "What are they for?" I asked. Silence even heavier than before. I sensed how uncomfortable everyone was and answered for myself. "I guess one is for pee-pee, the other for doo-doo and the third for ca-ca." A sigh of relief; no one had to answer my question. But I got the message—I wasn't supposed to ask "such" questions, though I didn't fully realize what "such" was about at that time. (Boston Women's Health Book Collective, *The New Our Bodies, Ourselves,* 1992)

In this chapter we tour the female sex organs. Even generally sophisticated students may fill in some gaps in their knowledge. Most of us know what a vagina is, but how many of us realize that only the female has an organ that is exclusively dedicated to pleasure? Or that a woman's passing of urine does not involve the vagina? How many of us know that a newborn girl already has all the **ova** she will ever produce?

As women readers encounter the features of their sexual anatomy in their reading, they may wish to examine their own genitals with a mirror. By following the text and the illustrations, students may discover some new anatomic features. They will see that their genitals can resemble those in the illustrations yet also be unique.

External Sex Organs

Taken collectively, the external sexual structures of the female are termed the pudendum or the **vulva**. Pudendum, because of its derivation, may be a less desirable term than *vulva*. Vulva is a Latin word that means "wrapper" or "covering." ***Question: What are the parts of the vulva?*** The vulva consists of the *mons veneris*, the *labia majora* and *minora* (major and minor lips), the *clitoris*, and the vaginal opening (see Figure 3.1). Figure 3.2 shows variations in the appearance of women's genitals.

Truth?Fiction?
Revisited

Pudendum derives from the Latin *pudendus*. It literally means "something to be ashamed of."

The Mons Veneris

Question: What is the mons veneris? The **mons veneris** consists of fatty tissue that covers the joint of the pubic bones in front of the body, below the abdomen and above the clitoris. At puberty the mons becomes covered with pubic hair that may be thick and curly but varies from person to person in waviness, texture, and color. The pubic hair captures the chemical secretions that exude from the vagina during sexual arousal. Their scent may allure lovers. The mons cushions a woman's body during

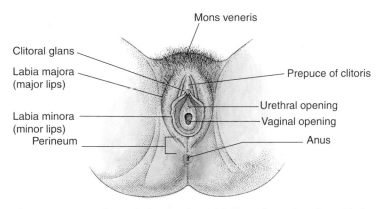

Figure 3.1. External Female Sex Organs. This figure shows the vulva with the labia opened to reveal the urethral and vaginal openings.

 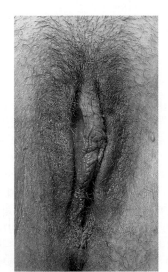 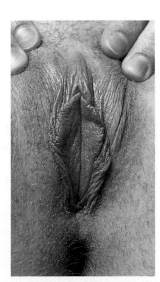

Figure 3.2. Normal Variations in the Vulva. The features of the vulva show a great deal of variation. A woman's attitude toward her genitals is likely to reflect her general self-concept and early childhood messages rather than the appearance of her vulva per se.

Pudendum (pyoo-DEN-dum) The external female genitals.

Ova Egg cells. (Singular: ovum.)

Vulva The external sexual structures of the female.

Mons veneris A mound of fatty tissue that covers the joint of the pubic bones in front of the body, below the abdomen and above the clitoris. (The name is a Latin phrase meaning hill or "mount of Venus," the Roman goddess of love. Also known as the *mons pubis,* or simply *mons.*)

Truth?Fiction?
Revisited

The historic view of women as unresponsive to sexual stimulation is ironic because women, not men, possess a sex organ—the clitoris—that is solely devoted to pleasurable sensations. The clitoris is the woman's most erotically charged organ; women most often masturbate through clitoral stimulation, not vaginal insertion.

Many males (and even some females) believe erroneously that for women urination and coitus occur through the same bodily opening. The confusion may arise from the fact that urine and semen both pass through the penis of the male or because the urethral opening lies near the vaginal opening.

Labia majora Large folds of skin that run downward from the mons along the sides of the vulva. (Latin for "large lips" or "major lips.")

Labia minora Hairless, light-colored membranes, located between the labia majora. (Latin for "small lips" or "minor lips.")

Clitoris A female sex organ consisting of a shaft and glans located above the urethral opening. It is extremely sensitive to sexual sensations.

sexual intercourse, protecting her and her partner from the pressure against the pubic bone that stems from thrusting. There is an ample supply of nerve endings in the mons, so that caresses can produce pleasurable sensations.

The Labia Majora

Question: What are the labia majora? The **labia majora** are large folds of skin that run downward from the mons along the sides of the vulva. In some women, the labia majora are thick and bulging. In others, they are thinner, flatter, and less noticeable. When close together, they hide the labia minora and the urethral and vaginal openings. The outer surfaces of the labia majora, by the thighs, are covered with pubic hair and darker skin than that found on the thighs or labia minora. The inner surfaces of the labia majora are hairless and lighter in color. They are amply supplied with nerve endings that respond to stimulation and can produce sexual pleasure. The labia majora also shield the inner female genitals. *Question: What are the labia minora?*

The Labia Minora

The **labia minora** are two hairless, light-colored membranes, located between the major lips. They surround the urethral and vaginal openings. The outer surfaces of the labia minora merge with the major lips. At the top they join at the prepuce (hood) of the clitoris. The labia minora differ in appearance from woman to woman. The labia minora of some women form protruding flower shapes that are valued greatly in some cultures, such as that of the Hottentots of Africa. (Hottentot women purposely elongate their labia minora by tugging at them.) Rich in blood vessels and nerve endings, the labia minora are highly sensitive to sexual stimulation. When stimulated they darken and swell, engorging with blood.

The Clitoris

What's the matter, papa? please don't stall.
Don't you know I love it and want it all?
I'm wild about that thing. Just give my bell a ring.
You pressed my button. I'm wild about that thing.
    "I'm Wild about That Thing," *recorded by Bessie Smith, 1929*

Worldwide, the clitoris is known by many names, from *bijou* (French for "jewel") to *pokhotnik* (Russian for "lust"). The Tuamotuan people of Polynesia have ten words for it, emblematic of their cultivated interest in female sexuality. *Question: What is the clitoris?* By any name, the clitoris is the only sex organ whose only known function is the experiencing of pleasure.

Clitoris (Figure 3.1) derives from the Greek word *kleitoris,* meaning "hill" or "slope." It receives its name from the manner in which it slopes upward in the shaft and forms a mound of spongy tissue at the glans. The body of the clitoris—the clitoral shaft—is about 1 inch long and ¼ inch wide. The clitoral shaft consists of erectile tissue that contains two spongy masses called **corpora cavernosa** ("cavernous bodies") that fill with blood (become engorged) and become erect in response to sexual stimulation. The stiffening of the clitoris is less apparent than the erection of the penis, because the clitoris does not swing free from the body. The **prepuce** (meaning "before a swelling"), or hood, covers the clitoral shaft. It is a sheath of skin formed by the upper part of the labia minora. The clitoral glans is a smooth, round knob or lump of tissue above the urethral opening. The glans is revealed by gently separating the labia minora and retracting the hood. It is highly sensitive to touch because of the rich supply of nerve endings.

The clitoris certainly has an "indirect" role in reproduction in that it is the female sex organ most sensitive to sexual sensation and thus a motivator of sexual activity. The size of the clitoris varies from woman to woman, just as the size of the penis varies among men. Because the clitoral glans is highly sensitive to touch, women usually prefer to be stroked or stimulated on the mons, or on the clitoral hood, rather than directly on the glans.

In some respects, the clitoris is the female counterpart of the penis. However, a survey of 373 Texas college students found that they had overwhelmingly been taught that the vagina was the counterpart to the penis (Ogletree & Ginsburg, 2000). Nevertheless, both organs—clitoris and penis—develop from the same embryonic tissue, which makes them similar in structure, or **homologous**. They are not fully similar in function, or **analogous**, however. Both organs receive and transmit sexual sensations, but the penis is directly involved in reproduction and excretion by serving as a conduit for sperm and urine, respectively.

Surgical removal of the clitoral hood is common among Moslems in the Near East and Africa. As we see in the nearby World of Diversity feature, it is a "rite of passage" to womanhood that leaves many scars—physical and emotional.

The Vestibule

Question: What is the vestibule? The word *vestibule*, which means "entranceway," refers to the area within the labia minora that contains the openings to the vagina and the urethra. The vestibule is richly supplied with nerve endings and is very sensitive to tactile or other sexual stimulation. *Question: What is the urethral opening?*

The Urethral Opening

Urine passes from the female's body through the **urethral opening** (see Figure 3.1), which is connected by a short tube (the urethra) to the bladder (see Figure 3.3). The urethral opening lies below the clitoral glans and above the vaginal opening. The urethral opening, urethra, and bladder are unrelated to the reproductive system.

The proximity of the urethral opening to the external sex organs can pose hygienic problems for sexually active women. The urinary tract, which includes the urethra, bladder, and kidneys, may become infected by bacteria from the vagina or rectum. Disease organisms may pass from the male's sex organs or hands to the urethral opening during sexual intercourse or foreplay. Anal intercourse followed by vaginal intercourse may transfer disease organisms from the rectum to the bladder. For similar reasons, women should first wipe the vulva, then the anus, when using the bathroom.

Cystitis is a bladder inflammation that may stem from any of these sources. Its symptoms include burning and frequent urination (also called *urinary urgency*). Pus

Corpora cavernosa Masses of spongy tissue in the clitoral shaft that become engorged with blood and stiffen in response to sexual stimulation. (Latin for "cavernous bodies.")

Prepuce (PREE-pyoose) The fold of skin covering the glans of the clitoris (or penis). (From Latin roots meaning "before a swelling.")

Homologous Similar in structure; developing from the same embryonic tissue.

Analogous Similar in function.

Urethral opening The opening through which urine passes from the female's body.

Cystitis An inflammation of the urinary bladder. (From the Greek *kystis,* meaning "sac.")

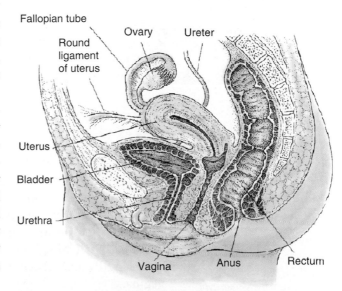

Figure 3.3. The Female Reproductive System. This cross section locates many of the internal sex organs that compose the female reproductive system. Note that the uterus is normally tipped forward.

Clitoridectomy—Cultural Practice or Genital Mutilation?

Despite hundreds of years of tradition, Hajia Zuwera Kassindja would not let it happen to her 17-year-old daughter, Fauziya. Hajia's own sister had died from it. So Hajia gave her daughter her inheritance from her deceased husband, which amounted to only $3,500 but left Hajia a pauper. Fauziya used the money to buy a phony passport and flee from the African country of Togo to the United States.

Upon arrival in the United States, Fauziya requested asylum from persecution. However, she was put into prison for more than a year. But then the Board of Immigration Appeals finally agreed that Fauziya was fleeing persecution, and she was allowed to remain in the United States.

From what had Hajia's sister died? From what was Fauziya escaping? *Clitoridectomy*. Cultures in some parts of Africa and the Middle East ritually mutilate or remove the clitoris, not just the clitoral hood. Removal of the clitoris, or **clitoridectomy**, is a rite of initiation into womanhood in many of these predominantly Islamic cultures. It is often performed as a puberty ritual in late childhood or early adolescence (not within a few days of birth, like male circumcision). In modern-day Egypt, the vast majority of female adolescents, aged 10 to 19, are circumcised (El-Gibaly et al., 2002).

The clitoris gives rise to feelings of sexual pleasure in women. Its removal is an attempt to ensure the girl's chastity, because it is assumed that uncircumcised girls are consumed with sexual desires. Cairo physician Said M. Thabit says "With circumcision we remove the external parts, so when a girl wears tight nylon underclothes she will not have any stimulation." What effects does it have on the sexuality of women? A study of 250 female patients from the Maternal and Childhood Centers of Ismailia, Egypt, found that those who were circumcised were 80% more likely to complain of dysmenorrhea, 49% more likely to complain of vaginal dryness during intercourse, 45% more likely to lack sexual desire, 49% less likely to be pleased by sex, and 61% more likely to have difficulty reaching orgasm (El-Defrawi et al., 2001).

But some groups in Egypt and in the Sudan simply perform clitoridectomies because it is a social custom that has remained unchallenged (Missailidis & Gebre-Medhin, 2000). It is usually done by women to women (Nour, 2000). Some perceive it as part of their faith in Islam. However, the Koran—the Islamic

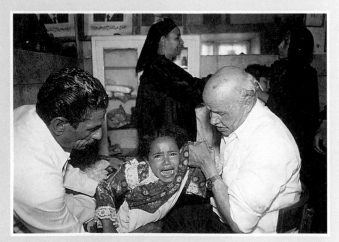

Clitoridectomy
Some predominantly Islamic cultures in Africa and the Middle East ritually remove the clitoris as a rite of initiation into womanhood. Novelist Alice Walker drew attention to the practice in her novel Possessing the Secret of Joy. *She has called for its abolition in her book and film,* Warrior Marks.

Clitoridectomy Surgical removal of the clitoris.

Gynecologist A physician who treats women's diseases, especially of the reproductive tract. (From the Greek *gyne*, meaning "woman.")

or a bloody discharge is common, and there may be discomfort above the pubic bone. These symptoms may disappear after several days, but consultation with a **gynecologist** is recommended, because untreated cystitis can lead to kidney infections. "Honeymoon cystitis" is caused by the tugging on the bladder and urethral wall that occurs during vaginal intercourse. It may occur upon beginning coital activity (though not necessarily on one's honeymoon) or upon resumption after lengthy abstinence. Figure 3.3 shows the close proximity of the urethra and vagina.

A few precautions may help women prevent serious inflammation of the bladder:

bible—does not authorize it (Nour, 2000). The typical young woman in this culture does not grasp that she is a victim. She assumes that clitoridectomy is part of being female. As one young woman told gynecologist Nawal M. Nour (2000), the clitoridectomy hurt but was a good thing, because now she was a woman.

In many locales, clitoridectomies are performed under unsanitary conditions without benefit of anesthesia. Medical complications are common, including infections, bleeding, tissue scarring, painful menstruation, and obstructed labor. The procedure is psychologically traumatizing.

An even more radical form of clitoridectomy, called *infibulation* or Pharaonic circumcision, is practiced widely in the Sudan. Pharaonic circumcision involves complete removal of the clitoris along with the labia minora and the inner layers of the labia majora. After removal of the skin tissue, the raw edges of the labia majora are sewn together. Only a tiny opening is left to allow passage of urine and menstrual discharge (Nour, 2000). The sewing together of the vulva is intended to ensure chastity until marriage. Medical complications are common, including menstrual and urinary problems, even death. After marriage, the opening is enlarged to permit intercourse. Enlargement is a gradual process that is often made difficult by scar tissue from the circumcision. Hemorrhaging and tearing of surrounding tissues are common consequences. It may take three months or longer before the opening is large enough to allow penile penetration. Mutilation of the labia is now illegal in the Sudan, although the law continues to allow removal of the clitoris. Some African countries, including Egypt, have outlawed clitoridectomies, although such laws are often unenforced.

More than 100 million women in Africa and the Middle East have undergone removal of the clitoris and the labia minora. Clitoridectomies remain common, even universal, in nearly 30 countries in Africa, in many countries in the Middle East, and in parts of Malaysia, Yemen, Oman, Indonesia, and the India-Pakistan subcontinent. Thousands of African immigrant girls living in European countries and the United States have also been mutilated (Nour, 2000).

Do not confuse male circumcision with the maiming inflicted on girls in the name of circumcision. Nour (2000) depicts the male equivalent of female genital mutilation as cutting off the penis. The Pulitzer Prize–winning, African American novelist Alice Walker drew attention to the practice in her best-selling novel *Possessing the Secret of Joy* and called for its abolition in her book and film *Warrior Marks*.

OUTLAWED

In 1996, the United States outlawed ritual genital mutilation within its borders. The government also directed American representatives to world financial institutions to deny aid to countries that have not established educational programs to bring an end to the practice. Yet calls from Westerners to ban the practice in parts of Africa and the Middle East have sparked controversy on grounds of "cultural condescension"—that people in one culture cannot dictate the cultural traditions of another. Yet for Alice Walker, "torture is not culture." As the debate continues, some 2 million African girls undergo clitoridectomy each year.

- Drinking two quarts of water a day to flush the bladder.
- Drinking orange or cranberry juice to maintain an acid environment that discourages growth of infectious organisms.
- Decreasing use of alcohol and caffeine (from coffee, tea, or cola drinks) that may irritate the bladder.
- Washing the hands prior to masturbation or self-examination.
- Washing one's partner's and one's own genitals before and after intercourse.
- Preventing objects that have touched the anus (fingers, penis, toilet tissue) from subsequently coming into contact with the vulva.
- Urinating soon after intercourse to help wash away bacteria.

The Vaginal Opening

When I was five or six, my mother told me about sex. I remember that I was confused about what my mother said, because somehow I couldn't conceptualize what the female vagina looked like. I was curious to see an actual vagina and not just how it looked diagramed in a book.

Morrison et al., 1980, p. 35

Question: What is the vaginal opening? One does not see an entire vagina, but rather the vaginal opening, or **introitus**, when one parts the labia minora. The introitus lies below and is larger than the urethral opening. Its shape resembles that of the **hymen**.

The hymen is a fold of tissue across the vaginal opening that is usually present at birth and may remain at least partly intact until a woman engages in coitus. For this reason the hymen has been called the "maidenhead." Its presence has been taken as proof of virginity, and its absence as evidence of coitus. However, some women are born with incomplete hymens, and other women's hymens are torn accidentally, such as during horseback riding, strenuous exercise or gymnastics—or even when bicycle riding. A punctured hymen is therefore poor evidence of coital experience. A flexible hymen may also withstand many coital experiences, so its presence does not guarantee virginity.

Figure 3.4 illustrates various vaginal openings. The first three show common shapes of hymens among women who have not had coitus. The fifth drawing shows a *parous* ("passed through") vaginal opening, typical of a woman who has delivered a baby. Now and then the hymen consists of tough fibrous tissue and is closed, or *imperforate,* as in the fourth drawing. An imperforate hymen may not be discovered until after puberty, when menstrual discharges begin to accumulate in the vagina. In these rare cases, a surgical incision will perforate the hymen. A woman may also have a physician surgically perforate her hymen if she would rather forgo the tearing and discomfort that may accompany her initial coital experiences. But this procedure is unnecessary for most women. They experience little pain during initial coitus despite old horror stories. A woman may also stretch the vaginal opening over several days in preparation for intercourse by inserting a finger and gently pressing downward toward the anus. After several repetitions, she may insert two fingers and repeat the process, spreading the fingers slightly after insertion.

Introitus The vaginal opening. (From the Latin for "entrance.")

Hymen A fold of tissue across the vaginal opening that is usually present at birth and remains at least partly intact until a woman engages in coitus. (Greek for "membrane.")

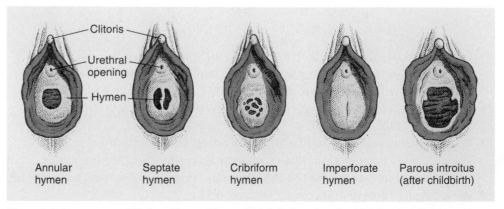

Figure 3.4. Appearance of Various Types of Hymens and the Introitus (at Right) as It Appears Following Delivery of a Baby

The hymen is found only in female horses and humans. It is not present in animal species closest to humans on the evolutionary scale, such as chimps and gorillas. The hymen remains something of a biological mystery, because it serves no apparent biological function.

The Perineum

Question: What is the perineum? The **perineum** incorporates the skin and underlying tissue between the vaginal opening and the anus. The perineum is rich in nerve endings. Stimulation of the area may heighten sexual arousal. Many physicians make a routine perineal incision during labor, called an **episiotomy**, to facilitate childbirth.

Structures That Underlie the External Sex Organs

Figure 3.5 shows what lies beneath the skin of the vulva. *Question: What structures are found beneath the vulva?* The vestibular bulbs and Bartholin's glands are active during sexual arousal and are found on both sides (shown on the right in Figure 3.5). Muscular rings (**sphincters**) that constrict bodily openings such as the vaginal and anal openings are also found on both sides.

The clitoral **crura** are wing-shaped, leglike structures that attach the clitoris to the pubic bone beneath. The crura contain corpora cavernosa, which engorge with blood and stiffen during sexual arousal.

The **vestibular bulbs** are attached to the clitoris at the top and extend downward along the sides of the vaginal opening. Blood congests them during sexual arousal, swelling the vulva and lengthening the vagina. This swelling contributes to coital sensations for both partners.

Bartholin's glands lie just inside the minor lips on each side of the vaginal opening. They secrete a couple of drops of lubrication just before orgasm. This lubrication is not essential for coitus. In fact, the fluid produced by the Bartholin's glands has no known purpose. If the glands become infected and clogged, however, a woman may notice swelling and local irritation. It is wise to consult a gynecologist if these symptoms do not fade within a few days.

It was once believed that the source of the vaginal lubrication or "wetness" that women experience during sexual arousal was produced by the Bartholin's glands. It is now known that engorgement of vaginal tissues during sexual excitement results in a form of "sweating" by the lining of the vaginal wall. During sexual arousal, the

Perineum The skin and underlying tissue that lies between the vaginal opening and the anus. (From Greek roots meaning "around" and "to empty out.")

Episiotomy A surgical incision in the perineum that may be made during childbirth to protect the vagina from tearing. (From the Greek roots *epision*, meaning "pubic region," and *tome*, meaning "cutting.")

Sphincters Ring-shaped muscles that surround body openings and open or close them by expanding or contracting. (From the Greek for "that which draws close.")

Crura Anatomical structures resembling legs that attach the clitoris to the pubic bone. (Singular: crus. A Latin word meaning "leg" or "shank.")

Vestibular bulbs Cavernous structures that extend downward along the sides of the introitus and swell during sexual arousal.

Bartholin's glands Glands that lie just inside the minor lips and secrete fluid just before orgasm.

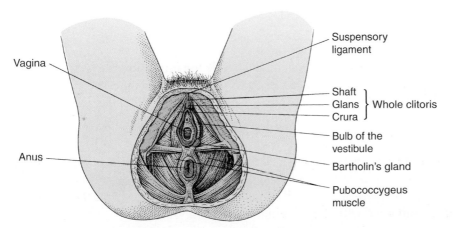

Vagina
Anus
Suspensory ligament
Shaft
Glans } Whole clitoris
Crura
Bulb of the vestibule
Bartholin's gland
Pubococcygeus muscle

Figure 3.5. Structures That Underlie the Female External Sex Organs. If we could see beneath the vulva, we would find muscle fibers that constrict the various body openings, plus the crura ("legs") of the clitoris, the vestibular bulbs, and Bartholin's glands.

Review: External Sex Organs

Reflect

How do people from your own sociocultural background regard the external female sexual organs? Are they seen as something of beauty or something to keep hidden? Explain.

Critical Thinking

Do you believe that disapproval of female circumcision by Americans and other Westerners shows cultural condescension or cultural insensitivity? Why or why not?

1. The word _____, which refers to the external female genitals, derives from a Latin word meaning "something to be ashamed of."

2. At puberty the _____ becomes covered with pubic hair.

3. The labia _____ are large folds of skin that run downward from the mons along the sides of the vulva.

4. The _____ is the only sex organ whose only known function is the experiencing of pleasure.

5. The clitoral shaft contains spongy masses called corpora _____ that become engorged and erect in response to sexual stimulation.

6. The clitoris and penis develop from the same embryonic tissue, which makes them (*Homologous* or *Analogous*?).

7. Urine passes from the female's body through the _____ opening.

8. The _____ is a fold of tissue across the vaginal opening that may remain at least partly intact until a woman engages in coitus.

9. During sexual arousal the pressure from _____ forces out moisture from small blood vessels in the vaginal wall to create lubrication.

pressure from this engorgement causes moisture from the many small blood vessels that lie in the vaginal wall to be forced out and to pass through the vaginal lining, forming the basis of the lubrication. In less time than it takes to read this sentence (generally within 10 to 30 seconds), beads of vaginal lubrication or "sweat" appear along the interior lining of the vagina in response to sexual stimulation, in much the same way that rising temperatures cause water to pass through the skin as perspiration.

Pelvic floor muscles permit women to constrict the vaginal and anal openings. They contract automatically, or involuntarily, during orgasm, and their tone may contribute to coital sensations.

Question: Now that we have examined the external female sexual organs, what are the internal female sex organs?

Internal Sex Organs

The internal sex organs of the female include the innermost parts of the vagina, the cervix, the uterus, and two ovaries, each connected to the uterus by a fallopian tube (see Figures 3.3 and 3.6). These structures comprise the female reproductive system.

The Vagina

Question: What is the vagina? The **vagina** extends back and upward from the vaginal opening (see Figure 3.3). It is usually 3 to 5 inches long at rest. Menstrual flow and babies pass from the uterus to the outer world through the vagina. During coitus, the penis is contained within the vagina.

The vagina is commonly pictured as a canal or barrel; but, when at rest, it is like a collapsed muscular tube. Its walls touch like the fingers of an empty glove. The vagina expands in length and width during sexual arousal. The vagina can also

Vagina The tubular female sex organ that contains the penis during sexual intercourse and through which a baby is born. (Latin for "sheath.")

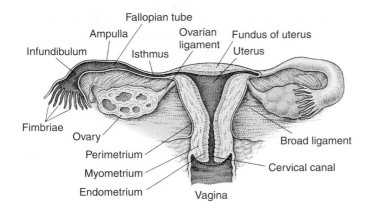

Fallopian tube
Ampulla
Ovarian ligament
Fundus of uterus
Infundibulum
Isthmus
Uterus
Fimbriae
Ovary
Perimetrium
Myometrium
Endometrium
Vagina
Broad ligament
Cervical canal

Figure 3.6. Female Internal Reproductive Organs. This drawing highlights the relationship of the uterus to the fallopian tubes and ovaries. Note the layers of the uterus, the ligaments that attach the ovaries to the uterus, and the relationship of the ovaries to the fimbriae of the fallopian tubes.

expand to allow insertion of a tampon, as well as the passage of a baby's head and shoulders during childbirth.

The vaginal walls have three layers. The inner lining, or *vaginal mucosa,* is made visible by opening the labia minora. It is a mucous membrane similar to the skin that lines the inside of the mouth. It feels fleshy, soft, and corrugated. It may vary from very dry (especially if the female is anxious about something like examinations) to very wet, in which case fingers slide against it readily. The middle layer of the vaginal wall is muscular. The outer or deeper layer is a fibrous covering that connects the vagina to other pelvic structures.

The vaginal walls are rich with blood vessels but poorly supplied with nerve endings. Unlike the sensitive outer third of the vaginal barrel, the inner two-thirds are so insensitive to touch that minor surgery may sometimes be performed on those portions without anesthesia. The entire vaginal barrel is sensitive to pressure, however, which can be experienced as pleasurable.

The vaginal walls secrete substances that help maintain the vagina's normal acidity (pH 4.0 to 5.0). Normally they taste salty, but their odor and taste may vary during the menstrual cycle. The secretions may contain substances that act as sexual attractants. Women who frequently **douche** or use feminine deodorant sprays may remove or mask substances that arouse sex partners. Douching or spraying may also alter the natural chemical balance of the vagina, which can increase the risk of infections. Feminine deodorant sprays can also irritate the vagina and evoke allergic reactions. The normal, healthy vagina cleanses itself through regular chemical secretions that are evidenced by a mild white or yellowish discharge.

Vaginitis refers to any vaginal inflammation, whether it is caused by an infection, birth control pills, antibiotics that alter natural body chemistry, an allergic reaction, chemical irritation, or lowered resistance, as may be caused by fatigue or poor diet. Changes in body chemistry or lowered resistance permit microscopic organisms normally found in the vagina to multiply to infectious levels. Vaginitis may be recognized by abnormal discharge, itching, burning of the vulva, and urinary urgency. Women with vaginitis are advised to seek medical attention, but let us note some suggestions that may help prevent vaginitis:

1. Wash your vulva and anus regularly with mild soap. Pat dry (taking care not to touch the vulva after dabbing the anus).
2. Wear cotton panties. Nylon underwear retains heat and moisture that cause harmful bacteria to flourish.
3. Avoid pants that are tight in the crotch.
4. Be certain that sex partners are well-washed. Condoms may also reduce the spread of infections from one's sex partner.

Douche Application of a jet of liquid to the vagina as a rinse. (From the Italian *doccia,* meaning "shower bath.")

Vaginitis Vaginal inflammation.

5. Use a sterile, water-soluble jelly such as K-Y jelly if artificial lubrication is needed for intercourse. Do *not* use Vaseline. Birth-control jellies can also be used for lubrication.

6. Avoid intercourse that is painful or abrasive to the vagina.

7. Avoid diets high in sugar and refined carbohydrates, because they alter the normal acidity of the vagina.

8. Women who are prone to vaginal infections may find it helpful to douche occasionally with plain water, a solution of 1 or 2 tablespoons of vinegar in a quart of warm water, or a solution of baking soda and water. Douches consisting of unpasteurized, plain (unflavored) yogurt may help replenish the "good" bacteria that are normally found in the vagina and that may be destroyed by use of antibiotics. Be careful when douching, and do not douche when pregnant or when you suspect you may be pregnant. Consult your physician before deciding to douche or to apply any preparations to the vagina.

9. Watch your general health. Eating poorly or getting insufficient rest will reduce your resistance to infection.

The Cervix

When someone first said to me two years ago, "You can feel the end of your own cervix with your finger," I was interested but flustered. I had hardly ever put my finger in my vagina at all, and felt squeamish about touching myself there, in that place "reserved" for lovers and doctors. It took me two months to get up nerve to try it, and then one afternoon, pretty nervously, I squatted down in the bathroom and put my finger in deep, back into my vagina. There it was, feeling slippery and rounded, with an indentation at the center through which, I realized, my menstrual flow came. It was both very exciting and beautifully ordinary at the same time. Last week I bought a plastic speculum so I can look at my cervix. Will it take as long this time? (Boston Women's Health Book Collective, 1992)

Question: What is the cervix? The **cervix** is the lower end of the uterus. Its walls, like those of the vagina, produce secretions that contribute to the chemical balance of the vagina. The opening in the middle of the cervix, or **os**, is normally about the width of a straw, although it expands to permit passage of a baby from the uterus to the vagina during childbirth. Sperm pass from the vagina to the uterus through the cervical canal. *Question: What should we know about cervical cancer?*

Cervical cancer is relatively uncommon in the United States, although there are about 12,000 new cases a year and 4,100 deaths (American Cancer Society, 2003). Cervical cancer is more common among women who have had many sex partners, who became sexually active at a relatively early age, who come from lower socioeconomic status, and who smoke (Duggirala et al., 2003). The mortality rate is more than twice as high for African American women as for European American women (National Cancer Institute, 2003). All women are at risk, however.

A **Pap test** examines a sample of cervical cells that are smeared on a slide to screen for cervical cancer and other abnormalities. The American Cancer Society (2003) recommends annual Pap tests along with a pelvic examination for women who are, or have been, sexually active or who have reached age 18. Most cases of cervical cancer can be successfully treated by surgery and **radiotherapy** if they are detected early. For women diagnosed with localized cancer, the survival rate is nearly 100% (American Cancer Society, 2003). Cervical cancer can also be prevented when

Cervix The lower end of the uterus. (Latin for "neck.")

Os The opening in middle of the cervix. (Latin for "mouth.")

Pap test A test of a sample of cervical cells that screens for cervical cancer and other abnormalities. (Named after the originator of the technique, Dr. Papanicolaou.)

Radiotherapy Treatment of a disease by X-rays or by emissions from a radioactive substance.

precancerous changes are detected by Pap test. The overall five-year survival rate is about 70%.

Vaccines are also under development that make women immune to the human papilloma virus (HPV), which is considered to be a key cause of cervical cancer. HPV comes in many forms, and one of them, HPV-16, is believed to lead to half the cases of cervical cancer. In a study of more than 2,300 young women reported in the *New England Journal of Medicine,* half, selected at random, were given a vaccine to immunize them against HPV-16, and half were given a placebo (Koutsky et al., 2002). The vaccine was fully effective in that none of the vaccinated women developed HPV infections or precancerous growths during a 17- to 27-month follow-up period, whereas 41 of the unvaccinated women became infected; and, of these, 9 showed precancerous cervical growths (which were then treated by the researchers).

The Uterus

Question: What is the uterus? The **uterus**, or womb (see Figures 3.3 and 3.6), is the organ in which a fertilized ovum implants and develops until birth. The uterus usually slants forward (is *antroverted*), although about 10% of women have uteruses that tip backward (are *retroverted*). In most instances a retroverted uterus causes no problems but some women with one find coitus in certain positions painful. A retroverted uterus normally tips forward during pregnancy. The uterus is suspended in the pelvis by flexible ligaments. In a woman who has not given birth, it is about 3 inches long, 3 inches wide, and 1 inch thick near the top. The uterus expands to house a fetus during pregnancy and shrinks after pregnancy, though not to its original size.

The uppermost part of the uterus is called the **fundus** (see Figure 3.6). The uterus is shaped like an inverted pear. If a ceramic model of a uterus were placed on a table, it would balance on the fundus. The central region of the uterus is called the body. The narrow lower region is the cervix, which leads downward to the vagina.

Like the vagina, the uterus has three layers (also shown in Figure 3.6). The innermost layer, or **endometrium**, is richly supplied with blood vessels and glands. Its structure varies according to a woman's age and phase of the menstrual cycle. Endometrial tissue is discharged through the cervix and vagina at menstruation. In some women, endometrial tissue may also grow in the abdominal cavity or elsewhere in the reproductive system. This condition is called **endometriosis**, and the most common symptom is menstrual pain. If untreated, it may lead to infertility.

Cancer of the endometrial lining is called endometrial cancer. *Question: What should we know about endometrial cancer?* The risk factors for endometrial cancer include obesity, a diet high in fats, early menarche or late menopause, history of failure to ovulate, and estrogen replacement therapy (Nelson et al., 2002). For women who obtain hormone replacement therapy (HRT), combining estrogen with progestin mitigates the risk of endometrial cancer (Nelson et al., 2002). Endometrial cancer is symptomized by abnormal uterine staining or bleeding, especially after menopause. The most common treatment is surgery (American Cancer Society, 2003). The five-year survival rate for endometrial cancer is up to 95% if it is discovered early and limited to the endometrium. (Endometrial cancer is usually diagnosed early because women tend to report postmenopausal bleeding to their doctors quickly.) The survival rate drops when the cancer invades surrounding tissues or metastasizes.

The second layer of the uterus, the **myometrium**, is well muscled. It endows the uterus with flexibility and strength and creates the powerful contractions that propel

Uterus The hollow, muscular, pear-shaped organ in which a fertilized ovum implants and develops until birth.

Fundus The uppermost part of the uterus. (*Fundus* is a Latin word meaning "base.")

Endometrium The innermost layer of the uterus. (From Latin and Greek roots meaning "within the uterus.")

Endometriosis A condition caused by the growth of endometrial tissue in the abdominal cavity or elsewhere outside the uterus and characterized by menstrual pain.

Myometrium The middle, well-muscled layer of the uterus. (*Myo-* stems from the Greek *mys,* meaning "muscle.")

a fetus outward during labor. The third or outermost layer, the **perimetrium**, provides an external cover.

Hysterectomy One woman in three in the United States has a **hysterectomy** by the age of 60. Most women who obtain them do so between the ages of 35 and 45. The hysterectomy is the second most commonly performed operation on women in this country. (Cesarean sections are the most common.) A hysterectomy may be performed when a woman develops cancer of the uterus, ovaries, or cervix or another disease that causes pain or excessive uterine bleeding. A **complete hysterectomy** involves the surgical removal of the ovaries, fallopian tubes, cervix, and uterus. It is usually performed to reduce the risk of cancer spreading throughout the reproductive system. A **partial hysterectomy** removes the uterus but spares the ovaries and fallopian tubes so that the woman continues to ovulate and produce adequate quantities of female sex hormones.

The hysterectomy can relieve symptoms associated with various gynecological disorders and improve the quality of life for many women (Kjerulff et al., 2000). However, many gynecologists believe that hysterectomy is recommended too often, before proper diagnostic steps are taken or when less radical interventions might alleviate the problem (Broder et al., 2000). We advise women whose physicians advise a hysterectomy to seek a second opinion before proceeding.

The Fallopian Tubes

Question: What are the fallopian tubes? The **fallopian tubes** are about 4 inches in length and extend from the upper end of the uterus toward the ovaries (see Figure 3.6). The part of each tube nearest the uterus is the *isthmus,* which broadens into the *ampulla* as it approaches the ovary. The outer part, or *infundibulum,* has fringelike projections called *fimbriae* that extend toward, but are not attached to, the ovary. Ova pass through the fallopian tubes on their way to the uterus. The fallopian tubes are not just passageways. They help nourish and conduct ova. The tubes are lined with tiny hairlike projections termed cilia ("lashes") that help propel ova through the tube at about 1 inch per day. Because ova must be fertilized within a day or two after they are released from the ovaries, fertilization usually occurs in the infundibulum within a couple of inches of the ovaries. The form of sterilization called tubal ligation ties off the fallopian tubes, so that ova cannot pass through them or become fertilized.

In an **ectopic pregnancy**, the fertilized ovum implants outside the uterus, most often in the fallopian tube where fertilization occurred. Ectopic pregnancies can eventually burst fallopian tubes, causing hemorrhaging and death. Ectopic pregnancies are thus terminated before the tube ruptures. They are not easily recognized, however, because their symptoms—missed menstrual period, abdominal pain, irregular bleeding—suggest many conditions. Any of these symptoms is an excellent reason for consulting a gynecologist. Women who are of advanced age, who have had pelvic inflammatory disease (PID), who have undergone tubal surgery, or who have used intrauterine devices (IUDs) are at increased risk of developing ectopic pregnancies (Women's-Health, 2003).

The Ovaries

Question: What are the ovaries? The two **ovaries** are almond-shaped organs that are each about 1½ inches long. They lie on either side of the uterus, to which they are attached by ovarian ligaments. The ovaries produce ova (egg cells) and the female sex hormones **estrogen** and **progesterone**. Estrogen is a generic term for several hormones (such as estradiol, estriol, and estrone) that promote the changes of puberty

---

Perimetrium The outer layer of the uterus. (From roots meaning "around the uterus.")

Hysterectomy Surgical removal of the uterus.

Complete hysterectomy Surgical removal of the ovaries, fallopian tubes, cervix, and uterus.

Partial hysterectomy Surgical removal of the uterus but not the ovaries and fallopian tubes.

Fallopian tubes Tubes that extend from the upper uterus toward the ovaries and conduct ova to the uterus. (After the Italian anatomist Gabriel Fallopio, who is credited with their discovery.)

Ectopic pregnancy A pregnancy in which the fertilized ovum implants outside the uterus, usually in the fallopian tube. (*Ectopic* derives from Greek roots meaning "out of place.")

Ovaries Almond-shaped organs that produce ova and the hormones estrogen and progesterone.

Estrogen A generic term for female sex hormones (including estradiol, estriol, estrone, and others) or synthetic compounds that promote the development of female sex characteristics and regulate the menstrual cycle. (From the roots meaning "generating" (*-gen*) and "estrus.")

and regulate the menstrual cycle. Estrogen also helps older women maintain cognitive functioning and feelings of psychological well-being (Ross et al., 2000). Progesterone also has multiple functions, including regulating the menstrual cycle and preparing the uterus for pregnancy by stimulating the development of the endometrium (uterine lining). Estrogen and progesterone levels vary with the phases of the menstrual cycle.

The human female is born with all the ova she will ever have (about 2 million), but they are immature in form. Of these, about 400,000 survive into puberty, each of which is contained in the ovary within a thin capsule, or **follicle**. During a woman's reproductive years, from puberty to menopause, only 400 or so ripened ova, typically 1 per month, will be released by their follicles for possible fertilization. How these ova are selected remains a mystery of nature.

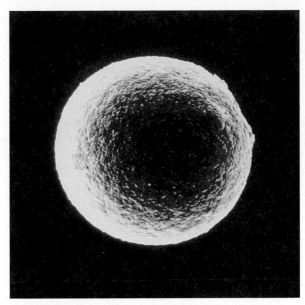

A Magnified Human Ovum (Egg Cell)

Ovarian Cancer Each year some 25,000 women in the United States are diagnosed with ovarian cancer, and about 14,000 die from it (American Cancer Society, 2003). *Question: What should we know about ovarian cancer?* Ovarian cancer most often strikes women between the ages of 40 and 70 and ranks as the fourth leading cancer killer of women, behind lung cancer, breast cancer, and colon cancer. Women most at risk are those with blood relatives who had the disease, especially a first-degree relative (mother, sister, or daughter). Other risk factors are also important, because about 9 women in 10 who develop ovarian cancer do not have a family history of it. Researchers have identified several risk factors that increase the chances of developing the disease: never having given birth, prolonged use of talcum powder between the anus and the vagina, infertility, a history of breast cancer, a diet rich in meat and animal fats, and cigarette smoking (Gnagy et al., 2000; Marchbanks et al., 2000). Questions have been raised as to whether the use of clomiphene, a fertility drug, increases the risk of ovarian cancer. On the other hand, use of acetaminophen (found in Tylenol and some other pain relievers—read the label) may cut the risk of ovarian cancer. Daniel Cramer and his colleagues (1998) studied the use of over-the-counter painkillers in 563 New England women who had ovarian cancer and 523 healthy New England women selected from the general population. They found that 8.8% of the healthy women used acetaminophen, as compared with 4.6% of the women with ovarian cancer.

Early detection is the key to fighting ovarian cancer. When it is detected before spreading beyond the ovary, 95% of victims survive. However, the overall five-year survival rate is about 50% (American Cancer Society, 2003). Unfortunately, ovarian cancer is often "silent" in the early stages, showing no obvious signs or symptoms. The most common sign is enlargement of the abdomen, which is caused by the accumulation of fluid. Periodic, complete pelvic examinations are important. The Pap test, which is useful in detecting cervical cancer, does not reveal ovarian cancer. The American Cancer Society (2003) advises women over the age of 40 to have a cancer-related checkup every year.

Surgery, radiation therapy, and drug therapy are treatment options. Surgery usually includes the removal of one or both ovaries, the uterus, and the fallopian tubes.

The Pelvic Examination

Women are advised to have an internal (pelvic) examination at least once a year by the time they reach their late teens (or earlier if they become sexually active) and

Progesterone A steroid hormone secreted by the corpus luteum or prepared synthetically that stimulates proliferation of the endometrium and is involved in regulation of the menstrual cycle. (From the root *pro-,* meaning "promoting," and the words *gestation, steroid,* and *one.*)

Follicle A capsule within an ovary that contains an ovum. (From a Latin word meaning "small bag.")

twice yearly if they are over age 35 or use birth-control pills. *Question: What happens during the pelvic examination?* The physician (usually a gynecologist) first examines the woman externally for irritations, swellings, abnormal vaginal discharges, and clitoral adhesions. The physician normally inserts a speculum to help inspect the cervix and vaginal walls for discharges (which can be signs of infection), discoloration, lesions, or growths. This examination is typically followed by a Pap test to detect cervical cancer. A sample of vaginal discharge may also be taken to test for the sexually transmitted infection (STI) gonorrhea.

To take a Pap smear, the physician will hold open the vaginal walls with a plastic or (hopefully prewarmed!) metal speculum so that a sample of cells (a "smear") may be scraped from the cervix with a wooden spatula (see Figure 3.7). Women should not douche prior to Pap tests or schedule them during menstruation, because douches and blood confound analysis of the smear.

The speculum exam is normally followed by a bimanual vaginal exam in which the index and middle fingers of one hand are inserted into the vagina while the lower part of the abdomen is palpated (touched) by the other hand from the outside. The physician uses this technique to examine the location, shape, size, and movability of the internal sex organs, searching for abnormal growths and symptoms of other problems. Palpation may be somewhat uncomfortable, but severe pain is a sign that something is wrong. A woman should not try to be "brave" and hide such discomfort from the examiner. She may only be masking a symptom (that is, depriving the physician of useful information). Physical discomfort is usually mild, however, and psychological discomfort may often be relieved by discussing it frankly with the examiner.

Finally, the physician should do a recto-vaginal examination in which one finger is inserted into the rectum while the other is inserted into the vagina. This procedure provides additional information about the ligaments of the uterus, the ovaries, and the fallopian tubes. The procedure also helps the physician evaluate the health of the rectum.

Although it may be somewhat uncomfortable, the pelvic examination is not ordinarily painful. It is normal for a woman who has not had one, or who is visiting a new doctor, to be anxious about the exam. The doctor should be reassuring if the woman expresses concern. If the doctor is not, the woman should feel free to consult another doctor. She should not forgo the pelvic examination itself, however. It is essential for early detection of problems.

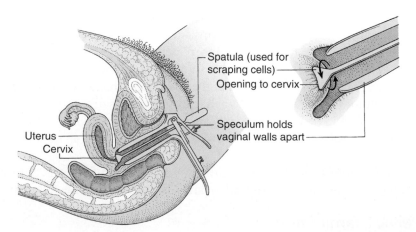

Figure 3.7. Use of the Speculum and Spatula during a Pelvic Examination. The speculum holds the vaginal walls apart while the spatula is used to gently scrape cells from the cervix. The Pap test screens for cervical cancer and other abnormalities.

Review: Internal Sex Organs

Reflect

Are the female sex organs more complex than you had believed? If so, how? Were any erroneous ideas corrected by the information in this section?

Critical Thinking

In the light of your own values, is the termination of an ectopic pregnancy an acceptable form of abortion? Why or why not?

10. The _____ walls have three layers.

11. _____ refers to any vaginal inflammation, regardless of the cause.

12. Sperm pass from the vagina to the uterus through the _____ canal.

13. A(n) _____ test examines cervical cells for cervical cancer and other abnormalities.

14. A fertilized ovum becomes implanted and develops with the _____.

15. The _____ is the second most commonly performed operation on women in the United States.

16. The _____ tubes extend from the uterus toward the ovaries and nourish and conduct ova.

17. The _____ produce ova and female sex hormones.

The Breasts

Some college women recall:

> I was very excited about my breast development. It was a big competition to see who was wearing a bra in elementary school. When I began wearing one, I also liked wearing see-through blouses so everyone would know. . . .

> My breasts were very late in developing. This brought me a lot of grief from my male peers. I just dreaded situations like going to the beach or showering in the locker room. . . .

> All through junior high and high school I felt unhappy about being "overendowed." I felt just too uncomfortable in sweaters—there was so much to reveal and I was always sure that the only reason boys liked me was because of my bustline. . . .

> By the time I was eleven I needed a bra. . . . The girls in my gym class in sixth grade laughed at me because my breasts were pretty big and I still didn't have a bra. I tried to cover myself up when I dressed and undressed. On my eleventh birthday my mom gave me a sailor blouse and inside was my first bra. . . . (It) was the best present I could have received. The bra made me feel a lot better about myself, but I was still unsure of my femininity for a long time. . . .
>
> *Morrison et al., 1980, pp. 66–70*

In some cultures the breasts are viewed merely as biological instruments for feeding infants. In our culture, however, breasts have taken on such erotic significance that a woman's self-esteem may become linked to her bustline.

Question: What are the breasts? The breasts are **secondary sex characteristics**. That is, like the rounding of the hips, they distinguish women from men, but they are not directly involved in reproduction. Each breast contains 15 to 20 clusters of milk-producing **mammary glands** (see Figure 3.8). Each gland opens at the nipple through its own duct. The mammary glands are separated by soft, fatty tissue. It is the amount of this fatty tissue, not the amount of glandular tissue, that largely determines the size of the breasts.

Secondary sex characteristics Traits that distinguish women from men but are not directly involved in reproduction.

Mammary glands Milk-secreting glands. (From the Latin *mamma,* which means both "breast" and "mother.")

Areola The dark ring on the breast that encircles the nipple.

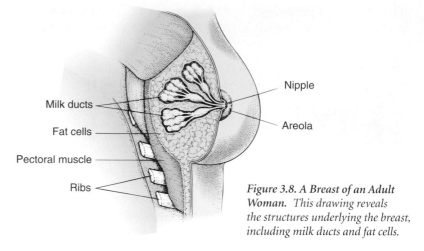

Figure 3.8. A Breast of an Adult Woman. This drawing reveals the structures underlying the breast, including milk ducts and fat cells.

The nipple, which lies in the center of the **areola**, contains smooth muscle fibers that make the nipple become erect when they contract. The areola, or area surrounding the nipple, darkens during pregnancy and remains darker after delivery. Oil-producing glands in the areola help lubricate the nipples during breast feeding. Milk ducts conduct milk from the mammary glands through the nipples. Nipples are richly endowed with nerve endings, so that stimulation of the nipples heightens sexual arousal for many women. Male nipples are similar in sensitivity.

Figure 3.9 shows some of the normal variations in the size and shape of the breasts of adult women. The sensitivity of the breasts to sexual stimulation is unrelated to their size. Small breasts may have as many nerve endings as large breasts, but they will be more densely packed.

Women can prompt their partners to provide breast stimulation by informing them that their breasts are sensitive to stimulation. They can also guide a partner's hands in ways that provide the type of stimulation they desire. The breasts vary in sensitivity with the phases of the menstrual cycle, and some women appear less responsive to breast stimulation than others. However, some less sensitive women may learn to enjoy breast stimulation by focusing on breast sensations during lovemaking in a relaxed atmosphere.

Breast Cancer

The first author's oldest daughter contracted breast cancer a couple of years ago. She was in her 30s, and a lump "suddenly" appeared in her mammography. She and the family dwelled in fear over the next couple of weeks as tissue from the tumor was

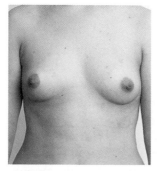
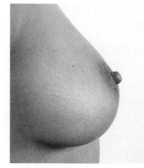
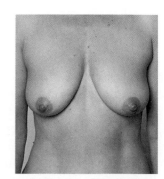

Figure 3.9. Normal Variations in the Size and Shape of the Breasts of Adult Women. The size and shape of the breasts have little bearing on ability to produce milk or on sensitivity to sexual stimulation. Breasts have become highly eroticized in our culture.

biopsied, found to be malignant, and arrangements were made to remove the breast. Given the "aggressiveness" of the tumor—the rapidity with which it had grown—every physician consulted recommended mastectomy (removing the breast) rather than lumpectomy (just removing the lump). The question arose as to whether or not she should have a prophylactic mastectomy of the healthy breast. A blood test determined that she did not possess gene mutations (BRCA1 or BRCA2[1]) that are connected with early-onset breast cancer (Wooster & Weber, 2003), and so the healthy breast was preserved. There was additional anxiety following the removal of the breast as tissues were examined to determine whether the cancer had spread within the breast or to lymph nodes. Fortunately, it had apparently remained within a duct despite the rapidity of its growth.

Then she dealt with the psychological issues of feeling unwhole, which were to some degree mitigated by attending a support group of women undergoing similar experiences. Reconstruction of the breast was an unexpected and lengthy process during which the muscles that normally underlie breasts were gradually ballooned out to surround and support a silicone implant. A new cosmetic nipple was constructed from thigh tissue. It was decided that she did not need chemotherapy or radiation, but she did go on tamoxifen, a drug that decreases the body's supply of estrogen—a factor in the development of cancerous tissue in the breast. There is no evidence of remaining malignant tissue, but we have not yet reached the "magical" five-year postsurgical survival date.

Question: What should we know about breast cancer? Breast cancer strikes nearly 211,000 women in the United States each year and takes about 40,000 lives (American Cancer Society, 2003). (An estimated 240 men also die of breast cancer annually.) The disease takes the lives of 2 to 3 of 10 women in the United States who develop it. It is not cancer in the breast that causes death, but rather its spread to vital body parts, such as the brain, bones, lungs, or liver.

Rates of breast cancer are rising slowly in the United States, at about 0.5% a year (American Cancer Society, 2003). More early cases of breast cancer are apparently being detected because of an increased use of **mammography**, a kind of X-ray that detects cancerous lumps in the breast. Advances in early detection and treatment have led to increased rates of recovery. The five-year survival rate for women whose breast cancers have not metastasized—that is, spread beyond the breast—is more than 90%, up from nearly 80% in the 1940s (American Cancer Society, 2003). The five-year survival rate drops to about 70% if the cancer has spread to the surrounding region and to about 20% if it has spread to distant sites in the body.

Risk Factors   Breast cancer is rare in women under age 25. The risk increases sharply with age. About four of five cases develop in women over the age of 50 (Armstrong et al., 2000). The National Cancer Institute (2003) estimates that from birth to age 40, 1 in 217 women will develop breast cancer. By age 50, the risk rises to 1 in 50. By age 60, it rises to 1 in 24, and by age 70, to 1 in 14.

Genetic factors are involved in breast cancer (Lichtenstein et al., 2000; Wooster & Weber, 2003). The risk of breast cancer is higher among women with a family history of the disease (Armstrong et al., 2000), although nobody in the author's daughter's family had developed breast cancer. A study of more than 100,000 women nurses showed that those with mothers or sisters who had breast cancer had nearly twice the chance of developing the disease themselves (Colditz et al., 1993). Women who had both

Mammography A special type of X-ray test that detects cancerous lumps in the breast.

---

1. Women who inherit BRCA1 or BRCA2 mutations have a 50% to 85% chance of developing breast cancer (American Cancer Society, 2003), as compared with one woman in eight or nine in the general population. They also have an increased risk of developing ovarian cancer.

a mother and a sister with the disease had between two and three times greater risk. British researcher Julian Peto (2002) followed 1,300 pairs of identical twins and 1,000 pairs of fraternal twins in which one member of the pair had developed breast cancer for several years. The identical twins of women with breast cancer stood a one in three chance of developing the disease themselves, as compared with one woman in nine in the general population. The sisters of fraternal twins with breast cancer were significantly less likely than sisters of identical twins to develop the disease, but more likely than women in the general population.

Genes for breast cancer appear to predict not only whether women will contract the disease but also how deadly it will be. A Dutch study reported in the *New England Journal of Medicine* found that only 5.5% of women whose cancers had a "good" genetic signature died within a decade of diagnosis and treatment, as compared with 45% of women with the most deadly genetic signatures (van de Vijver et al., 2002). Health professionals may soon be testing the genomes of women with breast cancer to help determine how aggressively they should treat the disease by means such as chemotherapy and radiation once the tumors have been removed surgically.

A key risk factor in breast cancer is prolonged exposure to estrogen, which stimulates breast development in young women and also the proliferation of breast cancer cells (Clemons & Goss, 2001; Gruber et al., 2002). The following all heighten the risk of breast cancer because they increase the woman's exposure to estrogen: early onset of menstruation (before age 14), late menopause (after age 55), delayed childbearing (after age 30), and never giving birth (American Cancer Society, 2003). Despite the fact that birth-control pills contain estrogen, reviews of the research conclude that, generally speaking, there is no connection between using the pill and breast cancer (Marchbanks et al., 2002). However, other research suggests that the pill may increase the risk of breast cancer in women with a family history of the disorder (Dawn et al., 2000; Grabrick et al., 2000). Exercise, by the way, may reduce the risk of breast cancer, presumably by decreasing the amount of fatty tissue in the body. Fat is connected with higher levels of estrogen production.

Heavy drinking of alcohol also heightens the risk of breast cancer (American Cancer Society, 2003; Singletary & Gapter, 2001). It remains unclear whether a high-fat diet contributes to breast cancer (Gruber et al., 2002). Nevertheless, higher amounts of fatty tissue in the body appear to be connected with breast cancer (American Cancer Society, 2003; Calle et al., 2003).

Does abortion increase a woman's risk of breast cancer? Some writers have speculated that because pregnancy decreases the risk of breast cancer, abortion will indirectly increase the risk (Malec, 2003).

Detection and Treatment   Women with breast cancer have lumps in the breast, *but most lumps in the breasts are not cancerous.* Most are either **cysts** or **benign** tumors called **fibroadenomas.** Breast cancer involves lumps in the breast that are **malignant.**

Early detection and treatment reduce the risk of mortality. The sooner cancer is detected, the less likely it is to have spread to critical organs.

Breast cancer may be detected in various ways, including breast self-examination ("BSE"), physical examination ("clinical breast examination," or "CBE"), and mammography. Through mammography, tiny, highly curable cancers can be detected—and treated—before they can be felt by touch. By the time a malignant lump is large enough to be felt by touch, it already contains millions of cells. It may even have metastasized—that is, splintered off to form colonies elsewhere in the body. A mam-

Cysts Saclike structures filled with fluid or diseased material.

Benign Doing little or no harm.

Fibroadenoma A benign, fibrous tumor.

Malignant Lethal; causing or likely to cause death.

African American Women and Breast Cancer

Overall, African Americans are more likely than European Americans to develop cancer. The case is somewhat different with breast cancer. As a group, African American women are somewhat less likely than European American women to de- velop breast cancer. However, when they do, they frequently do so at an earlier age. They tend to be diag- nosed with the disease somewhat later, and they are also more likely to die from it (American Cancer Soci- ety, 2003; Jetter, 2000). Some aspects of the racial differences, such as the tendency to be diagnosed later, may reflect less access to health care. On the other hand, genetic factors are also likely to be involved. It is usually estrogen that causes the proliferation of breast cancer cells, and thus some drugs, like tamoxifen, treat breast cancer by suppressing the body's supply of estrogen. However, African American women are more likely to develop tumors that are "estrogen- receptor negative." That is, they de- velop rapidly even in the absence of estrogen. These tumors are highly aggressive—that is, they grow very rapidly—and are a major factor in the higher mortality rate for African American women (American Can- cer Society, 2003; Jetter, 2000).

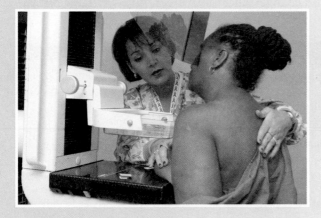

African American Women and Breast Cancer *African American women are generally less likely than European American women to develop breast cancer. But, when they do, the cancer tends to be more aggressive and deadly. The racial difference may be largely genetic.*

mography can detect tiny tumors before metastasis. One study found that 82% of women whose breast cancers were detected early by mammography survived for at least five years following surgery, as compared to 60% of those whose cancers were discovered later. Note that HRT can impair the accuracy of mammographic screen- ing (Kavanagh et al., 2000).

Early detection may offer another benefit. Smaller lumps can often be removed by **lumpectomy**, sparing the breast. More advanced cancers are likely to be treated by **mastectomy**.

Many drugs are also used to treat breast cancer, and others are in the research pipeline. For example, *tamoxifen* locks into the estrogen receptors of breast cancer cells, thereby blocking the effects of estrogen that would otherwise stimulate the cells to grow and proliferate. However, tamoxifen increases the risks of uterine cancer and of blood clots in the lungs, along with some other side effects. The risks of these side effects were lowest among women below the age of 50. The drug raloxifene (sold under the brand name Evista), which is intended to treat osteoporosis and prevent heart problems in postmenopausal women (Marwick, 2000), has also been shown to dramatically reduce the risk of breast cancer (Cummings et al., 1999). More- over, raloxifene does not appear to have the side effects associated with tamoxifen. (Nevertheless, after careful consideration and several consultations, the author's daughter was placed on tamoxifen and not raloxifene.) Other drugs, including Taxol, Herceptin, and many others, are also being studied for use against breast cancer. Ask your gynecologist for the latest research results and which drugs, if any, are right for you, given your risk of breast cancer, your age, and other factors.

Many women who have had mastectomies have had surgical breast implants to replace the tissue that has been removed. Other women have breast implants to

Lumpectomy Surgical removal of a lump from the breast.

Mastectomy Surgical removal of the entire breast.

Truth?Fiction?
Revisited

Monthly breast self-examinations (BSEs) are no longer recommended by the American Cancer Society. However, the "A Closer Look" on page 85 provides instructions for women who choose to engage in breast self-examination.

augment their breast size. Research suggests that breast implants appear to have no effect on the probability of developing breast cancer, rheumatoid arthritis, and a number of other health problems, casting doubts on previous studies that had implicated them in the development of these problems (Spiegel, 2001; Wooster & Weber, 2003). However, the issue remains controversial. Readers are advised to consult their gynecologists for the latest research evidence.

The American Cancer Society (2003) recommends that women have a clinical breast exam every three years when they are between 20 and 39 years of age and annually thereafter. Mammograms reduce the death rate from breast cancer in women age 50 and above by 25% to 30% (Chlebowski, 2000). The current guidelines of the American Cancer Society, and changes since 1997, are outlined in Table 3.1.

TABLE 3.1

Updated Breast Cancer Screening Guidelines: What Has Changed and Why

		Former guidelines (1997)	Updated guidelines and information (May 2003)	Explanation
Women at average risk	Mammography	Annually starting at age 40	No change from 1997 recommendation. There is a tremendous amount of additional, credible evidence of the benefit of mammography since 1997, especially regarding women in their 40s.	Women can feel confident about the benefits associated with regular screening mammography. However, mammography also has limitations: It will miss some cancers, and it sometimes leads to follow-up of findings that are not cancer, including biopsies.
	Clinical breast examination (CBE)	Every three years for women 20–39; annually for women 40 and older	CBE should be part of a woman's periodic health examination, about every three years for women in their 20s and 30s and annually for women 40 and older.	CBE is a complement to regular mammography screening and an opportunity for women and their health care providers to discuss changes in their breasts, risk factors, and early detection testing.
	Breast self-examination (BSE)	Monthly starting at age 20	Women should report any breast change promptly to their health care provider. Beginning in their 20s, women should be told about the benefits and limitations of BSE. It is acceptable for women to choose not to do BSE or to do it occasionally.	Research has shown that BSE plays a small role in detecting breast cancer compared with self-awareness. However, doing BSE is one way for women to know how their breasts normally feel and to notice any changes.
	Older women and women with serious health problems	Additional research is needed.	Continue annual mammography, regardless of age, as long as a woman does not have serious, chronic health problems. For women with serious health problems or short life expectancy, evaluate ongoing early detection testing.	There is a need to balance the potential benefits of ongoing screening mammography in women with limited longevity against the limitations. The survival benefit of a current mammogram may not be seen for several years.
Women known to be at increased risk	Women known to be at increased risk	Women with a family history of breast cancer should discuss guidelines with their doctors.	Women known to be at increased risk may benefit from earlier initiation of early detection testing and/or the addition of breast ultrasound or MRI.	The evidence available is only sufficient to offer general guidance. This guidance will help women and their doctors make more informed decisions about screening.

Source: American Cancer Society: http://www.cancer.org/docroot/NWS/content/NWS_1_1x_Updated_Breast_Cancer_Screening_Guidelines_Released.asp

In sum, more than ever is known about the development of breast cancer. Breast cancer that develops early, for example, is believed to be largely genetic, and genetic markers (BRCA1 or BRCA2 genes) for early-onset breast cancer can indicate whether a particular woman is at risk (ask your gynecologist). Prolonged exposure to estrogen is a known risk factor, because estrogen stimulates the proliferation of breast cancer cells as well as breast development in young women. Exercise is believed to reduce the risk of breast cancer by decreasing the amount of fat in the body. (Estrogen is produced by fat cells as well as by the ovaries.)

Some women with BRCA1 or BRCA2 genes that place them at high risk for breast cancer choose to have their breasts removed prophylactically—that is, to prevent development of breast cancer. Although the procedure is "radical," it appears to be effective (Meijers-Heijboer et al., 2000, 2001). On the other hand, there are the possibilities of problems with implants and reconstructive surgery, and some women are unhappy with the outcomes (Frost et al., 2000).

Mammography also allows for the detection of tiny, highly curable cancers before they can be felt by clinical examination or touch. Early detection allows many women to have small cancerous lumps removed by lumpectomy (surgical removal of the lump that contains the mass of cancer cells) rather than by mastectomy (removal of the entire breast).

An increasing arsenal of anti-breast-cancer medicines are also available or under development. For example, the drug *tamoxifen* locks into the estrogen receptors of

Review: The Breasts

Reflect

Feminist Germaine Greer wrote "The degree of attention which breasts receive, combined with the confusion about what the breast fetishists actually want, makes women unduly anxious about them. They can never be just right; they must always be too small, too big, the wrong shape, too flabby." How important is the size and shape of your breasts (or your partner's breasts) to you? Why?

CriticalThinking

The American Cancer Society no longer recommends that women need to conduct breast self-examinations as a means of detecting breast cancer early. Do you believe that it is a good idea for women to do breast self-exams anyhow? Why or why not?

18. The breasts are (*Primary* or *Secondary*?) sex characteristics.

19. Each breast contains 15 to 20 clusters of milk-producing _____ glands.

20. Milk _____ conduct milk from the mammary glands through the nipples.

21. Breast cancer strikes about _____ women in the United States each year.

22. The risk of breast cancer (*Increases* or *Decreases*?) with age.

23. The risk of breast cancer is (*Higher* or *Lower*?) among women with a family history of the disease.

24. A key risk factor in breast cancer is prolonged exposure to _____, which stimulates the proliferation of breast cancer cells.

25. (*African* or *European*?) Americans are more likely to die from breast cancer.

26. Through _____, curable breast cancers can be detected and treated before they can be felt by touch.

27. Smaller cancerous lumps can often be removed by _____, which leaves the non-diseased part of the breast intact.

28. Removal of the breast is termed _____.

Breast Self-Examination

Regular visits to a physician and mammograms provide the best protection against breast cancer, because they may lead to early detection and treatment. But many women find lumps themselves. It was previously recommended (as recently as 1997) that women conduct breast self-examinations (BSEs) at least once a month, but now the American Cancer Society considers BSEs to be optional. On the other hand, BSE may have psychological advantages for many women—empowering them to investigate their own bodies and to actively participate in their own disease prevention. Moreover, the American Cancer Society (2003) continues to recommend that women be "aware" of what is going on in their bodies. BSE would appear to be one useful way to cultivate this awareness.

The following instructions for breast self-examination are based on American Cancer Society guidelines (see Figure 3.10). Additional material on breast self-examination may be obtained from the American Cancer Society by calling 1-800-ACS-2345. However, women are advised to initiate BSEs with a health professional in order to determine their baseline "lumpiness" and to learn the proper technique.

1. *In the shower.* Examine your breasts during your bath or shower; hands glide more easily over wet skin. Keep your fingers flat and move gently over every part of each breast. Use the right hand to examine the left breast and the left hand for the right breast. Check for any lump, hard knot, or thickening.

2. *Before a mirror.* Inspect your breasts with your arms at your sides. Next, raise your arms high overhead. Look for any changes in the contour of each breast, a swelling, dimpling of skin, or changes in the nipple. Then rest your palms on your hips and press down firmly to flex your chest muscles. Your left and right breasts will not exactly match. Few women's breasts do. Regular inspection shows what is normal for you and will give you confidence in your examination.

3. *Lying down.* To examine your right breast, put a pillow or folded towel under your right shoulder. Place your right arm behind your head. This position distributes breast tissue more evenly on the chest. With your left hand, fingers flat, press gently with the finger pads (the top thirds of the fingers) of the three middle fingers in small circular motions around an imaginary clock face. Begin at the outermost top of your right breast for 12 o'clock, then move to 1 o'clock, and so on around the circle back to 12. A ridge of firm tissue in the lower curve of

breast cancer cells, thus blocking the effects of estrogen. Tamoxifen apparently reduces the probability of developing breast cancer by about 45% (Chlebowski, 2000). *Raloxifene* is used to treat osteoporosis and prevent heart problems in postmenopausal women (Marwick, 2000), but it also reduces the risk of breast cancer (Cummings et al., 1999). Other drugs including *Taxol* and *Herceptin* are being studied for use against breast cancer.

Your gynecologist should have the latest research results. Be proactive. Seize the opportunity to evaluate whether or not you have breast cancer. There are more treatment options than ever; the survival rates are higher than ever; and earlier detection is often connected with less radical treatments.

The Menstrual Cycle

Menstruation is the cyclical bleeding that stems from the shedding of the uterine lining (endometrium.) Menstruation takes place when a reproductive cycle has not led to the fertilization of an ovum. The word *menstruation* derives from the Latin *mensis*, meaning "month." The human menstrual cycle averages about 28 days in length.

Question: What is the menstrual cycle? The menstrual cycle is regulated by the hormones estrogen and progesterone and can be divided into four phases. During the first phase of the cycle, the *proliferative phase*, which follows menstruation, estrogen levels increase, causing the ripening of perhaps 10 to 20 ova (egg cells) within

Menstruation The cyclical bleeding that stems from the shedding of the uterine lining (endometrium).

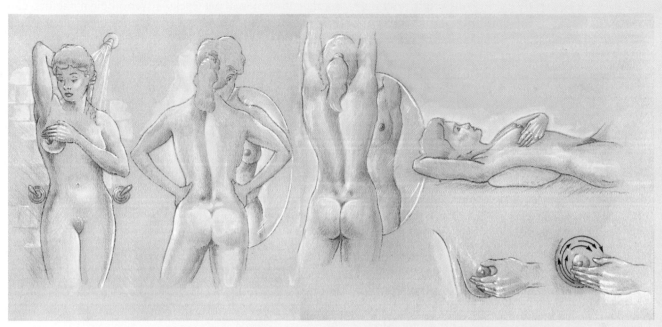

Figure 3.10. A Woman Examines Her Breast for Lumps

each breast is normal. Then move in 1 inch, toward the nipple. Keep circling to examine *every part of your breast,* including the nipple. This requires at least three more circles.

Now slowly repeat the procedure on your left breast. Place the pillow beneath your left shoulder, your left arm behind your head, and use the finger pads on your right hand.

After you examine your left breast fully, squeeze the nipple of each breast gently between your thumb and index finger. Any discharge, clear or bloody, should be reported to your doctor immediately.

their follicles and the proliferation of endometrial tissue in the uterus. During the second phase of the cycle, estrogen reaches peak blood levels, and **ovulation** occurs. Normally only 1 ovum reaches maturity and is released by an ovary during ovulation. Then the third phase—the *secretory,* or *luteal,* phase—of the cycle begins. The luteal phase begins right after ovulation and continues through the beginning of the next cycle.

The term *luteal phase* is derived from **corpus luteum**, the name given the follicle that releases an ovum. The corpus luteum functions as an **endocrine gland** and produces large amounts of progesterone and estrogen. Progesterone causes the endometrium to thicken, so that it will be able to support an embryo if fertilization occurs. If the ovum goes unfertilized, however, estrogen and progesterone levels plummet. These falloffs provide the trigger for the fourth phase, the *menstrual phase,* which leads to the beginning of a new cycle.

Ovulation may not occur in every menstrual cycle. Anovulatory ("without ovulation") cycles are most common in the years just after **menarche**. They may become frequent again in the years prior to menopause, but they may also occur irregularly among women in their 20s and 30s.

Although the menstrual cycle averages about 28 days, variations among women, and in the same woman from month to month, are quite common. Girls' cycles are often irregular for a few years after menarche but later assume reasonably regular patterns. Variations from cycle to cycle tend to occur during the proliferative phase that precedes ovulation. That is, menstruation tends to reliably follow ovulation by about 14 days. Variations of more than 2 days in the postovulation period are rare.

Ovulation The release of an ovum from an ovary.

Corpus luteum The follicle that has released an ovum and then produces copious amounts of progesterone and estrogen during the luteal phase of a woman's cycle. (From Latin roots meaning "yellow body.")

Endocrine gland A ductless gland that releases its secretions directly into the bloodstream.

Menarche The first menstrual period.

Hypothalamus A bundle of neural cell bodies near the center of the brain that are involved in regulating body temperature, motivation, and emotion.

Pituitary gland The gland that secretes growth hormone, prolactin, oxytocin, and others.

Hormone A substance secreted by an endocrine gland that regulates various body functions. (From the Greek *horman,* meaning "to stimulate" or "to goad.")

Testes The male gonads.

Although hormones regulate the menstrual cycle, psychological factors can influence the secretion of hormones. Stress can delay or halt menstruation. Anxiety that she may be pregnant and thus miss her period may also cause a woman to be late. Many women in otherwise good health stopped menstruating during imprisonment in Nazi concentration camps during World War II.

Regulation of the Menstrual Cycle

The menstrual cycle involves finely tuned relationships between structures in the brain—the **hypothalamus** and the **pituitary gland**—and the ovaries and uterus. All these structures are parts of the endocrine system, which means that they secrete chemicals directly into the bloodstream (see Figure 3.11). The ovaries and uterus are also reproductive organs. The chemicals secreted by endocrine glands are called **hormones.** (Other bodily secretions, such as milk, saliva, sweat, and tears, arrive at their destinations by passing through narrow, tubular structures in the body called ducts.)

Behavioral and social scientists are especially interested in hormones because of their behavioral effects. Hormones regulate bodily processes such as the metabolic rate, growth of bones and muscle, production of milk, metabolism of sugar, and storage of fats, among others. Several hormones play important roles in sexual and reproductive functions.

The gonads—the ovaries in the female and the **testes** (or testicles) in the male—secrete sex hormones directly into the bloodstream. The female gonads, the ovaries,

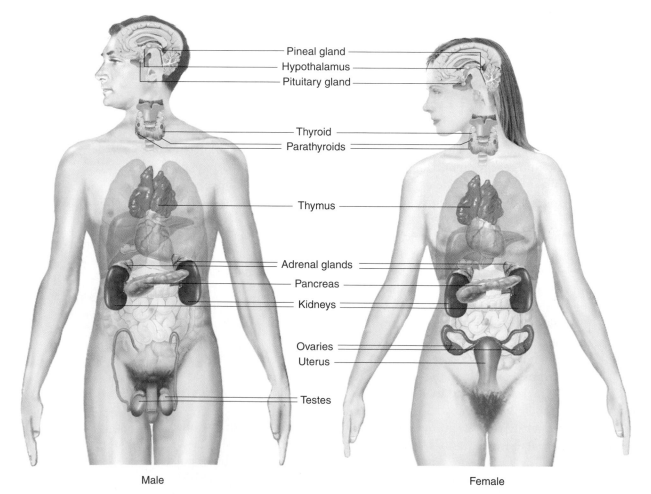

Male   Female

Figure 3.11. Major Glands of the Endocrine System. *The endocrine system consists of glands that secrete chemicals called hormones directly into the bloodstream.*

produce the sex hormones estrogen and progesterone. The male gonads, the testes, produce the male sex hormone **testosterone**. Males and females also produce sex hormones of the other gender but in relatively small amounts.

The hypothalamus is a pea-sized structure in the front part of the brain. It weighs about 4 to 5 grams and lies above the pituitary gland and below (hence the prefix *hypo-*, for "under") the thalamus. Despite its small size, it is involved in regulating many states of motivation, including hunger, thirst, aggression, and sex. For example, when the rear part of a male rat's hypothalamus is stimulated by an electric probe, the rat runs through its courting and mating sequence. It nibbles at a female's ears and at the back of her neck. When she responds, they copulate. Human sexuality is not so stereotyped or mechanical—although in the cases of some people who are highly routinized in their behavior, it may appear so.

The pituitary gland, which is about the size of a pea, lies below the hypothalamus at the base of the brain. Because many pituitary secretions regulate other endocrine glands, the pituitary has also been called the *master gland*. Pituitary hormones regulate bone and muscle growth and urine production. Two pituitary hormones are active during pregnancy and motherhood: **prolactin**, which stimulates production of milk, and **oxytocin**, which stimulates uterine contractions in labor and the ejection of milk during nursing. The pituitary gland also produces **gonadotropins** (literally, "that which 'feeds' the gonads") that stimulate the ovaries: **follicle-stimulating hormone** (**FSH**) and **luteinizing hormone** (**LH**). These hormones play central roles in regulating the menstrual cycle.

The hypothalamus receives information about bodily events through the nervous and circulatory systems. It monitors the blood levels of various hormones, including estrogen and progesterone, and releases a hormone called **gonadotropin-releasing hormone** (**Gn-RH**), which stimulates the pituitary to release gonadotropins. Gonadotropins, in turn, regulate the activity of the gonads. It was once thought that the pituitary gland ran the show, but it is now known that the pituitary gland is regulated by the hypothalamus. Even the "master gland" must serve another.

Phases of the Menstrual Cycle

The menstrual cycle has four stages or phases: proliferative, ovulatory, secretory, and menstrual (see Figure 3.12). It might seem logical that a new cycle begins with the first day of the menstrual flow, because this is the most clearly identifiable event of the cycle. Many women also count the days of the menstrual cycle beginning with the

Testosterone The male sex hormone that fosters the development of male sex characteristics and is connected with the sex drive.

Prolactin A pituitary hormone that stimulates production of milk.

Oxytocin A pituitary hormone that stimulates uterine contractions in labor and the ejection of milk during nursing.

Gonadotropins Pituitary hormones that stimulate the gonads. (Literally, "that which 'feeds' the gonads.")

Follicle-stimulating hormone (FSH) A gonadotropin that stimulates development of follicles in the ovaries.

Luteinizing hormone (LH) A gonadotropin that helps regulate the menstrual cycle by triggering ovulation.

Gonadotropin-releasing hormone (Gn-RH) A hormone secreted by the hypothalamus that stimulates the pituitary to release gonadotropins.

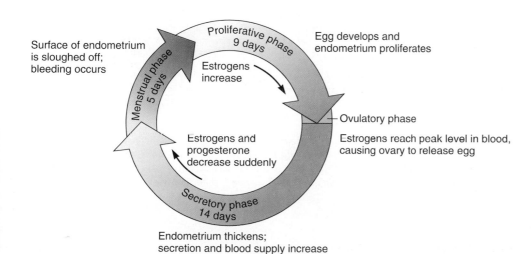

Figure 3.12. The Four Phases of the Menstrual Cycle. The menstrual cycle has proliferative, ovulatory, secretory (luteal), and menstrual phases.

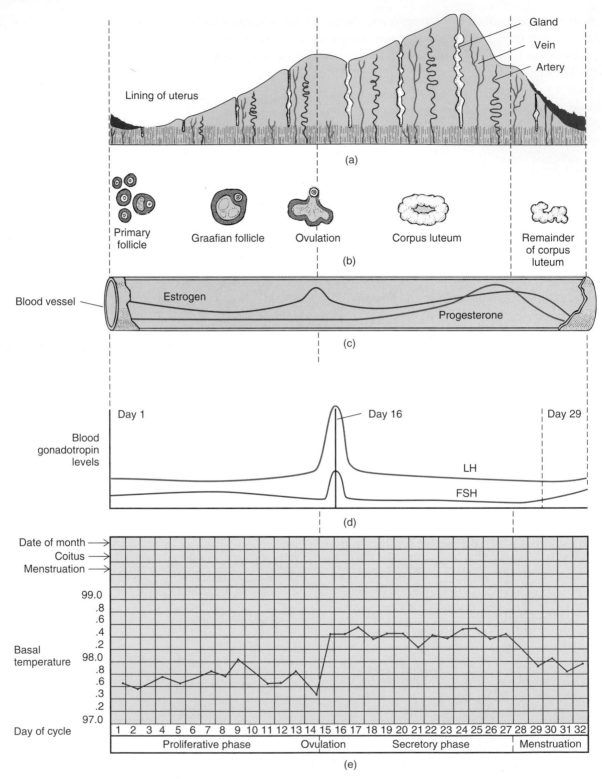

Figure 3.13. Changes That Occur During the Menstrual Cycle. This figure shows five categories of biological change: (a) changes in the development of the uterine lining (endometrium), (b) follicular changes, (c) changes in blood levels of ovarian hormones, (d) changes in blood levels of pituitary hormones, and (e) changes in basal temperature. Note the dip in temperature that is connected with ovulation.

onset of menstruation. Biologically speaking, however, menstruation is really the cul-
mination of the cycle. In fact, the cycle begins with the end of menstruation and the
initiation of a series of biological events that lead to the maturation of an immature
ovum in preparation for ovulation and possible fertilization.

The Proliferative Phase The first phase, or **proliferative phase**, begins with the end
of menstruation and lasts about 9 or 10 days in an average 28-day cycle (see Figures
3.12 and 3.13). During this phase the endometrium develops, or "proliferates." This
phase is also known as the *preovulatory* or *follicular* phase, because certain ovarian
follicles mature and the ovaries prepare for ovulation.

Low levels of estrogen and progesterone are circulating in the blood as menstruation draws to an end. When the hypothalamus senses a low level of estrogen in the
blood, it increases its secretion of Gn-RH, which in turn triggers the pituitary gland
to release FSH. When FSH reaches the ovaries, it stimulates some follicles (perhaps
10 to 20) to begin to mature. As the follicles ripen, they begin to produce estrogen.
Normally, however, only one of them—called the *graafian follicle*—will reach full
maturity in the days just preceding ovulation. As the graafian follicle matures, it
moves toward the surface of the ovary, where it will eventually rupture and release a
mature egg (see Figures 3.13 and 3.14).

Estrogen causes the endometrium in the uterus to thicken to about ⅛ inch.
Glands develop that would eventually nourish an embryo. Estrogen also stimulates
the appearance of a thin cervical mucus. This mucus is alkaline and provides a hos-
pitable, nutritious medium for sperm. The chances are thus increased that sperm
that enter the female reproductive system at the time of ovulation will survive.

The Ovulatory Phase During ovulation, or the **ovulatory phase**, the graafian follicle
ruptures and releases a mature ovum *near* a fallopian tube—not actually *into* a fallopian tube (see Figure 3.14). The other ripening follicles degenerate and are reabsorbed by the body. If two ova mature and are released during ovulation, and both
are fertilized, fraternal (nonidentical) twins will develop. Identical twins occur when
one fertilized ovum divides into two separate **zygotes**.

Ovulation is set into motion when estrogen production reaches a critical level.
The hypothalamus detects the high level of estrogen and triggers the pituitary to
release copious amounts of FSH and LH (see Figures 3.13 and 3.14). The surge of LH
triggers ovulation, which usually begins 12 to 24 hours after the level of LH in the
body has reached its peak. The synthetic hormone **clomiphene** is chemically similar
to LH and has been used by women who ovulate irregularly to induce reliable ovulation and thus increase the chances of conceiving.

Proliferative phase The
first phase of the menstrual
cycle, which begins with the
end of menstruation and
lasts about nine or ten days.
During this phase, the
endometrium proliferates.

Ovulatory phase The
second stage of the
menstrual cycle, during
which a follicle ruptures and
releases a mature ovum.

Zygote A fertilized ovum
(egg cell).

Clomiphene A synthetic
hormone that is chemically
similar to LH and induces
ovulation.

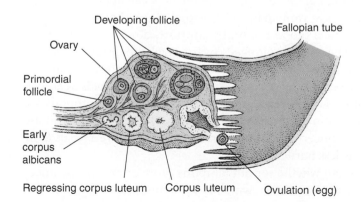

*Figure 3.14. Maturation and Eventual Decomposition of an
Ovarian Follicle. Many follicles develop and produce estrogen
during the proliferative phase of the menstrual cycle. Usually
only one, the graafian follicle, ruptures and releases an ovum.
The graafian follicle then develops into the corpus luteum, which
produces copious quantities of estrogen and progesterone. When
fertilization does not occur, the corpus luteum decomposes.*

Mittelschmerz Pain that occurs during ovulation. (German for "middle pain," reflecting the fact that the pain occurs midway between menstrual periods.)

Secretory phase The third phase of the menstrual cycle, which follows ovulation. Also referred to as the *luteal phase,* after the *corpus luteum,* which begins to secrete large amounts of progesterone and estrogen following ovulation.

A woman's *basal body temperature,* taken by oral or rectal thermometer, dips slightly at ovulation (see Figure 3.13) and rises by about 1°F on the day following ovulation. Many women use this information to help them conceive or avoid conceiving.

Some women have discomfort or cramping during ovulation, termed **mittelschmerz**. Mittelschmerz is sometimes confused with appendicitis. Mittelschmerz, however, may occur on either side of the abdomen, depending on which ovary is releasing an ovum. A ruptured appendix always causes pain on the right side.

The Secretory Phase The phase following ovulation is called the postovulatory or **secretory phase**. Some people refer to it as the *luteal phase,* which reflects the name given the ruptured (graafian) follicle—the *corpus luteum.* Figures 3.13 and 3.14 show the transformation of the graafian follicle into the corpus luteum.

Under the influence of LH, the corpus luteum, which has remained in the ovary, begins to produce large amounts of progesterone and estrogen. Levels of these hormones peak at around the 20th or 21st day of an average cycle (see Figure 3.13). These hormones cause the glands in the endometrium to secrete nutrients to sustain a fertilized ovum that becomes implanted in the uterine wall.

If implantation does not occur, the hypothalamus responds to the peak levels of progesterone by signaling the pituitary to stop producing LH and FSH. This feedback process is similar to that of a thermostat in a house reacting to rising temperatures by shutting down the furnace. The levels of LH and FSH decline rapidly, leading the corpus luteum to decompose. After its decomposition, levels of estrogen and progesterone fall precipitously. The corpus luteum sows the seeds of its own destruction: Its hormones signal the brain to shut down secretion of substances that maintain it.

The Menstrual Phase: An End and a Beginning The **menstrual phase** occurs when estrogen and progesterone levels decline to the point where they can no longer sustain the uterine lining. The lining then disintegrates and is discharged from the body along with the menstrual flow.

The low estrogen levels of the menstrual phase signal the hypothalamus to release Gn-RH, which in turn stimulates the pituitary to secrete FSH. FSH, in turn, prompts ovarian secretion of estrogen and the onset of another proliferative phase. Thus a new cycle begins. The menstrual phase is a beginning as well as an end.

Menstrual flow contains blood from the endometrium (uterine lining), endometrial tissue, and cervical and vaginal mucus. Although the flow can appear persistent and last for five days or more, most women lose only a total of 2 or 3 ounces of blood (4 to 6 tablespoonfuls). A typical blood donor, by contrast, donates 16 ounces of blood at a sitting. Extremely heavy or prolonged (over a week) menstrual bleeding may reflect health problems and should be discussed with a health professional.

Prior to 1933, women generally used external sanitary napkins or pads to absorb the menstrual flow. In that year, however, **tampons** were introduced. Tampons are inserted into the vagina and left in place to absorb menstrual fluid. Women who use tampons can swim without concern while menstruating, wear more revealing or comfortable apparel, and feel less burdened.

Questions have arisen about whether or not tampons cause or exacerbate infections, such as toxic shock syndrome (TSS), which is sometimes fatal. Signs of TSS

A World of Diversity

Historical and Cross-Cultural Perspectives on Menstruation

In Peru, they speak of a "visit from Uncle Pepe," whereas in Samoa, menstruation is referred to as "the boogie man." One of the more common epithets given menstruation through the course of history is "the curse." The Fulani of Upper Volta in Africa use a term for it that translates "to see dirt." Nationalism also rises to the call, with some nations blaming "the curse" on their historical enemies. In earlier times the French referred to menstruation as "the English" and to its onset as "the English are coming."

It is a common folk belief that menstruating women are contaminated. Men thus avoid contact with menstruating women for fear of their lives. To prevent their contaminating others, menstruating women in tribal societies may be dispatched to special huts on the fringe of the village. In the traditional Navajo Indian culture, for instance, menstruating women would be consigned to huts that were set apart from other living quarters. In many Islamic societies, a menstruating woman is considered polluted and is not permitted either to pray or to enter a mosque.

Women in industrialized nations are not consigned to special huts, but throughout the history of Western culture, menstruation has been seen as unclean, contaminating, and even magical.

Ancient societies—and some contemporary ones—have limited understanding of bodily processes, or else they rely on tradition more than science. Science teaches that there is no medical basis to fears of menstruating women and that there are no dangers in menstrual coitus.

We might laugh off these misconceptions as folly and ignorance, if it were not for their profound effect on women. Women who believe the myths about menstruation may see themselves as sources of pollution and endure anxiety, depression, and lowered self-esteem. Negative cultural beliefs concerning menstruation may also contribute to menstrual distress.

include fever, headache, sore throat, vomiting, diarrhea, muscle aches, rash, and dizziness. Peeling skin, disorientation, and a plunge in blood pressure may follow. TSS is caused by the *Staphylococcus aureus* ("staph") bacterium. In 1980, the peak year for cases of TSS, there were 344 recorded cases of TSS and 28 fatalities. Procter & Gamble removed its "extra absorbent" tampon Rely from the market when it was discovered that 71% of these TSS victims had used the product. A highly absorbent tampon that remains in place for 6 hours or more may create an ideal breeding ground for staph. The number of TSS cases has subsequently declined.

Although some researchers believe that concern over TSS has been exaggerated, many women now use regular rather than superabsorbent tampons. Some women alternate tampons with sanitary napkins during each day of menstruation. Some change their tampons three or four times a day. Other women have returned to external sanitary napkins. Still others use natural sponges. Women are encouraged to consult their health care providers about TSS.

Coitus during Menstruation

Many couples continue to engage in coitus during menstruation, but others abstain. Some people abstain because of religious prohibitions. Others express concern about the "fuss" or the "mess" of the menstrual flow. *Question: Is it harmful to engage in coitus during menstruation?* Despite traditional attitudes that associate menstruation with uncleanliness, there is no evidence that coitus during menstruation is physically

Menstrual phase The fourth phase of the menstrual cycle, during which the endometrium is sloughed off in the menstrual flow.

Tampon A cylindrical plug of cotton that is inserted into the vagina and left in place to absorb menstrual fluid. (A French word, meaning a gun barrel "plug.")

harmful to either partner. Ironically, menstrual coitus may be helpful to the woman. The uterine contractions that occur during orgasm may help relieve cramping by dispelling blood congestion. Orgasm achieved through masturbation may have the same effect.

Women may be sexually aroused at any time during the menstrual cycle. The preponderance of the research evidence, however, points to a peak in sexual desire in women around the time of ovulation.

Human coital patterns during the phases of the menstrual cycle apparently reflect personal decisions, not hormone fluctuations. Some couples may decide to increase their frequency of coitus at ovulation, in order to optimize the chances of conceiving, or to abstain during menstruation because of religious beliefs or beliefs linking menses with uncleanliness. Some may also increase their coital activity preceding menstruation to compensate for anticipated abstinence during menses or increase coital activity afterwards to make up for deprivation. In contrast, females of other species that are bound by the estrous cycle respond sexually only during estrus, except in relatively rare cases in which the female submits to sexual advances to fend off attacks from an aggressive male.

Menopause, Perimenopause, and the Climacteric

Menopause, or the "change of life," is the cessation of menstruation. Menopause is a process that most commonly occurs between the ages of 46 and 50 and lasts for about two years. However, it may begin any time between the ages of 35 and 60. There is at least one case of a woman who became pregnant at age 61. *Question: What are the differences between menopause, perimenopause, and the climacteric?*

The term **perimenopause** refers to the beginning of menopause and is usually characterized by 3 to 11 months of amenorrhea (lack of menstruation) or irregular periods (Bastian et al., 2003; Torpy et al., 2003). Perimenopause ends with menopause. Menopause, in other words, is a specific event in a longer-term process known as the **climacteric** ("critical period"). The term *climacteric* specifically refers to the gradual decline in the reproductive capacity of the ovaries. The climacteric generally lasts for about 15 years, from ages 45 to 60 or so. After about the age of 35, the menstrual cycles of many women shorten, from an average of 28 days to 25 days at age 40 and to 23 days by the mid-40s. By the end of her 40s, a woman's cycles often become erratic, with some periods close together and others missed.

In menopause, the pituitary gland continues to pour normal levels of FSH and LH into the bloodstream; but, for reasons that are not well understood, the ovaries gradually lose their capacity to respond. The ovaries no longer ripen egg cells or produce the sex hormones estrogen and progesterone.

The deficit in estrogen may lead to a number of unpleasant perimenopausal sensations, such as night sweats and hot flashes (suddenly feeling hot) and hot flushes (suddenly looking reddened) (Bastian et al., 2003; Dennerstein et al., 2000). Hot flashes and flushes may alternate with cold sweats, in which a woman feels suddenly cold and clammy. Anyone who has experienced "cold feet" or hands from anxiety or fear will understand how dramatic the shifting patterns of blood flow can be. Hot flashes and flushes stem largely from "waves" of dilation of blood vessels across the face and upper body. All of these sensations reflect "vasomotor instability." That is, there are disruptions in the body mechanisms that dilate or constrict the blood vessels to maintain an even body temperature. Additional signs of estrogen deficiency include dizziness, headaches, pains in the joints, sensations of tingling in the hands or feet, burning or itchy skin, and heart palpitations. The skin usually becomes drier.

Menopause The cessation of menstruation.

Perimenopause The beginning of menopause, as characterized by 3 to 11 months of amenorrhea or irregular periods.

Climacteric A long-term process, including menopause, that involves the gradual decline in the reproductive capacity of the ovaries.

There is some loss of breast tissue and decreased vaginal lubrication during sexual arousal. Women may also encounter sleep problems, such as awakening more frequently at night and having difficulty falling back to sleep. A Chinese study found that about one perimenopausal woman in six experienced migraine headaches (Wang et al., 2003).

Long-term estrogen deficiency has been linked to brittleness and porosity of the bones—a condition called **osteoporosis**. Bones break more readily, and some women develop so-called dowager's hump. Osteoporosis can be severely handicapping, even life threatening. The increased brittleness of the bones increases the risk of serious fractures, especially of the hip, and many older women never recover from these fractures (Marwick, 2000).

Estrogen deficiency also has psychological effects. It can impair cognitive functioning and feelings of psychological well-being (Ross et al., 2000; Yaffe et al., 2000).

Hormone Replacement Therapy (HRT)   Some women who experience severe physical symptoms have been helped by **hormone replacement therapy (HRT)**, which typically consists of synthetic estrogen and progesterone. *Question: What are the effects—and dangers—of hormone replacement therapy (HRT)?* Synthetic estrogen and progesterone are used to offset the losses of their naturally occurring counterparts. HRT may help reduce the hot flushes and other symptoms brought about by hormonal deficiencies during menopause (den Tonkelaar & Oddens, 2000). It is especially helpful in preventing the development of osteoporosis (Duenwald, 2002). Drinking milk, which is high in calcium, increases bone density among girls and is likely to help prevent against osteoporosis later in life. Calcium supplements also seem to be helpful in decreasing the number of bone fractures among postmenopausal women.

HRT is not without controversy. Although HRT has been helpful to many menopausal women, a study of more than 16,000 postmenopausal women aged 50 to 79 found that exposure to a combination of estrogen and progestin appears to significantly increase the risk of breast cancer (Chlebowski et al., 2003). (Progestin is used along with estrogen because estrogen alone exposes women to a significant risk of developing uterine cancer [Duenwald, 2002].) The Chlebowski study found that in addition to stimulating the growth of breast cancer, the combination of hormones also makes the tumors harder to detect, causing dangerous delays in diagnosis. During the course of the study, which was published in the *Journal of the American Medical Association,* of 8,506 women on HRT, 199 developed invasive breast cancers, as compared with 150 cases among the 8,102 women taking a placebo. Also, despite having yearly mammograms, 25.4% of the women who developed cancer while using HRT had cancers that had begun to metastasize, as compared with 16% of those taking the placebo. Because of such concerns, the number of women using HRT has dropped by about 50% within the past couple of years (Grady, 2003a). On the other hand, estrogen replacement apparently lowers the woman's risk of osteoporosis (Grady, 2003a, 2003b) and colon cancer (Grady, 2003b; Solomon & Dluhy, 2003).

Levels of LDL ("bad cholesterol") are known to rise among menopausal women, while levels of HDL ("good cholesterol") decrease (Hall et al., 2002). A number of studies suggest that HRT raises levels of HDL and lowers levels of LDL (Herrington et al., 2000; Nieto et al., 2000; Shlipak et al., 2000). Because high levels of LDL are connected with cardiovascular disease, it was believed, until recently, that HRT may reduce the risk of such disease in postmenopausal women. However, recent research reports show mixed results. The women in the Hormone Replacement Therapy trial

Not for Women Only
Osteoporosis is usually thought of as a health problem that afflicts older women, but men make up about 2 million of the 10 million people with osteoporosis in the United States. Men are at less risk for osteoporosis because they have larger, stronger bones than women. Osteoporosis is more likely to strike men who have low testosterone levels, use medications like steroids, smoke, drink heavily, and lead sedentary lives (Anderson et al., 2002).

Osteoporosis A condition caused by estrogen deficiency and characterized by a decline in bone density, such that bones become porous and brittle. (From the Greek *osteon,* meaning "bone," and the Latin *porus,* meaning "pore.")

Hormone replacement therapy (HRT) Replacement of naturally occurring estrogen or estrogen and progesterone with synthetic equivalents, following menopause.

A Closer Look

Myths about Menopause

Menopause is certainly a major life change for most women. For many women, menopause symbolizes the many midlife issues they face, including changes in appearance, sexuality, and health. Yet exactly what types of changes do we find? Many of us harbor misleading ideas about menopause—ideas that can be harmful to women. Consider the following myths and the realities. To which myths have you fallen prey?

- **Myth 1: Menopause is abnormal.** Of course not. Menopause is a normal development in women's lives.

- **Myth 2: The medical establishment considers menopause a disease.** No longer. Menopause is described as a "deficiency syndrome" today, referring to the decline in secretion of estrogen and progesterone. Unfortunately, the term *deficiency* also has negative meanings.

- **Myth 3: After menopause, women need complete replacement of estrogen.** Not necessarily. Some estrogen continues to be produced by the adrenal glands, fatty tissue, and the brain (Guzick & Hoeger, 2000).

- **Myth 4: Menopause is accompanied by depression and anxiety.** Not necessarily. A number of reviews of the literature have found no consistent relationship between menopause and these psychological symptoms (Avis, 2003; Kessler, 2003). (Outcomes may differ for women who have psychological problems prior to

Truth?Fiction?
Revisited

Despite the myth, many women do not have hot flashes at menopause. Among those who do, the flashes are often mild.

It is not true that menopause signals an end to women's sexual appetite. In fact, some women feel newly sexually liberated because of the separation of sex from reproduction.

of the Women's Health Initiative apparently ran a slightly *greater* risk of heart attacks and strokes (Fletcher & Colditz, 2002). Of the some 25,000 women in the study, nearly 1% of women using HRT developed such problems during the first year of HRT, but the risk tapered off rapidly during subsequent years. On the other hand, a study of nearly 165,000 British women aged 50 to 74 from the General Practice Research Database found that HRT, in the form of either pills or skin patches, did have cardioprotective effects (Varas-Lorenzo et al., 2000). What can we conclude? The fact of the matter is that research results on some issues with HRT are mixed, and others suggest caution (Grady, 2003b; Solomon & Dluhy, 2003). Women considering HRT are well advised to discuss the latest research findings with their gynecologists and to consider alternatives.

Breast cancer specialist Larry Norton (cited in Duenwald, 2002), of Memorial Sloan-Kettering Cancer Center in New York, notes that progestin alone prevents or lessens hot flashes in about 70% of women. Selective serotonin reuptake inhibitors (SSRIs) like Effexor, Paxil, and Prozac are also of help (Stearns et al., 2003). Women using SSRIs to treat hot flashes usually take half the dose used to treat depression, which is their major type of usage, although they are also helpful with premenstrual syndrome (PMS), premenstrual dysphoric disorder (PMDD), eating disorders, and some other problems.

Vaginal dryness can be treated with estrogens that are used locally—that is, placed in the vagina rather than the bloodstream, as hormones usually are. Creams (e.g., Estrace), suppositories (Vagifem), and a plastic ring (Estring) are available for the purpose.

The "designer estrogen" (meaning it is taken up by only certain estrogen receptors) raloxifene, like HRT, is of help with women with osteoporosis, but it apparently decreases rather than increases the risk of breast cancer. As another alternative, the bisphosphonates (Actonel or Fosamax) also help maintain bone strength.

menopause.) A Dutch study followed 2,103 females aged 46 to 54 for five years. During this time period, the number of women who reached postmenopausal status doubled, and the percentage of women reporting depression increased from 18.5% to 23.7% (Maartens et al., 2002). The increase is unlikely to be due to chance, but more than three out of four women in the study did not report significant levels of depression or anxiety at any time during the experience of menopause.

Much of a woman's response to menopause reflects its meaning to her, not physical changes (Hunter & O'Dea, 2001). Women who adopt the commonly held belief that menopause signals the beginning of the end of life may develop a sense of hopelessness about the future, which in turn can set the stage for depression. Women whose entire lives have centered around childbearing and child rearing are more likely to experience a sense of loss. Moreover, there is a cultural bias to explain depression and other problems of middle-aged women in terms of menopause, rather than to explore psychosocial factors.

- **Myth 5: At menopause, women experience debilitating hot flashes.** Not so.

- **Myth 6: A woman who has had a hysterectomy will not undergo menopause afterward.** It depends on whether or not the ovaries (the major producers of estrogen) were also removed. If they were not, menopause should proceed normally.

- **Myth 7: Menopause signals an end to a woman's sexual appetite.** Not at all!

- **Myth 8: A woman's general level of activity is lower after menopause.** Many postmenopausal women become peppier and more assertive.

Review: The Menstrual Cycle

Reflect

Do people from your sociocultural background tend to hold any particular attitudes toward menstruation? What are they? Do you share these attitudes? Explain.

CriticalThinking

Would a woman be justified in complaining that she is confused about the evidence concerning the effects of HRT? Do you find the evidence straightforward or confusing? Explain.

29. _____ is the cyclical bleeding that stems from the shedding of the uterine lining (endometrium).

30. The menstrual cycle is regulated by the hormones estrogen and _____ and is divided into four phases.

31. During the _____ phase, estrogen levels increase, causing the ripening of ova.

32. _____ occurs when estrogen reaches peak blood levels.

33. During the _____ phase, large amounts of progesterone produced by the corpus luteum cause the endometrium to thicken.

34. Dramatic (*Increases* or *Decreases*?) in estrogen and progesterone trigger the menstrual phase.

35. Stress (*Can* or *Cannot*?) delay or halt menstruation.

36. The pituitary gland produces _____ that stimulate the ovaries: FSH and LH.

37. The synthetic hormone _____ is chemically similar to LH and induces ovulation.

38. There (*Is* or *Is not*?) evidence that coitus during menstruation is physically harmful.

39. _____ is defined as the cessation of menstruation.

40. The term _____ refers to the beginning of menopause and is usually characterized by several months of amenorrhea or irregular periods.

41. A deficit in _____ may lead to perimenopausal sensations such as night sweats, hot flashes, and hot flushes.

42. The latest research suggests that HRT (*Increases* or *Decreases*?) the risk of breast cancer and offers no protection against heart disease.

Menstrual Problems

Although menstruation is a natural biological process, 50% to 75% of women experience some discomfort prior to or during menstruation (Sommerfeld, 2000). *Question: What kinds of menstrual problems do women experience?* The Self-Assessment on page 100 contains a list of commonly reported premenstrual symptoms. The problems we explore in this section include dysmenorrhea, mastalgia, menstrual migraine headaches, amenorrhea, premenstrual syndrome (PMS), and premenstrual dysphoric disorder (PMDD).

Dysmenorrhea

Pain or discomfort during menstruation, or **dysmenorrhea**, is the most common type of menstrual problem. Most women at some time have at least mild menstrual pain or discomfort. Pelvic cramps are the most common manifestation of dysmenorrhea. They may be accompanied by headache, backache, nausea, or bloated feelings. Women who develop severe cases usually do so within a few years of menarche. **Primary dysmenorrhea** refers to menstrual pain or discomfort in the absence of known organic pathology. Women with **secondary dysmenorrhea** have identified organic problems that are believed to cause their menstrual problems. Their pain or discomfort is caused by, or *secondary* to, these problems. Endometriosis, pelvic inflammatory disease, and ovarian cysts are just a few of the organic disorders that can give rise to secondary dysmenorrhea. Yet evidence is accumulating that supposed primary dysmenorrhea is often *secondary* to hormonal changes, although the precise causes have not been delineated. For example, menstrual cramps sometimes decrease dramatically after childbirth, as a result of the massive hormonal changes that occur with pregnancy.

Symptoms vary from person to person and also according to whether or not the woman has been pregnant. Women who have been pregnant report a lower incidence of menstrual pain but a higher incidence of premenstrual symptoms and menstrual discomfort.

Menstrual cramps appear to result from uterine spasms that may be brought about by copious secretion of hormones called **prostaglandins**. Prostaglandins apparently cause muscle fibers in the uterine wall to contract, as during labor. Most contractions go unnoticed, but powerful, persistent contractions are discomfiting in themselves and may temporarily deprive the uterus of oxygen, another source of distress. Women with more intense menstrual discomfort apparently produce higher quantities of prostaglandins. Prostaglandin-inhibiting drugs, such as ibuprofen, indomethacin, and aspirin are thus often of help. Menstrual pain may also be secondary to endometriosis.

Pelvic pressure and bloating may be traced to pelvic edema (Greek for "swelling")—the congestion of fluid in the pelvic region. Fluid retention can lead to a gain of several pounds, sensations of heaviness, and **mastalgia**—a swelling of the breasts that sometimes causes premenstrual discomfort. Masters and Johnson (1966) noted that orgasm (through coitus or masturbation) can help relieve menstrual discomfort by reducing the pelvic congestion that spawns bloating and pressure. Orgasm may also increase the menstrual flow and shorten this phase of the cycle.

Headaches frequently accompany menstrual discomfort. Most headaches (in both sexes) stem from simple muscle tension, notably in the shoulders, the back of the neck, and the scalp. Pelvic discomfort may cause muscle contractions, thus contributing to the tension that produces headaches. Women who are tense about their menstrual flow are thus candidates for muscle tension headaches. Migraine headaches may arise from changes in the blood flow in the brain, however. Migraines are typically limited to one side of the head and are often accompanied by visual difficulties.

Dysmenorrhea Pain or discomfort during menstruation.

Primary dysmenorrhea Menstrual pain or discomfort that occurs in the absence of known organic problems.

Secondary dysmenorrhea Menstrual pain or discomfort that is caused by identified organic problems.

Prostaglandins Hormones that cause muscle fibers in the uterine wall to contract, as during labor.

Mastalgia A swelling of the breasts that sometimes causes premenstrual discomfort.

Amenorrhea

Amenorrhea is the absence of menstruation and is a primary sign of infertility. **Primary amenorrhea** describes the absence of menstruation in a woman who has not menstruated at all by about the age of 16 or 17. **Secondary amenorrhea** describes delayed or absent menstrual periods in women who have had regular periods in the past. Amenorrhea has various causes, including abnormalities in the structures of the reproductive system, hormonal abnormalities, growths such as cysts and tumors, and psychological problems, such as stress. Amenorrhea is normal during pregnancy and following menopause. Amenorrhea is also a symptom of **anorexia nervosa**, an eating disorder characterized by an intense fear of putting on weight and a refusal to eat enough to maintain a normal body weight, which often results in extreme (and sometimes life-threatening) weight loss. Hormonal changes that accompany emaciation are believed responsible for the cessation of menstruation. Amenorrhea may also occur in women who exercise strenuously, such as competitive long-distance runners. It is unclear whether the cessation of menstruation in female athletes is due to the effects of strenuous exercise itself, to related physical factors such as low body fat, to the stress of intensive training, or to a combination of factors.

Premenstrual Syndrome (PMS) and Premenstrual Dysphoric Disorder (PMDD)

The term **premenstrual syndrome** (PMS) describes the combination of biological and psychological symptoms that may affect women during the four- to six-day interval that precedes their menses each month. For many women, premenstrual symptoms persist during menstruation. **Premenstrual dysphoric disorder** (PMDD) is a more technical term used as a diagnostic category by the American Psychiatric Association in its *Diagnostic and Statistical Manual.* PMDD is more severe than PMS, and is characterized by the symptoms shown in Table 3.2. The term is not always used precisely, and some make the mistake of confusing it with PMS (Smith et al., 2003). But the diagnosis of PMDD requires that five or more of the following symptoms be present most of the time during the week before the period and ending within a few days after period begins. At least one symptom must be one of the first

Amenorrhea The absence of menstruation.

Primary amenorrhea Lack of menstruation in a woman who has never menstruated.

Secondary amenorrhea Lack of menstruation in a woman who has previously menstruated.

Anorexia nervosa A psychological disorder of eating characterized by intense fear of putting on weight and refusal to eat enough to maintain normal body weight.

Premenstrual syndrome (PMS) A combination of physical and psychological symptoms (e.g., anxiety, depression, irritability, weight gain from fluid retention, and abdominal discomfort) that regularly afflicts many women during the four- to six-day interval that precedes their menses each month.

Premenstrual dysphoric disorder (PMDD) A diagnosis used by the American Psychiatric Association to describe cases of PMS that are characterized by severe changes in mood and impairment of functioning at work, at school or in social relationships.

TABLE 3.2

Symptoms of Premenstrual Dysphoric Disorder (PMDD)

1. Feelings of sadness, hopelessness, or worthlessness
2. Tension, anxious, feeling "on edge"
3. Notable changes in mood, including frequent crying
4. Persistent irritability and anger, often leading to increased interpersonal conflict
5. Lessened interest in usual activities, possibly with withdrawal from social relationships
6. Difficulty concentrating
7. Fatigue, lethargy, lack of energy
8. Notable changes in appetite, such as binge eating or craving certain foods
9. Hypersomnia (sleeping too much) or insomnia
10. Feeling overwhelmed or out of control
11. Other physical symptoms, for example, tenderness or swelling of the breasts, headaches, joint or muscle pain, feelings of bloating, weight gain

Source: DSM–IV–TR (2000). Washington, DC: American Psychiatric Association.

In order to diagnose PMDD, the *DSM–IV–TR* requires that symptoms have been present for most menstrual cycles over a given year. Five or more of the symptoms must be present most of the time during the week before the period and ending within a few days after period begins. At least one symptom must be one of the first four. The symptoms must notably impair functioning at work or school or in social activities and relationships.

Lifting "the Curse"—Should Monthly Periods Be Optional?

Women have been having menstrual periods for the 150,000 years or so that our species has been in existence, but only in the new millennium are we seriously considering making periods an option rather than a necessity. Health professionals have known for quite some time how the menstrual cycle is regulated by hormones, and they have realized that women can eliminate their periods by adjusting the hormones in their bloodstreams. But only now is the general public being made aware of the fact so that women can make informed decisions as to whether or not this option is right for them.

In an essay in the medical journal *The Lancet*, Charlotte Ellertson (2000), a reproductive health specialist at the Population Council, writes to women who experience difficult periods: "Health professionals and women ought to view menstruation as they would any other naturally occurring but frequently undesirable condition. This means providing those women who want it with safe and effective means to eliminate their menstrual cycles."

The fact is that the continuous use of oral contraceptives—in effect, tossing out the seven inactive pills that are usually packaged with the active 21 and taking the active tablets only—keeps sex hormone levels constant and eliminates menstruation. Although gynecologists sometimes let certain patients in on this trick—such as those wanting to avoid their periods on their honeymoons—they have generally not given women the option to suppress menstruation for long periods of time. Some doctors don't feel comfortable prescribing a relatively untested therapy and worry it could increase the pill's risks (Rako, 2003).

Is Menstruation Obsolete? *Use of hormones permits women to avoid having monthly periods. What are the benefits and risks of eliminating menstruation?*

But some gynecologists, endocrinologists, and contraceptive researchers are spreading the word about suppression of menstrual periods. "For many women there is a menstruation-associated health problem month after month and there is no reason they have to put up with it," says Dr. Sheldon Segal (cited in Sommerfeld, 2000), an endocrinologist at the Population Council and coauthor of the book *Is Menstruation Obsolete?* (Coutinho & Segal, 2003).

HEALTH BENEFITS

According to the American College of Obstetricians and Gynecologists, 50% to 75% of women suffer some

four. In addition, in order to diagnose PMDD, the *DSM* requires that symptoms have been present for most menstrual cycles over the past year and that they notably impair functioning at work or school or in social activities and relationships.

Nearly three women in four experience some premenstrual symptoms (Sommerfeld, 2000). A study of Chinese women in Taiwan, reported in a Scandinavian journal, reported that the most common symptoms of PMS are minor psychological discomfort, muscular tension, and aches or pains (Hsiao et al., 2002). The great majority of cases involve mild to moderate levels of discomfort. Only a small minority of women report menstrual symptoms severe enough to impair their social, academic, or occupational functioning and to thus be categorized at PMDD. PMS is not

physical or emotional discomfort during or right before their periods. Nearly 50% experience painful cramping. No periods mean no PMS and no cramps—and less monthly discomfort.

Women with endometriosis, which is caused by and made progressively worse by menstruation, may also benefit from skipping periods. The birth control pill has been shown to reduce the risk of endometrial cancer by 50% and ovarian cancer 40%.

SEASONALE—ONE PERIOD PER SEASON?

Seasonale, approved by the FDA in 2003, was the first oral contraceptive marketed specifically for the purpose of suppressing menstruation. Seasonale contains a combination of two hormones commonly used in other oral contraceptives, but in significantly lower doses—an estrogen (ethinyl estradiol) and a progestin (levonorgestrel). The pills are taken for 84 days rather than 21, and then a woman takes seven days off to menstruate. Seasonale works like conventional oral contraceptives by suppressing ovulation, thickening cervical mucus, and preventing the endometrium from thickening enough to enable a fertilized egg to embed itself (Russo, 2003). The hormones in Seasonale suppress growth of the endometrium entirely, causing periods to be lighter than usual. Many women involved in clinical trials had very light periods lasting about two days during their week of placebo pills or no periods at all (Russo, 2003).

Some doctors have concerns about the safety of using the pill for extended periods of time because they were not intended for that purpose (Rako, 2003). While studies have found the birth control pill safe for most women—with exceptions such as those who are over 35 and smoke or who have certain medical conditions such as heart disease, blood clots, or breast cancer—they have suggested that pill users have a slightly higher chance of developing blood clots in the veins and lungs, stroke, and heart attack.

"If you take it continuously, that's effectively increasing the amount of hormones someone gets by 25%. That will probably up the risks by that percentage," says Dr. Gerson Weiss (cited in Sommerfeld, 2000), chairman of the department of obstetrics and gynecology at New Jersey Medical School. "A potential increase in [blood clots] is probably the major [concern]." But Segal counters that the potential risks of continuous use of the pill are not all that different from those of the typical three-weeks-on, one-week-off regimen. He adds that women today are typically taking lower doses than in the past. Seasonale is also a low-dose pill.

A PERIOD-FREE FUTURE?

Dr. Elsimar Coutinho, a gynecology professor at Federal University of Bahia in Brazil, predicts that in future years women will only be having periods when they want to have them—for example, as part of cycles during which they wish to get pregnant.

Ellerston also envisions a period-free future: "Pills are more frequently being used for reasons other than contraception, for instance to control acne, and menstruation suppression might grow to be just another use for pills."

But Segal warns that continuous use of oral contraceptives is not all right for all women, and women should not attempt to suppress menstruation without consulting with their gynecologist.

unique to our culture. Researchers find premenstrual symptoms equally prevalent among women studied in the United States, Italy, and in the Islamic nation of Bahrain (Brody, 1992b).

The causes of PMS and PMDD are unclear, but evidence is accumulating for a biological basis. Researchers are looking to possible relationships between menstrual problems, including PMS and PMDD, and chemical imbalances in the body. Researchers have yet to find differences in levels of estrogen or progesterone between women with PMDD and those with PMS or no symptoms (Bäckström et al., 2003; Mortola, 1998). Research suggests that it is not the level of these hormones themselves that contributes to PMS and PMDD, but rather an abnormal response to

Self-Assessment

Do You Experience PMS or PMDD?[2]

Premenstrual syndrome (PMS) is a group of symptoms that may affect women for the period of about eight days prior to and during menstruation. Research evidence suggests that most women have some of these symptoms but that most often they are not severe enough to seriously impair daily functioning. When they do, they may qualify as PMDD. Women who have severe, even disabling, symptoms, are advised to discuss them with their gynecologists.

Do you experience PMS or PMDD? Complete the following questionnaire to gain insight into whether you do.

Directions: Following is a list of psychological and physical symptoms of PMS and PMDD. Indicate whether you encounter these symptoms and how severe they are by checking the appropriate box. Then turn to the answer key in Appendix A to assess your responses.

Part I: Psychological Symptoms of PMS	Do not have	Mild	Moderate	Severe	Disabling
Accident prone					
Depression					
Anxiety					
Panic					
Mood swings					
Crying spells					
Sudden anger					
Irritability					
Loss of interest in usual activities					
Difficulty concentrating					
Lack of energy					
Excessive use of alcohol					
Frustration					
Overeating or cravings for certain foods					
Insomnia or excessive sleeping					
Feelings of being out of control or overwhelmed					
Paranoia					
Part II: Physical Symptoms of PMS	Do not have	Mild	Moderate	Severe	Disabling
Migraines					
Breast tenderness					
Joint or muscle pain					
Stiffness					
Weight gain					
Feeling bloated					
Blurred vision					
Poor motor coordination					
Exhaustion					
Dark circles under the eyes					
Runny eyes					

the presence of these hormones (Schmidt et al., 1998). PMS and PMDD also appear to be linked with imbalances in neurotransmitters such as serotonin (Bäckström et al., 2003; Mortola, 1998). (Neurotransmitters are the chemical messengers in the nervous system.) Serotonin imbalances are also linked to changes in appetite. Women with PMS and PMDD show greater increases of appetite during the luteal phase than other women do. Another neurotransmitter, gamma-aminobutyric acid (GABA) also appears to be involved in premenstrual problems because medicines that affect the levels of GABA help many women with these problems (Bäckström et al., 2003; Mortola, 1998). PMS and PMDD may well be caused by a complex interaction between ovarian hormones and neurotransmitters (Bäckström et al., 2003; Mortola, 1998).

Only a generation ago, premenstrual disorders were seen as "a woman's lot"— something women must put up with. No longer. Today there are many treatment options. These include exercise, dietary control (for example, eating several small meals a day rather than two or three large meals; limiting salt and sugar; vitamin supplements), hormone treatments (usually progesterone), and medications that reduce anxiety or increase the amount of serotonin in the nervous system. You can get in touch with whether you have PMS, and how the symptoms affect you, by completing the nearby Self-Assessment. If you have severe or disabling symptoms, you may be diagnosable with PMDD. *Question: What can women do about PMS or PMDD?* Check with your gynecologist and consider the suggestions in the following section.

How to Handle Menstrual Discomfort

Most women experience some menstrual discomfort. Women with persistent menstrual distress may profit from the suggestions listed below. Researchers are exploring the effectiveness of these techniques in controlled studies. You might consider trying the techniques that sound right for you—all of them, if you wish. Try them for a few months to see if you reap any benefits.

1. Don't blame yourself! Menstrual problems were once erroneously attributed to women's "hysterical" nature. This is nonsense. Menstrual problems appear, in large part, to reflect hormonal variations or chemical fluctuations in the brain during the menstrual cycle. Researchers have not yet fully identified all the causal elements and patterns, but their lack of knowledge does not mean that women who have menstrual problems are hysterical.

2. Keep a menstrual calendar, so that you can track your menstrual symptoms systematically and identify patterns.

3. Develop strategies for dealing with days that you experience the greatest distress—strategies that will help enhance your pleasure and minimize the stress affecting you on those days (Hunter et al., 2002). Activities that distract you from your menstrual discomfort may be helpful. Go see a movie or get into that novel you've been meaning to read.

4. Ask yourself whether you harbor any self-defeating attitudes toward menstruation that might be compounding distress (Hunter et al., 2002). Do close relatives or friends see menstruation as an illness, a time of "pollution," a "dirty thing"? Have you adopted any of these attitudes—if not verbally, then in ways that affect your behavior, such as by restricting your social activities during your period?

Exercise as a Strategy for Coping with Menstrual Discomfort Some women find that vigorous exercise helps relieve menstrual discomfort.

5. See a gynecologist about your concerns, especially if you have severe symptoms. Severe menstrual symptoms can be secondary to medical disorders such as endometriosis and pelvic inflammatory disease (PID). Check it out.

6. Develop nutritious eating habits—and continue them throughout the entire cycle (that means always). Consider limiting intake of alcohol, caffeine, fats, salt, and sweets, especially during the days preceding menstruation. Research suggests that a low-fat, vegetarian diet reduces the duration and intensity of menstrual pain and the duration of premenstrual symptoms (Barnard et al., 2000).

7. Eat several smaller meals (or nutritious snacks) throughout the day, rather than a few highly filling meals.

8. Some women find that vigorous exercise—jogging, swimming, bicycling, fast walking, dancing, skating, even jumping rope—helps relieve premenstrual and menstrual discomfort. Evidence suggests that exercise helps to relieve and possibly prevent menstrual discomfort (Ling, 2000; Pearlstein & Steiner, 2000). By the way, develop regular exercise habits—don't seek to become solely a premenstrual athlete.

9. Check with your doctor about vitamin and mineral supplements (such as calcium and magnesium). Vitamin B6 appears to have helped some women (Chavez & Spitzer, 2002).

10. Ibuprofen (brand names: Medipren, Advil, Motrin, etc.) and other medicines available over the counter may be helpful for cramping. Prescription drugs such as anti-anxiety drugs (e.g., alprazolam) and anti-depressant drugs (selective serotonin reuptake inhibitors or SSRIs) may also be of help (Bäckström et al., 2003; Hunter et al., 2002; Stearns et al., 2003). "Anti-depressants" affect levels of neurotransmitters in a way that can be helpful for women with PMS or PMDD. Their benefits do not mean that women with PMS or PMDD are "basically" depressed. Ask your doctor for a recommendation.

11. Remind yourself that menstrual problems are time limited. Don't worry about getting through life or a career. Just get through the next couple of days.

In this chapter we have explored female sexual anatomy and physiology. In the following chapter, we turn our attention to the male.

Review: Menstrual Problems

Reflect

Do you (or your loved ones) experience PMS or PMDD? What are you (or they) doing about it? Why?

CriticalThinking

Critical thinkers avoid oversimplification. Explain how PMS and PMDD can have complex causes that involve both biological and psychological factors. Is there any significance in the fact that the research suggests that both medication and cognitive–behavioral therapy can be of help to women with PMS or PMDD?

43. The most common type of menstrual problem is pain during menstruation, which is termed _____.

44. Menstrual cramps appear to result from what may be caused by secretion of _____.

45. _____ is the absence of menstruation.

46. _____ syndrome (PMS) refers to a combination of biological and psychological symptoms that may affect women during the four- to six-day interval that precedes menstruation.

47. Premenstrual _____ disorder (PMDD) is the name given severe PMS that is accompanied by troublesome mood changes and that impairs functioning in school, on the job, or in relationships.

48. Selective _____ reuptake inhibitors (SSRIs) have been found to help many women who experience PMS or PMDD.

Recite

1. What are the parts of the vulva?	The female external sexual structures are collectively known as the vulva and consist of the mons veneris, labia majora and minora, the clitoris, the vestibule, and the vaginal opening.
2. What is the mons veneris?	The mons veneris consists of fatty tissue that covers the joint of the pubic bones in front of the body.
3. What are the labia majora?	The labia majora are large folds of skin that run downward from the mons along the sides of the vulva.
4. What are the labia minora?	The labia minora are hairless, light-colored membranes that surround the urethral and vaginal openings.
5. What is the clitoris?	The clitoris is the female sex organ that is most sensitive to sexual sensation, but it is not directly involved in reproduction.
6. What is the vestibule?	The vestibule contains the openings to the vagina and the urethra.
7. What is the urethral opening?	Urine passes from the female's body through the urethral opening.
8. What is the vaginal opening?	The vaginal opening, or introitus, lies below the urethral opening. The penis, babies, and the menstrual flow go through this opening.
9. What is the perineum?	The perineum is the area that lies between the vaginal opening and the anus.
10. What structures are found beneath the vulva?	These structures include the vestibular bulbs, Bartholin's glands, the sphincters, and the clitoral crura.
11. What are the internal female sex organs?	The internal female sex organs—or female reproductive system—include the innermost parts of the vagina, the cervix, the uterus, the ovaries, and the fallopian tubes.
12. What is the vagina?	Menstrual flow and babies pass from the uterus to the outer world through the vagina. During coitus, the vagina contains the penis.
13. What is the cervix?	The cervix is the lower end of the uterus. It contains an opening called the os.
14. What should we know about cervical cancer?	Cervical cancer is relatively uncommon but detectable via a Pap test. When detected early, the survival rate approaches 100%.
15. What is the uterus?	The uterus or womb is the pear-shaped organ in which a fertilized ovum implants and develops until birth. The uterine lining is called the endometrium.
16. What should we know about endometrial cancer?	Risk factors include obesity, a diet high in fats, lengthy exposure to estrogen, and estrogen-replacement therapy. For women obtaining HRT, combining estrogen with progestin lessens the risk. Early detection can lead to a 95% five-year survival rate.
17. What are the fallopian tubes?	Two fallopian tubes extend from the upper end of the uterus toward the ovaries. Ova pass through the fallopian tubes on their way to the uterus and are normally fertilized within these tubes.
18. What are the ovaries?	The ovaries lie on either side of the uterus and produce ova and the sex hormones estrogen and progesterone.
19. What should we know about ovarian cancer?	Ovarian cancer usually strikes women between the ages of 40 and 70. Women most at risk are those with first-degree blood relatives who had the disease, but most women who develop it do not have a family history. Risk factors include never giving birth, infertility, breast cancer, a diet rich in meat and animal fats, and cigarette smoking. Early detection is connected with a 95% survival rate.

Recite

20. What happens during the pelvic examination?	The gynecologist examines the woman externally for irritations, swellings, abnormal vaginal discharges, and clitoral adhesions. A speculum is used to inspect the cervix and vaginal walls for discharges, discoloration, lesions, or growths. This exam is usually followed by a Pap test.
21. What are the breasts?	The breasts are secondary sex characteristics that contain mammary glands. In some cultures the breasts are viewed as just a means for feeding infants. In our culture they have acquired erotic significance.
22. What should we know about breast cancer?	Women with breast cancer have lumps in the breast, but most lumps in the breasts are benign. Breast cancer may be detected by clinical breast examination (CBE), mammography, or breast self-examination (BSE). Risk factors include BRCA1 or BRCA2 mutations, exposure to estrogen, alcohol. When detected early, the five-year survival rate exceeds 90%.
23. What is the menstrual cycle?	Menstruation is the cyclical bleeding that stems from the shedding of the endometrium when a reproductive cycle has not led to the fertilization of an ovum. The menstrual cycle involves finely tuned relationships between the hypothalamus, the pituitary gland, and the ovaries and uterus. The cycle has four phases: proliferative, ovulatory, secretory, and menstrual. During the first phase, ova ripen within their follicles and endometrial tissue proliferates. During the second phase, ovulation occurs. During the third phase, the corpus luteum produces copious amounts of progesterone and estrogen that cause the endometrium to thicken. If the ovum goes unfertilized, a plunge in estrogen and progesterone levels triggers the fourth, or menstrual, phase.
24. Is it harmful to engage in coitus during menstruation?	There is no evidence that coitus during menstruation is harmful.
25. What are the differences between menopause, perimenopause, and the climacteric?	Menopause is the cessation of menstruation. Perimenopause is the beginning of menopause and is charactered by several months or irregular periods or amenorrhea. The climacteric is a multiyear process marked by declining levels of estrogen and ending in menopause.
26. What are the effects—and dangers—of hormone replacement therapy (HRT)?	HRT offsets losses of estrogen and progesterone and can help women with perimenopausal and postmenopausal symptoms, including night sweats, hot flashes, hot flushes, dry skin, loss of breast tissue, and decreased vaginal lubrication. However, HRT has been linked to an increased risk of breast and endometrial cancers, and apparently has no protective effect against heart disease.
27. What kinds of menstrual problems do women experience?	Dysmenorrhea—painful menstruation—is the most common menstrual problem, and pelvic cramps are the most common symptom. Amenorrhea—lack of menstruation—can be caused by problems such as abnormalities in the structures of the reproductive system, hormonal abnormalities, cysts, tumors, and stress. Premenstrual syndrome (PMS) occurs during the period prior to and for a few days during menstruation. It can be characterized by depression and anxiety, irritability, difficulty concentrating, migraines, breast tenderness, and bloating. Premenstrual dysphoric disorder (PMDD) is like a severe case of PMS, said to occur when symptoms are extreme and impair functioning in school, at work, or in relationships.
28. What can women do about PMS or PMDD?	PMS and PMDD can be alleviated to some degree by biological and psychological means. Medicines that may help include selective serotonin reuptake inhibitors (SSRIs) and drugs that relieve cramping. Psychological methods include examining attitudes toward menstruating, finding enjoyable activities, and remembering that symptoms are time-limited.

Chapter 4

Truth?Fiction?

T / F? The penis contains bone and muscle.

T / F? The father determines the baby's sex.

T / F? The sperm of the tiny fruit fly are longer than human sperm.

T / F? *Semen* is a synonym for *sperm*.

T / F? Morning erections reflect the need to urinate.

T / F? Men can will themselves to have erections.

T / F? The penis has a mind of its own.

T / F? Many men who are paralyzed below the waist can attain erection, engage in sexual intercourse, and ejaculate.

T / F? Men can have orgasms without ejaculating.

Male Sexual Anatomy and Physiology

Preview

From the earliest foundations of Western civilization, male-dominated societies elevated men and exalted male genitalia. The ancient Greeks carried oversized images of fish as **phallic symbols** in their Dionysian processions, which celebrated the wilder and more frenzied aspects of human sexuality. In the murky predawn light of Western civilization, humankind engaged in phallic worship. Phallic symbols played roles in religious worship and became glorified in art in the form of plows, axes, and swords.

The tradition of phallic worship became raised to higher aesthetic levels. The ancient Greeks adorned themselves with phallic rings and necklaces. In ancient Rome, celebrations were held to honor Venus, the goddess of love. The Romans outfitted a float in the shape of a large phallus and paraded it through the streets. There were no tributes to the female genitals. Even though Venus was being honored, no artisans devoted themselves to creating floats in the likeness of the vulva or the clitoris.

Men held their own genitals in such high esteem that it was common courtroom practice for them to swear to tell the truth with their hands on their genitals—as we swear to tell the truth in the name of God or by placing our hands on the Bible. The words **testes** and **testicles** derive from the same Latin word as "testify." The Latin *testis* means "a witness."

Even today, we see evidence of pride—indeed veneration!—of the male genitalia. Men with large genitals are accorded respect from their male peers and sometimes adoration from female admirers. Given these cultural attitudes, it is not surprising that young men (and some not-so-young men) belittle themselves if they feel that their penises do not measure up to some ideal. Boys who mature late may be ridiculed by their peers for their small genitals. Their feelings of inadequacy may persist into adulthood. Adult men,

too, may harbor doubts that their penises are large enough to satisfy their lovers. Or they may fear that their partners' earlier lovers had larger genitals.

In this chapter we examine male sexual anatomy and physiology, and we attempt to sort out truth from fiction. We see, for example, that, despite his lingering doubts, a man's capabilities as a lover do not depend on the size of his penis (at least within broad limits). For a man to judge his sexual prowess on the basis of locker-room comparisons makes about as much sense as choosing a balloon by measuring it when it is deflated.

In our exploration of male sexual anatomy and physiology, as in our exploration of female sexual physiology and anatomy, we begin with the external genitalia and then move inward. Once inside, we focus on the route of sperm through the male reproductive system.

External Sex Organs

Question: What are the external male sex organs? The external male sex organs include the penis and the scrotum (see Figures 4.1 and 4.2).

The Penis

> The penis mightier than the sword.
>
> *Mark Twain*

> Is that a gun in your pocket, or are you just glad to see me?
>
> *Mae West*

At first glance the **penis** may seem rather simple and obvious in its structures, particularly when compared to women's organs. This apparent simplicity may have contributed to cultural stereotypes that men are straightforward and aggressive, whereas women tend to be complicated, and perhaps, mysterious. Yet, as Figure 4.1 shows, the apparent simplicity of the penis is misleading. Much goes on below the surface. Gender stereotypes regarding anatomy are as misleading as those regarding personality (see Chapter 6).

Question: What are the functions and parts of the penis? The penis, like the vagina, is the sex organ used in sexual intercourse. Unlike the vagina, however, the penis serves as a conduit for urine. Semen and urine pass out of the penis through the urethral opening. The opening is called the urethral *meatus* (pronounced me-ATE-us), meaning "passage."

Rather than bones or muscles, the penis contains three cylinders of spongy material that run its length. The larger two of these cylinders, the **corpora cavernosa** (see Figure 4.1), lie side by side and function like the cavernous bodies in the clitoris. These cylinders fill up with blood and stiffen during sexual arousal. In addition, a **corpus spongiosum** (spongy body) runs along the bottom, or ventral, surface of the penis. It contains the penile urethra that conducts urine through the penis to the urinary opening (urethral meatus) at the tip. At the tip of the penis, the spongy body enlarges to become the glans, or head, of the penis.

All three cylinders consist of spongy tissue that swells (becomes engorged) with blood during sexual arousal, resulting in erection. The urethra is connected to the bladder, which is unrelated to reproduction, and to those parts of the reproductive system that transport semen.

The glans of the penis, like the clitoral glans, is extremely sensitive to sexual stimulation. Direct, prolonged stimulation can become irritating, even painful. Men generally prefer to masturbate by stroking the shaft of the penis rather than the glans, although some prefer the latter. The **corona**, or coronal ridge, separates the glans from the body of the penis. It is also quite sensitive to sexual stimulation. After the

Phallic symbols Images of the penis that are usually suggestive of generative power.

Testes The male sex glands, suspended in the scrotum, that produce sperm cells and male sex hormones. Singular: *testis.*

Testicles Testes.

Penis The male organ of sexual intercourse. (From the Latin for "tail.")

Corpora cavernosa Cylinders of spongy tissue in the penis that become congested with blood and stiffen during sexual arousal.

Corpus spongiosum The spongy body that runs along the bottom of the penis, contains the penile urethra, and enlarges at the tip of the penis to form the glans.

Corona The ridge that separates the glans from the body of the penis. (From the Latin for "crown.")

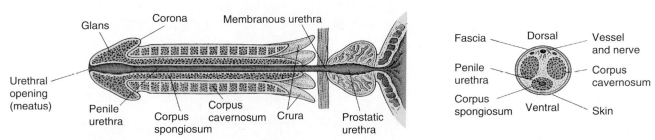

LONGITUDINAL SECTION

CROSS SECTION

Figure 4.1. The Penis. During sexual arousal, the corpora cavernosa and corpus spongiosum become congested with blood, causing the penis to enlarge and stiffen.

Truth?Fiction?
Revisited

Many mammals, including dogs, have penile bones that stiffen the penis to facilitate copulation. But, despite the slang term "boner," the human penis contains no bones. Nor, despite another slang term, "muscle," does the penis contain muscle tissue. However, muscles at the base of the penis, like the muscles surrounding the vaginal and urethral openings in women, are involved in controlling urination and ejaculation.

Frenulum The sensitive strip of tissue that connects the underside of the penile glans to the shaft. (From the Latin *frenum,* meaning "bridle.")

Root The base of the penis, which extends into the pelvis.

Shaft The body of the penis, which expands as a result of vasocongestion.

Foreskin The loose skin that covers the penile glans. Also referred to as the *prepuce.*

Circumcision Surgical removal of the foreskin of the penis. (From the Latin *circumcidere,* meaning "to cut around.")

glans, the parts of the penis that men tend to find most sensitive are the corona and an area on the underside of the penis called the **frenulum**. The frenulum is a thin strip of tissue that connects the underside of the glans to the shaft. Most men find the top part of the penis to be the least sensitive part.

The base of the penis, called the **root**, extends into the pelvis. It is attached to pelvic bones by leglike structures, called crura, that are like those that anchor the female's clitoris. The body of the penis is called the penile **shaft**. Unlike the clitoral shaft, it is free-swinging. Thus, when sexual excitement engorges the penis with blood, the result—erection—is obvious.

The skin of the penis is hairless and loose, allowing expansion during erection. It is fixed to the penile shaft just behind the glans. Some of it, however, like the labia minora in the female, folds over to partially cover the glans. This covering is the prepuce, or **foreskin**. It covers part or all of the penile glans just as the clitoral prepuce (hood) covers the clitoral shaft. The prepuce consists of loose skin that freely moves over the glans. However, smegma—a cheeselike, foul-smelling secretion—may accumulate below the prepuce, causing the foreskin to adhere to the glans.

Circumcision **Circumcision** is the surgical removal of the prepuce (Figure 4.3). *Question: What is the nature of the controversy surrounding male circumcision?* Advocates of male circumcision believe that it is hygienic because it eliminates a site where smegma might accumulate and disease organisms might flourish. Opponents believe circumcision is unnecessary because regular cleaning is sufficient to reduce the risk of these problems.

Male circumcision has a long history as a religious rite. Jews traditionally carry out male circumcision shortly after a baby is born. Circumcision is performed as a sign of the covenant between God and the people of Abraham. Muslims also have ritual circumcisions for religious reasons, although they are carried out within a few

Figure 4.2. The Male Reproductive System. *The external male sex organs include the penis and the scrotum.*

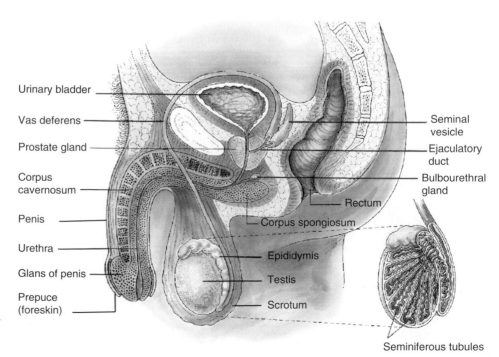

Urinary bladder
Vas deferens
Prostate gland
Corpus cavernosum
Penis
Urethra
Glans of penis
Prepuce (foreskin)

Seminal vesicle
Ejaculatory duct
Bulbourethral gland
Rectum
Corpus spongiosum
Epididymis
Testis
Scrotum

Seminiferous tubules

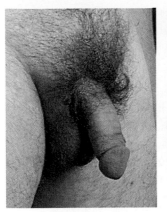  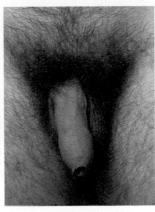

Figure 4.3. Normal Variations in the Male Genitals. *The penis and scrotum vary a good deal in appearance from one man to another. The penis in the photo to the right is uncircumcised.*

years of birth (Quereshi, 2003). Circumcision rates vary widely in the United States, from about 80% in the Midwest, where they are highest, to about 40% in the West, where they are lowest. Circumcision is uncommon elsewhere, except for the Muslim world. The rate is about 17% in Canada and 5% in England. Circumcision is quite rare elsewhere in Europe, in South America, and in non-Muslim Asia (Liptak, 2003).

According to the NHSLS study of 1,410 men aged 18 to 59, circumcision is most common among European American men (81%) and men whose mothers graduated from college (87%) (Laumann et al., 1997). Figure 4.4 compares the circumcision rates among various ethnic groups in the United States. The groups have some overlap; the great majority of Jews—for whom circumcision is a religious rite—are also European Americans.

Circumcision became widespread in the United States because medical research suggests that it lessens the risk of infections from urinary tract infections (Wiswell, 2003) to human papilloma virus (Castellsague et al., 2002) to HIV/AIDS (Bailey, 2000; Cohen, 2000; Halperin & Bailey, 1999). For example, Ann Buve (2000) of the Belgian Institute of Tropical Medicine compared the incidence of HIV infection in two African cities with high rates and two with low rates. In Yaoundé, Cameroon, and Cotonou, Benin, the prevalence of HIV among sexually active men was about 4% to 5%, and 99% of the men were circumcised. In Kisumu, Kenya, and Ndola, Zambia, where circumcision rates were much lower, the rates of HIV infection

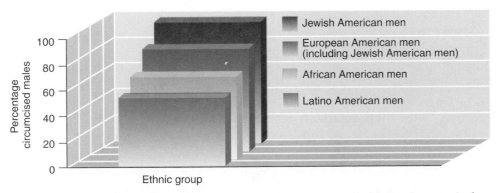

Figure 4.4. Who Is Circumcised? *Circumcision was most common among Jewish American men in the NHSLS study, for whom it is a religious rite, and among European American men in general, as compared with African American men and Latino Americans. Elsewhere in the world, circumcision is relatively rare except among Muslims, who also circumcise males for religious reasons.*

Source: Laumann et al., 1997.

Koro—Genital Retraction Syndrome

H. K. F., a 34-year-old Chinese man, felt the need to urinate while at the movies (ANRG, 2000). In the bathroom, he suddenly lost feeling in his genital region and developed fear that his penis was going to retract into his body. He went into a panic and his legs gave way. He sat on the floor, holding onto his penis to prevent it from retracting and waited a half hour, until the attack was over. He visited a health professional who assured him that his penis would not retract into his body and has not suffered another attack since.

H. K. F. had experienced Koro, otherwise known as genital retraction syndrome, a syndrome found in Malaysia, Indonesia, and China, in which men mistakenly believe that their penises will shrink and retract into their bodies. The anxiety they experience during an attack does cause the penis to shrink somewhat in size, but it does not retract into

the body—an anatomical impossibility. Koro is most likely to occur when a man attempts to urinate in the cold or while he is anxious—perhaps due to guilt over masturbating or visiting prostitutes—or worried about his sexual performance, or following an argument with his wife (ANRG, 2000).

The man will typically grab his genitals to prevent them from retracting. He may use mechanical devices like cords, chopsticks, clamps, or small weights to prevent retraction until he can find help. Koro is not all that common, but there was an "epidemic" of the problem, a sort of mass hysteria, that occurred among men in Singapore a few years ago.

Many men who experience Koro attacks, like H. K. F., profit from anatomical information and reassurance, as given by a health professional. In a couple of recent cases, men with attacks have also been

treated effectively with antidepressant medications (Kennedy & McDonough, 2002; Nakaya, 2002). The the reason for the effectiveness of these medications is not quite clear. Given that these were uncontrolled case studies, it is possible that the antidepressants worked like placebos—that is, "sugar pills"—and that the patients' belief that they would work was the "curative" agent.

Koro is one of a number of Chinese "culture-bound syndromes," which are believed to reflect loss (or fear of loss) of *yang*, a form of positive male energy which is balanced in nature by *ying*, or female energy. Nevertheless, there are some cases of Koro "spreading" to other cultures (Kennedy & McDonough, 2002). However, as contemporary health information becomes more widely spread, we will probably have fewer rather than more cases of Koro overall.

---

among sexually active men were about 26% to 27%. The protective effects of circumcision are likely to reflect a lower incidence of local inflammation and genital ulcers, both of which provide ports of entry for HIV, and the removal of cells in the foreskin—Langerhans cells—that are receptive to infection by HIV (Cohen, 2000; Szabo & Short, 2000).

Questions have also been raised about the *sexual* effects of circumcision. It is generally accepted that circumcision lessens sexual sensations (Liptak, 2003). Although circumcision lessens the risk of contracting cancer of the penis, STIs, and urinary tract infections (Wiswell, 2003), the procedure is extremely painful if it is not carried out with adequate anesthesia, and in 1999 the American Academy of Pediatrics issued a statement to the effect that the relatively higher risks of penis of the cancer and STIs were not sufficient to recommend that circumcision be carried out universally. Critics of circumcision also argue that it is not carried out with the informed consent of the person being operated on (who is usually only a few days old) (Liptak, 2003).

Physicians once agreed that circumcision is the treatment of choice for **phimosis**, a condition in which it is difficult to retract the foreskin from the glans. But today, only a small minority of males with phimosis are circumcised for that reason (Rickwood et al., 2000).

Phimosis An abnormal condition in which the foreskin is so tight that it cannot be withdrawn from the glans. (From the Greek *phimos,* meaning "muzzle.")

Penis Size

IRAS:	Am I not an inch of fortune better than she?
CHAIRMAN:	Well, if you were but an inch of fortune better than I, where would you choose it?
IRAS:	Not in my husband's nose.

William Shakespeare, Antony and Cleopatra

In our culture, the size of the penis is sometimes seen as a measure of a man's masculinity and his ability to please his sex partner. Shakespeare and other writers inform us that men have looked down at themselves for centuries, sometimes in delight but more often in chagrin. Men who are heralded for their sexual or reproductive feats are presumed to have more prominent "testaments" to their manhood. However, clinical experience with dysfunctional couples suggests that women are more likely to complain about their partners' ability to communicate or the emotional atmosphere of their relationships than the size of their partners' penises (Zilbergeld, 1999).

It may be of some comfort to note that even the smallest normal human penis is between three and four times the length of the phallus of the burly gorilla. Even so, the human penis does not merit comparison with the phallus of the blue whale. This ocean-dwelling mammal is about 100 feet from end to end and possesses a penis about 7 feet in length. When not in use, the penis is cached in the male's abdomen, which is a fortunate thing. If it were to trail down permanently, it might act as a rudder and confuse the animal's navigational ability.

Masters and Johnson (1966) reported that the penises of the 312 male subjects they studied generally ranged in length from 3½ inches to a little more than 4 inches when flaccid (soft). The average erect penis ranges from 5 to 7 inches in length (Reinisch, 1990). Erect penises differ less in size than flaccid (soft) penises do. Penises that are small when soft tend to gain more size when they become erect. Larger soft penises gain relatively less. Size differences in soft penises may thus be largely canceled out by erection.

Even when flaccid, the same penis can vary in size. Factors such as cold air or water, or emotions of fear or anxiety can cause the penis (along with the scrotum and testicles) to draw closer to the body, reducing its size. These factors sometimes trigger cases of Koro syndrome in Chinese culture, as we see in the nearby "A World of Diversity" feature. The flaccid penis may also grow in size in warm water or when the man is relaxed.

The Scrotum

Question: What is the scrotum? The **scrotum** is a pouch of loose skin that becomes covered lightly with hair at puberty. It has two compartments that hold the testes. Each testicle is held in place by a **spermatic cord**, a structure that contains the **vas deferens**, blood vessels and nerves, and the cremaster muscle. The **cremaster muscle** raises and lowers the testicle within the scrotum in response to temperature changes and sexual stimulation. (Sexual arousal draws the testes closer to the body.)

Sperm production is optimal at slightly below the 98.6 degrees Fahrenheit that is normal for most of the body. Scrotal temperature tends to be 5 to 6 degrees lower than body temperature. The scrotum is loose-hanging and flexible. It permits the testes and nearby structures to escape the higher body heat, especially in warm weather. In the middle layer of the scrotum is the **dartos muscle**, which, like the cremaster, contracts and relaxes reflexively in response to temperature changes. In cold weather, or when a man jumps into a body of cold water, it contracts to bring the testes closer to the body. In warm weather, it relaxes, allowing the testes to hang farther from the body. The dartos muscle also increases or decreases the surface area of

Scrotum The pouch of loose skin that contains the testes. (From the same linguistic root as the word *shred,* meaning "a long, narrow strip," and probably referring to the long furrows on the scrotal sac.)

Spermatic cord The cord that suspends a testicle within the scrotum and contains a vas deferens, blood vessels, nerves, and the cremaster muscle.

Vas deferens A tube that conducts sperm from the testicle to the ejaculatory duct of the penis. (From Latin roots meaning "a vessel" that "carries down.")

Cremaster muscle The muscle that raises and lowers the testicle in response to temperature changes and sexual stimulation.

Dartos muscle The muscle in the middle layer of the scrotum that contracts and relaxes in response to temperature changes.

Review: External Sex Organs

Reflect

Does your ethnic group have any particular attitudes or beliefs surrounding the practice of male circumcision? Do you share them? Explain.

CriticalThinking

What are the similarities and differences between male circumcision and female circumcision (clitoridectomy), as described in Chapter 3? Can one logically be in favor of one of these practices but opposed to the other?

1. The external male sex organs are the penis and the _____.

2. The penis, unlike the vagina, serves as a passageway for _____.

3. The corpora _____ fill with blood during sexual arousal, lengthening and stiffening the penis.

4. Circumcision is conducted by Jews and _____ for religious reasons.

5. The _____ muscle raises and lowers the testicle within the scrotum in response to sexual stimulation and changes in temperature.

---

the scrotum in response to temperature changes. Smoothing allows greater dissipation of heat in hot weather. Tightening or constricting the skin surface helps retain heat and gives the scrotum a wrinkled appearance in the cold.

The scrotum is developed from the same embryonic tissue that becomes the labia majora of the female. Thus, like the labia majora, it is quite sensitive to sexual stimulation. It is somewhat more sensitive than the top side of the penis but less so than other parts of the penis. (See Figure 4.2)

Internal Sex Organs

Question: What are the male internal sex organs? The male internal sex organs include the testes, the organs that manufacture sperm and testosterone; the system of tubes and ducts that conduct sperm through the male reproductive system; and the organs that help nourish and activate sperm and neutralize some of the acidity that sperm encounter in the vagina.

The Testes

The testes are the male gonads (*gonad* derives from the Greek *gone*, meaning "seed"). In slang, the testes are frequently referred to as "balls" or "nuts." These terms are considered vulgar, but they are reasonably descriptive. They also make it easier for many people to refer to the testes in informal conversation.

Question: What are the functions of the testes? The testes serve two functions analogous to those of the ovaries. They secrete sex hormones and produce mature **germ cells**. In the case of the testes, the germ cells are **sperm** and the sex hormones are **androgens**. The most important androgen is **testosterone**.

Testosterone Testosterone is secreted by **interstitial cells**, which are also known as **Leydig's cells**. Interstitial cells lie between the seminiferous tubules and release testosterone into the bloodstream (see Figure 4.5). Testosterone stimulates prenatal differ-

Germ cell A cell from which a new organism develops. (From the Latin *germen*, meaning "bud" or "sprout.")

Sperm The male germ cell. (From a Greek root meaning "seed.")

Androgens Male sex hormones. (From the Greek *andros*, meaning "man" or "males," and *-gene*, meaning "born.")

Testosterone A male steroid sex hormone.

Interstitial cells Cells that lie between the seminiferous tubules and secrete testosterone. (*Interstitial* means "set between.")

Leydig's cells Another term for *interstitial cells*.

entiation of male sex organs, sperm production, and development of **secondary sex characteristics**, such as the beard, a deep voice, and muscle mass.

In men, several endocrine glands—a feedback loop among the hypothalamus, pituitary gland, and testes (see Figure 4.6)—keep blood testosterone levels at a more or less even level, although there are slight variations with stress, time of day or month, and other factors. This contrasts with the peaks and valleys in levels of female sex hormones during the phases of the menstrual cycle.

The pituitary hormones, FSH and LH, which regulate the activity of the ovaries, also regulate the activity of the testes. FSH regulates the production of sperm. LH stimulates secretion of testosterone by interstitial cells. Low testosterone levels signal the hypothalamus to secrete the hormone, LH-releasing hormone (LH–RH). Like dominoes falling in a line, LH–RH causes the pituitary gland to secrete LH, which in turn stimulates the testes to secrete testosterone. LH is also known as *interstitial-cell-stimulating-hormone,* or ICSH.

When the level of testosterone in the blood system reaches a peak, the hypothalamus directs the pituitary gland *not* to secrete LH. This system for circling information around these three endocrine glands is called a *feedback loop.* This feedback loop is *negative.* That is, increases in hormone levels in one part of the system trigger another part to shut down and vice versa.

The testes usually range between 1 and 1¾ inches in length. They are about half as wide and deep. The left testicle usually hangs lower, because the left spermatic cord tends to be somewhat longer.

Sperm Each testicle is divided into many lobes, which are filled with winding **seminiferous tubules** (see Figure 4.2). Although packed into a tiny space, these tubules, placed end to end, would span the length of several football fields. Through **spermatogenesis**, these threadlike structures produce and store hundreds of billions of sperm over a lifetime.

Sperm cells develop through several stages. It takes about 72 days for the testes to manufacture a mature sperm cell. In an early stage, sperm cells are called **spermatocytes.** Each one contains 46 chromosomes, including one X and one Y sex chromosome. Each spermatocyte divides into two **spermatids**, each of which has 23 chromosomes. Half the spermatids have X sex chromosomes, and the other half have Y sex chromosomes. Looking something like tadpoles when examined under a microscope, mature sperm cells, called **spermatozoa**, each have a head, a cone-shaped midpiece, and a tail. The head is about 5 microns (1/50,000 of an inch) long

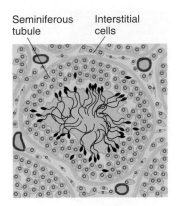

Seminiferous tubule   Interstitial cells

Figure 4.5. Interstitial Cells.
Testosterone is produced by the interstitial cells, which lie between the seminiferous tubules in each testis. Sperm (seen in the middle of the diagram) are produced within the seminiferous tubules.

Secondary sex characteristics Traits that distinguish the genders but are not directly involved in reproduction.

Seminiferous tubules Tiny, winding, sperm-producing tubes that are located within the lobes of the testes. (From Latin roots meaning "seed bearing.")

Spermatogenesis The process by which sperm cells are produced and developed.

Spermatocyte An early stage in the development of sperm cells, in which each parent cell has 46 chromosomes, including one X and one Y sex chromosome.

Spermatids Cells formed by the division of spermatocytes. Each spermatid has 23 chromosomes.

Spermatozoa Mature sperm cells.

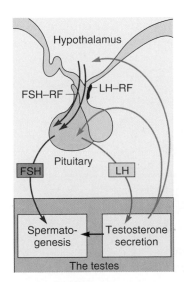

Figure 4.6. Hormonal Control of the Testes. *Several endocrine glands—the hypothalamus, the pituitary gland, and the testes—keep blood testosterone levels at a more or less constant level. Low testosterone levels signal the hypothalamus to secrete LH-releasing hormone (LH–RH). Like dominoes falling in line, LH–RH causes the pituitary gland to secrete LH, which in turn stimulates the testes to release testosterone. Follicle-stimulating hormone-releasing hormone (FSH–RH) from the hypothalamus causes the pituitary to secrete FSH which, in turn, causes the testes to produce sperm cells.*

Andropause and Chemistry: Must Testosterone Be Toxic?

Most of us are familiar enough with the phrase "raging hormones" when it comes to the alleged irritability shown by some women prior to menstruation and apparently related the fluctuations of sex hormones during the menstrual cycle. Yet men, too, could be said to be prey to "raging hormones." The male sex hormone testosterone is related to tendencies to dominate other people. There is research evidence that aggressive boys and college students have higher testosterone levels than their peers (Chance et al., 2000; Dabbs et al., 1996). For this reason, social commentator Anna Quindlen once wrote an article titled "Is Testosterone Toxic?" We will see that the answer to Anna Quindlen's question might be yes—that is, testosterone might well be toxic—but for reasons that she was not writing about.

Historically speaking, more research has been done with men's health problems than women's. Yet the problems related to low levels of sex hormones in men do not yet even have an agreed-upon name. *Andropause* suggests a falloff in androgens—male sex hormones. *Viropause* suggests a decline in virility, which is not a scientific term and suggests a general loss of ability. *Manopause* is a widely used but unscientific knockoff of the scientific term *menopause.*

For women, menopause is a time of relatively

Andropause? The term andropause *refers to the effects of the gradual decline in testosterone levels as men age. These effects, which frequently begin in the 50s, include reduced muscle strength, accumulation of fat, reduced energy, lowered fertility, and reduced erectile ability.*

distinct age-related declines in sex hormones and fertility. In men, the decline in the production of male sex hormones and fertility is more gradual (Tan & Culberson, 2003). It therefore is not surprising to find a man in his 70s or older fathering a child. However, many men in their 50s and 60s experience problems in achieving and maintaining erections (McElduff & Beange, 2003; Seidman, 2003), which may reflect

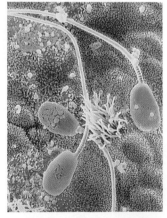

Human Sperm Cells Magnified Many Times

and contains the cell nucleus that houses the chromosomes. The midpiece contains structures that provide the energy that the tail needs to lash back and forth as it swims. Each sperm cell is about 50 microns (1/5,000 of an inch) long, one of the smallest cells in the body.

During fertilization, the 23 chromosomes from the father's sperm cell combine with the 23 chromosomes from the mother's ovum, furnishing the standard ensemble of 46 in the offspring. Among the 23 chromosomes borne by sperm cells is one sex chromosome—an X sex chromosome or a Y sex chromosome. Ova contain X sex chromosomes only. The union of an X sex chromosome and a Y sex chromosome

Figure 4.7. Age of Onset of Andropause. According to one study, andropause is most likely to initially affect men in the 50–60-year-old age range.

Source: Tan, R. S. Managing the andropause in aging men. Clinical Geriatrics. Retrieved March 23, 2002, from http://www.mmhc.com/cg/articles/CG9907/Tan.html

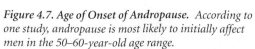

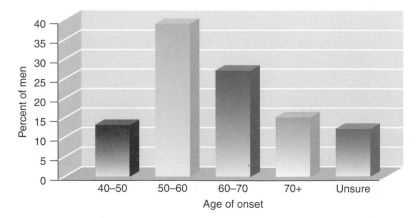

circulatory problems or have to do with hormone production. Figure 4.7 indicates the ages at which one group of researchers found symptoms of andropause to begin.

Sexual performance is only one part of the story. Figure 4.8 shows the frequencies with which a number of symptoms of andropause occur. Between the ages of 40 and 70, the typical American male loses 12 to 20 pounds of muscle, about 2 inches in height, and 15% of his bone mass. (Men as well as women are at risk for osteoporosis [Tan, 2001, 2002].) The percent of fat in the body nearly doubles. There is some loss in hearing and vision. There is loss of endurance as the cardiovascular system and lungs become less capable of adapting to exertion. Figure 4.8 indicates the frequency of some symptoms among a group of more than 300 men who were diagnosed with andropause.

Some of these changes can be slowed or even reversed. Exercise helps maintain muscle tone, keeps the growth of fatty tissue in check, and helps combat osteoporosis (Tan, 2002). A diet rich in calcium and vitamin D can help ward off bone loss in later life in both sexes. Hormone replacement may also help, but it is controversial.

Physicians in the United States write more than one million prescriptions for testosterone and related drugs for men each year, but the benefits are not fully proven, and the risks should make the caution lights blink (Vastag, 2003). Research suggests that testosterone replacement sometimes boosts strength, energy, and the sex drive as advertised, but it is connected with increased risks of prostate cancer and cardiovascular disease (Tan, 2002; Vastag, 2003). In fact, in 2002, the government decided not to proceed with a study of the effects of testosterone on aging men precisely because of these concerns (Kolata, 2002a). Dr. Richard Hodis (2002), director of the National Institute on Aging, comments, "In understanding the role of testosterone replacement, we are in many ways where we were decades ago with estrogen replacement with women. It is clear that we do not know enough to inform men and their doctors on the potential advantages or risks of hormone replacement."

As research in men's health progresses throughout the new millennium, perhaps we will develop "designer testosterone." Such a form or forms of testosterone would target the desired hormone receptors—those that contribute to strength, sexual performance, and a psychological sense of well being, but not to cancer and heart problems. Researchers are similarly searching for "designer estrogen"—forms of estrogen that will help women with perimenopausal and postmenopausal symptoms without increasing the risks of cancer and cardiac problems.

leads to the development of male offspring. Two X sex chromosomes combine to yield female offspring.

The testes are dynamos of manufacturing power, churning out about 1,000 sperm per second or 30 *billion* per year. Mathematically speaking, 10 to 20 ejaculations hold enough sperm to populate Earth. (Men are always so taken with themselves, notes the third author.)

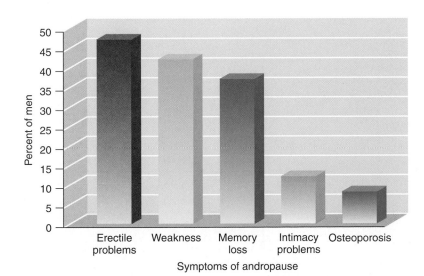

Figure 4.8. Frequency of Some Symptoms of Andropause. Andropause is most likely to be characterized by problems in attaining and maintaining an erection, weakness, and memory problems. The researchers' label "intimacy problems" refers to increased dependence of the man on his spouse and family. As testosterone goes down, men appear to be less likely to roam.

Source: Tan, R. S. Managing the andropause in aging men. Clinical Geriatrics. *Retrieved March 23, 2002, from* http://www.mmhc.com/cg/articles/CG9907/Tan.html

It is true that the father determines the baby's sex—through the presence of an X or Y sex chromosome.

The fruit fly's sperm are 1,000 times as long as human sperm (Miller & Pitnick, 2002). Remember that a human sperm cell is about 1/5,000 of an inch long and is one of the smallest cells in the body. In order to match the achievement of *Drosophila,* a man would have to produce sperm that are 100 to 120 feet long. The sperm of the tiny fruit fly are longer than the sperm of any mammal.

Researchers in Germany and at UCLA have discovered that sperm cells possess the same kind of receptors that the nose uses to sense odors (Wilkinson, 2003). Sperm may thus find their way to an egg cell by detecting its scent. In the future we may have contraceptives that prevent fertilization by blocking these receptors from sensing the odors of egg cells.

Sperm proceed from the seminiferous tubules through a maze of ducts that converge in a tube called the **epididymis**. The epididymis lies against the back wall of the testicle and stores sperm. The epididymis, some 2 inches in length, consists of twisted passages that would extend 10 to 20 feet if straightened. Sperm are inactive when they enter the epididymis. They continue to mature as they make their way through the epididymis for another two to four weeks.

The Vas Deferens

Each epididymis empties into a vas deferens (also called *ductus deferens*). *Question: What is the vas deferens?* The vas is a thin, cylindrical tube about 16 inches long that serves as a conduit for mature sperm. In the scrotum, the vas deferens lies near the skin surface within the spermatic cord. Therefore, a **vasectomy**, an operation in which the right and left vas deferens are severed, is a convenient means of sterilization. The tube leaves the scrotum and follows a circuitous path up into the abdominal cavity. Then it loops back along the rear surface of the bladder (see Figure 4.9).

The Seminal Vesicles

Question: What are the seminal vesicles? The two **seminal vesicles** are small glands, each about 2 inches long. They lie behind the bladder and open into the **ejaculatory ducts**, where the fluids they secrete combine with sperm (see Figure 4.9). The seminal vesicles were so named because they were mistakenly believed to be reservoirs for semen, rather than glands.

The fluid produced by the seminal vesicles is rich in fructose, a form of sugar, which nourishes sperm and helps them become active, or motile. Sperm motility is a major factor in male fertility. Before reaching the ejaculatory ducts, sperm are pro-

Epididymis A tube that lies against the back wall of each testicle and serves as a storage facility for sperm. (From Greek roots meaning "upon testicles.")

Vasectomy A sterilization procedure in which the vas deferens is severed, preventing sperm from reaching the ejaculatory duct.

Seminal vesicles Small glands that lie behind the bladder and secrete fluids that combine with sperm in the ejaculatory ducts.

Figure 4.9. Passage of Spermatozoa. Each testicle is divided into lobes that contain threadlike seminiferous tubules. Through spermatogenesis, the tubules produce and store hundreds of billions of sperm over the course of a lifetime. During ejaculation, sperm cells travel through the vas deferens, up and over the bladder, into the ejaculatory duct, and then through the urethra. Secretions from the seminal vesicles and the bulbourethral glands join with sperm to compose semen.

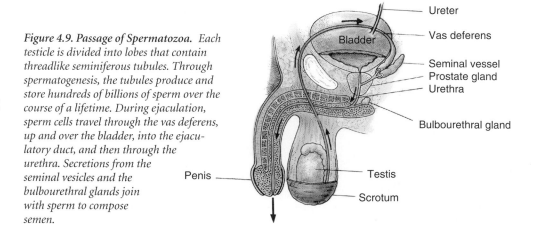

Big

Don't be fooled by his size. The tiny fruit fly, *Drosophila bifurca,* is only a fraction of an inch long. You can crush it easily with the tip of your finger. But this little insect holds the distinction of being number 1 in the *Guinness Book of Records* for length of sperm. He produces coiled sperm that stretch out to nearly 2½ inches, or 20 times the length of his own body! How does the fruit fly accomplish this feat? By devoting about 11% of his body weight to his testes.

There may be many more fruit flies than people, but fruit flies are no match for people in terms of numbers of sperm. Men can ejaculate several hundred million sperm at a time, whereas the fruit fly releases only about 50 (Miller & Pitnick, 2002). Moreover, human sperm are strong swimmers, whereas the rolled-up fruit fly sperm slowly unwinds in the female and apparently relies on transportation mechanisms within the female to reach its goal.

Why, the third author wishes to ask, must men be so competitive—even with fruit flies?

Drosophila Bifurca Although the fruit fly is only a fraction of an inch long, his sperm is 1,000 times longer than that of humans.

pelled along by contractions of the epididymis and vas deferens and by **cilia** that line the walls of the vas deferens. Once they become motile, they propel themselves by whipping their tails.

At the base of the bladder, each vas deferens joins a seminal vesicle to form a short ejaculatory duct that runs through the middle of the prostate gland (see Figure 4.9). In the prostate the ejaculatory duct opens into the urethra, which carries sperm and urine out through the tip of the penis.

The Prostate Gland

Question: What is the prostate gland? The **prostate gland** lies beneath the bladder and approximates a chestnut in shape and size (about ¾ inch in diameter). It contains muscle fibers and glandular tissue that secrete prostatic fluid. Prostatic fluid is milky and alkaline. It provides the characteristic texture and odor of the seminal fluid. The alkalinity neutralizes some of the acidity of the vaginal tract, prolonging the life span of sperm as seminal fluid spreads through the female reproductive system. The prostate is continually active in mature males, but sexual arousal further stimulates secretions. Secretions are conveyed into the urethra by a sievelike duct system. There the secretions combine with sperm and fluid from the seminal vesicles.

A vasectomy prevents sperm from reaching the urethra but does not cut off fluids from the seminal vesicles or prostate gland. A man who has had a vasectomy thus emits an ejaculate that appears normal but contains no sperm.

Cowper's Glands

Question: What are Cowper's glands? The two **Cowper's glands** are also known as the **bulbourethral glands**, in recognition of their shape and location. They lie below the prostate and empty their secretions into the urethra. During sexual arousal they

Ejaculatory duct A duct formed by the convergence of a vas deferens with a seminal vesicle through which sperm pass through the prostate gland and into the urethra.

Cilia Hairlike projections from cells that beat rhythmically to produce locomotion or currents.

Prostate gland The gland that lies beneath the bladder and secretes prostatic fluid, which gives semen its characteristic odor and texture.

Cowper's glands Structures that lie below the prostate and empty their secretions into the urethra during sexual arousal.

Bulbourethral glands Another term for *Cowper's glands.*

Review: Internal Sex Organs

Reflect

How are the testes analogous to the ovaries?

CriticalThinking

Does the evidence suggest that men undergo an "andropause" that is similar to menopause? Explain.

6. The _____ are the male gonads.

7. Testosterone is secreted by _____ cells.

8. The pituitary hormones, _____ and LH, regulate the activity of the testes as well as the ovaries.

9. The lobes of the testicles contain winding _____ tubules.

10. Spermatids have (*How many?*) chromosomes.

11. Each epididymis empties into a(n) _____ deferens.

12. The seminal vesicles produce a fluid that is rich in _____.

13. _____ fluid provides the characteristic texture and odor of seminal fluid.

14. _____ consists of sperm and the fluids contributed by several glands.

Truth?Fiction?
Revisited

Semen is *not* a synonym for sperm. Semen is the fluid that contains sperm and secretions that nourish and carry sperm.

secrete a drop or so of clear, slippery fluid that appears at the tip of the penis. The fluid may help buffer the acidity of the male's urethra and lubricate the urethral passageway, but not enough is produced to lubricate the vagina during intercourse.

Fluid from the Cowper's glands precedes the ejaculate and often contains sperm. Thus, coitus may lead to pregnancy even if the penis is withdrawn before ejaculation. For this reason, people who practice the "withdrawal method" of birth control are often called "parents."

Semen

Question: What is semen? Sperm and the fluids contributed by the seminal vesicles, the prostate gland, and the Cowper's glands make up **semen**, or whitish seminal fluid, which is expelled through the tip of the penis during ejaculation. The seminal vesicles secrete about 70% of the fluid that constitutes the ejaculate. The remaining 30% of seminal fluid consists of sperm and fluids produced by the prostate gland and the Cowper's gland. Sperm themselves account for only about 1% of the volume of semen. This is why men with vasectomies continue to ejaculate about as much semen as before, although their ejaculates are devoid of sperm.

Semen is the medium that carries sperm through much of the male's reproductive system and the reproductive tract of the female. Semen contains water, mucus, sugar (fructose), acids, and bases. It activates and nourishes sperm, and the bases help shield sperm from vaginal acidity. The typical ejaculate contains between 200 and 400 million sperm and ranges between 3 and 5 milliliters in volume. (Five milliliters is equal to about 1 tablespoon.) The quantity of semen decreases with age and frequency of ejaculation.

Semen The whitish fluid that constitutes the ejaculate, consisting of sperm and secretions from the seminal vesicles, prostate, and Cowper's glands.

Urologist A physician who specializes in the diagnosis and treatment of diseases of the urogenital system.

Health Problems of the Urogenital System

Because the organs that comprise the urinary and reproductive systems are near each other and share some "piping," they are referred to as the urinogenital or urogenital system. A number of health problems affect the urogenital system. The type of physician who specializes in their diagnosis and treatment is a **urologist**.

Urethritis

Question: What is urethritis? Men, like women, are subject to bladder and urethral inflammations, which are generally referred to as **urethritis**. The symptoms include frequent urination (urinary frequency), a strong need to urinate (urinary urgency), burning during urination, and a penile discharge. People with symptoms of urinary frequency and urinary urgency feel the pressing need to urinate repeatedly, even though they may have just done so and may have but another drop or two to expel. The discharge may dry on the urethral opening, in which case it may have to be peeled off or wiped away before it is possible to urinate. The urethra also may become constricted when it is inflamed, slowing or halting urination. It is a frightening sensation for a male to feel the urine rush from his bladder and then suddenly stop at the urethral opening!

Preventive measures for urethritis parallel those suggested for cystitis (bladder infection): drinking more water, drinking cranberry juice (4 ounces, two or three times a day), and lowering intake of alcohol and caffeine. Cranberry juice is highly acidic, and acid tends to eliminate many of the bacteria that can give rise to urethritis.

Cancer of the Testes

Question: What should we know about cancer of the testes? Cancer of the testicles remains a relatively rare form of cancer, accounting for about 7,600 new cases annually, or about 1% of all new cancers in men, and about 400 will die from it (American Cancer Society, 2003). It is the most common form of solid-tumor cancer to strike men between the ages of 20 and 34, accounting for nearly 10% of all deaths from cancer among men in that age group (American Cancer Society, 2003).

There is no evidence that testicular cancer results from sexual overactivity or masturbation. About 14% of men with testicular cancer had **cryptorchidism** as children, a condition in which one or both testicles fail to descend from the abdomen into the scrotum (American Cancer Society, 2003). Family history also increases the risk.

Although testicular cancer was generally fatal in earlier years, the prognosis today is quite favorable, especially for cases that are detected early. Treatments include surgical removal of the diseased testis, radiation, and chemotherapy. The survival rate among cases that are detected early, before the cancer has spread beyond the testes, is well above 90% (National Cancer Institute, 2003). Delayed treatment markedly reduces the chances of survival, because survival is connected with the extent to which the cancer has spread.

The surgical removal of a testicle may have profound psychological implications. Some men who have lost a testicle feel less "manly." Fears related to sexual performance can engender sexual dysfunctions. From a physiological standpoint, sexual functioning should remain unimpaired, as adequate quantities of testosterone are produced by the remaining testis.

The early stages of testicular cancer usually produce no symptoms, other than the mass itself. Because early detection is crucial to survival, men are advised to examine themselves monthly following puberty and to have regular medical checkups. Self-examination may also reveal evidence of sexually transmitted infections (STIs) and other problems.

Self-Examination of the Testes Self-examination (see Figure 4.10) is best performed shortly after a warm shower or bath, when the skin of the scrotum is most relaxed.

Urethritis An inflammation of the bladder or urethra.

Cryptorchidism A condition in which one of two testicles fails to descend from the abdomen into the scrotum.

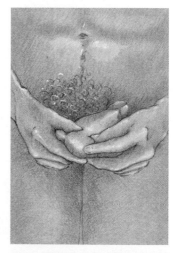

Figure 4.10. Self-Examination of the Testes

The man should exam the scrotum for evidence of pea-sized lumps. Each testicle can be rolled gently between the thumb and the fingers. Lumps are generally found on the side or front of the testicle. The presence of a lump is not necessarily a sign of cancer, but it should be promptly reported to a physician for further evaluation. The American Cancer Society (2003) and the National Cancer Institute (2003) list these warning signals:

1. Slight enlargement of one of the testicles.
2. Change in the consistency of a testicle.
3. Dull ache in the lower abdomen or groin. (Pain may be absent in cancer of the testes, however).
4. Sensation of dragging and heaviness in a testicle.

Disorders of the Prostate

The prostate gland is tiny at birth and grows rapidly at puberty. It may shrink during adulthood, but usually becomes enlarged past the age of 50.

Benign Prostatic Hyperplasia (BPH) The prostate gland becomes enlarged in about half the men past the age of 50 and 80% of men by age 80 (Prostatecare, 2003). *Question: What is benign prostatic hyperplasia?* **Benign prostatic hyperplasia** (BPH) is noncancerous enlargement of the prostate gland due to hormonal changes associated with aging rather than other causes, such as inflammation from sexually transmitted infections. Because the prostate surrounds the upper part of the urethra (see Figure 4.2), enlargement constricts the urethra, causing urinary frequency (including increased frequency of nocturnal urination), urinary urgency, and difficulty starting the flow of urine. Several treatments are available to relieve the pressure on the urethra and increase the flow of urine. Two types of drugs help men with BPH. The first type, 5ARIs (5-alpha reductase inhibitors), inhibits the production of the hormone DHT (a form of testosterone), which causes enlargement of the prostate. The 5ARIs shrink the prostate, provide long-term improvement of symptoms, and reduce the risk of severe urinary retention and the need for surgery. The second type is alpha-blockers, which act by relaxing the muscles of the bladder to improve the flow of urine, providing symptom relief. Part of the prostate is also sometimes surgically removed (Prostatecare, 2003).

Cancer of the Prostate Question: What should we know about prostate cancer? Prostate cancer is a serious and, unlike BPH, a life-threatening problem. About one man in six in the United States will develop prostate cancer at some time during his life (American Cancer Society, 2003). Prostate cancer is the second most common form of cancer among men, after skin cancer, and the second leading cause of cancer deaths in men, after lung cancer. There are about 221,000 new cases of prostate cancer each year in the United States, and nearly 39,000 men die from it (American Cancer Society, 2003).

Prostate cancer involves the growth of malignant prostate tumors that can metastasize to bones and lymph nodes if not detected and treated early. African American men are one third more likely than European American men to develop prostate cancer (National Cancer Institute, 2003). African American men have less access to health care than European American men do, so prostate cancer is diagnosed later among them, and they are twice as likely to die from it (American Cancer Society, 2003).

Benign prostatic hyperplasia Enlargement of the prostate gland due to hormonal changes associated with aging and characterized by symptoms such as urinary frequency, urinary urgency, and difficulty starting the flow of urine.

Researchers have identified intake of animal fat as a potential risk factor. Men whose diets are rich in animal fats, especially fats from red meat, have a substantially higher chance of developing advanced prostate cancer than do men with a low intake of animal fat. The incidence of prostate cancer also increases with age. More than 80% of cases of prostate cancer are diagnosed in men aged 65 or above (National Cancer Institute, 2003). Genetic factors are also apparently involved (Lichtenstein et al., 2000). Moreover, testosterone spurs the development of prostate cancer as well as BPH (American Cancer Society, 2003).

The early symptoms of cancer of the prostate may mimic those of benign prostate enlargement: urinary frequency and difficulty in urinating. Later symptoms include blood in the urine, pain or burning on urination, and pain in the lower back, pelvis, or upper thighs (National Cancer Institute, 2003). Most cases occur without noticeable symptoms in the early stages.

The American Cancer Society (2003) recommends that men receive annual digital rectal examinations (DREs) beginning at about age 50 (see Figure 4.11). African American men and other men at greater risk should begin at age 45. The physician inserts a finger into the rectum and feels for bumps or hard spots in the prostate gland. Unfortunately, many men are reluctant to undergo a rectal examination, even though it is only mildly uncomfortable and may save their lives. Some are embarrassed or reluctant to discuss urinary problems with their physicians. Some may resist the rectal examination because they associate rectal insertion with male–male sex. Still others fear that they may have cancer and choose to remain ignorant. Avoidance of, or ignorance of the need for, regular exams is a major contributor to the death rate from prostate cancer.

When a cancerous growth is suspected on the basis of a rectal examination or a PSA blood test, further testing is usually done via additional blood tests, ultrasound, or biopsy. PSA is a protein that helps transform a gel-like substance in the prostate gland to a liquid that transports sperm when it is ejaculated. In the diseased or enlarged prostate, PSA seeps into the blood at higher levels, giving higher test

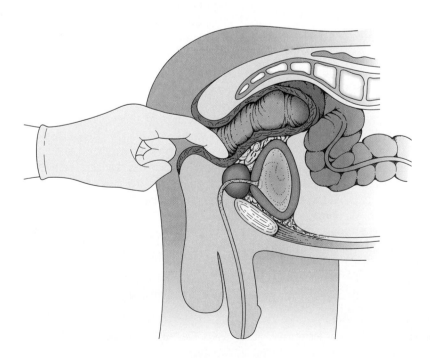

Figure 4.11. Digital Rectal Examination (DRE) for Prostate Cancer
Source: American Cancer Society, 2003.

Options—and Decisions—for Men with Prostate Cancer

Mayor Rudolph W. Giuliani of New York decided on a treatment for his prostate cancer, which was diagnosed in 2000, after months of private deliberation and public speculation. In mid-September, the mayor, along with his doctors at Mount Sinai Medical Center, announced he had received radioactive seed implants during an out-patient procedure earlier that day. But in deciding on a treatment, Mr. Giuliani said he had great difficulty weighing his choices. Doctors refer to the process as constructing a "decision tree" or "clinical pathway," as patients weigh each pro and con. Because the disease progresses at a relatively slow pace, men in the early stages can take some time to explore the expanding treatment options available to them.

Prostate cancer is usually detected and assessed with a combination of tests. These include a blood test for prostate specific antigen (PSA), recommended annually for men 50 and over (earlier for those at higher risk). Results under 4 nanograms per milliliter are considered normal. Results over 10 are high, and those between 4 and 10 are considered borderline.

Next comes the digital rectal exam (DRE), in which the doctor palpates the prostate gland with a finger to detect abnormalities. A transrectal ultrasound may also be used. If cancer is suspected, a needle biopsy is done of the gland and sometimes of nearby lymph nodes. If a tumor is detected, pathologists will "grade" two pieces of tissue and rate them from 1 to 5 on the Gleason scale, which determines the cancer's aggressiveness. The two scores are added together. Sums of 2 through 4 are considered low (slower growing), 5 and 6 are called intermediate, and 7 to 10 high, with the worst prognosis. Finally, doctors may do other tests to see if the cancer has spread. These include radionuclide bone scans, CAT scans (coaxial

tomography), and MRIs (magnetic resonance imaging).

Deciding on treatment can be daunting, partly because the options today are far better than 10 years ago. They include: improved surgery, with "nerve sparing" to help reduce incontinence and impotence; external-beam radiation, in which standard X-ray beams are directed at the prostate area; highly targeted proton radiation, in which where protons are "shaped" into beams to match the shape of the tumor and to eliminate damage of surrounding tissue; cryosurgery, or freezing of the cancerous cells; radioactive seed implants, in which rice-size pellets are injected into the prostate to kill cancer cells; new hormone treatments to block production of testosterone, which feeds cancer cells; combination therapies using two or more treatments at once; and "watchful waiting," in which patients seek no treatment, but simply monitor themselves for problems (a common practice in older patients).

And, new treatments continue to be developed in clinical trials around the country. Here are the stories of several men and the options they selected.

DAMON O. HARRIS, 50, CHOSE HORMONES, FOR SPREADING CANCER

Damon O. Harris spent much of the 1970s as a singer with the Temptations. But now Mr. Harris, in his 50s, spends time educating African American men about their higher-than-average risk of prostate cancer. Mr. Harris had never been screened for prostate cancer. But then he noticed a lingering pain. He had a DRE, and his PSA test came back at over 13. Within days, he was facing a cancer diagnosis. Mr. Harris began what he called "my crash course in Cancer 101. . . . I had little time to do research," he said. As it turned out, in his case, the decision was simple. "My cancer was metastatic," he said. "I opted for the best

Former Mayor Rudolph W. Giuliani of New York In 2000, New York's Mayor Rudy Giuliani decided to treat his prostate cancer with radioactive seed implants during an outpatient procedure. There are many treatments today for prostate cancer, and people with the disease must weigh the benefits and risks of each.

and only treatment available, which is hormone therapy."

Mr. Harris immediately began an oral medication, Casodex, to neutralize testosterone and other male hormones in his system, followed by weekly injections of Lupron, which shuts down new production of male hormones, like testosterone, needed for prostate growth. "I will be on it for the rest of my life," Mr. Harris said. The most severe side effects of hormone therapy are hot flashes, weight gain, and reduced sexual desire. Mr. Harris experienced all three. "I no longer have the hot flashes, for which I'm glad," he said. "But . . . they only last until your system adjusts." He exercises regularly to keep the weight off, and though his libido has changed, "I am still a man," he said. Mr. Harris is in "tentative remission," though frequent tests and scans "sadly remind me of my situation."

EUGENE WATERMAN, 71, CHOSE PROTON BEAM RADIATION

As a doctor, Eugene Waterman, 71, was especially aware of the risks of prostate

Source: Adapted from David Kirby (2000, October 3). More options, and decisions, for men with prostate cancer. *The New York Times* online.

cancer and the means of detecting it. Dr. Waterman, a semiretired psychiatrist, learned that his PSA had suddenly risen to 11, very high. A biopsy diagnosed cancer with an aggressive Gleason score of 8. Fearful of the risks of surgery, Dr. Waterman began researching proton-beam radiation therapy (PBRT). Unlike X-rays, the standard forms of external radiation, PBRT is highly specific and individualized. Protons can be "shaped" into a beam to match the exact shape of the tumor, whereas standard treatment—photons and electrons—reach surrounding healthy tissue.

"The side effects of radiation were mild," he said. "There was some fatigue at the end of the week and some diarrhea." He had some mild anal soreness, too, which was treated with a cortisone salve. But the treatment also involved hormone therapy, a Zoladex injection every three months for a year. The resulting testosterone depletion was difficult, Dr. Waterman said. Because the condition can lead to bone loss, he asked for a bone scan, and some borderline osteoporosis was found. Now he takes Fosomax twice a week.

But he also experienced hot flashes, 10 to 15 times a day. He suffered a complete loss of libido and sore, enlarged breasts. "But I have been off Zoladex for over a year," he said. "Testosterone levels are back to normal levels, and side effects have gone away." His sexual ability has returned with help from Viagra, Dr. Waterman said. "But desire is not as strong as it was." Today, his health is good, and his PSA has remained at 0.26 for the last year, though he realizes there is still a "50–50 chance" of eventual relapse.

THOMAS SELLERS, 50, HAD HIS PROSTATE REMOVED

Thomas Sellers, a 50-year-old resident of Brookline, Mass., is not only a prostate cancer survivor, he is also chief financial officer of the New England division of the American Cancer Society. As a cancer professional and an African American, Mr.

Sellers knew about the need to begin annual PSA tests at 45. A test showed that his PSA had leaped to 8.5. A biopsy confirmed cancer.

Ultimately, Mr. Sellers chose surgery, a nerve-sparing radical prostatectomy. Impotence, he said, worried him greatly, adding, "The likelihood of a cure because of early detection and the fact the cancer was still within the prostate outweighed fear of side effects." After surgery, Mr. Sellers wore a catheter for two weeks to drain urine. He took an eight-week medical leave and did not recover his full strength for six months, he said. He endured short-term incontinence, which he called disconcerting. "It took six months or more before I was completely dry, and nine months before I stopped wearing a pad," he said.

As for sexual activity, Mr. Sellers has some problems, despite the nerve-sparing, and he is "experimenting with Viagra, with intermittent success." But his cancer is cured, and his PSA is back to zero.

MELVIN S. KATZ, 56, RECEIVED RADIATION IMPLANTS

"I denied for eight months that anything was wrong with me," said Melvin S. Katz, a 56-year-old health care consultant from Forest Hills, N.Y. "I noticed symptoms in July and didn't do anything about it until the following March." By then, Mr. Katz's PSA had leapt to 91. A biopsy showed cancer with a Gleason score of 8. Only 48 at the time, he said he felt too young to have this "old man's disease."

Mr. Katz immediately went on combination hormone therapy (Eulexin plus Lupron) to halt the production of testosterone, the hormone that feeds prostate cancer. Mr. Katz chose high-dose external beam radiation five days a week for eight weeks at Columbia-Presbyterian Hospital. "It afforded me a quality of life," he explained, adding that side effects were mild. Three months after radiation, Mr. Katz stopped the hormones. . . . His PSA went from 0 to 25 in

just nine months, and he resumed hormone treatment. Then a biopsy showed lingering cancer. "I couldn't take any more external radiation, and surgery was risky because the radiation increased the chance of bleeding," he said.

His doctor at Columbia-Presbyterian suggested Palladium radioactive seed implants, and he agreed. The procedure was done under local anesthetic and lasted about an hour, while doctors injected rice-size pellets into his prostate. The radiation lasts for six to nine months, "and the only restriction is no little children or pregnant ladies on your lap," Mr. Katz said. Meanwhile, his PSA dropped from 25 to 0.9. Two years ago, he stopped the hormone therapy, replacing it with an herbal formula called PC-Spes, which Mr. Katz credited with lowering his PSA to 0.3, where it remains. But the implants "definitely had an impact," he said. "They killed most of the cancer, allowing me to stabilize and keep it under control with hormones and PC-Spes."

JOHN SOSDIAN, 79, DECIDED TO WATCH AND WAIT

John Sosdian, a 79-year-old retired Army electrician from Tinton Falls, N.J., began annual screenings for prostate cancer in 1992. Though Mr. Sosdian's PSA was slightly elevated, at 3.9, nothing abnormal was noted in a digital examination. For several years, his PSA remained in the 5 to 7 range and all exams were normal. Doctors thought the higher PSA numbers were explained by Mr. Sosdian's age. Then, in September 1999, the PSA jumped to 9.4, and a biopsy led to a cancer diagnosis. The tumor scored a 6 on the Gleason scale, showing a moderate growth rate, even though the digital examination still revealed nothing. Given Mr. Sosdian's age, surgery seemed risky. Mr. Sosdian's doctor recommended hormone therapy combined with radiation seed implants. But he also mentioned the idea of taking no action, something known as "watchful waiting."

(continues)

Mr. Sosdian carefully researched the side effects of each treatment and was discouraged by what he found. He discussed the treatment extensively with his wife, Lorette. "We agreed that watchful waiting was the best selection," he said, "because of my age and strong desire to maintain the relationship and lifestyle I have, which I treasure."

Mr. Sosdian has an exam every three months (with nothing abnormal detected) and a PSA test. Last April, the PSA was down to 6.6, and it has never risen above the 9.4 at diagnosis.

Mr. Sosdian will have a PSA test and an exam every three months and an ultrasound exam every 12 months for two years, followed by two PSAs and one

ultrasound each year after that. If he needs treatment, he said, he will opt for something called "Prost-R-cision," which uses irradiation to excise the prostate without cutting muscles and nerves, reducing the risks of incontinence and impotence.

readings. Early detection is important because treatment is most effective before the cancer has spread. Fifty-eight percent of cases of prostate cancer are discovered while they are still localized. The survival rate drops dramatically if the cancer has metastasized. Still, the overall survival rate has improved since the 1960s from 50% to more than 80% (American Cancer Society, 2003).

The most widely used treatment for prostate cancer is surgical removal of the prostate gland (Klein, 2000). However, surgical prostate removal may damage surrounding nerves, leading to problems in controlling the flow of urine or in erection or ejaculation (Stanford et al., 2000). Recently introduced surgical techniques tend to spare the surrounding nerves and reduce, but not eliminate, the risk of complications. Other treatments include radiation, hormone treatment, and anticancer drugs (Klein, 2000). Hormone treatment in the form of androgen (testosterone) suppression therapy and anticancer drugs may shrink the size of the tumor and relieve pain

Review: Health Problems of the Urogenital System

Reflect

Is any man you know reluctant to undergo regular screening (DRE and PSA testing) for cancer of the prostate? What are the sources of the reluctance? What arguments might you use to convince him to undergo screening?

CriticalThinking

If a man has a strong family history of prostate cancer, is there any point to his making an effort to watch his diet? Explain.

15. Bladder and urethral inflammations are usually called _____.

16. There (*Is* or *Is no*?) evidence that testicular cancer results from sexual overactivity or masturbation.

17. Benign prostatic hyperplasia (BPH) affects about _____ the men past the age of 50.

18. _____ blockers help with BPH by relaxing the muscles of the bladder to improve the flow of urine.

19. There are about _____ new cases of prostate cancer in the U.S.A. each year.

20. (*African* or *European*?) Americans are more likely than (*African* or *European*?) Americans to develop prostate cancer and to die from it.

21. The hormone _____ spurs the development of prostate cancer as well as BPH.

22. Prostate cancer can usually be detected early by means of digital _____ examination (DRE) and a blood test called a _____.

23. Prostate cancer is most often treated by means of _____.

24. Inflammation of the prostate gland is called _____.

25. Prostatitis is usually treated with _____.

for long periods of time. Men who have their prostate glands removed are more likely to experience urinary incontinence (loss of control over urination) and sexual dysfunction (trouble attaining erection) than men who use radiation (Potosky et al., 2000). But many physicians argue that surgery remains the better choice in terms of survival rates. Among older men with slow-growing prostate cancer, physicians often prefer "watchful waiting" to surgery. The men may live long enough to die from causes other than cancer. The treatment choices are explored further in the nearby "A Closer Look."

Prostatitis Question: What is prostatitis? Prostatitis is inflammation of the prostate, which can be caused by various infectious agents. The chief symptoms are an ache or pain between the scrotum and anal opening and painful ejaculation. Prostatitis is usually treated with antibiotics. Although aspirin and ibuprofen may relieve the pain, men with these symptoms should consult a physician. Painful ejaculation may discourage masturbation or coitus, which is ironic, because regular flushing of the prostate through ejaculation may be helpful in the treatment of prostatitis.

Male Sexual Functions

The male sexual functions of erection and ejaculation provide the means for sperm to travel from the male's reproductive tract to the female's. There the sperm cell and ovum unite to conceive a new human being. Of course, the natural endowment of reproduction with sensations of pleasure helps ensure that it will take place with or without knowledge of these biological facts.

Erection

Erection is caused by the engorgement of the penis with blood, such that the penis grows in size and stiffens. The erect penis is an efficient conduit, or funnel, for depositing sperm deep within the vagina.

Question: How does erection occur? In mechanical terms, erection is a hydraulic event. The spongy, cavernous masses of the penis are equipped to hold blood. Filling them with blood causes them to enlarge, like a sponge swells as it absorbs water. This simple description belies the fact that erection is a remarkable feat of biological engineering (there they go again, notes the third author) that involves the cooperation of the vascular (blood) system and the nervous system.

In a few moments—as quickly as 10 or 15 seconds—the penis can double in length, become firm, and shift from a funnel for passing urine to one that expels semen. Moreover, the bladder is closed off when the male becomes sexually aroused, decreasing the likelihood that semen and urine will mix.

What accounts for the firmness of an erection? The corpora cavernosa are surrounded by a tough, fibrous covering called the *tunica albuginea.* As the rubber of a balloon resists the pressure of pumped-in air, this housing resists expansion, causing the penis to rigidify. The corpus spongiosum, which contains the urethra, also engorges with blood during erection. It does not become hard, however, because it lacks the fibrous casing. The penile glans, which is formed by the crowning of the spongiosum at the tip of the penis, turns a dark purplish hue as it becomes engorged, but it too does not stiffen.

Erection is reversed when more blood flows out of the erectile tissue than flows in, restoring the pre-erectile circulatory balance and shrinking the erectile tissue

Prostatitis Inflammation of the prostate gland.

Erection The enlargement and stiffening of the penis as a consequence of engorgement with blood.

Truth?Fiction?
Revisited

It is not true that morning erections reflect the need to urinate. When the man awakens with both an erection and the need to urinate, he may mistakenly assume that the erection was caused by the pressure of his bladder.

Men cannot will themselves to have erections. People do not control sexual reflexes voluntarily, as they might lift an arm, but they can set the stage for them to occur by seeking sexual stimulation. Efforts to control sexual responses consciously by "force of will" can backfire and make it more difficult to become aroused (for example, to attain erection or vaginal lubrication).

or spongy masses. The erectile tissue thus exerts less pressure against the fibrous covering, resulting in loss of rigidity. Loss of erection occurs when sexual stimulation ceases, or when the body returns to a (sexual) resting state following orgasm. Loss of erection can also occur in response to anxiety or perceived threats. Loss of erection in response to threat can be abrupt, as when a man in the "throes of passion" suddenly hears a suspicious noise in the adjoining room, suggestive of an intruder. A man who fears that he will be unable to perform successfully may experience **performance anxiety** that can prevent him from achieving erection or lead to a loss of erection at penetration.

The male capacity for erection spans the life cycle. Erections are common in babies, even within minutes after birth. Evidence from ultrasound studies shows that male fetuses may have erections months prior to birth. Some men who are in their 80s and 90s continue to experience erections and engage in coitus.

Erections are not limited to the conscious state. Men have nocturnal erections every 90 minutes or so as they sleep. They generally occur during REM (rapid eye movement) sleep. REM sleep is associated with dreaming. It is so named because the sleeper's eyes dart about rapidly under the closed eyelids during this stage. Erections occur during most periods of REM sleep.

The mechanism of nocturnal erection appears to be physiologically based. That is, dreams may not have erotic content. Morning erections are actually nocturnal erections. They occur when the man is awakened during REM sleep, as by an alarm clock.

Spinal Reflexes and Sexual Response

Men may become sexually aroused by a range of stimuli, including tactile stimulation provided by their partners, visual stimulation (as from scanning photos of nudes on the Internet), or sexual fantasies. Regardless of the source of stimulation, the man's sexual responses, erection and ejaculation, occur by **reflex**.

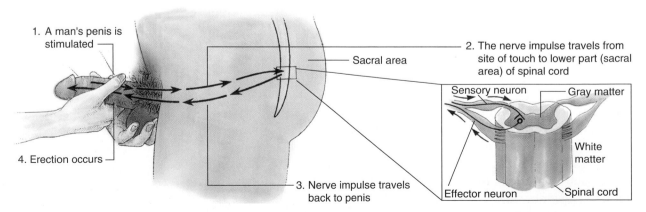

Figure 4.12. Reflexes. *Reflexes need not involve the brain, although messages to the brain may make us aware when reflexes are occurring. Reflexes are the product of "local government" in the spine.*

Question: What does it mean to say that erection and ejaculation are reflexes?
Sexual reflexes are automatic, unlearned responses to sexual stimulation. Examples
in women include vaginal lubrication and orgasm. We need not "try" to become
aroused. We need only expose ourselves to sexual stimulation and allow reflexes to do
the job for us.

The reflexes governing erection and ejaculation are controlled in the spinal cord.
They are thus called spinal reflexes. Erectile responses to direct stimulation such as
touching or licking involve a simple spinal reflex that does not require the direct participation of the brain (see Figure 4.12). Erections can also be initiated by the brain,
as when a man has sexual fantasies or catches a glimpse of an undressed woman. In
the case of the "no-hands" type of erections, stimulation from the brain travels to the
spinal cord, where the erectile reflex is triggered.

Tactile stimulation (touching) of the penis or nearby areas (lower abdomen,
scrotum, inner thighs) causes sensory neurons to transmit nerve messages (signals)
to an erection center in the lower back, in an area of the spinal cord called the
sacrum. The sacral erection center controls reflexive erections—that is, erections
occurring in response to direct stimulation of the penis and nearby areas. When
direct penile stimulation occurs, messages in the form of nerve impulses are received
by this erection center, which in turn sends impulses to the genitalia via nerves that
service the penis. These impulses cause arteries carrying blood to the corpora cavernosa and corpus spongiosum to dilate, so that more blood flows into these tissues; as
these tissues expand, the penis becomes erect.

The sacral erection center makes it possible for men whose spinal cords have
been injured or severed above the center to achieve erections (and ejaculate) in
response to direct tactile stimulation of the penis. Erection occurs even though their
injuries prevent nerve signals from reaching their brains. Because of the lack of communication between the genital organs and the brain, there are no sensations, but
many spinal-injured men report that sex remains psychologically pleasurable
because they can observe the responses of their partners.

The Role of the Brain If direct penile stimulation triggers erection at the spinal level,
what is the role of the brain? Although it may seem that the penis sometimes has a
mind of its own, the brain plays an important role in regulating sexual responses.

Tactile (touch) stimulation of the penis may trigger erection through the spinal
cord, but sexual sensations are then normally relayed to the brain, which generally
results in pleasure and perhaps in a decision to focus on erotic stimulation. The sight
of one's partner, erotic fantasies, memories, and so forth can result in messages being
sent by the brain through the spinal cord to the arteries servicing the penis, maintaining or strengthening the erection.

When the brain originates messages that trigger the erectile reflex, it transmits
nerve impulses to a second and higher erection center located in the upper back in
the lumbar region of the spinal cord. This higher spinal erection center serves as a
"switchboard" between the brain and the penis, allowing perceptual, cognitive, and
emotional responses to make their contributions. When the nerve pathways between
the brain and the upper spinal cord are blocked or severed, men cannot achieve erections in response to mental stimulation alone.

The brain can also stifle sexual response. A man who is highly anxious about his
sexual abilities may be unable to achieve an erection even with the most direct,
intense penile stimulation. Or a man who believes that sexual pleasure is sinful or
dirty may be filled with anxiety and guilt and be unable to achieve erection when he
is sexually stimulated by his partner.

Performance anxiety
Feelings of dread and
foreboding experienced in
connection with sexual
activity (or any other activity
that might be judged by
another person).

Reflex A simple, unlearned
response to a stimulus that is
mediated by the spine rather
than the brain.

Sacrum The thick, triangular
bone located near the
bottom of the spinal column.

Autonomic nervous system The division of the nervous system that regulates automatic bodily processes, such as heartbeat, pupil dilation, respiration, and digestion. Abbreviated *ANS*.

In some males, especially adolescents, the erectile reflex is so easily tripped that incidental rubbing of the genitals against his own undergarments, the sight of an attractive passerby, or a fleeting sexual fantasy produces erection. Spontaneous erections may occur under embarrassing circumstances, such as before classes change in junior or senior high school or on a public beach. In an effort to distract himself from erotic fantasies and to allow an erection to subside, many a male adolescent in the classroom has desperately renewed his interest in his algebra or foreign language textbook before the bell has rung. (A well-placed towel may serve in a pinch on the beach.)

As men mature they require more penile stimulation to achieve full erection. Partners of men in their 30s and 40s need not feel that their attractiveness has waned if their lovers no longer have instant "no-hands" erections when they disrobe. It takes men longer to achieve erection as they age, and direct stimulation becomes a more critical source of arousal.

The Role of the Autonomic Nervous System (ANS) Stimulation that brings about an erection can originate in the brain, but erection is not a voluntary response, like raising your arm. Whatever the original or dominant source of stimulation—direct penile stimulation or sexual fantasy—erection remains an unlearned, automatic reflex.

Automatic responses, such as erection, involve the division of the nervous system called the **autonomic nervous system** (ANS). *Autonomic* means "automatic." The ANS controls automatic bodily processes such as heartbeat, pupil dilation, respiration, and digestion. In contrast, voluntary movement (like raising an arm) is under the control of the *somatic* division of the nervous system.

Question: What are the roles of the sympathetic and parasympathetic branches of the ANS in erection and ejaculation? The ANS has two branches, the **sympathetic** and the **parasympathetic**. These branches have largely opposing effects; when they are activated at the same time, their effects become balanced out to some degree. In general, the sympathetic branch is in command during processes that involve a release of bodily energy from stored reserves, such as during running, performing some other athletic task, or being gripped by fear or anxiety. The sympathetic branch also governs the general mobilization of the body, such as by increasing the heart rate and respiration rate in response to threat.

The parasympathetic branch is most active during processes that restore reserves of energy, such as digestion. When we experience fear or anxiety, the sympathetic branch of the ANS quickens the heart rate. When we relax, the parasympathetic branch curbs the heart rate. The parasympathetic branch activates digestive processes, but the sympathetic branch inhibits digestive activity. Because the sympathetic branch is in command when we feel fear or anxiety, such stimuli can inhibit the activity of the parasympathetic system, possibly causing indigestion.

The divisions of the ANS play different roles in sexual arousal and response. The nerves that cause penile arteries to dilate during erection belong to the parasympathetic branch of the ANS. The parasympathetic system largely governs erection. The nerves governing ejaculation belong to the sympathetic branch, however. One implication of this division of neural responsibility is that intense fear or anxiety, which involves sympathetic nervous system activity, may inhibit erection by counteracting the activity of the parasympathetic nervous system. Since sympathetic arousal helps trigger ejaculation, anxiety or fear may also accelerate ejaculation, causing **premature ejaculation.**

The connection between emotions, sympathetic activity, and ejaculation can set up a vicious cycle. Anxiety in a sexual encounter may trigger premature ejaculation. During a subsequent sexual encounter, the man might fear recurrence of premature ejaculation. The fear may bring on the reality. He may face further sexual encounters with yet greater fear, possibly further hastening ejaculation—but possibly inhibiting erection. Methods for helping men with erectile dysfunction and premature ejaculation aim at reducing their levels of anxiety and thereby lessening sympathetic activity.

Erectile Abnormalities Some men find that their erect penises are slightly curved or bent. Some degree of curvature is normal, but men with **Peyronie's disease** have excessive curvature that can make erections painful. The condition is caused by buildup of fibrous tissue in the penile shaft. Although some cases of Peyronie's disease appear to clear up on their own, most require medical attention.

Some men experience erections that persist for hours or days. This condition is called *priapism,* after Priapus of Greek myth, the son of Dionysus and Aphrodite who personified male procreative power. Priapism is often caused by leukemia, sickle cell anemia, or diseases of the spinal cord, although in some cases the cause remains unknown. Priapism occurs when the mechanisms that drain the blood that makes the penis erect are damaged and so cannot return the blood to the circulatory system. Priapism may become a medical emergency, because erection prolonged beyond six hours can starve penile tissues of oxygen, leading to tissue deterioration. Medical intervention in the form of drugs or surgery may be required to reverse the condition.

Ejaculation

Question: How does ejaculation occur? Ejaculation, like erection, is a spinal reflex. It is triggered when sexual stimulation reaches a critical point or threshold. Ejaculation generally occurs together with **orgasm**, the sudden muscle contractions that occur at the peak of sexual excitement and result in the abrupt release of sexual tension that had built up during sexual arousal. Orgasm is generally pleasurable. *Ejaculation,* however, refers only to the expulsion of semen from the tip of the penis. Orgasm and ejaculation are *not* synonymous, however. For example, **paraplegics** can ejaculate if the area of the lower spinal cord that controls ejaculation is intact. They do not experience the subjective aspects of orgasm, however, because the sensations of orgasm do not reach the brain.

Ejaculation occurs in two stages. The first phase, often called the **emission stage**, involves contractions of the prostate, seminal vesicles, and the upper part of the vas deferens (the **ampulla**). The force of these contractions propels seminal fluid into the prostatic part of the urethral tract—a small tube called the **urethral bulb**—which balloons as muscles close at either end, trapping the semen. It is at this point that the man perceives orgasm as inevitable. The man feels that nothing can prevent ejaculation.

The second stage, which is often referred to as the **expulsion stage**, involves the propulsion of the seminal fluid through the urethra and out of the urethral opening at the tip of the penis. In this stage, muscles at the base of the penis and elsewhere contract rhythmically, expelling semen. The second stage is generally accompanied by the sensations of orgasm.

Sympathetic The branch of the ANS most active during emotional responses that spend the body's reserves of energy, such as fear and anxiety. The sympathetic ANS largely controls ejaculation.

Parasympathetic The branch of the ANS most active during processes that restore the body's reserves of energy, like digestion. The parasympathetic ANS largely controls erection.

Premature ejaculation A sexual dysfunction in which the male persistently ejaculates too early to afford the couple adequate sexual gratification.

Peyronie's disease An abnormal condition characterized by an excessive curvature of the penis that can make erections painful.

Orgasm The climax of sexual excitement.

Paraplegic A person with sensory and motor paralysis of the lower half of the body.

Emission stage The first phase of ejaculation, which involves contractions of the prostate gland, seminal vesicles, and the upper part of the vas deferens.

Ampulla A sac or dilated part of a tube or canal.

Urethral bulb The small tube that makes up the prostatic part of the urethral tract and that balloons out as muscles close at either end, trapping semen prior to ejaculation.

Expulsion stage The second stage of ejaculation, during which muscles at the base of the penis and elsewhere contract rhythmically, forcefully expelling semen and providing pleasurable sensations.

In ejaculation, seminal fluid is released from the urethral bulb and expelled by contractions of the pelvic muscles that surround the urethral channel and the crura of the penis. The first few contractions are most intense and occur at 0.8-second intervals. Subsequent contractions weaken. The interval between them increases. Seminal fluid is expelled in spurts during the first few contractions. In young men, seminal fluid may be propelled 12 to 24 inches. But in some men, semen travels but a few inches or oozes from the penile opening. The force of the expulsion varies with the condition of the man's prostate, his general health, and his age. There is some correspondence between the force of the expulsion and the pleasure of orgasm. More intense orgasms tend to accompany more forceful ejaculations.

Like erection, ejaculation is regulated by two centers in the spinal cord, one in the sacral region and one in the higher lumbar region. When sexual arousal reaches the point of ejaculatory inevitability, the lumbar ejaculatory center triggers the first stage of ejaculation, seminal emission. The lower, or sacral, ejaculatory center triggers the second stage of orgasm.

Although ejaculation occurs by reflex, a man can delay ejaculation by maintaining the level of sexual stimulation below the critical threshold, or "point of no return." Men who suffer from premature ejaculation have been successfully treated in programs that train them to learn to recognize their "point of no return" and maintain sexual stimulation below it. (Issues concerning the definition and treatment of premature ejaculation are explored in Chapter 15 on sexual dysfunction.) Recognizing the point of no return and keeping stimulation beneath the critical level can also prolong coitus and enhance sexual pleasure for couples even when the man does not experience premature ejaculation.

Retrograde Ejaculation In **retrograde ejaculation**, the ejaculate empties into the bladder rather than being expelled from the body. During normal ejaculation an external sphincter opens, allowing seminal fluid to pass out of the body. Another sphincter, this one internal, closes off the opening to the bladder, preventing the seminal fluid from backing up into the bladder. In retrograde ejaculation, the actions of these sphincters are reversed. The external sphincter remains closed, preventing the expulsion of the seminal fluid, while the internal sphincter opens, allowing the ejaculate to empty into the bladder. The result is an apparently dry orgasm. Retrograde ejaculation may be caused by prostate surgery (much less so now than in former years), drugs such as tranquilizers, certain illnesses, and accidents. Retrograde ejaculation is usually harmless in itself, because the seminal fluid is later discharged with urine. But infertility can result, and there may be changes in the sensations associated with orgasm. Persistent dry orgasms should be medically evaluated.

Male sexual functions, like female sexual functions, are complex. They involve the cooperation of the nervous system, the endocrine system, the cardiovascular system, and the musculoskeletal system. In Chapter 5 we learn more about how the female and male sex organs respond to sexual stimulation. In Chapter 6 we examine the similarities and differences between females and males with respect to sexual differentiation, behavior, and personality.

Retrograde ejaculation
Ejaculation in which the ejaculate empties into the bladder. (From the Latin *retrogradi,* meaning "to go backward.")

Review: Male Sexual Functions

Reflect

Since erection and ejaculation are reflexes, how is it that people can consciously cause them to happen?

CriticalThinking

Do you see any "deeper meaning" in the facts that erection and ejaculation in the male and vaginal lubrication and orgasm in the female can occur automatically? For example, do these biological facts suggest anything to you about the possible evolutionary history of humans? Explain.

26. _____ is caused by the engorgement of the penis with blood.

27. Erections are firm because the corpora cavernosa are surrounded by a fibrous covering called the _____ albuginea.

28. Erections are (*Common* or *Absent*?) in babies.

29. Erections usually occur during (*REM* or *NREM*?) sleep.

30. Morning erections (*Do* or *Do not*?) reflect the need to urinate.

31. Erection and ejaculation are automatic, unlearned responses to sexual stimulation called _____.

32. Men (*Can* or *Cannot*?) will themselves to have erections.

33. Erectile responses to direct stimulation such as touching or licking (*Do* or *Do not*?) require the participation of the brain.

34. There is an erection center in the lower back, in an area of the spinal cord called the _____.

35. When the brain originates messages that trigger erection, it transmits nerve impulses to a higher erection center located in the upper back in the _____ region of the spinal cord.

36. The _____ division of the ANS is involved in erection.

37. The _____ division of the ANS is involved in ejaculation.

38. Ejaculation usually occurs together with _____, the sudden muscle contractions that occur at the peak of sexual excitement and result in release of sexual tension.

39. The _____ stage of ejaculation involves contractions of the prostate, seminal vesicles, and the vas deferens.

40. The _____ stage of ejaculation involves the propulsion of seminal fluid out of the body.

Recite

1. What are the external male sex organs?	The external male sex organs include the penis and the scrotum, both of which are sensitive to sexual stimulation.
2. What are the functions and parts of the penis?	Semen and urine pass out of the penis through the urethral opening. The penis contains cylinders that fill with blood and stiffen during sexual arousal. There is little connection between the size of the penis and sexual performance.
3. What is the nature of the controversy surrounding male circumcision?	Circumcision—the surgical removal of the prepuce—has been carried out for religious and hygienic reasons. Research shows that circumcision makes a male less vulnerable to certain health problems; however, circumcision decreases sexual sensations, is painful, and—in infants—is carried out without the child's consent.
4. What is the scrotum?	The scrotum is the pouch of loose skin that contains the testes. Each testicle is held in place by a spermatic cord, which contains the vas deferens and the cremaster muscle.
5. What are the male internal sex organs?	The male internal sex organs consist of the testes, a system of tubes and ducts that conduct sperm, and organs that nourish and activate sperm.
6. What are the functions of the testes?	The testes serve two functions, analogous to those of the ovaries. They secrete male sex hormones (androgens) and produce germ cells (sperm). The hypothalamus, pituitary gland, and testes keep blood testosterone levels at more or less even levels through a hormonal negative feedback loop. Testosterone is produced by interstitial cells. Sperm are produced by seminiferous tubules. Sperm are stored and mature in the epididymis.
7. What is the vas deferens?	Each epididymis empties into a vas deferens that conducts sperm over (not through) the bladder.
8. What are the seminal vesicles?	The seminal vesicles are glands that open into the ejaculatory ducts where the fluids they secrete nourish sperm.
9. What is the prostate gland?	The prostate gland secretes fluid that provides the characteristic texture and odor of semen.
10. What are Cowper's glands?	During sexual arousal, the Cowper's glands secrete a drop or so of clear, slippery fluid that appears at the urethral opening.
11. What is semen?	Sperm and the fluids contributed by the seminal vesicles, prostate gland, and Cowper's glands make up semen, the whitish fluid that is expelled through the tip of the penis during ejaculation.
12. What is urethritis?	Men, like women, are subject to bladder and urethral inflammations, which are generally referred to as urethritis.

Recite

13. What should we know about cancer of the testes?

This is the most common form of solid-tumor cancer to strike young men between the ages of 20 and 34. Risk factors include cryptorchidism and family history. The survival rate for cases that are detected early (before metastasizing) is above 90%.

14. What is benign prostatic hyperplasia?

BPH is noncancerous enlargement of the prostate, which is caused by testosterone and connected with aging. It can be treated by drugs that shrink the prostate or improve the flow of urine, or by partial removal of the prostate.

15. What should we know about prostate cancer?

This is the second most common form of cancer in men and takes nearly 39,000 lives each year in the U.S.A. Risk factors include family history, aging, and eating animal fats; testosterone spurs growth of prostate cancer cells. Early detection is usually by means of a digital rectal examination (DRE) or blood test (PSA). Treatment options include, surgery, hormone treatments (that lower testosterone levels), radiation, anticancer drugs, freezing the tumor, and "watchful waiting."

16. What is prostatitis?

Prostatitis is inflammation of the prostate, which is usually treated with antibiotics.

17. How does erection occur?

Erection is the process by which caverns within the penis become engorged with blood, increasing the size of the penis and stiffening it. Erection occurs in response to sexual stimulation but is also common during REM sleep.

18. What does it mean to say that erection and ejaculation are reflexes?

Reflexes occur at the level of the spinal cord, without the brain being necessarily involved. There are two erection centers in the spinal cord. Although erection is a reflex, penile sensations are relayed to the brain, where they generally result in pleasure.

19. What are the roles of the sympathetic and parasympathetic branches of the ANS in erection and ejaculation?

Erection and ejaculation also involve the autonomic nervous system (ANS). The parasympathetic branch of the ANS largely governs erection, whereas the sympathetic branch largely controls ejaculation. Fear, which involves sympathetic activity, can inhibit erection yet trigger premature ejaculation.

20. How does ejaculation occur?

Ejaculation, like erection, is a reflex. It is triggered when sexual stimulation reaches a critical threshold. Ejaculation usually but not always occurs with orgasm, but the terms are not synonymous. The emission phase of ejaculation involves contractions of the prostate, seminal vesicles, and the upper part of the vas deferens. In the expulsion stage, semen is propelled through the urethra and out of the penis. In this stage, muscles at the base of the penis and elsewhere contract rhythmically, forcefully expelling semen. There are two ejaculation centers in the spinal cord. In retrograde ejaculation, the ejaculate empties into the bladder rather than being expelled from the body.

Chapter 5

Truth?Fiction?

T / F? The ancient Romans were so obsessed with offensive odors that they perfumed their horses.

T / F? The menstrual cycles of women who live together tend to become synchronized.

T / F? The primary erogenous zone is the brain.

T / F? "Spanish fly" will not turn your date on, but it may cure his or her warts.

T / F? Electrical stimulation of certain areas in the human brain can yield sensations similar to those of sexual pleasure and gratification.

T / F? Normal men produce estrogen, and normal women produce androgens.

T / F? Written descriptions of men's and women's experiences during orgasm cannot be differentiated.

T / F? Orgasms attained through sexual intercourse are more intense than those attained through masturbation.

Sexual Arousal and Response

Preview

What turns you on? What springs your heart into your mouth, tightens your throat, and opens the floodgates into your genitals? The sight of your lover undressing, a photo of Will Smith or Cameron Diaz, a sniff of musky perfume, a sip of wine?

Many factors contribute to sexual arousal. Some people are aroused by magazines with photographs of nude or seminude models that have been airbrushed to perfection. Some need only to imagine Hollywood's latest sex symbol. Some become aroused by remembrances of past lovers. Some are stimulated by sexual fantasies of flings with strangers.

People vary greatly in the cues that excite them sexually and in the frequency with which they experience sexual thoughts and feelings. Some young people seem perpetually aroused or arousable. Some people rarely or never entertain sexual thoughts or fantasies.

In this chapter we look at factors that contribute to sexual arousal and the processes that relate to sexual response. Because our experience of the world is initiated by our senses, we begin the chapter by asking: *Question: What are the roles of the senses in sexual arousal?*

Making Sense of Sex: The Role of the Senses in Sexual Arousal

We come to apprehend the world around us through our senses—vision, hearing, smell, taste, and the skin senses, which include that all-important sense of touch. Each of the senses plays a role in our sexual experience, but some senses play larger roles than others.

Vision: The Better to See You With

It was the face of Helen of Troy, not her scent or her melodic voice, that "launched a thousand ships." Men's and women's magazines are filled with pictures of comely members of the other sex.

In matters of sexual attraction, people seem to have more in common with birds than with fellow mammals such as dogs and cats. Birds identify prospective mates within their species on the basis of their plumage and other visual markings. People also tend to be visually oriented when it comes to sexual attraction. By contrast, dogs and cats are more attracted to each other on the basis of scents that signal sexual receptivity.

Visual cues can be sexual turn-ons. We may be turned on by the sight of a lover in the nude, disrobing, or dressed in evening wear. Lingerie companies hope to convince customers that they will enhance their sex appeal by wearing strategically concealing and revealing nightwear. Some couples find it arousing to observe themselves making love in an overhead mirror or on videotape. Some people find sexually explicit movies arousing. Others are bored or offended by them. Though both males and females can be sexually aroused by visually mediated erotica (a technical term for "porn flicks"), men are more interested in them.

Smell: Does the Nose Know Best?

Although the sense of smell plays a lesser role in governing sexual arousal in humans than in lower mammals, odors can be sexual turn-ons or turn-offs. Perfume companies, for example, bottle fragrances purported to be sexually arousing.

Most Westerners prefer their lovers to be clean and fresh smelling. People in our society learn to remove or mask odors by the use of soaps, deodorants, and perfumes or colognes. The ancient Egyptians invented scented bathing to rid themselves of offensive odors (Illes, 2000). Judith Illes (2000) notes that "Perfume . . . is often now considered a mere triviality, at best a room freshener or perhaps an expensive and romantic gift, an item of superfluous luxury, an item associated with women. For the ancient Egyptians, however, . . . fragrance and perfume were not only beautiful but were also vast fonts of spiritual and therapeutic potential."

Inclinations to find underarm or genital odors offensive may reflect cultural conditioning and not biological predispositions. In some societies, genital secretions are considered **aphrodisiacs**. And the underarms? *Question: Are there substances in genital or underarm secretions that function as aphrodisiacs?* Check out the nearby "Human Sexuality in the New Millennium" feature on **pheromones** for possible answers.

Menstrual Synchrony Research by several investigators suggests that exposure to other women's sweat can modify a woman's menstrual cycle (Morofushi et al., 2000). *Question: How does exposure to other women's sweat modify the menstrual cycle?* Let us examine some research on the subject and see.

Truth?Fiction?
Revisited

The ancient Romans had a passion for perfume. They would bathe in fragrances and even dab their horses and household pets.

Aphrodisiac Any drug or other agent that is sexually arousing or increases sexual desire. (From *Aphrodite*, the Greek goddess of love and beauty).

Pheromones Chemical substances secreted externally by certain animals, which convey information to, or produce specific responses in, other members of the same species. (From the Greek *pherien*, meaning "to bear [a message]" and *hormone*.)

The Search for a "Magic" Love Potion: On the Threshold?

For centuries people have searched for a love potion—a magical formula that could make other people fall in love with you or be strongly attracted to you. On the edge of the new millennium, some scientists suggest that such potions may already exist in the form of chemical secretions known as pheromones. Pheromones may enhance people's moods, have effects on fertility, and provide a basis for sexual communication below the level of conscious awareness.

Pheromones are odorless chemicals that in many animals are detected through a "sixth sense"—the *vomeronasal organ* (*VNO*). People possess VNOs in the mucous lining of the nose (Rodriguez et al., 2000). During prenatal development, the VNO shuttles sex hormones into the brain, aiding in the sexual differentiation of the embryo (Rodriguez et al., 2000). But before birth, the human VNO shrinks, and some researchers suggest that it stops working (Kouros-Mehr et al., 2001). But, if it does continue to work, it might detect pheromones and direct information about them to the hypothalamus, where they might affect sexual response (Cutler, 1999). Infants may also use pheromones to recognize their mothers, and adults might respond to them in seeking a mate. Lower animals use them to stimulate sexual response, organize food gathering, maintain pecking orders, sound alarms, and mark territories (Cutler, 1999). Pheromones induce mating behavior in insects. Male rodents such as mice are extremely sensitive to several kinds of pheromones (Leinders-Zufall et al., 2000). Male rodents show less sexual arousal when their sense of smell is blocked, but

How Much Sexual Communication Is Occurring below the Level of Conscious Awareness? *Research suggests that underarm secretions may make people more sexually attractive, even when others are unaware of sensing them. Are they drawn to each other's personal traits or to their pheromones?*

the role of pheromones in sexual behavior becomes less vital as one moves upward through the ranks of the animal kingdom.

Only a few years ago, most researchers did not believe that pheromones played a role in human behavior, but today this field of research has attracted new interest. In a typical study, Winnifred Cutler and her colleagues (1998) had heterosexual men wear a suspected male pheromone, whereas a control group wore a placebo. The men using the pheromone increased their frequency of sexual intercourse with their female partners but did not increase the frequency of masturbation. The researchers conclude that the substance increased the sexual attractiveness of the men to

Truth?Fiction?
Revisited

It is true that the menstrual cycles of women who live together tend to become synchronized—so long as the women's cycles are not being regulated by birth control pills.

In one study, women exposed to underarm secretions from other women, which contain steroids that may function as pheromones, showed converging shifts in their menstrual cycles (Preti et al., 1986). Similar synchronization of menstrual cycles has also been observed among women who share dormitory rooms. In another study, 80% of the women who dabbed their upper lips with an extract of perspiration from other women began to menstruate in sync with the cycles of the donors after about three menstrual cycles (Cutler, 1999). A control group, who dabbed their lips with alcohol, showed no changes in their menstrual cycles. In yet another study from this research group, the length of the cycles of women with unusually short or long cycles began to normalize when they were exposed to an extract of *male* underarm perspiration (Preti et al., 1986).

their partners, although they do not claim that it directly stimulated sexual behavior.

Other studies are also of interest. Consider experiments that exposed men and women to certain steroids (androstanedione produced by males and estratetraene produced by females) suspected of being pheromones. They found that both steroids enhanced the moods of women but not of men; the substances also apparently reduced feelings of nervousness and tension in women, but again, not in men (Grosser et al., 2000; Jacob et al., 2001; Jacob & McClintock, 2000). The findings about estratetraene are not terribly surprising. This substance is related to estrogen, and women tend to function best during the time of the month when estrogen levels are highest (Ross et al., 2000). The fact that the women responded positively to the androstanedione is of somewhat greater interest. Women may thus generally feel somewhat better when they are around men, even if the chemical substances that may be connected with their moods have not been shown to have direct sexual effects. Of course, being in a good (or better) mood could indirectly contribute to a woman's interest in sex.

In a double-blind experiment, 36 university women with a mean age of 28 were randomly assigned to wear a perfume laced with a suspected pheromone extracted from their underarm secretions or a placebo (McCoy & Pitino, 2002). The women recorded their sexual behaviors over three menstrual cycles (12 weeks). Three-quarters (74%) of the women who used the suspected pheromone showed significant increases in their frequency of sexual intercourse, sleeping next to a partner, formal dates, and female–male interactions characterized by kissing, petting, and other displays of

affection, as compared with one quarter (23%) of the users of the placebo. The researchers conclude that the suspected pheromone increased the women's attractiveness to men.

University of Pennsylvania biologists George Preti, Charles Wysocki, and their colleagues (2003) found that male perspiration has beneficial effects on women's moods. It induces feelings of relaxation and helps lessen stress. It even affects the menstrual cycle. The researchers extracted samples from the underarms of men who avoided using deodorant for a month. The samples were blended and applied to the upper lips on 18 women, aged 25 to 45. The women did not know the source or makeup of the chemicals on the swabs. The women then rated their moods over a six-hour period and reported feeling more relaxed and in better moods. Analysis of their blood revealed a rise in levels of luteinizing hormone (LH), which surges before ovulation. There was no indication that the women were sexually aroused, but it might be that men's perspiration provides "chemical communication" when they meet women, allowing them to coordinate reproductive efforts below the level of awareness. Charles Wysocki notes that "In a more sensual setting, exposure to these odors might facilitate the emergence of sexual mood or feelings." The researchers suggest that if they can isolate the active agent or agents in male perspiration, studies such as these might lead to new treatments for fertility, by affecting ovulation, and for premenstrual syndrome, by affecting the mood. Still, these substances do not directly stimulate behavior, as pheromones do with lower animals.

The Skin Senses: Sex as a Touching Experience

Our skin senses enable us to sense pain, changes in temperature, and pressure (or touch). Whatever the roles of vision and smell in sexual attraction and arousal, the sense of touch has the most direct effects on sexual arousal and response. Any region of that sensitive layer we refer to as skin can become eroticized. The touch of your lover's hand upon your cheek, or your lover's gentle massage of your shoulders or back, can be sexually stimulating. *Question: What are erogenous zones?*

Erogenous Zones **Erogenous** zones are parts of the body that are especially sensitive to tactile sexual stimulation—to strokes and other caresses. **Primary erogenous zones** are erotically sensitive because they are richly endowed with nerve endings. **Secondary erogenous zones** are parts of the body that become erotically sensitized through experience.

Erogenous zones Parts of the body that are especially sensitive to tactile sexual stimulation. (*Erogenous* is derived from roots meaning "giving birth to erotic sensations.")

Primary erogenous zones Erogenous zones that are particularly sensitive because they are richly endowed with nerve endings.

The Buds and the Bees

It may be that we should cover our children's eyes when bees are at work in the yard. Researchers at the Australian National University (ANU) have learned that bees who land on certain flowers are after something other than pollen. It turns out that some plants emit chemical secretions that mimic the pheromones of female bees ("Australia scientists," 2000). As a result, male bees try to mate with them. As a side effect, the bees transfer pollen from one plant to another, facilitating fertilization and the survival of these species of plants. No, there is no evidence that these plants are "trying" to dupe the bees (plants do not think); it just happens, evolutionarily speaking, that whatever genes contribute

to the development of these chemicals are likely to be transmitted to the next generation.

The kinds of plants that are "in on" the pheromone scam are orchids. One type is found in Europe, and nine types are found in Australia, where the bees are apparently especially active. These orchids produce the same hydrocarbon compounds that are found in the pheromones of the female bee. Aren't they lovely?

The power of the pheromones apparently overrides bees' vision. Even so, one of the researchers noted that "The bees will . . . only try mating with the flowers a few times each" (cited in "Australia

A Pheromonal Scam Australian researchers have discovered that certain orchids emit pheromones that mimic those of female bees. As a result, male bees attempt to mate with them (the flowers, that is). In the process, they pick up pollen and transfer it to other orchids, helping the orchids reproduce.

scientists," 2000). Better to learn late than never. (One imagines Dr. Evil suggesting, pinky in cheek, "Why don't the two of you get a room?")

Truth?Fiction?
Revisited

The brain is not an erogenous zone, because it is not stimulated directly by touch. (The brain processes tactile information from the skin, but it does not have sensory neurons to directly gather this information itself.) Part of the confusion may lie in the etymology (word origins) of the term *erogenous,* which would appear to apply to the brain. That is, the brain *can* "give birth" to erotic sensations through production of fantasy, erotic memories, and other thoughts.

Secondary erogenous zones Parts of the body that become erotically sensitized through experience.

Primary erogenous zones include the genitals; the inner thighs, perineum, buttocks, and anus; the breasts (especially the nipples); the ears (particularly the earlobes); the mouth, lips, and tongue; the neck; the navel; and, yes, the armpits. Preferences vary somewhat from person to person, reflecting possible biological, attitudinal, and experiential differences. Areas that are exquisitely sensitive for some people may produce virtually no reaction, or discomfort, in others. Many women, for example, report little sensation when their breasts are stroked or kissed. Many men are uncomfortable when their nipples are caressed. On the other hand (or foot), many people find the areas between their toes sensitive to erotic stimulation and enjoy keeping a toehold on their partners during coitus.

Secondary erogenous zones become eroticized through association with sexual stimulation. For example, a woman might become sexually aroused when her lover gently caresses her shoulders, because such caresses have been incorporated as a regular feature of the couple's lovemaking. A few of the women observed by Masters and Johnson (1966) reached orgasm when the smalls of their backs were rubbed.

People are also highly responsive to images and fantasies. This is why the brain is sometimes referred to as the primary sexual organ or an erogenous zone. Some women report reaching orgasm through fantasy alone (Kinsey et al., 1953). Men regularly experience erection and nocturnal emissions ("wet dreams") without direct stimulation of the genitals.

Taste: On Savory Sex

Taste appears to play a minor role in sexual arousal and response, unless we digress into puns and note that taste in the form of a zesty meal or a delicate wine may contribute to arousal. In any event, some people are sexually aroused by the taste of genital secretions, such as vaginal secretions or seminal fluid. We do not know, however, whether these secretions are laced with chemicals that have biologically arousing effects or whether arousal reflects the meaning that these secretions have to the individual. That is, we may learn to become aroused by, or to seek out, flavors or odors that have been associated with sexual pleasure. Others are turned off by them.

Hearing: The Better to Hear You With

The sense of hearing also provides an important medium for sexual arousal and response. Like visual and olfactory cues, sounds can be turn-ons or turn-offs. The sounds of one's lover, whether whispers, indications of pleasure, or animated sounds that may attend orgasm, may be arousing during the heat of passion. For some people, key words or vocal intonations may become as arousing as direct stimulation of an erogenous zone. Many people are aroused when their lovers "talk dirty." Spoken vulgarities spur their sexual arousal. Others find vulgar language offensive.

The sultry voices of screen sirens Lauren Bacall and Kathleen Turner have aroused the ardor of many a moviegoer.

A Touching Experience The sense of touch is intimately connected with sexual experience. The touch of a lover's hand on the cheek, or gentle massage, can be sexually stimulating. Certain parts of the body—called erogenous zones—have special sexual significance because of their response to erotic stimulation.

Review: Making Sense of Sex: The Role of the Senses in Sexual Arousal

Reflect

Do you find nude people to be sexually arousing? Why, or why not?

Critical Thinking

Would a person who uses a pheromone to enhance his or her sexual attractiveness be "playing fair"? Why or why not? (Critical thinkers pay attention to the definitions of terms. What does "playing fair" mean? In your answer you may want to compare using a pheromone with dying your hair, using perfume or cologne, and so on.)

1. Although people are visually oriented in terms of sexual attraction, dogs and cats rely more on the sense of _____.

2. (*Men* or *Women*?) appear to be more interested in pornography.

3. _____ are odorless chemicals that in many animals are detected through the vomeronasal organ.

4. Male rodents show (*More* or *Less*?) sexual arousal when their sense of smell is blocked.

5. The steroids androstanedione and estratetraene have been shown to enhance the moods of (*Men* or *Women*?).

6. An extract from women's underarm secretions (*Increases* or *Decreases*?) their sexual attractiveness to men.

7. The menstrual cycles of women who live together tend to _____.

8. _____ erogenous zones are erotically sensitive because they are richly endowed with nerve endings.

9. _____ erogenous zones become erotically sensitized through experience.

Teenagers may shriek at the music of groups such as Destiny's Child and 'NSYNC, just as their parents (and grandparents) did when they heard the Beatles, Frank Sinatra, Johnny Mathis, or the King himself (Elvis, that is). Of course, the sex appeal of these performers goes beyond the sounds that they produce.

Music itself can contribute to sexual arousal. Music can relax us and put us "in the mood" or have associations ("They're playing our song!"). Many couples find background music "atmospheric"—a vital accouterment of lovemaking.

Sounds can also be sexual turnoffs. Most of us would find funeral music a damper on sexual arousal. We may also be inhibited by scratchy, unnerving voices. Heavy metal rock might be a sexual turnoff to many (are your authors showing their age?), but it could help set the right tone for others.

Aphrodisiacs: Of Spanish Flies and Rhino Horns

The only known aphrodisiac is variety.

Marc Connolly

Question: What is an aphrodisiac? An aphrodisiac is a substance that arouses or increases one's capacity for sexual pleasure or response. You may have heard of "Spanish fly," an alleged aphrodisiac once extracted from a Spanish beetle. (The beetle from which it was taken, *Lytta vesicatoria,* is near extinction.) A few drops in a date's drink were believed to make you irresistible. Spanish fly is but one of many purported aphrodisiacs. It is toxic, however, not sexually arousing. Spanish fly is now synthesized—but not as an aphrodisiac.

We should also be concerned about an expectancy, or placebo effect, when evaluating the effectiveness of a purported aphrodisiac (Downs & Nazario, 2003). The belief that a substance has sexually stimulating effects may itself inspire sexual excitement. If a person tries a supposed aphrodisiac and feels sexually aroused, the person may well attribute the turn-on to the effects of the substance, even if the substance had no direct effect on sex drive.

Foods that in some way resemble male genitals have now and then been considered aphrodisiacs. They include oysters, clams, bull's testicles ("prairie oysters"), tomatoes, and "phallic" items such as celery stalks, bananas, and even ground-up rhinoceros, reindeer, and elephant horns (which is one derivation of the slang term "horny").

Even potatoes—both white and sweet—have been held to be aphrodisiacs. Yes, potatoes. Shakespeare echoed this belief when he wrote, "Let the sky rain potatoes . . . ; let a tempest of provocation come." None of these foods or substances has been shown to be sexually stimulating, however—not even deep-fried potato skins with cheddar cheese and bacon. Sadly, myths about the sexually arousing properties of substances drawn from rhinoceroses or elephants may be contributing to the rapidly diminishing numbers of these animals.

Other drugs and psychoactive substances may have certain effects on sexual arousal and response. The drug arginine, an amino acid extracted from the African yohimbe tree, does stimulate blood flow to the genitals (Downs & Nazario, 2003). However, its effects are limited and unreliable (Downs & Nazario, 2003). Fortunately, arginine does not appear to be toxic (Finley, 2003).

Amyl nitrate (in the form of "snappers" or "poppers") has been used mostly by gay men (and by some heterosexuals) in the belief that it heightens sensations of arousal and orgasm. Poppers dilate blood vessels in the brain and genitals, producing sensations of warmth in the pelvis and possibly facilitating erection and prolonging orgasm. Amyl nitrate does have some legitimate medical uses, such as helping reduce heart pain (angina) among cardiac patients. It is inhaled from ampules that "pop" open for rapid use when heart pain occurs. Poppers can cause dizziness, fainting, and migraine-type headaches, however. They should be taken only under a doctor's care for a legitimate medical need, not to intensify sexual sensations.

The drug Viagra was originally developed as a treatment for angina (heart pain) because it increases the blood flow to the heart—modestly. However, it also dilates blood vessels in the genital organs, thereby facilitating vasocongestion and erection—and, according to some reports, sexual response in women as well (Slovenko, 2001). Viagra is a treatment for erectile dysfunction (also termed *impotence*). Is Viagra also an aphrodisiac? It is a matter of definition. Although Viagra facilitates erection, it still takes a sexual turn-on for erection to occur. If an aphrodisiac is directly sexually arousing, Viagra is not an aphrodisiac.

But certain drugs do appear to have aphrodisiac effects, apparently because they act on the brain mechanisms controlling the sex drive. For example, drugs that affect brain receptors for the neurotransmitter dopamine, such as the antidepressant drug *bupropion* (trade name Wellbutrin) and the drug L-dopa used in the treatment of Parkinson's disease, can increase the sex drive (Modell et al., 2000; Segraves et al., 2001).

One recommendation that may truly backfire is based on a theory of the ancient Roman physician Galen. Galen believed, erroneously, that erection was a result of the penis filling up with air or "wind." Galen thus recommended spices, mainly peppers, carrots, asparagus, anise, mustard, nettles, and sweet peas—vegetables that were known to produce flatulence—as aphrodisiacs and as cures for male erectile problems (Downs & Nazario, 2003).

The most potent chemical "aphrodisiac" may be a naturally occurring substance in the body, the male sex hormone testosterone. It is the basic fuel of sexual desire in both males and females (Apperloo et al., 2003; S. Davis, 2000).

The safest and perhaps most effective method for increasing the sex drive may not be a drug or substance but proper diet and exercise. Regular exercise not only enhances general health; it also boosts energy and increases the sex drive in both sexes. Perhaps the most potent aphrodisiac of all is novelty. Partners can invent new ways of sexually discovering one another. They can make love in novel places, experiment with different techniques, wear provocative clothing, share or enact fantasies, or whatever their imaginations inspire.

The nearby "Human Sexuality in the New Millennium" feature reports the effects of a drug that is decidedly *not* an aphrodisiac: the so-called "date rape" drug.

Anaphrodisiacs

Aphrodisiacs are thought to stimulate a sexual response. ***Question: What kind of substance would have the opposite effect of an aphrodisiac?*** These would be substances like potassium nitrate (saltpeter), which have been considered inhibitors of sexual response, or **anaphrodisiacs**. Saltpeter, however, only indirectly dampens sexual arousal. As a diuretic that can increase the need for urination, it may make the thought of sex unappealing. It does not directly dampen sexual response, however.

Other chemicals do dampen sexual arousal and response. Tranquilizers and central nervous system depressants, such as barbiturates, can lessen sexual desire

Anaphrodisiacs Drugs or other agents whose effects are antagonistic to sexual arousal or sexual desire.

The "Date Rape" Drug: Decidedly *Not* an Aphrodisiac

An aphrodisiac works by stimulating sexual desire. Rophies, roofies, R2, roofenol, roachies, la rocha, Mexican valium, or whatever you call them do not directly stimulate sexual desire. They are more likely to put one to sleep or at least depress the nervous system to the point where the individual is helpless to resist. They became known as the "date rape" drug because these odorless and tasteless chemicals have been slipped into the drinks of unsuspecting women, lowering inhibitions (an effect of a depressed nervous system), rendering them incapable of resisting a sexual assault, and, when mixed with alcohol, sometimes causing blackouts that prevent the women from remembering exactly what happened to them.

The following questions and answers are provided by the Office on Women's Health in the U.S. Department of Health and Human Services.

WHAT IS THE "DATE RAPE" DRUG?

The "date rape" drug is the common name for Rohypnol, generically called flunitrazepam. Rohypnol is manufactured by Hoffman–La Roche and prescribed as a sleeping pill in countries outside of the United States. It is used as a short-term treatment for insomnia, as a sedative hypnotic, and a pre-anesthetic. It has physiological effects similar to Valium (diazepam), but is approximately ten times more potent. It is used also as an illicit drug, often in combination with other drugs, such as heroin, cocaine, and alcohol. Common names for Rohypnol include the following: rophies, roofies, R2, roofenol, Roche, roachies, la rocha, rope, rib, circles, Mexican valium, roach-2, roopies, and ropies. A similar drug is known as clonazepam (Klonopin in the United States and Rivotril in Mexico).

WHAT DOES ROHYPNOL LOOK LIKE?

Rohypnol tablets are white, scored on one side, with the word "ROCHE" and an encircled 1 or 2 (depending on the dosage) on the other. They are sold in presealed bubble packs of 1 or 2 mg doses. Rohypnol can often be dissolved in a drink, and undetectable.

IS ROHYPNOL LEGAL?

No, Rohypnol is not manufactured or sold legally in the United States. However, it is produced and sold legally by prescription in Europe and Latin America. It is smuggled into the United States by mail or delivery services.

WHO USES ROHYPNOL AND HOW?

Rohypnol use has been reported on every inhabited continent. It is often used in conjunction with other drugs. It is usually ingested orally but can be snorted. Teen use of Rohypnol is increasing. The most common pattern of use is by teenagers and young adults as an alcohol extender in an attempt to create a dramatic "high," most often in combination with beer, or as a drug to incapacitate a victim before a sexual assault.

WHY HAS THERE BEEN AN INCREASE IN TEEN USE OF ROHYPNOL?

First, Rohypnol is a low-cost drug, sold at less than $5.00 per tablet. Second, common misconceptions may explain the drug's popularity with young people: 1) many erroneously believe that the drug is unadulterated because it comes in presealed bubble packs— and therefore tamper-proof and safe; 2) many mistakenly think its use cannot be detected by urinalysis testing.

WHAT HAPPENS WHEN YOU TAKE ROHYPNOL? WHAT ARE THE SIDE EFFECTS?

Rohypnol intoxication is generally associated with impaired judgment and impaired motor skills and can make a victim unable to resist a sexual attack. The combination of alcohol and Rohypnol is also particularly hazardous because together their effects on memory and judgment are greater than the effects resulting from either taken alone. Effects begin within 30 minutes, peak within two hours, and can persist for up to eight hours. It is commonly reported that persons who become intoxicated on a combination of alcohol and flunitrazepam have "blackouts" lasting 8 to 24 hours following ingestion. Disinhibition (losing your social inhibitions) is another widely reported effect of Rohypnol, when taken alone or in combination with alcohol. Adverse effects of Rohypnol use include decreased blood pressure, memory impairment, drowsiness, visual disturbances, dizziness, confusion, gastrointestinal disturbances, and urinary retention.

IS ROHYPNOL ADDICTIVE?

Yes. Rohypnol can cause physical dependence. Withdrawal symptoms include headache, muscle pain,

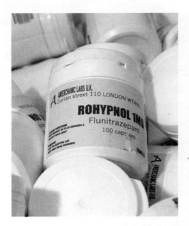

Rohypnol—The "Date Rape" Drug Rohypnol can be dissolved in an alcoholic or other drink and be undetectable. It is most often used by teenagers and young adults to create a more dramatic high from alcohol, but it is also used to incapacitate a woman before a sexual assault. Rohypnol intoxication impairs judgment and motor skills and can render the victim incapable of resisting a sexual attack. The combination of alcohol and Rohypnol is dangerous because their joint effects on memory, judgment, and the body are greater than those of either substance used alone. Although Rohypnol is frequently used as a prelude to sex, it is not an aphrodisiac.

confusion, hallucinations, and convulsions. Seizures may occur up to a week after cessation of use.

WHY IS ROHYPNOL CALLED THE "DATE RAPE" DRUG?

Rohypnol has been associated with date rape, and has also been called the "Forget Pill," "Trip-and-Fall," and "Mind-Erasers." In combination with alcohol, it can induce a blackout with memory loss and a decrease in resistance. Girls and women around the country have reported being raped after being involuntarily sedated with Rohypnol, which was often slipped into their drink by an attacker. The drug has no taste or odor, so the victims don't realize what is happening. About ten minutes after ingesting the drug, the woman may feel dizzy and disoriented, simultaneously too hot and too cold, or nauseated. She may experience difficulty speaking and moving and then pass out. Such victims have no memories of what happened while under the drug's influence.

ARE THERE OTHER "DATE RAPE" TYPE DRUGS?

Since about 1990, GHB (gamma-hydroxybutrate) has been abused in the United States for euphoric, sedative, and anabolic (body-building) effects. As with Rohypnol, GHB has been associated with sexual assault in cites throughout the country. Common names include "liquid ecstasy," "somatomax," "scoop," or "grievous bodily harm."

HOW CAN I AVOID BECOMING A VICTIM OF RAPE UNDER THE INFLUENCE OF ROHYPNOL OR GHB?

Here are a few suggestions for staying aware and alert:

- Be wary about accepting drinks from anyone you don't know well or long enough to trust. If you are accepting a drink, make sure it's from an unopened container and that you open it yourself.

- Don't put your drink down and leave it unattended, even to go to the restroom.

- Notify other females you know about the effects of this dangerous drug.

- If you think that you have been a victim, notify the authorities immediately.

FOR MORE INFORMATION

You can find out more about Rohypnol by contacting the National Women's Health Information Center (800-994-9662) or the following organizations:

National Institute on Drug Abuse
Phone: (888) NIH-NIDA
Internet Address:
http://www.nida.nih.gov/NIDAHome1.html

American Council for Drug Education
Phone: (800) 488-3784
Internet Address: http://www.acde.org/

American Society of Addiction Medicine
Phone: (301) 656-3920
Internet Address: http://www.asam.org/

Association for Medical Education and Research in Substance Abuse
Phone: (401) 444-1817
Internet Address: http://www.amersa.org/

This information was abstracted from fact sheets prepared by the National Institute on Drug Abuse (Rohypnol and GHB):

http://165.112.78.61/Infofax/RohypnolGHB.html.

and impair sexual performance. These drugs may paradoxically enhance sexual arousal in some people, however, by lessening sexual inhibitions or fear of possible repercussions from sexual activity. Antihypertensive drugs, which are used in the treatment of high blood pressure, may produce erectile and ejaculatory difficulties in men and reduction of sexual desire in men and women. Certain antidepressant drugs, such as fluoxetine (brand name: Prozac), amitriptyline (brand name: Elavil), and imipramine (brand name: Tofranil) appear to dampen the sex drive (Michelson et al., 2001). Antidepressants may also impair erectile response and delay ejaculation in men and orgasmic responsiveness in women (Michelson et al., 2001). (Because they delay ejaculation, some of these drugs are used to treat premature ejaculation.)

Nicotine, the stimulant in tobacco smoke, constricts the blood vessels. Thus it can impede sexual arousal by reducing the capacity of the genitals to become engorged with blood. Chronic smoking can also reduce the blood levels of testosterone in men, which can in turn lessen sex drive or motivation.

Antiandrogen drugs may have anaphrodisiac effects. They have been used in the treatment of deviant behavior patterns such as sexual violence and sexual interest in children, with some promising results (e.g., Roesler & Witztum, 2000).

Psychoactive Drugs

Psychoactive drugs, such as alcohol and cocaine, are widely believed to have aphrodisiac effects. *Question: Do any psychoactive drugs stimulate a sexual response?* Perhaps some do, but their effects may also reflect our expectations of them, or their effects on sexual inhibitions, rather than direct stimulation of sexual response.

Alcohol: The "Great Provoker of Three Things"   In Shakespeare's *Macbeth*, the following exchange takes place between Macduff and a porter:

> PORTER: . . . drink, sir, is a great provoker of three things.
> MACDUFF: What three things does drink especially provoke?
> PORTER: Marry,[1] sir, nose-painting,[2] sleep, and urine. Lechery,[3] sir, it provokes, and unprovokes; it provokes the desire, but it takes away the performance.

Small amounts of alcohol are stimulating, but large amounts curb sexual response. This fact should not be surprising because alcohol is a depressant. Alcohol reduces central nervous system activity. Large amounts of alcohol can severely impair sexual performance in both men and women.

People who drink moderate amounts of alcohol may feel more sexually aroused because of their expectations about alcohol, not because of its chemical properties (George et al., 2000). That is, people who expect alcohol to enhance sexual responsiveness may act the part. Expectations that alcohol serves as an aphrodisiac may lead men with problems achieving erection to turn to alcohol as a cure. The fact is that alcohol is a depressant, and a few drinks can reduce sexual potency rather than restore it.

Alcohol may also lower sexual inhibitions, because it allows us to ascribe our behavior to the effects of the alcohol rather than to ourselves. Alcohol is connected with a liberated social role and thus provides an excuse for dubious behavior. "It was

Antiandrogen A substance that decreases the levels of androgens in the bloodstream.

---

1. Contraction of the expression "By the Virgin Mary"; used by Elizabethans like Shakespeare to speak emphatically yet avoid disrespect to the Virgin Mary.

2. The reddening of the nose that occurs in many chronic alcoholics as a result of the bursting of small blood vessels.

3. Excessive indulgence of sexual desire. (Related to the German *lecken*, meaning "to lick.")

the alcohol," people can say, "not me." People may express their sexual desires and do things when drinking that they would not do when sober. For example, a person who feels guilty about sex may become sexually active when drinking because he or she can later blame the alcohol.

Binge drinking—defined as having five or more drinks in a row for a male, or four or more for a female (Naimi et al., 2003b)—is connected with high-risk sexual behavior, sexual promiscuity, and sexual assault (Abbey et al., 2001; Cooper, 2002; MacDonald et al., 2000; Vik et al., 2000). Nevertheless, binge drinking is on the rise in the United States (Naimi et al., 2003a). Forty-four percent of college students binge at least twice a month, and half this number binge three or more times every two weeks (Hingson et al., 2002).

Alcohol can also induce feelings of euphoria. Euphoric feelings may enhance sexual arousal and also wash away qualms about expressing sexual desires. Alcohol also appears to impair the ability to weigh information ("information processing") that might otherwise inhibit sexual impulses (MacDonald et al., 2000; Steele & Josephs, 1990). When people drink, they may be less able to foresee the consequences of misconduct and less likely to ponder their standards of conduct.

Hallucinogenics There is no evidence that marijuana and other hallucinogenic drugs directly stimulate sexual response. However, fairly to strongly intoxicated marijuana users claim to have more empathy with others, to be more aware of bodily sensations, and to experience time as passing more slowly. These sensations could heighten subjective feelings of sexual response. Some marijuana users report that the drug inhibits their sexual responsiveness, however (Wolman, 1985). The effects of the drug on sexual response may depend upon the individual's prior experiences with the drug, attitudes toward the drug, and the amount taken.

Other hallucinogenics, such as LSD and mescaline, have also been reported by some users to enhance sexual response. Again, these effects may reflect dosage level, as well as expectations, user experiences, attitudes toward the drugs, and altered perceptions.

What Are the Effects of Alcohol on Sexual Behavior? Small doses of alcohol can be stimulating, induce feelings of euphoria, and lower inhibitions, all of which could be connected with sexual interest and facilitate social and sexual behavior. Alcohol also reduces fear of consequences of engaging in risky behavior—sexual and otherwise. Alcohol also provides an excuse for otherwise unacceptable behavior, such as sexual intercourse on the first date (or upon a casual meeting). That is, drinkers can say, "It was the alcohol, not me." Alcohol is also expected to be sexually liberating, and people often live up to social and cultural expectations. Yet, as a depressant drug, large amounts of alcohol will biochemically dampen sexual response.

Stimulants Stimulants such as amphetamines ("speed," "uppers," "bennies," "dexies") have been reputed to heighten arousal and sensations of orgasm. High doses can give rise to irritability, restlessness, hallucinations, paranoid delusions, insomnia, and loss of appetite. These drugs generally activate the central nervous system but are not known to have specific sexual effects. Nevertheless, arousing the nervous system can contribute to sexual arousal (Palace, 1995). The drugs can also elevate the mood, and perhaps sexual pleasure is heightened by general elation.

Cocaine is a natural stimulant that is extracted from the leaves of the coca plant—the plant from which the soft drink Coca-Cola obtained its name. In fact, Coke—Coca-Cola, that is—contained cocaine as part of its original formula. Cocaine was removed from the secret formula in 1906. Cocaine is ingested in various forms, snorted as a powder, smoked in hardened rock form ("crack" cocaine) or in a free-base form, or injected directly into the bloodstream in liquid form. Cocaine produces a euphoric rush, which tends to ebb quickly. Physically, cocaine constricts blood vessels (reducing the oxygen supply to the heart), elevates the blood pressure, and accelerates the heart rate.

Review: Aphrodisiacs: Of Spanish Flies and Rhino Horns

Reflect

Have you done anything under the influence of alcohol or other drugs that you otherwise would not have done? What role did the drug play?

CriticalThinking

Agree or disagree with the following statement and support your point of view: Alcohol stimulates sexual desire and behavior.

10. A(n) _____ is a substance that arouses or increases one's capacity for sexual pleasure or response.

11. The effects of Spanish fly are due to _____ the urinary tract.

12. According to the _____ effect, belief that a substance will be sexually stimulating may inspire sexual excitement.

13. Foods such as oysters and bananas have been considered aphrodisiacs because they _____ male genitals.

14. The drug _____, extracted from the yohimbe tree, stimulates blood flow to the genitals.

15. Amyl nitrate, known generally as "_____," produces sensations of warmth in the pelvis and possibly facilitates erection.

16. The antidepressant drug _____ can increase the sex drive.

17. Potassium nitrate (saltpeter) is an anaphrodisiac that indirectly dampens sexual arousal by increasing the need to _____.

18. Tranquilizers and central nervous system depressants tend to (*Increase* or *Decrease*?) sexual desire and performance.

19. Antiandrogen drugs tend to have (*Aphrodisiac* or *Anaphrodisiac*?) effects.

20. Large amounts of alcohol (*Heighten* or *Lessen*?) sexual response.

21. Binge drinking is connected with (*Cautious* or *Indiscriminate*?) sexual behavior.

Despite the popular belief that cocaine is an aphrodisiac, frequent use can lead to sexual dysfunctions, such as difficulty attaining erection and ejaculating among males, decreased vaginal lubrication in females, and sexual apathy in both men and women (Weiss & Mirin, 1987). Some people do report initial increased sexual pleasure with cocaine use; however, that increase may reflect cocaine's loosening of inhibitions. Over time, though, regular users may become dependent on cocaine for sexual arousal or lose the ability to enjoy sex (Weiss & Mirin, 1987).

Sexual Response and the Brain: Cerebral Sex?

The brain may not be an erogenous zone, but it plays a central role in sexual functioning (Fisher, 2000). *Question: What is the role of the brain in sexual response?* Direct genital stimulation may trigger spinal reflexes that produce erection in the male and vaginal lubrication in the female without the direct involvement of the brain. The same reflexes may also be triggered by sexual stimulation that originates in the brain in the form of erotic memories, fantasies, visual images, and thoughts, however. The brain may also inhibit sexual responsiveness, as when we experience guilt or anxiety in a sexual situation, or when we suddenly realize in the midst of a sexual encounter that we have left the car lights turned on. Let us explore the brain mechanisms involved in sexual functioning.

Parts of the brain, in particular the cerebral cortex and the limbic system, play key roles in sexual functioning (Figure 5.1). Cells in the cerebral cortex fire (transmit messages) when we experience sexual thoughts, images, wishes, fantasies, and the like. Cells in the cerebral cortex interpret sensory information as sexual turn-ons or turn-offs. The sight of your lover disrobing, the anticipation of a romantic kiss, a

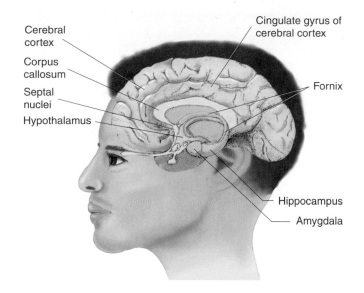

Cerebral cortex

Corpus callosum

Septal nuclei

Hypothalamus

Cingulate gyrus of cerebral cortex

Fornix

Hippocampus

Amygdala

Figure 5.1. Parts of the Brain Involved in Sexual Functioning. A view of the brain, split from top to bottom. Cells in the cerebral cortex transmit messages when we experience sexual thoughts and mental images. Cells in the cortex interpret sensory information as sexual turn-ons or turn-offs. The cerebral cortex may then transmit messages through the spinal cord that send blood coursing to the sex organs, leading to erection or vaginal lubrication. The limbic system lies along the inner edge of the cerebrum. When part of a male rat's hypothalamus is electrically stimulated, the rat engages in its courting and mounting routine. Klüver and Bucy (1939) found that destruction of areas of the limbic system triggered continuous sexual behavior in monkeys. Electrical stimulation of the hippocampus and septal nuclei produces erections in monkeys.

passing sexual fantasy, or an erotic photo can trigger the firing of cortical cells. These cells, in turn, transmit messages through the spinal cord that send blood rushing to the genitals, causing erection or vaginal lubrication. The cortex also provides the conscious sense of self. The cortex judges sexual behavior to be proper or improper, moral or immoral, relaxing or anxiety- or guilt-provoking.

Areas of the brain below the cortex, especially the limbic system, also play roles in sexual processes (Kimble, 1992). For example, when the rear part of a male rat's hypothalamus is stimulated by an electrical probe, the animal mechanically runs through its courting and mounting routine. It nibbles at the ears and the back of the neck of a female rat and mounts her when she responds. People, of course, are influenced by learning, fantasy, and values as well as simple brain (or spinal) stimulation.

The importance of the limbic system in the sexual behavior in animals was demonstrated in experiments by Heinrich Klüver and Paul Bucy of the University of Chicago in 1939. Klüver and Bucy reported that destruction of areas of the limbic system triggered persistent sexual behaviors that included masturbation and male–female and male–male mounting attempts. The monkeys even tried to mount the experimenters. For obvious ethical reasons, researchers have not injured or destroyed parts of people's brains to observe the effects on humans.

Classic research also reveals that electrical stimulation of the hippocampus and septum of the limbic system can produce erections in laboratory monkeys (McLean, 1976). Electrical stimulation of a pathway in the thalamus, moreover, produced a seminal discharge in these monkeys—without erection. Stimulation of certain areas in the thalamus and hypothalamus may induce ejaculation. Still, the precise relationships among brain structures that regulate erection and ejaculation in animals or humans have not been fully mapped out.

On Pushing the Right Buttons: Are There Pleasure Centers in the Brain?

Research with electrical probes suggests that "pleasure centers" may exist in and near the hypothalamus in other animals and perhaps even in people. Classic research found that when electrodes are implanted in certain parts of the limbic system, investigators find that laboratory animals such as rats (Olds, 1956; Olds & Milner, 1954)

Review: Sexual Response and the Brain: Cerebral Sex?

Reflect

If you could electrically stimulate a pleasure center in your brain and find as much pleasure as you do in sexual activity with another person, do you think you would bother to form romantic relationships? Why or why not?

CriticalThinking

If you electrically stimulate part of the rat's brain, it mechanically runs through a mating routine. Does it seem useful or wise to attempt to apply this research finding to humans?

22. Parts of the brain, in particular the cerebral cortex and the _____ system, play key roles in sexual functioning.

23. Cells in the _____ cortex transmit messages when we experience sexual thoughts and fantasies.

24. The cerebral cortex transmits messages through the _____ cord that send blood rushing to the genitals, causing erection or vaginal lubrication.

25. When the rear part of a male rat's _____ is stimulated by electricity, the animal runs through its sexual routine.

Truth?Fiction?
Revisited

It is apparently true that electrical stimulation of certain areas in the human brain can yield sensations similar to those of sexual pleasure and gratification. It is unclear whether these centers are responsible for sexual pleasure. But we might ask whether we would bother to develop sexual relationships if such centers could be stimulated directly. But before you run to the store for electrodes, consider that few researchers suggest that we will someday replace lovers with electronic kits.

will repeatedly press controls to receive bursts of electricity. Of course we cannot know what the rats experience, but people report that stimulation of these so-called pleasure centers led to feelings of sexual arousal and gratification.

Heath (1972) found that electrical stimulation of the septal region of the limbic system resulted in orgasmlike sensations in two people. Delgado (1969) reported that two female epileptic patients who received limbic stimulation as part of a diagnostic evaluation became sexually aroused by the stimulation:

> [One] reported a pleasant tingling sensation in the left side of her body "from my face down to the bottom of my legs." She started giggling and . . . [stated] that she enjoyed the sensation "very much." Repetition of these stimulations made the patient more communicative and flirtatious, and she ended by openly expressing her desire to marry the therapist. [The other patient reported] a pleasant sensation of relaxation and considerably increased her verbal output, which took on a more intimate character. [She] expressed her fondness for the therapist [whom she had just met], kissed his hands, and talked about her immense gratitude. (p. 145)

Sex Hormones: Do They "Goad" Us into Sex?

In a TV situation comedy, a male adolescent was described as a "hormone with feet." Ask parents why teenagers act the way they do, and you are likely to hear a one-word answer: hormones!

Question: How do hormones affect the sex drive and sexual response? Hormones are chemicals that are secreted by the ductless glands of the endocrine system directly into the bloodstream. The word *hormone* derives from the Greek *horman,* meaning "to stimulate" or "to goad." We could say that they very much goad us into sexual activity. Hormones also regulate various bodily functions, including growth and resistance to stress as well as sexual functions.

The hypothalamus and pituitary gland regulate gonadal secretion of sex hormones, specifically testosterone in males and estrogen and progesterone in females. At puberty a surge of sex hormones causes the blossoming of reproductive maturation: the sperm-producing ability of the testes in males and the maturation of ova and ovulation in females. Sex hormones released at puberty also cause the flowering of **secondary sex characteristics**. In males, the vocal cords lengthen (and the voice consequently lowers), and facial and pubic hair grow. In females, the breasts and hips become rounded with fatty tissue, and pubic hair grows.

Are Adolescents "Hormones with Feet"? Research shows that levels of androgens are connected with sexual interest in both male and female adolescents. Hormone levels are more likely to predict sexual behavior in adolescent males, however, perhaps because society places greater restraints on female sexuality.

Sex Hormones and Sexual Behavior: Organizing and Activating Influences

Sex hormones have organizing and activating effects on behavior. That is, they exert an influence on the type of behavior that is expressed (an *organizing* effect) and the frequency or intensity of the drive that motivates the behavior and the ability to perform the behavior (*activating* effects). For example, sex hormones predispose lower animals and possibly people toward stereotypical masculine or feminine mating behaviors (an organizing effect). They also facilitate sexual response and influence sexual desire (activating effects).

Though sex hormones clearly determine the sexual "orientations" and drives of many lower animals, their roles in human sexual behavior may be relatively more subtle and are not as well understood. Much of our knowledge of the organizing and activating effects of sex hormones comes from research with other species in which hormone levels were manipulated by castration or injection. Ethical standards prohibit such research with human infants, for obvious reasons.

The activating effects of testosterone can be clearly observed among male rats. For example, males who are castrated in adulthood and thus deprived of testosterone discontinue sexual behavior. If they are given injections of testosterone, however, they resume stereotypical male sexual behaviors, such as attempting to mount receptive females.

In rats, testosterone organizes or differentiates the brain in the masculine direction. As a result, adult male rats display stereotypical masculine behaviors upon activation by testosterone. Male fetuses and newborns normally have sufficient amounts of testosterone in their blood systems to organize their brains in the masculine direction. Female fetuses and newborns normally have lesser amounts of testosterone. Their brains thus become organized in a feminine direction. When female rats are prenatally exposed to large doses of testosterone, their sexual organs became somewhat masculinized, and they are predisposed toward masculine mating behaviors in adulthood (Kimble, 1992).

In rats and other rodents, sexual differentiation of the brain is not complete at birth. Female rodents who are given testosterone injections shortly before or shortly following birth (depending on the species) show typical masculine sexual patterns in

Secondary sex characteristics Physical traits that differentiate males from females but are not directly involved in reproduction.

adulthood, attempting to mount other females and resisting mounting by males (Ellis & Ames, 1987).

Questions remain about the organizing effects of sex hormones on human sexual behavior. Prenatal sex hormones are known to play a role in the sexual differentiation of the genitalia and of the brain structures, such as the hypothalamus. Their role in patterning sexual behavior in adulthood remains unknown, however. Some researchers have speculated that the brains of **transsexual** individuals may have been prenatally sexually differentiated in one direction, while their genitals were being differentiated in the other (Money, 1994). It has been speculated that prenatal sexual differentiation of the brain may also be connected with sexual orientation.

What of the activating effects of sex hormones on human sex drive and behavior? Though the countless attempts to extract or synthesize aphrodisiacs have failed to produce the real thing, men and women normally produce a genuine aphrodisiac—testosterone. Testosterone activates the sex drives of both men and women (Guzick & Hoeger, 2000).

Sex Hormones and Male Sexual Behavior

Male sex hormones are known to influence the sex drive and sexual response in nonhuman animals and men (Bialy & Sachs, 2002; Cooke et al., 2003). Evidence of the role for hormones in sex drive is found among men who have declines in testosterone levels as the result of chemical or surgical castration. Surgical castration (removal of the testes) is sometimes performed as a medical treatment for cancer of the prostate or other diseases of the male reproductive tract, such as genital tuberculosis. But some convicted sex offenders have voluntarily undergone castration as a condition of release.

Regardless of the reason for castration, men who are surgically or chemically castrated usually exhibit a gradual decrease in the incidence of sexual fantasies and loss of sexual desire (Bradford, 1998; Gijs & Gooren, 1996; Rösler & Witztum, 1998). They also gradually tend to lose the capacities to attain erection and to ejaculate—an indication that testosterone is important in maintaining sexual functioning as well as drive, at least in males. Castrated men show great variation in their sexual interest and functioning, however. Some continue to experience sexual desires and are able to function sexually for years, even decades. Learning appears to play a large role in determining continued sexual response following castration. Males who were sexually experienced before castration show a more gradual decline in sexual activity. Those who were sexually inexperienced at the time show relatively little or no interest in sex. Male sexual motivation and functioning thus involve an interplay of hormonal influences and experience.

Further evidence of the relationship between hormonal levels and male sexuality is found in studies of men with **hypogonadism,** a condition marked by abnormally low levels of testosterone production. Hypogonadal men generally suffer loss of sexual desire and a decline in sexual activity (McElduff & Beange, 2003). Here again, hormones do not tell the whole story. Hypogonadal men are capable of erection, at least for a while, even though their sex drives may wane. The role of testosterone as an activator of sex drives in men is further supported by evidence of the effects of testosterone replacement in hypogonadal men. When such men obtain testosterone injections, their sex drives, fantasies, and activity are often restored to former levels (Seidman, 2003; Tan & Culberson, 2003).

Transsexual A person with a gender-identity disorder who feels that he or she is really a member of the other sex and trapped in a body of the wrong sex.

Hypogonadism An abnormal condition marked by abnormally low levels of testosterone production.

Though minimal levels of androgens are critical to male sexuality, there is no one-to-one correspondence between hormone levels and the sex drive or sexual performance in adults. In men who have ample supplies of testosterone, sexual interest and functioning depend more on learning, fantasies, attitudes, memories, and other psychosocial factors than on hormone levels. At puberty, however, hormonal variations may play a more direct role in stimulating sexual interest and activity in males. Udry and his colleagues (Udry, 2001; Udry et al., 1985; Udry et al., 1986; Udry & Billy, 1987) found, for example, that testosterone levels predicted sexual interest, masturbation rates, and the likelihood of engaging in sexual intercourse among teenage boys. A positive relationship also has been found between testosterone levels in adult men and frequency of sexual intercourse (Dabbs & Morris, 1990). Moreover, drugs that reduce the levels of androgen in the blood system, called *antiandrogens,* lead to reductions in the sex drive and in sexual fantasies (Bradford, 1998).

Sex Hormones and Female Sexual Behavior

The female sex hormones estrogen and progesterone play prominent roles in promoting the changes that occur during puberty and in regulating the menstrual cycle. Female sex hormones do not appear to play a direct role in determining sexual motivation or response in human females, however.

In most mammals, females are sexually receptive only during estrus. Estrus is a brief period of fertility that corresponds to time of ovulation; and, during estrus, females are said to be "in heat." Estrus occurs once a year in some species; in others, it occurs periodically during the year in so-called sexual or mating seasons. Estrogen peaks at time of ovulation, so there is a close relationship between fertility and sexual receptivity in most female mammals. Women's sexuality is not clearly linked to hormonal fluctuations, however. Unlike females of most other species of mammals, the human female is sexually responsive during all phases of the reproductive (menstrual) cycle—even during menstruation, when ovarian hormone levels are low—and after menopause.

There is some evidence, however, that sexual responsiveness in women is influenced by the presence of circulating androgens, or male sex hormones, in their bodies. The adrenal glands of women produce small amounts of androgens, just as they do in males (Guzick & Hoeger, 2000). The fact that women normally produce smaller amounts of androgens than men does not mean that they necessarily have weaker sex drives. Rather, women appear to be more sensitive to smaller amounts of androgens. For women, it seems that less is more.

Women who receive **ovariectomies**, which are sometimes carried out when a hysterectomy is performed, no longer produce female sex hormones. Nevertheless, they continue to experience sex drives and interest as before. Loss of the ovarian hormone estradiol may cause vaginal dryness and make coitus painful, but it does not reduce sexual desire. (The dryness can be alleviated by a lubricating jelly or by estrogen-replacement therapy.) However, women whose adrenal glands *and* ovaries have been removed (so that they no longer produce androgens) gradually lose sexual desire. An active and enjoyable sexual history seems to ward off this loss, however, providing further evidence of the impact of cognitive and experiential factors on human sexual response.

Research provides further evidence on the links between testosterone levels and women's sex drives (Williams, 1999). In the studies by Udry and his colleagues mentioned earlier, androgen levels were also found to predict sexual interest among teenage girls. In contrast to boys, however, girls' androgen levels were unrelated to the likelihood of coital experience. Androgens apparently affect sexual desire in both

Ovariectomy Surgical removal of the ovaries.

Review: Sex Hormones: Do They "Goad" Us into Sex?

Reflect

Do you know people who have taken testosterone or estrogen for medical or other reasons? What were the reasons for using hormones? What were their effects?

CriticalThinking

Does the fact that male sex hormones are connected with the sex drive in both men and women mean that sex is basically a male function?

26. _____ are secreted by the ductless glands of the endocrine system.

27. Men (*Do* or *Do not?*) produce female sex hormones.

28. (*Primary* or *secondary?*) sex characteristics in males include the lengthening of the vocal cords.

29. The fact that sex hormones predispose animals toward masculine or feminine mating behaviors an (*Organizing* or *Activating?*) effect.

30. The hormone _____ activates the sex drives of both men and women.

31. Men with (*Hypogonadism* or *Hypergonadism?*) generally suffer loss of sexual desire and a decline in sexual activity.

32. Women whose _____ glands have been removed show reduction in sexual desire.

---

sexes, but sexual interest may be more likely to be directly translated into sexual activity in men than in women (Peplau, 2003). This sex difference may be explained by society's placement of greater restraints on female sexuality.

Other researchers report that women's sexual activity increases at points in the menstrual cycle when levels of androgens in the bloodstream are high (Guay, 2001; Morley & Perry, 2003). Another study was conducted with women whose ovaries had been surgically removed ("surgical menopause") as a way of treating disease. The ovaries supply major quantities of estrogen. Following surgery, the women in this study were treated either with estrogen-replacement therapy (ERT), with ERT *plus* androgens, or with a placebo (an inert substance made to resemble an active drug) (Sherwin et al., 1985). This was a double-blind study. Neither the women nor their physicians knew which drug the women were receiving. The results showed that the combination of androgens and ERT heightened sexual desire and sexual fantasies more than ERT alone or the placebo. The combination also helps women maintain a sense of psychological well-being (Guzick & Hoeger, 2000).

Androgens thus play a more prominent role than ovarian hormones in activating and maintaining women's sex drives. As with men, however, women's sexuality is too complex to be explained fully by hormone levels. For example, an active and enjoyable sexual history seems to ward off the loss of sexual interest that generally follows the surgical removal of the adrenal glands and ovaries.

Sexual Response

Although we may be culturally attuned to focus on sex differences rather than similarities, Masters and Johnson (1966) found that the physiological responses of men and women to sexual stimulation (whether from coitus, masturbation, or other sources) are quite alike. The sequence of changes in the body that takes place as men and women become progressively more aroused is referred to as the sexual response cycle. *Question: What is the Masters and Johnson sexual response cycle?*

The Four-Phase Masters and Johnson Sexual Response Cycle

Masters and Johnson divided the **sexual response cycle** into four phases: *excitement, plateau, orgasm,* and *resolution.* Figure 5.2 suggests the levels of sexual arousal associated with each phase.

Both males and females experience **vasocongestion** and **myotonia** early in the response cycle. Vasocongestion is the swelling of the genital tissues with blood, which causes erection of the penis and engorgement of the area surrounding the vaginal opening. The testes, nipples, and even earlobes become engorged as blood vessels in these areas dilate.

Myotonia refers to muscle tension. Myotonia causes voluntary and involuntary muscle contractions, which produce facial grimaces, spasms in the hands and feet, and eventually, the spasms of orgasm. Let us follow these and the other bodily changes that constitute the sexual response cycle.

Excitement Phase In younger men, vasocongestion during the **excitement phase** produces penile erection as early as 3 to 8 seconds after stimulation begins. Erection may occur more slowly in older men, but the responses are essentially the same. Erection may subside and return as stimulation varies. The scrotal skin thickens, losing its baggy appearance. The testes increase in size. The testes and scrotum become elevated.

In the female, vaginal lubrication may start 10 to 30 seconds after stimulation begins. Vasocongestion swells the clitoris, flattens the labia majora and spreads them apart, and increases the size of the labia minora. The inner two thirds of the vagina expands. The vaginal walls thicken and, because of the inflow of blood, turn from their normal pink to a deeper hue. The uterus becomes engorged and elevated. The breasts enlarge, and blood vessels near the surface become more prominent.

The skin may take on a rosy **sex flush** late in this phase. It varies with intensity of arousal and is more pronounced in women. The nipples may become erect in both sexes, especially in response to direct stimulation. Men and women show some increase in myotonia, heart rate, and blood pressure.

Sexual response cycle Masters and Johnson's model of sexual response, which consists of four phases.

Vasocongestion The swelling of the genital tissues with blood, which causes erection of the penis and engorgement of the area surrounding the vaginal opening.

Myotonia Muscle tension.

Excitement phase The first phase of the sexual response cycle, which is characterized by erection in the male, vaginal lubrication in the female, and muscle tension and increases in heart rate in both males and females.

Sex flush A reddish rash that appears on the chest or breasts late in the excitement phase of the sexual response cycle.

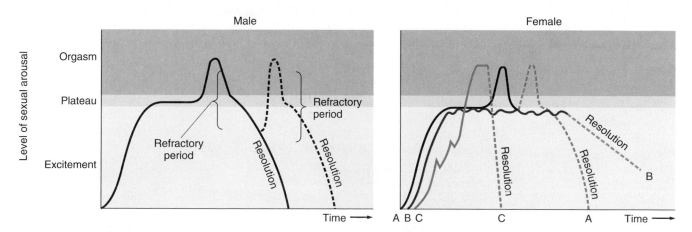

Figure 5.2. Levels of Sexual Arousal during the Phases of the Sexual Response Cycle. *Masters and Johnson divide the sexual response cycle into four phases: excitement, plateau, orgasm, and resolution. During the resolution phase, the level of sexual arousal returns to the prearoused state. For men there is a refractory period following orgasm. As shown by the broken line, however, men can become rearoused to orgasm once the refractory period is past and their levels of sexual arousal have returned to preplateau levels. Pattern A for women shows a typical response cycle, with the broken line suggesting multiple orgasms. Pattern B shows the cycle of a woman who reaches the plateau phase but for whom arousal is "resolved" without reaching the orgasmic phase. Pattern C shows the possibility of orgasm in a highly aroused woman who passes quickly through the plateau phase.*

Plateau phase The second phase of the sexual response cycle, which is characterized by increases in vasocongestion, muscle tension, heart rate, and blood pressure in preparation for orgasm.

Orgasmic platform The thickening of the walls of the outer third of the vagina, due to vasocongestion, that occurs during the plateau phase of the sexual response cycle.

Sex skin Reddening of the labia minora that occurs during the plateau phase.

Plateau Phase A plateau is a level region, and the level of arousal remains somewhat constant during the **plateau phase** of sexual response. Nevertheless, the plateau phase is an advanced state of arousal that precedes orgasm. Men in this phase show a slight increase in the circumference of the coronal ridge of the penis. The penile glans turns a purplish hue, a sign of vasocongestion. The testes are elevated further into position for ejaculation and may reach one and a half times their unaroused size. The Cowper's glands secrete a few droplets of fluid that are found at the tip of the penis (see Figure 5.3).

In women, vasocongestion swells the tissues of the outer third of the vagina, contracting the vaginal opening (thus preparing it to "grasp" the penis) and building the **orgasmic platform** (see Figure 5.4). The inner part of the vagina expands fully. The uterus becomes fully elevated. The clitoris withdraws beneath the clitoral hood and shortens. Thus a woman (or her partner) may feel that the clitoris has become lost. This may be mistaken as a sign that the woman's sexual arousal is waning, although it is actually increasing.

Coloration of the labia minora appears, which is referred to as the **sex skin**. The labia minora become a deep wine color in women who have borne children and bright red in women who have not. Further engorgement of the areolas of the breasts may make it seem that the nipples have lost part of their erection (see Figure 5.5). The Bartholin's glands secrete a fluid that resembles mucus.

About one man in four and about three women in four show a sex flush, which often does not appear until the plateau phase. Myotonia may cause spasmodic contractions in the hands and feet and facial grimaces. Breathing becomes rapid, like panting, and the heart rate may increase to 100 to 160 beats per minute. Blood pres-

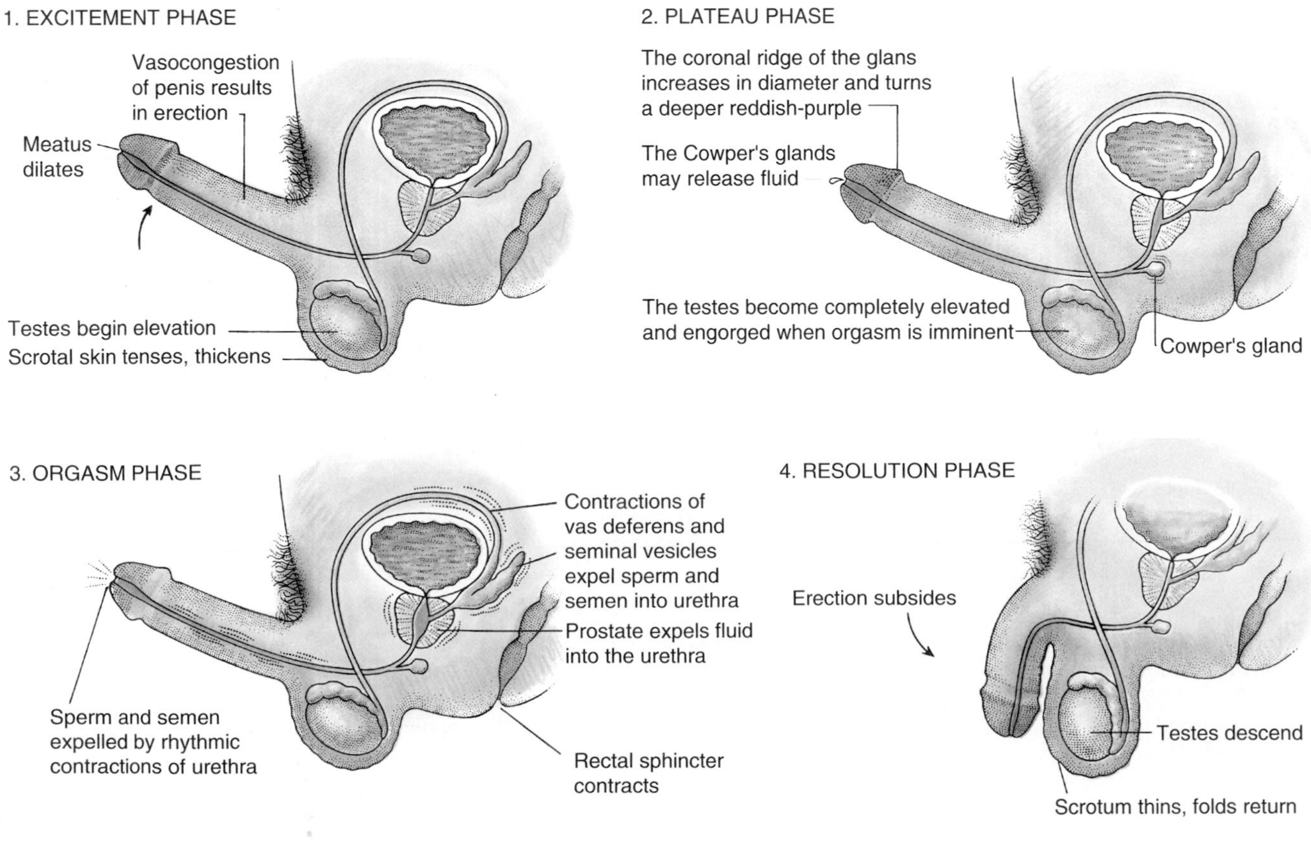

1. EXCITEMENT PHASE

Vasocongestion of penis results in erection

Meatus dilates

Testes begin elevation
Scrotal skin tenses, thickens

2. PLATEAU PHASE

The coronal ridge of the glans increases in diameter and turns a deeper reddish-purple

The Cowper's glands may release fluid

The testes become completely elevated and engorged when orgasm is imminent

Cowper's gland

3. ORGASM PHASE

Contractions of vas deferens and seminal vesicles expel sperm and semen into urethra

Prostate expels fluid into the urethra

Sperm and semen expelled by rhythmic contractions of urethra

Rectal sphincter contracts

4. RESOLUTION PHASE

Erection subsides

Testes descend

Scrotum thins, folds return

Figure 5.3. The Male Genitals during the Phases of the Sexual Response Cycle

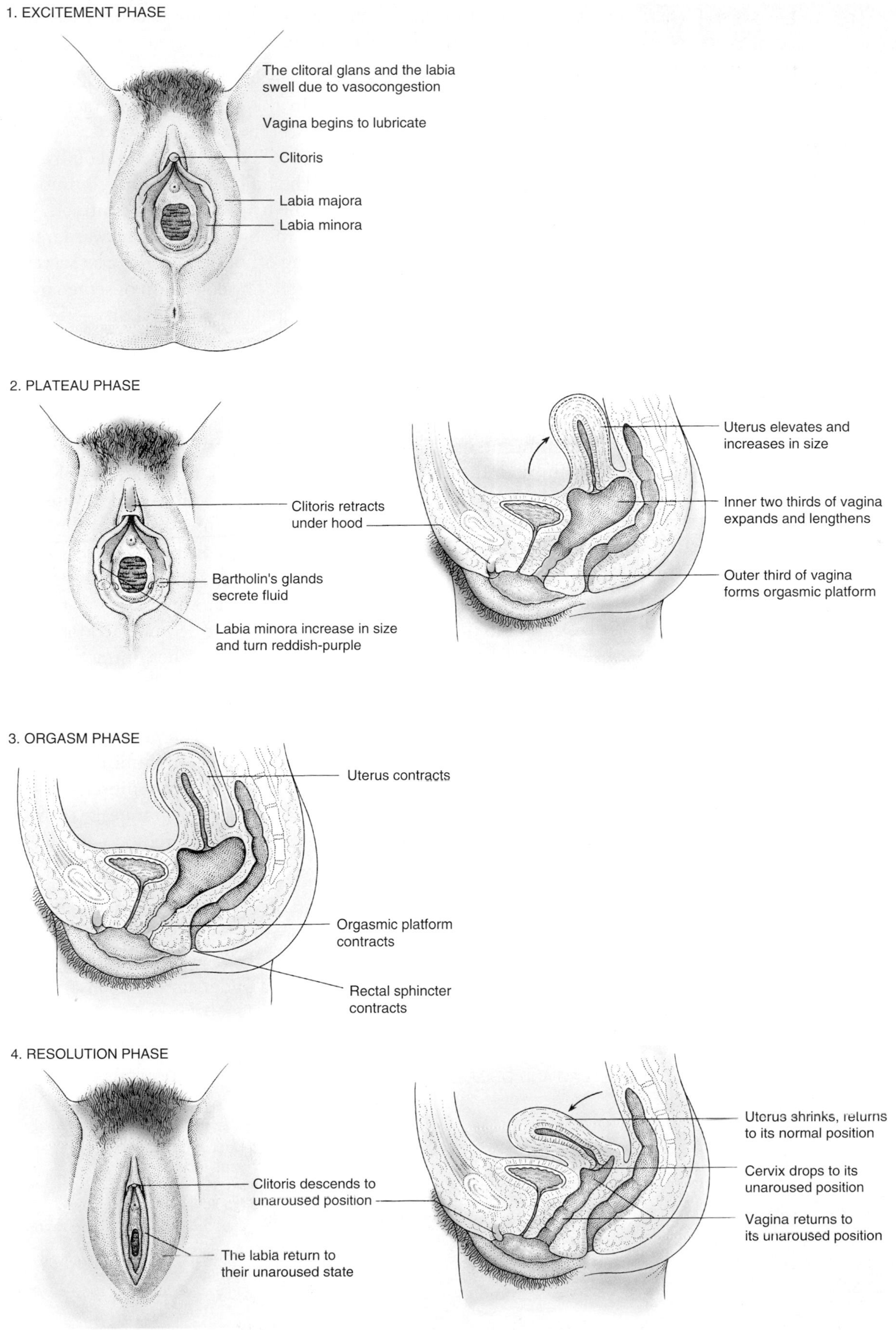

1. EXCITEMENT PHASE

The clitoral glans and the labia swell due to vasocongestion

Vagina begins to lubricate

Clitoris

Labia majora

Labia minora

2. PLATEAU PHASE

Clitoris retracts under hood

Bartholin's glands secrete fluid

Labia minora increase in size and turn reddish-purple

Uterus elevates and increases in size

Inner two thirds of vagina expands and lengthens

Outer third of vagina forms orgasmic platform

3. ORGASM PHASE

Uterus contracts

Orgasmic platform contracts

Rectal sphincter contracts

4. RESOLUTION PHASE

Clitoris descends to unaroused position

The labia return to their unaroused state

Uterus shrinks, returns to its normal position

Cervix drops to its unaroused position

Vagina returns to its unaroused position

Figure 5.4. The Female Genitals during the Phases of the Sexual Response Cycle

Truth?Fiction?
Revisited

Several studies suggest that written descriptions of women's and men's orgasms cannot be told apart. The orgasms of both may feel quite similar. In one study, 48 men and women provided written descriptions of orgasms. The researchers (Proctor et al., 1974) modified the language (for example, changing "penis" to "genitals") so that the authors' sexes would not be apparent. They then asked 70 "experts" (psychologists, gynecologists, etc.) to indicate the sex of each author. The ratings were no more reliable than guesswork—at least when they were altered to exclude language that gives away exactly which anatomic features are involved. (Thus, this Truth-or-Fiction item is only qualifiedly "true." Listen: Life is complex. Be tolerant.)

sure continues to rise. The increase in heart rate is usually less dramatic with masturbation than during coitus.

Orgasmic Phase The orgasmic phase in the male consists of two stages of muscular contractions. In the first stage, contractions of the vas deferens, the seminal vesicles, the ejaculatory duct, and the prostate gland cause seminal fluid to collect in the urethral bulb at the base of the penis (see Figure 5.3). The bulb expands to accommodate the fluid. The internal sphincter of the urinary bladder contracts, preventing seminal fluid from entering the bladder in a backward, retrograde ejaculation. The normal closing off of the bladder also serves to prevent urine from mixing with semen. The collection of semen in the urethral bulb produces feelings of ejaculatory inevitability—the sensation that nothing will stop the ejaculate from "coming." This sensation lasts for about 2 to 3 seconds.

In the second stage, the external sphincter of the bladder relaxes, allowing the passage of semen. Contractions of muscles surrounding the urethra and urethral bulb and the base of the penis propel the ejaculate through the urethra and out of the body. Sensations of pleasure tend to be related to the strength of the contractions and the amount of seminal fluid. The first 3 to 4 contractions are generally most intense and occur at 0.8-second intervals (5 contractions every 4 seconds). Another 2 to 4 contractions occur at a somewhat slower pace. Rates and patterns vary somewhat from man to man.

Orgasm in the female is manifested by 3 to 15 contractions of the pelvic muscles that surround the vaginal barrel. The contractions first occur at 0.8-second intervals, producing, as in the male, a release of sexual tension. Another 3 to 6 weaker and slower contractions follow. The spacing of these contractions is generally more variable in women than in men. The uterus and the anal sphincter also contract rhythmically. Uterine contractions occur in waves from the top to the cervix. In both sexes, muscles go into spasm throughout the body. Blood pressure and heart rate reach a peak, with the heart beating up to 180 times per minute. Respiration may increase to 40 breaths per minute.

Subjective Experience of Orgasm The sensations of orgasm have challenged the descriptive powers of poets. Words like "rush," "warmth," "explosion," and "release" do not adequately capture them. We may assume (rightly or wrongly) that others of our sex experience pretty much what we do, but can we understand the sensations of the other sex?

1. EXCITEMENT PHASE

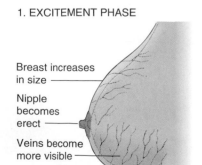

Breast increases in size

Nipple becomes erect

Veins become more visible

2. PLATEAU AND ORGASM PHASES

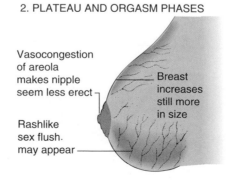

Vasocongestion of areola makes nipple seem less erect

Breast increases still more in size

Rashlike sex flush may appear

3. RESOLUTION PHASE

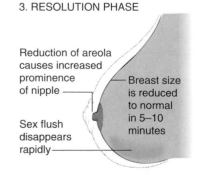

Reduction of areola causes increased prominence of nipple

Breast size is reduced to normal in 5–10 minutes

Sex flush disappears rapidly

Figure 5.5. The Breasts during the Phases of the Sexual Response Cycle

Resolution Phase The period following orgasm, in which the body returns to its prearoused state, is called the **resolution phase**. Following ejaculation, the man loses his erection in two stages. The first occurs in about a minute. Half the volume of the erection is lost as blood from the corpora cavernosa empties into the other parts of the body. The second stage occurs over a period of several minutes: The remaining tumescence subsides as the corpus spongiosum empties. The testes and scrotum return to normal size, and the scrotum regains its wrinkled appearance.

In women orgasm also triggers release of blood from engorged areas. In the absence of continued stimulation, swelling of the areolas decreases; then the nipples return to normal size. The sex flush lightens rapidly. In about 5 to 10 seconds the clitoris descends to its normal position. The clitoris, vaginal barrel, uterus, and labia gradually shrink to their prearoused sizes. The labia minora turn lighter (the "sex skin" disappears) in about 10 to 15 seconds.

Most muscle tension (myotonia) tends to dissipate within 5 minutes after orgasm in both men and women. Blood pressure, heart rate, and respiration may also return to their prearousal levels within a few minutes. About 30% to 40% of men and women find their palms, the soles of their feet, or their entire bodies covered with a sheen of perspiration. Both men and women may feel relaxed and satiated. However . . .

Although the processes by which the body returns to its prearousal state are similar in men and women, there is an important sex difference during the resolution phase. Unlike women, men enter a **refractory period** during which they are physiologically incapable of experiencing another orgasm or ejaculation (in much the same way that the flash attachment to a camera cannot be set off again immediately after it is used—it has to be recharged). The refractory period of adolescent males may last only minutes, whereas that of men age 50 and above may last from several minutes (yes, "it could happen") to a day. Women do not undergo a refractory period and so can become quickly rearoused to the point of repeated (multiple) orgasms if they desire and receive continued sexual stimulation (see Figure 5.2).

Myotonia and vasocongestion may take an hour or more to dissipate in people who are aroused but who do not reach orgasm. Persistent pelvic vasocongestion may cause "blue balls" in males—the slang term for a throbbing ache. Some men insist that their dates should consent to coitus, because it is unfair to stimulate them to the point where they have this condition. This condition can be relieved through masturbation as well as coitus, however—or allowed to dissipate naturally. Although it may be uncomfortable, it is not dangerous and should not be an excuse to pressure or coerce another person into any sexual activity. "Blue" sensations are not limited to men. Women, too, may experience unpleasant pelvic throbbing if they have become highly aroused and do not find release. Women, too, can relieve the throbbing through masturbation.

Question: Are there any other views of the sexual response cycle?

Kaplan's Three Stages of Sexual Response: An Alternative Model

Perhaps the only other view of the sexual response cycle that has received continued attention is the one proposed by Helen Singer Kaplan. Kaplan was a prominent sex therapist and author of several professional books (1974, 1979, 1987) on sex therapy. Whereas Masters and Johnson had proposed a four-stage model of sexual response, Kaplan developed a three-stage model consisting of (1) desire, (2) excitement, and (3) orgasm. Kaplan's model is an outgrowth of her clinical experience in working with people with sexual dysfunctions. She believes that their problems can best be

Resolution phase The fourth phase of the sexual response cycle, during which the body gradually returns to its prearoused state.

Refractory period A period of time following a response (e.g., orgasm) during which an individual is no longer responsive to stimulation (e.g., sexual stimulation).

classified according to these three phases. Kaplan's model makes it convenient for clinicians to classify sexual dysfunctions involving desire (low or absent desire), excitement (such as problems with erection in the male or lubrication in the female), and orgasm (such as premature ejaculation in the male or orgasmic dysfunction in the female).

Masters and Johnson view sexual response as composed of *successive* stages; the order is crucial and invariant. Kaplan treats her phases as relatively independent components of sexual response whose sequence is somewhat variable. For example, a person may experience sexual excitement and even orgasm, though sexual desire remains low.

Kaplan's model is noteworthy for designating desire as a separate phase of sexual response. Problems in lack of sexual interest or desire are among the most common brought to the attention of sex therapists.

Controversies about Orgasm

Few other topics in human sexuality have aroused more controversies over the years than orgasm. We do not have all the answers, but some intriguing research findings have shed light on some continuing controversies. *Questions: Are women capable of experiencing multiple orgasms? Are men?*

Multiple Orgasms Kinsey's reported that 14% of his female respondents regularly had **multiple orgasms**, surprising fellow scientists as well as the community at large (Kinsey et al., 1953). Many people were aghast that women could have more than one orgasm at a time. There were comments (mostly by men, of course!) that the women in the Kinsey surveys must be "nymphomaniacs" who were incapable of being satisfied with the "normal" complement of one orgasm per occasion. However, only 13 years later, Masters and Johnson (1966) reported that most if not all women are capable of multiple orgasms. Though all women may have a biological capability for multiple orgasms, not all women report them. A survey of 720 nurses showed that 43% reported experiencing multiple orgasms (Darling et al., 1991). A Canadian study of 202 married women aged 18 to 75 found that nearly half of them experienced multiple orgasms when they used a vibrator. They generally applied the vibrator to the clitoris and reported that orgasms experienced with the vibrator were more intense than other kinds. Two thirds of the women, by the way, used the vibrators in conjunction with sexual activity with their husbands.

It is difficult to offer a precise definition of multiple orgasm. In Masters and Johnson's view, multiple orgasm involves the occurrence of one or more *additional* orgasms following the first, within a short period of time and before the body has returned to a preplateau level of arousal. By this definition, a person would not have experienced a multiple orgasm if he or she had two or more successive orgasms that were separated by a return to a prearoused state or a preplateau (excitement stage) level of arousal.

By Masters and Johnson's definition, men are not capable of achieving multiple orgasms, because they enter a refractory period following ejaculation. Men who want more than one orgasm during one session may have to pause for a while. Yet women can maintain a high level of arousal between multiple orgasms and have them in rapid succession because women do not have a refractory period. Women can continue to have orgasms if they continue to receive effective stimulation (and, of course, are interested in continuing). Some men thus refrain from reaching orgasm until their partners have had the desired number. The differential capacity for multiple orgasms is one of the major sex differences in sexual response.

Multiple orgasms One or more additional orgasms following the first, which occur within a short period of time and before the body has returned to a preplateau level of arousal.

Some men have two or more orgasms without ejaculation ("dry orgasms") preceding a final ejaculatory orgasm. These men may not enter a refractory period following their initial dry orgasms and may therefore be able to maintain their level of stimulation at near-peak levels.

Masters and Johnson found that some women experienced 20 or more orgasms by masturbating. Still, few women have multiple orgasms during most sexual encounters, and many are satisfied with just one per occasion. Some women who have read or heard about female orgasmic capacity wonder what is "wrong" with them if they are content with just one. Nothing is wrong with them, of course: A biological capacity does not create a behavioral requirement.

How Many Kinds of Orgasms Do Women Have? One, Two, or Three? Question: How many kinds of orgasm do women experience? Until Masters and Johnson published their laboratory findings, many people believed that there were two types of female orgasm, as proposed by the psychoanalyst Sigmund Freud: the *clitoral orgasm* and the *vaginal orgasm.* Clitoral orgasms were achieved through direct clitoral stimulation, such as by masturbation. Clitoral orgasms were seen by psychoanalysts (mostly male psychoanalysts, naturally) as emblematic of a childhood fixation—a throwback to an erogenous pattern acquired during childhood masturbation.

The term *vaginal orgasm* referred to an orgasm achieved through coitus and was theorized to be a sign of mature sexuality. Freud argued that women achieve sexual maturity when they forsake clitoral stimulation for vaginal stimulation. This view would be little more than an academic footnote but for the fact that some adult women who continue to require direct clitoral stimulation to reach orgasm, even during coitus, have been led by traditional (generally male) psychoanalysts to believe that they are sexually "fixated" at an immature stage or are sexually inadequate.

Despite Freudian theory, Masters and Johnson (1966) were able to find only one kind of orgasm, physiologically speaking, regardless of the source of stimulation (manual–clitoral or penile–vaginal). By monitoring physiological responses to sexual stimulation, they found that the female orgasm involves the same biological events whether it is reached through masturbation, petting, coitus, or even stimulation of the breasts. Gertrude Stein wrote, "A rose is a rose is a rose." Biologically speaking, the same principle can be applied to orgasm: "An orgasm is an orgasm is an orgasm." In men, it also matters not how orgasm is achieved—through masturbation, petting, oral sex, coitus, or by fantasizing about a fellow student in chem lab. Orgasm still involves the same physiological processes: Involuntary contractions of the pelvic muscles at the base of the penis expel semen and release sexual tension. A woman or a man might prefer one source of orgasm to another—with a lover rather than by masturbation, or with one person rather than another, but the biological events that define orgasm remain the same.

Though orgasms attained through coitus or masturbation may be physiologically alike, there are psychological or subjective differences. (Were it not so, there would be fewer sexual relationships.) The coital experience, for example, is often accompanied by feelings of sexual attraction, lust, attachment, love, and connectedness with one's partner. Masturbation is more likely to be experienced as a sexual release.

The purported distinction between clitoral and vaginal orgasms also rests on an assumption that the clitoris is not stimulated during coitus. Masters and Johnson showed this assumption to be *false.* Penile coital thrusting draws the clitoral hood back and forth against the clitoris. Vaginal pressure also heightens blood flow in the clitoris, helping set the stage for orgasm (Lavoisier et al., 1995).

One might think that Masters and Johnson's research settled the question of whether or not there are different types of female orgasm. Other investigators, however, have proposed that there are distinct forms of female orgasm, yet not those suggested by psychoanalytic theory. For example, Singer and Singer (1972) suggested that there are three types of female orgasm: *vulval, uterine,* and *blended.* According to the Singers, the vulval orgasm represents the type of orgasm described by Masters and Johnson (1966). It involves *vulval* contractions—that is, contractions of the vaginal barrel. Consistent with the findings of Masters and Johnson (1966), they accept that a vulval orgasm remains the same regardless of the source of stimulation, clitoral or vaginal.

According to the Singers, the uterine orgasm does not involve vulval contractions. It occurs only in response to deep penile thrusting against the cervix. This thrusting slightly displaces the uterus and stimulates the tissues that cover the abdominal organs. The uterine orgasm is accompanied by a certain pattern of breathing: gasping or gulping of air is followed by an involuntary holding of the breath as orgasm approaches. When orgasm is reached, the breath is explosively exhaled. The uterine orgasm is accompanied by deep feelings of relaxation and sexual satisfaction.

The third type—blended orgasm—combines features of vulval and uterine orgasms. It involves both an involuntary breath-holding response and contractions of the pelvic muscles. The Singers note that the type of orgasm a woman experiences—vulval, uterine, or blended—depends on factors such as the parts of the body that are stimulated and the duration of stimulation. Each produces its own kind of satisfaction, and no type is necessarily better or preferable to another. The Singers' hypothesis of three distinct forms of female orgasm remains controversial.

The G Spot Question: What is the G spot? The **Grafenberg spot**, or G spot, is theorized to be a part of the vagina—a bean-shaped area in the anterior (front) wall that may have special erotic significance. The G spot is believed to lie about 1 to 2 inches from the vaginal entrance and to consist of a soft mass of tissue that swells from the size of a dime to a half dollar when stimulated (see Figure 5.6). The name derives from the gynecologist Ernest Grafenberg, who first suggested the possible erotic import of the area. The spot can be directly stimulated by the woman's or her partner's fingers or by penile thrusting in the rear entry or the female-superior positions. Some researchers suggest that stimulation of the spot produces intense erotic sensations and that, with prolonged stimulation, a distinct form of orgasm that is characterized by intense pleasure and, in some cases, a biological event formerly thought to be exclusively male: ejaculation (Perry & Whipple, 1981; Whipple & Komisaruk, 1988). These claims have been steeped in controversy.

In a laboratory experiment, Zaviacic and his colleagues (1988a, 1988b) found evidence of an ejaculate in 10 of 27 women studied. Some researchers believe that this fluid is urine that some women release involuntarily during orgasm. Others believe that it differs from urine (Zaviacic & Whipple, 1993). The nature of this fluid and its source remain unclear, but Zaviacic and Whipple (1993) suggest that it may represent a fluid that is released during sex by a "female prostate," a system of ducts and glands called *Skene's glands,* in much the same way that semen is released by the prostate gland in men. Zaviacic and Whipple suggest that "many women who

Grafenberg spot A part of the anterior wall of the vagina whose prolonged stimulation is theorized to cause particularly intense orgasms and a female ejaculation. Abbreviated *G spot.*

felt that they may be urinating during sex . . . [may be helped by] the knowledge that the fluid they expel may be different from urine and a normal phenomenon that occurs during sexual response" (1993, p. 149). Some women, however, may expel urine during sex, perhaps because of urinary stress incontinence (Zaviacic & Whipple, 1993). Zaviacic and Whipple also note that stimulation of the G spot may cause some women to ejaculate but not others.

Even supporters of the existence of the G spot admit that it is difficult to locate, because it is not apparent to the eye (Ladas et al., 1982). Terence Hines (2001) summarizes criticisms of the research into the G spot by noting that it is based on anecdotes and case studies with small numbers of subjects. Hines characterizes the evidence for the existence of the G spot as weak and unsupported by more rigorous anatomic and biochemical research. He dubs the G spot a "modern gynecologic myth." Critics also note that the entire anterior wall of the vagina, not just one area, is richly supplied with nerve endings and sensitive to erotic stimulation.

More research is needed to determine the scientific basis of the claims for different kinds of orgasm in women and whether specific sites in the vagina are especially sensitive to erotic stimulation.

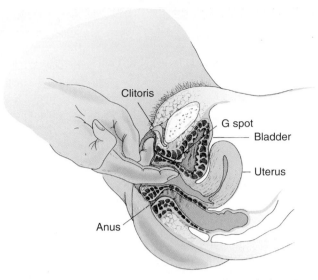

Figure 5.6. The Grafenberg Spot. *It is theorized that the "G spot" can be stimulated by fingers or by intercourse in the rear entry or the female-superior positions. Does stimulation of the G spot produce intense erotic sensations and a distinct form of orgasm?*

Review: Sexual Response

Reflect

Does the research finding that women but not men experience multiple orgasms challenge any prevailing views about female sexuality?

CriticalThinking

Historically speaking, the existence of the G spot was suggested at about the same time the women's movement was at its height. Can you think of any reasons why the existence—or lack of existence—of the G spot and a female ejaculate might have political as well as scientific overtones?

33. Masters and Johnson divided the sexual response cycle into _____ phases.

34. Sexual arousal is characterized by vasocongestion and _____ (muscle tension).

35. Erection and vaginal lubrication occur during the _____ phase of the sexual response cycle.

36. (*Men* or *Women*?) enter a refractory period following orgasm.

37. (*Men* or *Women*?) are capable of multiple orgasms.

38. In her three-stage sexual response cycle, Helen Singer Kaplan had one stage that Masters and Johnson did not have: _____.

39. Sigmund Freud believed that women could experience a clitoral or _____ orgasm.

40. Masters and Johnson found (*How many?*) kind(s) of orgasm.

41. Singer and Singer suggested that there are three types of female orgasm: *vulval, uterine,* and _____.

42. Gynecologist Ernest Grafenberg was first to suggest the existence of the "G spot" and that women as well as men could _____.

43. Evidence concerning the existence of the G spot is _____.

Recite

1. What are the roles of the senses in sexual arousal?

Each sense plays a role in sexual experience, but some play more of a role than others. Visual information plays a major role in human sexual attraction. Visual cues can be sexual turn-ons or turn-offs. Although the sense of smell plays a lesser role in governing sexual arousal in humans than in lower mammals, particular odors can be sexual turn-ons or turn-offs. The sense of touch has the most direct effects on sexual arousal and response. Taste appears to play only a minor role in sexual arousal and response. Like visual and olfactory cues, sounds can be turn-ons or turn-offs.

2. Are there substances in genital or underarm secretions that function as aphrodisiacs?

Many organisms are sexually aroused by naturally produced chemicals called pheromones, but their role in human sexual behavior remains somewhat controversial. On the other hand, there is research evidence that underarm secretions may make men and women more sexually attractive and that male underarm secretions have a positive effect on the moods of women.

3. How does exposure to other women's sweat modify the menstrual cycle?

Exposure to the odor of other women's sweat appears to cause the menstrual cycles of women who live together to become synchronized.

4. What are erogenous zones?

Erogenous zones are particularly sensitive to the sense of touch. Primary erogenous zones are particularly sensitive because they are richly endowed with nerve endings. Secondary erogenous zones are body parts that become erotically sensitized through experience.

5. What is an aphrodisiac?

An aphrodisiac is any substance that is sexually arousing or increases sexual desire. Alleged aphrodisiacs such as Spanish fly and foods that in some way resemble the genitals have not been shown to contribute to sexual arousal or response. The male sex hormone testosterone does heighten the sex drive in both males and females.

6. What kind of substance would have the opposite effect of an aphrodisiac?

Such substances would be anaphrodisiacs, such as amyl nitrate and antiandrogen drugs.

7. Do any psychoactive drugs stimulate a sexual response?

The alleged aphrodisiac effects of psychoactive drugs, such as alcohol and cocaine, may reflect our expectations or their effects on sexual inhibitions, rather than direct stimulation of sexual response. Alcohol is also connected with a liberated social role and thus provides an external excuse for dubious behavior. Some people report initial increased sexual pleasure with cocaine use, but frequent use can lead to sexual dysfunctions. The antidepressant drug Wellbutrin and L-dopa may have some aphrodisiacal properties.

Recite

8. What is the role of the brain in sexual response?

The cerebral cortex interprets sensory information as sexual turn-ons or turn-offs. The cortex transmits messages through the spinal cord that cause vasocongestion. Direct stimulation of parts of the limbic system causes erection and ejaculation in many male animals. Electrical stimulation of certain parts of the limbic system apparently yields sensations similar to those of sexual gratification.

9. How do hormones affect the sex drive and sexual response?

Sex hormones have organizing and activating effects on behavior. Men and women normally produce one genuine aphrodisiac: testosterone. Female sex hormones do not appear to play a direct role in determining sexual motivation or response in human females. Yet levels of testosterone in the bloodstream have been associated with sexual interest in women.

10. What is the Masters and Johnson sexual response cycle?

William Masters and Virginia Johnson found that the physiological responses of men and women to sexual stimulation are quite alike. Both experience vasocongestion and myotonia early in the response cycle. Sexual excitement is characterized by erection in the male and vaginal lubrication in the female. The plateau phase is an advanced state of arousal that precedes orgasm. The third phase of the sexual response cycle is characterized by orgasmic contractions of the pelvic musculature. Orgasm in the male occurs in two stages of muscular contractions. Orgasm in the female is manifested by contractions of the pelvic muscles that surround the vaginal barrel. During the resolution phase, the body returns to its prearoused state.

11. Are there any other views of the sexual response cycle?

Helen Singer Kaplan developed a three-stage model of sexual response consisting of desire, excitement, and orgasm. Kaplan's model makes it more convenient for clinicians to classify and treat sexual dysfunctions.

12. Are women capable of experiencing multiple orgasms? Are men?

Multiple orgasm is the occurrence of one or more additional orgasms following the first, within a short period of time and before the body has returned to a preplateau level of arousal. Most women, but few if any men, are capable of multiple orgasms.

13. How many kinds of orgasm do women experience?

Freud theorized the existence of two types of orgasm in women: clitoral and vaginal. Masters and Johnson found only one kind of orgasm among women. Singer and Singer suggested that there are three types of female orgasm: vulval, uterine, and blended.

14. What is the G spot?

The G spot—an allegedly distinct area within the anterior wall of the vagina—may have special erotic significance. Some researchers suggest that prolonged stimulation of the spot produces an orgasm that is characterized by intense pleasure in some women, by a type of ejaculation. The existence of the G spot and the nature of a woman's "ejaculate" remain in doubt.

Chapter 6

Truth?Fiction?

T / F? If male sex hormones were not present during critical stages of prenatal development, we would all develop external female sexual organs.

T / F? Seventeen of 18 boys who appeared to have female external sex organs suddenly developed male sex organs at puberty, when male sex hormones went to work.

T / F? The sex of a baby crocodile is determined by the temperature at which the egg develops.

T / F? Thousands of people have changed their sexes through sex-reassignment surgery.

T / F? Men act more aggressively than women do.

T / F? A 2½-year-old child may know that he is a boy but think that he can grow up to be a mommy.

Gender Identity and Gender Roles

Preview

We're halfway there. We've begun to raise our daughters more like sons—so now women are whole people. But fewer of us have the courage to raise our sons more like daughters. Yet until men raise children as much as women do—and are raised to raise children, whether or not they become fathers—they will have a far harder time developing in themselves those human qualities that are wrongly called "feminine," but are really those necessary to raise children: empathy, flexibility, patience, compassion, and the ability to let go.

Gloria Steinem, commencement speech at Smith College

Whatever women do they must do twice as well as men to be thought half as good. Luckily, this is not difficult.

Charlotte Whitton

I like men to behave like men—strong and childish.

French author *Françoise Sagan*

These remarks from war correspondents in the battle of the sexes signify key issues in the study of gender: gender roles, the actual differences between females and males, and the enduring problem of sexism. This chapter addresses the biological, psychological, and sociological aspects of gender. First we define **gender** as the psychological sense of being female or being male and the roles society ascribes to gender. Anatomic sex is based on, well, anatomy. But gender is a complex concept that is based partly on anatomy, partly on the psychology of the individual, and partly on culture and tradition.

Next we focus on sexual differentiation—the process by which males and females develop distinct reproductive anatomy. We then turn to gender roles—the clusters of behavior that are deemed "masculine" or "feminine" in a particular culture. The chapter examines research findings on sex differences. We next consider gender typing—the processes by which boys come to behave in line with what is expected of men (most of the time) and girls with what is expected of women (most of the time). We will also explore the concept of psychological androgyny, which applies to people who display characteristics associated with both gender roles in our culture.

Prenatal Sexual Differentiation

Question: How are males differentiated from females during prenatal development?
Over the years many ideas have been proposed to account for **sexual differentiation**. Aristotle believed that the anatomical difference between males and females was due to the heat of semen during sexual relations. Hot semen generated males, whereas cold semen made females[1] (National Center for Biotechnology Information, 2000). Others believed that sperm from the right testicle make females, but sperm from the left testicle make males.

According to the Bible, Adam was created first, and Eve issued forth from one of his ribs. From the standpoint of modern biological knowledge, as we will see, it would be more accurate to say that "Adams" (that is, males) develop from "Eves" (females).

When a sperm cell fertilizes an ovum, 23 **chromosomes** from the male parent normally combine with 23 chromosomes from the female parent. The **zygote**, the beginning of a new human being, is only 1/175 of an inch long. Yet, on this tiny stage, one's stamp as a unique individual has already been ensured—whether one will have black or blond hair, grow bald or develop a widow's peak, or become female or male.

The chromosomes from each parent combine to form 23 pairs. The 23rd pair are the sex chromosomes. An ovum carries an X sex chromosome, but a sperm cell can carry either an X or a Y sex chromosome. If a sperm cell with an X sex chromosome fertilizes the ovum, the newly conceived individual will have an XX sex chromosomal structure and normally develop as a female. If the sperm cell carries a Y sex chromosome, the child will normally develop as a male (XY).

After fertilization, the zygote divides repeatedly. After a few short weeks, one cell has become billions of cells. At about 3 weeks a primitive heart begins to drive blood through the embryonic bloodstream. At about 5 to 6 weeks, when the **embryo** is only ¼ to ½ inch long, primitive gonads, ducts, and external genitals whose sex cannot be distinguished visually have formed (see Figures 6.1, 6.2). Each embryo possesses primitive external genitals, a pair of sexually undifferentiated gonads, and

Gender The psychological state of being female or being male, as influenced by cultural concepts of gender-appropriate behavior. Compare and contrast the concept of gender with *anatomic sex,* which is based on the physical differences between females and males.

Sexual differentiation The process by which males and females develop distinct reproductive anatomy.

Chromosome One of the rodlike structures, found in the nucleus of every living cell, that carry the genetic code in the form of genes.

Zygote A fertilized ovum (egg cell).

Embryo The stage of prenatal development that begins with implantation of a fertilized ovum in the uterus and concludes with development of the major organ systems at about two months after conception.

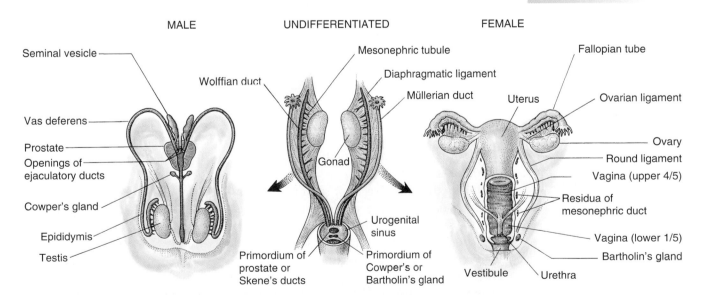

Figure 6.1. Development of the Internal Sexual Organs from an Undifferentiated Stage at about 5 or 6 Weeks Following Conception

---

1. Just a wee bit of stereotyping here—the hot-blooded male and the frigid female, notes the third author. Hopefully, we have moved beyond.

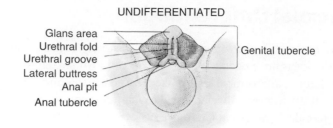

UNDIFFERENTIATED

Glans area
Urethral fold
Urethral groove
Lateral buttress
Anal pit
Anal tubercle

Genital tubercle

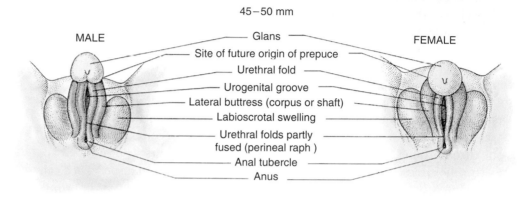

45–50 mm

MALE

FEMALE

Glans
Site of future origin of prepuce
Urethral fold
Urogenital groove
Lateral buttress (corpus or shaft)
Labioscrotal swelling
Urethral folds partly fused (perineal raph)
Anal tubercle
Anus

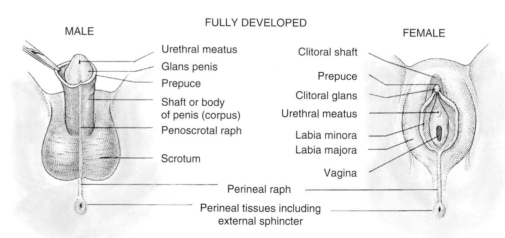

FULLY DEVELOPED

MALE

FEMALE

Urethral meatus
Glans penis
Prepuce
Shaft or body of penis (corpus)
Penoscrotal raph
Scrotum

Clitoral shaft
Prepuce
Clitoral glans
Urethral meatus
Labia minora
Labia majora
Vagina

Perineal raph
Perineal tissues including external sphincter

Figure 6.2. Development of the External Sexual Organs from an Undifferentiated Stage at about 5 or 6 Weeks Following Conception

two sets of primitive duct structures, the Müllerian (female) ducts and the Wolffian (male) ducts.

During the first 6 weeks or so of prenatal development, embryonic structures of both sexes develop along similar lines and resemble primitive female structures. At about the seventh week after conception, the genetic code (XX or XY) begins to assert itself, causing changes in the gonads, genital ducts, and external genitals. Genetic activity on the Y sex chromosome causes the testes to begin to differentiate (National Center for Biotechnology Information, 2000). Ovaries begin to differentiate if the Y chromosome is absent. The reproductive organs of some rare individuals who have only one X sex chromosome instead of the typical XY or XX arrangement also become female in appearance, because they too lack the Y sex chromosome. One could thus say that the basic blueprint of the human embryo is female. The genetic instructions in the Y sex chromosome cause the embryo to deviate from the female developmental course.

By about the seventh week of prenatal development, strands of tissue begin to organize into seminiferous tubules. Female gonads begin to develop somewhat later than male gonads. The forerunners of follicles that will bear ova are not found until the fetal stage of development, about 10 weeks after conception. Ovaries begin to form at 11 or 12 weeks.

Genetic Factors in Sexual Differentiation

Question: What roles do genes play in sexual differentiation? Some of the answers to this question are fascinating. For example, the interaction of a number of genes has led to the development of three different types of males in a crustacean and quite a complex mating strategy (Shuster & Sassaman, 1997). One sex-determining gene called "transformer" (*tra*) is needed in the development of female fruit flies. Chromosomal (XX) females with inactive *tra* attempt to mate with other females but they are attractive to males because they still emit female pheromones (Arthur et al., 1998). Researchers conclude that among fruit flies, sexual differentiation, sexual orientation, and sexual behavior are all determined by the interactions of genes (O'Dell & Kaiser, 1997). The SRY gene—which stands for sex-determining region Y gene—is also connected with sexual differentiation (Neerman-Arbez, 2003). In an article that could have been entitled "The Mouse That Roared," researcher Stephen Maxson (1998) reported that a number of genes that are involved in determining maleness in mice, including SRY, are also connected with aggressiveness. These studies suggest a role for genes in the determination of mating and other behavior patterns in humans. The studies with mice are of particular interest because human SRY is similar to the SRY of mice (National Center for Biotechnology Information, 2000). Nevertheless, people are also influenced by culture, values, experiences, and personal beliefs. In people there is only rarely a direct line between genetics and behavior, especially social behaviors such as mating and aggression.

SRY is also one of the molecules involved in sex determination in humans (National Center for Biotechnology Information, 2000). It binds to DNA, which is a strand of genes—the basic building blocks of heredity—and distorts it. The distortion alters the properties of the DNA and leads to the formation of the testes.[2] Another gene involved in sex determination has also been researched in mice: Sox 9. Sox 9 appears to regulate the expression of SRY (Overbeek, 1999). Females with XX sex chromosomal structure normally suppress the action of their own Sox 9, which in turn prevents the expression of SRY. However, when these XX mice are chemically prevented from turning off Sox 9, they develop as males—albeit sterile males. Sperm cells, therefore, are likely to be created by other genes, not Sox 9 and SRY.

The Role of Sex Hormones in Sexual Differentiation

Question: What role do sex hormones play in sexual differentiation? Once genes have done their work and testes develop in the embryo, they begin to produce androgens. Without male sex hormones, or **androgens**, we would all develop female external reproductive organs. The most important androgen, **testosterone**, spurs differentiation of the male (Wolffian) duct system (see Figure 6.1). Each Wolffian duct develops into an epididymis, vas deferens, and seminal vesicle. The external genitals, including the penis, begin to take shape at about the eighth week of development under

Androgens Male sex hormones.

Testosterone The male sex hormone that fosters the development of male sex characteristics and is connected with the sex drive.

---

2. The third author notes that this scientific finding seems to support the widely observed phenomenon that males are bent out of shape.

Inguinal canal A fetal canal that connects the scrotum and the testes, allowing their descent.

Cryptorchidism The condition defined by undescended testes. (From roots meaning (hidden testes.")

the influence of another androgen, *dihydrotestosterone* (DHT). MIS, a testicular hormone that is secreted during the fetal stage, prevents the Müllerian ducts from developing into the female duct system.

Small amounts of androgens are produced in female fetuses, but they are not normally sufficient to cause male sexual differentiation. In female fetuses, the relative absence of androgens causes degeneration of the Wolffian ducts and prompts development of female sexual organs. The Müllerian ducts evolve into fallopian tubes, the uterus, and the upper two thirds of the vagina. These developments occur even in the absence of female sex hormones. Although female sex hormones are crucial in puberty, they are not involved in fetal sexual differentiation. If a fetus with an XY sex chromosomal structure failed to produce testosterone, it would develop external female sexual organs, even though it would be infertile.

Descent of the Testes and the Ovaries

The testes and ovaries develop from slender structures high in the abdominal cavity. *Question: How do the testes and the ovaries descend from the abdominal cavity?* By about 10 weeks after conception, they have descended so that they are almost even with the upper edge of the pelvis. The ovaries remain there for the rest of the prenatal period. Later they rotate and descend farther to their adult position in the pelvis. About four months after conception, the testes normally descend into the scrotal sac via the **inguinal canal**. After their descent, the passageway closes.

In a small percentage of males, one or both testes remain undescended. They remain in the abdomen at birth. The condition is termed **cryptorchidism**. In most cases of cryptorchidism, the testes migrate to the scrotum during infancy. In still

---

Review: Prenatal Sexual Differentiation

Reflect

Given the anatomic differences between males or females, were you surprised to learn how similar female and male embryos are? Explain.

CriticalThinking

Critical thinkers do not oversimplify or overgeneralize. Consider this statement: In the absence of prenatal male sex hormones we would all develop as females. How is this statement an oversimplification or overgeneralization?

1. Sexual _____ is the process by which embryos develop into females or males.

2. At 5 to 6 weeks, embryos possess primitive external genitals, sexually undifferentiated gonads, Müllerian (*Female* or *Male*?) ducts, and Wolffian (*Female* or *Male*?) ducts.

3. Genetic activity on the (*X* or *Y*?) sex chromosome causes the testes to begin to differentiate.

4. Ovaries differentiate if the Y chromosome is (*Present* or *Absent*?).

5. Müllerian inhibiting substance (MIS) prevents the formation of (*Male* or *Female*?) internal reproductive organs.

6. In female fetuses, relative absence of androgens causes degeneration of the _____ ducts and development of female sexual organs.

7. The testes normally descend into the scrotal sac through the _____ canal.

other cases the testes descend by puberty. Men with undescended testes are usually treated through surgery or hormonal therapy, because they are at higher risk for cancer of the testes. Sperm production is also impaired because the undescended testes are subjected to a higher-than-optimal body temperature, causing sterility.

Abnormalities of the sex chromosomes can have profound effects on sexual characteristics, physical health, and psychological development. **Klinefelter syndrome**, a condition that affects about 1 in 500 males, is caused by an extra X sex chromosome, so the man has an XXY rather than an XY pattern. Men with this pattern fail to develop appropriate secondary sex characteristics. They have enlarged breasts, poor muscular development, and, because they fail to produce sperm, they are infertile. They also tend to be mildly retarded.

The brain, like the genital organs, undergoes prenatal sexual differentiation. Testosterone causes cells in the hypothalamus of male fetuses to become insensitive to the female sex hormone estrogen. In the absence of testosterone, as in female fetuses, the hypothalamus does develop sensitivity to estrogen.

Sensitivity to estrogen is important in the regulation of the menstrual cycle after puberty. The hypothalamus detects low levels of estrogen in the blood at the end of each cycle and initiates a new cycle by stimulating the pituitary gland to secrete FSH. FSH, in turn, stimulates estrogen production by the ovaries and the ripening of an immature follicle in an ovary.

Gender Identity

Question: What is gender identity? Our **gender identity** is our psychological awareness or sense of being male or being female and one of the most obvious and important aspects of our self-concepts. Gender identity, as we will see, is usually but not always with the individual's anatomic sex. **Sex assignment** (also called *gender assignment*) reflects the child's anatomic sex and usually occurs at birth. A child's sex is so important to parents that they may want to know "Is it a boy or a girl?" before they count fingers and toes.

Most children first become aware of their anatomic sex by about the age of 18 months. By 36 months, most children have acquired a firm sense of gender identity (Rathus, 2003).

Nature and Nurture in Gender Identity

Question: What determines gender identity? Are our brains biologically programmed along masculine or feminine lines by prenatal sex hormones? Does the environment, in the form of postnatal learning experiences, shape our self-concepts as males or females? Or does gender identity reflect an intermingling of biological and environmental influences?

Gender identity is almost always consistent with chromosomal sex. Such consistency does not certify that gender identity is biologically determined, however. We also tend to be reared as males or females, according to our anatomic sexes. How, then, might we sort out the roles of nature and nurture, of biology and the environment?

Investigators have found clues in the experiences of rare individuals, **intersexuals**, who possess the gonads of one sex but external genitalia that are ambiguous or typical of the other sex (Zucker, 1999). Intersexuals are sometimes reared as members of the other sex (the sex other than their chromosomal sex). Researchers have wondered whether the gender identity of these children reflects their chromosomal

Klinefelter syndrome A sex-chromosomal disorder caused by an extra X sex chromosome.

Gender identity One's belief that one is male or female.

Sex assignment The labeling of a newborn as a male or female. Also termed *gender assignment.*

Intersexual A person who possesses the gonads of one sex but external genitalia that are ambiguous or typical of the other sex. (Also termed *pseudohermaphrodite.*)

Hermaphrodite A person who possesses both ovarian and testicular tissue. (From the names of the male and female Greek gods *Hermes* and *Aphrodite*.)

Congenital adrenal hyperplasia A form of intersexualism in which a genetic female has internal female sexual structures but masculinized external genitals.

Androgen-insensitivity syndrome A form of intersexualism in which a genetic male is prenatally insensitive to androgens such that his genitals are not normally masculinized.

and gonadal sex or the sex to which they were assigned at birth, and according to which they were reared. Before going further, let us distinguish between true hermaphrodites and intersexuals.

Hormonal errors during prenatal development produce various congenital defects. Some individuals are born with both ovarian and testicular tissue. They are called **hermaphrodites**, after the Greek myth of the son of Hermes and Aphrodite, whose body became united with that of a nymph while he was bathing. True hermaphrodites may have one gonad of each sex (a testicle and an ovary), or gonads that combine testicular and ovarian tissue.

Regardless of their genetic sex, hermaphrodites often assume the gender identity and gender role of the sex assigned at birth. Figure 6.3 shows a genetic female (XX) with a right testicle and left ovary. This person married and became a stepfather with a firm male identity. The roles of biology and environment remain tangled, however, because true hermaphrodites have gonadal tissue of both sexes.

True hermaphroditism is extremely rare. More common is intersexualism, which occurs in perhaps 1 infant in 1,000. Intersexualism has given scientists an opportunity to examine the roles of nature (biology) and nurture (environmental influences) in the shaping of gender identity. Intersexuals have testes or ovaries, but not both. Unlike hermaphrodites, their gonads (testes or ovaries) match their chromosomal sex. Because of prenatal hormonal errors, however, their external genitals and sometimes their internal reproductive anatomy are ambiguous or resemble those of the other sex.

The most common form of female intersexualism is **congenital adrenal hyperplasia** (CAH), in which a genetic (XX) female has female internal sexual structures (ovaries), but masculinized external genitals (Berenbaum & Hines, 1992; Migeon & Donohue, 1991; Zucker, 1999; Zucker et al., 1996; see Figure 6.4). The clitoris is so enlarged that it may resemble a small penis. The syndrome occurs as a result of excessive levels of androgens. In some cases the fetus's own adrenal glands produce excess androgen (the adrenal glands usually produce low levels of androgen). In other cases mothers may have received synthetic androgens during their pregnancies. In the 1950s and 1960s, before these side effects were known, synthetic androgens were sometimes prescribed to help prevent miscarriages in women with histories of spontaneous abortions.

Swedish investigator Anna Servin and her colleagues (2003) studied gender-typed behaviors and interests in 26 girls aged 2 to 10 who had CAH and in 26 girls without CAH who were matched for age. Girls with CAH showed more interest in masculine-typed toys, such as transportation toys, and less interest in feminine-typed, such as dolls. The girls with CAH were also more likely to have boys as playmates and to desire masculine-typed careers. Parents rated the behavior of daughters with CAH as being more "boylike" than did parents of girls without CAH. The investigators did not find any evidence that the girls' parents influenced their play behavior. Servin and her colleagues interpret the results as supporting a hormonal contribution to differences in play between girls with and without CAH.

There are several varieties of **androgen-insensitivity syndrome**, another type of intersexualism. One involves genetic (XY) males who, due to a mutated gene, have lower-than-normal prenatal sensitivity to androgens (Adachi et al., 2000; Hughes, 2000). As a result, their genitals do not become normally masculinized. At birth their external genitals are feminized, including a small vagina, and their testes are undescended. Because of insensitivity to androgens, the male duct system (epididymis, vas deferens, seminal vesicles, and ejaculatory ducts) fails to develop. Nevertheless, the fetal testes produce Müllerian inhibiting substance (MIS), preventing the development of a uterus or fallopian tubes. Genetic males with androgen-insensitivity syndrome usually have no or sparse pubic and axillary (underarm) hair, because the development of hair in these locations is dependent on androgens.

Girls with partial androgen-insensitivity syndrome (PAIS) are also intersexuals. Partial androgen-insensitivity syndrome (PAIS) or complete androgen-insensitivity syndrome (CAIS) occurs in 1 in 2,000 to 5,000 girls. It occurs in girls with a single X sex chromosome and in girls with XX chromosomal structure who lose some X sex chromosome material. Girls with CAIS develop typical external genital organs, but their internal reproductive organs do not develop or function normally. By contrast, girls with PAIS develop masculinized external genitals and are sometimes raised as boys, sometimes as girls. A study by Melissa Hines and her colleagues (2003) compared 22 women with CAIS and single X sex chromosomal structure with 22 women who had the normal XX sex chromosomal structure. They found no differences between the women with CAIS and controls in self-esteem, general psychological well-being, gender identity, sexual orientation, gender-typed behavior patterns, marital status, personality traits, or hand preferences. The researchers conclude that two X sex chromosomes and ovaries are not essential to the development of feminine-typed behaviors in humans.

Dominican Republic syndrome is a form of intersexualism that was first documented in a group of 18 boys in two villages in the Dominican Republic (Imperato-McGinley et al., 1974). Dominican Republic syndrome is a genetic enzyme disorder that prevents testosterone from masculinizing the external genitalia. The boys were born with normal testes and internal male reproductive organs, but their external genitals were malformed. Their penises were stunted and resembled clitorises. Their scrotums were incompletely formed and resembled female labia. They also had partially formed vaginas. Because the boys resembled girls at birth, they were reared as females. At puberty, however, their testes swung into normal testosterone production, causing startling changes: Their testes descended, their voices deepened, their musculature filled out, and their "clitorises" expanded into penises. Of the 18 boys who were reared as girls, 17 shifted to a male gender identity. Sixteen of the 18 assumed a stereotypical masculine gender role. Of the remaining 2, 1 adopted a male gender identity but continued to maintain a feminine gender role, including wearing dresses. The other maintained a female gender identity and later sought sex-reassignment surgery to "correct" the pubertal masculinization. Despite being reared as girls, nearly all of these individuals made the transition to the male role without problem, suggesting the essential importance of biology in gender identity (Bailey, 2003b).

Many scientists conclude that gender identity is influenced by complex interactions of biological and psychosocial factors. But could the "complex-interaction" approach be a way of avoiding the hot-potato issue as to whether nature (biological factors) or nurture (psychosocial factors) is more important? To place the emphasis on nature is to lessen the role of personal choice and thus has major political consequences. Although some place relatively greater emphasis on psychosocial factors (Bradley et al., 1998; Money, 1994), others emphasize the role of biological factors (Collaer & Hines, 1995; Diamond, 1996; Legato, 2000; Servin et al., 2003). However, as noted in the nearby "A Closer Look" on "Boys Who Are Reared as Girls," the theory that newborns are psychosexually neutral and that gender identity depends mainly on environmental factors has had "rough sledding" in recent years.

In case you have had enough discussion of the complex issues surrounding the origins of sex and gender identity in human beings, consider the crocodile. Crocodile eggs do not carry sex chromosomes. The offspring's sex is determined by the temperature at which the eggs develop (Ackerman, 1991). Some (males) like it hot (at

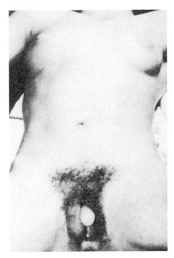

Figure 6.3. A Hermaphrodite. This genetic (XX) female has one testicle and one ovary and the gender identity of a male.

Figure 6.4. Intersexualism. In congenital adrenal hyperplasia, a genetic (XX) female has female internal sexual structures (ovaries) but masculinized external genitals.

Dominican Republic syndrome A form of intersexualism in which a genetic enzyme disorder prevents testosterone from masculinizing the external genitalia.

A Closer Look

Boys Who Are Reared as Girls

Are children "psychosexually neutral" at birth? Can you surgically reassign a boy as a female, rear him as a girl, and have him feel that he is truly a girl as the years go on? Will cosmetic surgery, female sex hormone treatments, and laces and ribbons do it? Or will he be maladjusted and his male gender identity sort of "break through"? No one has sought to answer these questions by randomly selecting male babies and reassigning their genders. Evidence on the matter derives from studies of children who have lost their penises or failed to develop them through accidents or unusual medical conditions.

GETTING DOWN TO CASES

For example, in 1967, one of a pair of male twins lost his penis as a result of a circumcision accident. As this case study is related by Colapinto (2000), the parents wondered what to do. Johns Hopkins sexologist John Money believed that gender identity was sufficiently malleable that the boy could undergo sex-reassignment surgery (have his testes removed and an artificial vagina constructed) and female hormone treatments and be successfully reared as a girl.

For a number of years, the case seemed to supply evidence for the view that children may be psychosexually neutral at birth. The sex-reassigned twin, unlike his brother, seemed to develop like a "real girl," albeit with a number of "tomboyish" traits. But at the age of 14, when "she" was informed about the circumcision accident and the process of sex reassignment, she immediately decided to pursue life as a male. As an adult, he recalled that he had never felt quite comfortable as a girl—a view confirmed by the recollections of his mother. At the age of 25, he married a woman and adopted her children. He reported being sexually attracted to women only. According to researchers such as Milton Diamond (1996), this outcome would appear to support the view that gender identity may be determined to a considerable extent in the uterus, as the fetal brain is being exposed to androgens.

ANOTHER FASCINATING CASE STUDY

Susan Bradley and her colleagues (1998) report on the development of another boy who suffered a circumcision accident in infancy. Again, John Money recommended sex reassignment, and the surgery was carried out at the age of 21 months. In this case, as Money found out in a follow-up at the age of 9, the individ-

Truth?Fiction?
Revisited

It is true that the sex of the crocodile is determined by the temperature at which the eggs develop.

Sex-reassignment surgery cannot implant the internal reproductive organs of the other gender. Therefore, it is not accurate to say that people have actually changed their sexes through sex-reassignment surgery. Instead, surgery creates the appearance of the external genitals typical of the other sex.

least in the mid-90s F), and some (females) like it not cold perhaps, but under the mid-80s F.

Transsexualism

In 1953 an ex-GI who journeyed to Denmark for a "sex-change operation" made headlines. She became known as Christine (formerly George) Jorgensen. Since then, thousands of **transsexuals** (also called *transgendered* people) have undergone sex-reassignment surgery.[3] *Question: What is transsexualism?*

Transsexualism is a condition in which the individual wishes to possess the anatomical features of people of the other sex and to live as a person of the other sex. Many transsexuals undergo hormone treatments and surgery to create the appearance of the external genitals typical of the other sex. This can be done more precisely with male-to-female than female-to-male transsexuals. After surgery people can participate in sexual activity and even attain orgasm. One survey found that two thirds of "new women" attained orgasm during sexual activity (Schroder & Carroll, 1999). But they cannot conceive or bear children.

---

3. This surgery has also been referred to as gender-reassignment surgery. In this text we are using the word "sex" to refer to anatomic sex and the word "gender" to refer to the psychological state of feeling male or female. To be consistent, then, the surgery would be reassigning one's sex, not one's gender.

ual was also tomboyish in behavior and personality traits but considered herself to be a girl.

She was interviewed subsequently at the ages of 16 and 26, and her situation had grown more complex. She considered herself to be bisexual and had sexual relationships with both men and women. However, when last interviewed, she had begun living with a woman in what the authors label a "lesbian" relationship. Of course, if one remembers that the individual has XY sex chromosomal structure, the relationship with the woman is not with a person of the same sex at all. On the other hand, the individual did retain the self-concept of being female.

A LARGER STUDY

These celebrated cases are far from the only ones. On May 12, 2000, researchers from the Johns Hopkins Hospital, including William G. Reiner, a psychiatrist and urologist, presented a paper on the subject to the Lawson Wilkins Pediatric

Endocrine Society Meeting in Boston. They recounted the development of 27 children who had been born without penises due to a rare condition called *cloacal exstrophy.* However, the children had normal testicles, male sex chromosomal structure, and male sex hormones.

Nevertheless, the sex of 25 of the 27 children was reassigned shortly after birth. They were surgically castrated and reared as girls by their parents. As the years went on, all 25—now 5 to 16 years old—showed the rough-and-tumble play considered stereotypical of males. Of the 25, 14 declared themselves to be males. Reiner (2000) suggests that "with time and age, children may well know what their gender is, regardless of any and all information and child-rearing to the contrary," he said. "They seem to be quite capable of telling us who they are." Reiner (2000) also noted that 2 of the 27 children who were not sex-reassigned fit in with male peers and appeared to be better adjusted than the children who were reassigned.

Marianne J. Legato (2000), a professor of medicine at Columbia University, believes that gender identity tends to be formed during the first trimester of pregnancy, even if children cannot verbally express their identities until a few years afterward. As Legato describes it, "When the brain has been masculinized by exposure to testosterone, it is kind of useless to say to this individual, 'You're a girl.' It is this impact of testosterone that gives males the feelings that they are men."

It should be noted that not all researchers, including Bradley and her colleagues (1998) agree as to the prominence of prenatal male sex hormones in the formation of gender identity. However, the view that newborns are psychosexually neutral and that gender identity depends mainly on nurture has become increasingly controversial in recent years.

What motivates transsexuals to live as people of the other sex? According to John Money (1994), transsexuals experience **gender dysphoria**. That is, they experience incongruity between their genital anatomy and their gender identity or role. Although they have the anatomic sex of one sex, they feel that they are members of the other. The discrepancy motivates them to wish to be rid of their own primary sex characteristics (their external genitals and internal sex organs) and to live as members of the other sex. A male-to-female transsexual perceives himself to be a female who, through some quirk of fate, was born with the wrong genital equipment. A female-to-male transsexual perceives herself as a man trapped in a woman's body.

Ray Blanchard (1988, 1989) and J. Michael Bailey (2003a, 2003b) have another view. Based on their extensive research with transsexuals, they contend that men who seek to become women tend to fall into other categories: either men who are extremely feminine or men who are sexually aroused by the idea of becoming a woman. The first category includes what Blanchard terms "**homosexual transsexuals**"—men who are extremely feminine gays and not fully satisfied by sexual activity with other males. The second category refers to males who are "**autogynephilic**," or sexually stimulated by fantasies of their own bodies as being female.

Although the prevalence of transsexualism remains unknown, it is thought to be relatively rare. The number of transsexuals in the United States is estimated to be below 50,000. Fewer than 20,000 are known to have undergone sex-reassignment surgery (Jones & Hill, 2002).

Homosexual transsexuals usually show cross-gender preferences in play and dress in early childhood. Some report that they felt they belonged to the other sex as long as they can remember. Some male-to-female transsexuals recall that, as children, they preferred playing with dolls, enjoyed wearing frilly dresses, and disliked

Transsexuals People who strongly desire to be of the other sex and live as a person of the other sex.

Gender dysphoria A sense of incongruity between one's anatomic sex and one's gender identity.

Homosexual transsexuals Extremely feminine gay males who seek sex reassignment.

Autogynephilic (aw-toe-gone-uh-FEE-lick) Descriptive of transsexuals who are sexually stimulated by fantasies that their own bodies are female. (From roots meaning "self," "woman," and "love" or "desire.")

Jayne Thomas, Ph.D.— In Her Own Words

"The 'Glass Ceiling,' male bashing, domestic violence, nagging, PMS, Viagra—these are but a few of the important issues examined in the Human Sexuality classes I instruct. As a participant-observer in my field, I see many of these topics aligning themselves as masculine/feminine or male/female. Ironically, I can both see and not see such distinctions. Certainly women have bumped up against, smudged (and in some cases even polished) this metaphorical limitation of women's advancement in the workplace (i.e., that 'Glass Ceiling'). And most assuredly men have often found themselves 'bashed' by angry women intent upon extracting a pound of flesh for centuries of felt unjust treatment. As previously mentioned, these distinctions between masculine and feminine, for me often become blurred; I must add that, having lived my life in both the roles of man and woman, I offer a rather unique perspective on masculinity and femininity.

GENDER IDENTITY DISORDER

"Gender Identity Disorder (GID) is defined by the American Psychiatric Association (1994) as a 'strong and persistent cross-gender identification [accompanied by] a persistent discomfort with his or her sex or sense of appropriateness in the gender role of that sex' (p. 537). All of my life, I harbored the strongest conviction that I was inappropriately assigned to the wrong gender—that of a man—when inside I knew myself to be a woman. Even so (and like so many other GIDs) I continued a life-long struggle with this deeply felt mistake; I was successful in school, became a national swimming champion, received my college degrees, married twice (fathering children in both marriages) and was respected as a competent and good man in the workplace. However, the persistently unrelenting wrongfulness of my life continued. Not until my fourth decade was I truly able to address my gender issue.

"Jay Thomas, Ph.D., underwent gender reassignment and officially became Jayne Thomas, Ph.D., in November of 1985, and what has transpired in the ensuing years has been the most enlightening of glimpses into the plight of humankind. As teachers we are constantly being taught by those we purport to instruct. My students, knowing my background (I share who I am when it is appropriate to do so), find me accessible in ways that many professors are not. Granted, I am continually asked the titillating questions that one watching *Geraldo* might ask and we do have fun with the answers (several years ago I even appeared on a few of the *Geraldo* shows). My students, however, are able to take our discussions beyond the sensational and superficial, and we enter into meaningful dialogue regarding sex differences in society and the workplace, sexual harassment, power and control issues in relationships, and

Jayne Thomas, Ph.D. *Jayne Thomas was chairperson of the Psychology Department of Los Angeles Mission College in Sylmar, California. She offered a comprehensive perspective on gender roles because she lived as both a man and a woman.*

what it really means to be a man or a woman.

CHALLENGING BOTH THE MASCULINE AND THE FEMININE

"Iconoclastically, I try to challenge both the masculine and feminine. 'I know something none of you women know or will ever know in your lifetime,' I can provocatively address the females in my audiences

rough-and-tumble play. They were often perceived by their peers as "sissy boys." Some female-to-male transsexuals report that as children they disliked dresses and acted much like "tomboys." They preferred playing "boys' games" and doing so with boys. Female transsexuals appear to have an easier time adjusting than male transsexuals (Selvin, 1993). "Tomboys" generally find it easier to be accepted by their peers than "sissy boys." Even in adulthood, it may be easier for a female transsexual to don men's clothes and "pass" as a slightly built man than it is for a brawny man to pass for a tall woman.

Sex Reassignment Surgery is one element of sex reassignment. Because the surgery is irreversible, health professionals conduct careful evaluations to determine that people seeking reassignment are competent to make such decisions and have thought

as Jayne. 'I once lived as a man and have been treated as an equal. You never have nor will you experience such equality.' Or, when a male student once came to my assistance in a classroom, fixing an errant video playback device and then strutting peacocklike back to his seat as only a satisfied male can, I teasingly commented to a nearby female student, 'I used to be able to do that.'

"Having once lived as a man and now as a woman, I can honestly state that I see profound differences in our social/ psychological/biological being as man and woman. I have now experienced many of the ways in which women are treated as less than men. Jay worked as a consultant to a large banking firm in Los Angeles and continued in that capacity as a woman following her gender shift. Amazingly the world presented itself in a different perspective. As Jay, technical presentations to management had generally been received in a positive manner and credit for my work fully acknowledged. Jayne now found management less accessible, credit for her efforts less forthcoming and, in general, found herself working harder to be well prepared for each meeting than she ever had as a male. As a man, her forceful and impassioned presentations were an asset; as a woman they definitely seemed a liability. On one occasion, as Jayne, when I passionately asserted my position regarding what I felt to be an important issue, my emotion and disappointment in not getting my point across (my voice showed my frustration) was met with a nearby colleague (a man) reaching to touch my arm with words of

reassurance, 'There, there, take it easy, it will be all right.' Believe me; that never happened to Jay. There was also an occasion when I had worked most diligently on a presentation to management only to find the company vice president more interested in the fragrance of my cologne than my technical agenda.

"Certainly there are significant differences in the treatment of men and women, and yet I continue to be impressed with how similar we two genders really are. Although I have made this seemingly enormous change in lifestyle (and it is immense in so many ways), I continue as the same human being, perceiving the same world through these same sensory neurons. The difference—I now find myself a more comfortable and serene being, than the paradoxical woman in a man's body, with anatomy and gender that have attained congruence.

ADJUSTING THE SHIFTING GENDER ROLES

"Does the shifting of gender role create difficulties in the GIDs life? Most assuredly it does. Family and intimate relationships rank highest among those issues most problematic for the transitioning individual to resolve. When one shifts gender role the effects of such a change are global; as ripples in a pond, the transformation radiates outward impacting all that have significantly touched the GID's life. My parents had never realized that their eldest son was dealing with such a lifelong problem. Have they accepted or do they fully understand the magnitude of

my issue? I fear not. After almost fifteen years of having lived as a female, my father continues to call me by my male name. I do not doubt my parents' or children's love for me, but so uninformed are we of the true significance of gender identity that a clear understanding seems light-years away. Often I see my clients losing jobs, closeness with family members, visitation rights with children, and generally becoming relegated to the role of societal outcast. Someone once stated that 'Everybody is born unique, but most of us die copies'—a great price my clients often pay for personal honesty and not living their lives a version of how society deems they should.

"Having lived as man and woman in the same lifetime one personal truth seems clear. Rather than each gender attempting to change and convert the other to their own side, as I often see couples undertaking to accomplish (women need be more logical and men more sharing of their emotions), we might more productively come together in our relationships building upon our gender uniqueness and strengths. Men and women have different perspectives, which can be used successfully to address life's issues."

Dr. Thomas taught and lectured at colleges and universities on the West Coast, sharing her views of masculine and feminine with her students, conducting workshops, and living out her experiment or *experience* of life. She passed away in 2002—a personal loss to your authors and to the community at large.

through the consequences. They usually require that the transsexual live openly as a member of the other sex for an extended trial period before surgery.

Once the decision is reached, a lifetime of hormone treatments is begun. Male-to-female transsexuals receive estrogen, which fosters the development of female secondary sex characteristics. It causes fatty deposits to develop in the breasts and hips, softens the skin, and inhibits growth of the beard. Female-to-male transsexuals receive androgens, which promote male secondary sex characteristics. The voice deepens, hair becomes distributed according to the male pattern, muscles enlarge, and the fatty deposits in the breasts and hips are lost. The clitoris may also grow more prominent. In the case of male-to-female transsexuals, "phonosurgery" can be done to raise the pitch of the voice (Brown et al., 2000).

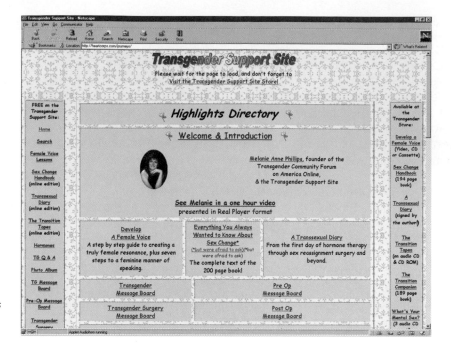

A Web Site That Helps Transgendered Individuals Adjust Numerous Web sites are available to help transsexuals adjust. The Web sites frequently have links to local support groups and commercial aspects (online stores).

Sex-reassignment surgery is largely cosmetic. Medical science cannot construct internal genital organs or gonads. Male-to-female surgery is generally more successful. The penis and testicles are first removed. Tissue from the penis is placed in an artificial vagina so that sensitive nerve endings will provide sexual sensations. A penis-shaped form of plastic or balsa wood is used to keep the vagina distended during healing.

In female-to-male transsexuals, the internal sex organs (ovaries, fallopian tubes, uterus) are removed, along with the fatty tissue in the breasts. Some female-to-male transsexuals engage in a series of operations, termed **phalloplasty**, to construct an artificial penis, but the penises don't work very well, and the procedures are costly. Therefore, most female-to-male transsexuals are content to have hysterectomies, mastectomies, and testosterone treatment (Bailey, 2003b).

Some transsexuals hesitate to undertake surgery because they are repulsed by the prospect of extreme medical intervention. Others forgo surgery so as not to jeopardize high-status careers or family relationships. Such people continue to think of themselves as members of the other sex, even without surgery.

Outcomes of Sex-Reassignment Surgery Following the introduction of sex-reassignment surgery in the United States in 1960s, most reports of postoperative adjustment were positive (Pauly & Edgerton, 1986). An influential study in the 1970s conducted at the Gender Identity Clinic at Johns Hopkins University was quite negative, however (Meyer & Reter, 1979). The study included a control group of transsexuals who did not receive sex-reassignment surgery. Psychological adjustment was more positive among transsexuals in the control group than among those who had undergone surgery.

In Canada, a follow-up study of 116 transsexuals (female-to-male and male-to-female) at least one year after surgery found that most of them were content with the results and were reasonably well adjusted (Blanchard et al., 1985). Positive results for surgery were also reported in a study of 141 Dutch transsexuals (Kuiper & Cohen-Kettenis, 1988). Nearly 9 of 10 male-to-female and female-to-male transsexuals in a study of 23 transsexuals reported they were very pleased with the results of their sex-reassignment surgery (Lief & Hubschman, 1993). Still another study (Abramowitz, 1986) reported that about two out of three cases showed at least some postoperative

Phalloplasty The surgical procedure of creating an artificial penis.

improvement in psychological adjustment. Social support contributes to postsurgical adjustment (Ross & Need, 1989).

Male-to-female transsexuals outnumber female-to-males, but postoperative adjustment is apparently more favorable for female-to-males. One reason may be that society is more accepting of women who desire to become men (Abramowitz, 1986). Female-to-male transsexuals tend to be better adjusted socially before surgery as well (Kockott & Fahrner, 1987), so their superior postoperative adjustment may be nothing more than a selection factor.

Programs across the country help transsexuals come to terms with themselves and adjust to living in a society in which they rarely feel welcome. One example is the Gender Identity Project in New York City's Greenwich Village, which sponsors meetings where transsexuals get together and share common concerns. Such programs help create a sense of community for a group of people who feel alienated from the larger society.

Psychotherapy has been a controversial topic with transsexuals because many therapists have aimed to convince preoperative transsexuals to change their minds (Jones & Hill, 2002). Transsexuals must usually obtain the consent of mental-health professionals before undergoing sex reassignment, and some professionals communicate the idea that they should learn to accept their anatomic sex (Raj, 2002). On the other hand, many transsexuals, including postoperative transsexuals, report that they have had positive experiences with therapists who show respect for them and help them adjust to their new lives (Rachlin, 2002).

Review: Gender Identity

Reflect

Do you remember learning that you were a girl or a boy? Did you share stereotypical preferences of toys and playmates? How did your preferences affect your identity and your self-esteem?

CriticalThinking

Explain why intersexuals provide researchers with a special opportunity to explore the origins of gender identity.

8. Our gender _____ is our awareness of being male or being female.

9. _____ assignment reflects the child's anatomic sex and usually occurs at birth.

10. _____ possess the gonads of one sex but their external genitalia are ambiguous or typical of the other sex.

11. People who are born with both ovarian and testicular tissue are called _____.

12. The gonads (testes or ovaries) of (*Intersexuals* or *Hermaphrodites*) match their chromosomal sex.

13. In congenital _____ hyperplasia (CAH), a genetic (XX) female has female internal sexual structures (ovaries), but masculinized external genitals.

14. Males with androgen _____ syndrome have an XY genetic code but lower-than-normal prenatal sensitivity to androgens.

15. Girls with (*Partial* or *Complete*?) androgen insensitivity syndrome develop typical external genital organs, but their internal reproductive organs do not develop or function normally.

16. Boys with Dominican Republic syndrome had a genetic enzyme disorder that prevented _____ from masculinizing the external genitalia.

17. Colapinto's report of a boy with XY sex chromosomal structure who underwent sex reassignment surgery and was reared as a girl after a circumcision accident suggests that gender identity (*Is* or *Is not*?) easily influenced by childrearing practices.

18. According to Money, transsexuals are motivated by gender _____.

19. However, Blanchard and Bailey believe that there are two types of transsexuals: _____ transsexuals and autogynephilic transsexuals.

Gender Roles and Stereotypes

"Why can't a woman be more like a man?" You may recall this lyric from the song that Professor Henry Higgins sings in the musical *My Fair Lady*. In the song the professor laments that women are emotional and fickle, whereas men are logical and dependable. The "emotional woman" is a stereotype. The "logical man" is also a stereotype—albeit more generous. Even emotions are stereotyped. People assume that women are more likely to experience feelings of fear, sadness, and sympathy, while men are more likely to experience anger and pride (Plant et al., 2000). *Question: What are stereotypes and gender roles?* A **stereotype** is a fixed, conventional—and often distorted—idea about a group of people. Sex assignment—our identification of ourselves as female or male—does not determine the roles or behaviors that are deemed masculine or feminine in our culture. Cultures have broad expectations for the personalities and behaviors of men and women that are termed **gender roles.**

The stereotypical feminine role includes traits such as gentleness, dependency, kindness, helpfulness, patience, and submissiveness. The masculine gender-role stereotype is one of toughness, gentlemanliness, and protectiveness. Females are generally seen as warm and emotional; males as independent, assertive, and competitive. The times are a-changing—somewhat. Women in our society are now almost as likely as men to be in the workforce, yet they also generally continue to bear the primary responsibilities for child rearing and homemaking. A survey of 30 countries confirmed that these gender role stereotypes are widespread (Williams & Best, 1994; see Table 6.1).

One of the effects of stereotyping is sexism, as we see in the following section.

Stereotype A fixed, conventional idea about a group of people.

Gender roles Complex clusters of expectations for males and females to behave.

Sexism The prejudgment that, because of her or his sex, a person will possess negative traits.

An Elementary School Teacher *If you think there is something wrong with this picture, it is because you have fallen prey to traditional gender role stereotypes. Tradition has prevented many women from seeking jobs in "male" preserves such as construction work, the military, and various professions. Tradition has also prevented many men from obtaining work in "female" domains such as secretarial work, nursing, and teaching at the elementary level.*

Sexism

We have all encountered the effects of sexism. *Question: What is sexism?* **Sexism** is the prejudgment that because of sex, a person will possess certain negative traits. These negative traits are assumed to disqualify the person for certain vocations or prevent him or her from performing adequately in these jobs or in some social situations.

Sexism may lead us to interpret the same behavior in prejudicial ways when performed by women or by men. A "sensitive" woman is simply sensitive, but a sensitive man may be seen as a "sissy." A woman may be perceived as polite, whereas a man showing the same behavior seems passive or weak. We may see a man as "self-assertive," but a woman who behaves in the same way as "pushy." We may look upon *him* as flexible but brand *her* fickle and indecisive. *He* may be rational, whereas *she* is cold. *He* is tough when necessary, but *she* is bitchy. When the businesswoman engages in stereotypical masculine behaviors, the sexist may brand her as abnormal or unhealthy.

Children develop stereotypes about the differences between "man's work" and "woman's work." Women have been historically excluded from "male occupations," and stereotypical expectations concerning "men's work" and "women's work" filter down to the primary grades. For example, according to traditional stereotypes, women are *not expected* to excel

---

TABLE 6.1

Gender Role Stereotypes in Thirty Nations from around the World

Stereotypes of Males		Stereotypes of Females	
Active	Opinionated	Affectionate	Nervous
Adventurous	Pleasure-seeking	Appreciative	Patient
Aggressive	Precise	Cautious	Pleasant
Arrogant	Quick	Changeable	Prudish
Autocratic	Rational	Charming	Self-pitying
Capable	Realistic	Complaining	Sensitive
Coarse	Reckless	Complicated	Sentimental
Conceited	Resourceful	Confused	Sexy
Confident	Rigid	Dependent	Shy
Courageous	Robust	Dreamy	Softhearted
Cruel	Sharp-witted	Emotional	Sophisticated
Determined	Show-off	Excitable	Submissive
Disorderly	Steady	Fault-finding	Suggestible
Enterprising	Stern	Fearful	Superstitious
Hardheaded	Stingy	Fickle	Talkative
Individualistic	Stolid	Foolish	Timid
Inventive	Tough	Forgiving	Touchy
Loud	Unscrupulous	Frivolous	Unambitious
Obnoxious		Fussy	Understanding
		Gentle	Unstable
		Imaginative	Warm
		Kind	Weak
		Mild	Worrying
		Modest	

Source of data: Williams & Best, 1994, p. 193, Table 1.

Psychologists John Williams and Deborah Best (1994) found that people in 30 countries largely agreed on what constituted masculine and feminine gender-role stereotypes.

---

in math. Exposure to such negative expectations may discourage women from careers in science and technology. Even when they choose a career in science or technology, women are often subject to discrimination in hiring, promotions, allocation of facilities for research, and funds to conduct research (Loder, 2000). Similarly, only recently have men begun to enter occupational domains previously restricted largely to women, such as secretarial work, nursing, and teaching in the primary grades. Only recently have the gates opened for women into traditionally masculine professions such as engineering, law, and medicine.

Sexism has psychologically unhealthful effects. One experiment found that women who were led to believe that sexism was pervasive reported lower self-esteem than women who were led to think that sexism was rare (Schmitt et al., 2003). In another experiment, men and women were led to believe that they were rejected from taking a course either due to sexism or personal reasons (Major et al., 2003). Attributing the rejection to prejudice rather than to personal deservingness had the effect of protecting their self-esteem ("It's not me, it's society").

Fortunately, it appears that education can modify traditional sexist attitudes. One study reported on the degree to which women's studies courses can help individuals become more aware of sexism and develop more egalitarian attitudes (Stake & Hoffman, 2001). In the study, 548 women's studies students completed questionnaires prior to and following the courses in areas such as openness to women's studies, egalitarian attitudes toward females and gender issues, and awareness of sexism

Web Sites Related to Gender Identity and Gender Roles

This is a support Web site for individuals who are transgendered (transsexual), or who are wondering whether they are transgendered.
http://www.heartcorps.com/journeys/

A directory of transgender organizations in various states with many links.
http://www.transgender.org/

Web site of the National Transgender Advocacy Coalition.
http://www.ntac.org/

An Australian support Web site for individuals who are transgendered.
http://host2.mbcomms.net.au/tg/satsg/

Web site of the Intersex Society of North America. The Web site is generally for individuals with ambiguous genitals, and the message is that people should feel free to be or remain what they are.
http://www.isna.org/

Web site of Femina, which has links to generally responsible Web sites "for, by, and about women." Issues include gender roles and sexism.
http://femina.cybergrrl.com/

and discrimination against females. As compared with students who did not take women's studies, the students in the courses reported increased awareness of sexism and other kinds of prejudice, more egalitarian attitudes toward women and other stigmatized groups, and more interest in engaging in activism for social causes.

In the next section, we see that gender-role stereotypes are also connected with sexual behavior.

Gender Roles and Sexual Behavior

Question: Have gender roles affected dating practices and sexual behavior? They most certainly have. Children learn at an early age that men usually approach women and initiate sexual interactions, whereas women usually serve as the "gatekeepers" in romantic relationships (Bailey et al., 2000b). In their traditional role as gatekeepers, women are expected to wait to be approached and to screen suitors. Men are expected to make the first (sexual) move and women to determine how far they will go.

The cultural expectation that men are initiators and women are gatekeepers is embedded within the larger stereotype that men are sexually aggressive and women are sexually passive. Men are expected to have a higher number of sexual partners than women do (Mikach & Bailey, 1999). Men not only initiate sexual encounters; they are expected to dictate all the "moves" thereafter, just as they are expected to take the lead on the dance floor. People who adhere to the masculine gender-role stereotype, whether male or female, are more likely to engage in risky (unprotected) sexual behavior (Belgrave et al., 2000). According to the stereotype, women are supposed to let men determine the choice, timing, and sequence of sexual positions and techniques. Unfortunately, the stereotype favors men's sexual preferences, denying women the opportunity to give and receive their preferred kinds of stimulation.

A woman may more easily reach orgasm in the **female-superior position**, but her partner may prefer the **male-superior position**. If the man is calling the shots, she may not have the opportunity to reach orgasm. Even the expression of her preferences may be deemed "unladylike."

The stereotypical masculine role also imposes constraints on men. Men are expected to take the lead in bringing their partners to orgasm, but they should not ask their partners what they like because they are expected to be natural experts. ("Real men" not only don't eat quiche; they also need not ask women how to make love.)

Female-superior position A coital position in which the woman is on top.

Male-superior position A coital position in which the man is on top.

Review: Gender Roles and Stereotypes

Reflect

Have you ever been guilty of engaging in, or been victimized by, sexism? What was the effect? How do you view the incident now?

CriticalThinking

Why would a researcher bother to study whether traditional gender-role stereotypes are found around the world?

20. A(n) _____ is a fixed, conventional idea about a group of people.

21. A broad cultural expectation as to how women and men should behave is termed a gender _____.

22. Gentleness is part of the stereotypical (*Masculine* or *Feminine?*) gender-role stereotype.

23. Cross-cultural research suggests that traditional gender-role stereotypes are (*Specific to our culture* or *Found around the world?*).

24. _____ is the prejudgment that a person will possess negative traits or be unqualified for certain vocations because of her or his sex.

25. Sexism is more likely to discourage (*Men* or *Women?*) from careers in science and technology.

Fortunately, more flexible attitudes are emerging. Women are becoming more sexually assertive, and men are becoming more receptive to expressing tenderness and gentleness. Still, the roots of traditional gender roles run deep.

According to another stereotype, men become sexually aroused at puberty and remain at the ready throughout adulthood. Women, however, do not share men's natural interests in sex, and a woman discovers her own sexuality only when a man ignites her sexual flame. Men must continue to stoke women's sexual embers, lest they die out. The stereotype denies that "normal" women have spontaneous sexual desires or are readily aroused.

Despite the stereotype, it is not clear that women are biologically less arousable than men; however, they are more likely to desire to limit sexual activity to committed relationships (Peplau, 2003). On the other hand, UCLA psychologist Letitia Anne Peplau (2003) finds consistent empirical support for the view that men generally have more sexual desire than women.

Questions remain as to the extent to which the sex differences associated with gender-role stereotypes reflect nature or the influences of culture and tradition. Sex differences are also vastly more pervasive than those involving sexual behavior, as we see next.

Sex Differences: *Vive la Différence* or *Vive la Similarité?*

If females and males were not anatomically different, this book would never have been written. *Question: But how do females and males differ in cognitive abilities, personality, and social behavior, if at all?*

Differences in Cognitive Abilities

Assessments of intelligence do not show overall sex differences in cognitive abilities (Halpern & LaMay, 2000). However, reviews of the research suggest that girls are somewhat superior to boys in verbal abilities, such as verbal fluency, ability to generate words that are similar in meaning to other words, spelling, knowledge of foreign languages, and pronunciation (Halpern, 1997, 2003). Far more boys than girls have reading problems, ranging from reading below grade level to severe disabilities.

Males seem to be somewhat superior in the ability to manipulate visual images in working memory. Males as a group excel in visual–spatial abilities of the sort used in math, science, and reading maps (Collaer & Nelson, 2002; Grön et al., 2000; Halpern & LaMay, 2000). They especially excel at mentally rotating geometric figures in space (see Figure 6.5). One study compared the navigation strategies of 90 male and 104 female university students (Dabbs et al., 1998). In giving directions, men more often referred to miles and directional coordinates (north, south, east, and west). Women were more likely to refer to landmarks and turning right or left.

Studies in the United States and elsewhere find that males generally obtain higher scores on math tests than females (Beller & Gafni, 2000; Gallagher et al., 2000; Halpern & LaMay, 2000; Leahey & Guo, 2001). Differences in problem solving are reflected on the mathematics test of the Scholastic Aptitude Test (SAT). The mean score is 500, and about two thirds of the test takers receive scores between 400 and 600. Twice as many boys as girls attain math scores over 500.

As you can imagine, research that establishes sex differences in cognitive abilities is quite controversial, because it appears to suggest that male ascendance in spheres involving visual–spatial skills and math is natural and permanent. Karen Kersting (2003), a reporter for the *Monitor on Psychology,* warns that any discussion of the issue can be a "political minefield." Nevertheless, investigators and commentators have noted the following:

1. Janet Hyde and a colleague (Hyde & Plant, 1995) argue that in most cases, sex differences in cognitive abilities are small. Some observers add that differences in verbal, mathematical, and spatial abilities are also growing smaller (Hyde et al., 1990; Maccoby, 1990; Voyer et al., 1995). However, psychologist J. Michael Bailey (2003b) of Northwestern University and others suggest that these differences are more robust than Hyde, Plant, and some others would have us believe. It is "politically correct" to attempt to minimize them, but political correctness does not necessarily make for scientific truth.

2. These sex differences are *group* differences. Variation in ability on tests of verbal or math skills is larger *within,* than between, the sexes (Maccoby, 1990). Despite differences between groups of boys and girls, millions of boys exceed the "average" girl in writing and spelling skills. Likewise, millions of girls outperform the "average" boy in problem-solving and spatial tasks. Males have produced their Shakespeares and females their Madame Curies.

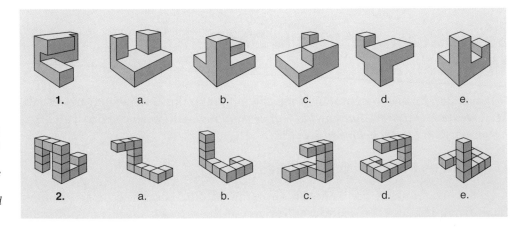

Figure 6.5. Rotating Geometric Figures in Space. Visual–spatial skills—for example, the ability to rotate geometric figures in space—are considered part of the male gender-role stereotype. But such sex differences are small and can be modified by training.

3. The small differences that may exist to some degree reflect environmental influences and cultural expectations (Fredricks & Eccles, 2002). Spatial and math skills are stereotyped in our culture as masculine, whereas reading skills are stereotyped as feminine. Women who are given just a few hours of training in spatial skills—for example, rotating geometric figures or studying floor plans—perform at least as well as men on tests of these skills (Baenninger & Elenteny, 1997; Lawton & Morrin, 1999). But in one study, girls performed more poorly on a difficult math test when they were told that the test had been shown to result in sex differences in scores—an experimental manipulation that may have made them more anxious about their performance (O'Brien & Crandall, 2003).

Are There Sex Differences in Cognitive Abilities? The physical differences between females and males are well established—and well celebrated! But are there cognitive differences between the genders? If so, what are they? How large are they? Are they the result of nature (heredity) or nurture (environmental influences such as educational experiences and cultural expectations)?

Differences in Personality

There are also many sex differences in personality. According to a meta-analysis of the research literature, females exceed males in extraversion, anxiety, trust, and nurturance (Feingold, 1994). Overall, however, differences in personality tend to be small (Bailey, 2003b). Males do tend to exceed females in assertiveness, tough-mindedness, and self-esteem. Your third author notes, with some displeasure, two factors that may largely account for the relatively lower self-esteem of females:

- Parents, on the average, prefer to have boys.
- Society has created an unlevel playing field in which females have to perform better than males to be seen as doing equally well.

Differences in Social Behavior

There are important sex differences in social behavior, particularly in matters concerning sex and aggression. Consider communication styles. Although we have been inundated with cartoons of suburban housewives gossiping across the fence or pouring endless cups of coffee when the "girls" drop by for a chat, the research shows that males dominate classroom discussions (Sadker & Sadker, 1994). As girls mature, it appears that they learn to "take a backseat" to boys and let the boys do most of the talking when they are in mixed-gender groups.

Women are more willing than men to disclose their feelings and personal experiences, however (Dindia & Allen, 1992). The stereotype of the "strong and silent" male may not discourage men from hogging the conversation, but it may inhibit them from expressing their personal feelings.

According to almost any measure that is used, men show more interest in sex than women do (Peplau, 2003). Women are more likely to want to combine sex with a romantic relationship (Peplau, 2003). A survey of more than 1,000 undergraduates by David Schmitt and his colleagues (2001) found that men also report being more interested than women in casual sex and in multiple sex partners.

Differences in Aggressiveness In most studies on aggression, males have been found to behave more aggressively than females (Felson, 2002; Hines & Saudino, 2003; Zeichner et al., 2003). As we will see, the key question is *why*?

Truth?Fiction?
Revisited

It is true that males tend to behave more aggressively than females do. In almost all cultures, it is the males who march off to war and who battle for fame, glory (and shaving-cream-commercial contracts in stadiums and arenas).

Differences in Willingness to Seek Health Care Men's life expectancies are seven years shorter, on the average, than women's. Part of the difference, according to surveys of physicians and of the general population, is due to women's greater willingness to seek health care (Courtenay, 2000). Men often let symptoms go until a problem that could have been prevented or readily treated becomes serious or life threatening. Women, for example, are much more likely to check themselves for breast cancer than men are to even recognize the symptoms of prostate cancer. Many men have a "bullet-proof mentality." They are too strong to see the doctor in their 20s, too busy in their 30s, and too frightened later on.

Review: Sex Differences: *Vive la Différence* or *Vive la Similarité?*

Reflect

Do any of the sex differences reported in the scientific literature surprise you? Why or why not?

CriticalThinking

Why do you think that some scientists suggest that it is "politically correct" to minimize sex differences in cognitive abilities? Is there "danger" in suggesting that sex differences exist in cognitive abilities? Explain.

26. Reviews of the research suggest that (*Males* or *Females*?) are somewhat superior in verbal abilities.

27. (*Males* or *Females*?) excel in visual–spatial abilities of the sort used in math, science, and reading maps.

28. (*Males* or *Females*) generally obtain higher scores on math tests.

29. According to a meta-analysis of the literature, (*Males* or *Females*?) excel in nurturance.

30. (*Males* or *Females*?) are more willing to disclose their feelings and personal experiences.

31. (*Males* or *Females*?) show more interest in sex.

32. (*Males* or *Females*?) are more likely to want to combine sex with a romantic relationship.

33. (*Males* or *Females*?) report being more interested in multiple sex partners.

34. (*Males* or *Females*?) behave more aggressively.

On Becoming a Man or a Woman: Gender Typing

We have chronicled the biological processes of sexual differentiation, and we have explored sex differences in cognitive abilities, personality, and social behavior. In this section we consider various explanations of **gender typing**, beginning with the biological.

Biological Perspectives

Question: How do biological approaches explain gender typing? Biological views on gender typing tend to focus on the roles of genetics and prenatal influences in pre-

Gender typing The process by which children acquire behavior that is deemed appropriate to their sex.

disposing men and women to gender-linked behavior patterns. Biological perspectives have also focused on the possible role of hormones in sculpting the brain during prenatal development.

The Evolutionary Perspective: It's Only Natural From the evolutionary perspective, the story of the survival of our ancient ancestors is etched in our genes. Genes that bestow attributes that increase an organism's chances of surviving to produce viable offspring are most likely to be transmitted to future generations. We thus possess the genetic remnants of traits that helped our ancestors survive and reproduce (Bjorklund & Kipp, 1996; Fisher, 2000). This heritage influences our social and sexual behavior as well as our anatomic features.

According to the evolutionary perspective, men's traditional roles as hunters and warriors and women's roles as caregivers and gatherers of fruits and vegetables are bequeathed to us in our genes. Men are better suited to war and the hunt because of physical attributes passed along since ancestral times. Upper-body strength, for example, would have enabled them to throw spears and overpower adversaries. Men also possess perceptual–cognitive advantages, such as superior visual–motor skills that favor aggression. Visual–motor skills would have enabled men to aim spears or bows and arrows.

Women, it is argued, are genetically predisposed to be empathic and nurturant because these traits enabled ancestral women to respond to children's needs and enhance the likelihood that their children would flourish and eventually reproduce, thereby transmitting their own genetic legacy to future generations. Prehistoric women thus tended to stay close to home, care for the children, and gather edible plants, whereas men ventured from home to hunt and raid their neighbors' storehouses.

The evolutionary perspective is steeped in controversy. Although scientists do not dispute the importance of evolution in determining physical attributes, many are reluctant to attribute complex social behaviors, such as aggression and gender roles, to heredity. The evolutionary perspective implies that stereotypical gender roles— men as breadwinners and women as homemakers, for example—reflect the natural order of things. Critics contend that among humans biology is not destiny, that behavior is not dictated by genes.

Prenatal Brain Organization Researchers have sought the origins of gender-typed behavior in the organization of the brain. Is it possible that the cornerstone of gender-typed behavior is laid in the brain before the first breath is taken?

The hemispheres of the brain are specialized to carry out certain functions (Shaywitz et al., 1995). In most people, the right hemisphere ("right brain") appears to be specialized to perform visual–spatial tasks. The "left brain" appears to be more essential to verbal functions, such as speech, in most people.

We know that sex hormones are responsible for prenatal sexual differentiation of the genitals and for the gender-related structural differences in the hypothalamus of the developing prenatal brain. Sexual differentiation of the brain may also partly explain men's superiority at spatial-relations tasks, such as interpreting road maps and visualizing objects in space. Testosterone in the brains of male fetuses spurs greater growth of the right hemisphere and slows the rate of growth of the left hemisphere. This difference may be connected with the ability to accomplish spatial-relations tasks, and even with preferences for childhood toys (Berenbaum & Hines, 1992).

Might boys' inclinations toward aggression and rough-and-tumble play also be prenatally imprinted in the brain? Some theorists argue that prenatal sex hormones may masculinize or feminize the brain by creating predispositions that are consistent with gender-role stereotypes, such as rough-and-tumble play and aggressive behavior in males (Collaer & Hines, 1995).

The Eye That Roves around the World?

One of the more controversial sex differences in the field of human sexuality is the suggestion that males are naturally polygamous, whereas females are naturally monogamous. If this were so, it would place a greater burden on societies in which men are expected to remain loyal to their mates. If the man strayed, after all, he could have the attitude, "Don't blame me. It's in my genes." Women, moreover, might wonder how realistic it is to expect that their partners will remain faithful.

Evolutionary psychologists have hypothesized a so-called *sexual strategies theory*, which holds that men and women differ in their long-term and short-term mating strategies, with men more interested in sexual variety in the short term (Barash & Lipton, 2001; Buss & Schmitt, 1993; Klusmann, 2002). In the long term, both males and females may seek a heavy investment in a relationship, feelings of love, companionship, and a sharing of resources. Even so, men are hypothesized to place more value on signals of fertility and reproductive value, as found in a woman's youth and physical appearance. But women are hypothesized to place relatively more value on a man's social status, maturity, and resources—cues that are relevant to his ability to provide over the long term. The qualities that men and women seek are believed to help solve adaptive problems that humans have faced over their evolutionary history.

But in the short term, men are more interested in one-night stands and relatively brief affairs. Women, evolutionarily speaking, would have little to gain from such encounters. Impregnation requires a long-term

commitment to child-rearing, and evolutionary forces would favor the survival of the children of women who created a long-term nurturing environment. But men would have a greater chance of contributing their genes to future generations by impregnating as many women as possible.

Because a "universal" form of behavior is more likely to be embedded in people's genes, the evolutionary theory of different sexual strategies would find support if males and females from various cultures showed similar sex differences in short-term mating strategies. In seeking just such evidence, David Schmitt (2003) supervised a survey of 16,288 people across 10 major regions of the world, including North America, South America, Western Europe, Eastern Europe, Southern Europe, Middle East, Africa, Oceania, South/Southeast Asia, and East Asia. He found indeed that sex differences in the desire for sexual variety were culturally universal.

Table 6.2 and Figure 6.6 reveal some of Schmitt's key findings as to the desire for variety in short-term and long-term relationships. When asked whether they would like to have more than one sex partner in the next month, men from all 10 areas of the world were significantly more likely than women to say that

Do Men around the World Have Roving Eyes? A study of 10 different areas of the world found that in every culture surveyed, men were more likely than women to desire multiple sex partners. According to the sexual strategies theory, this sex difference reflects human adaptation to environmental forces. Question for critical thinking: Does this research finding mean that it is "unnatural" to expect men to remain faithful to their partners?

they would. For example, 23.1% of North American men would like more than one partner, as compared with just 2.9% of North American women (Table 6.2). When asked about the mean (average) number of sex partners they would like to have over the next 30 years, men from every area said they would like to have significantly more sex partners than the women (Figure 6.6).

We cannot conclude that these research findings, intriguing as they are, "prove" the validity of the evolutionary approach to understanding sex differences in "sexual strategies." For example, we could point to details such as the fact that Oceanic women reported that they wanted more sex partners in the long term than did African men (Figure 6.6). We can also accept the universality of the finding but consider rival explanations for the data. For example, in a world with common global communication, it might not be surprising that there is worldwide overlap in gender roles. This overlap might affect the ways in which parents and cultural institutions influence children around the world.

The ideal model for demonstrating instinctive (inborn) behavior is to rear an individual in isolation from all other members of its species and then observe whether its behavior parallels or differs from that of other members of its species. For both practical and ethical reasons, this type of experiment has never been carried out with humans and most likely never will be. Therefore, the most we can expect are findings that are consistent with this sort of theorizing in humans, not findings that clearly prove them.

TABLE 6.2

Sex Differences in the Percentage of Men and Women Who Desire More Than One Sex Partner "in the Next Month" across Ten World Regions

World region	Percentage of Men Wanting More Than One Sexual Partner	Percentage of Women Wanting More Than One Sexual Partner
North America	23.1	2.9
South America	35.0	6.1
Western Europe	22.6	5.5
Eastern Europe	31.7	7.1
Southern Europe	31.0	6.0
Middle East	33.1	5.9
Africa	18.2	4.2
Oceania	25.3	5.8
South/Southeast Asia	32.4	6.4
East Asia	17.9	2.6

Source: Table 5. David P. Schmitt (2003). Universal sex differences in the desire for sexual variety: Tests from 52 nations, 6 continents, and 13 islands. *Journal of Personality and Social Psychology, 85*(1), 85–104.

The chances that any sex differences within a given region are due to chance is less than one in 1,000 ($p < .001$).

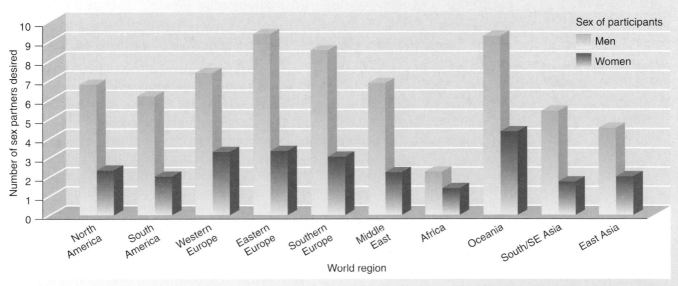

Figure 6.6. Mean Number of Sexual Partners Desired by Men and Women "in the Next 30 Years" across 10 World Regions

Source: David P. Schmitt (2003). Universal sex differences in the desire for sexual variety: Tests from 52 nations, 6 continents, and 13 islands. *Journal of Personality and Social Psychology, 85*(1), 85–104.

Psychological Perspectives

Question: How do psychological approaches explain gender typing? Developmentally speaking, children acquire awareness of gender-role stereotypes by the tender ages of 2½ to 3½ (Rathus, 2003). Both boys and girls generally agree, when asked to describe the differences between the genders, that boys build things, play with transportation toys such as cars and fire trucks, enjoy helping their fathers, and hit other children. Both boys and girls also agree that girls enjoy playing with dolls and helping their mothers cook and clean, and are talkative, dependent on others for help, and non-violent. They perceive the label "cruel" to be a masculine trait, whereas "cries a lot" is perceived as a feminine trait. By the time they are age 3, most children have become aware of the stereotypical ways in which men and women dress and the types of occupations that are considered appropriate for each (Rathus, 2003).

Psychologists have attempted to explain how children acquire such knowledge and adopt stereotypical behavior patterns in terms of psychodynamic, social-learning, and cognitive-developmental theories.

Psychodynamic Theory Sigmund Freud explained gender typing in terms of **identification**. Appropriate gender typing, in Freud's view, requires that boys come to identify with their fathers and girls with their mothers. Identification is completed, in Freud's view, as children resolve the **Oedipus complex** (sometimes called the Electra complex in girls).

According to Freud, the Oedipus complex occurs during the phallic period of psychosexual development, from the ages of 3 to 5. During this period the child develops incestuous wishes for the parent of the other gender and comes to perceive the parent of the same gender as a rival. The complex is resolved by the child's forsaking incestuous wishes for the parent of the other gender and identifying with the parent of the same gender. Through identification with the same-gender parent, the child comes to develop gender-typed behaviors that are typically associated with that gender. Children display stereotypical gender-typed behaviors earlier than Freud would have predicted, however. Even during the first year, boys are more independent than girls. Girls are more quiet and restrained. Girls show preferences for dolls and soft toys, and boys for hard transportation toys, by the ages of 1½ to 3 (Alexander, 2003). Because of their lack of empirical support, many researchers believe that Freud's views are now of historic interest only.

Social-Learning Theory Social-learning theorists explain the development of gender-typed behavior in terms of processes such as observational learning, identification, and socialization (Balter & Tamis-LeMonda, 1999; Fagot et al., 2000). Children can learn what is deemed masculine or feminine by observational learning, as suggested by the results of a classic experiment by Perry and Bussey (1979). In this study, 8- and 9-year-olds watched adult role models indicate preferences for each of 16 pairs of items—such as toy cows versus toy horses and oranges versus apples. But the children didn't know that the expressed preferences were made arbitrarily. The children then were asked to indicate their own preferences for the items represented in the pairs. The boys' choices agreed with the adult men's an average of 14 out of 16 times. Girls chose the pair item selected by the men, on the average, only 3 out of 16 times.

In social-learning theory, identification is seen as a continuous and learning process in which rewards and punishments influence children to imitate adult models of the same sex (Balter & Tamis-LeMonda, 1999; Fagot et al., 2000). In identification, the child not only imitates the behavior of the model but tries to become broadly like the model.

Identification
In psychoanalytic theory, the process of incorporating within ourselves our perceptions of the behaviors, thoughts, and feelings of others.

Oedipus complex
According to psychoanalytic theory, a conflict of the phallic stage in which the boy wishes to possess his mother sexually and perceives his father as a rival in love.

Socialization The process of guiding people into socially acceptable behavior patterns by means of information, rewards, and punishments.

Socialization also plays a role in gender typing (Balter & Tamis-LeMonda, 1999; Fagot et al., 2000). Almost from the moment a baby comes into the world, it is treated according to its gender. Parents tend to talk more to baby girls, and fathers especially engage in more roughhousing with boys. When children are old enough to speak, parents and other adults—even other children—begin to instruct children as to how they are expected to behave. Parents may reward children for behavior they consider gender-appropriate and punish (or fail to reinforce) them for behavior they consider inappropriate for their gender. Girls are encouraged to practice caretaking behaviors, which are intended to prepare them for traditional feminine adult roles. Boys are handed Legos or doctor sets to help prepare them for traditional masculine adult roles.

Fathers generally encourage their sons to develop assertive, instrumental behavior (that is, behavior that gets things done or accomplishes something) and their daughters to develop nurturant, cooperative behavior. Fathers are likely to cuddle their daughters gently. They are likely to carry their sons like footballs or toss them into the air. Fathers also tend to use heartier and harsher language with their sons, such as "How're yuh doin', Tiger?" and "Hey you, get your keester over here." Being a nontraditionalist, your first author made sure to toss his young daughters into the air, which raised immediate objections from the relatives, who chastised him for being too rough. This, of course, led him to modify his behavior. He learned to toss his daughters into the air when the relatives were not around.

Generally speaking, from an early age boys are more likely to receive toy cars and guns and athletic equipment and to be encouraged to compete aggressively. Even relatively sophisticated college students are likely to select traditionally masculine toys as gifts for boys and traditionally feminine toys for girls. Girls are spoken to more often, whereas boys are handled more frequently and more roughly. Whatever the biological determinants of sex differences in aggressiveness and verbal skills, early socialization experiences clearly contribute to gender typing.

Parental roles in gender typing are apparently changing. With more mothers working outside the home in our society, daughters are exposed to more women who represent career-minded role models than was the case in earlier generations. More

Gender Typing through Observational Learning
According to social-learning theory, people learn about the gender roles that are available to them—and expected of them—at an early age. Gender schema theory adds that once children have learned the expected gender roles (i.e., the gender schema of their culture), they blend these roles with their self-concepts. Their self-esteem comes to be dependent on their adherence to the expected gender roles.

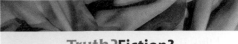

parents today are encouraging their daughters to become career minded and to engage in strenuous physical activities, such as organized sports. Many boys today are exposed to fathers who take a larger role than men used to in child care and household responsibilities.

Social-learning theorists believe that aggression is largely influenced by learning. Boys are permitted, even encouraged, to engage in more aggressive behavior than girls. Nonetheless, females are likely to act aggressively under certain conditions. Ann Frodi and her colleagues (1977) conducted a classic review of 72 studies of sex differences in aggression. All in all, females acted as aggressively as men when they were given the physical means to do so and believed that aggression was justified. In an influential review article, Maccoby and Jacklin commented on the socialization influences that discourage aggression in girls:

> Aggression in general is less acceptable for girls, and is more actively discouraged in them, by either direct punishment, withdrawal of affection, or simply cognitive training that "that isn't the way girls act." Girls then build up greater anxieties about aggression, and greater inhibitions against displaying it. (1974, p. 234)

Social-learning theorists have made important contributions to our understanding of how rewards, punishments, and modeling influences foster gender-typed behavior patterns. How do children integrate gender-role expectations within their self-concepts? And how do their concepts concerning gender influence their development of gender-typed behavior? Let us consider two cognitive approaches to gender typing that shed light on these matters: cognitive-developmental theory and gender schema theory.

Cognitive–Developmental Theory Psychologist Lawrence Kohlberg (1966) proposed a cognitive–developmental view of gender typing. From this perspective, gender typing is not the product of environmental influences that mechanically "stamp in" gender-appropriate behavior. Rather, children themselves play an active role. They form concepts, or **schemas**, about gender and then conform their behavior to their gender concepts. These developments occur in stages and are entwined with general cognitive development.

According to Kohlberg, gender typing entails the emergence of three concepts: *gender identity, gender stability,* and *gender constancy.* Gender identity is usually acquired by the age of 3. By the age of 4 or 5, most children develop a concept of **gender stability**—the recognition that people retain their genders for a lifetime.

The more sophisticated concept of **gender constancy** develops in most children by the age of 7 or 8. They recognize that gender does not change, even if people alter their dress or behavior. So gender remains constant even when appearances change. A woman who wears her hair short (or shaves it off) remains a woman. A man who dons an apron and cooks dinner remains a man.

According to cognitive–developmental theory, children are motivated to behave in gender-appropriate ways once they have established the concepts of gender stability and gender constancy. They then make an active effort to obtain information as to which behavior patterns are considered "masculine" and which "feminine" (Perry & Bussey, 1979). Once they obtain this information, they imitate the "gender-appropriate" pattern. So boys and girls who come to recognize that their genders will remain a fixed part of their identity will show preferences for "masculine" and "feminine" activities, respectively. Researchers find, for instance, that boys who had

Schema Concept; way of interpreting experience or processing information.

Gender stability The concept that people retain their genders for a lifetime.

Gender constancy The concept that people's genders do not change, even if they alter their dress or behavior.

achieved gender constancy played with an uninteresting gender-typed toy for a longer period of time than did boys who hadn't yet achieved gender constancy (Frey & Ruble, 1992). Both groups of boys played with an interesting gender-typed toy for about an equal length of time.

Cross-cultural studies of the United States, Samoa, Nepal, Belize, and Kenya find that the concepts of gender identity, gender stability, and gender constancy emerge in the order predicted by Kohlberg. However, gender-typed play often emerges at an earlier age than would be predicted by the cognitive–developmental theory. Many children make gender-typed choices of toys by the age of 2. Children as young as 18 months are likely to have developed a sense of gender identity, but gender stability and constancy are some years off. Gender identity alone thus seems sufficient to prompt children to assume gender-typed behavior patterns. Psychologist Sandra Bem (1983) also notes that Kohlberg's theory does not explain why the concept of gender plays such a prominent role in children's classification of people and behavior. Another cognitive view, gender schema theory, attempts to address these concerns.

Gender Schema Theory: An Information-Processing Approach Gender schema theory proposes that children develop a **gender schema** as a means of organizing their perceptions of the world (Bem, 1993). A gender schema is a cluster of mental representations about masculine and feminine physical qualities, behaviors, and personality traits. Gender gains prominence as a schema for organizing experience because of society's emphasis on it. Even young children start to mentally group people of the same sex according to the traits they believe represent them.

Children's gender schemas determine how important gender-typed traits are to them. Consider the dimension of *strength–weakness*. Children may learn that strength is connected with maleness and weakness with femaleness. (Other dimensions, such as *light–dark*, are not gender-typed and thus may fall outside children's gender schemas.) Children also gather that some dimensions, such as strong–weak, are more important to one sex (in this case, the male) than the other.

Once children acquire a gender schema, they begin to judge themselves according to traits considered appropriate to their sex (Fagot et al., 2000). In doing so, they blend their developing self-concepts with the prominent gender schema of their culture. Children with self-concepts that are consistent with the prominent gender schema of their culture are likely to develop higher self-esteem than children whose self-concepts are inconsistent. Jack learns that muscle strength is a characteristic associated with "manliness." He is likely to think more highly of himself if he perceives himself as embodying this attribute than if he does not. Alexis is likely to discover that the dimension of kindness–cruelty is more crucial than strength–weakness to the way in which women are perceived in society.

According to gender schema theory, gender identity itself is sufficient to inspire gender-appropriate behavior. Once children develop a concept of gender identity, they begin to seek information concerning gender-typed traits and try to live up to them. Jack will retaliate when provoked, because boys are expected to do so. Alexis will be "sugary and sweet" if such is expected of little girls. Thus, gender-typed behavior emerges earlier than would be proposed by cognitive-developmental theory.

Research suggests that children do process information according to a gender schema (Levy & Carter, 1989; Stangor & Ruble, 1989). Objects and activities pertinent to a child's own gender are better retained in memory. Boys, for example, do a better job of remembering transportation toys they have been shown previously, whereas girls are better at recalling dolls and other "feminine" objects (Bradbard & Endsley, 1984). In another study, Martin and Halverson (1983) showed elementary

Gender schema A cluster of mental representations about male and female physical qualities, behaviors, and personality traits.

Review: On Becoming a Man or a Woman: Gender Typing

Reflect

How do your recollections of the development of your own gender-typed behavior fit the theories described in this section? For example, do you recall making a conscious effort to behave in ways that are expected of people of your sex?

CriticalThinking

According to evolutionary theory, men have inherited a tendency to be interested in having multiple sex partners. Does this mean that it is "unnatural" for society to promote monogamous relationships?

35. Gender _____ refers to the processes by which children acquire behavior that is considered appropriate for their sex.

36. According to the _____ perspective, men's roles as hunters and warriors and women's roles as caregivers and gatherers are passed down to us in our genes.

37. According to sexual _____ theory, men and women differ in their long-term and short-term mating strategies.

38. According to evolutionary theory, (Men or Women?) would have little to gain from one-night stands and brief affairs.

39. According to Freudian theory, gender-typing is connected with resolution of the _____ complex.

40. However, children show preferences for gender-typed toys (Before or After?) resolution of the Oedipus complex would occur.

41. _____-learning theorists explain gender-typing in terms of observational learning, imitation, and socialization.

42. According to Kohlberg, gender typing involves the development of gender identity, gender stability, and gender _____.

43. A gender _____ is a cluster of mental representations about masculine and feminine traits.

44. According to gender schema theory, gender _____ is enough to inspire gender-appropriate behavior.

---

school children pictures of children involved in "gender-consistent" or "gender-inconsistent" activities. Gender-consistent pictures showed boys doing things like sawing wood and playing with trains. Girls were shown doing things like cooking and cleaning. Gender-inconsistent pictures showed models of the other sex involved in gender-typed endeavors. A week later, the children were asked whether boys or girls had engaged in each activity. Boys and girls both made errors recalling the sex of the models shown engaging in "gender-inconsistent" behavior.

In the following section, we see that Sandra Bem and Richard Lippa have also theorized that some people have traits that are stereotypical of both males and females and that they promote psychological adjustment to a complex society. *Question: How have Bem and Lippa reconstructed the concepts of masculinity and femininity?*

Psychological Androgyny and the Reconstruction of Masculinity–Femininity: The More Traits, the Merrier?

Most people think of masculinity and femininity as opposite ends of one continuum. People tend to assume that the more masculine a person is, the less feminine he or she must be, and vice versa. So a man who exhibits stereotypical feminine traits of nurturance, tenderness, and emotionality is often considered less masculine than other men. Women who compete with men in business are perceived not only as more masculine but also as less feminine than other women.

Some investigators, such as Sandra Bem (1993), argue that masculinity and femininity comprise separate personality dimensions. A person who is highly masculine, whether male or female, may also possess feminine traits—and vice versa. People who exhibit "masculine" assertiveness and instrumental skills (skills in the sciences and business, for example) along with "feminine" nurturance and cooperation fit both the masculine and feminine gender-role stereotypes. They are said to show **psychological androgyny** (see Figure 6.6). Assertiveness and instrumental skills are consistent with the masculine stereotype. Nurturance and cooperation are consistent with the feminine stereotype. People low in the stereotypical masculine and feminine traits are "undifferentiated," according to gender-role stereotypes.

People who are psychologically androgynous may be capable of summoning a wider range of masculine and feminine traits to meet the demands of various situations and to express their desires and talents. Researchers, for example, have found psychologically androgynous persons of both genders to show "masculine" independence under group pressures to conform and "feminine" nurturance in interactions with a kitten or baby (Bem, 1975; Bem et al., 1976). Psychologically androgynous adolescents are less likely to stereotype occupations as masculine or feminine (Kulik, 2000).

Many people who oppose the constraints of traditional gender roles may perceive psychological androgyny as a desirable goal. Some feminist writers, however, criticize psychological androgyny on grounds that the concept is defined in terms of, and thereby perpetuates, belief in the existence of masculine and feminine gender roles (Lott, 1985).

Other critics suggest that the so-called benefits of psychological androgyny can become confused with those of masculinity. The research evidence does show that psychologically androgynous people tend to have higher self-esteem and to be generally better adjusted psychologically than people who are feminine or undifferentiated (Whitley, 1983; Williams & D'Alessandro, 1994). That is, masculine traits such as assertiveness and independence may be related to psychological well-being, whether or not they are combined with feminine traits such as warmth, nurturance, and cooperation.

Psychologist Richard Lippa (2001) of California State University at Fullerton finds the model of psychological androgyny to be somewhat simplified. His research is based on surveys of personality traits and vocational interests. For example, in terms of vocational interests, he finds that traditional measures of "masculinity" tend to be positively related to interest in working with "things," whereas "femininity" is more related to working with people. In terms of personality traits, masculinity is more related to "instrumentality," or making things happen. Femininity is more related to expressiveness, or experiencing and expressing aspects of the emotional life. There are subordinate but interesting findings. For example, masculinity is also related to a heterosexual orientation, social dominance, and prejudice in men. Femininity is connected with behaviors that tend to provide the glue in interpersonal relationships. Keep in mind—again—that not all males are extremely "masculine," and not all females are overwhelmingly "feminine." Lippa, like many other researchers, has been attempting to define the nature and implications of the traditional cultural concepts (also called *constructs*) of masculinity and femininity. Perhaps it is fortunate that few of us are completely masculine or feminine, despite our anatomic sex.

In this chapter we have explored what it means to be female or to be male within a cultural setting such as ours. In the following chapter we consider how feelings of attraction and love develop between people of the other sex or people of the same sex.

Psychological androgyny A state characterized by possession of both stereotypical masculine traits and stereotypical feminine traits.

Review: Psychological Androgyny: The More Traits, the Merrier?

Reflect

Why might a woman be interested in seeking a psychologically androgynous man as a partner?

Critical Thinking

Explain the feminist argument against the concept of psychological androgyny.

45. Bem uses the term psychological _____ to describe individuals who show both stereotypical masculine and feminine traits and behaviors.

46. Adolescents who are psychologically androgynous are (*More* or *Less*?) likely to stereotype occupations as masculine or feminine.

47. Some critics argue that the apparent benefits of psychological androgyny actually reflect those of _____.

48. Lippa finds that measures of _____ tend to be positively related to interest in working with people.

49. Masculinity is related to social _____ in men.

Recite

1. **How are males differentiated from females during prenatal development?**

During the first six weeks or so of prenatal development, embryonic structures of both genders develop along similar lines and resemble primitive female structures, but then genes and sex hormones lead to the differentiation of female and male internal and external reproductive organs.

2. **What roles do genes play in sexual differentiation?**

At about the seventh week after conception, the genetic code (XX or XY) begins to assert itself, causing changes in the gonads, genital ducts, and external genitals. Abnormalities of the sex chromosomes can affect sexual characteristics, physical health, and psychological development, as in the case of Klinefelter syndrome.

3. **What role do sex hormones play in sexual differentiation?**

Testosterone spurs differentiation of the male (Wolffian) duct system. In the absence of testosterone, the Wolffian ducts degenerate, and female sex organs develop. Gender-specific changes occur in the hypothalamus during prenatal development. Testosterone causes cells in the hypothalamus of male fetuses to become insensitive to estrogen.

4. **How do the testes and the ovaries descend from the abdominal cavity?**

The testes and ovaries develop in the abdominal cavity. A few months after conception, the ovaries descend to the pelvic region, and the testes descend into the scrotal sac.

5. **What is gender identity?**

Gender identity is the psychological sense of being female or being male.

6. **What determines gender identity?**

Gender identity is almost always consistent with anatomic sex. However, research with intersexuals, such as (XX) individuals with congenital adrenal hyperplagia, and with attempts to reassign genetic (XY) males who have had circumcision accidents or were born with incomplete penises, suggests that prenatal exposure to androgens has powerful masculinizing effects on the brain as well as the genital organs.

7. **What is transsexualism?**

Transsexualism is the desire to have the genital organs of, and to live as, a member of the other sex. There is debate as to whether transsexuals experience gender dysphoria, as suggested by Money, or whether, as suggested by Blanchard and Bailey, they are highly effeminate gays (homosexual transsexualism), or are sexually excited by the idea of having the genitals of the other sex (autogynephilia). Many male-to-female transsexuals undergo hormone treatments and sex-reassignment surgery, but female-to-male transsexuals are often content with hysterectomy, mastectomy, and hormone treatments.

Recite

8. What are stereotypes and gender roles?

Cultures have broad expectations of men and women that are termed gender roles. In our culture the stereotypical female is seen as nurturant, gentle, dependent, kind, helpful, patient, and submissive. The stereotypical male is self-assertive, tough, competitive, gentlemanly, and protective.

9. What is sexism?

Sexism is the prejudgment that because of gender, a person will possess certain negative traits that disqualify him or her for certain vocations or prevent him or her from performing adequately in these jobs or in some social situations. Women have been historically excluded from "male occupations," and stereotypical expectations concerning "men's work" and "women's work" have dissuaded many from seeking occupations considered appropriate for people of the other sex.

10. Have gender roles affected dating practices and sexual behavior?

Gender roles have encouraged many males to take the initiative in approaching members of the other sex and in sexual activity itself.

11. How do females and males differ in cognitive abilities, personality, and social behavior?

Males tend to excel in math and spatial-relations skills, whereas females tend to excel in verbal skills. Stereotypical sex preferences for toys and play activities are in evidence at an early age. Males are more aggressive and more interested in sex than females. The extent and origins of all these sex differences are under debate.

12. How do biological approaches explain gender typing?

Biological views on gender typing focus on the roles of evolution, genetics, and prenatal influences in predisposing males and females to stereotypical behavior patterns. Evolutionary theory explains sex differences in terms of adaptation to environmental forces. Testosterone in the brains of male fetuses spurs greater growth of the right hemisphere, which may be connected with the ability to manage spatial-relations tasks.

13. How do psychological approaches explain gender typing?

Psychologists have attempted to explain gender typing in terms of psychodynamic, social-learning, and cognitive-developmental theories. Freud explained gender typing in terms of identification with the parent of the same gender through resolution of the Oedipus complex. Social-learning theorists explain the development of gender-typed behavior in terms of processes such as observational learning, identification, and socialization. According to Kohlberg, gender typing entails the emergence of three concepts: gender identity, gender stability, and gender constancy. Gender schema theory proposes that children blend their developing self-concepts with the prominent gender schema of their culture.

14. How have Bem and Lippa reconstructed the concepts of masculinity and femininity?

Bem and Lippa raise the issue as to whether masculinity and femininity comprise two independent personality dimensions rather than a single bipolar dimension. According to Bem, people who combine stereotypical masculine and feminine behavior patterns are psychologically androgynous. Lippa finds relationships between masculinity and instrumentality and between femininity and nurturance.

Chapter 7

Truth?Fiction?

T / F? Beauty is in the eye of the beholder.

T / F? College men would like women to be thinner than the women want to be.

T / F? People are regarded as more attractive when they are smiling.

T / F? Women who are randomly assigned names like Kathy and Jennifer are rated as more attractive than women assigned names like Harriet and Gertrude.

T / F? Physical appeal is the most important trait we seek in partners for long-term relationships.

T / F? "Opposites attract." We are more apt, that is, to be attracted to people who disagree with our views and tastes than to people who share them.

T / F? It is possible to be in love with someone who is not also a friend.

T / F? Committed couples can remain in love even after passion fades.

Attraction and Love— Binding Forces

Preview

Candy and Stretch. A new technique for controlling weight gain? No, these are the names of a couple who have just met at a camera club that doubles as a meeting place for singles.

Candy and Stretch stand above the crowd—literally. She is almost 6 feet tall, an attractive woman in her early 30s. He is more plain looking but "wholesome." He is in his late 30s and 6 feet 5 inches tall. Stretch has been in the group for some time. Candy is a new member. Let us follow them as they meet during a coffee break. As you will see, there are some differences between what they say and what they think.[1]

	THEY SAY	*THEY THINK*
STRETCH:	Well, you're certainly a welcome addition to our group.	(Can't I ever say something clever?)
CANDY:	Thank you. It certainly is friendly and interesting.	(He's cute.)
STRETCH:	My friends call me Stretch. It's left over from my basketball days. Silly, but I'm used to it.	(It's safer than saying my name is David Stein.)
CANDY:	My name is Candy.	(At least my nickname is. He doesn't have to hear Hortense O'Brien.)
STRETCH:	What kind of camera is that?	(Why couldn't a girl named Candy be Jewish? It's only a nickname, isn't it?)
CANDY:	Just this old German one of my uncle's. I borrowed it from the office.	(He could be Irish. And that camera looks expensive.)
STRETCH:	May I? (He takes her camera, brushing her hand and then tingling with the touch.) Fine lens. You work for your uncle?	(Now I've done it. Brought up work.)
CANDY:	Ever since college.	(Okay, so what if I only went for a year?)
	It's more than being just a secretary. I get into sales, too.	(If he asks what I sell, I'll tell him anything except underwear.)
STRETCH:	Sales? That's funny. I'm in sales, too, but mainly as an executive. I run our department.	(Is there a nice way to say used cars? I'd better change the subject.)
	I started using cameras on trips. Last time I was in the Bahamas, I took—	(Great legs! And the way her hips move—)
CANDY:	Oh! Do you go to the Bahamas, too? I love those islands.	(So I went just once, and it was for the brassiere manufacturers' convention. At least we're off the subject of jobs.)

---

1. Bach and Deutsch (1970).

STRETCH:

(She's probably been around. Well, at least we're off the subject of jobs.)

I did a little underwater work there last summer. Fantastic colors. So rich in life.

(And lonelier than hell.)

CANDY:

(Look at that build. He must swim like a fish. I should learn.)

I wish I'd had time when I was there. I love the water.

(Well, I do. At the beach, anyway, where I can wade in and not go too deep.)

So begins a relationship. Candy and Stretch have a drink and talk, talk, talk—sharing their likes and dislikes. Amazingly, they seem to agree on everything, from clothing to cars to politics. The attraction they feel is very strong, and neither of them is willing to turn the other off by disagreeing.

They fall in love. Weeks later they still agree on everything, even though there is one topic they avoid scrupulously: religion. Their different backgrounds became apparent once they exchanged last names. That doesn't mean they have to talk about it, however.

They delay introductions to their parents. The O'Briens and the Steins are narrow minded about religion. If the truth be known, so are Candy and Stretch. Candy errs by telling Stretch, "You're not like other Jews I know." Stretch also voices his feelings now and then. After Candy has nursed him through a cold, he remarks, "You know, you're very Jewish." Candy and Stretch play the games required to maintain the relationship. They tell themselves that their remarks were mistakes, and, after all, anyone can make mistakes. They were meant as compliments, weren't they? Yet each is becoming isolated from family and friends.

One of the topics they ignore is birth control. As a Catholic, Candy does not take oral contraceptives. (Stretch later claimed that he had assumed she did.) Candy becomes pregnant, and they get married. Only through professional help do they learn each other's genuine feelings. And on several occasions, the union comes close to dissolving.

How do we explain the goings-on in this tangled web of deception? Candy and Stretch felt strongly attracted to each other. What determines who is attractive? Why did Candy and Stretch pretend to agree on every-thing? Why did they put off introductions to their parents?

Two possible consequences of attraction are friendship and love. Candy and Stretch "fell in love." What *is* love? When the first author was a teenager, the answer was, "Five feet of heaven in a ponytail." However, this answer may lack scientific merit. We see that there are different forms of love and that our concepts of love are not universal.

Attraction: The Force That Binds?

Investigators define feelings of attraction as psychological forces that draw people together. Many factors enter into personal attraction. The first of these that we consider is physical appearance.

Physical Attractiveness: How Important Is Looking Good?

We might like to think of ourselves as so sophisticated that physical attractiveness does not move us. We might like to claim that sensitivity, warmth, and intelligence are more important to us. However, we may never learn about other people's personalities if they do not meet our minimal standards for physical attractiveness. *Question: Is physical attractiveness an important consideration in interpersonal attraction?* Research shows that physical attractiveness is a major determinant of interpersonal and sexual attraction (Langlois et al., 2000; Sangrador & Yela, 2000; Strassberg & Holty, 2003). Some researchers, in fact, contend that physical appearance is the key factor in consideration of partners for dates, sex, and long-term relationships (Hatfield & Sprecher, 1986).

Truth?Fiction?
Revisited

Beauty may not be completely in the eye of the beholder. Although personal tastes may vary within and across cultures, there are cultural standards for physical attractiveness.

Is Beauty in the Eye of the Beholder? Are our standards fully subjective, or is there broad agreement on what is attractive? Cross-cultural studies of preliterate societies have found that people universally want physically appealing partners (Ford & Beach, 1951). However, is that which appeals in one culture repulsive in others?

In certain African tribes, long necks and round, disklike lips are signs of feminine beauty. Women thus stretch their necks and lips to make themselves more appealing. Women of the Nama tribe persistently tug at their labia majora to make them "beautiful"—that is, prominent and elongated (Ford & Beach, 1951).

In our culture, taller men are considered to be more attractive by women (Pawlowski & Koziel, 2002). Undergraduate women prefer their dates to be about 6 inches taller than they are. Undergraduate men, on the average, prefer women who are about 4½ inches shorter (Gillis & Avis, 1980). Tall women are not viewed so positively. Shortness, though, is perceived to be a liability for both men and women (Jackson & Ervin, 1992).

Some women of Candy's stature find that shorter men are discouraged from asking them out. Some walk with a hunch, as if to minimize their height. A neighbor of the first and third authors refers to herself as 5 feet 13 inches tall.

Female plumpness is valued in many, perhaps most, preliterate societies (Anderson et al., 1992; Frayser, 1985). Wide hips and a broad pelvis are widely recognized as sexually appealing. In our culture, however, slenderness is in style. Some young women suffer from an eating disorder called **anorexia nervosa**, in which they literally starve themselves to conform to the contemporary ideal. Both females and males find slenderness (though not anorexic thinness) attractive, especially for females (Fallon & Rozin, 1985; Franzoi & Herzog, 1987; Rozin & Fallon, 1988).

The hourglass figure is popular in the United States. In one study, 87 African American college undergraduates—both male and female—rated women of average weight with a waist-to-hip ratio of 0.7 to 0.8 as most attractive and desirable for long-term relationships (Singh, 1994a; Streeter & McBurney, 2003). Neither very thin nor obese women were found to be as attractive, regardless of the waist-to-hip ratio. Findings were similar for a sample of 188 European American students (Singh, 1994b).

Cohen and Tannenbaum (2001) conducted an Internet study in which they posted various women's body shapes and asked lesbian and bisexual women to indi-

Anorexia nervosa
A potentially life-threatening eating disorder characterized by refusal to maintain a healthy body weight, intense fear of being overweight, a distorted body image, and, in females, lack of menstruation (amenorrhea.)

cate which were most sexually attractive to them. Respondents included 209 women self-identified as lesbian and 141 women self-identified as bisexual. The women, like heterosexual men, found women with a 0.7 waist-to-hip body ratio to be the most sexually attractive. However, they differed from the men in that their first choice was for *heavy* women with a 0.7 waist-to-hip body ratio and large breasts. Their second choice was for heavy women with the same waist-to-hip body ratio but with small breasts. The authors suggest that the women in this study were rejecting what they might view as societal emphasis on excessive slenderness.

Do men idealize the *Penthouse* centerfold? What size busts do men prefer? Researchers in one study showed young men and women a continuum of female figures that differed only in the size of the bust (Thompson & Tantleff, 1992). Men preferred women with large busts, but not nearly as large as those women *believed* that men would prefer.

Females and males both find obese people to be unattractive (Goode, 2000; Wade et al., 2000), but there are sex differences in impressions of the most pleasing body shape. On the average, college men think that their present physiques are close to ideal and appealing to women (Fallon & Rozin, 1985). College women generally see themselves as much heavier than the figure that is most alluring to men and heavier still than the figure they perceive as the ideal feminine form. But both are wrong about the preferences of the other sex.

People who are attractive know it. In one study, men and women rated each other for attractiveness and also rated themselves (Marcus & Miller, 2003). By and large, the individuals' self-ratings meshed with those by others, both female and male. Women's judgments were most closely related to how men perceived them, suggesting that they were reflecting men's opinions of them more so than women's.

How Behavior and Names Affect Perceptions of Physical Attractiveness: On the Importance of Not *Being Ernest. Question: What factors other than physical appearance contribute to the attractiveness?* Gender-role expectations may affect perceptions of attractiveness. For example, women are more likely to be attracted to socially dominant men than men are to be attracted to socially dominant women (Buunk et al., 2002). Women who viewed videos of prospective dates found men who acted outgoing and self-expressive more appealing than men who were passive (Riggio & Woll, 1984). Another study found that highly feminine women are more likely to be attracted to dominant "macho" men than less feminine women are (Maybach & Gold, 1994). Yet men who viewed videos in the Riggio and Woll (1984) study were put off by outgoing, self-expressive behavior in women. In yet another study, women rated videos of dominant college men (defined in this study as social control over a troublesome interaction with an instructor) as more appealing than submissive men. Again, male viewers were put off by similarly dominant women (Sadalla et al., 1987). Men are more likely to be jealous of socially dominant men, whereas women are more likely to be jealous of physically attractive women (Dijkstra & Buunk, 2002).

What Do You Look for in a Long-Term, Meaningful Relationship? Although personal qualities may assume more prominent roles in determining partner preferences in

Truth?Fiction?
Revisited

Men actually prefer women to be somewhat heavier than the women imagine they would. Women prefer their men to be a bit leaner than the men would have expected.

Both females and males rate the attractiveness of faces higher when they are smiling than when they are not smiling (O'Doherty et al., 2003). So there is reason to "put on a happy face" when you meet people socially or ask someone out.

Names also may affect perceptions of physical appeal. In one study, women who were randomly assigned names like Kathy, Jennifer, and Christine were rated more attractive than women assigned the names Harriet, Gertrude, and Ethel (Garwood et al., 1980). Seems silly, does it not? After all, our parents name us, and there need be no relationship between our names and our physical appeal. On the other hand, we may choose to keep our names or to use nicknames. So if you are unhappy with your name, why not assume a more popular nickname? Beginning college or a new job is an ideal time for doing so. Men, too, can doff their Sylvesters and Ernests, if they prefer. If you have an unusual name and are content with it, be yourself, however.

Wide-Eyed with . . . Beauty?

Some aspects of beauty seem to be largely cross-cultural. Research suggests that European Americans, African Americans, Asian Americans, and Latino and Latina Americans tend to agree on the facial features that they find to be attractive (Cunningham et al., 1995). They all prefer female faces with large eyes; greater distance between the eyes; small noses; narrower faces with smaller chins; high, expressive eyebrows; larger lower lips; and a well-groomed, full head of hair.

Consider the methodology of a study that compared the facial preferences of people in Japan and England. Perrett (1994) created computer composites of the faces of 60 women. Part A of Figure 7.1 is a composite of the 15 women who were rated the most attractive. He then used computer enhancement to exaggerate the differences between the composite of the 60—that is, the average face—and the composite of the 15 most attractive women. He found that both Japanese and British men deemed women with large eyes, high cheekbones, and narrow jaws to be the most attractive (Perret, 1994). Computer enhancement resulted in the image shown in Part B of Figure 7.1. The enhanced composite has still higher cheekbones and a narrower jaw than Part A. Part B was then rated as the most attractive image. Similar results were found for the image of a Japanese woman.

Cunningham and his colleagues (1995) reported historical anecdotes that suggest that the facial preferences of people as diverse as Europeans, Black Africans, Native Americans, Indians (in India, that is), and Chinese are quite consistent. They quoted from Charles Darwin's 1871 treatise, *The Descent of Man, and Selection in Relation to Sex*:

> Mr. Winwood Reade . . . who has had ample opportunities for observation [with Black Africans] who have never associated with Europeans is convinced that their ideas of beauty are, on the whole, the same as ours; and Dr. Rohlfs writes to me the same effect with respect to Borneo and the countries inhabited by the Pullo tribes. . . . Capt. Burton believes that a woman whom we consider beautiful is admired throughout the world.

Darwin believed that our physical preferences were largely inborn and related to survival of our species. What do you think? Do you believe that "their ideas of beauty are, on the whole, the same as ours"? Or do you think that research hasn't yet ferreted out significant cultural or ethnic differences that might exist? If there is ethnic consistency in these preferences, how would you explain them? For example, do you believe

- that they are coincidental?
- that there has been more exchange of ideas among cultures than has been believed?
- that there is something instinctive about them?

A   B

Figure 7.1. What Features Contribute to Facial Attractiveness? In both England and Japan, features such as large eyes, high cheekbones, and narrow jaws contribute to perceptions of the attractiveness of women. Part A is a computer composite of the faces of 15 women rated as the most attractive of a group of 60. Part B is a computer composite that exaggerates the features of these 15 women. That is, they are developed further in the direction that separates them from the average of the full group.

long-term relationships, physical appeal probably plays a "filtering" role. Unless a prospective date meets minimal physical standards, we might not look beneath the surface for "more meaningful" traits.

Nevid's results have been replicated in studies on attraction and on choice of mates. Women place relatively greater emphasis than men on traits like vocational status, earning potential, expressiveness, kindness, consideration, dependability, and fondness for children. Men give relatively more consideration to youth, physical attractiveness, cooking ability (can't they switch on the microwave by themselves?), and frugality (Howard et al., 1987; Sprecher et al., 1994). When it comes to mate selection, females in a sample of students from Germany and the Netherlands also emphasized the financial prospects and status of a potential mate, whereas males emphasized the importance of physical attractiveness (de Raad & Doddema-Winsemius, 1992). A study of more than 200 Korean college students found that in mate selection, women placed relatively more emphasis on education, jobs, and family of origin than men did (Brown, 1994). Men placed relatively more emphasis on physical attractiveness and affection. (Yes, men were more "romantic." Women were more pragmatic.)

Susan Sprecher and her colleagues (1994) surveyed a national probability sample of 13,017 English- or Spanish-speaking people, age 19 or above, living in households in the United States. In one section of their questionnaire, they asked respondents how willing they would be to marry someone who was older, younger, of a different religion, not likely to hold a steady job, not good looking, and so forth. Each item was followed by a 7-point scale in which 1 meant "not at all" and 7 meant "very willing." As shown in Table 7.1, women were more willing than men to marry someone who was not good looking. On the other hand, women were less willing to marry someone not likely to hold a steady job.

Truth?Fiction?
Revisited

It is not true that physical appeal is the most important trait we seek in partners for long-term relationships. Your second author conducted a survey of college men and women in the early 1980s and found that psychological characteristics such as warmth, fidelity, honesty, and sensitivity were rated higher in importance than physical attractiveness as desirable qualities in a prospective partner for a meaningful, long-term relationship (Nevid, 1984). Physical attractiveness won out when students were asked to consider the qualities that are most important in a partner for a sexual relationship. Overall, however, men placed greater emphasis on the physical characteristics of their partners for both types of relationships than did women. Women placed more value on qualities such as warmth, assertiveness, wit, and ambition. The single most highly desired quality students wanted in long-term partners was honesty. Honestly.

TABLE 7.1		
Sex Differences in Mate Preferences		
How willing would you be to marry someone who . . .	Men	Women
• was not "good-looking"?	3.41	4.42**
• was older than you by 5 or more years?	4.15	5.29**
• was younger than you by 5 or more years?	4.54	2.80**
• was not likely to hold a steady job?	2.73	1.62**
• would earn much less than you?	4.60	3.76**
• would earn much more than you?	5.19	5.93**
• had more education than you?	5.22	5.82**
• had less education than you?	4.67	4.08**
• had been married before?	3.35	3.44
• already had children?	2.84	3.11*
• was of a different religion?	4.24	4.31
• was of a different race?	3.08	2.84**

Source: Based on information in Susan Sprecher, Quintin Sullivan, & Elaine Hatfield (1994). Mate Selection Preferences: Gender Differences Examined in a National Sample. *Journal of Personality and Social Psychology, 66*(6), 1074–1080.

*Difference statistically significant at the .01 level of confidence.

**Difference statistically significant at the .001 level of confidence.

A World of Diversity

Sex Differences in Preferences in Mates across 37 Cultures

What do men in Nigeria, Japan, Brazil, Canada, and the United States have in common? For one thing, men in these countries report that they prefer mates who are younger than themselves. Buss (1994) reviewed survey evidence on the preferred age difference between oneself and one's mate in 37 cultures (representing 33 countries) in Europe, Africa, Asia, Australia, New Zealand, and North and South America. In every culture men preferred younger mates (the range was from 0.38 years to 6.45 years). Women, however, preferred older mates (the range was from 1.82 years to 5.1 years).

Sex differences in the preferred age of mates paralleled actual differences in age of men and women at the time of marriage. Men were between two and five years older on the average than their wives at the time of marriage. The smallest average age difference at marriage, 2.1 years, was found in Poland. The largest average difference, 4.92 years, was found in Greece. Men in the mainland United States averaged 2.71 years older than women at the time of marriage. In Canada, men were 2.51 years older than their mates, on the average.

Buss found that in all 37 cultures, men placed greater value on a prospective partner's "good looks" than did women. On the other hand, women in 36 of 37 cultures placed greater value on "good earning capacity" of prospective mates.

The consistency of Buss's findings lends credence to the notion that there are widespread sex differences in preferences with respect to age, physical characteristics, and financial status of prospective mates. Generally speaking, men place greater value on the physical attractiveness and relative youth of prospective mates. Women place relatively greater value on the earning capacity of prospective mates. Buss interpreted women's preferences for relatively older mates as additional evidence that women appraise future mates on the basis of their ability to provide for a wife and family, because age and income tend to be linked among men.

Despite these sex differences in preferences for mates, Buss found that both men and women placed greater weight on personal qualities than on looks or income potential of prospective mates. In *all* 37 cultures, the characteristics "kind, understanding" and "intelligent" were rated higher than earning power or physical attractiveness.

Are Preferences Concerning Attractiveness Inherited? On the surface, sex differences in perceptions of attractiveness seem unbearably sexist—and perhaps they are. Yet some evolutionary psychologists believe that evolutionary forces favor the continuation of sex differences in preferences for mates because certain preferred traits provide reproductive advantages (Bjorklund & Kipp, 1996; Fisher, 2000). Some physical features, like cleanliness, good complexion, clear eyes, good teeth, good hair, firm muscle tone, and a steady gait are universally appealing to both females and males (Ford & Beach, 1951). Perhaps they are markers of reproductive potential (Symons, 1995). Age and health may be relatively more important to a woman's appeal, because these characteristics tend to be associated with her reproductive capacity: the "biological clock" limits her reproductive potential. Physical characteristics associated with a woman's youthfulness, such as smooth skin, firm muscle tone, and lustrous hair, may thus have become more closely linked to a woman's appeal (Buss, 1994). A man's reproductive value, however, may depend more on how well he can provide for his family than on his age or physical appeal. The value of men as repro-

Beauty and Culture Can you find Mr. or Ms. Right among these people? Are your judgments of physical beauty based on universal standards or on your cultural experiences? Evolutionary psychologist David Buss found some nearly universal standards for beauty in his study of 37 cultures.

ducers, therefore, is more intertwined with factors that contribute to a stable environment for child rearing—such as economic status and reliability. Evolutionary psychologists argue that these sex differences in mate preferences may have been passed down through the generations as part of our genetic heritage (Buss, 1994; Symons, 1995).

Men's interest in younger women occurs in both preliterate and industrialized societies (Buss, 1994). Female jealousy of younger women is another thread that spans cultures. Sexual competition, according to Margaret Mead, generally involves

the struggle between stronger older men and weaker younger men or between more attractive younger women and more entrenched older ones. (Mead, 1967, p. 198)

The evolutionary view of sex differences in preferences for mates is largely speculative and not fully consistent with the evidence. Despite sex differences, both men and women report that they place greater weight on personal characteristics than on physical features in judging prospective mates (Buss, 1994). Many women, like men, still prefer physically appealing partners (Bixler, 1989). Women also tend to marry men similar to themselves in physical attractiveness as well as socioeconomic standing. Note also that older men are more likely than younger men to die from natural causes. From the standpoint of reproductive advantages, women would thus achieve greater success by marrying fit, younger males who are likely to survive during the child-rearing years than by marrying older, higher-status males. Moreover, similar cultural influences, rather than inherited dispositions, may explain commonalities across cultures in sex differences in mate preferences. For example, in societies in which women are economically dependent on men, a man's appeal may depend more on his financial resources than on his physical appeal.

The Matching Hypothesis: Who Is "Right" for You?

Do not despair if you are less than exquisite in appearance, along with most of us mere mortals. You may be saved from permanently blending in with the wallpaper by the effects of the **matching hypothesis.**

Question: What is the matching hypothesis? The matching hypothesis holds that people tend to develop romantic relationships with people who are similar to themselves in physical attractiveness rather than the local Will Smith or Jennifer Lopez look-alike.

Researchers have found that people who are involved in long-term relationships tend to be matched in physical attractiveness (Kalick, 1988). Young couples even tend to be matched in weight (Schafer & Keith, 1990). The central motive for seeking "matches" seems to be fear of rejection by more appealing people (Bernstein et al., 1983).

There are exceptions to the matching hypothesis. Now and then we find a beautiful woman in a relationship with a plain or ugly man (or vice versa). How do we explain it? What, after all, would *she* see in *him*? According to one study (Bar-Tal & Saxe, 1976), people judging "mismatched" pairs may tend to ascribe wealth, intelligence, or success to the man. We seek an unseen factor that will balance the physical

Matching hypothesis
The concept that people tend to develop romantic relationships with people who are similar to themselves in attractiveness.

Who Is Right for You? Research shows that people tend to pair off with others who are similar in physical characteristics and personality traits.

attractiveness of one partner. For some mismatched couples, similarities in attitudes and personalities may balance out differences in physical attractiveness.

More Than Beauty Matching applies not only to physical appeal. Our sex and marital partners tend to be like us in race and ethnicity, age, level of education, and religion. Consider some findings of the NHSLS study (Michael et al., 1994):

- The sex partners of nearly 94% of single European American men are European American women. About 2% of single European American men are partnered with Latina American women, 2% with Asian American women, and fewer than 1% with African American women.
- The sex partners of nearly 82% of African American men are African American women. Nearly 8% of African American men are partnered with European American women. Under 5% are partnered with Latina American women.
- About 83% of the women and men in the study chose partners within 5 years of their own age and of the same or a similar religion.
- Of all the women in the study, *not one* with a graduate college degree had a partner who had not finished high school.
- Men with a college degree almost never had sexual relationships with women with much more or much less education than they had.

Truth?Fiction?
Revisited

Actually, it is not true that "Opposites attract." We are actually *less* apt, that is, to be attracted to people who disagree with our views and tastes than to people who share them.

Attitudes: Do "Opposites Attract," or Do "Birds of a Feather Flock Together"?

Question: Do "opposites attract," or do "birds of a feather flock together"? Why do the great majority of us have partners from our own backgrounds? One reason is that marriages and other long-term relationships are made in the neighborhood and not in heaven (Michael et al., 1994). That is, we tend to live among people who are similar to us in background and thus come into contact with them. Another is that we are drawn to people who are similar in their attitudes. People similar in background are more likely to be similar in their attitudes. Similarity in attitudes and tastes is a key contributor to attraction, friendships, and love relationships (Cappella & Palmer, 1990; Griffin & Sparks, 1990; Laumann et al., 1994).

Let us also note a sex difference. Evidence shows that women place greater weight on attitude similarity as a determinant of attraction to a stranger of the other sex than do men, whereas men place more value on physical attractiveness (Feingold, 1991).

We also tend to *assume* that people we find attractive share our attitudes (Dawes, 1989; Marks et al., 1981). The physical attraction between Candy and Stretch motivated them to pretend that their preferences, tastes, and opinions coincided. They entered into an unspoken agreement not to discuss their religious differences. When sexual attraction is strong, perhaps we want to think that we can iron out all the kinks in the relationship. Although similarity may be important in determining initial attraction, compatibility appears to be a stronger predictor of maintaining an intimate relationship (Vinacke et al., 1988).

Reciprocity: If You Like Me, You Must Have Excellent Judgment

Has anyone told you that you are good-looking, brilliant, and emotionally mature to boot? That your taste is elegant? Ah, what superb judgment!

When we feel admired and complimented, we tend to return these feelings and behaviors. This is called **reciprocity**. *Question: What is the role of reciprocity in*

Reciprocity Mutual exchange.

"The (Electronic) Nearness of You"

Physical closeness, or proximity, has always been a factor in interpersonal attraction. People have always been drawn to the boy or girl next door (or next cave?). People tend to form romantic relationships with the people they meet in the neighborhood, in school, in their religious community, or on the job.

In the age of electronics, proximity is closer, yet it can also be farther away. It's as close as the monitor in front of your nose as you surf the net. Yet you can find yourself corresponding with, and perhaps feeling attracted to, people who are thousands of miles away.

When you meet somebody in person, you immediately observe what they look like, you hear their voices, and—according to some researchers—perhaps you get something like a sniff of their pheromones. But when you meet somebody in a chatroom or a computer-mediated multiuser dungeon, the cues that might spark interest are different. Mantovani (2001) notes that in the case of online relationships, the use of the written (keyboarded) language becomes more important; timing and the speed of writing and responding are crucial; and punctuation and those smiley-faced emoticons can all make a difference. But frequency of contact in the virtual world, as in the real world, plays a role (Levine, 2000; Montovani, 2001). Visiting the same chatroom repeatedly allows mutual awareness to develop and suggests similarity in interests.

Deb Levine (2000) notes that people are more likely to disclose intimate information about themselves on the Internet, perhaps because the actual—or unknown—distance between the parties provides a sense of security. Similarly, other people are quicker to reciprocate expressions of interest. Levine notes that flirting and erotic activity on the Internet can be extremely exciting, but they can also build unrealistic expectations and disqualify participants for relationships in the physical world. (Would you want to have a real-world relationship with someone who quickly enters sexual discussions online?)

Levine and Mantovani both warn that expressions of similarity are easy to feign on the net. Levine (2000) warns against becoming overly wrapped up in people who are reluctant to exchange sound files or pictures. And she adds that it makes sense to meet in the real world within a month or so to check out the accuracy of computer-mediated impressions—preferably in a safe, public place.

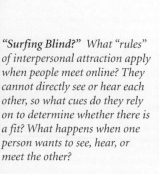

"Surfing Blind?" What "rules" of interpersonal attraction apply when people meet online? They cannot directly see or hear each other, so what cues do they rely on to determine whether there is a fit? What happens when one person wants to see, hear, or meet the other?

interpersonal attraction? Reciprocity is a potent determinant of attraction (Condon & Crano, 1988). We tend to be much more warm, helpful, and candid when we are with strangers who we believe like us (Clark et al., 1989; Curtis & Miller, 1986). We even tend to welcome positive comments from others when we know them to be inaccurate (Swann et al., 1987).

Review: Attraction: The Force That Binds?

Reflect

What do you look for in a romantic partner or a prospective mate? Why?

CriticalThinking

Do your own preferences in a romantic partner appear to support or repudiate evolutionary theory? Explain.

1. Research shows that physical _____ is a major determinant of interpersonal and sexual attraction.

2. In our culture, (*Taller* or *Shorter*?) men are considered to be more attractive by women.

3. (*Only males* or *Both females and males*?) find slenderness to be attractive.

4. In our culture, women with a waist-to-hip ratio of _____ are considered to be most attractive.

5. American males generally prefer women with (*Large* or *Small*?) eyes.

6. (*Both females and males* or *Only females*?) tend to prefer people of the other sex who are socially dominant.

7. A person's name (*Has* or *Does not have*?) an effect on perceptions of her or his attractiveness.

8. (*Women* or *Men*?) place relatively greater emphasis on traits like vocational status and reliability.

9. According to Sprecher's research, (*Women* or *Men*?) are more willing to marry someone who is not good-looking.

10. (*Women* or *Men*?) in Nigeria, Japan, Brazil, Canada, and the United States report that they prefer mates who are younger than themselves.

11. In all 37 cultures surveyed by Buss, (*Earning power, Physical attractiveness,* or *Kindness*?) was rated as the most important quality in a mate.

12. Evolutionary psychologists believe that evolutionary forces favor the continuation of sex differences in preferences for mates because preferred traits provide _____ advantages.

13. According to the _____ hypothesis, people tend to develop romantic relationships with people who are similar to themselves in physical attractiveness.

14. (*Similarity* or *Dissimilarity*?) in attitudes and tastes is a key contributor to attraction and love.

15. We tend to return or _____ feelings of liking.

Perhaps the power of reciprocity has enabled many couples to become happy with one another and reasonably well adjusted. By reciprocating positive words and actions, a person can perhaps stoke neutral or mild feelings into robust, affirmative feelings of attraction.

Attraction can lead to feelings of love. Let us now turn to that most fascinating topic.

Love: "The Morning and the Evening Star"?

For thousands of years, poets have sought to capture love in words. A 17th-century poet wrote that his love was like "a red, red rose." In Sinclair Lewis's novel *Elmer Gantry*, love is "the morning and the evening star." Love is beautiful and elusive. It shines, brilliant and heavenly. Passion and romantic love are also earthy and sexy, brimming with sexual desire.

Romantic love is hardly unique to our culture. Researchers report finding evidence of romantic love in 147 of the 166 different cultures they studied in a recent cross-cultural comparison (Jankowiak & Fischer, 1992). Romantic love occurs even in most preliterate societies.

Romantic love involves stories that we make up about ourselves, and stories in our culture (Sternberg et al., 2001). Our culture idealizes the concept of romantic love (Hatfield & Rapson, 2002; Hendrick & Hendrick, 2003). Thus we readily identify with the plight of the "star-crossed" lovers in *Romeo and Juliet* and *West Side Story,* who sacrificed for love. We learn that "love makes the world go round" and that "love is everything." Like other aspects of sexual and social behavior among humans, the concept of love must be understood within a cultural context. Luckily (or miserably), we have such a context in Western culture. . . .

The Greek Heritage

The concept of love can be traced back at least as far as the classical age of Greece. *Question: What concepts of love were held by the ancient Greeks?* The Greeks distinguished four concepts related to the modern meanings of love: *storge, agape, philia,* and *eros.*

Storge is loving attachment, deep friendship, or nonsexual affection. It is the emotion that binds friends and parents and children. Some scholars believe that even romantic love is a form of attachment that is similar to the types of attachments infants have to their mothers (Moore & Leung, 2002; Stephan & Bachman, 1999; Tucker & Anders, 1999).

Agape is similar to generosity and charity. It implies the wish to share one's bounty and is epitomized by anonymous donations of money. In relationships, it is characterized by selfless giving. Agape, according to Lee's research, is the kind of love least frequently found between adults in committed relationships.

Philia is closest in meaning to friendship. It is based on liking and respect, rather than sexual desire. It involves the desire to do and enjoy things with the other person and to see him or her when one is lonely or bored.

Eros is closest in meaning to our concept of passion. Eros was a character in Greek mythology (transformed in Roman mythology into Cupido, now called Cupid) who would shoot unsuspecting people with his love arrows, causing them to fall madly in love with the person who was nearest to them at the time. Erotic love embraces sudden passionate desire: "love at first sight" and "falling head over heels in love." Younger college students are more likely to believe in love at first sight and that "love conquers all" than older (and wiser?) college students (Knox et al., 1999a). Passion can be so gripping that one is convinced that life has been changed forever. This feeling of sudden transformation was captured by the Italian poet Dante Alighieri (1265–1321), who exclaimed upon first beholding his beloved Beatrice, "*Incipit vita nuova,*" which can be translated as "My life begins anew." Romantic love can also be earthy and sexy. In fact, sexual arousal and desire may be the strongest component of passionate or romantic love. Romantic love begins with a powerful physical attraction or feelings of passion and is associated with strong physiological arousal.

Unlike the Greeks, we tend to use the word *love* to describe everything from feelings of affection toward another to romantic ardor to sexual intercourse ("making love"). Still, different types or styles of love are recognized in our own culture, as we shall see.

Romantic Love in Contemporary Western Culture

The experience of *romantic love,* as opposed to loving attachment or sexual arousal per se, occurs within a cultural context in which the concept is idealized

---

Storge (STORE-gay) Loving attachment and nonsexual affection; the type of emotion that binds parents to children.

Agape (AH-gah-pay) Selfless love; a kind of loving that is similar to generosity and charity.

Philia (FEEL-yuh) Friendship love, which is based on liking and respect rather than sexual desire.

Eros The kind of love that is closest in meaning to the modern-day concept of passion.

(Berscheid, 2003; Hatfield & Rapson, 2002; Hendrick & Hendrick, 2003). ***Question: How does the concept of romantic love fit into Western culture?*** Western culture has a long tradition of idealizing the concept of romantic love, as represented, for instance, by romantic fairy tales that have been passed down through the generations. In fact, our exposure to the concept of romantic love may begin with hearing the fairy tales of Sleeping Beauty, Cinderella, and Snow White—along with their princes charming. Later perhaps, the concept of romantic love blossoms with exposure to romantic novels, television and film scripts, and the heady tales of friends and relatives.

During adolescence, strong sexual arousal along with an idealized image of the object of our desires leads us to label our feelings as love. We may learn to speak of "love" rather than "lust," because sexual desire in the absence of a committed relationship might be viewed as primitive or animalistic. Being "in love" ennobles attraction and sexual arousal, not only to society but also to oneself. Unlike lust, love can be discussed even at the dinner table. If others think we are too young to experience "the real thing"—which presumably includes knowledge of and respect for the other person's personality traits—our feelings may be called "puppy love" or a "crush."

Western society maintains much of the double standard toward sexuality. Thus, women are more often expected to justify sexual experiences as involving someone they love. Young men usually need not attribute sexual urges to love. So men are more apt to deem love a "mushy" concept. The vast majority of people in the United States nonetheless believe romantic love is a prerequisite for marriage or another kind of long-term or permanent relationship. Romantic love is rated by young people as the single most important reason for marriage (Roper Organization, 1985). You can explore your self-perceptions of being a romantic or a realist when it comes to love by completing the nearby Love Attitudes Scale.

When reciprocated, romantic love is usually a source of deep fulfillment and ecstasy (Hatfield & Rapson, 2002). How wonderful when love meets its match! When love is unrequited, however, it can lead to emptiness, anxiety, or despair. Romantic love can thus teeter between states of ecstasy and misery. Perhaps no other feature of our lives can lift us up as high or plunge us as low as romantic love.

Infatuation Versus "True Love": Will Time Tell? Perhaps you first noticed each other when your eyes met across a crowded room, like the star-crossed lovers in *West Side Story.* Or perhaps you met when you were both assigned to the same Bunsen burner in chemistry lab—less romantic but closer to the flame. However it happened, the meeting triggered such an electric charge through your body that you could not get him (or her) out of your mind. Were you truly in love, however, or was it merely a passing fancy? Was it infatuation or the "real thing"—a "true," lasting, and mutual love? How do you tell them apart?

Perhaps you don't, at least not at first. **Infatuation** is a state of intense absorption in or focusing on another person. It is usually accompanied by sexual desire, elation, and general physiological arousal or excitement. Some refer to passion as infatuation. Others dub it a "crush." Both monikers suggest that it is a passing fancy. In infatuation, your heart may pound whenever the other person draws near or enters your fantasies.

Infatuation A state of intense absorption in or focus on another person, which is usually accompanied by sexual desire, elation, and general physiological arousal or excitement; passion.

Infatuation or "True Love"? Infatuation is a state of intense absorption in another person. It is characterized by sexual longing and general excitement. Infatuation is often referred to as passion or as a crush. Infatuation is assumed to fade as relationships develop.

Self-Assessment

Are You a Romantic or a Realist? The Love Attitudes Scale

David Knox of East Carolina University contrasts romantic love with *realistic love*—the kind of love that is maintained across the years. Partners who share a realistic love have the blinders off. They accept and cherish each other, warts and all.

Knox (1983) developed the Love Attitudes Scale to evaluate the degree to which people hold a romantic or realistic view of love. How about you? Are you a realist or a romantic when it comes to matters of the heart? To find out, complete the scale, and then turn to the scoring key in the Appendix.

Directions: Circle the number that best represents your opinion on each item according to the following code. Add up your scores to arrive at a total score.

1 = Strongly agree (SA)
2 = Mildly agree (MA)
3 = Undecided (U)
4 = Mildly disagree (MD)
5 = Strongly disagree (SD)

1. Love doesn't make sense. It just is.   1 2 3 4 5
2. When you fall "head over heels" in love, it's sure to be the real thing.   1 2 3 4 5
3. To be in love with someone you would like to marry but can't is a tragedy.   1 2 3 4 5
4. When love hits, you know it.   1 2 3 4 5
5. Common interests are really unimportant; as long as each of you is truly in love, you will adjust.   1 2 3 4 5
6. It doesn't matter if you marry after you have known your partner for only a short time as long as you know you are in love.   1 2 3 4 5
7. If you are going to love a person, you will "know" after a short time.   1 2 3 4 5
8. As long as two people love each other, the educational differences they have really do not matter.   1 2 3 4 5
9. You can love someone even though you do not like any of that person's friends.   1 2 3 4 5
10. When you are in love, you are usually in a daze.   1 2 3 4 5
11. Love "at first sight" is often the deepest and most enduring type of love.   1 2 3 4 5
12. When you are in love, it really does not matter what your partner does because you will love him or her anyway.   1 2 3 4 5

13. As long as you really love a person, you will be able to solve the problems you have with that person.   1 2 3 4 5
14. Usually you can really love and be happy with only one or two people in the world.   1 2 3 4 5
15. Regardless of other factors, if you truly love another person, that is a good enough reason to marry that person.   1 2 3 4 5
16. It is necessary to be in love with the one you marry to be happy.   1 2 3 4 5
17. Love is more of a feeling than a relationship.   1 2 3 4 5
18. People should not get married unless they are in love.   1 2 3 4 5
19. Most people truly love only once during their lives.   1 2 3 4 5
20. Somewhere there is an ideal mate for most people.   1 2 3 4 5
21. In most cases, you will "know it" when you meet the right partner.   1 2 3 4 5
22. Jealousy usually varies directly with love; that is, the more you are in love, the greater your tendency to become jealous will be.   1 2 3 4 5
23. When you are in love, you are motivated by what you feel rather than by what you think.   1 2 3 4 5
24. Love is best described as an exciting rather than a calm thing.   1 2 3 4 5
25. Most divorces probably result from falling out of love rather than failing to adjust.   1 2 3 4 5
26. When you are in love, your judgment is usually not too clear.   1 2 3 4 5
27. Love often comes only once in a lifetime.   1 2 3 4 5
28. Love is often a violent and uncontrollable emotion.   1 2 3 4 5
29. When selecting a marriage partner, differences in social class and religion are of small importance compared with love.   1 2 3 4 5
30. No matter what anyone says, love cannot be understood.   1 2 3 4 5

Total Score the Love Attitudes Scale: _____

Source: Knox, D. (1983). *The Love Attitudes Inventory* (rev. ed.). Saluda, NC: Family Life Publications. Reprinted with permission.

For the first month or two, infatuation and the more enduring forms of romantic love are hard to differentiate. At first, both may be characterized by intense focusing or absorption. Infatuated people may become so absorbed that they cannot sleep, work, or carry out routine chores. Logic and reason are swept aside (Hatfield & Rapson, 2002). Infatuated people hold idealized images of their love objects and overlook their faults. Caution may be cast to the winds. In some cases, couples in the throes of infatuation rush to the altar, only to find a few weeks or months later that they are not well suited.

As time goes on, signs that distinguish infatuation from a lasting romantic love begin to emerge. The partners begin to view each other more realistically and determine whether or not the relationship should continue. Although the tendency to idealize one's lover is strongest at the outset of a relationship, we should note that a so-called "positive illusion" tends to persist in relationships (Martz et al., 1998). That is, we maintain some tendency to differentiate our partners from the average and also to differentiate the value of our relationships from the average.

Infatuation is based on feelings of passion but not on the deeper feelings of attachment and caring that typify a more lasting mutual love (Hatfield & Rapson, 2002). Although infatuation may be a passing fancy, it can be supplanted by the deeper feelings of attachment and caring that characterize enduring love relationships.

Note, too, that infatuation is not a necessary first step on the path to a lasting mutual love. Some couples develop deep feelings of love without ever experiencing the fireworks of infatuation (Barnes & Sternberg, 1997). Or sometimes one partner is infatuated while the other manages to keep his or her head below the clouds.

Contemporary Models of Love: Dare Science Intrude?

Despite the importance of love, scientists have historically paid little attention to it. Some people believe that love cannot be analyzed scientifically. Love, they maintain, should be left to the poets, philosophers, and theologians. Yet researchers are now applying the scientific method to the study of love. They recognize that love is a complex concept, involving many areas of experience—emotional, cognitive, and motivational (Berscheid, 2003). They have reinforced the Greek view that there are different kinds and styles of love. Let us consider some of the views of love that have emerged from modern theorists and researchers.

Love as Appraisal of Arousal Question: What is the model of love proposed by Berscheid and Walster? Social psychologists Ellen Berscheid and Elaine Hatfield (Berscheid, 2003; Berscheid & Walster, 1978; Hatfield & Rapson, 2002) define **romantic love** in terms of a state of intense physiological arousal and the cognitive appraisal of that arousal as love. The physiological arousal may be experienced as a pounding heart, sweaty palms, and butterflies in the stomach when one is in the presence of or thinking about one's love interest. Cognitive appraisal of the arousal means attributing it to some cause, such as fear or love. The perception that one has fallen in love is thus derived from several simultaneous events: (1) a state of intense physiological arousal that is connected with an appropriate love object (that is, a person, not an event like a rock concert), (2) a cultural setting that idealizes romantic love, and (3) the attribution of the arousal to feelings of love toward the person.

Styles of Love Question: What are the various "styles" of love? Some psychologists speak in terms of *styles* of love. Susan and Clyde Hendrick (2002) speak of love as a positive emotion that contributes to happiness, feelings of psychological well-being, and optimism about the future (2002). The Hendricks (2003) developed a Love Attitude Scale that suggests the existence of six styles of love. The following is a list of

Romantic love A kind of love characterized by feelings of passion and intimacy.

the styles. Each one is exemplified by statements similar to those on the original scale. As you can see, the styles owe a debt to the Greeks:

1. *Romantic love (eros):* "My lover fits my ideal." "My lover and I were attracted to one another immediately."
2. *Game-playing love (ludus):* "I keep my lover up in the air about my commitment." "I get over love affairs pretty easily."
3. *Friendship (storge, philia):* "The best love grows out of an enduring friendship."
4. *Logical love (pragma):* "I consider a lover's potential in life before committing myself." "I consider whether my lover will be a good parent."
5. *Possessive, excited love (mania):* "I get so excited about my love that I cannot sleep." "When my lover ignores me, I get sick all over."
6. *Selfless love (agape):* "I would do anything I can to help my lover." "My lover's needs and wishes are more important than my own."

Most people who are "in love" experience a number of these styles, but the Hendricks (1986) found some interesting sex differences in styles of love. College men are significantly more likely than college women to develop game-playing and romantic love styles. College women are more apt than college men to develop friendly, logical, and possessive love styles. (There were no sex differences in selfless love.) The Hendricks (2003) have also found that romantically involved couples tend to experience the same kinds of love styles. They also found evidence that couples with romantic and selfless styles of love are more likely to remain together. A game-playing love style leads to unhappiness, however, and is one reason that relationships come to an end.

Sternberg's Triangular Theory of Love **Question: What is Sternberg's triangular theory of love?** Psychologist Robert Sternberg (1986, 1988) offers a "triangular theory" of love that organizes the relationships among kinds of love discussed by many theorists, including passionate love, romantic love, and companionate love (Hatfield & Rapson, 2002; Hendrick & Hendrick, 2003). The three building blocks, or components, of loving experiences include

1. *Intimacy:* The experience of warmth toward another person that arises from feelings of closeness, bondedness, and connectedness to the other. Intimacy also involves the desire to give and receive emotional support and to share one's innermost thoughts with the other.
2. *Passion:* An intense romantic or sexual desire for another person, which is accompanied by physiological arousal.
3. *Commitment:* A component of love that involves *commitment* to maintain the relationship through good times and bad.

Sternberg's model is triangular in that various kinds of love can be conceptualized in terms of a triangle in which each vertex represents one of the building blocks (see Figure 7.2). The strength of each component can be represented by the shape of the triangle. For example, a love in which all three components were equally balanced—as in *consummate love*—would be represented by an equilateral triangle, as in Figure 7.2.

The Hendricks (2003) noted that couples who are romantically involved tend to share similar love styles. In terms of Sternberg's model, couples are well matched if they possess corresponding levels of passion, intimacy, and commitment (Drigotas

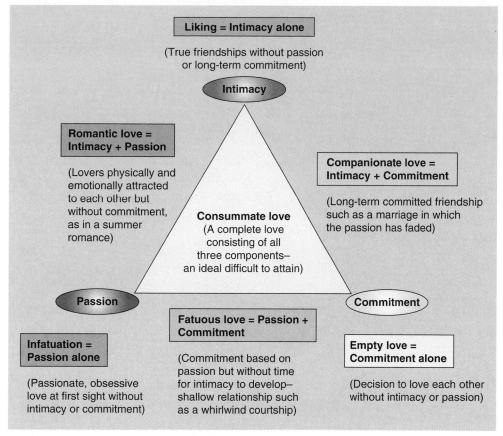

Figure 7.2. The Triangular Model of Love. *According to psychologist Robert Sternberg, love consists of three components, as shown by the vertices of this triangle. Various kinds of love consist of different combinations of these components. Romantic love, for example, consists of passion and intimacy. Consummate love—the cultural ideal—consists of all three.*

et al., 1999; Sternberg, 1988). Compatibility can be represented visually in terms of the congruence of the love triangles. Figure 7.3(A) shows a perfect match, in which the triangles are congruent. Figure 7.3(B) depicts a good match; the partners are similar in the three building blocks of love. Figure 7.3(C) shows a mismatch; major differences exist between the partners on all three components. Relationships

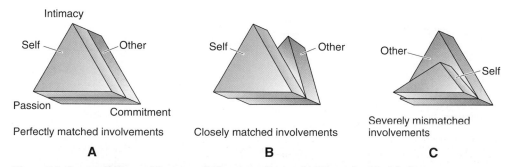

Figure 7.3. Compatibility and Incompatibility, According to the Triangular Model of Love.
Compatibility in terms of Sternberg's types of love can be represented as triangles. Part A shows a perfect match in which triangles are congruent. Part B depicts a good match; the partners are similar according to the three dimensions. Part C shows a mismatch. Major differences exist between the partners on all three components.

Self-Assessment

Sternberg's Triangular Love Scale

Which are the strongest components of your love relationship? Intimacy? Passion? Commitment? All three components? Two of them?

To complete the following scale, fill in the blank spaces with the name of one person you love or care about deeply. Then rate your agreement with each of the items by using a 9-point scale in which 1 = "not at all," 5 = "moderately," and 9 = "extremely." Use points in between to indicate intermediate levels of agreement between these values. Then consult the scoring key in the Appendix.

Intimacy Component

_____ 1. I am actively supportive of _____'s well-being.

_____ 2. I have a warm relationship with _____.

_____ 3. I am able to count on _____ in times of need.

_____ 4. _____ is able to count on me in times of need.

_____ 5. I am willing to share myself and my possessions with _____.

_____ 6. I receive considerable emotional support from _____.

_____ 7. I give considerable emotional support to _____.

_____ 8. I communicate well with _____.

_____ 9. I value _____ greatly in my life.

_____ 10. I feel close to _____.

_____ 11. I have a comfortable relationship with _____.

_____ 12. I feel that I really understand _____.

_____ 13. I feel that _____ really understands me.

_____ 14. I feel that I can really trust _____.

_____ 15. I share deeply personal information about myself with _____.

Passion Component

_____ 16. Just seeing _____ excites me.

_____ 17. I find myself thinking about _____ frequently during the day.

_____ 18. My relationship with _____ is very romantic.

_____ 19. I find _____ to be very personally attractive.

_____ 20. I idealize _____.

_____ 21. I cannot imagine another person making me as happy as _____ does.

_____ 22. I would rather be with _____ than anyone else.

_____ 23. There is nothing more important to me than my relationship with _____.

_____ 24. I especially like physical contact with _____.

_____ 25. There is something almost "magical" about my relationship with _____.

_____ 26. I adore _____.

_____ 27. I cannot imagine life without _____.

_____ 28. My relationship with _____ is passionate.

_____ 29. When I see romantic movies and read romantic books, I think of _____.

_____ 30. I fantasize about _____.

Commitment Component

_____ 31. I know that I care about _____.

_____ 32. I am committed to maintaining my relationship with _____.

_____ 33. Because of my commitment to _____, I would not let other people come between us.

_____ 34. I have confidence in the stability of my relationship with _____.

_____ 35. I could not let anything get in the way of my commitment to _____.

_____ 36. I expect my love for _____ to last for the rest of my life.

_____ 37. I will always feel a strong responsibility for _____.

_____ 38. I view my commitment to _____ as a solid one.

_____ 39. I cannot imagine ending my relationship with _____.

_____ 40. I am certain of my love for _____.

_____ 41. I view my relationship with _____ as permanent.

_____ 42. I view my relationship with _____ as a good decision.

_____ 43. I feel a sense of responsibility toward _____.

_____ 44. I plan to continue my relationship with _____.

_____ 45. Even when _____ is hard to deal with, I remain committed to our relationship.

Source: Sternberg, 1988. Reprinted by permission of Basic Books, Inc., Publishers, New York.

may run aground when partners are mismatched. A relationship may fizzle, rather than sizzle, when one partner experiences more passion than the other, or when one wants a long-term commitment when the other's idea of commitment is to stay the night.

According to the Sternberg model, various combinations of the three elements of love characterize different types of love relationships (see Figure 7.2 and Table 7.2). For example, *infatuation* (passionate love) is typified by strong sexual desire but not by intimacy and commitment. The partners may each feel passionate love for the other, or, as in the case of Tom, such feelings may go unrequited:

> Tom sat behind Lisa in physics class. Tom hated physics, but he could not say the same for Lisa. One look at her was enough to change his life. He had fallen madly in love with her. Instead of listening to the teacher or looking at the blackboard, he would gaze at Lisa throughout the class. Lisa was aware of this and was not happy about it. She did not much care for Tom, and when he tried to start a conversation with her, she moved on as quickly as possible. Tom's staring and his awkwardness in talking to her made her feel uncomfortable. Tom, on the other hand, could think of little else besides Lisa, and his grades began to suffer as he spent the time he should have been devoting to his homework thinking about her. He was a man obsessed. The obsession might have gone on for quite some time had not both Tom and Lisa graduated that June and gone to different colleges. Tom never saw Lisa again, and after several unanswered love letters, he finally gave up on her. (Sternberg, 1988, p. 123)

TABLE 7.2
Types of Love, According to Sternberg's Triangular Model

1. Nonlove	A relationship in which all three components of love are absent. Most of our personal relationships are of this type—casual interactions or acquaintances that do not involve any elements of love.
2. Liking	A loving experience with another person or a friendship in which intimacy is present, but passion and commitment are lacking.
3. Infatuation	A kind of "love at first sight" in which one experiences passionate desires for another person in the absence of both intimacy and commitment components of love.
4. Empty love	A kind of love characterized by commitment (to maintain the relationship) in the absence of either passion or intimacy. Stagnant relationships that no longer involve the emotional intimacy or physical attraction that once characterized them are of this type.
5. Romantic love	A loving experience characterized by the combination of passion and intimacy but without commitment.
6. Companionate love	A kind of love that derives from the combination of intimacy and commitment components of love. This kind of love often occurs in long-term relationships in which passionate attraction between the partners has died down and has been replaced by a kind of committed friendship.
7. Fatuous love	The type of love associated with whirlwind romances and "quickie marriages" in which the passion and commitment components of love are present, but intimacy is not.
8. Consummate love	The full or complete measure of love involving the combination of passion, intimacy, and commitment. Many of us strive to attain this type of complete love in our romantic relationships. Maintaining consummate love may be harder than achieving it.

Source: Adapted from Sternberg, 1988.

Truth?Fiction?
Revisited

It is indeed possible to be in love with someone who is not also a friend. Being in love can refer to states of passion or infatuation, whereas friendship is usually based on shared interests, liking, and respect.

It is true that couples can remain "in love" after passion fades; for example, they can experience companionate love. Companionate love need not be lacking in romance, however. Although passion may have ebbed, sexual pleasure can help strengthen bonds.

Liking is a basis for friendship. It consists of feelings of closeness and emotional warmth without passion or commitment. Liking is not felt toward passing acquaintances. It is reserved for people to whom one feels close enough to share one's innermost feelings and thoughts. We sometimes develop these intimate relationships without making the commitment to maintaining a long-term relationship that typifies other types of love, however. Liking may develop into a passionate love, however, or into a more committed form of love called *companionate love* by many writers, including Sternberg (1988), Clyde and Susan Hendrick (2003), and Elaine Hatfield (Hatfield & Rapson, 2002).

Should lovers also be friends, or are lovers and friends part of the twain that never meet? Candy and Stretch's relationship lacked the quality most often associated with true friendship: the willingness to share confidences. Despite their physical intimacy, their relationship remained so superficial that they couldn't even share information about their religious backgrounds.

Candy and Stretch were "in love" although they were far from friends. Friendship and passionate love do not necessarily overlap. There is nothing that prevents people in love from becoming good friends, however—perhaps even the best of friends. Sternberg's model recognizes that the intimacy we find in true friendships and the passion we find in love are blended in two forms of love—romantic love and consummate love. These love types differ along the dimension of commitment, however.

Romantic love has both passion and intimacy but lacks commitment. Romantic love may burn brightly and then flicker out. Or it may develop into a more complete love, called *consummate love,* in which all three components flower. Desire is accompanied by a deeper intimacy and commitment. The flames of passion can be stoked across the years, even if they do not burn quite as brightly as they once did. Consummate love is most special and certainly an ideal toward which many Westerners strive.

In *empty love,* by contrast, there is naught but commitment. Neither the warm emotional embrace of intimacy nor the flame of passion exists. With empty love, one's lover is a person whom one tolerates and remains with because of a sense of duty. Remaining in an empty-love relationship is often maintained either by personal prescription or social prescription (Cox et al., 1997). *Personal prescription* is based on the belief that one should persist in a relationship. *Social prescription* is based on the belief that one's friends or family members believe that it is right to persist in a relationship.

Sometimes a love relationship has both passion and commitment but lacks intimacy. Sternberg calls this *fatuous (foolish) love.* Fatuous love is associated with whirlwind courtships that burn brightly but briefly as the partners come to the realization that they are not well matched. Intimacy can develop in such relationships, but couples who rush into promises or marriage often find that the realities of their relationships give the lie to their expectations.

In *companionate love,* intimacy and commitment are strong, but passion is lacking. This form of love typifies long-term (so-called Platonic) relationships and marriages in which passion has ebbed but a deep and abiding friendship remains for those with whom our lives are entwined (Hatfield & Rapson, 2002; Hendrick & Hendrick, 2003).

The balance among Sternberg's three aspects of love is likely to shift through the course of a relationship. A strong dose of all three components—found in consummate love—typifies, for many of us, an ideal relationship. At the outset of a relationship, passions may be strong but intimacy weak. Couples may only first be getting to know each other's innermost thoughts and feelings. Time alone does not cause intimacy and commitment to grow, however. Some couples are able to peer into each other's deeper selves and form meaningful commitments at relatively early stages in their relationships. Yet some couples who have been together for many years may remain distant or waver in their commitment. Some couples experience only a faint flickering of passion early in the relationship. Then it becomes quickly extinguished. For some the flames of passion burn ever brightly. Yet many couples find that passion tends to fade while intimacy and commitment grow stronger.

Knowing about these components of love may help couples avoid pitfalls. Couples who recognize that passion exerts a strong pull early in a relationship may be less likely to let passion rush them into a long-term legal commitment. Couples who recognize that it is normal for passions to fade may avoid assuming that their love is at an end when it may, in fact, be changing into a deeper, more intimate and committed form of love. This knowledge may also encourage couples to focus on finding ways of rekindling the embers of romance, rather than looking to escape at the first signs that the embers have cooled.

In this chapter we have discussed interpersonal attraction—the force that initiates social contact. In the next chapter we follow the development of contacts into intimate relationships.

Review: Love: "The Morning and the Evening Star"?

Reflect

Have you ever been in love? How did you know that you were in love?

CriticalThinking

Why do you think that most people in the United States believe that people should get married only when they experience romantic love?

16. According to the ancient Greeks, _____ is the kind of love that defines attachment between parents and children.

17. The Greek concept of _____ is close in meaning to passion.

18. The concept of romantic love occurs within a cultural context in which it is _____.

19. Romantic _____ is rated by young people as the single most important reason for marriage.

20. _____ is a state of intense absorption in another person that is usually accompanied by sexual desire.

21. Infatuation has been likened to _____ love.

22. Berscheid and Walster assert that the perception that one has fallen in love is derived from intense physiological arousal, a cultural setting that idealizes romantic love, and the _____ of the arousal to feelings of love.

23. The Hendricks developed a love attitude scale that suggests the existence of _____ (*How many?*) styles of love among college students.

24. Sternberg offers a triangular theory of love with three components: intimacy, passion, and _____.

25. Couples are well matched if they experience corresponding levels of passion, _____, and commitment.

26. According to Sternberg, liking is characterized by _____ alone.

27. Companionate love in characterized by intimacy and _____.

28. _____ love is characterized by intimacy and passion.

Recite

1. Is physical attractiveness an important consideration in interpersonal attraction?

Physical attractiveness is a major determinant of sexual attraction. In our culture, slenderness is in style. Females and males both consider smiling faces more attractive. Socially dominant men, but not dominant women, are usually found attractive. Women place relatively greater emphasis on traits like vocational status and earning potential, whereas men give relatively more consideration to physical attractiveness. Some evolutionary psychologists believe that evolutionary forces favor such sex differences in preferred traits because these traits provide reproductive advantages.

2. What is the matching hypothesis?

According to the matching hypothesis, people tend to develop romantic relationships with people who are similar to themselves in attractiveness.

3. Do "opposites attract," or do "birds of a feather flock together"?

Research shows that despite the adage "opposites attract," similarity in attitudes and tastes is a strong contributor to attraction, friendships, and love relationships.

4. What is the role of reciprocity in interpersonal attraction?

Our feelings are warmer toward people who appear to like us. Through reciprocation of positive words and actions, neutral or mild feelings may be stoked into strong feelings of attraction.

5. What concepts of love were held by the ancient Greeks?

The Greeks had four concepts related to the modern meanings of love: storge (loving attachment, as between parents and children), agape (generosity and charity), philia (friendship, liking, respect), and eros (passion).

Recite

6. How does the concept of romantic love fit into Western culture?

Western culture has a long tradition of idealizing the concept of romantic love. Most people in the United States see romantic love as prerequisite to marriage. At first, infatuation and more enduring forms of romantic love may be indistinguishable.

7. What is the model of love proposed by Berscheid and Hatfield?

Berscheid and Hatfield define romantic love in terms of intense physiological arousal and cognitive appraisal of that arousal as love. Cultural belief in romantic love contributes to that labeling of arousal.

8. What are the various "styles" of love?

Hendrick and Hendrick suggest that there are six styles of love among college students: romantic love, game-playing love, friendship, logical love, possessive love, and selfless love.

9. What is Sternberg's triangular theory of love?

Sternberg suggests that there are three distinct components of love: intimacy, passion, and commitment. Various combinations of these components typify different kinds of love. Romantic love is characterized by the combination of passion and intimacy. Consummate love—the cultural ideal—is described by all three components. Relationships are more likely to last when the "triangles" that describe each individual's feelings tend to be congruent (to overlap).

Chapter 8

Truth?Fiction?

T / F? Small talk is an insincere method of opening a relationship.

T / F? Only phonies practice opening lines.

T / F? Swift self-disclosure of intimate information is the best way to deepen a new relationship.

T / F? People can have intimate relationships without being sexually intimate.

T / F? Many people remain lonely because they fear being rejected by others.

T / F? Conflict is destructive to a relationship.

T / F? "Love is all you need." That is, when partners truly love one another, they instinctively know how to satisfy each other sexually.

T / F? If you are criticized, the best course is to retaliate.

T / F? Relationships come to an end when the partners cannot resolve their differences.

Relationships and Communication

Preview

Will you, won't you, will you, won't you, will you join the dance?

Lewis Carroll, Alice in Wonderland

No man is an island, entire of it self.

John Donne, No Man Is an Island

"One, two. One, two." A great opening line? In the film *Play It Again, Sam,* Woody Allen plays Allan Felix, a social klutz who has just been divorced. Diane Keaton plays his platonic friend Linda. At a bar one evening with Linda and her husband, Allan Felix spots a young woman on the dance floor who is so attractive that he wishes *he* could have *her* children.

The thing to do, Linda prompts him, is to begin dancing, then dance over to her and "say something." With a bit more prodding, Linda convinces Allan to dance. It's so simple, she tells him. He need only keep time—"One, two, one, two."

"One, two," repeats Allan. Linda shoves him off to his dream woman.

Hesitantly, Allan dances up to her. Working up courage, he says, "One, two. One, two, one, two." He is ignored and finds his way back to Linda.

"Allan, try something more meaningful," Linda implores.

Once more, Allan dances nervously back toward the woman of his dreams. He stammers, "Three, four, three, four."

"*Speak* to her, Allan," Linda insists.

He dances up to her again and tries, "You interested in dancing at all?"

"Get lost, creep," she replies.

Allan dances rapidly back toward Linda. "What'd she say?" Linda asks.

"She'd rather not," he shrugs.

So much for "One, two, one, two" and, for that matter, "Three, four, three, four." Striking up a relationship requires some social skills, and the first few conversational steps can be big ones.

In this chapter we define the stages that lead to intimate relationships. We define intimacy and see that not all relationships—not even all long-term, committed relationships—achieve this level of interrelatedness. Moreover, some of us remain alone, and, perhaps, lonely. There are steps that people can take to overcome loneliness, however, as we illustrate in the pages ahead. Finally, we discuss satisfaction in relationships and enumerate ways of increasing satisfaction by enhancing communication skills.

The ABC(DE)'s of Romantic Relationships

Question: How do romantic relationships develop? Romantic relationships, like people, undergo stages of development. According to **social-exchange theory**, the development reflects the unfolding of social exchanges, which involve the rewards and costs of maintaining the relationship as opposed to dissolving it. During each stage, positive factors sway partners toward maintaining and enhancing their relationship. Negative factors incline them toward letting it deteriorate and end.

Numerous investigators have viewed the development of romantic relationships in terms of phases or stages (Berscheid & Reis, 1998; Dindia & Timmerman, 2003; Hendrick & Hendrick, 2000; Honeycutt & Cantrill, 2001; Levinger, 1980). From their work, we can build a five-stage **ABCDE model** of romantic relationships: (1) *Attraction*, (2) *Building*, (3) *Continuation*, (4) *Deterioration*, and (5) termination, or *Ending*.

Attraction occurs when two people become aware of each other and find one another appealing or enticing. We may find ourselves attracted to an enchanting person "across a crowded room," in a nearby office, or in a new class. We may meet others through blind dates, introductions by mutual friends, computer match-ups, or by "accident." According to the NHSLS study (Michael et al., 1994), married people are most likely to have met their spouses through mutual friends (35%) or self-introductions (32%) (see Figure 8.1). Other sources of introductions are family members (15%) and coworkers, classmates, or neighbors (13%). Unmarried couples also most commonly report meeting through mutual friends and self-introductions (Michael et al., 1994).

Being in a good mood apparently heightens feelings of attraction. George Levinger and his colleagues (Forgas et al., 1994) exposed 128 male and female moviegoers to either a happy or a sad film. Those shown the happy film reported more positive feelings about their partners and their relationships. (Think twice about what you take your date to see.)

Factors that motivate us to build relationships include similarity in physical attractiveness, similarity in attitudes, and mutual liking. Factors that deter building of relationships include lack of physical appeal, dissimilar attitudes, and lack of liking.

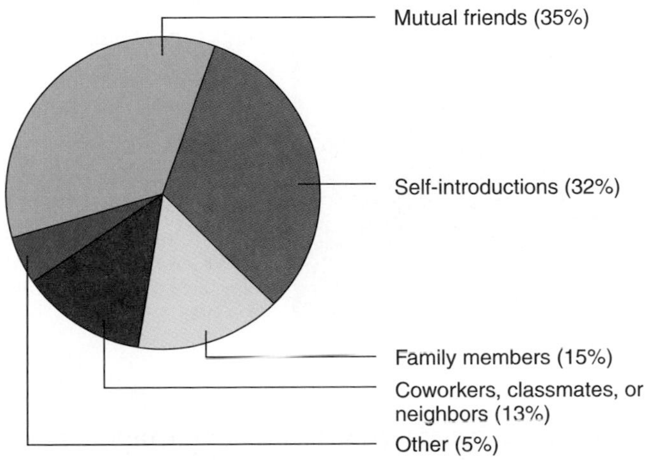

> **Social-exchange theory** The view that the development of a relationship reflects the unfolding of social exchanges—that is, the rewards and costs of maintaining the relationship as opposed to ending it.
>
> **ABCDE model** The view that romantic relationships encompass five stages or phases: attraction, building, continuation, deterioration, and ending.

Figure 8.1. How People Met Their Partners. *According to the NHSLS study (Michael et al., 1994), two-thirds of married people met their partners through either mutual friends or self-introductions. Mutual friends and self-introductions were also the main ways of meeting for unmarried couples in committed relationships.*

New Christian Take on the Old Dating Ritual

Casey Moss and Kara Price never dated each other, or anyone else. They never shared a meal alone, never talked about their dreams or plans. They never kissed and never held hands.

Yet two years ago, when Kara was 14 and Casey was 20 and heading off to medical school, they pledged their lives to each other in an improvised ceremony at their church that they called a betrothal. They exchanged matching signet rings, promised to be faithful, and considered their vows as binding as a marriage. Only then did they set about getting to know each other and thinking of themselves as a couple. With their parents' permission, they decided they could start holding hands.

While their story may seem a throwback to the Victorian age, Casey and Kara are actually on the front edge of a small but growing movement among conservative Christian youths who are rejecting the dominant culture's approach to dating and romance.

They are not simply saying no to premarital sex. They are essentially saying no to premarital romance. Convinced that dating causes emotional pain, broken promises, and sexual straying, they are trying to rewrite the rules for relationships.

Although a formal betrothal like Casey and Kara's is rare—even in conservative Christian circles some would consider their union extreme because of her youth—many people are promoting a similar hand-before-heart approach they call courtship. The commitment to marriage comes first, before a couple is allowed to begin drawing emotionally close. In some cases, they are little more than acquaintances. Even then they are chaperoned and kept accountable by parents, pastors, or responsible peers.

"There has been a big movement in the last several years of people going back to the old courtship model," said Brad A. Voyles, dean of student life at Belhaven College, an evangelical Christian school in Jackson, Mississippi. "You talk to the

Getting Married without Ever Having Dated? *Some conservative Christian couples in the United States are pledging themselves to one another without ever having dated—anyone. What are the advantages of doing so? What are the drawbacks?*

Many studies show that males tend to be more "romantic" (meaning *passionate*) than women in choosing whether to build relationships. For example, three German studies found that men are more likely than women to focus on sex and fun, whereas women are more likely to focus on issues such as communication ability and reciprocity (Hassebrauck, 2003). Thus, in male–male relationships, both partners are

parents to get permission to date the daughter, you don't go on dates by yourself but with groups of people, and dating is for the purpose of getting to know the other person with designs on getting married."

A variety of what are called biblical methods for finding a mate are gaining currency on Web sites, on the campuses of Christian colleges, and in a bevy of books inspired by Joshua Harris's volume *I Kissed Dating Goodbye* (Multnomah Books, 1997), which has sold more than 800,000 copies by the publisher's count and spawned a sequel, *Boy Meets Girl* (Multnomah, 2000).

Like many advocating these ideas, Mr. Harris grew up in the counterculture of Christian home schoolers who are accustomed to seeing themselves as mavericks cutting fresh paths in an ungodly society.

"What really drove my change of perspective on dating," said Mr. Harris, executive pastor at Covenant Life Church in Gaithersburg, Maryland, "was seeing how I had used and hurt different girls in relationships that didn't have a clear purpose and weren't about commitment or pursuing marriage."

Leading someone on is prohibited in the Bible, he said, citing a passage from First Thessalonians that warns against "defrauding." His first book opens with a bride's nightmare in which her groom stands at the altar, holding hands with the phantoms of all his previous girlfriends.

Joshua Goforth, a 22-year-old graphic artist in San Antonio who was schooled by his parents at home, said he observed his friends' habits and concluded early on that "dating is preparation for divorce." He explained: "You're winning a girl's heart, being emotionally or physically involved with her, and then when you're tired of it you just break it off and go to the next girl."

He noticed Noelle Wheeler, who is 24, at a home-schooling conference, and the two later found themselves working together intensively on a book project for a Christian publisher. Last November, he took Ms. Wheeler's father, Richard, out to breakfast at the local International House of Pancakes and nervously asked him for permission to begin to court his daughter. Mr. Wheeler said yes.

"I knew if I could trust his character then it would make a good marriage," said Mr. Wheeler, an evangelist who travels the country portraying Christian heroes in American history. "Because a marriage is built not on love, but on someone who has the character to withstand the storms that marriage brings, the arguments and the disagreements."

At their wedding in June, after saying "I do," the couple say they kissed for the first time in their lives. The kiss was celebrated by their church community as a triumph of Christian courtship.

But even to some like-minded Christian leaders, the revival of old-fashioned courtship rituals is both unrealistic and unnecessary. Jeramy Clark, a youth pastor at Tri-Lakes Chapel, a nondenominational church in Monument, Colorado, said, "Why do we think that just going back a few hundred years and doing it that way is any more godly than dating appropriately now?"

"To me it kind of seems like there's almost a lack of trust that two young people can keep themselves pure," said Mr. Clark, who wrote *I Gave Dating a Chance* (Waterbrook Press, 2000) as a rebuttal to Mr. Harris. "It's almost like, let's not give them the opportunity to make a mistake. I wonder at times, in families like that, whether their children are allowed to drive. There's safety risks when we enter into life, and we may get into a few fender benders along the way."

In his book, Mr. Clark advocates "Lordship dating" and encourages couples to set boundaries mindful of God's will for them to remain pure. He warns girls not to flirt, or brush against boys, or hug. If you must hug, he writes, "you can either put your hand out to protect your chest, or you can stand far enough away to make it a light hug."

Source: Reprinted from Laurie Goodstein (2001, September 5). New Christian take on the old dating ritual. *The New York Times online.*

likely to entertain sexual behavior relatively early. In female–female relationships, both partners are likely to be relatively cautious, unless they are revolting against female stereotypes. The German findings also fit with the evolutionary view that the male is more likely to be the initiator of sexual activity and that the female is more likely to be contemplating the value of the male as a reliable provider.

Therefore, it is not true that small talk is an insincere method of opening a relationship. Successful small talk encourages a couple to venture beneath the surface. At a get-together or a club, individuals may flit about from person to person, exchanging small talk, but now and then a couple finds common ground and pairs off.

Therefore, it is not true that only phonies practice opening lines. Actually, it can be helpful for *everyone* to practice opening lines.

It is not necessarily true that early disclosure of intimate information is the best way to deepen a new relationship. We may value "openness" in our relationships, but it may be a social mistake to open up about too much too soon.

Small talk A superficial kind of conversation that allows exchange of information but stresses breadth of topic coverage, rather than in-depth discussion.

Self-disclosure The revelation of personal, perhaps intimate, information.

Not-So-Small Talk: An Audition for Building a Relationship

Question: What is the role of small talk in building a relationship? **Small talk** enables people to probe one another during the early stages of building a relationship. It helps people find common ground—the overlapping of attitudes and interests—and to check out feelings of attraction (Knapp & Vangelista, 2000). Small talk stresses breadth of topic coverage rather than in-depth discussion. Engaging in small talk may seem "phony," but it is a legitimate trial balloon for a relationship.

"Opening Lines": How Do You Get Things Started?

Question: What is the role of the opening line in building a relationship? One kind of small talk is the greeting, or opening line. We usually precede greetings with eye contact and decide to try talking if eye contact is reciprocated. Avoidance of eye contact may mean that the person is shy, but it can also signify lack of interest. If you are interested in somebody, try a smile and eye contact. If the eye contact is reciprocated, try an opening line, or greeting. These include:

Verbal salutes, such as "Good morning."
Personal inquiries, such as "How are you doing?"
Compliments, such as "I like your outfit."
References to your mutual surroundings, such as "What do you think of that painting?" or "This is a nice apartment house, isn't it?"
References to people or events outside the immediate setting, such as "Have you been following the [local athletic team]?"
References to the other person's behavior, such as "I couldn't help noticing you were sitting alone" or "I see you out on this track every Saturday morning."
References to your own behavior, or to yourself, such as "Hi, my name is Allan Felix" (feel free to use your own name, if you prefer).

The simple "Hi" or "Hello" is very useful. A friendly glance followed by a cheerful hello ought to give you some idea of whether the attraction is reciprocated. If the hello is returned with a friendly smile and inviting eye contact, follow it up with another greeting, such as a reference to your surroundings, the other person's behavior, or your name.

Exchanging "Name, Rank, and Serial Number" Early exchanges are likely to include name, occupation, marital status, and hometown. This has been likened to exchanging "name, rank, and serial number" with the other person. Each person seeks a sociological profile of the other to discover common ground that may provide a basis for pursuing the conversation. An unspoken rule seems to be at work: "If I provide you with some information about myself, you will reciprocate by giving me an equal amount of information about yourself. Or . . . I'll tell you my hometown if you tell me yours" (Knapp & Vangelista, 2000). If the other person is unresponsive, she or he may not be attracted to you. But you may also be awkward in your approach or perhaps turn the other person off by disclosing too much about yourself at the outset.

Self-Disclosure: You Tell Me and I'll Tell You . . . Carefully

Question: What is the role of self-disclosure in building a relationship? **Self-disclosure,** or opening up, is central to building intimate relationships (Ben Ze'ev,

2003; Dindia & Timmerman, 2003). But what sort of information is it safe to disclose upon meeting someone? If you refuse to go beyond name, rank, and serial number, you may look uninterested or as though you are trying to keep things under wraps. But if you spill out the fact that you have a painful rash on your thigh, you may have disclosed too much too soon.

Research suggests that we should refrain from disclosing intimate information too rapidly. In a classic experiment, confederates of the researchers (Wortman et al., 1976) engaged in 10-minute conversations with study participants. Some confederates were "early disclosers," who shared intimate information early. Others, "late disclosers," shared intimate information toward the end of the conversation only. In both cases, the information was identical. Study participants then rated the disclosers. The early disclosers in this study were rated less mature, secure, well adjusted, and genuine than the late disclosers.

On the other hand, rapid self-disclosure seems to be something of a new norm when people meet in cyberspace (Ben-Ze'ev, 2003). Cyberspace allows for relative anonymity and enables people to control what they want to reveal—to safeguard their privacy even as they increase their emotional closeness and openness. The very nature of privacy changes in cyberspace, because matters that are usually kept under wraps tend to be discussed.

If the **surface contact** provided by small talk and initial self-disclosure has been mutually rewarding, partners in a relationship tend to develop feelings of liking for each other (Collins & Miller, 1994). Self-disclosure may build through the course of a relationship as partners come to trust each other enough to share intimate feelings.

Sex Differences in Self-Disclosure A woman complains to a friend, "He never opens up to me. It's like living with a stone wall." Women commonly declare that men are loath to express their feelings. Researchers find that masculine-typed individuals, whether male or female, tend to be less willing to disclose their feelings, perhaps in adherence to the traditional "strong and silent" masculine stereotype (Basow & Rubenfeld, 2003). A study by Susan Basow and Kimberly Rubenfeld (2003) found that feminine-typed individuals are more likely to be empathic and to listen to other people's troubles than masculine-typed individuals, regardless of their anatomic sex.

Factors that encourage continuation of relationships include seeking ways to introduce variety and maintain interest (such as trying out new sexual practices and social activities), showing evidence of caring and positive evaluation (such as sending birthday or Valentine's Day cards), trusting one's partner, perceiving fairness in the relationship, and experiencing feelings of general satisfaction. One of the developments in a continuing relationship is that of **mutuality**, which leads a couple to regard themselves as "we," not just two "I's" who happen to be in the same place at the same time (Neff & Harter, 2003). Mutuality favors continuation and further deepening of the relationship. Mutuality implies cognitive interdependence. Planning for the future in both little ways (What will I do this weekend?) and big ways (What will I do about my education and my career?) comes to include consideration of the needs and desires of one's partner. Cognitive interdependence is related to *intimacy,* as we will see in the following section.

Intimacy: Sharing Inmost Thoughts and Feelings

Question: What is intimacy? **Intimacy** consists of feelings of emotional connectedness with another person and the desire to share inmost thoughts and feelings. Partners in the throes of romantic love usually want to disclose everything to, and

Surface contact A probing phase of building a relationship in which people seek common ground and check out feelings of attraction.

Mutuality A phase in building a relationship in which members of a couple come to regard themselves as "we," no longer as two "I's" who happen to be in the same place at the same time.

Intimacy Feelings of closeness and connectedness that are marked by sharing of inmost thoughts and feelings.

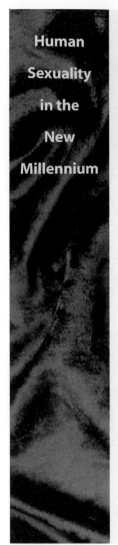

Human Sexuality in the New Millennium

In Modern E-Mail Romance, "Trash" Is Just a Click Away

One summer night, Jason Kellogg, a 24-year-old publishing assistant, left a bar in Brooklyn after spending a good deal of time talking with a woman he had met that evening. When he left the bar, his friends demanded the requisite information: How old is she? Is she from the area? Does she have any good-looking friends? And most important, did you get a phone number?

Mr. Kellogg hesitated on the last question. "Well, not exactly," he said. "She gave me her e-mail."

That was a first for Mr. Kellogg. He sent her an e-mail message a few days later, although nothing came of their correspondence. "I suppose it was better than a flat-out rejection," he said. "She was probably turned off by my bad spelling."

E-mail, which has long been an indispensable tool in business, is beginning to influence more romantic relationships as well. With more and more Americans in front of [computers] at work and spending time on them at home, e-mail is changing the ways people meet, court, and even break up.

"It's changed every aspect of dating," said Sherry Amatenstein, a dating expert for the iVillage online network (www.ivillage.com) and author of *The Q & A Dating Book* (Adams Media, 2000). "Our new technology is both boon and curse for the modern dater."

One reason for the change in etiquette from requesting a phone number to requesting an e-mail address is

How Will She Get Rid of Him? *Perhaps she will give him a phony e-mail address. Some women now use e-mail as a method of avoiding seeing people they do not want to go out with. They may give out their actual e-mail addresses but never respond, or they may give out seldom used or erroneous e-mail addresses. It's like giving out the wrong phone number. (Bye bye.)*

comfort, particularly for women. "It's safer than a phone number," said Brenda Ross, dating adviser for About.com and creator of the Dating Advice for Geeks Web (www.geekcheck.com) site. "With a few e-mails you can get some details, find out what a guy is like,

Truth?Fiction?
Revisited

People need not be *sexually* intimate to be emotionally intimate. Nor does sexual intimacy automatically create emotional intimacy. People who are sexually involved may not achieve emotional closeness. People can be more emotionally intimate with friends than with lovers.

know everything about, one another (Peven & Shulman, 1999). Along with sex, intimacy is one of the key ingredients in passionate relationships (Love & Brown, 1999). Feelings of intimacy and affection tend to grow as romantic relationships develop (Nieder & Sieffge-Krenke, 2001). Relationships also develop from being more casual and superficial to being relatively committed (Nieder & Sieffge-Krenke, 2001). Intimate relationships are also characterized by trust, caring, and acceptance.

Sternberg's (2003) triangular theory of love (see Chapter 7) regards intimacy as a basic component of romantic love. But people can be intimate and not in love, at least not in romantic love. Close friends and family members become emotionally intimate when they care deeply for each other and share their feelings and experiences.

Intimacy is important not only to interpersonal relationships but also to one's health. Researchers have found that intimacy fosters well-being and that its absence can be psychologically and physically harmful (Driver et al., 2003).

Intimacy and Self-Esteem Some social scientists suggest that getting to know and like yourself is an initial step toward intimacy with others. By coming to know and

and then decide if you want to go out with him. It takes a lot of pressure off."

Some women are now using e-mail as a way to avoid people they have no intention of ever going out with. In many instances, Ms. Ross said, a woman doesn't want to give out her phone number, but she also doesn't want to be pestered all night for it by some libidinous Neanderthal. Solution: give him your e-mail address and never respond, or give an e-mail address that you never use, an updating of the time-honored dating tradition of giving a wrong phone number. Eventually he will get the idea, and trashing an e-mail message is easier than dodging a phone call.

Many single people have found that e-mail can be a solution to another age-old dating problem—when to call? Ellen Lavery, a 25-year-old from Manhattan, found herself in that situation a few months ago, the morning after a party where she exchanged phone numbers and e-mail addresses with a man. "The next day, I would have absolutely considered a phone call too soon, too desperate," she said, "a severe violation of the three-day rule. So I shot him off a brief 'We should get together sometime' e-mail. It seemed more acceptable and less threatening, but not overbearing."

Traditionally, the first phone call can be more nerve-racking than transporting nuclear weapons across a rope bridge. You have to be on your toes: funny but not obnoxious, charming yet not hammy, deep but not psychotic, all on the spot. An e-mail message, however,

can go through multiple drafts; wording and tone can painstakingly be thought out, reviewed, edited and, if it's not quite right, sent back to committee. "I always show my e-mails to friends before I send them out," said Drew Brooks, a 25-year-old in Manhattan. "Involving other people is fun."

Single people who follow up on chance encounters with e-mail are finding that the awkward first stages of a relationship can be made easier online.

One reason relationships can move so far so fast over the Internet is the solitary nature of e-mail. "When you're e-mailing, you can be at home, cozy, in your pajamas," Ms. Amatenstein said. "It's so psychologically inviting, people say things they normally would not say."

Increasingly, people are also finding that the distance of e-mail simplifies one of the potentially messier tasks in a relationship: the breakup. "That's one great thing about e-mail," Mr. Brooks said. "There's no ramifications for you in just blowing someone off."

Not everyone sees it that way, though. Brenda Ross, whose former boyfriend broke up with her via e-mail, after they had talked about the possibility of marriage, said it was about the "lamest" thing a person could do. "E-mail is a great way to break up with someone," she said, "if you're a coward."

Source: Reprinted from Ed Boland (2000, October 19). In modern e-mail romance "trash" is just a click away. *The New York Times online.*

value yourself, you identify your own feelings and needs and develop the security to share them. Research suggests that partners with low self-esteem are more likely to harbor self-doubts that can interfere with the development and maintenance of romantic relationships (Murray & Holmes, 2000). For example, experiments show that when their partner is in a "bad mood," people with low self-esteem tend to feel more responsible for that mood, to feel more rejected, and, consequently, to behave in a more hostile manner (Bellavia & Murray, 2003). Yet people with high self-esteem seem to be more likely to use their partners' acceptance and approval as a way of maintaining their self-esteem when self-doubts arise (Murray et al., 2001). That is, even when we feel rather good about ourselves, we can come to rely on our partners' impressions of us.

Too much self-esteem can also be detrimental to a relationship if it takes the form of narcissism, or being wrapped up in oneself. Research shows that narcissists tend to play love games with their partners; they show less commitment and are more likely to have alternatives handy if relationships do not work out (Campbell et al., 2002). The same researchers found that self-esteem, as opposed to narcissism, was positively linked to romantic love.

Two other ingredients of an intimate relationship are trust and caring. Trust enables partners to feel confident that disclosing intimate feelings will not lead to ridicule or rejection. Trust usually builds gradually, as partners learn whether it is safe to share confidences.

A German study of 72 adolescents who were followed from the ages of 14 through 20 found that the quality of their relationships with their parents contributed to their ability to trust romantic partners (Seiffge-Krenke & Kuehnemund, 2001). Research also shows that people come to trust their partners when they see that their partners have made sincere investments in the relationship, as evidenced, for example, by making sacrifices to be with them, such as incurring the disapproval of their family (Rusbult & Van Lange, 2003; Wieselquist et al., 1999). Commitment and trust in a relationship can be seen as developing according to a model of **mutual cyclical growth:**

- Feelings that one needs one's partner promote commitment to and dependence on the relationship.
- Commitment to the relationship encourages the partners to do things that are good for the relationship (that is, to perform "pro-relationship acts").
- One's partner perceives the pro-relationship acts.
- Perception of the pro-relationship acts enhances the partner's trust in the other partner and in the relationship.
- Feelings of trust increase the partners' willingness to depend on the relationship.

Caring is an emotional bond that allows intimacy to develop. Caring means that partners try to satisfy each other's needs, gratify each other's interests, and make sacrifices, if necessary. Research shows that willingness to sacrifice is connected with commitment to the relationship, level of satisfaction in the relationship, and, interestingly, poor alternatives to the relationship (Van Lange et al., 1997). In other words, it may not be easy to find partners if one does not sacrifice for relationships. Is self-sacrifice thus self-serving (Finkenauer & Meeus, 2000)?

Because intimacy involves the sharing of inmost thoughts and feelings, honesty is a core feature of intimacy. A person need not be an "open book" to develop and maintain intimacy, however. Some aspects of experience are better kept even from one's most intimate partners, especially when they are embarrassing or threatening (Finkenauer & Hazam, 2000). For example, we would not expect partners to disclose every passing sexual fantasy. Nor would it be reasonable to expect intimate partners to divulge the details of past sexual experiences. Honesty means *saying what one means,* not providing hurtful details. Nor is intimacy established by frank but brutal criticism, even if it is honest.

Making a Commitment People may open up to strangers on airplanes or trains, or to health professionals, and still find it hard to talk openly with people to whom they are closest. Yet we know that we will not see the strangers again, or that the health professionals are required to keep our personal matters confidential. Truly intimate relationships are marked by commitment to maintain the relationship through thick and thin (Drigotas et al., 1999).

Numerous studies find that men tend to be more reluctant than women to make commitments. David Popenoe, co-director of the National Marriage Project at Rutgers University in New Jersey, conducted a study with 60 unmarried heterosexual men and found that the commonness of cohabitation is one reason why they are reluctant to make a commitment. In cohabitation, sex—traditionally a key reason for men to marry—is readily available. Popenoe (cited in Hussain, 2002) notes that "In a sense, with cohabitation he gets a quasi-wife without having to commit."

In committed relationships, a delicate balance exists between individuality and mutuality. In healthy unions, a strong sense of togetherness does not eradicate individuality. Partners in such relationships remain free to be themselves. Neither seeks

Mutual cyclical growth
The view that the need for one's partner promotes commitment; commitment promotes acts that enhance the relationship; and these acts build trust, increasing one's partner's commitment to the relationship.

to dominate or submerge himself or herself into the personality of the other. Each partner maintains individual interests, likes and dislikes, needs and goals.

Factors that can throw continuing relationships into a downward spiral include boredom, as in falling into a rut in leisure activities or sexual practices. Yet boredom does not always end relationships. Consider a study of 12 men who admitted to experiencing sexual boredom in long-term heterosexual relationships (Tunariu & Reavey, 2003). The men were not happy with sexual boredom, particularly in a culture in which men are viewed as highly sexual and romantic love is supposed to remain passionate. On the other hand, they viewed their boredom as a normal trade-off for so-called true love and long-term companionship.

Other factors that contribute to the discontinuation of a relationship include evidence of negative evaluation (such as bickering, and forgetting anniversaries and other important dates or pretending that they do not exist), lack of fairness in the relationship (such as one partner's always deciding how the couple will spend their free time), jealousy, and general dissatisfaction. *Question: How does jealousy affect relationships?*

Jealousy: Is the World a Real-Life *Temptation Island?*

> O! beware, my lord, of jealousy;
> It is the green-ey'd monster . . .
>
> *William Shakespeare,* Othello

Thus was Othello, the Moor of Venice, warned of jealousy in the Shakespearean play that bears his name. Yet Othello could not control his feelings and killed his beloved wife, Desdemona. The English poet John Dryden labeled jealousy a "tyrant of the mind." Anthropologists find evidence of jealousy in all cultures, although it may vary in amount and intensity across and within cultures. It appears to be more common and intense among cultures with a stronger *machismo* tradition, in which men are expected to display their virility. It is also powerful in cultures in which men view a woman's infidelity as a threat to their honor.

The emotion of jealousy accounts in part for the popularity of the reality TV show *Temptation Island.* On this show, people in committed relationships are exposed to attractive others, and the audience is apparently intrigued by the question of how much temptation the contestant on the show can withstand. No doubt, members of the audience also speculate on how much temptation they themselves could withstand.

Sexual jealousy is aroused when we suspect that an intimate relationship is threatened by a rival. Lovers can become jealous when others show sexual interest in their partners or when their partners show an interest (even a casual or nonsexual interest) in another. Jealousy can lead to loss of feelings of affection, feelings of insecurity and rejection, anxiety and loss of self-esteem, and feelings of mistrust of one's partner and potential rivals. Jealousy is one of the commonly mentioned reasons why relationships fail. Feelings of possessiveness, related to jealousy, also place stress on a relationship. In

How Do People's Partners Feel When Their Lovers Are Tempted by Rivals Like Those That Inhabit Temptation Island? *Does the opportunity to "spy on" another person's feelings of jealousy contribute to the popularity of reality TV shows like* Temptation Island? *How do we explain feelings of jealousy? What does jealousy do to an intimate relationship?*

Long-Distance Romance, Web Enabled

If you can't be with the one you love, get a Webcam.

At least, that's what Simon Wong, an engineer in California, and Chiunwei Shu, a student in Arizona, have done to make it easier to live in different states and still date each other. Mr. Wong and Ms. Shu, who met when Ms. Shu was visiting California, say they spend at least two hours every night with their Webcams trained on their bedrooms.

"It's cool," Mr. Wong said. "I'll be at home watching TV—and she's not here, so we can't hang out—and she'll be at home doing her thing, reading a book, and I can check out what she's doing."

Ms. Shu agreed. "If I'm studying, it's not bothering me," she said. "But we can both look up and smile at each other."

High-tech communication isn't just giving e-commerce a global outlook or letting adolescent gamers shoot at one another across town or across the country. Tools like instant messages, videoconferencing software, Web phones, and wireless communications are making it easier to keep love alive in long-distance relationships. Mr. Wong and Ms. Shu use NetMeeting, Microsoft's videoconferencing program, to gaze adoringly at each other over the Internet while they talk. They also keep in touch via instant messages and daily e-mail notes, usually with photos. Ms. Shu said she took a picture of herself and sent it to Mr. Wong every day so he could keep up to date on whether she looked happy, sad, or stressed. But aside from that analogue standby, the phone, videoconferencing is their favorite means of communication.

"If it weren't for the Internet," Mr. Wong said, "we wouldn't spend the same percentage of the day communicating—you simply can't talk on the phone all the time. But it's easy to spend two hours on NetMeeting. It actually feels like we hang out all the time." There is an added benefit, Mr. Wong said, laughing: "If the phone rings on her side, I can still play the jealous boyfriend," he said. "Like, 'Who's calling you?' Or if we're talking, I can see her expression—if she looks bored, I can say, 'Are you really interested in this conversation?'"

CALIFORNIA TO COSTA RICA TO BEIJING

Prentice Welch and Erika Lam, both 24, are old hands at using technology to keep in touch while they are apart. They have been sweethearts since high school but in 1997, Ms. Lam moved to Costa Rica for a year of college while Mr. Welch stayed in Davis, California. "That was before we knew about instant messaging," Ms. Lam said.

The two kept in touch by sending e-mail almost every day. Ms. Lam used an online florist to send Mr. Welch flowers, and he sent her the Web address for his basketball league's site so she could keep up with his games. (But she didn't check. "It took too long," she explained.)

Two years later, Mr. Welch moved to Beijing for the school year while Ms. Lam stayed in San Francisco. This time, instant messaging was more common, and they started doing that right away. "That was huge to be able to chat live," said Mr. Welch, now a computer operator in San Francisco, where he and Ms. Lam share a home. "We'd set up dates, when we'd meet online every other day. And sometimes I'd be online, sitting in a cafe in Beijing, and we'd bump into each other. That was so cool."

Ms. Lam and Mr. Welch said that while instant messaging had helped them stay in touch, high-tech communication could make things harder.

Keeping in Touch—Or at Least in Electronic Touch
When today's couples must be separated, many of them keep in touch by means of tools like instant messages, videoconferencing software, Web phones, and wireless communications. Some couples train Webcams on each other's bedrooms, not necessarily for sexual purposes but to maintain a kind of intimacy.

extreme cases jealousy can cause depression or give rise to spouse abuse, suicide, or, as with Othello, murder (Puente & Cohen, 2003; Vandello & Cohen, 2003). But milder forms of jealousy are not necessarily destructive to a relationship. They may even serve the positive function of revealing how much one cares for one's partner.

WHO WINS THE ARGUMENT? THE ONE WHO CAN TYPE FASTER

Ms. Lam said that conflict over international data lines could be hard to manage. "An argument in cyberspace is the worst," she said. "You never get a feeling of resolution."

Mr. Welch agreed. "And when we'd get in fights—as much of a fight as you can have typing rapidly at each other—she'd always win because she can type faster," he said.

The limits of the technology could prove frustrating. "Sometimes it made me want to cry," Ms. Lam said. "It was like, I can't touch you through the screen."

Both agreed that even though they felt connected when they were online, they had become lonely as soon as they turned away from the computer.

"I'd be in some smoky Internet cafe," Mr. Welch said with melancholy in his voice.

"And I'd be alone in my dark room," Ms. Lam said with a shudder.

They resolved that problem when Ms. Lam moved to Beijing to be with Mr. Welch after a five-month separation. The couple are expecting their first child in October, and they say their days of Internet connections are behind them. "Next time we go somewhere," Mr. Welch said as he took Ms. Lam's hand, "we'll go together."

NOT MAINTAINING A RELATIONSHIP, BUT ENDING ONE

For some people, the problem is not maintaining a relationship, but ending one. Ask Sun Kim, a 24-year-old research associate in a San Francisco cardiology laboratory. When her boyfriend moved to Korea last December for a consulting job, the two decided not to keep dating long distance but resolved to stay friends.

That, however, proved more difficult than it sounded. "While we were dating," Ms. Kim said, "he was really good at e-mailing. He worked in a dot-com and sat around in a cubicle and e-mailed me every day. He sent messages, stuff he found on the Internet, and he was the king of Egreetings." (Egreetings.com is an online greeting-card service.) When he moved to Korea, nothing changed.

"It was bad because we were supposed to be broken up," Ms. Kim said, "but he'd send flirty e-mails and use Net phones to call me from Korea—for free—all the time." She said her ex-boyfriend had also beamed a PocketSutra, a copy of the *Kama Sutra,* to her Handspring Visor.

"Geographically," Ms. Kim said, "the relationship changed, but most of it stayed the same through technology. It was like it was before, only I never saw him anymore. It was like, 'We're just friends, but I'm still going to be your virtual boyfriend.'"

BREAKING UP IS STILL HARD TO DO

Frequent instant messaging, or IM, sessions made the relationship drag out for months, Ms. Kim said, even though they were continents apart. "About six months after he left," Ms. Kim said, "I was ready to date other people. I told him that, and it turned into this big 'define the relationship' discussion over IM." The time lag between replies opened up room for confusion. "I'd ask a question," Ms. Kim said, "and he wouldn't respond right away, and I'd wonder: Is he offended? Away from his desk? Working?"

Nonetheless, Ms. Kim said she thought that her former boyfriend preferred the medium—lag time or no—to face-to-face discussion. "At one point in this weird breakup discussion over instant messaging," she said, "I said, 'You're probably so relieved we're doing this over IM,' and he said, 'Yeah, I am, actually.'

"Finally, I told him: 'I think it would be a good idea if we don't communicate like this anymore. Call me on the phone or don't contact me.' There was no response, so I logged off. He called a few days later, and he hadn't gotten the message. His Yahoo Messenger had been logging him on and off so he never got my message. He thought everything was fine."

She added: "It's hard to convey emotions over IM. If you're mad, it's hard to convey that in your tone without coming right out and saying, 'I'm mad at you.'"

"In general," she said, "technology makes it hard to have an old-fashioned breakup, where you never see or speak to each other again. I kind of miss the old-fashioned breakup."

Source: Reprinted from Sally McGrane (2000, August 31). Long-distance romance, Web enabled. *The New York Times online.*

For this reason, some investigators distinguish between "normal jealousy," which reflects occasional self-doubts and the belief that one's partner is attractive, and "obsessional jealousy," in which the individual, like Othello, is consumed by his or her fears of interference in the relationship (Marazziti et al., 2003).

Advice for Young Women: How to Prepare for Married Life

Many humorous e-mails make their way around the Net, so that now you see them and . . . now you see them again. The fourth or fifth time we received this anonymous e-mail, we decided to share it with you. It compares advice from a (genuine!) home economics textbook of the 1950s with the somewhat different advice a young woman might profit from today. It goes to show how the times, they have a-changed. Much!

What Advice Can We Give to This Young Couple? Shall we suggest that she plan ahead to have a delicious meal on the table when he comes home from his hard day of work? That she greet him with a ribbon in her hair to look as fresh as possible? That she do some picking up before he arrives so that their home will be his safe haven? (Perhaps not in the United States of the new millennium!)

	From the Home Economics Text: How to Prepare for Married Life, 1950s Style	The Updated Version for the Young Woman of the New Millennium
1. Have dinner ready.	Plan ahead, even the night before, to have a delicious meal on time. This is a way of letting him know that you have been thinking about him and are concerned about his needs. Most men are hungry when they come home, and the prospects of a good meal are part of the warm welcome needed.	Make reservations ahead of time. If your day becomes too hectic, just leave him a voice-mail message regarding where you'd like to eat and at what time. This lets him know that your day has been awful and gives him an opportunity to change your mood.
2. Prepare yourself.	Take 15 minutes to rest so you will be refreshed when he arrives. Touch up your make-up, put a ribbon in your hair, and be fresh looking. He has just been with a lot of work-weary people. Be a little gay and a little more interesting. His boring day may need a lift.	A quick stop at the Clinique counter on your way home will do wonders for your outlook and will keep you from becoming irritated every time he opens his mouth. (Don't forget to use his credit card.)
3. Clear away clutter.	Make one last trip through the main part of the house just before your husband arrives, gathering up schoolbooks, toys, paper, etc. Then run a dust cloth over the tables. Your husband will feel he has reached a haven of rest and order, and it will give you a lift too.	Call the housekeeper and tell her (or him!) that any miscellaneous items left on the floor by the children can be placed in the Goodwill box in the garage.

What causes jealousy? Experience and personality variables play roles. People may become mistrustful of their partners because former partners had cheated. People with low self-esteem may experience sexual jealousy because they become overly dependent on their partners. They may fear that they will not be able to find another partner if their present partner leaves.

Jealousy and Evolutionary Theory Sex differences in jealousy appear to support evolutionary theory. Males seem to be more upset by sexual infidelity, females by emotional infidelity (Shackelford et al., 2002). That is, males are made more insecure and angry when their partners have sexual relations with someone else. Females are made more insecure and angry when their partners become emotionally attached to someone else. Why? Evolutionary theory hypothesizes that sexual jealousy was shaped by natural selection as a method of ensuring males that their female partner's offspring is their own, and of ensuring females that their male partners will continue to provide resources to facilitate child rearing (Buss, 2003; Harris, 2003).

	From the Home Economics Text: How to Prepare for Married Life, 1950s Style	The Updated Version for the Young Woman of the New Millennium
4. Prepare the children.	Take a few minutes to wash the children's hands and faces if they are small, comb their hair, and (if necessary) change their clothes. They are little treasures, and he would like to see them playing the part.	Send the children to their rooms to watch television or play Nintendo. After all, both of them are from his previous marriage.
5. Minimize the noise.	At the time of his arrival, eliminate all noise of washer, dryer, or vacuum. Try to encourage the children to be quiet. Greet him with a warm smile and be glad to see him.	If you happen to be home when he arrives, be in the bathroom with the door locked.
6. Some DON'TS.	Don't greet him with problems or complaints. Don't complain if he's late for dinner. Count this as minor compared with what he might have gone through that day.	Don't greet him with problems and complaints. Let him speak first, and then your complaints will get more attention and remain fresh in his mind throughout dinner. Don't complain if he's late for dinner, simply remind him that the leftovers are in the fridge and that you left the dishes for him to do.
7. Make him comfortable.	Have him lean back in a comfortable chair or suggest he lie down in the bedroom. Have a cool or warm drink ready for him. Arrange his pillow and offer to take off his shoes. Speak in a low, soft, soothing, and pleasant voice. Allow him to relax and unwind.	Tell him where he can find a blanket if he's cold. This will really show you care.
8. Listen to him.	You may have a dozen things to tell him, but the moment of his arrival is not the time. Let him talk first.	But don't ever let him get the last word.
9. Make the evening his.	Never complain if he does not take you out to dinner or to other places of entertainment. Instead, try to understand his world of strain and pressure and his need to be home and relax.	Never complain if he does not take you out to dinner or other places of entertainment; go with a friend or go shopping. (Use his credit card.) Familiarize him with the phrase Girls' Night Out.
10. The Goal.	Try to make your home a place of peace and order where your husband can relax.	Try to keep things amicable without reminding him that he only *thinks* the world revolves around him. Obviously he's wrong.

Interestingly, the hypothesized sex difference in reactions to infidelity disappear when one's partner has an affair with someone of his or her own sex (Sagarin et al., 2003). Is it because the affair carries no threat of impregnation (a view that would be consistent with evolutionary theory)? Or is it because the victim consoles himself or herself by thinking that he or she really isn't competing in the same arena with the intruder? Are both explanations and other explanations possible?

And then there are some studies that fail to support evolutionary theory (Harris, 2000; DeSteno et al., 2002). However, the validity of these studies has also been challenged. Evolutionary theory remains in the forefront of approaches to understanding jealousy and (possible) sex differences in jealousy.

A Cognitive Perspective In recent years, cognitive theory has gained importance in many areas of the behavioral sciences, and sexual jealousy is no exception. In two studies, Stacie Bauerle and her colleagues (2002) presented 156 college undergraduates and 128 members of the general population with various scenarios in which their partners were unfaithful. By and large, jealousy increased when the individuals *attributed* their partner's infidelity to *internal* causes, such as clear personal choice. When they attributed the infidelity to *external* causes, such as alcohol or social pressure, the individuals in the study reported feeling significantly less jealous. ("Don't blame me; it was the alcohol.")

Many lovers—including many college students—play jealousy games. They let their partners know that they are attracted to other people. They flirt openly or manufacture tales to make their partners pay more attention to them, to test the relationship, to inflict pain, or to take revenge for a partner's disloyalty.

Responses to Deterioration of a Relationship

Question: What can partners do when a relationship begins to deteriorate? A relationship begins to fail when it becomes less rewarding than it was. Couples can respond to deterioration in *active* or *passive* ways. Active means of response include doing something that may enhance the relationship (such as working on improving communication skills, negotiating differences, or seeking professional help) or deciding to end the relationship. Passive methods of responding include merely waiting for something to happen, doing little or nothing. People can sit back and wait for the relationship to improve on its own (occasionally it does) or for the relationship to deteriorate to the point where it ends. ("Hey, these things happen.")

It is irrational (and damaging to a relationship) to assume that good relationships require no investment of time and effort. No two of us are matched perfectly. When problems arise, it is better to work to resolve them than to act as though they don't exist and hope that they will disappear of their own accord.

Breaking Up—Breaking Up Is (Often) Hard To Do

According to social-exchange theory, relationships draw to a close when the partners find little satisfaction in the affiliation, when the barriers to leaving the relationship are low (that is, the social, religious, and financial constraints are manageable), and especially when alternative partners are available. Problems in jealousy and communication are common reasons for ending a relationship. The availability of alternatives decreases one's commitment to a relationship (Knox et al., 1997a; Rusbult et al., 1998). This fact has been widely recognized throughout the ages, which is one reason why patriarchal cultures like to keep their women locked up—or, in the Middle East, literally "under wraps"—as much as possible.

Breaking up, as the song goes, can be hard to do—both for the person terminating the relationship and for the other party. For this reason, as noted in the "Human Sexuality in the New Millennium" feature "In Modern E-Mail Romance, 'Trash' Is Just a Click Away," some people break up via e-mail rather than in person or on the telephone.

Some people obviously take breaking up better than others. A study of more than 5,000 people, who responded to a survey on the Internet, found that anxious people were more likely to be highly preoccupied with the lost partner, to suffer more physical and emotional distress, to attempt to reestablish the relationship, and to be angry and vengeful (Davis et al., 2003). Emotionally secure individuals were most likely to seek social support among their friends and their families. Insecure individuals were most likely to turn to alcohol and drugs. A survey of 92 college undergraduates found that many believed they would grow from the experience of breaking up (Tashiro & Frazier, 2003). Individuals' "attributional styles" entered the picture: People who blamed themselves for the breakup experienced more stress than those who blamed external factors, such as the situation.

Breaking up is sometimes followed by stalking, or other "unwanted pursuit behaviors" (UPBs), such as unwelcome phone calls or e-mails, asking third parties about the person who dissolved the relationship, and following, threatening, or attacking that person or new partners of that person) (Davis et al., 2002; Langhinrichsen-Rohling et al., 2002). Jealousy, abusiveness, and physical violence in relationships are key predictors of unwanted pursuit (Puente & Cohen, 2003). Stalkers and violent individuals also tend to have a strong need to control others (Dye & Davis, 2003). We will see in the chapter on sexual coercion that a need to control other people is also connected with the violent crime of rape.

Various factors can prevent a deteriorating relationship from ending. For example, people who continue to find some sources of satisfaction, who are committed to maintaining the relationship, or who believe that they will eventually be able to overcome their problems are more likely to invest what they must to prevent the collapse.

The swan song of a relationship—moving on—is not always a bad thing. When people are highly incompatible, and when genuine attempts to preserve the relationship have failed, ending the relationship can offer each partner a chance for happiness with someone else.

Review: The ABC(DE)'s of Romantic Relationships

Reflect

Do you find it difficult to make small talk? Explain. Have you ever had trouble deciding how much intimate information to disclose to a dating partner? What are the dangers in disclosing too much too soon to a partner? Are there some things that you feel that you should never share with a partner?

CriticalThinking

Critical thinkers avoid oversimplifications and overgeneralizations. Explain how a critical thinker would answer this question: Is it a good thing or a bad thing when a relationship comes to an end?

1. According to social-_____ theory, the development of relationships reflects the unfolding of the rewards and costs of maintaining the relationship.

2. Partners are most likely to meet through mutual _____.

3. Factors that motivate us to build relationships include (*Similarity* or *Dissimilarity*?) in attitudes.

4. Studies show that (*Males* or *Females*?) tend to be more "romantic," in the sense of passionate, in choosing whether to build relationships.

5. In the early stages of a relationship, people probe each other with _____ contact.

6. _____ talk allows exchange of information but stresses breadth of topic coverage rather than in-depth discussion.

7. We usually precede verbal greetings with _____ contact.

8. Opening up, or self-_____, is central to building intimate relationships.

9. Researchers find that (*Feminine* or *Masculine*?)-typed individuals tend to be less willing to disclose their feelings.

10. The concept of _____ refers to the stage at which a couple regard themselves as "we," not two "I's."

11. _____ consists of feelings of emotional connectedness and the desire to share inmost thoughts and feelings.

12. A moderate amount of self-_____ promotes intimacy.

13. According to the model of mutual _____ growth, a partner makes commitments to a relationship and the other partner reciprocates.

14. _____ means *saying what one means,* not providing hurtful details.

15. (*Males* or *Females*?) are generally more reluctant to make a commitment to a relationship.

16. According to _____ theory, males are more upset by sexual infidelity, and females are more upset by emotional infidelity.

17. It is (*Rational* or *Irrational*?) to assume that good relationships require no investment of time and effort.

18. Jealousy, abusiveness, and violence in relationships are key predictors of unwanted _____ following the break up of a relationship.

Loneliness: "All the Lonely People, Where Do They All Come From?"

Many people start relationships because of loneliness. *Question: What is loneliness?* Loneliness and solitude (being alone) are not synonymous. Loneliness is a state of painful isolation, of feeling cut off from others (Long et al., 2003). Solitude, however, can be quite positive. Inner-directed solitude can be characterized by self-discovery and inner peace (Long et al., 2003). Outer-directed solitude can refer to spirituality or allow us to reflect on the world around us. Solitude is usually a matter of choice; loneliness is not.

Lonely people tend to spend a lot of time by themselves, eat dinner alone, spend weekends alone, and participate in few social activities. They are unlikely to date. Some lonely people report having many friends, but a closer look suggests that these "friendships" are shallow. Lonely people are unlikely to share confidences. Loneliness tends to peak during adolescence, when peer relationships begin to supplant family ties. A study of 90 adolescents aged 16 to 18 found that feelings of loneliness were connected with low self-confidence, introversion, unhappiness, and emotional instability (Cheng & Furnham, 2002). Loneliness is also often connected with feelings of depression. A study of 101 dating couples with a mean age of 21 found that poor relationships contributed to feelings of loneliness and to depression—even though the individuals had partners (Segrin et al., 2003).

Loneliness is connected with physical health problems as well as with psychological problems such as depression. One study, for example, found that lonely people had higher blood pressure than people who were not lonely (Hawkley et al., 2003). Lonely people also found stressful experiences to be more discomfiting, an observation that suggests the value of social support when we are undergoing stress (Hawkley et al., 2003). Social isolation has also been shown to predict cancer, cardiovascular disease, various other diseases, and a higher mortality rate (Hawkley & Cacioppo, 2003). It appears that one causal pathway between loneliness and illness involves stress. Stress impairs the functioning of the immune system, and lonely people perceive stress to be more aversive (Cacioppo et al., 2003).

Question: What are the causes of loneliness?

Loneliness or Solitude? Solitude can be a positive experience, allowing us to think or read or write. But loneliness is painful social isolation that can be detrimental to both our psychological and our physical health.

Causes of Loneliness

The causes of loneliness are many and complex. Lonely people tend to have several of the following characteristics:

1. *Lack of social skills.* Lonely people often lack the interpersonal skills to make friends or cope with disagreements.
2. *Lack of interest in other people.*
3. *Lack of empathy.* Empathy is a key aspect of satisfaction in romantic relationships (Cramer, 2003).
4. *Fear of rejection.*
5. *Failure to disclose personal information to potential friends* (Solano et al., 1982).
6. *Cynicism about human nature* (for example, seeing people as only out for themselves).
7. *Demanding too much too soon.* The lonely perceive other people as cold and unfriendly in the early stages of a relationship.
8. *General pessimism.* When we expect the worst, we often get . . . you guessed it.
9. *An external locus of control.* That is, lonely people do not see themselves as capable of taking their lives into their own hands and achieving their goals.

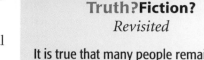

Truth?Fiction?
Revisited

It is true that many people remain lonely because they fear being rejected by others. This fear is often connected with self-criticism of social skills and expectations of failure in relating to others (Vorauer et al., 2003).

Coping with Loneliness

Helping professionals encourage lonely people develop more adaptive ways of thinking and behaving. Lonely people often have distorted views of others. They may have one or two unfortunate experiences and jump to the conclusion that people are generally selfish and not worth the effort of getting involved. Yes, some people *are* basically out for themselves, but the belief that everyone is selfish can perpetuate loneliness by motivating us to avoid others.

Question: What can you do to deal with loneliness in your own life? Here are some suggestions:

1. *Challenge your feelings of pessimism.* Adopt the attitude that things happen when you make them happen.
2. *Challenge your cynicism about human nature.* Yes, lots of people are selfish and not worth knowing, but if you assume that *all* people are like that, you can doom yourself to a lifetime of loneliness. Your task is to find people who possess the qualities that you value.
3. *Challenge the idea that failure in social relationships is unbearable and is thus a valid reason for giving up on them.* Sure, social rejection can be painful, but unless you happen to be George Clooney or Angelina Jolie, you may not appeal to everyone. We must all learn to live with some rejection. But keep looking for the people who possess the qualities you value and who will find things of equal value in you.
4. *Get out among people.* Sit down at a table with people in the cafeteria, not off in a corner by yourself. Smile and say hi to people who interest you. Practice opening lines for different occasions—and a few follow-up lines. Try them out in the mirror.
5. *Make numerous social contacts.* Join committees for student activities. Try intramural sports. Join social-action groups, such as environmental groups and community betterment groups. Join the photography club or the ski club. Get on the school yearbook or newspaper staff.

6. *Be assertive.* Express your genuine opinions.

7. *Become a good listener.* Ask people how they're doing. Ask them for their opinions about classes, politics, or the campus events of the day. Then actually *listen* to what they have to say. Tolerate diverse opinions; remember that no two of us are identical in our outlooks (not even your "perfectly" matched first and third authors). Maintain eye contact. Keep your face friendly. (No, you don't have to remain neutral and friendly if someone becomes insulting toward a religious or ethnic group.)

8. *Give people the chance to know you.* Exchange opinions and talk about your interests. Yes, you'll turn some people off—who doesn't?—but how else will you learn whether you and another person share common ground?

9. *Fight fair.* Friends will inevitably disappoint you, and you'll want to tell them about it. Do so, but fairly. You can start by asking if it's okay to be open about something. Then say, "I feel upset because you . . . ." You can ask your friend whether he or she realized that his or her behavior upset you. Try to work together to find a way to avoid recurrences. Finish by thanking your friend for helping you resolve the problem.

10. *Remember that you're worthy of friends.* It's true—warts and all. None of us is perfect. We're all unique, but you may connect with more people than you imagine. Give people a chance.

11. *Use your college counseling center.* Many thousands of students are lonely but don't know what to do about it. Others just cannot find the courage to approach others. College counseling centers are very familiar with the problem of loneliness, and you should consider them a valuable resource. You might even ask whether there's a group at the center for students seeking to improve their dating or social skills.

Review: Loneliness: "All the Lonely People, Where Do They All Come From?"

Reflect

Have you ever felt lonely? What did you do about feeling lonely? (Will you do something different now that you have read this section?)

Critical Thinking

How can we explain the connections between loneliness and physical health problems such as cancer and cardiovascular disease? Do the connections seem logical or far-fetched? Explain.

19. _____ is a state of painful isolation.

20. _____-directed solitude can be characterized by self-discovery and inner peace.

21. _____-directed solitude can refer to spirituality or allow us to reflect on the world around us.

22. A study of adolescents found that loneliness is connected with (*High* or *Low*?) self-confidence, introversion, unhappiness, and emotional (*Stability* or *Instability*?).

23. Lonely people have (*Higher* or *Lower*?) blood pressure than people who are not lonely.

24. Lonely people find stressful experiences to be (*More* or *Less*?) discomfiting.

25. Lonely people often fear _____ by other people.

26. Lonely people tend to have an (*Internal* or *External*?) locus of control.

Satisfaction in Relationships: Communication as a Key

Some relationships work out. Others don't. In Western culture, where people tend to form relationships with more than one partner as they develop, perhaps the majority of relationships draw to an end. Termination of a relationship, as noted earlier, is not necessarily a bad thing. As people spend time together, they learn more about whether they are well matched or poorly matched. Most also learn how to compromise to help build relationships and how to approach resolving conflicts in a constructive way.

Question: What factors contribute to satisfaction in relationships?

Truth?Fiction?
Revisited

It is not true that conflict is destructive to a relationship. The important thing is the way in which the couple attempts to resolve it.

Gottman's Research on Satisfaction in Relationships

John Mordechai Gottman and his colleagues (Driver et al., 2003; Gottman & Levenson, 1999; Gottman et al., 1998, 1999; Pasupathi et al., 1999) have extensively studied the factors that predict satisfaction in a relationship or the deterioration and ending of a relationship. Gottman focused mainly on married couples, particularly newlyweds, but his findings would appear to extend to unmarried couples in committed relationships, and perhaps to gay male and lesbian couples as well.

In one study, Gottman asked couples to resolve a conflict in their relationship and videotaped them as they did so. He also monitored their physiological responses, including their heart rates, sweating, and large motor movement, as they discussed the situation. It was found that deterioration of satisfaction in the relationship could be predicted by physiological measures, particularly on the part of the male. The calmer the couple's bodily responses, the more their relationship improved as time went on. On the other hand, couples whose hearts beat more rapidly, who sweated more, and who moved about agitatedly had relationships that deteriorated over the following three years.

Gottman also found that it was not the conflict itself—not even "hot conflict"—that hurt the relationship, although the couple were uncomfortable during the effort to resolve it. Gottman found that couples who were open and calm during the conflict tended to improve their satisfaction. Couples who were defensive and avoiding experienced deterioration in the relationship. A notable trait that contributed to deterioration was "stonewalling" by the male. Stonewalling means that there is little movement of the head, few if any nods, and few of the verbal acknowledgments made by listeners who are participating in a discussion. Deterioration of the relationship was also predicted by excessively agreeable, compliant behavior on the part of the female or by her verbalizing feelings of contempt. Facial expressions predicted deterioration, especially facial expressions that suggested disgust on the part of the female, fear on the face of the male, and then miserable smiles by both parties. These nonverbal behaviors were accompanied by more defensiveness, excuses, and denial of responsibility.

Stonewallers suffer not only in terms of their relationships. Stonewalling predicted loneliness after the relationship ended, and loneliness, in turn, was connected with deteriorating health.

Good outcomes for relationships could also be predicted by positive attributes during conflict, such as displays of humor, empathy, and affection; by mutual effort to solve problems; and by determination to listen to one's partner nondefensively. These positive elements kept physiological responses in check as well.

Truth?Fiction?
Revisited

Love is not all you need. You also need communication. Couples learn about each other's desires and needs through communication. Otherwise, this knowledge remains a mystery.

Other researchers have generally found evidence in support of Gottman's conclusions about couples in conflict. For example, Holman and Jarvis (2003) also found that the ways in which couples communicate to resolve conflicts are the key to the survival or termination of a relationship. Couples who validated each other's feelings in a respectful and helpful manner were most satisfied with their relationships. Couples who were hostile or explosive, or who attempted to avoid conflict, were less satisfied with their relationships.

We have examined certain pitfalls in attempting to resolve conflicts (or in avoiding attempting to resolve conflicts!). *Question: How can partners develop their communication skills to approach conflict resolution in a constructive manner?*

Communication Skills for Enhancing Relationships and Sexual Relations: How to Do It

Couple therapists and sex therapists might find less work if more couples communicated effectively about their sexual feelings. Unfortunately, when it comes to sex, *talk* may be the most overlooked four-letter word.

Many couples suffer for years because one or both partners are unwilling to speak up. Or problems arise when one partner misinterprets the other. Clear communication can take the guesswork out of relationships, avert misunderstandings, relieve resentments and frustrations, and increase sexual and general satisfaction with the relationship.

Obstacles to Sexual Communication   Why is it so difficult for couples to communicate about sex? There are several reasons.

Some couples believe that talking about sex is vulgar. But vulgarity, like beauty, is to some degree in the eye of the beholder. One couple's vulgarity may be another couple's love talk. Some people may maintain a Victorian belief that any talk about sex is not fit for mixed company, even between intimate partners. Sex, that is, is something you may do, but not something to be talked about. Other couples may be willing in principle to talk about sex but may find it difficult to actually do so because they lack an agreeable, common language.

How, for example, are they to refer to their genitals or to sexual activities? One partner may prefer to use coarse four-letter (or five-letter) words to refer to them. The other might prefer more clinical terms. A partner who prefers slang for the sexual organs might be regarded by the other as vulgar or demeaning. One who uses clinical terms, such as *fellatio* or *coitus,* might be regarded as, well, clinical. Some couples try to find a common verbal ground that is not vulgar at one extreme or clinical at the other. They might speak, for example, of "doing it" rather than "engaging in sexual intercourse." (The title of the Eddie Cantor musical of the 1930s suggests that some people once spoke of "making whoopie.") Or they might speak of "kissing me down there" rather than of practicing fellatio or cunnilingus.

Many couples also harbor irrational beliefs about relationships and sex, such as the notion that people should somehow *know* what their partners want, without having to ask. The common misconception that people should know what pleases their partners undercuts communication. Men, in particular, seem burdened with the stereotype that they should have a natural expertise at sex. Women may feel it is "unladylike" to talk openly about their sexual needs and feelings. Both partners may hold the idealized romantic notion that "love is all you need" to achieve sexual happiness.

A related irrational belief is that if our partners truly loved us, they would somehow "read our minds" and know what types of sexual stimulation we desire. Unfortunately, or fortunately, others cannot read our minds. We must assume the responsibility for communicating our preferences.

Some people communicate more effectively than others, perhaps because they are more sensitive to others' needs or because their parents served as good models as communicators. But communication skills can be acquired at any time. Learning takes time and work, but the following guidelines should prove helpful if you want to enhance your communication skills. These skills can also improve communication in areas of intimacy other than the sexual.

Getting Started How do you broach tough topics? Here are some ideas.

You can start by talking about talking. You can inform your partner that it is difficult for you to talk about problems and conflicts: "You know, I've always found it awkward to find a way of bringing things up" or "You know, I think other people have an easier time than I do when it comes to talking about some things." You can allude to troublesome things that happened in the past when you attempted to resolve conflicts. This approach encourages your partner to invite you to proceed.

Broaching the topic of sex can be difficult. Couples who gab endlessly about finances, children, and work, may clam up about sex. So it may be helpful to first agree to talk about talking about sex. You can admit that it is difficult to talk about sex. You can say that your sexual relationship is important to you and that you want to do everything you can to enhance it. Gently probe your partner's willingness to set aside time to talk about sex, preferably when you can dim the lights and avoid interruptions.

The "right time" may be when you are both relaxed, rested, and unpressed for time. The "right place" can be any place where you can enjoy privacy and speak undisturbed. Sex talk need not be limited to the bedroom. Couples may feel more comfortable talking about sex over dinner, when cuddling on the sofa, or when just relaxing together.

Another possibility is to request permission to raise an issue. You can say something like this: "There's something on my mind. Do you have a few minutes? Is now a good time to tell you about it?" Or you can say, "There's something that we need to talk about, but I'm not sure how to bring it up. Can you help me with it?"

You can also tell your partner that it is okay to point out ways in which you can become a more effective lover. For example, you can say, "I know that you don't want to hurt my feelings, but I wonder if I'm doing anything that you'd rather I didn't do?"

Listening Effective listening involves such skills as active listening, paraphrasing, the use of reinforcement, and valuing your partner even when the two of you disagree. To listen actively rather than passively, first adopt the attitude that you may actually learn something—or perceive things from another vantage point—by listening. You can learn more about active listening—and the controversy surrounding the procedure!—in the nearby "A Closer Look."

Even when you disagree with what your partner is saying, you can maintain good relations and keep channels of communication open by saying something like "I really appreciate your taking the time to try to work this out with me" or "I hope you'll think it's okay if I don't see things entirely in the same way, but I'm glad that we had a chance to talk about it."

When you disagree with your partner, do so in a way that shows that you still value your partner as a person. In other words, say something like "I love you very much, but it annoys me when you . . ." rather than "You're really contemptible for

The Active-Listening Controversy

A Closer Look

For decades, couples have listed communication problems as a prime cause of dissatisfaction in their relationships. Part of the problem, they have complained, is that their partners simply do not listen to them.

For this reason, couple therapists have suggested that couples use a technique that therapists themselves frequently use when listening to clients: active listening. Active listening involves recognizing that when your partner is speaking, it is helpful to do more than sit back passively. Sitting back passively can be confused with stonewalling, which is one of the behavior patterns that can lead to the termination of a relationship (Driver et al., 2003; Gottman & Levenson, 1999; Gottman et al., 1998, 1999; Pasupathi et al., 1999).

In other words, it is not helpful to stare off into space while your partner is talking or to offer a begrudging "mm-hmm" now and then just to be polite. Instead,

Is Actively Listening to Your Partner a Good Idea? *It might seem that the obvious answer is yes, because effective communication requires learning the other person's view of things. But be aware that John Gottman and his colleagues found some evidence that the specific form of listening that therapists term* active listening *can appear to be confrontational. Partners can listen actively by maintaining eye contact and modifying their facial expression to show that they understand their partner's feelings and ideas. They can ask helpful, nonconfrontational questions, such as "Did I disappoint you when I . . . ?" Tone of voice and sincerity are important.*

you can listen actively by maintaining eye contact and modifying your facial expression to show that you understand his or her feelings and ideas (Cole & Cole, 1999). For example, nod your head when appropriate.

Listening actively also involves asking helpful questions, such as "Would you please give me an example?" or "Was that good for you?"

An active listener does not simply hear what the other person is saying but also

doing . . . ." In this manner, you encourage your partner to disclose sensitive material without risk of attack or of losing your love or support.

Learning About Your Partner's Needs Listening is basic to learning about another person's needs, but sometimes it helps to go a few steps further. You can ask open-ended questions that allow for a broader exploration of issues, such as

"What do you like best about the way we make love?"
"Do you think that I do things to bug you?"
"Does it bother you that I go to bed later than you do?"
"Does anything disappoint you about our relationship?"
"Do you think that I do things that are inconsiderate when you're studying for a test?"

Closed-ended questions that call for a limited range of responses are most useful when you're looking for a simple yes-or-no type of response: "Would you rather make love with the stereo off?"

Self-disclosure is essential to developing intimacy. You can also use self-disclosure to learn more about your partner's needs, because communicating your own feelings and ideas invites reciprocation. For example, you might say, "There are times when I feel that I disappoint you when we make love. Should I be doing something differently?"

You can ask your partner to level with you about an irksome issue. You can say that you recognize that it might be awkward to discuss it but that you will try your

focuses attentively on the speaker's words and gestures to grasp meaning. Nonverbal cues may reveal more about the speaker's inner feelings than the spoken word. Good listeners do not interrupt, change the topic, or walk away when their partners are speaking.

Paraphrasing is another form of active listening that shows that you understand what your partner is trying to say. In paraphrasing, you recast or restate your partner's words to confirm your comprehension. For example, say if your partner says, "You hardly ever say anything when we're making love. I don't want you to scream or make obligatory grunts, or do something silly, but sometimes I wonder if I'm trying to make love to a brick wall." You can paraphrase this by saying something like "So it's sort of hard to know if I'm really enjoying it."

All of this made good common sense and was consistent with what was "known" by therapists for decades. But then in 1998, John M. Gottman and his

colleagues published a controversial study that was based on observations of the ways in which 130 newlywed couples went about trying to resolve conflicts. Gottman and his colleagues found that they could predict which couples would remain together and which would break up on the basis of their bodily responses to "discussing" their differences and what they said and did. The Gottman group reported that, contrary to popular opinion (among helping professionals), active listening did *not* help couples resolve conflicts and remain together. Instead, it was often perceived as confrontational and damaging to the relationship. The Gottman group also reported that the expression of anger was not necessarily damaging and—in a suggestion that outraged feminists—that females would be well advised to raise issues gently, so as not, perhaps, to bruise the male ego. On the other hand, the Gottman group did find support for encouraging males to be open to (nonabrasive?) suggestions from females.

The Gottman group received a great deal of criticism. Some of it referred to methodological flaws in their study, such as the facts that couples were not selected at random from the general population and that the investigators drew conclusions about cause and effect from correlational data (Stanley et al., 2000; see Chapter 2). Other critics noted that active listening, when carried out properly, does not appear to be confrontational, and that couples in therapy might benefit from more careful training in using the method (Cole & Cole, 1999; Hafen & Crane, 2003).

Is it dangerous to express anger when attempting to resolve conflict? Perhaps the answer lies in *how* the anger is expressed. When anger leads to stonewalling, character assassination, or physical confrontation, perhaps all therapists would agree that it is destructive. But if discussion can remain civil, it may be useful to recognize emotions—even negative emotions such as anger—for what they are.

best to listen conscientiously and not get too disturbed. You can also limit yourselves to one such difficult issue per conversation. If the entire emotional dam were to burst, the job of mopping up could be overwhelming.

Providing Information There are skillful ways of communicating information, including "accentuating the positive" and using verbal and nonverbal cues. It is irrational to expect that your partner can read your mind. He or she can tell when you're wearing a grumpy face, but your expression does not provide much information about your specific feelings. When your partner asks, "What would you like me to do?" don't say, "Well, I think you can figure out what I want" or "Just do whatever you think is best." Only you know what pleases you.

Let your partner know when he or she is doing something right! Speak up or find another way to express your appreciation. Accentuating the positive is rewarding and also informs your partner about what pleases you. In other words, don't just wait around until your partner does something wrong and then seize the opportunity to complain!

Sexual activity provides an excellent opportunity for direct communication. You can say something like "Oh, that's great" or "Don't stop." Or you can ask for feedback, as in "How does that feel . . . ?"

Feedback provides direct guidance about what is pleasing. Partners can also make specific requests and suggestions.

Sexual communication also occurs without words. Facial expressions and body language communicate likes and dislikes. Our partners may lean toward us or away from us when we touch them, or they may relax or tense up. In any case, they speak volumes in silence. The following exercises may help couples use nonverbal cues to communicate their sexual likes and dislikes.

1. *Taking turns petting.* Taking turns petting can help partners learn what turns one another on. Each partner takes turns caressing the other, stopping frequently enough to receive feedback by asking questions like "How does that feel?" The recipient is to provide feedback, which can be expressed verbally ("Yes, that's it—yes, just like that" or "No, a little lighter than that") or nonverbally, as in making appreciative or disapproving sounds. The knowledge gained through this exercise can be incorporated into the couple's regular pattern of lovemaking.

2. *Directing your partner's hand.* Gently guiding your partner's hand—to show your partner where and how you like to be touched—is a most direct way of communicating sexual likes. Women might show partners how to caress the breasts or clitoral shaft in this manner. Men might cup their partners' hands to show them how to stroke the penile shaft or caress the testes.

3. *Signaling.* Couples can use agreed-upon nonverbal cues to signal sexual pleasure. For example, one partner may rub the other in a certain way, or tap the other, to signal that something is being done right. The recipient of the signal takes mental notes and incorporates the pleasurable stimulation into the couple's lovemaking. This is a sort of "hit or miss" technique, but even near misses can be rewarding.

Making Requests A basic part of improving relationships or lovemaking is asking partners to change their behavior—to do something differently or to stop doing something that hurts or is ungratifying. The skill of making requests now comes to the fore.

Be specific in requesting changes. Telling your partner something like "I'd like you to be nicer to me" may accomplish little. Your partner may not know that his or her behavior is *not* nice and may not understand how to be "nicer." It is better to say something like "I would appreciate it if you would get coffee for yourself, or at least ask me in a more pleasant way." Or, "I really have a hard time with the way you talk to me in front of your friends. It's as if you're trying to show them that you have control over me or something." Similarly, it may be less effective to say "I'd like you to be more loving" than to say "When we make love, I'd like you to kiss me more and tell me how you care about me."

Of course, you can precede your specific requests with openers such as "There's something on my mind. Is this a good time for me to bring it up with you?"

You are more likely to achieve desired results by framing requests in *I*-talk than by heaping criticisms on your partner. For example, "I would like it if we spent some time cuddling after sex" is superior to "You don't seem to care enough about me to want to hold me after we make love." Saying "I find it very painful when you use a harsh voice with me" is probably more effective than "Sometimes people's feelings get hurt when their boyfriends [girlfriends] speak to them harshly in front of their friends or families."

You can try out *I*-talk in front of a mirror or with a confidante before using it with your partner. In this way, you can see whether your facial expression and tone of voice are consistent with what you are saying. Friends may provide constructive feedback.

Delivering Criticism Delivering criticism effectively is a skill. It requires focusing partners' attention on the problem without inducing resentment or reducing them to trembling masses of guilt or fear.

First, weigh your goals forthrightly. Is your primary intention to punish your partner, or are you more interested in gaining cooperation? If your goal is punishment, you may as well be coarse and disparaging, but expect to invite reprisals. If your goal is to improve the relationship, however, a tactful approach may be in order.

Deliver criticism privately—not in front of friends or family. Your partner has a right to be upset when you make criticism public. Making private matters public prompts indignation and cuts off communication.

Be specific about the *behavior* that disturbs you so that you bypass the trap of disparaging your partner's personality or motives. For example, you may be more effective by saying, "I could lose this job because you didn't write down the message" than by saying "You're completely irresponsible" or "You're a flake." Similarly, you may achieve better results by saying, "The bathroom looks and smells dirty when you throw your underwear on the floor" rather than "You're a filthy pig." Complain about specific, modifiable behavior rather than trying to overhaul another individual's whole personality.

Your partner will feel less threatened if you express displeasure in terms of your own feelings rather than by directly attacking his or her personality. Attacks often arouse defensive behavior, and sometimes retaliation. When confronting your partner for failing to be sensitive to your sexual needs when making love, it may be more effective to say, "You know, it really *upsets* me that you don't seem to care about my feelings when we make love" than to say, "You're so wrapped up in yourself that you never think about anyone else."

Keep criticism and complaints to the present. Think how many times have you been in an argument and heard things like "You never appreciated me!" or "Last summer you did the same thing!" Bringing up the past muddles current issues and heightens resentments. When your partner forgets to jot down a telephone message, it is more useful to note that "This was a vital phone call" than "Three weeks ago you didn't tell me about the phone call from Chris, and as a result I missed out on seeing *Terminator 17*." It's better to leave who did what to whom last year (or even last week) alone.

Avoid blunt criticisms or personal attacks and suggest constructive alternatives. Avoid saying, "You're really a lousy lover." Say instead, "Can I take your hand and show you what I'd like?"

Whenever possible, express criticism positively and combine it with a concrete request. When commenting on your partner's failure to display affection during lovemaking, say, "I love it when you kiss me. Please kiss me more" rather than "You never kiss me when we're in bed and I'm sick of it."

Receiving Criticism

> Honest criticism is hard to take, particularly from a relative, a friend, an acquaintance, or a stranger.
>
> *Franklin P. Jones*

Delivering criticism can be tricky, especially when you want to inspire cooperation. Receiving criticism can be even trickier. Nevertheless, the following suggestions offer some help.

When you hear "It's time you did something about . . . ," it is understandable if the hair on the backs of your arms does a headstand. After all, it's a blunt challenge. When we are confronted harshly, we are likely to become defensive and think of retaliating. But if your objective is to enhance the relationship, take a few moments to stop and think. To resolve conflicts, we need to learn about the other person's

concerns, keep lines of communication open, and find ways of changing problem behavior.

So when your partner says, "It's about time you did something about the bathroom," stop and think before you summon up your most menacing voice and say, "Just what the hell is that supposed to mean?" Ask yourself what you want to find out.

Just as it's important to be specific when delivering criticism, it helps if you encourage the other person to be specific when you are on the receiving end of criticism. In the example of the complaint about the bathroom, you can help your partner be specific and, perhaps, avert the worst by asking clarifying questions, such as "Can you tell me exactly what you mean?" or "The bathroom?"

Consider a situation in which a lover says something like "You're one of the most irritating people I know." Rather than retaliating and further harming the relationship, you can say something like "How about forgoing the character assassination and telling me what I did that's bothering you?" This response requests an end to insults and asks your partner to be specific.

Even when you disagree with a criticism, you can keep lines of communication open and show respect for your partner's feelings by acknowledging and paraphrasing the criticism.

On the other hand, if you are at fault, you can admit it. For example, you can say, "You're right. It was my day to clean the bathroom and it totally slipped my mind" or "I was so busy, I just couldn't get to it." Now the two of you should look for a way to work out the problem. When you acknowledge criticism, you cue your partner to back off and look for ways to improve the situation. What if your partner then becomes abusive and says something like "So you admit you blew it?" You might then try a little education in conflict resolution. You could say, "I admitted that I was at fault. If you're willing to work with me to find a way to handle it, great; but I'm not going to let you pound me into the ground over it."

Now, if you think that you were not at fault, express your feelings. Use *I*-talk and be specific. Don't seize the opportunity to angrily point out your partner's shortcomings. By doing so, you may shut down lines of communication.

Negotiating Differences   Negotiate your differences if you feel that there is merit on both sides of the argument. You may want to say something like "Would it help if I . . . ?" And if there's something about your obligation to clean the bathroom that seems totally out of place, perhaps you and your partner can work out an exchange—that is, you get relieved of cleaning the bathroom in exchange for tackling a chore that your partner finds equally odious.

If none of these approaches helps resolve the conflict, perhaps your partner is using the comment about the bathroom to express anger over other issues. You may find out by saying something like "I've been trying to find a way to resolve this thing, but nothing I say seems to be helping. Is this really about the bathroom, or are there other things on your mind?"

When Communication Is Not Enough: Handling Impasses   Communication helps build and maintain relationships, but sometimes partners have profound, substantial disagreements. In fact, it is normal to have disagreements from time to time. Even when their communication skills are superbly tuned, partners now and then reach an impasse. Couples who reach an impasse may find these suggestions helpful.

Research shows that taking one's partner's perspective (that is, looking at things from one's partner's point of view) during a dispute results in more positive feelings about the relationship and greater effort to respond in a constructive manner (Arriaga & Rusbult, 1998; Driver et al., 2003). Thus, if there is an impasse, ill feeling may be resolved by (honestly) saying something like "I still disagree with you, but I can understand why you take your position." But if you do not follow your partner's logic, you can say something like, "Please believe me: I'm trying very hard to look at this from your point of view, but I can't follow your reasoning. Would you try to help me understand your point of view?"

Sometimes when you reach a stalemate, it helps to allow the problem to "incubate" for a while. If you and your partner put the issue aside for a time, perhaps a resolution will dawn on one of you later on.

Although we tend to form relationships with people who share similar attitudes, there is never a perfect overlap. A partner who pretends to be your clone will most likely become a bore. Assuming that your relationship is generally rewarding and pleasurable, you may find it possible to tolerate some differences. Part of respecting other people is allowing them to be who they are. When we have a solid sense of who we are as individuals and what we stand for, we are more apt to tolerate differentness in our partners.

When all else fails, you can agree to disagree on various issues. You and your partner can remain solid, respected individuals even if you disagree from time to time.

Remember that disagreement itself is not necessarily destructive to a relationship—unless you are convinced that it must be. Two people cannot see everything in the same way. Failure to disagree *ever* will leave at least one partner feeling frustrated now and then. Conflict is nearly inevitable in a relationship. The key to satisfaction with the relationship is how the couple go about trying to resolve the conflict.

Review: Satisfaction in Relationships: Communication as a Key

Reflect

Do you have difficulty criticizing another person or accepting criticism? Why? How can you become better at delivering or receiving criticism?

Critical Thinking

Why is "active listening" controversial as a method for resolving conflict? Can you think of "unthreatening" uses of active listening?

27. Gottman studied the factors that predict satisfaction in a relationship by videotaping couples as they tried to resolve _____.

28. Gottman found that couples who remained _____ during discussion tended to improve their satisfaction.

29. Stonewalling by a male was connected with _____ of the relationship.

30. Clear _____ can take the guesswork out of relationships and enhance satisfaction.

31. Many people hold the _____ belief that their partner should *know* what they want.

32. There is controversy over whether _____ listening helps resolve conflicts.

33. _____ is a kind of active listening in which a partner restates what his or her partner is saying.

34. There is also controversy about whether it is dangerous to express the feeling of _____ in conflict resolution.

35. To deliver _____ effectively, do so privately and be specific.

36. If you cannot get past an impasse, you can agree to _____.

Recite

1. How do romantic relationships develop?

According to the "ABCDE" model of romantic relationships, they develop through five stages: attraction, building, continuation, deterioration, and ending.

2. What is the role of small talk in building a relationship?

Small talk enables individuals to learn whether they share interests, attitudes, and feelings of attraction with another person.

3. What is the role of the opening line in building a relationship?

The opening line—or greeting—enables individuals to begin surface contact with one another so that they can test whether they are matched and share feelings of attraction.

4. What is the role of self-disclosure in building a relationship?

Self-disclosure enables people to get below surface contact to determine whether they have things in common. Too little self-disclosure prevents development of intimacy; too much may appear to be socially inappropriate.

5. What is intimacy?

Intimacy involves feelings of emotional closeness with another person and the desire to share each other's inmost thoughts and feelings. Intimacy appears to require self-esteem, trust, caring, tenderness, honesty, and commitment.

6. How does jealousy affect relationships?

Jealousy is fear that a rival will intrude upon an intimate relationship. Some research suggests that males are more concerned when their partners have sexual relations with an outsider, whereas females are more concerned when their partners develop emotional closeness with an outsider. These findings are consistent with an evolutionary theory of jealousy.

7. What can partners do when a relationship begins to deteriorate?

Partners can take active means either to improve or to terminate the relationship, or they can sit back passively and let what happens happen.

Recite

8. What is loneliness?

Loneliness is a state of painful isolation, of feeling cut off from others. Solitude, by contrast, can be a positive experience.

9. What are the causes of loneliness?

The causes of loneliness include lack of social skills, lack of interest in other people, lack of empathy, fear of rejection, lack of self-disclosure, cynicism about human nature, demanding too much too soon, general pessimism, and an external locus of control.

10. What can you do to deal with loneliness in your own life?

People are helped to overcome loneliness by challenging self-defeating attitudes, developing social skills, and placing themselves among others rather than withdrawing socially.

11. What factors contribute to satisfaction in relationships?

Factors such as caring, lack of excessive jealousy, perceived fairness and mutual respect in the relationship, and ability to communicate in an open and calm manner are connected with satisfaction in relationships.

12. How can partners develop their communication skills to approach conflict resolution in a constructive manner?

Couples may find it difficult to talk about sex because of the lack of an agreeable common language or because they harbor irrational beliefs about relationships and sex. Therapists help couples develop communication skills such as getting started in communicating, listening to one's partner, learning about one's partner's needs, providing information, making requests, delivering and receiving criticism, and coping with impasses. Controversy exists over whether active listening helps couples communicate.

Chapter 9

Truth?Fiction?

T / F? Married people rarely if ever masturbate.

T / F? European American men are more likely to masturbate than African American men are.

T / F? Women who masturbate during adolescence are less likely to find gratification in marital coitus than women who do not.

T / F? Women are more likely to reach orgasm through sexual intercourse than through masturbation.

T / F? Most women masturbate by inserting a finger or other object into the vagina.

T / F? People who have sexual fantasies are likely to have sexual or social problems.

T / F? Lesbian couples commonly strap on dildos and engage in sexual intercourse with them.

T / F? Statistically speaking, oral sex is the norm for today's young couples.

T / F? African Americans are more likely than European Americans to engage in oral sex.

T / F? When lovers fantasize about other people, the relationship is in trouble.

T / F? Anal sex is more common among less well educated people.

Sexual Techniques and Behavior Patterns

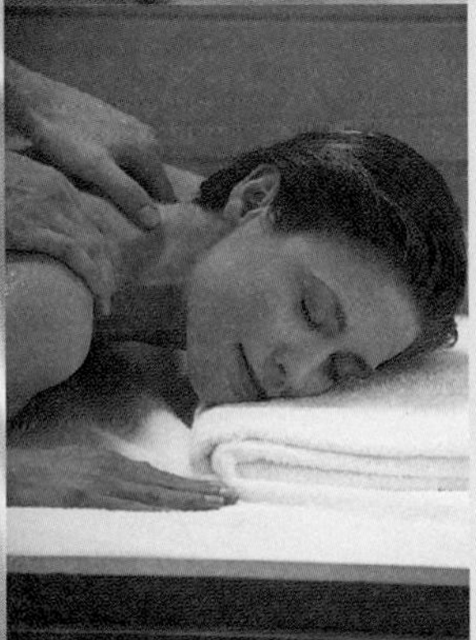

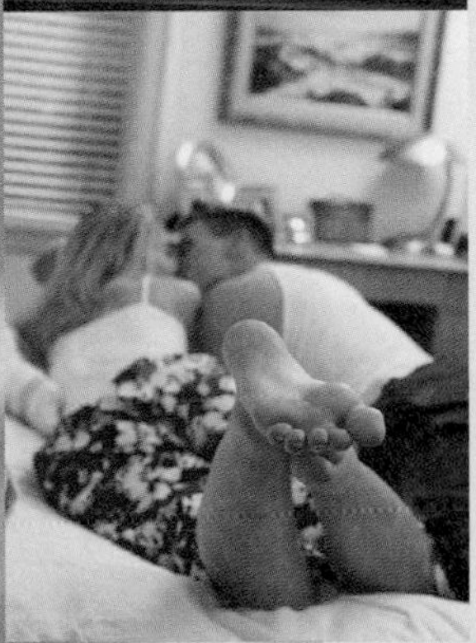

Preview

Solitary Sexual Behavior

Masturbation

A Closer Look: The Technology of Orgasm: "Hysteria," the Vibrator, and Women's Sexual Satisfaction

A World of Diversity: Sociocultural Factors and Masturbation

Use of Fantasy

Sexual Behavior with Others

Foreplay

Kissing

Touching

Stimulation of the Breasts

Oral–Genital Stimulation

A World of Diversity: Sociocultural Factors and Oral Sex

Sexual Intercourse: Positions and Techniques

*T*his is the chapter that describes sexual techniques and statistical breakdowns of "who does what with whom." There is great variety in human sexual expression. Some of us practice few, if any, of the techniques in the chapter. Some of us practice most or all of them. Some of us practice some of them some of the time. Our best knowledge of the prevalence of these techniques comes mainly from the sex surveys of Kinsey and the University of Chicago group. But even these surveys are plagued by problems such as not-fully-representative sampling, social desirability, and volunteer bias.

Readers of this textbook are as varied in their sexual values, preferences, and attitudes as is society in general. Some of the techniques discussed may thus strike some readers as indecent. Our aim is to provide information about the diversity of sexual expression. We are not seeking unanimity on what is acceptable. Nor do we pass judgments or encourage readers to expand their sexual repertoires.

The human body is sensitive to many forms of sexual stimulation. Yet we reiterate that biology is not destiny: A biological capacity does not impose a behavioral requirement. Cultural expectations, personal values, and individual experience—not only our biological capacities—determine our sexual behavior. What is right for you is right for *you*—not necessarily for your neighbor.

We begin by reviewing the techniques that people practice on their own to derive sexual pleasure: masturbation and sexual fantasy. We then consider techniques that involve a partner.

Solitary Sexual Behavior

Various forms of sexual expression do not require a partner or are not generally practiced in the presence of a partner. Masturbation is one of the principal forms of one-person sexual expression. *Question: What is masturbation?* Masturbation involves direct stimulation of the genitals. Other forms of individual sexual experience, such as sexual fantasy, may or may not be accompanied by genital stimulation.

Masturbation

> In solitude he pollutes himself, and with his own hand blights all his prospects for both this world and the next. Even after being solemnly warned, he will often continue this worse than beastly practice, deliberately forfeiting his right to health and happiness for a moment's mad sensuality.
>
> *J. H. Kellogg, M.D.,* Plain Facts for Old and Young, *1888*

The word *masturbation* derives from the Latin *masturbari,* from the roots for "hand" and "to defile." The derivation provides clues to historical cultural attitudes toward the practice. **Masturbation** may be practiced by manual stimulation of the genitals, perhaps with the aid of artificial stimulation, such as a vibrator. It may employ an object, such as a pillow or a **dildo,** that touches the genitals. Even before we conceive of sexual experiences with others, we may learn early in childhood that touching our genitals can produce pleasure.

Pleasure is not the only reason why people masturbate. Table 9.1 lists reasons for masturbation, according to the findings of the NHSLS study.

Question: How has masturbation been viewed in our culture? Within the Judeo-Christian tradition, masturbation has been strongly condemned as sinful (Bullough, 2002). Early Judeo-Christian attitudes toward masturbation reflected the censure that was applied toward nonprocreative sexual acts. In the Judeo-Christian tradition, masturbation has been referred to as "onanism," a name that is derived from the biblical story of Onan. According to the Book of Genesis (38:9–11), Onan was the secondborn son of Judah. Judah's first son, Er, had died without an heir. Biblical law required that if a man died without leaving a male heir, his brother must take the widow as a wife (a union called a levirate marriage) and rear their first son as his

Masturbation Sexual self-stimulation.

Dildo A penis-shaped object used in sexual activity.

TABLE 9.1		
Reasons for Masturbation (in Percents of Respondents Who Report Reason), According to the NHSLS Study		
Reasons for Masturbation	Men	Women
To relax	26%	32%
To relieve sexual tension	73	63
Partners are unavailable	32	32
Partner does not want to engage in sexual activity	16	6
Boredom	11	5
To obtain physical pleasure	40	42
To help get to sleep	16	12
Fear of AIDS and other STIs	7	5
Other reasons	5	5

Source: Adapted from Laumann, E. O., Gagnon, J. H., Michael, R. T., & Michaels, S. (1994). *The social organization of sexuality: Sexual practices in the United States.* Chicago: University of Chicago Press, Table 3.3, p. 86.

A Closer Look

The Technology of Orgasm: "Hysteria," the Vibrator, and Women's Sexual Satisfaction

Rachel Maines was going to write a book about needlework in the late nineteenth and early twentieth centuries. In the course of her research, she noticed advertisements for vibrators. She turned her attention to the meaning and use of vibrators in U.S. history and wound up writing a book called *The Technology of Orgasm: "Hysteria," the Vibrator, and Women's Sexual Satisfaction* (1999).

It turns out that genital massage to orgasm—often using a vibrator—was once a standard treatment for "hysteria," a health problem considered common in women. The treatment was usually carried out by a physician or a midwife. Genital massage would be used to bring the woman to "hysterical paroxysm" (orgasm, that is). The introduction of the vibrator in the 1880s made treatment more efficient.

Hysteria? What's that? In earlier centuries the diagnosis of hysteria would be made on the basis of symptoms such as anxiety, irritability, nervousness, pelvic swelling, heaviness in the abdomen (bloating), and fainting. There were other symptoms as well, including sexual fantasies and vaginal lubrication. The word *hysteria* derives from the Greek word for "uterus." The medical establishment believed that the uterus caused these symptoms by choking the patient because of sexual deprivation. Pregnancy would help; so would coitus. Single women were encouraged to get married, and married women were encouraged to get pregnant. Women without men might try horseback riding, use rocking chairs (yes, rocking chairs), or obtain genital massage. Maines found no evidence that physicians delighted in the task. Rather, they apparently relegated it to midwives whenever they could. Women, by the way, were not encouraged to masturbate as a way of achieving, uh, "hysterical paroxysm." Masturbation was seen as deviant and unhealthful. Use of the vibrator in the hands of the physician or midwife was seen as a medical treatment, not a sexual act (Heiman, 2000). An orgasm was a "hysterical crisis," not an orgasm.

It is obvious that the "symptoms of hysteria" are related to menstruation. Today we recognize that menstrual and premenstrual symptoms are associated with the secretion of sex hormones, but even as late as the mid-twentieth century, health professionals attributed a wide variety of mental disorders to hysteria. Therefore, the behaviors connected with the disorders—such as the development of physical symptoms in response to stress—were expected in women but surprising in men.

Psychologist Julia Heiman (2000) believes that the content and the sources cited by Maines deserve further scrutiny by other scholars. It is surprising that this piece of history has remained relatively hidden until now. Yet the book does have a solid list of references, along with illustrations of the vibrators and treatment tables. It would appear that the practice described by Maines did in fact occur. How widespread it was is still uncertain.

---

brother's heir. Judah thus directed Onan to "Go in unto thy brother's wife, and perform the duty of a husband's brother unto her, and raise up seed to thy brother." But Onan "spilled [his seed] upon the ground" during relations with his deceased brother's wife and was struck down by God for his deed.

Although "onanism" has come to be associated with Judeo-Christian condemnation of masturbation, Onan's act was one of **coitus interruptus**, not masturbation. Both acts, however, involve nonprocreative sex—spilling the seed. Moreover, Onan's punishment seems to have had more to do with his failure to fulfill his lawful obligations than with his spilling his seed. Whatever its biblical origins, masturbation is prohibited under Jewish law. St. Augustine was influenced by ancient Persian beliefs, which condemned all nonprocreative sexual activity as sinful (Bullough, 2002). Historians suspect that people in ancient times condemned sexual practices that did not lead to pregnancy because of the need for an increase in their numbers. The need for progeny is also linked to the widespread view that coitus in marriage is the only morally acceptable avenue of sexual expression.

Historical Medical Views of Masturbation St. Augustine's views were carried into medicine in the eighteenth century, and the medical profession "translated" sin into disease. Thus until recent times, masturbation was thought to be physically and mentally harmful, as well as degrading. The eighteenth-century physician Benjamin

Coitus interruptus The practice of withdrawing the penis prior to ejaculation during sexual intercourse.

Rush, a signer of the Declaration of Independence, believed that masturbation caused tuberculosis, "nervous diseases," poor eyesight, memory loss, and epilepsy.

Many clergy and medical authorities of the nineteenth century were persuaded that certain foods had a stimulating effect on the sex organs. Thus they advised parents to modify their children's diets to eliminate foods that were believed to excite the sexual organs, notably meat, coffee, tea, and chocolate. Parents should substitute "unstimulating" foods, most notably grain products. In the 1830s the Reverend Sylvester Graham developed a cracker, since called the graham cracker, to help people control their sexual impulses.

Yet another household name belongs to a man who made his mark by introducing a bland diet that was also intended to help people, especially youngsters, control sexual impulses. One of the more influential medical writers of the nineteenth century was the superintendent of the Battle Creek Sanatorium in Michigan, Dr. J. H. Kellogg (1852–1943), better known now as the creator of the modern breakfast cereal. Kellogg identified 39 "signs of masturbation," including acne, paleness, heart palpitations, rounded shoulders, weak backs, and convulsions. Kellogg, like Graham, believed that sexual desires could be controlled by a diet of simple foods, especially grains, including the corn flakes that have since borne his name. (We wonder how Kellogg would react to the energizing, sugar-coated cereals that now also bear his name.)

Many nineteenth-century physicians also advised parents to take measures to prevent their children from masturbating. Kellogg suggested that parents bandage or cage their children's genitals, or tie their hands (see Figure 9.1).

Several nineteenth-century scholars of sexuality joined the crusade against masturbation. Richard von Krafft-Ebing (in *Psychopathia Sexualis,* 1886) and Havelock Ellis (in *Studies in the Psychology of Sex,* 1900) condemned masturbation as psychologically dangerous. Krafft-Ebing linked masturbation to sexual orientation. Male masturbation, or so it was mistakenly believed, arrested the development of normal erotic instincts and led to **impotence** with women. Thus it encouraged male–male sexual activity.

Question: **Is *masturbation harmful?*** Despite this history, there is no scientific evidence that masturbation is harmful. Masturbation does not cause insanity, grow hair on the hands, or cause warts or any of the other psychological and physical ills once ascribed to it, save for rare injuries to the genitals due to rough stimulation. Nor is masturbation in itself psychologically harmful, although it may be a sign of an adjustment problem if people use masturbation as an exclusive sexual outlet when they have opportunities for sexual relationships. Sex therapists have even found therapeutic uses for masturbation. It has emerged as a treatment for individuals with low sexual desire and for women who have difficulty reaching orgasm (Coleman, 2002; Zamboni & Crawford, 2002; see Chapter 15).

Of course, people who consider masturbation wrong, harmful, or sinful may experience anxiety or guilt about masturbation (Kontula & Haavio-Mannila, 2002).

Impotence Recurrent difficulty in achieving or sustaining an erection sufficient to engage in sexual intercourse successfully. (The term has been replaced by the terms *male erectile disorder* and *erectile dysfunction,* as discussed in Chapter 15.)

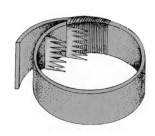

Figure 9.1. Devices Designed to Curb Masturbation. Because of widespread beliefs that masturbation was harmful, various contraptions were introduced in the nineteenth century to prevent the practice in children. Some of the devices were barbarous.

Sociocultural Factors and Masturbation

Few "forbidden" activities have been as widespread as masturbation. Nearly all of the adult men and about two-thirds of the adult women in the classic Kinsey studies (Kinsey et al., 1948, 1953) reported that they had masturbated at some time. The NHSLS study also found a gender gap in reported frequencies of masturbation (Laumann et al., 1994). Table 9.2 shows how study participants reported the frequency of masturbation "during the past 12 months," according to sex, age, marital status, level of education, religion, and race/ethnicity.

Overall, 37% of the men and 58% of the women who were sampled reported that they had *not* masturbated during the past year. Within every social category, men reported masturbating more frequently than women. Despite the sexual revolution, women may still find masturbation less acceptable than men do (Dantzker & Eisenman, 2003). Traditional women may still be subject to socialization pressures that teach that sexual activity for pleasure's sake is more of a taboo for women than for men (Dantzker & Eisenman, 2003). Then, too, women are more likely than men to pursue sexual activity within the context of a relationship.

Truth?Fiction?
Revisited

It is not true that married people rarely if ever masturbate.

African Americans are less likely—not more likely—than other ethnic groups to report masturbating over a 12-month period. Perhaps African American men are relatively more likely to adhere to traditional views concerning masturbation.

According to the Kinsey studies, women who had masturbated during adolescence were more likely, not less likely, to find gratification in sex with others in adulthood than women who had not.

Researchers also find that women achieve orgasm more reliably through masturbation than through coitus (Masters & Johnson, 1966; Young et al., 1998).

In Indian society, for example, it is commonly believed that masturbation leads to sexual impotence (Chakrabarti et al., 2002). Therefore, some Indian men experience extreme anxiety and fear as a result of masturbation, which sometimes leads to the lack of sexual response they dread. But these negative reactions are linked to their beliefs about masturbation, not to masturbation per se.

Question: Who masturbates? Despite some continued condemnation of masturbation, surveys indicate that most people in our society masturbate at some time. One difference since Kinsey's day is that individuals are now masturbating at earlier ages (Dekker & Schmidt, 2002). The incidence of masturbation has been, and remains, generally greater among men than among women. The above "World of Diversity" feature elaborates on masturbation among different groups.

Married people are less likely to have masturbated during the past 12 months than never-married and formerly married people. Nevertheless, only 43% of the married men and 63% of the married women sampled said that they did not masturbate at all during the past year.

People with more education—both female and male—reported more frequent masturbation. Perhaps people with more schooling are more likely to learn that masturbation itself is harmless or are less likely to follow traditional social restrictions. Traditional religious beliefs appear to restrain masturbation. Conservative Protestants are less likely to masturbate than liberal and moderate Protestants.

There appears to be a link between masturbation and orgasm during sex with others (Coleman, 2002). Kinsey and his colleagues had reported links between adolescent masturbation and sexual satisfaction in adulthood.

Correlational evidence does not suggest that adolescents should be encouraged to masturbate to foster sexual fulfillment in adulthood. A selection factor may explain the link (see Figure 9.2). That is, people who masturbate early may be generally more open to exploring their sexuality. These attitudes would carry over into adulthood and increase

TABLE 9.2				
Sociocultural Factors and Frequency of Masturbation During Past 12 Months, as Found in the NHSLS Study				
	Frequency of Masterbation (%)			
	Not at All		At Least Once a Week	
SOCIOCULTURAL CHARACTERISTICS	Men	Women	Men	Women
Total population	36.7	58.3	26.7	7.6
Age				
18–24	41.2	64.4	29.2	9.4
25–29	28.9	58.3	32.7	9.9
30–34	27.6	51.1	34.6	8.6
35–39	38.5	52.3	20.8	6.6
40–44	34.5	49.8	28.7	8.7
45–49	35.2	55.6	27.2	8.6
50–54	52.5	71.8	13.9	2.3
55–59	51.7	77.6	10.3	2.4
Marital Status				
Never married (not cohabiting)	31.8	51.8	41.3	12.3
Married	42.6	62.9	16.5	4.7
Formerly married (not cohabiting)	30.2	52.7	34.9	9.6
Education				
Less than high school	54.8	75.1	19.2	7.6
High school graduate	45.1	68.4	20.0	5.6
Some college	33.2	51.3	30.8	6.9
College graduate	24.2	47.7	33.2	10.2
Advanced degree	18.6	41.2	33.6	13.7
Religion				
None	32.6	41.4	37.6	13.8
Liberal or moderate Protestant	28.9	55.1	28.2	7.4
Conservative Protestant	48.4	67.3	19.5	5.8
Catholic	34.0	57.3	24.9	6.6
Race/Ethnicity				
European American	33.4	55.7	28.3	7.3
African American	60.3	67.8	16.9	10.7
Latino and Latina American	33.1	65.5	24.4	4.7
Asian American	38.7	—*	31.3	—*
Native American	—*	—*	—*	—*

Source: Adapted from Laumann, E. O., Gagnon, J. H., Michael, R. T., & Michaels, S. (1994). *The social organization of sexuality: Sexual practices in the United States.* Chicago: University of Chicago Press, Table 3.1, p. 82.

*Sample sizes too small to report findings.

the likelihood that women would seek the sexual stimulation they need to achieve sexual gratification. Adolescent masturbation may also set the stage for sexual satisfaction in adulthood by providing information about the types of stimulation that lead to sexual gratification.

In our efforts to correct misinformation about masturbation, let us not suggest that there is anything wrong with choosing *not* to masturbate. Although we may all be able to experience pleasure from self-stimulation (Pinkerton et al., 2003a), biology is not destiny. Readers are encouraged to make their own choices on the basis of their own values.

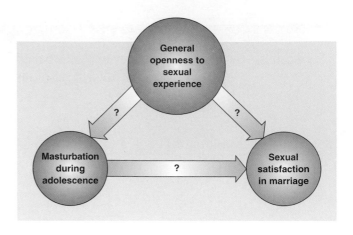

Figure 9.2. What Are the Connections Between Masturbation During Adolescence and Sexual Satisfaction in Marriage? There is a positive correlation between masturbation during adolescence and sexual satisfaction in marriage. What hypotheses can we make about the causal connections? Does experience with masturbation teach people about their sexual needs so that they are more likely to obtain adequate sexual stimulation in marriage? Are people who masturbate early generally more open to exploring their sexuality and learning about the types of stimulation that arouse them? Such attitudes might also increase the likelihood that people would seek the coital stimulation they need to achieve sexual gratification in marriage.

Masturbation Techniques Used by Males

> Sex is like bridge—if you don't have a good partner, you'd better have a good hand.
>
> *Bathroom graffiti*

Question: How do males masturbate? Although masturbation techniques vary widely, most men report that they masturbate by manual manipulation of the penis (see Figure 9.3). Kinsey and his colleagues (1948) reported that when masturbating, men typically take one or two minutes to reach orgasm. Men tend to grip the penile shaft with one hand, jerking it up and down in a milking motion. Some men move the whole hand up and down the penis, while others use just two fingers, generally the thumb and index finger. Men usually shift from a gentler rubbing action during the flaccid or semi-erect state of arousal to a more vigorous milking motion once full erection takes place. Men are also likely to stroke the glans and frenulum lightly at the outset, but their grip tightens and their motions speed up as orgasm nears. At orgasm, the penile shaft may be gripped tightly, but the glans has become sensitive, and contact with it is usually avoided. (Likewise, women usually avoid stimulating the clitoris directly during orgasm because of increased sensitivity.)

Some men use soapsuds (which may become irritating) as a lubricant for masturbation during baths or showers. Other lubricants, such as petroleum jelly or K-Y jelly, are less irritating and also more effective at reducing friction and simulating the moist conditions of coitus.

A few men prefer to masturbate by rubbing the penis and testicles against clothing or bedding (Kinsey et al., 1948). A few men rub their genitals against inflatable dolls sold in sex shops. These dolls may come with artificial mouths or vaginas that can be filled with warm water to mimic the sensations of coitus. Artificial vaginas are also for sale.

Some men strap vibrators to the backs of their hands. Electrical vibrators save labor but do not simulate the type of up-and-down motions of the penis that men favor. Hence, they are not used very often. Most men rely heavily on fantasy or erotic photos or videos but do not use sex-shop devices.

Figure 9.3. Male Masturbation. *Masturbation techniques vary widely, but most men report that they masturbate by manual manipulation of the penis. They tend to grip the penile shaft with one hand and jerk it up and down in a milking motion.*

Masturbation Techniques Used by Females   Question: How do females masturbate? Techniques of female masturbation also vary widely. In fact, Masters and Johnson reported never observing two women masturbate in precisely the same way. Even when the general technique was similar, women varied in the tempo and style of their self-caresses. But some general trends have been noted. Most women masturbate by massaging the mons, labia minora, and clitoral region with circular or back-and-forth motions (Kinsey et al., 1953). They may also straddle the clitoris with their fingers, stroking the shaft rather than the glans (see Figure 9.4). The glans may be lightly touched early during arousal, but because of its exquisite sensitivity, it is rarely stroked for any length of time during masturbation. Women typically achieve clitoral stimulation by rubbing or stroking the clitoral shaft or pulling or tugging on the vaginal lips. Some women also massage other sensitive areas, such as their breasts or nipples, with the free hand. Many women, like men, fantasize during masturbation (Leitenberg & Henning, 1995).

Kinsey and his colleagues (1953) found that only one in five women inserted objects into the vagina during masturbation. Some women experimented with vaginal insertion but gave it up as they became more familiar with their sexual anatomy and capabilities. Others practiced the technique because their male partners found it sexually stimulating to watch them. Still, some women reported erotic pleasure from deep vaginal penetration.

Truth?Fiction?
Revisited

In contrast to the male myth that women usually masturbate by simulating penile thrusting through the insertion of fingers or phallic objects into their vaginas, relatively few women actually do.

Figure 9.4. Female Masturbation.   Techniques of female masturbation vary so widely that Masters and Johnson reported never observing two women masturbating in precisely the same way. Most women masturbate by massaging the mons, labia minora, and clitoral region, however, either with circular or back-and-forth motions.

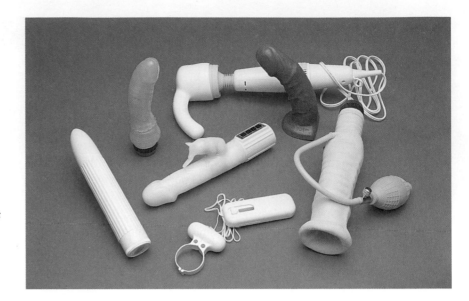

Figure 9.5. Electric Vibrators and Other Sex Toys. Both females and males use devices like these in the place of real penises, to try to increase the volume of the penis, or for other sexual ends. If they are to be used at all, they should be used with extreme caution.

Even when women use insertion, they usually precede or combine it with clitoral stimulation. Sex shops sell dildos, which women can use to rub their vulvas or to insert vaginally. Penis-shaped vibrators may be used similarly (McCaughey & French, 2001). Many women masturbate during baths; some spray their genitals with shower heads.

Handheld electrical vibrators (see Figure 9.5) provide a constant massaging action against the genitals. Some women find this type of stimulation too intense and favor vibrators that strap to the back of the hand, helping the fingers to vibrate during manual stimulation of the genitals. But this type of vibration may numb the hand attached to the vibrator. Women experiment with different vibrators to find one with the shape and intensity of vibration that suits them.

Use of Fantasy

Question: What is the role of fantasy in solitary sexual behavior? People may use sexual fantasies when they are alone or to heighten sexual excitement with a partner (Eggers, 2000; Leitenberg & Henning, 1995). Some couples find it sexually arousing to share fantasies or to enact them with their partners. Sexual fantasies may be experienced without sexual behavior, as in erotic dreams or daydreams. Masturbators often require some form of cognitive stimulation, such as fantasy or reading or viewing erotica, to increase their arousal to the point of orgasm.

There are many theories about sexual fantasies. One view, which apparently has little if any research evidence behind it, is that people who fantasize about sex are less likely to have enjoyable sex lives. That is, the fantasy takes the place of real sexual activity. But fantasies can also enhance sexual arousal, providing greater pleasure.

Question: Are sexual fantasies normal? Research suggests that sexual fantasies are normal in that most people have them—(even during sexual activity with someone else. They have fantasies either for their own sake or to heighten sexual arousal during activity with their partners (Leitenberg & Henning, 1995). Males seem to engage in sexual fantasies more frequently than females, but most females do so also—at least within our culture. A survey of 349 university students and employees, aged 18 to 70, who were involved in heterosexual relationships found that the great majority— 98% of the men and 80% of the women—reported sexual fantasies about someone *other* than their sex partner (Hicks & Leitenberg, 2001). These fantasies were more common among people who had been in their relationships longer, perhaps providing some sort of sexual novelty. Women were more likely than men to fantasize about *prior* sex partners, suggestive, perhaps, that they had less need to cognitively stray from familiar relationships. According to a *New York Times* poll, men are somewhat more likely than women—52% versus 40%—to think it is acceptable to fantasize about sex with someone other than their partner (Eggers, 2000).

Question: What does evolutionary theory have to say about sexual fantasies? Evolutionary theorists conjecture that women are relatively more likely to fantasize about the images of familiar lovers because female reproductive success in ancestral times was more likely to depend on an emotionally close, protective relationship with a reliable partner (Symons, 1995). Women can bear and rear relatively few offspring. Thus, they would have a relatively greater genetic investment than men in each reproductive opportunity.

Truth?Fiction?
Revisited

It is therefore not true that people who have sexual fantasies are likely to have sexual or social problems. The opposite may actually be true.

In keeping with gender-role stereotypes, the studies also found that males are more likely to fantasize about forcing women into sexual activity. Women are more likely to fantasize about being victimized (Donnelly & Fraser, 1998).

Researchers, by the way, use the frequency and variety of sexual fantasies as one measure of the sex drive (Baumeister et al., 2001). The sex drive and the frequency of sexual fantasizing are related to testosterone levels both in males and females. One study surveyed the frequency of sexual activity and sexual fantasies among women who had undergone oophorectomy and hysterectomy (Shifren et al., 2000). The women were administered various doses of testosterone or a placebo via skin patches. Women given higher doses of testosterone doubled or tripled their reported incidence of sexual fantasies, masturbation, and sexual intercourse.

Studies suggest that most of us consider sexual fantasies normal. One study surveyed 178 university students and staff and found that 84% of them reported having sexual fantasies at least occasionally during sexual intercourse (Cado & Leitenberg, 1990). Most of these individuals said that they believed that such fantasies were common, normal, moral, socially acceptable, and more beneficial than harmful. Still, about one-quarter of the sample reported feeling guilty about the fantasies. Those who felt most guilty were also most likely to experience sexual dissatisfaction and problems in their actual lives.

There are also "deviant" sexual fantasies, such as sadistic rape fantasies. Research evidence with the MMPI, a commonly used personality test, suggests that men who frequently have deviant sexual fantasies are more likely to be socially isolated and emotionally unstable (Curnoe & Langevin, 2002). Although there is a connection between our fantasy lives and our actual lives, the extent to which deviant sexual fantasies contribute to crimes involving sex and aggression is not completely clear. Nevertheless, many helping professionals work with men with deviant sexual fantasies in the hope that if they change their fantasies, the men will be less likely to commit crimes of violence (Leitenberg & Henning, 1995). And when it comes to fantasies about being victimized, Nancy Friday (1973) reports the following from a woman she interviewed:

> My fantasies are so personal, and the pleasure I get from them derives so much, I think, from the fact that they are private and locked away in my imagination, that I wouldn't dream of trying to make them come true. . . . But act my fantasies out? Make them come true? No, absolutely not. My real life's not what they're about; I don't want those things to really happen to me, I simply want to imagine what it would be like. So that's where they'll stay. (Friday, p. 288)

Review: Solitary Sexual Behavior

Reflect

What misinformation, if any, did you receive about masturbation as you were growing up? What was the source of the misinformation?

CriticalThinking

What kinds of information are available to help individuals decide whether masturbation and sexual fantasies are right or wrong for them? What type of information do you consider to be most important? Explain.

1. _____ is stimulation of one's own genitals to achieve sexual pleasure and release.

2. According to the NHSLS study, the most common reason for masturbating is to _____.

3. In the Judeo-Christian tradition, masturbation has been referred to as _____.

4. In his condemnation of masturbation, St. _____ was influenced by ancient Persian beliefs that condemned all nonprocreative forms of sexual activity.

5. Dr. _____ created the modern breakfast cereal as a means of helping people control sexual desires.

6. Surveys show that (*Men* or *Women*?) are more likely to masturbate.

7. People with more education are (*More* or *Less*?) likely to masturbate.

8. According to the NHSLS study, (*African* or *European*?) American men are more likely to masturbate.

9. According to the Kinsey studies, women who masturbated during adolescence were (*More* or *Less*?) likely to find gratification in sex with others in adulthood.

10. Most men report that they masturbate by _____ manipulation of the penis.

11. Most women (*Do* or *Do not*?) masturbate by inserting fingers or objects into the vagina.

12. Research suggests that (*Most* or *Only a few*?) people have sexual fantasies.

13. Surveys find that (*Males* or *Females*?) report more frequent use of sexual fantasies.

14. Men are (*More* or *Less*?) likely than women to fantasize about prior sex partners during sexual activity.

15. (*Men* or *Women*?) are more likely to fantasize about forcing people of the other sex into sexual activity.

Sexual Behavior with Others

Partners' feelings for one another, and the quality of their relationships, may be stronger determinants of their sexual arousal and response than the techniques that they employ. Partners are most likely to experience mutually enjoyable sexual interactions when they are sensitive to each other's sexual needs and incorporate techniques with which they are both comfortable. As with other aspects of sharing relationships, communication is the most important "sexual" technique. Let us begin our discussion of sex with others as many sexual episodes begin—with a discussion of foreplay. *Question: What is foreplay?*

Foreplay

Foreplay Physical interactions that are sexually stimulating and set the stage for intercourse.

Various forms of noncoital sex, such as cuddling, kissing, petting, and oral–genital contact, are used as **foreplay**. The pattern and duration of foreplay vary widely within and across cultures. Broude and Greene (1976) found that prolonged foreplay was the norm in about half of the societies in their cross-cultural sample. Foreplay was minimal in one in ten societies and virtually absent in about one-third of them.

Within the United States, there is a gender difference in the amount of foreplay desired. A survey of college students revealed that women wanted longer periods of foreplay (and "afterplay") than men did (Denny et al., 1984). Because women usually require a longer period of stimulation during sex with a partner to reach orgasm, increasing the duration of foreplay may increase female coital responsiveness.

Foreplay is not limited to the human species. Virtually all species of mammals, from horses and sheep to dogs and chimpanzees, engage in some kind of foreplay. Depending on the particular species, mating pairs may rub, playfully nip, lick, or nuzzle each other's genitals for minutes or hours preceding coitus (Geer et al., 1984).

Kissing, genital touching, and oral–genital contact may also be experienced as ends in themselves, not as preludes to coitus. Yet some people object to petting for petting's sake, equating it with masturbation as a form of sexual activity without a "product." Many people behave as though all sexual contact must lead to coitus, perhaps because of the importance that our culture places on it.

Kissing

Question: What is the role of kissing? Kissing is almost universal in our culture, but it occurs less often among the world's cultures than manual or oral stimulation of the genitals (Frayser, 1985). Kissing is unknown in some cultures, such as among the Thonga of Africa and the Siriono of Bolivia. Variations in styles of kissing also exist across cultures (Ford & Beach, 1951). Kissing is now practiced in Japan because of the influence of Western culture, but it was previously unknown there. Instead of kissing, the Balinese of the South Pacific bring their faces close enough to each other to smell each other's perfume and feel the warmth of each other's skin. This practice has been wrongly dubbed "rubbing noses" by Europeans. Among some preliterate societies, kissing consists of sucking the partner's lips and tongue and allowing saliva to pass from one mouth to the other.

Couples may kiss for its own enjoyment or as a prelude to intercourse, in which case it is a part of foreplay. In *simple kissing,* the partners keep their mouths closed. Simple kissing may develop into caresses of the lips with the tongue or into nibbling of the lower lip. In what Kinsey called *deep kissing,* which is also called French kissing or soul kissing, the partners part their lips and insert their tongues into each other's mouths. Some prefer the lips parted slightly. Others open their mouths widely.

Kissing may also be an affectionate gesture without erotic significance, as in kissing someone good-night. Some people are accustomed to kissing relatives and close friends affectionately on the lips. Others limit kissing relatives to the cheek. Sustained kissing on the lips and deep kissing are nearly always erotic gestures.

Kissing is not limited to the partner's mouth. Kinsey found that more than nine husbands in ten kissed their wives' breasts. Women usually prefer several minutes of body contact and gentle caresses before desiring to have their partner kiss their breasts or suck or lick their nipples. Women also usually do not prefer a hard sucking action unless they are highly aroused. Many women are reluctant to tell their partners that sucking hurts because they do not want to interfere with their partner's pleasure.

Other parts of the body are also often kissed, including the hands and feet, the neck and earlobes, the insides of the thighs, and the genitals themselves. When we kiss, we touch each other with our lips. *Question: What is the role of touching?*

Touching

Touching or caressing erogenous zones with the hands or other parts of the body can be highly arousing. Even simple hand-holding can be sexually stimulating for couples who are sexually attracted to one another. The hands are very rich in nerve endings.

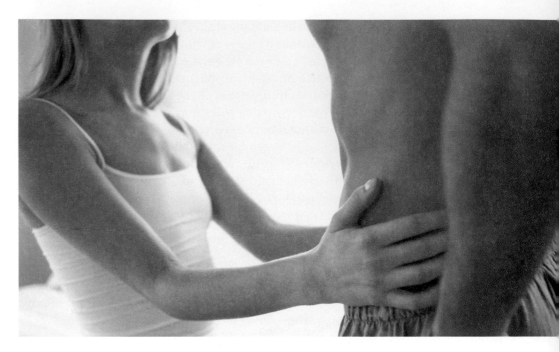

How Touching? *Touching is a common form of foreplay. Most people like manual or oral stimulation of the genital organs as a prelude to sexual intercourse.*

Touching is a common form of foreplay. Both men and women generally prefer manual or oral stimulation of the genitals as a prelude to intercourse. Women generally prefer that direct caressing of the genitals be focused around the clitoris but not directly on the extremely sensitive clitoral glans. Men sometimes assume (often mistakenly) that their partners want them to insert their finger or fingers into the vagina as a form of foreplay. But not all women enjoy this form of stimulation. Some women go along with it because it is what their partners want or is something they think their partners want. Ironically, men may do it because they assume that their partners want it. When in doubt, it would not hurt to *ask.* If you are not sure what to say, you can always blame us: "Listen, I read this thing in my human sexuality text, and I was wondering . . . ."

Masters and Johnson (1979) noted sex differences with respect to preferences in foreplay. Men typically prefer direct stroking of their genitals by their partner early in lovemaking. Women, however, tend to prefer that their partners caress their genitals after a period of general body contact that includes holding, hugging, and nongenital massage. This is not a hard and fast (or slow) rule, but it is consistent with other observations that men tend to be more genitally oriented than women. Women are more likely to view sex within a broader framework of affection and love.

Techniques of Manual Stimulation of the Genitals Here again, variability in technique is the rule, so partners need to communicate their preferences. The man's partner may use two hands to stimulate his genitals. One may be used to fondle the scrotum, by gently squeezing the skin between the fingers (taking care not to apply pressure to the testes themselves). The other hand may circle the coronal ridge and engage in gentle stroking of the penis, followed by more vigorous up and down movements as the man becomes more aroused.

The penis may also be gently rolled back and forth between the palms as if one were making a ball of clay into a sausage—increasing pressure as arousal progresses. Note that men who are highly aroused or who have just had an orgasm may find direct stimulation of the penile glans uncomfortable.

The woman may prefer that her partner approach genital stimulation gradually, following stimulation of other body parts. Genital stimulation may begin with light, stroking motions of the inner thighs and move on to the vaginal lips (labia) and the clitoral area. Women may enjoy pressure against the mons pubis from the heel of the hand, or tactile stimulation of the labia, which are sensitive to stroking motions. Clitoral stimulation can focus on the clitoral shaft or the region surrounding the shaft, rather than the clitoris itself, because of the extreme sensitivity of the clitoral glans to touch.

Moreover, the clitoris should not be stroked if it is dry, lest it become irritated. Because it produces no lubrication of its own, a finger may enter the outer portion of the vagina to apply some vaginal lubrication to the clitoral region.

Some, but not all, women enjoy having a finger inserted into the vagina, which can stroke the vaginal walls or simulate thrusting of the penis. Vaginal insertion is usually not preferred, if at all, until the woman has become highly aroused. Many women desire that their partners discontinue stroking motions while they are experiencing orgasm, but others wish stimulation to continue. Men and women may physically guide their partners' hands or otherwise express their preference of the types of strokes they find most pleasurable.

If a finger is to be inserted into the vagina, it should be clean. Fingernails should be well trimmed. Inserting fingers that have been in the anus into the vagina is dangerous. The fingers may transfer microbes from the woman's digestive tract, where they do no harm, to the woman's reproductive tract, where they can cause serious infections.

Some individuals engage in the sexual practice called "fisting." Fisting is the insertion of the fist or hand into the rectum, usually after the bowels have been evacuated with an enema. Fisting is more common among male–male than among male–female couples, and it carries the risk of infection or injury to the rectum or anus. A survey of 75 gay men in Australia found that fisting was usually done with gloves, although fingering was not (Richters et al., 2003).

Stimulation of the Breasts

Question: What is the role of stimulation of the breasts? Men are more likely to stimulate women's breasts than to have their own breasts fondled, even though the breasts (and especially the nipples) are erotically sensitive in both sexes. Most, but not all, women enjoy stimulation of the breasts. Masters and Johnson report that some women are capable of achieving orgasm from stimulation of the breasts alone.

The hands and the mouth can be used to stimulate the breasts and the nipples. Because the desired type and intensity of stimulation of the breasts vary from person to person, partners need to communicate their preferences.

Question: How do gay males and lesbians make use of stimulation of the breasts? Gay men apparently make more use of stimulation of their partner's nipples than heterosexual women do. Gay male couples tend to engage in sexual activities such as kissing, hugging, petting, mutual masturbation, fellatio, and anal intercourse. Masters and Johnson's (1979) laboratory observations of sexual relations between gay males showed that gay males spent a good deal of time caressing their partners' bodies before approaching the genitals (Figure 9.6). After hugging and kissing, 31 of 42 gay male couples observed by Masters and Johnson used oral or manual nipple stimulation.

Although some heterosexual men enjoy having their breasts and nipples stimulated by their partners, many—perhaps most—do not. Many men are unaware that their breasts are erotically sensitive. Others may feel uncomfortable receiving a form of stimulation that they have learned to associate with the stereotypical feminine sexual role.

Figure 9.6. Gay Males Hugging. *Masters and Johnson's observations suggest that gay males are likely to spend more time than heterosexual males in hugging their partners. Gay males are also more likely than heterosexual males to want their nipples to be caressed.*

Figure 9.7. Lesbians Holding One Another. *This position enables lesbians to hug one another and to reach one another's genitals. If the couple draws a bit closer, they can rub their genitals against one another's.*

Truth?Fiction?
Revisited

Images of lesbians strapping on dildos for vaginal penetration exist more in the imagination of uninformed heterosexual people than in the sexual repertoire of lesbian couples (Masters & Johnson, 1979). The emotional components of lovemaking—gentle touching, cuddling, and hugging—are important elements of sexual sharing in lesbian relationships.

Sexual techniques practiced by lesbians vary. Lesbian couples report kissing, manual and oral breast stimulation, and manual and oral stimulation of the genitals (Kinsey et al., 1953). Manual genital stimulation is the most common and frequent sexual activity among lesbian couples (Bell & Weinberg, 1978). Most lesbian couples also engage in genital apposition. That is, they position themselves so as to rub their genitals together rhythmically (Kinsey et al., 1953). Like gay males, lesbians spend a good deal of time holding, kissing, and caressing each other's bodies before they approach the breasts and genitals (Figure 9.7). By contrast, heterosexual males tend to move quickly to stimulate their partners' breasts or start directly with genital stimulation (Masters & Johnson, 1979).

Like heterosexual women, lesbians are less genitally oriented and less fixated on orgasm than are men. Lesbians generally begin stimulating their partners with more general genital stimulation rather than direct clitoral stimulation, whereas heterosexual males often begin by stimulating the clitoris (Masters & Johnson, 1979). Nor do lesbian couples generally engage in deep penetration of the vagina with fingers. Rather, they may use more shallow vaginal penetration, focusing stimulation on the vaginal lips and entrance.

Oral–Genital Stimulation

Question: What is oral–genital stimulation? Oral stimulation of the male genitals is called **fellatio**. Fellatio is referred to by slang terms such as "blow job," "sucking," "sucking off," or "giving head." Oral stimulation of the female genitals is called **cunnilingus**, which is referred to by slang expressions such as "eating" (a woman) or "going down" on her.

Question: Who engages in oral–genital stimulation? The popularity of oral–genital stimulation has increased dramatically since Kinsey's day, especially among young married couples. Kinsey and his colleagues (1948, 1953) found that at least 60% of married, *college-educated* couples had experienced oral–genital contact. Such experiences were reported by only about 20% of couples who had only a high school education and 10% who had only a grade school education.

According to the NHSLS study, the incidence of oral sex was higher in recent years (Laumann et al., 1994). About three of four men (77%) and two of three women (68%) reported playing the active role in oral sex during their lifetimes. Nearly four men in five (79%) and three of four women (73%) reported having been the recipients of oral–genital sex during their lifetimes. Among married couples, 80% of the men and 71% of the women have performed oral sex. Eighty percent of the men and 74% of the women have received oral sex. These are dramatic increases since Kinsey's day. Among young European American women (ages 18 to 36) in Kinsey's sample, 48% reported having engaged in fellatio. Fifty-one percent of their partners had engaged in cunnilingus.

Like touching, oral–genital stimulation can be used as a prelude to intercourse or as a sexual end in itself. If orgasm is reached through oral–genital stimulation, a partner may be concerned about tasting or swallowing the ejaculate. There is no evidence that swallowing semen is harmful to one's health, unless the man is infected with a sexually transmitted infection that can be transmitted via semen. But oral genital contact with the genitals of an infected partner, even without contact with semen, may transmit harmful organisms. Couples are thus advised to practice "safer sex" techniques (see Chapters 16 and 17) unless they know that they and their partners are free of sexually transmitted infections.

Techniques of Fellatio Although the word *fellatio* is derived from a Latin root meaning "to suck," sucking is generally not highly arousing. The up-and-down movements of the penis in the partner's mouth, and the licking of the penis, are generally the most stimulating. Gentle licking of the scrotum may also be highly arousing.

The mouth is stimulating to the penis because it contains warm, moist mucous membranes, as does the vagina. Muscles of the mouth and jaw can vary pressure and movements. Erection may be stimulated by gently pulling the penis with the mouth (being careful not to touch the penis with the teeth) and simultaneously providing manual stimulation.

Higher levels of sexual arousal or orgasm can be promoted by thrusting the penis in and out of the mouth. The speed of the motions can be varied, and manual stimulation near the base of the penis (firmly encircling the lower portion of the penis or providing pressure behind the scrotum) can also be stimulating.

Some people may gag during fellatio, a reflex that is triggered by pressure of the penis against the back of the tongue or against the throat. Gagging may be avoided if the man's partner grasps the shaft of the penis with one hand and controls the depth of penetration. Gagging is less likely to occur if the partner performing fellatio is on the top, rather than below, or if there is verbal communication about how deep the

Fellatio Oral stimulation of the male genitals.

Cunnilingus Oral stimulation of the female genitals.

Sociocultural Factors and Oral Sex

Table 9.3 shows the incidence of oral sex among men and women with various levels of education and from different racial/ethnic backgrounds in the NHSLS survey. Like masturbation, the incidence of oral sex correlates with level of education. That is, more highly educated individuals are more likely to have practiced oral sex. Why? Perhaps education encourages experimentation. Perhaps education dispels myths that nontraditional behavior patterns are necessarily harmful. Note also that

African American men and women were less likely to have engaged in oral sex than people from other racial/ethnic backgrounds. African American men and women were also less likely than other ethnic groups to report masturbating during the past 12 months. African Americans may adhere more strictly to traditional ideas about what kinds of sexual behavior are and are not proper.

Findings from a national survey of more than 3,000 sexually active men between the ages of 20 and 39

conducted by the Battelle Human Affairs Research Center in Seattle are consistent with the NHSLS findings. Seventy-five percent of the men reported performing oral sex. Seventy-nine percent reported receiving oral sex (Billy et al., 1993). Mirroring the racial differences observed by Laumann and his colleagues (1994), African American men in the Battelle survey were less likely than their European Americans to have performed or received oral sex.

Truth?Fiction?
Revisited

It is not true that African Americans are more likely than European Americans to engage in oral sex. A review of the research suggests that the opposite is more likely to be the case.

man should penetrate. Gagging may also be overcome by allowing gradually deeper penetration of the penis on successive occasions, while keeping the throat muscles relaxed.

Techniques of Cunnilingus Women can be highly aroused by their partner's tongue because it is soft, warm, and well lubricated. In contrast to a finger, the tongue can almost never be used too harshly. A woman may thus be more receptive to direct clitoral contact by a tongue. Cunnilingus provides such intense stimulation that many women find it to be the best means for achieving orgasm.

In performing cunnilingus, the partner may begin by kissing and licking the woman's abdomen and inner thighs, gradually nearing the vulva. Gentle tugging at or sucking of the labia minora can be stimulating, but the partner should take care not to bite. Many women enjoy licking of the clitoral region, and others desire sucking of the clitoris itself. The tongue may also be inserted into the vagina where it may imitate thrusting.

"69" The term *sixty-nine,* or *soixante-neuf* in French (pronounced swah-sahnt nuff), describes simultaneous oral–genital stimulation (see Figure 9.8). The numerals 6 and 9 are used because they resemble two partners who are upside-down and facing each other.

The "69" position has the psychologically positive feature of allowing couples to experience simultaneous stimulation, but it can be awkward if two people are not similar in size. Some couples avoid "69" because it deprives each partner of the opportunity to focus fully on receiving or providing sexual pleasure.

The "69" technique may be practiced side by side or with one partner on top of the other. There are no strict rules, and couples often alternate positions.

Abstaining from Oral Sex Despite the popularity of oral sex among couples today, those who desire to abstain have no reason to consider themselves abnormal.

TABLE 9.3				
Percent of NHSLS Study Respondents Who Report Experience with Oral Sex				
	Performed Oral Sex		Received Oral Sex	
	Men	Women	Men	Women
Education				
Less than high school	59.2	42.1	60.7	49.6
High school graduate	75.3	59.6	76.6	67.1
Some college	80.0	78.2	84.0	81.6
College graduate	83.7	78.9	84.6	83.1
Advanced college degree	80.5	79.0	81.4	81.9
Race/Ethnicity				
European American	81.4	75.3	81.4	78.9
African American	50.5	34.4	66.3	48.9
Latino and Latina American	70.7	59.7	73.2	63.7
Asian American	63.6	——*	72.7	——*

Source: Adapted from Laumann, E. O., Gagnon, J. H., Michael, R. T., & Michaels, S. (1994). *The social organization of sexuality: Sexual practices in the United States.* Chicago: University of Chicago Press, Table 3.6, p. 98.

*There were not enough Asian American women in the sample to report meaningful findings.

Figure 9.8. Simultaneous Oral–Genital Contact. The "69" position allows partners to engage in simultaneous oral–genital stimulation.

People offer various reasons for abstaining from oral sex. Although natural body odors may be arousing to some people, others are disturbed by the genital odors to which they are exposed. Some people object on grounds of cleanliness. They view the genitals as "dirty" because of their proximity to the urinary and anal openings. Concerns about offensive odors or cleanliness may be relieved by thoroughly washing the genitals beforehand.

Some prefer not to taste or swallow semen because they find it to be "dirty," sinful, or repulsive. Others are put off by the taste or texture. Semen has a salty taste and a texture similar to the white of an egg. If couples are to engage in unprotected oral sex, open discussion of feelings can enhance pleasure and diminish anxiety. For example, a man can be encouraged to warn his partner or remove his penis from her or his mouth when he is nearing ejaculation.

Let us dispel a couple of myths about semen. For one thing, it is impossible to become pregnant by swallowing semen. For another, semen is not fattening. The average amount of semen expelled in the ejaculate contains only about 5 Calories. On the other hand, it is not our intention to encourage swallowing of semen. The aesthetics of swallowing semen have little or nothing to do with concerns about pregnancy or weight. They involve the preferences of the individual.

A survey of college students found that shyness and embarrassment were the two reasons most frequently given for not engaging in oral sex (Gagnon & Simon, 1987). In one respect, oral sex is one of the most intimate types of lovemaking. After all, it provides a direct view of parts of the body we have been raised to keep private.

Sexual Intercourse: Positions and Techniques

Sexual intercourse, or *coitus* (from the Latin *coire*, which means "to go together"), is sexual activity in which the penis is inserted into the vagina. ***Question: What positions and techniques are used in sexual intercourse?*** Each position of sexual intercourse must allow the genitals to be aligned so that the penis is contained by the vagina. In addition to varying positions, couples also vary the depth and rate of thrusting (in-and-out motions) and of additional sexual stimulation.

Although the number of possible coital positions is virtually infinite, we will focus on four of the most commonly used positions: the male-superior (man-on-top) position, the female-superior (woman-on-top) position, the lateral-entry (side-entry) position, and the rear-entry position. We will also discuss anal intercourse, a sexual technique used by both male–female and male–male couples.

The Male-Superior (Man-on-Top) Position The male-superior position (this "superiority" is purely that of body position but has sometimes been taken as a symbol of male domination) has also been called the **missionary position**. In this position the partners face one another. The man lies above the woman, perhaps supporting himself on his hands and knees rather than applying his full weight against his partner (see Figure 9.9). Still, movement is easier for the man than for the woman, which suggests that he is responsible for directing their activity.

Many students of human sexuality suggest that it is preferable for the woman to guide the penis into the vagina, rather than having the man do so. The idea is that the woman can feel the location of the vaginal opening and determine the proper angle of entry. To accomplish this, the woman must feel comfortable "taking charge" of the couple's lovemaking. With the breaking down of the traditional stereotype of the female as passive, women are feeling more comfortable taking this role. On the other hand, if the couple prefers that the man guide his penis into his partner's vagina, the slight loss of efficiency need not trouble them, as long as he moves prudently to avoid hurting his partner.

The male-superior position has the advantage of permitting the couple to face one another so that kissing is easier. The woman may run her hands along her partner's body, stroking his buttocks and perhaps cupping a hand beneath his scrotum to increase stimulation as he reaches orgasm.

But the male-superior position makes it difficult for the man to caress his partner while simultaneously supporting himself with his hands. Therefore, the position

Missionary position
The coital position in which the man is on top. Also termed the *male-superior position.*

Figure 9.9. The Male-Superior Coital Position. *In this position the couple face one another. The man lies above the woman, perhaps supporting himself on his hands and knees rather than allowing his full weight to press against his partner. The position is also referred to as the missionary position.*

may not be favored by women who enjoy having their partners provide manual clitoral stimulation during coitus. This position can be highly stimulating to the man, which can make it difficult for him to delay ejaculation. The position also limits the opportunity for the woman to control the angle, rate, and depth of penetration. It may thus be more difficult for her to attain the type of stimulation she may need to achieve orgasm, especially if she favors combining penile thrusting with manual clitoral stimulation. Finally, this position is not advisable during the late stages of pregnancy. At that time the woman's distended abdomen would force the man to arch severely above her, lest he place undue pressure on her abdomen.

The Female-Superior (Woman-on-Top) Position In the female-superior position the couple face one another with the woman on top. The woman straddles the male from above, controlling the angle of penile entry and the depth of thrusting (see Figure 9.10). Some women maintain a sitting position; others lie on top of their partners. Many women vary their position.

In the female-superior position the woman is psychologically, and to some degree physically, in charge. She can move as rapidly or as slowly as she wishes with little effort, adjusting her body so as to vary the angle and depth of penetration. She can reach behind her to stroke her partner's scrotum or lean down to kiss him.

As in the male-superior position, kissing is relatively easy. This position has additional advantages. The man may readily reach the woman's buttocks or clitoris in order to provide manual stimulation. Assuming that the woman is shorter than he is, it is rather easy for him to stimulate her breasts orally (a pillow tucked behind his head may help). The woman can, in effect, guarantee that she receives adequate clitoral stimulation, either by the penis or manually by his hand or her own. This position thus facilitates orgasm in the woman. Because it tends to be less stimulating for the male, it may help him to control ejaculation. For these reasons this position is commonly used by couples who are learning to overcome sexual difficulties.

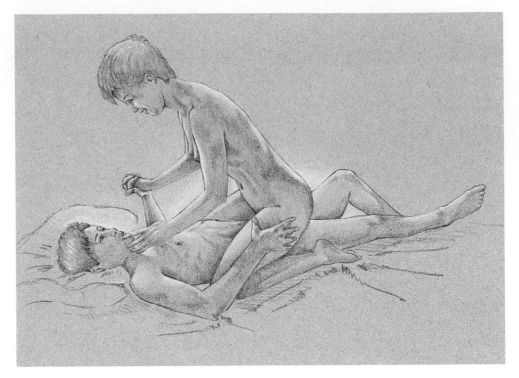

Figure 9.10. The Female-Superior Coital Position. *The woman straddles the male from above, controlling the angle of penile entry and the depth of thrusting. The female-superior position puts the woman psychologically and physically in charge. The woman can ensure that she receives adequate clitoral stimulation from the penis or the hand. The position also tends to be less stimulating for the male and may thus help him to control ejaculation.*

The Lateral-Entry (Side-Entry) Position In the lateral-entry position, the man and woman lie side by side, facing one another (see Figure 9.11). This position has the advantages of allowing each partner relatively free movement and easy access to the other. The man and woman may kiss freely, and they can stroke each other's bodies with a free arm. The position is not physically taxing, because both partners are resting easily on the bedding. Thus it is an excellent position for prolonged coitus or for coitus when couples are somewhat fatigued.

Let us note some disadvantages to this position. First, inserting the penis into the vagina while lying side by side may be awkward. Many couples thus begin coitus in another position and then change into the lateral-entry position—often because they wish to prolong coitus. Second, one or both partners may have an arm lying beneath the other that will "fall asleep" or become numb because of the constricted blood supply. Third, women may not receive adequate clitoral stimulation from the penis in this position. Of course, such stimulation may be provided manually (by hand) or by switching to another position after a while. Fourth, it may be difficult to achieve deeper penetration of the penis. The lateral position is useful during pregnancy (at least until the final stages, when the distension of the woman's abdomen may make lateral entry difficult).

The Rear-Entry Position In the rear-entry position, the man faces the woman's rear. In one variation (see Figure 9.12), the woman supports herself on her hands and knees while the man supports himself on his knees, entering her from behind. In another, the couple lie alongside one another and the woman lifts one leg, draping it backward over her partner's thigh. The latter position is particularly useful during the later stages of pregnancy.

The rear-entry position may be highly stimulating for both partners. Men may enjoy viewing and pressing their abdomens against their partner's buttocks. The man can reach around or underneath to provide additional stimulation of the clitoris or breasts, and she may reach behind (if she is on her hands and knees) to stroke or grasp her partner's testicles.

Figure 9.11. The Lateral-Entry Coital Position. *In this position the couple face each other side by side. Each partner has relatively free movement and easy access to the other. Because both partners rest easily on the bedding, it is an excellent position for prolonged coitus or for coitus when couples are fatigued.*

Potential disadvantages to this position include the following: First, this position is the mating position used by most other mammals, which is why it is sometimes referred to as *doggy style.* Some couples may feel uncomfortable about using the position because of its association with animal mating patterns. The position is also impersonal in the sense that the partners do not face one another, which may create a sense of emotional distance. Because the man is at the woman's back, the couple may feel that he is very much in charge—he can see her, but she cannot readily see him.

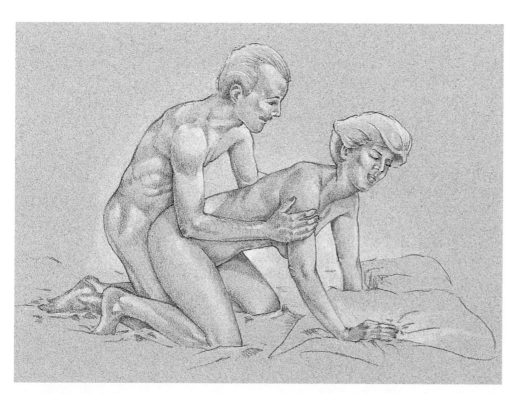

Figure 9.12. The Rear-Entry Coital Position. *The rear-entry position is highly erotic for men who enjoy viewing and pressing their abdomens against their partners' buttocks. Some couples feel uncomfortable about the position because of its association with animal mating patterns. The position is also impersonal in that the partners do not face one another. Moreover, some couples dislike the feeling that the man is psychologically in charge because he can see his partner but she cannot readily see him.*

Truth?Fiction?
Revisited

Evidence fails to show that coital fantasies are a sign of a troubled relationship.

Physically, the penis does not provide adequate stimulation to the clitoris. The penis also tends to pop out of the vagina from time to time. Finally, air tends to enter the vagina during rear-entry coitus. When it is expelled, it can sound as though the woman has passed air through the anus—a possibly embarrassing though harmless occurrence.

Use of Fantasy During Coitus Question: What is the role of sexual fantasies in sexual intercourse? As with masturbation, mental excursions into fantasy during coitus may be used to enhance sexual arousal and response (Bader, 2003; Boss & Maltz, 2001). Coital fantasies allow couples to inject sexual variety and even offbeat sexual escapades into their sexual activity without being unfaithful. Researchers find that most married people have engaged in coital fantasies (Bader, 2003; Boss & Maltz, 2001). In one study, 71% of the men and 72% of the women reported engaging in coital fantasies to enhance their sexual arousal (Zimmer et al., 1983). A survey of a sample of 178 students, faculty, and staff members at a college in Vermont found that 84% reported fantasizing at least occasionally during intercourse (Cado & Leitenberg, 1990). Nor does there appear to be any connection between sexual dissatisfaction with one's relationship and the use of coital fantasies (Davidson & Hoffman, 1986). Thus coital fantasies are not a form of compensation for an unrewarding sexual relationship.

Coital fantasies, like masturbation fantasies, run a gamut of themes. They include making love to another partner, group sex, orgies, images of past lovers or special erotic experiences, and making love in fantastic and wonderful places, among others.

Partners may be reluctant to share their coital fantasies or even to admit to them. This is especially true when the fantasy is about someone other than the partner. The fantasizer might fear being accused of harboring extramarital desires. Or the fantasizer might fear that the partner will interpret fantasies as a sign of rejection: "What's the matter, don't I turn you on anymore?" As noted in Chapter 8, one can be honest in a relationship without divulging every detail of one's past or one's sexual fantasies.

Anal Intercourse Questions: What is anal intercourse? Who engages in anal intercourse? Anal intercourse can be practiced by male–female couples and male–male couples. It involves insertion of the penis into the rectum. The rectum is richly endowed with nerve endings and is thus highly sensitive to sexual stimulation. Anal intercourse is also referred to as "Greek culture" or lovemaking in the "Greek style" because of bisexuality in ancient Greece among males. It is also the major act that comes under the legal definition of sodomy. Both women and men may reach orgasm through receiving the penis in the rectum and thrusting.

In anal intercourse, the penetrating male usually situates himself behind his partner. (He can also lie above or below his partner in a face-to-face position.) The receiving partner can supplement anal stimulation with manual stimulation of the clitoral region or penis to reach orgasm. Because the rectum produces no natural lubrication, people engaging in anal intercourse are advised to use an artificial lubricant, such as K-Y jelly.

Women often report wanting their partner's fingers in the anus at the height of passion or at the moment of orgasm. A finger in the rectum at the time of orgasm can heighten sexual sensation because the anal sphincters contract during orgasm. Although some men also want a finger in the anus, many resist because they associate anal penetration with the female role or with male–male sexual activity. However, the desire to be entered by one's partner is not necessarily connected with sexual orientation. A gay male or lesbian sexual orientation refers to the eroticization of members of one's own sex, not to the desire to penetrate or be penetrated.

Many couples are repulsed by the idea of anal intercourse. They view it as unnatural, immoral, or risky. Yet others find anal sex to be an enjoyable sexual variation, though perhaps not a regular feature of their sexual diet.

The NHSLS survey found that 1 man in 4 (26%) and 1 woman in 5 (20%) reported having engaged in anal sex at some time during their lives (Laumann et al., 1994). Yet only about 1 person in 10 (10% of the men and 9% of the women) had engaged in anal sex during the past year. As with oral sex, there was a higher incidence of anal sex among more highly educated people in the NHSLS survey. For example, about 30% of the male college graduates had engaged in anal sex, compared with 23% of male high school graduates. About 29% of the women with advanced college degrees had engaged in anal sex, compared with about 17% of the women who had graduated only from high school (Laumann et al., 1994). Education appears to be a liberating experience in sexual experimentation. About 1 in 5 men in one sample reported having engaged in anal intercourse (Billy et al., 1993). As in the NHSLS survey, anal intercourse was more commonly reported among better-educated men.

Religion appears to be a restraining influence on anal sex. About 34% of the men and 36% of the women in the NHSLS survey who said they had no religion reported engaging in anal sex during their lifetimes. Percentages for male Christians ranged from the lower to upper 20s, and for female Christians, from the midteens to the lower 20s (Laumann et al., 1994, p. 99). There were too few Jews in the sample to report meaningful figures for Jewish men and women.

Many couples kiss or lick the anus in their foreplay. This practice is called **anilingus**. Oral–anal sex carries a serious health risk, however, because microorganisms that cause intestinal diseases and various sexually transmitted infections can be spread through oral–anal contact.

Many couples today hesitate to engage in anal intercourse because of the fear of AIDS and other sexually transmitted infections (STIs). HIV and the microorganisms that cause STIs such as gonorrhea, syphilis, and hepatitis can be spread by anal intercourse. Cells in the rectum are especially susceptible to infection by some organisms, and small tears in the rectal tissues may allow other microbes to enter the recipient's blood system (see Chapter 16). Women also incur a greater risk of contracting HIV, the virus that causes AIDS, from anal intercourse than from vaginal intercourse— just as receptive anal intercourse in gay men carries a high risk of infection. However, partners who are both infection-free are at no risk of contracting STIs.

Not all gay males enjoy or practice anal intercourse. Of those who do, most alternate between being the inserter and being the insertee. Interviews with 51 gay men suggest that playing the inserter role in anal intercourse is sometimes associated with fantasies of domination, and the insertee role with fantasies of submission (Kippax & Smith, 2001). But some gays who practiced anal intercourse denied that sex had anything to do with power and with a dimension of activity–passivity; sex was about sharing.

In this chapter, we have observed many of the variations in human sexual expression. No other species shows such diversity in sexual behavior. People show diversity not only in sexual behavior but also in sexual orientation—which is the focus of the following chapter.

Truth?Fiction?
Revisited

Anal sex actually turns out to be *less* common among less well educated people. Perhaps education is a liberating influence on sexual experimentation.

Anilingus Oral stimulation of the anus.

Review: Sexual Behavior with Others

Reflect

How do your own attitudes and values affect the kinds of sexual practices with which you feel, or may feel, comfortable?

CriticalThinking

What is the connection between level of education and sexual practices such as oral sex and anal sex? How do you account for this relationship? Does the relationship affect your attitudes toward education? Explain.

16. Men usually desire (*Longer* or *Shorter*?) periods of foreplay than women do.

17. Kissing (*Is* or *Is not*?) almost universal in our culture.

18. In _____ kissing, partners part their lips and insert their tongues into each other's mouths.

19. Kinsey found that (*Most* or *Only a few*?) husbands kissed their wives' breasts.

20. (*Men, Women,* or *Both men and women*?) generally prefer manual or oral stimulation of the genitals prior to intercourse.

21. (*Men* or *Women*?) tend to prefer that their partners caress their genitals after a period of general body contact that includes holding, hugging, and nongenital massage.

22. _____ is the insertion of the fist or hand into the rectum.

23. The nipples are erotically sensitive in (*Women only* or *Both women and men*?). _____

24. _____ genital stimulation is the most common and frequent sexual activity among lesbian couples.

25. Oral stimulation of the male genitals is called _____.

26. Oral stimulation of the female genitals is called _____.

27. According to the NHSLS study, (*The majority* or *Only a minority*?) of men and women report engaging in oral–genital sex.

28. The _____-superior position for coitus has also been called the missionary position.

29. The _____-superior position facilitates orgasm in women.

30. The _____-entry position allows each partner relatively free movement and easy access to the other.

31. The _____-entry position permits men to view and press their abdomens against their partner's buttocks.

32. Evidence suggests that coital fantasies (*Are* or *Are not*?) a sign of a troubled relationship.

33. _____ intercourse involves insertion of the penis into the rectum.

Recite

1. What is masturbation?	Masturbation is self-stimulation of the genitals for purposes such as relieving sexual tension and obtaining sexual pleasure.
2. How has masturbation been viewed in our culture?	Within the Judeo-Christian tradition, masturbation has been condemned as sinful, as have been many other nonprocreative sexual acts. During the eighteenth and nineteenth centuries, many physical and psychological ills were ascribed to masturbation.
3. *Is* masturbation harmful?	Masturbation itself is rarely if ever physically harmful, although people whose values oppose masturbation may experience guilt and anxiety if they masturbate.
4. Who masturbates?	Surveys indicate that most people have masturbated at some point in their lives. Males are more likely than females to masturbate. European American males are more likely than African American males to masturbate.
5. How do males masturbate?	Males tend to masturbate by using a manual milking motion. Some males use vibrators.
6. How do females masturbate?	Females tend to stroke the mons and the area around the clitoral shaft. They usually do not insert fingers or objects into the vagina. Some females use dildos or vibrators.

Recite

7. What is the role of fantasy in solitary sexual behavior?

Sexual fantasies are often incorporated with masturbation or with sex with another person to heighten sexual response. Sexual fantasies range from the realistic to flights of fancy. Many people fantasize about sexual activities that they would not actually engage in.

8. Are sexual fantasies normal?

Sexual fantasies are normal in that most people have them and that they are not signs of psychological disorders or troubled relationships. However, some people oppose masturbation on religious grounds.

9. What does evolutionary theory have to say about sexual fantasies?

Evolutionary theory suggests that the male tendency to fantasize about novel and multiple partners, and the female tendency to fantasize about former lovers, represent mating strategies that helped people survive to reproductive age and rear children.

10. What is foreplay?

Foreplay involves kissing, touching, and other activities that heighten sexual arousal prior to coitus. Women usually desire longer periods of foreplay than men do.

11. What is the role of kissing?

Kissing is nearly universal in our culture but is not as popular around the world. Kissing signals intimacy, and prolonged, deep kissing can be sexually arousing in its own right.

12. What is the role of touching?

Touching or caressing erogenous zones can be highly arousing. Men typically prefer stroking of their genitals by their partner early in lovemaking. Women, however, tend to prefer that their genitals be caressed after a period of general body contact.

13. What is the role of stimulation of the breasts?

Most, but not all, women enjoy stimulation of the breasts by the hands and mouth as foreplay or in its own right.

14. How do gay males and lesbians make use of stimulation of the breasts?

Gay males and lesbians both tend to spend more time focusing on their partner's breasts and nipples than do heterosexuals.

15. What is oral–genital stimulation?

Fellatio is oral stimulation—kissing, licking sucking, and so on—of the male genitals. Cunnilingus is oral stimulation of the female genitals.

16. Who engages in oral–genital stimulation?

The popularity of oral–genital stimulation has increased dramatically since Kinsey's day such that the majority of couples today use it. European Americans are more likely than African Americans to use oral–genital stimulation.

17. What positions and techniques are used in sexual intercourse?

Couples today use a greater variety of coital positions than in Kinsey's time. Four of the most commonly used coital positions are the male-superior position, the female-superior position, the lateral-entry position, and the rear-entry position. The female-superior position allows the female to better obtain the stimulation needed to reach orgasm.

18. What is the role of sexual fantasies in sexual intercourse?

Sexual fantasies tend to heighten sexual excitement during coitus.

19. What is anal intercourse? Who engages in anal intercourse?

Anal intercourse is insertion of the penis into the rectum and may be carried out within heterosexual or gay relationships. Artificial lubrication facilitates anal intercourse.

Chapter 10

Truth?Fiction?

T / F? Gay males and lesbians would prefer to be members of the other sex.

T / F? Members of ethnic minority groups in the United States are more tolerant of homosexuals than are European Americans.

T / F? Gay males unconsciously fear women's genitals because they associate them with castration.

T / F? Most Americans would prefer that gay people be allowed to get married to one another.

T / F? Most Americans believe that gay people are born gay.

T / F? The American Psychiatric Association considers homosexuality to be a mental disorder.

T / F? Many gay couples have lifestyles similar to those of committed heterosexual couples and are as well adjusted.

Sexual Orientation

Preview

Mike and Sue Weinberg were out to dinner when their 6-year-old son, Jack, declared, "Mommy, I'm going to marry you." When Ms. Weinberg explained that she was already married, Jack persisted, "Then I'll marry Daddy."

"You can't marry Daddy," Ms. Weinberg said patiently, "He's a boy."

"But Mark and Kevin are boys," replied Jack, logic that his mother could not refute.

Mark Demich and Kevin Hengst, the couple across the street, are not actually married. Still, in the seven years they have lived in this Chicago suburb, they have become like the Buckinghams, the Therrons, the Siconolfis—just another young family in the neighborhood, socializing porch to porch on summer evenings.

Choosing the suburbs over the city, Mr. Demich and Mr. Hengst feared they would be The Gay Couple. But even in Wheaton—the seat of a reliably Republican county and home to an evangelical Christian college that until last year prohibited drinking and dancing—they have found plenty of company. Sixty gay men and lesbians turned out for a wine-tasting a few weeks ago. About 30 played softball at a local park on a recent Saturday.

Thirty miles away, in the Chicago area known as Boystown, which officials say is the nation's first city-designated gay business district, business owners and residents say the influx of young heterosexual families has rendered the neighborhood's name an anachronism. The gay bookstore now sells more children's books than "gay books."

In churches and in politics, the debate about homosexuality has focused recently on whether gays should be allowed to marry or whether gay sex should be legal. But in places like Wheaton and Boystown, people are sorting out more fundamental questions

about everyday life. As gays live openly with straights, they are confronting stereotypes about one another and testing comfort zones, with varying degrees of conflict and cooperation.

One step toward assimilation almost invariably prompts another toward rejection. As the Philadelphia Phillies became the latest Major League Baseball team to hold a "Gay Community Day," talk radio lit up with accusations that the all-American sport had sold its soul. When an openly straight woman won the Gay Pride Idol talent contest in San Francisco, gays cried foul.

Overall, though, those who study trends say that living side by side in more places—the 2000 Census showed gay couples living in 99.3% of the counties in the United States—has produced a tremendous shift in social attitudes over the past decade.

The General Social Survey, done by the University of Chicago, found that the percentage of people saying intercourse between people of the same sex is "always wrong" has dropped by 21 points in the last 10 years, from 77% to 56%. That was after almost no movement in the previous decade, said Tom W. Smith, director of the survey. Although opposition remains high, Mr. Smith said, the decline "is as large a social change as any ever."

Much survey data, Mr. Smith said, suggest that greater acceptance has come from more people knowing someone who is gay. "It's the same as racial equality," he said. "The point is to think of them as individuals, who are also coworkers, neighbors, someone who supports the local charity drive—to see people as people, except in this one little way they're different."[1]

This chapter is about **sexual orientation**. *Question: What is meant by sexual orientation?* Sexual orientation concerns the *direction* of one's romantic interests and erotic attractions—toward members of the same sex, the other sex, or both.

In this chapter, we see that homosexual people, like heterosexual people, struggle to incorporate their sexuality within their personal identity, to find lovers, and to establish satisfying lifestyles. In fact, gay civil unions are now permitted in a number of states, and, as this book goes to press, the Supreme Court of Massachusetts has ruled that gay marriages are constitutional in that state. Unlike heterosexual people, gay people in our culture face a backdrop of social intolerance, even if they commit themselves to long-term relationships.

---

1. Opening vignette adapted from Kate Zernike. (2003, August 24). The New Couples Next Door. *The New York Times online.*

Getting Oriented toward Sexual Orientation

One's sexual orientation consists of one's erotic attraction to, and interest in developing romantic relationships with, members of one's own or the other sex. *Question: What kinds of sexual orientation are there?* A **heterosexual orientation** is an erotic attraction to, and preference for developing romantic relationships with, members of the other sex. (Many homosexual people refer to heterosexual people as being *straight*, or as *straights*.)

A **homosexual orientation** is an erotic attraction to, and interest in forming romantic relationships with, members of one's own sex. The term *homosexuality* denotes sexual interest in members of one's own anatomic sex and applies to both men and women. Homosexual men are often referred to as **gay males**. Homosexual women are often called **lesbians**. Gay males and lesbians may also be referred to collectively as "gays" or "gay people." The term **bisexuality** describes an orientation in which one is sexually attracted to, and interested in forming romantic relationships with, both males and females.

Coming to Terms with Terms

Now that we have defined homosexuality, let us note that the term has become somewhat controversial. Some gay people object to it because they feel that it draws attention to sexual behavior. Moreover, the term carries a social stigma. As noted by the American Psychological Association's (1991) Committee on Lesbian and Gay Concerns, the word *homosexual* has also been historically associated with concepts of deviance and mental illness. It perpetuates negative stereotypes of gay people. Also, the term is often used to refer to men only. It thus renders lesbians invisible. Therefore, many people would prefer terms such as *gay male* or *lesbian sexual orientation*.

Then, too, the word *homosexual* is ambiguous in meaning. Does it refer to sexual behavior or to sexual orientation? In this book, your authors speak of male–female sexual behavior (not *heterosexual* behavior), male–male sexual behavior, and female–female sexual behavior to help distinguish sexual behavior from sexual orientation.

Sexual Orientation and Gender Identity

Question: Would homosexuals rather be members of the other sex? Because gay people are attracted to members of their own sex, some people assume that they would prefer to *be* members of the other sex. Like heterosexual people, however, the great majority of gay people have a gender identity that is consistent with their anatomic sex. J. Michael Bailey (2003b) writes that some "extremely gay" people become transsexuals—that is, adopt the lifestyle of people of the other sex within our culture. But feeling "trapped" in the body of the other sex is not part of the definition of being gay.

When heterosexuals think about homosexuals, they tend to focus almost exclusively on sexual aspects of male–male and female–female relationships. But the love relationships of homosexuals, like those of heterosexuals, involve more than sex. Homosexuals, like heterosexuals, spend only a small amount of their time in sexual activity. More basic to a gay male or lesbian sexual orientation is the formation of romantic attachments with members of one's own sex. These attachments, like male–female attachments, provide a framework for love and intimacy. Although sex-

---

Sexual orientation
The direction of one's sexual interests—toward members of the same sex, the other sex, or both.

Heterosexual orientation Erotic attraction to, and preference for developing romantic relationships with, members of the other sex.

Homosexual orientation Erotic attraction to, and preference for developing romantic relationships with, members of the same sex. (From the Greek *homos*, which means "same," not the Latin *homo*, which means "man").

Gay males Males who are erotically attracted to, and desire to form romantic relationships with, other males.

Lesbians Females who are erotically attracted to, and desire to form romantic relationships with, other females. (After *Lesbos*, the Greek island on which, legend has it, female–female sexual activity was idealized).

Bisexuality Erotic attraction to, and interest in developing romantic relationships with, males and females.

ual activity and love are common features of relationships, neither is a *necessary* prerequisite for a relationship. Sexual orientations are not defined by sexual activity per se, but rather by the *direction* of one's romantic interests and erotic attractions.

Classification of Sexual Orientation: Is Yes or No Enough?

Determining a person's sexual orientation might seem to be a clear-cut task. Some people are exclusively gay and limit their sexual activities to partners of their own sex. Others are strictly heterosexual and limit their sexual activities to partners of the other sex. Many people fall somewhere in between, however. *Questions: Where do we draw the line between a gay male and lesbian sexual orientation, on the one hand, and a heterosexual orientation, on the other? Where do we draw the line between these orientations and bisexuality?*

It is possible, indeed not unusual, for heterosexual people to have had some sexual experiences with people of their own sex. Eisenberg and Wechsler (2003) reported the results of a survey of more than 10,000 college students on 119 campuses; 6.1% of the students wrote that they had had sexual experiences with people of their own sex. As we will see, the number of 6% is probably twice that of the homosexuals in the population. In the absence of heterosexual outlets, adolescents and isolated populations such as prison inmates may have sexual experiences with people of their own sex while they maintain their heterosexual identities.

Gay males and lesbians, too, may engage in male–female sexual activity while maintaining a gay sexual orientation. Some gay males and lesbians marry members of the other sex but harbor unfulfilled desires for members of their own sex. Other people are bisexual but may not act on their attraction to members of their own sex (Edser & Shea, 2002).

Sexual orientation is not necessarily expressed in sexual behavior. Many people come to perceive themselves as gay or heterosexual long before they ever engage in sex with members of their own sex (Diamond, 2003a; Savin-Williams & Diamond, 2000). Some people, gay and heterosexual alike, adopt a celibate lifestyle for religious or ascetic reasons and abstain from sexual relationships.

People's erotic interests and fantasies may also shift over time. Gay males and lesbians may experience sporadic **heteroerotic** interests. Heterosexual people may have occasional **homoerotic** interests. Women's sexual orientations are apparently somewhat more flexible or plastic than men's, with women being somewhat more dependent on social experience (Bailey, 2003a; Diamond, 2000, 2002, 2003a). A classic survey of homosexuals found that about 50% of the lesbians who were sampled reported that they are sometimes attracted to men (Bell & Weinberg, 1978). Lisa M. Diamond (2003b) conducted a survey of lesbian and bisexual women that involved three interviews over a five-year period. She found that more than 25% of the women relinquished their lesbian or bisexual orientation as time went on. Half of these relabeled themselves as heterosexual, and the other half renounced any effort at self-labeling. Some heterosexual people report fantasies about sexual activity with people of their own sex (see Chapter 9). In their classic study of homosexuals, Masters and Johnson (1979) found that many gay people reported having fantasies about sexual activity with people of the other sex.

Attraction to people of the other sex and attraction to people of one's own sex may thus not always be mutually exclusive. People may have various degrees of sexual

Truth?Fiction?
Revisited

It is not true that gay males and lesbians in general would prefer to be members of the other sex. The gender identity of most homosexuals is consistent with their anatomic sex.

Heteroerotic Of an erotic nature and involving members of the other sex.

Homoerotic Of an erotic nature and involving members of one's own sex.

interest in, and sexual experience with, people of either sex. Kinsey and his colleagues recognized that the boundaries between gay male and lesbian sexual orientations, on the one hand, and a heterosexual orientation, on the other, are sometimes blurry. As Kinsey and his colleagues noted,

> The world is not to be divided into sheep and goats. . . . Only the human mind invents categories and tries to force facts into separated pigeonholes. The living world is a continuum in each and every one of its aspects. (1948, p. 639)

Kinsey and his colleagues (1948, 1953) found evidence of a continuum of sexual orientation among the people they surveyed, with bisexuality representing a midpoint between an exclusively heterosexual orientation and an exclusively gay male or lesbian sexual orientation. They conceived of a 7-point heterosexual–homosexual continuum, as shown in Figure 10.1. People are located on the continuum according to their patterns of sexual attraction and behavior. People in category 0 are considered exclusively heterosexual. People in category 6 are considered exclusively gay.

Question: What percentage of the population is gay? Kinsey and his colleagues reported that about 4% of men and 1% to 3% of women in their samples were exclusively gay (6 on their scale). A larger percentage of people were considered predominantly gay (scale points 4 or 5) or predominantly heterosexual (1 or 2 on their scale). All in all, Kinsey's data suggested that close to 10% of the U.S. population was gay or predominantly gay, a number that dramatically exceeds current estimates. Some were classified as equally gay and heterosexual in orientation and could be labeled bisexual (scale point 3). Most people were classified as exclusively heterosexual (scale point 0).

A 1993 Louis Harris poll found that 4.4% of men and 3.6% of women reported sexual activity with a member of their own sex within the past five years (Barringer, 1993b). Kinsey Institute director June Reinisch (1990) examined the available evidence and estimated that more than 25% of men in the United States had had a male–male sexual experience in their teens or adult years.

Statistics concerning *past* sexual activity with a member of one's own sex can be misleading. They may represent a single episode or a brief period of adolescent experimentation. Half of the men who reported male–male sexual activity in Kinsey's sample limited it to the ages of 12 to 14. Another third had male–male sexual experience by the age of 18, but not again.

Kinsey's research also showed that sexual behavior patterns can change, sometimes dramatically so. Sexual experiences or feelings involving people of one's own sex are common, especially in adolescence, and do not necessarily mean that one will engage in sexual activity exclusively with people of one's own sex in adulthood (Diamond, 2003).

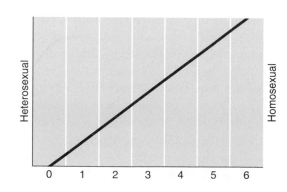

Figure 10.1. The Kinsey Continuum. *Kinsey and his colleagues conceived of a 7-point heterosexual–homosexual continuum that classifies people according to their homosexual behavior and the magnitude of their attraction to members of their own gender. People in category 0, who accounted for most of Kinsey's study participants, were considered exclusively heterosexual. People in category 6 were considered exclusively homosexual.*

The controversy over how many people are gay continues. Current estimates generally find lower percentages of gay people in the population than Kinsey did. Considering data drawn from studies conducted in the United States, Asia, and Pacific Island countries, Milton Diamond (1993) estimates that only about 5% of men and 2% to 3% of women across different cultures have engaged in sexual activity with someone of their own sex on at least one occasion since adolescence. Diamond and other researchers also find fewer people to have a bisexual orientation than to have a gay male or lesbian sexual orientation.

Research in the United States, Britain, France, and Denmark finds that about 3% of the men surveyed *identify* themselves as gay (Hamer et al., 1993; Laumann et al., 1994). About 2% of the U.S. women surveyed *identify* themselves as lesbians (Laumann et al., 1994). Surveys in the United States, Britain, and France find that larger numbers of men (5% to 11%) and women (2% to 4%) report *engaging in sexual behavior* with members of their own sex within the past five years (Sell et al., 1995). Surveys show that still larger numbers of men (8% to 9%) and women (8% to 12%) report some *sexual attraction* to members of their own sex, but no sexual interaction since the age of 15 (Sell et al., 1995).

Keep in mind that the following factors affect survey results:

- The ways in which the questions are phrased (for example, do they look into sexual identity, sexual behavior, or sexual attraction—and over what period of time?)
- The social desirability of the professed behavior
- The sex of the interviewer
- The manner in which the survey was conducted, such as by personal interviews, phone calls, or written surveys
- The biases of respondents, such as volunteer bias

Challenges to the Kinsey Continuum Alfred Kinsey believed that exclusive heterosexual and gay sexual orientations lay at opposite poles of one continuum. Therefore, the more heterosexual a person is, the less gay that person is, and vice versa. Viewing gay and heterosexual orientations as opposite poles of one continuum is akin to the traditional view of masculinity and femininity as opposite poles of one continuum, such that the more masculine one is, the less feminine, and vice versa. Viewing men and women as opposites has led to misunderstandings, even hostility, between the sexes (Bem, 1993).

Question: What alternatives are there to the Kinsey continuum? We may also regard masculinity and femininity as independent personality dimensions. Similarly, the view of gay people and heterosexuals as opposites has led to misunderstandings and hostility. Yet it may be that these sexual orientations are in fact separate dimensions, rather than polar opposites, at least for women.

Using the self-reporting of the content of erotic fantasies as an indication of sexual orientation, psychologist Michael Storms (1980) found evidence that there are separate dimensions of responsiveness to male–female sexual stimulation (heteroeroticism) and sexual stimulation that involves someone of the same sex (homoeroticism), as shown in Figure 10.2. According to this model, bisexuals are high on both dimensions, whereas people who are low on both are essentially asexual. According to Kinsey, bisexual individuals would be *less* responsive to stimulation by people of the other sex than heterosexual people are, but *more* responsive to stimulation by people of their own sex. But the two-dimensional model allows for bisexual individuals to be just as responsive to stimulation by people of the other sex as

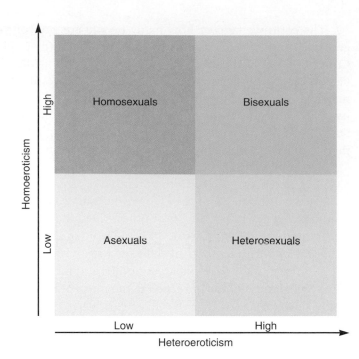

Figure 10.2. Heterosexuality and Homosexuality as Separate Dimensions. According to this model, homosexuality and heterosexuality are independent dimensions. One can thus be high or low on both dimensions at the same time. Most people are high on one dimension. Bisexuals are high on both dimensions. People who are low on both are considered asexual.

heterosexual people are *and* just as responsive to stimulation by people of their own sex as gay people are.

Using more complex kinds of measures, however, Richard Lippa and Sara Arad (1997) found that the two-dimensional model may hold only for women, if it is valid at all. They administered a variety of personality measures to 148 male and 246 female college undergraduates with a median age of 18. These measures included "masculine" instrumentality, "feminine" emotional expressiveness, and a number of other personality traits such as extraversion, agreeableness, conscientiousness, neuroticism (emotional instability), and openness to new experience. Students also completed a sexual behavior and attitude questionnaire that asked them about their sexual attraction to men and women, their emotional commitment in sexual relationships, their sex drive, and their interest in sexual fantasies and erotic stimuli. A mathematical grouping technique called factor analysis found four factors that characterized men's sexual behaviors and attitudes and four that characterized women's (see Table 10.1). They differed in important ways. Perhaps the most telling is that men seemed largely to fit the Kinsey model in that they showed a "bipolar" sexual orientation. That is, the more aroused they were by women, the less they were aroused by men, and vice versa. Women, by contrast, showed factors both for homosexuality and for heterosexuality. That is, whether or not they were aroused by men could be independent of whether or not they were aroused by other women, and vice versa. Interestingly, sexual behaviors and attitudes had little to do with the other personality measures.

Lippa and Arad's findings are consistent with research showing that women's sexual orientations are more flexible than men's and apparently more intertwined with their social experience (Bailey, 2003a; Diamond, 2000, 2002, 2003a). When we discuss **homophobia**, or hatred of homosexuals, we will see that men tend to be more homophobic than women. Homophobia is connected with traditional "tough" masculine attitudes. However, part of the reason for this sex difference in homophobia

Homophobia A cluster of negative attitudes and feelings toward gay people, including intolerance, hatred, and fear. (From Greek roots meaning "fear" [of members of the] "same" [sex].)

TABLE 10.1

Factors in Males' and Females' Sexual Behaviors and Attitudes

Males	Females
Bipolar sexual orientation	Homosexuality
Emotional commitment	Heterosexuality
Sex drive	Emotional commitment
Sexual fantasy	Sex drive

Source: Richard Lippa & Sara Arad (1997). The structure of sexual orientation and its relation to masculinity, femininity, and gender diagnosticity: Different for men and women. *Sex Roles, 37*(3–4), 187–208.

may be that heterosexual men have a more difficult time than heterosexual women understanding how any man could be attracted to a person of the same sex.

Bisexuality

To me, I never felt like I had a stronger attraction to men or women. I didn't have a problem identifying myself as gay, but I knew that wasn't the whole picture.

*A 29-year-old social worker from North Carolina
who fell in love with a woman and then had
a sexual relationship with his male roommate*

I don't limit myself to a guy or a girl. Whoever comes into my life, if we hit it off, great. That's happened with a lot of people I know. They'll say, "Guess what happened last night." It's very accepted.

A 22-year-old political science major

She finally came out of the closet and said, "Mom, there's this girl and she's the most gorgeous girl you've ever seen." I said, "You're only for girls?" She said, "No, it's not just the girls. I can see a really good-looking guy, too."

*The mother of a 19-year-old woman who uses a
computer bulletin board to meet other bisexuals*

Adapted from Gabriel, 1995b

Question: What is bisexuality? Bisexual people are sexually attracted to both males and females. Bisexual people are sometimes said to "swing both ways," or to be "A/C–D/C" (as in "alternating current" and "direct current"). Yet many have a somewhat stronger attraction to people of one sex than the other. In fact, Weinrich & Klein (2002) speak of bisexuals as falling into three categories: bi-gay, bi-straight, and bi-bi, meaning that some have a stronger leaning toward people of their own sex (bi-gays), some are more attracted to people of the other sex (bi-straights), and still others appear to be equally attracted to people of their own sex and of the other sex (bi-bi's). Depending on how one defines bisexuality, perhaps 1% to 4% of the population is bisexual. About 1% of the people (0.8% of the men and 0.9% of the women) surveyed in the NHSLS study (Laumann et al., 1994) reported having a bisexual *identity*. However, about 4% said they were sexually attracted to both women and men.

Biphobia Negative attitudes and feelings toward bisexual people, including intolerance, hatred, and fear.

Some gays (and some heterosexuals) believe that claims to bisexuality are a "cop-out" that people use to deny being gay. Perhaps they fear leaving their spouses or "coming out" (declaring their gay male or lesbian sexual orientation publicly). Others view bisexuality as a form of sexual experimentation with people of one's own sex by people who are mostly heterosexual. Surveys of more than 600 college undergraduates confirm that **biphobia**, or hatred of bisexuals, can be found in both the heterosexual and homosexual populations (Mulick & Wright, 2002).

But many avowed bisexuals and researchers assert that bisexuals can maintain erotic interests in, and romantic relationships with, members of both sexes. They insist that bisexuality is an authentic sexual orientation with its own developmental patterns, not just a "cover" for a gay male or lesbian sexual orientation (Brown, 2002; Weinrich & Klein, 2002).

Some bisexual people follow lifestyles that permit them to satisfy their dual inclinations. Others feel pressured by heterosexual and gay people alike to commit themselves one way or the other (Edser & Shea, 2002). Some gay people also mask their sexual orientation by adopting a bisexual lifestyle. That is, they get married but also enter into clandestine sexual liaisons with members of their own sex.

Still, it appears that many bisexual men remain reasonably comfortable in committed heterosexual relationships, such as marriages. An in-depth study of 20 married men who scored as bisexual on the Kinsey Scale found that they experienced some anxiety, some feelings of guilt, and some sense of loss, but not to the point where they suffered high levels of stress (Edser & Shea, 2002). By and large, the men were psychologically stable, and most of their marriages were in what the authors call "relatively good condition." The authors conclude that long-term committed relationships with women are a "viable option" for bisexual men. The authors were not moralistic; that is, they were not suggesting that bisexual men

Review: Getting Oriented toward Sexual Orientation

Reflect

Has your reading of this section changed your definition of homosexuality or your estimate of how many homosexuals there are in the population? Explain.

CriticalThinking

Why do some writers prefer to use the terms *male–male sexual behavior* and *female–female sexual behavior* instead of *homosexual behavior*?

1. One's sexual _____ consists of one's erotic attraction toward, and interest in developing romantic relationships with, members of one's own or the other sex.

2. A _____ orientation is an erotic attraction to members of one's own sex.

3. Homosexual men are often referred to as _____ males.

4. Homosexual women are often referred to as _____.

5. _____ are sexually attracted to both males and females.

6. Most gay people have a gender identity that is (*Consistent* or *Inconsistent*?) with their anatomic sex.

7. Women's sexual orientations are (*More* or *Less*?) flexible than men's.

8. _____ and his colleagues created a 7-point, bipolar heterosexual–homosexual continuum.

9. According to the NHSLS study, about _____% of men and _____% of women identify themselves as homosexuals.

10. Storms found evidence that hetero-eroticism and homoeroticism make up (*One* or *Two*?) dimension(s) of sexual responsiveness.

11. According to Lippa and Arad, the two-dimensional model may hold only for (*Men* or *Women*?).

12. Surveys show that biphobia is found among (*Heterosexuals only* or *Heterosexuals and homosexuals*?).

should seek committed relationships with women. They merely pointed out that such relationships can work.

Perspectives on Gay Male and Lesbian Sexual Orientations

Gay male and lesbian sexual orientations have existed throughout history. Attitudes toward these orientations have varied widely. They have been tolerated in some societies, openly encouraged in others, but condemned in most. In this section we review historical and other perspectives on gay male and lesbian sexual orientations. *Question: How has homosexuality been viewed historically?*

Historical Perspectives

In Western culture, few sexual practices have met with such widespread censure as sexual activities with members of one's own sex. Yet it was not always that way. In ancient Greece, for example, men frequently formed sexual relationships with adolescent males. "How can we know anything about the sex lives of Greeks who lived 2,500 years ago?" quips J. Michael Bailey (2003b, p. 126). "It is difficult enough to know about the sex lives of Americans today." Having posed the question, Bailey nevertheless goes on to describe such relationships between established men and adolescents at about the age of their first growing a beard. The main sexual activity depicted on Greek vases is that of the older male inserting his penis between the boy's thighs (not in the anus) and thrusting until he ejaculates.

A few centuries later, Bailey (2003b) continues, the Romans described highly feminine gay men who dressed flamboyantly, had showy hair styles and mannerisms, and cruised certain neighborhoods, searching for partners. The apostle Paul commented on this behavior as the key sign of the decadence of Rome, and the Christian Church assumed a strongly negative attitude toward homosexuality.

In the fifteenth century, Florence, a Christian city, was reputed to house numerous "sodomites." (Jews and Christians have traditionally referred to male–male sexual activity as the sin of Sodom. Hence the origins of the term *sodomy*, which generally alludes to anal intercourse and sometimes to oral–genital contact. According to the Book of Genesis, the city of Sodom was destroyed by God. Yet it is unclear what behavior incurred God's wrath. Pope Gregory III was not ambiguous, however, in his eighth-century account of the city's obliteration as a punishment for sexual activity with members of the same sex.) Sodomy was so common in Florence, and (theoretically) so disturbing to the city's governors, that they created "the Office of the Night" in 1432, which enabled the populace to anonymously accuse individuals of sodomy. During the 70 years that the Office was in operation, some 17,000 men were investigated as possible sodomites—nearly half of the male population of Florence throughout this period! Fewer than 3,000 were actually convicted, however, and those who were convicted were required to pay a fine rather than tossed into prison (Bailey, 2003b).

The Book of Leviticus was also clear in its condemnation:

> If a man lies with a man as with a woman, both of them have committed an abomination; they shall be put to death, their blood is upon them. (Leviticus 20:13)

Sexual activity with members of one's own sex was not the only sexual act considered sinful by the early Christians. Any nonprocreative sexual act was considered

Ethnicity and Sexual Orientation: A Matter of Belonging

Lesbians and gay men frequently suffer the slings and arrows of an outraged society. Because of societal prejudices, it is difficult for many young people to come to terms with an emerging lesbian or gay male sexual orientation. You might assume that people who have been subjected to prejudice and discrimination—members of ethnic minority groups in the United States—would be more tolerant of a lesbian or gay male sexual orientation.

In an article that addresses the experiences of lesbians and gay men from ethnic minority groups, Greene (1994) notes that it is difficult to generalize about ethnic groups in the United States. For example, African Americans may find their cultural origins in the tribes of West Africa, but they have also been influenced by Christianity and the local subcultures of their North American towns and cities. Native Americans represent hundreds of tribal groups, languages, and cultures. By and large, however, a lesbian or gay male sexual orientation is rejected by ethnic minority groups in the United States. Lesbians and gay males are pressured to keep their sexual orientations a secret or to move to communities where they can live openly without sanction.

Ethnicity and Sexual Orientation The experiences of lesbians and gay men can differ according to their ethnicity. For example, traditional Latino and Latina American culture includes strong differences in gender roles. Men are expected to support and defend the family. Women are expected to be submissive, respectable, and deferential to men. Latino and Latina American culture also often denies the sexuality of women. Thus, Latina American lesbians are multiply condemned—because they are lesbians, because they confront others with their sexuality, and because their independence from men is perceived as a threat to the tradition of male dominance.

Truth?Fiction?
Revisited

However, according to psychologist Beverly Greene (2000) of St. John's University, members of ethnic minority groups in the United States are less tolerant of homosexuals than are European Americans.

sinful, even within marriage. With the fall of the Roman Empire, the influence of Christianity spread across Western Europe. Christian beliefs were eventually encoded into secular law. By the late Middle Ages, most civil statutes throughout Western Europe contained penalties for nonprocreative sexual acts involving the discharge of semen, including oral or anal sex, masturbation, male–male sexual behavior, and bestiality. Male–male and female–female sexual practices continue to be condemned by most Christian and Jewish denominations and by Islam.

Our legal system, grounded in this religious tradition, maintains criminal penalties for sexual practices commonly associated with male–male and female–female sex, such as anal and oral sex. But

Within traditional Latino and Latina American culture, the family is the primary social unit. Men are expected to support and defend the family, and women are expected to be submissive, respectable, and deferential to men. Because women are expected to remain virgins until marriage, men sometimes engage in male–male sexual behavior without considering themselves gay (Greene, 1994). Latino and Latina American culture frequently denies the sexuality of women. Thus, women who label themselves lesbians are doubly condemned—because they are lesbians and because they are confronting others with their sexuality. Because lesbians are independent of men, most Latino and Latina American heterosexual people view Latina American lesbians as threats to the tradition of male dominance (Trujillo, 1991).

Asian American cultures emphasize respect for elders, obedience to parents, and sharp distinctions in gender roles (Chan, 1992). The topic of sex is generally taboo within the family. Asian Americans, like Latino and Latina Americans, tend to as-sume that sex is unimportant to women. Women are also considered less important than men. Open admission of a lesbian or gay male sexual orientation is seen as rejection of traditional cultural roles and as a threat to the continuity of the family line (Chan, 1992; Garnets & Kimmel, 1991). For all these reasons, it is not surprising that Asian American college students report being more homophobic than their European American counterparts (Lippincott et al., 2000).

Because many African American men have had difficulty finding jobs, gender roles among African Americans have been more flexible than those found among European Americans and most other ethnic minority groups (Greene, 2000). Nevertheless, the African American community appears to strongly reject gay men and lesbians, pressuring them to remain secretive about their sexual orientations (Gomez & Smith, 1990; Poussaint, 1990). Greene (2000) hypothesizes a number of factors that influence African Americans to be hostile toward lesbians and gay men. One is strong allegiance to Christian beliefs and Biblical scripture. Another is internalization of the dominant culture's stereotyping of African Americans as highly sexual beings. That is, many African Americans may feel a need to assert their sexual "normalcy."

Prior to the European conquest, sex may not have been discussed openly by Native Americans, but sex was generally seen as a natural part of life. Individuals who incorporated both traditional feminine and masculine styles were generally accepted and even admired. The influence of the religions of colonists led to greater rejection of lesbians and gay men, and this exerted pressure on them to move off the reservation to the big city (Greene, 1994). Thus Native American lesbians and gay men, like Asian American lesbians and gay men, often feel doubly removed from their families.

If any generalization is possible, it may be that lesbians and gay men find more of a sense of belonging in the gay community than in their ethnic communities.

much of the criminalization of male–male and female–female sex has been directed against men.

Question: How has homosexuality been viewed in other cultures?

Cross-Cultural Perspectives

Male–male sexual behavior has been practiced in many preliterate societies. In their review of the literature on 76 preliterate societies, Ford and Beach (1951) found that in 49 societies (64%), male–male sexual interactions were viewed as normal and deemed socially acceptable for some members of the group. The other 27 societies (36%) had sanctions against male–male sexual behavior. Nevertheless, male–male sexual activity persisted. In another cross-cultural analysis, Broude and Greene (1976) found that male–male sexual behavior was present but uncommon in 41% of a sample of 70 of the world's non-European societies. It was rare or absent in 59% of these societies. Broude and Greene also found evidence of societal disapproval and punishment of male–male sexual activity in 41% of a sample of 42 societies for which information was available.

In some societies, sexual activities are acceptable between older and younger males or between adolescents, but not between adult men. At the turn of the century, the Swans of North Africa expected all juvenile males to engage in sexual relations with older men. Fathers arranged for unmarried sons to be given to older men. Nearly all men were reported to have had such sexual relationships as boys. Later, between the ages of 16 and 20, they all married women.

Sexual activities between males are sometimes limited to rites that mark the young male's initiation into manhood. In some preliterate societies, semen is believed to boost strength and virility. Older males thus transmit semen to younger males through oral or anal sexual activities. Among the Sambian people of New Guinea, a tribe of warlike headhunters, 7- to 10-year-old males leave their parents' households and live in a "clubhouse" with other prepubertal and adolescent males. There they undergo sexual rites of passage. To acquire the fierce manhood of the headhunter, they perform fellatio on older males and drink semen (Bailey, 2003b). They are encouraged to take in as much semen as they can, as though it were mother's milk. Ingestion of semen is believed to give rise to puberty. Following puberty, adolescents are fellated by younger males. In their late teens or early twenties, however, young men are expected to take brides and enter into exclusively male–female sexual relationships.

These practices of Sambian culture might seem to suggest that the sexual orientations of males are fluid and malleable. The practices involve *behavior,* however, and not *sexual orientation.* Male–male sexual behavior among Sambians takes place within a cultural context that bears little resemblance to consensual male–male sexual activity in Western society. The prepubertal Sambian male does not *seek* sexual liaisons with other males. He is removed from his home and thrust into male–male sexual encounters by older males.

Little is known about female–female sexual activity in non-Western cultures. Evidence of female–female sexual behavior was found by Ford and Beach in only 17 of the 76 societies they studied. Perhaps female sexual behavior in general, not just sexual activity with other females, was more likely to be repressed. Perhaps women are less likely than men to develop sexual interests in, or romantic relationships with, members of their own sex. Whatever the reasons, this cross-cultural evidence is consistent with data from our own culture. Here, too, males are more likely than females to develop sexual interests in, or romantic relationships with, members of their own sex.

Cross-Species Perspectives

Many of us have observed other animals engaging in sexual behaviors that resemble male–male or female–female contacts among humans, such as mounting others of their own sex. *Question: What does sexual activity with members of the same sex signify in other species?*

A male baboon may present his rear and allow himself to be mounted by another male. This behavior may resemble anal intercourse among gay men. Is the behavior sexually motivated, however? Mounting behavior among male baboons may represent a type of dominance ritual in which lower-ranking males adopt a submissive (feminine) posture to ward off attack from dominant males (Nadler, 1990). (Some male–male acts among people also involve themes of dominance, as in the case of a dominant male prisoner forcing a less dominant one to submit to anal intercourse.) In other cases, male baboons may be seeking favors or protection from more dominant males (Nadler, 1990). Among juvenile animals, male–male behaviors may also be a form of play. Females may also attempt to mount other females, but here too, the motives may not be the same as those of humans.

Sexual motivation appears to play a role in some, but not all, male–male and female–female sexual interactions among animals. Fellatio and anal intercourse to ejaculation among juvenile male orangutans may be a case in point, as may be thrusting by one adult female gorilla against another. Some male–male encounters among rhesus monkeys also appear to be sexually motivated. However, researchers have not found prolonged, exclusive male–male sexual activity among monkeys and apes when male–female opportunities are available.

Attitudes toward Sexual Orientation in Contemporary Society

Toni, a 20-year-old lesbian college student, was incredulous that her parents believed she had *chosen* her sexual orientation. They saw her lesbianism as linked to the general rebelliousness that had been stirred by attending a school known for its "radical" image. Toni was infuriated that they believed that she would "get over" her lesbian sexual orientation once she decided to accept adult responsibilities.

The authors' files

Historically speaking, negative attitudes toward gay people have pervaded our society. At worst, male–male and female–female sexual behavior has been viewed as a crime against God or "nature." ***Question: What attitudes toward homosexuality do we find in contemporary American society?***

A national survey of males in their late teens (aged 15 to 19) showed that 9 of 10 felt that sex between men was "disgusting." Three of five could not even see themselves being friends with a gay man (Marsiglio, 1993b). Young males tend to be the harshest group in their judgments of gay people. A national poll conducted in June 1998 found that 59% of American adults believe that homosexuality is morally wrong, compared to 35% who say it is not wrong (Berke, 1998). (The remaining 6% had no answer or said they didn't know.)

Still, there are signs that Americans have grown more tolerant of gay people over the past few decades. For example, a poll conducted in June 1977 found that 56% of Americans said that gay people should have equal rights in terms of job opportunities (33% said they should not). By November 1996, 84% of Americans endorsed equal rights for gay people, and only 12% were opposed (Berke, 1998).

Gay "civil unions" have been with us for several years now, and Massachusetts' Supreme Court has ruled that gay marriages are to be permitted in that state. However, a *New York Times* poll found that only 28% of Americans agreed that "marriage between two people of the same sex should be legal" (Eggers, 2000).

An Associated Press poll conducted in the same year found that 34% supported gay marriages (Lester, 2000). But Americans are becoming more liberal on the issue: Whereas only 13% of people older than 70 in the Eggers (2000) article reported that such unions should be legal, 42% of those under the age of 30 endorsed them. The AP poll showed a similar age discrepancy: 54% of respondents aged 18 to 34 said gay people should be allowed to get married, compared with 14% of those over 65 (Lester, 2000).

The word *marriage* seems to be a major barrier. The Associated Press poll of a national sample of 1,012 adults in the United States split the sample so that half were asked whether they approved of gay people getting married, whereas the other half

were asked whether they approved of "domestic partnerships" that would give gay couples the same rights as married couples. As you can see in Table 10.2, more people approved of domestic partnerships than approved of marriage for gay couples. Despite the fact that a majority of those polled would not allow gay couples to form domestic partnerships that give partners the same rights as married partners, a majority would allow domestic partners specific rights, as shown in Table 10.3. That is, heterosexuals may be more wary of giving gays marriage certificates than of granting health benefits.

We began this section with the case of Toni, whose parents assumed that she would change her lesbian sexual orientation once she "outgrew" her rebelliousness. Toni's parents assumed that Toni had *chosen* to be gay, an assumption many people make. As we will see in the section on biological perspectives, research evidence is accumulating to support the view that inborn biological factors play a strong role in the development of sexual orientation. Interestingly, people who believe that sexual orientation is biologically determined and inborn are more tolerant of gay people than are those who see sexual orientation as stemming from upbringing or other

---

TABLE 10.2
Effect of Wording in a Poll on Gay Rights

Question	Percent saying "Should"	Percent saying "Should not"	Percent saying "Don't know"	Percent refusing to answer
In general, do you think gays and lesbians should or should not be allowed to be legally married?	34	51	11	3
In general, do you think gays and lesbians should or should not be allowed to form a domestic partnership that would give the same-sex couple the same rights and benefits as opposite-sex marriage?	41	46	11	3

Source: Will Lester (2000, May 31) Poll: Americans back some gay rights. *The Associated Press online.*

TABLE 10.3
Percent of Americans Who Would Approve of Certain Rights for Gay People in Domestic Partnerships

Would respondent approve of—	Percent in favor	Percent opposed	Percent who say "Don't know"	Percent who refuse to answer
Providing health coverage to gay partners?	53	37	7	3
Providing Social Security benefits to gay partners?	50	41	6	3
Providing inheritance rights to gay partners?	56	32	9	3

Source: Will Lester (2000, May 31). Poll: Americans back some gay rights. *The Associated Press online.*

environmental factors. Over the years, more people have believed in environmental rather than biological causes of sexual orientation (Berke, 1998), but the trend seems to be moving toward the inborn, biological point of view.

For example, a nationwide poll conducted in June of 1977 found that only 13% of Americans believed that gay people were "born with" their sexual orientation, compared to 56% who believed in environmental causes. In October of 1989, 18% of Americans said that gay people were born with their orientation, compared to 48% who believed in an environmental explanation. The Associated Press poll, conducted in 2000, found that 30% of Americans believe that gay people are born that way, compared to 46% who say they "choose" to be gay. More people are coming to look upon sexual orientation as something that one is born with. Thus fewer people are likely to believe that young people can be "seduced" into one sexual orientation or another.

One negative attitude we find toward homosexuality is called homophobia. *Question: What is homophobia?*

Homophobia Homophobia takes many forms, including

- Use of derogatory names (such as *queer, faggot,* and *dyke*)
- Telling disparaging "queer jokes"
- Barring gay people from housing, employment, or social opportunities
- Taunting (verbal abuse)
- **Gay bashing** (physical abuse)

Homophobia derives from root words meaning "fear of homosexuals." Although homophobia is more common among heterosexual people, gay people can also be homophobic.

Truth?Fiction?
Revisited

A majority of Americans still believe that gay people choose to be gay.

Gay bashing Violence against homosexuals.

Protesting Homophobia *Gay men and lesbians are frequently assaulted because of their sexual orientation. Hatred of gays is termed* homophobia, *although the roots of the word mean "fear of gays." Why do so many people hate gay men and lesbians? Why was college student Matthew Shepard killed by homophobes?*

Although some psychologists link homophobia to fears of a gay male or lesbian sexual orientation within oneself, homophobic attitudes may also be embedded within a cluster of stereotypical gender-role attitudes toward family life (Cotten-Huston & Waite, 2000). These attitudes support male dominance and the belief that it is natural and appropriate for women to sacrifice for their husbands and children (Cotten-Huston & Waite, 2000; Marsiglio, 1993b). People who have a strong stake in maintaining stereotypical gender roles may feel more readily threatened by the existence of the gay male or lesbian sexual orientation, because gay people appear to confuse or reverse these roles. Men have more of a stake in maintaining the tradition of male dominance, so perhaps it is not surprising that college men are more intolerant of gay males than college women are (Schellenberg et al., 1999).

Homophobic attitudes are more common among males who identify with a traditional male gender role and those who hold a fundamentalist religious orientation (Cotten-Huston & Waite, 2000; Marsiglio, 1993b). Similarly, researchers find that college students who hold a conservative political orientation tend to be more accepting of negative attitudes toward gay people than are liberal students (Cotten-Huston & Waite, 2000). Other studies of university samples find male students to be more homophobic than women (Kunkel & Temple, 1992; Schellenberg et al., 1999). In addition, business and science students at a Canadian University were more intolerant of gay people than students in the arts and social sciences (Schellenberg et al., 1999).

Heterosexual men are less tolerant of gay people than heterosexual women are (Kerns & Fine, 1994; Seltzer, 1992; Whitley & Kite, 1995). Perhaps some heterosexual men are threatened by the possibility of discovering male–male sexual impulses within themselves (Freiberg, 1995). Consistent with this view, heterosexual males tend to hold more negative attitudes toward gay men than toward lesbians (Kite, 1992).

At least some homophobic men may have homoerotic impulses of which they are unaware. Denial of these impulses may be connected with their fear and disapproval of gay males. Henry Adams and his colleagues (1996) showed men sexually explicit videotapes of male–female, female–female, and male–male sexual activity and measured their sexual response by means of the penile plethysmograph. The plethysmograph measures size of erection. Subjects were also asked to report how sexually aroused they felt in response to the videos. The men were also evaluated for their attitudes toward gay males. Men who were not homophobic were sexually aroused, according to their penile circumference, only by videos of male–female and female–female sexual activity. The homophobic viewers were also aroused, in terms of penile circumference, by the video of male–male sexual activity. However, the homophobic men reported that they did not *feel* aroused by the male–male sexual activity. Were they out of touch with their biological response, or was their biological response misleading?

Gay Bashing and the HIV/AIDS Epidemic Although strides toward social acceptance of gay people have been made since Kinsey's day, the advent of HIV/AIDS has added fuel to the fire of hatred and prejudice. When HIV/AIDS first appeared in North America, it primarily struck the gay male community. Some homophobes in the larger society believed that the epidemic was a plague inflicted by God to punish gay people for sinful behavior.

The advent of the epidemic has been accompanied by a dramatic rise in the incidence of gay bashing (Freiberg, 1995). Perhaps the epidemic serves as a pretext for some people to attack gay males, whom they blame for spreading the disease.

Gay bashing also occurs on college campuses. A large percentage (77%) of 121 lesbian and gay male undergraduate students in one survey at Pennsylvania State University reported they had been verbally insulted. Nearly one in three (31%)

reported being chased or followed (D'Augelli, 1992a). Nearly 20% said they had been physically assaulted. Most of the victimizers were fellow students. Few of these incidents were reported to the authorities.

Students, too, tend to hold gay men more responsible for behaviors that put themselves at risk of contracting HIV/AIDS. One study found that students assigned a greater amount of blame to a hypothetical person who had contracted HIV/AIDS when the person was identified as a gay male than when the person was identified as a heterosexual male (Anderson, 1992).

Sexual Orientation and the Law During the past generation, gay people have organized effective political groups to fight discrimination and to overturn the sodomy laws that have traditionally targeted them. Despite their success, sodomy laws are still on the books in many states. *Question: What are sodomy laws?* Sodomy laws prohibit "unnatural" sexual acts, even between consenting adults. Certain sexual acts that many gay people (and many heterosexual people) practice, such as anal intercourse and oral–genital contact, fall under the legal definition of sodomy in many states. Although sodomy laws are usually written to apply equally to all adults, the vast majority of prosecutions have been directed against gay people.

A 1986 Supreme Court decision (*Hardwick v. Bowers*) let stand a Georgia sodomy law that makes oral–genital or anal–genital sexual contact crimes punishable by up to 20 years in prison, even when engaged in by consenting adults. The decision was a setback to gay rights organizations, which had looked to the Supreme Court to overturn state sodomy laws.

However, in 2003, by a vote of 6 to 3, the Supreme Court reversed that decision by striking down a Texas law against "deviate sexual intercourse with another individual of the same sex." The Texas law "demeans the lives of homosexual persons," wrote Justice Anthony M. Kennedy, explaining the majority vote. Over the years, the Constitution's establishment of a right to privacy has been in conflict with laws against same-sex sexual behavior. Gay people "are entitled to respect for their private lives," Kennedy wrote further. In an interview, he added that "The state cannot demean their existence or control their destiny by making their private sexual conduct a crime."

Many other countries, including Mexico, Holland, Italy, Spain, England, France, and the Scandinavian countries, have also struck down laws against male–male and female–female sexual activity. As of 2004, when this book went to press, The Netherlands, Belgium, and Canada extended full marriage rights to same-sex couples. France, Germany, Finland, Sweden, Norway, Denmark, and Iceland allowed gay males and lesbians to enter into legal partnerships that in effect provided the protections and responsibilities of marriage. Nearly all developed countries were debating the issue of gay marriage.

Gay Activism Question: What is meant by gay activism? Gay activism is the joining together of gay people to achieve political ends. Nowhere in the United States have gay people been more politically effective than in San Francisco. They are well represented on the city police force and in other public agencies. The coming out of many gay people, and their flocking to more tolerant urban centers, has rendered them formidable political forces in these locales.

The Mattachine Society, named after gay medieval court jesters, was the first powerful gay rights organization. At first, membership was kept secret to protect members' social status in the community. Today members' names are published. The Mattachine Society now has chapters in most metropolitan areas. It publishes the *Mattachine Newsletter* and *Homosexual Citizen.* Another newsletter, the *Advocate,* is the nation's best-known gay newsletter.

Human Sexuality in the New Millennium

A First at *Bride's* Magazine: A Report on Same-Sex Unions

After 70 years of helping brides walk down the aisle, Condé Nast's *Bride's* magazine has crossed a threshold of its own. Its September–October 2003 issue contains a full-page article on same-sex weddings. This is the first time that any of the five top-selling bridal magazines has published such a feature.

The article, titled "Outward Bound" and written by David Toussaint, discusses recent developments in same-sex ceremonies. Gay and lesbian couples are interviewed about why they want their friends and community to recognize their unions publicly. The article also offers advice on how to be a good guest. It urges readers "not to panic" if they are invited to a gay wedding.

The story was discussed at an editorial meeting and was assigned after some discussion of whether the topic was appropriate for *Bride's* readers.

"We looked at what was happening in the wedding industry," says Millie Martini Bratten, the magazine's editor-in-chief and the editorial director of Condé Nast's Bridal Group. "We were hearing from various retailers that same-sex couples had become an important part of their gift registries," Ms. Bratten said. "And we were answering more readers' questions: 'If two women were getting married, what's the appropriate attire?'" She also noted that *The New York Times* and other newspapers had begun publishing notices of same-sex ceremonies.

Cathy Renna, news media director for the Gay and Lesbian Alliance Against Defamation, said every such article is an important step. "Maybe a cynical person would say they just want our business," Ms. Renna said. "But if you want to have a wedding, these are the publications you'll read. A story like this really energizes the gay and lesbian community."

Same-sex ceremonies have been covered for some time on Internet wedding sites. "Wow, they finally caught up," said Carley Roney, editor-in-chief and a co-founder of one such site, *TheKnot.com*, which claims more than two million visitors a month. The *Knot* has covered same-sex weddings since it began operating in 1997.

Editors at more than one national bridal magazine said that they also were considering articles on same-sex weddings, but added that business concerns remained a factor. So far, Condé Nast reports no adverse advertising reaction. Nina Lawrence, vice president and publisher of the Condé Nast Bridal Group, said she had not heard any complaints from her advertisers.

Ms. Lawrence noted that *Bride's* was trying to address generational changes in weddings and marriage ceremonies. The generation that is getting married now "is the most inclusive generation ever," she said. "If we were creating a product for people who were getting married 20 years ago, we'd be out of business."

Source: Reprinted from Bill Werde. (2003, July 28). A first at *Bride's* magazine: A report on same-sex unions. *The New York Times online.*

The largest lesbian organization is the Daughters of Bilitis, named after the Greek courtesan who was loved by the lesbian poet Sappho. The group provides a forum for sharing social experiences and pursuing equal rights. The organization's newsletter is the *Ladder*.

The AIDS epidemic has had a profound effect on the political agenda of gay rights organizations. These organizations combat the HIV/AIDS epidemic on several fronts:

1. They lobby for increased funding for HIV/AIDS research and treatment.
2. They educate the gay and wider communities about the dangers of high-risk sexual behavior.
3. They encourage gay men and others to adopt safer sex practices, including use of condoms.
4. They protect the civil rights of people with HIV/AIDS with respect to employment, housing, and medical and dental treatment.
5. They provide counseling and support services for people with HIV/AIDS.

Stereotypes and Sexual Behavior Among heterosexual people, sexual aggressiveness is linked to the masculine gender role. Sexual passivity is linked to the feminine role.

news

outward bound
Same-sex weddings step into the limelight

BY DAVID TOUSSAINT

Despite the media hype, when *The New York Times* made a groundbreaking decision last September to publish its first-ever same-sex wedding announcement, barely a ripple of controversy was heard. "Most readers took the decision in stride," says Toby Usnik, the paper's director of public relations. The item, in the Sunday Weddings/Celebrations section, was a simple ceremony notice from Daniel Gross and Steven Goldstein, two men who wanted to share their news with the world.

While gay couples have always been around, it wasn't until recently that they've begun to cement their relationships with formal celebrations, complete with officiants, cake-cuttings, even honeymoons. Gay men and women are out, loud, and proud about making a commitment. In other words, they're just like other couples in love.

taking the plunge
So why are more gays deciding to solidify their partnerships? Chalk it up to a natural progression and assertion of civil rights. "We simply did what all couples do in our society when they want to spend the rest of their lives together," says Marita Begley, 45, who in 1994 walked down the aisle with Leslie Becker, 44, in Glen Ridge, New Jersey. For Gross and Goldstein, it was the next big step in their decade-long romance. "The time was right," says Gross, 32, whose formal wedding to Goldstein, 40, was an elaborate weekend affair that included ceremonies in both Montreal and Lake Hero, Vermont. "We felt a wedding would demonstrate that our relationship is every bit as valid as anyone else's."

While public acknowledgment and acceptance is a key motivation for many same-sex couples, Evan Wolfson, executive director of the Freedom to Marry Collaborative (FMC), a national organization to end discrimination in civil marriage, believes that gay weddings also help part-

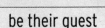

be their guest
You've just been invited to a gay wedding and your only reference point is the lesbian ceremony on *Friends*. Not to panic: Same-sex affairs can be nearly as traditional as heterosexual ones. "We told our guests to expect everything but the white dress," says Diamond, who wore a suit and registered for gifts. "My niece sang 'Here Come the Brides,'" says Candace Frede, 47, who had a civil union in Putney, Vermont, with Jean DeNiro, 52, last November. And don't be surprised if the couple shares a smooch. After all, says Goldstein, "we're just two guys in love."

ners who have, or want to have, children feel more connected to the world. "The family becomes a recognized union," he explains. "The hope of building a future, of counting on someone and having them count on you, is an enormous need in life whether you're gay or straight."

one love, one law?
In the United States, only Vermont allows gay and lesbian couples to enter into what's called a civil union, which gives them marital status under state, but not federal, law. For example, if a same-sex couple in Vermont has a civil union, they're eligible for the same healthcare benefits (covered by the state) as a heterosexual married couple. However, should one spouse die, the remaining partner would not be eligible for Social Security benefits (a federal program). A Vermont civil union has no legal clout in any other state and can be legally terminated by filing a dissolution document.

Since July 1, 2000, when Vermont enacted the law, more than 5,000 civil unions have been filed. Holland is the only country in the world that allows gays and lesbians to marry, though several others, including Canada, Germany, and South Africa, legally recognize same-sex partnerships.

pride and prejudice
Despite progress, gays and lesbians still face obstacles. "My father couldn't bring himself to attend our ceremony, in spite of his love for both of us," recalls Begley. "He's since passed away, but I believe he regretted his decision." Yet for every such tale, there's a happier story. "At holiday gatherings, our families expect us to be together now," says Laurence Diamond, 38, whose New York nuptials to Grant Schneider, 43, took place last September. "There's no longer a question that we're a couple." ●

GETTYIMAGES

The New Look of Bride's *Magazine?* The September/October issue of Bride's *contains an article about same-sex weddings. In it, gay and lesbian couples discuss why they want their unions to be recognized publicly.* Bride's *2003. Reprinted with permission.*

Some heterosexual people assume (often erroneously) that in gay male and lesbian relationships, one partner consistently assumes the masculine role in sexual relations, and the other the feminine role.

Many gay couples vary the active and passive roles, however. Among gay male couples, for example, roles in anal intercourse (*inserter* versus *insertee*) and in fellatio are often reversed. Contrary to popular assumptions, sexual behavior between lesbians seldom reflects distinct **butch–femme** gender roles. Most lesbians report providing and receiving oral–genital stimulation, alternating roles or simultaneously. Many gay people claim that the labels *masculine* and *feminine* merely reflect the "straight community's" efforts to pigeonhole them in terms that "straights" can understand.

Butch A lesbian who assumes a traditional masculine gender role.

Femme A lesbian who assumes a traditional feminine gender role.

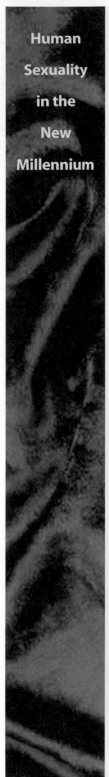

Human Sexuality in the New Millennium

Queer Guy with a Slob's Eye

In a classic scene from Robert Anderson's "Tea and Sympathy," a 1950's Broadway play about a teenage boy whose classmates taunt him for acting like a girl, the boy's closest straight buddy tries to teach him to walk like a man. Of course, the boy can't get it right. He walks back and forth across the room, aping his friend, but failing to swagger and glare convincingly. Finally, he is saved from his ruinous girlishness only by the headmaster's wife, who seduces him, saying famously, "Years from now, when you talk about this—and you will—be kind."

I thought of this scene while I watched a recent episode of *Queer Eye for the Straight Guy,* in which the roles in "Tea and Sympathy" are reversed. This time, instead of a straight man showing his nelly friend how to "butch it up," five gay men surround a hopelessly

Inherently Hip? Jai Rodriguez of Bravo channel's "Queer Eye for the Straight Guy."

unfashionably straight guy named Butch and get him in touch with what one of the Fab Five calls "the inner Butch."

"The tables have turned with a vengeance," as Tennessee Williams might have said, camping it up. But the straight men who submit themselves to public makeovers by a team of gay men are not your stereotypical playground bullies. In the two episodes I saw, both guys were good-natured and easygoing. And the show's fashion-savvy gay men are smart, immaculate and handsome. Which is why I begin to mistrust *Queer Eye for the Straight Guy.* If this is reality TV, why aren't the straight guys hostile and punctilious and the gay men sloppy and depressed? "All the gay men I know are terrible slobs, including you," my mother told me, when she called to discuss the show. "Do you think you could get them to clean up your apartment?" Indeed, the show insists on reinforcing the stereotype that gay guys are groomed and charming and slender and witty, and no more than 35 years old. Yet here I sit in my Megadeth T-shirt, dirt broke, middle-aged, downing a carton of vanilla ice cream and spilling it on my computer keyboard.

Some gay men dress down to look "street," but I'm not a chic slob, I'm a real one. My apartment is designed like a bowling alley, with the furniture pushed against the walls, except where it can be used to cover carpet stains.

And many gay people are equally unstylish. In fact, the most gorgeously well-mannered person I know is a masculine straight man from Queens, an amateur boxer who flicks lint from my sweater every time I see him.

I'd like to be the straight guy who gets cleaned up on TV. Then I might look like a convincing gay man, the kind of ingratiating homosexual America loves enough to grant equal rights, like Will on "Will and Grace." Unfortunately, when I go shopping, it's not because I'm eager to find just the right tuxedo shirt from DKNY, but because I compulsively spend money I don't have on nothing I really need: boxed sets of CD's of soundtracks from Kurosawa films; handmade Vietnamese percussion instruments; every edition of "Macbeth," including all the opera versions.

Biological Perspectives

Questions: Is sexual orientation an inborn trait that is transmitted genetically, like eye color or height? Does it reflect hormonal influences? Biological perspectives focus on the possible roles of evolution, genetics, and hormonal influences in shaping sexual orientation.

When I feel the urge to be surrounded by smart, stylish homosexuals, I call my gay girlfriends. The hippest gays I know are all women; and nobody is as diabolically sloppy as a messy straight woman. But it is hard to imagine a network or even a cable TV show that would cast five sassy, beautiful lesbians and send them to the appalling homes of distracted straight girls to put things in order.

Queer Eye for the Straight Guy comes at a moment when lesbians and gay men seem to have reached a public relations peak. First the Supreme Court ruled that antisodomy laws are unconstitutional. Then America's Episcopal Church approved its first openly gay bishop. Now Bravo is sending friendly gay guys into the homes of all-American men and showing them how to shop.

Reviewers have called the show "subversive," because it shows gay men touching straight guys in intimate places—the inseam, the sideburn—without being beaten up or legislated against. We can all get along if we would just let our gay brothers give us fashion tips, the show seems to say. Yet I wonder how surprising it is for television to feature a bunch of "fabulous" gay guys whose sole desire is to make the world a better place for straight men.

After all, *Queer Eye for the Straight Guy* is not about what gay men do so much as it is about how straight men feel. It flatters heterosexuals by putting them where they already are, at the center of the action.

And while some straight people might agree that we can all do what we want in our own bedrooms—especially if we want to have cute gay guys choose our wallpaper—gays and lesbians may be enjoying a short-lived exhilaration over a few recent social and political gains. With both George Bush and the Vatican making statements opposing gay marriage, same-sex marriage is likely to be an explosive and divisive issue in the coming presidential election.

In the meantime, is *Queer Eye for the Straight Guy* creating a new "common ground" where gay men and straight men can bond? No doubt it is, for some people—in particular, for television executives and advertisers impressed with the show's ratings. To me, however, the most touching aspect of the show is its

plain proof that all men, straight or gay, yearn to be praised by a guy. Though the makeover artists are sometimes catty about their straight pals, mostly, they are achingly sincere.

"How do you feel now?" they ask their buddy, Butch, as they cut his hair, paint his apartment, choose his outfits, and get his art work shown for the first time at a New York gallery. "Is there an emotion that comes through for you?" In another episode, they rescue a cuddly mensch named Adam from his careless heterosexual habits.

"Does that feel good, Adam?" they ask him, as he takes a mud bath, learns to tie a tie. "How does it feel?" And the straight guys, so masculine that even their names evoke über-men—"Butch," everybody's high school dream date; "Adam," the father of us all—mumble and burble, sighing with contentment.

There is love in the room; it is somehow very Iron John. Indeed, each episode I watched devolved into a combo frat party/encounter group. First there was the buddy bash: six guys (one straight and five gays) piled into a big van, hanging together, doing what guys do. Afterward, knocking back beers, they had their Oprah moment. One of them, singled out for an affirmation, got patted on the back. "You look incredible," his pals said, circling him. "You look fantastic."

Anybody with a father has learned how difficult it can sometimes be to get a man to pay attention to you. The subversive charge of *Queer Eye for the Straight Guy* may not be its homo/hetero get-together, but its demonstration that all men want contact with other men. Of course, you can learn the same thing from a hockey game.

Still, I think of the show's grooming guru, Kyan, asking his buddy Adam if anyone had ever taught him how to shave, and Adam's mumbled reply, "No, unh-unh, no."

In that moment, it seemed like five gay dads had been beamed down to planet Earth to give men what they really want: a father who's not afraid to pat your head and say, "Atta boy."

Source: Reprinted from John Weir. (2003, August 10). Queer guy with a slob's eye. *The New York Times online.*

The Evolutionary Perspective It might seem odd that evolutionary theorists have endeavored to explain gay male and lesbian sexual orientations. After all, gay males and lesbians are not motivated to engage in sexual activity with members of the other sex. How, then, can gay and lesbian sexual orientations confer any evolutionary advantage?

To answer the question, we must look to the group or the species rather than the individual. Kirkpatrick (2000) suggests that male–male and female–female sexual behavior derive from individual selection for reciprocal *altruism*. That is, strong male–male and female–female alliances have advantages for group survival in that they bind group members together emotionally. This hypothesis remains speculative.

Genetics and Sexual Orientation Considerable evidence exists that gay male and lesbian sexual orientations run in families (Bailey et al., 2000a; Dawood et al., 2000; Kendler et al., 2000; Rahman & Wilson, 2003). Twin studies shed light on the possible role of heredity (Bailey, 2003b). **Monozygotic (MZ) twins**, or identical twins, develop from a single fertilized ovum and share 100% of their heredity. **Dizygotic (DZ) twins**, or fraternal twins, develop from two fertilized ova. Like other brothers and sisters, DZ twins share only 50% of their heredity. Thus if a gay male or lesbian sexual orientation were transmitted genetically, it should be found about twice as often among identical twins of gay people as among fraternal twins. Because MZ and DZ twins who are reared together share similar environmental influences, differences in the degree of **concordance** for a given trait between the types of twin pairs are further indicative of genetic origins. Several studies have identified gay men who had either identical (MZ) or fraternal (DZ) twin brothers in order to examine the prevalence of a gay male sexual orientation in their twin brothers. In one of the most carefully conducted twin studies, about 52% of identical (MZ) twin pairs were found to be "concordant" (in agreement) for a gay male sexual orientation, compared with 22% of fraternal (DZ) twins and only 11% of adoptive brothers (Bailey, 2003a; Bailey & Pillard, 1991). Bear in mind that MZ twins are more likely than DZ twins to be dressed alike and treated alike. Thus, their greater concordance for a gay sexual orientation may at least in part reflect environmental factors (Kendler et al., 2000).

Researchers have found evidence linking a region on the X sex chromosome to a gay male sexual orientation (Bailey et al., 1999). One group of researchers (Hamer et al., 1993) found that gay males in a sample of 114 gay men were more likely to have gay male relatives on their mothers' side of the family than would be expected on the basis of the prevalence of a gay male sexual orientation in the general population. Yet these gay males did not have a greater than expected number of gay male relatives on the paternal side of the family. This pattern of inheritance is consistent with genetic traits, such as hemophilia, that are linked to the X sex chromosome, which men receive from their mothers.

The researchers then examined the X chromosome in 40 pairs of gay male, nontwin brothers. In 33 of the pairs, the brothers had identical DNA markers on the end tip of the X chromosome. For brothers overall in the general population, about half would be expected to have inherited this chromosomal structure. It is suspected, therefore, that this chromosomal region may hold a gene that predisposes men to a gay male sexual orientation.

The researchers cautioned that they had not found a particular gene linked to sexual orientation, just a general location where the gene may be found. Nor do scientists know how such a gene, or combination of genes, might account for sexual orientation. Perhaps a particular gene or gene governs the development of proteins that sculpt parts of the brain in ways that favor the development of a gay male sexual orientation. On the other hand, a number of the gay brothers, 7 of the 40 pairs, did *not* share the chromosomal marker.

Hormonal Influences and Sexual Orientation Sex hormones strongly influence the mating behavior of other species (Crews, 1994). Researchers have thus looked into possible hormonal factors in determining sexual orientation in humans.

Monozygotic (MZ) twins Twins who develop from the same fertilized ovum. Identical twins.

Dizygotic (DZ) twins Twins who develop from different fertilized ova. Fraternal twins.

Concordance Agreement.

Testosterone is essential to male sexual differentiation. Thus, levels of testosterone and its by-products in the blood and urine have been studied as possible influences on sexual orientation. Research has failed to connect sexual orientation in either sex with differences in the levels of either male or female sex hormones in adulthood (Friedman & Downey, 1994). In adulthood, testosterone appears to have **activating effects**. That is, it affects the intensity of sexual desire, but not the preference for partners of the same or the other sex (Whalen et al., 1990).

What of the possible *prenatal* effects of sex hormones? Pregnant rats in experiments were given anti-androgen drugs that block the effects of testosterone. When the drugs were given during critical periods in which the fetuses' brains were becoming sexually differentiated, male offspring were likely to show feminine mating patterns as adults (Ellis & Ames, 1987). The adult males became receptive to mounting attempts by other males and failed to mount females.

Do prenatal sex hormones play a similar role in determining sexual orientation in people? There is suggestive evidence. For example, Meyer-Bahlburg and his colleagues (1995) interviewed groups of women exposed prenatally to DES, a synthetic estrogen. They found that these women were more likely to be rated as lesbian or bisexual than women who were not exposed to DES. The genitals of gay people differentiate prenatally in accord with their chromosomal sex. However, it remains possible that imbalances in prenatal sex hormones may cause brain tissue to be sexually differentiated in one direction even though the genitals are differentiated in the other (Collaer & Hines, 1995). Moreover, as we will see later, butch lesbians may differ somewhat biologically from femme lesbians.

The Structure of the Brain Evidence suggests that there may be structural differences between the brains of heterosexual and gay men. In 1991 Simon LeVay, a neurobiologist at the Salk Institute in La Jolla, California, carried out autopsies on the brains of 35 AIDS victims—19 gay men and 16 (presumably) heterosexual men. He found that a segment of the hypothalamus—specifically, the *third interstitial nucleus of the anterior hypothalamus*—in the brains of the gay men was less than half the size of the same segment in the heterosexual men. The same brain segment was larger in the brain tissues of heterosexual men than in brain tissues obtained from a comparison group of 6 presumably heterosexual women. No significant differences in size were found between the brain tissues of the gay men and the women, however.

LeVay's findings are intriguing but preliminary. We do not know, for example, whether the structural differences found by LeVay are innate. Nor do the findings prove that biology is destiny. As Richard Nakamura, a scientist with the National Institute of Mental Health, commented, "This [LeVay's findings] shouldn't be taken to mean that you're automatically [gay] if you have a structure of one size versus a structure of another size" (Angier, 1991).

The belief that sexual orientation is innate or inborn has many adherents—in both the scientific and general communities. Support for the possible influences of prenatal hormonal factors in "sculpting" the brain in a masculine or feminine direction is based largely on animal studies, however. Direct evidence with people is lacking. We must also be careful in generalizing results from other species to our own.

Psychological Perspectives

Questions: Do family relationships play a role in the origins of sexual orientation? What are the effects of childhood sexual experiences? Psychoanalytic theory and learning theory provide two of the major psychological approaches to understanding the origins of sexual orientation.

Activating effects Those effects of sex hormones that influence the level of the sex drive, but not sexual orientation.

Truth?Fiction?
Revisited

Therefore, the idea that "castration anxiety" in gay males is aroused by knowledge of male–female intercourse has not been scientifically demonstrated.

Psychoanalytic Views Sigmund Freud, the originator of psychoanalytic theory, believed that children are naturally open to all forms of sexual stimulation. However, through proper resolution of the Oedipus complex, a boy will forsake his incestuous desires for his mother and come to identify with his father. As a result, his erotic attraction to his mother will eventually be transferred to more appropriate *female* partners. A girl, through proper resolution of her Electra complex, will identify with her mother and seek erotic stimulation from men when she becomes sexually mature.

In Freud's view, a gay male or lesbian sexual orientation results from failure to resolve the Oedipus complex successfully by identifying with the parent of the same sex. In men, faulty resolution of the Oedipus complex is most likely to result from the so-called classic pattern of an emotionally "close-binding" mother and a "detached–hostile" father. A boy reared in such a family may come to identify with his mother and even to "transform himself into her" (Freud, 1922/1959, p. 40). He may thus become effeminate and develop sexual interests in men.

Freud believed that unresolved **castration anxiety** plays a role in a gay male sexual orientation. By the time the Oedipus complex takes effect, the boy will have learned from self-stimulation that he can obtain sexual pleasure from his penis. In his youthful fantasies, he associates this pleasure with mental images of his mother. Similarly, he is likely to have learned that females do not possess a penis. The psychoanalyst theorizes that somewhere along the line, the boy may also have been warned that his penis will be removed if he plays with himself. From all this, the boy may surmise that females—including his mother—once had penises, but that they were removed.

During the throes of the Oedipus complex, the boy unconsciously comes to fear that his father, his rival in love for the mother, will retaliate by removing the organ that the boy has come to associate with sexual pleasure. His fear causes him to repress his sexual desire for his mother and to identify with the potential aggressor—his father. The boy thus overcomes his castration anxiety and is headed along the path toward adult heterosexuality.

If the Oedipus complex is not successfully resolved, castration anxiety may persist. When sexually mature, the man will not be able to tolerate sex with women. Their lack of a penis will arouse unconscious castration anxiety within himself.

The Electra complex in little girls follows a somewhat different course. Freud believed that little girls become envious of boys' penises, because they lack their own. Jealousy leads little girls to resent their mothers, whom they blame for their anatomic "deficiency," and to turn from their mothers to their fathers as sexual objects. They now desire to possess the father, because the father's penis provides what they lack. But incestuous desires bring the girl into competition with her mother. Motivated by fear that her mother will withdraw her love if the desires persist, the girl normally represses them and identifies with her mother. She supplants her childhood desire for a penis with a desire to marry a man and bear children. The baby, emitted from between her legs, serves as the ultimate penis substitute.

A nagging problem of Freudian theory is that many of its concepts, such as castration anxiety and penis envy, are believed to operate at an unconscious level. As such, they lie beyond the scope of scientific observation and measurement. Moreover, as pointed out by Friedman and Downey (2001), viewing childhood sexuality from the vantage point of adulthood, as happens in psychoanalysis, can provide a distorted view of what really took place—especially when the analyst is motivated to find support for his or her theory.

Castration anxiety
In psychoanalytic theory, a man's fear that his genitals will be removed. Castration anxiety is an element of the Oedipus complex and, in Freud's view, is implicated in the directionality of erotic interests.

Research evidence provides another perspective on the issue of the family relationships of gay sons. Richard Pillard and his colleagues (Pillard & Weinrich, 1986; Pillard, 1990) found that gay males described themselves as more distant from their fathers during childhood than did heterosexual controls or the gay men's own heterosexual brothers. The gay men in their sample also reported greater closeness to their mothers. Still, the father's psychological distance from the son may have reflected the *son's* alienation from *him,* not the reverse. That is, the son may have been so attached to his mother, or so uninterested in traditional masculine activities, that he rebuffed paternal attempts to engage him in conventional father–son activities.

Learning Theories Learning theorists agree with Freud that early experiences play an important role in the development of sexual orientation. They focus on the role of reinforcement of early patterns of sexual behavior, however, rather than on the resolution of unconscious conflicts. People generally repeat pleasurable activities and discontinue painful ones. Thus, people may learn to engage in sexual activity with people of their own sex if childhood sexual experimentation with them is connected with sexual pleasure.

If sexual motivation is high, as it tends to be during adolescence, and the only outlets are with others of one's own sex, adolescents may experiment sexually with them. If these encounters are pleasurable, and heterosexual experiences are unpleasant, a firmer gay male or lesbian sexual orientation may develop (Gagnon & Simon, 1973). Conversely, pain, anxiety, or social disapproval may be connected with early contacts with people of one's own sex. In such cases, the child may learn to inhibit feelings of attraction to people of his or her own sex and develop a firmer heterosexual orientation.

Although learning may play a role in the development of a gay male or lesbian sexual orientation, learning theorists have not identified specific learning experiences that would lead to these orientations. Moreover, most adolescent encounters with people of the same sex, even if pleasurable, do not lead to an adult gay male or lesbian sexual orientation. Many heterosexual people have had adolescent encounters with members of their own sex that did not sway their adult orientations. This is true even of people whose early sexual interactions with the other sex were fumbling and frustrating. Moreover, the overwhelming majority of gay males and lesbians were aware of sexual interest in people of their own sex *before* they had sexual encounters with them, pleasurable or otherwise (Bell et al., 1981; Savin-Williams & Diamond, 2000).

Gender Nonconformity

Question: What is gender nonconformity? Gender nonconformity is failure to conform to the gender-role stereotype that is consistent with one's anatomic sex. On average, gay males tend to be somewhat feminine and lesbians to be somewhat masculine, but there is a good deal of variation within each group (Bailey, 2003b; Bailey et al., 1997; Dawood et al., 2000). Thus it seems that stereotypes of the effeminate gay male and the masculine lesbian are exaggerated. Gender nonconformity begins in childhood. Gay males and lesbians are more likely than heterosexuals to report childhood behavior stereotypical of the other sex (Bailey & Zucker, 1995; Singh et al., 1999). Many gay males and lesbians recall acting and feeling "different" from their childhood peers. Many gay males from a variety of groups, such as prisoners, psychiatric patients, and members of gay rights organizations report that they avoided participating in competitive sports as children, were more fearful of physical injury, and were more likely to avoid getting into fights, than heterosexual males (Dawood et al.,

2000). Some gay males recall feeling different as early as age 3 or 4. Feelings of differentness were often related to behavior that is stereotypical of the other sex.

Gay males are also more likely to recall feeling more sensitive than their heterosexual peers during childhood (Isay, 1990). They cried more easily. Their feelings were more readily hurt. They had more artistic interests. They had fewer male buddies but more female playmates. Gay males were more likely than their heterosexual counterparts to have preferred "girls' toys." They preferred playing with girls to playing with trucks or guns or engaging in rough-and-tumble play (Dawood et al., 2000). Their preferences often led to their being called "sissies." Gay men also recall more cross-dressing during childhood. They preferred the company of older women to that of older men and engaged in childhood sex play with other boys rather than with girls.

Gender Nonconformity and the Butch–Femme Dimension There is also evidence of masculine-typed behavior among lesbians as children (Bailey & Zucker, 1995). Lesbians as a group were more likely than heterosexual women to perceive themselves as having been "tomboys." They were more likely to have preferred rough-and-tumble games than to play with dolls and enjoyed wearing boy's clothing rather than "cutesy" dresses.

An important study by Devendra Singh and colleagues (1999) relates gender nonconformity in lesbians to the butch–femme dimension and biological factors. The investigators compared self-identified butch and femme lesbians on various personality, behavioral, and biological measures. They found that butch lesbians were significantly more likely than femme lesbians to recall gender-atypical behavioral preferences in childhood. Butch lesbians also had higher waist-to-hip ratios and higher testosterone levels in their saliva, both of which are more typical of males. The Singh group suggests that their findings support the validity of the butch–femme distinction and that the distinction may be caused by differences in exposure to prenatal androgens (male sex hormones).

Childhood Effeminacy and a Gay Male Sexual Orientation How might extreme childhood effeminacy lead to a gay male sexual orientation? Those who support an environmental view speculate that the social detachment of these boys from male peers and role models (especially fathers) creates strong, unfulfilled cravings for male affection. This craving then leads them to seek males as partners in sex and love relationships in adolescence and adulthood. Alan Bell of the Kinsey Institute believes that self-perceptions of differentness and social distance from other males during childhood lead these boys to develop erotic attractions that differ from those of other boys. These are erotic attractions toward members of their own sex.

Of course, there is another possibility, as suggested by the research of J. Michael Bailey and his colleagues (Bailey et al., 2000; Dawood et al., 2000): Gender nonconformity appears to be somewhat heritable. Moreover, if a tendency toward homosexuality is inherited, gender nonconformity could also be an expression of that tendency.

All in all, the origins of a gay male or lesbian sexual orientation remain mysterious and complex—just as mysterious as the origins of heterosexuality. In reviewing theories and research, we are left with the impression that sexual orientation is unlikely to have a single cause. Sexual orientation appears to spring from multiple origins, including biological and psychosocial factors (Strickland, 1995). Genetic and biochemical factors (such as hormone levels) may affect the prenatal organization of the brain. These factors may predispose people to a certain sexual orientation. But it may be that early socialization experiences are also necessary to give rise to a gay male, lesbian, heterosexual, or bisexual sexual orientation. The precise influences and interactions of these factors have so far eluded researchers.

Review: Perspectives on Gay Male and Lesbian Sexual Orientations

Reflect

What are the attitudes of most people from your background toward gay males and lesbians? Do you share these attitudes? Explain.

Critical Thinking

Some people believe that sexual orientation is inborn; others believe that it represents the choice of the individual. Why are people who believe sexual orientation is inborn more tolerant of homosexuals?

13. In ancient _____, men frequently formed sexual relationships with adolescent males.

14. The "Office of the _____" was established in fifteenth-century Florence to help identify "sodomites."

15. The early _____ considered any nonprocreative sexual act sinful.

16. To acquire the fierce manhood of the headhunter, young Sambians drink _____.

17. Over the past few decades, people in the United States have become (*More* or *Less*?) tolerant of homosexuals.

18. The term _____ derives from roots meaning "fear of homosexuals."

19. Homophobia is associated with beliefs in (*Equality of the sexes* or *Male dominance*?).

20. Heterosexual men are (*More* or *Less*?) tolerant of gay people than heterosexual women are.

21. In 2003, the Supreme Court (*Supported* or *Struck down*?) a Texas law against "deviate sexual intercourse with another individual of the same sex."

22. The _____ Society was the first powerful gay rights organization.

23. Monozygotic (MZ) twins are (*More* or *Less*?) likely to be concordant for homosexuality than dizygotic (DZ) twins.

24. Research evidence links a region on the _____ sex chromosome to a gay male sexual orientation.

25. The male offspring of pregnant rats who were given anti-androgen drugs were likely to show (*Masculine* or *Feminine*?) mating patterns as adults.

26. Psychoanalytic theory relates homosexuality to faulty resolution of the _____ or _____ complex.

27. _____ theorists focus on the role of reinforcement of early patterns of sexual behavior in the development of sexual orientation.

28. Gay males and lesbians are more likely than heterosexuals to report childhood behavior stereotypical of the (*Same* or *Other*?) sex.

29. (*Butch* or *Femme*?) lesbians have higher testosterone levels in their saliva.

Adjustment of Gay Males and Lesbians

Question: Is homosexuality a mental disorder? Until 1973, a gay male sexual orientation and a lesbian were in and of themselves considered to be mental illnesses by the American Psychiatric Association and were listed as such in their diagnostic manual. But in that year, the members of the association voted to drop a gay male sexual orientation and a lesbian sexual orientation from its list of mental disorders,[2] although a diagnostic category remains for people with persistent and marked distress about their sexual orientation (American Psychiatric Association, 2000).

Many members of the organization objected to the vote, arguing that it was politically motivated. Could the American Medical Association vote to drop cancer as a physical illness, they asked? Those who raised this kind of objection maintain the belief that homosexuality is a disorder.

2. We use the words *mental* and *psychological* interchangeably when we are talking about "mental health" (or "psychological health") or "mental disorders" ("psychological disorders").

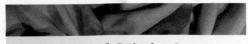

Question: Are homosexuals more likely than heterosexuals to suffer from mental disorders? For a number of years, research evidence seemed to suggest that gay males and lesbians were not any more likely than heterosexuals to suffer from mental disorders such as anxiety, depression, and schizophrenia (Reiss, 1980). Some researchers even pointed out that, overall, gay men and lesbians were more likely to be more highly educated than most Americans (Cronin, 1993). Yet some more recent, carefully controlled studies have found that gay males and lesbians are more likely than heterosexuals to experience feelings of anxiety and depression and that they are more prone to suicide (Bagley & D'Augelli, 2000; Cochran et al., 2003; Meyer, 2003). Gay males, moreover, are more likely to have eating disorders (anorexia nervosa and bulimia nervosa) than heterosexual males (Ferguson et al., 1999).

Psychologist J. Michael Bailey (1999) of Northwestern University has carefully reviewed the issues surrounding the origins and correlates of homosexuality, and he wrote an interesting article about these recent studies in *Archives of General Psychiatry.* Bailey did not dispute the findings themselves. He did, however, have a great deal to say about their implications.

First, Bailey (1999) noted that many of the psychiatrists who had objected to the 1973 vote of the American Psychiatric Association were likely to claim vindication. "Aha!" they would say. "I told you so." Something, that is, was wrong with homosexuality. Bailey also noted that some social conservatives were likely to say that the troubles of homosexuals resulted from their "choice" of an immoral lifestyle. "If you make your bed, you must lie in it," they might argue. Needless to say, Bailey does not consider these interpretations to be warranted by the evidence. Bailey proposes four possible interpretations:

1. Societal oppression causes the greater incidence of depression and suicidality found among gay males and lesbians. "Surely," writes Bailey, "it must be difficult for young people to come to grips with their homosexuality in a world where homosexual people are often scorned, mocked, mourned, and feared." Coming out is difficult at best, and gay males and lesbians, especially as adolescents, are likely to have few friends and to encounter a great deal of homophobia.

2. Bailey acknowledges the possibility that homosexuality is a departure from the most common path of development and, as such, could be associated with other differences, some of which may lead to anxiety, depression, and other psychological problems. Bailey does not "push for" this view but mentions it because it is a possibility. He does say that "Considerably more research would be necessary to validate the general hypothesis." Moreover, even if homosexuality is a departure from the more common path of development, this "departure" does not make the gay male or lesbian a "bad" person. As an example, consider the fact that nearsightedness is a departure from normal development but that we do not stigmatize nearsighted people.

3. A third possibility is connected with the view that sexual orientation may reflect atypical levels of sex hormones (particularly androgens) during prenatal development. In such a case, gay males might be prone to psychological disorders that typically afflict women, and lesbians to disorders that more typically affect men. For example, women are more likely than men to experience anxiety and depression, and gay males are more likely than heterosexual males to experience these problems. Lesbians should then be more likely than other

women to be diagnosed with antisocial personality disorder, a problem that is more often found in men. But so far, there is insufficient evidence for a general "reversal" of psychological health issues.

4. Bailey also suggests the possibility that psychological health problems among homosexual people reflects lifestyle differences that are connected with differences in sexual orientation. He notes that gay males are much more likely than heterosexual males to have eating disorders and also notes that "the gay male culture emphasizes physical attractiveness and thinness, just as the heterosexual culture emphasizes female physical attractiveness and thinness." (The incidence of eating disorders among gay males could also be connected with atypical levels of prenatal hormones, as discussed previously.) In this regard, we can also note that about half of the professional male dancers in the United States are gay (Bailey & Oberschneider, 1997) and that eating disorders are especially common among dancers, who strive to remain thin at all costs.

We should emphasize that Bailey insists that we must obtain more evidence before arriving at any judgments about why gay males and lesbians are more prone to mental or psychological health problems and suicidal ideas. Nevertheless, it is clear that gay males and lesbians do encounter stress from societal oppression and rejection. It is also clear that the adjustment of gays is connected with conflict over their sexual orientation (Simonsen et al., 2000).

There are also connections between lifestyle and health—physical and psychological—among gay males and lesbians and among heterosexual people. Gay men and lesbians occupy all socioeconomic and vocational levels and follow a variety of lifestyles. In their classic research, Bell and Weinberg (1978) found variations in adjustment in the gay community that seem to mirror the variations in the heterosexual community. Gay people who lived with partners in stable, intimate relationships —so-called close couples—were about as well adjusted as married heterosexual couples. Older gay people who lived alone and had few sexual contacts were more poorly adjusted. So, too, are many heterosexual people who have similar lifestyles. All in all, Bell and Weinberg found that differences in adjustment were more likely to reflect the lifestyle of the individual than his or her sexual orientation.

Most gay males and lesbians who share close relationships with their partners are satisfied with the quality of their relationships. Researchers find that heterosexual and gay couples report similar levels of satisfaction with their relationships (Kurdek & Schmitt, 1986; Peplau & Cochran, 1990). Gay males and lesbians in enduring relationships generally report high levels of love, attachment, closeness, caring, and intimacy (Peplau & Cochran, 1990).

As with heterosexual people, not all of the relationships of gay people are satisfying. Among both groups, satisfaction is higher when both partners feel that the benefits they receive from the relationship outweigh the costs (Veniegas & Peplau, 1997). Like heterosexual people, gay men and lesbians are happier in relationships in which they share power and make joint decisions (Veniegas & Peplau, 1997).

Treatment of Gay Male and Lesbian Sexual Orientations

Questions: *Should helping professionals try to help homosexuals change their sexual orientation? Does "conversion therapy" work?*

Despite the judgment of the American Psychiatric Association, some people—including some homosexuals—still view a gay male or a lesbian sexual orientation as an illness. If it is an illness, then it is something to be "cured," perhaps by medical or psychological means. However, the great majority of gay men and lesbians do not seek professional assistance to change their sexual orientations. Most see their sexual orientations as integral parts of their personal identities. Bell and Weinberg (1978) found only a few gay people who were interested in changing their sexual orientation—even if a "magic pill" were available to bring about the change (see Table 10.4). Only a minority of Bell and Weinberg's sample had *ever* considered discontinuing male–male or female–female sexual activity.

A few gay males and lesbians do express an interest in changing their orientations, however, for such reasons as religious beliefs or the desire to create a typical family life (Haldeman, 2002; Rosik, 2003). But because doing so is relatively rare, many helping professionals believe that gay males and lesbians would not wish to change their sexual orientation if it were not for social pressure and prejudice. Haldeman (2002) notes that the very availability of such "therapy" contributes to the social devaluation of homosexuals and bisexuals. A so-called middle position might be that some gay males and lesbians want to change their orientations for "legitimate" reasons and that therapists should make themselves available to help them do so (Beckstead, 2001; Rosik, 2003). But Richard-Jay Green (2003) argues that most gay people who seek to change their sexual orientations are highly ambivalent about their wishes, and that people who are exclusively homosexual are unlikely to be able to change their pattern of sexual attraction. The controversy continues.

Nonetheless, a few therapists have reported changing the sexual orientations of some individuals. Among the best known of these, Masters and Johnson (1979), employed methods used to treat sexual dysfunctions (see Chapter 15) to "reverse" clients' gay male or lesbian sexual orientations. For example, they involved gay males in a graded series of pleasurable activities with women, such as massage and genital stimulation. Masters and Johnson reported failure rates of 20% for the gay men and 23% for the lesbians they treated in their therapy program. At a 5-year follow-up, more than 70% of the clients continued to engage in male–female sexual activity (Schwartz & Masters, 1984). For many reasons, however, these patients do not seem to represent the general gay population:

- Most of them were bisexuals. Only about one in five engaged exclusively in male–male or female–female sexual activities.
- More than half were married.
- All were highly motivated to switch their sexual orientations.

Regardless of these people's changes in sexual behavior, remember that sexual behavior is not the equivalent of sexual orientation. There is thus no evidence that

---

TABLE 10.4

Percentages of Gay People Who Wish They Had Received a "Magic Heterosexuality Pill" at Birth or Could Receive One Today

	European American males	African American males	European American females	African American females
Desire magic pill at birth?	28	23	16	11
Desire magic pill today?	14	13	5	6

Source: Reprinted by permission of Simon & Schuster from Bell, A. P., & Weinberg, M. S. (1978). *Homosexualities: A study of diversity among men and women.* New York: Simon & Schuster, p. 339.

Review: Adjustment of Gay Males and Lesbians

Reflect

What is your reaction to the way in which the American Psychiatric Association modified its classification of homosexuals? Explain.

Critical Thinking

We live in a society that is generally prejudiced against homosexuals. Is it possible, therefore, to know whether a homosexual who asks for help in changing his or her sexual orientation is acting of his or her own free will?

30. Until 1973, a homosexual orientation was considered to be a mental illness by the American _____ Association.

31. Recent, carefully controlled studies find that homosexuals are (*More* or *Less*?) likely than heterosexuals to experience anxiety and depression.

32. Bell and Weinberg found that gay _____ couples were about as well adjusted as married heterosexual couples.

33. Bell and Weinberg found that a (*Majority* or *Minority*?) of gay people wished they were heterosexual.

34. Masters and Johnson changed the sexual (*Behavior* or *Orientation*?) of some homosexuals.

Masters and Johnson changed their clients' sexual *orientation*. That is, many gay people engage in sexual activities with people of the other sex. Nevertheless, they still prefer to have such relationships with people of their own sex.

On the other hand, psychiatrist Robert Spitzer addressed the American Psychiatric Association in 2001, informing them of interviews with some 200 men and women who said that they had experienced a significant shift from homoerotic to heteroerotic attraction and sustained the change for five years. The issue of whether exclusively gay people can change their sexual orientation, rather than just their behavior, remains hotly debated.

Coming Out: Coming to Terms with Being Gay

Because of the backdrop of social condemnation and discrimination, gay males and lesbians in our culture often struggle to come to terms with their sexual orientation. *Question: What is meant by "coming out"?* Gay men and lesbians usually speak of the process of accepting their sexual orientation as "coming out" or as "coming out of the closet." Coming out is a two-pronged process: coming out to oneself (recognizing one's gay male or lesbian sexual orientation) and coming out to others (declaring one's orientation to the world). Coming out can create a sense of pride in one's sexual orientation and foster the ability to form emotionally and sexually satisfying relationships with gay male or lesbian partners.

Coming Out to Oneself

Many gay people have a difficult time coming to recognize, let alone accept, their sexual orientation. Some have even considered or attempted suicide because of problems in self-acceptance (Bagley & D'Augelli, 2000):

> It (suicidal thinking) was because of my homosexuality. I was completely depressed that my homosexuality was leading me nowhere. My life seemed to be

going around in a circle. I was still fighting against recognition of my homosexuality. I knew what I was but I didn't want to be.

[I had] the feeling that homosexuality was a hopeless existence. I felt there was no future in it, that I was doomed to be alone. And from my Catholic background, I felt that homosexuality was very evil. (Bell & Weinberg, 1978, p. 202)

Consider the experience of a New Zealand gay adolescent who was subjected to merciless taunting until his parents pulled him out of school. "He threw a ball like a girl does," said a hot-line worker (cited in Shenon, 1995), "and the hassling just wouldn't stop. He was hassled nonstop from the day he got to that school until the day he left."

According to Ritch Savin-Williams and Lisa Diamond (2000), the development of sexual identity in gay males and lesbians involves four steps or features: attraction to members of the same sex, self-labeling as gay or lesbian, sexual contact with members of the same sex, and disclosure of one's sexual orientation to other people. The researchers by and large found a 10-year gap between initial attraction to members of one's own sex, which tended to occur at about the age of 8 or 9, and disclosure of one's orientation to other people, which usually occurred at about age 18. In keeping with sex differences noted in Chapter 6, females were more likely to focus on the emotional or romantic aspects of their budding feelings. Males were more likely to focus on the sexual aspects. Males—who are generally more open than females to sexual experimentation—were likely to become involved in sexual activity with other males before they labeled themselves as gay. Females, on the other hand, were more likely to label themselves as lesbians before pursuing relationships with other females.

Self-labeling of oneself as gay or lesbian can be a daunting task. Two researchers in human sexuality note that

Youths with emerging identities that are gay, lesbian, or bisexual, living in generally hostile climates, face particular dilemmas. They are well aware that in many secondary schools the words "fag" and "dyke" are terms of denigration and that anyone who is openly gay, lesbian, or bisexual is open to social exclusion and psychological and physical persecution. Some of their families too will express negative feelings about people who are gay, lesbian, or bisexual; youths in such families may be victimized if they disclose that they are not heterosexual. (Bagley & D'Augelli, 2000)

For some people, coming to recognize and accept a gay male or lesbian sexual orientation involves gradually stripping away layers of denial. For others it may be a sudden awakening. Long-standing sexual interests in members of one's own sex may rush into focus on a particular person, as happened with a graduate student named David:

In college [David's] closest friend was gay. Although this friend had wanted to have sex with David and the attraction was mutual, David still could not associate this attraction with a sexuality that was not acceptable to him. In his first year of graduate school, when he was about 23, he fell in love and then suddenly and with a great sense of relief recognized and acknowledged to himself that he was homosexual. He then had sex for the first time and has subsequently been . . . open about his sexuality. (Isay, 1990, p. 295)

Recognition of a gay sexual orientation may be only the first step in a lifelong process of sexual identity formation. Acceptance of being gay becomes part of one's self-definition (Isay, 1990). The terms *gay, lesbian,* and *homosexual identity* refer to the subjective sense of being homosexual.

COMING OUT: COMING TO TERMS WITH BEING GAY

Coming Out to Others

There are different patterns of coming out to others. Coming out occasionally means an open declaration to the world. More often a person may inform only one or a few select people. The person might tell friends but not family members.

Many gay men and lesbians remain reluctant to declare their sexual orientation, even to friends and family. Disclosure is fraught with the risk of loss of jobs, friendships, and social standing (Bagley & D'Augelli, 2000; Griffith & Hebl, 2002). On the other hand, if the organization where the individual works is generally supportive of gays, coming out can be related to greater job satisfaction and less anxiety (Griffith & Hebl, 2002).

Gay men and lesbians often anticipate negative reactions from informing family members, including denial, anger, and rejection (Bagley & D'Augelli, 2000). Family members and loved ones may refuse to hear or be unwilling to accept reality, as Martha Barron Barrett notes in her book *Invisible Lives*, which chronicles the lives of a sample of lesbians in the United States:

> Parents, children, neighbors, and friends of lesbians deny, or compartmentalize, or struggle with their knowledge in the same way the women themselves do. "My parents know I've lived with my partner for six years. She goes home with me. We sleep in the same bed there. The word *lesbian* has never been mentioned." "I told my mother and she said, 'Well, now that's over with. We don't need to mention it again.' She never has, and that was ten years ago. I don't know if she ever told my father." A husband may dismiss it as "just a phase," a boyfriend may interpret it as a sexual tease, a straight woman may believe "she's just saying that because she couldn't get a man."
>
> The strong message is, "Keep it quiet." Many lesbians do that by becoming invisible. . . . They (lesbians) leave their lesbian persona at home when they go to work on Monday morning. On Friday they don it again. That weekend at home, the flip side of the double life, is what most of heterosexual society never sees. (Barrett, 1990, p. 52)

Some families are more accepting. They may in fact have had suspicions and prepared themselves for such news. Then, too, many families are initially rejecting but eventually come to at least grudging acceptance that a family member is gay.

Review: Coming Out: Coming to Terms with Being Gay

Reflect

Do you know anyone who "came out"? Was it a surprise? How did people react? Did you learn anything about people from observing the process?

Critical Thinking

How do you account for the differences between the ways in which males and females come out?

35. Homosexuals speak of the process of accepting their sexual orientation as "_____ out."

36. According to Savin-Williams and Diamond, the development of sexual identity in homosexuals involves four steps: attraction to members of the _____ sex, self-labeling as gay or lesbian, sexual contact with members of the same sex, and _____ of one's sexual orientation.

37. Many homosexuals fear coming out to _____ because of risk of loss of a job or friendships.

"Don't Ask, Don't Tell"—Far from Clear as a Bell

In 2000, the Pentagon issued a report criticizing the military's implementation of its policy on gays and vowed to roll out a massive training program aimed at reducing the level of anti-gay harassment in the armed services. As part of the new effort, military leaders will be instructed explicitly that they should never ask about a person's sexual orientation, no matter what the circumstance. "The question, 'Are you homosexual?' is never in order. Ever," Bernard Rostker, undersecretary of defense for personnel and readiness, said emphatically at a Pentagon news conference. "The days of the witch hunt, the days of stakeouts, are over."

The new policy was spurred by a survey conducted by the Defense Department's inspector general that found that harassment of gay men and

What Is the Sexual Orientation of These Soldiers? During Bill Clinton's presidency, a "don't ask, don't tell" policy was adopted toward gay people in the military. If they divulge their sexual orientation, they may be removed from the military, but superiors are not allowed to ask them about it.

Gay Lifestyles

One of the mistakes that laypeople (and some researchers) make is to treat gay people as though they were all the same. According to Bell and Weinberg (1978), gay people do not adopt a single, stereotypical lifestyle. That is why the authors termed their report *Homosexualities: A Study of Diversity Among Men and Women*. **Question: What kinds of lifestyles are adopted by gay people?** Variations in sexual expression exist within and across sexual orientations. Descriptions of gay and heterosexual lifestyles must consider individual differences.

Gay men and lesbians in larger U.S. urban centers can usually look to gay communal structures to provide services and support. These include gay rights organizations and gay-oriented newspapers, magazines, bookstores, housing cooperatives, medical services, and other support services (Gagnon, 1990). The gay community provides a sense of acceptance and belonging that gay people do not typically find in society at large.

Restrictions on gay people serving in the armed services has been a continuing controversy. In 1993, President Clinton encountered opposition when he sought to follow through on his campaign pledge to permit gay men and women to serve openly in the military. As a compromise measure, he instituted a "don't ask, don't tell" policy. It permits gay males and lesbians to serve so long as they do not publicly express or reveal their sexual orientation. Moreover, military officials are prohibited

lesbians is commonplace and widely tolerated in the U.S. military. The survey found that 80% of those questioned had heard offensive comments about gays within the previous year.

The proposal to eliminate anti-gay behavior was the recommendation of a panel convened to review the military's "don't ask, don't tell" policy toward gays. The policy arose after President Clinton failed to persuade Congress and the Pentagon to allow gays to serve openly and holds that gays can serve in the military as long as they don't reveal their sexual orientation.

As part of the 13-point anti-harassment plan, the panel called for improving training to clear up misconceptions about the policy, for measuring the effectiveness of the new training, and for making commanders responsible for implementing the policy correctly. The panel's "Anti-Harassment Action Plan" stated that the Pentagon should make it clear that "commanders and leaders will be held accountable for failure to enforce this directive."

The Army released its own report on the command climate at Fort Campbell, Kentucky, where a gay soldier was beaten to death in 1999 by another soldier wielding a baseball bat and shouting anti-gay epithets. That murder had provoked questioning by many, including Clinton, of whether the "don't ask, don't tell" policy is really working. Overall, the Army report portrays the unit in which Pvt. Barry Winchell served—D Company, 2nd Battalion, 502nd Infantry Regiment, 101st Airborne Division—as demoralized, lacking in the required number of officers, with some soldiers drinking heavily and an abusive top sergeant. But the Army report clears the chain of command above that sergeant. When Winchell reported to the company commander that the sergeant had called him a "faggot," the report says, the commander counseled the sergeant. General Eric K. Shinseki, the Army chief of staff, said that the abusive sergeant ultimately was moved.

In detailing its program, the DiBattiste panel borrowed some key phrases used often by those opposed to permitting openly gay service members. For example, the panel stated as an "overarching principle" that treating individuals with dignity and respect is "essential to good order and discipline." Opponents often argue that permitting openly gay soldiers will undercut military discipline. Similarly, the panel turned another argument of the opponents on its head by stating that anti-gay harassment undercuts "unit cohesion."

Generally, the panel's strategy appears to have been to adopt much of the approach the military has used to counter discrimination against black and female service personnel. Yet a major difference remains: Those programs deal with obvious, visible characteristics, while the program the Pentagon is about to embark on is intended to train the troops to respect people who can't identify themselves.

Source: Adapted from Ricks, T. E. (2000, July 22). Pentagon vows to enforce "don't ask." *The Washington Post online,* p. A01.

from inquiring about the sexual orientation of recruits. As noted in the nearby "A Closer Look," the policy has required adjustment over the years.

Gay rights organizations fight for acknowledgment of the rights of gay people to participate fully in society—to teach in public schools, to adopt children, to get married, and to serve openly and proudly in the military. Cafés and social clubs provide places where gay men and lesbians can socialize and be open about their sexual orientations. Organizations such as New York's Gay Men's Health Crisis (GMHC) provide medical, social, and psychological assistance to gay males who have been afflicted by HIV/AIDS.

Not all gay people feel that they are a part of the "gay community" or participate in gay rights organizations, however. For many, their sexual orientation is a part of their identity, but not a dominant theme that governs their social and political activities.

Lifestyle Differences between Gay Males and Lesbians

Researchers have consistently found that gay males are more likely than lesbians to engage in casual sex with many partners. Lesbians more often confine their sexual activity to a committed, affectionate relationship (Bell & Weinberg, 1978; Peplau & Cochran, 1990). In their classic research, Bell and Weinberg reported that 84% of gay males, compared to about 7% of lesbian women, report having had more than 50 partners in their lifetimes. Seventy-nine percent of gay males in their study,

A Lesbian Couple and Their Child Many gay couples, such as this one, have children. Sometimes the children derive from earlier marriages. Sometimes they are adopted. Some lesbians are artificially inseminated or else engage in sexual intercourse for the purpose of becoming pregnant. And then again . . . in 2004, as reported in the journal Nature (Vol. 428, pages 860–864), Japanese researcher Tomohiro Kono and his colleagues actually created mice from the genetic material of two mothers. The name of the article is a bit bland, considering the subject matter: "Birth of parthenogenetic mice that can develop to adulthood." The article leads to speculation as to whether a day may come when two dads or two moms can actually have children who share their genetic material.

Truth?Fiction?
Revisited

It is true that many gay couples have lifestyles similar to those of married heterosexual couples and are as well adjusted. Bell and Weinberg refer to them as *close couples.*

Cruising The name homosexuals give to searching for a sex partner.

compared to only 6% of lesbians, reported that more than half of their partners were strangers. Even gay males within committed relationships have more permissive attitudes toward extracurricular sexual activity than lesbians do (Blumstein & Schwartz, 1990; Peplau & Cochran, 1990).

Traditionally, the gay bar was an arena for making sexual contacts (Bell & Weinberg, 1978). **Cruising** is the name gay people give to searching for a sex partner, principally for casual sex. One can "cruise," and one can "be cruised." Gay males were more likely than lesbians to cruise in public places, such as gay bars. Lesbians were more likely to find partners among friends, at work, and at informal social gatherings.

Today, with the threat of contracting HIV/AIDS hanging over every casual sexual encounter, many gay bathhouses, long a setting for casual sexual contacts, have closed down—or have been closed down by authorities. In the early days of the HIV/AIDS epidemic, when being infected with HIV was in effect a death sentence, many gay males changed their behavior to minimize the danger of their contracting or spreading HIV/AIDS. As a group, gay males became more likely to limit or avoid unprotected anal and oral sex, especially with new partners. However, the advent of effective treatments for HIV/AIDS has apparently led some gays, and some heterosexuals, to again throw caution to the winds. They have become more likely to engage in unprotected sex with multiple partners (Demmer, 2002; Katz et al., 2002; Ostrow et al., 2002).

Research also shows that extracurricular sexual activity is common among gay male couples. One study surveyed 943 gay males and 1,510 married heterosexual males who had been living with a partner for 2 to 10 years. Four of five (79%) of the gay males reported sex with another partner during the preceding year, compared to only 11% of the heterosexual males (Blumstein & Schwartz, 1990). Among couples who had been together for longer than 10 years, 94% of gay men reported extracurricular activity at some time during their primary relationships.

Variations in Gay Lifestyles

Bell and Weinberg (1978) found that about three out of four gay couples they studied could be classified according to one of five lifestyles: *close couples, open couples, functionals, dysfunctionals,* and *asexuals.* **Close couples** strongly resembled married couples. They evidenced deep emotional commitment and few outside sexual relationships. Almost three times as many lesbians (28%) as gay males (10%) lived in such committed, intimate relationships. Gay people living in close relationships showed fewer social and psychological problems than those with any other lifestyle.

The partners that Bell and Weinberg described as **open couples** lived together but engaged in clandestine affairs. Gay people living as open couples were not as well adjusted as close couples. Nevertheless, their overall adjustment was similar to that of heterosexual people. Still other gay people lived alone and had sexual contacts with numerous partners—a kind of "swinging singles" gay lifestyle. Some of those who lived alone, **functionals**, appeared to have adapted well to their swinging lifestyle and were sociable and well adjusted. Others, called **dysfunctionals**, had sexual, social, or psychological problems. Dysfunctionals were often anxious and unhappy, and many found it difficult to form intimate relationships. **Asexuals** also lived alone but were distinguished by having few sexual contacts. Asexuals tended to be older than gay people in the other groups. Although they did not have the adjustment problems of dysfunctionals, they too did not form intimate relationships. Despite their being largely asexual in terms of behavior, their sexual orientation was clearly gay.

Homosexuals, like heterosexuals, have many different styles of life. Things are no simpler in the gay world than in the straight world. And the reasons why some people are homosexual remain no clearer than the reasons why most people are heterosexual.

Close couples Bell and Weinberg's term for gay couples whose relationships resemble marriage in their depth of commitment and exclusiveness.

Open couples Bell and Weinberg's term for gay couples who live together but engage in secret affairs.

Functionals Bell and Weinberg's term for gay people who live alone, have adapted well to a swinging lifestyle, and are sociable and well adjusted.

Dysfunctionals Bell and Weinberg's term for gay people who live alone and have sexual, social, or psychological problems.

Asexuals Bell and Weinberg's term for gay people who live alone and have few sexual contacts.

Review: Gay Lifestyles

Reflect

What did you learn about gay males and lesbians from this chapter? What misinformation has been corrected? What is completely new to you?

CriticalThinking

How do you account for the sex differences in the lifestyle preferences of gay males and lesbians?

38. Gay males are (*More* or *Less*?) likely than lesbians to engage in casual sex with many partners.

39. _____ is what gay people call searching for a sex partner for casual sex.

40. The advent of effective treatments for HIV/AIDS has led some gays to become (*More* or *Less*?) likely to engage in unprotected sex.

41. Bell and Weinberg's _____ couples resemble married couples in their lifestyle.

42. _____ couples live together but have secret affairs.

Recite

1. What is meant by sexual orientation?

Sexual orientation concerns the direction of one's sexual and romantic interests—toward members of the same gender, the other gender, or both.

2. What kinds of sexual orientation are there?

Heterosexuals are attracted to members of the other sex. Homosexuals—gay males and lesbians—are attracted to members of the same sex.

3. Would homosexuals rather be members of the other sex?

Most homosexuals are content with their sex; that is, their gender identity is consistent with their anatomic sex. Some extremely feminine gay males may wish to have the body of a woman.

4. Where do we draw the line between a gay male and lesbian sexual orientation, on the one hand, and a heterosexual orientation, on the other? Where do we draw the line between these orientations and bisexuality?

Kinsey and his colleagues constructed a 7-point bipolar continuum to describe people who are exclusively heterosexual, exclusively homosexual, or somewhere in between. Bisexuals occupied the midpoint of this continuum.

5. What percentage of the population is gay?

The best evidence we have suggests that about 3% of American males are exclusively gay and about 2% of American women are exclusively lesbian.

6. What alternatives are there to the Kinsey continuum?

Storms suggested that attraction to people of the other sex and attraction to people of the same sex could be independent dimensions. Research by Lippa and Arad suggests that men tend to be bipolar in terms of their erotic interests, whereas for women, heterosexuality and homosexuality may indeed be independent dimensions.

7. What is bisexuality?

Bisexuality is sexual attraction to people of the other sex and to people of the same sex.

8. How has homosexuality been viewed historically?

The Judeo–Christian and Islamic traditions frown on homosexuality and other forms of nonprocreative sex. Ancient Greek men often entered into sexual relationships with adolescent males. Homosexuality was highly prevalent in fifteenth-century Florence.

9. How has homosexuality been viewed in other cultures?

Most preliterate societies oppose homosexuality. In a few societies, male–male sexual behavior is encouraged at an early age, but males are expected to establish male–female relationships later on.

10. What does sexual activity with members of the same sex signify in other species?

Same-sex sexual activity can be a way of establishing and maintaining "pecking orders" in some species.

11. What attitudes toward homosexuality do we find in contemporary American society?

Most Americans oppose same-sex sexual behavior but are growing more tolerant. Most oppose gay marriages but endorse granting gay people equal rights to jobs and housing.

Recite

12. What is homophobia?

Homophobia literally translates as "fear of homosexuals" but is used to mean hatred of homosexuals. Men are more likely than women to be homophobic. The HIV/AIDS epidemic has contributed to homophobia and gay bashing.

13. What are sodomy laws?

These are laws against anal intercourse and oral–genital contact. They have been enforced against gay males more often than against male–female couples.

14. What is meant by gay activism?

Gay activism is the joining together of gay people to achieve political ends. Gays have lobbied for rights to jobs and housing and for research on HIV/AIDS.

15. Is sexual orientation an inborn trait that is transmitted genetically, like eye color or height? Does it reflect hormonal influences?

Research with MZ and DZ twins suggests that genetic factors play a role in the development of sexual orientation. Prenatal sex hormones are also believed to play a role; for example, female embryos exposed to androgens tend to develop into individuals who exhibit more masculine behavior patterns. Butch lesbians also have higher saliva levels of testosterone than femme lesbians.

16. Do family relationships play a role in the origins of sexual orientation? What are the effects of childhood sexual experiences?

It is unclear whether gay males are more likely than heterosexual males to have had distant relationships with their fathers and close-binding mothers. Sexual reinforcement at an early age does not appear to be a causal factor in the development of sexual orientation.

17. What is gender nonconformity?

Gender nonconformity is assumption of the gender-related behaviors that are stereotypical of the other sex. Many gay males were effeminate in childhood, and many lesbians were tomboys.

18. Is homosexuality a mental disorder?

No, although until 1973 the American Psychiatric Association considered it to be.

19. Are homosexuals more likely than heterosexuals to suffer from mental disorders?

Homosexuals are more likely than heterosexuals to experience anxiety and depression and to have suicidal thoughts. Bailey notes that social prejudice may contribute to the psychological problems but allows that the problems may also reflect atypical patterns of development.

20. Should helping professionals try to help homosexuals change their sexual orientation? Does "conversion therapy" work?

Most professionals agree that homosexuals who request conversion therapy are ambivalent in their feelings and influenced by social prejudice. Evidence is mixed as to whether conversion therapy changes sexual orientation or just sexual behavior.

21. What is meant by "coming out"?

Coming out to oneself is a gradual process in which the individual eventually comes to accept his or her homosexual orientation. Coming out to others is, for many, an anxiety-evoking process characterized by fear of social disapproval, loss of a job, and the like.

22. What kinds of lifestyles are adopted by gay people?

Gay people adopt varied lifestyles. Lesbians tend to form deep romantic attachments and committed relationships, whereas gay males are relatively more likely to seek out multiple partners. "Close couples" of either sex form committed, exclusive relationships.

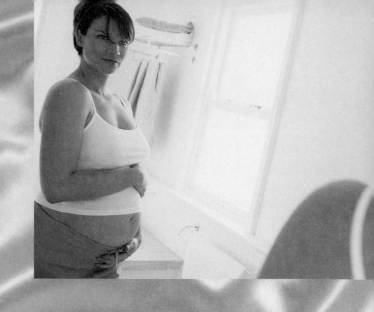

Chapter 11

Truth?Fiction?

T / F? Prolonged athletic activity may decrease fertility in the male.

T / F? A "test-tube baby" is grown in a laboratory dish throughout the 9-month gestation period.

T / F? There is an all-female species of lizard that lays unfertilized eggs that develop into identical females generation after generation.

T / F? Morning sickness is a sign that a pregnancy is progressing normally.

T / F? For the first week after conception, a fertilized egg cell is not attached to its mother's body.

T / F? Pregnant women can have one or two alcoholic beverages a day without harming their babies.

T / F? The way that the umbilical cord is cut determines whether the baby will have an "inny" or an "outy."

T / F? In the United States, nearly 1 birth in 4 is by cesarean section.

T / F? Couples should abstain from sexual activity for at least 6 weeks after childbirth.

Conception, Pregnancy, and Childbirth

Preview

On a balmy day in October, Elaine and her partner Dennis rush to catch the train to their jobs in the city. Elaine's workday is outwardly the same as any other. Within her body, however, a drama is unfolding. Yesterday, hormones had caused an ovarian follicle to rupture, releasing its egg cell, or ovum. Like all women, Elaine possessed at birth all the ova she would ever have, each encased in a follicle. How this particular follicle was selected to ripen and release its ovum this month remains a mystery. But for the next day or so, Elaine will be capable of conceiving.

The previous morning Elaine had used her ovulation-timing kit, which showed that she was about to ovulate. So later that night, Elaine and Dennis had made love, hoping that Elaine would conceive. Dennis ejaculated hundreds of millions of sperm within Elaine's vagina. Only a few thousand survived the journey through the cervix and uterus to the fallopian tube that contained the ovum, released just hours earlier. Of these, a few hundred remained to bombard the ovum. One succeeded in penetrating the ovum's covering, resulting in conception. From a single cell formed by the union of sperm and ovum, a new life begins to form. The **zygote** is but 1/175 of an inch across—a tiny beginning for the drama about to take place.

Elaine is age 37. Four months into her pregnancy, Elaine obtains **amniocentesis** in order to check for the presence of chromosomal abnormalities, such as **Down syndrome**.

(Down syndrome is more common among children born to women in their late 30s and older.) Amniocentesis also indicates the sex of the fetus. Although many parents prefer to know the sex of their baby before it is born, Elaine and Dennis ask their doctor not to inform them. "Why ruin the surprise?" Dennis tells his friends. So Elaine and Dennis are left to debate boys' names and girls' names for the next few months.

Conception: Against All Odds

Question: What is conception? Conception is the union of a sperm cell and an ovum. On the one hand, conception is the beginning of a new human life. Conception is also the end of a fantastic voyage, however, in which a viable ovum, one of only several hundred that will mature and ripen during a woman's lifetime, unites with one of several hundred *million* sperm produced by the man in the average ejaculate.

Ova carry X sex chromosomes. Sperm carry either X or Y sex chromosomes. Girls are conceived from the union of an ovum and an X-bearing sperm, boys from the union of an ovum and a Y-bearing sperm. Sperm that bear Y sex chromosomes appear to be faster swimmers than those bearing X sex chromosomes. This is one of the reasons why between 120 and 150 boys are conceived for every 100 girls. What seem to be natural balancing factors favor the survival of female fetuses, however. Male fetuses are more likely to be lost in a **spontaneous abortion**, which often occurs during the first month of pregnancy. In many cases of early spontaneous abortion, the woman never realizes that she had been pregnant. Despite spontaneous abortions, boys still outnumber girls at birth. Boys suffer from a higher incidence of infant mortality, however. Thus the numbers of boys and girls in the population are further equalized by the time they mature to the point of pairing off.

The 200 to 400 million sperm in an average ejaculate may seem excessive, given that only 1 can fertilize an egg. Only 1 in 1,000 will ever arrive in the vicinity of an ovum, however. Millions deposited in the vagina simply flow out of the woman's body because of gravity, unless she remains prone for quite some time. Normal vaginal acidity kills many more. Many surviving sperm swim against the current of fluid coming from the cervix, through the os and into the uterus. Surviving sperm may reach the fallopian tubes 60 to 90 minutes after ejaculation. About half the sperm end up in the wrong tube—that is, the one not containing the egg. Perhaps some 2,000 sperm find their way into the right tube. Fewer still manage to swim the final 2 inches against the currents generated by the cilia that line the tube.

The journey of sperm may be blind but not random. Ova secrete a chemical that attracts sperm. Sperm cells have been shown to have odor receptors (Donner & Babcock, 2003; Spehr et al., 2003). It is thus conceivable (pardon the pun) that sperm are attracted to ova through a variation of the sense of smell.

Fertilization normally occurs in a fallopian tube. (Figure 11.1 shows sperm swarming around an egg in a fallopian tube.) Ova contain chromosomes, proteins, fats, and nutritious fluid and are surrounded by a gelatinous layer called the **zona pellucida**. This layer must be penetrated if fertilization is to occur. Sperm that have completed their journey secrete the enzyme **hyaluronidase**, which briefly thins the zona pellucida, enabling one sperm to penetrate. Once a sperm has entered, the zona pellucida thickens, locking other sperm out. The corresponding chromosomes in the sperm and ovum line up opposite each other. Conception occurs as the chromosomes from the sperm and ovum combine to form 23 new pairs, which carry a unique set of genetic instructions.

Optimizing the Chances of Conception

Couples may wish to optimize their chances of conceiving during a particular month so that birth occurs at a certain time. Others may have trouble conceiving and may want to maximize their chances for a few months before seeing a fertility specialist. Fairly simple procedures can increase the chances of conceiving for couples without serious fertility problems.

Zygote A fertilized ovum.

Amniocentesis A procedure for drawing off and examining fetal cells in the amniotic fluid to determine whether various disorders are present in the fetus.

Down syndrome A chromosomal abnormality that leads to mental retardation and is caused by an extra chromosome on the 21 pair.

Spontaneous abortion The sudden, involuntary expulsion of the embryo or fetus from the uterus before it is capable of independent life.

Zona pellucida A gelatinous layer that surrounds an ovum. (From roots meaning "zone that light can shine through.")

Hyaluronidase An enzyme that briefly thins the zona pellucida, enabling one sperm to penetrate. (From roots meaning "substance that breaks down a glasslike fluid.")

Figure 11.1. Human Sperm Swarming Around an Ovum in a Fallopian Tube. *Fertilization normally occurs in a fallopian tube, not in the uterus. Sperm secrete the enzyme* hyaluronidase, *which thins the layer surrounding the ovum, allowing one sperm cell to penetrate.*

The ovum can be fertilized for about 4 to 20 hours after ovulation (Wilcox et al., 2000). Sperm are most active within 48 hours after ejaculation, so one way to optimize the chances of conception is to engage in coitus within a few hours of ovulation. There are several ways to predict ovulation.

Using the Basal Body Temperature Chart Few women have perfectly regular cycles, so they can only guess when they are ovulating (Wilcox et al., 2000). A basal body temperature (BBT) chart (Figure 11.2) can provide a more reliable estimate.

Body temperature is fairly even before ovulation. Early morning temperature is usually below 98.6°F. But just before ovulation, basal temperature dips slightly. Then, on the day after ovulation, temperature tends to rise by about 0.4°F to 0.8°F and to remain higher until menstruation. A woman can detect these changes by tracking her temperature after awakening in the morning but before rising from bed. Thermometers that provide finely graded readings, such as electronic digital thermometers, best detect the minor changes. The couple record the woman's temperature and the day of the cycle (as well as the day of the month) and indicate whether they have engaged in coitus. With regular charting for 6 months, the woman may learn to predict the day of ovulation more accurately—assuming that her cycles are fairly regular.

Opinion is divided on whether it is better for couples to have coitus every 24 hours or every 36 to 48 hours for the several-day period during which ovulation is expected. More frequent coitus around the time of ovulation may increase the chances of conception. Relatively less frequent coitus (every 36 to 48 hours) leads to a higher sperm count during each ejaculation. Most fertility specialists recommend that couples seeking to conceive a baby have intercourse once every day or two during the week in which the woman expects to ovulate. Men with lower than normal sperm counts may be advised to wait 48 hours between ejaculations.

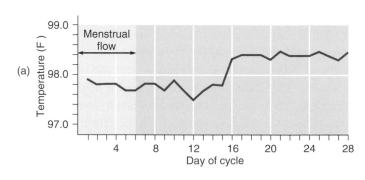

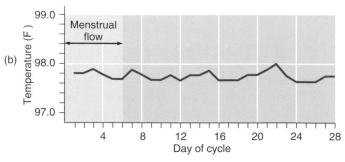

Figure 11.2. A Basal Body Temperature (BBT) Chart. *Because most women have somewhat irregular menstrual cycles, they may not be able to predict ovulation perfectly. The basal body temperature (BBT) chart helps them to do so. Body temperature is fairly even before ovulation but dips slightly just before ovulation. On the day following ovulation, temperature rises about 0.4°F to 0.8°F above the level before ovulation.*

Analyzing Urine or Saliva for Luteinizing Hormone Over-the-counter kits are more accurate than the BBT method and predict ovulation by analyzing the woman's urine or saliva for the surge in luteinizing hormone (LH) that precedes ovulation by about 12 to 24 hours.

Tracking Vaginal Mucus Women can track the thickness of their vaginal mucus during the menstrual cycle by rolling it between their fingers and noting changes in texture. The mucus is thick, white, and cloudy during most phases of the cycle. It becomes thin, slippery, and clear for a few days before ovulation. A day or so after ovulation the mucus again thickens and becomes opaque.

Additional Considerations Coitus in the male-superior position allows sperm to be deposited deeper in the vagina and minimizes leakage of sperm out of the vagina due to gravity. Women may improve their chances of conceiving by lying on their backs and drawing their knees close to their breasts after ejaculation. This position, perhaps aided by use of a pillow to support the buttocks, may prevent sperm from dripping out and elevate the pool of semen in relation to the cervix. Gravity thus works for, rather than against, conception. A woman may also improve the odds of conception by lying still for 30 to 60 minutes after ejaculation.

Women with severely retroverted or "tipped" uteruses may profit from supporting themselves on their elbows and knees and having their partners enter them from behind. Again, this position helps prevent semen from dripping out.

The man should penetrate as deeply as possible just before ejaculation, hold still during ejaculation, and then withdraw slowly in a straight line to avoid dispersing the pool of semen.

Selecting the Sex of Your Child(?)

Parents have wished that they could select the sex of their children for thousands of years. In many cultures, one sex—usually male—has been preferred over the other. In other cases, parents who already have girls (or boys) would like to be able to "balance" their family by having a boy (or girl). Then, too, there are sex-linked diseases that show up only in sons. In such cases, parents would feel safer if they could choose to have daughters.

Question: How do people attempt to select the sex of their children? Folklore is replete with methods (Kalb, 2004). Some cultures advised coitus under the full moon to conceive boys. The Greek philosopher Aristotle suggested that making love during a north wind would beget sons. A south wind would produce daughters. Sour foods were once suggested for parents desirous of having boys. Those who wanted girls were advised to consume sweets. Husbands who yearned to have boys might be advised to wear their boots to bed. The thesis that the right testicle was responsible for seeding boys was popular at one time. Eighteenth-century French noblemen were advised to have their left testicles removed if they wanted to sire sons. It goes without saying that none of these methods worked (but we will say it anyhow).

These methods, or non-methods, would supposedly lead to the conception of children of the desired sex. However, methods applied after conception have also been used, such as the abortion of fetuses because of their sex. There are also many cultures in which infanticide has been used. Because boys have usually been considered more desirable than girls, female infanticide has been more common than male infanticide.

Today, more reliable and less drastic methods seem to be in the offing.

A World of Diversity

Clinics' Pitch to Indian Émigrés: It's a Boy

The pitch could not be more direct. The intended audience could not be more specific. "Desire a Son?" asked an advertisement in recent editions of *India Abroad,* a weekly newspaper for Indian expatriates in the United States and Canada.

"Choosing the sex of your baby: new scientific reality," declared another in the same publication. A third ad ran in both *India Abroad* and the North American edition of *The Indian Express.* "Pregnant?" it said. "Wanna know the sex of your baby right now?"

Some people would call it niche marketing—an effort by companies to promote their products to one of the country's fastest-growing ethnic groups. But the products in question are not chewing gum or financial services. They are procedures to preselect the sex of a child or to identify the sex of the fetus early in pregnancy. And the target market is immigrants from India, where sex-determination tests were outlawed years ago in a still unsuccessful effort to thwart the widespread practice of aborting female fetuses.

Such ads would be illegal in India, which has struggled for years to discourage women from exploiting medical technology to assure themselves of giving birth to boys (Ban on prenatal scans, 2003). Now, Indians in the United States and Canada find themselves being courted by companies that promise to help do just that. It is a strange twist on the usual immigrant tug of war between old customs and new choices, the wrinkle being that new freedoms may help perpetuate an age-old preference for boys.

To be singled out as a market for sex-selection procedures distresses many Indian-Americans. So does the casual merchandising of techniques that claim to increase the odds of having a male child. The subject is so sensitive—and so evocative of painful debates about free choice and abortion back in India—that *India Abroad* abruptly dropped all three ads after the newspaper's owner learned about them.

In conversations prompted by the appearance of the sex-selection ads, many Indian and South Asian immigrants also said that traditional bias against female children ran deep. In India, it is responsible for a widening sex gap, with the number of girls per 1,000 boys dropping to

Do Couples from Developing Countries Such as India and China Want Boys or Girls? By and large, they prefer boys. Boys are traditionally expected to support their parents in later adulthood, and in some cases, only males can inherit. Sex-selection procedures do not guarantee that couples will achieve their wishes, but they appear to offer better-than-chance probabilities. Sex-selection procedures are banned in India, where the number of male births considerably outnumbers that of female births even though the government is attempting to change age-old traditions.

Shettles's Approach Sperm bearing the Y sex chromosome are smaller than those bearing the X sex chromosome and are faster swimmers. But sperm with the X sex chromosome are more durable. From these assumptions, Landrum Shettles derived a number of strategies for choosing the sex of one's children (Kalb, 2004). For example, to increase the chances of having a boy, the couple should engage in coitus on the

927 from 962 in just 20 years. The 2002 census found that in the states of Haryana and Punjab the ratio of girls below the age of 6 had fallen to 90 for every 100 boys, from 95 in 1991. In Haryana there were 86 females for 100 males (Ban, 2003).

But while many people in India are trying to stamp out the tradition, the openness of the American medical marketplace could help prolong it. "As immigrants, we really had a chance of starting with a clean, fresh slate," said Shamita Das Dasgupta, a founder of a group that provides counseling for abused South Asian women. "But we also know that's not possible because we bring our own baggage with us.

"So it makes me scared when something like this happens with impunity, where people are saying, 'We are offering a service the community will practice anyway,'" Dr. Das Dasgupta added. "These practitioners are taking advantage of a practice that is totally misogynous, and unless the good-thinking people of our community stand up and let their voices be heard, such practices will continue happening."

In many cultures, a boy is particularly valued as a breadwinner who will support his parents in their old age; often only a son can inherit property. A girl is seen as a burden who requires a costly dowry when she marries. The attitudes are so deeply ingrained that they often persist after immigration.

There is no sign yet that Indian immigrants seeking male children are flocking to the American companies that offer sex-selection procedures, which work on the assumption that sperm carrying the male chromosome can be separated before insemination from those carrying the female chromosome. But doctors at clinics in the New York City area said that Indian immigrants, as well as immigrants from elsewhere in Asia, made up a fast-growing part of their clientele.

"The ethnic groups that are moving in—from the Asian subcontinent and China—have a tradition of wanting boys," said Dr. Andrew Y. Silverman, the medical director of sex-selection centers. "Just from my own patient population, I'm seeing an increase in those kinds of patients. That's why I started advertising in *India Abroad*."

In India, recently released census figures suggested that female fetuses were being regularly aborted despite efforts to restrict access to prenatal tests (Ban, 2003). The ban against sex-determination tests is feeble and abortions are virtually unregulated. Radiologists travel the countryside from clinic to clinic with their compact ultrasound machines. The desire for boys, experts said, cuts across lines of wealth and class and may have intensified with a trend in India, and among immigrants to the United States, toward having smaller families.

Indians are not the only immigrant group to be offered sex-selection procedures so directly. Chinese immigrants in New York City can find a sex-selection clinic right in Manhattan's Chinatown, where Dr. Robert M. Nyein started offering the Ericsson sperm-separation technique as part of his gynecological practice about four years ago. Nearly all the Chinese immigrants who come to him, said Dr. Nyein, want boys.

China, like India, has a long tradition of favoring male children, a tradition that has been exacerbated by the country's current one-child policy. Last year, however, Hong Kong, which has its own legislature, banned sex selection except when parents want to prevent the transmission of certain hereditary diseases.

Counselors who work with South Asian families said that whether it comes from family or culture or personal desire, the pressure on immigrant couples to have at least one male child is as intense here as in their native countries. "I find so many people crying and saying, 'This is the second child and it's also a girl and now I'll have a big problem,'" said Nahar Alam, a Bangladeshi-born counselor for an advocacy group for South Asian women.

Source: Reprinted from Susan Sachs (2001, August 15). Clinics' pitch to Indian émigrés: It's a boy. *The New York Times*, pp. A1, B6.

day of ovulation and the man should be penetrating deeply at the moment of ejaculation. To increase the chances of having a girl, the couple should engage in coitus two days or more before ovulation, and the man should ejaculate at a shallow depth of penetration. However, other researchers have not found these methods to be effective (Kalb, 2004).

Sperm-Separation Procedures Sperm-separation procedures have also been in use. One is based on the relative swimming rates of Y- and X-bearing sperm. Another relies on the differences in electrical charges of the two types of sperm to separate them. Still another relies on the fact that sperm carrying the Y sex chromosome have about 2.8% less genetic material (DNA) than sperm carrying the X sex chromosome (Kalb, 2004). Edward Fugger (1998) and his colleagues managed to pass some 200 million human sperm in an ejaculation through a "DNA detector" and sort them on this basis. The cell sorter lined up the sperm individually in a stream, and then they were separated according to the amount of DNA they contained. Mothers were then artificially inseminated with the "proper" sperm. The results: The method may be able to create a female baby on about 85% of attempts, a male baby on about 65% of attempts. The method is more effective with cows and horses, because among these animals there is a larger difference (one of about 4%) in the amount of DNA between male and female sex-chromosome-bearing sperm (Kalb, 2004).

Preimplantation Genetic Diagnosis (PGD) PGD is the most reliable new kid on the sex-selection block.[1] PGD was originally developed to detect genetic disorders (Kalb,

Review: Conception: Against All Odds

Reflect

How can you use the information presented in this section to increase or decrease the chances of pregnancy?

CriticalThinking

Sex-selection methods raise many moral and ethical questions. Many people wonder whether people have the "right" to select the sex of their children, either for religious reasons or because sex selection is usually sexist (that is, males are usually preferred). Where do you stand on the issue? Why?

1. _____ is the union of a sperm cell and an ovum.
2. More (*Boys* or *Girls*?) are conceived.
3. Sperm cells have _____ receptors that help them locate ova.
4. Fertilization normally occurs in a _____ tube.
5. Sperm secrete the enzyme _____, which thins the zona pellucida, enabling the ovum to be penetrated.
6. The ovum can be fertilized for a number of hours after _____.
7. Just before ovulation, basal temperature (*Increases* or *Decreases*?).
8. Kits predict ovulation by analyzing the woman's urine or saliva for the surge in _____ hormone.
9. Vaginal mucus becomes _____ for a few days before ovulation.
10. Coitus in the (*Female* or *Male*?) superior position increases the chances of conceiving.
11. One sperm-separation procedure relies on the fact that sperm bearing (*X* or *Y*?) sex chromosomes are faster swimmers.

---

1. The third author would like to know whether the first two authors could have made this sentence any uglier.

2004). In this method, health professionals fertilize ova *in vitro* (in a laboratory dish). Perhaps 6 to 8 embryos are conceived in this manner. After a few days of cell division, a cell is extracted from each embryo. The sex chromosomal structure of the cell is examined under a microscope to determine whether the embryo is female or male. The embryos of the desired sex are implanted in the woman's uterus, where one or more can grow to term. As a sex-selection method, PGD is fool proof. On the other hand, it is medically invasive and expensive, and, as we will see in the secton on *in vitro fertilization* (IVF), successful implantation cannot be guaranteed (Kalb, 2004).

The future is likely to bring even more efficient and affordable methods for the sex selection of infants. For that reason, we are very likely to have to cope with moral and ethical questions related to the procedures.

Infertility and Alternative Ways of Becoming Parents

For couples who want children, few problems are more frustrating than inability to conceive. Physicians often recommend that couples try to conceive on their own for 6 months before seeking medical assistance. The term **infertility** is usually not applied until the failure to conceive has persisted for more than a year, but women above the age of 35 are advised to seek professional help within 6 months of unsuccessful attempts to become pregnant (American Infertility Association, 2002).

Infertility concerns millions of Americans. ***Questions: What are the causes of infertility? How are couples helped to have children?*** Because the incidence of infertility increases with age, it is partially the result of a rise in the number of couples who postpone childbearing until their 30s and 40s (Brody, 2002a; Merck Manual, 2002). All in all, about 15% of American couples have fertility problems (American Infertility Association, 2002). However, about half of them eventually succeed in conceiving a child (Brody, 2002a). Many treatment options are available, ranging from drugs that stimulate ovulation to newer reproductive technologies, such as in vitro fertilization.

Male Fertility Problems

Although most concerns about fertility have traditionally centered on women, the problem lies with the man in about 30% of cases. In about 20% of cases, problems are found in both partners (Hatcher, 2001; Howards, 1995).

Fertility problems in the male reflect abnormalities such as these:

1. Low sperm count
2. Irregularly shaped sperm—for example, malformed heads or tails
3. Low sperm **motility**
4. Chronic diseases such as diabetes, as well as infectious diseases such as sexually transmitted diseases
5. Injury to the testes
6. An **autoimmune response**, in which antibodies produced by the man deactivate his own sperm
7. A pituitary imbalance and/or thyroid disease

Problems in producing normal, abundant sperm may be caused by genetic factors, advanced age, hormonal problems, diabetes, injuries to the testes, varicose veins in the scrotum, drugs (alcohol, narcotics, marijuana, tobacco), blood pressure medications, environmental toxins, excess heat, and stress. Sperm production gradually

Infertility Inability to conceive a child.

Motility Self-propulsion. A measure of the viability of sperm cells.

Autoimmune response The production of antibodies that attack naturally occurring substances that are (incorrectly) recognized as being foreign or harmful.

declines with age, but normal aging does not cause infertility. Men in late adulthood father children, even though conception may require more attempts.

Low sperm count (or the absence of sperm) is the most common problem. Sperm counts of 40 million to 150 million sperm per milliliter of semen are considered normal. A count of fewer than 20 million is generally regarded as low. Sperm production may be low among men with undescended testes that were not surgically corrected before puberty. Frequent ejaculation can reduce sperm counts. Sperm production may also be impaired in men whose testicles are consistently 1 or 2 degrees above the typical scrotal temperature of 94°F to 95°F. Frequent hot baths and tight-fitting underwear can also reduce sperm production, at least temporarily. Some men may encounter fertility problems from prolonged athletic activity, use of electric blankets, or even long, hot baths. In such cases the problem can be readily corrected. Male runners with fertility problems are often counseled to take time off to increase their sperm counts.

Sometimes the sperm count is adequate, but prostate, hormonal, or other factors deprive sperm of motility or deform them. Motility can also be hampered by scar tissue from infections. Scarring may prevent sperm from passing through parts of the male reproductive system, such as the vas deferens. To be considered normal, sperm must be able to swim for at least 2 hours after coitus and most (60% or more) must be normal in shape.

Sperm counts have been increased by surgical repair of varicose veins in the scrotum. Microsurgery can also open blocked passageways that prevent the outflow of sperm (Brody, 2002a; Schroeder-Printzen, et al., 2000). Researchers are investigating the effects on sperm production of special cooling undergarments. One device, a kind of athletic supporter that is kept slightly damp with distilled water, has been approved by the Federal Drug Administration. Seventy percent of the men whose infertility is due to higher-than-normal scrotal temperatures achieve increased sperm count and quality by wearing cooling undergarments (Leary, 1990; Silber, 1991).

Artificial Insemination The sperm of men with low sperm counts can be collected and quick-frozen. The sperm from multiple ejaculations can then be injected into a woman's uterus at the time of ovulation. This is one kind of **artificial insemination**. The sperm of men with low sperm motility can also be injected into their partners' uteruses, so that the sperm begin their journey closer to the fallopian tubes. Sperm from a donor can be used to artificially inseminate a woman whose partner is completely infertile or has an extremely low sperm count. The child then bears the genes of one of the parents, the mother. A donor can be chosen who resembles the man in physical traits and ethnic background.

A variation of artificial insemination has been used with some men who have very low (or zero!) sperm counts in the semen, immature sperm, or immotile sperm. Immature sperm can be removed from a testicle via a thin needle and then directly injected into an egg in a laboratory dish. The method has even been successful with a few men who have only tailless spermatids in the testes.

Artificial insemination
The introduction of sperm into the reproductive tract through means other than sexual intercourse.

Female Fertility Problems

The major causes of infertility in women include the following:

1. Irregular ovulation, including failure to ovulate
2. Obstructions or malfunctions of the reproductive tract, which are often caused by infections or diseases involving the reproductive tract

3. Endometriosis
4. Declining hormone levels of estrogen and progesterone that occur with aging and may prevent the ovum from becoming fertilized or remaining implanted in the uterus

Some 10% to 15% of female infertility problems stem from failure to ovulate. Many factors can play a role in failure to ovulate, including hormonal irregularities, malnutrition, genetic factors, stress, and chronic disease. Failure to ovulate may occur in response to low levels of body fat, as in the cases of women with eating disorders and athletes (Frisch, 1997).

Ovulation may often be induced by the use of fertility drugs such as *clomiphene* (Clomid). Clomiphene stimulates the pituitary gland to secrete FSH and LH, which in turn stimulates maturation of ova. Clomiphene leads to conception in most cases of infertility that are due *solely* to irregular or absent ovulation (Reinisch, 1990). But because infertility can have multiple causes, only about half of women who use clomiphene become pregnant. Another infertility drug, Pergonal, contains a high concentration of FSH, which directly stimulates maturation of ovarian follicles. Like clomiphene, Pergonal has high success rates with women whose infertility is due to lack of ovulation. Clomiphene and Pergonal have been linked to multiple births, including quadruplets and even quintuplets (Gleicher et al., 2000). The CDC (Centers for Disease Control and Prevention, 2000c) estimates that 43% of the triplet and higher-order multiple births in the United States result from such fertility treatments. However, fewer than 10% of such pregnancies result in multiple births.

Local infections that scar the fallopian tubes and other organs impede the passage of sperm or ova. Such infections include pelvic inflammatory disease—an inflammation of the woman's internal reproductive tract that can be caused by various infectious agents, such as the bacteria responsible for gonorrhea and chlamydia (see Chapter 16).

In **endometriosis**, cells break away from the uterine lining (the endometrium) and become implanted and grow elsewhere. When they develop on the surface of the ovaries or fallopian tubes, they may block the passage of ova or impair conception. About 1 case in 6 of female sterility is believed to be due to endometriosis. Hormone treatments and surgery sometimes reduce the blockage enough so that the woman can conceive. A physician may suspect endometriosis during a pelvic exam, but it is diagnosed with certainty by **laparoscopy**. A long, narrow tube is inserted through an incision in the navel, permitting the physician to inspect the organs in the pelvic cavity visually. The incision is practically undetectable.

Suspected blockage of the fallopian tubes may also be checked by a **Rubin test** or a **hysterosalpingogram** (sometimes shortened to "hysterogram"). In a Rubin test, carbon dioxide gas is blown through the cervix. Its pressure is then monitored to determine whether it flows freely through the fallopian tubes into the abdomen or is trapped in the uterus. In the more common hysterosalpingogram, the movement of an injected dye is monitored by X-rays. This procedure may be uncomfortable.

Several methods help many couples with problems, such as blocked fallopian tubes, bear children.

In Vitro Fertilization   When Louise Brown was born in England in 1978 after being conceived by the method of *in vitro* fertilization (IVF), the event made headlines around the world. Louise was dubbed the world's first "test-tube baby." However, conception took place in a laboratory dish (not a test tube), and the embryo was implanted in the mother's uterus, where it developed to term. Before *in vitro fertilization*, fertility drugs are administered to stimulate the ripening of ova. Ripe ova are then surgically removed from an ovary and placed in a laboratory dish along with the

Endometriosis
An abnormal condition in which endometrial tissue is sloughed off into the abdominal cavity rather than out of the body during menstruation. The condition is characterized by abdominal pain and may cause infertility.

Laparoscopy A medical procedure in which a long, narrow tube (laparoscope) is inserted through an incision in the navel, permitting the visual inspection of organs in the pelvic cavity. (From the Greek *lapara*, meaning "flank.")

Rubin test A test in which carbon dioxide gas is blown through the cervix and its progress through the reproductive tract is followed to determine whether the fallopian tubes are blocked.

Hysterosalpingogram A test in which a dye is injected into the reproductive tract and its progress is tracked by X-rays to determine whether the fallopian tubes are blocked. (From roots meaning "record of," "uterus," and "fallopian tubes.")

***In vitro* fertilization (IVF)** A method of conception in which mature ova are surgically removed from an ovary and placed in a laboratory dish along with sperm.

A Closer Look

Sex and the Single Lizard

Some years back, a scandalous book broke on the scene—*Sex and the Single Woman.* A somewhat different scandal has now emerged in the animal world. It could be dubbed "Sex and the Single Lizard."

National Geographic reports the discovery of a most unusual all-female species of lizard found in South America and the West Indies. At time for re-production, no males need apply. With no male contact, the lizards lay un-fertilized eggs. The hatchlings develop into identical females generation after generation (Cole, 1995). Why? They

derive all of their hereditary material from their mothers. The scientific name of the species is *Gymnophthalmus underwoodi.* (We include the scientific name so that you will think there is some important academic value attached to this "A Closer Look" feature.)

The lizards are hybrids of two species of lizard, each of which reproduces normally—that is, by having male lizards fertilize the females' eggs.

The third author notes that she has three perfect daughters and no sons. The first author does not wish to discuss the matter further.

A Chip Off the Old . . . Mommy
There is a species of lizard that obtains all its genetic material from Mother. Yes, there is no generation gap.

Truth?Fiction?
Revisited

It is not true that a "test-tube baby" is grown in a large laboratory dish throughout the 9-month gestation period. A test-tube baby is conceived in a laboratory dish (which is similar to a test tube, perhaps), but the zygote is then placed in the mother's uterus to become implanted and develop to term.

Yes, there really is an all-female species of lizard that lays unfertilized eggs that develop into identical females generation after generation.

father's sperm. Fertilized ova are then injected into the mother's uterus to become implanted in the uterine wall.

Laura Schieve and her colleagues (1999) studied nearly 10,000 births from IVF and found that the greatest success rates were achieved when professionals attempted to implant two embryos: 43% among 20- to 29-year-olds and 36% among 30- to 34-year-olds. For each age group, multiple births (of DZ twins) occurred in about half of the cases.

GIFT In **gamete intrafallopian transfer (GIFT)**, sperm and ova are inserted together into a fallopian tube for fertilization. Unlike in vitro fertilization, conception occurs in a fallopian tube rather than a laboratory dish.

ZIFT **Zygote intrafallopian transfer (ZIFT)** involves a combination of IVF and GIFT. Sperm and ova are combined in a laboratory dish. After fertilization, the zygote is placed in the mother's fallopian tube to begin its journey to the uterus for implantation. ZIFT has an advantage over GIFT in that the fertility specialists can ascertain that fertilization has occurred before insertion is performed.

Donor IVF "l tell her Mommy was having trouble with, I call them ovums, not eggs," says a 50-year-old female therapist in Los Angeles (cited in Stolberg, 1998a). "I say that I needed these to have a baby, and there was this wonderful woman and she was willing to give me some, and that was how she helped us. I want to be honest that we got pregnant in a special way."

That special way is termed **donor IVF**. In this variation of the IVF procedure, the ovum is taken from another woman, fertilized, and then injected into the uterus or fallopian tube of the intended mother. The procedure is used when the intended mother does not produce ova. The number of births in which this method is used has been mushrooming in recent years (Stolberg, 1998a).

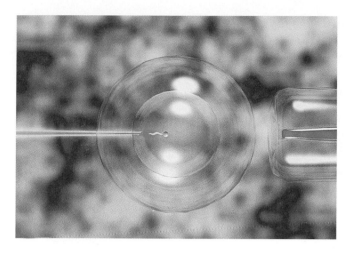

Intracytoplasmic Sperm Injection ICSI is sometimes used when the man has too few sperm for in vitro fertilization (IVF) or when IVF fails. As shown in the photograph, a thin (very thin!) needle injects a single sperm directly into an ovum.

Embryonic Transfer **Embryonic transfer** can be used with women who do not produce ova of their own. A woman volunteer is artificially inseminated by the male partner of the infertile woman. Five days later the embryo is removed from the volunteer and inserted within the uterus of the mother-to-be, where it is hoped it will become implanted.

Intracytoplasmic Sperm Injection **Intracytoplasmic sperm injection (ICSI)** can be used when the man has too few sperm for IVF or when IVF fails. ICSI injects a sperm cell directly into an ovum. However, research with Belgian and Australian children who were conceived by ICSI or by IVF suggest that these methods may be associated with an increase in birth defects (Hansen et al., 2002). Such defects include heart, stomach, kidney, and bladder problems, cleft palate, hernia, and, in boys, malformation of the penis (Wennerholm et al., 2000).

Review: Infertility and Alternative Ways of Becoming Parents

Reflect

Do you know any people who adopted a child or any child who was adopted? How would you describe the experiences of adopting a child or knowing one is adopted?

CriticalThinking

Do some or all methods of overcoming infertility strike you as being "unnatural"? Explain. Would your judgment about whether these methods are natural affect your willingness to try one or more of them? Explain.

12. Couples are labeled infertile if they have been trying unsuccessfully to conceive for _____.

13. About _____% of American couples have fertility problems.

14. The most common male fertility problem is _____.

15. In _____ insemination, sperm is injected into the uterus at the time of ovulation.

16. Ovulation can often be induced by the use of fertility drugs such as _____.

17. In _____, cells break away from the uterine lining and grow elsewhere in the abdomen.

18. In _____ (IVF), conception occurs in a laboratory dish, and embryos are implanted in the uterus.

19. In _____ (ICSI), a single sperm is injected directly into an ovum.

Gamete intrafallopian transfer (GIFT) A method of conception in which sperm and ova are inserted into a fallopian tube to encourage conception.

Zygote intrafallopian transfer (ZIFT) A method of conception in which an ovum is fertilized in a laboratory dish and then placed in a fallopian tube.

Donor IVF A variation of in vitro fertilization in which the ovum is taken from one woman, fertilized, and then injected into the uterus or fallopian tube of another woman.

Embryonic transfer A method of conception in which a woman volunteer is artificially inseminated by the male partner of the intended mother, after which the embryo is removed from the volunteer and inserted within the uterus of the intended mother.

Intracytoplasmic sperm injection (ICSI) A method of conception in which a single sperm is injected directly into an ovum.

Surrogate mother
A woman who is impregnated, through artificial insemination, with the sperm of a prospective father, carries the embryo and fetus to term, and then gives the child to the prospective parents.

Surrogate Motherhood A **surrogate mother** is artificially inseminated by the husband of the infertile woman and carries the baby to term. The surrogate signs a contract to turn the baby over to the infertile couple. Such contracts have been invalidated in some states, however, so that surrogate mothers in these states cannot be compelled to hand over the babies.

Adoption Adoption is another way for people to obtain children. Despite occasional conflicts that pit adoptive parents against biological parents who change their minds about giving up their children, most adoptions result in the formation of loving new families. Many Americans find it easier to adopt infants from other countries or with special needs.

Pregnancy

Women react to pregnancy in different ways. For those who are psychologically and economically prepared, pregnancy may be greeted with joyous celebration. But an unwanted pregnancy may evoke feelings of fear and hopelessness, as occurs with many teenagers.

In this section we examine biological and psychological aspects of pregnancy: signs of pregnancy, prenatal development, complications, effects of drugs and sex, and the psychological experiences of pregnant women and fathers. *Question: What are the early signs of pregnancy?*

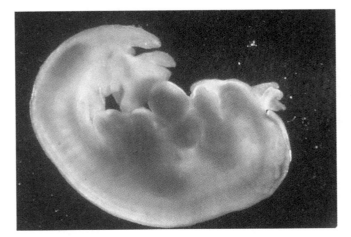

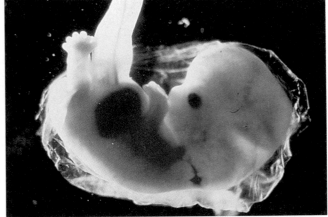

Prenatal Development Developmental changes are most rapid and dramatic during prenatal development. Within a few months, a human embryo and then fetus increases from a fraction of an ounce to several pounds in weight, and from one cell to billions of cells.

Early Signs of Pregnancy

For many women the first sign of pregnancy is missing a period. But some women have irregular menstrual cycles or miss a period because of stress. Missing a period is thus not a fully reliable indicator. Some women experience cyclic bleeding or spotting during pregnancy, although the blood flow is usually lighter than normal. If a woman's BBT remains high for about 3 weeks after ovulation, there is reason to suspect pregnancy even if she spots 2 weeks after ovulation.

Pregnancy Tests

You may have heard your parents say that they learned your mother was pregnant by means of the "rabbit test," in which a sample of the woman's urine was injected into a laboratory animal. This procedure, which was once commonly used to confirm pregnancy, relied on the fact that women produce **human chorionic gonadotropin (HCG)** shortly after conception. HCG causes rabbits, mice, and rats to ovulate.

Today, pregnancy can be confirmed in minutes by tests that directly detect HCG in the urine as early as the third week of pregnancy. A blood test—the *beta subunit HCG radioimmunoassay* (RIA)—can detect HCG in the woman's blood as early as the eighth day of pregnancy, about 5 days preceding her expected period.

Over-the-counter home pregnancy tests are also available. They too test the woman's urine for HCG and are intended to be used as early as 1 day after a missed period. Laboratory-based tests are considered 98% or 99% accurate. Home-based tests performed by laypeople are somewhat less accurate. Women are advised to consult their physicians if they suspect that they are pregnant or wish to confirm a home pregnancy test result.

About a month after a woman misses her period, a health professional may be able to confirm pregnancy by pelvic exam. Women who are pregnant usually show **Hegar's sign**. Hegar's sign is softness of a section of the uterus between the uterine body and the cervix, which may be palpated (felt) by the woman's physician by placing a hand on the abdomen and two fingers in the vagina.

Early Effects of Pregnancy

Question: What are the early effects of pregnancy? Just a few days after conception, a woman may note tenderness of the breasts. Hormonal stimulation of the mammary glands may make the breasts more sensitive and cause sensations of tingling and fullness.

Morning sickness, which may actually occur throughout the day, consists of nausea, food aversions, and vomiting that many women experience during pregnancy. Women carrying more than one child usually experience more nausea. Although called morning sickness, nausea and vomiting during pregnancy can occur any time during the day or night and are not a "sickness" at all, but rather a perfectly normal part of pregnancy (Flaxman & Sherman, 2000). There is some evidence that the nausea and vomiting experienced by pregnant women reflect bodily changes that promote the development of the placenta (Huxley, 2000). Evolutionary biologists Samuel Flaxman and Paul Sherman (2000) reviewed records of some 20,000 pregnancies and reported in the *Quarterly Review of Biology* that morning sickness was associated with a healthy outcome, including lower incidences of miscarriage and stillbirth. The researchers suggest that the food aversions that may accompany morning sickness protect the mother and fetus from likely sources of toxins and disease-causing agents, which are most commonly found in spoiled meat. Although it may have provided an evolutionary advantage, the usefulness of morning sickness has

Human chorionic gonadotropin (HCG) A hormone produced by women shortly after conception, which stimulates the corpus luteum to continue to produce progesterone. The presence of HCG in a woman's urine indicates that she is pregnant.

Hegar's sign Softness of a section of the uterus between the uterine body and the cervix, which indicates that a woman is pregnant.

Morning sickness Symptoms of pregnancy, including nausea, aversions to specific foods, and vomiting.

waned over the millennia, especially with the advent of refrigeration to help store foods safely.

All this is of little consolation to pregnant women. In some cases, morning sickness is so severe that the woman cannot eat regularly and must be hospitalized to ensure that she and the fetus receive adequate nutrition. In milder cases, having small amounts of food in the stomach throughout the day is helpful. Many woman find that eating a few crackers at bedtime and before getting out of bed in the morning helps. Other women profit from medication. Many medications are available today, and women are advised to discuss the situation with their obstetricians rather than just assuming that they have to tough it out on their own. Morning sickness usually—but not always—subsides by about the twelfth week of pregnancy.

Pregnant women may experience greater-than-normal fatigue during the early weeks and may sleep longer and fall asleep more readily than usual. Frequent urination, which may also be experienced, is caused by pressure from the swelling uterus on the bladder.

Miscarriage

Miscarriage
A spontaneous abortion.

Question: Why do some pregnancies end in miscarriage? **Miscarriages** have many causes, including chromosomal defects in the fetus and abnormalities of the placenta and uterus. Miscarriage is more common among older mothers (Stein & Susser, 2000). About 3 in 4 miscarriages occur in the first 16 weeks of pregnancy, and most of these occur in the first 7 weeks. Some miscarriages occur so early that the woman does not know she was pregnant.

After a miscarriage, a couple may feel a deep sense of loss and undergo a period of mourning. Emotional support from friends and family often help the couple cope with the loss. In most cases, women who miscarry can carry subsequent pregnancies to term.

Sex During Pregnancy

Question: Is it safe to have sex during pregnancy? Most health professionals agree that coitus is safe throughout pregnancy until the start of labor, provided that the pregnancy is developing normally and the woman has no history of miscarriages. Women who experience bleeding or cramps during pregnancy may be advised by their obstetricians not to engage in coitus.

Masters and Johnson (1966) reported an initial decline in sexual interest among pregnant women during the first trimester. There is increased interest during the second trimester and another decline in interest during the third. Many women show declines in sexual interest and activity during the first trimester because of fatigue, nausea, or misguided concerns that coitus will harm the embryo or fetus. Also during the first trimester, vasocongestion may cause tenderness of the breasts, discouraging fondling and sucking. One study found that 90% of 570 women were engaging in coitus at 5 months into their pregnancies (Byrd et al., 1998). Researchers in Israel reported a gradual decline in sexual interest and frequency of intercourse and orgasm during pregnancy among a sample of 219 women. The greatest decline occurred during the third trimester (Hart et al., 1991). Pain during intercourse is also commonly reported, especially in the third trimester.

As the woman's abdominal region swells, the popular male-superior position becomes unwieldy. The female-superior, lateral-entry, and rear-entry positions are common alternatives. Manual and oral sex can continue as usual.

Some women are concerned that the uterine contractions of orgasm may dislodge an embryo. Such concerns are usually unfounded, unless the woman has a history of miscarriage or is currently at risk of miscarriage. Women and their partners are advised to consult their obstetricians for the latest information.

Psychological Changes during Pregnancy

Question: What psychological changes take place during pregnancy? A woman's psychological response to pregnancy reflects her desire to be pregnant, her physical changes, and her attitudes toward these changes. Women with the financial, social, and psychological resources to meet the needs of pregnancy and child rearing may welcome pregnancy. Some describe it as the most wondrous experience of their lives. Other women may question their ability to handle their pregnancies and childbirth. Or they may fear that pregnancy will interfere with their careers or their mates' feelings about them. In general, women who want to have a baby and chose to become pregnant are better adjusted during their pregnancies.

The first trimester may be difficult for women who are ambivalent about pregnancy. At that stage symptoms like morning sickness are most pronounced, and women must come to terms with being pregnant. The second trimester is generally less tempestuous. Morning sickness and other symptoms have largely vanished. It is not yet difficult to move about, and the woman need not yet face the delivery. Women first note fetal movement during the second trimester, and for many the experience is stirring:

> I was lying on my stomach and felt—something, like someone lightly touching my deep insides. Then I just sat very still and . . . felt the hugeness of having something living growing in me. Then I said, No, it's not possible, it's too early yet, and then I started to cry. . . . That one moment was my first body awareness of another living thing inside me. (*The New Our Bodies, Ourselves,* 1992)

Review: Pregnancy

Reflect

Do you know of any sexually active woman who has missed a period? How did the woman react to missing the period? Why?

CriticalThinking

How would you explain the relationship between a woman's experience of the physical aspects of pregnancy and her desire to have a child? Why might some women consider "morning sickness" a blessing and other women consider it a curse?

20. Women produce human chorionic _____ (HCG) shortly after conception.

21. Pregnant women usually show _____ sign, which is softness of a section of the uterus between the uterine body and the cervix.

22. There is some evidence that "morning sickness" reflects bodily changes that promote the development of the _____.

23. Miscarriages often reflect _____ defects in the fetus.

24. Women show most interest in sexual activity during the _____ trimester.

25. Some expectant fathers experience morning sickness and vomiting—a reaction termed _____ pregnancy.

During the third trimester it is normal, especially for first-time mothers, to worry about the mechanics of delivery and whether the child will be normal. The woman becomes increasingly heavy and literally "bent out of shape." It may become difficult to get up from a chair or out of bed. She must sit farther from the steering wheel when driving. Muscle tension from supporting the extra weight in her abdomen may cause backaches. She may feel impatient in the days and weeks just before delivery.

Men, like women, respond to pregnancy according to the degree to which they want the child. Many men are proud and look forward to the child with great anticipation. In such cases, pregnancy may bring parents closer together. But fathers who are financially or emotionally unprepared may consider the pregnancy a "trap." Now and then an expectant father experiences some signs of pregnancy, including morning sickness and vomiting. This reaction is termed **sympathetic pregnancy**.

Prenatal Development

Sympathetic pregnancy The experiencing of a number of signs of pregnancy by the father.

Germinal stage The period of prenatal development before implantation in the uterus.

Period of the ovum Germinal stage.

Blastocyst A stage within the germinal stage of prenatal development, at which the embryo is a sphere of cells surrounding a cavity of fluid.

Embryonic disk The platelike inner part of the blastocyst, which differentiates into the ectoderm, mesoderm, and endoderm of the embryo.

Trophoblast The outer part of the blastocyst, from which the amniotic sac, placenta, and umbilical cord develop.

We can date pregnancy from the onset of the last menstrual cycle before conception, which makes the normal gestation period 280 days. We can also date pregnancy from the date at which fertilization was assumed to have taken place, which normally corresponds to 2 weeks after the beginning of the woman's last menstrual cycle. In this case, the normal gestation period is 266 days.

Once pregnancy has been confirmed, the delivery date may be calculated by *Nagele's rule*:

- Jot down the date of the first day of the last menstrual period.
- Add 7 days.
- Subtract 3 months.
- Add 1 year.

For example, if the last period began on November 12, 2005, adding 7 days yields November 19, 2005. Then subtracting 3 months yields August 19, 2005. Adding 1 year gives a "due date" of August 19, 2006. Few babies are born exactly when they are due,[2] but the great majority are delivered during a 10-day period that spans the due date.

Stages of Prenatal Development

Shortly after conception, the single cell that results from the union of sperm and egg begins to multiply—becoming 2 cells, then 4, then 8, and so on. During the weeks and months that follow, tissues, structures, and organs begin to form, and the fetus gradually takes on the shape of a human being. By the time the fetus is born, it consists of hundreds of billions of cells—more cells than there are stars in the Milky Way galaxy. Prenatal development can be divided into three periods: the *germinal stage*, which corresponds to about the first 2 weeks, the *embryonic stage*, which coincides with the first 2 months, and the *fetal stage*. We also commonly speak of prenatal development in terms of 3 trimesters of 3 months each. *Question: What happens during the stages of prenatal development?*

---

2. The first and third authors wish to boast, however, that their daughters Allyn and Jordan were born precisely on their due dates. At least one of them has been just as compulsive ever since. The second author adds that he and his wife Judy had their son Michael within 1 day of the due date. (Close, but no cigar, notes the first author.)

The Germinal Stage Within 36 hours after conception, the zygote divides into 2 cells. It then divides repeatedly, becoming 32 cells within another 36 hours as it continues its journey to the uterus. It takes the zygote perhaps 3 or 4 days to reach the uterus. This mass of dividing cells then wanders about the uterus for perhaps another 3 or 4 days before it begins to become implanted in the uterine wall. Implantation takes about another week. This period from conception to implantation is termed the **germinal stage**, or the **period of the ovum** (see Figure 11.3).

Several days into the germinal stage, the cell mass takes the form of a fluid-filled ball of cells, which is called a **blastocyst**. Already some cell differentiation has begun. Cells begin to separate into groups that will eventually become different structures. Within a thickened mass of cells that is called the **embryonic disk**, two distinct inner layers of cells are beginning to form. These cells will become the embryo and eventually the fetus. The outer part of the blastocyst, called the **trophoblast**, consists of several membranes from which the amniotic sac, placenta, and umbilical cord eventually develop.

Implantation may be accompanied by some bleeding, which results from the usual rupturing of some small blood vessels that line the uterus. Bleeding can also be a sign of a miscarriage—although most women who experience implantation bleeding do not miscarry but go on to have normal pregnancies and deliver healthy babies.

The Embryonic Stage The period from implantation to about the eighth week of development is called the **embryonic stage**. The major organ systems of the body begin to differentiate during this stage.

Development of the embryo follows two trends—**cephalocaudal** and **proximodistal**. The apparently oversized heads depicted in Figure 11.4 represent embryos and fetuses at various stages of prenatal development. Growth of the head (the cephalic region) takes precedence over the growth of the lower parts of the body. You can also think of the body as containing a central axis that coincides with the spinal

Truth?Fiction?
Revisited

It is true that for the first week after conception, a fertilized egg cell is not attached to its mother's body. Later it becomes implanted in the uterine wall.

Embryonic stage
The stage of prenatal development that lasts from implantation through the eighth week and is characterized by differentiation of the major organ systems.

Cephalocaudal From the head downward. (From Latin roots meaning "head" and "tail.")

Proximodistal From the central axis of the body outward. (From Latin roots meaning "near" and "far.")

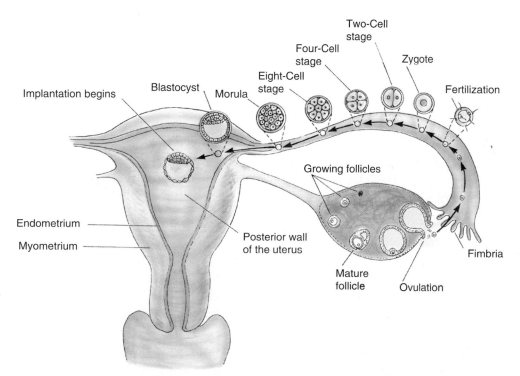

Figure 11.3. The Ovarian Cycle, Conception, and the Early Days of the Germinal Stage. *The zygote first divides about 36 hours after conception. Continuing division creates the hollow sphere of cells termed the blastocyst. The blastocyst normally becomes implanted in the wall of the uterus.*

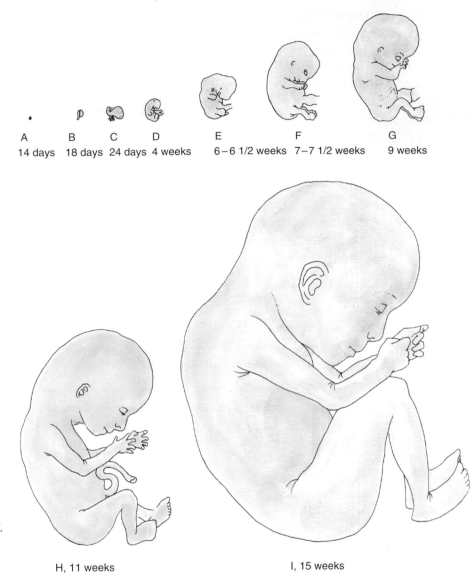

A   B   C   D   E   F   G
14 days   18 days   24 days   4 weeks   6–6 1/2 weeks   7–7 1/2 weeks   9 weeks

H, 11 weeks

I, 15 weeks

Figure 11.4. Human Embryos and Fetuses. Development is cephalocaudal and proximodistal. Growth of the head takes precedence over the growth of the lower parts of the body.

Ectoderm The outermost cell layer of the newly formed embryo, from which the skin and nervous system develop.

Neural tube A hollow area in the blastocyst from which the nervous system will develop.

Endoderm The inner layer of the newly formed embryo, from which the lungs and digestive system develop.

cord. The growth of the organ systems that lie close to this axis (that is, *proximal* to the axis) takes precedence over the growth of those that lie farther away toward the extremities (that is, *distal* to the axis). Relatively early maturation of the brain and organ systems that lie near the central axis allows these organs to facilitate further development of the embryo and fetus.

As the embryonic stage unfolds, the nervous system, sensory organs, hair, nails, and teeth and the outer layer of skin begin to develop from the outer layer of cells, or **ectoderm**, of the embryonic disk. By about 3 weeks after conception, two ridges appear in the embryo. The ridges fold together to form the **neural tube**. This tube develops into the nervous system. The inner layer of the embryonic disk is called the **endoderm**. From this layer develop the respiratory and digestive systems, and organs such as the liver and the pancreas. A short time later in the embryonic stage, the middle layer of cells, or **mesoderm**, differentiates and develops into the reproductive, excretory, and circulatory systems, as well as the skeleton, the muscles, and the inner layer of the skin.

During the third week of development, the head and blood vessels begin to form. By the fourth week, a primitive heart begins to beat and pump blood in an embryo that measures but a fifth of an inch in length. The heart will normally continue to beat without rest for every minute of every day for the better part of a century. By the end of the first month of development, we can see the beginnings of the arms and legs—"arm buds" and "leg buds." The mouth, eyes, ears, and nose begin to take shape. The brain and other parts of the nervous system begin to develop.

The arms and legs develop in accordance with the proximodistal principle. First the upper arms and legs develop. Then the forearms and lower legs. Then the hands and feet form, followed by webbed fingers and toes by about 6 to 8 weeks into development. The webbing is gone by the end of the second month. By this time the head has become rounded, and the limbs have elongated and separated. Facial features are visible. All this has occurred in an embryo that is about 1 inch long and weighs 1/30 of an ounce. During the second month, nervous impulses also begin to travel through the developing nervous system.

The embryo—and, later, the fetus—develop within a protective environment in the mother's uterus called the **amniotic sac**, which is surrounded by a clear membrane. The embryo and fetus are suspended within the sac in **amniotic fluid**. The amniotic fluid acts like a shock absorber. It cushions the embryo from damage that might result from the mother's movements. The fluid also helps maintain a steady temperature.

Nutrients and waste products are exchanged between mother and embryo (or fetus) through a mass of tissue called the **placenta**. The placenta is unique in origin. It develops from material supplied by both mother and embryo. Toward the end of the first trimester, it becomes a flattish, round organ about 7 inches in diameter and 1 inch thick—larger than the fetus itself. The fetus is connected to the placenta by the **umbilical cord**. The mother is connected to the placenta by the system of blood vessels in the uterine wall. The umbilical cord develops about 5 weeks after conception and reaches 20 inches in length. It contains two arteries through which maternal nutrients reach the embryo. A vein transports waste products back to the mother.

The circulatory systems of mother and embryo do not mix. A membrane in the placenta permits only certain substances to pass through, such as oxygen (from the mother to the fetus); carbon dioxide and other wastes (from the embryo or fetus to the mother, to be eliminated by the mother's lungs and kidneys); nutrients; some microscopic disease-causing organisms; and some drugs, including aspirin, narcotics, alcohol, and tranquilizers.

The placenta is also an endocrine gland. It secretes hormones that preserve the pregnancy, stimulate the uterine contractions that induce childbirth, and help prepare the breasts for breastfeeding. Some of these hormones may also cause the signs of pregnancy. HCG (human chorionic gonadotropin) stimulates the corpus luteum to continue to produce progesterone. The placenta itself secretes increasing amounts of estrogen and progesterone. Ultimately, the placenta passes from the woman's body after delivery. For this reason it is also called the "afterbirth."

The Fetal Stage The fetal stage begins by the ninth week and continues until birth. By about the ninth or tenth week, the fetus begins to respond to the outside world by turning in the direction of external stimulation. By the end of the first trimester, the major organ systems, the fingers and toes, and the external genitals have been formed. The sex of the fetus can be determined visually. The eyes are clearly distinguishable.

During the second trimester the fetus increases dramatically in size, and its organ systems continue to mature. The brain now contributes to the regulation of basic body functions. The fetus increases in weight from 1 *ounce* to 2 *pounds* and grows from about 4 to 14 inches in length. Soft, downy hair grows above the eyes and

Mesoderm The central layer of the embryo, from which the bones and muscles develop.

Amniotic sac The sac containing the fetus.

Amniotic fluid Fluid within the amniotic sac that suspends and protects the fetus.

Placenta An organ connected to the fetus by the umbilical cord. The placenta serves as a relay station between mother and fetus, allowing the exchange of nutrients and wastes.

Umbilical cord A tube that connects the fetus to the placenta.

on the scalp. The skin turns ruddy because of blood vessels that show through the surface. (During the third trimester, layers of fat beneath the skin will give the red a pinkish hue.)

Usually by the middle of the fourth month the mother can feel the first fetal movements. By the end of the second trimester, the fetus moves its limbs so vigorously that the mother may complain of being kicked—often at 4:00 A.M. It opens and shuts its eyes, sucks its thumb, alternates between periods of wakefulness and sleep, and perceives lights and sounds. The fetus also does somersaults, which the mother will definitely feel. Fortunately, the umbilical cord will not break or strangle the fetus, no matter what acrobatic stunts the fetus performs.

Near the end of the second trimester the fetus approaches the **age of viability**. Still, only a minority of babies born at the end of the second trimester who weigh under 2 pounds will survive—even with intense medical efforts.

During the third trimester, the organ systems continue to mature and enlarge. The heart and lungs become increasingly capable of maintaining independent life. Typically, during the seventh month the fetus turns upside down in the uterus so that it will be head first, or in a **cephalic presentation**, for delivery. But some fetuses do not turn during this month. If such a fetus is born prematurely it can have either a **breech presentation** (bottom first) or a shoulder-first presentation, which can complicate problems of prematurity. The closer to term (the full 9 months) the baby is born, the more likely it is that the presentation will be cephalic. If birth occurs at the end of the eighth month, the odds are overwhelmingly in favor of survival.

During the final months of pregnancy, the mother may become concerned that the fetus seems to be less active than before. Most of the time this change in activity level is normal. The fetus has grown so large that it is cramped, and its movements are restricted.

Environmental Influences on Prenatal Development

Advances in scientific knowledge have made us more aware of the changes that take place during prenatal development. They have also heightened our awareness of the problems that can occur and what might be done to prevent them. *Question: How do environmental factors affect prenatal development?* These include the mother's diet, maternal diseases and disorders, and the mother's use of drugs.

The Mother's Diet It is a common misconception that the fetus will take what it needs from its mother. Actually, malnutrition in the mother can adversely affect fetal development. Women who are too slender risk preterm deliveries and having babies who are low in birthweight (Cnattingius, 1998). Pregnant women who are adequately nourished are more likely to deliver babies of average or above average size. Their infants are also less likely to develop colds and serious respiratory disorders. However, maternal *obesity* is linked with a higher risk of stillbirth (Cnattingius, 1998).

A woman can expect to gain at least 20 pounds during pregnancy because of the growth of the placenta, amniotic fluid, and the fetus itself. Most women will gain 25 pounds or so. Overweight women may gain less. Slender women may gain 30 pounds. Regular weight gains are most desirable, about ½ pound a week during the first half of pregnancy and about 1 pound a week during the second half.

Maternal Diseases and Disorders Environmental influences or agents that can harm the embryo or fetus are called **teratogens**. These include drugs taken by the mother, such as alcohol and even aspirin, as well as substances produced by the mother's body, such as Rh-positive antibodies. Other teratogens include the metals lead and mercury, radiation, and disease-causing organisms such as viruses and bacteria.

Age of viability The age at which a fetus can sustain independent life.

Cephalic presentation Emergence of the baby head first from the womb.

Breech presentation Emergence of the baby feet first from the womb.

Teratogens Environmental influences or agents that can damage an embryo or fetus. (From the Greek *teras,* meaning "monster.")

Although many disease-causing organisms cannot pass through the placenta to infect the embryo or fetus, some extremely small organisms, such as those that cause syphilis, measles, mumps, and chicken pox, can. Some disorders, such as toxemia, are not transmitted to the embryo or fetus but can adversely affect the environment in which it develops.

Critical Periods of Vulnerability The time at which exposure to a particular teratogen can cause the greatest harm is termed a **critical period of vulnerability**. Critical periods correspond to the times at which the structures that are most affected by the teratogens are developing (see Figure 11.5). The heart, for example, develops rapidly from the third to the fifth week after conception. It may be most vulnerable to certain teratogens at this time. The arms and legs, which develop later, are most vulnerable from the fourth through the eighth week of development. Because the major organ systems differentiate during the embryonic stage, the embryo is most vulnerable to the effects of teratogens during this stage (Koren et al., 1998). Let us now consider some of the most damaging effects of specific maternal diseases and disorders.

Rubella (German Measles) Rubella is a viral infection. Women who contract rubella during the first month or two of pregnancy, when rapid differentiation of major organ systems is taking place, may bear children who are deaf or who develop mental retardation, heart disease, or cataracts. The risk of these defects declines as pregnancy progresses.

Nearly 85% of women in the United States had rubella as children and so acquired immunity. Women who do not know whether they have had rubella may be tested. If they are not immune, they can be vaccinated *before pregnancy*. Inoculation

Critical period of vulnerability A period of time during which an embryo or fetus is vulnerable to the effects of a teratogen.

Rubella A viral infection that can cause mental retardation and heart disease in an embryo. Also called *German measles*.

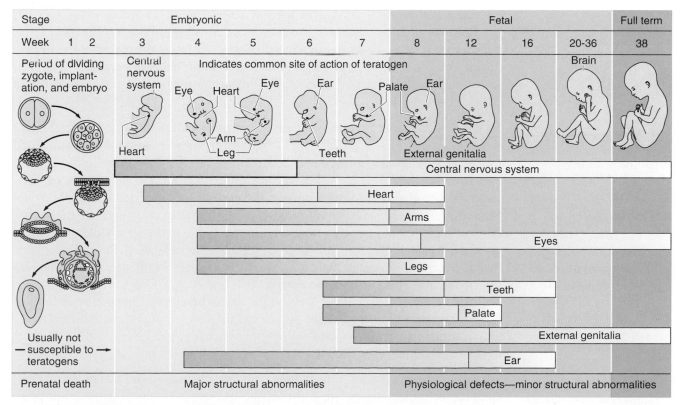

Figure 11.5. Critical Periods in Prenatal Development. *The developing embryo is most vulnerable to teratogens when the organ systems are taking shape. The periods of greatest vulnerability of organ systems are shown in gray. Periods of lesser vulnerability are shown in yellow.*

Preventing Your Baby from Being Infected with HIV

Pregnant women with HIV/AIDS or other sexually transmitted infections (STIs) should discuss them with their doctors. They can take measures to help protect their babies. For example, zidovudine reduces the amount of HIV in the mother's bloodstream. Infected women who use zidovudine during pregnancy reduce the rate of HIV infection in their neonates by two thirds (Mofenson, 2000). In one study, 8% of the babies born to women who obtained zidovudine became infected with HIV, compared to 25% of babies whose mothers did not obtain zidovudine (Connor et al., 1994).

The European Mode of Delivery Collaboration Trial of 400 mothers infected with HIV compared the use of C-section versus vaginal delivery as a means of decreasing the risk of transmission of HIV to the baby (Ricci et al., 2000). All mothers received zidovudine during pregnancy. Half were randomly assigned to deliver vaginally, the other half by C-section. The rate of HIV infection among the babies was 10.6% for those delivered vaginally, compared with 1.7% for those delivered by C-section. Thus the combination of zidovudine and C-section cut the chance that an infected mother will transmit HIV to her baby to about 1 in 50.

For up-to-date information on HIV/AIDS, call the National AIDS Hotline at 1-800-342-AIDS. If you want to receive information in Spanish, call 1-800-344-SIDA.

during pregnancy is considered risky because the vaccine causes a mild case of the disease in the mother, which can affect the embryo or fetus. Increased awareness of the dangers of rubella during pregnancy and of the protective effects of inoculation has led to a dramatic decline in the number of children born in the United States with defects caused by rubella, from about 20,000 cases in 1964–1965 to 28 in the year 2000 (CDC, 2001a).

Syphilis Maternal **syphilis** may cause miscarriage or **stillbirth** or may be passed along to the child in the form of congenital syphilis. Congenital syphilis can impair the vision and hearing, damage the liver, or deform the bones and teeth.

Routine blood tests early in pregnancy can reveal syphilis and other problems. Because the bacteria that cause syphilis do not readily cross the placental membrane during the first months of pregnancy, the fetus will probably not contract syphilis if an infected mother is treated successfully with antibiotics before the fourth month of pregnancy.

HIV/AIDS **Acquired immunodeficiency syndrome** (AIDS) is caused by the *human immunodeficiency virus* (HIV). HIV is blood-borne and is sometimes transmitted through the placenta to infect the fetus. The rupturing of blood vessels in mother and baby during childbirth provides another opportunity for transmission of HIV. *However, the majority of babies born to mothers who are infected with HIV do not become infected themselves.* Using antiviral medication can also minimize the probability of transmission (see the above "Human Sexuality in the New Millennium" feature). HIV can also be transmitted to children by breastfeeding. Research suggests that about half of infected newborns are infected while in the uterus, and half are infected during childbirth (Mofenson, 2000; Wood et al., 2000).

African American children account for more than half of the pediatric cases of HIV/AIDS, and Latino and Latina Americans account for almost one quarter (CDC, 2003). Inner-city neighborhoods, where there is widespread intravenous drug use, have been hard hit (CDC, 2003).

Toxemia **Toxemia** is a life-threatening condition characterized by high blood pressure. It may afflict women late in the second or early in the third trimester of pregnancy. The first stage is termed *pre-eclampsia*. It is diagnosed by protein in the urine, swelling from fluid retention, and high blood pressure, and it may be mild. As

Syphilis A sexually transmitted disease caused by a bacterial infection.

Stillbirth The birth of a dead fetus.

Acquired immunodeficiency syndrome (AIDS) A sexually transmitted disease that destroys white blood cells in the immune system, leaving the body vulnerable to various "opportunistic" diseases.

Toxemia A life-threatening condition that is characterized by high blood pressure.

pre-eclampsia worsens, the mother may have headaches and vision problems from high blood pressure, along with abdominal pain. If left untreated, the disease may progress to the final stage, *eclampsia*. Eclampsia can lead to maternal or fetal death. Babies born to women with toxemia are often undersized or premature.

Toxemia appears to be linked to malnutrition. Ironically, undernourished women may gain weight rapidly through fluid retention, but their swollen appearance may discourage them from eating. Pregnant women who gain weight rapidly but have not increased their food intake should consult their obstetricians.

Ectopic Pregnancy In an **ectopic pregnancy**, the fertilized ovum implants itself somewhere other than in the uterus. Most ectopic pregnancies occur in a fallopian tube ("tubal pregnancies") when the ovum is prevented from moving into the uterus because of obstructions caused by infections. Ectopic pregnancies are more common among older women (Stein & Susser, 2000). If ectopic pregnancies do not abort spontaneously, they must be removed by surgery or use of medicines such as methotrexate, because the fetus cannot develop to term. Delay in removal may cause hemorrhaging and the death of the mother. A woman with a tubal pregnancy will not menstruate but may notice spotty bleeding and abdominal pain.

Rh Incompatibility In **Rh incompatibility**, antibodies produced by the mother are transmitted to a fetus or newborn infant. *Rh* is a blood protein found in some people's red blood cells. Rh incompatibility occurs when a woman who does not have this blood factor, and is thus *Rh-negative*, is carrying an *Rh-positive* fetus, which can happen if the father is Rh-positive. The negative–positive combination is found in about 10% of U.S. marriages. However, it becomes a problem only in a minority of the resulting pregnancies. In such cases the mother's antibodies attack the red blood cells of the fetus, which can cause brain damage or death. Rh incompatibility does not usually adversely affect a first child because women will usually not yet have formed antibodies to the Rh factor.

Because mother and fetus have separate circulatory systems, it is unlikely that Rh-positive fetal red blood cells will enter the Rh-negative mother's body. The probability of an exchange of blood increases during childbirth, however, especially when the placenta becomes detached from the uterine wall. If an exchange of blood occurs, the mother will then produce antibodies to the baby's Rh-positive blood. The mother's antibodies may enter the fetal bloodstream and cause a condition called *fetal erythroblastosis*, which can result in anemia, mental deficiency, or even the death of the fetus or newborn infant.

Fortunately, blood-typing of pregnant women significantly decreases the threat of uncontrolled erythroblastosis. If an Rh-negative mother is injected with the vaccine Rhogan within 72 hours after delivering an Rh-positive baby, she will not develop the dangerous antibodies and thus will not pass them on to the fetus in a subsequent pregnancy. A fetus or newborn child at risk for erythroblastosis may also receive a preventive blood transfusion, in order to remove the mother's Rh-positive antibodies from its blood.

Drugs Taken by the Mother (and the Father) Some widely used drugs, including nonprescription drugs, are linked with birth abnormalities. In the 1960s the drug thalidomide was marketed to pregnant women as a presumably safe treatment for nausea and insomnia. However, the drug caused birth deformities, including stunted or missing limbs (Koren et al., 1998). Maternal use of illegal drugs such as cocaine and marijuana may also place the fetus at risk.

Paternal use of certain drugs also may endanger the fetus. One question is whether drugs alter the genetic material in the father's sperm. The use of certain substances

Ectopic pregnancy
A pregnancy in which the fertilized ovum becomes implanted somewhere other than in the uterus.

Rh incompatibility
A condition in which antibodies produced by a pregnant woman are transmitted to the fetus and may cause brain damage or death.

by those who come into contact with a pregnant woman can harm the fetus. For example, the mother's inhalation of second-hand tobacco or marijuana smoke can hurt the fetus.

Several antibiotics may harm a fetus, especially if they are taken during certain periods of fetal development. Tetracycline may yellow the teeth and deform the bones (Koren et al., 1998). Other antibiotics have been implicated in deafness and jaundice. Acne drugs such as Accutane can cause physical and mental handicaps in the children of women who use them during pregnancy. Antihistamines, used commonly for allergies, may deform the fetus.

If you are pregnant, or suspect that you are, it is advisable to consult your obstetrician before taking any and all drugs, not just prescription drugs. Your obstetrician can usually direct you to a safe and effective substitute for a drug that could harm a fetus.

Hormones The hormones progestin and DES have sometimes been used to help women at risk of miscarriage maintain their pregnancies. When taken at about the time that sex organs differentiate, progestin—which is similar in composition to male sex hormones, can masculinize the external sex organs of embryos with female (XX) sex chromosomal structures. Progestin taken during the first trimester has also been linked to increased levels of aggressive behavior during childhood.

DES (short for *diethylstilbestrol*), a powerful estrogen, was given to many women at risk for miscarriage from the 1940s through the 1960s to help maintain their pregnancies. DES is suspected of causing cervical and testicular cancer in some of the children whose mothers used it when pregnant (Koren et al., 1998). Other problems have been reported as well. Daughters whose mothers used DES during their pregnancies have a higher-than-expected rate of miscarriages and premature deliveries. It was once suspected that men who were exposed prenatally to DES had higher-than-expected rates of infertility. However, research reveals no connection between in utero exposure to DES and male infertility (Wilcox et al., 1995). DES users themselves appear to be at high risk of some serious medical problems, such as breast cancer (Greenberg et al., 1984).

Vitamins Many pregnant women are prescribed daily doses of multivitamins to maintain their own health and to promote the development of a healthy pregnancy. "Too much of a good thing" may be hazardous, however. High doses of vitamins such as A, B_6, D, and K have been linked to birth defects. Vitamin A excesses have been linked to cleft palate and eye damage, whereas excesses of vitamin D are linked to mental retardation.

Narcotics Narcotics such as heroin and methadone can readily pass from mother to fetus through the placental membrane. Narcotics are addictive. Fetuses of mothers who use them regularly during their pregnancies can become addicted in utero. At birth, such babies may undergo withdrawal and show muscle tension and agitation. Women who use narcotics are advised to notify their obstetricians so that measures can be taken to aid the infants before and after delivery.

Tranquilizers and Sedatives The tranquilizers Librium and Valium cross the placental membrane and may cause birth defects such as harelip. Sedatives, such as the barbiturate *phenobarbital,* are suspected of decreasing testosterone production and causing reproductive problems in the sons of women who use them during pregnancy.

Marijuana The active ingredient in marijuana, THC, readily crosses the placenta. Research into the cognitive effects of maternal prenatal use of marijuana suggests that there may be no impairment in global intellectual functioning per se (Fried &

DES Diethylstilbestrol: an estrogen that was once given to women at risk for miscarriage to help maintain pregnancy.

Smith, 2001). However, problem solving and decision making may be affected. A study (Goldschmidt et al., 2000) of the behavioral problems of 635 10-year-olds who had been exposed to maternal use of marijuana in utero found that prenatal use of marijuana was significantly related to increased hyperactivity, impulsivity, and problems in paying attention.

Alcohol Mothers who drink heavily during pregnancy expose the fetus to greater risk of birth defects, infant mortality, sensory and motor problems, and mental retardation (Astley & Clarren, 2001; Schonfeld et al., 2001). Nearly 40% of children whose mothers drank heavily during pregnancy develop **fetal alcohol syndrome (FAS)**. FAS is a cluster of symptoms typified by developmental lags and characteristic facial features, such as an underdeveloped upper jaw, flattened nose, and widely spaced eyes. Infants with FAS are often smaller than average and have smaller than average brains. They may be mentally retarded, lack coordination, and have deformed limbs and heart problems.

Although research suggests that light drinking is unlikely to harm the fetus in most cases (Jacobson & Jacobson, 1994), FAS has been found even among the children of mothers who drank only 2 ounces of alcohol a day during the first trimester (Astley & Clarren, 2001). Moreover, individual sensitivities to alcohol may vary widely. The critical period for the development of the facial features associated with FAS seems to be the first 2 months of prenatal development, when the head is taking shape.

Cigarette Smoking Cigarette smoke contains chemicals such as carbon monoxide and the stimulant nicotine that are transmitted to the fetus. It also reduces the amount of oxygen received by the fetus (Gruslin et al., 2000). Maternal smoking increases the risk of spontaneous abortion and of complications during pregnancy such as premature rupturing of the amniotic sac, stillbirth, premature birth, low birthweight, and early infant mortality (Haslam & Draper, 2001; Tizabi et al., 2000). The health risks generally increase with the amount smoked.

Truth?Fiction?
Revisited

It has not been shown that pregnant women can have one or two alcoholic beverages a day without harming their babies. No safe minimal amount of drinking for pregnant women has been determined.

Fetal alcohol syndrome (FAS) A cluster of symptoms caused by maternal drinking, in which the child shows developmental lags and characteristic facial features such as an underdeveloped upper jaw, flattened nose, and widely spaced eyes.

Don't Do It! Smoking cigarettes and pregnancy do not mix. Maternal smoking has been shown to increase the risk of spontaneous abortion and of complications during pregnancy. It is connected with premature rupturing of the amniotic sac, stillbirth, premature birth, low birthweight, infant mortality, and delayed intellectual development in the child.

Maternal smoking may also impair intellectual development. In one study, women who smoked during pregnancy were 50% more likely than women who did not to have children whose intelligence test scores placed them in the mentally retarded range (that is, beneath an IQ score of 70) when the children were 10 years old (Drews et al., 1996).

Low birthweight is a common risk factor for infant disease, mortality, and learning problems in school (O'Keeffe et al., 2003). Maternal smoking during pregnancy more than doubles the risk of low birthweight (Haslam & Draper, 2001). The combination of smoking and drinking alcohol places the child at greater risk of low birthweight than either practice alone (Day & Richardson, 1994). Maternal smoking affects the fetal heart rate and increases the risk of sudden infant death syndrome (SIDS) (Gordon et al., 2002; Pollack, 2001). Maternal smoking has also been linked to reduced lung function in newborns (Hanrahan et al., 1992) and to asthma in childhood (Martinez et al., 1992). Evidence also points to reduced attention spans, hyperactivity, and lower IQs and achievement test scores in children exposed to maternal smoking during and after pregnancy (Barr et al., 1990).

Smoking by the father (or other household members) may be dangerous to a fetus because second-hand smoke (smoke exhaled by the smoker or emitted from the tip of a lit cigarette) may be absorbed by the mother and passed along to the fetus. Passive exposure to second-hand smoke during infancy is also linked to increased risk of SIDS (Gordon et al., 2002).

Most American women of reproductive age drink alcohol, at least occasionally. More than 1 in 4 smokes. Many do not suspend drug use until they learn that they are pregnant, which may not occur until weeks into the pregnancy. Many women are unwilling or unable to change their drug use habits even after learning they are pregnant.

Our clinical experience suggests that it may be easier for women to quit if they consider quitting as limited to the terms of their pregnancies, rather than as permanent. Then, of course, if they should remain abstinent after delivery, perhaps they will not be disappointed.

Other Agents X-rays increase the risk of malformed organs in the fetus, especially within a month and a half after conception. (Ultrasound has *not* been shown to harm the embryo or fetus.)

Chromosomal and Genetic Abnormalities

Not all of us have the normal complement of chromosomes. Some of us have genes that threaten our health or our existence (see Table 11.1). *Question: What kinds of disorders are caused by chromosomal and genetic abnormalities?*

Down Syndrome Children with Down syndrome have characteristic round faces; wide, flat noses; and protruding tongues. They often suffer from respiratory problems and heart malformations, problems that tend to claim their lives by middle age—the "prime of life" for most of us. People with Down syndrome are also moderately mentally retarded, but they usually can learn to read and write. With a little help from family and social agencies, they may hold jobs and lead largely independent lives.

The risk of a child's having Down syndrome increases with the mother's age (Brody, 2002a; CDC, 2002a; see Table 11.2). Down syndrome is usually caused by an extra chromosome on the 21st pair. In most cases, Down syndrome is transmitted by the mother. The inner corners of the eyes of people with the syndrome have a

TABLE 11.1

Some Chromosomal and Genetic Abnormalities

Health Problem	Comments
Cystic fibrosis	A genetic disease in which the pancreas and lungs become clogged with mucus, which impairs respiration and digestion.
Down syndrome	A condition characterized by an extra chromosome on the 21st pair. A child with Down syndrome has a characteristic fold of skin over the eye and mental retardation. The risk of having a child with the syndrome increases as parents increase in age.
Hemophilia	A sex-linked disorder in which blood does not clot properly.
Huntington's chorea	A fatal neurological disorder whose onset occurs in middle adulthood.
Neural tube defects	Disorders of the brain or spine, such as *anencephaly,* in which part of the brain is missing, and *spina bifida,* in which part of the spine is exposed or missing. Anencephaly is fatal shortly after birth, but some spina bifida victims survive for a number of years, though with severe handicaps.
Phenylketonuria	A disorder in which children cannot metabolize phenylalanine, which builds up in the form of phenylpyruvic acid and causes mental retardation. The disorder can be diagnosed at birth and controlled by diet.
Retina blastoma	A form of blindness caused by a dominant gene.
Sickle-cell anemia	A blood disorder that mostly afflicts African Americans, in which deformed blood cells obstruct small blood vessels, decreasing their capacity to carry oxygen and heightening the risk of occasionally fatal infections.
Tay-Sachs disease	A fatal neurological disorder that primarily afflicts Jews of East European origin.

downward-sloping crease of skin that gives them a superficial likeness to Asians. This is why the syndrome was once dubbed *mongolism,* a moniker that has since been rejected because of its racist overtones.

Sickle-cell Anemia and Tay-Sachs Disease Sickle-cell anemia and Tay-Sachs disease are genetic disorders that are most likely to afflict certain racial and ethnic groups. Sickle-cell anemia is most prevalent in the United States among African Americans. One of every 375 African Americans is affected by the disease, and 8% are carriers of the sickle-cell trait (Ashley-Koch et al., 2000). In sickle-cell anemia, the red blood cells assume a sickle shape—hence the name—and they form clumps that obstruct narrow blood vessels and diminish the supply of oxygen. As a result, victims can suffer problems ranging from swollen, painful joints to potentially lethal pneumonia

TABLE 11.2

Risk of Giving Birth to an Infant with Down Syndrome, According to Age of the Mother

Age of Mother	Probability of Down Syndrome in the Child
20	1 in 1,667
30	1 in 953
40	1 in 106
49	1 in 11

Sources: American Infertility Association, 2002; Centers for Disease Control, 2002a.

Recessive trait A trait that is not expressed when the gene or genes involved have been paired with dominant genes. Recessive traits are transmitted to future generations, however, and are expressed if they are paired with other recessive genes.

and heart and kidney failure. Infections are a leading cause of death among those with the disease.

Tay-Sachs disease is a fatal neurological disease of young children. Only 1 in 100,000 people in the United States is affected, but among Jews of Eastern European background the figure rises steeply to 1 in 3,600 (Khoury et al., 2000). The disease is characterized by degeneration of the central nervous system and gives rise to retardation, loss of muscle control and paralysis, blindness, and deafness. Victims seldom live beyond the age of 5.

Sex-Linked Genetic Abnormalities Some genetic defects, such as hemophilia, are sex linked, in that they are carried only on the X sex chromosome. They are transmitted from generation to generation as **recessive traits**. Females, each of whom has two X sex chromosomes, are less likely than males to be afflicted by sex-linked disorders, because the genes that carry the disorder would have to be present on both of their sex chromosomes for the disorder to be expressed. Sex-linked disorders are more likely to afflict sons of female carriers because they have only one X sex chromosome, which they inherit from their mothers. England's Queen Victoria was a hemophilia carrier and transmitted the condition to many of her children, who in turn carried it into several ruling families of Europe. For this reason, hemophilia has been dubbed the "royal disease."

Averting Chromosomal and Genetic Abnormalities Question: How do health professionals determine whether children will have chromosomal or genetic abnormalities? Guided by information about a couple's medical background and family history of genetic defects, genetic counselors help couples appraise the risks of passing along genetic defects to their children. Some couples who face a high risk of passing along genetic defects to their children decide to adopt. Other couples decide to have an abortion if the fetus is determined to have certain abnormalities.

Various medical procedures are used to detect the presence of these disorders in the fetus. *Amniocentesis* is usually performed about 4 months into pregnancy but is sometimes done earlier. Fluid is drawn from the amniotic sac (or "bag of waters") with a syringe. Fetal cells in the fluid are grown in a culture and examined under a microscope for the presence of biochemical and chromosomal abnormalities. *Chorionic villus sampling* (CVS) is performed at about 10 weeks. A narrow tube is used to snip off material from the chorion, which is a membrane that contains the amniotic sac and fetus. This material is analyzed. The risks of amniocentesis and CVS are comparable (Simpson, 2000). The tests detect Down syndrome, sickle-cell anemia, Tay-Sachs disease, spina bifida, muscular dystrophy, Rh incompatibility, and other conditions. The tests also identify the sex of the fetus.

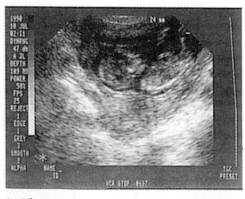

An Ultrasound Image An ultrasound image of the second author's son, Michael, at 12 weeks following conception. The head and upper torso (facing upward) can be seen by those of you willing to look for many hours in the upper middle section of the image. Michael was handsome even then, his father points out. The first and third author note that they did not insist on including their own boring ultrasound photos in this text.

In ultrasound, high-pitched sound waves are bounced off the fetus, like radar, revealing a picture of the fetus on a TV monitor and allowing the obstetrician to detect certain abnormalities. Obstetricians also use ultrasound to locate the fetus during amniocentesis in order to lower the probability of injuring it with the syringe.

Parental blood tests can suggest the presence of problems such as sickle-cell anemia, Tay-Sachs disease, and neural tube defects. Still other tests examine fetal DNA and can indicate the presence of Huntington's chorea, cystic fibrosis, and other disorders. Blood tests also now make it possible to detect Down syndrome during the first trimester.

Review: Prenatal Development

Reflect

Do you know anyone who smoked or drank heavily during pregnancy? Was she aware of the problems that these behaviors could cause? Did she say anything about them? If so, what? What was your reaction. Explain.

CriticalThinking

Why do some women aged 35 and above decide to have amniocentesis, and others decide not to do so? Where do you stand on the issue? Explain.

26. The normal gestation period is _____ days.

27. Prenatal development can be divided into the _____ stage, the embryonic stage, and the fetal stage.

28. Several days into the germinal stage, the cell mass takes the form of a fluid-filled ball of cells called a _____.

29. Bleeding during implantation is (*Normal* or *Abnormal*?).

30. The major organ systems begin to differentiate during the _____ stage.

31. During the embryonic stage, the nervous system, sensory organs, and outer layer of skin begin to develop from the _____ of the embryonic disk.

32. The arms and legs develop in accordance with the _____ principle.

33. The embryo develops within a protective environment called the _____ sac.

34. Nutrients and wastes are exchanged between mother and embryo through the _____.

35. The fetus is connected to the placenta by the _____ cord.

36. The mother usually senses fetal movements by the middle of the _____ month.

37. The baby is usually born in a _____ presentation.

38. Most women gain about _____ pounds during pregnancy.

39. _____ are environmental influences or agents that can harm the embryo or fetus.

40. The times when exposure to particular teratogens can cause the greatest harm are termed _____ periods of vulnerability.

41. Toxemia is a life-threatening condition characterized by (*High* or *Low*?) blood pressure.

42. In Rh _____, antibodies produced by the mother are transmitted to a fetus or newborn infant.

43. Acne drugs such as _____ can cause handicaps in the children of women who use them during pregnancy.

44. _____ is suspected of causing cervical and testicular cancer in children whose mothers used it during pregnancy.

45. Nearly 40% of children whose mothers drink heavily during pregnancy develop _____ (FAS).

46. Maternal smoking is connected with _____ abortion and impaired intellectual development.

47. _____ syndrome is usually caused by an extra chromosome on the 21st pair.

48. _____-cell anemia and Tay-_____ disease are genetic disorders that are most likely to afflict certain racial and ethnic groups.

49. In _____, fluid is drawn from the amniotic sac, and fetal cells are cultured and examined for chromosomal abnormalities.

Childbirth

Question: What events lead to childbirth? Early in the ninth month of pregnancy, the fetus's head settles in the pelvis. This shift is called "dropping" or "lightening." The woman may actually feel lighter because of lessened pressure on the diaphragm. About a day or so before the beginning of labor, the woman may notice blood in her vaginal secretions because fetal pressure on the pelvis may rupture superficial blood vessels in the birth canal. Tissue that had plugged the cervix, possibly preventing entry of infectious agents from the vagina, becomes dislodged. There is a resultant discharge of bloody mucus. At about this time, 1 woman in 10 also has a rush of warm "water" from the vagina. The "water" is amniotic fluid, and it means that the amniotic sac has burst. Labor usually begins within a day after rupture of the amniotic sac. For most women the amniotic sac does not burst until the end of the first stage of childbirth. Other signs of impending labor include indigestion, diarrhea, abdominal cramps, and an ache in the small of the back. Labor begins with the onset of regular uterine contractions.

The first uterine contractions are relatively painless and are called **Braxton-Hicks contractions**, or false labor contractions. They are false because they do not widen the cervix or advance the baby through the birth canal. They tend to increase in frequency but are less regular than labor contractions. Real labor contractions, by contrast, become more intense when the woman moves around or walks.

The initiation of labor may involve the secretion of hormones by the fetal adrenal and pituitary glands that stimulate the placenta and the mother's uterus to secrete **prostaglandins**. Prostaglandins stimulate the uterine musculature to contract. It would make sense for the fetus to have a mechanism for signaling the mother that it is mature enough to sustain independent life. The mechanisms that initiate and maintain labor are not fully understood, however. Later in labor the pituitary gland releases **oxytocin**, a hormone that stimulates contractions strong enough to expel the baby.

Stages of Childbirth

Childbirth begins with the onset of labor and has three stages. *Question: What happens during the stages of childbirth?*

The First Stage In the first stage, uterine contractions cause the cervix to **efface** and **dilate** to about 4 inches (10 cm) in diameter, so that the baby may pass. Stretching of the cervix causes most of the pain of childbirth. A woman may experience little or no pain if her cervix dilates easily and quickly. The first stage may last from a couple of hours to more than a day. Twelve to 24 hours of labor is considered about average for a first pregnancy. In later pregnancies, labor takes about half this time.

The initial contractions are usually mild and spaced widely, at intervals of 10 to 20 minutes. They may last 20 to 40 seconds. As time passes, contractions become more frequent, long, strong, and regular.

Transition is the process that occurs when the cervix becomes almost fully dilated and the baby's head begins to move into the vagina, or birth canal. Contractions usually come quickly during transition. Transition generally lasts 30 minutes or less and is often accompanied by feelings of nausea, chills, and intense pain.

The Second Stage The second stage of childbirth follows transition and begins when the cervix has become fully dilated and the baby begins to move into the vagina and first appears at the opening of the birth canal (see Figure 11.6). The woman may be taken to a delivery room for the second stage of childbirth. The second stage is shorter than the first stage. It lasts from a few minutes to a few hours and ends with the birth of the baby.

Each contraction of the second stage propels the baby farther along the birth canal (vagina). When the baby's head becomes visible at the vaginal opening, it is said to have *crowned*. The baby typically emerges fully a few minutes after crowning.

Braxton-Hicks contractions So-called false labor contractions that are relatively painless.

Prostaglandins Uterine hormones that stimulate uterine contractions.

Oxytocin A pituitary hormone that stimulates uterine contractions.

Efface To become thin.

Dilate To open or widen.

Transition The process during which the cervix becomes nearly fully dilated and the head of the fetus begins to move into the birth canal.

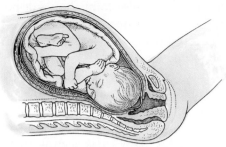

1. The second stage of labor begins

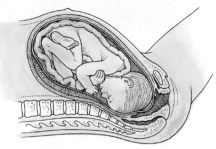

2. Further descent and rotation

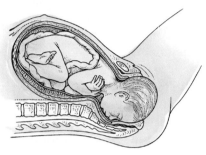

3. The crowning of the head

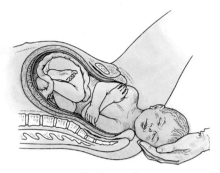

4. Anterior shoulder delivered

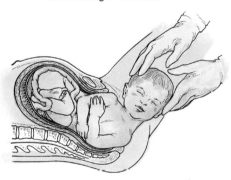

5. Posterior shoulder delivered

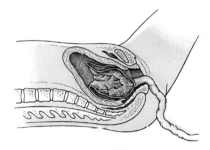

6. The third stage of labor begins with separation of the placenta from the uterine wall

Figure 11.6. The Stages of Childbirth. In the first stage, uterine contractions efface and dilate the cervix to about 4 inches so that the baby may pass through. The second stage begins with movement of the baby into the birth canal and ends with birth of the baby. During the third stage, the placenta separates from the uterine wall and is expelled through the birth canal.

An **episiotomy** may be performed on the mother when the baby's head has crowned. The purpose is to prevent the random tearing of the **perineum** that can occur if it becomes extremely effaced. Episiotomies are controversial, however (Roberts, 2000). The incision can cause infection and pain and may create discomfort and itching as it heals. In some cases the discomfort interferes with coitus for months. Prenatal massage of the perineum can sometimes avert the necessity of episiotomy (Eason et al., 2000; Johanson, 2000). For these and other reasons, an article in *Obstetrics & Gynecology* recommends that "Episiotomy should no longer be routine" (Eason & Feldman, 2000). And apparently, it isn't. A national survey reported in *Obstetrics & Gynecology* found that the overall episiotomy rate dropped from nearly 70% to about 19% over the past two decades (Goldberg et al., 2002).

Episiotomy A surgical incision in the perineum that widens the birth canal, preventing random tearing during childbirth.

Perineum The area between the vulva and the anus.

It is not true that the cutting of the umbilical cord determines whether the baby will have an "inny" or an "outy." The cord dries and falls off on its own.

Even so, physicians generally agree that episiotomy should be performed if the baby's shoulders are too wide to emerge without causing tearing, or if the baby's heartbeat drops for an extended period of time (Eason & Feldman, 2000). Yet one study found that the strongest predictor of whether a physician will use episiotomy is his or her customary practice, not the condition of the woman in labor or of the baby (Robinson et al., 2000). (When interviewing obstetricians, ask how often he or she performs an episiotomy!)

With or without an episiotomy, the baby's passageway to the external world is a tight fit. As a result, the baby's facial features and the shape of its head may be temporarily distended. The baby may look as if it has been through a prizefight. Its head may be elongated, its nose flattened, and its ears bent. Although parents may be concerned about whether the baby's features will assume a more typical shape, they almost always do.

The Third Stage The third, or placental, stage of childbirth may last from a few minutes to an hour or more. During this stage, the placenta is expelled. Detachment of the placenta from the uterine wall may cause some bleeding. The uterus begins the process of contracting to a smaller size. The attending physician sews up the episiotomy or any tears in the perineum.

In the New World As the baby's head emerges, mucus is cleared from its mouth by means of suction aspiration to prevent the breathing passageway from being obstructed. Aspiration is often repeated once the baby is fully delivered. (Newly delivered babies are no longer routinely held upside down to help expel mucus. Nor is the baby slapped on the buttocks to stimulate breathing, as in old films.)

Once the baby is breathing adequately, the umbilical cord is clamped and severed about 3 inches from the baby's body. (After the birth of your first and third authors' third child, your first author was invited by the obstetrician to cut the umbilical cord—but your third author seized the scissors and cut the umbilical cord herself, squirting blood on the obstetrician's glasses. "Who gave the obstetrician the right to determine who would cut the umbilical cord!" she wanted to know.) The stump of the umbilical cord dries and falls off in its own time, usually in 7 to 10 days.

While the mother is in the third stage of labor, the nurse may perform procedures on the baby, such as placing drops of silver nitrate or an antibiotic ointment into the eyes. This procedure is required by most states to prevent bacterial infections in the newborn's eyes. Typically the baby is also footprinted and (if the birth has taken place in a hospital) given an identification bracelet. Because neonates do not manufacture vitamin K on their own, the baby may also receive an injection of the vitamin to ensure that her or his blood will clot normally in case of bleeding.

Methods of Childbirth

Until the twentieth century, childbirth usually occurred at home and involved the mother, a midwife, family, and friends. *Question: What methods of childbirth are used today?* These days, women in the United States and Canada typically give birth in hospitals attended by obstetricians who use surgical instruments and anesthetics to protect mothers and children from infection, complications, and pain. Medical procedures save lives but also make childbearing more impersonal. Social critics argue that these procedures have medicalized a natural process—that they have usurped control over women's bodies and, through the use of drugs, denied many women the experience of giving birth.

Anesthetized Childbirth

> In sorrow thou shalt bring forth children.
>
> *Genesis 3:16*

The Bible suggests that the ancients saw suffering as a woman's lot. But during the past two centuries, science and medicine have led to the expectation that women should experience minimal discomfort during childbirth. Today only about 10% of American women use no anesthesia (Jameson, 2000).

General anesthesia first became popular when Queen Victoria of England delivered her eighth child under chloroform in 1853. General anesthesia, like the chloroform of old, induces unconsciousness. The drug sodium pentothal, a barbiturate, induces general anesthesia when it is injected into a vein. Barbiturates may also be taken orally to reduce anxiety while the woman remains awake. Women may also receive tranquilizers such as Valium or narcotics such as Demerol to help them relax and to blunt pain without inducing sleep.

Anesthetic drugs, as well as tranquilizers and narcotics, decrease the strength of uterine contractions during delivery. They may thus delay the process of cervical dilation and prolong labor. They also weaken the woman's ability to push the baby through the birth canal. And because they cross the placental membrane, they also lower the newborn's overall responsiveness.

Regional or **local anesthetics** block pain in parts of the body without generally depressing the mother's alertness or putting her to sleep. In a *pudendal block,* the external genitals are numbed by local injection. In an *epidural block* and a *spinal block,* an anesthetic injected into the spinal canal temporarily numbs the mother's body below the waist. To prevent injury, the needles used for these injections do not come into contact with the spinal cord itself. Although local anesthesia decreases the responsiveness of the newborn baby, there is little evidence that medicated childbirth has serious, long-term consequences on children.

Natural Childbirth Partly as a reaction against the use of anesthetics, English obstetrician Grantly Dick-Read endorsed **natural childbirth** in his 1944 book *Childbirth Without Fear.* Dick-Read argued that women's labor pains were heightened by their fear of the unknown and by the resulting muscle tension. Many of Dick-Read's contributions came to be accepted practice in modern preparation for childbirth, such as the emphasis on informing women about the biological aspects of reproduction and childbirth, the encouragement of physical fitness, and the teaching of relaxation and breathing exercises.

Prepared Childbirth: The Lamaze Method The French obstetrician Fernand Lamaze visited the Soviet Union in 1951 and found that many Russian women bore babies without anesthetics and without reporting a great deal of pain. Lamaze returned to Western Europe with some of the techniques the women used; they are now termed the **Lamaze method,** or *prepared childbirth.* Lamaze (1981) argued that women can learn to conserve energy during childbirth and reduce the pain of uterine contractions by associating the contractions with other responses, such as thinking of pleasant mental images such as beach scenes or engaging in breathing and relaxation exercises.

A pregnant woman typically attends Lamaze classes with a "coach"—usually the father—who will aid her in the delivery room by timing contractions, offering

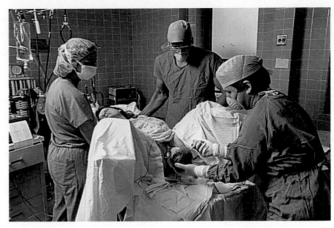

Coming into the World
Childbirth progresses through three stages. In the first stage, uterine contractions efface and dilate the cervix so that the baby may pass through. The second stage lasts from a few minutes to a few hours and ends with the birth of the baby. During the third stage, the placenta is expelled.

General anesthesia
The use of drugs to put people to sleep and eliminate pain, as during childbirth.

Local anesthesia
Anesthesia that eliminates pain in a specific area of the body, as during childbirth.

Natural childbirth
A method of childbirth in which women use no anesthesia but are given other strategies for coping with discomfort and are educated about childbirth.

Lamaze method
A childbirth method in which women learn about childbirth, learn to relax and to breathe in patterns that conserve energy and lessen pain, and have a coach (usually the father) present at childbirth. Also termed *prepared childbirth.*

emotional support, and coaching her in the breathing and relaxation exercises. The woman and her partner also receive more general information about childbirth. The father is integrated into the process, and many couples report that their marriages are strengthened as a result.

The Lamaze method is flexible about the use of anesthetics. Many women report some pain during delivery and obtain anesthetics. However, the Lamaze method appears to help women to gain a greater sense of control over the delivery process.

Cesarean Section In a **cesarean section**, the baby is delivered via surgery rather than naturally through the vagina. The term *section* is derived from the Latin for "to cut." Julius Caesar is said to have been delivered in this way, but health professionals believe this unlikely. In a cesarean section (C-section for short) the woman is anesthetized, and incisions are made in the abdomen and uterus so that the surgeon can remove the baby. The incisions are then sewn up and the mother can begin walking, often on the same day, although generally with some discomfort for a while. Although most C-sections are without complications, some cause urinary tract infections, inflammation of the wall of the uterus, blood clots, or hemorrhaging (ACOG, 2003). All in all, women who have C-sections are four times as likely to experience a pregnancy-related death (35.9 deaths per 100,000 deliveries) as women who deliver vaginally (9.2 deaths per 100,000) (ACOG, 2003).

C-sections are most likely to be advised when normal delivery is difficult or threatening to the health of the mother or child. Vaginal deliveries can become difficult if the baby is large, if the mother's pelvis is small or misshapen, if she is tired or weakened, or if she is aging (Roberts, 2000). Herpes and HIV infections in the birth canal can be bypassed by C-section. C-sections are also likely to be performed if the baby presents for delivery in the breech position (feet downward) or the **transverse position** (lying crosswise) or if the baby is in distress.

Use of the C-section has mushroomed. Nearly 1 of every 4 births (24%) is currently by C-section (USDHHS, 2003). Compare this figure to about 1 in 20 births in 1965. Much of the increase in the rate of C-sections reflects advances in medical technology, such as use of fetal monitors that allow doctors to detect fetal distress; fear of malpractice suits; financial incentives for hospitals and physicians; and, simply, current medical practice patterns. Yet some women request C-sections to avoid the discomforts of vaginal delivery or to control the timing of the delivery (Cohen & Feig, 2003). Critics claim that many C-sections are unnecessary, and the USDHHS believes that a rate of 15 per 100 births would be more appropriate (ACOG, 2003). But many obstetricians are concerned that a political push to lower the C-section rate could be dangerous ("After years of decline," 2000). Despite the often justified reasons for doing C-sections, one of the reasons remains "doctors' habits" ("After years of decline," 2000).

Some women who have C-sections experience negative emotional consequences. A meta-analysis of the results of studies on women who have C-sections reported that they are generally less satisfied with the birth process, are less likely to breastfeed, and interact somewhat less with their newborn babies (DiMatteo et al., 1996). But it has not been shown that C-sections are connected with significant, enduring emotional consequences for mothers or their children.

Medical opinion formerly held that once a woman had a C-section, subsequent deliveries also had to be by C-section. Otherwise, uterine scars might rupture during labor. Research has shown that rupture is rare, however. In one study, only 10 of 3,249 women who chose to try vaginal delivery after a previous C-section had a uterine rupture (McMahon et al., 1996). Moreover, there were no maternal deaths. In any

Cesarean section
A method of childbirth in which the fetus is delivered through a surgical incision in the abdomen.

Transverse position
A crosswise birth position.

event, only about 1 woman in 4 (23.4%) who have previously had a C-section deliver subsequent babies vaginally ("After years of decline," 2000).

Consumer advocates advise pregnant women who would like to deliver vaginally, if possible, to ask about the rates of C-sections when they are choosing a physician and a hospital ("After years of decline," 2000). Women can try to choose obstetricians who have lower rates or who are open to a second opinion for elective surgery. But it should not be forgotten that there are excellent reasons for having C-sections. It makes no sense to avoid a C-section for "political" reasons if vaginal delivery might put the mother or the baby at risk.

Laboring through the Birthing Options: Where Should a Child Be Born?

Women today have some choice in where they are going to give birth. *Questions: Where should a woman deliver her child? (And why?)* Options include home delivery, a special birthing suite, a typical hospital labor room, and, of course, a tub or pool. Women can select from a menu of obstetricians, midwives, and doulas. They can bring in aromatherapy and yoga.

American women appear to be searching for some sort of family atmosphere— a natural, nonmedicalized childbirth—even though only 10% of them avoid using anesthetics. Nurse-midwives have found themselves more busy, and so have doulas (nonprofessionals who offer support during childbirth but don't perform deliveries). Today's mothers are also not as willing as their own mothers to surrender control to an obstetrician. Hospitals and birthing centers are happy to oblige, because satisfied customers are likely to return for future deliveries and other medical services—for their families as well as for themselves.

State-of-the-Art Birthing and Competition Duke University Medical Center in Durham, North Carolina, is a case in point. Health professionals there recognized that although they offered high-quality care, they weren't emitting the warm fuzzies of competing hospitals. "We realized that changes needed to be made if we were going to survive," noted medical director Dr. William Herbert (cited in Stenson, 2000). "Our rooms were far inferior in terms of the amenities and expectations that people have now. They want a very home-like atmosphere that's family friendly, to celebrate delivery."

Thus Duke opened a birthing center within its hospital—21 private LDRPs— rooms that offer labor, delivery, recovery, and postpartum care, wrapped into one. The rooms are decorated like hotel suites, with hardwood floors, TVs, refrigerators, and private baths. Fathers and families can use day beds to spend the night. Bassinets allow the baby to stay with Mom and Dad after being born. Rather than transfer women from room to room during labor, the LDRP reduced the hassle for both the mother and medical staff. But Herbert adds that if a woman needs a C-section, she is transferred to a nearby operating room, like any other woman with complications.

LDRPs have all the equipment needed for uncomplicated births, tucked out of sight but within easy reach of doctors and nurses. Duke's emergency services are just down the hall, however, because many doctors worry about delivering babies in free-standing birthing centers that have no nearby surgical facilities.

How About Birth at Home? Each year in the United States, there are about 8 maternal deaths for every 100,000 live births. In developing countries, the number rises to 480 deaths per 100,000 births. The lower American death rate reflects access to quality health care, although African American women, with less access, die during childbirth at a rate double that of European Americans.

Childbirth Advice Is Just Keystrokes Away

You're pregnant and it's midnight. You've just felt a couple of abdominal twinges and you're a little worried. You know your obstetrician's probably asleep and since you still have a couple of weeks to go before the baby's due, you don't want to rush out to the emergency room. Right now, some good, solid medical information would be ever so reassuring.

If you've got an Internet connection, help could be just a few keystrokes away. These days, the Web is teeming with birth-related sites. The Net-savvy mother-to-be can research labor issues, find a childbirth class, chat with other expectant women and shop for everything from pregnancy vitamins to maternity fitness wear.

Of course, as with everything that appears on the Web, there's a certain amount of drivel and misinformation. So MSNBC has rounded up some experts to help you find the best places to dock your surfboard.

For trustworthy medical advice, you should probably stick to sites that are affiliated with either an academic institution or an established professional organization, suggests Dr. David Toub, director of quality improvement at Keystone Mercy Health Plan and a member of the department of obstetrics and gynecology at the Pennsylvania Hospital in Philadelphia.

One such site, Intelihealth, a joint venture between Johns Hopkins Medical Institutions and Aetna, offers its own experts and links to many reputable sources of information, says Dr. Pamela Yoder, medical director of women's health, obstetrics and gynecology, and maternal–fetal medicine at Provena Covenant Medical Center at the University of Illinois.

Another option is to seek sites that have input from recognized experts, such as Obgyn.net. This site also contains chats and forums that focus on such subjects as pregnancy, birth and breastfeeding.

When she was pregnant, Dr. Kelly Shanahan often drifted over to Obgyn.net's forums to talk with other mothers-to-be about such topics as swollen ankles. "Sometimes it's good to be able to vent to other people in the same situation," says Shanahan, a physician in private practice and chair of obstetrics and gynecology at the Barton Memorial Hospital in South Lake Tahoe, California.

And after the baby was born, Shanahan frequented the chat for new moms. "I may be an obstetrician, but I didn't know diddley about what to do with babies once they're out of the uterus," she says. "It was really helpful to get hints from other moms on how to cope with a newborn."

Another good site for conversation about pregnancy and baby-rearing is iVillage.com, Shanahan says. "This site also has an expert question and answer section," she adds.

When it comes to bulletin boards, women should remember that anyone can post anything, experts say.

"My impression is that UseNet has a lot of unmoderated free-for-alls that post incorrect, even libelous information," Toub says. "A recent troll on Sci.Med, for example, showed it contained postings that claimed that ACOG was covering up the 'truth' about obstetricians crushing fetal skulls and creating shoulder dystocia during vaginal deliveries."

In other words, the medical oriented newsgroup has some not-so-correct advice mixed in with its information, he said.

Delivering at Home?

If you think you might want to deliver at home, consider checking out midwives listed on the Internet. But, "as with anything else on the Web, the key is to look carefully at the motivations and credentials of the person posting the information," cautions Cheri Van

Many health professionals frown on home births because labor and delivery can be unpredictable. Home birth presents less of a threat for women who have already had uncomplicated pregnancies, but the risk still surpasses that of giving birth in a hospital.

A certified nurse-midwife assesses a woman's risk for complications and the availability of nearby emergency care before agreeing to help with a home birth. But most nurse-midwives work alongside obstetricians in hospitals. They may handle low-risk births, with an obstetrician nearby. Midwives, unlike obstetricians, remain with the woman through the entire process, helping her to relax, using massage, yoga,

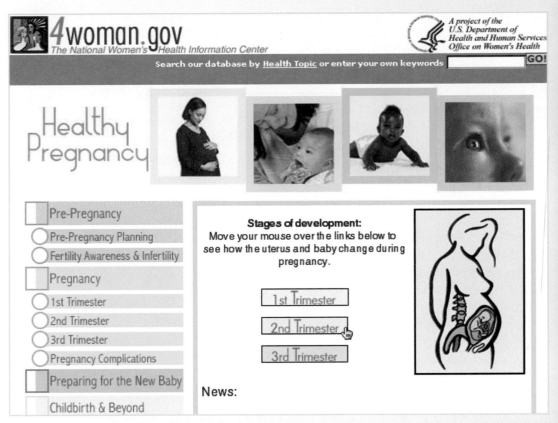

4woman.gov
The National Women's Health Information Center

A project of the
U.S. Department of
Health and Human Services
Office on Women's Health

Search our database by Health Topic or enter your own keywords   GO!

Healthy Pregnancy

- Pre-Pregnancy
- Pre-Pregnancy Planning
- Fertility Awareness & Infertility
- Pregnancy
- 1st Trimester
- 2nd Trimester
- 3rd Trimester
- Pregnancy Complications
- Preparing for the New Baby
- Childbirth & Beyond

Stages of development:
Move your mouse over the links below to see how the uterus and baby change during pregnancy.

1st Trimester
2nd Trimester
3rd Trimester

News:

Surfing Online for Information About Pregnancy and Childbirth Today's women can find everything from advice from obstetricians to fitness wear for pregnant women online.

Hoover, a midwife who practices at Stanford University in Palo Alto, California. "Responsible midwives will disclose their background, credentials and a way to contact them for more information."

A good starting place is the American College of Nurse-Midwives, Van Hoover suggests. Another good site is Childbirth.org, according to Dr. R. Daniel Braun, a clinical professor in the department of obstetrics and gynecology at the Indiana University School of Medicine in Indianapolis. "If you are going to have a home delivery this is an excellent site," Braun says. "The site is run by a doula. But remember that it is biased towards the 'natural' delivery."

Childbirth Classes

If you're looking for childbirth classes, there are plenty of listings on the Web, Van Hoover says. But again, women should be asking a few questions, she adds. For example, you might want to [ask], "Where did the instructors get their training?" Van Hoover suggests.

(continues)

and other techniques to ease pain and anxiety. Midwives appeal to many because they seem to be open to alternative techniques.

Doulas Nonprofessional doulas can help because they are patient advocates. They are especially helpful when women do not have partners of their own.

And How About Water Birth? Most American health professionals admit that labor in water can be safe if the tub has been adequately disinfected, but they're skeptical. Infants occasionally drown.

Human Sexuality in the New Millennium

"Which professional organizations do they belong to? Do they believe there is only one right way to give birth or are they flexible and individualized in their approach?"

Ultimately, it could be the Web's easy shopping that you use the most.

One-Stop Shopping

For Shanahan, retail on the Web made all the difference. "I live in a rural community in the mountains," says Shanahan, who gave birth in December. "And getting out of here in the winter can sometimes be a problem."

One of Shanahan's favorite finds was a site marketing fitness wear for pregnant women. This site also contains information on exercise during pregnancy, including the recommendations of the American College of Obstetricians and Gynecologists (ACOG).

If you'd like to order vitamins or disposable diapers, for that matter, you might try Drugstore.com's pregnancy page, Shanahan suggests. The site also has accurate medical information, she says.

Another commercial site that provides expert information and advice is the Babycenter's birth and labor section. The site offers information on a variety of topics. You just select from the menu and click. Often sections are written by experts, whose biographies are readily available. And everything on the site is reviewed by a board that includes several ob-gyns.

Here you can also get answers to practical questions, like, "What should I take to the hospital?" or "When is it too late to change obstetricians?" The site includes discussions about the various types of childbirth classes, and an interactive survey designed to help you figure out which kind of class would best fit your needs.

And if you were looking for insight on whether you could have contractions without being in labor, text under the heading "false labor" at the Babycenter site could put your mind at ease.

SOME OF THE BEST WEB SITES

The American College of Obstetricians and Gynecologists
www.acog.org/

American College of Nurse-Midwives
www.midwife.org/

Doulas of North America
www.dona.com/

Intelihealth
www.intelihealth.com/

Obgyn.net
www.obgyn.net/

iVillage.com
www.parentsplace.com/pregnancy/

Childbirth.org
www.childbirth.org/

Fitness Wear for Pregnant Women
www.fitmaternity.com/index.html

Drugstore.com
www.drugstore.com/

Birth and labor section of Babycenter.com
www.babycenter.com/birthandlabor/

Reprinted from Linda Carroll (2000). Childbirth advice keystrokes away: How to find the best Web sites. *MSNBC online.*

Hense there are many options. Does it make sense to be prepared for worst-case scenarios even as we do everything we can to make the birthing experience pleasant?

Birth Problems

Most deliveries are uncomplicated, or "unremarkable" in the medical sense—although childbirth is the most remarkable experience of many parents' lives. Problems can and do occur, however. *Question: What are some of the problems encountered at birth?* Some of the most common birth problems are anoxia and the birth of preterm and low-birthweight babies.

Anoxia Prenatal **anoxia** can cause various problems in the neonate and affect later development. It leads to complications such as brain damage and mental retardation. Prolonged anoxia during delivery can also result in cerebral palsy and possibly death.

The baby is supplied with oxygen through the umbilical cord. Passage through the birth canal squeezes the umbilical cord. Temporary squeezing, like holding one's breath for a moment, is unlikely to cause problems. (In fact, slight oxygen deprivation at birth is not unusual, because the transition from receiving oxygen through the umbilical cord to breathing on its own may not happen immediately after the baby emerges.) Anoxia can result if constriction of the cord is prolonged, however. Prolonged constriction is more likely to occur with a breech presentation, because the baby's head presses the umbilical cord against the birth canal during delivery. Fetal monitoring can help detect anoxia early, however, before damage occurs. A C-section can be performed if the fetus appears to be in distress.

Preterm and Low-Birthweight Children A neonate is considered to be premature, or **preterm**, if born before 37 weeks of gestation. The normal period of gestation is 40 weeks. Prematurity is generally linked with low birthweight, because the fetus normally makes dramatic gains in weight during the last weeks of pregnancy.

Regardless of the length of its gestation period, a newborn baby is considered to have a low birthweight if it weighs less than 5 pounds (about 2,500 grams). Preterm and low-birthweight babies face a heightened risk of infant mortality from causes ranging from asphyxia and infections to sudden infant death syndrome (SIDS) (Berger, 2000; Kramer et al., 2000). Neurological and developmental problems are also common among preterm infants, especially those born at or prior to 25 weeks of gestation (Wood et al., 2000).

Twins and other multiple birth groupings are more likely to be of low birthweight than individual births (Blickstein et al., 2000). There is also a relationship between prematurity and the spacing of babies. Women who have babies less than 18 months or more than 59 months apart have the highest risk of premature infants (Fuentes-Afflick & Hessol, 2000). On the other hand, it is common for women carrying more than one child to deliver prematurely, apparently because the babies are running out of space.

Preterm babies are relatively thin because they have not yet formed the layer of fat that accounts for the round, robust appearance of most full-term babies. Their muscles are immature, weakening their sucking and breathing reflexes. Also, in the last weeks of pregnancy, fetuses secrete **surfactant** that prevents the walls of their airways from sticking together. Muscle weakness and incomplete lining of the airways with surfactant can cause a cluster of problems known as **respiratory distress syndrome**, which is responsible for many neonatal deaths. (Today, surfactant replacement therapy is extending the possibilities of survival in preterm infants [Cole, 2000].) Preterm babies may also suffer from underdeveloped immune systems, which leave them more vulnerable to infections.

Preterm infants usually remain in the hospital for a time. There they can be monitored and placed in incubators that provide a temperature-controlled environment and offer some protection from disease. If necessary, they may also receive oxygen. Although remarkable advances are being made in our ability to help preterm babies survive, the likelihood of developmental disabilities continues to increase dramatically for babies who are born at 25 weeks of gestation or earlier (Cole, 2000).

Anoxia Oxygen deprivation.

Preterm Born before 37 weeks of gestation.

Surfactants Substances that prevent the walls of the airways from sticking together.

Respiratory distress syndrome A cluster of breathing problems, including weak and irregular breathing, to which preterm babies are especially vulnerable.

Review: Childbirth

Reflect

Do you know people who have used different methods of childbirth, such as natural childbirth or the Lamaze method? What were their experiences like?

CriticalThinking

Critical thinkers tackle controversial issues. What are the pros and cons of the following aspects of childbirth: episiotomy, use of anesthesia, and home delivery?

50. The first uterine contractions are usually false and are called _____ contractions.

51. Pituitary _____ stimulates contractions strong enough to expel the baby.

52. In the first stage of childbirth, uterine contractions _____ and _____ the cervix.

53. _____ occurs when the cervix becomes almost fully dilated and the baby's head begins to move into the birth canal.

54. The _____ stage of childbirth begins when the baby first appears at the opening of the birth canal.

55. An _____ may be performed to prevent random tearing of the perineum, but the procedure is controversial.

56. During the third stage of childbirth, the _____ is expelled.

57. Today about _____% of American women use no anesthesia.

58. _____ anesthesia induces unconsciousness.

59. In the _____ method, women are taught to conserve energy during childbirth and reduce the pain of contractions by engaging in breathing and relaxation exercises.

60. About _____% of American women today deliver by C-section.

61. C-sections (*Increase* or *Decrease*?) the likelihood that a baby will be infected with herpes or HIV during delivery.

62. The lure of the birthing center or midwife is (*Increased safety* or *Homelike atmosphere*?).

63. _____ is absence of oxygen.

64. Anoxia occurs during delivery when the _____ cord is constricted.

65. Preterm and low-_____ babies face a heightened risk of infant mortality.

66. Weakness and incomplete lining of the airways with surfactant can cause _____ distress syndrome.

The Postpartum Period

The weeks after delivery are called the **postpartum** period. The first few days postpartum are frequently happy ones. The long wait is over, as are the discomforts of childbirth. However, according to the American Psychiatric Association, about 70% of new mothers have periods of tearfulness, sadness, and irritability that the association refers to as "baby blues" (2000, p. 423).

Maternal Depression

Question: What kinds of emotional problems do women experience during the postpartum period? These problems include the baby blues and more serious mood disorders ("postpartum-onset mood episodes"), which occasionally include "psychotic features" (American Psychiatric Association, 2000). These problems are far-flung; researchers have found that they occur with similar frequency in China, Turkey, Guyana, Australia, and South Africa (Affonso et al., 2000; Cooper et al., 1999; Guelseren, 1999; Lee et al., 2001).

Baby blues affect the majority of women in the weeks after delivery. Researchers believe they are caused by the hormonal changes that accompany and follow delivery (Guelseren, 1999; Morris, 2000). They last for about 10 days and are not severe enough

Postpartum Following birth.

to impair the mother's functioning. Don't misunderstand; the baby blues are seriously upsetting and not to be dismissed (as in "Oh, you're just experiencing what most women experience"). The point is that most women can get through them even though they're pretty awful at times, partly because they know that the baby blues will pass.

As many as 1 in 5 to 10 women encounters a more serious mood disorder called **postpartum depression (PPD)**. PPD begins within 4 weeks after delivery and may linger for weeks or months. PPD symptoms include serious sadness, feelings of hopelessness and helplessness, feelings of worthlessness, difficulty concentrating, and major changes in appetite (usually loss of appetite) and sleep patterns (frequently insomnia). There can also be severe fluctuations in mood, with women sometimes feeling elated. Some women show obsessive concern with the well-being of their babies at this time.

Many researchers suggest that PPD is caused by the interactions of biological (mainly hormonal) and psychological factors, including a precipitous drop in estrogen levels (Johnstone et al., 2001). PPD, like baby blues, may be worsened by concerns about all the life changes that motherhood creates and about whether one will be a good mother (Grazioli & Terry, 2000; Ritter, 2000). Marital problems and having a sick or unwanted baby heighten the likelihood and severity of PPD (Terry et al., 1996; Zelkowitz & Milet, 1996). But the focus today is on the biological, because there are major changes in body chemistry during and after pregnancy, and because women around the world seem to experience similar disturbances in mood, even when their life experiences and support systems are very different from those we find in the United States.

According to the American Psychiatric Association (2000), postpartum mood episodes are accompanied by "psychotic features" (loss of touch with reality) in 1 woman in 500 to 1,000. Very rarely, women experience delusions that the infant is possessed by the devil or that they must kill the infant.

Women who experience PPD may profit from psychotherapy or drugs. Drugs that increase estrogen levels or antidepressants may help. Most women get over PPD on their own. At the very least, women need to know that the problem is not unusual and does not necessarily mean that there is something seriously wrong with them or that they are not living up to their obligations.

Breastfeeding versus Bottle-Feeding

The majority of mothers in the United States today—about 3 in 5—breastfeed their children (American Academy of Pediatrics, 2002). However, only about 1 woman in 5 continues to breastfeed after 6 months, and the American Academy of Pediatrics (2002) recommends that women breastfeed for a year or more.

Question: Why do women bottle-feed or breastfeed their children? One reason why a woman may bottle-feed her baby is that she returns to the workforce shortly following childbirth. Some choose to share feeding chores with the father, who is equally equipped to prepare and hold a bottle, but not to breastfeed. Other women find breastfeeding inconvenient or unpleasant. Long-term comparisons of breastfed and bottle-fed children show few, if any, significant differences. HIV (the AIDS virus) can be transmitted to infants by breast milk. According to UN estimates, one third of the infants with HIV around the world were infected via breast milk (United Nations Special Session on AIDS, 2001). Moreover, when undernourished mothers in developing countries breastfeed, their babies can become malnourished (Crossette, 2000).

On the other hand, breastfeeding reduces the general risk of infections to the baby by transmitting the mother's antibodies to the baby. Breastfeeding also reduces

Postpartum depression Persistent and severe mood changes during the postpartum period, involving feelings of despair and apathy and characterized by changes in appetite and sleep, low self-esteem, and difficulty concentrating.

the incidence of allergies in babies, particularly in allergy-prone infants (American Academy of Pediatrics, 2002; Kramer et al., 2001; Lawrence et al., 2001). Uterine contractions that occur during breast-feeding help return the uterus to its typical size. (Breastfeeding delays resumption of normal menstrual cycles but is not a perfectly reliable birth-control method.)

The hormones prolactin and oxytocin are involved in breastfeeding. **Prolactin** stimulates production of milk, or **lactation**, 2 to 3 days after delivery. Oxytocin causes the breasts to eject milk and is secreted in response to suckling. When an infant is weaned, secretion of prolactin and oxytocin is discontinued, and lactation comes to an end.

Should a woman breastfeed her baby? The issue is largely political (Law, 2000). Much of the literature on breastfeeding has little to do with the advantages of breast milk or formula, but with occupational and domestic arrangements, child day care, mother–infant bonding, and the politics of domestic decision making. Although breastfeeding benefits both mother and infant, each woman must weigh the pluses and minuses for herself.

Questions: When do ovulation and menstruation resume? When can women safely resume sexual activity?

Resumption of Ovulation and Menstruation

For close to a month after delivery, women experience a reddish vaginal discharge called **lochia**. A nonnursing mother does not resume actual menstrual periods until 2 to 3 months postpartum. The first few cycles are likely to be irregular. Many women incorrectly assume that they will resume menstruating following childbirth by having a menstrual period and ovulating 2 weeks later, but in most cases the opposite is true. Ovulation precedes the first menstrual period after childbirth. Thus, a woman may become pregnant before the menstrual phase of her first postpartum cycle. Some women who suffered premenstrual syndrome before their pregnancies find that their periods give them less discomfort after the birth of their children.

Resumption of Sexual Activity

The resumption of coitus depends on a couple's level of sexual interest, the healing of episiotomies or other injuries, fatigue, the recommendations of obstetricians, and, of course, tradition. Obstetricians usually advise a 6-week waiting period for safety and comfort. One study of 570 women found that they actually resumed sexual intercourse an average of 7 weeks after childbirth (Byrd et al., 1998).

Women typically prefer to delay coitus until it becomes physically comfortable, generally when the episiotomy or other lacerations have healed and the lochia has ended. This may take several weeks. Women who breastfeed may also find that they have less vaginal lubrication, and the dryness can cause discomfort during coitus. K-Y jelly or other lubricants may help in such cases.

The return of sexual interest and resumption of sexual activity may take longer for some couples than for others. Sexual interest depends more on psychological than on physical factors. Many couples encounter declining sexual interest and activity in the first year following childbirth, generally because child care can sap energy and limit free time. Generally speaking, couples whose sexual relationships were satisfying before the baby arrived tend to show greater sexual interest and to resume sexual activity earlier than those who had less satisfying relationships beforehand. (No surprise.)

Prolactin A pituitary hormone that stimulates production of milk. (From roots meaning "for milk.")

Lactation Production of milk by the mammary glands.

Lochia A reddish vaginal discharge that may persist for a month after delivery. (From the Greek *lochios,* meaning "of childbirth.")

Review: The Postpartum Period

Reflect

How have women you know reacted emotionally in the hours, days, and weeks following childbirth?

CriticalThinking

What are the "political" issues involved in breastfeeding versus bottle-feeding?

67. About _____% of new mothers have periods of tearfulness, sadness, and irritability that are termed "baby blues."

68. Researchers believe baby blues are caused by _____ changes during and after delivery.

69. More serious _____ (PPD) begins within 4 weeks after delivery and may linger for weeks or months.

70. In 1 woman of 500 to 1,000, postpartum mood episodes are accompanied by "_____ features" (loss of touch with reality).

71. Breastfeeding reduces the general risk of infections to the baby by transmitting the mother's _____.

72. The hormone _____ stimulates production of milk.

73. The first few menstrual cycles following childbirth tend to be (*Regular* or *Irregular*?).

74. Obstetricians usually advise that couples wait for _____ weeks after delivery before resuming intercourse.

Recite

1. **What is conception?**

   Conception is the union of a sperm cell and an ovum. Fertilization normally occurs in a fallopian tube. Between 120 and 150 boys are conceived for every 100 girls, but male fetuses have a higher rate of miscarriage. Chromosomes from the sperm cell align with chromosomes in the egg cell, combining to form 23 new pairs.

2. **How do people attempt to select the sex of their children?**

   Methods have been developed for sorting male (Y) and female (X) sperm cells. Shettles suggested methods based on the swimming rates and other characteristics of X- and Y-bearing sperm cells. Others have developed methods based on the electrical charges of sperm cells and on the bulk of their genetic material. Use of these methods raises profound ethical questions.

3. **What are the causes of infertility? How are couples helped to have children?**

   Male fertility problems include low sperm count and motility, infections, and trauma to the testes. Female fertility problems include failure to ovulate, infections, endometriosis, and obstructions in the reproductive tract. Fertility drugs help regulate ovulation. Artificial insemination may be done with the sperm from multiple ejaculations of a man with a low sperm count or with that of a donor. In vitro fertilization (IVF) may be used when the fallopian tubes are blocked. Embryonic transplant transfers the embryo into a host uterus, as when the mother cannot produce ova.

4. **What are the early signs of pregnancy?**

   Early signs include a missed period, presence of HCG in the blood or urine, and Hegar's sign. Pregnancy tests detect the presence of human chorionic gonadotropin (HCG) in the woman's urine or blood.

5. **What are the early effects of pregnancy?**

   Early effects include tenderness in the breasts and morning sickness. Morning sickness is believed to be associated with healthy pregnancy.

6. **Why do some pregnancies end in miscarriage?**

   Miscarriages have many causes, including chromosomal defects in the fetus and abnormalities of the placenta and uterus.

7. **Is it safe to have sex during pregnancy?**

   Most health professionals agree that in most cases, coitus is safe until the start of labor. An exception would be the case of threatened miscarriage.

(continues)

Recite

8. What psychological changes take place during pregnancy?

A woman's psychological response to pregnancy reflects her desire to be pregnant, her physical changes, and her attitudes toward these changes. Men, like women, respond to pregnancy according to the degree to which they want the child.

9. What happens during the stages of prenatal development?

During the germinal stage, the zygote divides but does not gain in mass. It travels to the uterus, where it becomes implanted. The mass becomes a fluid-filled ball of cells called a blastocyst. The embryo and fetus exchange nutrients and wastes with the mother through the placenta. The umbilical cord connects the fetus to the placenta. The embryonic stage lasts from implantation until about the eighth week of development, a time during which the major body organ systems differentiate. Development follows cephalocaudal and proximodistal trends. The fetal stage lasts from the end of the embryonic stage until birth. The second trimester is characterized by maturation of organs and gains in size. By the end of the second trimester, the fetus opens and shuts its eyes, sucks its thumb, alternates between periods of wakefulness and sleep, and responds to light and sounds. During the third trimester, the heart and lungs become capable of sustaining independent life.

10. How do environmental factors affect prenatal development?

Maternal malnutrition is linked with low birthweight, prematurity, and cognitive problems. Maternal diseases and disorders can harm the embryo and are called teratogens. Women who contract rubella may bear children who suffer from deafness, retardation, heart disease, or cataracts. Syphilis can cause miscarriage or stillbirth. Babies born to mothers who are infected with HIV (the AIDS virus) may become infected during birth. Toxemia, characterized by high blood pressure, is connected with preterm or undersized babies. In Rh incompatibility, antibodies produced by the mother can kill the fetus or cause brain damage. Teratogens are most harmful during critical periods when certain organs are developing. The antibiotic tetracycline can cause yellowed teeth and bone abnormalities in children. Children of women who used DES to maintain their pregnancies are at risk for cervical or testicular cancer. Maternal addiction to heroin is linked to low birthweight and prematurity, and fetuses can be born addicted. Heavy maternal use of alcohol is linked to fetal alcohol syndrome (FAS). Maternal cigarette smoking deprives the fetus of oxygen and is linked with low birthweight, stillbirth, and learning problems.

11. What kinds of disorders are caused by chromosomal and genetic abnormalities?

Chromosomal abnormalities become more likely as parents age. Mental retardation is common in many such disorders. Down syndrome is caused by an extra chromosome on the 21st pair. Disorders that arise from abnormal numbers of sex chromosomes are called sex-linked. Sickle-cell anemia is most common among African Americans. Tay-Sachs disease is a fatal disease of the nervous system that is most common among children in Jewish families of East European origin.

12. How do health professionals determine whether children will have chromosomal or genetic abnormalities?

In amniocentesis, fetal cells found in amniotic fluid are cultured to detect genetic abnormalities. Chorionic villus sampling (CVS) is similar to amniocentesis but is conducted earlier. Ultrasound is used to track the growth of the fetus and find structural abnormalities. Parental blood tests can reveal the presence of recessive genes for disorders such as sickle-cell anemia and Tay-Sachs disease.

13. What events lead to childbirth?

Early in the ninth month, the head of the fetus settles in the pelvis. The first uterine contractions are "false" Braxton-Hicks contractions. A day or so before labor begins, pelvic pressure from the fetus may rupture blood vessels in the birth canal so that blood appears. Some women have a

Recite

rush of amniotic fluid because the amniotic sac has burst. Fetal hormones stimulate the placenta and the uterus to secrete prostaglandins, which cause labor contractions. Then the pituitary gland releases oxytocin, which stimulates contractions strong enough to expel the baby.

14. What happens during the stages of childbirth?

Childbirth begins with the onset of regular contractions of the uterus, which efface and dilate the cervix, causing most of the pain of childbirth. During transition, the cervix is almost fully dilated and the head of the fetus begins to move into the birth canal. The second stage begins when the baby appears at the opening of the birth canal and ends with the birth of the baby. When the baby's head has crowned, an episiotomy—which has become controversial—may be performed to prevent random tearing of the perineum. Once the baby's head emerges from the mother's body, mucus is removed from its mouth by suction. The umbilical cord is cut. The third stage expels the placenta.

15. What methods of childbirth are used today?

General anesthesia puts the woman to sleep but also decreases the strength of uterine contractions and lowers the responsiveness of the baby. Regional or local anesthetics deaden pain in areas of the body without putting the mother to sleep. Dick-Read promoted natural childbirth; he encouraged educating women about reproduction, physical fitness, and relaxation and breathing exercises. The Lamaze method uses breathing and relaxation exercises, along with a "coach" who aids the mother. A cesarean section delivers a baby surgically through the abdomen. C-sections are most likely to be advised if the baby is large or in distress, or if the mother's pelvis is small or she is weak. Herpes and HIV infections in the birth canal can often be bypassed by C-section.

16. Where should a woman deliver her child? (And why?)

Women have choices in childbirth—home delivery, birthing suites, traditional labor room, use of a doula. Birthing suites can provide homelike surroundings with hospital backup available.

17. What are some of the problems encountered at birth?

Prenatal oxygen deprivation—anoxia—can damage the nervous system and kill the baby. Anoxia can be caused by immaturity of the baby's respiratory system and pressure against the umbilical cord during birth. Risks for preterm and low-birthweight babies include mortality and delayed development. If babies do not yet secrete surfactants, they may develop respiratory distress syndrome.

18. What kinds of emotional problems do women experience during the postpartum period?

Women may encounter baby blues and postpartum depression, which, at worst, can include psychotic symptoms. These problems are found around the world and may reflect hormonal changes following birth. Support and certain medications can be of help.

19. Why do women bottle-feed or breastfeed their children?

Breastfeeding is connected with fewer infections and allergic reactions in the baby than bottle-feeding. Long-term studies show few differences between children whose parents used one or the other feeding method, however. Therefore, for many women the issue of convenience takes center stage.

20. When do ovulation and menstruation resume?

The first few menstrual cycles following childbirth are likely to be irregular.

21. When can women safely resume sexual activity?

Obstetricians usually advise a 6-week waiting period following childbirth before resuming coitus. Couples need not wait this long to enjoy other kinds of sexual activity.

Chapter 12

Truth?Fiction?

T / F? Ancient Egyptians used crocodile dung as a contraceptive.

T / F? There is an oral contraceptive that can be taken the morning after unprotected intercourse.

T / F? Sterilization operations can be surgically reversed.

T / F? Contraceptives not only prevent conception; they also prevent the spread of sexually transmitted infections.

T / F? Testosterone can be used as a male contraceptive.

T / F? Abortions were legal in the newly founded United States.

T / F? The D&C is the most widely used abortion method in the United States.

Contraception and Abortion

Preview

Contraception

Methods of Contraception

Abortion

It was a stifling day in July 1912. Margaret Sanger (1883–1966), a nurse practitioner, was summoned to the house of a woman near death from a botched self-induced abortion. Her husband had called a doctor, and the doctor sent for Sanger. Together, doctor and nurse worked feverishly through the days and nights that followed to stem an infection that had taken hold in the woman. Sanger later commented,

> Never had I worked so fast, never so concentratedly. The sultry days and nights were melted into a torrid inferno. It did not seem possible there could be such heat, and every bit of food, ice, and drugs had to be carried up three flights of stairs. . . .

After two interminable weeks, the woman began to recover. Her neighbors, who had feared the worst, came to express their joy. But the woman, who smiled wanly at those who came to see her, appeared more depressed and anxious than would be expected of someone who was recovering from a grave illness. By the end of the third week, when Sanger prepared to leave her patient, the woman, Mrs. Sachs, voiced the fear that was haunting her. Her face registered deep despair as she explained to Sanger that she dreaded becoming pregnant again and facing a choice between attempting another abortion, which she feared might kill her, and bearing a baby whose care it was beyond her means to support. She pleaded for information about contraception, but Sanger could offer none. In 1912 it was a crime even for health professionals like Margaret Sanger to dispense information about contraceptives. Abortions, too, were illegal. Sanger tried to comfort her and promised to return to talk again (Reed & Lampe, 2003).

Three months later she received another urgent call. It was Mr. Sachs. His wife was sick again—from the same cause. As Sanger recalled,

> For a wild moment I thought of sending someone else, but actually, of course, I hurried into my uniform, caught up my bag, and started out. All the way I longed for a subway wreck, an explosion, anything to keep me from having to enter that home again. But nothing happened, even to delay me. I turned into the dingy doorway and climbed the familiar stairs once more. The children were there, young little things.
>
> Mrs. Sachs was in a coma and died within ten minutes. I folded her still hands across her breast, remembering how they had pleaded with me, begging so humbly for the knowledge which was her right. I drew a sheet over her pallid face. Jake was sobbing, running his hands through his hair and pulling it out like an insane person. Over and over again he wailed, "My God! My God! My God!" (Sanger, 1938)

Today, partly because of the work of Margaret Sanger, who went on to become a key advocate for birth control, information about contraceptives is disseminated freely throughout the United States.

Methods of birth control include contraception and abortion. ***Question: What is contraception?*** The term *contraception* refers to techniques that prevent conception. The term *abortion* refers to the termination of a pregnancy before the embryo or fetus is capable of surviving outside the womb, as we see later in the chapter.

Contraception

People have been devising means of contraception ever since they became aware of the relationship between coitus and conception. Ironically, the safest and most effective method of contraception is also the least popular: abstinence. The Bible contains many references to contraceptive techniques, including vaginal sponges and contraceptive concoctions. It also refers to *coitus interruptus*, or withdrawal. The story of Onan, for example, implies knowledge of the withdrawal method.

Ancient Egyptian methods of birth control included douching with wine and garlic after coitus, and soaking crocodile dung in sour milk and stuffing the mixture deep within the vagina. The dung blocked the passage of many—if not all—sperm through the cervix and also soaked up sperm. The dung may also have done its job through a social mechanism. It may have discouraged all but the most ardent suitors.

Greek and Roman women placed absorbent materials within the vagina to absorb semen. The use of sheaths, or coverings for the penis, has a long history. Sheaths worn over the penis as decorative covers can be traced to ancient Egypt (1350 BCE). Sheaths of linen were first described in European writings in 1564 by the Italian anatomist Fallopius (from whom the name of the fallopian tube is derived). Linen sheaths were used, without success, as a barrier against syphilis. The term **condom** was not used to describe penile sheaths until the eighteenth century. At that time, sheaths made of animal intestines became popular as a means of preventing sexually transmitted infections and unwanted pregnancies. Among the early advocates of condoms as a method of contraception was the Italian adventurer and writer Giovanni Casanova (1725–1798). We now associate his name with men who are known for their amorous adventures. James Boswell (1740–1795), the biographer of Samuel Johnson, described his use of "armor," or condoms, in his graphic *London Journal.* On one occasion, however, he was so enamored with a street prostitute that he neglected to don his armor and contracted gonorrhea. Condoms made of rubber (hence the slang "rubbers") were introduced shortly after Charles Goodyear invented vulcanization of rubber in 1843. Many other forms of contraception were also widely used in the nineteenth century, including withdrawal, vaginal sponges, and douching.

Truth?Fiction?
Revisited

It is true that ancient Egyptians used crocodile dung as a contraceptive. (No comment.)

Coitus interruptus
A method of contraception in which the penis is withdrawn from the vagina prior to ejaculation. Also referred to as the *withdrawal method.*

Condom A sheath made of animal membrane or latex that covers the penis during coitus and serves as a barrier to sperm after ejaculation.

Contraception in the United States: The Legal Battle

As methods of contraception grew more popular in the nineteenth century, opponents waged a battle to make contraception illegal. *Question: What happened during the legal battle over contraception in the United States?* One powerful opponent of contraception was Anthony Comstock, who served for a time as the secretary of the New York Society for the Suppression of Vice. Comstock lobbied successfully for passage of a federal law in 1873—the Comstock Law—that prohibited the dissemination of birth-control information through the mail on the grounds that it was "obscene and indecent." Many states passed even more restrictive laws. They outlawed the passage of such information from one person to another, even from physician to patient.

Consider the resistance that Margaret Sanger met when she challenged the laws restricting the dissemination of information about contraception (Reed & Lampe, 2003). In 1914 she established the National Birth Control League, which published the magazine *The Woman Rebel. Rebel* did not publish birth-control information but challenged the view that it was obscene. Nevertheless, charges were brought against Sanger, and she fled to Europe before her trial. During her self-imposed exile, she visited birth-control clinics in the Netherlands. When the charges against her in the

A Closer Look

Talking with Your Partner about Contraception

When is the right time to discuss contraception? On a first date? When you are invited to meet your partner's family? When you are lost in amorous embraces? Broaching the topic can be awkward. *Not* broaching it can be disastrous. Often a man responds to news that his partner is pregnant by saying something like this: "But I thought you were using *something*!"

Technically speaking, the right time to discuss birth control is *anytime* that allows your contraceptive to become effective before you engage in coitus. That can mean weeks or months before, if you decide to use a prescription contraceptive such as the birth-control pill, the IUD, the diaphragm, or the cervical cap. Or it can mean a few moments before coitus, if you decide to use a condom and have one ready. Despite the obvious advantages of deciding upon contraception before coitus, the issue is often broached, if it is broached at all, only after the partners become sexually intimate. Practically speaking, it is awkward—and perhaps presumptuous!—to discuss contraception when you meet or are on a first date. But at the very least, it is advisable to prepare oneself for the possibility of coitus. The man or woman may bring along a condom. The woman may already be on the pill, or have an IUD in place, or carry a diaphragm.

Talking about contraception helps many couples make the transition from a casual relationship to an intimate one. Talking enables partners to share responsibility for their behavior. As a result, the woman is less likely to be resentful that the responsibility rests entirely on her.

Yes, it can be awkward or difficult to raise the topic. Couples may not feel that their relationship is secure enough. They might think, "We'll cross that bridge when we come to it." Not planning ahead, however, prevents the effective use of contraceptives that require advance planning. Couples who choose to discuss contraception before engaging in coitus may benefit from these communication guidelines:

1. *Pick a strategic time and place.* Choose a time when the two of you are alone and free of distractions. Pick a place that is comfortable and private.

2. *Couch your discussion in terms of your feelings about your partner and your relationship.* Talk about your general feelings toward your partner and your general relationship before you narrow in on contraception.

3. *Don't apologize for raising the topic.* You may feel embarrassed talking about sensitive topics like birth control. But you need not apologize for bringing up the subject. Apologizing suggests that you think you are doing something wrong.

4. *Raise the subject in a way that encourages candid discussion.* Use open-ended questions to explore your partner's attitudes. Say something like "I think our relationship has reached the point where we need to talk about contraception. I know we're not sleeping together yet, but some forms of contraception require advanced planning. Have you been thinking about it?"

5. *Explore options.* Don't make demands of your partner. Don't say, "Since we may start sleeping together, I think you should go on the pill." Rather, say something like "I know that many different types of contraceptives are available. Why don't we discuss which method might be best for us if we become intimate?" Use the opportunity to explore each other's views about birth control in general and specific techniques in particular.

United States were dropped in 1916, Sanger returned and established a birth-control clinic in Brooklyn, New York. The clinic was closed by the police, and Sanger was arrested. Released on bail, she reopened the clinic and was thereupon sentenced to 30 days in jail. She successfully appealed the sentence. In 1918 the courts ruled that physicians must be allowed to provide information that might aid in the cure and prevention of disease. Dismantling of the Comstock Law had begun. With the financial support of a wealthy friend, Katherine Dexter McCormack, Sanger spurred research into the use of hormones as one approach to contraception. In 1960, only 6 years before Sanger's death, oral contraception—"the pill"—was finally marketed in the United States. In 1965 the Supreme Court struck down the last impediment to free use of contraception: a law preventing the sale of contraceptives in Connecticut (*Griswold v. Connecticut*, 1965). In 1973 abortion was in effect legalized by the Supreme Court in the case of *Roe v. Wade*, permitting women to terminate unwanted pregnancies.

Today, contraceptives are advertised in popular magazines and sold through vending machines in college dormitories. U.S. history is not a one-way road to unrestricted use of birth control, however. Recent Supreme Court decisions have set aside bits and pieces of *Roe v. Wade,* giving the states more discretion over the regulation of abortion and restricting access to abortions for minors. Use of **artificial contraception** continues to be opposed by many groups, including the Roman Catholic Church. Yet many individual Catholics, including many priests, hold liberal attitudes toward contraception.

Methods of Contraception

There are many methods of contraception, including oral contraceptives (the pill), Norplant, intrauterine devices (IUDs), diaphragms, cervical caps, spermicides, condoms, douching, withdrawal (*coitus interruptus*), timing of ovulation (rhythm), and some devices under development.

Oral Contraceptives ("The Pill")

Question: What is "the pill"? An **oral contraceptive** is commonly referred to as a birth-control pill or simply as "the pill." However, there are many kinds of birth-control pills that vary in the type and dosages of hormones they contain. Birth-control pills fall into two major categories: combination pills and minipills.

Combination pills (such as Ortho-Novum, Ovcon, and Loestrin) contain a combination of synthetic forms of the hormones estrogen and progesterone (progestin). Most combination pills provide a steady dose of synthetic estrogen and progesterone. Other combination pills, called *multiphasic* pills, vary the dosage of these hormones across the menstrual cycle to reduce the overall dosages to which the woman is exposed and possible side effects. The **minipill** contains synthetic progesterone (progestin) only.

Artificial contraception A method of contraception that applies a human-made device.

Oral contraceptive A contraceptive, consisting of sex hormones, that is taken by mouth.

Combination pill A birth-control pill that contains synthetic estrogen and progesterone.

Minipill A birth-control pill that contains synthetic progesterone but no estrogen.

Available only by prescription, oral contraceptives are used by more than one quarter of women in the United States who use reversible (nonsterilization) forms of contraception (Angier, 1993a). Birth-control pills are the most popular forms of contraception among single women of reproductive age (Gilbert, 1996).

How They Work Women cannot conceive when they are already pregnant because their bodies suppress maturation of egg follicles and ovulation. The combination pill fools the brain into acting as though the woman were already pregnant, so that no additional ova mature or are released. If ovulation does not take place, a woman cannot become pregnant.

In a normal menstrual cycle, low levels of estrogen during and just after the menstrual phase stimulate the pituitary gland to secrete FSH, which in turn stimulates the maturation of ovarian follicles. The estrogen in the combination pill inhibits FSH production, so follicles do not mature. The progesterone (progestin) inhibits the pituitary's secretion of LH, which would otherwise lead to ovulation. The woman continues to have menstrual periods, but there is no unfertilized ovum to be sloughed off in the menstrual flow.

The combination pill is taken for 21 days of the typical 28-day cycle. Then, for 7 days, the woman takes either no pill at all or an inert placebo pill to maintain the habit of taking a pill a day. The sudden drop in hormone levels causes the endometrium to disintegrate and menstruation to follow 3 or 4 days after the last pill has been taken. Then the cycle is repeated.

The progestin in the combination pill also increases the thickness and acidity of the cervical mucus. The mucus thus becomes a more resistant barrier to sperm and inhibits development of the endometrium. Therefore, even if an egg were somehow to mature and become fertilized in a fallopian tube, sperm would not be likely to survive the passage through the cervix. Even if sperm were somehow to succeed in fertilizing an egg, the failure of the endometrium to develop would mean that the fertilized ovum could not become implanted in the uterus. Progestin may also impede the progress of ova through the fallopian tubes and make it more difficult for sperm to penetrate ova.

The minipill contains progestin but no estrogen. Minipills are taken daily through the menstrual cycle, even during menstruation. They act in two ways. They thicken the cervical mucus to impede the passage of sperm through the cervix, and they render the inner lining of the uterus less receptive to a fertilized egg. Thus, even if the woman does conceive, the fertilized egg will pass from the body rather than becoming implanted in the uterine wall. It contains no estrogen, so the minipill does not usually prevent ovulation. The combination pill, by contrast, works directly to prevent ovulation. Because ovulation and fertilization may occur in women who use the minipill, some people see use of the minipill as an early abortion method. Others reserve the term *abortion* for methods of terminating pregnancy after successful implantation has occurred.

Effectiveness of Birth-Control Pills The failure rate associated with perfect use of the birth-control pill is very low—0.5% or less, depending on the type of pill (see Table 12.1). The failure rate increases to 3% in typical use. Failures can occur when women forget to take the pill for 2 days or more, when they do not use backup methods when they first go on the pill, and when they switch from one brand to another. But forgetting to take the pill even for a single day may alter the woman's hormonal balance, allowing ovulation—and fertilization.

Reversibility Use of oral contraceptives may temporarily reduce fertility after they are discontinued but is not associated with permanent infertility. Nine of 10 women begin ovulating regularly within 3 months of suspending use (Reinisch, 1990). Users of the pill who frequently start and stop usage may later incur fertility problems, however (Reinisch, 1990). When a woman appears not to be ovulating after going off the pill, a drug such as clomiphene is often used to induce ovulation.

Advantages and Disadvantages The great advantage of oral contraception is that when used properly, it is nearly 100% effective. Unlike many other forms of contraception, such as the condom or diaphragm, its use does not interfere with sexual spontaneity or diminish sexual sensations. The sex act need not be interrupted, as it would be by use of a condom.

Birth-control pills may also have some *healthful* side effects. They appear to reduce the risk of pelvic inflammatory disease (PID), benign ovarian cysts, and fibrocystic (benign) breast growths. The pill regularizes menstrual cycles and reduces menstrual cramping and premenstrual discomfort. The pill may also be helpful in the treatment of iron-deficiency anemia and facial acne. The combination pill reduces the risks of ovarian and endometrial cancer, even for a number of years after the woman has stopped taking it (Gnagy et al., 2000; Hatcher, 2001; Narod et al., 1998). The pill's protective effects against ovarian cancer increase with the length of use (Gnagy et al., 2000).

The pill does have some disadvantages. The pill provides no protection against STIs. Moreover, it may reduce the effectiveness of antibiotics used to treat STIs. Going on the pill requires medical consultation, so a woman must plan to begin using the pill at least several weeks before becoming sexually active or before discontinuing the use of other contraceptives and must incur the expense of medical visits. Polly A. Marchbanks and her colleagues (2002) compared 4,575 women with breast cancer with 4,682 controls and found no increased risk for breast cancer among women who were using or had used oral contraceptives. Moreover, the pill did not increase the risk of breast cancer in women with a family history of the disorder.

The main drawbacks of birth-control pills are potential side effects and possible health risks. Although there is a good deal of research that suggests that the pill is safe for healthy women, in 2000 the American College of Obstetricians and Gynecologists released a bulletin suggesting caution in women with various preexisting medical conditions. These include hypertension, diabetes, migraine headaches, fibrocystic breast tissue, uterine fibroids, and elevated cholesterol level (Voelker, 2000).

The estrogen in combination pills may produce side effects such as nausea and vomiting, fluid retention (feeling bloated), weight gain, increased vaginal discharge, headaches, tenderness in the breasts, and dizziness. Many of these side effects are temporary. When they persist, women may be switched from one pill to another, perhaps to one with lower doses of hormones. Pregnant women produce high estrogen levels in the corpus luteum and placenta. The combination pill artificially raises levels of estrogen, so it is not surprising that some women who use it have side effects that mimic the early signs of pregnancy, such as weight gain or nausea ("morning sickness"). Weight gain can result from estrogen (through fluid retention) or progestin (through increased appetite and development of muscle). Oral contraceptives may also increase blood pressure in some women, but clinically significant elevations are rare in women using the low-dose pills that are available today (Hatcher, 2001). Still, it is wise for women who use the pill to have their blood pressure checked regularly. Women who encounter problems with high blood pressure from taking the pill are usually advised to switch to another form of contraception.

Many women who use oral contraceptives experience hormone withdrawal symptoms during times when they do not take the pill (Sulak et al., 2000). These include headaches, pelvic pain, bloating, and breast tenderness.

Many women have avoided using the pill because of the risk of blood clots. The lower dosages of estrogen found in most types of birth-control pills on the market today are associated with much lower risk of blood clots than was the case in the 1960s and 1970s, when higher dosages were used (Gilbert, 1996). Still, women who are at increased risk for blood clotting, such as women with a history of circulatory problems or stroke, are typically advised not to use the pill.

Women who are considering using the pill need to discuss the benefits and risks with their health care providers. For the great majority of young, healthy women in their 20s and early 30s, the pill is unlikely to cause blood clots or other cardiovascular problems (Hatcher, 2001). Although research has found the pill to be safe for most women who do not smoke and are younger than 35, pill users may have a slightly higher chance than nonusers of developing blood clots in the veins and lungs, stroke, and heart attack (Rako, 2003).

Some women should not be on the pill at all (Calderone & Johnson, 1989; Hatcher, 2001; Reinisch, 1990). These include women who have had circulatory problems or blood clots and those who have suffered a heart attack or stroke or have a history of coronary disease, breast or uterine cancer, undiagnosed genital bleeding, liver tumors, or sickle-cell anemia (because of associated blood-clotting problems). Because of their increased risk of cardiovascular problems, caution should be exercised when the combination pill is used with women over 35 years of age who smoke (Hatcher, 2001). Nursing mothers should also avoid using the pill; the hormones may be passed to the baby in the mother's milk.

Because the risks of cardiovascular complications generally increase with age, many women over the age of 35 have been encouraged by their gynecologists to use other forms of birth control. However, the American College of Obstetricians and Gynecologists believes that healthy nonsmokers can use oral contraceptives safely at least until the age of 45.

The pill may also have psychological effects. Some users report depression or irritability. Switching brands or altering doses may help. Evidence is lacking concerning the effects of lower-estrogen pills on sexual desire.

Progestin fosters male secondary sex characteristics, so women who take the minipill may develop acne, facial hair, thinning of scalp hair, reduction in breast size, vaginal dryness, and missed or shorter periods. Irregular bleeding, or so-called breakthrough bleeding, between menstrual periods is a common side effect of the minipill. Irregular bleeding should be brought to the attention of a health professional. Because they can produce vaginal dryness, minipills can hinder vaginal lubrication during intercourse, decreasing sexual sensations and rendering sex painful.

Researchers have also examined suspected links between use of the pill and certain forms of cancer, especially breast cancer, because breast cancer is sensitive to hormonal changes. Results from several large-scale studies show no overall increase in the rates of breast cancer among pill users, but it is possible that some subgroups of women who use the pill may be at increased risk (Hatcher, 2001). The evidence linking use of the pill with increased risk of cervical cancer is mixed, some studies show such a link and others show none (Hatcher, 2001).

Women considering the pill are advised to have a thorough medical evaluation to rule out preexisting conditions that might make its use unsafe. The evaluation should include a detailed medical and family history, and a physical exam including a Pap smear, assessment of blood pressure, screening for STIs, urinalysis, breast and pelvic exams, and possibly an EKG (electrocardiogram). Women who begin to use the pill, regardless of their age or risk status, should pay attention to changes in their physical condition, have regular checkups, and promptly report any physical complaints or unusual symptoms to their physicians.

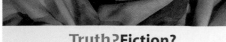

"Morning-After" Pills The term *morning-after pill,* or postcoital contraceptive, actually refers to several types of pills that have high doses of estrogen and progestin. Because they are not taken regularly, they do not prevent ovulation from occurring. Instead, they stop fertilization from taking place or prevent the fertilized egg from implanting itself in the uterus. In that respect, then, they represent an early abortion technique. However, 65% of the respondents in a national poll taken by *The New York Times* said they would consider morning-after pills a form of birth control; fewer than 20% considered them an abortion method (Goldberg & Elder, 1998).

Morning-after pills are most effective when taken within 72 hours after ovulation. Women who wait to see whether they have missed a period are no longer candidates for the morning-after pill. Depending on the brand, four, six, or eight pills are prescribed.

Question: What is the morning-after pill? Morning-after pills have a higher hormone content than most birth-control pills. For this reason, nausea is a common side effect, occurring in perhaps 70% of users. Nausea is usually mild and passes within a day or two after treatment, but it can be treated with antinausea medication (Hatcher, 2001).

Morning-after pills are certainly not recommended as a regular form of birth control. They are *one-time* forms of emergency protection (Hatcher, 2001), which may be most appropriate to use following rape or when regular contraceptive devices fail (for example, if a condom breaks or a diaphragm becomes dislodged). The morning-after pill generally prevents implantation of a zygote, but health professionals caution that when it fails, the fetus may be damaged by exposure to the hormones that the pill contains.

Norplant

Question: What is Norplant? The contraceptive implant *Norplant* consists of six matchstick-sized silicone tubes that contain progestin and are surgically embedded in a woman's upper arm. More than 1 million women in the United States used Norplant after its approval by the FDA, but it was taken off the market in 2002 because it was associated with unpredictable bleeding and other problems (Berger, 2002). Norplant, like the pill, relied on female sex hormones to suppress fertility. But rather than the woman taking a pill once a day, tubes implanted in her body released a small, steady dose of progestin into her bloodstream, providing continuous contraceptive protection for as long as 5 years (Hatcher, 2001). The progestin in the Norplant system suppressed ovulation and thickened the cervical mucus so that sperm could not pass.

Intrauterine Devices (IUDs)

Camel drivers setting out on long desert journeys once placed round stones in the uteruses of female camels to prevent them from becoming pregnant and lost to service. The stones may have acted as primitive **intrauterine devices (IUDs)**. *Question: What is the IUD?* IUDs are small objects of various shapes that are inserted into the uterus. IUDs have been used by humans since Greek times. Today, they are inserted into the uterus by a physician or nurse practitioner and are usually left in place for a year or more. Fine plastic threads or strings hang down from the IUD into the vagina, so that the woman can check to see that it remains in place.

IUDs are used by about 2 million women in the United States and by more than 100 million women around the world (Hatcher, 2001). Most of them live in China,

Intrauterine device (IUD) A small object that is inserted into the uterus and left in place to prevent conception.

where nearly 1 in 3 married women uses an IUD during her childbearing years. By contrast, IUDs are used by only about 3% of women in committed relationships in the United States. American women in committed relationships are more than twice as likely as single women to use an IUD (Hatcher, 2001).

IUDs achieved their greatest popularity in the United States in the 1960s and 1970s. Then there was a sharp decline in their use during the 1980s after a popular model, the Dalkon Shield, was linked to a high incidence of pelvic infections and tubal infertility (Hatcher, 2001).

Figure 12.1 shows two IUDs: the Progestasert T, which releases small quantities of progesterone (progestin) daily, and the Copper T 380A (ParaGard), a T-shaped, copper-based device. Because the Progestasert T must be replaced annually, and any insertion carries some risk of infection, health authorities recommend the use of the ParaGard device, which can be used for upwards of 8 years, unless the woman is allergic to copper (Hatcher, 2001).

How They Work We do not know exactly how IUDs work. A foreign body, such as the IUD, apparently irritates the uterine lining. This irritation gives rise to mild inflammation and to the production of antibodies that may be toxic to sperm or fertilized ova and/or may prevent fertilized eggs from becoming implanted. Inflammation may also impair proliferation of the endometrium—another impediment to implantation. Progestin released by the Progestasert T also has effects like the progestin-only minipill: It lessens the likelihood of fertilization and implantation. Action on fertilized ova may be considered to constitute an early abortion. Because IUDs may not prevent fertilization, people who oppose abortion, regardless of how soon it occurs after conception, also oppose the IUD.

Effectiveness The failure rate associated with typical use of the Progestasert T is about 2% (see Table 12.1). Most failures occur within 3 months of insertion, often because the device shifts position or is expelled. ParaGard is the most effective IUD. The first-year failure rate in typical use is 0.8%.

The IUD may irritate the muscular layer of the utcrine wall, causing contractions that expel it through the vagina. The device is most likely to be expelled during

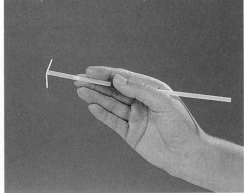

Figure 12.1. Two IUDs: The Progestasert T and the Copper T 380A (ParaGard). The Progestasert T releases small quantities of progesterone (progestin) daily. The Copper T 380A is a T-shaped, copper-based device.

menstruation, so users are advised to check their sanitary napkins or tampons before discarding them. Women who use IUDs are advised to check the string several times a month to ensure that the IUD is in place. Spontaneous expulsions occur in 2% to 10% of users within the first year of use (Hatcher, 2001). Women who have not borne children have a higher expulsion rate (about 7%) than women who have (3%). Some family-planning clinics advise women to supplement their use of IUDs with other devices for the first 3 months, when the risks of a shift in position or expulsion are greatest.

Anti-inflammatory drugs, such as aspirin, and antibiotics may also decrease IUD effectiveness. Because many physicians recommend an aspirin every other day as a way of helping prevent certain kinds of cancer (Marcus, 1995), women are advised to discuss these issues with their gynecologists.

Reversibility IUDs may be removed readily by professionals. Nine out of 10 former IUD users who wish to do so become pregnant within a year (Hatcher, 2001).

Advantages and Disadvantages The IUD has three major advantages: (1) It is highly effective; (2) it does not diminish sexual spontaneity or sexual sensations; and (3) once it is in place, the woman need not do anything more to prevent pregnancy (other than checking that it remains in place). The small risk of failure is reduced in effect to zero if the couple also use an additional form of birth control, such as the diaphragm or condom.

The IUD also does not interfere with the woman's normal hormonal production. Users continue to produce pituitary hormones that stimulate ovarian follicles to mature and rupture, thereby releasing mature ova and producing female sex hormones.

If IUDs are so effective and relatively "maintenance-free," why are they not more popular? One reason is that insertion can be painful. Another reason is side effects. The most common side effects are excessive menstrual cramping, irregular bleeding (spotting) between periods, and heavier than usual menstrual bleeding (Hatcher, 2001). These side effects generally occur shortly following insertion and are among the primary reasons why women ask to have the device removed. A more serious concern is the possible risk of pelvic inflammatory disease (PID), a serious disease that can become life threatening if left untreated (Hatcher, 2001). Women who use the IUD may have an increased risk of PID (Hatcher, 2001). The risk of infection is associated more with the insertion of the device (bacteria may enter the woman's reproductive tract during insertion) than with use of the device itself.

PID can produce scar tissue that blocks the fallopian tubes, causing infertility. Women with pelvic infections should not use an IUD (Hatcher, 2001). Women who have risk factors for PID may also wish to consider the advisability of an IUD. Risk factors include a recent episode of gonorrhea or chlamydia, recurrent episodes of these STIs, sexual contact with multiple partners, and sexual contact with a partner who has had multiple sexual partners. All in all, the IUD may be best suited to women who have completed their families and are advised not to use oral contraceptives.

Another risk in using an IUD is that the device may perforate (tear) the uterine or cervical walls, which can cause bleeding, pain, and adhesions and can become life threatening. Perforations are usually caused by improper insertion and occur in perhaps 1 case in 1,000 (Reinisch, 1990). IUD users are also at greater risk for ectopic pregnancies, both during and after usage, and for miscarriage. Ectopic pregnancies occur in about 5% of women who become pregnant while using an IUD (Hatcher, 2001). IUD use is not recommended for women with a history of ectopic pregnancy. Women who become pregnant while using the IUD stand about a 50–50 chance of miscarriage (Hatcher, 2001).

Despite the fact that the IUD irritates uterine tissues, there is no evidence that IUD users run a greater risk of cancer. Long-term data on the health effects of IUD use are limited, however.

Another drawback to the IUD is its cost. The typical cost of an IUD insertion in a family-planning clinic is a few hundred dollars. Potential expulsion of the IUD presents yet another disadvantage. Moreover, the IUD, like the pill, offers no protection against STIs. Finally, like the pill, IUDs place the burden of contraception entirely on the woman.

The Diaphragm

Diaphragms were once used by about one third of U.S. couples who practiced birth control. When invented in 1882, they were a breakthrough. Their popularity declined only in the 1960s with the advent of the pill and the IUD. Today, fewer than 5% of women in committed relationships use the diaphragm (Hatcher, 2001).

Question: What is the diaphragm? The diaphragm is a shallow cup or dome made of thin latex rubber (see Figure 12.2). The rim is a flexible metal ring covered with rubber. Diaphragms come in different sizes to allow a precise fit.

Diaphragms are available by prescription and must be fitted to the contour of the vagina by a health professional. Several sizes and types of diaphragms may be tried during a fitting. Women practice insertion in a health professional's office so that they can be guided as needed.

How It Works The diaphragm is inserted and removed by the woman, much like a tampon. It is akin to a condom in that it forms a barrier against sperm when placed snugly over the cervical opening. Yet it is unreliable as a barrier alone. Thus, the diaphragm should be used in conjunction with a spermicidal cream or jelly. The diaphragm's main function is to keep the spermicide in place.

How It Is Used The diaphragm should be inserted no more than 2 hours before coitus, because the spermicides that are used may begin to lose effectiveness beyond this time. Some health professionals, however, suggest that the diaphragm may be inserted up to 6 hours preceding intercourse. (It seems reasonable to err on the side of caution and assume that there is a 2-hour time limit.) The woman or her partner places a tablespoonful of spermicidal cream or jelly on the inside of the cup and spreads it inside the rim. (Cream spread outside the rim might cause the diaphragm to slip.) The woman opens the inner lips of the vagina with one hand and folds the diaphragm with the other by squeezing the ring. She inserts the diaphragm against the cervix, with the inner side facing upward (see Figure 12.3). Her partner can help insert the diaphragm, but the woman is advised to check its placement. Some women prefer a plastic insertion device, but most find it easier to insert the diaphragm without it. The diaphragm should be left in place *at least 6 hours* to allow the spermicide to kill sperm remaining in the vagina (Hatcher, 2001). It should not be left in place for longer than 24 hours, to guard against toxic shock syndrome (TSS).

After use, the diaphragm should be washed with mild soap and warm water and stored in a dry, cool place. When cared for properly, a diaphragm can last about 2 years. Women may need to be refitted after pregnancy or after a change in weight of about 10 pounds or more.

Effectiveness If it is used consistently and correctly, the failure rate of the diaphragm is estimated to be 6% during the first year of use (see Table 12.1). In typical use, however, the failure rate is believed to be three times as high—18%. Some women become pregnant because they do not use the diaphragm during every coital experience. Others may insert it too early or not leave it in long enough. The diaphragm

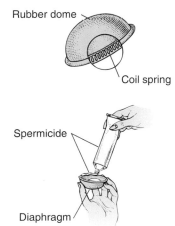

Rubber dome

Coil spring

Spermicide

Diaphragm

Figure 12.2 A Diaphragm. The diaphragm is a shallow cup or dome made of latex. Diaphragms must be fitted to the contour of the vagina by a health professional. The diaphragm forms a barrier to sperm but should be used in conjunction with a spermicidal cream or jelly.

Diaphragm A shallow rubber cup or dome, fitted to the contour of a woman's vagina, that is coated with a spermicide and inserted prior to coitus to prevent conception.

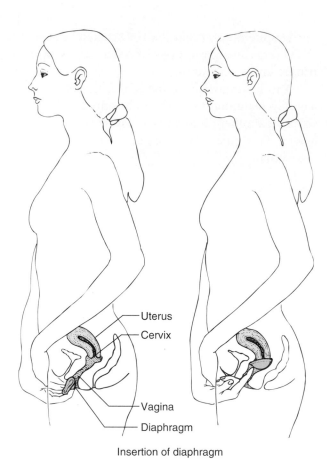

— Uterus
— Cervix
— Vagina
— Diaphragm

Insertion of diaphragm

Figure 12.3. Insertion and Checking of the Diaphragm. *Women are instructed in insertion of the diaphragm by a health professional. In practice, a woman and her partner may find joint insertion an erotic experience.*

may not fit well, or it may slip—especially if the couple is acrobatic. A diaphragm may develop tiny holes or cracks. Women are advised to inspect the diaphragm for signs of wear and to consult their health professionals when in doubt. Effectiveness also is seriously compromised when the diaphragm is not used along with a correctly applied spermicide.

Reversibility The effects of the diaphragm are fully reversible. In order to become pregnant, the woman simply stops using it. The diaphragm has not been shown to influence subsequent fertility.

Advantages and Disadvantages The major advantage of the diaphragm is that when used correctly, it is a safe and effective means of birth control and does not alter the woman's hormone production or reproductive cycle. The diaphragm can be used as needed, whereas the pill must be used daily and the IUD remains in place whether or not the woman engages in coitus. Another advantage is the virtual absence of side effects. The few women who are allergic to the rubber in the diaphragm can switch to a plastic model.

The major disadvantage is the high pregnancy rate associated with typical use. Nearly 1 in 5 typical users (18%) of the diaphragm combined with spermicidal cream or jelly becomes pregnant during the first year of use (Hatcher, 2001). Another disadvantage is the need to insert the diaphragm prior to intercourse, which the couple may find disruptive. The woman's partner may find the taste of the spermicides used in conjunction with the diaphragm to be unpleasant during oral sex. The pressure exerted by the diaphragm against the vaginal and cervical walls may also irritate the urinary tract and cause urinary or even vaginal infections. Switching to a different size diaphragm or one with a different type of rim may help alleviate this problem. About 1 woman or man in 20 may develop allergies to the particular spermicide that is used, which can lead to irritation of the genitals. This problem may also be alleviated by switching to another brand.

Spermicides

Question: What are spermicides? Spermicides are agents that kill sperm. They come in different forms, including jellies and creams, suppositories, aerosol foam, and a contraceptive film. Spermicides should be left in place in the vagina (no douching) for several hours after coitus (Hatcher, 2001).

How They Are Used Spermicidal jellies, creams, foam, and suppositories should be used no more than 60 minutes preceding coitus to provide for maximum effectiveness (Cates & Raymond, 1998). Spermicidal jellies and creams come in tubes with plastic applicators that introduce the spermicide into the vagina (see Figure 12.4). Spermicidal foam is a fluffy white cream with the consistency of shaving cream. It is contained in a pressurized can and is introduced with a plastic applicator in much the same way as spermicidal jellies and creams.

Vaginal suppositories are inserted into the upper vagina, near the cervix, where they release spermicide as they dissolve. Unlike spermicidal jellies, creams, and foam, which become effective immediately when applied, suppositories must be inserted no less than 10 to 15 minutes before coitus so that they have sufficient time to dissolve (Hatcher, 2001).

Spermicidal film consists of thin, 2-inch-square sheets that are saturated with spermicide. When placed in the vagina, they dissolve into a gel and release the spermicide. The spermicidal film should be inserted at least 5 minutes before intercourse to allow time for it to melt and for the spermicide to be dispersed. It remains effective for upwards of 1 hour. Some users have noted that the film has a tendency to adhere to the fingertips, which makes it difficult to insert correctly.

How They Work Spermicides coat the cervical opening, blocking the passage of sperm and killing sperm by chemical action.

Effectiveness In typical use, the first-year failure rate of spermicides used alone is 21 pregnancies per year per 100 users (Hatcher, 2001). When used correctly and consistently, the failure rate is estimated to drop to about 6 pregnancies per 100 users in the first year. All forms of spermicide are more effective when they are combined with other forms of contraception, such as the condom.

Reversibility Spermicides have not been linked with any changes in reproductive potential. Couples who wish to become pregnant simply stop using them.

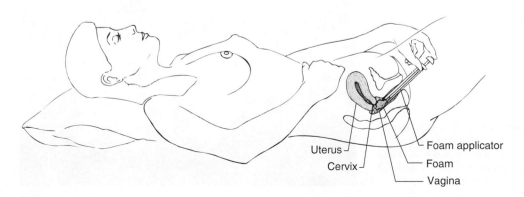

Uterus
Cervix
Foam applicator
Foam
Vagina

Figure 12.4. The Application of Spermicidal Foam. Spermicidal jellies and creams come in tubes with plastic applicators. Spermicidal foam comes in a pressurized can and is applied with a plastic applicator in much the same way as spermicidal jellies and creams.

Advantages and Disadvantages The major advantages of spermicides are that they do not alter the woman's natural biological processes and that they are applied only as needed. Unlike a diaphragm, they do not require a doctor's prescription or a fitting. They can be bought in virtually any drugstore, and the average cost per use of the foam variety is modest—about 50 cents.

The major disadvantage is the high failure rate among typical users. Foam often fails when the can is not shaken enough, when too little is used, when it is not applied deeply enough within the vagina near the cervix, or when it is used after coitus has begun.

Spermicides are generally free of side effects but occasionally cause vaginal or penile irritation. Irritation is sometimes alleviated by changing brands. Some partners find the taste of spermicides unpleasant. (Couples can engage in oral sex before applying spermicides.) Spermicides may pose a danger to an embryo, so women who suspect that they are pregnant are advised to suspend use until they find out for certain.

It was once thought that spermicides that contain nonoxynol-9 might provide some protection against STIs such as HIV/AIDS, genital herpes, trichomoniasis ("trich"), syphilis, and chlamydia. Yet a controlled experiment in Africa did not find that nonoxynol-9 afforded any protection against disease-causing agents (Roddy et al., 1998). Further research suggests that nonoxynol-9 is actually harmful as a **microbicide** (Perriëns, 2000). (Microbicides are chemical substances that kill viruses and bacteria. They are applied vaginally or rectally prior to sexual intercourse in the form of gels, creams, suppositories, or films. Any number of chemicals will kill viruses and bacteria; the challenge is to develop agents that will kill the microbes without harming the person using them.) UNAIDS oversaw a trial of the effectiveness of the spermicide as a means of preventing HIV infection among African and Thai prostitutes. It turned out that the group using nonoxynol-9 actually had a significantly *higher* rate of HIV infection (15%) than the group using the placebo (10%) (Stephenson, 2000b). Joseph Perriëns (2000), head of the UNAIDS microbicide effort, suggested that the local ulceration (irritation) caused by nonoxynol-9 might have made the vaginal tract an easier port of entry for HIV.

The Contraceptive Sponge

Microbicide A chemical substance that kills viruses and bacteria.

The contraceptive sponge (brand name: Today) was taken off the market by the manufacturer in 1995 because FDA inspectors had found some problems in production, including bacterial contamination. The manufacturer decided that it would be too costly to modify procedures to meet FDA objections.

Is He "Spongeworthy"? In the TV series Seinfeld, *Elaine learned that her favorite contraceptive device, the contraceptive sponge, was going off the market. She bought up as many as she could and then, in view of her limited supply, considered whether a potential lover was "spongeworthy."*

In 1995 the sponge made something of a splash on the *Seinfeld* TV show. The character Elaine, learning that her favorite method of contraception was going off the market, scavenged to buy as many as she could. Then, with her limited supply, she decided whether a beau was "spongeworthy."

As of this writing, the contraceptive sponge may be making some sort of comeback. It is available in Canada and possibly over the Internet. Before using it, we strongly recommend checking with your gynecologist.

Question: What is the contraceptive sponge? The contraceptive sponge is a soft, disposable device. Unlike the diaphragm, the sponge does not need to be fitted. Like the diaphragm, it provides a barrier that holds a spermicide, but the spermicide is built in. The sponge can also be inserted into the vagina several hours before coitus and has the additional advantage of absorbing sperm. It is odorless and tasteless, and users found it less drippy than the diaphragm. On the negative side, about 1 user in 20 (male and female) is mildly irritated by the spermicide. There is also a remote chance of toxic shock syndrome (TSS): 1 case arose for every 4 *million* days of use.

The Cervical Cap

Question: What is the cervical cap? The cervical cap, like the diaphragm, is a dome-shaped rubber cup. It comes in different sizes and must be fitted by a health professional. It is smaller than the diaphragm, however—about the size of a thimble—and is meant to fit snugly over the cervical opening.

How It Is Used Like the diaphragm, the cap is intended to be used with a spermicide applied inside it. When inserting it, the woman (or her partner) fills the cap about a third full of spermicide. Then, squeezing the edges together, the woman inserts the cap high in the vagina, so that it presses firmly against the cervix. The woman can test the fit by running a finger around the cap to ensure that the cervical opening is covered. It should be left in place for at least 8 hours after intercourse. The cap provides continuous protection for upwards of 48 hours without the need for additional spermicide. To reduce the risk of toxic shock syndrome, the cap should not be left in place longer than 48 hours. Like the diaphragm, the cap should be cleaned after use and checked for wear and tear. When cared for properly, the cap should last for upwards of 3 years.

How It Works Like the diaphragm, the cervical cap forms a barrier and also holds spermicide in place against the cervix. It prevents sperm from passing into the uterus and fallopian tubes and kills sperm by chemical action.

Effectiveness The failure rate in typical use is estimated to be high, ranging from 18% in women who have not borne children to 36% in women who have (Hatcher, 2001). Failures may be attributed, at least in part, to the cap's becoming dislodged and to changes in the cervix during the menstrual cycle, which can cause the cap to fit less snugly over it.

Reversibility There is no evidence that the cervical cap affects fertility.

Advantages and Disadvantages Like the diaphragm, the cap is a mechanical device that does not affect the woman's hormonal production or reproductive cycle. The cap may be especially suited to women who cannot support a diaphragm because of lack of vaginal muscle tone. Because of concern that the cap may irritate cervical tissue, however, users are advised to have regular Pap tests.

Some women find the cap uncomfortable. The cap can also become dislodged during sexual activity or lose its fit as the cervix changes over the menstrual cycle. Side effects include urinary tract infections and allergic reactions or sensitivities to the rubber or spermicide. Other disadvantages include the expense and inconvenience of being fitted by a health professional. Moreover, some women are shaped so that the cap does not remain in place. For these reasons, and because they may be hard to obtain, cervical caps are not very popular in the United States.

Condoms

Question: What are condoms? Condoms are also called "rubbers," "safes," **prophylactics** (because latex condoms protect against STIs), and "skins" (referring to those that are made from lamb intestines). Condoms lost popularity with the advent of the pill and the IUD. They are less effective than the pill or IUD, may disrupt sexual spontaneity, and can decrease coital sensations because they prevent the penis from actually touching the vaginal wall.

Condoms have been making a comeback, however, because those made of latex rubber can help prevent the spread of HIV/AIDS and other STIs and, to a lesser extent, because of concerns about side effects of the pill and the IUD. Largely because of concerns about HIV/AIDS and other STIs, the use of condoms among single women has mushroomed.

Condom advertisements have appeared in mainstream media, including magazines such as *People* and *Cosmopolitan,* and on major TV networks. In one TV commercial, a man and a woman are shown hurriedly undressing. The man tells the woman that he forgot to bring a condom with him. She then tells him that he'd best forget it (making love, that is). Whether the media campaign will increase condom usage remains to be seen.

The renewed popularity of condoms has also been spurred by the increased assertiveness of contemporary women. They make the point (which should be obvious, but all too often is not) that contraception is as much the man's responsibility as the woman's. Condoms alter the psychology of sexual relations. By using a condom, the man assumes much of the responsibility for contraception. Condoms are the only contraceptive device worn by men and the only readily reversible method of contraception that is available to them. Condoms are inexpensive and can be obtained without prescription from pharmacies, family-planning clinics, rest rooms, and even vending machines in some college dormitories.

Some condoms are made of latex rubber. Thinner, more expensive condoms ("skins") are made from the intestinal membranes of lambs. The latter allow greater sexual sensation but do not protect as well against STIs. Only latex condoms are effective against HIV (the AIDS virus). Condoms made of animal intestines have pores large enough to permit HIV and other viruses, such as the one that causes hepatitis B, to pass through (Hatcher, 2001). A few condoms are made from other materials, such as plastic (polyurethane). Questions remain about the effectiveness of polyurethane condoms. Some condoms have plain ends. Others have nipples, or reservoirs (see Figure 12.5), that catch semen and may help prevent the condom from bursting during ejaculation.

How They Work A condom is a cylindrical sheath that serves as a barrier, preventing the passage of sperm and disease-carrying microorganisms from the man to his partner. It also helps prevent infected vaginal fluids (and microorganisms) from entering the man's urethral opening or penetrating through small cracks in the skin of the penis.

How They Are Used The condom is rolled onto the penis once erection is achieved and before contact between the penis and the vagina (see Figure 12.6). If the condom is *not* used until moments before the point of ejaculation, sperm-carrying fluid from the Cowper's glands or from preorgasmic spasms may already have passed into

Prophylactic An agent that protects against disease.

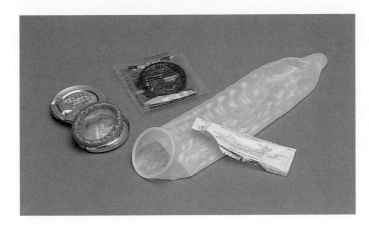

Figure 12.5. Condoms. Some condoms are plain-tipped, whereas others have nipples or reservoirs that catch semen and may help prevent the condom from bursting during ejaculation. Latex condoms form effective barriers to HIV (the tiny AIDS virus).

the vagina. Nor does the condom afford protection against STIs if it is fitted after penetration.

Condoms sometimes fall off or break. Between 1% and 2% of condoms break or fall off during intercourse or when the man is withdrawing the penis afterward (Hatcher, 2001). Condoms also sometimes slip down the shaft of the penis without falling off. To use a condom most effectively and to help prevent it from either breaking or falling off, a couple should observe the following guidelines:[1]

- Use a condom each and every time you have intercourse. Inexperienced users should also practice putting on a condom before they have occasion to use one with a partner.
- Handle the condom carefully, making sure not to damage it with your fingernail, teeth, or sharp objects.
- Place the condom on the erect penis before it touches the vulva.
- Uncircumcised men should pull back the foreskin before putting on the condom.
- If you use a spermicide, place some inside the tip of the condom before placing the condom on the penis. You may also wish to use additional spermicide applied by an applicator inside the vagina to provide extra protection, just in case the condom breaks.
- Do not pull the condom tightly against the tip of the penis.
- For a condom without a reservoir tip, leave a small empty space—about a half-inch—at the end of the condom to hold semen, yet do not allow any air to be trapped at the tip. Some condoms come equipped with a reservoir (nipple) tip that will hold semen.
- Unroll the condom all the way to the bottom of the penis.
- Ensure that adequate vaginal lubrication during intercourse is present, using lubricants if necessary. But use only water-based lubricants such as contraceptive jelly or K-Y jelly. Never use an oil-based lubricant that can weaken the latex material, such as petroleum jelly (Vaseline), cold cream, baby oil or lotion, mineral oil, massage oil, vegetable oil, Crisco, hand or body lotions, and most skin creams. Do not use saliva as a lubricant because it may contain infectious organisms, such as viruses.
- If the condom breaks during intercourse, withdraw the penis immediately, put on a new condom, and use more spermicide.
- After ejaculation, carefully withdraw the penis while it is still erect.

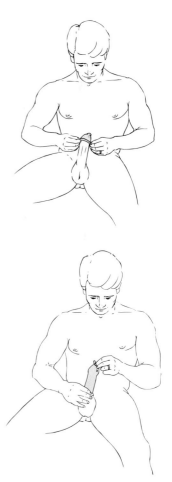

Figure 12.6. Applying a Condom. First the rolled-up condom is placed on the head of the penis, and then it is rolled down the shaft of the penis. If a condom without a reservoir tip is used, a one-half-inch space should be left at the tip for the ejaculate to accumulate.

---

1. Adapted from the Centers for Disease Control pamphlet, *Condoms and sexually transmitted Diseases . . . especially AIDS* (HHS Publication FDA 90-4329) and other sources.

- Hold the rim of the condom firmly against the base of the penis as the penis is withdrawn, to prevent the condom from slipping off.
- Remove the condom carefully from the penis, making sure that semen doesn't leak out.
- Check the removed condom for tears or cracks. If any are found, immediately apply a spermicide containing nonoxynol-9 directly to the penis and within the vagina. Wrap the used condom in a tissue, and discard it in the garbage. (Condoms can be hard to flush down the toilet.) Wash your hands thoroughly with soap and water.

Since condoms can be eroded by exposure to body heat or other sources of heat, they should not be kept for any length of time in a pocket or the glove compartment of a car. Nor should a condom be used more than once. Here are some other things you should *never* do with a condom:

- Never use teeth, scissors, or sharp fingernails to open a package of condoms. Open the condom package carefully to avoid tearing or puncturing the condom.
- Never test a condom by inflating it or stretching it.
- Never use a condom after its expiration date.
- Never use damaged condoms. Condoms that are sticky, gummy, discolored or brittle, that appear otherwise damaged, or that show signs of deterioration should be considered damaged.
- Never use a condom if the sealed packet containing the condom is damaged, cracked, or brittle, because the condom itself may be damaged or defective.
- Do not open the sealed packet until you are ready to use the condom. A condom contained in a packet that has been opened can become dry and brittle within a few hours, causing it to tear more easily. The box that contains the condom packets, however, may be opened at any time.
- Never use the same condom twice. Use a new condom if you switch the site of intercourse, such as from the vagina to the anus, or from the anus to the mouth, during a single sexual act.
- If you want to carry a condom with you, place it in a loose jacket pocket or purse, not in your pants pocket or in a wallet held in your pants pocket, where it might be exposed to body heat.
- Never buy condoms from vending machines that are exposed to extreme heat or placed in direct sunlight.

Effectiveness In typical use, the failure rate of the male condom is estimated at 12% (see Table 12.1). That is, 12 women out of 100 whose partners rely on condoms alone for contraception can expect to become pregnant during the first year of use. This rate drops dramatically if the condom is used correctly and combined with the use of a spermicide (Warner & Hatcher, 1998). The effectiveness of a condom and spermicide combined rivals that of the birth-control pill when used correctly and consistently.

Reversibility The condom is simply a mechanical barrier to sperm and does not compromise fertility. Therefore, a couple who wish to conceive a child simply discontinue its use.

Advantages and Disadvantages Condoms have the advantage of being readily available. They can be purchased without prescription. They require no fitting and can remain in sealed packages until needed. They are readily discarded after use. The combination of condoms and spermicides containing the ingredient nonoxynol-9 increases contraceptive effectiveness. Some condoms contain this spermicidal agent as a lubricant. When in doubt, ask a pharmacist.

Condoms do not affect production of hormones, ova, or sperm. Women whose partners use condoms ovulate normally. Men who use them produce sperm and ejaculate normally. With all these advantages, why are condoms not more popular?

One disadvantage of the condom is that it may render sex less spontaneous. The couple must interrupt lovemaking to apply the condom. Condoms may also lessen sexual sensations, especially for the man. Latex condoms do so more than animal membrane sheaths. Condoms also sometimes slip off or tear, allowing sperm to leak through.

On the other hand, condoms are almost entirely free of side effects. They offer protection against STIs that is unparalleled among contraceptive devices. They can also be used without prior medical consultation. Both partners can share putting on the condom, which makes it an erotic part of their lovemaking, not an intrusion. The use of textured or ultrathin condoms may increase sensitivity, especially for the male. Thus many couples find that the advantages outweigh the disadvantages. Sex in the age of HIV/AIDS has given condoms a new respectability, even a certain trendiness. Note, for example, the new "designer colors" and styles on display at your local pharmacy. Advertisers now also target women in their ads, suggesting that women, like men, can come prepared with condoms.

It is tempting to claim that the condom has a perfect safety record and no side effects. Let us settle for "close to perfect." Some people have allergic reactions to the spermicides with which some lubricated condoms are coated or that the woman may apply. In such cases the couple may need to use a condom without a spermicidal lubricant or stop using supplemental spermicides. Some people are allergic to latex.

Women have an absolute right to insist that their male sex partners wear latex condoms if their partners are not latex-sensitive. STIs such as gonorrhea and chlamydia (see Chapter 16) do far more damage to a woman's reproductive tract than to a man's. Condoms can help protect women from vaginitis, pelvic inflammatory disease (PID), infections that can harm a fetus or cause infertility, and, most important, HIV/AIDS.

Douching

Many couples believe that if a woman **douches** shortly after coitus, she will not become pregnant. *Question: What is douching?* Women who douche for contraceptive purposes often use syringes to flush the vagina with water or a spermicidal agent. The water is intended to wash sperm out; the spermicides, to kill them. Douching is ineffective, however, because large numbers of sperm move beyond the range of the douche seconds after ejaculation. In addition, squirting a liquid into the vagina may even propel sperm *toward* the uterus. Douching, at best, has a failure rate among typical users of 40% (Reinisch, 1990), too high to be considered reliable.

Regular douching may also alter the natural chemistry of the vagina, increasing the risk of vaginal infection. In short, douching is a "nonmethod" of contraception.

Douche To rinse or wash the vaginal canal by inserting a liquid and allowing it to drain out.

The Withdrawal Method (*Coitus Interruptus*)

Question: What is the withdrawal method? In the withdrawal method, the man removes his penis from the vagina before ejaculating. Withdrawal has a first-year failure rate among typical users of about 20% (Kowal, 1998). There are several reasons for these failures. The man may not withdraw in time. Even if the penis is withdrawn just before ejaculation, some ejaculate may still fall on the vaginal lips, and sperm may find their way to the fallopian tubes. Active sperm may also be present in the *pre*-ejaculatory secretions of fluid from the Cowper's glands, a discharge of which the man is usually unaware and cannot control. These sperm are capable of fertilizing an ovum even if the man withdraws before orgasm. Because of its unreliability and high failure rate, withdrawal, like douching, is generally considered a nonmethod of contraception.

Fertility Awareness (Rhythm) Methods

Question: What is the rhythm method? There are actually several rhythm methods, but all of them rely on fertility awareness—that is, awareness of the occurrence of the fertile segments of the woman's menstrual cycle. Terms such as *natural birth control* and *natural family planning* also refer to these methods. The essence of such methods is that coitus is avoided on days when conception is most likely. Fertility awareness methods are used by a small minority of women, more so by women in committed relationships. Because the rhythm method does not employ artificial devices, it is acceptable to the Roman Catholic Church.

How They Work A number of rhythm methods are used to predict the likelihood of conception. They are the mirror images of the methods that couples use to increase their chances of conceiving (see Chapter 11). Methods for enhancing the chances of conception seek to predict time of ovulation so the couple can arrange to have sperm present in the woman's reproductive tract at about that time. As methods of *birth control,* rhythm methods seek to predict ovulation so that the couple can *abstain* from coitus when the woman is fertile.

The Calendar Method The **calendar method** assumes that ovulation occurs 14 days prior to menstruation. The couple abstains from intercourse during the period that begins 3 days prior to day 13 (because sperm are unlikely to survive for more than 72 hours in the female reproductive tract) and ends 2 days after day 15 (because an unfertilized ovum is unlikely to remain receptive to fertilization for longer than 48 hours). The period of abstention thus covers days 10 to 17 of the woman's cycle (Wilcox et al., 2000).

When a woman has regular 28-day cycles, predicting the period of abstention is relatively straightforward. Women with irregular cycles are generally advised to chart their cycles for 10 to 12 months to determine their shortest and longest cycles. The first day of menstruation counts as day 1 of the cycle. The last day of the cycle is the day preceding the onset of menstruation.

Consider a woman whose cycles vary from 23 to 33 days. In theory she will ovulate 14 days before menstruation begins. (To be safe, she should assume that ovulation will take place anywhere from 13 to 15 days before her period.) Applying the rule of "3 days before" and "2 days after," she should avoid coitus from day 5 of her cycle, which corresponds to 3 days before her earliest expected ovulation (computed by subtracting 15 days from the 23 days of her shortest cycle and then subtracting 3 days), through day 22, which corresponds to 2 days after her latest expected ovulation (computed by subtracting 13 days from the 33 days of her longest cycle and then adding 2 days). Another way of determining this period of abstention would be to subtract 18 days from the woman's shortest cycle to determine the start of the "unsafe" period and 11 days from her longest cycle to determine the last "unsafe" day. The woman in the example has irregular cycles. She thus faces an 18-day abstention period each month—quite a burden for a sexually active couple.

Most women who follow the calendar method need to abstain from coitus for at least 10 days during the middle of each cycle. Moreover, the calendar method cannot ensure that the woman's longest or shortest menstrual cycles will occur during the 10- to 12-month period of baseline tracking. Some women, too, have such irregular

Calendar method
A fertility awareness (rhythm) method of contraception that relies on prediction of ovulation by tracking menstrual cycles, typically for a 10- to 12-month period, and assuming that ovulation occurs 14 days prior to menstruation.

cycles that the range of "unsafe" days cannot be predicted reliably even when baseline tracking is extended.

The Basal Body Temperature (BBT) Method In the **basal body temperature (BBT) method**, the woman tracks her body temperature upon awakening each morning to detect the small changes that occur directly before and after ovulation. A woman's basal body temperature sometimes dips slightly just before ovulation and then tends to rise between 0.4°F and 0.8°F just before, during, and after ovulation. It remains elevated until the onset of menstruation. (The rise in temperature is caused by the increased production of progesterone by the corpus luteum during the luteal phase of the cycle.) Thermometers that provide finely graded readings, such as electronic thermometers, are best suited for determining minor changes. A major problem with the BBT method is that it does not indicate the several *unsafe* preovulatory days during which sperm deposited in the vagina may remain viable. Rather, the BBT method indicates when a woman *has* ovulated. Thus, many women use the calendar method to predict the number of "safe" days prior to ovulation and the BBT method to determine the number of "unsafe" days after. A woman would avoid coitus during the "unsafe" preovulatory period (as determined by the calendar method) and then for 3 days when her temperature rises and remains elevated. A drawback of the BBT method is that changes in body temperature may also result from factors unrelated to ovulation, such as infections, sleeplessness, or stress. For this reason, some women triple-check themselves by also tracking their cervical mucous.

The Cervical Mucous (Ovulation) Method The **ovulation method** tracks changes in the **viscosity** of the cervical mucous. Following menstruation, the vagina feels rather dry. There is also little or no discharge from the cervix. These dry days are relatively safe. Then a mucous discharge appears in the vagina that is first thick and sticky, and white or cloudy in color. Coitus (or unprotected coitus) should be avoided at the first sign of any mucous. As the cycle progresses, the mucous discharge thins and clears, becoming slippery or stringy, like raw egg white. These are the **peak days**. This mucous discharge, called the *ovulatory mucous,* may be accompanied by a feeling of vaginal lubrication or wetness. Ovulation takes place about 1 day after the last peak day (about 4 days after this ovulatory mucous first appears). Then the mucous becomes cloudy and tacky once more. Intercourse may resume 4 days following the last peak day.

One problem with the mucous method is that some women have difficulty detecting changes in the mucous discharge. Such changes may also result from infections, certain medications, or contraceptive creams, jellies, or foam. Sexual arousal may also induce changes in viscosity.

Ovulation-Prediction Kits Predicting ovulation is more accurate with an ovulation-prediction kit. Kits allow women to test their urine daily for the presence of luteinizing hormone (LH). LH levels surge about 12 to 24 hours prior to ovulation. Ovulation-prediction kits are more accurate than the BBT method. Some couples use these kits to enhance their chances of conceiving a child by engaging in coitus when ovulation appears imminent. Others use them as a means of birth control to find out when to avoid coitus. When used correctly, ovulation-predicting kits are highly accurate.

Ovulation kits are expensive and require that the woman's urine be tested each morning. Nor do they reveal the full range of the unsafe *preovulatory* period during which sperm may remain viable in the vagina. A couple might thus choose to use the kits to determine the unsafe period following ovulation, and the calendar method to determine the unsafe period preceding ovulation.

Basal body temperature (BBT) method A fertility awareness method of contraception that relies on prediction of ovulation by tracking the woman's temperature during the course of the menstrual cycle.

Ovulation method A fertility awareness method of contraception that relies on prediction of ovulation by tracking the viscosity of the cervical mucous.

Viscosity Stickiness, consistency.

Peak days The days during the menstrual cycle during which a woman is most likely to be fertile.

Effectiveness The estimated first-year failure rate in typical use is 20%, which is high but no higher than that for the use of such contraceptive devices as the cervical cap and the female condom (see Table 12.1). Still, perhaps 1 in 5 typical users will become pregnant during the first year of use. (You may have heard the joke "What do you call people who use the rhythm method?" "Parents!") Fewer failures occur when these methods are applied conscientiously, when a combination of rhythm methods is used, and when the woman's cycles are quite regular. Restricting coitus to the postovulatory period can reduce the pregnancy rate to 1% (Jennings et al., 1998). The trick is to determine when ovulation occurs. The pregnancy rate can be reduced to practically zero if rhythm methods are used with other forms of birth control, such as the condom or diaphragm.

Advantages and Disadvantages Because they are a natural form of birth control, rhythm methods appeal to many people who, for religious or other reasons, prefer not to use artificial means. No devices or chemicals are used, and there are no side effects. They cause no loss of sensation, as condoms do. Nor is there disruption of lovemaking, as with condoms, diaphragms, or foam, although lovemaking could be said to be quite "disrupted" during the period of abstention. Rhythm methods are inexpensive, except for ovulation-prediction kits. Both partners may share the responsibility for rhythm methods. The man, for example, can take his partner's temperature or assist with the charting. All rhythm methods are fully reversible.

A disadvantage is the fact that the reliability of rhythm methods is low. Rhythm methods may be unsuitable for women with irregular cycles. Women with irregular cycles who ovulate as early as a week after their menstrual flows can become pregnant even if they engage in unprotected intercourse only when they are menstruating, because some sperm remaining in a woman's reproductive tract may survive for up to 8 days and fertilize an ovum that is released at that time. Moreover, the rhythm method requires abstaining from coitus for several days, or perhaps weeks, each month. Rhythm methods also require that records of the menstrual cycle be kept for many months prior to implementation. Unlike diaphragms, condoms, and spermicides, rhythm methods cannot be used at a moment's notice. Finally, rhythm methods do not offer any protection whatsoever against STIs.

Sterilization

Question: What is sterilization? The term **sterilization** refers to procedures that permanently make the individual incapable of fertilizing a partner or of conceiving. Many people decide to be sterilized when they plan to have no children or no more children. With the exception of abstinence, sterilization is the most effective form of contraception. Yet the prospect of sterilization arouses strong feelings because a person is transformed all at once, and presumably permanently, from someone who might be capable of bearing children to someone who cannot. This transformation often involves a profound change in self-concept. These feelings are especially strong in men and women who link fertility to their sense of masculinity or femininity.

Still, more than a million sterilizations are performed in the United States each year. It is the most widely used form of birth control among couples in committed relationships age 30 and above.

Male Sterilization The male sterilization procedure used today is the **vasectomy**. About 500,000 vasectomies are performed each year in the United States. More than 15% of men in the United States have had vasectomies.

A vasectomy is usually carried out in a doctor's office, under local anesthesia, in 15 to 20 minutes. Small incisions are made in the scrotum. Each vas is cut, a small

Sterilization Surgical procedures that render people incapable of reproduction without affecting sexual activity.

Vasectomy The surgical method of male sterilization in which sperm are prevented from reaching the urethra by cutting each vas deferens and tying it back or cauterizing it.

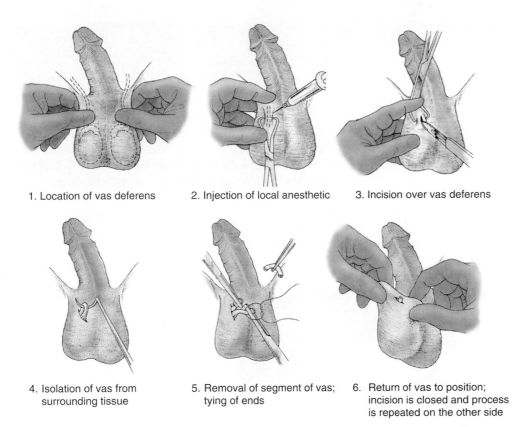

1. Location of vas deferens   2. Injection of local anesthetic   3. Incision over vas deferens

4. Isolation of vas from surrounding tissue   5. Removal of segment of vas; tying of ends   6. Return of vas to position; incision is closed and process is repeated on the other side

Figure 12.7. Vasectomy. The male sterilization procedure is usually carried out in a doctor's office, using local anesthesia. Small incisions are made in the scrotum. Each vas deferens is cut, and the ends are tied off or cauterized to prevent sperm from reaching the urethra. Sperm are harmlessly reabsorbed by the body after the operation.

segment is removed, and the ends are tied off or cauterized (to prevent them from growing back together) (see Figure 12.7). Sperm can no longer reach the urethra and are reabsorbed by the body.

The man can usually resume sexual relations within a few days. Because some sperm may be present in his reproductive tract for a few weeks, however, he is best advised to use an additional contraceptive method until his ejaculate has a sperm count of zero. Some health professionals recommend that the man have a follow-up sperm count a year after his vasectomy, to ensure that the segments of the vas deferens have not rejoined.

Vasectomy does not diminish sex drive or result in any change in sexual arousal, erectile or ejaculatory ability, or sensations of ejaculation. No significant differences have been found among men in sexual satisfaction, marital satisfaction, communication, and frequency of sexual intercourse before and after vasectomy (Hofmeyr & Greeff, 2002). Male sex hormones and sperm are still produced by the testes. Without a passageway to the urethra, however, sperm are no longer expelled with the ejaculate. Because sperm account for only about 1% of the ejaculate, the volume of the ejaculate is not noticeably different.

Over the years there has been some concern about whether vasectomy raises the risk of prostate cancer. Two studies of more than 73,000 men who had undergone vasectomies found that men who had had vasectomies more than 20 years earlier faced a slightly increased risk of prostate cancer (Altman, 1993a; Giovannucci et al., 1993a, 1993b). A New Zealand study took another approach, comparing the incidence of vasectomy among more than 900 men who had had prostate cancer with

Selecting a Method of Contraception

If you believe that you and your partner should use contraception, how will you determine which method is right for you? There is no simple answer. What is right for your friends may be wrong for you. You and your partner will make your own selections, but here are some issues you may want to consider:

1. *Convenience.* Is the method convenient? The convenience of a method depends on a number of factors:

Does it require a device that must be purchased in advance? If so, can it be purchased over the counter as needed, or are a consultation with a doctor and a prescription required? Will the method work at a moment's notice, or (as with the birth-control pill) will it require time to reach maximum effectiveness? Some couples feel that few things dampen ardor and spontaneity more quickly than the

need to pay attention to a contraceptive device in the heat of passion. Use of contraceptives such as the condom and the diaphragm need not interrupt sexual activity, however. Both partners can share in applying the device. Some couples find that this becomes an erotic aspect of their lovemaking.

2. *Moral acceptability.* A method that is morally acceptable to one person may be objectionable to another. For

Selecting a Method of Contraception
Should you and your partner use contraception? If so, how can you determine which method is right for you? Issues you may want to consider include convenience, effectiveness, moral acceptability, safety, reversibility, and cost. Other issues include whether the method allows you and your partner to share the responsibility and whether it also affords protection from STIs.

Vasovasotomy The surgical method of reversing vasectomy in which the cut or cauterized ends of the vas deferens are sewn together.

Tubal sterilization The most common method of female sterilization, in which the fallopian tubes are surgically blocked to prevent the meeting of sperm and ova. Also called *tubal ligation.*

Minilaparotomy A kind of tubal sterilization in which a small incision is made in the abdomen to provide access to the fallopian tubes.

that among a matched group of about 1,100 who had not (Cox et al., 2002). The researchers found absolutely no difference in the rate of vasectomy between the two groups, even when they adjusted their findings for social class, religious affiliation, and family history of prostate cancer. In sum, vasectomy appears to be connected with either no increased risk or a slightly increased risk of prostate cancer. Individuals considering vasectomy should discuss the most recent available findings with their physicians.

Vasectomy is nearly 100% effective. Fewer than 2 pregnancies occur during the first year among 1,000 couples in which the man has undergone a vasectomy (see Table 12.1). The few failures stem from sperm remaining in the male's genital tract shortly after the operation or from the rejoining of the segments of a vas deferens.

Reversibility is simple in concept but not in practice. Thus, vasectomies should be considered permanent. In an operation to reverse a vasectomy, called a **vasovasotomy**, the ends of the vas deferens are sewn together, and in a few days they grow together. Estimates of success at reversal, as measured by subsequent pregnancies, range from 16% to 79% (Hatcher, 2001). Some vasectomized men develop antibodies that attack their own sperm. The production of antibodies does not appear to

example, some oral contraceptives prevent fertilization; others allow fertilization to occur but then prevent implantation of the fertilized ovum in the uterus. In the second case, the method of contraception may be considered to produce a form of early abortion, which is likely to concern people who object to abortion no matter how soon after conception it occurs. Yet the same people may have no moral objection to preventing fertilization.

3. *Cost.* Methods vary in cost. Some more costly methods involve devices (such as the diaphragm, the cervical cap, and the IUD) or hormones (pills) that require medical visits in addition to the cost of the devices themselves. Other methods, such as rhythm methods, are essentially free.

4. *Sharing responsibility.* Most forms of birth control place the burden of responsibility largely, if not entirely, on the woman. The woman must consult with her doctor to obtain birth-control pills or other prescription devices such as diaphragms, cervical caps, and IUDs. The woman must take birth-control pills reliably or check to see that her IUD remains in place.

Some couples prefer methods that allow for greater sharing of responsibility, such as alternating use of the condom and diaphragm. A man can also share the responsibility for the birth-control pill by accompanying his partner on her medical visits, sharing the expense, and helping her remember to take her pill.

5. *Safety.* How safe is the method? What are the side effects? What health risks are associated with its use? Can your partner's health or comfort be affected by its use?

6. *Reversibility.* In most cases, the effects of birth-control methods can be fully reversed by discontinuing their use. In other cases, reversibility may not occur immediately, as with oral contraceptives. One form of contraception, sterilization, should be considered irreversible, although many attempts at reversal have been successful.

7. *Protection against sexually transmitted infections (STIs).* Birth-control methods vary in the degree of protection they afford against STIs such as gonorrhea, chlamydia, and HIV/AIDS. This is especially important to people

who are sexually active with one or more partners who are *not known* to be free of infectious diseases.

8. *Effectiveness.* Techniques and devices vary widely in their effectiveness in actual use. Despite the widespread availability of contraceptives, about 2 of 3 pregnancies in the United States are unplanned, and of these, about half result from contraceptive failures (Angier, 1993a). The failure rate for a particular method is the percentage of women who become pregnant when using the method for a given period of time, such as during the first year of use. Most contraceptive methods are not used correctly all or even much of the time. Thus it is instructive to compare the failure rate among people who use a particular method or device *perfectly* (consistently and correctly) with the failure rate among *typical* users. Failure rates among typical users are often considerably higher because of incorrect, unreliable, or inconsistent use. Table 12.1 shows the failure rates, continuation rates, reversibility, and degree of protection against STIs associated with various contraceptive methods.

endanger the man's health (Hatcher, 2001), but it may contribute to infertility following reconnection.

No deaths due to vasectomy have been reported in the United States (Reinisch, 1990). Few documented complications of vasectomies have been reported in the medical literature. Minor complications are reported in 4% or 5% of cases, however. They typically involve temporary local inflammation or swelling after the operation. Ice packs and anti-inflammatory drugs, such as aspirin, may help reduce swelling and discomfort. More serious but rarer medical complications include infection of the epididymis.

Truth?Fiction?
Revisited

The truth is that some *but not all* contraceptives prevent sexually transmitted infections as well as conception.

Female Sterilization Nearly 4 in 10 women (39%) under the age of 45 and in committed relationships have been surgically sterilized (U.S. Bureau of the Census, 2000). **Tubal sterilization**, also called *tubal ligation,* is the most common method of female sterilization. Tubal sterilization prevents ova and sperm from passing through the fallopian tubes. Several hundred thousand tubal sterilizations are performed each year in the United States.

The two main surgical procedures for tubal sterilization are *minilaparotomy* and *laparoscopy.* In **minilaparotomy**, a small incision is made in the abdomen, just above

TABLE 12.1

Approximate Failure Rates of Various Methods of Birth Control (in percentage of women using the method who become pregnant within the first year of use)

Method	% of Women Experiencing an Accidental Pregnancy within the First Year of Use		% of Women Continuing Use at 1 Year[3]	Reversibility	Protection against Sexually Transmitted Infections (STIs)
	Typical Use[1]	Perfect Use[2]			
Chance[4]	85	85		yes (unless fertility has been impaired by exposure to an STI)	no
Spermicides[5]	26	6	43	yes	no
Periodic Abstinence	20		67	yes	no
Calendar		9			
Ovulation Method		3			
Sympto-Thermal[6]		2			
Post-Ovulation		1			
Withdrawal	19	4		yes	no
Cervical Cap[7]					
Parous Women[8]	40	30	45	yes	some
Nulliparous Women[9]	20	9	58	yes	some
Diaphragm[7]	20	6	58	yes	some
Condom alone					
Female (Reality)	21	5	56	yes	yes
Male	14	3	63	yes	yes
Pill	3		72	yes	no, but may reduce the risk of PID[10]
Progestin Only		0.5			
Combined		0.1			
IUD					
Progestasert	2.0	1.5	81	yes, except if fertility is impaired	no, and may increase the risk of PID
ParaGard Cop- perT 380A	0.8	0.6	78		
Depo-Provera	0.3	0.3	70	yes	no
Norplant (6 capsules)	0.05	0.05	85	yes	no
Female Sterilization	0.5	0.5	100	questionable	no
Male Sterilization	0.15	0.10	100	questionable	no

[1]Among typical couples who initiate use of a method (not necessarily for the first time), the percentage who experience an accidental pregnancy during the first year if they do not stop use for any other reason.

[2]Among couples who initiate a method (not necessarily for the first time) and who use it perfectly (both consistently and correctly), the percentage who experience an accidental pregnancy during the first year if they do not stop use for any other reason.

[3]Among couples attempting to avoid pregnancy, the percentage who continue to use a method for 1 year.

[4]The percentages failing in columns (2) and (3) are based on data from populations where contraception is not used and from women who cease using contraception in order to become pregnant. Among such populations, about 89% become pregnant within 1 year. This estimate was lowered slightly (to 85%) to represent the percentage who would become pregnant within 1 year among women now relying on reversible methods of contraception if they abandoned contraception altogether.

[5]Foams, creams, gels, vaginal suppositories, and vaginal film.

[6]Cervical mucus (ovulation) method supplemented by calendar in the pre-ovulatory and basal body temperature in the post-ovulatory.

[7]With spermicidal cream or jelly.

[8]Pelvic inflammatory disease.

[9]Women who have borne children.

[10]Women who have not borne children.

Sources: For failure rates and percentages of women discontinuing use, adapted from Hatcher (2001) and Hatcher et al. (1994). Information on reversibility and protection against STIs added.

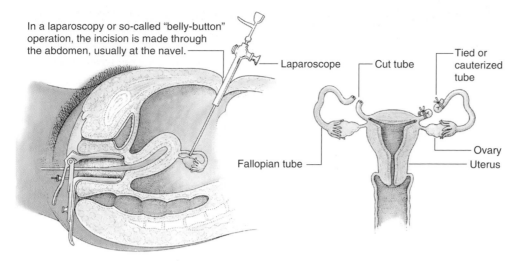

In a laparoscopy or so-called "belly-button" operation, the incision is made through the abdomen, usually at the navel.

Laparoscope

Fallopian tube

Cut tube

Tied or cauterized tube

Ovary

Uterus

Figure 12.8. Laparoscopy. *In this method of female sterilization, the surgeon approaches the fallopian tubes through a small incision in the abdomen just below the navel. A narrow instrument called a* laparoscope *is inserted through the incision, and a small section of each fallopian tube is cauterized, cut, or clamped to prevent ova from joining with sperm.*

the pubic hairline, to provide access to the fallopian tubes. Each tube is cut and either tied back or clamped with a clip. In **laparoscopy** (see Figure 12.8), sometimes called "belly button surgery," the fallopian tubes are approached through a small incision in the abdomen just below the navel. The surgeon uses a narrow, lighted viewing instrument called a *laparoscope* to locate the tubes. A small section of each of the tubes is cauterized, cut, or clamped. The woman usually returns to her daily routine in a few days and can resume coitus when it becomes comfortable. In an alternative sterilization procedure, **culpotomy**, the fallopian tubes are approached through an incision in the back wall of the vagina.

None of these methods disrupts sex drive or sexual response. Surgical sterilization does not induce premature menopause or alter the woman's production of sex hormones. The menstrual cycle is undisturbed. The unfertilized egg is simply reabsorbed by the body, rather than being sloughed off in the menstrual flow.

A **hysterectomy** also results in sterilization. A hysterectomy is a major operation that is commonly performed because of cancer or other diseases of the reproductive tract; it is inappropriate as a method of sterilization. Hysterectomy carries the risks of major surgery and, when the ovaries are removed along with the uterus, it induces a "surgical menopause" because the woman no longer produces female sex hormones.

Female sterilization is highly effective in preventing pregnancy, although slightly less effective than male sterilization. Overall, about 1 woman in 200 (0.4%) becomes pregnant in the first year following a tubal sterilization (Hatcher, 2001), most likely as the result of a failed surgical procedure or an undetected pregnancy at the time of the procedure. Like vasectomy, tubal ligation should be considered irreversible. Reversals are successful, as measured by subsequent pregnancies, in 43% to 88% of cases (Hatcher, 2001). Reversal is difficult and costly, however.

Some women incur medical complications. The most common complications are abdominal infections, excessive bleeding, inadvertent punctures of nearby organs, and scarring. The use of general anesthesia (typical in laparoscopies and in

Truth?Fiction?
Revisited

Not all sterilization operations can be surgically reversed. Sterilization is not advised for individuals who believe that they might later change their minds about becoming pregnant.

Laparoscopy Tubal sterilization by means of a *laparoscope,* which is inserted through a small incision just below the navel and used to cauterize, cut, or clamp the fallopian tubes. Sometimes referred to as "belly button surgery."

Culpotomy A kind of tubal sterilization in which the fallopian tubes are approached through an incision in the back wall of the vagina.

Hysterectomy Surgical removal of the uterus. (*Not* appropriate as a method of sterilization.)

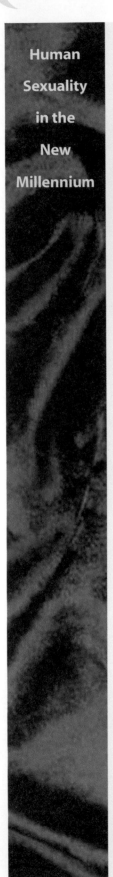

Human Sexuality in the New Millennium

Where Is the Perfect Contraceptive? The Search Goes On

The search continues—the search for the perfect contraceptive. It is difficult to say precisely what that contraceptive will look like, but it will be safe and effective, and it will not interfere with sexual spontaneity or sexual pleasure.

Early in the third millennium, that contraceptive does not yet seem to be within our grasp. However, it appears that we will be making advances in mechanical and chemical barrier methods, systems for delivering hormones, intrauterine devices (IUDs), and methods for men (such as a male pill).

MECHANICAL BARRIER METHODS

Mechanical barriers have the advantage of not introducing chemicals into people's circulatory systems. On the other hand, they have sometimes been cumbersome and, in the case of the male condom, have reduced sexual sensations and spontaneity. Moreover, the male condom is "male-controlled," and there is the desire for more female-controlled devices. One, the female condom, is already on the market.

The Female Condom

The female condom consists of a polyurethane (plastic) sheath that is used to line the vagina during intercourse. It is held in place at each end by a flexible plastic ring. The female condom provides a secure but flexible shield that barricades against sperm but allows the penis to move freely within the vagina during coitus. It can be inserted as much as 8 hours before intercourse and should be removed soon afterward and discarded (Hatcher, 2001).

Like the male condom, the female condom may offer some protection against STIs. Women can use the female condom if their partners refuse to wear a male condom. But many women note that the female condom is bulky and difficult to insert. Naming the device *Reality* suggests that it may be used most widely by women faced with the reality of male partners who refuse to use condoms themselves or who fail to use them consistently or properly.

The female condom (brand name: Reality) carries a warning label that it appears to be less effective than the male latex condom in preventing pregnancies and transmission of STIs. During test trials, the pregnancy

rate was estimated to range between 21% and 26%, but it is estimated to be as low as 5% among cautious users (Hatcher, 2001). Evidence concerning the effectiveness of the female condom in providing protection against STIs is scarce.

Lea's Shield

This diaphragmlike device comes in one size that fits all women (Berger, 2002). It has a valve that allows air to escape when it is put in place, creating suction that keeps it in close contact with the cervix. The valve permits uterine and cervical fluid to drain but prevents the passage of sperm.

The Silicone Diaphragm

A diaphragm made of silicone promises to be more comfortable and easy to use than other models.

Nonlatex Male Condoms

The latex condom is often not used because it interferes with sexual spontaneity and pleasure. Condoms made of animal intestine provide more sexual sensations, but they permit the passage of some infectious organisms, including HIV. A polyurethane condom that allows more sexual sensations but prevents passage of HIV is currently on the market, and other nonlatex condoms are under development.

CHEMICAL BARRIER METHODS

New spermicides are under development—chemical barriers that will adhere better to the vaginal wall but cause less irritation. Such devices will take the form of contraceptive film, sponges, and so on. One sponge now available in Canada, Protectaid, uses low levels of active ingredients so to avoid irritating the woman.

Let us note parenthetically that the search is on for chemical barriers that will kill disease organisms, such as HIV, but not harm sperm. To date, however, no microbicide that does not damage sperm has been found.

HORMONAL METHODS FOR WOMEN

Hormonal methods, such as "the pill," have excellent track records for women in terms of effectiveness and safety, and they remain extremely popular (Berger, 2002). New hormone preparations that are available or under development take the form of vaginal rings, subdermal implants, suppositories, long-acting injections (such as Depo-Provera), and hormone pills or injections for men.

The Skin Patch

One new hormonal method is a skin patch that is worn 3 weeks each month and can be readily replaced by the woman. The Ortho Evra patch, introduced by Ortho-McNeil Pharmaceuticals in 2002, is already highly popular. The skin patch is a convenient means of receiving a continuous dose of hormones without having to remember to take a pill.

The Vaginal Ring

The vaginal ring delivers hormones through the skin. It can be worn in the vagina for 3 months before replacement. Shaped like a diaphragm, the ring contains either a combination of estrogen and progestin or progestin only.

Improved Implants

Implanon is a single implant, compared with Norplant's six. Implanon, like the now-defunct Norplant, uses progestin and can be expected to cause some irregular bleeding. Implanon is also intended to be removed after 3 years (rather than Norplant's 5), for optimal spacing between children.

Depo-Provera

Depo-Provera (medroxyprogesterone acetate) is a long-acting, synthetic form of progesterone that works as a contraceptive by inhibiting ovulation. The progesterone signals the pituitary gland in the brain to stop producing hormones that would lead to the release of mature ova by the ovaries. Administered by injection once every 3 months, Depo-Provera is an effective form of contraception, with reported failure rates of less than 1 pregnancy per 100 women during the first year of use (Hatcher, 2001). The drug may produce side effects such as weight gain, menstrual irregularity, and spotting between periods. Use of Depo-Provera has also been linked to osteoporosis, a condition involving bone loss that can cause bones to become brittle and to fracture easily.

Designer Hormones

Research is under way to find "designer" hormone preparations that act more specifically to prevent conception without acting on other bodily systems.

Designer hormones would have fewer side effects and would carry less risk of fostering the growth of cancerous cells.

HORMONAL METHODS FOR MEN

Male sex hormones such as testosterone have shown promise in reducing sperm production. The pituitary gland normally stimulates the testes to produce sperm. Testosterone suppresses the pituitary, in turn suppressing sperm production. Men who have received injections of testosterone or progestin have shown declines in sperm production. Potential complications include an increased risk of prostate cancer. Testosterone also appears to increase cholesterol levels in the bloodstream, which may heighten the risk of cardiovascular disease.

Nevertheless, testosterone-delivery systems for men are under development. Eventually they will provide protection by reducing the sperm count for months or years. One current method being tested in pilot studies involves injections of progestin every 3 months and, because progestin lowers the sex drive in men, implants of testosterone every 4 months (Male contraceptive tests positive, 2003).

One "male pill" under development includes testosterone and progestogen (Cohen, 1998). This pill is 95% effective in reducing the sperm counts to levels at which impregnation is highly unlikely, and it may be available within a few years.

OTHER METHODS FOR MEN

Another approach to male contraception was suggested when investigators in China found extremely low birth rates in communities in which cottonseed oil was used in cooking. They extracted from the cotton plant a drug, *gossypol,* that shows promise as a male contraceptive. Chinese studies reveal the drug to be nearly 100% effective in preventing pregnancies. The drug appears to nullify sperm production without affecting hormone levels or the sex drive. However, the toxic effects of gossypol have limited its acceptability as a male contraceptive.

Some men are infertile because they produce antibodies that destroy their own sperm. It is also speculated that vasectomy causes some men's bodies to react to their own sperm as foreign substances and

(continues)

Human Sexuality in the New Millennium

produce antibodies. This is an immunological response to sperm. Some researchers have suggested that it may be possible to develop ways to induce the body to produce such antibodies. Ideally, this procedure would be reversible.

Applying ultrasound waves to the testes has been shown to produce reversible sterility in laboratory rats, dogs, and monkeys. No one is quite certain how ultrasound induces temporary sterilization. Moreover, its safety has not been demonstrated. A Chinese researcher has developed an electronic device that emits impulses that kill sperm and make a man sterile for up to a month ("China develops," 1998). The device is gaining some followers in China. It remains to be seen whether interest will spread to the West.

INTRAUTERINE DEVICES (IUDs)

Use of existing IUDs has been connected with problems such as expulsion, cramping, and irritation or perforation of the uterus. Under development is a "frameless" IUD that would eliminate pressure against the uterus, thus minimizing cramping. The copper-releasing sleeves would be anchored by a poly-propylene thread rather than by a frame.

Mirena, introduced in 2001, releases the chemical levonorgestrel. It is highly effective and proves up to a decade of protection against conception. Mirena is less likely than other IUDs in use to cause bleeding, and it may be helpful in avoiding PID. Its main disadvantage is that it is much more expensive than copper devices.

IMMUNOCONTRACEPTIVES

Many chemicals are under development that will cause the body's immune system to prevent fertilization. For example, antigens may be developed for use with women that act on sperm or the zona pellucida of ova.

"Vaccines" for men that shut down production of both sperm and testosterone or of sperm alone are under development. A vaccine that shuts down testosterone production would have to be used along with testosterone supplements. Therefore, it would be better to shut down just sperm production. A vaccine based on follicle-stimulating hormone (FSH) might do the job.

THE ULTIMATE CONTRACEPTIVE DEVICE

Wouldn't it be wonderful if people—female or male—could take a pill that would suspend fertility, with no side effects, until they took another pill that reversed the situation and made it possible for them to conceive again? Such an arrangement would be perfectly effective and perfectly safe. It would not interfere with sexual spontaneity. It would be quickly reversible if and when couples changed their minds about conceiving.

That pill may be awhile off, but researchers are thinking about it.

Source: The material on methods for women is reprinted from Leslie Berger (2002, December 10). After long hiatus, new contraceptives emerge. *The New York Times.*

Truth?Fiction?
Revisited

It is true that testosterone can be used as a male contraceptive.

some minilaparotomies) poses additional risks, as in any major operation. (Most of the deaths that are attributed to tubal sterilization actually result from the anesthesia [Reinisch, 1990]. The overall death rate is quite small, however—2 to 5 deaths per 100,000 operations.)

Advantages and Disadvantages of Sterilization The major advantages of sterilization are effectiveness and permanence. Sterilization is nearly 100% effective. Following surgery, the couple need not do anything more to prevent conception. Permanence is also its major drawback, however. People sometimes change their minds about wanting to have children.

Sterilization procedures create varying risks of complications following surgery, with women generally incurring greater risks than men. Another disadvantage of sterilization is that it affords no protection against STIs. People who are sterilized may still wish to use condoms and spermicides for protection against STIs.

Review: Methods of Contraception

Reflect

What method or methods of birth control do you find medically and ethically acceptable? Why?

CriticalThinking

Is the use of the minipill or the IUD a method of contraception or of abortion? Does it matter? Explain your views.

7. A(n) _____ contraceptive is commonly referred to as a birth-control pill, or "the pill."

8. Combination pills contain estrogen and _____.

9. The _____ contains progesterone only.

10. The combination pill fools the brain into acting as though the woman is _____.

11. The _____ in the combination pill inhibits FSH production.

12. When used properly, oral contraception is nearly _____% effective.

13. The combination pill (*Increases* or *Reduces*?) the risks of ovarian and endometrial cancer.

14. Progestin fosters (*Female* or *Male*?) secondary sex characteristics.

15. The morning-after pill (*Does* or *Does not*?) prevent ovulation.

16. Morning-after pills have a (*Higher* or *Lower*?) hormone content than most birth-control pills.

17. Norplant consists of tubes that contain _____ progestin and are embedded in a woman's arm.

18. The most common side effect of Norplant was unpredictable menstrual _____.

19. The IUD may work by irritating the _____ lining.

20. The IUD (*Does* or *Does not*?) affect the woman's normal hormone production.

21. The _____ is a shallow rubber dome that should be used along with a spermicide.

22. _____ are agents that kill sperm.

23. Spermicides that contain nonoxynol-9 (*Do* or *Do not*?) provide some protection against STIs such as HIV/AIDS.

24. Like the diaphragm, the _____ cap forms a barrier and holds spermicide in place.

25. _____ are also called "rubbers," "safes," prophylactics, and "skins."

26. Condoms made of latex (*Can* or *Cannot*?) prevent the transmission of HIV.

27. Douching is considered to be an (*Effective* or *Ineffective*?) method of birth control.

28. In the _____ method, the man removes his penis from the vagina before ejaculating.

29. _____ methods rely on awareness of the fertile segments of the woman's menstrual cycle.

30. The _____ method assumes that ovulation occurs 14 days prior to menstruation.

31. In the _____ body temperature (BBT) method, the woman tracks her body temperature to detect the small changes that occur before and after ovulation.

32. The ovulation method tracks changes in the _____ of the cervical mucus.

33. Ovulation-prediction kits allow women to test their urine for the presence of _____ hormone (LH).

34. The male sterilization procedure is called the _____.

35. Vasectomy (*Does* or *Does not*?) Lower the sex drive or change erectile or ejaculatory ability.

36. Tubal _____ is the most common method of female sterilization.

37. The main surgical procedures for tubal sterilization are minilaparotomy and _____.

Abortion

"When I was young, I felt it myself, that it was wrong to kill a baby," said Maria (cited in Lewin, 1998a). Maria is a 17-year-old Latina American high school student who lives in Houston. She is waiting to be seen at an abortion clinic. "But when I got to be a teenager, and started having sex, things looked different. It's more complicated when it's your own life. I want to go to college, and I know that having a baby now, without a husband or anything, would make that very hard."

Maria is not all that unusual among young people in the United States today. Abortion has little to do with politics to her. The *Roe v. Wade* decision occurred 8 years before Maria was born. Like half the adults in the United States, Maria believes that abortion is murder (Goldberg & Elder, 1998). But like one third of the Americans who say abortion is murder, Maria believes that abortion is an acceptable solution to a very bad situation.

Question: What is meant by abortion? In common usage, the term *abortion* usually refers to an **induced abortion** (in contrast to a spontaneous abortion, or miscarriage), or the purposeful termination of a pregnancy. Perhaps more than any other contemporary social issue, induced abortion (hereafter referred to simply as abortion) has divided neighbors and family members into opposing camps.

Thirty-seven million abortions worldwide are performed each year. In the United States, the abortion rate increased steadily from the early 1970s through 1980, leveled off somewhat in the 1980s, reached a peak in about 1990, when there were about 1.4 million abortions, and has declined to about 1.2 million abortions per year more recently (CDC, 2000g). The great majority of abortions in the United States—nearly 90%—occur during the first trimester. This is when they are safest for the woman and least costly.

About 43% of women in the United States have a voluntary abortion at some time (Davis, 2000). Some 80% of them are single (Lewin, 1998a). Nearly half of them have had a previous abortion. Nearly half are mothers who already bear family responsibilities (Russo et al., 1992). They are young: Nearly 75% of them are under 30. Sixty percent of them are European American. About 1 in 3 (35%) is African American. Nearly 1 in 6 is Latina American.

Abortion is practiced widely in Canada, Japan, Russia, and many European nations. It is less common in developing nations, largely because of sparse medical facilities. Abortion is rarely used as a primary means of birth control. It usually comes into play when other methods have failed.

There are many reasons why women have abortions, including psychological factors as well as external circumstances. Abortion is often motivated by a desire to reduce the risk of physical, economic, psychological, and social disadvantages that the woman perceives for herself and her present and future children should she take the pregnancy to term (Russo et al., 1992).

The national debate over abortion has been played out in recent years against a backdrop of demonstrations, marches, and occasional acts of violence, such as firebombing of abortion clinics and even murder. The right-to-life (pro-life) movement asserts that human life begins at conception and thus views abortion as the murder of an unborn child (Sagan & Dryan, 1990). Some in the pro-life movement brook no exception to their opposition to abortion. Others would permit abortion to save the mother's life or when a pregnancy results from rape or incest.

The pro-choice movement contends that abortion is a matter of personal choice and that the government has no right to interfere with a woman's right to terminate

Induced abortion The purposeful termination of a pregnancy before the embryo or fetus is capable of sustaining independent life. (From the Latin *abortio*, meaning "that which is miscarried.")

Self-Assessment

Pro-Choice or Pro-Life? Where Do You Stand?

What does it mean to be "pro-life" on the abortion issue? What does it mean to be "pro-choice"? Which position is closer to your own views on abortion?

The *Reasoning about Abortion Questionnaire* (RAQ) (Parsons et al., 1990) assesses agreement with pro-life or pro-choice lines of reasoning about abortion. To find out which position is closer to your own, indicate your level of agreement or disagreement with each of the following items by circling the number that most accurately represents your feelings. Then refer to the Appendix to interpret your score.

5 = Strongly Agree   2 = Disagree
4 = Agree   1 = Strongly Disagree
3 = Mixed Feelings

1. Abortion is a matter of personal choice. 5 4 3 2 1
2. Abortion is a threat to our society. 5 4 3 2 1
3. A woman should have control over what is happening to her own body by having the option to choose abortion. 5 4 3 2 1
4. Only God, not people, can decide if a fetus should live. 5 4 3 2 1
5. Even if one believes that there may be some exceptions, abortion is still basically wrong. 5 4 3 2 1
6. Abortion violates an unborn person's fundamental right to life. 5 4 3 2 1
7. A woman should be able to exercise her rights to self-determination by choosing to have an abortion. 5 4 3 2 1
8. Outlawing abortion could take away a woman's sense of self and personal autonomy. 5 4 3 2 1
9. Outlawing abortion violates a woman's civil rights. 5 4 3 2 1
10. Abortion is morally unacceptable and unjustified. 5 4 3 2 1
11. In my reasoning, the notion that an unborn fetus may be a human life is not a deciding issue in considering abortion. 5 4 3 2 1
12. Abortion can be described as taking a life unjustly. 5 4 3 2 1
13. A woman should have the right to decide to have an abortion based on her own life circumstances. 5 4 3 2 1
14. If a woman feels that having a child might ruin her life, she should consider an abortion. 5 4 3 2 1
15. Abortion could destroy the sanctity of motherhood. 5 4 3 2 1
16. An unborn fetus is a viable human being with rights. 5 4 3 2 1
17. If a woman feels she can't care for a baby, she should be able to have an abortion. 5 4 3 2 1
18. Abortion is the destruction of one life for the convenience of another. 5 4 3 2 1
19. Abortion is the same as murder. 5 4 3 2 1
20. Even if one believes that there are times when abortion is immoral, it is still basically the woman's own choice. 5 4 3 2 1

a pregnancy. Pro-choice advocates argue that women are free to control what happens within their bodies, including pregnancies.

Question: When does human life begin?

When Does Human Life Begin?

The question of when human life begins is one that you will have to answer for yourself. We can only note that moral concerns about abortion often turn on the question of when human life begins. For some Christians, the matter revolves around when they believe the fetus obtains a soul.

In his thesis on *ensoulment,* the thirteenth-century Christian theologian Saint Thomas Aquinas wrote that a male fetus does not acquire a human soul until 40 days

Abortion Views Contradictory

A *Los Angeles Times* poll of a national sample of 2,071 Americans found that the majority—57%—believe abortion is murder, yet more than two-thirds believe that the decision to have an abortion should be left to a woman and her doctor (Poll, 2000). Polls such as these are full of apparent contradictions. For example 65% of the respondents opposed a constitutional amendment to ban abortion, yet only 43% supported the *Roe v. Wade* Supreme Court decision that established a right to abortion based on privacy. And more than half of those who consider abortion to be murder nevertheless think that women should have the right to choose.

"I don't think I personally would have an abortion. But . . . I don't know that it's fair to make someone go through that—an unwanted pregnancy," said a respondent from Florida (Poll, 2000). "I just feel it's a personal choice with a lot of gray areas."

Susan Carroll, a researcher at Rutgers University, said many Americans are simply reluctant to impose their views on other people. "Most Americans are in favor of letting people make their own individual choices," she said (Poll, 2000).

About two-thirds of respondents believe that abortion should be illegal after the first trimester. More than 80% supported abortion when a woman's health was at risk; nearly two-thirds supported it when the fetus might have an abnormality; but only about half supported abortion when the issue was the emotional health of the mother.

Truth?Fiction?
Revisited

It is true that abortions were legal in the United States prior to the Civil War—until the point in the pregnancy when the woman sensed fetal movements.

after conception, a female fetus not until after 80 days. Scientists, too, have attempted to define when human life can be said to begin. Astronomer Carl Sagan, for example, wrote that fetal brain activity can be considered a scientific marker of human life (Sagan & Druyan, 1990). Brain activity is needed for thought, the quality that is considered most "human" by many. Brain-wave patterns typical of children do not begin until about the 30th week of pregnancy. Before then, the human fetus lacks the brain architecture to begin thinking (Sagan & Druyan, 1990). Of course, this line of reasoning raises the question of whether fetal brain-wave activity can be equated with thought. (What would a fetus "think" about?) Moreover, some argue that a newly fertilized ovum carries the *potential* for human thought in the same way that the embryonic or fetal brain does. It could even be argued that sperm cells and ova are living things in that they carry out the biological processes characteristic of cellular life. All in all, the question of when *human* life begins is a matter of definition that is apparently not answerable by science.

Historical and Legal Perspectives on Abortion

Question: How have various societies reacted to abortion? Societal attitudes toward abortion have varied across cultures and times in history. Abortion was permitted in ancient Greece and Rome, but women in ancient Assyria were impaled on stakes for attempting abortion. The Bible does not specifically prohibit abortion (Sagan & Dryan, 1990). For much of its history, the Roman Catholic Church held to Thomas Aquinas's belief that ensoulment of the fetus did not occur for at least 40 days after conception. In 1869, Pope Pius IX declared that human life begins at conception. Thus an abortion at any stage of pregnancy became murder in the eyes of the church and grounds for excommunication.

Abortion was legal in the United States from 1607 to 1828 (Hitt, 1998). Women were permitted to terminate a pregnancy until "quickening" occurred (the point at which the woman was first able to feel the fetus stirring within her). More restrictive abortion laws emerged because of a national desire to increase the population and because of concerns voiced by physicians about protecting women from botched abortions (Hitt, 1998). By 1900, virtually all states in the union had enacted legislation banning abortion *at any point* during pregnancy, except when necessary to save the woman's life.

Abortion laws remained essentially unchanged until the late 1960s, when some states liberalized their abortion laws under mounting public pressure. Then, in 1973, the U.S. Supreme Court in effect legalized abortion nationwide in the landmark *Roe v. Wade* decision. *Roe v. Wade* held that a woman's right to an abortion was protected under the right to privacy guaranteed by the Constitution. The decision legalized abortions for any reason during the first trimester. In its ruling, the Court also noted that a fetus is not considered a person and is thus not entitled to constitutional protection. The Court ruled that states may regulate a woman's right to have an abortion during the second trimester to protect her health, as in requiring her to obtain an abortion in a hospital rather than a doctor's office. The Court also held that when a fetus becomes viable, its rights override the mother's right to privacy. Because the fetus may become viable early in the third trimester, states may prohibit third-trimester abortions, except when an abortion is necessary to protect a woman's health.

Since *Roe v. Wade,* most states have also enacted laws requiring parental consent or notification before a minor may have an abortion. About two-thirds of adults in the United States believe that parental permission should be required before teenage girls can have abortions (Carlson, 1990). But many pregnant teenage girls, especially those living in families with alcoholic or abusive parents, fear telling their parents that they are pregnant.

Parental-consent laws have widespread popular support. Four out of 5 adults approve of such provisions, including many supporters of abortion rights (Goldberg & Elder, 1998). With or without the rules, most girls seeking abortion do consult their parents. On the other hand, a survey reported in the *Journal of the American Medical Association* found that 48% of a sample of 950 girls visiting Planned Parenthood said that they would stop using all of the organization's services if their parents were notified of the visits (Reddy et al., 2002).

Attitudes toward Legalized Abortion National public opinion polls taken since *Roe v. Wade* have consistently shown that a majority of people in the United States support the decision legalizing abortion (Goldberg & Elder, 1998). Catholics, Jews, and Protestants differ little in support for abortion (Goldberg & Elder, 1998). On the other hand, African Americans are less likely than European Americans to support abortion. Researchers find that higher levels of education are associated with pro-choice attitudes. Reduced support for legal abortion is associated with religious commitment, conservative attitudes on premarital sex, and belief in having large families (Lynxwiler & Gay, 1994).

Most people in the United States favor legalized abortion, but not under all circumstances. A national poll by *The New York Times* found that 61% of Americans believe that abortion should be permitted during the first trimester (Figure 12.9), but 70% said that abortion was unacceptable if the purpose was to prevent the child from interfering with the woman's career (Goldberg & Elder, 1998). Only 42% felt that abortion was justified to prevent interference with a teenaged girl's education. But there was strong support for abortion when the woman was raped, her health was endangered, or there was the strong possibility of a deformity in the baby. People with more years of education were more accepting of abortion (Figure 12.10). People who said that religion was extremely important to them were less tolerant of abortion than those who said that religion was not so important. Elizabeth Cook (1998), author of a book about abortion entitled *Between Two Absolutes,* suggests that

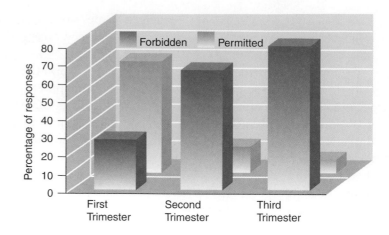

Figure 12.9. Responses to the Question "Should a Woman Be Permitted or Forbidden to Have an Abortion During the (First, Second, or Third) Trimester of Pregnancy?" Respondents to The New York Times *poll were less permissive of abortion during the later stages of pregnancy.*

a consensus about abortion may be emerging—that abortion should be allowed under some circumstances but is not to be taken lightly. Three-quarters of the sample opposed a constitutional amendment that would ban abortion. Most Americans clearly want the individual to have the right to an abortion, even if they disapprove of it.

Many people in the pro-choice movement argue that if abortions were to be made illegal again, thousands of women, especially poor women, would die or suffer serious physical consequences from botched or nonsterile abortions. People in the pro-life movement counter that alternatives to abortion such as adoption are available to pregnant women. Pro-choice advocates argue that the debate about abortion should be framed not only by notions of the mother's right to privacy but also by the issue of the quality of life of an unwanted child. They argue that minority and physically or mentally disabled children are often hard to place for adoption. These children may spend their childhoods being shuffled from one foster home to another. Pro-life advocates counter that killing a fetus eliminates any potential that it might have, despite hardships, of living a fruitful and meaningful life.

Roe v. Wade is not in the personal memories of most women who choose to have abortions in the United States today (Rubin, 2000). Many of them have a hard time believing that abortion was ever illegal and cannot imagine what it would mean if abortion were to be made illegal again.

Says a 19-year-old woman from Chicago who is waiting in an abortion clinic: "I've never heard anything about *Roe v. Wade.* I know there is tension between different groups and that there are people who are really, really against abortion. My

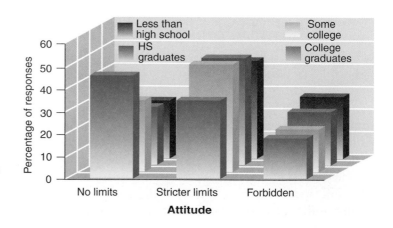

Figure 12.10. Attitudes toward Abortion and Level of Education. Respondents to The New York Times *poll with more years of education were more likely to say that abortion should be generally available (no limits). People with fewer years of education were more likely to say that abortion should not be permitted (forbidden).*

mom is totally against it. If she knew I was here, Wow! I can't even imagine what it was like when abortion was illegal. I just opened up the phone book. People definitely take it for granted today. I think of the movie 'Dirty Dancing.' I never understood why she was so sick, but it was because she got an illegal abortion" (Lewin, 1998a).

Says Sirena, a 24-year-old woman from Brooklyn who has two young children and has had three abortions: "I don't think there could ever be a time when abortion would be illegal. No one would let that happen. There would be too many girls throwing babies in the garbage or abusing their kids. But there's always going to be people who are against abortion, like my sister, and people who are pro-choice, like me. It's always been the same and it's always going to be" (Lewin, 1998a).

Methods of Abortion

Regardless of the moral, legal, and political issues that surround abortion, there are many abortion methods. *Question: What abortion methods are in use today?*

Vacuum Aspiration Vacuum aspiration, or suction curettage, is the safest and most common method of abortion. It accounts for more than 90% of abortions in the United States. It is relatively painless and inexpensive. It can be done with little or no anesthesia in a medical office or clinic, but only during the first trimester. Later, thinning of the uterine walls increases the risks of perforation and bleeding.

In the procedure the cervix is usually dilated first by insertion of progressively larger curved metal rods, or "dilators," or by insertion, hours earlier, of a stick of seaweed called *Laminaria digitata. Laminaria* expands as it absorbs cervical moisture, providing a gentler means of opening the os. Then an angled tube connected to an aspirator (suction machine) is inserted through the cervix into the uterus. The uterine contents are then evacuated (emptied) by suction (Figure 12.11). Possible complications include perforation of the uterus, infection, cervical lacerations, and hemorrhaging, but these are rare.

Vacuum aspiration
Removal of the uterine contents by suction. An abortion method used early in pregnancy. (From the Latin *aspirare,* meaning "to breathe upon.")

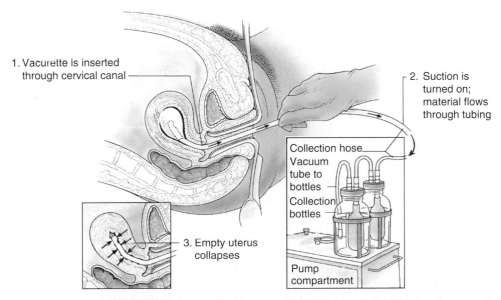

Figure 12.11. Vacuum Aspiration. This is the safest and most common method of abortion, but it can be performed only during the first trimester. An angled tube is inserted through the cervix into the uterus, and the uterine contents are then evacuated (emptied) by suction.

Partial-Birth Abortion

Most Americans believe that early abortions should be permitted, but there is great concern over the late-term surgical abortion method generally known as "partial-birth abortion" and referred to medically as an "intact dilation and extraction" or "intact D and X." In partial-birth abortion, the cervix is dilated and a fetus that may be 10 inches long is extracted from the mother through the birth canal. Brain tissue is destroyed to terminate rapidly any life functions in the fetus.

Support of abortion rights drops off rapidly as the stages of pregnancy progress (see Figure 12.9). Most people who support early first-trimester abortion oppose partial-birth abortion because of its timing. However, many pro-choice people argue in favor of partial-birth abortions for at least two reasons. One is that they are relatively rare and are usually performed when the health of the mother is at stake. Another is the "slippery slope" argument, or fear that women's surrendering the right

to have a partial-birth abortion could eventually lead to their surrendering the right to have other kinds of abortions.

The general attitudes of the medical profession toward the partial-birth abortion may be reflected in the fact that the procedure is not to be found in medical books (Hitt, 1998). As this book goes to press, Congress has passed a bill to outlaw partial-birth abortion, and the law may well be challenged in the Supreme Court (Stolberg, 2003).

Dilation and Curettage (D&C) The **D&C** was once the customary method of performing abortions. It now accounts for only a small number of abortions in the United States. It is usually performed 8 to 20 weeks following the last menstrual period (LMP). Once the cervix has been dilated, the uterine contents are scraped from the uterine lining with a blunt scraping tool.

D&C's are carried out in a hospital, usually under general anesthesia. The scraping increases the chances of hemorrhaging, infection, and perforation. Because of these risks, D&C's have largely been replaced by the vacuum aspiration method. D&C's are still used to treat various gynecological problems, however, such as abnormally heavy menstrual bleeding.

Dilation and Evacuation (D&E) The **D&E** is used most commonly during the second trimester, when vacuum aspiration alone would be too risky. The D&E combines suction and the D&C. First the cervix is dilated. The cervix must also be dilated more fully than with vacuum aspiration to allow for passage of the larger fetus. Then a suction tube is inserted to remove some of the contents of the uterus. But suction alone cannot safely remove all uterine contents, so the remaining contents are removed with forceps. A blunt scraper may also be used to scrape the uterine wall to make sure that the lining has been removed fully. Like the D&C, the D&E is usually performed in the hospital under general anesthesia. Most women recover quickly and relatively painlessly. In rare instances, however, complications can arise. These include excessive bleeding, infection, and perforation of the uterine lining (Thompson, 1993).

Inducing Labor by Intra-amniotic Infusion Second-trimester abortions are sometimes performed by chemically inducing premature labor and delivery. The procedure, which must be performed in a hospital, is called instillation, or **intra-amniotic infusion**. It is usually performed when fetal development has progressed beyond the point at which other methods are deemed safe. A saline (salt) solution or a solution of prostaglandins (hormones that stimulate uterine contractions during labor) is injected into the amniotic sac. Prostaglandins may also be administered by vaginal suppository. Uterine contractions (labor) begin within a few hours after infusion. The fetus and placenta are expelled from the uterus within the next 24 or 48 hours.

Intra-amniotic infusion accounts for only a small number of abortions. Medical complications, risks, and costs are greater with this procedure than with other meth-

D&C Abbreviation for *dilation and curettage,* an operation in which the cervix is dilated and uterine contents are then gently scraped away.

D&E Abbreviation for *dilation and evacuation,* an abortion method in which the cervix is dilated prior to vacuum aspiration.

Intra-amniotic infusion An abortion method in which a substance is injected into the amniotic sac to induce premature labor. Also called *instillation.*

ods of abortion. Overly rapid labor can tear the cervix, but previous dilation of the cervix with *Laminaria* lessens the risk. Perforation, infection, and hemorrhaging are rare if prostaglandins are used, but about half the recipients experience nausea and vomiting, diarrhea, or headaches. Saline infusion can cause shock and even death if the solution is carelessly introduced into the bloodstream.

Hysterotomy The **hysterotomy** is, in effect, a cesarean section. Incisions are made in the abdomen and uterus, and the fetus and uterine contents are removed. Hysterotomy may be performed during the late second trimester, between the 16th and 24th weeks after the last menstrual period. It is performed very rarely, usually only when intra-amniotic infusion is not advised. A hysterotomy is major surgery that must be carried out under general anesthesia in a hospital. Hysterotomy involves risks of complications from the anesthesia and the surgery itself.

Abortion Drugs RU-486 (mifepristone) induces early abortion by blocking the effects of progesterone. Progesterone is the hormone that stimulates proliferation of the endometrium, allowing implantation of the fertilized ovum and, subsequently, development of the placenta.

RU-486 must be used within 49 days of the beginning of the woman's last menstrual period (FDA approves, 2000). The typical course is for the woman to take three mifepristone pills. Two days later, she is given a second oral drug, misoprostol, that causes uterine contractions to expel the embryo. There is also usually a follow-up visit within 2 weeks to make sure that the abortion is complete and the woman is well.

Supporters of RU-486 argue that it offers a safe, noninvasive substitute for more costly and unpleasant abortion procedures (Christin-Maitre et al., 2000). Supporters also note that RU-486 may reduce the numbers of women who die each year from complications from self-induced abortions. Such women are usually too poor to avail themselves of legally sanctioned abortion facilities. Or else they live in Third World countries that lack adequate medical services. On the other hand, an 18-year-old died in the United States after using RU-486, apparently from an infection caused by fragments of the fetus left inside the uterus (Teen dies, 2003).

As the abortion debate continues, so does research into the use of other drugs (Christin-Maitre et al., 2000). A combination of the cancer drug methotrexate and misoprostol can also be used to terminate early pregnancy (Ngai et al., 2000). Methotrexate is toxic to the trophoblastic tissue of the embryo, and—as in combination with RU-486—misoprostol causes the uterus to expel the embryo.

Psychological Consequences of Abortion

The woman who faces an unwanted pregnancy may experience a range of negative emotions, including fear, anger directed inward ("How could I let this happen?"), guilt ("What would my parents think if they knew I was having an abortion?"), and ambivalence ("Will I regret it if I have an abortion? Will I regret it more if I don't?")

Consider the comments of Yardena, a 22-year-old woman who is the mother of a 3-year-old, had an abortion at the age of 16, and was waiting to be seen at the Planned Parenthood clinic when she learned that she was pregnant again: "I'm not pro-choice—I'm anti-abortion. I still have negative feelings about abortion, and I love children, but this is something I have to do at this point in my life" (Lewin, 1998a).

A 19-year-old college student says, "I don't like the idea of abortion being used as birth control. This is my first time [at the clinic] and my last. If I get pregnant again, which I won't, I'm having the child. That will mean I was stupid twice. Once is all right, but not the same mistake twice."

Hysterotomy An abortion method in which the fetus is removed by cesarean section.

Whether to have an abortion is typically a painful decision—perhaps the most difficult decision a woman will ever make. Even women who apparently make the decision without hesitation may regret it later. Although the woman's partner is often overlooked in the research on abortion, he may experience similar feelings.

Women's reactions depend on various factors, including the support they receive from others (or the lack thereof) and the strength of their relationships with their partners (Ring-Cassidy & Gentles, 2002; Williams, 2001). Women with greater support from their male partners or parents tend to show a more positive emotional reaction following an abortion. Generally speaking, the sooner the abortion occurs, the less stressful it is. Women who have a difficult time reaching an abortion decision, who blame the pregnancy on their character, who have lower coping ability, and who have less social support experience more distress following abortion.

Many men are very concerned and supportive of their partners. Others seek to detach themselves from the situation. And of course there are some cases in which the identity of the father is unknown. Some men consider pregnancy the woman's responsibility: "She's the one who let herself get pregnant." Some men reproach the woman for failing to take precautions. No wonder feminists insist that men share full responsibility for pregnancies.

All right. We know that abortion continues to be a political football. We know that people on both sides of the issue cite moral and social reasons why their views are correct. But what of the experiences of women who have abortions? How do they react? We reported a couple of anecdotes at the beginning of this section, but let's forget about anecdotes. We can all point to people who are well-adjusted following abortion and to others who are "a mess." What do the carefully conducted surveys tell us?

Frankly, their results are less than crystal clear. Consider one survey reported in *Archives of General Psychiatry* (Major et al., 2000) of several hundred women who showed up at one of three sites for a first-trimester abortion. More than 1,000 women were approached at random as they arrived at the clinic, and 882 (85%) agreed to be followed for 2 years so that their responses could be assessed at various times. Of these 882, 442 were actually followed for the 2 years. As you can see in Figure 12.12, the majority (72%) said they were satisfied with their decision to have the abortion. A majority said they would make the same decision if they had it to do over (69%) and that they had experienced more benefit than harm from having the abortion (72%). Moreover, 4 out of 5 women (80%) were *not* depressed.

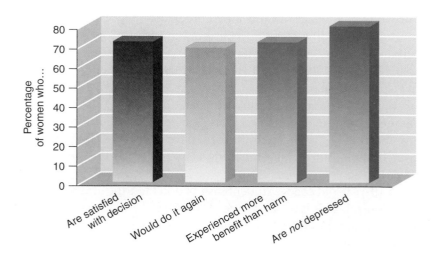

Figure 12.12. Women's Psychological Adjustment Two Years after Having Had an Abortion. Of several hundred respondents to an Archives of General Psychiatry *survey (Major et al., 2000), 72% of those who had had an abortion reported being satisfied with their decision 2 years after the fact. How do you interpret this finding? Do you focus on the fact that the great majority of women are satisfied with their choice or on the fact that significant numbers of women (28%) are not?*

Note that you can interpret these findings in any way that you like. Pro-choice advocates can say that the great majority of women appear to be psychologically well-adjusted 2 years after having an abortion. But pro-life advocates can say that significant numbers of women are not. To see what we mean, assume that the percentages reported in this study are accurate predictors of the adjustment of all women in the United States who have had abortions. Also assume that there are 1 million abortions per year. With these assumptions in place, 720,000 women (72%) every year will say they are satisfied with their decision 2 years later. But 280,000 women

Review: Abortion

Reflect

One of the issues concerning abortion is whether it is the taking of a human life. How do *you* define *human life*? When do *you* believe human life begins? At conception? When the embryo becomes implanted in the uterus? When the fetus begins to assume a human shape or develops human facial features? When the fetus is capable of sustaining independent life? Do your beliefs have anything to do with the concept of ensoulment? Explain.

CriticalThinking

How is it that research concerning the psychological effects of abortion on the mother can be interpreted in different ways by pro-life and pro-choice people? As an intellectual exercise, can you argue for and against each point of view?

38. An _____ abortion, in contrast to a spontaneous abortion, is the purposeful termination of a pregnancy.

39. The majority of abortions in the United States occur during the _____ trimester.

40. The pro-_____ movement asserts that abortion is the murder of an unborn child.

41. The pro-_____ movement argues that access to abortion is a woman's right.

42. For many Christians, the question of when human life begins revolves around when they believe the fetus obtains a _____.

43. In 1869, Pope Pius IX declared that human life begins at _____.

44. Abortion (*Was* or *Was not?*) legal in the United States prior to the Civil War.

45. A majority of people in the United States (*Support* or *Oppose?*) the Supreme Court decision legalizing abortion.

46. Vacuum _____, or suction curettage, is the safest and most common method of abortion.

47. With the D&C, the _____ is dilated and uterine contents are scraped from the uterine lining.

48. The D&E combines _____ and the D&C.

49. In intra-amniotic _____, a solution of prostaglandins is injected into the amniotic sac.

50. _____-birth abortion is a late-term surgical abortion method in which the cervix is dilated and a fetus is removed through the birth canal.

51. _____ tissue is destroyed to terminate life functions in the fetus.

52. The hysterotomy is a _____ section.

53. RU-486 induces early abortion by blocking the effects of _____.

will *not* say they are satisfied with their decision. Similarly, 310,000 women (31%) each year will *not* be able to say they would do it again, and 280,000 women each year will *not* be able to say that they found the effects of the abortion to be more beneficial than harmful.

Our conclusion is that both sides are correct. The great majority of women appear to be psychologically well adjusted a couple of years after having an abortion. It is also true that hundreds of thousand of women per year cannot say that they are satisfied with their decision to have an abortion. In other words, numbers alone do not tell the whole story. There is no simple answer to questions about the psychological effects of having an abortion.

What *is* clear is that neither side is entitled to make overgeneralized, extreme claims. Pro-choice advocates cannot claim that women who have abortions suffer no psychological ill effects. (Some women do.) Nor can pro-life advocates argue that having an abortion has devastating psychological effects on women. (Most women who have abortions are well adjusted.)

Recite

1. What is contraception?	Contraception is any technique that prevents a sperm cell and ovum from uniting.
2. What happened during the legal battle over contraception in the United States?	In the United States, Anthony Comstock lobbied successfully for passage of a federal law in 1873 that prohibited the dissemination of birth-control information through the mail on the grounds that it was obscene and indecent. In 1918 the courts ruled that physicians must be allowed to disseminate information that might aid in the cure and prevention of diseases. Dismantling of the Comstock Law had begun.
3. What is "the pill"?	Birth-control pills include combination pills and minipills. Combination pills contain estrogen and progestin and fool the brain into acting as though the woman is already pregnant, so that no additional ova mature or are released. Minipills contain progestin, thicken the cervical mucus to impede the passage of sperm through the cervix, and render the inner lining of the uterus less receptive to a fertilized egg. Oral contraception is nearly 100% effective. The main drawbacks are side effects and potential health risks. "Morning-after" pills prevent implantation of a fertilized ovum in the uterus.
4. What is the morning-after pill?	This is a pill with high hormone content that prevents fertilization or implantation.
5. What is Norplant?	Norplant consists of tubes containing progestin that are surgically embedded under the skin of the woman's upper arm. Norplant provides continuous contraceptive protection for as long as 5 years.
6. What is the IUD?	The intrauterine device (IUD) apparently irritates the uterine lining, causing inflammation and the production of antibodies that may be toxic to sperm or fertilized ova and/or may prevent fertilized eggs from becoming implanted. The IUD is highly effective, but there are possible troublesome side effects and the potential for serious health complications.
7. What is the diaphragm?	The diaphragm covers the cervix and should be used with a spermicidal cream or jelly. It must be fitted by a health professional.
8. What are spermicides?	Spermicides block the passage of sperm and kill sperm. Their failure rate is high.
9. What is the contraceptive sponge?	The contraceptive sponge absorbs sperm and also contains a spermicide.
10. What is the cervical cap?	Like the diaphragm, the cap covers the cervix and is most effective when used with a spermicide.

Recite

11. What are condoms?

Latex condoms afford protection against STIs as well as conception. Condoms are the only contraceptive device worn by men and the only readily reversible method of contraception that is available to men.

12. What is douching?

Douching, or washing one's vagina after coitus, is ineffective as a contraceptive because large numbers of sperm may pass beyond the range of the douche within seconds after ejaculation.

13. What is the withdrawal method?

Withdrawal—pulling out before ejaculating—requires no special equipment but has a high failure rate.

14. What is the rhythm method?

There are several rhythm methods, each of which relies on awareness of the occurrence of fertile segments of the woman's menstrual cycle. Rhythm methods include the calendar method, the basal body temperature method, and the cervical mucous method. Their failure rate is high in typical use, especially when women have irregular cycles.

15. What is sterilization?

Sterilization is a permanent method of contraception, although it may be reversed in many cases. The male vasectomy cuts the vas deferens and is usually carried out under local anesthesia. Female sterilization methods—called tubal sterilization or tubal ligation—prevent ova and sperm from passing through the fallopian tubes.

16. What is meant by abortion?

The term *abortion* typically refers to induced or purposeful abortion, as opposed to miscarriage (spontaneous abortion).

17. When does human life begin?

People disagree about when human life begins. Some argue that it begins at conception, others when the fetus becomes viable, and still others sometime in between, as, for example, when neural activity begins in the fetal brain.

18. How have various societies reacted to abortion?

In colonial times and through the mid-nineteenth century, women in the United States were permitted to terminate a pregnancy at any time before "quickening" occurred. More restrictive abortion laws were enacted after the Civil War. In 1973, the U.S. Supreme Court in effect legalized abortion nationwide in the landmark *Roe v. Wade* decision.

19. What abortion methods are in use today?

Abortion methods in use today include vacuum aspiration, D&C, D&E, induction of labor by intra-amniotic infusion, hysterotomy, and drugs such as RU-486. Partial-birth abortion is the most controversial method.

Chapter 13

Truth?Fiction?

T / F? Many boys are born with erections.

T / F? Infants often engage in pelvic thrusting at 8 to 10 months of age.

T / F? Most children learn the facts of life from parents or from school sex-education programs.

T / F? Sex education encourages sexual activity among children and adolescents.

T / F? The country of Iran is more explicit and detailed than the United States in its sex education programs.

T / F? Nocturnal emissions in boys accompany erotic dreams.

T / F? Petting is practically universal among adolescents in the United States.

T / F? About 800,000 adolescent girls in the United States become pregnant each year.

T / F? In some school districts, condoms are distributed to adolescents without parental consent.

Sexuality in Childhood and Adolescence

Preview

My heart leaps up when I behold
    A rainbow in the sky:
So was it when my life began;
So is it now I am a man;
So be it when I shall grow old,
    Or let me die!
The Child is father of the Man;
And I could wish my days to be
Bound each to each by natural piety.

—William Wordsworth, "My Heart Leaps Up When I Behold"

What a life it would be, indeed, were our hearts to swell with the wonders of the world throughout our days. In this chapter we begin our chronicle of sexual behavior across the life span, and we see the ways in which the child is father of the man. Within children's personal and social experiences lie the seeds of adult sexual competence and self-esteem—or the seeds of incompetence, guilt, and shame. In the next chapter we shall see that our sexuality remains an integral part of our lives *throughout* our lives—one that can make our hearts leap up for all our days.

Infancy (0 to 2 Years): The Search for the Origins of Human Sexuality

Question: What sexual behaviors do we find among fetuses and newborns? Quite a few, actually. Imaging techniques such as ultrasound have shown, for example, that male fetuses have erections. Fetuses of both sexes suck their fingers. The sucking reflex enables babies to gain nourishment, which is necessary for survival. But as Sigmund Freud theorized, infants may also reap sensual pleasure from sucking fingers, pacifiers, nipples, or whatever else fits into the mouth. None of this is surprising, given the sensitivity of the mouth's mucous lining.

Stimulation of the genitals in infancy may also produce sensations of pleasure. Parents who touch their infants' genitals while changing or washing them may discover the infants smiling or becoming excited. Infants discover the pleasure of self-stimulation (masturbation) for themselves when they gain the capacity to manipulate their genitals with their hands.

Truth?Fiction?
Revisited

It is true that many boys are born with erections. Erection is a reflex that begins to operate early in life.

It is true that infants often engage in pelvic thrusting at 8 to 10 months of age. However, thrusting may not mean the same thing in infants as in adults.

The Infant's Capacity for Sexual Response

Boys not only have erections in utero. Many are also born with erections. Most have erections during the first few weeks.

Signs of sexual arousal in infant girls, such as vaginal lubrication, are less readily detected. Yet evidence of lubrication and genital swelling has been reported (Martinson, 1976).

Do not interpret children's reflexes according to adult concepts of sexuality, however. The reflexes of lubrication and erection do not necessarily signify "interest" in sex. We cannot say what, if anything, infants' reflexes "mean" to them.

Pelvic Thrusting Pelvic thrusting is observed in infant monkeys, apes, and humans. These observations led ethologist John Bowlby (1969) to suggest that infantile sexual behavior may be the rule in mammals, not the exception. Thrusting has been observed in humans at 8 to 10 months of age and may be an expression of affection. Typically, the infant clings to the parent, nuzzles, and thrusts and rotates the pelvis for several seconds.

Orgasm At least some infants seem capable of sexual responses that closely resemble orgasm. Kinsey and his colleagues (1953) noted that baby boys show behaviors that resemble orgasm as early as 5 months, baby girls as early as 4 months. Orgasms in boys are similar to those in men—but lacking ejaculation. Ejaculation occurs only after puberty.

Masturbation

Masturbation is typical for infants and young children and tends to start between 6 and 12 months. Infants often masturbate by rubbing the genitals against a soft object, such as a towel, bedding, or a doll. As they mature and become capable of more coordinated hand movements, infants may prefer manual stimulation of the genitals.

Masturbation to orgasm is rare until the second year (Reinisch, 1990). Some children begin masturbating to orgasm later. Some never do. All in all, however, orgasm from masturbation is found frequently among children, as among adults (Reinisch, 1990).

Sexual Curiosity

Children play "Doctor" and show their curiosity about the sexual anatomy of other people in other ways, such as wanting to be present while a parent is taking a shower or bath. The question is, when does this sort of sexual curiosity develop? A study of 26 German children and their parents found that children frequently develop sexual curiosity in infancy, sometimes as early as 12 to 15 months of age.

Genital Play

Children in the United States typically do not engage in genital play with others until about the age of 2. Then, as an expression of their curiosity about their environment and other people, they may investigate other children's genitals or may hug, cuddle, kiss, or climb on top of them. None of this need cause concern. Spiro (1965) describes 2-year-olds at play in an Israeli kibbutz:

> Ofer [a boy] and Pnina [a girl] sit side by side on chamber pots. . . . Ofer puts his foot on Pnina's foot, she then does the same—this happens several times. . . . Finally, Pnina shifts her pot away, then moves back, then away . . . they laugh. . . . Pnina stands up, lies on the table on her stomach, . . . Ofer pats her buttocks. . . . Ofer kicks Pnina gently, and they laugh . . . Pnina touches and caresses Ofer's leg with her foot . . . says "more more" . . . . Ofer stands, then Pnina stands, both bounce up and down . . . both children are excited, bounce, laugh together . . . Pnina grabs Ofer's penis, and he pushes her away . . . she repeats, he pushes her away, and turns around . . . . Pnina touches his buttocks. (p. 225)

There is no reason to infer that Ofer and Pnina were seeking sexual gratification. Rough-and-tumble play, including touching the genitals, is common among children.

Bed-Sharing

An issue that causes concern among many parents is whether it is "safe" for infants to share their beds. Parents have several motives for sharing their beds with infants, including the fact that infants are more likely to get back to sleep in their parents' beds when they awaken in the night and that it makes breast-feeding easier at odd hours. But there is also the fear that allowing infants to spend the night with parents may have adverse effects on their sexual development.

Little research has been done on the issue, but one 18-year longitudinal study is of special interest. The researchers followed a newborn infant to the age of 18 in 205 families (Okami et al., 2002). They found that the children who shared beds with their parents during infancy showed superior intellectual development at the age of 6 years, compared with children who did not share beds with their parents. The advantage of bed-sharing essentially disappeared by the age of 18. Most instructive is the finding that no sexual problems were connected with bed-sharing, at any age. Therefore, it would appear that research evidence does not support the view that parents need to avoid sharing their beds with their children.

Sexual Orientation of Parents

Questions have also been raised about the effects of gay parents on the sexual orientation of their children. A Scandinavian research group supported the findings of most studies of the issue. The group analyzed the findings of 23 studies of 615 children reared from infancy by gay and lesbian parents and 387 control children reared by heterosexual parents (Anderssen et al., 2002). Outcome measures included emo-

Review: Infancy (0 to 2 Years): The Search for the Origins of Human Sexuality

Reflect

How would you respond if you observed your infant masturbating? Why?

Critical Thinking

Why is it difficult to interpret the meaning of pelvic thrusting in infants?

1. Stimulation of the genitals in infancy (*Does* or *Does not?*) produce sensations of pleasure.

2. Boys (*Can* or *Cannot?*) be born with erections.

3. Lubrication and erection are automatic responses called _____.

4. Pelvic thrusting has been observed in humans as early as _____ of age.

5. Masturbation tends to start between _____ and _____ months of age.

6. Children begin to engage in genital play with others at about the age of _____.

7. There (*Is* or *Is not?*) research evidence that bed-sharing with infants harms their personal or sexual development.

8. Children reared by homosexual parents (*Do* or *Do not?*) differ from other children in their sexual orientation and gender-typed behavior patterns.

tional stability, sexual orientation, gender-typed behavior, adjustment, gender identity, and intellectual functioning. The children reared by homosexual parents did not differ from controls on any of the variables, including sexual orientation and gender-typed behavior patterns.

Early Childhood (3 to 8 Years)

SUSAN: Once my younger sister and I were over at a girl friend's house playing in her bedroom. For some reason she pulled her pants down and exposed her rear to us. We were amazed to see she had an extra opening down there we didn't know about. My sister reciprocated by pulling her pants down so we could see if she had the same extra opening. We were amazed at our discovery, our mothers not having mentioned to us that we had a vagina!

CHRISTOPHER: Nancy was a willing playmate, and we spent many hours together examining each other's bodies as doctor and nurse. We even once figured out a pact that we would continue these examinations and watch each other develop. That was before we had started school. (Morrison et al., 1980, p. 19)

These recollections from early childhood illustrate children's interest in sexual anatomy and behavior. *Question: What types of sexual behaviors do we find among children in early childhood?* One finding is that children often show each other their bodies. The unwritten rule seems to be "I'll show you mine if you'll show me yours."

Masturbation

KIM: I began to masturbate when I was 3 years old. My parents . . . tried long and hard to discourage me. They told me it wasn't nice for a young lady to have her hand between her legs.

At What Age Does Curiosity about Sex Develop?
Children are naturally inquisitive about sexual anatomy and sexual behavior. Much curiosity is triggered when they become aware that males and females differ in anatomy.

How Should Parents React to Children Who Masturbate?

Few parents today believe that children who masturbate set the stage for physical and mental maladies. Still, some parents react with concern, disgust, or shock when their children masturbate.

Parents who are unaware that masturbation is commonplace among children may erroneously assume that children who masturbate are oversexed or aberrant. The parent may pull a child's hands away and scold her or him. Some may even slap the child's hand. Once the child is capable of understanding speech, the parent may say things like "Don't touch down there! That's a bad thing to do. Stop doing that." Threats and punishments may be used. Or parents may fail to acknowledge the behavior openly but move the hands away from the genitals or pick up the child whenever he or she is discovered masturbating.

Sex educators Mary Calderone and Eric Johnson (1989) argue that

punishment will not stop children from masturbating. It may cause them to become secretive and guilty about it, however. Sex guilt tends to persist and may impede sexual pleasure in marriage. June Reinisch (1990), director of the Kinsey Institute, notes that

> Parents who scowl, scold, or punish in response to a child's exploring his or her genitals may be teaching the child that this kind of pleasure is wrong and that the *child* is "bad" for engaging in this kind of behavior. This message may hinder the ability to give and receive erotic pleasures as an adult and ultimately interfere with the ability to establish a loving and intimate relationship. (p. 248)

Calderone, Johnson, and Reinisch concur that children need to learn that masturbation in public is not acceptable in our culture, however. Calderone and Johnson suggest that the child who

masturbates in front of others can be told something like this:

> I'm glad you've found your body feels good, but when you want to touch your body that way, it's more private to be in your room by yourself. (p. 138)

Reinisch adds that parents are important shapers of their children's sexuality and, more broadly, of their self-esteem. Acknowledging the child's sexuality, rather than rejecting and discouraging it, can strengthen children's self-esteem, build a positive body image, and encourage competence and assertiveness.

Not all authorities, and certainly not all parents, endorse such views. Some object to masturbation on religious or moral grounds. Others feel uncomfortable or conflicted about masturbation themselves. Parents must decide for themselves how best to react when they discover their children masturbating.

> When I was five I remember my mother discovering that I masturbated with a rag doll I slept with. She was upset, but she didn't make a big deal about it. She just told me in a matter-of-fact way, "Do you know that what you're doing is called masturbating?" That didn't make much sense to me, except I got the impression she didn't want me to do it. (Morrison et al., 1980, pp. 4–5)

Because of the difficulties in conducting research into childhood sexuality, statistics on masturbation and other sexual activities are largely speculative. Parents may not wish to answer questions about their children's sexual behavior. Or they may want to present their children as little "gentlemen" and "ladies" by underreporting their sexual activity. Their biases may lead them not to perceive genital touching as masturbation. Many parents will not even allow their adolescents to be interviewed about sex (Kaiser Family Foundation, 2003), let alone younger children. And when we try to look back as adults, our memories may be inaccurate.

A study by psychologist William Friedrich (1998) of the Mayo Institute relied on interviews with the mothers of more than 1,100 children. The goal of the study was to establish what kinds of sexual behaviors can normally be expected in childhood, in order to help educators and other professionals determine when sexual behavior might be suggestive of childhood sexual abuse. The study did not provide data about masturbation per se, but, as shown in Table 13.1, it offered some insight into how many children touch their "private parts." Friedrich suggests that behavior that occurs in at least 20% of children is normal from a statistical point of view.

TABLE 13.1		
Some Sexual Behaviors Common in Childhood		
	Boys	Girls
Ages 2–5		
Touches or tries to touch mother's or other women's breasts	42.4%	43.7%
Touches private parts when at home	60.2	43.8
Tries to look at people when they are nude or undressing	26.8	26.9
Ages 6–9		
Touches private parts when at home	39.8	20.7
Tries to look at people when they are nude or undressing	20.2	20.5
Ages 10–12		
Is very interested in the opposite sex	24.1	28.7

Source of data: William M. Friedrich. Cited in Susan Gilbert (1998, April 7). New light shed on normal sexual behavior in a child. *The New York Times*, p. F7.

Male–Female Sexual Behavior

ALICIA: On my birthday when I was in the second grade, I remember a classmate, Tim, walked home with a friend and me. He kept chasing me to give me kisses all over my face, and I acted like I didn't want him to do it, yet I knew I liked it a lot; when he would stop, I thought he didn't like me anymore. (Morrison et al., 1980, pp. 21, 29)

Three- and 4-year-olds commonly express affection through kissing. Curiosity about the genitals increases in this stage. Sex games like "show" and "playing doctor" may begin earlier, but they become common between the ages of 6 and 10 (Reinisch, 1990). Much of this sexual activity takes place in same-sex groups, although mixed-sex sex games are not uncommon. Children may show their genitals to each other, touch each other's genitals, or masturbate together.

Male–Male and Female–Female Sexual Behavior

ARNOLD: When I was about 5, my cousin and I . . . went into the basement and dropped our pants. We touched each other's penises, and that was it. I guess I didn't realize the total significance of the secrecy in which we carried out this act. For later . . . my parents questioned me . . . and I told them exactly what we had done. They were horrified and told me that that was definitely forbidden. (Morrison et al., 1980, p. 24)

Despite Arnold's parents' "horror," same-sex sexual play in childhood does not foreshadow adult sexual orientation (Reinisch, 1990). It may, in fact, be more common than heterosexual play. It typically involves handling the other child's genitals, although it may include oral or anal contact. It may also include an outdoor variation of the game of "show" in which boys urinate together and see who can reach farthest or highest.

Review: Early Childhood (3 to 8 Years)

Reflect

Have you "caught" or observed children playing "Doctor"? What was your reaction? Why?

CriticalThinking

Why is it difficult to obtain accurate information about sexual behavior in childhood?

9. Statistics concerning the incidence of masturbation in children are (*Accurate* or *Speculative*?)

10. The Friedrich study found that about _____% of 2- to 5-year-olds touch their "private parts" when at home.

11. About _____% of 2- to 5-year-olds try to look at people who are nude or undressing.

12. Three- and 4-year-olds commonly express affection through _____.

13. Sex games like "show" and "playing doctor" become common between the ages of _____ and _____.

14. Same-sex sexual play in childhood (*Does* or *Does not*?) foreshadow adult sexual orientation.

We will end this section with the memories of a woman when she was on the edge of preadolescence.

> When I was 8 and had just learned about menstruation, I fashioned a small sanitary napkin for [my Barbie doll] out of neatly folded tissues. Rubber bands held it in place. "Look," said my bemused mother, "Barbie's got her little period. Now she can have a baby."[1] I was disappointed, but my girlfriends snickered in a way that satisfied me. You see, we all wanted Barbie to be, well, dirty.
>
> Our Barbies had sex, at least our childish version of it. They hugged and kissed the few available boy dolls we had—clean-cut and oh-so-square Ken, the more relaxed and sexy Allan. Our Barbies also danced, pranced and strutted, but mostly they stripped. An adult friend tells me how she used to put her Barbie's low-backed bathing suit on backward, so the doll's breasts were exposed. I dressed mine in her candy-striped baby-sitter's apron—and nothing else. Girls respond intuitively to the doll's sexuality, and it lets them play out those roles in an endlessly compelling and yet ultimately safe manner. (McDonough, 1998, p. 70)

Preadolescence (9 to 13 Years)

Question: How does sexual behavior in preadolescence differ from that of earlier stages of development? Some of the pertinent behaviors are sexually related rather than sexual per se. For example, during preadolescence children typically form relationships with a close "best friend" that enable them to share secrets and confidences. The friends are usually of the same sex. Preadolescents also tend to socialize with larger networks of friends in sex-segregated groups. At this stage, boys are likely to think that girls are "dorks." To girls at this stage, *dork* is too nice an epithet to apply to most boys.

Preadolescents grow increasingly preoccupied with and self-conscious about their bodies. Peers pressure preadolescents to conform to dress codes, the "proper"

---

1. Yes, yes, we know that the first several cycles of most girls are anovulatory (and so they cannot get pregnant), but we are recounting what someone *said*. So far as we know, it is difficult for Barbie dolls to get pregnant under the best of circumstances.

slang, and group norms concerning sex and drugs. Peer disapproval can be an intense punishment.

Sexual urges are experienced by many preadolescents but may not emerge until adolescence. Sigmund Freud had theorized that sexual impulses are hidden ("latent") during preadolescence, but many preadolescents are quite active sexually.

Masturbation

> PAUL: When I was about 10, stories about masturbation got me worried. A friend and I went to a friend's older brother whom we respected and asked, "Is it really bad?" His reply stuck in my mind for years. "Well, it's like a bottle of olives—every time you take one out, there is one less in there." We were very worried because we thought we'd run out before we got to girls. (Morrison et al., 1980, pp. 6–8)

Kinsey and his colleagues (1948, 1953) reported that masturbation is the primary means of achieving orgasm during preadolescence for both boys and girls. They found that 45% of males and 15% of females masturbated by age 13. Although the frequencies of masturbation reported by Kinsey and his colleagues are suspect, other studies agree that adolescent males are more likely to masturbate than adolescent females (Pinkerton et al., 2002). As noted by Steven Pinkerton and his colleagues (2002), the frequency of masturbation is connected with social norms that appear to hold that masturbation is more acceptable or normal for males than for females.

Male–Female Sexual Behavior

Preadolescent sex play often involves mutual display of the genitals, with or without touching. Such sexual experiences are quite common and do not appear to impair future sexual adjustment (Leitenberg et al., 1989).

Although preadolescents tend to socialize in same sex groups, interest in the other sex among heterosexuals tends to increase gradually as they approach puberty. Group dating and mixed-sex parties often provide preadolescents with their first exposure to heterosexual activities. Couples may not begin to pair off until early or middle adolescence.

Male–Male and Female–Female Sexual Behavior

Much preadolescent sexual behavior among members of the same sex is simply exploration. Some incidents reflect lack of availability of partners of the other sex. As with younger children, preadolescent experiences with children of the same sex may be more common than heterosexual experiences (Leitenberg et al., 1989). These activities are usually limited to touching of each other's genitals or mutual masturbation. Most same-sex sexual experiences involve single episodes or short-lived relationships and do not reflect the individual's sexual orientation.

Question: Generally speaking, how do preadolescents learn about sex?

Sex Education and Miseducation: More Than "Don't"

> Imagine teaching driving the same way sex education is taught. You'd be told never to drive or ride as a passenger because you could be injured and go to the hospital. No one would ever take a car out. (Mark Miller, 1998)

Talking with Your Children about Sex

"Daddy, where do babies come from?"

"What are you asking me for? Go ask your mother."

Most children do not find it easy to talk to their parents about sex (National Campaign to Prevent Teenage Pregnancy, 2003). It may be no easier for the parents. Only about one-quarter of the children investigated in one study had done so (National Campaign to Prevent Teenage Pregnancy, 2003). Children and adolescents usually find it easier to approach their mothers than their fathers. Many receive *mis*information from their friends, and misinformed teenagers run a higher risk of unwanted pregnancies and STIs (Ben-Zur, 2003).

Yet most young children are curious about where babies come from, about what makes little girls different from little boys, and so on. Parents who avoid answering such questions convey their own uneasiness about sex and may teach children that sex is something to be ashamed of, not something they should discuss openly.

Some parents resist talking about sex with their children because they are insecure in their own knowledge. But parents need not be sex experts to talk to their children about sex. Parents can turn to books in the local bookstore to fill in gaps in knowledge, or to books that are intended for parents to read to their children. They can admit that they do not know the answer to a particular question. Children often respect parents who display such honesty.

In answering children's questions, parents need to think about what children can understand. The 4-year-old who wants to know where babies come from is probably not interested in detailed biological information. It may be enough to say, "From Mommy's uterus" and then point to the abdominal region. Why say "tummy"? "Tummy" is wrong and confusing.

In their *Family Book about Sexuality*, Calderone and Johnson (1989) offer some pointers:

1. *Be willing to answer questions about sex.* Parents who respond to their

children's questions about sex by saying, "Why do you want to know that?" squelch further questioning. The child is likely to interpret the parent's response as meaning "You shouldn't be interested in that."

2. *Use appropriate language.* As children develop awareness of their sexuality, they need to learn the names of their sex organs. They also need to learn that the "dirty words" that others use to refer to the sexual parts of the body are not acceptable in most situations, because they carry emotional connotations that can arouse negative feelings.

Nor should parents use "silly words" to describe sexual organs:

Another way parents send out negative messages about sexuality is by using silly words (or no words at all) to describe sexual anatomy. Whether they call genitals "pee-pee" or "privates" or nothing at all, parents are telling children that these body parts are significantly

Truth?Fiction?
Revisited

It is not true that most children learn the facts of life from parents or from school sex education programs. Most children learn about sex from peers. Is the lamp on the street corner the key guiding light for U.S. youth?

Preadolescents and adolescents could be said to learn about sex through a combination of education and miseducation. Mark Miller is a graduate of Brown University's program in sexuality and society. He and scholars of human sexuality lament the approaches of most sex education programs. Says Anke Ehrhardt (1998), a psychiatry professor at Columbia University, "In other countries, sex education is put in a positive context of loving relationships, but here we spread fear. And it hasn't worked. We have a much higher rate of teen pregnancy."

As noted in Table 3.2, adolescents and young adults in the Kaiser Family Foundation study reported that they were somewhat more likely to receive information about sex from friends and media sources—TV shows, films, magazines, and the Internet—than from sex education classes or their parents (Kaiser Family Foundation, 2003). We have to wonder about the representativeness of the sample because the parents of minors were available to provide permission to interview them. Young people with more distant or less available parents might obtain relatively more information from friends and the media, and less from their parents.

different, embarrassing, mysterious, or taboo compared to such other body parts as the eyes, nose, and knees, which have names openly used in conversation. (Reinisch, 1990, p. 248)

3. *Give advice in the form of information that the child can use to make sound decisions, not as an imperial edict.* State your convictions, but label them as your own rather than something you are trying to impose on your child. "Laying down the law" is not likely to be as effective as providing information and encouraging discussion. Reinisch (1990) suggests combining information about sex with expressions of the parents' values and beliefs.

Parents of teenage children often react to sexual experimentation with threats or punishments, which may cause adolescents to rebel or tune them out. Or the adolescent may learn to associate sex with fear and anger, which may persist even in adult relationships. Parents may find it more constructive to convey concern about the consequences of children's actions in a loving and nonthreatening way that invites an open response.

Say, for example, "I'm worried about the way you are experimenting, and I'd like to give you some information that you may not have. Can we talk about it?" (Calderone & Johnson, 1989, p. 141).

4. *Share information in small doses.* Pick a time and place that feel natural for such discussions, such as when the child is preparing for bed or when you are riding in the car.

5. *Encourage the child to talk about sex.* Children may feel embarrassed about talking about sex, especially with family members. Make the child aware that you are always available to answer questions. Be "askable." But let the child postpone talking about a sensitive topic until the two of you are alone or the child feels comfortable. Books about sexuality may help a child open up. They can be left lying around or given to the child with a suggestion such as "This is a good book about sex, or at least I thought so. If you read it, then maybe we can talk about it" (Calderone & Johnson, 1989, p. 136).

6. *Respect privacy rights.* Most of us, parents and children alike, value our

privacy at certain times. A parent who feels uncomfortable sharing a bathroom with a child can simply tell the child that Daddy or Mommy likes to be alone when using the bathroom. Or the parent might explain, "I like my privacy, so please knock and I'll tell you if it's okay to come in. I'll do the same for you" (Calderone & Johnson, 1989, p. 137). This can be said without a scolding or harsh tone. Privacy rights in the bedroom can be established by saying, in a clear and unthreatening way, "Please knock when the door's closed and wait to be invited in" (Calderone & Johnson, 1989, p. 138). But it is just as important for the parent to respect the child's rights to privacy. The child is likely to feel grateful for the respect and to show respect in return.

Adolescents offer parents some additional advice on how to communicate with them (Pistella & Bonati, 1999):

1. Treat teenagers as equals.
2. Increase your knowledge about the lifestyles of today's teenagers and the peer pressures they experience.
3. *Listen.*

TABLE 13.2

Percent of Adolescents and Young Adults (Ages 13 to 24) Who Say They Have Learned "A Lot" or "Some" from the Following Sources

Friends	76%
Media sources (movies, magazine, Internet)	72
Sex education classes	68
Parents	68
Boyfriends, girlfriends, or partners	65
Doctors or other health care providers	58
Brothers and sisters	39

Source: Kaiser Family Foundation, Holt, T., Greene, L., & Davis, J. (2003). *National survey of adolescents and young adults: Sexual health knowledge, attitudes and experiences.* Menlo Park, CA: Henry J. Kaiser Family Foundation. Table 30, p. 37.

U.S. Falls Behind in Sex Education

Iran may let 9-year-old girls get married, but it could still teach the United States something about sex education, Population Action International said in a report issued in 2022. Well-meaning adults trying to protect children and teenagers from sexual activity are actually keeping vital knowledge from them, and this is true around the world, the report from the nonprofit family-planning advocacy group says.

Only the Netherlands has an exemplary policy, the group said, citing statistics that show the Dutch reap benefits from their policies that include exceptionally low rates of teenage pregnancy, HIV infection in youth and sexually transmitted infections (STIs).

"Iran has a relatively strong public health system through which family planning and maternal health services are widely delivered," Margaret Greene, who helped write the report, told a news conference. "In the United States we are increasingly headed toward a politicized content

Sex Education Despite the availability of sex education in most schools, many young people still learn about sex from their peers. Survey data show that most parents want sex education to cover abstinence, avoiding pregnancy, sexually transmitted infections, abortion, and sexual orientation. However, we may do a poorer job of teaching our children about sex than most European nations do, and even Iran!

Truth?Fiction?
Revisited

There is no evidence that sex education encourages sexual activity among children and adolescents.

It is true that the country of Iran is more explicit and detailed than the United States in its sex education programs.

Today, nearly all states mandate or recommend sex education, although its content and length varies widely. Most programs emphasize biological aspects of puberty and reproduction. Few deal with abortion, masturbation, sexual orientation, or sexual pleasure.

Sex education in the schools, especially about value-laden topics, remains a source of controversy. Some people argue that sex education ought to be left to parents and religious authorities. But the data suggest that the real alternatives to the schools are peers and the corner newsstand, which sells more copies of "adult" magazines than of textbooks. Many parents are also concerned that teaching subjects such as sexual techniques and contraception encourages sexual experimentation. Yet research does not show that sex education increases sexual experimentation (Blake et al., 2003; Kirchheimer & Smith, 2003).

Many school programs that offer information about contraception and other sensitive topics are limited to high school juniors and seniors. But sexual experimentation often begins earlier (Ehrhardt, 1998). Accurate information in preadolescence might prevent sexual mishaps. Many teens, for example, erroneously believe that a female cannot get pregnant from her first coital experience. Others believe that douching protects them from pregnancy and disease.

with no guarantee of medical accuracy . . . whereas Iran has developed age-appropriate sex materials that are very accurate and explicit," Greene said. "I'd say there is far less hypocrisy in this area."

The group cited moves in Congress, where a House of Representatives panel endorsed funding "abstinence only" sex education, defeating opponents who called for a broader sex education curriculum providing information on birth control and STIs. The panel also dropped wording in the bill that would require sex education programs to be backed by scientific research.

BLOCKED MOVES

The group also points out, however, that Iran's religious leaders recently blocked moves to raise the legal age of marriage for girls from 9 to 15 and

that Iran's sex education programs assume that all sexually active couples are married.

The problem in most countries is that they do not respect the ability of adolescents to make wise decisions for themselves, said James Waggoner, president of Advocates for Youth, which supported the report. "Too many policymakers subscribe to the caricature of adolescents as mere hormone-driven accidents waiting to happen," Waggoner said.

The groups especially attacked abstinence-only education programs, which teach only that sex before marriage is wrong and do not offer any information to teens who may be having sex anyway. The result can be deadly, Waggoner said: "Our HIV rate for young men is 3 times higher than in the Netherlands. Our rate for teen births is 11 time higher than in the Netherlands. Our teen

gonorrhea rate is 74 times higher than in the Netherlands."

Many studies have shown that open sex education that includes information about contraception and that also attempts to build self-esteem can lower sexual activity rates and result in fewer pregnancies and cases of disease, the report says.

"We have over 87 percent of Americans who believe there should be comprehensive sex education in schools (see Table 13.3), and we have a Congress that does not support this in their legislation," Population Action International president Amy Coen said. "It is a battle between religious conservatives and the rest of the country and the rest of the world."

Source: Adapted from U.S. falls behind in sex education, study finds (2002, April 26). Washington, DC: Reuters.

TABLE 13.3

What American Parents Want from Sex Education

Percentage of parents who say sex education should cover . . .	
HIV/AIDS and other sexually transmitted infections	98%
Abstinence; what to do in cases of rape or sexual assault; how to talk with parents about sex	97
How to deal with pressure to have sex and the emotional consequences of sex	94
How to be tested for HIV and other sexually transmitted infections	92
The basics of reproduction and birth control	90
How to talk with a partner about birth control and sexually transmitted infections	88
How to use condoms	85
How to use and where to get other birth control	84
Abortion	79
Sexual orientation and homosexuality	76

Source: Kaiser Family Foundation; reported in Diana Jean Schemo (2000, October 4). Survey finds parents favor more detailed sex education. *The New York Times,* pp. A1, A27.

Review: Preadolescence (9 to 13 Years)

Reflect

How did you learn about sex? Would you want your own children to learn about sex in the same way? Why or why not?

Critical Thinking

Do you approve or disapprove of sex education in the schools? What topics should sex education cover? Explain.

15. Preadolescents tend to socialize with friends of the (*Same* or *Other*?) sex.

16. Preadolescents become (*More* or *Less*?) self-conscious about their bodies.

17. _____ pressure induces preadolescents to conform to dress codes and standards of behavior.

18. Kinsey reported that _____ is the primary means of achieving orgasm during preadolescence.

19. Adolescent (*Males* or *Females*?) are more likely to masturbate.

20. Preadolescent sex play often involves mutual _____ of the genitals.

21. During preadolescence, sexual experiences with children of the (*Same* or *Other*?) sex may be more common.

22. Adolescents are most likely to learn about sex from _____.

Adolescence

Question: What is adolescence? This is not a trick question. *Adolescence* is actually a technical term. Adolescence is bounded at its beginning by the advent of puberty and at its end by the capacity to take on adult responsibilities. In our society adolescents are "neither fish nor fowl," as the saying goes—neither children nor adults. Adolescents may be able to reproduce and be taller than their parents, but they may not be allowed to get a driver's license or attend R-rated films. They are prevented from working long hours and must usually stay in school until age 16. They cannot marry until they reach the "age of consent." The message is clear: Adults see adolescents as impulsive and as needing to be restricted for "their own good." Given these restrictions, a sex drive that is heightened by surges of sex hormones, and media inundation with sexual themes, it is not surprising that many adolescents are in conflict with their families about going around with certain friends, about sex, and about using the family car (Pettit, 2003).

Adolescence Adolescence begins with puberty. Many adults see adolescents as impulsive, as needing to be controlled for "their own good." However, adolescents have a sex drive that is heightened by surges of sex hormones, and they are flooded with sexual themes in the media. Therefore, it is not surprising that many of them are in conflict with their families about issues of autonomy and sexual behavior.

Puberty

Question: It was noted that adolescence begins with puberty. What is puberty?
Puberty begins with the appearance of **secondary sex characteristics** and ends when the long bones make no further gains in length (see Table 13.4). The appearance of strands of pubic hair is often the first visible sign of puberty. Pubic hair tends to be light colored, sparse, and straight at first. Then it spreads and grows darker, thicker, and coarser. Puberty also involves changes in **primary sex characteristics**. Once puberty begins, most major changes occur within 3 years in girls and within 4 years in boys.

Reproduction becomes possible toward the end of puberty. The two principal markers of reproductive potential are **menarche** in the girl and the first ejaculation in the boy. But these events may not signify immediate fertility.

Girls typically experience menarche between the ages of 10 and 18. In the mid-1800s, European girls typically achieved menarche by about age 17 (see Figure 13.1). The age of menarche has declined sharply since then among girls in Western nations, probably because of improved nutrition and health care. In the United States, by the 2000s the average age of menarche had dropped to about 12.1 years for African American girls and to 12.6 years for European American girls (Anderson et al., 2003).

The **critical fat hypothesis** suggests that girls must reach a certain body weight (perhaps 103 to 109 pounds) to trigger pubertal changes such as menarche, and children today tend to achieve larger body sizes sooner. Body fat might play a crucial role because fat cells secrete leptin. Leptin is a chemical that would then signal the body to secrete a cascade of hormones that increase the levels of estrogen in the body. In the Anderson (2003) study, higher body weight was associated with earlier menarche. It is also known that menarche comes later to athletes, who have a lower percentage of body fat (Frisch, 1997).

Pubertal Changes in the Female First menstruation, or menarche, is the most obvious sign of puberty in girls. Yet other, less obvious changes have already set the stage for menstruation. Between 8 and 14 years of age, release of FSH by the pituitary gland causes the ovaries to begin to secrete estrogen. Estrogen has several major effects on pubertal development. For one, it stimulates the growth of breast tissue ("breast buds"), perhaps as early as age 8 or 9. The breasts usually begin to enlarge during the tenth year.

Estrogen promotes the growth of the uterus and the thickening of the vaginal lining. It also stimulates growth of fatty and supporting tissue in the hips and buttocks. This tissue and the widening of the pelvis cause the hips to become rounded and permit childbearing. But the growth of fatty deposits and connective tissue varies considerably. Some women may have pronounced breasts; others may have relatively large hips.

Small amounts of androgens produced by the female's adrenal glands, along with estrogen, stimulate development of pubic and underarm hair, beginning at about age 11. Excessive androgen production can darken or thicken facial hair.

Estrogen causes the labia to grow during puberty, but androgens cause the clitoris to develop. Estrogen stimulates growth of the vagina and uterus. Estrogen typically brakes the female growth spurt some years before that of the male. Girls deficient in estrogen during their late teens may grow quite tall, but most tall girls owe their stature to normal, genetically determined variations, not estrogen deficiency.

Estrogen production becomes cyclical in puberty and regulates the menstrual cycle. Following menarche, a girl's early menstrual cycles are typically **anovulatory**. Girls cannot become pregnant until ovulation occurs, which may lag behind

Puberty The stage of development during which reproduction first becomes possible. Puberty begins with the appearance of *secondary sex characteristics* and ends when the long bones make no further gains in length. (From the Latin *puber,* meaning "of ripe age.")

Secondary sex characteristics Physical characteristics that differentiate males and females and that usually appear at puberty but are not directly involved in reproduction, such as the bodily distribution of hair and fat, development of the muscle mass, and deepening of the voice.

Primary sex characteristics Physical characteristics that differentiate males and females and are directly involved in reproduction, such as the sex organs.

Menarche The onset of menstruation; first menstruation. (From the Greek roots *men,* meaning "month," and *arche,* meaning "beginning.")

Critical fat hypothesis The view that girls must reach a certain body weight to trigger pubertal changes such as menarche.

Anovulatory Without ovulation.

TABLE 13.4

Stages of Pubertal Development*

In Females	
Beginning sometime between ages 8 and 11	Pituitary hormones stimulate ovaries to increase production of estrogen. Internal reproductive organs begin to grow.
Beginning sometime between ages 9 and 15	First the areola (the darker area around the nipple) and then the breasts increase in size and become more rounded. Pubic hair becomes darker and coarser. Growth in height continues. Body fat continues to round body contours. A normal vaginal discharge becomes noticeable. Sweat and oil glands increase in activity, and acne may appear. Internal and external reproductive organs and genitals grow, making the vagina longer and the labia more pronounced.
Beginning sometime between ages 10 and 16	Areola and nipples grow, often forming a second mound sticking out from the rounded breast mound. Pubic hair begins to grow in a triangular shape and to cover the center of the mons. Underarm hair appears. Menarche occurs. Internal reproductive organs continue to develop. Ovaries may begin to release mature eggs capable of being fertilized. Growth in height slows.
Beginning sometime between ages 12 and 19	Breasts near adult size and shape. Pubic hair fully covers the mons and spreads to the top of the thighs. The voice may deepen slightly (but not as much as in males). Menstrual cycles gradually become more regular. Some further changes in body shape may occur into the young woman's early 20s.

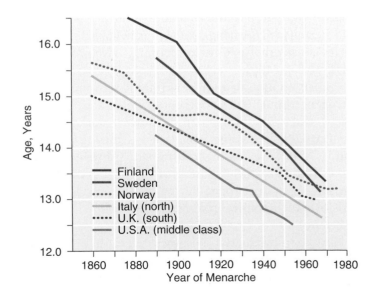

Figure 13.1. Age at Menarche. *The age at menarche has been declining since the mid-1800s among girls in Western nations, apparently because of improved nutrition and health care. Menarche may be triggered by the accumulation of a critical percentage of body fat.*

TABLE 13.4 Continued

Stages of Pubertal Development*

In Males	
Beginning sometime between ages 9 and 15	The testicles begin to grow.
	The skin of the scrotum becomes redder and coarser.
	A few straight pubic hairs appear at the base of the penis.
	Muscle mass develops, and the boy begins to grow taller.
	The areola grows larger and darker.
Beginning sometime between ages 11 and 16	The penis begins to grow longer.
	The testicles and scrotum continue to grow.
	Pubic hair becomes coarser and more curled and spreads to cover the area between the legs.
	The body gains in height.
	The shoulders broaden.
	The hips narrow.
	The larynx enlarges, resulting in a deepening of the voice.
	Sparse facial and underarm hair appears.
Beginning sometime between ages 11 and 17	The penis begins to increase in circumference as well as in length (though more slowly).
	The testicles continue to increase in size.
	The texture of the pubic hair becomes more like an adult's.
	Growth of facial and underarm hair increases.
	Shaving may begin.
	First ejaculation occurs.
	In nearly half of all boys, gynecomastia (breast enlargement) occurs; it then decreases in a year or two.
	Increased skin oils may produce acne.
Beginning sometime between ages 14 and 18	The body nears final adult height, and the genitals achieve adult shape and size, with pubic hair spreading to the thighs and slightly upward toward the belly.
	Chest hair appears.
	Facial hair reaches full growth.
	Shaving becomes more frequent.
	For some young men, further increases in height, body hair, and muscle growth and strength continue into their early 20s.

---

* This table is a general guideline. Changes may appear sooner or later than shown and do not always appear in the indicated sequence.

Source: Copyright © 1990 by the Kinsey Institute for Research in Sex, Gender, and Reproduction. From *The Kinsey Institute new report on sex*.

menarche by as much as 2 years. At first ovulation may not be reliable, so a girl may be relatively infertile. Some teenagers are highly fertile soon after menarche, however.

Pubertal Changes in the Male At puberty the hypothalamus signals the pituitary to increase production of FSH and LH. These releasing hormones stimulate the testes to increase their output of testosterone. Testosterone prompts growth of the male genitals: the testes, scrotum, and penis. It fosters differentiation of male secondary sex characteristics: the growth of facial, body, and pubic hair and the deepening of the voice. Testicle growth, in turn, accelerates testosterone production and pubertal changes. The testes continue to grow, and the scrotal sac becomes larger and hangs

Truth?Fiction?
Revisited

Despite the term *wet dreams,* nocturnal emissions need not accompany boys' erotic dreams.

loosely from the body. The penis widens and lengthens, and pubic hair appears.

By age 13 or 14, erections become frequent. Indeed, many junior high school boys dread being caught between classes with erections or being asked to stand before the class. Under the influence of testosterone, the prostate and seminal vesicles—the organs that produce semen—increase in size, and semen production begins. Boys typically experience their first ejaculation by age 13 or 14, most often through masturbation. There is much variation, however. First ejaculations may occur as early as age 8 or not until the early 20s (Reinisch, 1990). Mature sperm are not usually found in the ejaculate until about a year after the first ejaculation, at age 14 on average. But sperm may be present in the first ejaculate, so pubertal boys should not assume that they have an infertile "grace period" following their first ejaculation. About a year after first ejaculation, boys may also begin to experience **nocturnal emissions**, which are also called "wet dreams" because of the belief that nocturnal emissions accompany erotic dreams—which need not be so.

Underarm hair appears at about age 15. Facial hair is at first a fuzz on the upper lip. A beard does not appear for another 2 or 3 years. Only half of U.S. boys shave (of necessity) by age 17. The beard and chest hair continue to develop past the age of 20. At age 14 or 15, the voice deepens because of the growth of the **larynx** and the lengthening of the vocal cords. Development is gradual, and the voices of adolescent boys sometimes crack embarrassingly.

Boys and girls undergo general growth spurts during puberty. Girls usually shoot up before boys. Individuals differ, however, and some boys experience these growth spurts sooner than some girls.

Increases in muscle mass produce increases in weight. The shoulders and the circumference of the chest widen. At the age of 18 or so, men stop growing taller because estrogen prevents the long bones from making further gains in length. Males normally produce some estrogen in the adrenal glands and testes. Nearly one in two boys experiences temporary enlargement of the breasts, or **gynecomastia**, during puberty; this condition is also caused by estrogen.

In both females and males, sex hormones course through the bloodstream in copious amounts, giving rise to a relatively strong sex drive. *Question: What sexual outlets do adolescents find?*

Masturbation

Masturbation is a major sexual outlet during adolescence. About half of the adolescent boys (46%) in Coles and Stokes's (1985) national survey of 1,067 teenagers and about a quarter of the girls (24%) reported masturbating. Surveys consistently show the same sex difference: Boys are more likely than girls to masturbate (Larsson & Svedin, 2002).

A southern California survey of 641 teenagers showed that boys who masturbate do so two to three times a week, on the average, compared to about once a month for girls (Hass, 1979). Researchers find no links between adolescent masturbation and early sexual activity (for example, frequency of intercourse, number of different partners, or age upon first intercourse) and sexual adjustment during young adulthood (Leitenberg et al., 1993). Some teens still think of masturbation as shameful.

Male–Female Sexual Behavior

Young people today start dating and going out earlier than in past generations. Teens who date earlier (by age 14) are more likely to engage in coitus during high school

Nocturnal emission Involuntary ejaculation of seminal fluid while asleep. Also referred to as a "wet dream," although the individual need not be dreaming about sex, or dreaming at all, at the time.

Larynx A structure of muscle and cartilage at the upper end of the trachea that contains the vocal cords; the voice box.

Gynecomastia Overdevelopment of a male's breasts. (From the Greek roots *gyne,* meaning "woman," and *mastos,* meaning "breast.")

Human
Sexuality
in the
New
Millennium

Keeping Teenagers in Line Online

A divorced mother of two teenagers in Livingston, New Jersey, finally realized that her 14-year-old son's online habits called for drastic steps. For months he had been glued to the family computer at all hours, getting into online quarrels. His grades were sinking, and letters from America Online were piling up, citing violations of its policy against vulgar language in its forums.

His mother tried parental-control software, but he circumvented it within minutes. She tried closing the family's America Online account several times; feigning her voice, he had it reopened. She installed hardware requiring a password to be entered to start the computer; he reconfigured the circuitry to get back in. One night, in desperation, she slept with the power cord under her pillow.

Then she took the computer away. For seven months she hid the computer tower in the trunk of her car, covered with blankets. Finally, she said, "he got it back, with the explicit understanding that I have the passwords to all his screen names." Since then she has been vigilant in inspecting the cache of Web sites he has visited and checking the Recycle Bin for signs of trouble.

"He certainly improved my computer skills," she said.

Teenagers, the moment you have been dreading has arrived: Parents are starting to get a clue about the Internet, and they are more and more determined to gain control of where you go, what you read, whom you talk to, and how you behave online. The Internet age is ushering in a new mode of parental oversight, one in which Mom and Dad draw Web-based boundaries, issue computer curfews and worry about whether their hack-happy youngsters are making trouble.

Granted, many parents would still not know a motherboard from Mother Hubbard, but that doesn't mean they are not trying. In a survey by the Pew Internet and American Life Project, a nonprofit research center, more than 60% of parents reported that they checked to see which Web sites their teenagers had visited. About 60% of the 754 parents surveyed also said that they had set time limits for Internet use. In a survey of 774 parents conducted for Disney Online, 71% said they had set rules about what kinds of content their children could see online, and 88% said they had forbidden Internet access in the bedroom (a rule that the mother in Livingston swears by).

(Continues on pages 444–445)

A BATTLE FOR CONTROL

Parents' Tactics

- Enforcing time limits by installing software like TooMuchPC (*www.blairsoft.com*) and PC TimeCop (*www.parental-control-software.com*).
- Recording the keystrokes their children have typed in by using software like ChildSafe (*www.webroot.com/childsafe1.htm*).
- Using AOL's parental controls or installing filtering software.
- Setting up parent-only passwords that must be entered to log on.
- Checking for misbehavior by searching temporary Internet files or the Web browser history log or rooting through the desktop Recycle Bin.

Teenagers' Tactics

- Switching screens or minimizing windows when Mom enters the room.
- Forgoing the family's America Online account in favor of free e-mail sources like Hotmail.
- Arguing that their schoolwork requires more time online.
- Complaining that filtering software blocks too many educational sites.
- Clearing out the temporary Internet files, clearing the Web browser History log and emptying the Recycle Bin before logging off, to erase traces of where they have been.

Where Is This Adolescent Going (Online) Today?
Because the sex sites are all but countless, that's the question many parents would like to have answered. Many parents have developed strategies for snooping, and many adolescents have developed strategies for evading detection.

Some parents say they have no qualms about reading their children's e-mail by logging in under their screen names. Others report that they have learned to distinguish between the pause-laden typing patterns that signal that their children are doing homework and the frenetic tap-tap-tap of instant messaging. It is the modern equivalent of listening furtively at the bathroom door after the teenager drags the phone in there for a private conversation.

Roni Murillo, a mother in Syosset, New York, said she has "sneak-in times" when she tries to read the instant messages sent and received by her 15-year-old son, who once got a citation from AOL for posting a note containing profanity in a professional-wrestling forum. "I have to do it," she said, though abashedly. "I've seen other kids answer him with all these curses. There is no way to monitor that unless you are right there."

The snooping does not sit well with those snooped upon. Checking e-mail In boxes is considered the most flagrant privacy violation. "That's just wrong," said Freddie Alvarez, a 16-year-old from Islip, New York, who said he bought his own computer so he can use it whenever he wants. Other teenagers liken the e-mail box to a diary in arguing for their right to privacy.

Jen Albanese, 16, from Bergenfield, New Jersey, uses command keys to minimize her instant-messaging screen whenever her mother walks into the room. "She'll be like over my shoulder, saying, 'Jen what are you doing? Why did you put that screen down?'" she said.

The primary threats driving them to set rules, many parents say, are online pornography and child predators. But 45% of the parents surveyed by Pew said they also worried that their children might be the instigators of misbehavior such as online threats or hacking. Many parents report that boys seem more inclined than girls to get into trouble. Surveys may validate their concerns. In an online poll conducted by Scholastic News Zone,

an educational Web site, almost half of the 47,235 respondents, in grades 1 through 8, said they did not consider hacking a crime, even though unauthorized entry into computer networks is illegal. In Pew's study, about 9% of boys ages 15 to 17 reported that they had sent prank e-mail or an "e-mail bomb," which clogs people's e-mail In boxes with dozens or hundreds of copies of the same message.

Even when their teenagers seem to have no inclination toward computer mischief, parents have another concern: the sheer amount of time the children spend online. Robert and Marilyn Pohn of Chicago require their 15-year-old daughter and 12-year-old son to seek permission before going online and check to ensure that they are using the computer only for schoolwork. Lauren, their daughter, seems resigned to the restrictions, remarking that the situation could be worse: "I have a friend who has an hour on Fridays. That's it. She's not happy."

David Blair, a software programmer and father of two teenagers in Fairfield, Iowa, decided that rules were not enough. He designed a shareware program called TooMuchPC that enables parents to set an automated timer that shuts down the computer at specific times or after a specified number of hours. In his house, where the computer is in the family office, a little window pops up on the screen when one of his children has been on the machine for an hour, to signal that it is the sibling's turn. His daughter, he said, "is addicted to ICQ," the instant-messaging tool, and used to fight over the computer with her brother, who wanted to play Soldier of Fortune. Now harmony reigns. "It is great," he said. "It eliminated all those arguments."

Addiction to instant messaging may not seem serious, of course, given the stories about teenagers' getting into far worse trouble. A wave of attacks that crippled access to some of the Internet's busiest sites in 2000, including CNN.com, Yahoo, Amazon, and eBay,

Truth?Fiction?
Revisited

It is true that petting is practically universal among adolescents in the United States.

(Miller et al., 1986). Teens who initiate sexual intercourse earlier are also less likely to use contraception and more likely to incur an unwanted pregnancy. If the young woman decides to keep her baby, she is more likely to have to leave school and to scuttle educational and vocational plans. Early dating does not always lead to early coitus, however. Nor does early coitus always lead to unwanted pregnancies. Still, some young women find their options in adulthood restricted by a chain of events that began in early adolescence.

turned out to be the handiwork of a 15-year-old from Montreal who called himself Mafiaboy. As a minor, he faces up to 2 years in detention.

Dennis Moran, an 18-year-old in New Hampshire who went by the online name coolio, is serving 9 months in jail for defacing DARE, an anti-drug Web site, with pro-drug slogans and images. In April, a 15-year-old in Connecticut was charged with hacking into government computer systems that track the movements of Air Force planes.

The image of the teenage hacker hunched over his bedroom computer has existed for some 20 years now. The difference today is that not only are vast numbers of children online, but many parents also are heavy Internet users themselves, both at work and at home, and are therefore at least aware of what their children might be doing. Chris Goggans, a founding member of a 1980s hacking group called Legion of Doom, said he was the only person in his family to have a computer back then—"I got mine from mowing lawns," he said—and his parents never used one. Eventually federal agents learned of Mr. Goggans's online snooping and obtained a warrant to search his computer. (He was never charged with a crime, he said.) His parents had until then been largely oblivious to his online activity.

"They knew something interesting was going on," said Mr. Goggans, 32, who is now an independent security consultant in northern Virginia. "They got phone calls from people who were obviously long-distance, people I'd met in bulletin boards. But as long as I was on the computer and not on the streets knocking over mailboxes, there were no indicators that there was anything negative in what was going on."

Some parents today are still oblivious—either to the online activities of their children or to the implications of those activities. Sarah Gordon, a senior research fellow at Symantec, has talked with several parents in analyzing the behavior of people who write computer viruses. She said she was dismayed to hear fathers saying that their sons' activities were "cool."

As a result, Ms. Gordon counts herself among a handful of security experts, including Mr. Goggans, who are trying to get parents to think beyond time limits, Internet filters, and computer confiscation. They hope to persuade parents and schools to teach children about the repercussions of their actions online.

One of the leaders of that crusade is Winn Schwartau, author of "Internet and Computer Ethics for Kids (and Parents and Teachers Who Haven't Got a Clue)." Mr. Schwartau said the book's aim was to get parents to ask themselves this question: "It's 3:30 p.m.–do you know where your children are in cyberspace?" He said he started working on the book years ago when he realized that his daughter, who is now 16, might not understand the hazards of hacking. Then last summer he discovered that his son, Adam, then 9, had stolen a friend's AOL password to read her e-mail. "I blew a minor gasket," he said.

In an interview, Adam still sounded surprised that his actions—which had begun with his secretly writing his friend Holly's password on a piece of paper as she used the computer—caused such consternation. "I was just bored, it was summer," he said. When Holly found out, he said, "she kind of kicked me."

Some parents are convinced that online discipline, combined with some poking around for verification, is the only strategy that will keep their teenagers in line online. Ms. Murillo, the mother of the 15-year-old in Syosset, said her next challenge would be the new computer that her son will be getting before school starts. "God knows what will happen then," she said. "But I'll be watching. God knows I'll be watching."

Source: Adapted from Lisa Guernsey. (2001, July 19). Looking for clues in junior's keystrokes. *The New York Times,* pp. G1, G9.

Petting Many adolescents use petting to express affection, satisfy their curiosities, heighten their sexual arousal, and reach orgasm while avoiding pregnancy and maintaining virginity.

An overwhelming majority (97%) of teenagers sampled in the Coles and Stokes (1985) survey had engaged in kissing (a form of light petting) by the age of 15. Girls tended to engage in kissing earlier than boys, perhaps because girls tend to mature faster. By age 13, 73% of the girls and 66% of the boys had engaged in kissing. Surveys also find that girls are more likely than boys to be forced into sexual activities such as petting and to feel guilty about it (Larsson & Svedin, 2002).

TABLE 13.5

Percentage of Never-Married Males Aged 15 to 19 Who Report Ever Having Engaged in Various Sexual Activities

	N	Masturbated by a female	Received oral sex from female	Gave oral sex to female	Had anal intercourse	Had vaginal intercourse
All Respondents						
Total	1,297	53	49	49	11	55
Age						
15–16	606	38	33	24	7	37
17–19	691	63	62	50	13	68
Race/Ethnicity						
European American	474	53	51	42	9	50
African American	360	52	47	21	16	78
Latino American	426	48	44	37	16	58

Source of data: Gary J. Gates & Freya L. Sonenstein. (2000). Heterosexual genital sexual activity among adolescent males. *Family Planning Perspectives, 32*(6): 295–297, 304.

Oral Sex Table 13.5 highlights some of the results of a national survey reported by Gary Gates and Freya Sonenstein (2000). The incidence of oral sex increases with age. European American and Latino American males are more likely to have engaged in cunnilingus than African American males. Some adolescent couples use oral sex as a means of birth control. As one 17-year-old New York girl put it, "That's what we used to do before we could start having sex, because we didn't have protection and stuff" (Coles & Stokes, 1985, p. 60).

Premarital Intercourse As we enter the new millennium, surveys find that about half of the high school students in the United States are sexually active (CDC, 2000e; Gates & Sonenstein, 2000). However, as noted in Table 13.5, African American males (78%) are more likely than Latino American males (58%) and European American males (50%) to have engaged in sexual intercourse.

The incidence of premarital intercourse for females has increased dramatically since Kinsey's day. In Kinsey's time, the sexual double standard held firm. Women were expected to remain virgins until marriage, but society looked the other way for men. By the age of 20, 77% of the single men but only 20% of the single women reported that they had engaged in premarital coitus. Of those still single by age 25, the figures rose to 83% for men but to only 33% for women. The discrepancy between males and females is partly explained by the fact that men were often sexually initiated by prostitutes (Hunt, 1974). Rates of premarital coitus among young women should not be confused with promiscuity. Kinsey found that 53% of the females who had engaged in premarital coitus did so with one partner only (Kinsey et al., 1953).

Let us pose another question that is not meant as a trick question: *Question: Why do adolescents engage in premarital sexual intercourse?*

Motives for Intercourse Having sex means more than having sex. Premarital intercourse is actually motivated by a number of factors. Sex hormones, of course—especially testosterone—activate sexual arousal. Thus the pubertal surge of hormones directly activates sexual arousal, at least among boys (Brooks-Gunn & Furstenberg,

1989). Hormonal changes may also have indirect effects on sexual experimentation (Brooks-Gunn & Furstenberg, 1989). About half of the men (51%) and one-quarter of the women (24%) in the NHSLS study reported that their primary reason for the first coital experience was curiosity, or "readiness for sex" (Michael et al., 1994, p. 93).

Hormonal changes stoke the development of secondary sex characteristics. Adolescents whose secondary sex characteristics develop early may begin dating earlier, which may increase the likelihood of their progressing toward sexual intercourse at an earlier age. Some early maturers are pressured into dating or sex—whether they are psychologically ready or not.

Many psychological motives are involved in sexual activity, including love, desire for pleasure, conformity to peer norms, seeking peer recognition, and the desire to dominate someone (Browning et al., 2000; O'Donnell et al., 2003). Many adolescents engage in sexual intercourse because of feelings of love (Browning et al., 2000). The NHSLS study found that affection for the partner was the primary reason for first intercourse among nearly half (48%) of the women and one-quarter (25%) of the men sampled (Michael et al., 1994). Betsy believed that she was in love:

> I was seventeen when I had my first sexual experience. I had been going out with my boyfriend for about five months, during which time he had been continually pressuring me to have sex. He made it seem as though I had to comply or he would end the relationship. Because I was deeply in love with him (or so I thought), I allowed it to happen. (Copyright © 1991 by McIntyre, Formichella, Osterhout, and Gresh by arrangement with Avon Books, p. 64)

Adolescents may consider intercourse a sign of maturity, a way for girls to reward a boyfriend for remaining loyal, or a means of punishing parents (McBride et al., 2003; O'Donnell et al., 2003). Some adolescents engage in coitus in response to peer pressure, especially from close friends (O'Donnell et al., 2003). Adolescents whose friends have engaged in sexual intercourse are more likely to engage in intercourse themselves.

Sometimes the pressure comes from dating partners. About one-quarter (24%) of the women sampled in the NHSLS study said that they went along with intercourse only for the sake of their partners (Michael et al., 1994):

> MEGAN (18, California): I have felt pressure before. My first boyfriend pressured me because he knew I loved him and that he could take advantage of my feelings. I was blinded by my feelings and I had sex with him. I hated it.

> AMY (18, Washington, D.C.): I was sexually pressured by my second boyfriend. He didn't love me, but he did want to have sex. I helped him sneak into my room in the middle of the night. Just before we were about to have sex, I realized that it wasn't something I wanted to do. I wanted my first time to be with someone I loved and who loved me. I stopped him, although he tried everything to get me to say yes. The next day we broke up, and I couldn't have been happier. (Copyright © 1991 by McIntyre, Formichella, Osterhout, and Gresh by arrangement with Avon Books, pp. 4–6)

About 8% of the men in the NHSLS study say they went along with intercourse for the sake of their partners (Michael et al., 1994). As one young man describes it:

> MATT (18, New York): My girlfriend pressured me and I didn't handle it very well. I submitted so she wouldn't be mad or disappointed. (Copyright © 1991 by McIntyre, Formichella, Osterhout, and Gresh by arrangement with Avon Books, p. 65x)

A
Closer
Look

The First Time

MARK: *As we had no place to go, we went out into the woods with several blankets and made love. It was like something out of a Woody Allen movie. I couldn't get my pants off because I was shaking from nerves and from the cold. The nerves and cold made it all but impossible for me to get an erection and then after I had and we made love I couldn't find the car keys.*

AMY: *My first sexual experience occurred after the Junior Prom in high school in a car at the drive-in. We were both virgins, very uncertain, but very much in love. We had been going together since eighth grade. The experience was somewhat painful. I remember wondering if I would look different to my mother the next day. I guess I didn't because nothing was said.(Morrison et al., 1980, p. 608)*

For those who do not remain celibate, there must be a first time. Given the inexperience and awkwardness of at least one member of the couple, and frequent feelings of guilt and fear, it is not surprising that most people, like Mark and Amy, don't get it quite right the first time. Adolescent boys and girls often report different concerns about first intercourse. The girl is more likely to be concerned about whether she is doing the right thing. The boy is more likely to be concerned about whether he is doing the thing right. Women are more likely than men to be physically and psychologically disappointed with the experience and to feel guilty afterwards (Darling et al., 1992; Sprecher et al., 1995). One study of 300 sexually experienced college students found that only 28% of the women considered their first encounter physically or psychologically satisfying. Yet 81% of college men were physically satisfied,

and 67% were psychologically satisfied (Darling & Davidson, 1986).

Negative attitudes among women toward their first coital experience may have cultural roots. A comparison between American and Swedish women showed that American women reported more negative emotional reactions to their first premarital coitus (Schwartz, 1993). In general, the Swedish have more permissive attitudes about sex than do people in the United States. Negative emotional consequences of first intercourse reflect cultural norms or standards as well as the act itself. Of course, it is also possible that Swedish men are more responsive to their partners' needs.

Coles and Stokes (1985) found that most adolescent boys (60%) reported feeling "glad" after their first intercourse (see Table 13.6). Most adolescent girls (61%) expressed ambivalence. About 1

Factors in Premarital Intercourse Many young people abstain from premarital coitus for religious or moral reasons (Belgrave et al., 2000). Family influences are important determinants of adolescent sexual experience (National Campaign to Prevent Teenage Pregnancy, 2003). Other reasons include fear of being caught, of pregnancy, or of disease.

Studies of African American and European American adolescent females have found that girls who are not sexually active, or who engage in less risky sexual activities, tend to be younger and more career oriented, to live in two-parent households, to hold more conservative values about sexuality, and to be more influenced by fam-

TABLE 13.6

Feelings about First Intercourse (percentage)

	Sorry	Ambivalent	Glad	No Feelings
Males	1	34	60	5
Females	11	61	23	4

Source: Sex and the American teenager by R. Coles and G. Stokes. Copyright © 1985 by Rolling Stone Press. Reprinted by permission of HarperCollins Publishers.

in 10 girls (11%) reported feeling "sorry," compared to only 1% of boys. Some females feel guilty about ending their virginity. Others find first intercourse painful or uncomfortable, in part because of the tearing of the hymen, in part because penetration may have been rushed or forced. The pain was more than one 15-year-old New York girl had anticipated:

[I] wasn't expecting it to hurt that much. It was like total pain. Even after the first minutes of pain, it's still like you're too sure to enjoy anything. I didn't expect that at all. (Coles & Stokes, 1985, p. 74)

Yet for some, the quality of the relationship tempered pain:

We were both so excited. We hadn't been able to sleep the night before. I can't remember that much leading up to it, but we had sex a few times—I guess about three times—that night. He really enjoyed it; I found it emotionally nice, but painful. It was like a good hurt, but still it hurt; it was un-comfortable. But it was something we both felt really good about. (Coles & Stokes, 1985, p. 74)

Young women are more likely to find their first coital experience satisfying when their partners are loving, gentle, and considerate (Weiss, 1983).

First intercourse is often awkward, even fumbling. The partners are still learning about their own sexual responses and how to please each other:

KAREN (23, New York): I had sexual intercourse for the first time at age 18. My boyfriend and I had been going out for a year. For several months before we had intercourse we engaged in a lot of petting but not much genital contact. I was the more aggressive partner and I was the one who suggested we have intercourse. It was very awkward; the first time we tried, he couldn't get in. (Copyright © 1991 by McIntyre, Formichella, Osterhout, and Gresh by arrangement with Avon Books, pp. 50–51)

Let us note some sex differences in choice of first partners. For first-time intercourse, survey evidence shows that females are more likely than males to report having been in a committed relationship with their partners (Darling et al., 1992; Sprecher et al., 1995). In the study of some 1,600 college students by Susan Sprecher and her colleagues (1995), 60% of the women reported that their first partner was someone they were dating seriously, compared to 36% of the men. Men were more likely than women (23% versus 8%) to engage in first intercourse with someone they had been seeing for less than a week. Men experienced more pleasure, largely because they were more likely to reach orgasm. Women experienced more guilt. These sex differences are consistent with the traditional double standard that accords greater sexual freedom to men. Men are expected to "sow their wild oats" with casual partners. Women are expected to "save themselves" for a man with whom they share strong emotional ties and an enduring relationship.

ily values and religion (Belgrave et al., 2000; Langille & Curtis, 2002). Teens who have higher educational goals and do better in school are less likely to engage in coitus than less academically oriented teens (Belgrave et al., 2000). Adolescents who begin dating earlier are also more likely to progress through stages of petting to coitus (Belgrave et al., 2000).

The relationship between teens and their parents is crucial (Belgrave et al., 2000; Langille & Curtis, 2002). Adolescents whose parents are permissive and impose few rules and restrictions are more likely to engage in premarital intercourse (Mundy, 2000). Parents who show interest in their children's behavior and communicate their concerns and expectations with understanding and respect may best influence their children to show sexual restraint (National Campaign to Prevent Teenage Pregnancy, 2003).

Male–Male and Female–Female Sexual Behavior

Question: How common is male–male and female–female sexual behavior in adolescence? About 5% of the adolescents in the Coles and Stokes (1985) national survey reported sexual experiences with people of their own sex. More than 9 out of 10 experiences among adolescents of the same sex are between peers. Seduction of adolescents by gay male and lesbian adults is relatively rare. Most adolescent sexual encounters with people of the same sex are transitory. They most often include mutual masturbation, fondling, and genital display.

Ethnicity, Teenagers, and HIV/AIDS

"I was young and stupid. I wasn't scared of anything. It was just about having fun. I didn't listen to older people. I thought they didn't know what they were talking about."

—*Shernika, 16*

"I was scared. I was like, 'I shouldn't have done this.' But he didn't look like nothing was wrong with him."

—*George, 14*

"Everybody I've been with, I knew a long time, since childhood. I didn't think they'd have something like that."

—*Dicki, 16*

They heard endless warnings about the dangers of intravenous drug use, about the wisdom of using condoms. Many even knew older relatives, neighbors, and friends who had died because of AIDS.

But somehow, it didn't add up. Not me, they said. Couldn't happen to me.

And so a 16-year-old girl became infected with HIV because she had unprotected sex with a friend. A 14-year-old boy never took his condom out of its wrapper, and now he is HIV-positive. A 16-year-old girl trusted her boyfriend, a drug user. She shouldn't have.

The experiences of African American teenagers are far from unique. African American youths have become the new face of HIV, making up about two-thirds of the new cases among people under 25, according to recent studies by the CDC (2000b, 2000e).

"The disease is disappearing from the mainstream and becoming a disease of kids who are disenfranchised anyway," said Lawrence D'Angelo, who runs the Burgess Clinic for HIV-infected adolescents at Children's Hospital in Washington.

Risky sexual behavior is nothing new among young people. But medical professionals find it disturbing that the risk-taking continues, despite extensive educational campaigns, and that African American youths are paying an especially high price. That is a major change from the early 1980s, when gay European American men made up the majority of young people infected with HIV.

Much to Think About *Adolescents need to think about the possibilities of unwanted pregnancy and of contracting HIV/AIDS and other STIs when they make decisions about sexual behavior.*

"For many of our kids, HIV has become just one of the many problems in their lives, like are they going to get a good meal, who are they

Many gay males and lesbians, of course, develop a firm sense of being gay during adolescence. Coming to terms with adolescence is often a difficult struggle, but it is often more intense for gay people (Baker, 1990) (see Chapter 10). Adolescents can be particularly cruel in their stigmatization, referring to gay peers as "homos," "queers," "faggots," and so on. Many adolescent gays therefore feel isolated and lonely and decide to cloak their sexual orientation. Many do not express their sexual orientation at all until after their high school years.

Adding to the strain of developing a gay identity in a largely hostile society is the threat of AIDS, which is all the more pressing a threat to young gay males because of the toll that AIDS has taken on the gay male community (Baker, 1990).

going to live with, are they going to school?" D'Angelo said.

D'Angelo and Ligia Peralta, who treats HIV-infected adolescents in Baltimore, began to notice the change in the 1990s when growing numbers of young African American women, most of them poor, began entering their programs.

"Theoretically, they do understand the risks," said Peralta, who runs Star Track, an HIV and AIDS clinic for adolescents at the University of Maryland Medical Center in Baltimore. "However, from there to recognizing that my partner, the person that I choose, may be infected with HIV, there's the major disconnect."

The disease is spread casually among young people, the doctors have found in the course of conducting a long-term HIV study. Once infected youths discover that they have HIV, many are unwilling to admit it to sexual partners. D'Angelo said that only about half tell their regular partners that they are HIV-positive, and almost none bothers to tell an occasional partner.

And with a stigma still attached to homosexuality in some communities, young African American men who have sex with other men tend to be less likely than their European American peers to identify themselves as gay, which may result in their ignoring HIV-prevention messages aimed at gay men, said Helene Gayle, director of the CDC's National Center for HIV, STI, and TB Prevention. "I think it means we have to make sure our prevention messages are keeping pace with the times and keeping pace with the population at risk," Gayle said.

THE PERSONAL FABLE

Some say yet another factor—the sense that young people have that they can live forever—also is at work. "All youth—rich, poor, black, white—have this sense of invincibility, invulnerability," says Ronald King (2000), executive director of the HIV Community Coalition of Metropolitan Washington, explaining why many adolescents who know the risks still expose themselves to HIV infection.

The developmental psychologist Jean Piaget noted that adolescents appear to believe in a **personal fable**—the conviction that one's feelings and ideas are special, even unique, and that they are invulnerable. The personal fable is apparently connected with adolescent behavior patterns such as showing off and taking risks. Many adolescents have an "It can't happen to me" attitude; they assume they can smoke without risk of cancer or engage in sexual activity without risk of STIs or pregnancy.

Peralta and D'Angelo have found that adolescent girls in all groups are especially vulnerable to STIs, such as HIV, because the cervix at their age is not fully mature and is more susceptible to infection. Also, many of the young men and women in both programs were sexually abused as children and became sexually active at a young age. Most of the women also were infected by men 10 to 20 years older.

Although some national studies show that condom use has increased among young people in recent years and that they are delaying sex until their mid-teens, a recent survey of 4,500 patients at Children's Hospital showed that the average age when boys begin having sex is 12; for girls, the average age is 13.

Source: Adapted from Frazier, L. (2000, July 16). The new face of HIV is young, black. *The Washington Post*, p. C01.

Teenage Pregnancy

Question: How common is teenage pregnancy in the United States? About 8% to 10% of American girls ages 15 to 19 become pregnant each year (Bernstein, 2004). This amounts to nearly 1 in 5 sexually active girls and nearly 800,000 pregnancies a year, resulting in about 500,000 births (CDC, 2000e, 2000f; Ventura et al., 2001).

Although these figures are cause for concern, the rate of births for teenagers actually dropped by 28% since its 1990 peak (Bernstein, 2004). Some pregnant teenagers plan their pregnancies, but the great majority do not. Nine in 10 pregnancies among unmarried teenagers are unplanned (Centers for Disease Control, 2000e).

Personal fable The belief that one's feelings and ideas are special and that one is invulnerable.

Truth?Fiction?
Revisited

It is true that about 800,000 adolescent girls in the United States become pregnant each year.

The consequences of unplanned teenage pregnancies can devastate young mothers, their children, and society at large. Poverty, joblessness, and lack of hope for the future are recurrent themes in adolescent pregnancy. Half of teenage mothers quit school and go on public assistance. Few receive consistent emotional or financial help from the fathers, who generally cannot support themselves, much less a family. Working teenage mothers earn half as much as those who give birth in their 20s (CDC, 2000e). Barely able to cope with one baby, many mothers who give birth at age 15 or 16 have at least one more baby by the time they are 20. Among teenage girls who become pregnant, nearly 1 in 5 will become pregnant again within a year. More than 3 in 10 will have a repeat pregnancy within 2 years.

The children of teenage mothers are at greater risk of physical, emotional, and intellectual problems in their preschool years as a consequence of poor nutrition and health care, family instability, and inadequate parenting (Coley & Chase-Lansdale, 1998). They are more aggressive and impulsive as preschoolers than are children of older mothers. They do more poorly in school. They are also more likely to suffer maternal abuse or neglect.

Question: What factors contribute to the incidence of teenage pregnancy? There are many. They include a loosening of traditional taboos on adolescent sexuality in the mainstream culture, impaired family relationships, problems in school, emotional problems, misunderstandings about reproduction, and lack of contraception. Some adolescent girls believe that a baby will elicit a commitment from their partners or fill an emotional void. Some become pregnant as a way of rebelling against their parents. Some poor teenagers view early childbearing as the best of the severely limited options they perceive for their futures. But the largest number become pregnant because of misunderstandings about reproduction and contraception or by miscalculating the odds of conception. Many teens who are relatively well informed about contraception fail to use it consistently.

More attention has been focused on teenage mothers, but young fathers bear equal responsibility for teenage pregnancies. A survey based on a nationally representative sample of 1,880 young men ages 15 through 19 showed that socioeconomically disadvantaged young men in particular appeared to view paternity as a source of self-esteem and were consequently more likely than more affluent young men to say that fathering a child would make them feel like a real man and that they would be pleased, or at least not as upset, with an unplanned pregnancy (Marsiglio, 1993a). Consistent with these attitudes, poor young men were less likely to have used an effective method of contraception during their most recent sexual experience.

Contraceptive Use Among Sexually Active Teens Sexually active teenagers use contraception inconsistently, if at all (Mundy, 2000). Contraception is most likely to be used by teens in stable, monogamous relationships (Baker et al., 1988). But even teens in monogamous relationships tend to use ineffective methods of contraception or to use effective methods inconsistently.

Various factors determine use of contraceptives. Teenage girls who engage in more frequent intercourse are more likely to use contraception and to use more effective methods. Teens whose peers use contraceptives are more likely to use them themselves (O'Donnell et al., 2003). Older teenagers are more likely than younger ones to use con-

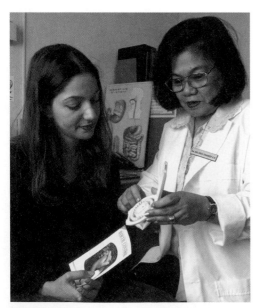

Preventing Teenage Pregnancy Even with the recent decline in the rate of pregnancy among teenagers, hundreds of thousands of girls in the United States aged 15 to 19 become pregnant each year. Teenage mothers are more likely to live in poverty and to receive welfare than other girls their age. Half of them quit school and rely on public assistance. Few receive meaningful help from the fathers.

traception (O'Donnell et al., 2003). Younger teens who are sexually active may be less likely to use contraception because they lack information about contraception and because they do not always perceive the repercussions of their actions (O'Donnell et al., 2003). Younger teens may also have less access to contraceptives.

Poor family relationships and communication with parents are associated with inconsistent contraceptive use (McBride et al., 2003; National Campaign to Prevent Teen Pregnancy, 2003). Poor performance in school and low educational ambitions predict irregular contraceptive use as well as early sexual initiation.

When asked to explain why they don't use contraceptives, sexually active teens often cite factors such not having intercourse often enough to use it and the fact that it gets in the way of sexual spontaneity (Mundy, 2000). Some teenagers get "carried away" and do not wish to disrupt sex by obtaining or applying contraceptives.

Myths also decrease the likelihood of teenager's using birth control. Some adolescents believe that they are too young to become pregnant. Others believe that pregnancy results only from repeated coitus or will not occur if they are standing up. Still other adolescents simply do not admit to themselves that they are engaging in coitus.

Teenagers who focus on the long-term consequences of their actions are more likely to use contraceptives. The quality of the relationship is also a factor. Satisfaction with the relationship is associated with more frequent intercourse *and* more consistent use of contraception (Bernstein, 2004). More consistent contraceptive use is found in relationships in which the young woman takes the initiative in making decisions and resolving conflicts.

Question: What can be done to prevent teenage pregnancy?

Combating Teenage Pregnancy One of the interesting factors in teenage pregnancy is that parents tend to underestimate the influence they have on their teenagers. According to a National Campaign to Prevent Teen Pregnancy (2003) poll of several thousand teenagers, 88% said that it would be easier for them to postpone sex and avoid pregnancy if they could have more open discussions with their parents! Yet nearly 1 teen in 4 (23%) said that they had never discussed sex, contraception, or pregnancy with their parents. Memo to parents: Talk to your kids.

Other means for combating teenage pregnancy include universal sex education, free contraceptive services, and dissemination of information about sex and contraception through schools and the media. Given the effects of sex education in other industrialized countries, many helping professionals believe that the rate of teenage pregnancy and the spread of STIs in the United States could be curtailed through sex education about contraception and provision of contraceptives.

Pregnancy-prevention programs in the schools range from encouraging teens to delay sex ("saying no to early sex") to providing information about contraception to distributing condoms or referring students to contraceptive clinics (Santelli et al., 2003). Most sex educators recommend abstinence to their students as the best way to prevent pregnancy and HIV/AIDS. But 3 out of 4 large school districts in the United States provide some instruction about the methods of contraception and the use of condoms to prevent the spread of HIV/AIDS and other STIs.

Susan Blake and her colleagues (2003) surveyed more than 4,000 high school students in Massachusetts. About 20% of their schools made condoms available to students. The survey revealed that distributing condoms did not increase the percentage of students who were sexually active; however, it led to more consistent use of condoms among students who were already sexually active.

Douglas Kirby, who has extensively studied the relationship between schools' distribution of condoms to students and the students' sexual behaviors summarizes the effects as follows: "Actually, multiple studies consistently show that making condoms available to students does not increase any measure of their sexual behavior—whether the teens have sex, how frequently they have it, or the number of partners they have. And some studies, including one that I conducted involving thousands of Seattle high school students, show, as Susan [Blake's] study does, that the percentage of teens having sex declined after condoms were made available to them" (cited in Kirchheimer & Smith, 2003).

Remember, too, that parents are highly influential when it comes to advising their teenagers about sex (National Campaign to Prevent Teen Pregnancy, 2003). The Washington, D.C. Campaign to Prevent Teen Pregnancy is working to cut the rate of teenage pregnancy by encouraging parents and other adults to discuss the issues involved with teenagers (Donovan, 2000). The Web site of the Campaign has links to information and resources on teen pregnancy. For more information, go to www.teenpregnancydc.org.

Review: Adolescence

Reflect

What factors led to becoming sexually active or remaining abstinent among the adolescents you knew in high school?

CriticalThinking

Where do you stand on the issue of whether school districts should make contraceptive devices available to students? Explain your views.

23. Adolescence is bounded at its beginning by _____ and at its close by the capacity to take on adult responsibilities.

24. Puberty begins with the appearance of _____ sex characteristics.

25. Principal markers of reproductive potential are _____ in the girl and first _____ in the boy.

26. The critical _____ hypothesis suggests that girls must reach a certain body weight to trigger menarche.

27. FSH causes the ovaries to begin to secrete _____.

28. Estrogen production becomes cyclical in puberty and regulates the _____ cycle.

29. FSH and LH stimulate the testes to increase their output of _____.

30. _____ emissions are also called "wet dreams," although they may not accompany erotic dreams.

31. _____ is a major sexual outlet during adolescence.

32. Petting (*Is* or *Is Not*?) practically universal among adolescents in the United States.

33. The incidence of premarital oral sex has (*Increased* or *Decreased*?) since Kinsey's time.

34. About _____ of the high school students in the United States are sexually active.

35. Adolescents whose friends have engaged in coitus are (*More* or *Less*?) likely to engage in intercourse themselves.

36. Teens who have higher educational goals are (*More* or *Less*?) likely to engage in coitus than less academically oriented teens.

37. Nearly 1 in _____ sexually active 15- to 19-year-old girls in the United States becomes pregnant each year.

38. The rate of births for teenagers (*Increased* or *Decreased*?) over the past decade.

39. Sexually active teenagers use contraception (*Consistently* or *Inconsistently*?).

40. Most sex educators recommend _____ to students as the best way to prevent pregnancy and HIV/AIDS.

41. A survey of Massachusetts high schoolers by Blake and colleagues reported that distributing condoms (*Did* or *Did not*?) increase the percentage of students who were sexually active.

Recite

1. **What sexual behaviors do we find among fetuses and newborns?**

Male fetuses have erections; male and female fetuses suck their fingers. Stimulation of the genitals in infancy may produce sensations of pleasure. Pelvic thrusting has been observed as early as 8 months of age. Masturbation may begin at 6 to 12 months. Some infants seem capable of sexual responses that resemble orgasm. Bed-sharing has no effect on sexual development. Gay and lesbian parents are no more likely than heterosexuals to have gay or lesbian children.

2. **What types of sexual behaviors do we find among children in early childhood?**

Statistics concerning the incidence of masturbation at ages 3 to 8 is speculative. In early childhood, children show curiosity about the genitals and may play "doctor." Same-sex sexual activity play may be more common than heterosexual play and does not foreshadow sexual orientation.

3. **How does sexual behavior in preadolescence differ from that of earlier stages of development?**

Preadolescents tend to socialize with same-sex peers and to become self-conscious about their bodies. Masturbation is the primary means of achieving orgasm during preadolescence for both sexes. Preadolescent sex play often involves mutual display of the genitals, with or without touching. Much preadolescent same-sex sexual behavior involves sexual exploration and is short-lived.

4. **Generally speaking, how do preadolescents learn about sex?**

Despite the increased availability of sex education programs, friends remain a major source of sexual information.

5. **What is adolescence?**

Adolescence is bounded at its beginning by the advent of puberty and at its end by the capacity to take on adult responsibilities.

6. **It was noted that adolescence begins with puberty. What is puberty?**

Pubertal changes are ushered in by sex hormones. Puberty begins with the appearance of secondary sex characteristics and ends when the long bones make no further gains in length. Once puberty begins, most major changes in primary sex characteristics occur within 3 years in girls and within 4 years in boys.

7. **What sexual outlets do adolescents find?**

Masturbation is a major sexual outlet during adolescence. Adolescents today date and "go steady" earlier than in past generations, a change that has apparently increased the incidence of teenage pregnancy. Many adolescents use petting as a way of achieving sexual gratification without becoming pregnant or ending their virginity. The incidence of premarital intercourse, especially for females, has increased dramatically since Kinsey's day.

8. **Why do adolescents engage in premarital sexual intercourse?**

Sexual gratification is one reason, but adolescents are also curious about sex and subject to peer pressure.

9. **How common is male–male and female–female sexual behavior in adolescence?**

A minority of adolescents report sexual experience with people of the same sex—in 9 of 10 cases, with agemates. Most of these sexual encounters are transitory. Coming to terms with adolescence is often more intense for gay males and lesbians, largely because of stigmatization.

10. **How common is teenage pregnancy in the United States?**

About 800,000 adolescents in the United States become pregnant each year.

11. **What factors contribute to the incidence of teenage pregnancy?**

Factors include lack of closeness with parents, low interest and achievement in academics, and inconsistent use of contraceptives.

12. **What can be done to prevent teenage pregnancy?**

Prevention may involve better communication with parents and, for sexually active teenagers, reliable use of contraceptives.

Chapter 14

Truth? Fiction?

T / F? "Singlehood" (forgive the word) has become a more common U.S. lifestyle over the past few decades.

T / F? Divorced people are more likely than never-married people to cohabit.

T / F? In the ancient Hebrew and Greek civilizations, wives were viewed as their husbands' property.

T / F? Men are more romantic than women.

T / F? Most of today's sophisticated young people see nothing wrong with an occasional extramarital fling.

T / F? Few women can reach orgasm after the age of 70.

T / F? People who are paralyzed because of spinal cord injuries cannot become sexually aroused or engage in sexual intercourse.

Sexuality in Adulthood

Preview

Americans entering adulthood today face a wider range of sexual choices and lifestyles than those available to earlier generations. The sexual revolution loosened traditional constraints on sexual choices, especially for women. Couples experiment with lifestyles that would have been unthinkable in earlier generations. An increasing number of young people choose to remain single as a way of life, not merely as a way station preceding the arrival of Mr. or Ms. Right.

In this chapter, we discuss diverse forms of adult sexuality in the United States today, including singlehood, marriage, and alternative lifestyles such as cohabitation, open marriage, and group marriage. Let us begin as people begin—with singlehood.

Question: What are the trends in the numbers of people remaining single?

Singlehood

Recent years have seen a sharp increase in the numbers of single young people in our society. "Singlehood," not marriage, is now the most common lifestyle among people in their early 20s. Marriages may be made in heaven, but many Americans are saying heaven can wait. By the end of the millennium, 1 woman in 4 and 3 men in 10 in the United States 15 years of age and older had never married. Half a century earlier, in 1950, 1 woman in 5 and about 1 man in 4 aged 15 and above had never been married. The rate of marriages had also fallen off. More than 4 men in 5 (84%) in the 20-to-24 age range were unmarried, up from 55% in 1970 (Census, 2001). By 2000, the number of single women in this age group had grown to 73% from 36% in 1970 (Census, 2001).

Question: Why do people remain single? Several factors contribute to the increased proportion of singles. For one thing, more people are postponing marriage to pursue educational and career goals. Many young people are deciding to "live together" (cohabit), at least for a while, rather than getting married. Also, as you can see in Table 14.1, people are getting married later. The typical man in the United States gets married at about age 27 today, compared with age 23 just 50 years earlier (Census, 2001). The typical woman gets married today at about age 25; 50 years earlier, the typical woman married at age 20.

Single-mother family groups increased to 26% of all families from 12% three decades earlier (Census, 2001). Some of these women started their families as single mothers, but the increased prevalence of divorce also swells the ranks of single mothers.

Single people encounter less social stigma today. Although they are less likely today to be perceived as socially inadequate or as failures, some unmarried people

Truth?Fiction?
Revisited

It is true that "singlehood" has become a more common American lifestyle over the past few decades. More people are remaining single into their 20s and 30s than was the case a generation or two ago.

TABLE 14.1

Estimated Median Age at First Marriage, by Sex: 1890 to 2000

Year	Males	Females
2000	26.8	25.1
1990	26.1	23.9
1980	24.7	22.0
1970	23.2	20.8
1960	22.8	20.3
1950	22.8	20.3
1940	24.3	21.5
1930	24.3	21.3
1920	24.6	21.2
1910	25.1	21.6
1900	25.9	21.9
1890	26.1	22.0

Source: U.S. Bureau of the Census, Current Population Reports, Series P20-514, "Marital status and living arrangements: March 1998 (update)," and earlier reports. U.S. Bureau of the Census Internet release date: January 7, 1999; Census: Americans marry later in life (June 29, 2001). The Associated Press.

Singles *There is no single "singles scene." Although some singles meet in singles' bars, many meet in more casual settings, such as the neighborhood laundromat. Some singles advertise online or in newspapers or magazines.*

Serial monogamy
A pattern of involvement in one exclusive relationship after another, as opposed to engaging in multiple sexual relationships at the same time.

Celibacy Complete sexual abstinence. (Sometimes used to describe the state of being unmarried, especially in the case of people who take vows to remain single.)

still encounter stereotypes. Men who have never married may be suspected of being gay. Single women may feel that men perceive them as "loose." Nor are women over the age of 30 likely to be regarded as "spinsters" anymore (Edwards, 2000); see findings of a *Time*/CNN poll in Figure 14.1.

Many single people do not choose to be single. Some remain single because they have not yet found Mr. or Ms. Right. Yet many young people see singlehood as an alternative, open-ended way of life—not a temporary stage that precedes marriage. Because career options for women have expanded, they are not as financially dependent on men as their mothers and grandmothers. A number of career women, like career-oriented men, choose to remain single (at least for a time) to focus on their careers.

Singlehood is not without its problems. Many single people are lonely. Some singles express concerns about a lack of a steady, meaningful social relationship. Others, usually women, worry about their physical safety. Some people who live alone find it difficult to satisfy their needs for intimacy, companionship, sex, and emotional support. Despite these concerns, most singles are well adjusted and content. Singles who have a greater number of friends and a supportive social network tend to be more satisfied with their lifestyles.

There is no single "singles scene." Single people differ in their sexual interests and lifestyles. Many achieve emotional and psychological security through a network of intimate relationships with friends. Most are sexually active and practice **serial monogamy**. Other singles have a primary sexual relationship with one steady partner but occasional brief flings. A few, even in this age of AIDS, are "swinging singles." That is, they pursue casual sexual encounters, or "one-night stands."

Some singles remain celibate, either by choice or for lack of opportunity. People choose **celibacy** for a number of reasons. Nuns and priests do so for religious reasons. Others believe that celibacy allows them to focus their energies and attention on

---

- In 1963, 83% of American women aged 25 to 55 were married, compared with about 65% today.

- When asked what they missed most because of being single, 75% of women said companionship, and only 4% said sex.

- Even as the birthrate has been falling among teenagers, it has been climbing among single adult women—up 15% since 1990 among women in their 30s.

- When single women were asked whether they would consider rearing a child on their own, 61% of those aged 18 to 49 said yes.

- Single women are an economic force. About a fifth of all home sales were to unmarried women, up from 10% in 1985.

- Only 34% of single women said they would settle for less than a perfect mate if they couldn't find one, as compared with 41% of men.

Figure 14.1. Some Results of a **Time**/CNN *Poll, Year 2000.* *Single adult women in the United States are more self-confident and selective than ever before. They are assuming many of the social, economic, and sexual freedoms that had formerly been reserved for single men.* Source of data: *Tamala Edwards (2000).*

Review: Singlehood

Reflect

Is remaining single an option for you? Why, or why not?

CriticalThinking

People face a variety of sources of pressure to get married. Which arguments for getting married, or for remaining single, make sense to you? Why?

1. Recent years have seen a(n) (*Increase* or *Decrease?*) in the numbers of young people who remain single.
2. The typical American male gets married at about age _____, the typical woman at about _____.
3. Single-mother family groups make up about _____% of all families.
4. Many women remain single today because they are not as _____ dependent on men as women used to be.
5. There is (*More* or *Less?*) social stigma attached to being single today.
6. Most single people (*Are* or *Are not?*) sexually active and practice _____ monogamy.

work or to commit themselves to an important cause. They see celibacy as a temporary accommodation to other pursuits. Others remain celibate because they view sex outside of marriage as immoral. Still others remain celibate because they find the prospects of sexual activity aversive or unalluring, or because of fears of STIs.

Cohabitation: Darling, Would You Be My POSSLQ?

> There is nothing I would not do
> If you would be my POSSLQ
> —*Charles Osgood*

POSSLQ? Question: So what's a POSSLQ? POSSLQ is the unromantic abbreviation that was introduced by the U.S. Bureau of the Census to refer to **cohabitation**. It stands for *People of Opposite Sex Sharing Living Quarters* and applies to unmarried couples who live together.

Some social scientists believe that cohabitation has become accepted within the social mainstream. Whether or not this is so, society in general has become more tolerant. We seldom hear cohabitation referred to as "living in sin" or "shacking up" any longer. People today are more likely to refer to cohabitation with value-free expressions such as "living together." Perhaps the current tolerance reflects society's adjustment to the increase in the numbers of cohabiting couples. Or perhaps the numbers of cohabiting couples have increased as a consequence of tolerance.

Question: Who cohabits?

Trends in Cohabitation

The numbers of households consisting of an unmarried adult male and female couple living together in the United States quadrupled over the past 25 years (Smock, 2000). They grew from about 1.6 million couples in 1980 to 3.2 million couples in

Cohabitation Living together as though married but without legal sanction.

Cohabitation *Cohabitation was once referred to as "living in sin," but it has become an increasingly common lifestyle. Some sociologists predict that cohabitation will replace marriage as the nation's most popular lifestyle sometime during the first century of the new millennium.*

Truth?Fiction?
Revisited

It is true that divorced people are more likely than never-married people to cohabit. The experience of divorce may make some people more willing to share their lives than their bank accounts—the second or third time around.

1990 and about 5.5 million couples today (Marquis, 2003; Smock, 2000). The population of the United States has also grown throughout this period, but not nearly at the same pace. The numbers of cohabiting couples increased by 72% in the decade from 1990 to 2000 alone (Marquis, 2003).

Although much attention is focused on college students living together, cohabitation is actually more prevalent among less well educated and less affluent people (Willis & Michael, 1994). The cohabitation rate is about twice as high among African American couples as among European American couples.

More than half (56%) of the marriages that took place during the past decade were preceded by living together (Smock, 2000). It also turns out that nearly 55% of the couples who cohabit wind up getting married, which has led some social scientists to suggest that cohabitation, for many, is a new stage of engagement. Even so, about 40% of these couples get divorced later on, so "trial marriage" may not provide couples with as much information as they need about each other.

We are reaching a time when we can say that half of the people living in the United States have cohabited at some time. For example, about half of women in their late 30s in the United States report having cohabited (Smock, 2000). Children are nearly as common in cohabiting households as among married couples (Marquis, 2003). Nearly half of the divorced people who are cohabiting with new partners have children in the household (Smock, 2000). At least 1 out of 3 households with never-married cohabiting couples also have children living with them.

Question: Why do people cohabit? For many reasons. Cohabitation, like marriage, is an alternative to the loneliness that can accompany living alone. Romantic partners may have deep feelings for each other but not be ready to get married. Some couples prefer cohabitation because it provides a consistent relationship without the legal entanglements of marriage (Hussain, 2002; Marquis, 2003).

Willingness to cohabit is related to more liberal attitudes toward sexual behavior, less traditional views of marriage, and less traditional views of gender roles (Hussain,

2002; Marquis, 2003; Smock, 2000). For example, divorced people are more likely than people who have never been married to cohabit (Smock, 2000). Cohabitors are less likely than noncohabitors to attend church regularly (Laumann et al., 1994).

Many cohabitors are less committed to their relationships than married people are (Hussain, 2002; Marquis, 2003). Ruth, an 84-year-old woman, has been living with her 85-year-old partner for 4 years. "I'm a free spirit," she says. "I need my space. Sometimes we think of marriage, but then I think that I don't want to be tied down" (cited in Steinhauer, 1995, p. C7).

Ruth's comments are of interest because they counter stereotypes of women and older people. However, it is more often the man who is unwilling to make a commitment (Peplau, 2003). Mark, a 44-year-old computer consultant, lives with Nancy and their 7-year-old daughter, Janet. Mark says, "We feel we are not primarily a couple but rather primarily individuals who happen to be in a couple. It allows me to be a little more at arm's length. Men don't like committing, so maybe this is just some sort of excuse" (cited in Steinhauer, 1995, p. C7). David Popenoe of Rutgers University notes that many men cohabit because they get a "quasi-wife" without having to make a commitment (Hussain, 2002).

Economic factors come into play as well. Emotionally committed couples may decide to cohabit because of the economic advantages of sharing household expenses. Cohabiting individuals who receive public assistance (Social Security or welfare checks) risk losing support if they get married (Hussain, 2002; Marquis, 2003). Some older people live together rather than marrying because of resistance from adult children. Some children fear that a parent will be victimized by a needy senior citizen. Others may not want their inheritances to come into question or may not want to decide where to bury the remaining parent. Younger couples may cohabit secretly to maintain parental support that they might lose if they were to get married or to reveal their living arrangements.

Question: What happens to people who cohabit?

Cohabitation and Later Marriage: Benefit or Risk?

Cohabiting couples may believe that cohabitation will strengthen eventual marriage by helping them iron out the kinks in their relationship. Yet cohabitors who later marry also run a serious risk of getting divorced. According to Pamela Smock's (2000) survey at the Institute for Social Research at the University of Michigan, 40% of couples who cohabited before tying the knot got divorced later on. Cohabitors who marry may run a greater—not lesser—risk of divorce than noncohabitors. Some studies suggest that the likelihood of divorce within 10 years of marriage is nearly twice as great among married couples who cohabited before marriage (Smock, 2000).

Why might cohabiting couples run a greater risk of divorce than couples who did not cohabit prior to marriage? Do not assume that cohabitation *causes* divorce. We must always be cautious about drawing causal conclusions from correlational data. Note that none of the couples in these studies were *randomly assigned* to cohabitation or noncohabitation. Therefore, *selection factors*—the factors that lead some couples to cohabit and others not to cohabit—may explain the results (see Figure 14.2). Cohabitors tend to be more committed to personal independence (Hussain, 2002; Marquis, 2003; Smock, 2000). They also tend to be less traditional and less religious than noncohabitors. All in all, people who cohabit prior to marriage tend to be less committed to the values and interests traditionally associated with the institution of marriage. The attitudes of cohabitors, not cohabitation itself, may account for their higher rates of marital dissolution.

Commitment
to personal
independence

Less commitment to
marriage as an
institution

Low religiosity

?   ?

Cohabitation
prior to
marriage   ?   Divorce

Figure 14.2. Does Cohabitation Prior to Marriage Increase the Risk of Eventual Divorce? There is a correlational relationship between cohabitation prior to marriage and the risk of divorce later on. Does cohabitation increase the risk of divorce, or do other factors—such as a commitment to personal independence—contribute to both the likelihood of cohabitation and eventual divorce?

Review: Cohabitation: Darling, Would You Be My POSSLQ?

Reflect

Do you know people who are living together without being married? What is their motivation for doing so? How do most people from their sociocultural background feel about cohabitation? Why?

CriticalThinking

Research shows that cohabitors who get married run a greater risk of divorce than noncohabitors. Can you think of at least two possible explanations for this finding?

7. The term _____ refers to the lifestyle in which unmarried couples live together.

8. Society has become (*More* or *Less*?) tolerant of cohabitation over the past couple of generations.

9. About _____ couples cohabit today in the United States.

10. Cohabitation is more prevalent among (*More* or *Less*?) well educated and (*More* or *Less*?) affluent people.

11. (*More* or *Less*?) than half of the marriages that took place during the past decade were preceded by living together.

12. Willingness to cohabit is related to (*Traditional* or *Liberal*?) attitudes toward sexual behavior and marriage.

13. Popenoe notes that many men cohabit because they get a "quasi-wife" without having to make a _____.

14. In Smock's survey, about _____% of couples who cohabited before marrying got divorced later on.

Marriage: Tying the Knot

Truth?Fiction?
Revisited

It is true that in the ancient Hebrew and Greek civilizations, wives were viewed as their husbands' property.

Question: Does marriage remain popular? Apparently, it does. Despite the growing incidence of cohabitation in the United States and other Western nations, marriage is found in all human societies. Most people in every known society, sometimes nearly all, get married at least once.

Marriage remains our most common lifestyle, but not by much! In the year 2000, 52% of the families in the United States were headed by married couples, down from 55% in 1990 (Armas, 2000). But people still view marriage as permanent. A *New York Times* poll asked, "If you got married today, would you expect to stay married for the rest of your life?" and 86% of respondents answered yes (Eggers, 2000). Only 11% said no. In some cultures, such as among the Hindu of India, marriage is virtually universal, with more than 99% of the females eventually marrying. However, cohabitation is also becoming wide-

A Closer Look

Historical Perspectives on Marriage

Marriage has a long and varied history. The ancient Hebrews, Greeks, and Romans lived in patriarchies in which men dominated most aspects of life. The wife was considered part of the husband's property: a chattel whose responsibilities consisted of child rearing and homemaking. Marriages were usually arranged by men, sometimes for financial or political gain. In classical Greece, men would turn to high-class prostitutes for sensual sex and sophisticated conversation—not to their wives.

The Christian tradition also has a patriarchal foundation. Male dominance was legitimized by biblical scripture, as we can see in this passage from the New Testament: "Wives, submit to your own husbands, as unto the Lord. For the husband is the head of the wife, as Christ is the head of the church" (Ephesians 5:23–24).

Patriarchal traditions in Western culture weakened with time, and women came to be viewed as loving companions rather than chattels. They became recognized as being capable of profiting from education. But the notion that a married woman might seek fulfillment through a career unrelated to her husband's needs is a recent development. The idea that women have a right to sexual fulfillment is also new. As late as the nineteenth century, marital sex was largely seen as a means for producing children and satisfying the man's needs.

Although marital roles in modern society have changed, some couples still adhere to traditional gender roles that ascribe breadwinning responsibilities to the husband and child care and homemaking roles to the wife. American couples today are more likely to share or even reverse marital roles, however. Table 14.2 lists some of the features of traditional and so-called modern marriages.

spread in the United States. University of Wisconsin researcher Larry Bumpass estimates that nationwide, half of the adult population under age 40 is cohabiting. He estimates that sometime within the next decade, half of the adult population under the age of 50 will be cohabiting.

Question: Why, then, do people get married?

TABLE 14.2

A Comparison of Traditional and Modern Marriages

Traditional Marriage	Modern Marriage
The emphasis is on ritual and traditional roles.	The emphasis is on companionship.
Couples do not live together before marriage.	Couples may live together before marriage.
The wife takes the husband's last name.	The wife may choose to keep her maiden [or birth] name.
The husband is dominant; the wife is submissive.	Neither spouse is dominant or submissive.
The roles for the husband and the wife are specific and rigid.	Both spouses have flexible roles.
There is one income (the husband's).	There may be two incomes; that is, the couple may share the breadwinning role. In many cases, the woman is the breadwinner.
The husband initiates sexual activity; the wife complies.	Either spouse may initiate (or refuse) sex.
The wife cares for the children.	The parents share child-rearing chores.
Education is considered important for the husband, not for the wife.	Education is considered equally important for both spouses.
The husband's career determines the location of the family residence.	The career of either spouse may determine the location of the family residence.

Source: From D. Knox & C. Schacht (2002). *Choices in relationships—An introduction to marriage and the family,* 7th ed. Belmont, CA: Wadsworth.

Why Do People Marry?

People marry for many reasons, even in this era of cohabitation. Marriage meets personal and cultural needs. It legitimizes sexual relations and provides a legal sanction for deeply committed relationships. It permits the maintenance of a home life and provides an institution in which children can be supported and socialized. Marriage restricts sexual relations so that a man can be assured—or at least assume—that his wife's children are his. Marriage permits the orderly transmission of wealth from one family to another and from one generation to another. As late as the seventeenth and eighteenth centuries, most European marriages were arranged by the parents, generally on the basis of how the marriage would benefit the families.

Notions such as romantic love, equality, and the radical concept that men as well as women would do well to aspire to the ideal of faithfulness are recent additions to the structure of marriage in Western society. Not until the nineteenth century did the notion of love as a basis for marriage become widespread in Western culture.

Today, because more people believe that premarital sex is acceptable between two people who feel affectionate toward each other, the desire to engage in sexual intercourse is less likely to motivate marriage. But marriage provides a sense of emotional and psychological security and opportunities to share feelings, experiences, and ideas with someone with whom one forms a special attachment. Desires for companionship and intimacy are key goals in marriage today.

Broadly speaking, people today want to get married because they believe that they will be happier. A Gallup poll suggests that their optimism may be well founded (Chambers, 2000). The poll found that married people are more likely than single people to report that they are "fairly happy" or "very happy" (see Table 14.3).

Question: We've been talking about marriages between one man and one woman. What other kinds of marriage are there?

Types of Marriage

There are several types of marriage. Among male and female couples, we have two types: monogamy and polygamy. In **monogamy**, a husband and wife are wed only to each other. But let us not confuse monogamy, which is a form of matrimony, with sexual exclusivity. People who are monogamously wed often do have extramarital affairs, as we shall see, but they are married to one person at a time. In **polygamy**, a person has more than one spouse (of the other sex) and is permitted sexual access to each of them. In **gay marriage**, an individual is married to someone of the same sex.

Polygyny has been the most prevalent form of polygamy among the world's preliterate societies (Ford & Beach, 1951; Frayser, 1985). **Polyandry** is relatively rare (see Chapter 1). In polygynous societies, including many Islamic societies, men are permitted to have multiple wives. Practically speaking, in many cases, only wealthy men can afford to support multiple wives and the children of these unions. But few societies have enough women to allow most men to have multiple wives (Harris & Johnson, 2000; Whitten, 2001).

As noted in Chapter 10, The Netherlands, Belgium, and Canada extended full marriage rights to same-sex couples in 2003, and many other Western nations allow

Monogamy Marriage to one person.

Polygamy Simultaneous marriage to more than one person.

Gay marriage Marriage to a person of the same sex.

Polygyny A form of marriage in which a man is married to more than one woman at the same time.

Polyandry A form of marriage in which a woman is married to more than one man at the same time.

TABLE 14.3

Percent Who Report They Are "Very Happy," According to Marital Status

	Married	Unmarried
Total	57%	36%
Men	53	35
Women	62	37

Source: Chris Chambers (2000, October 13). Americans are overwhelmingly happy and optimistic about the future of the U.S. Marital status strongly affects both happiness and optimism. Princeton, NJ: Gallup News Service.

gay males and lesbians to enter into legal partnerships that provide the rights and responsibilities of marriage. Some states in this country now permit "civil unions" between same-sex partners. Polls of the opinions of Americans about allowing gay marriage are "all over the map." A recent poll in California found that the public opposed gay marriage by about 50% to 42% of the population (half in California, 2003). In the same year, residents of Massachusetts supported gay marriage by 50% to 44% of those sampled (Phillips, 2003). But there are two important trends worth nothing: First, younger people, especially college students, are more supportive of gay marriage than older and less well educated people. Second, majorities in most areas polled would allow gays to enter into civil contracts that are similar to marriage, even if they define the term *marriage* to exclude gay unions.

Marriages are generally based on the expectation of sexual exclusivity. Alternative or nontraditional lifestyles, however, such as **open marriages** and **group marriages**, permit intimate relationships with people outside the marriage. Such alternative lifestyles attracted a flurry of attention during the heyday of the sexual revolution in the 1970s, but even then they were more often talked about than practiced (Harris & Johnson, 2000; Whitten, 2001). Today, they find still fewer adherents.

Although the ideal of the traditional marriage remains strong in our culture, men are somewhat more likely than women to express an interest in lifestyles that permit greater sexual freedom (Knox & Schacht, 2002). (Why is the third author not surprised?) But even most of those who have tried lifestyles such as cohabitation, open marriage, or group marriage enter into traditional marriages at some time.

All in all, most adults in the United States still seem to feel about marriage the way Winston Churchill felt about democracy: It's flawed, laden with problems, and frustrating—but preferable to the alternatives.

Question: All right, now we know about types of marriages. How do we select the individuals *we marry?*

Whom Do We Marry?: Are Marriages Made in Heaven or in the Neighborhood?

Most preliterate societies regulate the selection of spouses in some way. The universal incest taboo proscribes matings between close relatives. Societal rules and customs also determine which people are desirable mates and which are not.

In Western cultures, mate selection is presumably free. Parents seldom arrange marriages, although they may still encourage their child to date that wonderful son or daughter of the solid churchgoing couple who live down the street. Nevertheless, factors such as race, social class, and religion often determine the categories of people within which we seek mates (Laumann et al., 1994). People in our culture tend to marry others from the same geographic area and social class. Because neighborhoods are often made up of people from a similar social class, storybook marriages like Cinderella's are the exception to the rule.

Because we make choices, we tend to marry people who attract us. According to the matching hypothesis, as noted in Chapter 7, these people are often similar to us in physical attractiveness and attitudes, even in minute details. We are more often than not similar to our mates in characteristics such as height, weight, personality traits, and intelligence. We also tend to think about whether potential mates are likely to meet our material, sexual, and psychological needs.

The concept of "like marrying like" is termed **homogamy**. Most of the time, we also marry people of the same racial/ethnic background, educational level, and religion. Only 40 years ago three-fifths (59%) of Americans believed that marriage between African Americans and European Americans should be illegal, and it was so

Open marriage
A marriage that is characterized by the personal privacy of the spouses and the agreed-upon liberty of each spouse to form intimate relationships, which may include sexual relationships, with people other than the spouse.

Group marriage A social arrangement in which three or more people share an intimate relationship. Group marriages are illegal in the United States.

Homogamy The practice of marrying people who are similar in social background and standing. (From the Greek roots *homos*, meaning "same," and *gamos*, meaning "marriage.")

in 42 states at one time or another (Kristof, 2002). Only in 1967 did the Supreme Court invalidate these state laws. Mixed-race marriages in the United States now number about 1.5 million and are doubling every 10 years or so (Kennedy, 2003; Kristof, 2002). In recent years, nearly 40% of Asian Americans and 6% of African Americans have married European Americans (Kennedy, 2003; Kristof, 2002).

We also tend to follow *age homogamy* (Michael et al., 1994). Age homogamy—the selection of a partner who falls in one's own age range—may reflect the tendency to marry early in adulthood. Persons who marry late or who remarry tend not to select partners so close in age. Bridegrooms tend to be 2 to 5 years older than their wives, on the average, in European, North American, and South American countries (Buss, 1994).

Some marriages also show a **mating gradient**. The stereotype has been that an economically established older man would take an attractive, younger woman as his wife. But by and large, with boring predictability, we are attracted to and marry the boy or girl (almost) next door. Most marriages seem to be made not in heaven, but in the neighborhood.

Who Has His Head in the Clouds? (Hint: The Question Is **Not** *Phrased in Sexist Language)* When it comes to picking a mate, men tend to be the romantics, women the pragmatists. Men are more likely to believe that each person has one true love whom they are destined to find (Peplau, 2003). Men are more likely to believe in love at first sight. Women, on the other hand, are more likely to value financial security as much as passion. Women are more likely to believe that they could form a loving relationship with many individuals. Women are also less likely to believe that love conquers all—especially economic problems.

There's a rumor that marriage has something to do with sex. *Question: What kinds of patterns of sexual activity do we find in marriage?*

Marital Sexuality

Patterns of marital sexuality vary across cultures, yet anthropologists have noted some common threads (Harris & Johnson, 2000; Whitten, 2001). Privacy for sexual relations is valued in nearly all cultures. Most cultures also place restrictions on coitus during menstruation, during at least some stages of pregnancy, and for a time after childbirth.

Until the sexual revolution of the 1960s and 1970s, Western culture could have been characterized as restrictive, even toward marital sex. We usually think of the sexual revolution in terms of the changes in sexual behaviors and attitudes that occurred among young, unmarried people, but it also ushered in profound changes in marital sexuality. Compared to Kinsey's "pre-revolution" samples from the late 1930s and 1940s, married couples today engage in coitus more frequently, with greater variety, and for longer periods of time. They report greater sexual satisfaction. The sexual revolution helped dislodge the view that sexual pleasure is meant for men and that it is the duty of women to satisfy their husbands' sexual needs. Adult cable channels have brought sexually explicit films into middle-class suburban homes.

Scientific findings were also liberalizing influences. Kinsey's and Masters and Johnson's findings that normal women are capable not only of orgasm but also of multiple orgasms punctured traditional beliefs that sexual gratification was the birthright of men alone. TV shows, films, and radio talk shows began to portray women as sexual initiators who enjoy sex. The affluence of the post–World War II years also encouraged more young people to pursue a college education and live away

Mating gradient The tendency for women to "marry up" (in social or economic status) and for men to "marry down."

from home. College liberates not only through exposure to great books and scientific knowledge, but also through the challenging of students' attitudes by bright, knowledgeable peers from different backgrounds.

The development of effective contraceptives separated sex from reproduction. Motives for sexual pleasure became more open. All these liberalizing forces have led to changes in the frequency of marital sex and in techniques of foreplay and coitus since Kinsey's day.

Changes in Duration and Techniques of Foreplay Married women in Kinsey's sample reported an average (median) length of foreplay of about 12 minutes. This figure rose to nearly 15 minutes among the wives in the *Playboy* survey (Hunt, 1974). Kinsey found that men at lower educational levels engaged in briefer periods of foreplay, generally lasting only a minute or two before penetration. The length of foreplay rose to 5 to 15 minutes among college-educated men. In a dramatic shift in sophistication since Kinsey's day, Hunt found that the typical duration of foreplay in the 1970s was 15 minutes for college-educated and noncollege males alike. Foreplay was relatively longer in duration among younger married couples than their elders, however.

Marital foreplay has also become more varied since Kinsey's day. Couples in more recent surveys report using a wider variety of foreplay techniques, including oral stimulation of the breasts and oral–genital contact (Laumann et al., 1994).

Changes in Frequency of Marital Coitus How frequently do married couples engage in coitus? Table 14.4 summarizes results from the Kinsey surveys. The frequency of coitus was clearly negatively related to age. That is, older couples engaged in coitus less frequently.

The data reported by the NHSLS study do not allow a direct comparison with the Kinsey figures. As shown in Table 14.5, however, the overwhelming majority of married men and women in the United States report engaging in sexual relations either a few times per month or two to three times a week (Laumann et al., 1994). The average is seven times a month (Michael et al., 1994, p. 136). These figures are not notably different from Kinsey's.

Kinsey and the University of Chicago group (who conducted the NHSLS study) did not find strong links between coital frequency and educational level. Studies consistently find that the frequency of sexual relations declines with age, however (Call et al., 1995; Laumann et al., 1994). At the ages of 50 to 59, for example, people reported an average of four to five times per month (Laumann et al., 1994). Regardless

---

TABLE 14.4

Median Weekly Frequency of Marital Coitus, Male and Female Estimates Combined, According to the Kinsey Surveys

Age	Frequency
16–25	2.45
26–35	1.95
36–45	1.40
46–55	0.85
55–60	0.50

Source: Kinsey et al., 1948, 1953.

TABLE 14.5

Frequency of Marital Sexual Relations during the Past Year, According to NHSLS Study

Frequency of Sexual Relations	Men (%)	Women (%)
Not at all	1.3	3.0
A few times a year	12.8	11.9
A few times a month	42.5	46.5
Two to three times a week	36.1	31.9
Four or more times a week	7.3	6.6

Source: Adapted from Laumann, E. O., Gagnon, J. H., Michael, R. T., & Michaels, S. (1994). *The social organization of sexuality: Sexual practices in the United States.* Chicago: University of Chicago Press, Table 3.4, pp. 88–89.

of a couple's age, sexual frequency also appears to decline with years of marriage. There would appear to be a novelty effect.

Changes in Techniques and Duration of Coitus In coitus, as in foreplay, the marital bed since Kinsey's day has become a stage on which the players act more varied roles. Today's couples use greater variety in coital positions.

Kinsey's study participants mainly limited coitus to the male-superior position. As many as 70% of Kinsey's males used the male-superior position exclusively (Kinsey et al., 1948). Perhaps 3 couples in 10 used the female-superior position frequently. One in 4 or 5 used the lateral-entry position frequently, and about 1 in 10 used the rear-entry position. Younger and more highly educated men reported greater variety, however.

An often overlooked but important difference between Kinsey's and current samples involves the length of intercourse. In Kinsey's time it was widely believed that the "virile" man ejaculated rapidly during intercourse. Kinsey estimated that most men reached orgasm within 2 minutes after penetration, many within 10 or 20 seconds. Kinsey recognized that women usually took longer to reach orgasm through coitus, and that some clinicians were already asserting that a man's ejaculation was "premature" unless he delayed it until "the female (was) ready to reach orgasm" (1948, p. 580).

Even today's less-educated couples appear to be more sophisticated than Kinsey's in their recognition of the need for sexual variety and their focus on exchanging sexual pleasure rather than rapidly reaching orgasm (Michael et al., 1994). According to the NHSLS study, the "duration of the last sexual event" of 3 out of 4 married couples was 15 minutes to an hour. Some 8% to 9% of couples exceeded an hour (Michael et al., 1994). (About 1 unmarried, noncohabiting couple in 3 made love for an hour or more, suggesting that novelty and youth have their motivational aspects.)

Now we know about patterns of sexual activity among married people. *Question: But are married people sexually satisfied?*

Sexual Satisfaction One index by which researchers measure sexual satisfaction is orgasmic consistency. Men tend to reach orgasm more consistently than women do. After 15 years of marriage, 45% of the wives in Kinsey's study reported reaching orgasm 90% to 100% of the time. After 15 years of marriage, 12% of the wives in Kinsey's study had not experienced orgasm.

Orgasmic consistency now seems higher than in Kinsey's day. The NHSLS study found that more than 90% of the men and about 70% of the women reported reaching orgasm "always" or "usually" with their primary partner during the 12 months prior to the survey (Laumann et al., 1994; Michael et al., 1994) (see Table 14.6). Fully 3 out of 4 men (75%) and nearly 3 women in 10 (28.6%) reported reaching orgasm on every occasion (not shown in Table 14.6). Only 2% of the married women reported never reaching orgasm with their husbands during the past year (not shown).

Women in their 40s were somewhat more likely to reach orgasm consistently than younger and older women. Perhaps women in their 40s have had more time to get in touch with their sexuality and may be more secure in their relationships than younger women are. The falloff for women and men in their 50s may be biologically related. The nature of the relationship is a factor for women. Married women were most likely to reach orgasm consistently, followed by cohabiting women and then noncohabiting women. Security in the relationship apparently promotes orgasmic consistency. There do not seem to be notable racial or ethnic differences.

Orgasm is not the only way of measuring pleasure or satisfaction in marital sex. The NHSLS study asked participants whether they had been extremely physically satisfied with their primary partners during the past year. It is apparent, from Table

TABLE 14.6

Sociocultural Factors and Sexual Satisfaction in Primary Relationship During Last Year (in Percents)

Sociocultural Characteristics	Always or Usually Had an Orgasm with Partner		Has Been Extremely Physically Satisfied with Partner		Has Been Extremely Emotionally Satisfied with Partner	
	Men	Women	Men	Women	Men	Women
Age						
18–24	92%	61%	44%	44%	41%	39%
25–29	94	71	50	39	46	40
30–39	97	70	45	41	39	38
40–49	97	78	44	42	38	42
50–59	91	73	53	32	52	32
Marital Status						
Noncohabiting	94	62	39	40	32	31
Cohabiting	95	68	44	46	35	44
Married	95	75	52	41	49	42
Race/Ethnicity*						
European American	96	70	47	40	43	38
African American	90	72	43	44	43	38
Latino and Latina American	96	68	51	39	43	39

Source: Combined from Laumann, E. O., Gagnon, J. H., Michael, R. T., & Michaels, S. (1994). *The social organization of sexuality: Sexual practices in the United States.* Chicago: University of Chicago Press, Table 3.7, pp. 116–117; and Michael, R. T., Gagnon, J. H., Laumann, E. O., & Kolata, G. (1994). *Sex in America: A definitive survey.* Boston: Little, Brown, Table 9, pp. 128–129.

*The numbers of Asian Americans and Native Americans were too small to report reliable statistics.

14.6, that men and women are comparable in general physical satisfaction—about 47% and 41%, respectively. Orgasm, then, is not a guarantee of satisfaction. And lack of orgasm is not necessarily a sign of dissatisfaction.

The emotional satisfaction in a marital relationship is also linked to sexual satisfaction. Table 14.6 shows that about 40% of men and women report being extremely emotionally satisfied with their primary partners. Closer relationships are connected with more consistent orgasm.

Extramarital Sex

> Women seek soul mates; men seek playmates. Women believe that their affair is justified when it is for love; men, when it's *not* for love.
>
> —*Janis Abrahms Spring (1997)*

It's next door and it's in the White House—Bill Clinton and Monica Lewinsky, Bill Cosby and a "friend," Kobe Bryant and a woman in Colorado. Journalist Eric Alterman (1997) writes that adultery is everywhere today. When French President François Mitterand died, his wife, his mistress, and his illegitimate daughter were numbered among the mourners. Alterman mentions the examples of Kelly Flinn (who was forced to resign from the armed services), Frank Gifford (who retired from

Extramarital Affairs *President Bill Clinton remained in office despite numerous well-publicized extramarital affairs. Basketball star Kobe Bryant admitted to "consensual sex" with a woman in Colorado, although he was being prosecuted for sexual assault as this book went to press.*

Monday Night Football in 1998), Bill Cosby (who admitted to an affair but denied that the woman's daughter was his child), and actor Eddie Murphy.

> ***Questions: Why do people engage in extramarital sex? What are its effects on a marriage?***

Some people engage in extramarital sex for variety (Lamanna & Riedmann, 1997). Some have affairs to break the routine of a confining marriage. Others enter affairs for reasons similar to the nonsexual reasons that adolescents often have for sex: as a way of expressing hostility toward a spouse or retaliating for injustice. Husbands and wives who engage in affairs often report that they are not satisfied with, or fulfilled by, their marital relationships. Curiosity and desire for personal growth are often more prominent motives than marital dissatisfaction. Middle-aged people may have affairs to boost their self-esteem or to prove that they are still attractive.

Many times the sexual motive is less pressing than the desire for emotional closeness. Some women say they are seeking someone whom they can talk to or communicate with (Lamanna & Riedmann, 1997). There is a notable gender difference here (Peplau, 2003). According to Janis Abrahms Spring, author of *After the Affair,* women are usually seeking "soul mates," whereas men are seeking "playmates." Women tend to justify affairs when they are for love, but men do so when the affair is *not* for love. Witness the fact that 77% of women who have had affairs, compared to 43% of men, cite love as their justification (Townsend, 1995). Men who have had affairs are more likely than women—75% versus 55%—to cite a need for sexual excitement as a justification (Glass & Wright, 1992).

These data support the view, expressed repeatedly throughout this text, that women are less accepting of sex without emotional involvement (Peplau, 2003). Men are more likely than women to distinguish between sex and love, whereas women see love and sex as going together in such a way that falling in love justifies sex (Peplau, 2003). Men (whether single, married, or cohabiting) are also generally more approving of extramarital affairs than women are (Glass & Wright, 1992). But note that these are all *group* differences. Many individual men are interested primarily in the extramarital relationship rather than in the sex per se. Similarly, many women are out for the sex and not the relationship.

Earlier, we read about patterns of sexual activity in marriage. ***Question: What patterns of extramarital sex do we find?***

Patterns of Extramarital Sex Let us begin with a few definitions. **Extramarital sex** is usually conducted without the spouse's knowledge or approval. Secret affairs are referred to as **conventional adultery**, infidelity, or simply cheating. Conventional adultery runs the gamut from the "one-night stand" to the affair that persists for years. (Bill Clinton's affair with Gennifer Flowers is alleged to have persisted for a dozen years.) In **consensual adultery**, extramarital relationships are conducted openly—that is, with the knowledge and consent of the partner. In what is called **swinging**, **comarital sex**, or *mate-swapping*, the partner participates.

How many people "cheat" on their spouses? Viewers of TV talk shows may get the impression that everyone cheats, but surveys paint a different picture. In surveys conducted between 1988 and 1996 by the respected National Opinion Research Center, about 1 husband in 4 or 5, and 1 wife in 8, admitted to marital infidelity (Alterman, 1997; "Cheating," 1993). Similarly, more than 90% of the married women and 75% of the married men in the NHSLS study reported remaining loyal to their spouses (Laumann et al., 1994). The vast majority of people who were cohabiting also reported that they were sexually faithful to their partners while they were living together (Laumann et al., 1994). Similarly, the overwhelming majority—86%—of respondents to a *New York Times* poll reported that they were "absolutely certain" that their partners were faithful to them (Eggers, 2000). What can we conclude? Perhaps two things: One is that men are about twice as likely as women to admit to affairs. The other is that only a minority of married people admit to affairs.

Those are the conclusions, but note that we said "*admit* to affairs." Having presented the percentages of reported extramarital sex, we point out that these reports cannot be verified. People may be reluctant to reveal that they have cheated on their spouses even when they are assured of anonymity. There is likely to be an overall tendency to underreport the incidence of extramarital sex.

Why are people reluctant to admit that they have cheated on their spouses? *Question: What are our attitudes toward extramarital sex?*

Attitudes toward Extramarital Sex The sexual revolution does not seem to have changed attitudes toward extramarital sex. About 9 out of 10 Americans say that affairs are "always wrong" or "almost always wrong" (Alterman, 1997). Some 3 out of 4 Americans say that extramarital sex is "always wrong" (Berke, 1997). Another 1 in 7 say it is "almost always wrong." Only about 1% say that extramarital sex is "not at all wrong." Most married couples embrace the value of monogamy as the cornerstone of their marital relationship (Blumstein & Schwartz, 1990).

Effects of Extramarital Sex Question: What are the effects of infidelity? The discovery of infidelity can evoke anger, jealousy, even shame. Feelings of inadequacy and doubts about one's attractiveness and desirability may surface. Infidelity may be seen by the betrayed spouse as a serious breach of trust and intimacy. Marriages that are not terminated in the wake of the disclosure may survive in a damaged condition (Charny & Parnass, 1995).

The harm an affair does to a marriage may reflect the meaning of the affair to the individual and his or her spouse. Deborah Lamberti, director of a counseling and psychotherapy center in New York City, points again to women's traditional intertwining of sex with relationships and argues that "Men don't view sex with another person as a reason to leave a primary relationship" (1997, pp. 131–132). Women may recognize this and be able to tell themselves that their husbands are sleeping with someone else just for physical reasons. But women are more concerned about

---

Truth?Fiction?
Revisited

It is not true that most of today's sophisticated young people see nothing wrong with an occasional extramarital fling. The sexual revolution never extended to extramarital affairs—at least among the majority of married people.

Extramarital sex Sexual relations between a married person and someone other than his or her spouse.

Conventional adultery Extramarital sex that is kept hidden from one's spouse.

Consensual adultery Extramarital sex that is engaged in openly with the knowledge and consent of one's spouse.

Swinging A form of consensual adultery in which both spouses share extramarital sexual experiences. Also referred to as *mate-swapping*.

Comarital sex Swinging; mate-swapping.

"Someone to Watch over Me"? Yes–Snoopware!

We went to the SpectorSoft Web site (*www.spectorsoft .com*) and the ad shown here leapt at us from our monitor. Spector Pro is an example of "snoopware." Imagine that a phone-answering machine secretly recorded everything you said on it and then sent the audio clips to your spouse or parents or boss. It's as if a private investigator were standing behind you with a video camera and shooting a running record over your shoulder of everything that comes across your monitor—every Web site, every e-mail, every instant message, every file opened, every password, every credit card number, every sales transaction. It has been said that you can learn nearly everything you need to know about someone by going through his or her electronic garbage. Snoopware not only goes through your electronic garbage; it also makes a record of everything you write or save. Privacy is a thing of the past. Snoopware is the most successful voyeur of them all.

Spy software was originally used primarily by law enforcement agencies and large corporations. But Spector Pro, eBlaster, Cyber Snoop, the 007 Stealth Activity Recorder and Reporter, and similar spy programs are available to consumers today. Spector Pro was originally designed to permit parents to track the Web sites and chat rooms visited by their children. But the main customers today are suspicious spouses, mistrustful bosses, and private investigators.

STEALTH MODE

The program's "stealth mode" is truly frightening. Only the person who installed it knows that it is peeping in the background. When the object of investigation is gone, the investigator keyboards a secret combination of keys (Crtl-Alt-Shift-S, all held at once) and a password. Everything that showed up on the user's monitor is then played back. Like the stealth fights and bombers, the program is invisible to the computer user's personal radar. It isn't listed on any directory (don't bother instructing your computer to "find" a program with *Spector Pro* or *snoop* in the title). Even expert teenage hackers won't locate it. (eBlaster is intended for people who do not have regular access to their target's computer. It hides in the background, like Spector Pro, and then regularly sends a secret e-mail with the revealing information to whatever address is specified by the installer. The reports are sent when the target is connected to the Internet. It leaves no e-mail trail. It doesn't use the modem to dial the Internet itself; dialing could alert the target that there's more here than meets the eye and ear).

Spector Pro and similar programs are not Web filters like SurfWatch and Net Nanny, which prevent employees and children from accessing porno and other undesirable sites on the Net. Rather, they spy on people who erroneously assume that as long as no one made of flesh and blood is watching them, the images that flash across their monitor are known to them alone.

TESTIMONIALS

To those who are offended by the very existence of this software, SpectorSoft offers customer testimonials like the following:

- A Nashville woman used Spector Pro to discover that her husband regularly visited porno sites and sex-related chat rooms. Spector Pro replayed messages he sent to women he met online, proposing liaisons and bragging about extramarital affairs throughout his marriage. The woman's

remaining monogamous. Therefore, if a woman is sleeping with another man, she may already have a foot out the door, so to speak. Alterman (1997) also notes that a wife's affair may be an unforgivable blow to the husband's ego or pride. A woman may be more likely to see the transgression as a threat to the structure of her life.

If a person has an affair because the marriage is deeply troubled, the affair may be one more factor that speeds its dissolution. The effects on the marriage may depend on the nature of the affair. It may be easier to understand that a spouse has fallen prey to an isolated, unplanned encounter than to accept an extended affair (Charny & Parnass, 1995). In some cases the discovery of infidelity stimulates the couple to work to improve their relationship.

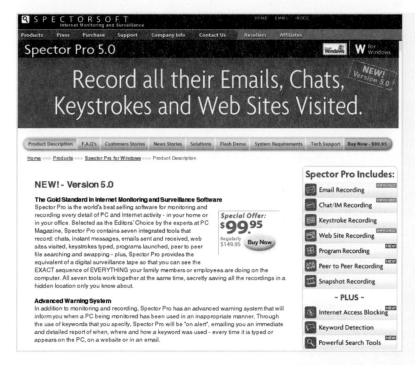

"Snoopware" It has been said that you can learn almost anything about people by going through their garbage. *"Snoopware"* rummages through electronic garbage, making a record of everything the target writes or looks at or saves. Someone could install such software on your computer without your knowledge.

divorce lawyer plopped dozens of pages of printouts in his lap, all time-stamped by the software. "Spector Pro is no different than going out and hiring a private investigator," she said (cited in Lewis, 2000). "All it is is a more sophisticated way of doing something women and men have done for centuries."

- A Kansas man installed Spector Pro on his wife's computer. The snoopware dutifully recorded e-mails between his wife and her boyfriend. They revealed not only the affair but also the boyfriend's wish to harm the husband physically. When confronted with the Spector Pro record, his wife agreed to a divorce, moved out of town, and surrendered custody of the children without a fight.

- In yet another case, a woman hired a private investigator to check out her fiancé. He installed the

software on the fiancé's computer and revealed that he was a philanderer. The marriage didn't happen.

MORAL AND LEGAL QUESTIONS

Spector Pro raises many moral and legal questions. The legality of snoopware has not been adequately tested, but there are some obvious parallels between snoopware and tapping someone's phone line.

"Based on my reading of different state statutes, it is not clear if it is illegal or not," says Mike Godwin (cited in Lewis, 2000), the lawyer who wrote *Cyber Rights: Defending Free Speech in the Digital Age.* But "If someone ever installed this software on my computers in my home without my permission or knowledge," he would take them to court.

Divorce

My wife and I were considering a divorce, but after pricing lawyers we decided to buy a new car instead.

—*Henny Youngman*

Whenever I date a guy, I think, is this the man I want my children to spend their weekends with?

—*Rita Rudner*

Question: How many marriages end in divorce? At least half of the marriages in the United States end in divorce (Carrère et al., 2000; Laumann et al., 1994). The divorce rate in the United States rose steadily through much of the twentieth century before leveling off in the 1980s. About one-quarter (26%) of children below the age of 18 live in single-parent households. Divorced women outnumber divorced men, in part because men are more likely to remarry following divorce. *Question: Why do people get divorced?*

The relaxation of legal restrictions on divorce, especially the introduction of the so-called no-fault divorce, has made divorces easier to obtain. Until the mid-1960s, adultery was the only legal grounds for divorce in New York State. Other states were equally strict. But now no-fault divorce laws have been enacted in nearly every state, allowing a divorce to be granted without a finding of marital misconduct. The increased economic independence of women has also contributed to the rising divorce rate. More women today have the economic means of breaking away from a troubled marriage. Today, more people consider marriage an alterable condition than in prior generations.

People today also hold higher expectations of marriage than did their parents or grandparents. They expect marriage to be personally fulfilling as well as an institution for family life and rearing children. Most people want to be happy in marriage. The most common reasons given for a divorce today are problems in communication and a lack of understanding. Key predictors of divorce today include a husband's criticism, defensiveness, contempt, and stonewalling—not lack of financial support (Carrère et al., 2000; Gottman et al., 1998).

Why do Americans believe that the divorce rate has risen so high? A *Time*/CNN Poll asked a national sample, "Which is the main reason for the increase in the number of divorces?" Answers are shown in Table 14.7. Respondents were almost equally split in their answer to the question "Do you believe it should be harder than it is for married couples to get a divorce?" Half (50%) said yes, and 46% said no.

All right, half of marriages end in divorce. *Question: What is the cost of divorce for the couple and the children?*

The Cost of Divorce Divorce is usually connected with financial and emotional problems. When a household splits, the resources often cannot maintain the earlier standard of living for each partner. Divorce hits women in the pocketbook harder than men. According to a Population Reference Bureau report, a woman's household income drops by about 24% (Bianchi & Spain, 1997). A man's declines by about 6%. Women who have not pursued a career may have to struggle to compete with younger,

---

TABLE 14.7

Americans' Opinions about the Main Reason for the Increase in the Divorce Rate, According to a National *Time*/CNN Poll

Reason	Percent of Respondents Citing Reason as Main Reason
Marriage is not taken seriously by the couples	45%
Society has become more accepting of divorced people	15
It is easier to get divorced than it used to be	10
People who get divorced are selfish	9
Changes in the earning power of women and men	7
All of the above	9

Source of Data: Kirn, Walter (1997, August 18). The ties that bind. *Time,* pp. 48–50.

Effects of Divorce on Chinese and African Children

Studies of Chinese and African children find that children of divorced parents in other cultures experience problems similar to those that such children experience in the United States. One Chinese study matched 58 children of divorced parents with 116 children from intact families according to gender, age, and social class. Children whose parents were divorced were more likely than the other children to have physical complaints ("My stomach hurts," "I feel nauseous"), to encounter social problems, and to act aggressively (Liu et al., 2000). Another Chinese study found that divorce decreases the quality of parent–child relationships, interferes with parental concern over the children's education, and creates financial hardship—all of which impair the well-being of the child (Sun, 2001). A third Chinese study shows that divorce compromises the academic and social functioning of Chinese and American children in similar ways (Zhou et al., 2001).

A study of children and their mothers in Botswana, Africa, showed similar results (Maundeni, 2000). Most of the mothers and children in this study reported that divorce led to economic hardship, causing some children to feel inferior to children with greater resources. Financial worries and feelings of resentment and betrayal among children of divorced parents led to social and emotional problems.

Apparently, there is no safe place for divorce, as far as the children are concerned.

more experienced workers. Divorced mothers often face the combined stress of assuming sole responsibility for child rearing and the need to increase their incomes. Divorced fathers may find it difficult to pay alimony and child support while establishing a new lifestyle.

Divorce can also prompt feelings of failure as a spouse and parent, loneliness and uncertainty about the future, and depression. Married people appear to be better able to cope with the stresses and strains of life, perhaps because they can lend each other emotional support. Divorced and separated people have the highest rates of physical and mental illness (Carrère et al., 2000; Gottman et al., 1998). They also have high rates of suicide (Carrère et al., 2000; Gottman et al., 1998). On the other hand, divorce may permit personal growth and renewal—an opportunity to take stock of oneself and establish a new, more rewarding life.

Children are often the biggest losers when parents get a divorce (Ellis, 2000). Yet chronic marital conflict is also connected with psychological distress in children and adolescents (Ellis, 2000; Erel & Burman, 1995; Harold et al., 1997). Boys have greater problems adjusting to conflict or divorce, such as conduct problems at school and increased anxiety and dependence. Children whose parents are divorced are more likely to have psychological problems and conduct disorders, to have lower self-esteem, to abuse drugs and alcohol, and to do poorly in school (Amato, 2001; Chao et al., 2001; O'Connor et al., 2000). There are individual differences in all of this, and boys tend to fare worse than girls (Grych et al., 2000), but by and large, the fallout for children is worst during the first year after the breakup, and

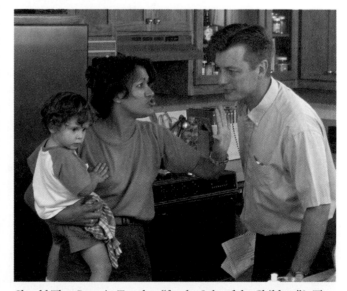

Should They Remain Together "for the Sake of the Children"? *The research seems to suggest that children may fare better when parents who are in regular conflict separate. The key issue appears to be how the parents interact in the presence of the children, not whether they get a divorce.*

children tend to rebound after a couple of years or so. Judging on the basis of a number of case studies, however, Wallerstein and Blakeslee (1989) reported that even some apparently well-adjusted "children of divorce" developed problems in early adulthood, especially lack of trust in their partners' commitments.

Researchers attribute children's problems following divorce not only to the divorce itself but also to a consequent decline in the quality of parenting. Children's adjustment is enhanced when both parents maintain parenting responsibilities and set aside their differences long enough to agree on child-rearing practices (Ellis, 2000). Children of divorced parents also benefit when their parents avoid saying negative things about each other in the children's presence.

Despite the difficulties in adjustment, most divorced people eventually bounce back. Most remarry. Among older people, divorced men are more likely than divorced women to remarry—in part because men usually die earlier than women (and so fewer prospective husbands are available), in part because older men tend to remarry younger women.

Review: Marriage: Tying the Knot

Reflect

Do most people from your sociocultural background approve or disapprove of divorce as a remedy for an unhappy marriage? Do you agree with their beliefs? Explain.

CriticalThinking

Agree or disagree with the following statement, and support your answer: Marriage is an old-fashioned, outdated lifestyle that has become irrelevant for today's sophisticated young people.

15. Marriage (*Is* or *Is not*?) our most common lifestyle among adults.

16. Most Americans surveyed (*Do* or *Do not*?) view marriage as permanent.

17. Among the ancient Hebrews, Greeks, and Romans, the wife was considered the husband's _____.

18. One of the features of a (*Traditional* or *Modern*?) marriage is that the wife often chooses to keep her birth name.

19. Marriage facilitates the orderly transmission of _____ from one family to another and from one generation to another.

20. According to a recent Gallup poll, (*Married* or *Unmarried*?) people are more likely to report that they are happy.

21. In _____, a woman and man are wed only to each other.

22. In _____ marriage, an individual is married to someone of the same sex.

23. Americans are generally more supportive of the concept of (*Gay marriage* or *Civil unions among gays*?).

24. The phenomenon of "like marrying like" is termed _____.

25. (*Men* or *Women*?) are more likely to believe in love at first sight.

26. Compared to Kinsey's samples from the late 1930s and 1940s, married couples today engage in coitus (*More* or *Less*?) frequently.

27. Couples today use a (*Wider* or *Narrower*?) variety of foreplay techniques than in Kinsey's day.

28. Married people appear to achieve (*Greater* or *Lesser*?) orgasmic consistency than in Kinsey's day.

29. According to the NHSLS study, married women reach orgasm (*More* or *Less*?) consistently than cohabiting women and noncohabiting women.

30. More (*Men* or *Women*?) justify affairs by claiming that love is the motive.

31. (*Women* or *Men*?) are more likely to have extramarital affairs.

32. A (*Majority* or *Minority*?) of Americans disapprove of extramarital affairs.

33. The divorce rate in the United States (*Rose* or *Declined*) over the past century.

34. Until the mid-1960s, _____ was the only legal grounds for divorce in New York State.

35. (*Boys* or *Girls*?) have greater problems adjusting to parental conflict or divorce.

36. Remarriages are (*More* or *Less*?) likely than first marriages to end in divorce.

But remarriages are even more likely than first marriages to end in divorce (Lown & Dolan, 1988). One reason is the selection factor. Divorced people are relatively less inclined than others to persist in a troubled marriage. Many divorced people who remarry are also encumbered with alimony and child-support payments that strain new marriages. Many bring children from their earlier marriages to their new ones.

Because of the high incidence of divorce and remarriage, the stepfamily is becoming a more common family unit in the United States. Many stepfamilies disband, often because of conflict over stepchildren, such as parental favoritism for their own (Golish, 2003; Hofferth & Anderson, 2003). However, among remarriages that survive, the level of personal happiness in family members can be as high as it was in the original marriages (Braithwaite et al., 2001).

Sex in the Later Years

Which is the fastest growing segment of the U.S. population? People age 65 and above. More than 30 million people in the United States are senior citizens, and their number is growing fast. This "graying" of the United States may have a profound effect on our views of older people, especially concerning their sexuality. Many people in our culture see sexual activity as appropriate only for the young. This belief falls within a constellation of unfounded cultural myths about sexuality among older people, which includes the notions that older people are sexless, that older people with sexual urges are abnormal, and that older men with sexual interests are "dirty old men" (Walz, 2002). *Question: What sex-related changes take place in the body and in behavior during the later years?*

Researchers find that sexual daydreaming, sex drive, and sexual activity tend to decline with age, whereas negative sexual attitudes tend to increase (Barnett & Dunning, 2003). However, research does not support the belief that people lose their sexuality as they age. Nearly all (95%) of the older people in one sample reported that they liked sex, and 75% reported that orgasm was essential to their sexual fulfillment (Starr & Weiner, 1981). People who are exposed to cultural views that sex among older people is deviant may renounce sex as they age, however. Those who remain sexually active may be bothered by guilt (Trudel et al., 2000).

Sexual activity among older people, as among other groups, is influenced not only by physical structures and changes but also by psychological well-being, feelings of intimacy, and cultural expectations.

Physical Changes

Although many older people retain the capacity to respond sexually, physical changes do occur as the years pass (see Table 14.8). If we are aware of them, we will not view them as abnormal or find ourselves unprepared to cope with them. Many potential problems can be averted by changing our expectations or making some changes to accommodate the aging process.

Let us not begin this section with a deeply biological focus on changes in cells, hormones, and the like. Let's talk, first, about what happens when we look in the mirror. Many of us are saddened or dismayed by the obvious physical changes that take place as we age. We develop wrinkles. Our hair turns gray. Our muscle tone decreases. We tend to put on weight, especially if we do not exercise regularly. All in all, we are likely to feel that we are less attractive than we were. And the fact is that our partners may find us to be less attractive. Nevertheless, in enduring intimate relationships, feelings of love, intimacy, and sharing a life together can outweigh all of those

TABLE 14.8	
Changes in Sexual Arousal Often Associated with Aging	
Changes in the Female	Changes in the Male
Reduced myotonia (muscle tension)	Longer time to erection and orgasm
Reduced vaginal lubrication	Need for more direct stimulation for erection and orgasm
Reduced elasticity of the vaginal walls	Less semen emitted during ejaculation
Smaller increases in breast size during sexual arousal	Erections may be less firm
Reduced intensity of muscle spasms at orgasm	Testicles may not elevate as high into the scrotum
	Less intense orgasmic contractions
	Lessened feeling of a need to ejaculate during sex
	Longer refractory period

Source: Copyright © 1990 by The Kinsey Institute for Research in Sex, Gender, and Reproduction. From *The Kinsey Institute new report on sex.* Reprinted with permission from St. Martin's Press, New York, NY.

changes and feelings. But if we are single in our later years, perhaps because of divorce or becoming widowed, the future, including the sexual future, may appear to be more bleak.

Yet, as we will see, older people can also lead sexually fulfilling lives. In fact, if they fine-tune their expectations, they may find themselves leading some of the most sexually fulfilling years of their lives (Trudel et al., 2000). Having noted these concerns, let us now catalogue many of the physical changes that occur in women and men as they grow older.

Changes in the Female Many of the physical changes in women stem from decline in the production of estrogen around the time of menopause. The vaginal walls lose much elasticity and the thick, corrugated texture of the childbearing years. They grow paler and thinner. Thus coitus may become irritating. The thinning of the walls may also place greater pressure against the bladder and urethra during coitus, leading in some cases to symptoms of urinary urgency and burning urination. The condition may persist for days.

Sexuality in Late Adulthood *Are older people sexually active? If they are, are they abnormal or deviant? Although young people frequently find it difficult to imagine older people engaging in sexual activity, it is normal to retain sexual interest and activity for a lifetime.*

The vagina also shrinks in size. The labia majora lose much of their fatty deposits and become thin. The introitus becomes relatively constricted, and penile entry may become somewhat difficult. This "problem" has a positive aspect: Increased friction between the penis and vaginal walls may heighten sexual sensations. The uterus decreases in size after menopause and no longer becomes so congested during sexual arousal. Following menopause, women also produce less vaginal lubrication, and the lubrication that is produced may take minutes, not seconds, to appear. Lack of adequate lubrication is also a major reason for painful coitus.

Many of these changes may be slowed or reversed through estrogen-replacement therapy, although estrogen replacement has become quite controversial (see Chapter 3). Natural lubrication may also be increased through more elaborate foreplay. The need for more foreplay may encourage the man to become a more considerate lover. (Older men, too, are likely to need more time to become aroused.) An artificial lubricant can also ease problems posed by difficult entry or painful thrusting.

Women's breasts show smaller increases in size with sexual arousal as they age, but the nipples still become erect. Because the muscle tone of the urethra and anal sphincters decreases, the spasms of orgasm become less powerful and fewer in number. Thus orgasms may feel less intense. The uterine contractions that occur during orgasm may become discouragingly painful for some postmenopausal women. Despite these changes, women can retain their ability to achieve orgasm well into their advanced years. The subjective experience of orgasm also remains highly satisfying, despite the lessened intensity of muscular contractions.

Changes in the Male Age-related changes tend to occur more gradually in men than in women and are not clearly connected with any one biological event, as they are with menopause in the woman (Barnett & Dunning, 2003). Male adolescents may achieve erection in a matter of seconds through sexual fantasy alone. After about age 50, men take progressively longer to achieve erection. Erections become less firm, perhaps because of lowered testosterone production (Perry et al., 2001). Older men may require minutes of direct stimulation of the penis to achieve an erection. Couples can adjust to these changes by extending the length and variety of foreplay.

Most men remain capable of erection throughout their lives. Erectile dysfunction is not inevitable with aging. Men generally require more time to reach orgasm as they age, however, which may also reflect lowered testosterone production. In the eyes of their sex partners, however, delayed ejaculation may make them better lovers.

The testes often decrease slightly in size and produce less testosterone with age. Testosterone production usually declines gradually from about age 40 to age 60 and then begins to level off. However, the decline is not inevitable and may be related to the man's general health. Sperm production tends to decline as the seminiferous tubules degenerate, but viable sperm may be produced quite late in life. Men in their 70s, 80s, and 90s have fathered children.

Nocturnal erections tend to diminish in intensity, duration, and frequency as men age, but they do not normally disappear in healthy men (Perry et al., 2001). The refractory period tends to lengthen with age. An adolescent may require only a few minutes to regain erection and ejaculate again after a first orgasm, whereas a man in his 30s may require half an hour. Past age 50, the refractory period may increase to several hours.

Older men produce less ejaculate, and it may seep rather than shoot out. Although the contractions of orgasm still begin at 0.8-second intervals, they become

Truth?Fiction?
Revisited

It is not true that few women can reach orgasm after the age of 70. Actually, healthy women can retain the capacity for orgasm well into their advanced years.

weaker and fewer. Still, the number and strength of spasms do not translate precisely into subjective pleasure. An older male may enjoy orgasm as thoroughly as he did at a younger age. Attitudes and expectations can be as important as the contractions themselves.

An 82-year-old man commented on his changing sexual abilities:

> I come maybe once in every three sexual encounters these days with my wife. My erection comes and goes, and it's not a big concern to us. I get as much pleasure from touching and thrusting as I do from an ejaculation. When I was younger it was inconceivable to me that I might enjoy sex without an orgasm, but I can see now that in those days I missed out on some pleasure by making orgasm such a focus. (Gordon & Snyder, 1989, p. 153)

Following orgasm, erection subsides more rapidly than it does in a younger man. A study of 65 healthy men aged 45 to 74 showed an age-related decline in sexual desire, arousal, and activity. Yet there were no differences between younger and older men in level of sexual satisfaction or enjoyment (Schiavi et al., 1990).

Patterns of Sexual Activity

Despite the decline in certain physical functions, older people can continue to lead a fulfilling sex life. In fact, years of sexual experience may more than compensate for any diminution in physical responsiveness (Barnett & Dunning, 2003; Trudel et al., 2000). A Roper Starch poll of 1,292 people in the United States aged 60 and above found that 74% of the men and 70% of the women who had remained sexually active said they were as satisfied or *more* satisfied with sex than they were in their 40s (Leary, 1998). Unfortunately, people who overreact to expected changes in sexual response may conclude that their sex lives are over and give up on sexual activity or even on expressing any physical affection.

Ninety-four percent of the men and 84% of the women in Kinsey's samples remained sexually active at the age of 60. Half of the 60- to 91-year-olds surveyed by Starr and Weiner (1981) reported sexual relations on a regular basis—and half of these, at least once a week. A study of 200 healthy 80- to 102-year-olds reported that 30% of the women and 62% of the men still engaged in intercourse (Bretschneider & McCoy, 1988). A study of 100 older men in England found that the key factor in whether they continued to engage is sexual activity was the availability of a partner, not physical condition (Jones et al., 1994). Sex therapist Helen Singer Kaplan (1990) concluded,

> The loss of sexuality is not an inevitable aspect of aging. . . . The results of these studies are remarkable in their consensus: Without exception, each investigator found that, providing they are in good health, the great majority of people remain sexually functional and active on a regular basis until virtually the end of life. Or, to put it more succinctly, 70% of healthy 70-year-olds remain sexually active, and are having sex at least once a week, and typically more often than that. . . .
>
> Although it is widely believed that sex no longer matters after middle age, the opposite is true, and sex often becomes *more* and not *less* important as a person grows older. Because sex is among the last pleasure-giving biological processes to deteriorate, it is potentially an enduring source of gratification at a time when these are becoming fewer and fewer, and a link to the joys of youth. These are important ingredients in the [older] person's emotional well-being. (pp. 185, 204)

Coital frequency tends to decline with age (Trudel et al., 2000). Several factors play a role in declining activity, including physical problems, boredom, and cultural attitudes toward sex among the aging. Despite general trends, sexuality among older people is variable (Knox & Schacht, 2002). Many older people engage in intercourse, oral sex, and masturbation at least as often as when younger; some become disgusted by sex; others simply lose interest.

But coital frequency is not synonymous with sexual satisfaction. In a Canadian study of 215 married people who were middle-aged and older (51 to 81 years of age), those aged 65 or above showed lower coital frequency than younger respondents (Libman, 1989). But no sizable differences emerged in the level of sexual satisfaction between older and younger groups.

The frequency of masturbation also generally declines with age for both men and women, although an increase may occur following a marital separation, divorce, or death of a spouse. Still, continued masturbation was reported by nearly half (46%) among a sample of people aged 60 to 91 (Starr & Weiner, 1981).

Couples may accommodate to the physical changes of aging by broadening their sexual repertoire to include more diverse forms of stimulation. Many respondents to a *Consumer Reports* survey reported using oral–genital stimulation, sexual fantasy, sexually explicit materials, anal stimulation, vibrators, and other sexual techniques to offset problems in achieving lubrication or erection (Brecher, 1984). Sexual satisfaction may be derived from manual or oral stimulation, cuddling, caressing, and tenderness, as well as from intercourse to orgasm.

The availability of a sexually interested and supportive partner may be the most important determinant of continued sexual activity. Many women discontinue sexual activity because of the death of their husbands. Women's life expectancy exceeds men's by an average of 7 years.

Review: Sex in the Later Years

Reflect

What are your own attitudes toward sexual activity among older people? Is sex something "meant" for young people? Does or did the thought of your parents engaging in sexual activity disturb you? Explain.

Critical Thinking

Why is it that among older people, the availability of a sexually interested and supportive partner may be the most important determinant of continued sexual activity?

37. Many of the physical changes in older women stem from decline in the production of _____.

38. Orgasms feel (*More* or *Less*?) intense.

39. After about age 50, erections become (*More* or *Less*?) firm.

40. Erectile dysfunction (*Is* or *Is not*?) inevitable with aging.

41. Older people (*Can* or *Cannot*?) continue to lead a fulfilling sex life.

Sex and Disability

Like older people, people with disabilities (especially those whose physical disabilities render them dependent on others) are often seen as sexless and childlike (Nosek et al., 1994). Such views are based on misconceptions about the sexual functioning of people with disabilities. Some of these myths and stereotypes may be eroding, however, in part because of the success of the civil and social rights movements of the disabled in the 1970s and the attention focused on the sexuality of people with disabilities in films such as *Coming Home, Born on the Fourth of July,* and *My Left Foot.* **Question: How do physical disabilities affect sexual functioning?**

A person may have been born with or acquire a bodily impairment or may suffer a loss of function or a disfiguring change in appearance. Although the disability may require the person to make adjustments in order to perform sexually, most people with disabilities have the same sexual needs, feelings, and desires as people without disabilities. Their ability to express their sexual feelings and needs depends on the physical limitations imposed by their disabilities, their adjustment to their disabilities, and the availability of partners. The establishment of mature sexual relationships generally demands some distance from one's parents. Therefore, people with disabilities who are physically dependent on their parents may find it especially difficult to develop sexual relationships. Parents who acknowledge their children's sexual development can be helpful by facilitating dating. Far too often, parents become overprotective:

> Adolescent disabled girls have the same ideas, hopes, and dreams about sexuality as able-bodied girls. They will have learned the gender role expectations set for them by the media and others and may experience difficulty if they lack more substantive educational information about sexuality and sex function. In addition their expectations may come in conflict with the family, which may have consistently protected or overindulged the child and not permitted her to "grow up." . . . In many cases the families are intensely concerned about the sexual and emotional vulnerability of the daughter and hope that "nothing bad" will happen to her. They may, therefore, encourage her to wear youthful clothing and to stay a safe little girl. The families can mistakenly assume there may be no sexual life ahead of her and protect her from this perceived bitter reality with youthful clothing and little-girlish ways. The result can be, of course, that the young emerging woman may become societally handicapped in learning how to conduct herself as a sexual woman. She will be infantilized. (Cole, 1988, pp. 282–283)

In such families, young people with disabilities get the message that sex is not for them. As they mature, they may need counseling to help them recognize the normalcy of their sexual feelings and to help them make responsible choices for exploring their sexuality.

Physical Disabilities

According to Margaret Nosek and her colleagues (1994), sexual wellness, among the disabled, as among the population at large, involves five factors:

- Positive sexual self-concept; seeing oneself as valuable sexually and as a person
- Knowledge about sexuality
- Positive, productive relationships

- Coping with barriers to sexuality (social, environmental, physical, and emotional)
- Maintaining the best possible general and sexual health, given one's limitations

This model applies to all of us, of course. Let us now consider aspects of specific physical disabilities and human sexuality.

Cerebral Palsy **Cerebral palsy** does not generally impair sexual interest, capacity for orgasm, or fertility (Reinisch, 1990). Depending on the nature and degree of muscle spasticity or lack of voluntary muscle control, however, afflicted people may be limited to certain types of sexual activities and coital positions.

The importance of sex education for disabled people is highlighted by a case of a man with cerebral palsy:

> A 40-year-old man with moderate cerebral palsy came to see me for sexual counseling. When asked why he came for counseling, he said, "I think I'm old enough to learn about sex." He was college educated, fully employed, and had been living by himself, away from his parents, for three years. In questioning him further, I found that the extent of his sexual knowledge was he knew he had a penis but knew nothing about the human sexual response or about female anatomy. When I asked him if any "white, sticky stuff" ever came out of his penis, he replied, "Yes, and doesn't that have something to do with my cerebral palsy?" (Knight, 1989, p. 186)

People with disabilities such as cerebral palsy often suffer social rejection during adolescence and perceive themselves as unfit for or unworthy of intimate sexual relationships, especially with people who are not disabled. They are often socialized into an asexual role. Counseling can help them understand and accept their sexuality, promote a more positive body image, and provide the social skills to establish intimate relationships.

Spinal Cord Injuries People who suffer physical disabilities as the result of traumatic injuries or physical illness must not only learn to cope with their physical limitations but also adjust to a world designed for nondisabled people. Spinal cord injuries affect about 6,000 to 10,000 people annually in the United States (Seftel et al., 1991). The majority of persons who suffer disabling spinal cord injuries are young, active males. Automobile or pedestrian accidents account for about half of these cases. Other common causes include stabbing or bullet wounds, sports injuries, and falls. Depending on the location of the injury to the spinal cord, a loss of voluntary control (paralysis) can occur in either the legs (*paraplegia*) or all four limbs (*quadriplegia*). A loss of sensation may also occur in parts of the body that lie beneath the site of injury. Most people who suffer such injuries have relatively normal life spans, but the quality of their lives is profoundly affected.

The effect of spinal cord injuries on sexual response depends on the site and severity of the injury. Men have two erection centers in the spinal cord: a higher center in the lumbar region that controls psychogenic erections and a lower one in the sacral region that controls reflexive erections. When damage occurs at or above the level of the lumbar center, men lose the capacity for psychogenic erections, the kinds of erections that occur in response to mental stimulation alone, such as when viewing erotic films or fantasizing. They may still be able to achieve reflexive erections from direct stimulation of the penis, because these erections are controlled by the sacral erection center located in a lower portion of the spinal cord. However, they cannot feel any genital sensations because the nerve connections to the brain are

Cerebral palsy
A muscular disorder that is caused by damage to the central nervous system (usually prior to or during birth) and characterized by spastic paralysis.

severed. Men with damage to the sacral erection center lose the capacity for reflexive erections but can still achieve psychogenic erections so long as their upper spinal cords remains intact (Spark, 1991). Overall, researchers find that about 3 of 4 men with spinal cord injuries are able to achieve erections but only about 1 in 10 continues to ejaculate naturally (Spark, 1991). Others can be helped to ejaculate with the aid of a vibrator (Szasz & Carpenter, 1989). Their brains may help to fill in some of the missing sensations associated with coitus and even orgasm. When direct stimulation does not cause erection, the woman can insert the limp penis into the vagina and gently thrust her hips, taking care not to dislodge the penis.

Although the frequency of sexual activity among spinal-cord-injured men tends to decline following the injury (Alexander et al., 1993), a study of almost 1,300 men with these injuries found that about 1 out of 3 (35%) continued to engage in sexual intercourse (Spark, 1991). Only about 1 in 5 of the men received any kind of sexual counseling to help him adjust sexually to his disability. The men typically reported increased interest in alternative sexual activities, especially those involving areas above the level of the spinal injury, such as the mouth, lips, neck, and ears.

Retention of sexual response in women also depends on the site and severity of the spinal cord injury. Women may lose the ability to experience genital sensations or to lubricate normally during sexual stimulation. However, sensations in the breasts may not be affected, making the breasts more erotogenic. Most women with spinal cord injuries can engage in coitus, become impregnated, and deliver vaginally. A survey of 68 spinal-cord-injured women showed that about half were able to achieve orgasm in response to audiovisual erotic material combined with manual genital stimulation (Sipski et al., 2001). Spinal-cord-injured women can heighten their sexual pleasure by using sexual imagery and manual stimulation (Sipski et al., 2001).

Couples facing the challenge of spinal cord injury may expand their sexual repertoire to focus less on genital stimulation (except to attain the reflexes of erection and lubrication) and more on the parts of the body that retain sensation. Stimulation of some areas of the body, such as the ears, the neck, and the breasts (in both men and women) can yield pleasurable erotic sensations.

Sensory Disabilities Sensory disabilities, such as blindness and deafness, do not directly affect genital responsiveness. Still, sexuality may be affected in many ways. A person who has been blind since birth or early childhood may have difficulty understanding a partner's anatomy. Sex education curricula have been designed specifically to enable visually impaired people to learn about sexual anatomy via models. Anatomically correct dolls may be used to simulate positions of intercourse.

People who are deaf often lack knowledge about sex. Their ability to comprehend the social cues involved in forming and maintaining intimate relationships may also be impaired. Sex education programs based on sign language are helping many people with hearing impairments become more socially perceptive as well as more knowledgeable about the physical aspects of sex. People with visual and hearing impairments often lack self-esteem and self-confidence, problems that make it difficult for them to establish intimate relationships. Counseling may help them become more aware of their sexuality and develop social skills.

Other Physical Disabilities and Impairments Specific disabilities pose particular challenges to, and impose particular limitations on, sexual functioning. **Arthritis** may make it difficult or painful for affected individuals to bend their arms, knees,

Arthritis A progressive disease that is characterized by inflammation and pain in the joints.

and hips during sexual activity. Coital positions that minimize discomfort and the application of moist heat to the joints before sexual relations may be helpful.

A male amputee may find that he is better balanced in the lateral-entry or female-superior position than in the male-superior position. A woman with limited hand function may find it difficult or impossible to insert a diaphragm and may need to request assistance from her partner or switch to another contraceptive. Sensitivity to each other's needs is as vital to couples in which one member has a disability as it is to nondisabled couples.

Speaking of sensitivity, let us turn to other psychological issues. *Question: How do psychological disabilities affect sexual functioning?*

Psychological Disabilities

People with psychological disabilities, such as mental retardation, are often stereotyped as incapable of understanding their sexual impulses. Retarded people are sometimes assumed to maintain childlike innocence through their lives or to be devoid of sexuality. Some stereotype retarded people in the opposite direction: as having stronger-than-normal sex drives and being incapable of controlling them (Reinisch, 1990). Some mentally retarded people do act inappropriately—by masturbating publicly, for example. The stereotypes are exaggerated, however, and even many mentally retarded people who act inappropriately can be trained to follow social rules (Reinisch, 1990).

Parents and caretakers often discourage retarded people from learning about their sexuality or teach them to deny or suppress their sexual feelings. Although the physical changes of puberty may be delayed in mentally retarded people, most develop normal sexual needs. Most are capable of learning about their sexuality and can be guided into rewarding and responsible intimate relationships.

Review: Sex and Disability

Reflect

Do you know of anyone with a physical or psychological disability who got married or became involved in an intimate relationship? Are you aware of any particular problems that the couple experienced? How did things work out?

Critical Thinking

Why do people tend to assume that individuals with serious physical or psychological disabilities are "sexless" or unaffected by sexual feelings?

42. Cerebral _____ does not generally impair sexual interest, capacity for orgasm, or fertility.

43. The majority of persons who suffer disabling spinal cord injuries are (*Males* or *Females*?).

44. Men have _____ (How many?) erection centers in the spinal cord.

45. A (*Majority* or *Minority*?) of men with spinal cord injuries are able to achieve erections.

46. Most women with spinal cord injuries (*Can* or *Cannot*?) become pregnant.

47. Most mentally retarded people (*Can* or *Cannot*?) learn about their sexuality and be guided into rewarding intimate relationships.

One of the greatest impediments to sexual fulfillment among people with disabilities is difficulty in finding a loving and supportive partner. Some people engage in sexual relations with people with disabilities out of sympathy. By and large, however, the partners are other people with disabilities or nondisabled people who have overcome stereotypes that portray disabled people as undesirable. Many partners have had some prior positive relationship with a person with a disability, usually during childhood. Experience facilitates acceptance of the idea that a disabled person can be desirable. Depending on the nature of the disability, the nondisabled partner may need to be open to assuming a more active sexual role to compensate for the limitations of the partner with the disability. Two partners with disabilities need to be sensitive to each other's needs and physical limitations. People with disabilities and their partners may also need to expand their sexual repertoires to incorporate ways of pleasuring each other that are not fixated on genital stimulation.

The message is simple: Sexuality may enrich the lives of nearly all adults at virtually any age.

Recite

1. What are the trends in the numbers of people remaining single?	Recent years have seen a sharp increase in the numbers of single young people in our society.
2. Why do people remain single?	Reasons include increased permissiveness toward premarital sex and, particularly for women, the desire to become established in a career. Some people remain single or celibate for religious reasons. No one lifestyle characterizes single people.
3. What's a POSSLQ?	A POSSLQ is a person of the opposite sex sharing living quarters. The term is used by the U.S. Census Bureau.
4. Who cohabits?	Cohabitation is more prevalent among less well educated and less affluent people.
5. Why do people cohabit?	Some couples prefer cohabitation because it provides a consistent intimate relationship without the legal and economic entanglements of marriage. Some emotionally committed couples cohabit because of the economic advantages of sharing household expenses.
6. What happens to people who cohabit?	Cohabitors who later marry may run a greater risk of divorce than noncohabitors, perhaps because of a selection factor; that is, cohabitors tend to be more liberal than people who do not live together before getting married.
7. Does marriage remain popular?	Marriage is found in all human societies and is our most common lifestyle.
8. Why do people get married?	Throughout Western history, marriages have legitimized sexual relations, sanctioned the permanence of a deeply committed relationship, provided for the orderly transmission of wealth, and facilitated child rearing. In Western society today, romantic love is seen as an essential aspect of marriage.
9. We've been talking about marriages between one man and one woman. What other kinds of marriage are there?	The major types of marriages between men and women are monogamy and polygamy. Polygamy includes polygyny and polyandry. Gay marriages are now recognized in several Western nations. Open marriages permit each partner open companionship and personal privacy, which may allow sexual intimacy with others. In a group marriage, three or more people share an intimate relationship.

Recite

10. How do we select the individuals we marry?

People in the United States tend to marry within their geographic area and social class. They tend to marry people who are similar in physical attractiveness, who share similar attitudes, and who seem likely to meet their material, sexual, and psychological needs.

11. What kinds of patterns of sexual activity do we find in marriage?

Married couples today engage in coitus more frequently and for longer durations of time than in Kinsey's day. They report higher levels of sexual satisfaction and engage in a greater variety of sexual activities.

12. Are married people sexually satisfied?

American women today are more likely to reach orgasm through marital sex than in Kinsey's day. Wives take more active sexual roles than in Kinsey's day.

13. Why do people engage in extramarital sex?

People may have affairs for sexual variety, to punish their spouses, to achieve emotional closeness with someone, or to prove that they are attractive.

14. What patterns of extramarital sex do we find?

Extramarital sex is usually conducted without the spouse's knowledge or approval. Secret affairs are termed conventional adultery, infidelity, or simply "cheating." Conventional adultery runs the gamut from "one-night stands" to affairs that persist for years. In consensual adultery, extramarital relationships are conducted with the knowledge and consent of the partner. In swinging, or *mate-swapping,* the partner participates. The incidence of extramarital sex remains unknown, but it appears that men are more likely than women to have affairs.

15. What are our attitudes toward extramarital sex?

Extramarital sex continues to be viewed negatively by the majority of married people in our society.

16. What are the effects of infidelity?

The discovery of infidelity can evoke anger, jealousy, shame, and divorce. Affairs typically damage marriages.

17. How many marriages end in divorce?

About half of the marriages in the United States end in divorce.

18. Why do people get divorced?

Reasons include relaxed restrictions on divorce, greater financial independence among women, and the idea that marriages should be happy.

19. What is the cost of divorce for the couple and the children?

Divorce is often associated with financial and emotional problems, however. Divorce can give rise to feelings of failure and depression and can make it difficult to rear children. Yet divorce can be preferable to remaining married, even for the sake of the children, if conflict persists.

20. What sex-related changes take place in the body and in behavior during the later years?

As the years go on and bodies change, partners may become less attractive to one another. It becomes more difficult for males to attain and maintain erections, and for females to lubricate. Many potential problems can be averted by changing expectations and making changes to accommodate aging.

21. How do physical disabilities affect sexual functioning?

Cerebral palsy does not usually impair sexual interest, capacity for orgasm, or fertility, but afflicted people may be limited to certain types of sexual activities and coital positions. People with spinal cord injuries may be paralyzed and lose sensation below the waist. They often respond reflexively to direct genital stimulation. Sensory disabilities do not directly affect sexual response but may impair sexual knowledge and social skills.

22. How do psychological disabilities affect sexual functioning?

Most mentally retarded people can learn the basics of their own sexuality and develop responsible intimate relationships.

Chapter 15

Truth?Fiction?

T / F? Sexual dysfunctions are rare.

T / F? Only men can reach orgasm too early.

T / F? The most common cause of painful intercourse in women is vaginal infection.

T / F? Sex therapy teaches a man with erectile disorder how to will an erection.

T / F? A doctor made a somewhat unusual presentation to a medical convention by dropping his pants to reveal an erection.

T / F? Many sex therapists recommend masturbation as the treatment for women who have never been able to reach orgasm.

T / F? A man can be prevented from ejaculating by squeezing his penis when he feels that he is about to ejaculate.

Sexual Dysfunctions

Preview

Types of Sexual Dysfunctions

Sexual Desire Disorders

Sexual Arousal Disorders

Orgasmic Disorders

Sexual Pain Disorders

A World of Diversity: Inis Beag and Mangaia—Worlds Apart

Origins of Sexual Dysfunctions

Organic Causes

Psychosocial Causes

A World of Diversity: An Odd Couple: Koro and Dhat Syndromes

Treatment of Sexual Dysfunctions

The Masters-and-Johnson Approach

The Helen Singer Kaplan Approach

A Closer Look: How Do You Find a Qualified Sex Therapist?

Sexual Desire Disorders

Sexual Arousal Disorders

Orgasmic Disorders

Human Sexuality in the New Millennium: Thinking Critically about Buying Viagra and Other Drugs Online

Human Sexuality in the New Millennium: Development of Biological Treatments of Sexual Dysfunctions in Women

Sexual Pain Disorders

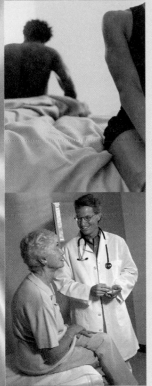

Derek, 39, and his wife Pam, 37, had not attempted sexual intercourse for 5 years. Sexual relations had been limited to fondling, caressing, and occasional oral–genital contact. They had given up attempting intercourse because of Derek's difficulty in attaining and sustaining erections. But recently they had begun trying again. Some nights Derek would have an erection enabling him to penetrate, only to find that he quickly lost the erection. Many nights he was unable to perform at all. Each failure was another blow to his self-esteem. Pam worried that he could not perform because he was no longer attracted to her.

Terry, 24, has decided she is built differently from friends and women she reads about. They all reach orgasm, it seems, at the drop of a hat. But she has never managed "one of those things." Her husband David, also 24, is considerate, but Terry knows that he, too, is frustrated and feels guilty with every ejaculation. Why should he enjoy sex if Terry cannot? Terry and David anticipate sex with fear rather than pleasure, and David has been having difficulty attaining erection. Terry wonders whether she should try to fake orgasm to hold on to him. But she fears she would not know how.

(The Authors' Files)

Derek and Terry have sexual dysfunctions. ***Question: What are sexual dysfunctions?*** **Sexual dysfunctions** are persistent or recurrent problems in becoming sexually aroused or reaching orgasm. Many of us have sexual problems from time to time. Men occasionally have difficulty obtaining an erection or ejaculate more quickly than they would like. Women occasionally have difficulty becoming lubricated or reaching orgasm. But sexual dysfunctions, by contrast, are persistent and cause significant distress.

People with sexual dysfunctions may avoid sexual opportunities for fear of failure. They may anticipate that sex will result in frustration or pain rather than pleasure and gratification. Because our culture emphasizes sexual competence, people with sexual dysfunctions may feel inadequate or incompetent, feelings that diminish their self-esteem (Fishman & Mamo, 2001). They may also experience guilt, shame, frustration, depression, and anxiety.

Sexual dysfunctions
Persistent or recurrent difficulties in becoming sexually aroused or reaching orgasm.

Many people with sexual dysfunctions find it difficult to talk about them, even with spouses or helping professionals. A woman who cannot reach orgasm with her husband may not want to "make a fuss." A man may find it difficult to admit erectile problems to his physician during a physical exam. Many physicians are also uncomfortable talking about sex and may never ask about it.

Question: How common are sexual dysfunctions? We do not have precise figures on their occurrence. The most accurate information may be based on the National Health and Social Life Survey (Laumann et al., 1994) (see Table 15.1). The NHSLS group asked respondents whether there had been a period of several months during the past year when they lacked interest in sex, could not reach orgasm, reached orgasm too rapidly, had pain during sex, did not enjoy sex, were anxious about their sexual performance, had trouble obtaining or maintaining an erection (for men), or had trouble lubricating (for women). Women more often reported painful sex, lack of pleasure, inability to reach orgasm, and lack of desire. Men were more likely to report reaching orgasm too soon and anxiety about their performance. A national telephone survey found that perhaps 1 woman in 4 is seriously distressed about her sexuality or her sexual relationship (Bancroft et al., 2003). However, the NHSLS study suggested that 43% of women had a sexual dysfunction (Laumann et al., 1994). Moreover, Rosen and Laumann (2003) argue that the telephone survey was inferior in methodology to the face-to-face interviews of the NHSLS study.

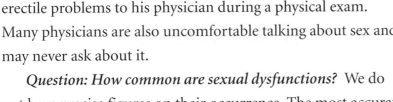

Truth?Fiction?
Revisited

It is not true that sexual dysfunctions are rare. Although there is disagreement about exactly how many people have sexual dysfunctions, they appear to be quite common.

TABLE 15.1

Sexual Dysfunctions Reported within the Past Year, According to the NHSLS Study

	Men (%)	Women (%)
Pain during sex	3.0	14.4
Sex not pleasurable	8.1	21.2
Unable to reach orgasm	8.3	24.1
Lack of interest in sex	15.8	33.4
Anxiety about performance*	17.0	11.5
Reaching climax too early	28.5	10.3
Unable to keep an erection**	10.4	—
Having trouble lubricating	—	18.8

*Anxiety about performance is not itself a sexual dysfunction. However, it figures prominently in sexual dysfunctions.

**Incidence increases with age, and the NHSLS figures may be an underestimate.

Source: Adapted from Tables 10.8A and 10.8B, pages 370 and 371, in Laumann, E. O., Gagnon, J. H., Michael, R. T., & Michaels, S. (1994). *The social organization of sexuality: Sexual practices in the United States.* Chicago: University of Chicago Press.

Types of Sexual Dysfunctions

The most widely used system of classification of sexual dysfunctions is based on the American Psychiatric Association's (2000) *Diagnostic and Statistical Manual of Mental Disorders (DSM)*. The DSM proposes four categories of sexual dysfunctions:

1. **Sexual desire disorders.** These involve lack of interest in sex or aversion to sexual contact.
2. **Sexual arousal disorders.** Sexual arousal is mainly characterized by erection in the male and vaginal lubrication and swelling of the external genitalia in the female. In men, sexual arousal disorders involve difficulty in obtaining or sustaining erections sufficient to engage in sexual intercourse. In women, they typically involve insufficient lubrication.
3. **Orgasmic disorders.** Men or women may have difficulty reaching orgasm or may reach orgasm more quickly than they would like. Women are more likely to encounter difficulties reaching orgasm. Men are more likely to reach orgasm too quickly (to experience premature ejaculation).
4. **Sexual pain disorders.** Both men and women may suffer from **dyspareunia** (painful intercourse). Women may experience **vaginismus**, or involuntary contraction of muscles that surround the vaginal barrel, preventing penetration by the penis or making it painful.

Sexual dysfunctions are classified as lifelong or acquired. (Acquired dysfunctions follow a period of normal functioning.) Dysfunctions are also classified as generalized or situational. *Generalized* dysfunctions occur in all situations. *Situational* dysfunctions affect sexual functioning only in some situations, such as during intercourse but not masturbation, or with one partner but not another. If a man has never been able to obtain erection during sexual relations with a partner but can do so during masturbation, his dysfunction is lifelong and situational.

Sexual Desire Disorders

Question: What are sexual desire disorders? Sexual desire disorders involve lack of sexual desire or aversion to genital sexual activity. People with little or no sexual interest or desire are said to have *hypoactive sexual desire disorder.* They often report an absence of sexual fantasies. Lack of desire is more common among women than among men (Bancroft et al., 2003; Laumann et al., 1994). Nevertheless, the belief that men are always eager for sex is a myth.

Lack of sexual desire does not imply that a person is unable to achieve erection, lubricate adequately, or reach orgasm. Some people with low sexual desire can become sexually aroused and reach orgasm when stimulated adequately. Many enjoy sexual activity, even if they are unlikely to initiate it. Many appreciate the affection and closeness of physical intimacy but have no interest in genital stimulation.

Hypoactive sexual desire is one of the most commonly diagnosed sexual dysfunctions, yet there is no clear consensus among clinicians and researchers concerning the definition of low sexual desire. How much sexual interest or desire is "normal"? There is no standard level of sexual desire—no 98.6° reading on the "sexual thermometer." Lack of desire is usually considered a problem when couples recognize that their level of sexual interest has gotten so low that little remains. The lack of desire is often limited to one partner. When one member of a couple is more interested in sex than the other, sex therapists often recommend that couples try to compromise. They also try to uncover and resolve problems in the relationship that may dampen sexual ardor.

Sexual desire disorders Sexual dysfunctions in which people have persistent or recurrent lack of sexual desire or aversion to sexual contact.

Sexual arousal disorders Sexual dysfunctions in which people persistently or recurrently fail to become adequately sexually aroused to engage in or sustain sexual intercourse.

Orgasmic disorders Sexual dysfunctions in which people persistently or recurrently have difficulty reaching orgasm or reach orgasm more rapidly than they would like, despite attaining a level of sexual stimulation of sufficient intensity to normally result in orgasm.

Sexual pain disorders Sexual dysfunctions in which people persistently or recurrently experience pain during coitus.

Dyspareunia A sexual dysfunction characterized by persistent or recurrent pain during sexual intercourse. (From roots meaning "badly paired.")

Vaginismus A sexual dysfunction characterized by involuntary contraction of the muscles surrounding the vaginal barrel, preventing penile penetration or making penetration painful.

A debate is under way about when to consider lack of sexual desire among women a dysfunction (Basson, 2002; Bean, 2002). The literature on sex differences strongly suggests that women, in general, are less interested in sex than men are (Peplau, 2003). This is not to suggest that there is anything wrong with women who experience strong, regular sexual urges. On the other hand, some researchers note that the definition of lack of desire as a dysfunction, as applied to women, attempts to impose on women a male model of what is normal (Bean, 2002). Keep in mind that lack of desire usually does not come to the health practitioner's attention unless one partner is more desirous of sex than the other. That is usually the situation in which the less-interested partner is exposed to the possibility of being labeled with a dysfunction.

Biological and psychosocial factors—hormonal deficiencies, depression, dissatisfaction with one's relationship, and so on—contribute to lack of desire (Frohlich & Meston, 2002). Among the medical conditions that diminish sexual desire are testosterone deficiencies, thyroid overactivity or underactivity, and temporal lobe epilepsy. Sexual desire is stoked by testosterone, which is produced by men in the testes and by both men and women in the adrenal glands (Tuiten et al., 2000). Women may experience less sexual desire when their adrenal glands are surgically removed. Low sexual interest, along with erectile difficulties, are also common among men with **hypogonadism**, which is treated with testosterone (Lue, 2000).

Researchers find men with hypoactive sexual desire disorder to be older than women with the disorder (Ghizzani, 2003; Morley & van den Berg, 2000). A gradual decline in sexual desire, among men, may be explained in part by the reduction in testosterone levels that occurs in middle and later life (Morley & van den Berg, 2000; Perry et al., 2001). But women's sexual desire may also decline with age because of physical and psychological changes, as we will see (Kingsberg, 2002). Abrupt changes in sexual desire are more often explained by psychological and interpersonal factors such as depression, stress, and problems in the relationship (Bancroft et al., 2003; Frohlich & Meston, 2002; Graham, 2003).

Psychological problems can contribute to low sexual desire (Bancroft et al., 2003; Ghizzani, 2003). Anxiety is the most commonly reported factor. Anxiety may dampen sexual desire, including performance anxiety (anxiety over being evaluated negatively), anxiety involving fears of pleasure or loss of control, and deeper sources of anxiety related to fears of injury. Depression is a common cause of lack of desire (Frohlich & Meston, 2002). A history of sexual assault has also been linked to low sexual desire.

Some medications, including those used to control anxiety or hypertension, may reduce desire. Changing medications or doses may restore the person's previous level of desire.

Sexual Aversion Disorder People with low sexual desire may have little or no interest in sex, but they are not repelled by genital contact. Some people, however, find sex disgusting or aversive and avoid genital contact.

Some researchers consider sexual aversion to be a *sexual phobia* or *sexual panic state* with intense, irrational fears of sexual contact and a pressing desire to avoid sexual situations (Kaplan, 1987). A history of erectile problems can cause sexual aversion in men. Men with such histories may be anxious in sexual situations because such situations trigger feelings of failure and shame. Their partners may also develop an aversion to sexual contact because of this anxiety and because of their own frustration. A history of sexual trauma, such as rape or childhood sexual abuse or incest, often figures prominently in cases of sexual aversion, especially in women.

Hypogonadism
An endocrine disorder that reduces the output of testosterone.

Sexual Arousal Disorders

When we are sexually stimulated, our bodies normally respond with **vasocongestion**, which produces erection in the male and vaginal lubrication in the female. *Question: What are sexual arousal disorders?* People with sexual arousal disorders fail to achieve or sustain the lubrication or erection necessary for coital activity. Or they lack the feelings of sexual pleasure or excitement that normally accompany sexual arousal (American Psychiatric Association, 2000).

Problems of sexual arousal have sometimes been labeled *impotence* in the male and *frigidity* in the female. But these labels are pejorative, so many professionals prefer to use less threatening, more descriptive terms.

Male Erectile Disorder Sexual arousal disorder in the male is called **male erectile disorder** or *erectile dysfunction.* It is characterized by persistent difficulty in achieving or maintaining an erection sufficient to allow the completion of sexual activity. In most cases the failure is limited to sexual activity with partners, or with some partners and not others. It can thus be classified as *situational.* In rare cases the dysfunction is found during any sexual activity, including masturbation. In such cases, it is considered *generalized.* Some men with erectile disorder are unable to attain an erection with their partners. Others can achieve erection but not sustain it (or recover it) long enough for penetration and ejaculation.

As many as 30 million men in the United States experience some degree of erectile dysfunction (Goldstein, 1998). The incidence of erectile disorder increases with age (Ghizzani, 2003), although there is great disagreement on how many men are affected. The NHSLS group reported that difficulty keeping an erection increases from about 6% in the 18- to 24-year-old age group to about 20% in the 55- to 59-year-old age group. Another study reported that about 3% of men in their 50s had difficulty obtaining or maintaining erections and that this figure rose to about 35% for men in their 70s (Blanker et al., 2001). But urologist Irwin Goldstein (1998)

Vasocongestion
Engorgement of blood vessels with blood, which swells the genitals and breasts during sexual arousal.

Male erectile disorder
Persistent difficulty achieving or maintaining an erection sufficient to allow the man to engage in or complete sexual intercourse. Also termed *erectile dysfunction.*

The Emotional Toll of Erectile Dysfunction Male erectile disorder or erectile dysfunction is characterized by persistent difficulty in achieving or maintaining an erection sufficient to allow the completion of sexual activity. As many as 30 million men in the United States experience some degree of erectile dysfunction, and its incidence increases with age. Occasional erectile problems are common and may be caused by fatigue, alcohol, or anxiety about a new partner. But fear of recurrence can create a vicious cycle, in which anxiety leads to failure, and failure heightens anxiety.

found that nearly *half* the men aged 40 to 70 in a Massachusetts survey reported problems in obtaining and maintaining erections—at least now and then. We cannot account for these discrepancies between studies. We can only suggest that erectile disorder may be more common than is generally believed. Drugs used to treat the disorder sell quite briskly, although perhaps only a minority of men with erectile disorder use them.

Erectile disorder usually develops after a period of normal functioning. Many men engage in years of successful coitus before the problem begins. Occasional problems in achieving or maintaining erection are quite common. Fatigue, alcohol, anxiety over impressing a new partner, and other factors may account for a transient episode. Even an isolated occurrence can lead to a persistent problem if the man fears recurrence, however. The more anxious and concerned the man becomes about his sexual ability, the more likely he is to suffer **performance anxiety**. This anxiety can contribute to repeated failure, and a vicious cycle of anxiety and failure may develop.

A man with erectile problems may try to "will" an erection, which can compound the problem. Each failure may further demoralize and defeat him. He may ruminate about his sexual inadequacy, setting the stage for yet more anxiety. His partner may try to comfort and support him by saying things like "It can happen to anyone," "Don't worry about it," or "It will get better in time." But attempts at reassurance may be to no avail. As one client put it,

> I always felt inferior, like I was on probation, having to prove myself. I felt like I was up against the wall. You can't imagine how embarrassing this (erectile failure) was. It's like you walk out in front of an audience that you think is a nudist convention and it turns out to be a tuxedo convention. (The Authors' Files)

The vicious cycle of anxiety and erectile failure may be interrupted if the man recognizes that occasional problems are normal and does not overreact. The emphasis in our culture on men's sexual prowess may spur them to view occasional failures as catastrophes rather than as transient disappointments, however. Viewing occasional problems as an inconvenience, rather than a tragedy, may help avert the development of persistent erectile difficulties.

Performance anxiety is a prominent cause of erectile disorder. So are other psychological factors such as depression, low self-esteem, and problems in the relationship. Biological factors can also play a causal role, as we shall see.

Female Sexual Arousal Disorder Women may encounter persistent difficulties becoming sexually excited or sufficiently lubricated in response to sexual stimulation. In some cases these difficulties are lifelong. In others they develop after a period of normal functioning. In some cases, difficulties are pervasive and occur during both masturbation and sex with a partner. More often they occur in certain situations. For example, they occur with some partners and not with others, or during coitus but not during oral–genital sex or masturbation.

Female sexual arousal disorder often accompanies other sexual disorders such as hypoactive sexual desire disorder and orgasmic disorders. Despite problems in becoming sexually aroused, women with sexual arousal disorders can often engage in coitus. Vaginal dryness may produce discomfort, however.

Female sexual arousal disorder, like its male counterpart, may have physical causes. A thorough evaluation by a medical specialist (a urologist in the case of a male, a gynecologist in the case of a female) is recommended. Any neurological, vascular, or hormonal problem that interferes with the lubrication or swelling response of the vagina to sexual stimulation may contribute to female sexual arousal disorder. For example, diabetes mellitus may diminish sexual excitement in women

Performance anxiety
Anxiety concerning one's ability to perform behaviors, especially behaviors that may be evaluated by other people.

by damaging the nerves and blood vessels serving the clitoral region. Reduced estrogen production can also result in vaginal dryness.

Female sexual arousal disorder more commonly has psychological causes, however. In some cases, women harbor deep-seated anger and resentment toward their partners. They thus find it difficult to turn off these feelings when they go to bed. In other cases, sexual trauma is implicated. Survivors of sexual abuse often find it difficult to respond sexually to their partners. Childhood sexual abuse is especially prevalent in cases of female sexual arousal disorder (Bean, 2002; Fishman & Mamo, 2001). Feelings of helplessness, anger, or guilt—and even flashbacks of the abuse—may surface when the woman begins sexual activity, dampening her ability to become aroused. Other psychosocial causes include anxiety or guilt about sex and ineffective stimulation by the partner (Bean, 2002; Fishman & Mamo, 2001).

Orgasmic Disorders

Question: What are orgasmic disorders? These include (1) female orgasmic disorder, (2) male orgasmic disorder, and (3) premature ejaculation. In female or male orgasmic disorder, the woman or man is persistently delayed in reaching orgasm or does not reach orgasm at all, despite achieving sexual stimulation of sufficient intensity to normally result in orgasm. The problem is more common among women than among men. In some cases a person can reach orgasm without difficulty while engaging in sexual relations with one partner, but not with another.

Female Orgasmic Disorder Women with female orgasmic disorder are unable to reach orgasm or have difficulty reaching orgasm following what would usually be an adequate amount of sexual stimulation. Women who have never achieved orgasm through any means are sometimes described as **anorgasmic** or *pre*orgasmic.

A woman who reaches orgasm through masturbation or oral sex may not necessarily reach orgasm during coitus with her partner. Penile thrusting during coitus may not provide sufficient clitoral stimulation to facilitate orgasm. An orgasmic disorder may be diagnosed, however, if orgasm during coitus was impaired by factors such as sexual guilt or performance anxiety. Women who try to force an orgasm may also find themselves unable to do so. They may assume a **spectator role** and observe rather than fully participate in their sexual encounters. "Spectatoring" may further decrease the likelihood of orgasm.

Male Orgasmic Disorder Male orgasmic disorder has also been termed *delayed ejaculation, retarded ejaculation,* or *ejaculatory incompetence.*[1] The problem may be lifelong or acquired, generalized or situational. There are very few cases of men who have never ejaculated. In most cases the disorder is limited to coitus. The man may be capable of ejaculating during masturbation or oral sex but find it difficult, if not impossible—despite high levels of sexual excitement—to ejaculate during intercourse. There is a myth that men with male orgasmic disorder and their female partners enjoy his condition, because it enables him to "go on forever" (Dekker, 1993). Actually, the experience is frustrating for both partners.

Male orgasmic disorder is relatively infrequent in the general population and in clinical practice, where it is among the least frequently diagnosed disorders (Dekker, 1993). Research on the problem has been scarce (Dekker, 1993), and only a few indi-

Anorgasmic Never having reached orgasm. (Literally, "without orgasm.")

Spectator role A role, usually taken on because of performance anxiety, in which people observe rather than fully participate in their sexual encounters.

---

1. Just as we find such terms as *impotence* and *frigidity* unnecessarily pejorative, we prefer to use the more clinical-sounding but less offensive *male orgasmic disorder* or *delayed ejaculation* rather than *retarded ejaculation* or *ejaculatory incompetence.*

vidual or multiple case reports have appeared in the literature (e.g., Masters & Johnson, 1970; Rathus, 1978).

Male orgasmic disorder may be caused by physical problems such as multiple sclerosis or neurological damage that interferes with neural control of ejaculation. It may also be a side effect of certain drugs. Various psychological factors, including performance anxiety, sexual guilt, and hostility toward the partner, may play a role. Helen Singer Kaplan (1974) suggests that some men with male orgasmic disorder may be unconsciously "holding back" their ejaculate from their partners because of underlying hostility or resentment. Masters and Johnson (1970) found that men with this problem frequently have strict religious backgrounds that may leave a residue of unresolved guilt about sex, inhibiting ejaculation. Emotional factors such as fears of pregnancy and anger toward one's partner can also play a role.

As with other sexual dysfunctions, men with orgasmic disorder and their partners may "try harder." But trying harder may worsen rather than help sexual problems. Sexual relations become a job to get done, a chore rather than an opportunity for pleasure and gratification.

Premature Ejaculation A second type of male orgasmic disorder, premature ejaculation, was the most common male sexual dysfunction reported in the NHSLS study (see Table 15.1). Men with **premature ejaculation** ejaculate too rapidly to permit their partners or themselves to enjoy sexual relations fully. The degree of prematurity varies. Some men ejaculate during foreplay or even at the sight of their partner disrobing. But most ejaculate either just prior to or immediately upon penetration, or following a few coital thrusts (Byers & Grenier, 2003).

Just what constitutes *prematurity*? Some definitions focus on a particular time period during which a man should be able to control ejaculation. Is ejaculation within 30 seconds of intromission premature? Within 1 minute? Within 10 minutes? There is no clear timetable. Some scholars argue that the focus should be on whether the couple is satisfied with the duration of coitus, rather than on a specific time period (Byers & Grenier, 2003).

Helen Singer Kaplan (1974) suggested that the label "premature" should be applied to cases in which men persistently or recurrently lack voluntary control over their ejaculations. This may sound like a contradiction in terms, because ejaculation is a reflex, and reflexes need not involve thought or conscious control. Kaplan means, however, that a man may control his ejaculation by learning to regulate the amount of sexual stimulation he experiences so that it remains below the threshold at which the ejaculation reflex is triggered.

Rapid Female Orgasm: Can Women Reach Orgasm Too Quickly? The female counterpart to premature ejaculation, *rapid orgasm*, is so rarely recognized as a problem that it is generally ignored by clinicians and is not classified as a sexual dysfunction in the DSM system. Still, some women experience orgasm rapidly and show little interest in continuing sexual activity so that their partners can achieve gratification. Many women who reach orgasm rapidly are open to continued sexual stimulation and capable of experiencing successive orgasms, however.

Sexual Pain Disorders

For most of us, coitus is a source of pleasure. For some of us, however, coitus gives rise to pain and discomfort. *Question: What are sexual pain disorders?*

Dyspareunia One sexual pain disorder, dyspareunia, or painful coitus, afflicts both men or women. Dyspareunia is a common sexual dysfunction and a common complaint of women seeking gynecological services.

Premature ejaculation
A sexual dysfunction in which ejaculation occurs with minimal sexual stimulation and before the man desires it.

A World of Diversity

Inis Beag and Mangaia—Worlds Apart

Let us invite you on a journey to two islands that are a world apart—sexually as well as geographically. The sexual attitudes and practices within these societies will shed some light on the role of cultural values in determining what is sexually normal and what is sexually dysfunctional.

Our first stop is the island of Inis Beag, which lies off the misty coast of Ireland. From the air, Inis Beag is a green jewel, fertile and inviting. At ground level things do not appear quite so warm, however.

The residents of this Irish folk community do not believe that it is normal for women to experience orgasm. Anthropologist John Messenger (1971), who visited Inis Beag in the 1950s and 1960s, reported that any woman who finds pleasure in sex—especially the intense waves of pleasure that can accompany orgasm—is viewed as deviant. *Should women on Inis Beag, then, be diagnosed as orgasmically impaired?*

Premarital sex is all but unknown on Inis Beag. Prior to marriage, men and women socialize apart. Marriage comes relatively late—usually in the middle 30s for men and the middle 20s for women. Mothers teach their daughters that they will have to submit to their husbands' animal cravings in order to obey God's injunction to "be fruitful and multiply." *After this indoctrination, women show little interest in sex. Should they be diagnosed as having hypoactive sexual desire disorder?*

The women of Inis Beag need not be overly concerned about frequent sexual intercourse, however, because the men of the island believe, erroneously, that sexual activity will drain their strength. Consequently, men avoid sex on the eve of sporting activity or strenuous work. Because of taboos against nudity, married couples engage in intercourse with their underclothes on. Intercourse takes place in the dark—literally as well as figuratively.

During intercourse the man takes the male-superior position. The male is always the initiator. Foreplay is brief, rarely involving manual stimulation of the breasts and never including oral stimulation of the genitals. *Should people who have difficulty becoming sexually aroused under these circumstances be diagnosed as having sexual arousal disorders?* The man ejaculates as rapidly as possible, in the belief that he is the only partner with sexual needs and to spare his wife as best he can. Then he turns over and rapidly falls asleep. Once more the couple have done their duty. *Given that the man ejaculates rapidly, should he be diagnosed as having premature ejaculation?*

Our next stop is Mangaia. Mangaia is a Polynesian pearl of an island. It lifts languidly out of the blue waters of the Pacific. It lies on the other side of the world from Inis Beag—in more ways than one. From an early age, Mangaian boys and girls are encouraged to get in touch with their own sexuality through sexual play and masturbation (Marshall, 1971). At about the age of 13, Mangaian boys are initiated into manhood by adults who instruct them in sexual techniques. Mangaian males are taught the merit of bringing their female partners to multiple orgasms before ejaculating.

Truth?Fiction?
Revisited

The most common cause of painful intercourse in women is not vaginal infection. It is lack of adequate lubrication.

Pain is usually a sign that something is wrong. Dyspareunia may result from physical causes, emotional factors, or an interaction of the two (Meana & Binik, 1994). The most common cause of coital pain in women is inadequate lubrication. In such a case, additional foreplay or artificial lubrication may help. Vaginal infections or sexually transmitted diseases (STIs) may also produce coital pain, however. Allergic reactions to spermicides, even the latex material in condoms, can give rise to coital pain or irritation. Pain during deep thrusting may be caused by endometriosis or pelvic inflammatory disease (PID), by other diseases or structural disorders of the reproductive organs, or by penile contact with the cervix.

Psychological factors such as unresolved guilt or anxiety about sex or the lingering effects of sexual trauma may also be involved. These factors may inhibit lubrication and cause involuntary contractions of the vaginal musculature, making penetration painful or uncomfortable.

Polynesia Cultural expectations affect our judgments about what kinds of sexual behavior are functional and what kinds are dysfunctional. Some Polynesian cultures are sexually permissive. They encourage children to explore their sexuality. Men may be expected to bring their partners to orgasm several times before ejaculating. In such cultures, should men who ejaculate before their partners have multiple orgasms be diagnosed with premature ejaculation? (*Paul Gauguin,* And the gold of their bodies. *Photo: B. Hatala. Musée d'Orsay, Paris, France. Courtesy of Réunion des Musées Nationaux/Art Resources, NY.*)

Girls, too, learn techniques of coitus from their elders. Typically they are initiated by an experienced male relative. Mangaians look on virginity with disdain, because virgins do not know how to provide sexual pleasure. Thus, the older relative makes his contribution to the family by initiating the girl.

Mangaians, by the way, expressed concern when they learned that many European and U.S. women do not regularly experience orgasm during coitus. Orgasm is apparently universal among Mangaian women. Therefore, Mangaians could only assume that Western women suffered from some abnormality of the sex organs. *Do they?*

All in all, the sharp contrasts between Inis Beag and Mangaia illustrate how concepts of normality are embedded within a cultural context. Behavior that is judged to be normal in one culture may be regarded as abnormal in another. How might our own cultural expectations influence our judgments about sexual dysfunction?

Are Mangaian males who ejaculate before their partners have multiple orgasms suffering from premature ejaculation?

Boys practice their new techniques with girlfriends on secluded beaches or beneath the listing fronds of palms. They may visit girlfriends in the evening in the huts where they sleep with their families. Parents often listen for their daughters to laugh and gasp so that they will know that they have reached orgasm with a visiting young man, called a "sleepcrawler." Usually they pretend to be asleep so as not to interfere with courtship and impede their daughters' chances of finding a suitable mate. Daughters may receive a nightly succession of sleepcrawlers.

Painful intercourse is less common in men and is generally associated with genital infections that cause burning or painful ejaculation. Smegma under the penile foreskin of uncircumcised men may also irritate the penile glans during sexual contact.

Vaginismus Another sexual pain disorder, vaginismus, involves involuntary contraction of the pelvic muscles that surround the outer third of the vaginal barrel. Vaginismus occurs reflexively during attempts at vaginal penetration, making entry by the penis painful or impossible. The muscle contractions are accompanied by fear of penetration. Some women with vaginismus are unable to tolerate penetration by any object, including a finger, tampon, or a physician's speculum. The prevalence of vaginismus is unknown.

The woman with vaginismus usually is not aware that she is contracting her vaginal muscles. In some cases, husbands of women with vaginismus develop erectile disorder after repeated failures at penetration.

Vaginismus is caused by a psychological fear of penetration, rather than by a physical injury or defect (Leiblum & Rosen, 2000). Women with vaginismus often have histories of sexual trauma, rape, or botched abortions that resulted in vaginal injuries. They may desire sexual relations. They may be capable of becoming sexually aroused and achieving orgasm. However, fear of penetration triggers an involuntary spasm of the vaginal musculature at the point of penile insertion. Vaginismus can

TABLE 15.2

Differences between European Americans and African Americans in the Incidence of Current Sexual Problems (respondents reporting the problem within the past year)

	European American Men (%)	African American Men (%)	European American Women (%)	African American Women (%)
Pain during sex	3.0	3.3	14.7	12.5
Sex not pleasurable	7.0	15.2	19.7	30.0
Unable to reach orgasm	7.4	9.9	23.2	29.2
Lack of interest in sex	14.7	20.0	30.9	44.5
Anxiety about performance	16.8	23.7	10.5	14.5
Reaching climax too early	27.7	33.8	7.5	20.4
Unable to keep an erection	9.9	14.5	—	—
Having trouble lubricating	—	—	20.7	13.0

Source: Adapted from Tables 10.8A and 10.8B, pages 370 and 371, in Laumann, E. O., Gagnon, J. H., Michael, R. T., & Michaels, S. (1994). *The social organization of sexuality: Sexual practices in the United States.* Chicago: University of Chicago Press.

Review: Types of Sexual Dysfunctions

Reflect

There is no consensus among clinicians and researchers concerning the definition of low sexual desire. How much sexual interest or desire would seem to be normal to you? Why?

CriticalThinking

When does a sexual problem become a sexual dysfunction? Where do you draw the line? How can concern about a sexual problem make it into a dysfunction?

1. Sexual _____ are persistent or recurrent problems in becoming sexually aroused or reaching orgasm.

2. Women are (*More* or *Less*?) likely than men to have trouble reaching orgasm.

3. Women are (*More* or *Less*?) likely than men to be anxious about their sexual performance.

4. Sexual desire disorders involve lack of sexual desire or _____ to genital sexual activity.

5. Sexual desire is stoked by the hormone _____.

6. Vasocongestion produces erection in the male and _____ in the female.

7. The incidence of erectile disorder (*Increases* or *Decreases*?) with age.

8. _____ mellitus may lessen sexual response in women as a consequence of degeneration of nerves and damage to blood vessels.

9. Women who have never reached orgasm by any means are termed _____.

10. Retarded ejaculation is now known more technically as male _____ disorder.

11. _____ ejaculation is the most common male sexual dysfunction reported in the NHSLS study.

12. The sexual pain disorder _____ may occur in both men and women.

13. _____ involves involuntary contraction of the muscles that surround the outer part of the vaginal barrel.

also be a cause or an effect of dyspareunia. Women who experience painful coitus may develop a fear of penetration. Fear then leads to the development of involuntary vaginal contractions. Vaginismus and dyspareunia may also give rise to, or result from, erectile disorder in men (Speckens et al., 1995). Feelings of failure and anxiety can overwhelm both partners.

Table 15.2 shows differences between European Americans and African Americans in the incidence of recently reported sexual dysfunctions and other problems, according to the NHSLS study (Laumann et al., 1994). African American men report a higher incidence than European American men of sexual dysfunctions. African American women report a higher incidence of most sexual dysfunctions, with the exceptions of painful sex and trouble lubricating.

Origins of Sexual Dysfunctions

Because sexual dysfunctions involve the sex organs, it was once assumed that they stemmed largely from organic or physical causes. Today it is widely believed that many cases reflect psychosocial factors such as sexual anxieties, lack of sexual knowledge, or dissatisfaction with one's relationship. Many cases involve a combination of organic and psychological factors.

Organic Causes

Question: What organic factors are involved in sexual dysfunctions? Physical factors such as fatigue and lowered testosterone levels can dampen sexual desire and reduce responsiveness. Fatigue may lead to erectile disorder and orgasmic disorder in men, and to inadequate lubrication and orgasmic disorder in women. But these will be isolated incidents unless the person attaches too much meaning to them and becomes concerned about future performances. Painful coitus, however, often reflects underlying infections. Medical conditions that affect orgasmic functioning include heart disease, diabetes mellitus, multiple sclerosis, spinal cord injuries, complications from surgery (such as removal of the prostate in men), hormonal problems, and use of some medicines, such as those used to treat hypertension and psychiatric disorders. Edward Laumann and his colleagues (1999) found that poor health can contribute to all kinds of sexual dysfunctions in men, but mostly to sexual pain in women.

Organic factors may be involved in as many as 80% of cases of sexual dysfunction (Brody, 1998c). But psychological factors such as anger and depression may prolong or worsen the problem (Feldman et al., 1994).

Organic causes of erectile disorder affect the flow of blood to and through the penis—a problem that becomes more common as men age—or damage the nerves involved in erection (Goldstein, 1998, 2000). Erectile problems can arise when clogged or narrow arteries leading to the penis deprive the penis of oxygen (Lipshultz, 1996). For example, erectile disorder is common among men with diabetes mellitus, a disease that can damage blood vessels and nerves. Eric Rimm (2000) of the Harvard School of Public Health studied 2,000 men and found that erectile dysfunction was connected with a large waist, physical inactivity, and drinking too much alcohol (*or* not having any alcohol!). The common condition among these men may be high cholesterol levels. Cholesterol can impede the flow of blood to the penis just as it impedes the flow of blood to the heart. Another study connects erectile dysfunction with heart disease and hypertension (Johannes et al., 2000). One or two drinks per day, exercise, and weight loss all help lower cholesterol levels.

We're not recommending that abstinent readers take up drinking to ward off or treat erectile problems. Try weight control and regular exercise. The findings of the

Massachusetts Male Aging Study suggest that men who exercise regularly seem to ward off erectile dysfunction (Derby, 2000). Men who burned 200 calories or more a day in physical activity, an amount that can be achieved by briskly walking for 2 miles, cut their risk of erectile dysfunction about in half. Exercise seems to prevent clogging of arteries, keeping them clear for the flow of blood into the penis.

Nerve damage resulting from prostate surgery may impair erectile response. Former senator and presidential candidate Bob Dole encountered erectile problems following removal of his prostate gland. Erectile disorder may also result from multiple sclerosis (MS), a disease in which nerve cells lose the protective coatings that facilitate transmission of neural messages. MS has also been implicated in male orgasmic disorder.

The bacteria that cause syphilis, a sexually transmitted infection, can invade the spinal cord and affect the cells that control erection, resulting in erectile dysfunction. Chronic kidney disease, hypertension, cancer, emphysema, and heart disease can all impair erectile response. So can endocrine disorders that impair testosterone production (Ralph & McNicholas, 2000).

Women also develop vascular or nervous disorders that impair genital blood flow, reducing lubrication and sexual excitement, rendering intercourse painful, and reducing their ability to reach orgasm. As with men, these problems become more likely as women age.

People with sexual dysfunctions are generally advised to undergo a physical examination to determine whether their problems are biologically based. Men with erectile disorder may be evaluated in a sleep center to determine whether they attain erections while asleep. The technique is termed nocturnal penile **tumescence** (NPT). Healthy men usually have erections during rapid-eye-movement (REM) sleep, which occurs every 90 to 100 minutes. Men with organically based erectile disorder often do not have nocturnal erections.

Prescription drugs and illicit drugs account for many cases of erectile disorder. Antidepressant medication and antipsychotic drugs may impair erectile functioning and cause orgasmic disorders (Ashton et al., 2000; Michelson et al., 2000). Tranquilizers such as Valium and Xanax may cause orgasmic disorder in either men or women. Some drugs used to treat high blood pressure can impair erectile response (Ralph & McNicholas, 2000). Switching to other blood pressure drugs or adjusting doses may help. Other drugs that can lead to erectile disorder include adrenergic blockers, diuretics, cholesterol-lowering drugs ("statins"), anticonvulsants, anti-Parkinson drugs, and dyspepsia and ulcer-healing drugs (Ralph & McNicholas, 2000).

Central nervous system depressants such as alcohol, heroin, and morphine can reduce sexual desire and impair sexual arousal. Narcotics also depress testosterone production, thereby reducing sexual desire and leading to erectile failure. Marijuana use has been associated with reduced sexual desire and performance (Wilson et al., 2000).

Regular use of cocaine can cause erectile disorder or male orgasmic disorder and reduce sexual desire in both women and men (Rawson et al., 2002). Some people report increased sexual pleasure from initial use of cocaine, but repeated use can lead to dependency on the drug for sexual arousal. Long-term use may compromise the ability to experience sexual pleasure.

Despite the fact that alcohol can impair sexual arousal on a given occasion, Laumann and his colleagues (1999) found no general relationship between alcohol consumption and the experiencing of sexual dysfunctions. However, problems can arise when people misattribute the sexually dampening effects of depressants such as alcohol to causes within themselves. In other words, if you are unable to perform sex-

Tumescence Swelling; erection. (From the Latin *tumere*, meaning "to swell." *Tumor* has the same root.)

ually when you have had a few drinks and do not know that alcohol can depress your performance, you may believe that something is wrong with you. This belief can create anxiety at your next sexual opportunity, and that anxiety can prevent normal functioning. A second failure may set off a vicious cycle in which self-doubts prompt anxiety, and anxiety results in repeated failure and more anxiety.

Psychosocial Causes

Question: What psychosocial factors are connected with sexual dysfunctions? These include cultural influences, economic problems, psychosexual trauma, a gay sexual orientation, dissatisfaction with one's relationship, lack of sexual skills, irrational beliefs, and performance anxiety (Laumann et al., 1999).

Cultural Influences Children reared in sexually repressive cultural or home environments may learn to respond to sex with feelings of anxiety and shame, rather than anticipation and pleasure. People whose parents instilled in them a sense of guilt over touching their genitals may find it difficult to accept their sex organs as sources of pleasure.

In most cultures, sexual pleasure has traditionally been a male preserve. Young women may be reared to believe that sex is a duty to be performed for their husbands, not a source of personal pleasure. Although the traditional double standard may have diminished in the United States in recent years, girls may still be exposed to relatively more repressive attitudes. Women are more likely than men in our culture to be taught to suppress their sexual desires. Self-control and vigilance—not sexual awareness and acceptance—become identified as feminine virtues. Women reared with such attitudes may be less likely to learn about their sexual potentials or express their erotic preferences to their partners.

Many women who are exposed to negative attitudes about sex during childhood and adolescence find it difficult to suddenly view sex as a source of pleasure and satisfaction as adults. A lifetime of learning to turn themselves off sexually may impair sexual arousal and enjoyment when an acceptable opportunity arises (Bean, 2002; Fishman & Mamo, 2001).

Psychosexual Trauma Women and men who were sexually victimized in childhood are more likely to experience difficulty in becoming sexually aroused (Laumann et al., 1999). Learning theorists focus on the role of conditioned anxiety in explaining sexual dysfunctions. Sexual stimuli come to elicit anxiety when they have been paired with traumatic experiences, such as rape, incest, or sexual molestation. Unresolved anger, misplaced guilt, and feelings of disgust also make it difficult for victims of sexual trauma to respond sexually, even years later and with loving partners.

Sexual Orientation Some gay males and lesbians test their sexual orientation by developing heterosexual relationships, even marrying and rearing children with partners of the other sex. Others may wish to maintain the appearance of heterosexuality to avoid the social stigma sometimes attached a gay sexual orientation. In such cases, problems with heterosexual partners can reflect a lack of heteroerotic interests (Laumann et al., 1999).

Ineffective Sexual Techniques In some relationships, couples fall into a narrow sexual routine because one partner controls the timing and sequence of sexual techniques. A woman who remains unknowledgeable about the erotic importance of her clitoris may be unlikely to seek direct clitoral stimulation. A man who responds to one erectile failure by trying to force an erection may be unintentionally setting himself up for repeated failure. The couple who fail to communicate their sexual

An Odd Couple: Koro and Dhat Syndromes

Many men in the United States are concerned that their penises are too small. However, they are not usually concerned that their genitals will retract into their bodies. Some people in the United States still believe that men should avoid sex on the eve of an athletic event, because sex "saps the body's strength." This belief has a counterpart in the country of India.

Let us consider two Far Eastern sexual disorders: Koro syndrome and Dhat syndrome.

KORO SYNDROME

Koro syndrome is found primarily in China and some other Far Eastern countries. People with Koro syndrome fear that their genitals are shrinking and retracting into the body, a problem that they believe will be fatal. Koro syndrome has been identified mainly in young men, although some cases have also been reported in women. People with Koro syndrome show signs of acute anxiety, including profuse sweating, breathlessness, and heart palpitations. Men with the disorder have been known to use mechanical devices, such as chopsticks, to try to prevent the penis from retracting into the body.

Koro syndrome has been traced as far back as 3000 BCE. Epidemics involving hundreds or thousands of people have been reported in China, Singapore, Thailand, and India (Tseng et al., 1992). In Guangdong Province in China, an epidemic involving more than 2,000 people occurred during the 1980s. Guangdong residents who did not fall victim to Koro were less superstitious and more intelligent than those who did (Tseng et al., 1992).

Reassurance by a health professional that fears that the genitals will retract into the body are unfounded often put an end to Koro episodes. In any event, episodes tend to pass with time.

DHAT SYNDROME

Dhat syndrome is found among young Asian Indian males and involves excessive fears over the loss of seminal fluid during nocturnal emissions (Shukla & Singh, 2000). Some men with Dhat syndrome also believe (incorrectly) that semen mixes with urine and is excreted by urinating. Dhat syndrome has been associated with erectile dysfunction, apparently because of concern about loss of semen fluid through ejaculation.

There is a widespread belief within Indian culture (and other Near and Far Eastern cultures) that the loss of semen is harmful because it depletes the body of physical and mental energy (Shukla & Singh, 2000). Therefore, men with Dhat syndrome may visit physician after physician to find help in preventing nocturnal emissions or the imagined loss of semen mixed with urine.

"In India," notes Akhtar (1988), "semen is considered to be the elixir of life, in both a physical and mystical sense. Its preservation is supposed to guarantee health and longevity" (p. 71). Many Hindus believe that it takes "40 meals to form one drop of blood; 40 drops of blood to fuse and form one drop of bone marrow, and 40 drops of this produce one drop of semen" (Akhtar, 1988, p. 71). Some Indian males thus fear involuntary loss of the fluid through nocturnal emissions (Shukla & Singh, 2000).

preferences or to experiment with new techniques may find themselves losing interest. Brevity of foreplay and coitus may contribute to female orgasmic disorder.

Emotional Factors Orgasm involves a sudden loss of voluntary control. Fear of losing control or "letting go" may block sexual arousal. Other emotional factors, especially depression, are often implicated in sexual dysfunctions (Ralph & McNicholas, 2000). Depression can contribute to lack of sexual desire (Frohlich & Meston, 2002). Stress can also interfere with sexual interest and response.

Problems in the Relationship Problems in the relationship are not easily left at the bedroom door (Fish et al., 1994; Leiblum & Rosen, 2000). Couples usually find that sex is no better than other facets of their relationship. Couples who harbor resentments toward one another may make sex their arena of combat. They may fail to

A Vicious Cycle? Conflict in the Relationship and Lack of Sexual Desire Conflicts in a relationship may dampen sexual interest. Lack of sexual interest may then further strain the relationship.

become aroused by their partners or "withhold" orgasm to make their partners feel guilty or inadequate.

Troubled relationships are usually characterized by poor communication. Partners who have difficulty communicating in general may be unlikely to communicate their sexual desires to each other. The following case highlights how sexual dysfunctions can develop against the backdrop of a troubled relationship:

> After living together for six months, Paul and Petula are contemplating marriage. But a problem has brought them to a sex therapy clinic. As Petula puts it, "For the last two months he hasn't been able to keep his erection after he enters me." Paul is 26, a lawyer; Petula, 24, is a buyer for a large department store. They both grew up in middle-class, suburban families, and they were introduced through mutual friends and began having intercourse, without difficulty, a few months into their relationship. At Petula's urging, Paul moved into her apartment, although he wasn't sure he was ready for such a step. A week later he began to have difficulty maintaining his erection during intercourse, although he felt strong desires for his partner. When his erection waned, he would try again, but would lose his desire and be unable to achieve another erection. After a few times like this, Petula would become so angry that she began striking Paul in the chest and screaming at him. Paul, who at 200 pounds weighed more than twice as much as Petula, would just walk away, which angered Petula even more.
>
> It became clear that sex was not the only trouble spot in their relationship. Petula complained that he preferred to be with his friends and go to baseball games than spend time with her. When they were together at home, he would become absorbed in watching sports events on television, and showed no interest in activities she enjoyed—attending the theater, visiting museums, etc. Since there was no evidence that the sexual difficulty was due to either organic problems or depression, a diagnosis of male erectile disorder was given. Neither Paul nor Petula was willing to discuss their nonsexual problems with a therapist. Although the sexual problem was treated successfully with a form of sex therapy modeled after techniques developed by Masters and Johnson [see discussion later in the chapter] and the couple later married, Paul's ambivalence continued well into their marriage, and there were recurrences of sexual problems as well. (Adapted from Spitzer et al., 1989, pp. 149–150)

Even though couples in committed and supportive relationships may develop strategies for overcoming sexual problems, couples in conflicted relationships may derive little benefit from consulting health professionals (Leiblum & Rosen, 2000).

Lack of Sexual Skills Sexual competency involves sexual knowledge and skills that are acquired through learning. We generally learn what makes us and others feel good through trial and error and by talking and reading about sex. Some people may not develop sexual competency because of a lack of opportunity to acquire knowledge and experience—even within a committed relationship. People with sexual dysfunctions may have been reared in families in which discussions of sexuality were off limits and early sexual experimentation was harshly punished.

Irrational Beliefs Psychologist Albert Ellis (1962, 1977) points out that irrational beliefs and attitudes may contribute to sexual dysfunctions. Negative feelings such as anxiety and fear, Ellis submits, do not stem directly from the events we experience but, rather, from our interpretations of these events. If a person encounters a certain event, such as an erectile or orgasmic disorder, on a given day and then *believes* that the event is awful or catastrophic, he or she will exaggerate feelings of disappointment and set the stage for future problems.

Performance Anxiety Anxiety—especially performance anxiety—plays an important role in sexual dysfunctions. Performance anxiety occurs when a person becomes overly concerned with how well he or she performs a certain act or task. Performance anxiety may place a dysfunctional individual in a spectator rather than a performer role. Rather than focusing on erotic sensations and allowing reflexes such as erection, lubrication, and orgasm to occur naturally, he or she focuses on self-doubts and thinks, "Will I be able to do it this time? Will this be another failure?"

Performance anxiety can set the stage for a vicious cycle in which a sexual failure increases anxiety. Anxiety then leads to repeated failure, and so on. Sex therapists emphasize the need to break this vicious cycle by removing the need to perform.

Review: Origins of Sexual Dysfunctions

Reflect

Are there any sexual attitudes common to people of your sociocultural background that can give rise to sexual problems or dysfunctions? What are the attitudes? Do you share these attitudes? Explain.

CriticalThinking

Given our cultural values, why might it lead to a problem in a relationship if a woman were to exhibit sexual competence?

14. Organic causes of erectile disorder affect the flow of _____ to and through the penis.

15. Rimm found that erectile dysfunction was connected with high levels of _____.

16. _____ medication may cause orgasmic disorders.

17. Repeated use of _____ can lead to dependency on the drug for sexual arousal.

18. Children reared in sexually _____ environments may learn to respond to sex with anxiety and shame rather than pleasure.

19. In most cultures, sexual pleasure has traditionally been a (*Male* or *Female*?) preserve.

20. Sexual stimuli come to elicit _____ when they have been paired with traumatic experiences such as sexual molestation.

21. Briefness of foreplay and coitus may contribute to female _____ disorder.

22. Sexual competency involves sexual _____ and skills.

23. Albert Ellis points out that _____ beliefs and attitudes may contribute to sexual dysfunctions.

24. Performance anxiety may place a dysfunctional individual in a _____ role rather than a performer role.

In men, performance anxiety can inhibit erection while also triggering a premature ejaculation. (Erection, mediated by the parasympathetic nervous system, can be blocked by activation of the sympathetic nervous system in the form of anxiety. Because ejaculation, like anxiety, is mediated by the sympathetic nervous system, arousal of this system in the form of anxiety can increase the level of stimulation and thereby heighten the potential for premature ejaculation.)

In women, performance anxiety can reduce vaginal lubrication and contribute to orgasmic disorder. Women with performance anxieties may try to force an orgasm, only to find that the harder they try, the more elusive it becomes.

Treatment of Sexual Dysfunctions

When Kinsey conducted his surveys in the 1930s and 1940s, there was no effective treatment for sexual dysfunctions. At the time, the predominant model of therapy for sexual dysfunctions was long-term psychoanalysis. Psychoanalysts believed that the sexual problem would abate only if unconscious conflicts presumed to lie at the root of the problem were resolved through long-term therapy. Evidence of the effectiveness of psychoanalysis in treating sexual dysfunctions is still lacking, however.

Since that time, cognitive and behavioral models of short-term treatment, collectively called sex therapy, have emerged. *Question: What is sex therapy?* **Sex therapy** aims to modify dysfunctional cognitions (beliefs and attitudes) and behavior as directly as possible. Sex therapists also recognize the roles of childhood conflicts and the quality of the partners' relationship. Therefore, they draw on various forms of therapy, as needed (Kleinplatz, 2003; Leiblum & Rosen, 2000).

Although the particular approaches vary, sex therapies aim to

1. Change self-defeating beliefs and attitudes
2. Teach sexual skills
3. Enhance sexual knowledge
4. Improve sexual communication
5. Reduce performance anxiety

Sex therapy usually involves both partners, although individual therapy is preferred in some cases. Therapists find that granting people "permission" to experiment sexually or discuss negative attitudes toward sex helps many people overcome sexual problems without the need for more intensive therapy.

Biological treatments have also been emerging for various sexual dysfunctions. Most public attention has been focused on Viagra, a drug that is helpful in most cases of erectile dysfunction. But competitors to Viagra and biological treatments for premature ejaculation, female orgasmic dysfunction, and lack of sexual desire are also emerging.

In this section we will explore both psychological and behavioral approaches to the treatment of sexual dysfunctions. Let us begin with the groundbreaking work of Masters and Johnson. *Question: What is the Masters-and-Johnson approach to sex therapy?*

The Masters-and-Johnson Approach

Masters and Johnson pioneered the use of direct behavioral approaches to treating sexual dysfunctions (Masters & Johnson, 1970). A female–male therapy team focuses on the couple as the unit of treatment during a 2-week residential program. Masters and Johnson consider the couple, not the individual, dysfunctional. A couple may

Sex therapy A collective term for short-term behavioral models for treatment of sexual dysfunctions.

describe the husband's erectile disorder as the problem, but this problem is likely to have led to problems in the couple—that is, in the relationship—by the time they seek therapy. Similarly, a man whose wife has an orgasmic disorder is likely to be anxious about his ability to provide effective sexual stimulation.

The dual-therapist team approach permits each partner to discuss problems with someone of his or her own gender. It reduces the chance of therapist bias in favor of the female or male partner. It enables each partner to hear concerns expressed by another member of the other gender. Anxieties and resentments are aired, but the focus of treatment is behavioral change. Couples perform daily sexual homework assignments, such as **sensate focus exercises**, in the privacy of their own rooms.

Sensate focus sessions are carried out in the nude. Partners take turns giving and receiving stimulation in nongenital areas of the body. Without touching the breasts or genitals, the giver massages or fondles the receiving partner in order to provide pleasure under relaxing and nondemanding conditions. Because genital activity is restricted, there is no pressure to "perform." The giving partner is freed to engage in trial-and-error learning about the receiving partner's sensate preferences. The receiving partner is also freed to enjoy the experience without feeling rushed to reciprocate or obliged to perform by becoming sexually aroused. The receiving partner's only responsibility is to direct the giving partner as needed. In addition to these general sensate focus exercises, Masters and Johnson used specific assignments designed to help couples overcome particular sexual dysfunctions.

Masters and Johnson were pioneers in the development of sex therapy, yet many sex therapists have departed from the Masters-and-Johnson format. Many do not treat clients in an intensive residential program. Many question the necessity of female–male therapist teams. Researchers find that one therapist is about as effective as two, regardless of her or his gender. Nor does the therapeutic benefit seem to depend to any great extent on whether the sessions are conducted within a short period of time, as in the Masters-and-Johnson approach, or spaced over time (Segraves & Althof, 1998). Some success has also been reported in minimal-contact programs in which participants are given written instructions rather than live therapy sessions (Mohr & Beutler, 1990). Therapists have also departed from the Masters-and-Johnson approach by working individually with preorgasmic women rather than with the couple. Group treatment programs have also been used successfully in treating female orgasmic disorder (Killmann et al., 1987).

The Helen Singer Kaplan Approach

Question: What is the Kaplan approach to sex therapy? Kaplan (1974) calls her approach *psychosexual therapy.* Psychosexual therapy combines behavioral and psychoanalytic methods. Kaplan, as noted, believes that sexual dysfunctions have both *immediate* causes and *remote* causes (underlying intrapsychic conflicts that date from childhood). Kaplan begins therapy with the behavioral approach. She focuses on improving the couple's communication, eliminating performance anxiety, and fostering sexual skills and knowledge. She uses a brief form of insight-oriented therapy when it appears that remote causes impede response to the behavioral program. In so doing, she hopes to bring to awareness unconscious conflicts that are believed to have stifled the person's sexual desires or responsiveness. Although Kaplan reports a number of successful case studies, there are no controlled studies demonstrating that the combination of behavioral and insight-oriented, or psychoanalytic, techniques is more effective than the behavioral techniques alone. Let us now consider some of the specific techniques that sex therapists have introduced in treating several of the major types of sexual dysfunctions.

Sensate focus exercises Exercises in which sex partners take turns giving and receiving pleasurable stimulation in nongenital areas of the body.

How Do You Find a Qualified Sex Therapist?

How would you find a qualified sex therapist if you had a sexual dysfunction? You might find advertisements for "sex therapists" in the Yellow Pages. But beware. Most states do not restrict usage of the term *sex therapist* to recognized professionals. In these states, anyone who wants to use the label may do so, including quacks and prostitutes.

Thus, it is essential to determine that a sex therapist is a member of a recognized profession (such as psychology, social work, medicine, or marriage and family counseling) who has had training and supervision in sex therapy. Professionals are usually licensed or certified by their states. All states require licensing of psychologists and physicians, but some states do not license social workers or couple therapists. If you have questions about the license laws in your state, contact your state's professional licensing board. The ethical standards of these professions prohibit practitioners from claiming expertise in sex therapy without suitable training.

If you are uncertain how to locate a qualified sex therapist in your area, you may obtain names of local practitioners from various sources, such as your university or college psychology department, health department, or counseling center; a local medical or psychological association; a family physician; or your instructor. You may also seek services from a sex therapy clinic affiliated with a local medical center or medical school in your area. Many such clinics charge for services on a sliding scale, depending on your income level. You may also contact the American Association of Sex Educators, Counselors, and Therapists (AASECT), a professional organization that certifies sex therapists. This association can provide you with the names of certified sex therapists in your area. It is located at 11 Dupont Circle, N.W., Washington, DC.

Ethical professionals are not annoyed or embarrassed if you inquire about (1) what their profession is, (2) where they earned their advanced degree,

(3) whether they are licensed or certified by the state, (4) their fees, (5) their plans for treatment, and (6) the nature of their training in human sexuality and sex therapy. If the therapist hems and haws, asks why you are asking such questions, or fails to provide a direct answer, go elsewhere.

Professionals are also restricted by the ethical principles of their professions from engaging in unethical practices, such as sexual relations with their clients. The nature of therapy creates an unequal power relationship between therapist and client. The therapist is perceived as an expert whose suggestions are likely to carry great authority. Clients may thus be vulnerable to exploitation by therapists who misuse their therapeutic authority. Let's be absolutely clear here: There is no therapeutic justification for a therapist to engage in sexual activity with a client. Any therapist who makes a sexual overture toward a client, or tries to persuade a client to engage in sexual relations, is acting unethically.

Sexual Desire Disorders

Question: How do professionals treat sexual desire disorders? Some therapists help kindle the sexual appetites of people with hypoactive sexual desire by prescribing self-stimulation exercises combined with erotic fantasies (Leiblum & Rosen, 2000). Sex therapists may also assist dysfunctional couples by prescribing sensate focus exercises, enhancing communication, and expanding the couple's repertoire of sexual skills. Sex therapists recognize that hypoactive sexual desire is often a complex problem that requires more intensive treatment than do problems of the arousal or orgasm phases (Leiblum & Rosen, 2000). Helen Singer Kaplan (1987) argues that insight-oriented approaches are especially helpful in the treatment of hypoactive sexual desire and sexual aversion to uncover and resolve deep-seated psychological conflicts.

Some cases of hypoactive sexual desire in men involve hormonal deficiencies, especially deficiencies in testosterone. Testosterone replacement therapy works with about half of men who have low testosterone levels (Rakic et al., 1997). Among women, as among men, lack of sexual desire can be connected with low levels of androgens, and testosterone shows promise in heightening desire (Munarriz, R., et al., 2002; Tuiten et al., 2000).

If lack of desire is connected with depression, sexual interest may rebound when the depression lifts. Treatment in such cases may involve psychotherapy or chemotherapy, not sex therapy per se. When problems in the relationship are involved, couple therapy may be indicated. Once interpersonal problems are ironed out, sexual interest may return.

Treatment of sexual aversion disorder may involve a multifaceted approach, including biological treatments such as the use of medications to reduce anxiety and psychological treatments designed to help the individual overcome the underlying sexual phobia. Couple therapy may be used in cases in which sexual aversions arise from problems in relationships (Gold & Gold, 1993). Sensate focus exercises may be used to lessen anxiety about sexual contact. Fears may also need to be overcome through behavioral exercises in which the client learns to manage the stimuli that evoke fears of sexual contact.

Bridget, 26, and Bryan, 30, had been married for four years but had never consummated their relationship because Bridget would panic whenever Bryan attempted coitus with her. While she enjoyed foreplay and was capable of achieving orgasm with clitoral stimulation, her fears of sexual contact were triggered by Bryan's attempts at vaginal penetration. The therapist employed a program of gradual exposure to the feared stimuli to give Bridget the opportunity to overcome her fears in small, graduated steps. First she was instructed to view her genitals in a mirror when she was alone—this in order to violate her long-standing prohibition against looking at and enjoying her body. Although this exercise initially made her feel anxious, with repeated exposure she became comfortable performing it and then progressed to touching her genitals directly. When she became comfortable with this step, and reported experiencing pleasurable erotic sensations, she was instructed to insert a finger into the vagina. She encountered intense anxiety at this step and required daily practice for two weeks before she could tolerate inserting her finger into her vagina without discomfort. Her husband was then brought into the treatment process. The couple was instructed to have Bridget insert her own finger in her vagina while Bryan watched. When she was comfortable with this exercise, she then guided his finger into her vagina. Later he placed one and then two fingers into her vagina, while she controlled the depth, speed, and duration of penetration. When she felt ready, they proceeded to attempt penile penetration in the female superior position, which allowed her to maintain control over penetration. Over time, Bridget became comfortable enough with penetration that the couple developed a normal sexual relationship. (Adapted from Kaplan, 1987, pp. 102–103)

Sexual Arousal Disorders

There are male and female sexual arousal disorders. *Question: How do professionals treat sexual arousal disorders?*

Erectile Disorder Male sexual arousal disorder is also known as erectile disorder. Men with erectile disorder may ask their therapists to "teach" them or "show" them how to obtain an erection. Some of our clients have asked us to tell them what fantasies they should entertain to obtain an erection or how they should touch their partners or be touched. Erection is a reflex, however, not a skill. A man need not learn how to have an erection any more than he need learn how to breathe.

In sex therapy, women who have trouble becoming lubricated and men with erectile problems learn that they need not "do" anything to become sexually aroused. As long as their problems are psychologically and not organically based, they need only receive sexual stimulation under relaxed circumstances, so that anxiety does not inhibit natural reflexes.

In order to reduce performance anxiety, the partners engage in nondemanding sexual contacts—contacts that do not demand lubrication or erection. They may start with nongenital sensate focus exercises in the style of Masters and Johnson. After a couple of sessions, sensate focus extends to the genitals. The position shown in Figure 15.1 allows the woman easy access to her partner's genitals. She repeatedly "teases" him to erection and allows the erection to subside. Thus she avoids creating performance anxiety that could lead to loss of erection. By repeatedly regaining his erection, the man loses the fear that loss of erection means it will not return. He learns also to focus on erotic sensations for their own sake. He experiences no demand to perform, because the couple is instructed to refrain from coitus.

When the dysfunctional partner can reliably achieve sexual excitement (denoted by erection in the male and lubrication in the female), the couple does not immediately attempt coitus, for this might rekindle performance anxiety. Rather, the couple engages in a series of nondemanding, pleasurable sexual activities, eventually culminating in coitus.

In Masters and Johnson's approach, the couple begin coitus after about 10 days of treatment. The woman teases the man to erection while she is sitting above him, straddling his thighs. When he is erect, she inserts the penis—to avoid fumbling attempts at entry—and moves slowly back and forth in a *nondemanding* way. Neither attempts to reach orgasm. If erection is lost, teasing and coitus are repeated. Once the

Truth?Fiction?
Revisited

It is not true that sex therapy teaches a man with erectile disorder how to will an erection. Men with erectile disorder are actually taught that it is not possible to will an erection. One can only set the stage for erection (or vaginal lubrication) to occur and then allow it to happen reflexively.

Figure 15.1. The Training Position Recommended by Masters and Johnson for Treatment of Erectile Disorder and Premature Ejaculation. By lying in front of her partner, who has his legs spread, the woman has ready access to his genitals. In one part of a program designed to overcome erectile disorder, she repeatedly "teases" him to erection and allows the erection to subside. Thus she avoids creating performance anxiety that could lead to loss of erection. Through repeated regaining of erection, the man loses the fear that loss of erection means it will not return.

Truth?Fiction?
Revisited

It is true that a doctor dropped his pants to reveal an erection at a medical convention. He was demonstrating the effects of alprostadil.

couple become confident that erection can be retained—or reinstated if lost—they may increase coital thrusting gradually to reach orgasm.

Biological Approaches to Treatment of Erectile Disorder The world's attention has recently been focused on biological approaches to treating erectile disorder. Perhaps the opening shot in the biological war against erectile disorder rang out in 1983, when a speaker made a somewhat unusual presentation to his audience at a medical convention. He dropped his trousers to reveal an erection. The erection was the result not of sexual stimulation or sexual fantasies, but of the injection of a drug called *alprostadil* into his penis. Alprostadil is a vasodilator; it relaxes the muscles surrounding the arteries in the penis, allowing more blood to flow in, thus increasing vasocongestion and causing erection. The speaker—a urologist—was giving a "live" demonstration of a biological method of treating erectile disorder.

Biological or biomedical approaches are helpful in treating erectile disorder, especially when organic factors are involved. Treatments include surgery, medication, and vacuum pumps (see Table 15.3).

Surgery There are two main types of surgery: vascular surgery and the installation of penile implants. *Vascular surgery* can help in cases in which the blood vessels that supply the penis are blocked or in which structural defects in the penis restrict blood flow (Cowley & Rogers, 1997). An arterial bypass operation reroutes vessels around the blockage.

TABLE 15.3	
Biological Treatments of Erectile Problems	
Surgery	
Vascular Surgery	Helps when blood vessels that supply the penis are blocked.
Penile Implants	May be used when other treatments fail because of biological problems.
Medication	
Hormone Therapy	Helps men and women with abnormally low levels of male sex hormones.
Injections	Muscle relaxants such as *alprostadil* and *phentolamine* are injected into the corpus cavernosum of the penis, relaxing the muscles that surround the arteries in the penis, allowing the vessels to dilate and blood to flow more freely.
Suppository	Alprostadil is inserted into the tip of the penis in gel form.
Oral Medication	Oral forms of several compounds—sildenafil (Viagra), vardenafil (Levitra), and tadalafil (Cialis)—relax the muscles that surround the small blood vessels in the penis, allowing them to dilate so that blood can flow into them more freely. Apomorphine (Uprima) increases brain levels of the neurotransmitter dopamine. (Parkinson's disease is caused by the death of dopamine-producing cells and is often accompanied by erectile dysfunction. Men who use drugs that treat Parkinson's disease by increasing dopamine levels often have erections as side effects.)
Vacuum Pump	
Vacuum Pump	A *vacuum constriction device* creates a vacuum when it is held over the penis. The vacuum induces erection by increasing the flow of blood into the penis. Rubber bands around the base of the penis maintain the erection.

A *penile implant* may be used when other treatments fail. Implants are either malleable (semirigid) or inflatable. The semirigid implant is made of rods that remain in a *permanent* semirigid position. It is rigid enough for intercourse but permits the penis to hang reasonably close to the body at other times. The inflatable type requires that cylinders be implanted in the penis. A fluid reservoir is placed near the bladder, and a tiny pump is inserted in the scrotum. To attain erection, the man squeezes the pump, releasing fluid into the cylinders. When the erection is no longer needed, a release valve returns the fluid to the reservoir, deflating the penis. The inflatable implant more closely duplicates the normal processes of tumescence and detumescence. Some adverse side effects of penile implants have been reported, including destruction of erectile tissue, impairing the man's ability to have normal erections. Penile implants do not affect sex drive, sexual sensations, or ejaculation.

Implant surgery is irreversible. Therefore, the National Institutes of Health recommend that penile implants be used only when less invasive techniques, such as sex therapy and medication, are unsuccessful.

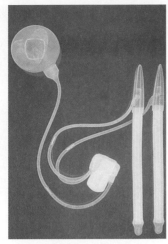

A Penile Implant. Penile implants provide erection when the man's cardiovascular system does not do the job. Cylinders are implanted in the penis, and a fluid reservoir (top left) is placed near the bladder. A pump (lower middle) is typically inserted in the scrotum. Squeezing the pump forces fluid into the cylinders, inflating the penis. A release valve returns the fluid to the reservoir, deflating the penis.

Medication There are several ways in which medication can be used to help men with erectile problems. For example, hormone (testosterone) treatments help restore the sex drive and erectile ability in many men with abnormally low levels of testosterone (Lue, 2000; Rakic et al., 1997). Hormone therapy does not appear to help men with normal hormone levels.

The muscle relaxants *alprostadil* (brand names Caverject and Edex) and *phentolamine* (Invicorp) can be injected into the corpus cavernosum of the penis. These chemicals relax the muscles that surround the small blood vessels in the penis. The vessels dilate and allow blood to flow in more freely. Alprostadil erections last for an hour or more and occur whether or not there is sexual stimulation. A physician teaches the man how to inject himself. If phentolamine is used along with the protein VIP, erection only occurs when sexual stimulation is applied.

Injections are most effective for men with problems in the transmission of nerve signals that regulate erection (Altman, 1995c). They are less effective for men with vascular problems that restrict the flow of blood into the penis.

Injections may have side effects, including pain from the injection itself and prolonged, painful erections (*priapism*) (Ralph & McNicholas, 2000). Many men find the idea of penile injections distasteful (the "wince factor") and refuse them.

Alprostadil is also available as a suppository in gel form (brand name MUSE). It is then inserted into the tip of the penis by an applicator. The suppository helps men get around the "wince" factor that many experience with injections (Padma-Nathan et al., 1997). "Putting a needle in your penis is not everybody's idea of foreplay," notes Dr. John Seely (Kolata, 2000b).

Other medications are taken orally. For example, the oral form of sildenafil is sold as Viagra, and the oral form of vardenafil is sold as Levitra. The oral form of tadalafil (Cialis) becomes effective in about half an hour and lasts up to 36 hours. Users in France dubbed it "the weekend pill." The drug apomorphine (Uprima) heightens brain levels of dopamine, a neurotransmitter involved in erection, and is available in the United Kingdom and advertised online (do not use it without consulting your physician). Researchers became aware of the potential benefits of dopamine-enhancing drugs through research with Parkinson's disease. Parkinson's is apparently caused by the death of dopamine-producing cells and is connected with loss of motor coordination and erectile dysfunction. L-dopa and other drugs that are used to treat Parkinson's raise dopamine levels and frequently have the "side effect" of erection (Kolata, 2000b).

Viagra was hailed as a miracle drug when it hit the market in early 1998. It sold faster than any new drug had ever sold. The stock of Pfizer Company, which

Erection Wars? *In an effort to reassure men with erectile dysfunction who fear that it may be unmanly to use Viagra, Levitra, or Cialis, marketers are recruiting athletic superstars like NASCAR driver Mark Martin to endorse their products.*

produces Viagra, shot up after the appearance of the drug. A study published in the *New England Journal of Medicine* tested the effects of Viagra on more than 800 men with erectile dysfunction due both to psychological causes and to a number of organic causes (Goldstein et al., 1998). In one phase of the study, 69% of attempts to engage in intercourse were successful for men taking Viagra, compared to 22% for men taking a placebo. Viagra and its chemical cousins Levitra and Cialis are currently locked in an epic struggle. All are endorsed by youngish athletes, apparently to make it appear more "manly" to use them.

Vacuum Pumps Sounding like something from the "What will they think of next?" category, a *vacuum constriction device* (VCD) helps men achieve erections through vacuum pressure. The device (brand name: ErecAid) consists of a cylinder connected to a hand-operated vacuum pump. It creates a vacuum when it is held over the limp penis. The vacuum induces erection by increasing the flow of blood into the penis. Rubber bands around the base of the penis can maintain the erection for as long as 30 minutes.

The VCD has been used successfully by men with both organically and psychologically based erectile failure. However, side effects such as pain and black-and-blue marks are common. The rubber bands prevent normal ejaculation, so semen remains trapped in the urethra until the bands are released. The quality of the erections produced by the device is also considered inferior to that of spontaneous erections.

Where Do We Go from Here? It would appear that oral medications (pills) will be the most popular biological treatment of erectile problems. They are helpful with most men and avoid the "wince factor." Viagra, Levitra, and Cialis have side effects, though, such as migraine headaches, flushing, and some others. The migraines are not surprising, because they are related to increased blood flow, and these drugs are not precise enough to direct blood only to the genitals. Soon after Viagra was approved by the FDA, there were scattered reports of men with cardiovascular problems experiencing heart attacks. A carefully conducted study of the effects of Viagra on 14 older men with at least one severely constricted coronary artery suggests that Viagra by itself is not the problem (Herrmann et al., 2000). In this study, reported in the prestigious *New England Journal of Medicine* (www.nejm.com), Viagra was not shown to have adverse effects on the blood supply to the heart. Ironically, Viagra, which dilates blood vessels, is now being considered by some for use as a heart *medicine*.

Female Sexual Arousal Disorder Psychological treatments for female sexual arousal disorder parallel those for orgasmic disorder and are discussed in the following pages. Here let us briefly note that they involve sex education (labeling the parts, discussing their functions, and explaining how to arouse them), searching out and coping with possible cognitive interference (such as negative sexual attitudes), creating nondemand situations in which sexual arousal may occur, and—when appropriate—working on problems in the relationship.

Yet many cases of female sexual arousal disorder reflect impaired blood flow to the genitals, just as in erectile disorder. Female sexual arousal involves vaginal lubrication, which permits sexual intercourse without a great deal of pain-causing friction. Lubrication is made possible by vasocongestion—the flow of blood into the genitals. Lack of lubrication can reflect the physical effects of aging, menopause, or surgically induced menopause, as through surgery.

Sometimes all that is necessary to deal with lack of lubrication is an artificial lubricant such as K-Y Jelly. But lessened blood flow to the genitals can also sap sexual pleasure and, as a consequence, lessen a woman's desire for sex.

Just as biological treatments for erectile disorder are mushrooming, so are biological treatments for female sexual arousal disorder. Sadly—and certainly because of the lesser amount of attention that has historically been paid to women's health problems—the development of treatments has lagged several paces behind the development of treatments for men. Ironically, the treatments that are emerging are highly similar to those that help men with erectile disorder.

For example, drugs identical or similar to those used for men are being investigated for use with women (Leland, 2000). Many trials have been undertaken with Viagra for women. Researchers are also developing alprostadil (the vasodilator) for use with women, largely in the form of creams that are inserted into the vagina to enhance the flow of blood and hence lubrication.

There is a perfect parallel in the area of lack of sexual desire for women who are low in sexual desire because of low levels of "male" sex hormones. As an aside, we might begin to wonder out loud whether we should stop referring to estrogen as a female sex hormone and to testosterone as a male sex hormone. They are both produced by both women and men—although in different quantities—and both are intricately involved with women's and men's health, sexual functioning, and other kinds of behavior. In any event, testosterone skin patches can be used by women who lack sexual desire because they lack adequate quantities of testosterone (Guzick & Hoeger, 2000; Shifren et al., 2000).

There is even a device—*Eros*—that is a parallel to the vacuum pump used by some men with erectile disorder. It is a clitoral device that was approved by the Food and Drug Administration in 2000 and is available by prescription. The clitoris swells during sexual arousal because of vasocongestion, and vasocongestion increases clitoral sexual sensations, thus moving somewhat in step with sexual interest and lubrication. The device creates gentle suction over the clitoris, increasing vasocongestion and sexual sensations (Leland, 2000; see Figure 15.2).

Orgasmic Disorders

Question: How do professionals treat orgasmic disorders? Because orgasmic disorders are relatively rare among men, our response will focus mainly on women. Women who have never experienced orgasm often harbor negative sexual attitudes that cause anxiety and inhibit sexual response. Treatment in such cases may first address these attitudes.

Masters and Johnson use a couples-oriented approach in treating anorgasmic women. They begin with sensate focus exercises. Then, during genital massage and, later, during coitus, the woman guides her partner in the caresses and movements that she finds sexually exciting. Taking charge helps free the woman from the traditional role of the passive, subordinate female.

Masters and Johnson recommend a training position (see Figure 15.3) that gives the man access to his partner's breasts and genitals. She can guide his hands to show him the types of stimulation she enjoys. The genital play is *nondemanding*. The goals are to learn to provide and enjoy effective sexual stimulation, not to reach orgasm. The clitoris is not stimulated early, because doing so may produce a high level of stimulation, even hurt, before the woman is prepared.

Figure 15.2. A Clitoral Device That Stimulates Genital Vasocongestion in Women by Creating Gentle Suction over the Clitoris

Human Sexuality in the New Millennium

Thinking Critically about Buying Viagra and Other Drugs Online

Viagra is a prescription drug. Many men who might otherwise use Viagra are reluctant to discuss erectile dysfunction with their physicians. The anonymity of doing things on the Net is a lure—you don't have to admit your personal worries to your doctor face to face. Some men, unfortunately, do not even have a regular physician. What to do?

Many have discovered that by searching *Viagra* on the Net, they can find many Web sites where they can "consult" with online physicians, obtain a prescription, and order the drug for home delivery. Easy! A few questions and a fee, and they've got it. But is it wise? Perhaps, perhaps not.

Prescriptions are needed for various drugs because physicians are better equipped than most laypeople to diagnose an individual's health problems, understand the chemical nature and side effects of the drugs that are available for treatment, and predict how the drugs will affect the individual patient. The physicians are also usually prepared to deal with the unexpected effects of the drugs, and there can be many.

So ask yourself what kind of physician will prescribe drugs online, without personally knowing the patient. Is it possible that some of them would have difficulty establishing private practices or getting jobs in hospitals? If you have a question about the drug once you use it, will you be able to get back to the prescriber easily for an answer, or will you wind up making an embarrassed call to your own physician—or a trip to the emergency room?

You will find that many of the sites are online pharmacies that also advertise Propecia for treatment of hair loss, drugs that reverse the loss of pubic hair (yes, pubic hair), weight control drugs that prevent the absorption of some of the fat in food (such as Xenical), herbal supplements, and so on. What you will tend to hit in your search are chemical armories of weapons that sound as if they can stop you from aging, or even reverse the aging process. It may sound as if they will help you remain (or regain your status as) a studmuffin. But the fact is that medical science isn't there yet.

While surfing the Net, you will also come across sites that claim to have "natural" preparations (including a variety of herbs) that are as effective as Viagra, but without the side effects and without the need to get a prescription. Use some critical thinking: Are you convinced of the effectiveness and safety of these preparations? Because they are foods (sort of) rather than drugs, they escape the scrutiny of the Food and Drug Administration. That is, the government is not watching over them. Be warned.

In sum, even if it is convenient to buy a drug online, you are well advised to get your prescription face to face—from a doctor you know and trust.

Figure 15.3. The Training Position for Nondemanding Stimulation of the Female Genitals. This position gives the man access to his partner's breasts and genitals. She can guide his hands to show him the types of stimulation she enjoys.

Should You Buy Viagra Online? *Many Web sites enable men to consult with physicians and order Viagra online. Is it wise to purchase Viagra—or any other prescription drug—online? Prescriptions are needed for drugs when the person's diagnosis is in question and when the drugs have side effects. Physicians are better equipped than most laypeople to diagnose health problems, understand the chemical composition and effects of drugs, and predict how drugs will affect the individual.*

After a number of occasions of genital play, the couple undertake coitus in the female-superior position (see Figure 15.4). This position allows the woman freedom of movement and control over her genital sensations. The couple engage in several sessions of deliberately slow thrusting to sensitize the woman to sensations produced by the penis and break the common counterproductive pattern of desperate, rapid thrusting.

Orgasm cannot be willed or forced. When a woman receives effective stimulation, feels free to focus on erotic sensations, and knows that nothing is being demanded of her, she will generally reach orgasm. Once the woman is able to attain orgasm in the female-superior position, the couple may extend their sexual repertoire to other positions.

Masters and Johnson prefer working with the couple in cases of anorgasmia, but other sex therapists prefer to begin working with the woman individually through masturbation (Leiblum & Rosen, 2000). Masturbation provides women opportunities to learn about their own bodies at their own pace. It frees them of the need to rely on partners or to please partners. The sexual pleasure they experience helps counter lingering sexual anxieties. Although there is some variation among therapists, the following elements are commonly found in directed-masturbation programs:

1. *Education.* The woman and her partner (if she has one) are educated about female sexuality.

Figure 15.4. Coitus in the Female-Superior Position. *In treatment of female orgasmic disorder, the couple undertake coitus in the female-superior position after a number of occasions of genital play. This position allows the woman freedom of movement and control over her genital sensations. She is told to regard the penis as her "toy." The couple engage in several sessions of deliberately slow thrusting to sensitize the woman to sensations produced by the penis and break the common counterproductive pattern of desperate, rapid thrusting.*

2. *Self-exploration.* Self-exploration is encouraged as a way of increasing the woman's sense of body awareness. She may hold a mirror between her legs to locate her sexual anatomic features.

3. *Self-massage.* Once the woman feels comfortable about exploring her body, she creates a relaxing setting for self-massage. She chooses a time and place where she is free from external distractions. She begins to explore the sensitivity of her body to touch, discovering and repeating the caresses she finds pleasurable. Nonalcohol-based oils and lotions may be used to enhance the sensuous quality of the massage and to provide lubrication for the external genitalia. Some women use their dominant hand to stimulate their breasts, while the other hand massages the genitals. During the first few occasions, the woman does not attempt to reach orgasm, so as to prevent performance anxiety.

4. *Giving oneself permission.* The woman may be advised to challenge lingering guilt and anxiety about masturbation. For example, she might repeat to herself, "This is my body. I have a right to learn about my body and receive pleasure from it."

5. *Use of fantasy.* Arousal is heightened through the use of sexual images, fantasies, and fantasy aids, such as erotic written or visual materials.

6. *Use of a vibrator.* A vibrator may be recommended to provide more intense stimulation, especially for women who find that manual stimulation is insufficient.

7. *Involvement of the partner.* Once the woman is capable of regularly achieving orgasm through masturbation, the focus may shift to her sexual relationship with her partner. Nondemanding sensate focus exercises may be followed by nondemanding coitus. The female-superior position is often used. It enables the woman to control the depth, angle, and rate of thrusting. She thus ensures that she receives the kinds of stimulation she needs to reach orgasm.

Our focus has been on sexual techniques, but it is worth noting that employing a combination of approaches that focus on sexual techniques and underlying interpersonal problems may be more effective than focusing on sexual techniques alone, at least for couples whose relationships are troubled (Leiblum & Rosen, 2000).

Male Orgasmic Disorder Treatment of male orgasmic disorder generally focuses on increasing sexual stimulation and reducing performance anxiety (Leiblum & Rosen, 2000). Masters and Johnson instruct the couple to practice sensate focus exercises for several days, during which the man makes no attempt to ejaculate. The couple is then instructed to bring the man to orgasm in any way they can, usually manually. Once the man can ejaculate in his partner's presence, she brings him to the point at which he is about to ejaculate. Then, in the female-superior position, she inserts the penis and thrusts vigorously to bring him to orgasm. If he loses the feeling that he is about to ejaculate, the process is repeated. Even if ejaculation occurs at the point of penetration, it often helps break the pattern of inability to ejaculate within the vagina.

Premature Ejaculation In the Masters-and-Johnson approach, sensate focus exercises are followed by practice in the training position shown in Figure 15.1. The woman teases her partner to erection and uses the **squeeze technique** when he indicates that he is about to ejaculate. She squeezes the tip of the penis, which temporarily prevents ejaculation. This process is repeated three or four times in a 15- to 20-minute session before the man purposely ejaculates.

In using the squeeze technique, the woman holds the penis between the thumb and first two fingers of the same hand. The thumb presses against the frenulum. The fingers straddle the coronal ridge on the other side of the penis. Squeezing the thumb and forefingers together fairly hard for about 20 seconds (or until the man's urge to ejaculate passes) prevents ejaculation. The erect penis can withstand fairly strong pressure without discomfort, but erection may be partially lost.

After 2 or 3 days of these sessions, Masters and Johnson have the couple begin coitus in the female-superior position because it creates less pressure to ejaculate. The woman inserts the penis. At first she contains it without thrusting, allowing the man to get used to intravaginal sensations. If he signals that he is about to ejaculate, she lifts off and squeezes the penis. After some repetitions, she begins slowly to move backward and forward, lifting off and squeezing as needed. The man learns gradually to tolerate higher levels of sexual stimulation without ejaculating.

The "stop–start" method for treating premature ejaculation was introduced by urologist James Semans (1956). The method can be applied to manual stimulation or coitus. For example, the woman can manually stimulate her partner until he is about to ejaculate. He then signals her to suspend sexual stimulation and allows his arousal to subside before stimulation is resumed. This process enables the man to recognize the cues that precede his point of ejaculatory inevitability, or "point of no return," and to tolerate longer periods of sexual stimulation. When the stop-start technique is applied to coitus, the couple begin with simple vaginal containment with no pelvic thrusting, preferably in the female-superior position. The man withdraws if he feels he is about to ejaculate. As the man's sense of control increases, thrusting can begin, along with variations in coital positions. The couple again stop when the man signals that he is approaching ejaculatory inevitability.

Biological Approaches to Treatment of Premature Ejaculation Pilot studies have recently appeared in which drugs generally used for psychological problems have been helpful in treating premature ejaculation. One, clomipramine, is normally used to treat people with obsessive-compulsive disorder or schizophrenia. However, in a pilot study with 15 couples, low doses of clomipramine helped men engage in coitus five times longer than usual without ejaculating (Althof, 1994). So-called

Truth?Fiction?
Revisited

Many sex therapists do recommend masturbation as a treatment for women who have never been able to reach orgasm. Masturbation allows women (and men) to get in touch with their own sexual responses without relying on a partner.

It is true that a man can be prevented from ejaculating by squeezing his penis when he feels that he is about to ejaculate. This is the so-called squeeze technique.

Squeeze technique
A method for treating premature ejaculation whereby the tip of the penis is squeezed temporarily to prevent ejaculation.

Development of Biological Treatments of Sexual Dysfunctions in Women

A key trend in the treatment of sexual problems is their accelerating "medicalization." Impressive advances are being made in biomechanical methods and drugs (Kleinplatz, 2003). As women age, they, like men, experience a reduced flow of blood to the genital region. The clitoris becomes less engorged during sexual arousal and may be connected with feelings of lessened sexual arousal overall. Postmenopausal women experience vaginal dryness because of drop-off in the secretion of estrogen (Berman & Berman, 2001; Fishman & Mamo, 2001). Large numbers of middle-aged and older women say that they have lost interest in sex or have difficulty becoming aroused. Table 15.4 is an overview of methods in use or under development.

It is of interest that many of the methods that have been helpful with men also hold promise for women. For example, drugs that enhance the flow of blood into the genital region, such as Viagra, may enhance the sexual experiences of women as well as men. Many women report greater vaginal lubrication and stronger orgasms after using Viagra (Berman, 2000; Berman et al., 2001). Table 15.5 shows the results of a study with 35 women (Berman, 2000). Another study treated 48 middle-aged women with sexual arousal disorder with Viagra over a 6-week period (Berman et al., 2001). Results revealed increased genital blood flow and vaginal lubrication. The women self-reported greater sexual desire and arousal, less difficulty reaching orgasm, less vaginal pain, and more sexual satisfaction.

Pilot studies with 500 European women ("Women might mark millennium," 1998) also found drugs that enhance the flow of blood to the genitals to be quite effective. A number of pharmaceutical companies are developing Viagra-like drugs for women—drugs with names such as VasoFem, Alista, and FemProx (Leland, 2000).

But a study of 577 women found that Viagra was no more effective than a placebo (sugar pill) in increasing sexual desire among women (Basson, 2000). Berman (2000) also found sexual desire per se to be the least changed variable in her study. Prior to treatment, 52% of the women in her study reported low sexual desire, and this percentage fell to only 45% after treatment. Sexual desire, of course, involves the quality of relationships as well as biological factors. But Viagra dramatically reduced problems related to biological arousal, such as lack of lubrication and painful sex (see Table 15.5). Drugs such as Viagra are more effective at helping with the biological than with the psychological aspects of sexual relationships.

Also consider a typical study of the effects of androgen replacement therapy with older women (Munarriz et al., 2002). The women reported a significant increase in sexual desire, vaginal lubrication, and orgasm, along with normalization in blood values of androgens, including testosterone. However, there were side effects related to the effects of male sex hormones. For example, 11% of the women showed increased facial hair, and 5% developed acne.

Although the "medicalization" of sex therapy continues, no pill and no biomechanical device will enhance the quality of a relationship. If people have serious problems with their partners, popping a pill is unlikely to solve them.

---

antidepressant drugs have also been helpful in treatment of premature ejaculation (Waldinger et al., 2001, 2002; Meston & Frohlich, 2000).

Why do drugs used to treat psychological problems help with premature ejaculation? The psychological problems are frequently connected with imbalances in body chemicals, such as **neurotransmitters**—the chemical messengers of the brain. Neurotransmitters are also involved in other bodily functions, including ejaculation. The antidepressant drugs (fluoxetine, paroxetine, and sertraline) all work by increasing the action of the neurotransmitter serotonin. Serotonin, in turn, may inhibit the ejaculatory reflex (Meston & Frohlich, 2000; Shipko, 2000). It remains to be seen whether medications continue to show positive effects and to compare their effectiveness with psychological sex therapy techniques.

Neurotransmitter
A chemical that transmits messages from one brain cell to another.

Sexual Pain Disorders

There are two major sexual pain disorders: dyspareunia and vaginismus. *Question: How do professionals treat sexual pain disorders?*

TABLE 15.4

Biological Treatments in Use or under Investigation to Help Women with Sexual Dysfunctions

Method	How Used	Effect	Current Status
Alprostadil	Gel, cream	May improve blood flow to the clitoris, enhancing arousal.	Studies under way.
DHEA	Pill	May boost sex drive by increasing testosterone levels.	Available by prescription. Available as a dietary supplement, though experts caution against unsupervised use. Studies under way.
Eros	Hand-held device that applies gentle suction to the clitoris.	Promotes blood flow to the clitoris, enhancing arousal.	Available by prescription. (See Figure 15.2 on page 517.)
Estrogen	Pill, patch, gel, cream	Counters vaginal dryness.	Available by prescription.
PDE5 inhibitors	Pill	May improve blood flow to the clitoris, enhancing arousal.	Viagra, Levitra, and Cialis available by prescription. Studies under way for treating women's sexual problems.
Testosterone	Pill, patch, gel, cream	May boost sex drive.	Available by prescription. Studies under way for treating women's sexual problems.
VasoFem, Alista, FemProx	Viagra-like drugs	May improve blood flow to the clitoris, enhancing arousal.	Studies under way for treating women's sexual problems.
Yohimbine with nitric oxide	Pill	May improve blood flow to the clitoris, enhancing arousal.	Studies under way.

TABLE 15.5

Impact of Sildenafil (Viagra) on the Posthysterectomy Sexual Complaints of Women in the Berman (2000) Study

	Before Using Viagra	After Using Viagra
Low sexual sensations	100%	22%
Inability to reach orgasm	100	18
Little or no sexual desire	52	45
Little or no lubrication	67	40
Pain or discomfort during sex	68	33

Source of data: Berman, L. (2000). Paper presented to the annual meeting of the American Urological Association, Atlanta, GA. Cited in "Women, too, may benefit from Viagra." (2000, May 1). Web posted by CNN.

Dyspareunia Dyspareunia, or painful intercourse, generally calls for medical intervention to assess for and treat any underlying physical problems, such as urinary tract genital infections, that might give rise to pain (Laumann et al., 1999). When dyspareunia is caused by vaginismus, treatment of vaginismus through a behavioral approach, described below, may eliminate pain.

Vaginismus Vaginismus is generally treated with behavioral exercises in which plastic vaginal dilators of increasing size are inserted to help relax the vaginal musculature. A gynecologist may first demonstrate insertion of the narrowest dilator. Later the woman herself practices insertion of wider dilators at home. The woman increases the size of the dilator as she becomes capable of tolerating insertion and containment (for 10 or 15 minutes) without discomfort or pain. The woman herself—not her partner or therapist—controls the pace of treatment (Leiblum & Rosen, 2000). The woman's or her partner's fingers (first the littlest finger, then two fingers and so on) may be used in place of the plastic dilators, with the woman controlling the speed and depth of penetration. When the woman is able to tolerate dilators (or fingers) equivalent in thickness to the penis, the couple may attempt coitus. Still, the woman should control insertion. Circumstances should be relaxed and nondemanding. The idea is to avoid resensitizing her to fears of penetration. Because vaginismus often occurs among women with a history of sexual trauma, such as rape or incest, treatment for the psychological effects of these experiences may also be in order (Leiblum & Rosen, 2000).

Review: Treatment of Sexual Dysfunctions

Reflect

If you had a sexual dysfunction, do you think that you would be willing to participate in sex therapy? Explain.

CriticalThinking

One researcher writes that the treatment of sexual dysfunctions is becoming "medicalized." What does that mean? Do you agree or disagree? Explain.

25. Sex therapy involves _____ and behavioral models of short-term treatment.

26. Sex therapy aims to change dysfunctional behavior (*Directly* or *By giving people insight into the childhood origins of their problems*?).

27. The _____-and-Johnson approach uses a female–male therapy team.

28. Masters and Johnson prescribe _____ focus exercises.

29. Helen Singer Kaplan combined behavioral and _____ methods.

30. _____ sexual desire may involve hormonal deficiencies, especially that of androgens.

31. Erection and lubrication are (*Reflexes* or *Skills*?).

32. In order to reduce _____ anxiety, partners engage in nondemanding sexual contacts.

33. Vacuum pumps are used with (*Men only, Women only,* or *Both men and women*?) to increase blood flow to the genitals.

34. Penile implant surgery is (*Reversible* or *Irreversible*?).

35. Viagra's recently marketed chemical cousin is called _____.

36. Some sex therapists use masturbation to treat female _____ disorder.

37. The squeeze technique and stop–start techniques are methods for treating _____ ejaculation.

38. A series of plastic dilators is used to treat _____.

Recite

1. **What are sexual dysfunctions?**

Sexual dysfunctions are persistent or recurrent difficulties in becoming sexually aroused or reaching orgasm.

2. **How common are sexual dysfunctions?**

Although there are no precise figures on the incidence of sexual dysfunctions, they appear to be somewhat more common among women than among men. Men are more likely to experience rapid orgasm and performance anxiety. Women are more likely to experience lack of desire, difficulty reaching orgasm, and painful sex.

3. **What are sexual desire disorders?**

These disorders involve dysfunctions in sexual desire, interest, or drive, in which the person experiences a lack of sexual desire or an aversion to genital sexual contact.

4. **What are sexual arousal disorders?**

In men, sexual arousal disorders involve recurrent difficulty in achieving or sustaining erections sufficient to engage in sexual intercourse successfully. In women, they typically involve failure to become sufficiently lubricated.

Recite

5. What are orgasmic disorders?

These involve having difficulty reaching orgasm or reaching orgasm too soon. Women are more likely to encounter difficulties reaching orgasm, whereas men are more likely to experience premature ejaculation.

6. What are sexual pain disorders?

These disorders include dyspareunia, or painful coitus, and vaginismus, which is characterized by involuntary contraction of the muscles surrounding the vaginal barrel, making penetration difficult and painful.

7. What organic factors are involved in sexual dysfunctions?

Fatigue may lead to erectile disorder in men and to orgasmic disorder and dyspareunia in women. Dyspareunia often reflects vaginal infections and STIs. Organic factors are believed to be involved in more than half of cases of erectile disorder. Medications and other drugs, such as drugs for high blood pressure and depression, may also impair sexual functioning.

8. What psychosocial factors are connected with sexual dysfunctions?

Psychosocial factors connected with sexual dysfunctions include cultural influences, psychosexual trauma, a gay sexual orientation, dissatisfaction with the relationship, lack of sexual skills, irrational beliefs, and performance anxiety. Children reared in sexually repressive cultural or home environments may learn to respond to sex with anxiety and shame rather than with sexual arousal and pleasure. Many people do not acquire sexual competencies because of lack of opportunity to acquire knowledge and experience, even within a committed relationship. Irrational beliefs and attitudes, such as excessive needs for approval and perfectionism, may also contribute to sexual problems. Performance anxiety may place a dysfunctional individual in a "spectator" rather than performer role.

9. What is sex therapy?

Sex therapy is a cluster of cognitive and behavioral methods that aim to modify dysfunctional behavior directly by changing self-defeating beliefs and attitudes, fostering sexual skills and knowledge, enhancing sexual communication, and suggesting behavioral exercises to enhance sexual stimulation while reducing performance anxiety.

10. What is the Masters-and-Johnson approach to sex therapy?

Masters and Johnson pioneered the direct, behavioral approach to treating sexual dysfunctions. They employ a male-and-female therapy team during an in-residence program, which focuses on the couple as the unit of treatment. Sensate focus exercises are used to enable the partners to give each other pleasure in a nondemanding situation and then allow sexual response to proceed "naturally."

11. What is the Kaplan approach to sex therapy?

Kaplan's *psychosexual therapy* combines behavioral and psychoanalytic methods. She attempted to get at the distant roots of current sexual problems as well as to treat the problems directly.

12. How do professionals treat sexual desire disorders?

Some sex therapists help kindle the sexual appetites of people who lack sexual desire through prescribing self-stimulation exercises combined with erotic fantasies. Androgens also heighten the sex drive in people with androgen deficiencies.

13. How do professionals treat sexual arousal disorders?

Men and women with impaired sexual arousal receive sexual stimulation from their partners under relaxed circumstances, so that anxiety does not inhibit their natural reflexes. Biological treatments such as the drugs Viagra and Levitra are also used with male erectile disorder, and there are several other biological approaches. Some biological approaches that help males also appear to have applications with females.

14. How do professionals treat orgasmic disorders?

The Masters-and-Johnson technique uses a couples-oriented approach in treating anorgasmic women. Other sex therapists prefer a program of directed masturbation to enable women to learn about their own bodies at their own pace and free them of the need to rely on partners or to please partners. Premature ejaculation is usually treated with the squeeze technique or the stop–start method. Biological treatment methods for female orgasmic disorder, such as using sildenafil, and for premature ejaculation, such as using selective serotonin reuptake inhibitors, are under development.

15. How do professionals treat sexual pain disorders?

Dyspareunia, or painful intercourse, is generally treated by ensuring that the female is adequately lubricated or using medical intervention, as in the case of local infections. Vaginismus is generally treated with plastic vaginal dilators of increasing size.

Chapter 16

Truth?Fiction?

T / F? Most women who contract gonorrhea do not develop symptoms.

T / F? Christopher Columbus brought more than beads, blankets, and tobacco back to Europe from the New World: He also brought syphilis.

T / F? Gonorrhea and syphilis can be contracted from toilet seats in public rest rooms.

T / F? If a syphilitic sore goes away by itself, the infection does not require medical treatment.

T / F? Men can develop vaginal infections.

T / F? As you are reading this page, you are engaged in search-and-destroy missions against foreign agents within your body.

T / F? Most people who are infected by HIV remain symptom-free and appear healthy for years.

T / F? Genital herpes can be transmitted only during flare-ups of the infection.

Sexually Transmitted Infections

Preview

*H*arold and Carin, both 20, have been dating for several months. They feel strong sexual attraction toward each other but have hesitated to become sexually intimate because of fears about AIDS. Harold believes that using condoms is no guarantee against infection and wants the two of them to be tested for HIV, the virus that causes AIDS. Carin has resisted undergoing an HIV test, partly because she feels insulted that Harold fears that she may be infected and, frankly, partly in fear of the test results. She has heard that symptoms may not develop for years after infection. She wonders whether she might have been infected by one of the men with whom she slept in the past.

Keisha has genital herpes. A 19-year-old pre-law student, she has had no recurrences since the initial outbreak 2 years earlier. But she knows that herpes is a lifelong infection and may recur periodically from time to time. She also knows that she may inadvertently pass the herpes virus along to her sex partners, even to the man she eventually marries. She has begun thinking seriously about Steve, a man she has been dating for the past month. She would like to tell him that she has herpes before they become sexually intimate. Yet she fears that telling him might scare him off.

José, 21, a math and computer science major, is planning a career in computer operations, hoping one day to run the computer systems for a large corporation. He lives off-campus with several of his buddies in a run-down house they've dubbed the "Nuclear Dumpsite." He has been dating Maria, a theater major, for several months. They have begun having sexual relations and have practiced "safer sex"—at least most of the time. During the past week he noticed a burning sensation while urinating. It seems to have passed now, so he figures that it was probably nothing to worry about. But he's not sure and wonders whether he should see a doctor.

Harold, Carin, Keisha, and José express some of the fears and concerns of a generation of young people who are becoming sexually active at a time when the threat of HIV/AIDS and other **sexually transmitted infections (STIs)** hangs over every sexual decision.

An Epidemic

Question: How common are STIs? STIs are rampant. HIV/AIDS is indeed a scary thing, a very scary thing. But HIV/AIDS is only one of many STIs. Other STIs actually pose wider threats. There are about 40,000 new cases of HIV/AIDS each year (CDC, 2003), compared with 4 million new cases of the bacterial infection chlamydia (CDC, 2002b). *Human papilloma virus* (HPV) (the organism that causes genital warts) is estimated to be present in at least 20% of Americans over the age of 12 and in at least one-third of college women (Baer et al., 2000).

College students have become reasonably well informed about HIV/AIDS. However, many are unaware that chlamydia can go undetected for years. Moreover, if it is left untreated, it can cause pelvic inflammation and infertility. Most college students appear to be ignorant about HPV and its links to genital warts and cervical cancer (Baer et al., 2000). Yet the Centers for Disease Control and Prevention (CDC, 2003) estimates that as many as 1 million new cases of HPV infection occur each year in the United States—more than syphilis, genital herpes, and HIV/AIDS combined. Whereas 800,000 to 900,000 million Americans are thought to be infected with HIV, an estimated 50 to 60 million are infected with other STI-causing viruses, such as those responsible for genital warts, herpes, and hepatitis.

Who Is at Risk? Evidence suggests that young people are more sexually active than ever before. Thus, it is as important as ever that they be aware of the risks involved and take responsibility for their sexual health.

STIs are transmitted through sexual means, such as vaginal or anal intercourse or oral sex. They were formerly called *sexually transmitted diseases* (STDs) and, before that, *venereal diseases* (VDs)—after Venus, the Roman goddess of love.

Some STIs can be (and often are) spread through nonsexual contact as well. For example, HIV/AIDS and viral hepatitis may be spread by sharing contaminated needles. And yes, a few STIs (such as "crabs") may be picked up from bedding or other objects, such as moist towels, that harbor the infectious organisms that cause these STIs.

The World Health Organization (WHO) estimates that at least 333 million people around the world are stricken with curable STIs each year (UNAIDS, 2002). The United States is believed to have the highest rate of infection by STIs in the industrialized world. In a recent year, for example, 150 cases of gonorrhea were reported per 100,000 people in the United States, compared with 18.6 per 100,000 in Canada and 3 per 100,000 in Sweden.

In the United States, 10 to 15 million new cases of STIs are reported to the disease control centers each year, including 2.5 million adolescents (about 1 in 6). At least 1 in 4 Americans is likely to contract an STI at some point in life. And 2 cases out of 3 occur in people under the age of 25.

Some people have STIs and do not realize it. Ignorance is not bliss, however. Some STIs may not produce noticeable symptoms, but they can be harmful if left untreated. STIs can also be painful and, in the cases of HIV/AIDS, advanced syphilis, and the cervical cancer that can follow infection with HPV, lethal. Hundreds of thousands of women become infertile each year because of STIs that are spreading through their reproductive system. Overall, STIs are believed to account for 15% to 30% of cases of infertility among women. In addition to their biological effects, STIs exact an emotional toll and strain relationships to the breaking point.

Sexually transmitted infections (STIs) Infections that are communicated through sexual contact. (Some, such as HIV/AIDS, can also be transmitted in other ways.)

A Closer Look

Talking with Your Partner about STIs

Many people find it hard to talk about STIs with their partners. As one young woman explained,

It's one thing to talk about being responsible . . . and a much harder thing to do it at the very moment. It's just plain hard to say to someone I am feeling very erotic with, "Oh, yes, before we go any further, can we have a conversation about STI?" It's hard to imagine murmuring into someone's ear at a time of passion, "Would you mind slipping on this condom or using this cream just in case one of us has [an STI]?" Yet it seems awkward to bring it up any sooner if it's not clear between us that we want to make love. (Boston Women's Health Book Collective, 1992)

Because talking about STIs with sex partners can be awkward, many people just wing it (Montano et al., 2001). They assume that their partners are free of STIs and hope for the best. Some people act as if not talking about HIV/AIDS and other STIs will cause them to go away. But the microbes that cause AIDS, herpes, chlamydia, genital warts, and other STIs will not go away simply because we ignore them.

Imagine yourself in this situation: You've gone out with Chris a few times and you're keenly attracted. Chris is attractive, bright, and witty; shares some of your attitudes; and, all in all, is a powerful turn-on. Now the evening is winding down. You've been cuddling, and you think you know where things are heading.

Something clicks in your mind! You realize that as wonderful as Chris is, you don't know every place Chris has "been." As healthy as Chris looks and acts, you don't know what's swimming around in Chris's bloodstream. Chris may not know either. In a moment of pent-up desire, Chris may also (there is no way to put this delicately) *lie* about not being infected or about past sexual experiences.

What do you say now? How do you protect yourself without turning Chris off? Ah, the clumsiness! If you ask about condoms or STIs, it is sort of making a verbal commitment to have sexual relations, and perhaps you're not exactly sure that's what your partner intends. Even if it's clear that's where the two of you are heading, will you seem too straightforward? Will you kill the romance?

The spontaneity of the moment? Sure you might—life has its risks. But which is riskier: an awkward moment or being infected with a fatal illness? Let's put it another way: Are you *really* willing to die for sex? Given that few responses are perfect, here are some things you can try:

1. You might say something like this: "I've brought something and I'd like to use it . . ." (referring to a condom).

2. Or you can say, "I know this is a bit clumsy" [you are assertively expressing a feeling and asking permission to pursue a clumsy topic; Chris is likely to respond with "That's okay," or "Don't worry—what is it?"] "but the world isn't as safe as it used to be, and I think we should talk about what we're going to do."

Your partner hasn't been living in a cave. Your partner is also aware of the dangers of STIs and ought to be working with you to make things safe and unpressured. If your partner is pressing for unsafe sex and is inconsiderate of your feelings and concerns, you need to reassess whether you want to be with this person. Perhaps you can do better.

Why the surge in the incidence of STIs? One is the increased numbers of young people who engage in coitus. Many of them fail to use latex condoms consistently, if at all (Montano et al., 2001). Some people do not use condoms because the woman is on the pill. Although birth-control pills are reliable methods of contraception, they do not prevent STIs. Another reason is that some infections, like chlamydia, may have no symptoms. Therefore, some infected individuals unwittingly pass them on to others. Other risk factors include early sexual involvement and sex with multiple partners. Drug use is also associated with an increased risk of STIs (CDC, 2000h; Wagstaff et al., 2000). People who abuse drugs are more likely than others to engage in risky sexual practices. Moreover, certain forms of drug use, such as needle sharing, can directly transmit infectious organisms such as HIV. Another risk factor, ironically, is the success of new drugs in treating HIV/AIDS. As a result, many individuals who had become more cautious in their sexual behavior have once again thrown caution to the winds (Dilley et al., 2003).

Self-Assessment

STI Attitude Scale

Do your attitudes toward sexually transmitted infections lead you to take risks that increase the chances of your contracting one? The STI Attitude Scale (Yarber et al., 1989) was constructed to measure the attitudes of young adults toward STIs and provide insight into these questions.

To complete the questionnaire, read each statement carefully. Record your reactions by circling the responses according to this code:

SA = Strongly Agree   D = Disagree
A = Agree   SD = Strongly Disagree
U = Undecided

Interpret your responses by referring to the scoring key in the Appendix.

1. How one uses her or his sexuality has nothing to do with STI. SA A U D SD
2. It is easy to use the prevention methods that reduce one's chances of getting an STI. SA A U D SD
3. Responsible sex is one of the best ways of reducing the risk of STI. SA A U D SD
4. Getting early medical care is the main key to preventing harmful effects of STI. SA A U D SD
5. Choosing the right sex partner is important in reducing the risk of getting an STI. SA A U D SD
6. A high rate of STI should be a concern for all people. SA A U D SD
7. People with an STI have a duty to get their sex partners to medical care. SA A U D SD
8. The best way to get a sex partner to STI treatment is to take him or her to the doctor with you. SA A U D SD
9. Changing one's sex habits is necessary once the presence of an STI is known. SA A U D SD
10. I would dislike having to follow the medical steps for treating an STI. SA A U D SD
11. If I were sexually active, I would feel uneasy doing things before and after sex to prevent getting an STI. SA A U D SD
12. If I were sexually active, it would be insulting if a sex partner suggested we use a condom to avoid STI. SA A U D SD
13. I dislike talking about STI with my peers. SA A U D SD
14. I would be uncertain about going to the doctor unless I was sure I really had an STI. SA A U D SD
15. I would feel that I should take my sex partner with me to a clinic if I thought I had an STI. SA A U D SD
16. It would be embarrassing to discuss STI with one's partner if one were sexually active. SA A U D SD
17. If I were to have sex, the chance of getting an STI makes me uneasy about having sex with more than one person. SA A U D SD
18. I like the idea of sexual abstinence (not having sex) as the best way of avoiding STI. SA A U D SD
19. If I had an STI, I would cooperate with public health persons to find the sources of STI. SA A U D SD
20. If I had an STI, I would avoid exposing others while I was being treated. SA A U D SD
21. I would have regular STI checkups if I were having sex with more than one partner. SA A U D SD
22. I intend to look for STI signs before deciding to have sex with anyone. SA A U D SD
23. I will limit my sex activity to just one partner because of the chances I might get an STI. SA A U D SD
24. I will avoid sexual contact any time I think there is even a slight chance of getting an STI. SA A U D SD
25. The chance of getting an STI would not stop me from having sex. SA A U D SD
26. If I had a chance, I would support community efforts toward controlling STI. SA A U D SD
27. I would be willing to work with others to make people aware of STI problems in my town. SA A U D SD

Source: Yarber, W. L., Torabi, M. R., & Veenker, C. H. (1989). Development of a three-component sexually transmitted diseases attitude scale. *Journal of Sex Education & Therapy, 15:*36–49. Reprinted with permission.

Review: An Epidemic

Reflect

What problems would you expect to encounter in discussing STIs with a partner? How could you handle them?

Critical Thinking

Why do you think the United States has the largest incidence of STIs in the industrialized world?

1. Many college students are not aware of the link between _____ and cervical cancer.
2. STIs were formerly called _____ diseases.
3. About _____ million people around the world are stricken with curable STIs each year.
4. STIs are believed to account for _____ % of cases of infertility among women.

Education is critical to curtailing the epidemic of STIs among young people (Montano et al., 2001). The goals are to promote responsible sexual decision making and to alter risky behavior. However, education may not be enough. If education is to change their behavior, young people must also *want* to practice prevention and risk-reduction strategies (Benotsch & Kalichman, 2002).

Bacterial Infections

Bacteria Plural of *bacterium,* a class of one-celled microorganisms that have no chlorophyll and can give rise to many illnesses. (From the Greek *baktron,* meaning "stick," referring to the fact that many bacteria are rod-shaped.)

Gonorrhea An STI caused by the *Neisseria gonorrhoeae* bacterium and characterized by a discharge and burning urination. Left untreated, gonorrhea can give rise to pelvic inflammatory disease (PID) and infertility. (From the Greek *gonos,* meaning "seed," and *rheein,* meaning "to flow," referring to the fact that in ancient times the penile discharge characteristic of the illness was erroneously interpreted as a loss of seminal fluid.)

Question: What are bacteria? **Bacteria** are one-celled microorganisms, some of which are essential to human life and some of which are harmful. Bacteria play vital roles in our bodies' digestive systems. Bacteria are essential to fermentation. Without bacteria, there would be no wine. Unfortunately, bacteria also cause many diseases such as pneumonia, tuberculosis, and meningitis—along with the common STIs gonorrhea, syphilis, and chlamydia.

Gonorrhea

Question: What is gonorrhea? **Gonorrhea**—also known as "the clap" or "the drip"—was once the most widespread STI in the United States, but it has been replaced by chlamydia. The rate of infection declined substantially from the mid-1980s through the mid-1990s, apparently because of safer sexual practices. However, the rate surged by about 9% in the late 1990s, possibly because of advances in the treatment of HIV/AIDS. As HIV/AIDS becomes less frightening, people may engage in more spontaneous sexual behavior and increase the rate of STIs (CDC, 2000d). About 800,000 to 900,000 new cases of gonorrhea are now reported each year. Most new cases are contracted by people between the ages of 20 and 24.

Gonorrhea is caused by the gonococcus bacterium (see Table 16.1). A penile discharge that was probably gonorrhea is described in ancient Egyptian and Chinese writings and is mentioned in the Old Testament (*Leviticus* 15). Ancient Jews and Greeks assumed that the discharge was an involuntary loss of seminal fluid. In about 400 BCE, the Greek physician Hippocrates suggested that the loss stemmed from excessive sex, or "worship" of Aphrodite (whom the Romans would later rename *Venus*). The term *gonorrhea* is attributed to the Greek physician Galen, who lived in the second century CE. Albert L. S. Neisser identified the gonococcus bacterium that bears his name in 1879: *Neisseria gonorrhoeae.*

TABLE 16.1

Causes, Modes of Transmission, Symptoms, Diagnosis, and Treatment of Major Sexually Transmitted Infections (STIs)

STI and Pathogen	Modes of Transmission	Symptoms	Diagnosis	Treatment
		Bacterial Diseases		
Gonorrhea ("clap," "drip"): gonococcus bacterium (*Neisseria gonorrhoeae*)	Transmitted by vaginal, oral, or anal sexual activity, or from mother to newborn during delivery	In men, yellowish, thick penile discharge, burning urination	Clinical inspection, culture of sample discharge	Antibiotics: ceftriaxone, ciprofloaxacin, cefixime, ofloxacin
		In women, increased vaginal discharge, burning urination, irregular menstrual bleeding (most women show no early symptoms)		
Syphilis: *Treponema pallidum*	Transmitted by vaginal, oral, or anal sexual activity, or by touching an infectious chancre	In primary stage, a hard, round, painless chancre or sore appears at site of infection within 2 to 4 weeks. May progress through secondary, latent, and tertiary stages, if left untreated	Primary-stage syphilis is diagnosed by clinical examination and by examination of fluid from a chancre in a dark-field test. Secondary-stage syphilis is diagnosed by blood test (the VDRL).	Penicillin; or doxycycline, tetracycline, or erythromycin for nonpregnant penicillin-allergic patients
Chlamydia and nongonococcal urethritis (NGU): *Chlamydia trachomatis* bacterium; NGU in men may also be caused by *Ureaplasma urealyticum* bacterium and other pathogens	Transmitted by vaginal, oral, or anal sexual activity; to the eye by touching one's eyes after touching the genitals of an infected partner, or to newborns passing through the birth canal of an infected mother	In women, frequent and painful urination, lower abdominal pain and inflammation, and vaginal discharge (but most women are symptom-free)	The Abbott Testpack analyzes a cervical smear in women; in men, an extract of fluid from the penis is analyzed	Antibiotics: azithromycin, doxycycline, ofloxacin, amoxicillin
		In men, symptoms are similar to, but milder than, those of gonorrhea—burning or painful urination, slight penile discharge (most men are also symptom-free)		
		Sore throat may indicate infection from oral–genital contact.		
		Vaginal Infections		
Bacterial vaginosis: *Gardnerella vaginalis* bacterium and others	Can arise by overgrowth of organisms in vagina, allergic reactions, etc.; also transmitted by sexual contact	In women, thin, foul-smelling vaginal discharge, irritation of genitals, and mild pain during urination	Culture and examination of bacterium	Metronidazole, clindamycin
		In men, inflammation of penile foreskin and glans, urethritis, and cystitis		
		Both sexes may be symptom-free.		

(continues)

TABLE 16.1 Continued

Causes, Modes of Transmission, Symptoms, Diagnosis, and Treatment of Major Sexually Transmitted Infections (STIs)

STI and Pathogen	Modes of Transmission	Symptoms	Diagnosis	Treatment
Vaginal Infections Continued				
Candidiasis (moniliasis, thrush, "yeast infection"): *Candida albicans*— a yeastlike fungus	Can arise by overgrowth of fungus in vagina; may also be transmitted by sexual contact or by sharing a washcloth with an infected person	In women, vulval itching; white, cheesy, foul-smelling discharge; soreness or swelling of vaginal and vulval tissues In men, itching and burning on urination, or a reddening of the penis	Diagnosis usually made on basis of symptoms	Single-dose oral fluconazole, or suppositories of miconazole, clotrimazole, or butaconazole; modification of use of other medicines and chemical agents; keeping infected area dry
Trichomoniasis ("trich"): *Trichomonas vaginalis,* a protozoan (one-celled animal)	Almost always transmitted sexually	In women, foamy, yellowish, odorous vaginal discharge; itching or burning sensation in vulva. Many women are symptom-free. Men are usually symptom-free, but mild urethritis is possible.	Microscopic examination of a smear of vaginal secretions, or of culture of the sample (latter method preferred)	Metronidazole
Viral Diseases				
Oral herpes: *Herpes simplex virus-type 1 (HSV-1)*	Touching, kissing, sexual contact with sores or blisters; sharing cups, towels, toilet seats	Cold sores or fever blisters on the lips, mouth, or throat; herpetic sores on the genitals	Usually clinical inspection	Over-the-counter lip balms, cold-sore medications; check with your physician, however.
Genital herpes: *Herpes simplex virus-type 2 (HSV-2)*	Almost always by means of vaginal, oral, or anal sexual activity; most contagious during active outbreaks of the disease	Painful, reddish bumps around the genitals, thighs, or buttocks; in women, may also be in the vagina or on the cervix. Bumps become blisters or sores that fill with pus and break, shedding viral particles. Other possible symptoms: burning urination, fever, aches and pains, swollen glands; in women, vaginal discharge	Clinical inspection of sores; culture and examination of fluid drawn from the base of a genital sore	There is no cure, but the antiviral drugs acyclovir, famciclovir, and valacyclovir may provide relief and prompt healing over; people with herpes often profit from counseling and group support as well.
Viral hepatitis: hepatitis A, B, C, and D type viruses	Sexual contact, especially involving the anus (especially hepatitis A); contact with infected fecal matter; transfusion of contaminated blood (especially hepatitis B and C)	Ranges from being symptom-free to mild flulike symptoms and more severe symptoms, including fever, abdominal pain, vomiting, and "jaundiced" (yellowish) skin and eyes	Examination of blood for hepatitis antibodies; liver biopsy	Treatment usually involves bed rest, intake of fluids, and, sometimes, antibiotics to ward off bacterial infections that might take hold because of lowered resistance. Alpha interferon is sometimes used in treating hepatitis C.

(continues)

	TABLE 16.1 Continued			
	Causes, Modes of Transmission, Symptoms, Diagnosis, and Treatment of Major Sexually Transmitted Infections (STIs)			
STI and Pathogen	Modes of Transmission	Symptoms	Diagnosis	Treatment
		Viral Diseases Continued		
Acquired immunodeficiency syndrome (AIDS): *Human immunodeficiency virus (HIV)*	HIV is transmitted by sexual contact; by infusion with contaminated blood; from mother to fetus during pregnancy, or through childbirth or breast-feeding	Infected people may initially have no symptoms or develop mild flulike symptoms, which may then disappear for many years prior to the development of "full-blown" AIDS. The symptoms of full-blown AIDS include fever, weight loss, fatigue, diarrhea, and opportunistic infections such as rare forms of cancer (Kaposi's sarcoma) and pneumonia (PCP)	Blood, saliva, or urine tests detect HIV antibodies. More expensive tests confirm the presence of the virus (HIV) itself. The diagnosis of HIV/AIDS is usually made on the basis of antibodies, a low count of CD4 cells, and/or the presence of indicator diseases.	There is no cure for HIV infection or AIDS. Treatment ("HAART") is a "cocktail" of antiviral drugs including a protease inhibitor and nucleoside analogues such as Zidovudine. New drugs such as fusion inhibitors are also joining the arsenal.
Genital warts (venereal warts): *Human papilloma virus (HPV)*	Transmission is by sexual and other forms of contact, such as with infected towels or clothing	Appearance of painless warts, often resembling cauliflowers, on the penis, foreskin, scrotum, or internal urethra in men; or on the vulva, labia, wall of the vagina, or cervix in women. May occur around the anus and in the rectum of both genders	Clinical inspection	Methods include cryotherapy (freezing), podophyllin, trichloroacetic acid (TCA) or bichloroacetic acid (BCA), burning, and surgical removal
		Ectoparasitic Infestations		
Pediculosis ("crabs"): *Phthirus pubis (pubic lice)*	Transmission is by sexual contact, or by contact with an infested towel, sheet, or toilet seat	Intense itching in pubic area and other hairy regions to which lice can attach	Clinical examination	Lindane (brand name: Kwell)—a prescription shampoo; nonprescription medications containing pyrethrins or piperonal butoxide (brand names: RID, Triple X)
Scabies: *Sarcoptes scabiei*	Transmission is by sexual contact, or by contact with infested clothing or bed linen, towels, and other fabrics	Intense itching; reddish lines on skin where mites have burrowed in; welts and pus-filled blisters in affected areas	Clinical inspection	Lindane (Kwell)

Source: Adapted from Rathus, S. A. (2005). *Psychology: Concepts and connections,* 9th ed. Belmont, CA: Wadsworth.

Transmission Gonococcal bacteria require a warm, moist environment, like that found along the mucous membranes of the urinary tract in both genders or the cervix in women. Outside the body, they die in about a minute. There is no evidence that gonorrhea can be picked up from public toilet seats or by touching dry objects. In rare cases, gonorrhea is contracted by contact with a moist, warm towel or sheet used immediately beforehand by an infected person. Gonorrhea is nearly always

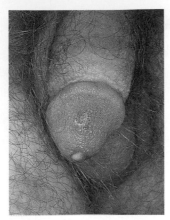

Figure 16.1. Gonorrheal Discharge. Gonorrhea in the male often causes a thick, yellowish, puslike discharge from the penis.

transmitted by unprotected vaginal, oral, or anal sexual activity, or from mother to newborn during delivery.

A person who performs fellatio on an infected man may develop **pharyngeal gonorrhea**, which produces a throat infection. Mouth-to-mouth kissing and cunnilingus are less likely to spread gonorrhea. The eyes provide a good environment for the bacterium. Thus, a person whose hands come into contact with infected genitals and who inadvertently touches his or her eyes afterward may infect them. Babies have contracted gonorrhea of the eyes (**ophthalmia neonatorum**) when passing through the birth canals of infected mothers. This disorder may cause blindness, but it has become rare because the eyes of newborns are treated routinely with silver nitrate or penicillin ointment, which are toxic to gonococcal bacteria.

A gonorrheal infection may be spread from the penis to the partner's rectum during anal intercourse. A cervical gonorrheal infection can be spread to the rectum if an infected woman and her partner follow vaginal intercourse with anal intercourse. Gonorrhea is less likely to be spread by vaginal discharge than by penile discharge.

Gonorrhea is highly contagious. Women stand nearly a 50% chance of contracting gonorrhea after one exposure. Men have a 25% risk of infection (Hatcher, 2001). The risks to women are apparently greater because women retain infected semen in the vagina. The risk of infection increases with repeated exposure.

Symptoms Most men experience symptoms within 2 to 5 days after infection. Symptoms include a penile discharge that is clear at first (Figure 16.1). Within a day it turns yellow to yellow-green, thickens, and becomes puslike. The urethra becomes inflamed, and urination is accompanied by a burning sensation. Some 30% to 40% of males have swelling and tenderness in the lymph glands of the groin. Inflammation and other symptoms may become chronic if left untreated.

The initial symptoms of gonorrhea usually abate within a few weeks without treatment, leading people to think of gonorrhea as being no worse than a bad cold. However, the gonococcus bacterium usually continues to damage the body internally.

The primary site of infection in women is the cervix, where it causes **cervicitis**. Cervicitis may cause a yellowish to yellow-green, puslike discharge that irritates the vulva. If the infection spreads to the urethra, women may also note burning urination. However, about 80% of the women who contract gonorrhea are **asymptomatic**—that is, they have no symptoms—during the early stages of the infection. Because many infected women do not seek treatment until symptoms develop, they may innocently infect another sex partner.

When gonorrhea is not treated early, it may spread through the urogenital systems in both genders and strike the internal reproductive organs. In men, it can lead to **epididymitis**, which can cause fertility problems. Swelling and feelings of tenderness or pain in the scrotum are the principal symptoms of epididymitis. Fever may also be present. Occasionally the kidneys are affected.

In women, the bacterium can spread through the cervix to the uterus, fallopian tubes, ovaries, and other parts of the abdominal cavity, causing **pelvic inflammatory disease** (PID) (Wingood & DiClemente, 2002). Symptoms of PID include cramps, abdominal pain and tenderness, cervical tenderness and discharge, irregular menstrual cycles, coital pain, fever, nausea, and vomiting. PID may also occur without symptoms. Regardless of symptoms, PID can cause scarring that blocks the fallopian tubes, leading to infertility. PID is a serious illness that requires aggressive treatment with antibiotics. Surgery may be needed to remove infected tissue. Unfortunately, many women become aware of a gonococcal infection only when they develop PID. These consequences are all the more unfortunate because gonorrhea, when diagnosed and treated early, clears up rapidly in over 90% of cases.

Pharyngeal gonorrhea A gonorrheal infection of the pharynx (the cavity leading from the mouth and nasal passages to the larynx and esophagus) that is characterized by a sore throat.

Ophthalmia neonatorum A gonorrheal infection of the eyes of newborn children who contract the disease by passing through an infected birth canal. (From the Greek *ophthalmos*, meaning "eye.")

Cervicitis Inflammation of the cervix.

Asymptomatic Without symptoms.

Epididymitis Inflammation of the epididymis.

Diagnosis and Treatment Diagnosis of gonorrhea involves clinical inspection of the genitals by a physician (a family practitioner, urologist, or gynecologist) and the culturing and examination of a sample of genital discharge.

Antibiotics are the standard treatment for gonorrhea. Penicillin was once the favored antibiotic, but the rise of penicillin-resistant strains of *Neisseria gonorrhoeae* has necessitated the use of alternative antibiotics (Hatcher, 2001). An injection of the antibiotic ceftriaxone is often recommended. Other antibiotics that are used to treat gonorrhea include ciprofloxacin, and ofloxacin (CDC, 2002a, 2002b). Because gonorrhea and chlamydia often occur together, people who are infected with gonorrhea are usually also treated for chlamydia through the use of another antibiotic (Hatcher, 2001). The sex partners of people with gonorrhea should also be examined.

Syphilis

Nobody wanted to be associated with **syphilis.** In Naples they called it "the French disease." In France it was "the Neapolitan disease." Many Italians called it "the Spanish disease," but in Spain they called it "the disease of Española" (modern Haiti).

In 1530 the Italian physician Girolamo Fracastoro wrote a poem about Syphilus, a shepherd boy. Syphilus was afflicted with the disease as retribution for insulting the sun god Apollo.

Question: What is syphilis? Syphilis is an STI that is caused by a bacterium isolated in 1905 by the German scientist Fritz Schaudinn: *Treponema pallidum* (*T. pallidum*, for short) (see Figure 16.2). The name contains roots meaning a "faintly colored (pallid) turning thread," describing the corkscrewlike shape of the microscopic organism. Because of its spiral shape, *T. pallidum* is also called a *spirochete*, from Greek roots meaning "spiral" and "hair."

The Origins of Syphilis The origins of syphilis are controversial. The Columbian theory holds that Christopher Columbus returned to Spain from his first voyage to the West Indies (1492–1493) with more than beads, blankets, and tobacco. Then,

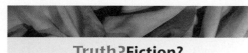

Truth?Fiction?
Revisited

It is true that most women who contract gonorrhea do not have noticeable symptoms. However, they may develop serious health problems later on.

Pelvic inflammatory disease Inflammation of the pelvic region—possibly including the cervix, uterus, fallopian tubes, abdominal cavity, and ovaries—that can be caused by organisms such as *Neisseria gonorrhoeae.* Its symptoms are abdominal pain and tenderness, nausea, fever, and irregular menstrual cycles. The condition may lead to infertility. Abbreviated *PID.*

Syphilis An STI that is caused by the *Treponema pallidum* bacterium and may progress through several stages of development— often from a chancre to a skin rash to damage to the cardiovascular or central nervous systems. (From the Greek *siphlos,* meaning "maimed" or "crippled.")

Figure 16.2. **Treponema pallidum.** Treponema pallidum *is the bacterium that causes syphilis. Because of the spiral shape,* T. pallidum *is also called a spirochete.*

Truth?Fiction?
Revisited

It is apparently not the case that Christopher Columbus brought syphilis back to Europe from the New World, although this theory was believed by many until it was refuted in the 1990s.

It is not true that gonorrhea and syphilis can be contracted from toilet seats in public rest rooms. Pubic lice can be contracted in this manner, however, as we will see later.

It is not true that the infection does not require medical treatment if a syphilitic chancre (sore) goes away by itself. The belief that medical treatment is unnecessary if the symptoms of an STI disappear by themselves is unfounded. Both gonorrhea and syphilis, for example, can damage the body even when their early symptoms have abated.

Chancre A sore or ulcer.
Congenital syphilis A syphilis infection that is present at birth.

from Spain, Spanish mercenaries may have carried the disease to Naples when they were hired to protect that city from French invaders. Then the French army may have contracted syphilis from prostitutes, who also practiced their profession with the Spaniards and Neapolitans. Sailors may have eventually spread syphilis to the East.

It is generally accepted that Columbus exhibited symptoms of advanced syphilis when he died in 1506. However, evidence reported in 1992 shows that syphilis existed in Europe prior to the voyages of Columbus (Wilford, 1992).

The incidence of syphilis decreased in the United States with the introduction of penicillin. But there has been a recent resurgence in rates of syphilis to about 10,000 cases per year as the advent of effective drugs for HIV/AIDS has contributed to a new wave of risky sexual behavior among many individuals (Dilley et al., 2003). Although syphilis is less widespread than it once was, its effects can be extremely harmful. They include heart disease, blindness, confusion, and death. Syphilis killed the painter Paul Gauguin.

Transmission Syphilis, like gonorrhea, is most often transmitted by vaginal or anal intercourse or by oral–genital or oral–anal contact with an infected person. The spirochete is usually transmitted when open lesions on an infected person come into contact with the mucous membranes or skin abrasions of the partner's body during sexual activity. Syphilis may also be contracted by touching an infectious **chancre**, but not from using the same toilet seat as an infected person.

Pregnant women may transmit syphilis to their fetuses, because the spirochete can cross the placental membrane. Miscarriage, stillbirth, or **congenital syphilis** may result. Congenital syphilis may impair vision and hearing or deform bones and teeth. Blood tests are administered routinely during pregnancy to diagnose syphilis in the mother so that congenital problems in the baby may be averted. The fetus will probably not be harmed if an infected mother is treated before the fourth month of pregnancy.

Symptoms and Course of Illness Syphilis develops through several stages. In the first stage, or *primary stage* of syphilis, a painless chancre (a hard, round, ulcerlike lesion with raised edges) appears at the site of infection 2 to 4 weeks after contact. When women are infected, the chancre usually forms on the vaginal walls or the cervix. It may also form on the external genitalia, most often on the labia. When men are infected, the chancre usually forms on the penile glans. It may also form on the scrotum or penile shaft. If the mode of transmission is oral sex, the chancre may appear on the lips or tongue (see Figure 16.3). If the infection is spread by anal sex, the rectum may be the site of the chancre. The chancre disappears within a few weeks, but if the infection remains untreated, syphilis will continue to work within the body.

The *secondary stage* begins a few weeks to a few months later. A skin rash develops, consisting of painless, reddish, raised bumps that darken after a while and burst, oozing a discharge. Other symptoms include sores in the mouth, painful swelling of joints, a sore throat, headaches, and fever. A person with syphilis may thus wrongly assume that he or she has the flu.

These symptoms also disappear. Syphilis then enters the *latent stage* and may lie dormant for 1 to 40 years. But spirochetes continue to multiply and burrow into the circulatory system, central nervous system (brain and spinal cord), and bones. The person may no longer be contagious to sex partners after several years in the

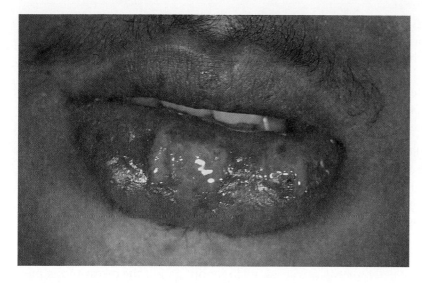

Figure 16.3. Syphilis Chancre. The first stage, or primary stage, of a syphilis infection is marked by the appearance of a painless sore or chancre at the site of the infection.

latent stage, but a pregnant woman may pass along the infection to her newborn at any time.

In many cases the disease eventually progresses to the late stage, or *tertiary stage*. A large ulcer may form on the skin, muscle tissue, digestive organs, lungs, liver, or other organs. This destructive ulcer can often be successfully treated, but still more serious damage can occur as the infection attacks the central nervous system or the cardiovascular system (the heart and the major blood vessels). Either outcome can be fatal. **Neurosyphilis** can cause brain damage, resulting in paralysis or the mental illness called **general paresis**.

The primary and secondary symptoms of syphilis inevitably disappear. Infected people may thus be tempted to believe that they are no longer at risk and may fail to see a doctor. This is unfortunate, because failure to eradicate the infection through proper treatment may eventually lead to dire consequences.

Diagnosis and Treatment Primary-stage syphilis is diagnosed by clinical examination. If a chancre is found, fluid drawn from it can be examined under a microscope. The spirochetes are usually quite visible. Blood tests are not definitive until the secondary stage begins. The most frequently used blood test is the **VDRL**. The VDRL tests for the presence of **antibodies** to *Treponema pallidum* in the blood.

Penicillin is the treatment of choice for syphilis, although for people allergic to penicillin, doxycycline and some other antibiotics can be used (Hatcher, 2001). Sex partners of persons infected with syphilis should also be evaluated by a physician.

Chlamydia

Question: What is chlamydia? Chlamydia, another bacterial STI, is more common than gonorrhea and syphilis in the United States (Hatcher, 2001). Chlamydia infections are caused by the *Chlamydia trachomatis* bacterium, a parasitic organism that can survive only within cells. This bacterium can cause several different types of inflammation, including *nongonococcal urethritis* (NGU) in men and women, *epididymitis* (inflammation of the epididymis) in men, and *cervicitis* (infection of the cervix), *endometritis* (inflammation of the endometrium), and PID in women (Hatcher, 2001).

Nearly 4 million new chlamydia infections occur each year (CDC, 2002b). The incidence of chlamydia infections is especially high among teenagers and college students (CDC, 2000h; Montano et al., 2001).

Neurosyphilis A syphilitic infection of the central nervous system, which can cause brain damage and death.

General paresis A progressive form of mental illness caused by neurosyphilis and characterized by gross confusion.

VDRL The test that is named after the Venereal Disease Research Laboratory of the U.S. Public Health Service and tests for the presence of antibodies to *Treponema pallidum* in the blood.

Antibodies Specialized proteins produced by the white blood cells of the immune system in response to disease organisms and other toxic substances. Antibodies recognize and attack the invading organisms or substances.

Transmission *Chlamydia trachomatis* is usually transmitted through vaginal or anal sexual intercourse. *Chlamydia trachomatis* may also cause an eye infection if a person touches his or her eyes after handling the genitals of an infected partner. Oral sex with an infected partner can infect the throat. Newborns can acquire potentially serious chlamydia eye infections as they pass through the cervix of an infected mother during birth. Even newborns delivered by cesarean section may be infected if the amniotic sac breaks before delivery.

Symptoms Chlamydia infections usually produce symptoms that are similar to, but milder than, those of gonorrhea. In men, *Chlamydia trachomatis* can lead to non-gonococcal urethritis (NGU). *Urethritis* is an inflammation of the urethra. NGU refers to forms of urethritis that are not caused by the gonococcal bacterium. (NGU is generally diagnosed only in men. In women, an inflammation of the urethra caused by *Chlamydia trachomatis* is called a chlamydia infection or simply chlamydia.) NGU was formerly called nonspecific urethritis, or NSU. Many organisms can cause NGU. *Chlamydia trachomatis* accounts for about half of the cases among men (Hatcher, 2001).

NGU in men may give rise to a thin, whitish discharge from the penis and some burning or other pain during urination. These contrast with the yellow-green discharge and more intense pain produced by gonorrhea. There may be soreness in the scrotum and feelings of heaviness in the testes. NGU is about two to three times as prevalent among American men as gonorrhea (Hatcher, 2001). Young male adults are at the highest risk of contracting gonorrhea and NGU, presumably because of their high levels of sexual activity (Montano et al., 2001).

In women, chlamydial infections usually give rise to infections of the urethra or cervix (Wingood & DiClemente, 2002). Women, like men, may experience burning when they urinate, genital irritation, and a mild (vaginal) discharge. Women are also likely to encounter pelvic pain and irregular menstrual cycles. The cervix may look swollen and inflamed. But as many as 25% of men and 70% of women infected with chlamydia have no noticeable symptoms (Hatcher, 2001; Wingood & DiClemente, 2002). For this reason, chlamydia has been dubbed the "silent disease." Symptom-free people may go untreated and unknowingly pass their infections to new partners. In women, an untreated chlamydial infection can spread throughout the reproductive system, leading to PID and scarring the fallopian tubes, resulting in infertility (Wingood & DiClemente, 2002). About half of the more than 1 million annual cases of PID are attributed to chlamydia (Hatcher, 2001). Women exposed to *Chlamydia trachomatis* also stand a greater chance of undergoing an ectopic (tubal) pregnancy.

Untreated chlamydial infections can also damage the internal reproductive organs of men. About 50% of cases of epididymitis are caused by chlamydial infections (Hatcher, 2001). Yet only about 1% or 2% of men with untreated NGU caused by *Chlamydia trachomatis* go on to develop epididymitis. The long-term effects of untreated chlamydial infections in men remain undetermined.

Chlamydial infections also frequently occur together with other STIs, most often gonorrhea. Nearly half of cases of gonorrhea involve coexisting chlamydial infections (Hatcher, 2001).

Diagnosis and Treatment Various tests are used in the laboratory or the physician's office to verify a diagnosis of chlamydia in women (CDC, 2002b). The tests analyze a cervical smear and are highly reliable. In men, a swab may be inserted through the penile opening to extract fluid that is analyzed for the presence of *Chlamydia trachomatis.*

Antibiotics other than penicillin are highly effective in eradicating chlamydia infections. These include azithromycin, doxycycline, ofloxacin, and amoxicillin

(Hatcher, 2001). Sex partners are treated when possible to prevent the infection from bouncing back and forth (Hatcher, 2001). Both partners may be unaware that they are infected and oblivious to the internal damage the infection is causing. Because of the risks posed by untreated chlamydial infections, especially to women, and the high rate of symptom-free infections, many physicians screen young women for chlamydia during regular checkups.

Other Bacterial Infections

Question: Are there any other bacterial STIs? Several other types of bacterial STIs occur in the United States and Canada, though less frequently. These include chancroid, shigellosis, granuloma inguinale, and lymphogranuloma venereum.

Chancroid Chancroid, or "soft chancre," is caused by the bacterium *Haemophilus ducreyi.* It is more commonly found in the tropics and Eastern nations than in Western countries. The chancroid sore consists of a cluster of small bumps or pimples on the genitals, perineum (the area of skin that lies between the genitals and the anus), or the anus itself. These lesions usually appear within 7 days of infection. Within a few days the lesion ruptures, producing an open sore or ulcer. Several ulcers may merge with other ulcers, forming giant ulcers. There is usually an accompanying swelling of a nearby lymph node. In contrast to the syphilis chancre, the chancroid ulcer has a soft rim (hence the name) and is painful in men. Women frequently do not experience any pain and may be unaware of being infected (Wingood & DiClemente, 2002). The bacterium is typically transmitted through sexual or bodily contact with the lesion or its discharge. Diagnosis is usually confirmed by culturing the bacterium, which is found in pus from the sore, and examining it under a microscope. Antibiotics are usually effective in treating the disease (Hatcher, 2001).

Shigellosis Shigellosis is caused by the *Shigella* bacterium and is characterized by fever and severe abdominal symptoms, including diarrhea and inflammation of the large intestine. About 25,000 cases of shigellosis are reported each year in the United States. Shigellosis can result from food poisoning, but it is also often contracted by oral contact with infected fecal material, which may stem from oral–anal sex. Shigellosis often resolves itself, but people with the disease may become severely dehydrated from the diarrhea. Severe cases are usually treated with antibiotics.

Granuloma Inguinale Rare in the United States, **granuloma inguinale**, like chancroid, is more common in tropical regions. It is caused by the bacterium *Calymmatobacterium granulomatous* and is not as contagious as many other STIs. Primary symptoms are painless red bumps or sores in the groin area that ulcerate and spread. Like chancroid, it is usually spread by intimate bodily or sexual contact with a lesion or its discharge. Diagnosis is confirmed by microscopic examination of tissue of the rim of the sore. Numerous antibiotics are effective in treating this disease (Hatcher, 2001).

Lymphogranuloma venereum (LGV) Lymphogranuloma venereum (LGV) is another tropical STI that occurs only rarely in the United States and Canada. Some U.S. soldiers returned from Vietnam with cases of LGV. It is caused by several strains of the *Chlamydia trachomatis* bacterium. LGV usually enters the body through the penis, vulva, or cervix, where a small, painless sore may form. The sore may go unnoticed, but a nearby lymph gland in the groin swells and grows tender. Other symptoms mimic those of flu: chills, fever, and headache. Other possible symptoms include backache (especially in women) and arthritic complaints (painful joints). If LGV is untreated, growths and fistulas in the genitals and elephantiasis of the legs and

Chancroid An STI caused by the *Haemophilus ducreyi* bacterium. Also called *soft chancre.*

Shigellosis An STI caused by the *Shigella* bacterium.

Granuloma inguinale A tropical STI caused by the *Calymmatobacterium granulomatous* bacterium.

Lymphogranuloma venereum A tropical STI caused by the *Chlamydia trachomatis* bacterium.

Review: Bacterial Infections

Reflect

Why should people *not* be relieved when the symptoms of a sexually transmitted disease "disappear"?

Critical Thinking

Can you apply concepts of evolutionary theory to explain why a bacterial disease may "become" resistant to penicillin?

5. Bacteria are made up of _____ cell(s).

6. The most common STI caused by a bacterium is _____.

7. _____ is also known as "the clap" or "the drip."

8. Gonorrhea (*Can* or *Cannot*?) be picked up from public toilet seats.

9. Babies sometimes contract gonorrhea of the eyes (called _____ neonatorum) while being born.

10. Symptoms of gonorrhea include a penile _____.

11. The primary site of gonorrheal infection in women is the _____.

12. Syphilis is caused by the *Treponema* _____ bacterium.

13. During the first stage of syphilis, a painless _____ appears.

14. During the tertiary stage, _____ can cause brain damage.

15. The blood test most frequently used to diagnose syphilis is the _____.

16. *Chlamydia trachomatis* can cause _____ urethritis (NGU).

17. Gonorrhea and chlamydia can both lead to pelvic _____ disease in women.

18. Bacterial diseases are usually treated with _____.

---

genitals may occur. Diagnosis is made by skin tests and blood tests. Antibiotics are the usual treatment (Hatcher, 2001).

Vaginal Infections

Question: What is a vaginal infection? A vaginal infection or inflammation is technically termed **vaginitis.** Vaginitis is typically characterized by genital irritation or itching and burning during urination, but the most common symptom is an odorous discharge.

Most cases of vaginitis are caused by organisms that reside in the vagina or by sexually transmitted organisms. Organisms that reside in the vagina may overgrow when the environmental balance of the vagina is upset by factors such as birth-control pills, antibiotics, dietary changes, excessive douching, or nylon underwear or pantyhose. (See Chapter 3 for ways to reduce the risk of vaginitis.) Still other cases are caused by sensitivities or allergic reactions to various chemicals.

The great majority of vaginal infections involve bacterial vaginosis (BV), candidiasis (commonly called a "yeast" infection), or trichomoniasis ("trich"). Bacterial vaginosis is the most common form of vaginitis, followed by candidiasis and then by trichomoniasis, but some cases involve combinations of the three (Wingood & DiClemente, 2002).

The microbes that cause vaginal infections in women can also infect the man's urethral tract. A "vaginal infection" can be passed back and forth between sex partners.

Bacterial Vaginosis

Question: What is bacterial vaginosis? Bacterial vaginosis (BV—formerly called *nonspecific vaginitis*) is most often caused by overgrowth of the bacterium *Gardnerella vaginalis* (Wingood & DiClemente, 2002). The bacterium is mainly transmitted sex-

Vaginitis Any type of vaginal infection or inflammation.

Bacterial vaginosis A form of vaginitis usually caused by the *Gardnerella vaginalis* bacterium.

ually. The most characteristic symptom in women is a thin, foul-smelling vaginal discharge, but infected women often have no symptoms. Diagnosis requires culturing the bacterium in the laboratory. Besides causing troublesome symptoms in some cases, BV may increase the risk of various gynecological problems, including infections of the reproductive tract (Wingood & DiClemente, 2002). Oral treatment with metronidazole (brand name: Flagyl) is recommended and is effective in most cases. Topical treatments with metronidazole or clindamycin are also effective. But recurrences are common.

Questions remain about whether a male partner should also be treated. The bacterium can usually be found in the urethra of a symptom-free male (Wingood & DiClemente, 2002). Being symptom-free, the male may unknowingly pass the bacterium on to others.

Truth?Fiction?
Revisited

It is not literally true that men can develop vaginal infections. Only women have vaginas. However, the microbes that cause these infections in women may also cause problems for men.

Candidiasis

Question: What is candidiasis? Candidiasis is an STI caused by a yeastlike fungus, *Candida albicans.* It is also known as moniliasis, as thrush, or simply as a yeast infection. Candidiasis commonly produces soreness, inflammation, and intense (sometimes maddening!) itching around the vulva that is accompanied by a thick, white, curdlike vaginal discharge (see Figure 16.4). Yeast generally produces no symptoms when the vaginal environment is normal. Yeast infections can also occur in the mouth in both men and women and in the penis in men.

Infections most often arise from changes in the vaginal environment that allow the fungus to overgrow. Factors such as the use of antibiotics, birth-control pills, or intrauterine devices (IUDs), pregnancy, and diabetes may alter the vaginal balance, enabling the fungus that causes yeast infections to grow to infectious levels. Wearing nylon underwear and tight, restrictive, poorly ventilated clothing may also set the stage for a yeast infection.

Diet may play a role in recurrent yeast infections. Reducing intake of substances that produce excessive excretion of urinary sugars (such as dairy products, sugar, and artificial sweeteners) apparently reduces the frequency of recurrent yeast infections. Eating daily a pint of yogurt that contains active bacterial (*Lactobacillus acidophilus*) cultures may reduce the rate of recurrent infections.

Candidiasis can be passed back and forth between sex partners through vaginal intercourse. It may also be passed back and forth between the mouth and the genitals through oral–genital contact and infect the anus through anal intercourse. However, most infections in women are believed to be caused by an overgrowth of "yeast" normally found in the vagina, not by sexual transmission. Still, it is advisable to evaluate partners simultaneously. Whereas most men with *Candida* have no symptoms, some may develop NGU or a genital thrush that is accompanied by itching and burning during urination or by reddening of the penis. Candidiasis may also be transmitted nonsexually, as between women who share a washcloth.

Authorities agree that at least half of adult women will experience at least one episode of candidiasis by their mid-20s (Marrazzo, 2003). About 25% of these will have recurrent infections. A single dose of oral fluconazole, or vaginal suppositories or creams containing miconazole, clotrimazole, or butaconazole are recommended for treatment

Candidiasis A form of vaginitis caused by a yeastlike fungus, *Candida albicans.*

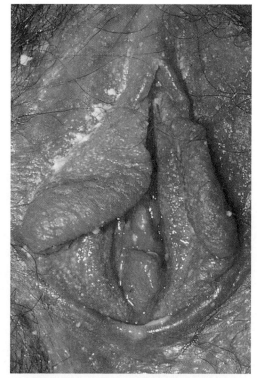

Figure 16.4. Candidiasis. A *"yeast infection" is caused by the* Candida albicans *fungus and causes soreness, inflammation, and itching around the vulva, accompanied by a thick white vaginal discharge.*

(Hatcher, 2001; Wingood & DiClemente, 2002). Many of these treatments are sold over the counter. Ask the pharmacist which preparations contain these medicines (or read the labels). We advise women with vaginal complaints to consult their physicians before using any of these medications to ensure that they receive the proper diagnosis and treatment.

Trichomoniasis

Question: What is trichomoniasis? **Trichomoniasis** ("trich") is the most common parasitic STI. It is caused by *Trichomonas vaginalis,* a one-celled parasite. There are 2 to 3 million cases a year among women in the United States (Wingood & DiClemente, 2002). Symptoms include burning or itching in the vulva, mild pain during urination or coitus, and an odorous, foamy whitish to yellowish-green discharge. Some infected women report lower abdominal pain. Many women notice symptoms appearing or worsening during, or just following, their menstrual periods. Trichomoniasis facilitates the transmission of HIV (Wingood & DiClemente, 2002) and is also linked to the development of tubal adhesions that can result in infertility. As with many other STIs, many infected women have no symptoms.

Candidiasis often reflects the overgrowth of organisms normally found in the vagina, but trich is nearly always sexually transmitted. Because the parasite can survive for several hours on moist surfaces outside the body, trich can be communicated from contact with infected semen or with vaginal discharges on towels, washcloths, and bedclothes. This parasite is one of the few disease agents that can be picked up from a toilet seat, but it would have to come into contact with the penis or vulva.

Trichomonas vaginalis can cause NGU in the male, who may experience a slight penile discharge that is usually noticeable prior to first urination in the morning. There may be tingling, itching, and other irritating sensations in the urethral tract. But most infected men are symptom-free and can unwittingly transfer the organism to other sex partners. Diagnosis is frequently made by microscopic examination of a smear of a woman's vaginal fluids.

Except during the first 3 months of pregnancy, trichomoniasis is usually treated in both women and men with metronidazole (brand name: Flagyl). Both partners are treated when possible, whether or not they report symptoms, and the success rate approaches 100% (Hatcher, 2001; Wingood & DiClemente, 2002).

Trichomoniasis A form of vaginitis caused by the protozoan *Trichomonas vaginalis.*

Review: Vaginal Infections

Reflect

How can women attempt to prevent vaginal infections?

CriticalThinking

Critical thinkers pay attention to definitions of terms. What does it mean to say that men "have" a vaginal infection?

19. _____ is defined as any kind of vaginal infection or inflammation.

20. Vaginitis can be caused when organisms that reside in the vagina _____.

21. _____ is commonly called a yeast infection.

22. _____ is commonly called "trich."

23. _____ vaginosis is most often caused by overgrowth of *Gardnerella vaginalis.*

24. A common symptom of candidiasis is a white _____.

25. Candidiasis (*May* or *May not?*) be transmitted when women share a washcloth.

26. *Trichomonas vaginalis* is a _____-celled parasite.

Viral Infections

Question: What is a virus? Viruses are tiny particles of DNA surrounded by a protein coating. They are incapable of reproducing on their own. When they invade a body cell, however, they can direct the cell's own reproductive machinery to spin off new viral particles that spread to other cells, causing infection. Our immune systems defeat many viruses, and many others are not lethal. In this chapter we discuss viral STIs, some of which are indeed deadly: HIV/AIDS, herpes, viral hepatitis, genital warts, and molluscum contagiosum.

HIV/AIDS

Question: What is HIV/AIDS? HIV is the acronym for **human immunodeficiency virus**, the virus that causes AIDS. AIDS is the acronym for **acquired immunodeficiency syndrome**. AIDS is considered fatal, although there are currently many people living with HIV/AIDS, thanks to the development of powerful antiviral medications. For people in industrialized nations such as the United States and Canada, Western European nations, and Japan, HIV/AIDS may become a chronic but manageable condition, like diabetes. But for many millions in developing nations, where medications are too expensive or too difficult to deliver, HIV/AIDS may remain a death sentence.

HIV attacks and disables the immune system, the body's natural line of defense, stripping it of its ability to fend off disease-causing organisms. HIV is believed to have originated in Africa in the 1930s as a virus that infected, but was not lethal to, chimpanzees (simian immunodeficiency virus, or SIV). The chimpanzees are believed to have become infected by eating SIV-infected monkeys (Bailes et al., 2003; Paraskeris et al., 2003). A protein in the cells of monkeys makes them immune to HIV (Goff, 2004; Kolata, 2004). SIV mutated into HIV either in the chimp or after it infected humans. However, it stayed in remote Africa until it was spread worldwide by the development of large cities, the global economy, and jet travel (Hillis, 2000).

Prevalence of HIV/AIDS Although Hillis (2000) identifies the "birthdate" of HIV as 1931, AIDS was not described in the medical journals until 50 years later—in 1981. Early in the new millennium, 800,000 to 900,000 Americans are living with HIV/AIDS (CDC, 2003). More than half a million Americans have died from it (CDC, 2003). AIDS has become the fifth leading cause of death among Americans aged 25 to 44 (Feig, 2003). The incidence of HIV/AIDS is increasing most rapidly among women, people of color (see Table 16.2), people who share needles when they inject drugs,

Human immuno-deficiency virus (HIV) A sexually transmitted virus that destroys white blood cells in the immune system, leaving the body vulnerable to life-threatening diseases.

Acquired immuno-deficiency syndrome (AIDS) A condition caused by the human immuno-deficiency virus (HIV) and characterized by destruction of the immune system, which strips the body of its ability to fend off life-threatening diseases.

TABLE 16.2		
AIDS Cases by Race or Ethnicity		
Race or Ethnicity	Number of AIDS Cases	Percentage
European American (not Latino or Latina American)	364,458	41.2%
African American (not Latino or Latina American)	347,491	39.3
Latino and Latina American	163,940	18.6
Asian/Pacific Islander	6,924	0.8
American Indian/Alaska Native	2,875	0.3
Race/Ethnicity Unknown	887	0.1

Source of data: Centers for Disease Control and Prevention (2003). U.S. HIV and AIDS cases reported through December 2002. *HIV/AIDS Surveillance Report.* Year-end edition, Vol. 14, No. 2.

A World of Diversity

Killer of Dreams

KWAMHLANGA, SOUTH AFRICA— One of the great mysteries to me about AIDS in Africa has been this: Why do people not take precautions during sex even when they see friends and relatives dying?

It's easy for Westerners to say that widespread promiscuity is the root of the AIDS problem in Africa, where the virus is transmitted mainly by heterosexual contact. And there's definitely something to that. But the reasons for reckless promiscuity go beyond hormones, and I came to understood them better near this town of KwaMhlanga in the northeastern part of South Africa, in the tin shack where Gertrude Tobela frets about her teenage daughter.

Ms. Tobela, 34, slim and quick to smile—and now to cry—is the first in her family to graduate from elementary school, high school or college.

Two years ago, she was at the top of her world, preparing to graduate from the university, have her second child and join the middle class.

Now she is another African widow, poor, dying and heartbroken because she cannot protect her children from the same fate. She is but one of 30 million Africans with HIV/AIDS (24 will die of it while you're reading this column), but her tale underscores how HIV in Africa is not just a virus but also a self-replicating cycle of AIDS, poverty and hopelessness.

Ms. Tobela's world began to collapse when her husband, Simon, an electrician, was found to have AIDS. Then she tested positive for HIV, apparently after getting it from him. And her newborn son, Victor, turned out to have caught the virus from her.

Her husband died last year, and she is now too sick to hold a job. She survives on $22.50 a month in government child support and spends her time wondering about who should raise Victor after her death.

"I think maybe if I die first, before him, then maybe my mother can take Victor," she says, her voice catching.

Ms. Tobela seems typical of Africa's AIDS victims. In Africa, 58% of HIV carriers are female, and among teenagers with HIV, more than 75% are girls. This is largely because of an explosion in quasi-prostitution between young girls and older men.

"It's not just promiscuity," said Blanche Pitt, director of the South Africa office of the African Medical and Research Foundation. "It's poverty. It's desperation."

and people who engage in unprotected, male–female sex. Here are some facts about HIV/AIDS around the world (CDC, 2003; UNAIDS, 2002):

- As of 2003, 42 million people were estimated to be living with HIV/AIDS (see Figure 16.5). Of these, 38.6 million were adults. 19.2 million were women, and 3.2 million were children under the age of 15.
- In developed nations, where more than half a million people are receiving antiretroviral drugs, 25,000 people died of AIDS in 2002. In Africa, where only 30,000 are receiving these drugs, more than 2 million people died of AIDS.
- An estimated 70 million people will die of HIV/AIDS-related diseases over the next two decades, unless developed nations spend what is necessary to bring antiretroviral drugs to undeveloped nations.
- An estimated 5 million people were infected with HIV in 2002, including 2 million women and 800,000 children under the age of 15.
- During 2002, AIDS killed an estimated 3.1 million people, including 1.2 million women and 610,000 children under the age of 15.
- Women are becoming increasingly affected by HIV. Approximately half, or 19.2 million, of the 38.6 million adults living with HIV/AIDS worldwide are women.

In the United States, AIDS is predominantly found among men who engage in sexual activity with other men (about 59%) or share needles when injecting drugs (24%) (CDC, 2003; see Table 16.3). However, male–female sexual contact is the

As young women become infected, so do their babies. One-fifth of pregnant women in southern Africa have HIV, and worldwide, 800,000 babies a year get HIV from their mothers.

Ms. Tobela managed to talk in a composed way about her death and Victor's. But she broke down when I asked about her 14-year-old daughter, Thabang (she has a different surname, which I'll keep to myself).

"My daughter left me because she wants liberty," Ms. Tobela said, weeping. "She is so sexually active, and she stays in bars and rental rooms."

It began in June, when Thabang began coming home late. Ms. Tobela screamed at her and then beat her, but it did no good. The girl ran off to live with her grandmother but then stayed away for days at a time. After the grandmother beat Thabang as well, she ran away again.

I searched the town for Thabang and finally found her at a relative's house. She is very pretty, with a fondness for makeup, well spoken and smart. I told her that her mom scolded her only because she loved her. Thabang began to cry.

"She doesn't love me," she said fiercely. "If she did, she would talk to me instead of beating me. She wouldn't say these things about me. She would accept my friends." Thabang insisted that while her friends slept with men for cash or gifts, she did not.

Why would girls who have seen what AIDS can do commit suicide by sex?

Part of the answer is that the disease carries a mechanism for perpet-uating itself: It first devastates families financially and emotionally, then leaves adults unable to mind their children, and finally breeds crippling despair. Death, poverty and hopelessness so suffuse Ms. Tobela's tin shack that I can imagine them impelling a mixed-up 14-year-old girl into the arms of older men for a few coins.

When a girl's mother and brother are dying, when a family's middle-class dreams collapse in a ramshackle hut, when there isn't enough money to pay for Victor's visits to the doctor—when a girl's world is shattering in slow motion—she doesn't know what to live for.

And so AIDS insinuates itself into the next generation.

Source: Nicholas D. Kristof (2003, October 4). Killer of dreams. *The New York Times.*

---

fastest-growing exposure category in the United States. Among women, male–female sexual contact now accounts for more than half of cases (CDC, 2003; see Table 16.3).

The Immune System and HIV/AIDS AIDS is caused by a virus that attacks the body's **immune system**—the body's natural line of defense against disease-causing organisms. The immune system combats disease in several ways. It produces white blood

> **Immune system** A term for the body's complex of mechanisms for protecting itself from disease-causing agents such as pathogens.

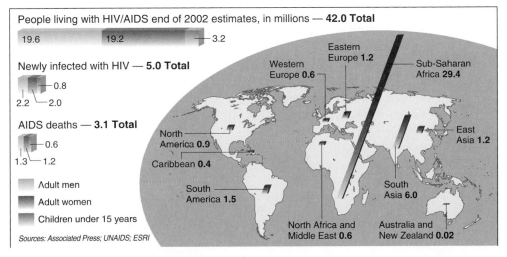

Figure 16.5. HIV/AIDS around the World. Sub-Saharan African has been hardest hit by the HIV/AIDS epidemic, but the epidemic has found its way around the world.

TABLE 16.3			
Number of Adolescents and Adults with AIDS by Exposure Category			
Exposure Category	Male	Female	Total
Men who have sex with men	420,790	–	420,790
Injecting drug use	172,351	67,917	240,268
Men who have sex with men and inject drugs	59,719	–	59,719
Heterosexual contact	50,793	84,835	135,628
Other	14,350	6,519	20,869
Totals	718,003	159,721	877,274

Source of data: Centers for Disease Control and Prevention (2003). U.S. HIV and AIDS cases reported through December 2002. *HIV/AIDS Surveillance Report.* Year-end edition, Vol. 14, No. 2.

Truth?Fiction?
Revisited

It is true that as you read this page, you are engaged in search-and-destroy missions against foreign agents within your body. The white cells in your immune system continuously seek and destroy foreign pathogens within your body.

Pathogen An agent, especially a microorganism, that can cause a disease. (From the Greek *pathos,* meaning "suffering" or "disease," and *genic,* meaning "forming" or "coming into being.")

Leukocytes White blood cells that are essential to the body's defenses against infection. (From the Greek *leukos,* meaning "white" and *kytos,* meaning "a hollow" and used in combination with other word forms to mean *cell.*)

cells that envelop and kill **pathogens** such as bacteria, viruses, and funguses; worn out body cells; and cancer cells. White blood cells are called **leukocytes.** Leukocytes engage in microscopic search-and-destroy missions. They identify and eradicate foreign agents and debilitated cells.

Leukocytes recognize foreign agents by their surface fragments. The surface fragments are termed **antigens** because the body reacts to their presence by developing specialized proteins, or antibodies. Antibodies attach themselves to the foreign bodies, inactivate them, and mark them for destruction. (Infection by HIV may be determined by examining the blood, saliva, or urine for the presence of antibodies.)

Rather than marking pathogens for destruction or war against them, special "memory lymphocytes" are held in reserve. Memory lymphocytes can remain in the bloodstream for years, and they form the basis for a quick immune response to an invader the second time around.[1]

Another function of the immune system is to promote **inflammation.** When you suffer an injury, blood vessels in the region initially contract to check bleeding. Then they dilate. Dilation expands blood flow to the injured region, causing the redness and warmth that characterize inflammation. The elevated blood supply also brings in an army of leukocytes to combat invading microscopic life forms, such as bacteria, that might otherwise use the local injury to establish a beachhead for their assault on the body.

Effects of HIV on the Immune System Spikes (technically known as "gpl20" spikes) on the surface of HIV allow it to bind to sites on cells in the immune system. Like other viruses, HIV uses the cells it invades to spin off copies of itself. HIV uses the enzyme *reverse transcriptase* to cause the genes in the cells it attacks to make proteins that the virus needs in order to reproduce.

HIV attacks the immune system by destroying a type of lymphocyte called the CD4 cell (see Figure 16.6).[2] The CD4 cell is the "quarterback" of the immune system. CD4 cells "recognize" invading pathogens and signal B-lymphocytes or B-cells—

---

1. Vaccination is the placement of a weakened form of an antigen in the body, which activates the creation of antibodies and memory lymphocytes. Smallpox has been annihilated by vaccination, and researchers are trying to develop a vaccine against the virus that causes HIV/AIDS.

2. CD4 cells are also known as T4 cells or helper T-cells.

another kind of white blood cell—to produce antibodies that inactivate pathogens and mark them for annihilation. CD4 cells also signal another class of T-cells, called killer T-cells, to destroy infected cells. By attacking and destroying helper T-cells, HIV disables the very cells on which the body relies to fend off diseases. As HIV cripples the body's defenses, the individual develops infections that would not otherwise take hold. Cancer cells might also proliferate. Although the CD4 cells appear to be its main target, HIV also attacks other types of white blood cells.

> **Truth?Fiction?**
> *Revisited*
>
> It is true that most people who are infected by HIV remain symptom-free for years.

The blood normally contains about 1,000 CD4 cells per cubic millimeter. The numbers of CD4 cells may remain at about this level for years following HIV infection. Many people show no symptoms and appear healthy while CD4 cells remain at this level. Then, for reasons that are not clearly understood, the levels of CD4 cells begin to drop off, although symptoms may not appear for a decade or more. As the numbers of CD4 cells decline, symptoms generally increase, and people fall prey to diseases that their weakened immune systems are unable to fight off. People become most vulnerable to opportunistic infections when the level of CD4 cells falls below 200 per cubic millimeter.

Progression of HIV/AIDS HIV follows a complex course once it enters the body. Shortly following infection, the person may experience mild flulike symptoms—fatigue, fever, headaches, muscle pain, lack of appetite, nausea, swollen glands, and possibly a rash. Such symptoms usually disappear within a few weeks, and people may dismiss them as a case of flu. People who enter this symptom-free or carrier state generally look and act well and do not realize that they are carrying an infectious virus. Thus, they can unwittingly pass the virus on to others.

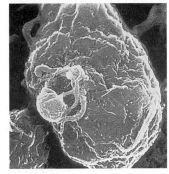

Figure 16.6 HIV (the AIDS Virus) Attacks a White Blood Cell. *HIV progressively weakens the immune system, leaving the body vulnerable to infections and diseases that would otherwise be fended off.*

Most people who are infected with HIV remain symptom-free for years. Others enter a symptomatic state (previously labeled *AIDS-related complex,* or ARC) that is typically characterized by symptoms such as chronically swollen lymph nodes and intermittent weight loss, fever, fatigue, and diarrhea. This symptomatic state does not constitute full-blown AIDS, but it shows that HIV is undermining the integrity of the immune system.

Even during the years when HIV appears to be dormant, billions of viral particles are being spun off. In a seesaw battle, the great majority of them are wiped out by the immune system. Eventually, in nearly all cases, the balance tips in favor of HIV. Then the virus's numbers swell. Perhaps a decade or more after the person is infected with HIV, the virus begins to overtake the immune system. It obliterates the cells that house it and spreads to other cells of the immune system. About half of people with HIV develop AIDS within 10 years of initial infection. For this reason, people who know that they are infected with HIV may feel that they are carrying time bombs within them.

AIDS is called a *syndrome* because it is characterized by a variety of different symptoms. The beginnings of full-blown cases of AIDS are often marked by such symptoms as swollen lymph nodes, fatigue, fever, night sweats, diarrhea, and weight loss (a "wasting syndrome") that cannot be attributed to dieting or exercise. AIDS is connected with the appearance of diseases such as Pneumocystis carinii pneumonia (PCP), Kaposi's sarcoma (a form of cancer), toxoplasmosis of the brain (an infection of parasites), or *herpes simplex* with chronic ulcers. These are termed **opportunistic diseases** because they are not likely to emerge unless a weakened immune system gives them the opportunity.

About 10% of people with AIDS have the wasting syndrome. Wasting is the unintentional loss of more than 10% of a person's body weight and is connected with

Antigen A protein, toxin, or other substance to which the body reacts by producing antibodies. (Combined word formed from *anti*body *gen*erator.)

Inflammation Redness and warmth that develop at the site of an injury, reflecting the dilation of blood vessels that permits the expanded flow of leukocytes to the region.

Opportunistic diseases Diseases that take hold only when the immune system is weakened and unable to fend them off. Kaposi's sarcoma and Pneumocystis carinii pneumonia (PCP) are examples of opportunistic diseases found in people with AIDS.

Could This Couple Be Transmitting HIV? *HIV is a blood-borne virus that is transmitted via various bodily fluids, including blood, semen, and vaginal fluids. However, the Centers for Disease Control and Prevention (CDC) have not found that HIV occurs in infectious quantities in saliva.*

HIV/AIDS, some other infections, and cancer. It appears that people with HIV/AIDS who waste away do so because they take in less energy, not because they burn more calories.

As HIV/AIDS progresses, the individual grows thinner and more fatigued. He or she becomes unable to perform ordinary life functions and falls prey to opportunistic infections. If left untreated, AIDS almost always results in death within a few years.

Transmission HIV can be transmitted by certain contaminated bodily fluids—blood, semen, vaginal secretions, and breast milk. The first three of these may enter the body through vaginal, anal, or oral–genital intercourse with an infected partner. An African study that followed seropositive mothers and their babies for 2 years found that the probability of transmission of HIV via breast milk was about 16.2% (1 in 6) (Nduati et al., 2000). Other avenues of infection include sharing a hypodermic needle with an infected person (as do many people who inject drugs), transfusion with contaminated blood, transplants of organs and tissues that have been infected with HIV, artificial insemination with infected semen, or being stuck by a needle used previously on an infected person. HIV may enter the body through tiny cuts or sores in the mucous lining of the vagina, the rectum, and even the mouth. These cuts or sores can be so tiny that the individuals are not aware of them.

Transmission of HIV through kissing, even prolonged kissing or "French" kissing, is considered unlikely. When a person injects drugs, a small amount of his or her blood remains inside the needle and syringe. If the person is infected with HIV, the virus may be found in the blood remaining in the needle or syringe. Others who use the needle inject the infected blood into their bloodstream. HIV can also be spread by sharing needles used for other purposes, such as injecting steroids, ear piercing, and tattooing.

HIV can also be transmitted from mother to fetus during pregnancy or from mother to child through childbirth or breast-feeding (Mofenson, 2000; Wood et al., 2000). Transmission is most likely during childbirth.

Male-to-female transmission through vaginal intercourse is about twice as likely as female-to-male transmission (CDC, 2003; see Table 16.2), partly because more of the virus is found in the ejaculate than in vaginal secretions. A man's ejaculate may also remain for many days in the vagina, providing greater opportunity for infection to occur. Male–female or male–male anal intercourse is especially risky because it often tears or abrades rectal tissue, facilitating entry of the virus into the bloodstream (Caceres & van-Griensven, 1994).

Male–female transmission via sexual intercourse is the primary route of HIV infection in Africa, Latin America, and Asia. Worldwide, male–female sexual intercourse accounts for the majority of cases of HIV/AIDS (UNAIDS, 2002). In the United States, many cases of male–female transmission occur among people who inject drugs and their sex partners.

In the early years of the AIDS epidemic, HIV spread rapidly among hemophiliacs who had unknowingly been transfused with contaminated blood. But blood supplies are now routinely screened for HIV. Medical authorities now consider the risk of HIV transmission through transfusion of screened blood to be negligible if not entirely absent (Klein, 2000).

HIV may be spread by donor semen, such as that used in artificial insemination. Cases have also been reported of women who have become infected with hepatitis B, gonorrhea, trichomoniasis ("trich"), and chlamydia by donor semen.

Factors Affecting the Risk of Sexual Transmission Some people seem more likely to communicate HIV, and others seem to be especially vulnerable to HIV infection. Why, for instance, are some people infected by one sexual contact with an infected partner, whereas others are not infected during months or years of unprotected sex? Several factors appear to affect the risk of HIV infection and the development of AIDS:

- The probability of sexual transmission rises with the number of sexual contacts with an infected partner.
- The probability of transmission is affected by the type of sexual activity. Anal intercourse, for example, provides a convenient port of entry for HIV because it often tears or abrades the rectal lining.
- The amount of virus in semen also affects the probability of infection. The quantity of HIV in the semen peaks shortly after initial infection and when full-blown AIDS develops.
- STIs such as genital warts, gonorrhea, trichomoniasis, and chlamydia inflame the genital region, which heightens the risk of sexual transmission of other STIs. STIs that produce genital ulcers, such as syphilis and genital herpes, may heighten vulnerability to HIV infection by allowing the virus to enter the circulatory system through the ulcers.
- Circumcision lowers the risk of infection, in part because circumcised men are less likely to have genital ulcers (Auvert et al., 2001; Hirozawa, 2001). Moreover, HIV cannot accumulate under the folds of the foreskin in men who have been circumcised. Cells in the foreskin may be particularly vulnerable to HIV infection (Cohen, 2000). A study conducted in India found that seven times as many uncircumcised men as circumcised men were infected with HIV. (Reynolds et al., 2004).
- Genetic factors may also be at work. About 1% of people of Western European descent have inherited from both parents a gene that prevents HIV from entering cells in the immune system and, as a consequence, are apparently immune to HIV infection. Perhaps 20% of individuals of Western European descent have inherited the gene from one parent; HIV disease appears to progress more slowly in these people. Some prostitutes in Thailand and Africa, where HIV infection has been running rampant, also appear to be immune to HIV infection (Royce et al., 1997).

How HIV Is Not Transmitted There is much misinformation about the transmission of HIV. Let us consider some of the ways in which HIV is *not* transmitted:

1. *HIV is not transmitted from donating blood.* AIDS cannot be contracted by donating blood because needles are discarded after a single use. Unfortunately, many people have avoided donating blood because of unfounded fears of HIV transmission.

2. *HIV is not transmitted through casual, everyday contact.* There is no evidence of transmission of HIV through hugging someone, shaking hands, bumping into strangers on buses and trains; handling money, doorknobs, or other objects that have been touched by infected people; sharing drinking fountains, public telephones, public toilets, or swimming pools; or trying on clothing that has been worn by an infected person. Nor is HIV known to be transmitted by contact with urine, feces, sputum, sweat, tears, or nasal secretions, unless blood is clearly visible in these fluids. (Still, should you need to clean up someone's urine, feces, nasal secretions, and especially blood, it would be wise to use rubber gloves and wash your hands thoroughly immediately afterwards.)

3. *HIV is not transmitted by insect bites.* HIV is not transmitted by mosquito bites or bites by other insects such as bedbugs, lice, or flies). Nor can you get HIV from contact with animals.

4. *HIV is not transmitted by airborne germs or contact with contaminated food.* People do not contract HIV from contact with airborne germs, as by sneezing or

Seropositive Having a pathogen or antibodies to that pathogen in the bloodstream.

Seronegative Lacking a pathogen or antibodies to that pathogen in the bloodstream.

coughing, or by contact with contaminated food or eating food prepared by a person infected with HIV.

5. *HIV is not transmitted through sharing work or home environments.* HIV has not been shown to be transmitted from infected people to family members or others they live with through any form of casual contact, such as hugging or touching, or through sharing bathrooms, food, or eating utensils, as long as there is no exchange of blood or genital secretions. No cases of HIV transmission have been documented to arise from nonsexual contact in schools or in the workplace.

Diagnosis of HIV Infection and AIDS The enzyme-linked immunosorbent assay (ELISA for short) is one widely used test for HIV. ELISA takes a number of days to yield results and does not directly detect HIV. Instead, it reveals HIV antibodies. Rapid tests such as OraQuick indicate the presence of HIV antibodies within 20 minutes. People may show an antibody response to HIV long before they develop symptoms of infection. A positive (**seropositive**) test result means that antibodies were found and usually[3] indicates that the person is infected with HIV. A negative (**seronegative**) outcome means that antibodies to HIV were not detected.

ELISA can be performed on samples of blood, saliva, or urine. OraQuick is based on a blood sample obtained by pricking the finger with a needle. The saliva test OraSure, provides results within 20 minutes and has been shown to be 99% accurate (McNeil, 2004). Although HIV antibodies can be detected in saliva, HIV itself is not found in measurable quantities. This is why kissing is not considered an avenue of transmission of HIV. Saliva is absorbed by a cotton pad on a stick that is placed between the lower gum and the cheek. The saliva undergoes analysis in a laboratory. When people show evidence of the presence of HIV antibodies, the presence of the virus itself can be confirmed by more expensive tests, such as the Western blot test or the PCR (polymerase chain reaction) test.

Treatment of HIV/AIDS For many years, researchers were frustrated by failure in the effort to develop effective vaccines and treatments for HIV/AIDS. There is still no safe, effective vaccine, but recent developments in drug therapy have raised hopes in the area of treatment.

Potential HIV/AIDS vaccines are being tested on people and animals (Barouch et al., 2000; Nabel & Sullivan, 2000). Several vaccines have proved effective in animal trials but not in humans (Barouch et al., 2000; Ho, 1995). The ideal vaccine against AIDS would be safe, be inexpensive, and confer lifetime protection against all strains of the disease.

Today many drugs are used to combat HIV/AIDS. They offer a good deal of hope to people with HIV/AIDS, including pregnant women who are infected with HIV.

Zidovudine (previously referred to as AZT) has been the most widely used HIV/AIDS drug. Zidovudine is one of a number of so-called nucleoside analogues that inhibit replication (reproduction) of HIV by targeting the enzyme called reverse transcriptase. Other nucleoside analogues include ddI, ddC, d4T, and 3TC. Zidovudine in many cases delays the progression of the infection and increases the blood count of CD4 cells. HIV-infected pregnant women who use zidovudine reduce the rate of HIV infection in their newborns by two-thirds (Connor et al., 1994). Zidovudine helps prevent transmission during childbirth by reducing the amount of the virus in the mother's bloodstream. Only 8% of the babies born to the zidovudine-treated women became infected with HIV, compared to 25% of babies

---

3. But not always! Fetuses, for example, may receive antibodies from infected mothers, but not the virus itself. Some fetuses, however, do become infected with the virus.

whose mothers were untreated. Zidovudine is generally used for 26 weeks prior to childbirth. However, using zidovudine for even the final few weeks cuts the transmission rate of HIV from mother to child by half (Meyer, 1998). Thus, it can be effective even when the mother has not sought prenatal treatment early in her pregnancy. Because zidovudine is expensive, briefer treatment may be of most help in developing nations.

The results of the European Mode of Delivery Collaboration Trial on the efficacy of elective C-section versus vaginal delivery show that C-section further decreases the risk of maternal transmission of HIV to the baby (Ricci et al., 2000). The study enlisted about 400 seropositive mothers. All mothers received zidovudine during pregnancy. Half of the mothers were assigned at random to deliver vaginally, and half by C-section. The HIV infection rate was 10.6% for babies delivered vaginally (similar to the 8% reported by Meyer, 1998) and 1.7% for babies delivered by C-section. Thus, the combination of zidovudine during pregnancy and C-section cuts the chance that a seropositive mother will transmit HIV to her baby to about 1 in 50.

Other drugs that block the replication of HIV include *protease inhibitors.* Protease inhibitors block reproduction of HIV by targeting the protease enzyme. A combination or "cocktail" of antiviral drugs including zidovudine, another nucleoside analogue, and a protease inhibitor has become the standard treatment for HIV/AIDS (Gallant, 2000). This combination—referred to as **HAART** (for "highly active antiretroviral therapy")—decreases the likelihood that HIV will develop resistance to treatment. It has reduced HIV below detectable levels in many infected people (Lederman & Valdez, 2000). It has created hope that AIDS will become increasingly manageable, a chronic health problem as opposed to a terminal illness. However, HAART is expensive, and many people who could benefit from it cannot afford it. The side effects of these medicines can be unpleasant. They include nausea and, in the case of protease inhibitors, unusual accumulations of fat, such as "buffalo humps" in the neck.

HAART has worked wonders to date (Lederman & Valdez, 2000). It has cut the U.S. death rate from HIV/AIDS-related causes by about 75% since the mid- to late 1990s (CDC, 2003). Yet even when HIV has been reduced to "undetectable levels" by ordinary means, scientists have been able to use methods of close scrutiny to locate it in "resting" (nonreplicating) CD4 cells (Lederman & Valdez, 2000). Therefore, HAART is not a cure. In fact, HAART-resistant strains of HIV may evolve as HAART

HAART (pronounced *HEART*) The acronym for "highly active antiretroviral therapy," which refers to the combination, or "cocktail," of drugs used to treat HIV/AIDS.

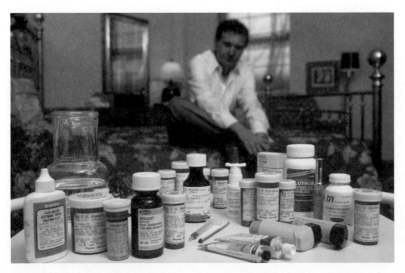

HAART HAART *is the acronym for "highly active antiretroviral therapy." It refers to a combination, or "cocktail," of antiviral drugs—including zidovudine, another nucleoside analogue, and a protease inhibitor— that has become the standard treatment for HIV/AIDS. The combination of drugs decreases the likelihood that HIV will develop resistance to drug therapy. HAART has reduced blood levels of HIV to below-detectable levels in many infected individuals. However, it is expensive, there are side effects, and it does not work for everyone.*

is being used. For this and other reasons, many HIV-infected people go on helpful drug "vacations" after using HAART for a number of months or years. Promising results are also reported in treating the opportunistic infections (such as PCP and fungal infections) that take hold in people with weakened immune systems.

Newer drugs are also being developed. Fusion inhibitors, for example, attack HIV during yet another phase in its reproductive cycle. Research suggests that fusion inhibitors, although expensive, will be useful against mutations of HIV that resist the HAART "cocktail" (Lalezari et al., 2003; Tashima & Carpenter, 2003).

Despite the advent of HAART and the ongoing development of newer drugs, nearly 10,000 people in the United States still die of AIDS each year (CDC, 2003). The Centers for Disease Control and Prevention (CDC, 2003) attributes these deaths to lack of early testing and treatment for some people, to failure of some people with HIV/AIDS to follow HAART treatment regimens, and, in some cases, to treatment failure. People who assume that HIV/AIDS is no longer a deadly syndrome need to recognize that HAART does not help everyone with HIV/AIDS and that newer drugs, such as fusion inhibitors, are not a guarantee of successful treatment. Ironically, however, the advent of HAART has increased the frequency of risky sexual behavior by some people (Dilley et al., 2003).

Unfortunately, the advances in treatment in the United States do not extend to everyone in the world—and not even to everyone in the United States. Among women in the United States today, the risks of HIV/AIDS fall most heavily on poor women, mostly African American and Latina American women, who live in urban areas. African American and Latina American women account for nearly three-quarters of women with AIDS in the United States, although they make up only about one-quarter of the female population (CDC, 2003; see Table 16.3).

Prevention What can we do to curb the spread of HIV/AIDS? Given the lack of a vaccine or cure, prevention is our best hope. Our discussion of prevention will focus on sexual transmission, but other efforts have been made to prevent transmission of HIV from mother to child, through injection of drugs, and through blood transfusions. For example, HIV-infected women are advised to avoid breast-feeding. Zidovudine given to the mother, and other measures, such as C-section, decrease the probability of transmission through childbirth (Ricci et al., 2000). Zidovudine and other drugs given to newborn babies further lessen their risk of being infected with HIV during childbirth (Taha et al., 2003). The screening of potential blood donors and sperm donors has reduced the probability of transmission via blood transfusion and artificial insemination. We have been less successful in reducing the risk of infection through unsafe sexual contact.

Most prevention efforts focus on education. Sexually active people have been advised to alter their sexual behavior by practicing abstinence, by limiting their sexual experiences to a lifelong monogamous relationship, or by practicing "safe sex"—which, as we shall see, could more accurately be dubbed "safer sex."

For the latest information on HIV/AIDS, call the government AIDS hotline: 1-800-342-AIDS. The call is free and anonymous. We expand our discussion of prevention of HIV/AIDS in the section entitled "Prevention of STIs: It's More than Safer Sex."

Genital Herpes

Question: What is genital herpes? Genital herpes is an STI caused by the *herpes simplex* virus. The hysteria that surrounded the rapid spread of genital herpes in the 1970s and 1980s died down in the wake of the AIDS epidemic. Nevertheless, there

are 200,000 to 500,000 new cases of genital herpes each year. The Centers for Disease Control and Prevention (CDC, 2001b) estimate that as many as 45 million Americans aged 12 and older may be infected with genital herpes.

Once you get herpes, it's yours for life. After the initial attack, it remains an unwelcome guest in your body. It finds a cozy place to lie low until it stirs up trouble again. It causes recurrent outbreaks that often happen at the worst times, such as around final exams. This is because stress can depress the functioning of the immune system and boost the likelihood of outbreaks.

You can also pass the infection along to sex partners for the rest of your life. Flare-ups may continue to recur, sometimes with annoying frequency. On the other hand, some people have no recurrences. Still others have mild, brief recurrences that become less frequent over time.

Different types of herpes are caused by variants of the *Herpes simplex* virus. The most common type, **herpes simplex virus type 1** (HSV-1 virus) causes oral herpes. Oral herpes is characterized by cold sores or fever blisters on the lips or mouth. It can also be transferred to the genitals by the hands or by oral–genital contact (CDC, 2001b). **Genital herpes** is caused by a related but distinct virus, the **herpes simplex virus type 2** (HSV-2). This virus produces painful shallow sores and blisters on the genitals. HSV-2 can also be transferred to the mouth through oral–genital contact. Both types of herpes can be transmitted sexually.

Transmission Herpes can be transmitted through oral, anal, or vaginal sexual activity with an infected person (CDC, 2001b). The herpes viruses can also survive for several hours on toilet seats or other objects, where they can be picked up by direct contact. Oral herpes is easily contracted by drinking from the same cup as an infected person, by kissing, even by sharing towels. But genital herpes is usually spread by coitus or by oral or anal sex.

One problem is that many people do not realize that they are infected. They can thus unknowingly transmit the virus through sexual contact. And many of the people who know they are infected don't realize that they can pass along the virus even when they have no noticeable outbreak (CDC, 2001b). Although genital herpes is most contagious during active flare-ups, it can also be transmitted when an infected partner has no symptoms (genital sores or feelings of burning or itching in the genitals). Any intimate contact with an infected person carries some risk of transmission of the virus, even if the infected person never has another outbreak. People may also be infected with the virus and have no outbreaks, yet pass the virus along to others.

Herpes can be spread from one part of the body to another by touching the infected area and then touching another body part. One potentially serious result is a herpes infection of the eye: **ocular herpes**. Thorough washing with soap and water after touching an infected area may reduce the risk of spreading the infection to other parts of the body. Still, it is best to avoid touching the infected area altogether, especially if there are active sores.

Women with genital herpes are more likely than the general population to have miscarriages. Passage through the birth canal of an infected mother can infect babies with genital herpes, damaging or killing them. Obstetricians thus often perform cesarean sections if the mother has active lesions or **prodromal symptoms** at the time of delivery. Herpes can also place women at greater risk of genital cancers, such as cervical cancer. (All women, not just women with herpes, are advised to have regular pelvic examinations, including Pap tests for early detection of cervical cancer.)

herpes simplex **virus type 1** The virus that causes oral herpes, which is characterized by cold sores or fever blisters on the lips or mouth. Abbreviated HSV-1.

Genital herpes An STI caused by the *Herpes simplex* virus type 2 and characterized by painful shallow sores and blisters on the genitals.

herpes simplex **virus type 2** The virus that causes genital herpes. Abbreviated HSV-2.

Ocular herpes A herpes infection of the eye, usually caused by touching an infected area of the body and then touching the eye.

Prodromal symptoms Warning symptoms that signal the onset or flare-up of a disease. (From the Greek *prodromos,* meaning "forerunner.")

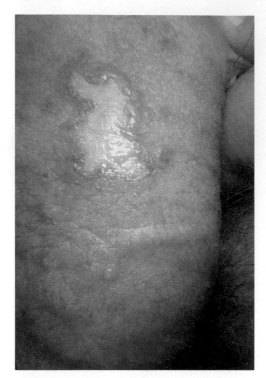

Figure 16.7. Herpes Lesion on the Male Genitals. Herpes lesions or sores can appear on the genitals in both men and women. In contrast to the syphilis chancre, they can be quite painful. Herpes is most likely to be transmitted during outbreaks of the disease (when the sores are present, that is), but it can be transmitted at other times as well. Stress increases the likelihood of outbreaks. Antiviral drugs tend to decrease the frequency, duration, and discomfort of outbreaks.

Symptoms Genital lesions or sores appear about 6 to 8 days after infection with genital herpes. At first they appear as reddish, painful bumps, or papules, along the penis or the vulva (see Figure 16.7). They may also appear on the thighs or buttocks, in the vagina, or on the cervix. These papules turn into groups of small blisters that are filled with fluid containing infectious viral particles. The blisters are attacked by the body's immune system (white blood cells). They fill with pus, burst, and become extremely painful, shallow sores or ulcers that are surrounded by a red ring. People are especially infectious during such outbreaks, because the ulcers shed millions of viral particles. Other symptoms may include headaches and muscle aches, swollen lymph glands, fever, burning urination, and a vaginal discharge. The blisters crust over and heal in 1 to 3 weeks. Internal sores in the vagina or on the cervix may take 10 days longer than external (labial) sores to heal. Physicians thus advise infected women to avoid unprotected intercourse for at least 10 days following the healing of external sores.

Although the symptoms disappear, the disease does not. The virus remains in the body, burrowing into nerve cells in the base of the spine, where it may lie dormant for years or a lifetime. The infected person is least contagious during this dormant stage. For reasons that remain unclear, in most cases the virus becomes reactivated and gives rise to recurrences. Recurrences may be related to factors such as infections (as in a cold), stress, fatigue, depression, exposure to the sun, and hormonal changes, such as those that occur during pregnancy or menstruation. Recurrences tend to occur within 3 to 12 months of the initial episode and to affect the same part of the body.

Symptoms of oral herpes include sores or blisters on the lips, the inside of the mouth, the tongue, or the throat. Fever and feelings of sickness may occur. The gums may swell and redden. The sores heal over in about 2 weeks, and the virus retreats into nerve cells at the base of the neck, where it lies dormant between flare-ups.

Diagnosis and Treatment Genital herpes is first diagnosed by clinical inspection of herpetic sores or ulcers in the mouth or on the genitals. A sample of fluid may be taken from the base of a genital sore and cultured in the laboratory to detect the growth of the virus.

There is encouraging news about the development of a vaccine, called Simplirix, against genital herpes (Laino, 2000). In pilot studies, the vaccine is reported to have prevented herpes outbreaks in more than 70% of women who had not previously had cold sores or genital herpes. The herpes virus that causes cold sores ironically confers some protection against genital herpes, and the vaccine does not help women who have already contracted genital herpes. It remains unclear why the vaccine has been ineffective with men.

Viruses, unlike the bacteria that cause gonorrhea or syphilis, do not respond to antibiotics. Antiviral drugs such as acyclovir (brand name: Zovirax), famciclovir, and valacyclovir can relieve pain, speed healing, and reduce the duration of viral shedding (Hatcher, 2001). Acyclovir can be applied directly to the sores in ointment form, but it must be taken orally, in pill form, to help combat internal lesions in the vagina or on the cervix. Oral administration of antiviral drugs may reduce the severity of the initial episode and, if taken regularly, the frequency and duration of recurrent outbreaks (Hatcher, 2001). On the other hand, users may develop tolerance for these drugs, meaning that larger doses must be used to maintain effectiveness (Drew, 2000).

Warm baths, loosely fitting clothing, aspirin, and cold, wet compresses may relieve pain during flare-ups. People with herpes are advised to maintain regular sleeping habits and to learn to manage stress.

Coping with Genital Herpes The psychological problems connected with herpes can be more distressing than the physical effects of the illness. The prospect of a lifetime of recurrences and concerns about infecting one's sex partners exacerbate the emotional impact of herpes. People with herpes often feel angry, especially toward those who transmitted the disease to them. They may feel anxious about making a long-term commitment or bearing children:

> After the first big episode of herpes, I felt distant from my body. When we began lovemaking again, I had a hard time having orgasms or trusting the rhythm of my responses. I shed some tears over that. I felt my body had been invaded. My body feels riddled with it; I'm somehow contaminated. And there is always that lingering anxiety: is my baby okay? It's unjust that the birth of my child may be affected. (Boston Women's Health Book Collective, 1992)

Most people with herpes learn to cope. Some are helped by support groups that share ways of living with the disease. A caring and trusting partner is important. Joanne, a 26-year-old securities analyst, kept her herpes a secret from Jonathan during the first month they were dating. But when they approached the point of becoming sexually intimate, she felt obligated to tell him that she carried the virus:

> "I feared that telling him would scare him off. After all, who wants to have a relationship with someone who can give them herpes? After the first few dates I felt that this was the person I could spend the rest of my life with. I knew he also felt the same way. I had to tell him before things became too intense between us. Believe me, it wasn't easy blurting it out. He wasn't shocked or anything, although he did ask me all kinds of questions about it. I remember telling him that I got recurrences about once a year or so for about a week at a time. I told him that there was always the potential that I could infect him but that we would play it safe and avoid having sex whenever I had an outbreak. I also told him that even at other times I couldn't guarantee that it would be perfectly safe. He said at first that he needed some time to think about it. But later, that very night in fact, he called to tell me that he didn't want this to come between us and that we should try to make our relationship work."
>
> Joanne and Jonathan were married about six months later. A year after that their daughter Andrea was born. Jonathan remains uninfected. Joanne's occasional outbreaks are treated with acyclovir ointment and pass within a week or so. (The Authors' Files)

The attitudes of people with herpes also play a role in their adjusting. People who view herpes as a manageable illness or problem, not as a medical disaster or character deficit, seem to find it easier to cope.

Viral Hepatitis

Question: What is viral hepatitis? Viral hepatitis refers to various types of liver infections (**hepatitis** is an inflammation of the liver) that are caused by viruses. The major types are *hepatitis A* (formerly called infectious hepatitis), *hepatitis B* (for-

Hepatitis An inflammation of the liver. (From the Greek *hepar,* meaning "liver.")

merly called serum hepatitis), *hepatitis C* (formerly called hepatitis non-A, non-B), and *hepatitis D.*

Most people with hepatitis have no symptoms. When symptoms do appear, they often include **jaundice**, feelings of weakness and nausea, loss of appetite, abdominal discomfort, whitish bowel movements, and brownish or tea-colored urine. The symptoms of hepatitis B tend to be more severe and long-lasting than those of hepatitis A or C. In about 10% of cases, hepatitis B can lead to chronic liver disease. Hepatitis C tends to have milder symptoms but often leads to chronic liver disease such as cirrhosis or cancer of the liver. Hepatitis D—also called *delta hepatitis* or type D hepatitis—occurs only in the presence of hepatitis B. Hepatitis D, which has symptoms similar to those of hepatitis B, can produce severe liver damage and often leads to death.

The hepatitis A virus is transmitted through contact with infected fecal matter found in contaminated food or water and by oral contact with fecal matter, as through oral–anal sexual activity (licking or mouthing the partner's anus). (It is largely because of the risk of hepatitis A that restaurant employees are required to wash their hands after using the toilet.) Eating raw infested shellfish is also a common means of transmitting hepatitis A.

Hepatitis B can be transmitted sexually through anal, vaginal, or oral intercourse with an infected partner; through transfusion with contaminated blood supplies; by the sharing of contaminated needles or syringes; and by contact with contaminated saliva, menstrual blood, nasal mucus, or semen. The sharing of razors, toothbrushes, or other personal articles with an infected person can transmit hepatitis B. Hepatitis C and hepatitis D can be transmitted sexually or through contact with contaminated blood. A person can transmit the viruses that cause hepatitis even if he or she is unaware of having any symptoms of the disease.

Hepatitis is usually diagnosed by testing blood samples for the presence of hepatitis antigens and antibodies. There is no cure for viral hepatitis. Bed rest and fluids are usually recommended until the acute stage of the infection subsides, generally in a few weeks. Full recovery may take months. A vaccine provides protection against hepatitis B and also against hepatitis D, because, as we have noted, hepatitis D can occur only if hepatitis B is present (Hatcher, 2001).

Genital Warts

Question: What are genital warts? **Genital warts** are an STI that is caused by the *human papilloma virus* (HPV). HPV is the world's most common sexually transmitted infectious agent; signs of infection are found in nearly half of the adult women in some countries (Grady, 2002). Half or more of the sexually active college women in the United States are infected with HPV. Although the warts may appear in visible areas of the skin, in most cases they appear in areas that cannot be seen, such as on the cervix in women or in the urethra in men. They occur most commonly among people in the 20- to 24-year-old age range (Grady, 2002). Within a few months following infection, the warts are usually found in the genital and anal regions. Women are more susceptible to HPV infection because cells in the cervix divide swiftly, facilitating the multiplication of HPV. Women who initiate coitus prior to the age of 18 and who have many sex partners are particularly susceptible to infection (Grady, 2002). It is estimated that nearly half of the sexually active teenage women in some American cities are infected with HPV (Grady, 2002).

Genital warts are similar to common plantar warts—itchy bumps that vary in size and shape. Genital warts are hard and yellow-gray when they form on dry skin.

Jaundice A yellowish discoloration of the skin and the whites of the eyes. (From the Old French *jaune,* meaning "yellow.")

Genital warts An STI that is caused by the human papilloma virus and takes the form of warts that appear around the genitals and anus.

They take on pink, soft, cauliflower shapes in moist areas such as the lower vagina (see Figure 16.8). In men they appear on the penis, foreskin, and scrotum and in the urethra. They appear on the vulva, along the vaginal wall, and on the cervix in women. They can also occur outside the genital area—for example, in the mouth; on the lips, eyelids, or nipples; around the anus; or in the rectum.

Genital warts may not produce any symptoms, but those that form on the urethra can cause bleeding or painful discharges. HPV has been implicated in cancers of the genital organs, particularly cervical cancer and penile cancer (Koutsky et al., 2002). Nearly all cases of cervical cancer are linked to HPV (Grady, 2002). Men who have been circumcised are significantly less likely to carry HPV than men who have not been circumcised (Castellsague et al., 2002). All in all, it would seem wise for women to safeguard themselves from HPV-related cervical cancer by limiting the number of their sex partners (to reduce their risk of exposure to HPV), thinking about the extracurricular sexual activities of their mates, and having regular Pap smears.

HPV can be transmitted sexually through skin-to-skin contact during vaginal, anal, or oral sex. It can also be transmitted by other forms of contact, such as touching infected towels or clothing. The incubation period may vary from a few weeks to a couple of years.

Freezing the wart (*cryotherapy*) with liquid nitrogen is a preferred treatment. One alternative treatment involves painting or coating the warts over several days with podofilox solution or gel, imiquimod cream, trichloroacetic acid (TCA), or bichloroacetic acid (BCA) (Hatcher, 2001). An alcohol-based podophyllin solution causes the warts to dry up and fall off. Unfortunately, although the warts themselves may be removed, treatment does not rid the body of the virus (Hatcher, 2001). There may thus be recurrences. Podophyllin is not recommended for use with pregnant women or for treatment of warts that form on the cervix. The warts can also be treated by a doctor with electrodes (burning) or surgery (by laser or surgical removal).

Inspired by the discovery of molecules that inform the immune system that the virus is present, researchers are attempting to develop a vaccine for HPV (Reaney, 1998). For the time being, however, prevention means using latex condoms, which help reduce the risk of contracting HPV (Montano et al., 2001). They do not eliminate the risk entirely, because the virus can be transmitted from areas of the skin not protected by condoms, such as the scrotum. People with active warts should probably avoid sexual contact until the warts are removed and the area heals completely.

Figure 16.8. Genital Warts. Genital warts are caused by the human papilloma virus (HPV) and may have a cauliflowerlike appearance. Many—perhaps most—cases occur where they can go visually undetected. HPV is implicated in cervical cancer, and women should be checked regularly for genital warts and other possibly "silent" STIs.

Molluscum Contagiosum

Question: What is molluscum contagiosum? **Molluscum contagiosum** is an STI that is characterized by painless raised lesions that appear on the genitals, buttocks, thighs, or lower abdomen and are caused by a pox virus. Pinkish in appearance with a waxy or pearly top, the lesions usually appear within 2 or 3 months of infection. Most infected people have between 10 and 20 lesions, although the number of lesions can range from 1 to 100 or more. The lesions are generally not associated with serious complications and often disappear on their own within 6 months. Or they can be treated by squeezing them (like "popping" a blackhead) to exude the whitish center plug. Solutions of podophyllin, trichloroacetic acid (TCA), or silver nitrate are also used. Freezing with liquid nitrogen (*cryotherapy*) can be employed to remove the lesions. However, do not try to treat any lesions on your own. See your doctor.

Molluscum contagiosum An STI is caused by a pox virus that causes painless raised lesions to appear on the genitals, buttocks, thighs, or lower abdomen.

Review: Viral Diseases

Reflect

Do you favor distribution of condoms in the public schools as a means of attempting to prevent the transmission of HIV/AIDS? Do you support the distribution of free hypodermic needles to people who inject drugs? Explain.

CriticalThinking

Do STIs have any bearing on the decision whether to have a male baby circumcised?

27. Viruses are tiny particles of _____.

28. AIDS is caused by the human _____ virus (HIV).

29. HIV disables the body's _____ system.

30. The surface fragments of pathogens are termed _____.

31. HIV destroys a type of lymphocyte called the _____ cell.

32. AIDS is connected with _____ diseases that would not be likely to emerge except for the disabled immune system.

33. HIV can be transmitted by blood, _____, vaginal secretions, or breast milk.

34. Worldwide, (*Male–female* or *Male–male*?) sexual intercourse accounts for most cases of HIV/AIDS.

35. Circumcision (*Raises* or *Lowers*?) the risk of infection by HIV.

36. HAART is the abbreviation for "highly active _____ therapy."

37. Genital herpes is caused by the *Herpes* _____ virus type 2 (HSV-2).

38. HSV-2 produces painful _____ on the genitals.

39. Viruses (*Do* or *Do not*?) respond to antibiotics.

40. _____ is an inflammation of the liver.

41. Hepatitis _____ can be transmitted sexually through anal, vaginal, or oral intercourse.

42. The *human papilloma virus* (HPV) causes genital _____.

43. HPV has been linked to cancers of the cervix and _____.

44. HPV (*Can* or *Cannot*?) be transmitted by touching infected towels or clothing.

Ectoparasitic Infestations

Question: What are ectoparasites? **Ectoparasites**, as distinguished from *endoparasites,* live on the outer surfaces of animals (*ecto* means "outer"). *Trichomonas vaginalis* is an endoparasite (*endo* means "inner"). Ectoparasites are larger than the agents that cause other STIs. In this section we consider two types of STIs caused by ectoparasites: pediculosis and scabies.

Pediculosis

Figure 16.9. Pubic Lice.
Pediculosis is an infestation by pubic lice (Phthirus pubis.) *Pubic lice are commonly called "crabs" because of their appearance under a microscope.*

Question: What is pediculosis? **Pediculosis** is the name given to an infestation of a parasite whose proper Latin name, *Phthirus pubis* (pubic lice), sounds rather too dignified for these bothersome (dare we say ugly?) creatures that are better known as "crabs." Pubic lice are commonly called "crabs" because, under the microscope, they are somewhat similar in appearance to crabs (see Figure 16.9). They belong to a family of insects called biting lice. Another member of the family, the human head louse, is an annoying insect that clings to hair on the scalp and often spreads among schoolchildren.

In the adult stage, pubic lice are large enough to be seen with the naked eye. They are spread sexually but can also be transmitted by contact with an infested towel, sheet, or—yes—toilet seat. They can survive for only about 24 hours without a human host, but they may deposit eggs that can take up to 7 days to hatch in bedding

or towels. Therefore, all bedding, towels, and clothes that have been used by an infested person must be either washed in hot water and dried on the hot cycle, or dry-cleaned to ensure that they are safe. Fingers may also transmit the lice from the genitals to other hair-covered parts of the body, including the scalp and armpits. Sexual contact should be avoided until the infestation is eradicated.

Itching, ranging from the mildly irritating to the intolerable, is the most prominent symptom of a pubic lice infestation. The itching is caused by the "crabs" attaching themselves to the pubic hair and piercing the skin to feed on the blood of their hosts. (Yecch!) The life span of these insects is only about 1 month, but they are prolific egg-layers and may spawn several generations before they die. An infestation can be treated effectively with a prescription medication, a 1% solution of lindane (brand name: Kwell), which is available as a cream, lotion, or shampoo. Nonprescription medications containing pyrethrins or piperonyl butoxide (brand names: RID, Triple X, and others) will also do the job. Kwell is not recommended for use by pregnant or lactating women. A careful reexamination of the body is necessary after several days of treatment to ensure that all lice and eggs were killed.

Scabies

Question: What is scabies? **Scabies** (short for *Sarcoptes scabiei*) is a parasitic infestation caused by a tiny mite that may be transmitted through sexual contact or contact with infested clothing, bed linen, towels, and other fabrics. The mites attach themselves to the base of pubic hair and burrow into the skin, where they lay eggs and subsist for the duration of their 30-day life span. Like pubic lice, scabies are often found in the genital region and cause itching and discomfort. They are also responsible for reddish lines (created by burrowing) and sores, welts, or blisters on the skin. Unlike lice, they are too tiny to be seen by the naked eye. Diagnosis is made by detecting the mite or its by-products on microscopic examination of scrapings from suspicious-looking areas of skin. Scabies are most often found on the hands and wrists, but they may also appear on the genitals, buttocks, armpits, and feet. They do not appear above the neck—thankfully!

Ectoparasites Parasites that live on the outside of the host's body—in contrast to *endo*parasites, which live within the body. (From the Greek *ektos,* meaning "outside.")

Pediculosis A parasitic infestation by pubic lice (*Phthirus pubis*) that causes itching.

Scabies A parasitic infestation caused by a tiny mite (*Sarcoptes scabiei*) that causes itching.

Review: Ectoparasitic Infestations

Reflect

If pubic lice can be transmitted by contact with an infested toilet seat, why is it referred to as a sexually transmitted infection?

CriticalThinking

Do you believe that it is a good idea that medications for ectoparasites are available without prescription? Discuss the pros and cons.

45. Ectoparasites live on the (*Inner* or *Outer?*) surfaces of animals.

46. Pubic _____ are commonly referred to as crabs.

47. Pubic lice (*Can* or *Cannot?*) be transmitted by contact with an infested toilet seat.

48. _____ is the abbreviation of *Sarcoptes scabiei.*

Scabies, like pubic lice, may be treated effectively with 1% lindane (Kwell). The entire body from the neck down must be coated with a thin layer of the medication, which should not be washed off for 8 hours. But lindane should not be used by women who are pregnant or lactating. To avoid reinfection, sex partners and others in close bodily contact with infected individuals should also be treated. Clothing and bed linen that the infected person has used must be washed and dried on the hot cycle or dry-cleaned. As with "crabs," sexual contact should be avoided until the infestation is eliminated.

Prevention of STIs: More than Safer Sex

Prevention is the best way to control the spread of STIs, especially those for which there is no cure or vaccine. Prevention of even one case of an STI can prevent its spread to others—perhaps eventually to you.

Question: How can we prevent STIs? There are many things that individuals can do to lower the risk of contracting STIs. As you will see, safer sex is only one aspect of prevention.

Abstinence or Monogamy

> I don't even masturbate anymore. I'm so afraid I'll give myself something. I just want to be friends with myself.
>
> —*Richard Lewis*

The only fully effective strategies to prevent the sexual transmission of STIs are abstinence and maintaining a monogamous sexual relationship with an uninfected partner. If you are celibate, or if you and your sex partner are not infected and neither of you engages in sexual activity with anyone else, you have little to be concerned about. Many people are sexually active and have not committed themselves to a monogamous relationship, however. Even for those who seek monogamous relationships, there must always be that "first time."

Be Knowledgeable about the Risks Be aware of the risks of STIs. Many of us try to put the dangers of STIs out of our minds, especially in moments of passion. Make a pact with yourself to refuse to play the dangerous game of pretending that the dangers of STIs do not exist or that you are somehow immune.

Knowledge about HIV transmission does not always translate into behavioral change, such as increased use of latex condoms (which can block the transmission of HIV) and other safer-sex practices. In fact, knowledge about transmission of HIV and other STIs is not reliably related to condom use (Hartung et al., 2002; Lin & Wang, 2003; Mansergh et al., 2002; Pinkerton et al., 2003b). Despite widespread efforts to educate the public about the dangers of unprotected sex, negative attitudes toward using condoms persist, especially among males. Consider the litany of complaints we come across: "They reduce sexual pleasure. . . . They're a nuisance to put on. . . . They cost too much. . . . They interrupt sex," and so on.

If virtually all young people in the United States are aware of the sexual transmission of HIV, why do so many continue to engage in risky sexual behavior? For one thing, teenagers do not perceive risky behavior to be as dangerous as adults do. This generalization extends to drinking, smoking, failure to use seat belts, and drag racing, as well as to sexual behavior (CDC, 2000e). Young people also profit from being taught specific skills to protect themselves from engaging in risky behaviors, such as communication skills for discussing safer-sex with their partners, assertiveness skills for ensuring that their needs and interests are respected by their partners, social skills to resist peer pressures, and proper use of condoms (Montano et al., 2001). Greater efforts are needed to reverse peer norms that discourage condom use. For example, it may be advisable for adolescents themselves to support and teach condom use to their peers (Montano et al., 2001).

Researchers have identified several factors that underlie risky sexual behavior among young people:

1. *Perceived low risk of infection.* One of the major stumbling blocks in promoting safer-sex practices is that many young heterosexuals perceive a low risk of contracting HIV (Ironson et al., 2002; Wingood & DiClemente, 2002). People who perceive themselves as being at low risk are less likely to alter their behavior.

   Given the current low rate of known infections among heterosexuals who do not inject drugs, many heterosexuals may perceive risky sexual practices as a reasonable gamble (Ironson et al., 2002; Montano et al., 2001). Heterosexuals who have never had a friend or relative with HIV/AIDS may dismiss it as a problem that affects other types of people. Even gay men may subscribe to the "I'm not the type" fallacy and underestimate their personal risks.

2. *Negative attitudes toward condom use.* Many factors discourage condom use (Montano et al., 2001). Some people feel embarrassed to buy them. For others, the risk of being infected with HIV seems to fly out of their minds whenever the opportunity for sex arises. Some claim that applying a condom dampens romantic ardor in moments of passion by requiring an interruption of the sexual act. Some people just regard them as too much of a fuss. Many men say that condoms deprive them of sexual pleasure. Unless such obstacles to using condoms are overcome, efforts to stem the tide of HIV infection may be thwarted.

Talking about Preventing Transmission of HIV/AIDS and other STIs
Most people do not find it easy to talk frankly about preventing STIs, but what is the alternative?

3. *Myth of personal invulnerability.* Some people subscribe to a myth of personal invulnerability and believe that they are somehow immune to HIV/AIDS and other diseases. Even students who are generally well informed about STIs may think of themselves as personally immune. One junior at the University of Miami (Ohio) explained to an interviewer why she did not insist that her partners use a condom: "I have an attitude—it may be wrong—that any guy I would sleep with would not have AIDS." The adventurous spirit that we often associate with youth may confer a dangerous sense of immortality and a greater willingness to take risks (CDC, 2000h; King, 2000). Perceptions of personal invulnerability help to explain why AIDS education does not always translate into behavioral change.

Even people who do not believe themselves to be immune may underestimate their risk of being infected with HIV (van der Velde et al., 1994). This finding holds true for poor inner-city residents (Hobfoll et al., 1993) as well as college students (Goldman & Harlow, 1993). People tend to view themselves as luckier than the norm. (After all, don't you believe that you alone hold the winning lottery ticket?) Moreover, because the transmission of HIV through casual male–female sexual encounters is an infrequent event, people who regularly engage in risky sexual practices and so far have remained uninfected may be lulled into a false sense of security.

Remain Sober Alcohol and other drugs increase the likelihood of engaging in risky sexual behavior (Centers for Disease Control and Prevention, 2000a; MacDonald et al., 2000).

Inspect Yourself and Your Partner Inspect yourself for a discharge, bumps, rashes, warts, blisters, chancres, sores, lice, or foul odors. Do not expect to find telltale signs of an HIV infection, but infected people often have other STIs. Check out any unusual feature with a physician before you engage in sexual activity.

You may be able to work an inspection of your partner into foreplay—a reason for making love the first time with the lights on. In particular, a woman may hold her partner's penis firmly, pulling the loose skin up and down, as if "milking" it. Then she can check for a discharge at the penile opening. The man may use his fingers to detect any sign of a vaginal discharge. Other visible features of STIs include herpes blisters, genital warts, syphilitic chancres or rashes, and pubic lice.

If you find anything that doesn't look, feel, or smell right, bring it to your partner's attention. Treat any unpleasant odor as a warning sign. Your partner may not be aware of the symptom and may be carrying an infection. If you notice any suspicious signs, refrain from further sexual contact until your partner has the chance to seek a medical evaluation. It is advisable to be informed about the common signs and symptoms of STIs, but you need not become a medical expert. Even if your concerns prove groundless, you can resume sexual relations without the uncertainty that you would have had if you had ignored them.

Of course, your partner may become defensive or hostile if you express a concern that he or she may be carrying an STI. Try to be empathic. The social stigma attached to people with STIs makes it difficult to accept the possibility of infection. It may be appropriate to point out that STIs are quite common (among college students, bank officers, military personnel, or . . . fill in the blank) and that many people are unaware that they carry them.

But for your sake as well as your partner's, if you are not sure that sex is safe, stop. Think carefully about the risks, and seek expert advice.

Use Latex Condoms Latex condoms are effective in blocking nearly all sexually transmissible organisms. Improper use or inconsistent use is a common reason for failures in using condoms to prevent STI transmission (Hatcher, 2001). Yet even when used properly, condoms may be of limited or no value against disease-causing organisms that are transmitted externally, such as those that cause herpes, genital warts, and ectoparasitic infestations.

Condoms made from animal membranes ("skins") are less effective as barriers against STI-causing organisms (they contain pores that allow tiny microbes, including HIV, to penetrate). Even latex condoms are not 100% effective in preventing the transmission of HIV and other STIs. Condoms (and the people who use them) are fallible. Condoms can break or slip off.

Use Barrier Devices When Practicing Oral Sex (Fellatio or Cunnilingus) If you decide to practice oral sex, use a condom before practicing fellatio and a dental dam (a square piece of latex rubber used by dentists during oral surgery) to cover the vagina before engaging in cunnilingus.

Avoid High-Risk Sexual Behaviors Avoid unprotected vaginal intercourse (intercourse without a latex condom). Unprotected anal intercourse is one of the riskiest practices. Other high-risk behaviors include unprotected oral–genital activity, oral–anal activity, insertion of a hand or fist ("fisting") into someone's rectum or vagina, or any activity in which you or your partner would come into contact with the other's blood, semen, or vaginal secretions. If you do engage in anal–genital sex and are uncertain whether you or your partner is infected, use a latex condom. Oral–anal sex, or anilingus (sometimes called *rimming*), should be avoided because of the potential of transmitting microbes between the mouth and the anus.

Also avoid sexual contact with people with STIs, people who practice high-risk sexual behaviors, people who inject drugs, prostitutes, and people who frequent prostitutes.

Wash the Genitals before and after Sex Washing the genitals before and after sex removes a quantity of potentially harmful agents. Washing together may be incorporated into erotic foreplay. Right after intercourse, washing with soap and water may help reduce the risk of infection. Do not, however, deceive yourself into believing that washing your genitals is an effective substitute for safer sex. Most STIs are transmitted internally. Washing is useless against them.

Douching right after coitus might have some limited benefits for women. But frequent douching should be avoided because it may change the vaginal flora and encourage the growth of infectious organisms.

Have Regular Medical Checkups A sexually active person should have health examinations regularly—at least once a year. Many community clinics and family-planning centers scale their charges to ability to pay. Checkups are a small investment to make in one's own health. Many people are symptomless carriers of STIs, especially of chlamydial infections. Medical checkups enable them to learn about and receive treatment for disorders that might otherwise go unnoticed. Many physicians advise routine testing of asymptomatic young women for chlamydial infections to prevent the hidden damage that can occur if the infection goes untreated.

Discuss Whether You and Your Partner Should Undergo Testing before Initiating Sexual Relations Some couples reach a mutual agreement to be tested for HIV and other STIs before they initiate sexual relations. (Some people simply insist that their prospective partners be tested before they initiate sexual relations.) But many people resist testing or feel insulted when their partners raise the issue. People usually assume that they are free of STIs if they are symptom-free and have been reasonably selective in their choice of partners. But STIs happen to the "nicest people," and the absence of symptoms is no guarantee of freedom from infection. Unless you have been celibate or involved in a monogamous relationship with an uninfected partner, you should consider yourself at risk of carrying or contracting an infectious STI.

Engage in Noncoital Sexual Activities Other forms of sexual expression, such as hugging, massage, caressing, mutual masturbation, and rubbing bodies together without vaginal, anal, or oral contact, are low-risk ways of finding sexual pleasure, so long as semen and vaginal fluids do not come into contact with mucous membranes or breaks in the skin. Many sexologists refer to such activities as **outercourse** to distinguish them from sexual intercourse. Sharing sexual fantasies can be very titillating, as can taking a bath or shower together. Vibrators, dildos, and other "sex toys" may also be erotically stimulating and carry a low risk of infection, if they are washed thoroughly with soap and water before use and between uses by two people.

Consult Your Physician If You Suspect That You Have Been Exposed to an STI If you think that you may have been exposed to an STI, such as HIV, see a doctor as soon as possible. Many STIs are detectable in the early stages of development and can be successfully treated. If HIV is in your bloodstream, there is some chance that it may be eradicated before it infects cells in the immune system. If you are infected with HIV, early treatment may keep virus levels low and prevent you from developing AIDS. Early intervention may also prevent the damage that can occur when an STI spreads to vital body organs. Be sensitive to any physical changes that may be symptomatic of STIs. Talk to a health professional when in doubt.

Get to Know Your Partner before Initiating Sexual Relations Be selective in your choice of sex partners. Having sex with multiple partners—especially "one-night stands"—increases your risk of sexual contact with an infected person. It also robs you of the opportunity to get to know your partner well enough to determine whether he or she has participated in high-risk sexual practices or has had sex partners in the past who practiced high-risk behaviors.

Avoid Other High-Risk Behaviors Avoid contact with bodily substances (blood, semen, vaginal secretions, fecal matter) from other people. Do not share hypodermic needles, razors, cuticle scissors, or other implements that could contain another person's blood. Be careful when handling wet towels, bed linen, or other material that might contain bodily substances.

Outercourse Forms of sexual expression (such as massage, hugging, caressing, mutual masturbation, and rubbing bodies together) that do not involve the exchange of body fluids. (Contrast with *intercourse.*)

Sources of Help

Do you have questions about the signs and symptoms of STIs? Do you need assistance in coping with an STI? A number of organizations have established telephone hotlines that provide anonymous callers with information. Some organizations publish newsletters and other material to help people with particular diseases cope more effectively.

National Toll-Free Hotlines for Information about AIDS and Other STIs These hotlines provide information about AIDS and other STIs, as well as referral sources. You don't have to give your name or identify yourself to obtain information.

National AIDS Hotline, Centers for Disease Control AIDS Hotline: (800) 342-AIDS: Information and referral resources nationwide, 24 hours a day.
National STI Hotline: 1-800-227-8922 (in California, 800-982-5883) (A hotline sponsored by the American Social Health Association that dispenses information about STI symptoms and refers callers to local STI clinics that provide confidential, minimal cost or no-cost treatment.)
Spanish AIDS/SIDA Hotline: (800) 344-7432
AIDS Hotline for Teens: (800) 234-TEEN
AIDS Hotline for the Hearing Impaired: (800) 243-7889
Canadian Toll-Free Hotline (Toll free in Canada): AIDS Committee of Toronto: (800) 267-6600

Where to Obtain Help or Information about Herpes

National Herpes Hotline: (919) 361-8488
The Helper is a newsletter published by HELP (Herpetics Engaged in Living Productively), an organization that helps people with herpes cope with the disease. For copies of the newsletter, and for the address of the HELP chapter closest to you, either call the National STI Hotline (1-800-227-8922) or write to HELP, Herpes Resource Center, P.O. Box 13827, Research Triangle Park, NC 27709.
Herpes Resource Center, Box 100, Palo Alto, CA 94302

Review: Prevention of STIs: More than Safer Sex

Reflect

Why doesn't knowledge of methods of transmission and the effects of STIs reliably result in behavioral change?

CriticalThinking

What is the difference between being *exposed* to HIV and being *infected* with HIV? Why does the difference matter?

49. The only completely effective ways to prevent the sexual transmission of STIs are _____ and the maintenance of a monogamous relationship with an uninfected partner.

50. Most Americans (*Are* or *Are not*?) aware of the dangers of HIV/AIDS and how it is transmitted.

51. One problem in promoting safer sex is that many young heterosexuals see themselves as being at (*High* or *Low*?) risk of contracting HIV.

52. Many men say that condoms (*Increase* or *Decrease*?) their sexual pleasure.

53. People tend to (*Overestimate* or *Underestimate*?) their risk of being infected with HIV.

54. Condoms made out of _____ block nearly all sexually transmissible organisms.

Recite

1. How common are STIs?

More than 13 million people in the United States contract a sexually transmitted infection (STI) each year. Although public attention has been riveted on HIV/AIDS for two decades, other STIs (such as chlamydia and genital warts) pose wider threats.

2. What are bacteria?

Bacteria are one-celled microorganisms. Some are essential to human life, but others cause a variety of illnesses.

3. What is gonorrhea?

Gonorrhea is caused by the *Neisseria gonorrhoeae* bacterium. For men, symptoms include a penile discharge and burning urination. Most women are asymptomatic. If left untreated, gonorrhea can attack the internal reproductive organs and lead to PID in women. Gonorrhea is treated with antibiotics.

4. What is syphilis?

Syphilis is caused by the *Treponema pallidum* bacterium. Syphilis undergoes several stages of development, beginning with a painless chancre. Although it can lie dormant for many years, it may eventually be lethal. At any stage, syphilis can be treated with antibiotics.

5. What is chlamydia?

Chlamydia, or chlamydial infections, are the most common bacterial STIs and are caused by the *Chlamydia trachomatous* bacterium. The symptoms of chlamydial infections resemble those of gonorrhea but tend to be milder. Chlamydial infections also respond to antibiotics.

6. Are there any other bacterial STIs?

Yes. These include chancroid, shigellosis, granuloma inguinale, and lymphogranuloma venereum.

7. What is a vaginal infection?

Vaginitis is characterized by a foul-smelling discharge, genital irritation, and burning during urination. Most cases involve bacterial vaginosis, candidiasis, or trichomoniasis.

8. What is bacterial vaginosis?

Bacterial vaginosis is characterized by local irritation and is usually caused by the *Gardnerella vaginalis* bacterium.

9. What is candidiasis?

Candidiasis is caused by a yeastlike fungus, *Candida albicans.* Infections usually arise from changes in the vaginal environment that allow the fungus to overgrow. But these infections can then be transmitted sexually back and forth between partners.

10. What is trichomoniasis?

"Trich" is caused by a one-celled animal (a protozoan) called *Trichomonas vaginalis.*

11. What is a virus?

Viruses are particles of DNA that reproduce by invading a body cell and directing the cell's own reproductive machinery to spin off new viral particles.

12. What is HIV/AIDS?

The number of people worldwide who are infected with HIV (the human immunodeficiency virus) stands at 40 to 50 million. AIDS (acquired immunodeficiency syndrome) is caused by HIV, which attacks the body's immune system. As HIV disables the body's natural defenses, the person becomes vulnerable to opportunistic diseases—such as serious infections and cancers—

Recite

that are normally held in check. HIV is a blood-borne virus that is also found in semen, vaginal secretions, and breast milk. Common avenues of transmission include sexual intercourse, transfusion with contaminated blood, sharing a hypodermic needle with an infected person, childbirth, and breast-feeding. HIV infection is usually diagnosed through tests of blood, saliva, or urine. There is no cure or safe and effective vaccine for HIV/AIDS. The most effective form of treatment as this book goes to press is HAART, which uses a combination of antiviral agents.

13. What is genital herpes?

Oral herpes is caused by the *herpes simplex* virus type 1 (HSV-1). Genital herpes is caused by the *herpes simplex* virus type 2 (HSV-2), which produces painful shallow sores and blisters on the genitals. A vaccine helps prevent women from contracting genital herpes but is ineffective with men. Antiviral drugs can relieve pain and speed healing during flare-ups.

14. What is viral hepatitis?

There are several types of hepatitis, and they are caused by different hepatitis viruses. Most cases of hepatitis are transmitted sexually or by contact with contaminated blood or fecal matter.

15. What are genital warts?

Genital warts are caused by the human papilloma virus (HPV). HPV has been linked to cancers of the genital tract. Freezing the wart is a preferred treatment for removal of the wart, but the virus remains in the body afterward.

16. What is molluscum contagiosum?

This viral STI, caused by a pox virus, causes an outbreak of painless raised lesions on the genitals, buttocks, thighs, or lower abdomen. The lesions usually disappear on their own, without serious complications, within 6 months.

17. What are ectoparasites?

Ectoparasites, as contrasted with endoparasites, are parasites that live on the outside of the body.

18. What is pediculosis?

Pediculosis ("crabs") is caused by pubic lice (*Phthirus pubis*). Pubic lice attach themselves to pubic hair and feed on the blood of their hosts, which often causes itching. Infestations can be treated with a prescription medication (lindane) or with nonprescription medications containing pyrethrins or piperonal butoxide.

19. What is scabies?

Scabies (*Sarcoptes scabiei*) is a parasitic infestation of a tiny mite that causes itching. Scabies, like pubic lice, is treated with lindane.

20. How can we prevent STIs?

Strategies for preventing STIs include abstinence, monogamy, inspecting oneself and one's partner, using latex condoms, avoiding high-risk sex, washing the genitals before and after sex, having regular medical checkups, and getting to know one's partner before engaging in sexual activity.

Chapter 17

Truth?Fiction?

T / F? King Henry III of France insisted on being considered a woman and on being referred to as "Her Majesty."

T / F? Nude sunbathers are exhibitionists.

T / F? People who enjoy watching their mates undress are voyeurs.

T / F? Exhibitionists and voyeurs are never violent.

T / F? Some people cannot become sexually aroused unless they are bound, flogged, or humiliated by their sex partners.

T / F? It is considered normal to enjoy some mild forms of pain during sexual activity.

T / F? There is a subculture in the United States in which sexual sadists and sexual masochists form liaisons to inflict and receive pain and humiliation during sexual activity.

Atypical Sexual Variations

Preview

Aimee's life is mostly nothing but Net. Aimee is a 29-year-old accountant who lives on the coast of North Carolina. She looks like the girl next door, with her red hair and freckles, but 5,000 or so strangers stop by for an intimate encounter every day. Not at her house, but at her Web site, *http://acamgirl.com*. Aimee is one of the Web's more familiar faces (Figure 17.1). Life in front of the four webcams in her house is her way of life. "I don't regret it for a second," she says (cited in Taylor, 2000).

Why is Aimee such a draw? She alerts (should we say "warns"?) the visitor to her Web site that this is not an "adult site." There is no nudity, no sex. The cameras update the pictures regularly, and most of them are downright boring. The more exciting activities are rolling around the floor with her dogs, playing the guitar, and working at her computer. Or one might find Aimee lying on her sofa.

But it isn't all watching; it's interactive. The visitor can chat with Aimee via microphone while he (or she) watches. The site also has Aimee's own writings, including her diary ("Daily Scribbles"), and the e-mail comments of some of the visitors (the "Freak of the Week" feature). Here's a sample comment from a "freak":

Aimee is the biggest male basher I have ever known. Her little web picture has her showing mega (and boy do I mean MEGA!!!!!) cleavage, when I asked her to show it, she got all bent out of shape. If you advertise something...you better be able to back it up......got it!!! Do you see something wrong here? Really...I'm not a hating person, I like to live and have fun, but when you have a person like Aimee always judging and putting people down...it makes you want to reach through the screen and choke the living s✶✶✶ out of her!!!!!

Why does Aimee do it? What motivates her? Why does she take the chance of arousing people who write this kind of e-mail? Aimee says that living with endless voyeurism is the price she pays for the chance to have people read her writings. "You draw them in with the camera, and then they'll stay and read your stuff," she explains (Taylor, 2000). Of course, she also garners a great deal of attention, as in *Time* magazine and in this book.

Even if Amy's motivation is, uh, literary, there are thousands of Web sites where people—male, female,

Figure 17.1. Aimee's Home Page, http://acamgirl
.com. *Aimee has some 5,000 visitors who drop
in to watch her every day. Is she an* exhibitionist?
Are her electronic visitors voyeurs? *What are the true
definitions of these terms? What are the origins of
exhibitionistic and voyeuristic behavior?*

couples, trios, etc.—are happy to expose their bodies and engage in sex acts while the
visitor watches. A Yankelovich poll found, in fact, that many Americans would not mind
engaging in sexual activities in front of a camera (see Table 17.1).

Many webcam sites are adult pay sites, where visitors pay a fee and ask the "actor" (who
is usually female) in front of the webcam to engage in various kinds of sexual acts. The
motivation of most such "actors" is simple: money.

The case of Aimee raises a number of
questions. Aimee exposes aspects of her life to
thousands of strangers. Could she be considered
an *exhibitionist?* And what about the people who
stop by her Web site and those of others with
webcams? Are they *voyeurs?* Is what Aimee and
her visitors are doing "normal," or is it abnormal
or deviant? In this chapter we explore a number
of sexual and sexually related behaviors that
deviate from the norm in one sense or another.
But first let us consider in depth the question of
how we define normality.

TABLE 17.1
Percentage of Adult Americans Who Say They Would Allow a TV Show to Film Them . . .

In pajamas	31%
Kissing	29
Crying	26
Having an argument	25
Drunk	16
Naked	8
Having sex	5

Source of data: Yankelovich Partners telephone poll of 1,218 adult Americans for
Time/CNN. Reported in James Poniewozik et al. (2000, June 26). We like to watch:
Led by the hit *Survivor*, voyeurism has become TV's hottest genre. Why the passion
for peeping? *Time, 155*(26): 56–62.

Question: How do we determine what kind of behavior is normal and what is deviant or abnormal?

Normal versus Deviant Sexual Behavior

One common approach to defining normality is based on a statistical norm. From this perspective, rare or unusual sexual behaviors are considered abnormal or deviant. The statistical approach may seem value-free, because the yardstick of normality is based on the frequency of behavior, not on judgments about its social acceptability. Engaging in coitus while standing, or more than 7 times a week, might be considered deviant by this standard. So might maintaining a full erection between ejaculations, but most couples would probably not complain about it.

Moreover, our choice of what behaviors to subject to statistical comparison is not divorced from our underlying values. We tend to consider sexual behaviors abnormal or deviant, for example, when they run counter to our religious values, when they make most of us wince (such as sadism or masochism), or when they seem inexplicable (such as being turned on more by a woman's shoe than by the woman herself). Behaviors that run counter to someone's religious values may be common enough, but that individual might label them deviant because they deviate from what the person has been led to believe is normal (or "proper").

What is considered normal in one culture or at a particular time may be considered abnormal in other cultures and at other times. A gay male or lesbian sexual orientation was considered abnormal throughout most of Western history and was once labeled a mental disorder by the American Psychiatric Association. But in 1973, classification of a gay male or lesbian sexual orientation as a mental disorder was dropped from the association's diagnostic and statistical manual (the DSM). What is "normal" behavior for the female adolescent Trobriand islander (see Chapter 1) might be considered deviant—even *nymphomaniacal*—by Western cultural standards.

In our own culture, sexual practices such as oral sex and masturbation were once considered deviant or abnormal. Today, however, they are practiced so widely that few people would label them as deviant. Concepts of "normalcy" and "deviance," then, reflect the mores and customs of a particular culture at a given time.

Review: Normal versus Deviant Sexual Behavior

Reflect

Do you consider sexual practices such as oral sex and masturbation to be deviant or abnormal? Why or why not?

Critical Thinking

Why is statistical rarity an inadequate standard for considering a sexual practice to be normal or abnormal?

1. From the _____ perspective, rare sexual behaviors are abnormal or deviant.

2. A gay male or lesbian sexual orientation was considered (*Normal* or *Abnormal*?) throughout most of Western history.

Another basis for determining sexual deviance is to classify sexual practices as deviant when they involve the persistent preference for nongenital sexual outlets (Seligman & Hardenburg, 2000). If a man prefers fondling a woman's panties to engaging in sexual relations with her, or prefers to masturbate against her foot rather than engaging in coitus, his behavior is likely to be labeled deviant.

Because of the confusing array of meanings of the terms *deviant* and *abnormal*, some professionals speak about unusual patterns of sexual arousal or behavior as "atypical variations" in sexual behavior, rather than as "sexual deviations." Atypical patterns of sexual arousal or behavior that become problematic in the eyes of the individual or society are labeled *paraphilias* by the DSM (2000). Clinicians consider paraphilias to be mental disorders. But milder forms of these behaviors may be practiced by many people and fall within the normal spectrum of human sexuality.

Question: What are paraphilias?

The Paraphilias

Paraphilias involve sexual arousal in response to unusual stimuli such as children or other nonconsenting persons (such as unsuspecting people whom one watches or to whom one exposes one's genitals), nonhuman objects (such as shoes, leather, rubber, or undergarments), or pain or humiliation (Seligman & Hardenburg, 2000). The psychiatric diagnosis of paraphilia requires that the person have acted on the urges or be distinctly distressed by them.

People with paraphilias usually feel that their urges are insistent, demanding, or compulsory (Seligman & Hardenburg, 2000). They may describe themselves as overcome by them now and then. People with paraphilias tend to experience their urges as beyond their control, in much the same way that drug addicts and compulsive gamblers see themselves as helpless in the face of irresistible urges. For these reasons, theorists have speculated that paraphilias may represent a type of sexual compulsion or an addiction.

Paraphilias vary in severity. In some cases the person can function sexually in the absence of the unusual stimuli and seldom if ever acts on his or her deviant urges. In other cases the person resorts to paraphilic behavior only in times of stress. In more extreme forms, the person repeatedly engages in paraphilic behavior and may become preoccupied with thoughts and fantasies about these experiences. In such cases the person may not be able to become sexually aroused without either fantasizing about the paraphilic stimulus or having it present. For some people, paraphilic behavior is the only means of attaining sexual gratification.

The person with a paraphilia typically replays the paraphilic act in sexual fantasies to stimulate arousal during masturbation or sexual relations. It is as though he or she is mentally replaying a videotape of the paraphilic scene. But the scene grows stale after a while, and the individual feels the need to perform another paraphilic act to make a new "video."

Some paraphilias are mostly harmless and victimless, such as *fetishism* and crossdressing to achieve sexual arousal (*transvestic fetishism*). Even being humiliated by one's partner may be relatively harmless if the partner consents. Other paraphilic behaviors, such as exposing oneself in public or enticing children into sexual relations, do have victims and may cause harm, sometimes severe physical or psychological harm. They are also against the law. Sexual sadism, in which sexual arousal is connected to hurting or humiliating another person, can be a most harmful paraphilia when it is forced upon a nonconsenting person. Some brutal rapes involve sexual sadism.

Paraphilia A diagnostic category used by the American Psychiatric Association to describe atypical patterns of sexual arousal or behavior that become problematic in the eyes of the individual or society, such as fetishism and exhibitionism. The urges are recurrent and either are acted on or are distressing to the individual. (From Greek roots *para-*, meaning "to the side of," and *philos*, meaning "loving.")

Fetishism A club-goer licks the toes and platform shoe of another at Zenwarp, a goth/alien/vampire/fetish-themed club at the Limelight nightclub in Manhattan.

Fetishism A paraphilia in which an inanimate object such as an article of clothing or items made of rubber, leather, or silk elicit sexual arousal.

Partialism A paraphilia related to fetishism in which sexual arousal is exaggeratedly associated with a particular body part, such as feet, breasts, or buttocks.

Transvestism A paraphilia in which a person repeatedly cross-dresses to achieve sexual arousal or gratification or is troubled by persistent, recurring urges to cross-dress. (From the Latin roots *trans-*, meaning "cross," and *vestis*, meaning "garment.") Also known as *transvestic fetishism*.

All paraphilias except sexual masochism are believed to occur almost exclusively among men (Seligman & Hardenburg, 2000). The prevalence of paraphilias in the general population remains unknown, because people are generally unwilling to talk about them. Much of what we have learned about paraphilias derives from the reported experiences of people who have been apprehended for performing illegal acts (such as exposing themselves in public) and of the few who have voluntarily sought help. The characteristics of people who have not been identified or studied remain virtually unknown.

We discuss the major types of paraphilia in this chapter, beginning with fetishism. The one exception is *pedophilia*. In pedophilia, children become the objects of sexual arousal. Pedophilia often takes the form of sexual coercion of children, as in incest and sexual molestation. It is discussed in Chapter 18 as a form of sexual coercion. *Question: What is fetishism?*

Fetishism

The roots of the word *fetish* come from the French *fétiche*, which is thought to derive from the Portuguese *feitico*, meaning "magic charm." The "magic" in this case lies in an object's ability to arouse a person sexually. In **fetishism**, an inanimate object elicits sexual arousal. Articles of clothing (for example, women's panties, bras, lingerie, stockings, gloves, shoes, or boots) and materials made of rubber, leather, silk, or fur are among the more common fetishistic objects. Leather boots and high-heeled shoes are especially popular ones.

The fetishist may act on the urges to engage in fetishistic behavior, such as masturbating by stroking an object or while fantasizing about it, or he may be distressed about such urges or fantasies but not act upon them. In a related paraphilia, **partialism**, people are excessively aroused by a particular body part, such as the feet, breasts, or buttocks.

Most fetishes and partialisms are harmless. Fetishistic practices are nearly always private and involve masturbation or are incorporated into coitus with a willing partner. Only rarely have fetishists coerced others into paraphilic activities. Yet some partialists have touched parts of women's bodies in public. And some fetishists commit burglaries to acquire the fetishistic objects. Now and then we hear of someone who has stolen hundreds of pairs of women's shoes, for example.

Fetishism appears to include *transvestism*. *Question: What is transvestism?*

Transvestism

Transvestism may be viewed as a type of fetish. Whereas other fetishists become sexually aroused by handling the fetishistic object while they masturbate, transvestites become excited by wearing articles of clothing—the fetishistic objects—of the other gender. A fetishist may find either the object per se or sex involving the object to be erotically stimulating. For the transvestite, the object is sexually alluring only when it is worn. Nearly all transvestites are males. Transvestism has been described among

Transvestism *Transvestites cross-dress for purposes of obtaining sexual arousal and gratification. Are women who wear blue jeans engaging in transvestic activity?*

heterosexual and gay males. Many are married and otherwise masculine in behavior and dress.

Transvestism may overlap with transsexualism, but it is not quite the same. First let us note that some transvestites and some transsexuals appear to be motivated by **autogynephilia**—a condition in which the individual is sexually stimulated by fantasies that their own bodies are female (Bailey, 2003b). But there are differences between transvestites and transsexuals. Transvestites are usually adequately gratified by cross-dressing and masturbating or engaging in sexual activity with others while cross-dressing. They may also find it highly gratifying to masturbate while fantasizing about episodes of cross-dressing. But many transvestites have masculine gender identities and do not seek to change their anatomic sex. Yet some male transvestites are gay or show some aspects of a feminine gender identity. Transsexuals usually cross-dress because they are uncomfortable with the attire associated with their anatomic sex and truly wish to be members of the other sex. For this reason, as noted in Chapter 6, transsexuals may seek sex reassignment.

Like fetishism in general, the origins of transvestism remain obscure. Evidence of biological hormonal and neurological abnormalities in transvestism is mixed (Bailey, 2003b). Family relationships may play a role. Some researchers report that transvestites are more likely than other people to be oldest children or only children (Schott, 1995). Transvestites may also report closer relationships with their mothers than with their fathers (Schott, 1995). Some transvestites report a history of "petticoat punishment" during childhood. That is, they were humiliated by being dressed in girl's attire. Some authorities have speculated that the adult transvestite might be attempting psychologically to convert humiliation into mastery by achieving an erection and engaging in sexual activity despite being attired in female clothing (Geer et al., 1984).

Cross-dressing has occurred in other cultures and has been reported in historical accounts of figures such as King Henry III of France. This sixteenth-century monarch wanted to be considered a woman and to be referred to as "Her Majesty" (Geer et al., 1984). But cross-dressing may occur in other cultures for reasons other than sexual arousal. In the case of Henry III, it appears that transsexualism, not transvestism, was involved.

Autogynephilia A fetish in which men are sexually stimulated by fantasies that their own bodies are female. Autogynephilia is found in some transsexuals as well as some fetishists. (From roots meaning "self," "woman," and "love" or "desire.")

A Closer Look

Archie: A Case of Transvestism

Many transvestites are married and engage in sexual activity with their wives. Yet they seek additional sexual gratification through dressing as women, as in the case of Archie.

Archie was a 55-year-old plumber who had been cross-dressing for many years. There was a time when he would go out in public as a woman, but as his prominence in the community grew, he became more afraid of being discovered in public. His wife Myrna knew of his "peccadillo," especially because he borrowed many of her clothes. She urged him to stay at home, offering to help him with his "weirdness." For many years his paraphilia had been restricted to the home.

The couple came to the clinic at the urging of the wife. Myrna described how Archie had imposed his will on her for 20 years. Archie would wear her undergarments and masturbate while she told him how disgusting he was. (The couple also regularly engaged in

"normal" sexual intercourse, which Myrna enjoyed.) The cross dressing had come to a head because a teenage daughter had almost walked into the couple's bedroom while they were acting out Archie's fantasies.

With Myrna out of the consulting room, Archie explained how he grew up in a family with several older sisters. He described how underwear had been perpetually hanging to dry in the home's single bathroom. As an adolescent Archie experimented with rubbing against articles of underwear and then with trying them on. On one occasion a sister walked in while he was modeling panties before the mirror. She told him he was a "dredge to society," and he straightaway experienced unparalleled sexual excitement. He masturbated when she left the room, and his orgasm was the strongest of his young life.

Archie did not think that there was anything wrong with wearing women's undergarments and masturbating. He

was not about to give it up, regardless of whether it destroyed his marriage. Myrna's main concern was finally separating herself from Archie's "sickness." She didn't care what he did any more, so long as he did it by himself. "Enough is enough," she said.

That was the compromise the couple worked out. Archie would engage in his fantasies by himself. He would do so when Myrna was not at home, and she would not be told of his activities. He would also be very, very careful to choose times when the children would not be around.

Six months later the couple were together and content. Archie had replaced Myrna's input into his fantasies with transvestic–sadomasochistic magazines. Myrna said, "I see no evil, hear no evil, smell no evil." They continued to have sexual intercourse. After a while, Myrna forgot to check to see which underwear had been used.

Truth?Fiction?
Revisited

It is true that King Henry III of France insisted on being considered a woman. The king appears to have been transsexual.

Some men cross-dress for reasons other than sexual arousal and so are not "true transvestites." Some men make a living by impersonating women such as Marilyn Monroe and Madonna on stage and are not motivated by sexual arousal. Among some segments of the gay male community, it is fashionable to masquerade as women. Gay men do not usually cross-dress to become sexually stimulated, however.

Transvestic behaviors may range from wearing a single female garment when alone to sporting dresses, wigs, makeup, and feminine mannerisms at a transvestite club. Some transvestites become sexually aroused by masquerading as women and attracting the interest of unsuspecting males. They sometimes entice these men or string them along until they find some excuse to back out before their anatomic sex is revealed. The great majority of transvestites do not engage in antisocial or illegal behavior. Most practice their sexual predilection in private and would be horrified or embarrassed to be discovered by associates while dressed in female attire.

Although some transvestites persuade their female partners to permit them to wear feminine attire during their sexual activities, most keep their transvestic urges and activities to themselves. A survey of 504 transvestite men showed that most had kept their transvestism a secret from their wives-to-be, hoping that they would not be bothered by their urge to cross-dress once they were married (Weinberg & Bullough, 1986, 1988). But the urges continued into marriage, and the wives eventually discovered them. Seventy of the wives were interviewed (Bullough & Weinberg, 1989). The wives tended to react with confusion, surprise, or shock to discover their husbands' cross-dressing. Most tried to be understanding at first. Some assisted their husbands in their cross-dressing, such as by helping them apply makeup. Yet the longer the women were married, the more negative their attitudes toward their mates' cross-dressing became. Even so, the wives generally became tolerant in time, if not supportive.

Another study of 21 male heterosexual cross-dressers from New England yielded similar results (Reynolds & Caron, 2000). Most wives were tolerant, but many who found out about their husbands' cross-dressing years into the marriage felt betrayed and angry. A common worry of the wives was that outsiders would learn about their husbands' behavior.

Exhibitionism

If fetishism is often victimless, the same cannot be said for exhibitionism. *Question: What is exhibitionism?* **Exhibitionism** ("flashing") consists of persistent, powerful urges and sexual fantasies involving exposing one's genitals to unsuspecting strangers for the purpose of achieving sexual arousal or gratification. The urges are either acted upon or are disturbing to the individual. Exhibitionists are nearly always males.

What we know of exhibitionists, as with most other people with paraphilias, is almost entirely derived from studies of men who have been apprehended or treated by mental health professionals. Such knowledge may yield a biased picture of exhibitionists, because relatively few reported incidents result in apprehension and conviction. Studies in England, Guatemala, the United States, and Hong Kong suggest that fewer than 20% of occurrences are reported to the police (Cox, 1988). The characteristics of most perpetrators may thus differ from those of people who have been available for study.

The prevalence of exhibitionism in the general population is unknown, but a survey of 846 college women at nine randomly selected American universities found exposure to exhibitionism to be widespread. A third of the women indicated that they had run into a "flasher" (Cox, 1988). A majority of the women had been approached for the first time (some had been approached more than once) by 16 years of age. Only 15 of the women had reported these incidents to the police. The clinical definition of exhibitionism involves exposure to a stranger, but about a third (36%) of the incidents among the college women were committed by acquaintances, relatives, or "good friends."

The archetypal exhibitionist is young, unhappily married, and sexually repressed. An exhibitionist may claim that marital coitus is reasonably satisfactory but that he also experiences the compulsion to expose himself to strangers. Many exhibitionists are single, however. They typically have difficulty relating to women and have been unable to establish meaningful heterosexual relationships.

Exhibitionism usually begins before age 18 (DSM, 2000). The urge to exhibit oneself, if not the actual act, usually begins in early adolescence, generally between the ages of 13 and 16 (Freund et al., 1988). The frequency of exhibitionism declines markedly after the age of 40 (DSM, 2000). The typical exhibitionist does not attempt further sexual contact with the victim. Thus, he does not usually pose a physical threat (DSM, 2000).

The police sometimes trivialize exhibitionism as a "nuisance crime," but the psychological consequences among victims, especially young children, indicate that exhibitionism is not victimless. Victims may feel violated and may experience recurrent images or nightmares. They may harbor misplaced guilt that they had unwittingly

Exhibitionism
A paraphilia characterized by persistent, powerful urges and sexual fantasies involving exposing one's genitals to unsuspecting strangers for the purpose of achieving sexual arousal or gratification.

Michael: A Case of Exhibitionism

Michael was a 26-year-old, handsome, boyish-looking married male with a 3-year-old daughter. He had spent about one-quarter of his life in reform schools and in prison. As an adolescent he had been a fire-setter. As a young adult, he had begun to expose himself. He came to the clinic without his wife's knowledge because he was exposing himself more and more often—up to three times a day—and he was afraid that he would eventually be arrested and thrown into prison again.

Michael said he liked sex with his wife, but it wasn't as exciting as exposing himself. He couldn't prevent his exhibitionism, especially now, when he was between jobs and worried about where the family's next month's rent was coming from. He loved his daughter more

than anything and couldn't stand the thought of being separated from her.

Michael's method of operation was as follows: He would look for slender adolescent females, usually near the junior high school and the senior high school. He would take his penis out of his pants and play with it while he drove up to a girl or a small group of girls. He would lower the car window, continuing to play with himself, and ask them for directions. Sometimes the girls didn't see his penis. That was okay. Sometimes they saw it and didn't react. That was okay, too. But when they saw it and became flustered and afraid, that was best of all. He would start to masturbate harder, and now and then he managed to ejaculate before the girls had departed.

Michael's history was unsettled. His father had left home before he was born, and his mother had drunk heavily. He was in and out of foster homes throughout his childhood, "all over" the capital district area of New York State. Before he was 10 years old, he was involved in sexual activities with neighborhood boys. Now and then the boys also forced neighborhood girls into petting, and Michael had mixed feelings when the girls got upset. He felt bad for them, but he also enjoyed it. A couple of times, girls had seemed horrified at the sight of his penis, and it had made him "really feel like a man. To see that look, you know, with a girl, not a woman, but a girl—a slender girl, that's what I'm after."

enticed the exhibitionist. They may blame themselves for reacting excessively or for failing to apprehend the perpetrator. They may also develop fears of venturing out on their own.

Geer and his colleagues (1984) see exhibitionism as a means of expressing hostility toward women. Exposure may be an attempt by the exhibitionist to strike back at women because of a belief that women have wronged him or damaged his self-esteem by failing to notice him or take him seriously. The direct expression of anger may be perceived as too risky, so the exhibitionist vents his rage by humiliating a defenseless stranger. The urge to expose himself often occurs when the exhibitionist feels that his masculinity has been insulted. Some evidence suggests that exhibitionists are attempting to assert their masculinity by evoking a response from victims. A number of exhibitionists have reported that they hoped women would enjoy the experience and be impressed with the size of their penises (Langevin et al., 1979).

Other studies show exhibitionists to be shy, dependent, passive, lacking in sexual and social skills, and even inhibited (Dwyer, 1988). They tend to be self-critical, to have doubts about their masculinity, and to suffer from feelings of inadequacy and inferiority (Dwyer, 1988). Many have had poor relationships with their fathers and have overprotective mothers (Dwyer, 1988). Exhibitionists who are socially shy or inadequate may be using exhibitionism as a substitute for the intimate relationships they cannot develop.

The preferred victims are typically girls or young women (Freund & Blanchard, 1986). The typical exhibitionist drives up to, or walks in front of, a stranger and exposes his penis. In one sample of 130 exhibitionists, about half reported that they always or nearly always had erections when they exposed themselves (Langevin et al., 1979). After his victim has registered fear, disgust, confusion, or surprise, an exhibitionist will typically cover himself and flee. He usually masturbates, either while

A Closer Look

How to Respond to an Exhibitionist

It is understandable for an unsuspecting woman who is exposed to an exhibitionist to react with shock, surprise, or fear. Unfortunately, her display of shock or fear may reinforce the flasher's tendencies to expose himself. She may fear that the flasher, who has already broken at least one social code, is likely to assault her physically as well. Fortunately, most exhibitionists do not seek actual sexual contact with their victims and run away before they can be apprehended by the police or passers-by.

Some women respond with anger, insults, or even pronouncements that the offender should feel ashamed. A display of anger may reinforce exhibitionism. We do not recommend that the victim insult the flasher, lest it provoke a violent response. Although most exhibitionists are not violent, some have considered or attempted rape (Langevin, 2003; Price et al., 2002).

When possible, showing no reaction or simply continuing on one's way may be the best response. If women do desire to respond to the flasher, they might calmly say something like "You really need professional help. You should see a professional to help you with this problem." In any case, they should promptly report the incident to police, so that authorities can apprehend the offender.

exposing himself or shortly afterward, while thinking about the act and the victim's response (DSM, 2000). Some exhibitionists ejaculate during the act. Most of the 238 exhibitionists in a Canadian study reported masturbating to orgasm while exposing themselves or afterward while fantasizing about it (Freund et al., 1988).

Exhibitionists and some other people with paraphilias may find that the risk of being caught heightens their erotic response because it precipitates a rush of stress hormones that are chemically similar to testosterone (Haake et al., 2003). The exhibitionist may even purposefully increase the risk, such as by always exposing himself in the same location in his own, easily identifiable car.

Courts tend to be hard on exhibitionists, partly because there is evidence that some exhibitionists progress to more serious crimes of sexual aggression (Price et al., 2002). Still, the majority of exhibitionists apparently do not become rapists or child molesters.

Definitions of exhibitionism also bring into focus the boundaries between normal and abnormal behavior. Are exotic dancers (stripteasers) or nude sunbathers exhibitionists? Aren't they also exposing themselves to strangers? But exotic dancers—male or female—remove their clothes to sexually excite or entertain an audience that is paying to watch them. Their motive is (usually) to earn a living. Sunbathers in their "birthday suits" may also seek to arouse others, not themselves. Of course, they may also be seeking an all-over tan or trying to avoid feeling encumbered by clothing. In any case, stripteasers and sunbathers do not expose themselves to *unsuspecting* others. Thus these behaviors are not regarded as exhibitionistic.

It is also normal to become sexually excited while stripping before one's sex partner. Such stripping is done to excite a willing partner, not to surprise or shock a stranger.

Truth?Fiction?
Revisited

It is not true that nude sunbathers are exhibitionists—at least not in terms of the clinical definition of the disorder. Exhibitionists seek to become sexually aroused by exposing themselves to unsuspecting victims, not to show themselves off.

Obscene Telephone Calling

Like exhibitionists, obscene phone callers (nearly all of whom are male) seek to become sexually aroused by shocking their victims. *Question: What do we know about obscene telephone calling?* Whereas an exhibitionist exposes his genitals to

Telephone scatologia
A paraphilia characterized by the making of obscene telephone calls. (From the Greek *skatos,* meaning "excrement.)

produce the desired response, the obscene phone caller "exposes" himself verbally by uttering obscenities and sexual provocations to a nonconsenting person. Because of such similarities, obscene telephone calling is sometimes considered a subtype of exhibitionism. The DSM (2000) labels this type of paraphilia **telephone scatologia** (lewdness).

Relatively few obscene callers are women (Price et al., 2002). Women who are charged with such offenses are generally motivated by rage for some actual or fantasized rejection, rather than by the desire for sexual arousal. They use the phone to hurl sexual invectives against men whom they feel have wronged them. By contrast, male obscene phone callers are generally motivated by a desire for sexual excitement and usually choose their victims randomly from the phone book or by chance dialing. They typically masturbate during the phone call or shortly afterward. Most obscene telephone callers also engage in other paraphilic acts, especially voyeurism and exhibitionism (Price et al., 2001, 2002).

There are many patterns of obscene phone calling. Some callers limit themselves to obscenities. Others make sexual overtures. Some just breathe heavily into the receiver. Others describe their masturbatory activity to their victims. Some profess to have previously met the victim at a social gathering or through a mutual acquaintance. Some even represent themselves as "taking a sex survey" and ask a series of personally revealing questions.

The typical obscene phone caller is a socially inadequate heterosexual male who has had difficulty forming intimate relationships with women. The relative safety and anonymity of the telephone may shield him from the risk of rejection. A reaction of shock or fright from his victims may fill him with feelings of power and control that are lacking in his life, especially in his relationships with women. The obscenities may vent the rage that he holds against women who have rejected him.

Obscene phone calls are illegal, but it has been difficult for authorities to track down perpetrators. Call tracing can help police track obscene or offending phone callers. Call tracing works in different ways in different locales. Caller ID shows the caller's telephone number on a display panel on the receiving party's telephone. In some locales, people can program their telephone service so that a caller who calls from a private number or one without caller ID receives a message stating that the recipient accepts calls only from people who identify their phone numbers or names. These services may deter some obscene callers, but others may use public phones instead of their home phones. Check with your local telephone company if you are interested in these services.

What should a woman do if she receives an obscene phone call? Advice generally parallels that given to women who are victimized by exhibitionists. Above all, women are advised to remain calm and not to reveal shock or fright, because such reactions tend to reinforce the caller and increase the probability of repeat calls. Women may be best advised to say nothing at all and gently hang up the receiver. A woman might alternatively offer a brief response that alludes to the caller's problems before hanging up. She might say in a calm but strong voice, "It's unfortunate you have this problem. I think you should seek professional help." If she should receive repeated calls, the woman might request an unlisted number or contact the police about tracing the calls. Many women list themselves only by their initials in the phone directory in order to disguise their gender. But because this practice is so widespread, obscene callers may surmise that people listed by initials are women living alone.

Voyeurism could be considered the "flip side of the coin" of exhibitionism. *Question: What is voyeurism?*

Voyeurism

Voyeurism involves strong, repetitive urges to observe unsuspecting strangers who are nude, undressing, or involved in sexual relations (DSM, 2000). The voyeur becomes sexually aroused by watching and typically does not seek sexual relations with the "victim." Like fetishism and exhibitionism, voyeurism is found almost exclusively among males. It usually begins before age 15 (DSM, 2000).

The voyeur may masturbate while peeping or afterward while replaying the incident in his mind. The voyeur may fantasize about sex with the observed person but have no intention of actually seeking sexual relations with her.

Are people voyeurs who become sexually aroused by the sight of their lovers undressing? What about people who enjoy watching pornographic films or stripteasers? No, no, and no. The people being observed are not unsuspecting strangers. The lover knows that his or her partner is watching. Porn actors and strippers know that others will be viewing them. They would not be performing if they did not expect or have an audience.

It is normal for men and women to be sexually stimulated by the sight of other people who are nude, undressing, or engaged in sexual activity (Montemurro et al., 2003). Women who attend male strip clubs also enjoy "bonding" with their friends and other women at the clubs (Montemurro et al., 2003). But true voyeurs want to peep on *unsuspecting* strangers.

Voyeurs are also known as "peepers" or *peeping Toms.* Why "peeping Toms"? According to an old English legend, Lady Godiva asked the townspeople not to look upon her while she rode horseback in the nude to protest the oppressive tax that her husband, a landowner, had imposed on them. A tailor named Tom of Coventry was the only townsperson not to grant her request.

Voyeurs often put themselves in risky situations in which they face the prospect of being caught. They may risk injury by perching in trees or otherwise assuming precarious positions to catch a preferred view of their target. They will occupy rooftops and fire escapes in brutal winter weather. Peepers can be exceedingly patient. They may wait hour after hour, night after night, for a furtive glimpse of the target. One 25-year-old, recently married man secreted himself in his mother-in-law's closet, waiting for her to disrobe. Part of the sexual excitement seems to stem from the risks voyeurs run. The need for risk may explain why voyeurs are not known to frequent nude beaches or nudist camps where it is acceptable to look (though not to stare) at nude people.

Although most voyeurs are nonviolent, some commit violent crimes such as assault and rape (Langevin, 2003). Voyeurs who break into and enter homes or buildings, or who tap at windows to gain the attention of victims, are among the more dangerous.

Compared to other types of sex offenders, voyeurs tend to be less sexually experienced and are less likely to be married (Gebhard et al., 1965). Like exhibitionists, voyeurs tend to harbor feelings of inadequacy and to lack social and sexual skills (Dwyer, 1988). They may thus have difficulty forming romantic relationships with women. For this shy and socially inadequate type of voyeur, "peeping" affords sexual gratification without risk of rejection. Yet not all voyeurs are socially awkward and inept with women.

Truth?Fiction?
Revisited

It is not true that people who enjoy watching their mates undress are voyeurs. In such cases the person who is disrobing is knowingly and willingly observed, and the watcher's enjoyment is completely normal. Voyeurs target unsuspecting victims.

It is incorrect to say that exhibitionists and voyeurs are never violent. Exhibitionistic and voyeuristic activities per se do not involve outright violence, but some exhibitionists and voyeurs have been known to be violent, and they may, if provoked or angered, react violently.

Voyeurism A paraphilia characterized by strong, repetitive urges and related sexual fantasies of observing unsuspecting strangers who are naked, disrobing, or engaged in sexual relations. (From the French verb *voir,* meaning "to see.")

Shooting Private Parts in Public Places

Police have this warning for Washington, DC, women: Beware of geeks bearing tiny cameras.

In what they describe as a growing trend, police are beginning to catch video voyeurs trying to shoot private parts in public places. These men are aiming the latest compact camcorders up women's skirts in crowded stores and shopping malls, parks, and fairs—and often posting the pictures on the Internet.

Fairfax County, Virginia, police arrested a 21-year-old man who was holding a palm-sized video camera under a woman's dress at a Tower Records store. At a Hecht's department store in Alexandria, police nabbed a 19-year-old man toting a bulky VHS video camera. He was angling for similar shots in the china department,

they said. At the Fairfax Fair, a man was arrested for videotaping from a camera bag dangling on a long strap down to his ankles.

"I had one guy who was doing it on Metro trains," said Alexandria Detective Harold Duquette, who tracked the suspect's movements across the region by watching days' worth of his video-tapes. "I mean, he was in D.C. (District of Columbia). He was in tunnels. He was sitting on benches. He had one lady reading the newspaper."

"UPSKIRT SITES"

What began as a small photo gallery on the Internet a couple of years ago has rapidly expanded to a multitude of "Up-skirt" sites, including one devoted entirely

to shots taken up skirts in Maryland, said Duquette.

Through the Internet, many of these video peepers learn about new techniques and exchange stories, Duquette added. The most popular method, is concealing a small video camera in a shoulder bag, with the lens pointing out of the top. The bag is either dangled under a woman's skirt or set on the ground next to her.

A LACK OF LAWS

Because the phenomenon is so new, there are few laws on the books to deal with it. Officials in Washington, DC, and Maryland say they do not have a law that specifically fits the crime, unless the person assaults the victims or stalks

---

Truth?Fiction?
Revisited

It is true that some sexual masochists cannot become sexually aroused unless they are bound, flogged, or humiliated by their sex partners.

Sexual masochism
A paraphilia characterized by the desire or need for pain or humiliation to enhance sexual arousal so that gratification may be attained. (From the name of Leopold von Sacher-Masoch.)

Bondage Ritual restraint, as by shackles, as practiced by many sexual masochists.

Sexual Masochism

Although pleasure and pain may seem like polar opposites, some people experience sexual pleasure through having pain or humiliation inflicted on them by their sex partners. *Question: What is sexual masochism?* People who associate experiencing pain or humiliation with sexual arousal are "into" **sexual masochism**. A sexual masochist either acts upon or is distressed by persistent urges and sexual fantasies involving the desire to be bound, flogged, humiliated, or made to suffer in some way by a sexual partner in order to achieve sexual excitement. In extreme cases the person is incapable of becoming sexually aroused unless pain or humiliation is incorporated into the sexual act.

Sexual masochism is the only paraphilia that is found among women with some frequency (DSM, 2000). Even sexual masochism is much more prevalent among men than among women, however. Male masochists may outnumber females by a margin of 20 to 1 (DSM, 2000).

The word *masochism* is derived from the name of the Austrian storyteller Leopold von Sacher-Masoch (1835–1895). He wrote tales of men who derived sexual satisfaction from having a female partner inflict pain on them, typically by flagellation (beating or whipping).

Sexual masochists may derive pleasure from various types of punishing experiences, including being restrained (a practice known as **bondage**), blindfolded (sensory bondage), spanked, whipped, or made to perform humiliating acts, such as walking around on all fours and licking the boots or shoes of the partner, or being subjected to vulgar insults. Some masochists have their partners urinate or defecate on them. Some masochists prefer a particular source of pain. Others seek an assort-

them. Peeping Tom statutes relate to peering into dwellings, not up skirts.

In Virginia, police are using a relatively new state law–"unlawful filming, videotaping or photographing of another"–to prosecute people caught putting their lenses where they're not wanted. The statute, a misdemeanor with a maximum penalty of 12 months in jail, applies to circumstances in which victims had a "reasonable expectation of privacy."

"Next time I go to the mall," said Kim Chinn, a Prince William County police spokeswoman, "I'm wearing jeans."

Source: Adapted from Patricia Davis (1998, June 9). Peeping Toms with videocams plague malls. *The Washington Post online.* Copyright © 1998 The Seattle Times Company.

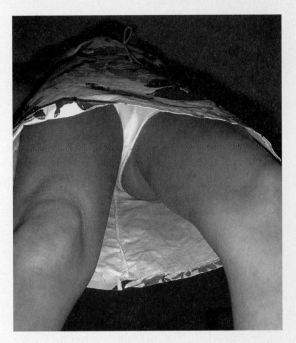

Shooting Private Parts in Public Places In places like the malls in the suburbs surrounding Washington, DC, police are beginning to catch people who are trying to shoot private parts in public places. They aim compact camcorders up women's skirts in crowded stores and shopping malls, parks, and fairs. Sometimes they post the pictures on the Internet. Often the pictures wind up for sale on sex sites.

ment. But we should not think that sexual masochists enjoy types of pain that do not involve sex. Sexual masochists are no more likely than anyone else to derive pleasure from the pain they experience when they stub their toes or touch a hot stove. Pain must be part of an elaborate sexual ritual to provide erotic gratification.

Sexual masochists and **sexual sadists** often form sexual relationships to meet each other's needs. Some sexual masochists enlist the services of prostitutes or obtain the cooperation of their regular sexual partners to enact their masochistic fantasies.

It may seem contradictory for pain to become connected with sexual pleasure. The association of sexual arousal with mildly painful stimuli is actually quite common, however. Kinsey and his colleagues (1953) reported that perhaps as many as 1 person in 4 has experienced erotic sensations from being bitten during lovemaking. The eroticization of mild forms of pain (love bites, hair pulls, minor scratches) may fall within the normal range of sexual variation. Pain from these sources increases overall bodily arousal, which may enhance sexual excitement. Some of us become sexually excited when our partners "talk dirty" to us or call us vulgar names. When the urge to experience pain for purposes of sexual arousal becomes so persistent or strong that it overshadows other sources of sexual stimulation, or when the masochistic experience causes physical or psychological harm, we may say that the boundary between normality and abnormality has been breached.

Baumeister (1988a) proposes that independent and responsible selfhood become burdensome or stressful at times. Sexual masochism provides a temporary reprieve from the responsibilities of independent selfhood. It is a blunting of one's ordinary

Truth?Fiction?
Revisited

It is in fact considered normal to enjoy some mild forms of pain during sexual activity. Love bites, hair pulls, and minor scratches are examples of sources of pain that are considered to fall within normal limits.

Sexual sadists People who become sexually aroused by inflicting pain or humiliation on others.

Hypoxyphilia A practice in which a person seeks to enhance sexual arousal, usually during masturbation, by becoming deprived of oxygen. (From the Greek root *hypo-,* meaning "under.")

Sexual sadism A paraphilia characterized by the desire or need to inflict pain or humiliation on others to enhance sexual arousal so that gratification is attained. (From the name of the Marquis de Sade.)

Sadomasochism A mutually gratifying sexual interaction between consenting sex partners in which sexual arousal is associated with the infliction and receipt of pain or humiliation. Commonly known as S&M.

level of self-awareness that is achieved by "focusing on immediate sensations (both painful and pleasant) and on being a sexual object" (Baumeister, 1988a, p. 54).

Sexual masochism can range from relatively benign to potentially lethal practices such as **hypoxyphilia.** Hypoxyphiliacs put plastic bags over their heads, nooses around their necks, or pressure on their chests to deprive themselves temporarily of oxygen and enhance their sexual arousal. They usually fantasize that they are being strangled by a lover. They try to discontinue oxygen deprivation before they lose consciousness, but some miscalculations result in death by suffocation or strangulation (Blanchard & Hucker, 1991; Cosgray et al., 1991).

Sexual Sadism

Sexual sadism seems to be the flip side of the coin of sexual masochism. *Question: What is sexual sadism?* **Sadism** is named after the infamous Marquis de Sade (1774–1814), a Frenchman who wrote tales of becoming sexually aroused by inflicting pain or humiliation on others. The virtuous Justine, the heroine of his best-known novel of the same name, endures terrible suffering at the hands of fiendish men. She is at one time bound and spread-eagled so that bloodhounds can savage her. She then seeks refuge with a surgeon who tries to dismember her. Later she falls into the clutches of a saber-wielding mass murderer, but Nature saves her with a timely thunderbolt.

Sexual sadism is characterized by persistent, powerful urges and sexual fantasies involving the inflicting of pain and suffering on others to achieve sexual excitement or gratification. The urges are acted on or are disturbing enough to cause personal distress. Some sexual sadists cannot become sexually aroused unless they make their sex partners suffer. Others can become sexually excited without such acts.

Some sadists hurt or humiliate willing partners, such as prostitutes or sexual masochists. Others—a small minority—stalk and attack nonconsenting victims.

Sadomasochism Sadomasochism (S&M) involves *mutually gratifying sexual interactions* between *consenting partners.* Occasional S&M is quite common among the general population. Couples may incorporate mild or light forms of S&M in their lovemaking now and then, such as mild dominance and submission games or gentle physical restraint. It is also not uncommon for lovers to scratch or bite their partners to heighten their mutual arousal during coitus. They generally do not inflict severe pain or damage, however.

Twenty-two percent of the men and 12% of the women surveyed by Kinsey and his colleagues (1953) reported at least some sexual response to sadomasochistic stories. Although some milder forms of sadomasochism may fall within the boundaries of normal sexual variation, sadomasochism becomes pathological when such fantasies are acted upon in ways that become destructive, dangerous, or distressing to oneself or others, as we find in the following case example:

Geoffrey Rush as the Marquis de Sade, in the Film Quills *Sexual sadism is a fascinating topic in literature and among social and behavioral scientists. Why is it that some individuals do not obtain sexual gratification unless it is at the expense of others whom they subject to pain or humiliation? Why are sadists almost invariably male?*

A 25-year-old female graduate student described a range of masochistic experiences. She reported feelings of sexual excitement during arguments with her husband when he would scream at her or hit her in a rage. She would sometimes taunt him to make love to her in a brutal fashion, as though she were being raped. She found the brutality and sense of being punished to be sexually stimulating. She had also begun having sex with strange men and enjoyed being physically punished by them during sex more than any other type of sexual stimulus. Being beaten or whipped produced the most intense sexual experiences she had ever had. Although she recognized the dangers posed by her sexual behavior, and felt somewhat ashamed about it, she was not sure that she wanted treatment for "it" because of the pleasure that it provided her. (Adapted from Spitzer et al., 1989, pp. 87–88)

In one subculture, sadomasochism is the preferred or even the exclusive form of sexual gratification. People in this subculture seek one another out through mutual contacts, S&M social organizations, or personal ads in S&M magazines. The S&M subculture has spawned magazines and clubs catering to people who describe themselves as "into S&M," as well as sex shops that sell sadomasochistic paraphernalia. These include leather restraints and leather face masks that resemble the ancient masks of executioners.

Participants in sadomasochism often engage in highly elaborate rituals involving dominance and submission. Rituals are staged, as though they were scenes in a play (Weinberg et al., 1984). In the "master and slave" game, the sadist leads the masochist around by a leash. The masochist performs degrading or menial acts. In bondage and discipline (B&D), the dominant partner restrains the submissive partner and flagellates (spanks or whips) or sexually stimulates the submissive partner. The erotic appeal of bondage seems connected with controlling or being controlled.

Various types of stimulation may be used to administer pain during S&M encounters, but pain is not always employed. When it is, it is usually mild or moderate. Psychological pain, or humiliation, is perhaps as common as physical pain. Pain may also be used symbolically, as in the case of a sadist who uses a harmless, soft rubber paddle to spank the masochist. Hence, the erotic appeal of pain for some S&M participants may derive from the ritual of control rather than from the pain itself (Weinberg, 1987).

Extreme forms of pain, such as torture or severe beatings, are rarely reported by sadomasochists (Breslow et al., 1985). Masochists may seek pain, but they usually avoid serious injury and dangerous partners (Baumeister, 1988b).

S&M participants may be heterosexual, gay, or bisexual (Breslow et al., 1986). They may assume either the masochistic or the sadistic role, or they may alternate roles depending on the sexual script. People who seek sexual excitement by enacting both sadistic and masochistic roles are known as *sadomasochists.* In heterosexual relationships the partners may reverse traditional gender roles. The man may assume the submissive or masochistic role, and the woman may take the dominant or sadistic role (Reinisch, 1990).

A survey of S&M participants drawn from ads in S&M magazines found that about 3 out of 4 were male and about 1 in 4 were female (Breslow et al., 1985). Most were married. Women respondents engaged in S&M more often and had more partners than men. (Apparently a greater number of men than women seek partners for S&M.)

The causes of sexual masochism and sadism, as of other paraphilias, are unclear. Ford and Beach (1951) speculated that humans may possess a physiological capacity to experience heightened sexual arousal from the receipt or infliction of pain (which may explain the prevalence of love bites). Mild pain may heighten physiological

Truth?Fiction?
Revisited

It is true that there is a subculture in the United States in which sexual sadists and sexual masochists form liaisons to inflict and receive pain and humiliation during sexual activity. This S&M subculture is catered to by sex shops, magazines, and Web sites.

arousal in both aggressor and victim, adding to the effects of sexual stimulation. Yet intense pain is likely to decrease rather than increase sexual arousal.

Pain may also have more direct biological links to pleasure. Natural chemicals called *endorphins,* similar to opiates, are released in the brain in response to pain and produce feelings of euphoria and general well-being. Perhaps, then, pleasure is derived from pain because of the release or augmentation of endorphins (Weinberg, 1987). This theory fails to explain the erotic appeal of sadomasochistic encounters that involve minimal or symbolic pain, however. Nor does it explain the erotic appeal to the sadist of inflicting pain.

Whatever their causes, the roots of sexual masochism and sadism apparently date to childhood. Sadomasochistic behavior commonly begins in early adulthood, but sadomasochistic fantasies are likely to have been present during childhood (DSM, 2000; Breslow et al., 1986).

Frotteurism

Some people who use the subway run into pickpockets. Some women who use the subway find themselves victimized by frotteurs. *Question: What is frotteurism?* **Frotteurism** (also known as "mashing") is rubbing against or touching a nonconsenting person. As with other paraphilias, a diagnosis of frotteurism requires either acting upon these urges or being distressed by them. Mashing has been reported exclusively among males (DSM, 2000).

Most mashing takes place in crowded places, such as buses, subway cars, or elevators. The man finds the rubbing or the touching, not the coercive nature of the act, to be sexually stimulating. While rubbing against a woman, he may fantasize a consensual, affectionate sexual relationship with her. Typically the man incorporates images of his mashing within his masturbation fantasies. A practice related to mashing is **toucherism**: fondling nonconsenting strangers.

Mashing may be so fleeting and furtive that the woman may not realize what has happened. Mashers thus stand little chance of being caught. Consider the case of a man who victimized a thousand or so women within a decade but was arrested only twice:

> Charles, 45, was seen by a psychiatrist following his second arrest for rubbing against a woman in the subway. He would select as his target a woman in her 20s as she entered the subway station. He would then position himself behind her on the platform and wait for the train to arrive. He would then follow her into the subway car and when the doors closed would begin bumping his penis against her buttocks, while fantasizing that they were enjoying having intercourse in a loving and consensual manner. About half of the time he would ejaculate into a plastic bag that he had wrapped around his penis to prevent staining his pants. He would then continue on his way to work. Sometimes when he hadn't ejaculated he would change trains and seek another victim. While he felt guilty for a time after each episode, he would soon become preoccupied with thoughts about his next encounter. He never gave any thought to the feelings his victims might have about what he had done to them. While he was married to the same woman for 25 years, he appears to be rather socially inept and unassertive, especially with women. (Adapted from Spitzer et al., 1989, pp. 106–107)

Although this masher was married, many mashers have difficulty forming relationships with women and are handicapped by fears of rejection. Mashing provides sexual contact in a relatively nonthreatening context.

Frotteurism A paraphilia characterized by recurrent, powerful sexual urges and related fantasies involving rubbing against or touching a nonconsenting person. (From the French *frotter,* meaning "to rub.")

Toucherism A practice related to frotteurism and characterized by the persistent urge to fondle nonconsenting strangers.

Other Paraphilias

The paraphilias we have been discussing, fetishism through frotteurism, are the most common. But there are others. *Question: What less common paraphilias are there?*

Zoophilia A person with **zoophilia** experiences repeated, intense urges and related fantasies involving sexual contact with animals. As with other paraphilias, the criteria for this diagnosis are that the urges be acted upon or cause personal distress. A child or adolescent who shows some sexual response to an occasional episode of rough-and-tumble play with the family pet is not displaying zoophilia.

The term *bestiality* applies to actual sexual contact with an animal. Human sexual contact with animals, mythical and real, has a long history. Michelangelo's painting *Leda and the Swan* depicts the Greek god Zeus taking the form of a swan to mate with a woman, Leda. Zeus was also portrayed as taking the form of a bull or serpent to mate with humans. In the Old Testament, God is said to have put to death people who had sexual relations with animals. The Greek historian Herodotus notes that goats at the Egyptian temple at Mendes were trained to copulate with people.

Although the prevalence of zoophilia in the general population is unknown, Kinsey and his colleagues (1948, 1953) found that about 8% of the men and 3% to 4% of the women interviewed admitted to sexual contacts with animals. Men more often had sexual contact with farm animals, such as calves and sheep. Women more often reported sexual contacts with household pets. Men were more likely to masturbate or copulate with the animals. Women more often reported general body contact. People of both genders reported encouraging the animals to lick their genitals. A few women reported that they had trained a dog to engage in coitus with them. Urban–rural differences also emerged. Rates of bestiality were higher among boys reared on farms. Compared with only a few city boys, 17% of farm boys had reached orgasm at some time through sexual contact with dogs, cows, and goats. These contacts were generally restricted to adolescence, when human outlets were not available. Still, adults sometimes engage in sexual contacts with animals, generally because of curiosity or novelty or for a sexual release when human partners are unavailable. Whether such contacts constitute zoophilia depends on their frequency and intensity or on whether they cause the person distress. In most cases, true zoophilia is associated with deep-seated psychological problems and difficulties developing intimate relationships with people.

Necrophilia In **necrophilia**, a rare paraphilia, a person desires sex with corpses. Three types of necrophilia have been identified (Rosman & Resnick, 1989). In *regular necrophilia*, the person has sex with a deceased person. In *necrophilic homicide*, the person commits murder to obtain a corpse for sexual purposes. In *necrophilic fantasy*, the person fantasizes about sex with a corpse but does not actually carry out necrophilic acts. Necrophiles often obtain jobs that provide them with access to corpses, such as working in cemeteries, morgues, or funeral homes. The primary motivation for necrophilia appears to be the desire to sexually possess a completely unresisting and nonrejecting partner (Rosman & Resnick, 1989). Many necrophiles are clearly mentally disturbed.

Less Common Paraphilias In **klismaphilia**, sexual arousal is derived from use of enemas. Klismaphiles generally prefer the receiving role to the giving role. Klismaphiles may have derived sexual pleasure in childhood from the anal stimulation provided by parents giving them enemas.

Zoophilia A paraphilia characterized by persistent or repeated sexual urges and related fantasies involving sexual contact with animals.

Necrophilia A paraphilia characterized by desire for sexual activity with corpses. (From the Greek *nekros*, meaning "dead body.")

Klismaphilia A paraphilia in which sexual arousal is derived from use of enemas.

Human Sexuality in the New Millennium

"Cybersex Addiction"—A New Psychological Disorder?

Sex is the hottest topic among adult users of the Internet. Studies show that fully a third of all visits are directed to sexually oriented Web sites, chat rooms, and news groups.

For most people these forays into cybersex are relatively harmless recreational pursuits, but experts in the field say that the affordability, accessibility, and anonymity of the Internet are fueling a brand new psychological disorder—cybersex addiction—that appears to be spreading with astonishing rapidity and bringing turmoil to the lives of those affected.

Writing in the journal *Sexual Addiction and Compulsivity* (*http://www.tandf.co.uk/journals/titles/10720162.html*), psychologist Al Cooper and his colleagues (2000) report that many of the men and women who now spend dozens of hours each week seeking sexual stimulation from their computers deny that they have a problem and refuse to seek help until their marriages and/or their jobs are in serious jeopardy.

For some people, the route to compulsive use of the Internet for sexual satisfaction is fast and short, said Dr. Mark Schwartz of Masters and Johnson. "Sex on the Net is like heroin," he said. "It grabs them and takes over their lives. And it's very difficult to treat because the people affected don't want to give it up."

Those most strongly hooked on Internet sex are likely to spend hours each day masturbating to pornographic images or having "mutual" online sex with someone contacted through a chat room. Occasionally, they progress to actual affairs with sex partners they meet online.

Cooper and his colleagues (1999, 2000) conducted the largest and most detailed survey of online sex. Cooper calls the Net "the crack cocaine of sexual compulsivity." The survey, conducted online among 9,265 men and women who admitted surfing the Net for sexually oriented sites, indicated that at least 1% were seriously hooked on online sex. The survey found that

Do People Become Addicted to Cybersex? *According to Dr. Mark Schwartz of the Masters and Johnson Institute, "Sex on the Net is like heroin" for some people. "It grabs them and takes over their lives." Some people spend hours each day masturbating to pornographic images they find online or engaging in "mutual" online sex with someone they contact through a chat room. Is getting hooked on cybersex a safe kind of "addiction"? What do you think?*

as many as a third of Internet users have visited some type of sexual site.

"This is a hidden public health hazard exploding, in part, because very few are recognizing it as such or taking it seriously," Dr. Cooper wrote in the journal article.

According to Dr. Cooper, who works at the San Jose Marital and Sexuality Center in Santa Clara, California, cybersex compulsives are just like drug addicts. They "use the Internet as an important part of their sexual acting out, much like a drug addict who has a 'drug of choice,'" and often with serious harm to their home lives and livelihood. Especially vulnerable to becoming hooked on Internet sex, he wrote, are "those users whose sexuality may have been suppressed and limited all their lives [but who] suddenly find an infinite supply of sexual opportunities" on the Internet.

A second survey conducted by Dr. Jennifer Schneider, a physician in Tucson, Arizona, among 94 family

Coprophilia A paraphilia in which sexual arousal is attained in connection with feces. (From the Greek *copros,* meaning "dung.")

In **coprophilia**, sexual arousal is connected with feces. The person may desire to be defecated on or to defecate on a sex partner. The association of feces with sexual arousal may also be a throwback to childhood. Many children appear to obtain anal sexual pleasure by holding in and then purposefully expelling feces. It may also be that the incidental connection between erections or sexual arousal and soiled diapers during infancy eroticizes feces.

members affected by cybersex addiction reveals that the problem can arise even among people in loving marriages with ample sexual opportunities. "Sex on the Net is just so seductive and it's so easy to stumble upon it," she said. "People who are vulnerable can get hooked before they know it."

To those who say a behavioral compulsion is not a true addiction, Dr. Schneider responds with a definition of addiction that would clearly apply to cybersex abusers: "Loss of control, continuation of the behavior despite significant adverse consequences, and preoccupation or obsession with obtaining the drug or pursuing the behavior." Although behavioral addictions involve no external drugs, research suggests that they may cause changes in brain chemicals, such as the release of endorphins, that help to perpetuate the behavior.

The sexual stimulation and release obtained through cybersex also contribute to the pursuit of the activity, Dr. Schwartz said. He wrote, "Intense orgasms from the minimal investment of a few keystrokes are powerfully reinforcing." He added, "Cybersex affords easy, inexpensive access to a myriad of ritualized encounters with idealized partners."

Some cybersex addicts develop a conditioned response to the computer and become sexually aroused even before turning it on, Dr. Putnam said. This can exacerbate the problem for people whose jobs involve work on a computer. "Simply sitting down to work at the computer can start a sexual response that may facilitate online sexual activities," he wrote in the journal.

As with other addictions, tolerance to cybersex stimulation can develop, prompting the addict to take more and more risks to recapture the initial high, Dr. Schneider said. Online viewing that began as a harmless recreation can become an all-consuming activity and can even lead to real sexual encounters with people met online.

Cybersex compulsives can become so involved with their online activities that they ignore their partners and children and risk their jobs. In Dr. Cooper's survey, 20% of the men and 12% of the women reported that they had used computers at work for some sexual pursuits. Many companies now monitor employees' online activities, and repeated visits to sexually oriented sites have cost people their jobs.

To those who say, "What's the harm? They're not risking disease or death," Dr. Schneider, who has written extensively on sexual addiction, responds that the damage to a cybersex addict's life and family can be as devastating as that caused by compulsive gambling or addiction to alcohol or drugs. In her survey, 91 women and 3 men in committed relationships said they had experienced serious adverse consequences, including broken relationships, from their partners' cybersex addictions. Partners commonly reported feeling betrayed, devalued, deceived, ignored, abandoned and unable to compete with a fantasy.

Among them was a 34-year-old woman who had been married for 14 years to a minister who she discovered was compulsively seeking sexual satisfaction by visiting pornographic sites on the Internet. "How can I compete with hundreds of anonymous others who are now in our bed, in his head?" the woman wrote. "Our bed is crowded with countless faceless strangers, where once we were intimate."

Children, too, often become victimized by cybersex addiction in a parent. As Dr. Schneider noted, children can stumble upon the pornographic material left on or near the computer or walk in on a parent masturbating at the computer. Several mothers in her survey were worried because their husbands surfed the Net while supposedly watching their children, who got to view the pornography and sometimes the masturbation.

As Dr. Putnam put it, "Once people get hooked on cybersex, they tend to put themselves at risk and do things they wouldn't ordinarily do."

Source: Adapted from Brody, J. E. (2000, May 16). Cybersex gives birth to a psychological disorder. *The New York Times,* pp. F7, F12.

In **urophilia,** sexual arousal is associated with urine. As with coprophilia, the person may desire to be urinated on or to urinate on a sexual partner. Also like coprophilia, urophilia may have childhood origins. Stimulation of the urethral canal during urination may become associated with sexual pleasure. Or urine may have become eroticized by experiences in which erections occurred while the infant was clothed in a wet diaper.

Urophilia A paraphilia in which sexual arousal is associated with urine.

Review: The Paraphilias

Reflect

Are the women on your campus who enjoy dressing in men's-style clothing, such as blue jeans, to be considered transvestites? Why, or why not?

CriticalThinking

Critical thinkers pay closer attention to definitions. Why are (most) stripteasers and nude sunbathers *not* exhibitionists?

3. _____ involve sexual arousal in response to unusual stimuli, objects, or pain or humiliation.

4. The diagnosis of paraphilia requires that the person either have acted on the urges or be _____ by them.

5. Paraphilias such as fetishism and cross-_____ (transvestic fetishism) are generally victimless.

6. In sexual _____, sexual excitement is connected to harming another person.

7. Most paraphilias occur among (*Men* or *Women*?).

8. In _____, an inanimate object evokes sexual arousal.

9. In _____, people are excessively aroused by a specific body part, such as feet.

10. _____ become sexually aroused by wearing articles of clothing of the other sex.

11. _____ involves exposing one's genitals to strangers to achieve sexual gratification.

12. A survey of college women found that

about _____ had run into a "flasher."

13. Exhibitionism usually begins (*After* or *Before*?) age 18.

14. According to the text, stripteasers (*Are* or *Are not*?) exhibitionists.

15. In the DSM, obscene telephone calling is termed telephone _____.

16. _____ involves urges to observe unsuspecting strangers who are naked, disrobing, or engaged in sexual relations.

17. It is (*Normal* or *Abnormal*?) to be sexually stimulated by the sight of other people who are nude, undressing, or engaged in sexual relations.

18. People who associate the receipt of pain with sexual arousal are called sexual _____.

19. _____ is named after the infamous Marquis de Sade.

20. _____ is abbreviated S&M.

21. _____ is also known as "mashing."

22. In _____, a person desires sex with corpses.

Theoretical Perspectives

The paraphilias are fascinating and perplexing variations in sexual behavior. We may find it difficult to understand how people can become sexually excited by fondling an article of clothing or by cross-dressing. It may also be difficult to identify with people who feel compelled to exhibit their genitals or to rub their genitals against unsuspecting victims in crowded places. Perhaps we can recognize some voyeuristic tendencies in ourselves, but we cannot imagine peeping through binoculars while perched in a nearby tree or, for that matter, risking the social and legal consequences of being discovered in the act. Nor might we understand how people can become sexually turned on by inflicting or receiving pain. Let us consider explanations that have been advanced from various theoretical perspectives.

Biological Perspectives

Researchers are investigating whether there are biological factors in paraphilic behavior. *Question: What is the biological perspective on paraphilias?* The biological perspective looks into factors such as the endocrine system (hormones) and the nervous system in paraphilic behavior.

Because testosterone is linked to sex drive, researchers have focused on differences in testosterone levels between people with paraphilias and people without them. One study found evidence of some hormonal differences between a group of 16 male exhibitionists and controls (Lang et al., 1989). Although no differences in overall levels of testosterone were found, researchers reported that exhibitionists evidenced significantly elevated levels of the measure of testosterone believed to be most closely linked to sex drive. The implication would be that exhibitionists may have biologically elevated sex drives, although the results would not address why exhibitionists expose themselves to achieve, or in response to, sexual arousal.

Other studies appear to confirm that many paraphilics do have higher-than-normal sex drives (Haake et al., 2003; Kafka, 2003). A German study, for example, found that people with parahilias had shorter refractory periods after orgasm by masturbation than most men and experienced a higher frequency of sexual fantasies and urges (Haake et al., 2003). Kafka (2003) refers to this heightened sex drive as *hypersexual desire*—the opposite of hypoactive sexual desire disorder (see Chapter 15). Bradford concurs and believes that paraphilics of this type could be considered to have *hyperactive sexual desire disorder.*

But these studies address the strength of the sex drive, not the direction it takes. A more recent study used the electroencephalograph (EEG) to investigate electrical responses in the brain among paraphilics and control subjects. They measured what is termed "evoked electrical potentials" to erotic stimuli in a sample of 62 right-handed men, half of whom were considered normal in terms of their sexual fantasies and behaviors (the control subjects), and half of whom had been diagnosed as paraphilic (fetishistic and sadomasochistic) (Waismann et al., 2003). The men were shown three sets of 57 slides each in random order—57 paraphilic slides that portrayed depicting fetishistic and sadomasochistic themes, 57 "normal" slides that depicted nude women, coitus, and oral sex, and 57 neutral slides of landscapes, street scenes, and the like. An electrical response labeled "P600" was determined to be the best indicator of sexual arousal in the men. It was found that the main site for evoking the P600 response to "normal" sexual stimuli was on the right side of the brain. The main site for paraphilic stimuli was the left, frontal part of the brain. Paraphilic men showed a significantly greater response than control subjects in the P600 response in the left, frontal part of the brain. Moreover, control subjects were more likely to differentiate between paraphilic and normal stimuli on the right side of the brain.

Another neurological study may offer some insight into masochism. A research team from Massachusetts General Hospital found that the same neural circuits in the brain are often activated either by painful or by pleasurable stimuli (Becerra et al., 2001). The researchers discovered that a painfully hot (115°F) stimulus to the hand activated areas of the brain believed to involve "reward" circuitry. The researchers had set out to find ways to help chronic pain patients, not to investigate sexual masochism, but their findings certainly have implications for masochism.

Psychologist J. Michael Bailey (2003a) believes that as time goes on, we will learn more about potential biological foundations of paraphilic behavior. Better understanding of these atypical patterns of sexual behavior may lead to the development of more effective treatments.

Psychoanalytic Perspectives

Psychoanalytic theory has attempted explanations of a number of sexual matters. *Question: What is the psychoanalytic perspective on paraphilias?* Psychoanalytic theory suggests that paraphilias are psychological defenses, usually against unresolved castration anxiety dating to the Oedipus complex (Fenichel, 1945; Horne, 2003). Perhaps the sight of a woman's vagina threatens to arouse castration anxiety in the transvestite, reminding him that women do not have penises and that he might suffer the same fate. Sequestering his penis beneath women's clothing symbolically asserts that women *do* have penises, which provides unconscious reassurance against his own fears of castration. By exposing his genitals, perhaps the exhibitionist unconsciously seeks reassurance that his penis is secure. It is as if he were asserting, "Look! I have a penis!" Shock or surprise on the victim's face confirms that his penis exists, temporarily relieving castration anxiety. Perhaps masturbation with an object such as a shoe enables the fetishist to gratify his sexual desires while keeping a safe distance from the dangers that he unconsciously associates with sexual contact with women. Or the fetishistic object itself—the shoe—may unconsciously symbolize the penis. Are sadists attempting to defend themselves against unconscious feelings of impotence by inflicting pain on others?

The paraphilias have provided a fertile ground for psychoanalytic theories. However, such evidence as there is consists of case studies and anecdotes, which are open to interpretation. Unconscious mechanisms cannot be directly observed or measured. Psychoanalytic theories remain interesting but speculative hypotheses about the origins of the paraphilias.

Learning-Theory Perspectives

Learning theorists, like psychoanalytic theorists, believe that experience plays a major role in the development of sexual preferences. *Question: What are learning-theory perspectives on paraphilias?* Learning theorists generally believe that fetishes and other paraphilias are learned behaviors that are acquired through experience. An object may acquire sexually arousing properties through association with sexual arousal or orgasm. According to Alfred Kinsey and his colleagues (1953),

> Even some of the most extremely variant types of human sexual behavior may need no more explanation than is provided by our understanding of the processes of learning and conditioning. Behavior which may appear bizarre, perverse, or unthinkably unacceptable to some persons, and even to most persons, may have significance for other individuals because of the way in which they have been conditioned. (pp. 645–646)

According to the conditioning model, a boy who glimpses his mother's stockings hanging on the towel rack while he is masturbating may develop a fetish for stockings. Orgasm in the presence of the object reinforces the erotic connection, especially if it occurs repeatedly.

Breslow (1989) proposed a learning-theory explanation that describes the development of paraphilias in terms of the gradual acquisition of sexual arousal to an unusual object or activity through its incorporation in masturbatory fantasies. A transvestite, for example, may have achieved an erection while trying on his mother's panties in childhood. Panties are then incorporated into masturbatory fantasies and reinforced by orgasm. The paraphilic object or activity is repeatedly used as a masturbatory aid, strengthening the erotic bond.

McGuire and his colleagues (1965) report a case that provides some support for the role of learning in the development of exhibi-

Is Her Behavior Appropriate or Inappropriate?
Many theorists suggest that early learning experiences contribute to the development of paraphilias. Is this woman's interaction with her young child of the sort that can lead to sexual problems as the child matures?

tionism. Two young males were surprised by an attractive woman while urinating. Although they were embarrassed at the time, their memories of the incident were sexually stimulating, and they masturbated repeatedly while fantasizing about it. The fantasies persisted, possibly reinforced by frequent orgasms. After a while, the young men purposely began to expose themselves to rekindle the high level of sexual excitement. Still, only a small percentage of men who have been discovered while exposed have become exhibitionists.

Friedrich & Gerber (1994) studied five adolescent boys who practiced hypoxyphilia and found extensive early histories of choking in combination with physical or sexual abuse. The combination seems to have encouraged each of the boys to associate choking with sexual arousal.

Learning explanations of sexual masochism focus on the pairing of sexual excitement with punishment. For example, a child may be punished when discovered masturbating. Or a boy may reflexively experience an erection if his penis accidentally rubs against the parent's body as he is being spanked. With repeated encounters like these, pain and pleasure may become linked in the person's sexual arousal system.

Many exhibitionists, voyeurs, frotteurs, and other people with paraphilias have few interpersonal skills in relating to women and may avoid "normal" social interactions with them for fear of rejection. Their furtive, paraphilic behaviors may provide sexual release without risk of rejection and may be maintained because they are the only source of sexual gratification.

Modeling or observational learning may also play a role in the development of some cases. Parents, for example, may inadvertently model exhibitionistic behavior to young sons, which can lead the sons to eroticize the act of exposing themselves. Young people may also read books or magazines or view films or TV programs with paraphilic content. Media may give them the idea of trying paraphilic behavior, and they may find it exciting, especially if acts such as exhibitionism or voyeurism provide a rush or adrenaline.

Sociological Perspectives

Psychoanalytic theory and learning theory are psychological theories that focus on the mental processes and behavior of the individual. *Question: What are sociological perspectives on paraphilic behavior?* Sociological perspectives tend to focus on the effects of the group and of society in general on individual and group behavior. For example, although most people indulge paraphilias privately, sexual masochists and sadists require a partner. Most sadomasochists learn S&M rituals, make sexual contacts, acquire sexual paraphernalia, and confirm their sadomasochistic self-identities within what is termed an *S&M subculture*—a loosely connected network of S&M clubs, specialty shops, organizations, magazines, and so on. But the S&M subculture exists in the context of the larger society, and its rituals mirror widely based social and gender roles.

Martin Weinberg (1987) proposes a sociological model that focuses on the social context of sadomasochism. S&M rituals generally involve some form of dominance and submission. Weinberg attributes their erotic appeal to the opportunity to reverse the customary power relationships that exist between males and females and between social classes. Within the confines of the carefully scripted S&M encounter, the meek can be powerful and the powerful can be meek. People from lower social classes or in menial jobs may be drawn to S&M so that they can enact a dominant role. Dominance and submission games allow people to accentuate or reverse the gender stereotypes that identify masculinity with dominance and femininity with submissiveness. Even so, interviews with, and observations of, sadomasochists suggest that

Review: Theoretical Perspectives

Reflect

Which of the theoretical perspectives presented here seems to be most scientific to you? Why?

CriticalThinking

If people with paraphilias have powerful urges to engage in deviant behavior as a consequence of biological forces or unconscious fears, can they be expected to control their behavior?

23. Several studies suggest that many people with paraphilias have (*Higher* or *Lower*?)-than-normal sex drives.

24. An EEG study found that the main site for evoking a "P600" response to normal sexual stimuli was on the (*Right* or *Left*?) side of the brain.

25. Psychoanalytic theory suggests that paraphilias may be defenses against unresolved _____ anxiety.

26. According to learning theory, an object may acquire sexually arousing properties through _____ with sexual arousal or orgasm.

27. Breslow proposed that the development of paraphilias involves the gradual acquisition of sexual arousal to an unusual object or activity through its incorporation into _____ fantasies.

28. Learning explanations of sexual masochism focus on pairing sexual excitement with _____.

29. Weinberg proposes a _____ model that attributes the erotic appeal of S&M encounters to the opportunity to reverse the customary power relationships that exist in society.

30. Money and Lamacz believe that childhood experiences etch a _____ in the brain that determines what types of stimuli and activities become sexually arousing.

Lovemap A pattern in the brain, wherein is etched a representation of the idealized lover and the idealized erotic activity with the lover.

most often dominance–submission relationships tend to be consistent with traditional masculine and feminine gender roles in society (Damon, 2002; Santtila et al., 2002). Although there are many exceptions, men more often tend to be dominant and women to be submissive in S&M rituals.

An Integrated Perspective: The "Lovemap"

Like other sexual patterns, paraphilias may have multiple biological, psychological, and sociocultural origins (Seligman & Hardenburg, 2000). Might our understanding of them thus be best approached from a theoretical framework that incorporates multiple perspectives? John Money (2000), for example, traces the origins of paraphilias to childhood. He believes that childhood experiences etch a pattern in the brain, called a **lovemap**. *Question: What is a lovemap?* This lovemap determines the types of stimuli and activities that become sexually arousing to the individual. In the case of paraphilias, lovemaps become distorted or "vandalized" by early traumatic experiences, such as incest, antisexual upbringing, and abuse or neglect.

Research suggests that voyeurs and exhibitionists often were the victims of childhood sexual abuse (Lee et al., 2002). Not all children exposed to such influences develop paraphilic compulsions, however. For reasons that remain unknown, some children who are exposed to such influences appear to be more vulnerable to developing distorted lovemaps than are others. A genetic predisposition, hormonal factors, brain abnormalities, or a combination of these and other factors may play a role in determining one's vulnerability to vandalized lovemaps.

Treatment of the Paraphilias

The treatment of these atypical patterns of sexual behavior raises a number of issues. First, people with paraphilias usually do not want or seek treatment, at least not voluntarily. They often deny that they are offenders, even after they are apprehended and convicted. They are generally seen by mental health workers only when they come into conflict with the law or at the urging of their family members or sexual partners who have discovered them performing the paraphilic behavior or found evidence of their paraphilic interests.

Paraphilic behavior is a source of pleasure, so many people are not motivated to give it up. The individual typically perceives his problems as stemming from society's intolerance, not from feelings of guilt or shame.

Second, helping professionals may encounter ethical problems when they are asked to contribute to a judicial process by trying to persuade a sex offender that he (virtually all are male) *ought* to change his behavior. Helping professionals traditionally help clients clarify or meet their own goals; it is not their role to impose societal goals on the individual. Many helping professionals believe that the criminal justice system, not they, ought to enforce social standards.

The third issue is a treatment problem. Therapists realize that they are generally less successful with resistant or recalcitrant clients. Unless the motivation to change is present, therapeutic effort is often wasted.

The fourth problem is the issue of perceived responsibility. Sex offenders almost invariably claim that they are unable to control their urges and impulses. Such claims of uncontrollability are often self-serving and may lead others to treat offenders with greater sympathy and understanding. Most therapies, however, are based on the belief that whatever causes may have led to the problem behavior, and however difficult it may be to resist these unusual sexual urges, accepting personal responsibility for one's actions is a prelude to change. Thus, if therapy is to be constructive, it is necessary to break through the client's personal mythology that he or she is powerless to control his or her behavior.

Despite these issues, many offenders are referred for treatment by the courts. A few seek therapy themselves because they have come to see how their behavior harms themselves or others. Let us consider some of the ways in which therapists treat people with these atypical sexual behavior patterns.

We shall consider psychological and biological approaches to the treatment of people with paraphilias. *Question: What psychological approaches are used to treat paraphilias?* The major psychological approaches that have been used to treat the paraphilias are psychoanalysis and cognitive–behavioral therapy.

Psychoanalytic Psychotherapy

Psychoanalysis focuses on resolving the unconscious conflicts that are believed to originate in childhood and to give rise in adulthood to pathological problems such as paraphilias. The aim of therapy is to help bring unconscious conflicts, principally Oedipal conflicts, into conscious awareness so that they might be worked through in the light of the individual's adult personality (Laws & Marshall, 2003).

Although some favorable case results have been reported, psychoanalytic therapy of the paraphilias has not been subjected to experimental analysis. We thus do not know whether successes are due to the psychoanalytic treatment itself or to other factors, such as spontaneous improvement or a client's willingness to change.

Cognitive–Behavioral Therapy

Whereas traditional psychoanalysis tends to entail a lengthy process of exploration of the childhood origins of problem behaviors, **cognitive–behavioral therapy** is relatively briefer and focuses directly on changing behavior. Cognitive–behavioral therapy has spawned a number of techniques to help eliminate paraphilic behaviors and strengthen appropriate sexual behaviors. These techniques include systematic

Cognitive–behavioral therapy Therapy that attempts to change directly the ways in which people view events and respond to them, relying frequently on the application of principles of learning.

Systematic desensitization

A method for terminating the connection between a stimulus (such as a fetishistic object) and an inappropriate response (such as sexual arousal to the paraphilic stimulus). Muscle relaxation is practiced in connection with each stimulus in a series of increasingly arousing stimuli, so that the person learns to remain relaxed (and not sexually aroused) in their presence.

Aversion therapy

A method for terminating undesirable sexual behavior in which the behavior is repeatedly paired with an aversive stimulus such as electric shock so that a conditioned aversion develops.

Covert sensitization

A form of aversion therapy in which thoughts of engaging in undesirable behavior are paired repeatedly with imagined aversive stimuli.

Pedophiles
Persons with pedophilia, a paraphilia involving sexual interest in children.

Social-skills training

Behavior therapy methods for building social skills through a therapist's coaching and through practice.

Orgasmic reconditioning
A method for strengthening the connection between sexual arousal and appropriate sexual stimuli (such as fantasies about an adult of the other gender) by repeatedly pairing the appropriate stimuli with orgasm.

desensitization, aversion therapy, social skills training, covert sensitization, and orgasmic reconditioning, to name a few (Krueger & Kaplan, 2002).

Systematic desensitization attempts to break the link between the sexual stimulus (such as a fetishistic stimulus) and the inappropriate response (sexual arousal). The client is first taught to relax selected muscle groups in the body. Muscle relaxation is then paired repeatedly with each of a series of progressively more arousing paraphilic images or fantasies. Relaxation comes to replace sexual arousal in response to each of these stimuli, even the most provocative. In one case study, a fetishistic transvestite who had become attracted to his mother's lingerie at age 13 was taught to relax when presented with audiotaped scenes representing transvestite or fetishistic themes (Fensterheim & Kantor, 1980). He played such tapes daily while remaining relaxed. He later reported a complete absence of transvestite thoughts or activities.

In **aversion therapy**, the undesirable sexual behavior (for example, masturbation to fetishistic fantasies) is paired repeatedly with an aversive stimulus (such as a harmless but painful electric shock or a nausea-inducing chemical) in the hope that the client will develop a conditioned aversion to the paraphilic behavior.

Covert sensitization is a variation of aversion therapy in which paraphilic fantasies are paired with an aversive stimulus in imagination. In one study of 38 **pedophiles** and 62 exhibitionists, more than half of whom were court referred, subjects were treated by pairing imagined aversive odors with fantasies of the problem behavior (Maletzky, 1980). They were instructed to fantasize pedophiliac or exhibitionistic scenes. Then,

> At a point . . . when sexual pleasure is aroused, aversive images are presented. . . . Examples might include a pedophiliac fellating a child, but discovering a festering sore on the boy's penis, an exhibitionist exposing to a woman but suddenly being discovered by his wife or the police, or a pedophiliac laying a young boy down in a field, only to lie next to him in a pile of dog feces. (Maletzky, 1980, p. 308)

Maletzky used this treatment weekly for 6 months and then followed it with booster sessions every 3 months over a 3-year period. The procedure resulted in at least a 75% reduction in the deviant activities and fantasies for over 80% of the study participants at follow-up periods of up to 36 months. At a 25-year follow-up of 7,275 sex offenders who received similar treatment, Maletzky and Steinhauser (2002) found that benefits were maintained for many of the exhibitionists but for fewer of the pedophiles. However, fewer than 50% of the original participants could be contacted after this much time had passed.

Social-skills training focuses on helping the individual improve his ability to relate to the other gender. The therapist might first model a desired behavior, such as how to ask a woman out on a date or how to handle a rejection. The client might then role-play the behavior, with the therapist playing the part of the woman. Following the role-play enactment, the therapist would provide feedback and additional guidance and modeling to help the client improve his skills. This process would be repeated until the client mastered the skill.

Orgasmic reconditioning aims to increase sexual arousal to socially appropriate sexual stimuli by pairing culturally appropriate imagery with orgasmic pleasure. The person is instructed to become sexually aroused by masturbating to paraphilic images or fantasies. But as he approaches the point of orgasm, he switches to appropriate imagery and focuses on it during orgasm. In a case example, Davison (1977) reports reduction of sadistic fantasies in a 21-year-old college man. The client was instructed to attain an erection in any way he could, even through the use of the sadistic fantasies he wished to eliminate. But once erection was achieved, he was to masturbate while looking at photos of *Playboy* models. Orgasm was thus paired with nonsadistic images. These images and fantasies eventually acquired the capacity to elicit sexual arousal. Orgasmic reconditioning is often combined with other techniques, such as social-skills training, so that more desirable social behaviors can be strengthened as well (Adams et al., 1981).

Although behavior therapy techniques tend to have higher reported success rates than most other methods, they too are limited by reliance on uncontrolled case studies. Without appropriate controls, we cannot isolate the effective elements of therapy or determine that the results were not due merely to the passage of time or to other factors not related to the treatment. It is possible that clients who are highly motivated to change may succeed in doing so with *any* systematic approach.

In many ways the treatment of sexual problems is becoming more "medicalized" (Kleinplatz, 2003). *Question: What medical approaches are used to treat paraphilias?*

Medical Approaches

There is no medical "cure" for the paraphilias. No drug or surgical technique eliminates paraphilic urges and behavior. Yet some progress has recently been reported in using selective serotonin reuptake inhibitors (SSRIs), which are used mainly as antidepressants, in treating exhibitionism, voyeurism, and fetishism (Bradford, 2001; Roesler & Witztum, 2000). Why SSRIs? In addition to treating depression, SSRIs have been helpful in treating obsessive–compulsive disorder, a type of emotional disorder involving recurrent obsessions (intrusive ideas) and/or compulsions (urges to repeat a certain behavior or thought). Paraphilic behavior has an obsessive–compulsive quality. People with paraphilias often experience intrusive, repetitive thoughts or images of the paraphilic object or stimulus, such as mental images of young children. Many also report feeling compelled to carry out the paraphilic acts repeatedly. Paraphilias may belong to what researchers have dubbed an obsessive–compulsive spectrum of behaviors.

People who experience such intense urges that they are at risk of committing sexual offenses may be helped by **anti-androgen drugs**, which reduce the level of testosterone in the bloodstream (Bradford, 2001; Roesler & Witztum, 2000). Testosterone is closely linked to sex drive and interest. Medroxyprogesterone acetate (MPA) (trade name: Depo-Provera), which is administered in weekly injections, is the anti-androgen that has been used most extensively in the treatment of sex offenders. In men, anti-androgens reduce testosterone to a level that is typical of a prepubertal boy (Bradford, 2001). They consequently reduce sexual desire and the frequency of erections and ejaculations (Bradford, 2001).

Depo-Provera suppresses the sexual appetite in men. It can lower the intensity of sex drive and erotic fantasies and urges so that the man may feel less compelled to act upon them (Roesler & Witztum, 2000). Anti-androgens do not, however, eliminate all paraphilic urges or completely change a person's sexual behavior.

The use of anti-androgens is sometimes incorrectly referred to as *chemical castration*. Surgical castration, the surgical removal of the testes, has sometimes been performed on convicted rapists and violent sex offenders (Roesler & Witztum, 2000). Surgical castration eliminates testicular sources of testosterone. Anti-androgens suppress, but do not eliminate, testicular production of testosterone. Also, unlike surgical castration, the effects of anti-androgens can be reversed when the treatment is terminated.

Evidence suggests that anti-androgens help some people when they are used in conjunction with psychological treatment (Roesler & Witztum, 2000). The value of anti-androgens has been limited by high refusal and dropout rates, however (Roesler & Witztum, 2000). Questions also remain concerning side effects.

Anti-androgen drug
A chemical substance that reduces the sex drive by lowering the level of testosterone in the bloodstream.

Although we have amassed a great deal of information from research on atypical variations in sexual behavior, our understanding of them and our treatment approaches to them remain less than satisfactory.

Review: Treatment of the Paraphilias

Reflect

Is it ethical for mental health professionals to work with clients who do not want treatment?

CriticalThinking

Which methods of therapy aim to work by reducing the sex drive in general, and which aim to replace sexual response to socially inappropriate stimuli with sexual response to appropriate stimuli?

31. People with paraphilias usually (*Want* or *Do not want?*) treatment.

32. Therapists are generally (*More* or *Less?*) successful with resistant clients.

33. _____ focuses on resolving unconscious conflicts that are believed to originate in childhood.

34. _____ therapy focuses on directly changing behavior.

35. Systematic _____ attempts to break the link between the sexual stimulus and sexual arousal by pairing muscle relaxation with paraphilic images or fantasies.

36. In _____ therapy, paraphilic behavior is paired with a painful stimulus.

37. Orgasmic _____ aims to increase the individual's response to socially appropriate sexual stimuli by pairing culturally appropriate imagery with orgasmic pleasure.

38. Selective serotonin reuptake inhibitors (SSRIs) are used mainly as _____ but have been helpful in treating some cases of exhibitionism, voyeurism, and fetishism.

39. _____ drugs act by reducing the level of testosterone in the bloodstream.

Recite

1. How do we determine what kind of behavior is normal and what is deviant or abnormal?

Statistical rarity contributes to the impression that behavior is abnormal but is not an adequate standard. Moreover, what is considered normal in one culture or at a particular time may be considered abnormal in other cultures and at other times. Some atypical patterns of sexual arousal or behavior become problematic in the eyes of the individual or society and are labeled *paraphilias.*

2. What are paraphilias?

Paraphilias involve sexual arousal in response to unusual stimuli such as children or other nonconsenting persons, certain objects, or pain or humiliation. The psychiatric diagnosis of paraphilia requires that the person have acted on these persistent urges or be distinctly distressed by them. Except in the case of sexual masochism, paraphilias are believed to occur almost exclusively among men.

3. What is fetishism?

In fetishism, an inanimate object comes to elicit sexual arousal. In partialism, people are inordinately aroused by a particular body part, such as the feet.

4. What is transvestism?

Whereas other fetishists become sexually aroused by handling the fetishistic object while they masturbate, transvestites become excited by wearing articles of clothing—the fetishistic objects—of the other sex. Many transvestites may be motivated by *autogynephilia*—the fantasy of possessing women's bodies.

Recite

5. What is exhibitionism?	An exhibitionist experiences the compulsion to expose himself to strangers. Most exhibitionists do not attempt further sexual contact with the victim, but some do pose a physical threat.
6. What do we know about obscene telephone calling?	The obscene phone caller is motivated to become sexually aroused by shocking his victim. Such callers typically masturbate during the phone call or shortly afterward.
7. What is voyeurism?	Voyeurs become sexually aroused by watching and usually do not seek sexual relations with the target. The voyeur may masturbate while peeping or afterward while engaging in voyeuristic fantasies. Some exhibitionists and voyeurs harbor feelings of inadequacy and poor self-esteem and lack social and sexual skills.
8. What is sexual masochism?	Sexual masochists associate the receipt of pain or humiliation with sexual arousal. Sexual masochists and sexual sadists sometimes form liaisons to meet each other's needs.
9. What is sexual sadism?	Sexual sadism is characterized by persistent, powerful urges and sexual fantasies involving the inflicting of pain and suffering on others to achieve sexual excitement or gratification. Sexual sadists may be quite dangerous, especially when they seek nonconsenting "partners." Sadomasochists enjoy playing both sadistic and masochistic roles.
10. What is frotteurism?	Most frotteuristic acts—rubbing against nonconsenting persons, also known as mashing—take place in crowded places, such as buses, subway cars, and elevators.
11. What less common paraphilias are there?	Zoophiles desire to have sexual contact with animals. Necrophiles desire to have sexual contact with dead bodies.
12. What is the biological perspective on paraphilias?	Investigators who have adopted the biological perspective have determined that many people with paraphilias have higher-than-normal sex drives. Their brains may also respond differently to paraphilic and "normal" sexual stimuli.
13. What is the psychoanalytic perspective on paraphilias?	Classical psychoanalytic theory suggests that paraphilias in males are psychological defenses against castration anxiety.
14. What are learning-theory perspectives on paraphilias?	Some learning theorists have argued that unusual stimuli may acquire sexually arousing properties through association with sexual arousal or orgasm. Unusual stimuli may gradually acquire sexually arousing properties through incorporation into masturbatory fantasies. Watching or reading about paraphilias in the media may also encourage some people to try them.
15. What are sociological perspectives on paraphilic behavior?	According to Weinberg's sociological model, the erotic appeal of S&M rituals may result from the opportunity to reverse the customary power relationships that exist between men and women and between the social classes in society.
16. What is a lovemap?	Money and Lamacz theorize that childhood experiences etch a pattern in the brain—a *lovemap*—that determines what types of stimuli and activities become sexually arousing. In the case of paraphilias, these lovemaps become distorted by early traumatic experiences.
17. What psychological approaches are used to treat paraphilias?	Psychoanalysis aims to bring unconscious Oedipal conflicts that prompt paraphilic behavior into awareness so that they can be worked through in adulthood. Cognitive–behavioral therapy attempts to eliminate paraphilic behaviors through techniques such as systematic desensitization, aversion therapy, social-skills training, covert sensitization, and orgasmic reconditioning.
18. What medical approaches are used to treat paraphilias?	Selective serotonin reuptake inhibitors (SSRIs), which are usually used as antidepressants, tend to depress sexual response and have been used with some paraphilic individuals. By reducing the sex drive, anti-androgen drugs also help people who have difficulty combating paraphilic urges.

Chapter 18

Truth?Fiction?

T / F? A woman is raped every 10 minutes in the United States.

T / F? The prevalence of rape is 10 times greater in the United States than in Japan.

T / F? The majority of rapes are committed by strangers in deserted neighborhoods or darkened alleyways.

T / F? Ten times as many women as men are raped in the United States.

T / F? Men who rape other men are gay.

T / F? Many women say no when they mean yes.

T / F? Most rapists are mentally ill.

T / F? Women who encounter a rapist should attempt to fight him off.

T / F? Father–daughter incest is the most common type of incest.

Sexual Coercion

Preview

*I*t seems that the media are in a constant feeding frenzy over incidents of sexual assault and sexual harassment involving celebrities, highly placed politicians, and members of the armed services. In the early 1990s, the spotlight was on the rape trials of William Kennedy Smith and boxer Mike Tyson, and on the Senate confirmation hearings of Supreme Court nominee Clarence Thomas, who faced charges of sexual harassment leveled by a former assistant, Anita Hill. A few years later, the spotlight shifted to an affair between Bill Clinton and a young White House intern named Monica Lewinsky. Many argued that their relationship constituted sexual harassment because of the disparity in their power, even though Lewinsky was a willing partner.

There has been no let up in the new millennium. As this book goes to press, L.A. Lakers star Kobe Bryant is about to stand trial for rape in Colorado. High school football players in the New York suburb of Long Island are being tried for raping and sodomizing new team members as part of an initiation rite (Healy, 2003). University of Colorado football players have been accused of raping a female teammate.

Then there's "Gropegate." The new governor ("governator"?) of California, Arnold Schwarzenegger, has been accused of sexual harassment—of groping (fondling) more than a dozen women against their will a number of years ago.

It has also been charged that the Air Force Academy had "traditions" that encouraged or legitimized the sexual assault of female cadets. A number of women cadets left the academy, officers have resigned, and policies have been changed (Janofsky & Schemo, 2003).

Arnold Schwarzenegger as "Terminator" and as Governor of California During the 2003 gubernatorial campaign in California, Arnold Schwarzenegger was accused by several women of "groping" (fondling) them while movies were being filmed several years earlier. The scandal was dubbed "Gropegate" in the press.

And then there were the stories that flooded the media of American priests who sexually abused children. For example, the Boston Archdiocese was reported to have received over 1,000 complaints of child sexual abuse over the past several decades and to have turned a blind eye to the charges (Sex Abuse Victims, 2003). All in all, more than 4,000 priests have been accused nationwide (Goodstein, 2004), and some Roman Catholics have wondered whether the church's requirement that priests remain celibate has contributed to the problem (Adams, 2003). Lastly, as this book goes to press, pop star Michael Jackson has been charged with several counts of child molestation (Broder, 2003).

All in all, a team of professional writers could not have developed more scandalous material, but the plots and the characters in these media series are very real. Many observers wince as they see aspects of themselves—either as aggressors or as victims—laid bare before the public.

This chapter is about sexual coercion. In it we discuss rape and other forms of sexual pressure, including sexual harassment. Sexual coercion also includes *any* sexual activity between an adult and a child. Even when children cooperate, sexual relations with children are coercive because children are below the legal age of consent.

Rape: The Most Intimate Crime of Violence

During the school year, you talk to people it has happened to, even upperclass-men, and they all say the same thing. They tell you to expect getting raped, and if it doesn't happen to you, you're one of the rare ones. They say if you want a chance to stay here, if you want to graduate, you don't tell. You just deal with it.

—Sharon Fullilove (cited in Janofsky & Schemo, 2003)

The women at the Air Force Academy, like another half a million American women each year, were victimized by a most common crime of violence. **Question: What is rape?** **Rape** has its sexual aspects—ugly and grossly sexual aspects, indeed—but it is also the subjugation of women by men by force or threat of force (Mardorossian, 2002; Rozee & Koss, 2001).

For the first few thousand years of history, the only rapes that were punished were those that defiled virgins. These rapes were considered crimes against property (virgins being the property of their fathers), not crimes against persons. In ancient Babylonia, rape laws applied to married women as well. Babylonian law required the assailant *and his victim* to be bound and thrown into a river. As the injured party (after all, *his* property had been damaged), the husband could choose to let his wife drown or to save her. Blaming the victim of rape is thus an age-old tradition. The ancient Hebrews stoned to death a married woman who was raped, along with her assailant. In the ancient Babylonian and Hebrew cultures, the wife was seen as guilty of adultery. Virgins who were raped within the protection of the city gates were also stoned by the Hebrews. It was thought that they could have maintained their purity by crying out.

The current definition of rape varies from state to state. **Forcible rape** is usually defined as sexual intercourse with a nonconsenting person by the use of force or the threat of force. **Statutory rape** is sexual intercourse with a person who is below the age of consent, even if the person cooperates.

Traditionally, a man could not be convicted for raping his wife, even though he might have forced her to submit to sexual activity by physical power or threats. This marital exclusion was derived from the English common law that held that a woman "gives herself over" to her husband when she becomes his wife and cannot retract her consent. Today, however, most states have rape statutes that permit the prosecution of husbands who rape their wives.

Rape laws are now also applied to men who rape men and to women who coerce men into sexual activity or assist men in raping other women. Forcible rape is a form of **sexual assault**. Even when a sexual attack does not meet the legal definition of rape, as in the case of forced penetration of the anus by an object such as a bottle or a broom handle, it can be prosecuted as sexual assault.

Incidence of Rape

Question: How common is rape? The government's National Crime Victimization Survey (U.S. Department of Justice, 2003) estimates that 225,320 women were sexually assaulted in 2001. This figure included 76,850 rapes and 62,620 attempted rapes. This means that a woman was reported to be raped about every 7 minutes on the average. Men—6,770 of them—were also victimized by rape.

But such reports tend to seriously underreport the incidence of rape. They largely rely on crime statistics. However, the majority of rapes are not reported to the police or prosecuted (Fisher et al., 2003; Watts & Zimmerman, 2002). Many women choose not to report assaults because of concern that they will be humiliated by the

Rape Sexual intercourse that takes place as a result of force or threats of force, rather than consent. (The legal definition of rape varies from state to state.) See also *forcible rape* and *statutory rape.*

Forcible rape Sexual intercourse with a non-consenting person effected by the use of force or the threat of force.

Statutory rape Sexual intercourse with a person who is below the age of consent. Sexual intercourse under such conditions is considered statutory rape even though the person attacked may cooperate.

Sexual assault Any sexual activity that involves the use of force or the threat of force.

criminal justice system. Others fear reprisal from their families or the rapist. Some simply assume that the offender will not be apprehended or prosecuted. Because they live in a culture in which women are often expected to "suffer in silence," Mexican American women are even more likely than European American women to remain quiet about rape and sexual abuse (Lira et al., 1999).

There are two reasons why even the National Crime Victimization Survey underestimates the incidence of rape in the United States (Watts & Zimmerman, 2002). First, many women mistakenly believe that coercive sex is rape only when the rapist is a stranger. Second, many women mistakenly assume that only forced vaginal penetration is defined as rape, whereas many states define rape more broadly. All in all, the weight of the evidence suggests that between 1 in 7 and 1 in 4 women in the United States are raped during their lifetimes (Koss & Kilpatrick, 2001). The prevalence of reported rapes in the United States is about seven times greater than that in Great Britain and more than ten times greater than that in Japan (*Newsweek,* 1990). Later we consider some of the cultural influences that make our society a breeding ground for rape.

Women of all ages, races, and social classes are raped, but young women are at greater risk. Women of ages 16 to 24 are two to three times more likely to be raped than older women (U.S. Department of Justice, 2003).

Question: What kinds of rape are there?

Types of Rapes

One of the central myths about rape in our culture is that most rapes are perpetrated by strangers lurking in dark alleyways or by intruders who climb through open windows in the middle of the night. The truth is that most women are raped by men they know—often by men they have come to trust. Figure 18.1 shows that only 4% of the women in the NHSLS study were "forced to do something sexual that they did not want to do" by a stranger. According to the U.S. Department of Justice (2003), about two-thirds of rapes are committed by acquaintances of the victim. The types of rape include stranger rape, acquaintance rape, date rape, gang rape, male rape, marital rape, and rape by females.

Stranger Rape **Stranger rape** is rape committed by an assailant (or assailants) not previously known to the person attacked. The stranger rapist often selects targets who seem vulnerable—women who live alone, who are older or retarded, who are walking down deserted streets, or who are asleep or intoxicated. After choosing a target, the rapist may search for a safe time and place to commit the crime—a deserted, run-down part of town, or a darkened street.

Truth?Fiction?
Revisited

It is true that in the United States a woman is raped at least every 10 minutes. Every 6 minutes is closer to the truth.

It is true that the prevalence of rape is 10 times greater in the United States than in Japan. (That is, the prevalence of *reported* rape is more than ten times greater in the United States.)

It is not true that the majority of rapes are committed by strangers in deserted neighborhoods or darkened alleyways. Actually, most women are raped by men they know, not by strangers.

Stranger rape Rape that is committed by an assailant previously unknown to the person who is assaulted.

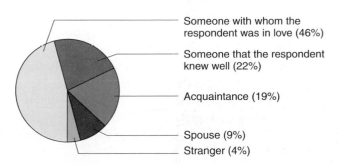

- Someone with whom the respondent was in love (46%)
- Someone that the respondent knew well (22%)
- Acquaintance (19%)
- Spouse (9%)
- Stranger (4%)

Figure 18.1. Women's Relationships with Men Who Forced Them to Do Something Sexual That They Did Not Want to Do. Only 4% of the sexual assaults reported in the NHSLS study were perpetrated by strangers. (*Source:* Adapted from Laumann, E. O., Gagnon, J. H., Michael, R. T., & Michaels, S. [1994]. *The social organization of sexuality: Sexual practices in the United States.* Chicago: University of Chicago Press, Figure 9.3, p. 338.)

Acquaintance Rape Women are more likely to be raped by men they know, such as classmates, fellow office workers, and even their brothers' friends, than by strangers (Schafran, 1995). **Acquaintance rapes** are much less likely than stranger rapes to be reported to the police (Fisher et al., 2003). One reason is that rape survivors may not perceive sexual assaults by acquaintances as rapes. Only about one-quarter of the women in a national college survey who had been sexually assaulted saw themselves as rape victims (Koss et al., 1987; Koss & Kilkpatrick, 2001; Rozee & Koss, 2001). Despite increased public awareness of acquaintance rape, many still think of rapists as strangers lurking in shadows and believe that a woman should be able to resist a sexual advance unless the man uses a weapon. Acquaintance rapists themselves tend to rationalize their behavior by subscribing to myths such as the traditional view that men are expected to assume a sexually aggressive role in dating and the belief that rapists are strangers. Even when acquaintance rapes are reported to police, they may be treated as "misunderstandings" or lovers' quarrels rather than as violent crimes.

Date Rape Date rape is a form of acquaintance rape. Studies of college women show a consistent trend: 10% to 20% of women report being forced into sexual intercourse by dates (Koss & Kilpatrick, 2001; Tang et al., 1995). These figures hold at the Chinese University of Hong Kong as well as in the United States (Tang et al., 1995). In one U.S. study, most reported date rapes were committed by men whom the women had known for nearly a year on the average (Muehlenhard & Linton, 1987). Rapes were more likely to occur when the couple had too much to drink and then parked in the man's car or went back to his residence. The man tended to perceive his partner's willingness to return home with him as a signal of sexual interest, even if she resisted his advances. Most of the men ignored the women's protests and overcame their resistance by force. None used a weapon. Only a few used threats of violence.

Men who commit date rape may believe that acceptance of a date indicates willingness to have sexual relations. They may think that women should reciprocate with coitus if they are taken to dinner. Other men assume that women who frequent places such as singles bars are expressing tacit agreement to engage in sex with men who show interest in them. Some date rapists believe that a woman who resists advances is just "playing hard to get" so that she will not look "easy." They interpret resistance as coyness. It is a ploy in the cat-and-mouse game that typifies the "battle of the sexes" to them. They may believe that when a woman says no, she means yes, especially when a sexual relationship has already been established (Monson et al., 2000; Osman, 2003).

According to Roy Baumeister and his colleagues (2001, 2002), perpetrators and victims view sexual assaults in very different ways. Women see themselves as overpowered and deeply hurt. Men often focus on their own feelings, ignoring those of the victim, and act on their sexual frustration when the woman says it's time to call it quits. The more the man focuses on his own wants and ignores those of the woman, the more likely he is to commit rape (Bushman et al., 2003). In these cases, the motive may be largely sexual, but the man remains a violent criminal who refuses to take no for an answer.

The issue of consent lies at the heart of whether a sexual act is rape. Unlike cases of stranger rape, date rape occurs within a context in which sexual relations could occur voluntarily. Thus, the issue of consent can become murky. Juries and judges are often faced with a woman plaintiff who alleges that the male defendant, who may appear neatly dressed and looking like the boy next door, forced her into sexual relations against her will. As in the Mike Tyson and Kobe Bryant court appearances, the defendant may admit that sexual intercourse took place but claim that it was consensual. Judges and juries then have to distinguish among shades of meaning regarding "consent."

Acquaintance rape
Rape by an acquaintance of the person who is assaulted.

Charges of date rape often come down to his word against hers. Her word often becomes less persuasive in the eyes of the jury if it was clear that she had participated in consensual acts beforehand, such as sharing dinner, attending the movies together, accompanying him to his home, sharing a drink alone, and perhaps kissing or petting (Maxwell et al., 2003; Osman, 2003). The issue becomes even further clouded by the fact that some survivors of date rape continue their relationships, and even marry, the perpetrators.

The problem of date rape has been brought under closer public scrutiny in recent years. "Take Back the Night" marches have become a common form of student protest on college campuses against the sexual misconduct of men. Many colleges have mandated date rape seminars and workshops.

The Gang Rape In their classic study of rape, Groth and Birnbaum (1979) relate the story of Kurt, a 23-year-old European American, married father of three who was involved in a number of rapes with a friend, Pete:

> I always looked up to Pete and felt second-class to him. I felt I owed him and couldn't chicken out on the rapes. I worshiped him. He was the best fighter, lover, water-skier, motorcyclist I knew. Taking part in the sexual assaults made me feel equal to him. . . . I didn't have any friends and felt like a nobody. . . . He brought me into his bike club. He made me a somebody.
>
> I'd go to a shopping center and find a victim. I'd approach her with a knife or a gun and then bring her to him. He'd rape her first and then I would. . . . We raped about eight girls together over a four-month period. (p. 113)

By participating in a gang rape, the follower, like Kurt, is attempting to conform to the stereotype of the tough, competent, "masculine" he-man. Followers, however, may fortify the courage of the instigator of the act. One of Groth and Birnbaum's planners of such an assault remarks, "Having a partner is like having something to

Charged with Rape. Basketball superstar Kobe Bryant was charged in 2003 with raping a woman in Colorado. He admitted to adultery but claimed that the sex was consensual.

Taking Back the Night. Whose fault is it if a woman is raped when she goes out alone at night? Many women—and men who care about women—have marched to demonstrate their disgust with the men who might assault women out walking by themselves, and toward a society that too often blames the victim for what happens to her.

A Closer Look

Anatomy of a Date Rape: Ann and Jim

Date rape is a pressing concern on college campuses, where thousands of women have been raped by men they knew or had dated, and where there is much controversy about exactly what constitutes date rape. Consider the case of Ann:

I first met him at a party. He was really good looking and he had a great smile. I wanted to meet him but I wasn't sure how. I didn't want to appear too forward. Then he came over and introduced himself. We talked and found we had a lot in common. I really liked him. When he asked me over to his place for a drink, I thought it would be OK. He was such a good listener, and I wanted him to ask me out again.

When we got to his room, the only place to sit was on the bed. I didn't want him to get the wrong idea, but what else could I do? We talked for a while and then he made his move. I was so startled. He started by kissing. I really liked him so the kissing was nice.

But then he pushed me down on the bed. I tried to get up and I told him to stop. He was so much bigger and stronger. I got scared and I started to cry. I froze and he raped me.

It took only a couple of minutes and it was terrible, he was so rough. When it was over he kept asking me what was wrong, like he didn't know. He had just forced himself on me and he thought that was OK. He drove me home and said he wanted to see me again. I'm so afraid to see him. I never thought it would happen to me.

College men on dates frequently perceive their dates' protests as part of an adversarial sex game (Bernat et al., 1999). One male undergraduate said "Hell, no" when asked whether a date had consented to sex. He added, "but she didn't say no, so she must have wanted it, too. . . . It's the way it works" (Celis, 1991). Consider the comments of Jim, the man who raped Ann:

Combating Rape on Campus
Many colleges and universities have instituted rape-awareness programs to combat the problem of rape on campus. What is the prevalence of rape on your campus? What are you going to do about it?

I first met her at a party. She looked really hot, wearing a sexy dress that showed off her great body. We started talking right away. I knew that she liked me by the way she kept smiling and touching my arm while she was speaking. She seemed pretty relaxed so I asked her back to my place for a drink. . . . When she said yes, I knew that I was going to be lucky!

When we got to my place, we sat on the bed kissing. At first, everything was great. Then, when I started to lay her down on the bed, she started twisting and saying she didn't want to. Most women don't like to appear too easy, so I knew that she was just going through the motions. When she stopped struggling, I knew that she would have to throw in some tears before we did it.

She was still very upset afterwards, and I just don't understand it! If she didn't want to have sex, why did she come back to the room with me? You could tell by the way she dressed and acted that she was no virgin, so why she had to put up such a big struggle I don't know.

Accepting a date is not the equivalent of consenting to coitus. Accompanying a man to his room or apartment is not the equivalent of consenting to coitus. Nor are kissing and petting the equivalent of consenting to coitus. When the woman says no, the man is obligated to take no for an answer.

drink. I felt braver. I felt stronger. This gave me the courage to do something I might not have done on my own" (1979, p. 112).

Exercise of power is a major motive behind gang rapes, although some attackers may also be expressing anger against women. Gang members often believe that once women engage in coitus they are "whores." Thus, each offending gang member may become more aggressive as he takes his turn.

The Koss college survey (Koss et al., 1987) showed that sexual assaults involving a group of assailants tend to be more vicious than individual assaults (Gidycz & Koss, 1990). Relatively few survivors of gang rape reported the attack to police or sought support from a crisis center.

Male Rape The prevalence of male rape is unknown because most assaults are not reported. The U.S. Department of Justice (2003) estimates that 1 in 10 rape survivors is a man. Most men who rape other men are heterosexual. Their motives tend to include domination and control, revenge and retaliation, sadism and degradation, and (when the rape is carried out by a gang member) status and affiliation (Krahe et al., 2003). Sexual motives may be absent.

Most male rapes occur in prison settings, but some occur outside prison walls. Males are more often attacked by multiple assailants, are held captive longer, and are more often reluctant to report the assault. After all, victimization does not fit the male stereotype of capacity for self-defense. Men are expected to be not only strong but also silent. Nevertheless, male rape survivors may suffer traumatic effects similar to those suffered by female survivors (Krahe et al., 2003).

Truth?Fiction?
Revisited

It is true that 10 times as many women as men are raped in the United States. It is *not* true that men who rape other men are gay. Most men who rape other men are heterosexual.

Marital Rape Marital rapes are probably more common than date rapes because a sexual relationship has already been established (Monson et al., 2000; Osman, 2003). A "traditional" husband may believe that he is entitled to sex with his wife any time he wishes. He may be less willing to accept a rebuff. He may believe it is his wife's duty to satisfy his sexual needs even when she is uninterested. However, men who are more highly educated and less prone to accepting traditional stereotypes about sexual relationships are less likely to commit marital rape (Basile, 2002).

Marital rape has been largely unreported and is often not recognized by survivors as actually being rape (Monson et al., 2000). Women may also fail to report marital rape because of fear that no one will believe them.

Motives for marital rape vary. Some men use sex to dominate their wives. Others degrade their wives through sex, especially after arguments. Sexual coercion often occurs within a context of a pattern of marital violence, battering, and physical intimidation (Johnson, 2003). In some cases, though, violence is limited to the sexual relationship (Peacock, 1998). Some men see sex as the solution to marital disputes. They think that if they can force their wives into sex, "Everything will be OK."

Survivors of marital rape may be as fearful of serious injury or death as survivors of stranger rape. The long-term effects of marital rape on survivors are also similar to those experienced by survivors of stranger rape, including fear, depression, and sexual dysfunctions (Bergen, 1998; Mahoney & Williams, 1998; Peacock, 1998). Moreover, the woman who is raped by her husband usually continues to live with her assailant and may fear repeated attacks.

Rape by Women Rape by women is rare. When it does occur, it often involves aiding or abetting men who are attacking another woman. Rape by women may occur in gang rape, when women may follow male leaders to gain their approval. In such cases, a woman may be used to lure another woman to a reasonably safe place for the rape. Or the woman may hold the other woman down while she is assaulted.

But some men have been raped by women. Sarrel and Masters (1982) reported 11 cases of men who were sexually assaulted by women, including one case of a 37-year-old man who was coerced into sexual intercourse by two women who accosted him at gunpoint. In another case, a 27-year-old man fell asleep in his hotel room with a woman he had just met in a bar and then awakened to find that he was bound to his bed, gagged, and blindfolded. He was then forced into sexual intercourse with four different women, who threatened him with castration if he did not perform satisfactorily. Rape of a man may not be recognized as rape in states that adhere to a legal definition that requires forced vaginal penetration of a woman by a man. In such

cases, the assailant or assailants may be charged under other statutes governing physical or sexual assaults.

Rape is common in the United States. *Question: What social and cultural factors contribute to the high frequency of rape in the United States?*

Social Attitudes, Myths, and Cultural Factors That Encourage Rape

Many people believe a number of myths about rape, such as "Women say no when they mean yes," "All women like a man who is pushy and forceful," "The way women dress, they are just asking to be raped," and "Rapists are crazed by sexual desire" (Maxwell et al., 2003; Osman, 2003). Yet another myth is that deep down inside, women want to be raped. The belief that women desire to be overpowered by men and forced into sexual relations is a rationalization for violence (Powell, 1996).

Rape myths create a social climate that legitimizes rape. Although both men and men are susceptible to rape myths, researchers find that college men show greater acceptance of rape myths than do college women (Maxwell et al., 2003; Van Wie & Gross, 2001). Men also cling more stubbornly to myths about date rape than do women, even following date rape education classes designed to challenge these views (Maxwell et al., 2003). Such myths do not occur in a social vacuum. They are related to other social attitudes, including gender-role stereotyping, perception of sex as adversarial, and acceptance of violence in relationships. The nearby questionnaire will help you determine whether you harbor myths that legitimize rape.

Many observers contend that our society breeds rapists by socializing males into socially and sexually dominant roles (Bernat et al., 1999; Davis & Liddell, 2002; Holcomb et al., 2002). Males are often reinforced from childhood for aggressive and competitive behavior. Gender typing may also lead men to reject "feminine" traits such as tenderness and empathy that might restrain aggression (Davis & Liddell, 2002; Shultz et al., 2000).

Research with college students supports the connection between stereotypical masculine identification and tendencies to rape or condone rape. Studies have compared students who believe strictly in traditional gender roles with students who hold less rigid attitudes. The "traditionalists" express a greater likelihood of committing rape, are more accepting of violence against women, are more likely to blame rape survivors, and are more aroused by depictions of rape (Check & Malamuth, 1983; Raichle & Lambert, 2000). College men who more closely identify with the traditional masculine gender role more often report engaging in verbal sexual coercion and forcible rape (Bernat et al., 1999; Shultz et al., 2000).

Do the lessons learned in competitive sports predispose young American males to sexual violence (Holcomb et al., 2002)? Boys are often exposed to coaches who emphasize winning at all costs. They are taught to be dominant and to vanquish their opponents, even if winning means injuring or "taking out" the opposition. Does this philosophy carry over from the playing field into relationships with women?

Sexual behavior and sports in our culture are linked through common idioms. A young man may be taunted by his friends after a date with a woman with such questions as "Did you score?" or, more bluntly, "Did you get in?" Consider, for example, the aggressive competitiveness with which this male college student views dating relationships between men and women:

A man is supposed to view a date with a woman as a premeditated scheme for getting the most sex out of her. Everything he does, he judges in terms of one

Self-Assessment
Cultural Myths That Create a Climate That Supports Rape

The following statements are based on a questionnaire by Martha Burt (1980). Read each statement and indicate whether you believe it to be true or false by circling the T or the F. Then turn to the key in Appendix B to learn about the implications of your answers.

T F   1. A woman who goes to the home or apartment of a man on their first date implies that she is willing to have sex.

T F   2. Any female can get raped.

T F   3. One reason why women falsely report a rape is because they need to call attention to themselves.

T F   4. Any healthy woman can successfully resist a rapist if she really wants to.

T F   5. When women go around braless or wearing short skirts and tight tops, they are just asking for trouble.

T F   6. In the majority of rapes, the victim is promiscuous or has a bad reputation.

T F   7. If a girl engages in necking or petting and she lets things get out of hand, it is her own fault if her partner forces sex on her.

T F   8. Women who get raped while hitchhiking get what they deserve.

T F   9. A woman who is stuck-up and thinks she is too good to talk to guys on the street deserves to be taught a lesson.

T F   10. Many women have an unconscious wish to be raped and may then unconsciously set up a situation in which they are likely to be attacked.

T F   11. If a woman gets drunk at a party and has intercourse with a man she's just met there, she should be considered "fair game" to other males at the party who want to have sex with her too, whether she wants to or not.

T F   12. Many women who report a rape are lying because they are angry and want to get back at the man they accuse.

T F   13. Many, if not most, rapes are merely invented by women who discovered they were pregnant and wanted to protect their reputation.

criterion—"getting laid." He's supposed to constantly pressure her to see how far he can get. She is his adversary, his opponent in a battle, and he begins to view her as a prize, an object, not a person. While she's dreaming about love, he's thinking about how to conquer her. (Powell, 1991, p. 55)

Psychological Characteristics of Rapists: Who Are They?

Although sexual aggressiveness may be embedded within our social fabric, not all men are equally vulnerable to such cultural influences. Personal factors are thus also involved. *Question: What psychological factors characterize rapists?* Are rapists mentally disturbed? Retarded? Driven by insatiable sexual urges?

Much of our knowledge about the psychological characteristics of rapists derives from studies of samples of incarcerated rapists. One conclusion that emerges is that there is no single type of rapist. Rapists vary in their psychological characteristics, family backgrounds, mental health, and criminal histories (Prentky & Knight, 1991). Generally speaking, rapists are no less intelligent or more mentally ill than other people (Renzetti & Curran, 1989). Many rapists show no evidence of psychological disturbance (Dean & de Bruyn-Kops, 1982). This does not mean that their behavior is "normal." It means that most rapists are in control of their behavior and know it is illegal.

Truth?Fiction?
Revisited

It is not true that most rapists are mentally ill, even though their crimes might strike observers as being "sick."

A Closer Look

The (Highly Controversial!) Evolutionary View of Rape

According to evolutionary theory, those traits that help an individual reach sexual maturity and reproduce are more likely to be passed on to future generations. Could one such trait in males be sexual aggressiveness? Could sexual aggressiveness be somehow embedded in the human genetic code?

According to evolutionary psychologists, it might just be true. One argument is that rape is a common—even "normal"—way of mating in many species (Archer & Vaughan, 2001). Evolutionary psychologists accept the view that prior to civilization, males who were more sexually aggressive were generally more likely to transmit their genes to future generations (Fisher, 2000; Koss, 2003; Thornhill & Palmer, 2000). Modern-day society, by contrast, may regard personal qualities such as intelligence and reliability and social

behaviors such as maintaining lasting relationships as being more important than brute strength. Modern society has also outlawed sexual aggression—viewing it as a crime against the woman who is victimized, rather than as a crime against the "property" of some other man. But modern society and the current legal system are relatively new things on the planet, and the human genetic code has evolved over millions of years. There might thus remain a "natural" tendency for males to be more sexually aggressive than females and to try to take what they want.

Although the evolutionary perspective may view sexual coerciveness in men as "natural," many or most evolutionary psychologists also tend to agree that rape is inexcusable and criminal in modern society and that males can *choose* not to be aggressive (Koss, 2003). Yes, it is

conceivable that men carry genes that now and then give rise to aggressive impulses, some of which involve sexual encounters. But men also carry other genes that enable them to picture themselves in the place of the victim and choose *not* to behave aggressively. Empathy—that is, experiencing the feelings of another person—may be more common in women than in men, but it is not absent in men and can also be cultivated in men, as has been shown by numerous rape prevention programs (Davis & Liddell, 2002; Hall & Barongan, 1997; Holcomb et al., 2002; O'Donohue et al., 2003).

We do not "accept" the natural aggressiveness of predators such as snakes and large cats by walking unarmed into the jungle. Why should we accept aggressiveness in other people, whether it is natural or not?

Some rapists feel socially inadequate and report that they cannot find willing partners. Some lack social skills and avoid social interactions with women (Overholser & Beck, 1986). Others are no less skillful socially than nonrapists in the same socioeconomic group, however (Segal & Marshall, 1985). Some rapists are basically antisocial and have long histories of violent behavior (Knight et al., 1991). They tend to act on their impulses, regardless of the cost to the person they attack. The use of alcohol may also dampen self-restraint and spur sexual aggressiveness.

For some rapists violence and sexual arousal become intermeshed. Thus, they seek to combine sex and violence to enhance their sexual arousal (Quinsey et al., 1984). Some rapists are more sexually aroused than other men (as measured by the size of erections) by verbal descriptions, films, or audiotapes that portray themes of rape (Barbaree & Marshall, 1991). Other researchers, however, have failed to find deviant patterns of arousal in rapists (e.g., Baxter et al., 1986; Hall, 1989). These researchers find that, as a group, rapists, like most other people, are more aroused by stimuli depicting mutually consenting sexual activity than by rape stimuli.

Studies of incarcerated rapists may be criticized on grounds that the samples may not represent the total population of rapists. It is estimated that fewer than 4% of rapists are caught and eventually imprisoned (Gibbs, 1991). Most rapes are committed by acquaintances. Acquaintance rapists are even less likely than stranger rapists to be arrested, convicted, and incarcerated.

To offset this methodological concern, researchers have turned to the survey method to study men who anonymously report that they have engaged in sexually coercive behaviors, including rape, but have not been identified by the criminal justice system. Harney and Muehlenhard (1991) summarized research findings on self-identified sexually aggressive men. These men are more likely than other men to

- Condone rape and violence against women
- Hold traditional gender-role attitudes
- Be sexually experienced
- Be hostile toward women
- Engage in sexual activity in order to express social dominance
- Be sexually aroused by depictions of rape
- Be irresponsible and lack a social conscience
- Have peer groups, such as fraternities, that pressure them into sexual activity

The Motives of Rapists: The Search for Types Although sexual arousal is an obvious and important element in rape, some researchers argue that sexual desire is not the basic motivation for rape (Gebhard et al., 1965; Groth & Birnbaum, 1979). Other researchers find that sexual motivation plays a key role in acquaintance and date rapes (Baumeister et al., 2002; Bushman et al., 2003). On the basis of their clinical work with more than 1,000 rapists, Groth and Birnbaum believe that there are three basic kinds of rape: anger rape, power rape, and sadistic rape.

- *Anger rape.* The **anger rape** is a vicious, unplanned attack that is triggered by anger and resentment toward women. Anger rapists usually employ more force than is needed to obtain compliance. The people they rape are often coerced into performing degrading and humiliating acts. Typically, the anger rapist reports that he had suffered humiliations at the hands of women and used the rape as a means of revenge.
- *Power rape.* The man who commits a **power rape** is motivated by the desire to control and dominate the woman he rapes (Mardorossian, 2002). Sexual gratification is secondary. The power rapist is attempting "to resolve disturbing doubts about [his] masculine identity and worth, [or] to combat deep-seated feelings of insecurity and vulnerability" (Groth & Hobson, 1983, p. 165).
- *Sadistic rape.* The **sadistic rape** is a ritualized, savage attack. Some sadists bind their victims and subject them to humiliating and degrading experiences and threats. Some torture or murder their victims. Mutilation is common. Groth (1979) estimated that about 40% of rapes are anger rapes, 55% are power rapes, and 5% are sadistic rapes.

Adjustment of Rape Survivors

Many women who are raped fear for their lives during the attack. Whether or not weapons or threats are used, the experience of being dominated by an unpredictable and threatening assailant is terrifying. The woman does not know whether she will survive and may feel helpless to do anything about it. ***Question: How do survivors adjust to being raped?*** After being raped, many survivors enter a **crisis**.

Many survivors are traumatized in the days and weeks following their rape (Koss et al., 2002, 2003). They have trouble sleeping and cry frequently. They tend to report eating problems, cystitis, headaches, irritability, mood changes, anxiety and depression, and menstrual irregularity. They may become withdrawn, sullen, and mistrustful. People in the United States tend to believe that women who are raped are at least partly to blame for the assault; therefore, some survivors experience feelings of guilt and shame. Emotional distress tends to peak in severity by about 3 weeks following the assault and generally remains high for about a month before beginning to abate about a month or two later (Koss et al., 2002, 2003). Many survivors encounter more lasting problems. A study of women in the military who had survived rape and

Anger rape A vicious, unplanned rape that is triggered by feelings of intense anger and resentment toward women.

Power rape Rape that is motivated by the desire to control and dominate the person assaulted.

Sadistic rape A highly ritualized, savage rape in which the person who is attacked is subjected to painful and humiliating experiences, threats and/or torture.

Crisis A highly stressful situation that can involve shock, loss of self-esteem, and lessened capacity for making decisions.

"Honor" Killings: Blaming the Victim—to Death

This is a story about women . . . that begins with a man. His name is Ghazi al Marine. He had been married just 3 months—the happiest months of his life, he told us—when a killer came to their home and shot his wife.

"She was lying in that corner," he says, pointing. "The blood was everywhere."

That night, police arrested her brother. Apparently, he murdered his sister to preserve his family's honor—an honor was stained when she was raped 3 years ago. From the time she was raped until her marriage, she had lived in a prison. Not because she had done anything wrong but because, like dozens of other women, she needed to be protected from her family.

The reputation of a family in certain countries rests on the reputation of its women. All it takes for violence to be justified is for a woman to be seen with a man she is not related to, for her to reject an unwanted suitor or even to be the victim of a sexual crime.

In Jordan, more than 30 women a year are killed in the name of "honor," amounting to one-third of the nation's murders. In Pakistan, human rights organizations say, thousands of women and girls are stabbed, shot, maimed, or burned each year.

In Bangladesh, a typical punishment is sulfuric acid thrown in the woman's face. "Why did they do this to us?" asks Bina Akhtar in a *20/20* interview. "We didn't harm anyone." "It's the male feeling that they are responsible and authorized to control women's lives and bodies," says

physical abuse found psychological and health-related problems a decade after the assault (Sadler et al., 2000). Some survivors suffer physical injuries and sexually transmitted infections, even HIV/AIDS.

Survivors may also encounter problems at work, such as difficulty relating to coworkers or bosses or trouble concentrating. Work adjustment, however, usually returns to normal levels within a year (Calhoun & Atkeson, 1991). Relationships with spouses or partners may also be impaired. Disturbances in sexual functioning are common and may last for years or a lifetime. Survivors often report a lack of sexual desire, fears of sex, and difficulty becoming sexually aroused (Koss et al., 2002, 2003).

Most women fail to report sexual assaults to police. Why? The reasons include fear of retaliation, the social stigma attached to the survivors of rape, doubts that others will believe them, feelings that it would be hopeless to try to bring charges against the perpetrator, concerns about negative publicity, and fears about the emotional distress to which they would be subjected if the case were to go to trial (Fisher et al., 2003).

Post-traumatic stress disorder A type of stress reaction brought on by a traumatic event and characterized by flashbacks of the experience in the form of disturbing dreams or intrusive recollections, a sense of emotional numbing or restricted range of feelings, and heightened body arousal. Abbreviated PTSD.

Rape and Psychological Disorders Rape survivors are at higher-than-average risk of developing anxiety disorders and depression, and of abusing alcohol and other substances (Koss et al., 2002, 2003). One anxiety disorder common among rape survivors is **post-traumatic stress disorder** (PTSD) (Koss et al., 2003). PTSD is brought on by exposure to a traumatic event and is often seen in soldiers who were in combat (American Psychiatric Association, 2000). People with PTSD may have flashbacks to the traumatic experience, disturbing dreams, emotional numbing, and nervousness. PTSD may persist for years. The person may also develop fears of situations connected with the traumatic event. For example, a woman who was raped on an elevator may develop a fear of riding elevators by herself. Researchers also report that women who blame themselves for the rape tend to suffer more severe depression and adjustment problems, including sexual problems (Koss et al., 2002).

Asthma Khadar, a Jordanian human rights lawyer.

The men who commit these crimes know they will probably never be punished. The few who are arrested show very little remorse

"I'm proud that I killed her," says one man in prison. "I'm ashamed that she was my sister." These men will serve a few months in prison, at most, for the murder of a mother, a sister, a daughter, a wife.

"Most of the time," says Nazrin Huk, a Bangladeshi women's rights activist, "people who throw acid get away with it. Most people think, 'Oh, we can, you know, nothing is going to happen to us.'"

Protests in some of these countries have produced some signs of change. For the first time, Pakistan's President, Pervez Musharraf, has made this promise: "Pakistan will treat honor killings as murder."

In Jordan, the king and queen have vowed to end the practice. The courts have begun in a few cases to issue longer sentences for honor crimes.

Ghazi al Marine has told his lawyer he will fight in the courts to make sure that his wife did not die in vain. But will he get justice?

"I hope so," he says. "He should be hanged . . . like everyone who kills a woman."

The honor crimes continue, but there is now at least the possibility for justice. And just a little less acceptance of violence in the name of honor.

Source: Reprinted with permission from Sheila MacVicar (2000, June 5). Crimes in the name of honor. www.abcnews.com.

If You Are Raped . . . Elizabeth Powell (1996) offers several suggestions to follow if you should be raped:

1. Don't change anything about your body—don't wash, don't even comb your hair. Leave your clothes as they are. Otherwise you could destroy evidence.
2. Strongly consider reporting the incident to police. You may prevent another woman from being assaulted, and you will be taking charge, starting on the path from victim to survivor.
3. Ask a relative or friend to take you to a hospital, if you can't get an ambulance or a police car. If you call the hospital, tell them why you're requesting an ambulance, in case they are able to send someone trained to deal with rape cases.
4. Seek help in an assertive way. Seek medical help. Injuries you are unaware of may be detected. Insist that a written or photographic record be made to document your condition. If you decide to file charges, the prosecutor may need this evidence to obtain a conviction.
5. Question health professionals. Ask about your biological risks. Ask what treatments are available. Ask for whatever will help make you comfortable. Call the shots. Demand confidentiality if that's what you want. Refuse what you don't want.

You may also wish to call a rape hotline or rape crisis center for advice, if one is available in your area. A rape crisis volunteer may be available to accompany you to the hospital and help see you through the medical evaluation and police investigation if you report the attack. It is not unusual for rape survivors to try to erase the details of the rape from their minds. However, trying to remember details clearly will permit you to provide an accurate description of the rapist to the police, including his clothing, type of car, and so on. This information may help police apprehend the rapist and assist in the prosecution.

Treatment of Rape Survivors

Question: How can we help survivors of rape? The treatment of survivors typically involves helping the woman (the vast majority are female) through the crisis following the attack and then working to foster long-term adjustment (Hensley, 2002). Crisis intervention typically provides the survivor with support and information and encourages her to express her feelings and develop strategies for coping with the trauma. Psychotherapy, involving group or individual approaches, can help the survivor cope with the emotional consequences of rape, avoid self-blame, improve self-esteem, validate the welter of feelings surrounding the experience, and establish or maintain loving relationships. Therapists also recognize the importance of helping the rape survivor mobilize social support. Family, friends, religious leaders, and health care specialists are all potential sources of help. However, as among the ancient Babylonians, women often find that those from whom they seek support—including family members and clergy—frequently blame them for being attacked (Filipas & Ullman, 2001; Sheldon & Parent, 2002). In major cities and many towns, concerned men and women have formed rape crisis centers and hotlines, peer counseling groups, and referral agencies geared to assessing and meeting survivors' needs after the assault. Some counselors are specially trained to mediate between survivors of rape and their loved ones—husbands, lovers, and so forth. These counselors help people to discuss and work through the often complex emotional legacy of rape. Phone numbers for these services can be obtained from feminist groups (for example, your local office of the National Organization for Women [NOW]), the police department, or the telephone directory.

Helping survivors adjust is one thing. *Question: How can we prevent rape?*

Rape Prevention

The elimination of rape will require massive changes in cultural attitudes and socialization processes. Educational intervention on a smaller scale may reduce its incidence, however. Many colleges and universities offer coeducational programs about date rape that have apparently reduced the incidence of date rape (Davis & Liddell, 2002; Holcomb et al., 2002; O'Donohue et al., 2003; Shultz et al., 2000). These programs are aimed at developing empathy for the victim by explaining the damage done by rape, exposing traditional cultural myths that endorse rape, and clarifying the borders between encouraging a date to have sex and rape.

Until the basic cultural attitudes that support rape change, however, "rape prevention" means that women take a number of precautions. Why should women be advised to take measures to avoid rape? Is not the very listing of such measures a subtle way of blaming the woman if she should fall prey to an attacker? No! To provide information is not to blame the person who is attacked. The rapist is *always* responsible for the assault.

As discussed in *The New Our Bodies, Ourselves* (Boston Women's Health Book Collective, 1992), women can take certain precautions to help protect themselves:

- Establish a set of signals with other women in the building or neighborhood.
- List yourself in the phone directory and on the mailbox by your first initials only.
- Use dead-bolt locks.
- Lock windows, and install iron grids on first-floor windows.
- Keep doorways and entries well lit.
- Keep your keys handy when approaching the car or the front door.
- Do not walk by yourself after dark.

- Avoid deserted areas.
- Do not allow men you do not know into your house or apartment without first checking their credentials.
- Keep your car doors locked and the windows up.
- Check out the back seat of your car before entering.
- Don't live in a risky building. (We realize that this suggestion may be of little use to poor women who have relatively little choice in where they live.)
- Don't give rides to hitchhikers (including women hitchhikers).
- Don't converse with strange men on the street.
- Shout "Fire!" not "Rape!" People are likely to flock to fires but to avoid scenes of violence.

Powell (1996) adds the following suggestions for avoiding date rape:

Truth?Fiction?
Revisited

It is unclear whether women who encounter a rapist should attempt to fight off the assailant. Women must make their own decisions about whether to resist a rapist physically, taking into account their assessment of the rapist, the situation, and their ability to resist.

- Communicate your sexual limits to your date. Tell your partner how far you would like to go so that he will know what the limits are. For example, if your partner starts fondling you in ways that make you uncomfortable, you might say, "I'd prefer if you didn't touch me there. I really like you, but I prefer not to get so intimate at this point in our relationship."
- Meet new dates in public places, and avoid driving with a stranger or a group of people you've met. When meeting a new date, drive in your own car and meet your date at a public place. Don't drive with strangers or offer rides to strangers or groups of people. In some cases of date rape, the group disappears just prior to the assault.
- State your refusal definitively. Be firm in refusing a sexual overture. Look your partner straight in the eye. The more definite you are, the less likely it is that your partner will misinterpret your wishes.
- Become aware of your fears. Note any fears of displeasing your partner that might stifle your assertiveness. If your partner is truly respectful of you, you need not fear an angry or demeaning response. But if your partner is not respectful, it is best to become aware of it and end the relationship right there.
- Pay attention to your "vibes." Trust your gut-level feelings. Many victims of acquaintance rape said afterward that they had had a strange feeling about the man but failed to pay attention to it.
- Be especially cautious if you are in a new environment, such as college or a foreign country. You may be especially vulnerable to exploitation when you are becoming acquainted with a new environment, different people, and different customs.
- If you have broken off a relationship with someone you don't really like or feel good about, don't let him into your place. Many so-called date rapes are committed by ex-lovers and ex-boyfriends.

Confronting a Rapist: Should You Fight, Flee, or Plead? What if you are accosted by a rapist? Should you try to fight him off, flee, or plead with him to stop? Some women have thwarted attacks by pleading or crying. Screaming may be effective in warding off some attacks (Byers & Lewis, 1988). Running away sometimes works, but running may not be effective if the woman is outnumbered by a group of assailants (Gidycz & Koss, 1990). No single suggestion is likely to work in all cases.

Self-defense training may help women become better prepared to fend off an assailant. Yet physical resistance may spur some rapists to become more aggressive

Review: Rape: The Most Intimate Crime of Violence

Reflect

Have you ever been involved in a discussion about when sexual activity becomes rape? If a woman pets with a man in the nude and then says no when he attempts intercourse, is he guilty of rape if he forces her? Explain.

Critical Thinking

Agree or disagree with the following statement, and support your answer: A woman who walks in a dangerous neighborhood or talks to a stranger invites what she gets.

1. Many social scientists view rape as an act of _____ violence that is more connected with domination, anger, power, and sadism than with sex.

2. For the first few thousand years of history, rapes were considered crimes against _____.

3. _____ rape consists of sexual intercourse with a person who is below the age of consent.

4. Studies tend to (*Overreport* or *Underreport?*) the incidence of rape.

5. The prevalence of rape in the United States is (*Greater* or *Less?*) than that in Great Britain and Japan.

6. Most women are raped by (*Strangers* or *Acquaintances?*).

7. Rapes by (*Acquaintances* or *Strangers?*) are more likely to be reported to the police.

8. _____ appears to be the major motive behind gang rapes.

9. A husband (*Can* or *Cannot?*) be charged with raping his wife.

10. Rape myths create a social climate that _____ rape.

11. Social critics contend that our society breeds rapists by _____ males into socially and sexually dominant roles.

12. Generally speaking, rapists (*Are* or *Are not?*) mentally ill.

13. Rapists are more likely than other men to hold (*Traditional* or *Nontraditional?*) gender-role attitudes.

14. According to Groth and Birnbaum, the _____ rape is a ritualized, savage attack.

15. _____ is among the most frequent emotional reactions to sexual assault.

(Powell, 1996). Women who resist increase their chances of preventing the completion of a rape, but resistance also increases the odds of their being injured.

It may be difficult, if not impossible, for people to think through their options clearly and calmly when they are attacked. Rape experts recommend that women practice alternative responses to a rape attack. Thompson (1991) suggests that effective self-defense is built upon the use of multiple strategies, ranging from attempts to avoid potential rape situations (such as by installing home security systems or by walking only in well-lit areas), to acquiescence when active resistance would seem too risky, to the use of more active verbal or physical forms of resistance in some low-risk situations.

Sexual Abuse of Children

Many view sexual abuse of children as among the most heinous of crimes. Children who are sexually assaulted often suffer social and emotional problems that impair their development and persist into adulthood, affecting their self-esteem and their ability to form intimate relationships.

No one knows how many children are sexually abused. Although most sexually abused children are girls, one-quarter to one-third are boys (Edwards et al., 2003). Interviews with 8,667 adult members of an HMO suggest that the prevalence of sexual abuse among boys is about 18% and among girls is about 25% (Edwards et al., 2003). These estimates may underrepresent the actual prevalence, because people may fail to report such incidents as a consequence of faulty memories, shame, or embarrassment.

Question: What is sexual abuse of children? Sexual abuse of children ranges from exhibitionism, kissing, fondling, and sexual touching to oral sex and anal intercourse and, with girls, vaginal intercourse. Acts such as touching children's sexual organs while changing or bathing them, sleeping with children, or appearing nude before them are open to interpretation and often are innocent (Haugaard, 2000). Sexual contact between an adult and a child is abusive, even if the child is willing, because children are legally incapable of consenting to sexual activity. Although the age of consent varies among the states, sexual relations between adults and children under the age of consent are a criminal offense in every state.

Voluntary sexual activity *between children* of similar ages is not sexual abuse. Children often engage in consensual sex play with peers or siblings, as in "playing doctor" or in mutual masturbation. Although such experiences may be recalled in adulthood with feelings of shame or guilt, they are not typically as harmful as experiences with adults. When the experience involves coercion, or when the other child is significantly older or in a position of power over the younger child, the sexual contact may be considered sexual abuse.

Questions: Which children are sexually abused? Who abuses them?

Patterns of Abuse

Children from stable, middle-class families appear to be generally at lower risk of encountering sexual abuse than children from poorer, less cohesive families (Edwards et al., 2003). In most cases, children who are sexually abused are not accosted by the proverbial stranger lurking in the school yard. Most molesters are close to them: relatives, steprelatives, family friends, and neighbors (Edwards et al., 2003).

Parents who discover that their child has been abused by a family member are often reluctant to notify authorities. Some may feel that such problems are "family matters" that are best kept private. Others may be reluctant to notify authorities for fear that it may shame the family or that they may be held accountable for failing to protect the child. The decision to report the abuse to the police depends largely on the relationship between the abuser and the person who discovers the abuse. In a Boston community survey, none of the parents whose children were sexually abused by family members notified the authorities. By contrast, 23% of the parents whose children had been abused by acquaintances notified the authorities; 73% of the parents whose children were abused by strangers did so (Finkelhor, 1984).

Typically, the child initially trusts the abuser. Physical force is seldom needed to gain compliance, largely because of the child's helplessness, gullibility, and submission to adult authority. Whereas most sexually abused children are abused only once, those who are abused by family members are more likely to suffer repeated abuse.

Genital fondling is the most common type of abuse (Edwards et al., 2003). In one sample of women who had been molested in childhood, most of the contacts involved genital fondling (38% of cases) or exhibitionism (20% of cases). Intercourse occurred in only 4% of cases (Knudsen, 1991). Repeated abuse by a family member, however, commonly follows a pattern that begins with affectionate fondling during the preschool years, progresses to oral sex or mutual masturbation during the early school years, and culminates in sexual penetration (vaginal or anal intercourse) during preadolescence or adolescence.

Abused children rarely report the abuse, often because of fear of retaliation from the abuser or because they believe they will be blamed for it. Adults may suspect abuse if a child shows sudden personality changes or develops fears, difficulties in

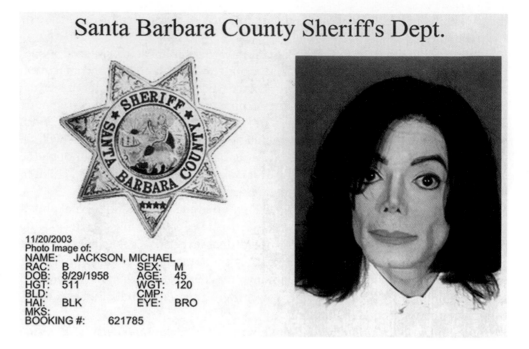

Charged with Child Molestation Pop star Michael Jackson was charged with child molestation in 2003. More than 60 police officers suddenly descended on his California estate, "Neverland," searching for evidence. A decade earlier, Jackson settled out of court a case that might also have involved child molestation (Broder, 2003). What motivates adults to seek sexual activity with children?

school, or problems eating or sleeping. A pediatrician may discover physical signs of abuse during a medical exam. The average age at which most children are first sexually abused ranges from 6 to 12 years for girls and from 7 to 10 years for boys (Knudsen, 1991).

Types of Abusers Researchers find that the overwhelming majority of people who sexually abuse children (both boys and girls) are males (Edwards et al., 2003). Although most child abusers are adults, some are adolescents. Adolescent male sex offenders are more likely than other adolescents to have been molested themselves as boys. Some adolescent sex offenders may be imitating their own victimization. Adolescent child molesters also tend to feel socially inadequate and to be fearful of social interactions with age-mates of the other gender (Katz, 1990).

Although the great majority of sexual abusers are male, the number of female sexual abusers may be greater than has been generally believed (Banning, 1989). Many female sexual abusers may go undetected because society accords women a much freer range of physical contact with children than it does men. A woman who fondles a child might be seen as affectionate, or at worst seductive, whereas a man would be more likely to be perceived as a child molester (Banning, 1989).

What motivates a woman to sexually abuse children, even her own children? Some female abusers have histories of becoming dependent on, or being rejected by, abusive males (Matthews et al., 1990). Some appear to have been manipulated into engaging in sexual abuse by their husbands. Others appear to have unmet emotional needs and low self-esteem and may have been seeking acceptance, closeness, and attention through sexual acts with children. Some, motivated by unresolved feelings of anger, revenge, powerlessness, or jealousy, may view their own and others' children as safe targets for venting these feelings. Some view their crimes as expressions of love.

The great majority of child molesters are male. Why? Banning (1989), arguing within a sociocultural framework, suggests that males in our culture are socialized into seeking partners who are younger and weaker, whom they can easily dominate. This pattern of socialization may take the extreme form of development of sexual interest in children and adolescent girls, who because of their age are more easily dominated than adult women.

Sexual interest in children may also be motivated by unusual patterns of sexual arousal. This brings us to pedophilia. *Question: What is pedophilia?*

Pedophilia

Pedophilia is a paraphilia (see Chapter 17) in which an adult finds children to be the preferred and sometimes exclusive objects of sexual desire. The prevalence of pedophilia in the general population is unknown. Some pedophiles are so distressed by their urges that they never act on them. Many, however, molest young children and adolescents, often repeatedly. Some pedophiles are responsible for large numbers of sexual assaults on children. One study of 232 convicted pedophiles showed that they had each molested an average of 76 children (Abel et al., 1989). Incarcerated pedophiles have usually committed many more offenses than those for which they were convicted.

The Monster in the Bedroom.
Not all monsters are make-believe. Some, like the perpetrators of incest, are members of the family.

Although pedophiles are sometimes called child molesters, not all child molesters are pedophiles. Pedophilia involves persistent or recurrent sexual attraction to children. Some molesters, however, may seek sexual contacts with children only when they are under unusual stress or lack other sexual outlets. Thus, they do not meet the clinical criteria for a diagnosis of pedophilia.

Pedophiles are almost exclusively male (Cooper et al., 1990). Some pedophiles are sexually attracted only to children. Others are sexually attracted to adults as well. Some pedophiles limit their sexual interest in children to incestuous relationships with family members. Others abuse children to whom they are not related. Some pedophiles limit their sexual interest in children to looking at them or undressing them. Others fondle them or masturbate in their presence. Some manipulate or coerce children into oral, anal, or vaginal intercourse.

Children tend not to be worldly-wise. They can often be "taken in" by pedophiles who tell them that they would like to "show them something," "teach them something," or do something with them that they will "like." Some pedophiles seek to gain the child's affection and discourage the child from disclosing the sexual activity by showering the child with attention and gifts. Others threaten the child or the child's family to prevent disclosure.

There is no consistent personality profile of the pedophile (Okami & Goldberg, 1992). Most pedophiles do not fit the common stereotype of the "dirty old man" in the trench coat who hangs around school yards. Most are otherwise law-abiding, well-respected citizens, generally in their 30s and 40s. Many are married or divorced, with children of their own.

Research suggests that sexual attraction to children may be more common than is generally believed. Researchers in one study administered an anonymous survey to a sample of 193 college men (Briere & Runtz, 1989). A high percentage of the students—21%—admitted to having been sexually attracted to small children. Nine percent reported sexual fantasies involving young children. Five percent reported masturbating to such fantasies. Seven percent reported that there was some likelihood that they would have sex with a young child if they knew they could avoid detection and punishment. Fortunately, most people with such erotic interests never act on them.

Pedophilia may have complex and varied origins. Some pedophiles who are lacking in social skills may turn to children after failing to establish gratifying relationships with adult women (Overholser & Beck, 1986). Research generally supports the stereotype of the pedophile as weak, passive, and shy—a socially inept, isolated man

Pedophilia A type of paraphilia that is defined by sexual attraction to unusual stimuli: children. (From the Greek *paidos,* meaning "child," not the Latin *pedis,* meaning "foot.")

who feels threatened by mature relationships (Ames & Houston, 1990). Some pedophiles were sexually abused as children. Cycles of abuse may be perpetuated from generation to generation if children who are sexually abused become victimizers or partners of victimizers as adults.

Some pedophiles engage in incestuous relationships with their own children. Some of these pedophiles are very dominant, others very passive. Few are found between these extremes (Ames & Houston, 1990). *Question: What is incest?*

Incest: Breaking Taboos

Incest involves people who are related by blood, or *consanguineous.* The law may also proscribe coitus between, say, a stepfather and stepdaughter. Although a few societies have permitted incestuous pairings among royalty, all known cultures have some form of an incest taboo.

Perspectives on the Incest Taboo Speculations about the origin of incest taboos abound. One explanation holds that the incest taboo developed because it was adaptive for ancient humans to prevent the harmful effects of inbreeding that may result when genetic defects or diseases are carried within family bloodlines (Leavitt, 1990). Our ancient ancestors lacked knowledge of the mechanisms of genetics, but they may have observed that certain diseases or defects tend to run in families. Evidence suggests that the offspring of close relatives bear an increased rate of genetic diseases, mental retardation, and other physical abnormalities (Ames & Houston, 1990). Inbreeding may also be counterproductive to survival because it reduces the amount of genetic variation in the gene pool. Therefore, it can reduce the ability of the population to adapt to changes in the environment.

Other theorists explain the incest taboo in terms of the role that it may play in maintaining stability in the family and establishing kinship ties within the larger social grouping (Harris & Johnson, 2003; Whitten, 2001). The anthropologist Bronislaw Malinowski (1927), for example, argued that the incest taboo serves to reduce sexual competition within the family. If left uncontrolled, competition would create rivalry and hostility such that the family might be unable to function as a social unit. Because the family unit fosters survival of a society, the incest taboo may have developed as a means of keeping the family intact.

Cooperation theory emphasizes the importance to the survival of the society of cooperative ties between family groups (Harris & Johnson, 2003; Whitten, 2001). Society is complex. Its survival requires the cooperation of large numbers of people. Marriage establishes kinship ties that lessen suspiciousness and hostility between family groups and foster cooperation. According to cooperation theory, the incest taboo was established to help ensure that people would marry outside their own families and thus create cohesive communities. Such theories are fascinating but remain speculative.

Types of Incest Most of our knowledge of incestuous relationships concerns father–daughter incest. Why? Most identified cases involve fathers who were eventually incarcerated.

About 1% of a sample of women in five American cities reported a sexual encounter with a father or stepfather (Cameron et al., 1986). But brother–sister incest, not parent–child incest, is the most common type of incest (Waterman & Lusk, 1986). Brother–sister incest is also believed to be greatly underreported, possibly because it tends to be transient and is apparently less harmful than parent–child incest. Finkelhor (1990) found that 21% of the college men in his sample, and 39% of the college women, reported incestuous relationships with a sibling of the other sex. Only 4% reported an incestuous relationship with their fathers. Incest between

Incest Marriage or sexual relations between people who are so closely related (by "blood") that sexual relations are prohibited and punishable by law. (From the Latin *in-,* meaning "not," and *castus,* meaning "chaste.")

siblings of the same sex is rare, and mother–daughter incest is the least common form of incest (Waterman & Lusk, 1986).

Let us further consider the two most common incest patterns, father–daughter incest and brother–sister incest.

Father–Daughter Incest Father–daughter incest often begins with affectionate cuddling or embraces and then progresses to teasing sexual play, lengthy caresses, hugs, kisses, and genital contact, even penetration. In some cases genital contact occurs more abruptly, usually when the father has been drinking or has been arguing with his wife. Force is not typically used to gain compliance, but daughters are sometimes physically overcome and injured by their fathers.

Truth?Fiction?
Revisited

It is not true that father–daughter incest is the most common type of incest. Father–daughter incest may be the most highly publicized variety of incest, but brother–sister incest is more common.

Brother–Sister Incest In sibling incest, the brother usually initiates sexual activity and assumes the dominant role. Some younger brothers and sisters may view their sexual activity as natural experimentation and not know that it is taboo.

Evidence on the effects of incest between brothers and sisters is mixed. In a study of college undergraduates, those who reported childhood incest with siblings did not reveal more evidence of sexual adjustment problems than other undergraduates (Greenwald & Leitenberg, 1989). Sibling incest is most likely to be harmful when it is forced or when parental response is harsh.

Family Factors in Incest Incest frequently occurs within the context of general family disruption, as in families in which there is spouse abuse, a dysfunctional marriage, or alcoholic or physically abusive parents (Alter-Reid et al., 1986; Sirles & Franke, 1989). Stressful events in the father's life, such as the loss of a job or problems at work, often precede the initiation of incest (Waterman, 1986).

Fathers who abuse older daughters tend to be domineering and authoritarian with their families (Waterman, 1986). Fathers who abuse younger, preschool daughters are more likely to be passive, dependent, and low in self-esteem. As Waterman (1986) notes,

> [The fathers] may need soothing and comforting, and may feel especially safe with preschool children: "I felt safe with her. . . . I didn't have to perform. She was so little that I knew she wouldn't and couldn't hurt me."

Marriages in incestuous families tend to be characterized by an uneven power relationship between the spouses. The abusive father is usually dominant. Another thread that frequently runs through incestuous families is a troubled sexual relationship between the spouses. The wife often rejects the husband sexually (Waterman, 1986).

In their classic research, Gebhard and his colleagues (1965) found that many fathers who committed incest with their daughters were religiously devout, fundamentalist, and moralistic. Perhaps such men, when sexually frustrated, are less likely to seek extramarital and extrafamilial sexual outlets or to turn to masturbation as a sexual release. In many cases the father is under stress but does not find adequate emotional and sexual support from his wife (Gagnon, 1977). He turns to a daughter as a wife surrogate, often when he has been drinking alcohol (Gebhard et al., 1965). The daughter may become, in her father's fantasies, the "woman of the house." This fantasy may become his justification for continuing the incestuous relationship. In some incestuous families, a role reversal occurs. The abused daughter assumes many of the mother's responsibilities for managing the household and caring for the younger children.

Incestuous abuse is often repeated from generation to generation. One study found that in 154 cases of children who were sexually abused within the family, more

A Closer Look

How Child Sexual Abuse May Set the Stage for Psychological Disorders in Adulthood

One way in which child sexual abuse may set the stage for psychological disorders in adulthood is by increasing people's bodily responses to stress (Altemus et al., 2003; Bremner et al., 2003). Responses to stress are typically measured in terms of the reactivity of the endocrine system, which produces hormones (particularly stress hormones such as ACTH and cortisol), and the autonomic nervous system, which affects the heart rate and other signs of stress, such as sweating and blood pressure.

For example, a study by Christine Heim and her colleagues (2000, 2002) recruited 49 generally healthy women with an average age of 35. Twenty-seven of the women reported childhood physical and/or sexual abuse in interviews; 22 did not. Twenty-three of the women were currently diagnosed with major depression; 26 were not. All 49 women were exposed to a stressor that has been shown to heighten the release of stress hormones and autonomic nervous system reactions. The women had to think about and make a public speech that included mental arithmetic. Meanwhile, their levels of stress hormones and heart rates were being assessed. As shown in Table 18.1, the presence of depression alone did not distinguish women who were depressed (group B) from women who were not (group A). However, women who reported a history of child abuse (groups C and D) were significantly more likely to show higher blood levels of ACTH and cortisol in response to the stressor than women who did not report a history of abuse (groups A and B). Group D, consisting of women who reported a history of abuse and who were also diagnosed with major depression, showed significantly higher levels of stress hormones and heart rate than all other groups. Therefore, the combination of early abuse and current depression apparently makes the body most sensitive to stress. But even among women who were not depressed, the history of abuse was connected with greater reactivity of the endocrine system and the autonomic nervous system.

Other studies of adult women who had experienced childhood sexual abuse reported similar findings (e.g., Bremner et al., 2003). These studies suggest that child sexual abuse may promote a bodily reactivity to stress that endures well into adulthood, setting the stage for physical as well as psychological problems.

---

than a third of the male offenders and about half of the mothers had either been abused themselves or were exposed to abuse as children (Faller, 1989b).

Sociocultural factors, such as poverty, overcrowded living conditions, and social or geographic isolation, contribute to incest in some families (Waterman, 1986). Sibling incest may be encouraged by the crowded living conditions and open sexuality that occur among some economically disadvantaged families.

We have considered the factors that contribute to the sexual abuse of children. *Question: What are the effects of sexual abuse on children?*

Effects of Sexual Abuse on Children

The effects of sexual abuse are variable, and there is no single identifiable syndrome that emerges from sexual abuse (Resick, 2003; Saywitz et al., 2000). Nevertheless, sexual abuse often inflicts great psychological harm on the child, whether it is perpetrated by a family member, an acquaintance, or a stranger. Children who are sexually abused may suffer from a variety of short- and long-term psychological complaints, including anger, depression, anxiety, eating disorders, inappropriate sexual behavior, aggressive behavior, self-destructive behavior, sexual promiscuity, drug abuse, suicide attempts, post-traumatic stress disorder, low self-esteem, sexual dysfunction, mistrust of others, and feelings of detachment (Edwards et al., 2003). Sexual abuse may also have physical effects such as genital injuries and may cause psychosomatic problems such as stomachaches and headaches.

Abused children commonly "act out." Younger children have tantrums or display aggressive or antisocial behavior. Older children turn to substance abuse (Herrera & McCloskey, 2003; Kendler et al., 2000). Some abused children become withdrawn and retreat into fantasy or refuse to leave the house. Regressive behaviors, such as

TABLE 18.1		
Responses of Women with or without a History of Child Abuse to a Stressor		
	Women Who Are Not Experiencing a Major Depressive Episode	Women Who Are Experiencing a Major Depressive Episode
Women with No History of Child Abuse	**GROUP A–12 WOMEN** Endocrine System: ACTH peak: 4.7 parts/liter Cortisol peak: 339 parts/liter Autonomic Nervous System: Heart rate: 78.4/minute	**GROUP B–10 WOMEN** Endocrine System: ACTH peak: 5.3 parts/liter Cortisol peak: 337 parts/liter Autonomic Nervous System: Heart rate: 83.8/minute
Women with a History of Child Abuse	**GROUP C–14 WOMEN** Endocrine System: ACTH peak: 9.3 parts/liter Cortisol peak: 359 parts/liter Autonomic Nervous System: Heart rate: 82.2/minute	**GROUP D–13 WOMEN** Endocrine System: ACTH peak: 12.1 parts/liter Cortisol peak: 527 parts/liter Autonomic Nervous System: Heart rate: 89.7/minute

Source of data: Heim, C., et al. (2000). Pituitary-adrenal and autonomic responses to stress in women after sexual and physical abuse in childhood. *Journal of the American Medical Association, 284*: 592–597.

thumb sucking, fear of the dark, and fear of strangers, are also common among sexually abused children. On the heels of the assault and in the ensuing years, many survivors of childhood sexual abuse—like many rape survivors—show signs of post-traumatic stress disorder. They have flashbacks, nightmares, numbing of emotions, and feelings of estrangement from others (Herrera & McCloskey, 2003).

The sexual development of abused children may also be shaped in dysfunctional ways. For example, the survivor may become prematurely sexually active or promiscuous in adolescence and adulthood (Browning, 2002; Herrera & McCloskey, 2003; Kendler et al., 2000). Researchers find that adolescent girls who are sexually abused tend to engage in consensual coitus at earlier ages than nonabused peers (Browning, 2002; Herrera & McCloskey, 2003).

Researchers generally find more similarities than differences between the genders with respect to the effects of sexual abuse in childhood (Edwards et al., 2003). For example, both boys and girls tend to suffer fears and sleep disturbance. There are some sex differences, however. The most consistent sex difference appears to be that boys more often "externalize" their problems, perhaps by becoming more physically aggressive. Girls more often "internalize" their difficulties, such as by becoming depressed (Edwards et al., 2003).

Late adolescence and early adulthood seem to be especially difficult periods for survivors of childhood sexual abuse. Studies of women in these age groups reveal more psychological and social problems in abused women (Herrera & McCloskey, 2003; Kendler et al., 2000). Women who blame themselves for the abuse apparently have lower self-esteem and more depression than those who do not (Edwards et al., 2003). The nearby "A Closer Look" feature suggests a biological link between sexual abuse in childhood and psychological problems in adulthood.

Sexual abuse of children is a devastating crime. *Question: How can we prevent it?*

Online Registries of Sex Offenders: Boon or Boondoggle?

Congress began requiring states to maintain registries of sex offenders in 1996. States are now going further by posting the information, along with photos of the offenders and ugly details of their offenses, on Web pages. Anyone with a computer and modem can access them. "It's the wave," said Scott Matson (cited in Zielbauer, 2000), a researcher with the Center for Sex Offender Management. "Everyone's doing it now."

Supporters of the Web postings argue that bringing community notification to the Internet is an important and easy way to spread information on dangerous sex offenders. Putting information about sex offenders online "should make sex offenders think twice before offending again in Wisconsin, and that should certainly make this state a safer place," said Governor Tommy G. Thompson (Zielbauer, 2000) when he announced Wisconsin's intention to create an online registry.

Critics argue that these online registries can stigmatize and victimize marginal offenders, even preventing them from getting help. Thus, they may eventually be responsible for the commission of more sex crimes than they prevent. Critics note that the sites do not explain how to protect children or evaluate the danger the offenders represent. David A. D'Amora, director of a treatment program for sexual abusers, believes that "Just throwing a bunch of things up on a screen is like throwing gasoline on a fire" (Zielbauer, 2000). For example, online registries have led to retributive violence against sex offenders. Ex-offenders have been harassed by neighbors, evicted by landlords, fired from their jobs, even beaten by mobs. Some examples:

- In 2000, two men beat a convicted child molester with a baseball bat in Florida. They threatened to kill him if he approached any children in the neighborhood.
- In 1999, four men in Dallas beat a 27-year-old retarded man whose address was erroneously listed on Texas's online registry.
- In 1998, a Linden, New Jersey, man, after receiving a police flier, fired bullets from a .45-caliber handgun into the house of a paroled rapist and was charged with aggravated assault.
- Also in 1998, residents of a trailer park in the state of Washington burned down a mobile home days before a released sex offender was to move into it.

The registration of information about sex offenders on the Internet is "evolutionary, . . . awkward and painful," says Roxanne Lieb, director of the Washington State Institute for Public policy (Zielbauer, 2000). "I think it's important to remember that at least what we started with was not knowing, and that is worse."

"I think that when violent criminals are placed back in the community, the community has every right to know who they are and what they did," said Marc Klaas (Zielbauer, 2000), whose daughter was kidnaped and strangled by a sex offender. "You wouldn't want to hire a baby sitter, would you, that had spent years in prison for a violent crime. If you were a single mother, you certainly wouldn't want to start dating one of those characters. Community notification creates some kind of outer control on these individuals. If people know who they are, they're going to be more careful than if people don't know who they are."

Prevention of Sexual Abuse of Children

Many of us were taught by our parents never to accept a ride or an offer of candy from a stranger. However, many instances of sexual abuse are perpetrated by a familiar adult, often a family member or friend (Zielbauer, 2000). Prevention programs help children understand what sexual abuse is and how they can avoid it. A national survey showed that 2 out of 3 children in the United States have participated in school-based sex abuse prevention programs (Goleman, 1993). In addition to learning to avoid strangers, children need to recognize the differences between acceptable touching, as in an affectionate embrace or pat on the head, and unacceptable or "bad" touching. Even children of elementary school age can learn the distinction between "good touching and bad touching." School-based programs can help prepare children to handle an actual encounter with a molester (Goleman, 1993). Children who receive training are more likely to use strategies such as running away, yelling, or saying no when they are threatened by an abuser. They are also more likely to report incidents to adults.

Researchers recognize that children can easily be intimidated or overpowered by adults or older children. Children may be unable to say no in a sexually abusive situation, even though they want to and know it is the right thing to do. Although children may not always be able to prevent abuse, they can be encouraged to tell someone about it. Most prevention programs emphasize teaching children messages such as "It's not your fault," "Never keep a bad or scary secret," and "Always tell your parents about this, especially if someone says you shouldn't tell them."

Children also need to be alerted to the types of threats they might receive for disclosing the abuse. They are more likely to resist threats if they are reassured that they will be believed if they disclose the abuse, that their parents will continue to love them, and that they and their families will be protected from the molester.

School-based prevention programs focus on protecting the child. In most states, teachers and helping professionals are required to report suspected abuse to authorities. Tighter controls and better screening are needed to monitor the hiring of day care employees. Administrators and teachers in preschool and day care facilities also need to be educated to recognize the signs of sexual abuse and to report suspected cases. Treatment programs to help people who are sexually attracted to children *before* they commit abusive acts would also be of use.

Treatment of Survivors of Sexual Abuse

Question: What can be done to help survivors of sexual abuse? Because the majority of cases of sexual abuse go unreported during childhood, psychotherapy in adulthood often becomes the first opportunity for survivors to confront lingering feelings of pain, anger, and misplaced guilt. Group or individual therapy can help improve survivors' self-esteem and ability to develop intimate relationships. Social support is an important factor in helping survivors of childhood sexual abuse maintain their self-esteem and minimize the stress they experience (Hyman et al., 2003).

Review: Sexual Abuse of Children

Reflect

How would you attempt to teach a child the difference between "good touching" and "bad touching"?

CriticalThinking

Why do you think that most cases of child sexual abuse are not reported to the authorities?

16. Most sexually abused children are (*Boys* or *Girls*?).

17. Sexual contact between an adult and a child (*Is* or *Is not*?) abusive when the child is willing.

18. Voluntary sexual activity *between children* of similar ages (*Is* or *Is not*?) sexual abuse.

19. Most children who are sexually abused are accosted by (*Strangers* or *Acquaintances*?).

20. _____ is the most common type of sexual child abuse.

21. The majority of people who sexually abuse children are (*Males* or *Females*?).

22. _____ involves persistent or recurrent sexual attraction to children.

23. Research generally supports the stereotype of the pedophile as socially (*Skilled* or *Unskilled*?).

24. _____ involves sexual activity with people who are related by blood, or *consanguineous.*

25. Malinowski argued that the incest taboo serves to reduce sexual _____ within the family.

26. _____ incest is the most common type of incest.

27. Incest often occurs within the context of family _____.

28. Children of elementary school age children (*Are* or *Are not*?) too young to learn the distinction between "good touching and bad touching."

Many therapists recommend a multicomponent treatment approach, which may involve individual therapy for the child, mother, and father; group therapy for the adolescent or even preadolescent survivor; art therapy or play therapy for the younger child (such as using drawings or puppets to express feelings); marital counseling for the parents; and family therapy for the entire family.

Treatment of Rapists and Child Molesters

Question: How shall we treat rapists and child molesters? Before we attempt to answer that question, let's ask another: Just what does *treatment* mean? When a helping professional treats someone, the goal is usually to help that individual. When we speak of treating a sex offender, the goal is as likely, or more likely, to be to help society by eliminating the problem behavior.

Rapists and child molesters are criminals, not patients. Most convicted rapists and child molesters are incarcerated as a form of punishment, not treatment. They may receive psychological treatment or rehabilitation in prison to help prepare them for release and reentry into society, however. The most common form of treatment is group therapy, which is based on the belief that although offenders may fool counselors, they do not easily fool one another (Kaplan, 1993). Yet the great majority of incarcerated sex offenders receive little or no treatment in prison (Goleman, 1992). In California, for example, which has 15,000 incarcerated sex offenders, treatment has been provided in but one experimental program for only 46 rapists and child molesters (Goleman, 1992).

The results of prison-based treatment programs are mixed at best. Consider a Canadian study of 54 rapists who participated in a treatment program. Following release from prison, 28% were later convicted of a sexual offense, and 43% were convicted of a violent offense (Rice et al., 1990). Treatment also failed to curb recidivism among a sample of 136 child molesters (Rice et al., 1991).

More promising findings resulted from innovative programs in prison facilities in California and Vermont (Goleman, 1992). In the Vermont program, the average rate of conviction for additional sex crimes following release was reduced by at least half in a group of sex offenders who took part in the treatment program, compared to a control group who did not. These innovative programs used a variety of techniques. Empathy training was used to increase the offender's sensitivity to his victims. One empathy exercise had offenders write about their crimes from the perspective of the victim. The technique of covert sensitization was used to help offenders resist deviant sex fantasies, which often lead to deviant behavior. The offender would pair, in his imagination, scenes involving rape and molestation with aversive consequences. An exhibitionist, for example, might be asked to practice imagining that he is about to expose himself and is discovered in the act by his parents. A child molester might fantasize about sexually approaching a child, only to find himself confronted by police officers.

Another approach uses medical interventions such as castration to reduce testosterone levels and, consequently, offenders' sex drives. Experts do not agree on whether castration helps sex offenders control their sexual urges (Roesler & Witztum, 2000). Many castrated rapists report lowered sex drives, as might be expected from the reductions in testosterone production that result from removal of the testes. They may retain sexual interest and remain capable of erection, however. And some do repeat their crimes. Other researchers report lower recidivism rates among castrated offenders than among other offenders.

Surgical castration is an extreme measure. It raises ethical concerns because of its invasive character and irreversibility. Anti-androgen drugs such as Depo-Provera

Review: Treatment of Rapists and Child Molesters

Reflect

How do you feel about the posting of the names, photos, and addresses of known sex offenders on Web sites? Explain.

CriticalThinking

Agree or disagree with the following statement, and support your answer: We should punish sex offenders and not worry about "treating" them.

29. Rapists and child molesters are (*Criminals* or *Mental patients*?).

30. The most common form of treatment for rapists and child molesters is _____ therapy.

31. _____ training is used to increase the offender's sensitivity to his victims.

32. Medical interventions such as surgical or chemical _____ reduce the sex drives of offenders.

---

chemically reduce testosterone levels (Roesler & Witztum, 2000). Unlike surgical castration, "chemical castration"—via anti-androgen drugs—is reversible (Roesler & Witztum, 2000).

Sexual Harassment

Many Americans were spellbound by the Michael Douglas–Demi Moore film *Disclosure*. In the film, Demi Moore plays Michael Douglas's supervisor. She uses her power over him to harass him into sexual activity.

Question: What is sexual harassment?

Sexual harassment can be difficult to define (Lewin, 1998b). For example, President Bill Clinton was accused of sexually touching, or "groping," a resistant White House volunteer named Kathleen Willey and of placing her hand on his penis (Lewin, 1998b). Such behavior would clearly constitute sexual harassment. But Clinton also engaged in fellatio with a young White House intern, Monica Lewinsky. Although Lewinsky participated voluntarily, some critics note that the White House *is* a workplace and that Clinton's power over the intern caused their interaction to constitute sexual harassment.

For legal purposes, sexual harassment in the workplace is usually defined as the "deliberate or repeated unsolicited verbal comments, gestures, or *physical contact*[1] of a sexual nature that is considered to be unwelcome by the recipient" (U.S. Merit Systems Protection Board, 1981, p. 2). Examples of sexual harassment can range from unwelcome sexual jokes, overtures, suggestive comments, and sexual innuendos to outright sexual assault and may include behaviors such as the following (Powell 1996):

- Verbal harassment or abuse
- Subtle pressure for sexual activity
- Remarks about a person's clothing, body, or sexual activities
- Leering at or ogling a person's body
- Unwelcome touching, patting, or pinching
- Brushing against a person's body
- Demands for sexual favors accompanied by implied or overt threats concerning one's job or student status

Sexual harassment
Deliberate or repeated unsolicited verbal comments, gestures, or physical contact of a sexual nature that is unwelcome to the recipient.

---

1. Our italics.

- Physical assault. The idea here is that sexual assault, of the kind of which President Clinton was accused, would be sexual harassment but could also be much more

Both men and women can commit, and both can be subjected to, sexual harassment. However, despite the plot of the film *Disclosure*, about 99% of harassers are men.

Charges of sexual harassment are often ignored or trivialized by coworkers and employers. The victim may hear, "Why make a big deal out of it? It's not like you were attacked in the street." Evidence shows, however, that persons subjected to sexual harassment *do* suffer from it. Many report reactions such as anxiety, irritability, lowered self-esteem, and anger. Some find harassment on the job so unbearable that they resign. College women have dropped courses, switched majors, or changed graduate programs or even colleges because they were unable to stop professors from sexually harassing them (Fitzgerald, 1993a, 1993b).

One reason why sexual harassment is so stressful is that, as with so many other forms of sexual exploitation or coercion, the blame tends to fall on the victim (Powell, 1996). Some harassers seem to believe that charges of harassment were exaggerated or that the victim "overreacted" or "took me too seriously." In our society, women are expected to be "nice"—to be passive and not make a scene. The woman who asserts her rights may be seen as "strange" and disturbing or as a troublemaker. "Women are damned if they assert themselves and victimized if they don't" (Powell, 1991, p. 114).

Sexual harassment sometimes has more to do with the abuse of power than with sexual desire (Tedeschi & Felson, 1994). Relatively few cases of sexual harassment involve outright requests for sexual favors. Most involve the expression of power as a tactic to control or frighten someone, usually a woman. The harasser is usually in a dominant position and abuses that position by exploiting the victim's vulnerability. Sexual harassment may be used as a tactic of social control. It may be a means of keeping women "in their place." This is especially so in work settings that are traditional male preserves, such as the firehouse, the construction site, or the military academy. Sexual harassment reflects resentment and hostility toward women who venture beyond the boundaries of the traditional feminine role (Fitzgerald, 1993b).

Sexual harassment is not confined to the workplace or the university. It may also occur between patients and doctors and between therapists and clients. Therapists may use their power and influence to pressure clients into sexual relations. Such harassment may be disguised, expressed in terms of the "therapeutic benefits" of sexual activity.

Two settings where sexual harassment occurs are in the workplace and on campus.

Sexual Harassment in the Workplace

Question: How does sexual harassment occur in the workplace? Harassers in the workplace can be employers, supervisors, coworkers, or clients of a company. In some cases, clients make unwelcome sexual advances to employees and these overtures are ignored or approved of by the boss. If a worker asks a coworker for a date and is refused, it is not sexual harassment. If the coworker persists with unwelcome advances and does not take no for an answer, however, the behavior crosses the line and becomes harassment.

Perhaps the most severe form of sexual harassment, short of an outright assault, involves an employer or supervisor who demands sexual favors as a condition of employment or advancement. In 1980, the Equal Employment Opportunity Commission drafted a set of guidelines that expanded the definition of sexual harassment in the workplace to include any behavior of a sexual nature that interferes with an individual's work performance or creates a hostile, intimidating, or offensive work environment.

In 1986, the U.S. Supreme Court recognized sexual harassment as a form of sex discrimination under Title VII of the Civil Rights Act of 1964. It held that employers could be held accountable if such behavior was deemed to create a hostile or abusive work environment or to interfere with an employee's work performance. A 1993 Supreme Court ruling held that a person need not have suffered psychological damage to sue an employer on grounds of sexual harassment ("Court, 9-0," 1993). Moreover, employers can be held responsible not only for their own actions, but also for sexual harassment by their employees when the employer either knew *or should have known* that harassment was taking place and failed to eliminate it promptly (McKinney & Maroules, 1991). To protect themselves, many companies and universities have developed programs to educate workers about sexual harassment, have established mechanisms for dealing with complaints, and have imposed sanctions against harassers.

Under the law, persons subjected to sexual harassment can obtain a court order to have the harassment stopped, to have their jobs reinstated (when they have lost them by resisting sexual advances), to receive back pay and lost benefits, and to obtain monetary awards for the emotional strain inflicted by the harassment. However, proving charges of sexual harassment is generally difficult because there are usually no corroborating witnesses or evidence. As a result, relatively few persons who encounter sexual harassment in the workplace file formal complaints or seek legal remedies. Like people subjected to other forms of sexual coercion, persons experiencing sexual harassment often do not report the offense for fear that they will not be believed or will be subjected to retaliation. Some fear that they will be branded as troublemakers or that they will lose their jobs.

How common is sexual harassment in the workplace? Two-thirds of the men interviewed by the *Harvard Business Review* said that reports of sexual harassment in the workplace were exaggerated (Castro, 1992). *However,* a survey by *Working Woman* magazine showed that more than 90% of the Fortune 500 companies had received complaints of sexual harassment from their employees. More than one-third of the companies had been sued on charges of sexual harassment. A survey of federal employees by the U.S. Merit System Protection Board found that 42% of females and 14% of males reported instances of sexual harassment (DeWitt, 1991). Overall, as many as 1 in 2 women encounters some form of sexual harassment on the job or on campus. Research overseas finds that about 70% of the women who work in Japan and 50% of those who work in Europe have encountered sexual harassment (Castro, 1992). Sexual harassment against women is more common in workplaces in which women have traditionally been underrepresented (Fitzgerald, 1993b), such as the construction site and the shipyard.

Sexual Harassment on Campus

Question: How does sexual harassment occur on campus? Estimates of the frequency of sexual harassment of college students vary widely across studies. Overall, 25% to 30% of students report at least one incident of sexual harassment in college, and males are about twice as likely as females to commit sexual harassment (Menard et al., 2003). The federal law prohibiting sex discrimination in academic institutions permits students to sue their schools for monetary damages for sexual harassment.

Sexual harassment on campus usually involves the less severe forms of harassment, such as sexist comments and sexual remarks, as well as come-ons, suggestive looks, propositions, and light touching (Menard et al., 2003). Relatively few acts involve the use of direct pressure for sexual intercourse. Most students who encounter sexual harassment do not report the incident. If they do, it is usually to a confidant, not to a person in authority.

Most forms of harassment involve unequal power relationships between the harasser and the person harassed. *Peer harassment* occurs between people who are equal in power, as in the cases of repeated sexual taunts from fellow employees, students, or colleagues. The harasser may even have less formal power than the person harassed. For example, women professors have been sexually harassed by students—in cases in which the traditional social dominance of the male may override the academic position of the woman, at least in the mind of the offender.

One common form of harassment by students, reported by nearly one-third of the female professors polled in one survey, involves sexist remarks. Other common forms of harassment include obscene phone calls, undue attention, and sexual remarks. Outright sexual advances are reported by a few professors (Grauerholz, 1989). Male faculty and staff members may also be subjected to harassment. Of 235 male faculty members polled at one university, 6% reported being sexually harassed by a student (Fitzgerald et al., 1988).

Sexual harassment also occurs long before students get to college. A nationwide survey of high school and junior high school students found that many boys and girls had encountered harassment in the form of others grabbing or groping them or subjecting them to sexually explicit putdowns when they were walking through school hallways (Henneberger, 1993).

The picture that emerges from a 1993 Louis Harris nationwide poll of teenagers in grades 8 through 11 indicates that sexual taunts and advances have become part of an unwelcome ritual for many students, especially girls, as they make their way through the hallways and stairwells of high schools (Barringer, 1993c; Henneberger, 1993). More than 2 of 3 of the girls, and more than 4 out of 10 of the boys, reported being touched, grabbed, or pinched at school. Furthermore, 2 out of 3 boys and about 1 out of 2 girls reported harassing other students. Many of the harassers (41% of the boys and 31% of the girls) viewed their actions as "just part of school life" and "no big deal." Unwelcome sexual comments and advances had a negative impact on both boys and girls, but especially on girls. One in 3 girls who experienced sexual harassment at school reported that it made them feel that they didn't want to go to school. Some 28% said that sexual harassment had made it more difficult for them to pay attention in class, and 20% said it had lowered their grades.

How to Resist Sexual Harassment

What would you do if you were sexually harassed by an employer or a professor? How would you handle it? Would you try to ignore it and hope that it would stop? *Question: How can one resist sexual harassment?* We offer some suggestions, adapted from Powell (1996), that may be helpful. Recognize, however, that responsibility for sexual harassment always lies with the perpetrator and with the organization that permits sexual harassment to take place, *not* with the person subjected to the harassment.

1. *Convey a professional attitude.* Harassment is often stopped cold by responding to the harasser with a businesslike, professional attitude.

2. *Discourage harassing behavior, and encourage appropriate behavior.* Harassment may also be stopped cold by shaping the harasser's behavior. Your reactions to the harasser may encourage businesslike behavior and discourage flirtatious or suggestive behavior. If a harassing professor suggests that you come back after school to review your term paper so that the two of you will be undisturbed, set limits assertively. Tell the professor that you'd feel more comfortable discussing the paper during regular office hours. Remain task-oriented. Stick to business. The harasser should quickly get the message that you insist on maintaining a

strictly professional relationship. If the harasser persists, do not blame yourself. You are responsible only for your own actions. When the harasser persists, a more direct response may be appropriate: "Professor Jones, I'd like to keep our relationship on a purely professional basis, okay?"

3. *Avoid being alone with the harasser.* If you are being harassed by your professor but need some advice about preparing your term paper, approach him or her after class when other students are milling about, not privately during office hours. Or bring a friend to wait outside the office while you consult the professor.

4. *Maintain a record.* Keep a record of all incidents of harassment to use as documentation in the event that you decide to lodge an official complaint. The record should include the following: (1) where the incident took place, (2) the date and time, (3) what happened, including the exact words that were used, if you can recall them, (4) how you felt, and (5) the names of witnesses. Some people who have been subjected to sexual harassment have carried a hidden tape recorder during contacts with the harasser. Such recordings may not be admissible in a court of law, but they are persuasive in organizational grievance procedures. Using a hidden tape recorder may be illegal in your state, however. Be sure to check the law.

5. *Talk with the harasser.* It may be uncomfortable to address the issue directly with a harasser, but doing so puts the offender on notice that you are aware of the harassment and want it to stop. It may be helpful to frame your approach in terms of a description of the specific offending actions (for example, "When we were alone in the office, you repeatedly attempted to touch me or brush up against me"), your feelings about the offending behavior ("It made me feel like my privacy was being violated. I'm very upset about this and haven't been sleeping well"); and what you would like the offender to do ("So I'd like you to agree never to attempt to touch me again, okay?"). Having a talk with the harasser may stop the harassment. If the harasser denies the accusations, it may be necessary to take further action.

6. *Write a letter to the harasser.* Set down on paper a record of the offending behavior, and put the harasser on notice that the harassment must stop. Your letter might (1) describe what happened ("Several times you have made sexist comments about my body"), (2) describe how you feel ("It made me feel like a sexual object when you talked to me that way"), and (3) describe what you would like the harasser to do ("I want you to stop making sexist comments to me").

7. *Seek support.* Support from people you trust can help you through the often trying process of resisting sexual harassment. Talking with others allows you to express your feelings and to receive emotional support, encouragement, and advice. In addition, it may strengthen your case if you have the opportunity to identify and talk with other people who have been harassed by the offender.

8. *File a complaint.* Companies and organizations are required by law to respond reasonably to complaints of sexual harassment. In large organizations, a designated official (sometimes an ombudsman, affirmative action officer, or sexual harassment advisor) is usually charged with handling such complaints. Set up an appointment with this official to discuss your experiences. Ask about the grievance procedures in the organization and about your right to confidentiality. Have available a record of the dates of the incidents, what happened, how you felt about it, and so on.

   The two major government agencies that handle charges of sexual harassment are the Equal Employment Opportunity Commission (look under the government section of your phone book for the telephone number of the nearest office) and your state's Human Rights Commission (listed in your phone book under state or municipal government). These agencies may offer advice on how you can protect your legal rights and proceed with a formal complaint.

9. *Seek legal remedies.* Sexual harassment is illegal and actionable. If you are considering legal action, consult an attorney familiar with this area of law. You may be entitled to back pay (if you were fired for reasons arising from the sexual harassment), job reinstatement, and punitive damages.

In closing, we do not ask what survivors of rape, incest, and sexual harassment can do to recover from the harm that has been done to them. We ask what we will *all* do to reshape society so that sex is no longer used as an instrument of power, coercion, and violence.

Review: Sexual Harassment

Reflect

Imagine that you are sexually harassed and want to report it, but a friend advises, "Why make such a fuss? Is it really worth it? After all, complaining could backfire." How would you respond?

CriticalThinking

Agree or disagree with the following statement, and support your answer: Because of all the publicity, people who are intolerant of normal sexual advances, or who want to punish their supervisors, are now crying sexual harassment.

33. Sexual _____ is usually defined as unsolicited verbal comments, gestures, or physical contact of a sexual nature that is unwelcome by the recipient.

34. The great majority of people who commit sexual harassment are (*Men* or *Women*?).

35. One reason why sexual harassment is stressful is that people tend to blame the _____.

36. Sexual harassment often reflects resentment toward women who venture beyond the traditional (*Masculine* or *Feminine*?) role.

37. The U.S. Supreme Court has recognized sexual harassment as a form of sex discrimination.

38. The (*Majority* or *Minority*?) of victims of sexual harassment seek legal help.

39. Most forms of harassment involve unequal _____ relationships between the harasser and the victim.

Recite

1. What is rape?

The definition of rape varies from state to state but usually refers to a crime of violence in which the perpetrator obtains sexual intercourse with a nonconsenting person by the use or threat of force. Statutory rape involves sexual intercourse with a willing person who is unable to provide consent, as in the case of being too young.

2. How common is rape?

Surveys suggest that there are about half a million rapes and sexual assaults each year in the United States. Many rapes go unreported.

3. What kinds of rape are there?

The types of rapes include stranger rape, acquaintance rape, marital rape, gang rape, male rape, and rape by females. Women are more likely to be raped by men they know than by strangers. Most male rapes occur in prison settings. Husbands who rape their wives can be prosecuted under the rape laws in many states.

4. What social and cultural factors contribute to the high frequency of rape in the United States?

Social attitudes such as gender-role stereotyping, seeing sex as adversarial, and acceptance of violence in interpersonal relationships all help create a climate that encourages rape. Social critics argue that our society breeds rapists by socializing males to be socially and sexually aggressive and dominant.

5. What psychological factors characterize rapists?

Incarcerated rapists vary in their psychological characteristics. Self-identified sexually aggressive men are more likely than other men to condone rape and violence against women, to have

Recite

traditional gender-role attitudes, to be hostile toward women, to engage in sexual activity to express social dominance, to be sexually aroused by rape, to lack a social conscience, and to have peer groups (such as fraternities) that pressure them into sexual activity. Groth and Birnbaum identified three basic kinds of rape: anger rape, power rape, and sadistic rape.

6. How do survivors adjust to being raped?

Rape survivors often experience stress disorders (acute stress disorder and post-traumatic stress disorder (PTSD).

7. How can we help survivors of rape?

Treatment of rape survivors typically involves supporting them through the crisis period following the attack and then helping to foster their long-term adjustment.

8. How can we prevent rape?

Rape prevention involves educating society at large and encouraging women to take a number of precautions. Whether or not women take precautions to prevent rape, however, the rapist is always the one responsible for the assault.

9. What is sexual abuse of children?

Any form of sexual contact between an adult and a child is abusive, even if force or physical threat is not used, because children are legally incapable of consenting to sexual activity with adults.

10. Which children are sexually abused? Who abuses them?

Sexual abuse of children, like rape and other forms of sexual coercion, cuts across all socioeconomic classes. In most cases, the molesters are close to the children they abuse—relatives, step-relatives, family friends, and neighbors. Genital fondling is the most common type of abuse. Like rape, sexual abuse of children is underreported.

11. What is pedophilia?

Pedophilia is a type of paraphilia in which adults are sexually attracted to children. Pedophiles are almost exclusively male.

12. What is incest?

Incest is marriage or sexual relations between people who are so closely related that sex is prohibited and punished. Several theories have been advanced to explain the development of the incest taboo, including theories based on the dangers of inbreeding, the role played by the taboo in maintaining stability in the family, and cooperation theory. Father–daughter incest is most likely to be reported and prosecuted, but brother–sister incest is the most common type of incest. Incest frequently occurs within the context of general family disruption.

13. What are the effects of sexual abuse on children?

Children who are sexually abused often suffer social and emotional problems that impair their development and persist into adulthood, affecting their self-esteem and their ability to form intimate relationships.

14. How can we prevent sexual abuse of children?

In addition to learning to avoid strangers, children need to learn the difference between acceptable touching, such as an affectionate embrace or pat on the head, and unacceptable or "bad" touching. Children who may not be able to prevent abuse may nevertheless be encouraged to tell someone about the experience.

15. What can be done to help survivors of sexual abuse?

Psychotherapy may help adult survivors of sexual abuse improve their self-esteem and ability to develop intimate relationships. Special programs provide therapeutic services to abused children and adolescents.

16. How shall we treat rapists and child molesters?

Methods include prison-based rehabilitation programs, often in the form of group therapy and chemical (via anti-androgen drugs) or surgical castration.

17. What is sexual harassment?

Sexual harassment involves "deliberate or repeated unsolicited verbal comments, gestures, or physical contact of a sexual nature that [is] unwelcome [to] the recipient."

18. How does sexual harassment occur in the workplace?

Sexual harassment is often an expression of unequal power relationships. It may be used as a tactic to keep women "in their place," especially in work settings that are traditional male preserves.

19. How does sexual harassment occur on campus?

About 25% to 30% of students report at least one incident of sexual harassment in college. Professors may also be harassed by students. Sexual harassment below the college level has become an unwelcome ritual that many junior and senior high school students endure.

20. How can one resist sexual harassment?

There is no guaranteed way to put an end to sexual harassment, but some approaches that have helped many individuals are conveying a professional attitude, avoiding being alone with the harasser, keeping a record of incidents, and seeking legal remedies.

Chapter 19

Truth?Fiction?

T / F? Prostitution is illegal throughout the United States.

T / F? The massage and escort services advertised in the Yellow Pages are fronts for prostitution.

T / F? Most female prostitutes were sexually abused as children.

T / F? Typical customers of prostitutes have difficulty forming sexual relationships with other women.

T / F? Only males are sexually aroused by pornography.

T / F? Pornography causes violence against women.

T / F? One-quarter of Internet surfing is surfing for sex.

The World of Commercial Sex

Preview

Prostitution—Sex on the Run

Pornography and Obscenity

A few years ago, England's floppy-haired actor Hugh Grant was caught with a prostitute in a BMW on Hollywood's Sunset Boulevard. Why? His girlfriend was supermodel Elizabeth Hurley, who at the time was promoting the perfume called "Pleasures." Grant exemplified good looks, charm, innocence, and success. Still, he sought the sexual services of a woman for hire.

Why, indeed. Why have millions of men (and some women) paid for sex throughout the ages? In the caverns of Wall Street, brokers and traders sell stocks and other financial instruments that drive the nation's commercial enterprises. On the floor of Chicago's Board of Trade, brokers trade commodities—soybeans, corn, wheat, and other goods. Prices go up, prices go down, responding to the law of supply and demand. On street corners a few short blocks from these financial institutions another sort of commerce takes place. In New York City and Chicago, as in Hollywood and the nation's smaller towns and villages, prostitutes exchange sex for money or for goods such as drugs.

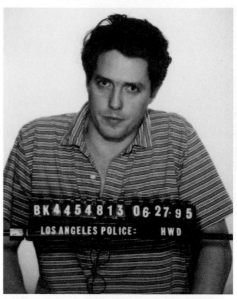

British Actor Hugh Grant in L.A. *Why would the handsome and popular actor Hugh Grant seek the services of a streetwalker? Especially when his significant other at the time was supermodel Elizabeth Hurley? As we will see in this chapter, there are many reasons.*

Sex as commerce runs the gamut from adult movie theaters and bookshops to strip shows, sex toy shops, erotic hotels and motels, escort/outcall services, "massage parlors," "900" telephone services, cybersex (e.g., sex over the Internet), and the use of sex appeal in advertisements for products. The "world of commercial sex is a kind of X-rated amusement park—Disneyland for Adults" (Edgley, 1989, p. 372).

Prostitution—Sex on the Run

Hugh Grant ran afoul of the law because prostitution is illegal in California. *Question: What is prostitution?* **Prostitution** is the sale of sexual activity for money. Prostitution is illegal everywhere in the United States except for some rural counties in Nevada, where it is restricted to state-licensed brothels.

Soliciting the services of a prostitute is also illegal in many states. Police rarely crack down on customers, or "johns," however. (Hugh Grant came to their attention because he was engaging in a "lewd act" in a car parked on a public street.) The few who are arrested are usually penalized with a small fine. On occasion, the names of convicted johns are published in local newspapers, which may deter men who fear publicity. On the other hand, some believe that Hugh Grant's indiscretion *boosted* receipts for his film *Nine Months,* which opened a few days later. Although prostitutes and their clients can be male or female, most prostitutes are female and virtually all customers are male.

Prostitution is often called "the world's oldest profession"—for good reason. It can be traced at least to ancient Mesopotamia, where temple prostitution flourished. The Greek historian Herodotus noted that all women in the city were expected to put in some time at the temple. They would offer their bodies to passing strangers, who would make a "religious" donation.

Prostitution flourished in medieval Europe and during the sexually repressive Victorian period in the nineteenth century. Then, as now, the major motive for prostitution was economic. Many poor women were drawn to prostitution as a means of survival. In Victorian England, prostitution was widely regarded as a necessary outlet for men to satisfy their sexual appetites. It was widely believed that women did not enjoy sex. Therefore, it was thought better for a man to visit a prostitute than to "soil" his wife with his carnal passions.

In the nineteenth-century United States, married and unmarried men frequented prostitutes regularly. Use of prostitution cut across all economic and social boundaries. Prostitution most often occurred within two contexts: sexual initiation for males and regular brothel visitation.

Incidence of Prostitution in the United States

Question: How widespread is prostitution? No one knows how many prostitutes there are in the United States, but it appears that there are hundreds of thousands. Prostitutes are found in the streets, brothels, and adult films; on the Internet; and in the phone book and classified ads.

Almost two-thirds of the European American males in Kinsey's sample (Kinsey et al., 1948) reported visiting a prostitute at least once. About 15% to 20% visited them regularly. The use of prostitutes varied with educational level, however. By the age of 20, about 50% of Kinsey's non-college-educated single males, but only 20% of his college-educated males, had visited a prostitute. By the age of 25, the figures swelled to about two-thirds for non-college-educated males but only to slightly above 25% for college men.

Kinsey's data foreshadowed a falling off of experience with prostitutes that seems linked to the decay of the sexual double standard. Young men in recent generations appear to be less likely to visit prostitutes than those in Kinsey's day, because they are more likely to become sexually initiated with their girlfriends. As Edgley (1989) put

Prostitution The sale of sexual activity for money or goods of value, such as drugs. (From the Latin *prostituere,* meaning "to cause to stand in front of." The implication is that one is offering one's body for sale.)

The Joy of Amsterdam's Red-Light District: A Police Guide

Rule No. 1, according to the new police guide for tourists to Amsterdam's red-light district, is: Have FUN, but act in a NORMAL manner.

Tolerant. Within limits. How very Dutch.

- Rule No. 6: PROSTITUTION. No pictures of the women.
- Rule No. 8: Soft drugs, NOT UNDER 18.
- And No. 10: Parking is NOT FREE.

"This brochure is NORMAL," insisted Superintendent Klaas Wilting, chief police spokesman, who must have repeated the word *normal* 30 times in an hour-long conversation about the brief brochure. He denied that the police felt defensive about publishing it. But he was distinctly irked that the FOREIGN press had taken such an interest. Here we go again, he implied: the old stereotype of Amsterdam as SIN CITY.

Actually, the guide is fairly subdued. Most of it is the kind of common-sense advice dished out by the police everywhere: watch out for pickpockets, don't play balletje (Amsterdam's three-card monte), resist those drunken impulses to take off all your clothes and jump into the canals.

Although it contains a map, it is not the usual guide, per se. It doesn't say which "coffee shops" sell the best marijuana, which live-sex shows are liveliest, or which bordellos have the prettiest women. In fact, it is virtually impossible to find such information in print here. Most tourist guides to the Netherlands devote pages to the Vermeers in the Rijksmuseum but scant sentences to the red-light district, even though it is unlikely the Vermeers get five million visitors a year.

SO, WHERE IS IT?

So what's the most common inquiry at the Amsterdam Tourist Service on Damrak Street?

"'Where is the red-light district?'" answered Djawehly Pelupessy, who works behind the counter. "They blush, we tell them, then they walk away fast. They're shy. They don't want to admit they want to see the women in the windows."

Toine Rodenburg, who manages the Banana Bar, the Erotic Museum, Theater Casa Rosso; and other district landmarks, accuses the city of being "ambivalent or even hypocritical" toward the reality that sex lures far more visitors than culture.

"They take the taxes without saying thank you," he complained. "They put up signs everywhere saying 'Rijksmuseum' or 'Anne Frank House,' but there's only one for the red-light district, like it's something horrible. As if Amsterdam was all about tulips and wooden shoes. It's not. It's about freedom."

If it seems hard to tell whether the guide was written by a police officer or by a fed-up resident, it is because the answer to both questions is yes. The author, Officer Willem Schild, has patrolled this libertarian Arcadia for 12 years and, like Mr. Rodenburg, lives there. "That's me on the cover," he said proudly, pointing to the grinning policeman on a motorbike beside an Erotic Museum sign.

The guide reflects neighborhood thinking, repeated by everyone from Officer Schild to Erik Blom, a law student who sells tickets to the Moulin Rouge show, to Theodoor van Boven, founder of the Condomerie condom boutique. If the district has a problem, they say, it is not the law-abiding women sitting in pink windows wearing only fetching smiles and eye-popping underwear. Nor is it the mellowed-out hashish dealers who sit giggling with their coffee shop customers, debating which of Bob Marley's tunes was his chef-d'oeuvre.

Rather, if there is a problem in this district of 300-year-old gabled buildings and expensive real estate housing doctors, lawyers, and plenty of families, it is the street drug dealers who sell heroin—or cough drops ground up to look like heroin—and those tourists, American spring break kids or English stag party louts who jump into the canals, howl their drunken lungs out at 4 A.M. and punch each other silly.

BLUE-RINSE GRANDMOTHERS AT THE CASA ROSSO

Nobody really minds the middle-class tour groups that fill the sex shows in theaters that are cleaner and better lighted than many Off Broadway houses. Mr. Rodenburg seems to revel in the groups—often

Amsterdam's Red-Light District Prostitution is legal in Amsterdam's red-light district. Tourists wend their way through the narrow streets by the canals, doing "window shopping." Prim grandmothers sometimes join the audiences at the live sex shows. District landmarks include the Erotic Museum and the Casa Rosso. Along with the nearby Rembrandts, Rubens, and van Goghs, the district is so thoroughly ingrained in Amsterdam's culture that the police have issued a guide to enjoying the district—safely.

featuring blue-rinse grandmothers and other unexpected spectators—that flock to his Theater Casa Rosso. By prior arrangement with tour guides, he confided, the loudest-mouthed man in each group is the person selected by a leather-clad lady with whips to join her on stage—to his embarrassment and the general hilarity of his fellow tourists.

Superintendent Wilting's guide seems to be written in the same spirit of tolerance for human indulgence, while noting that despite popular notions about Amsterdam, the place does have rules.

ALL DRUGS ARE NOT EQUAL

"Cocaine, heroin, LSD, ecstasy, etc. are strictly forbidden," the guide notes. "These drugs are always FAKE (washing powder, sugar, rat poison, vitamin C). On top of that, you may be forced to hand over your wallet." A small amount of marijuana for personal use can legally be con-

sumed in a coffee shop, the leaflet says, adding, "When you feel sick after smoking, or eating spice cake, drink lots of water with sugar."

There is also a discreet hint about prostitutes: "If you visit one of the women, we would like to remind you they are not always women." But, here too, the guide demands decorum: "Don't shout or use bad language toward these women. SHOW SOME RESPECT."

That section was the most heavily edited by the department, Officer Schild said. He had advised tourists that the women charge $25 to $50 for 20 minutes, paid in advance. "So make a clear deal at the door and don't be too drunk to get things done," he had written. "Time is money for the ladies."

The department felt that was a bit *too* helpful, he said, although his precinct house's biggest headaches are frustrated drunks who get angry. All the women have alarm buttons,

and the police then have to run or bicycle over to sort out the fight.

He also had a warning about "smart shops," which sell herbs that supposedly boost intelligence or virility, along with hallucinatory psilocybin mushrooms, which can mix badly with alcohol. "People think they're eagles and try to fly out of their hotel rooms," Officer Schild said. But the department is trying to ban smart shops, which also sell drug paraphernalia, so it did not want them included.

Officer Schild said he got to put in 95% of what he had hoped for, and [he] takes the pamphlet around himself to bars and restaurants. "In the Netherlands," Superintendent Wilting noted, "we talk about the problems. We don't put them away."

Source: Reprinted with permission from McNeil, D. G., Jr. (2000, July 21). The joy of the red-light district: A police guide. *The New York Times online.*

A Streetwalker. It is estimated that several hundred thousand prostitutes work in the United States. Some prostitutes—called streetwalkers—*ply their trade by literally walking the streets and hawking their wares to pedestrians and those who drive by. Others, who may be connected with "massage" or "escort" services let their customers' fingers do the walking through the Yellow Pages. Still others advertise online.*

it, "An old and hallowed economic principle was at work; those who charge for a service cannot compete with those who give it away" (p. 392). Increased concern about sexually transmitted infections, especially HIV/AIDS, has also limited the use of prostitutes. Nevertheless, prostitution continues to flourish.

Types of Female Prostitutes

Female prostitutes—commonly called *hookers, whores, working girls,* or *escorts*—are usually classified according to the settings in which they work. ***Question: What kinds of prostitutes are there?*** The major types of prostitutes today are streetwalkers; brothel or "house" prostitutes, many of whom work in massage parlors; and "escorts," or call girls (many prostitutes today have their customers "let their fingers do the walking through the Yellow Pages"). Traditional brothel prostitution is less common today than it was before World War II.

Streetwalkers Part of the mystery about Hugh Grant was why he would seek the services of any prostitute. Another part of it was why he would seek out a **streetwalker**.

Although most prostitutes are streetwalkers, streetwalkers occupy the bottom rung in the hierarchy of prostitutes. They earn the lowest incomes and are usually the least desirable. They also incur the greatest risk of abuse by customers and **pimps**. Streetwalkers tend to come from poverty and to have had unhappy childhoods (Dalla, 2003). Many are survivors of rape, sexual abuse, or incest (Medrano et al., 2003). Many are teenage runaways who turn to prostitution to survive.

Streetwalkers operate in the open. They are thus more likely than other prostitutes to draw attention to themselves and risk arrest. To avoid arrest, streetwalkers may be indirect about their services. They may ask passers-by if they are interested in "a good time" or "some fun" rather than sex per se. In many cities, streetwalkers dress in revealing or provocative ways.

The prostitute is often stereotyped as a sexually unresponsive woman who feigns sexual arousal with johns while she keeps one eye glued to the clock. Most street prostitutes in a Philadelphia sample, however, reported that some forms of sex with customers were "very satisfying" (Savitz & Rosen, 1988). More than 60% of the prostitutes reported experiencing orgasm with customers at least occasionally. Most prostitutes also reported that they had enjoyable sexual relationships in their private lives and were regularly orgasmic. Not surprisingly, they garnered more sexual enjoyment from their personal relationships than from their customers.

In most locales, penalties for prostitution involve small fines or short jail terms. Many police departments, besieged by drug peddling and violent crimes, consider prostitution a "minor" or "nuisance" crime. Many prostitutes find the criminal justice system a revolving door. They pay the fine. They spend a night or two in jail. They return to the streets.

A bar prostitute is a variation of the streetwalker. She approaches men in a bar she frequents, rather than on the streets. Payoffs to bar owners or managers secure their cooperation, although the women are sometimes tolerated because they draw customers. Some streetwalkers work X-rated, or "adult," movie houses and may service their patrons in their seats with manual or oral sex. Payoffs may secure the cooperation of the management.

Many streetwalkers support a pimp (Williamson & Cluse-Tolar, 2002). A pimp acts as lover–father–companion–master. He provides streetwalkers with protection, bail, and sometimes room and board, in exchange for a high percentage of their earn-

Streetwalkers Prostitutes who solicit customers on the streets.

Pimps Men who serve as agents for prostitutes and live off their earnings. (From the Middle French *pimper,* meaning "to dress smartly.")

ings. Still, prostitutes are often physically abused by their pimps, who may use threats and beatings as means of control (Williamson & Cluse-Tolar, 2002).

Streetwalkers do not stay in the business ("the life") very long (Edgley, 1989). Some make the transition to a traditional life or get married. Others die young from drug abuse, disease, suicide, or physical abuse at the hands of pimps or customers. Survivors become less marketable with age.

Streetwalkers who work hotels and conventions generally hold a higher status than those who work the streets or bars. Clients are typically conventioneers or businessmen traveling away from home. The hotel prostitute must be skilled in conveying subtle messages to potential clients without drawing the attention of hotel management or security. They usually provide sexual services in the client's hotel room. Some hotel managers will tolerate known prostitutes (usually for a payoff under the table), so long as the woman conducts herself discreetly.

Brothel Prostitution Many brothel prostitutes occupy a middle status between streetwalkers and call girls in the hierarchy of prostitutes. They work in a brothel or, more commonly today, in a massage parlor.

The life of the brothel (or "house") prostitute is usually neither as lucrative as that of the call girl nor as degrading as that of the streetwalker. Some prostitutes associated with massage parlors or working for escort services may not consider themselves "real prostitutes" because they do not walk the streets and because they work for businesses that present a legitimate front. *Cathouse, bordello, cat wagon, parlor house, whorehouse, joy house, sport house, house of ill repute*—these are but a handful of the names given to houses in which prostitutes work. The heyday of the brothel is all but over in the United States. Formal brothels today are rare, except in Nevada, where they are legal but regulated. Brothel prostitutes split their fees with management. In addition to their "split," they receive free room and board. They are on duty 3 weeks a month and on call 24 hours a day during that time. When a customer arrives, they step into the living room "lineup." After one has been chosen, they wait again, resting, reading, or watching television.

Some brothel prostitutes lead lives of degradation (Jeffreys, 1998). Many poor Asian women have been recently lured to the United States by promises of the good life. Upon arrival, they have found themselves enslaved in brothels—working for tips and not allowed to leave. Such a brothel was recently closed by police at 208 Bowery in New York City. It housed more than 30 women smuggled from Thailand and came to the attention of the police when one woman jumped from a window (Goldberg, 1995).

The Massage Parlor Nature abhors a vacuum. "Massage parlors" have sprung up from coast to coast to fill the vacuum created by the departure of the brothels. Many massage parlors are legitimate establishments that provide massage—and only massage—to customers. Masseuses and masseurs are licensed in many states, and laws prohibit them from offering sexual services. Many localities require that the masseuse or masseur keep certain parts of her or his body clothed (some masseuses in suburban Detroit wear a scarf or a garter to comply) and not touch the client's genitals.

Many massage parlors serve as fronts for prostitution, however. They are often found in malls in middle-class suburbs, where there is ample parking. In these establishments, clients typically pay fees for a standard massage and then tip the workers for "extras."

Massage parlor prostitutes generally offer manual stimulation of the penis ("a local"), oral sex, or less frequently, coitus ("full service"). Some massage parlor prostitutes are better educated than streetwalkers and brothel workers and would not work in those other venues.

Escort Services If Hugh Grant had hired an "escort," we probably would never have learned of it. Conventioneers and businessmen are more likely to turn to the listings for "massage" and "escort services" in the telephone directory or under the personal ads in local newspapers than to seek hotel prostitutes. Services that provide "outcall" send masseuses (or masseurs) or escorts to the hotel room.

Escort services are typically (but not always) fronts for prostitution. Escort services are found in every major American city and present themselves as legitimate business providing escorts for men. Indeed, one will find female companionship for corporate functions and for unattached men traveling away from home under "escort services." Many escort services provide only prostitution, however, and clients of other escort services sometimes negotiate sexual services after formal escort duties are completed—or in their stead.

Many prostitutes who work for escort services come from middle-class backgrounds and are well educated—the better to hold their own in social conversation. Escort services may establish arrangements with legitimate companies to provide "escorts" for visiting customers or potential clients. Escort services also provide female escorts to "entertain" at conventions. Because of her high-society background, Sidney Biddle Barrow, the so-called Mayflower Madam, attracted a great deal of publicity when it was discovered that she ran an exclusive "escort service" in New York City in the 1980s.

Call Girls **Call girls** occupy the highest status on the social ladder of female prostitution. Many of them advertise as escorts. Call girls tend to be the most attractive and well-educated prostitutes and tend to charge more for their services. Many come from middle-class backgrounds (Edgley, 1989). Many call girls work on their own so that they need not split their income with an escort service or massage parlor. Consequently, they can lead a luxurious lifestyle when business is good, living in expensive neighborhoods and wearing stylish clothes, and can be selective about their customers. Yet they incur expenses for answering services, laundry, and payoffs to landlords, to doormen, and sometimes to police.

Call girls may escort their clients to dinner and social functions, providing not only sex but also charming and gracious conversation (Edgley, 1989). Call girls can give clients the feeling that they are important and attractive. They may simulate sexual pleasure and create the illusion that time does not matter. It does, of course. To the call girl, as to other entrepreneurs, time is money.

Call girls may receive clients in their apartments ("incalls") or make "outcalls" to clients' homes and hotels. Some call girls trade or sell "black books" that list clients and their sexual preferences. To protect themselves from the police and from abusive clients, call girls may insist on reviewing a client's business card or learning his home telephone number before personal contact is made. They may investigate whether the customer is in fact the person he purports to be.

We now have some ideas of the various kinds of prostitutes. *Question: How do prostitutes become involved in "the life"?*

Getting into "The Life"

No single factor explains entry into female prostitution, but poverty and sexual and/or physical abuse figure prominently in the backgrounds of the majority of female prostitutes (Bamgbose, 2002; Medrano et al., 2003). They often come from conflict-ridden or single-parent homes in poor urban areas or rural farming communities.

Call girls Prostitutes who arrange for their sexual contacts by telephone. *Call* refers both to telephone calls and to being "on call."

For young women of impoverished backgrounds and marginal skills, the life of the prostitute may seem alluring. It is an alternative to the menial and dismal work that is otherwise available. On the basis of their studies of streetwalkers in Milwaukee, Romensko and Miller (1989) concluded that

> Poverty, and the many concomitants of poverty manifest in American society, were the factors pushing these women into the world of illicit work. Conversely, the bright lights, money, and independence that the street seemingly offered—things that were largely absent from these women's lives prior to their entrance into street life—were enticements that drew women to street life. (p. 112)

Researchers find a high level of psychological disturbance among prostitutes. Melissa Farley and her colleagues (1998) interviewed nearly 500 prostitutes from the United States, Europe, Africa, and Asia and found that nearly two-thirds of them could be diagnosed with **post-traumatic stress disorder** (PTSD). Only 5% of the general population have PTSD, and only 20% to 30% of combat veterans. The incidence of PTSD was the same for streetwalkers and brothel workers, although brothel prostitutes encountered less violence (Zuger, 1998). The prostitutes also developed high numbers of medical problems beyond STIs. Some 90% said that they wanted to leave "the life."

Cross-cultural evidence from a study of 41 prostitutes in Belgium showed similar patterns of psychopathology (de Schampheleire, 1990). Compared to other women (female flight attendants), streetwalkers in the Belgian study were more fearful, anxious, resentful, and depressed. They also had poorer relationships with their families and were in poorer health. In a study in the United States, teenage female prostitutes were more likely than normal female adolescents or delinquents who did not engage in prostitution to show signs of psychological disturbance and to have been placed in special-education classes in school (Gibson et al., 1988).

Poverty accounts for the entry of young women into prostitution in many countries. In some Third World nations, such as Thailand, many rural, impoverished parents in effect sell daughters to recruiters who place them in brothels in cities (Bamgbose, 2002; Gomes do Espirito & Etheredge, 2003). Many of the women send home whatever money they can and also work hard to try to pay off the procurers and break free of their financial bonds.

In the United States and Canada, many initiates into prostitution are teenage runaways. The family backgrounds of teenage runaways vary in socioeconomic status. Some come from middle-class or affluent homes, whereas others are reared in poverty. However, family discord and dysfunction frequently set the stage for their entry into street life and prostitution (Dalla, 2003; Medrano et al., 2003).

Some teenagers who have endured sexual abuse or incest learn how to detach themselves emotionally from sex to survive unwanted sexual experiences. The transition to prostitution may represent an extension of this unfortunate learning experience. Although teenage prostitutes may turn to prostitution primarily for money, Price (1989) recognized that survivors of sexual abuse or incest may also be attracted to prostitution because they have learned that sex can win them attention or love from adults:

> For a lonely adolescent, attention from tricks or a sugar daddy is not all that different from the attention he or she received at home. In fact, it may be preferable, as there may not be any physical abuse involved. (p. 84)

Not all sexually abused children become prostitutes, of course. Only 12% of one sample of predominantly female 16- to 18-year-olds who had been sexually abused

Post-traumatic stress disorder A type of stress reaction brought on by a traumatic event and characterized by flashbacks of the experience in the form of disturbing dreams or intrusive recollections, a sense of emotional numbing or restricted range of feelings, and heightened body arousal. Abbreviated PTSD.

became involved in prostitution (Seng, 1989). Abused children who run away from home are much more likely to become involved in prostitution than those who do not (Seng, 1989). Runaways are also more likely to become drug and alcohol abusers.

"Johns"—The Customers of Female Prostitutes

Hugh Grant was a "john" or a "trick." That is how many prostitutes refer to their customers. Terms such as *patron, meatball, sucker,* and *beefbuyer* are also heard.

Question: Who are "johns" or "tricks"? Men who use female prostitutes come from all walks of life and represent all socioeconomic and racial groups. Most patrons are "occasional johns." Examples include traveling salesmen or military personnel who are stopping over in town without their regular sex partners. Men are more interested than women in sexual novelty or variety (Barash & Lipton, 2001; Klusman, 2002; Schmitt, 2003), and variety may provide a major motive for occasional johns.

"Habitual johns" use prostitutes as their major or exclusive sexual outlet. Some habitual johns have never established an intimate sexual relationship. Some wealthy men who wish to avoid intimate relationships habitually patronize call girls.

"Compulsive johns" feel driven to prostitutes to meet some psychological or sexual need. They may repeatedly resolve to stop using prostitutes but feel unable to control their compulsions. Some compulsive johns suffer from a **whore–Madonna complex**. They see women as either sinners or saints. They permit themselves to enjoy sex only with prostitutes or would ask only prostitutes to engage in acts such as fellatio. They see marital sex as an obligation.

Motives for Using Prostitutes There appear to be six common motives for using prostitutes:

1. *Sex without negotiation.* The research on sex differences suggests that men have a stronger sex drive than women do (Peplau, 2003). Prostitution sort of evens things up by making women available at the whim of the man. By turning to prostitutes, men need not spend the time, effort, and money involved in dating and getting to know someone for the sake of sexual activity. Hugh Grant might have wanted sex, and his girlfriend was a continent and an ocean away. The streetwalker was willing to supply sex in the absence of a relationship.

2. *Sex without commitment.* The research on sex differences also shows that men are more willing than women to engage in sexual activity in the absence of a commitment (Peplau, 2003). Prostitutes require no commitment from the man other than payment for services rendered.

3. *Sex for eroticism and variety.* Many prostitutes offer "something extra" in the way of novel or kinky sex—for example, oral sex, use of costumes (such as leather attire), and S&M rituals (such as B&D). Men may desire such activity but not obtain it with their regular partners. Men, as noted, are also more interested than women in sexual variety (Barash & Lipton, 2001; Klusman, 2002; Schmitt, 2003), and prostitutes provide variety or novelty in sex partners.

4. *Prostitution as sociability.* In the nineteenth and early twentieth centuries, the brothel served not only as a place to obtain sex, but also as a kind of "stopping off" place between home and work. Sex was sometimes secondary to the companionship and conversation men would find in brothels, especially in the "bawdy houses" of the old West. (Similarly, women who attend male strip clubs

Whore–Madonna complex A rigid stereotyping of women as either sinners or saints.

enjoy "bonding" with their friends at the clubs, as well as the show [Montemurro et al., 2003].)

5. *Sex away from home.* The greatest contemporary use of prostitution occurs among men who are away from home, as among businessmen at conventions and sports fans at out-of-town events. In these typical all-male preserves, peer pressure may encourage sexual adventures.

6. *Problematic sex.* People who have physical disabilities or disfiguring conditions sometimes seek the services of prostitutes because of difficulty attracting other partners or because of fear of rejection. (One prostitute at a Nevada brothel said that she was a favorite of the management because she accepted johns with cerebral palsy.) Some lonely men who lack sex partners may seek prostitutes as substitutes.

Truth?Fiction?
Revisited

It is not true that typical customers of prostitutes have difficulty forming sexual relationships with other women. Many men often turn to prostitutes for sexual variety or because they seek sexual activity when they are away from home.

All the prostitutes we have been discussing are female. *Questions: Do males also work as prostitutes? What do we know of them?*

Male Prostitution

Males do also work as prostitutes. Some have female clients, but most have male clients. Male prostitutes who service female clients—*gigolos*—are rare. Gigolos' clients are typically older, wealthy, unattached women. Gigolos may serve as escorts or as surrogate sons for the women, and they may or may not offer sexual services. Many gigolos are struggling actors or models.

The overwhelming majority of male prostitutes service gay men. Males who service males are called **hustlers**. Their patrons are typically called **scores**. Hustlers average 17 to 18 years of age and become initiated into prostitution at an average age of 14 (Coleman, 1989). They typically have less than 11th-grade educations and few, if any, marketable skills. The majority come from working-class and lower-class backgrounds. Many male prostitutes, like many female prostitutes, come from families troubled by conflict, alcoholism, and/or physical or sexual abuse (Minichiello et al., 2001).

Hustlers may be gay, bisexual, or heterosexual in orientation. In a large-scale Australian study, half of the male prostitutes surveyed described themselves as being gay (Minichiello et al., 2001). About one-third (31%) said they were bisexual, and 5.5% considered themselves "straight."

A Norwegian study surveyed all adolescents aged 14 to 17 in public and private schools in Oslo, the capital of the country (Pedersen & Hegna, 2003). The response rate was 94% (10,828 students). About 1.4% of the sample had sold sexual favors, including three times as many boys as girls. Of these, half had done so more than 10 times. Prostitution was found to be connected with initiation of sexual intercourse at an early age, conduct problems, abuse of alcohol and other drugs (including heroin), and physical and sexual abuse. The male prostitutes reported that many of their clients were gay or bisexual. The adolescents did not reliably use condoms, which placed them at risk of contracting HIV/AIDS and other STIs.

The major motive for male prostitution, like female prostitution, is money (Minichiello et al., 2001; Zhou et al., 2002). Running away from home is a common entry point for male as well as female prostitutes.

People engage in some risky activities. *Question: What is the role of prostitution in the transmission of HIV and other STIs?*

Hustlers Men who engage in prostitution with male customers.

Scores Customers of hustlers.

Japan Journal: Schoolgirls as Sex Toys

A disturbing national pastime has taken root in Japan: a male obsession with schoolgirls dressed in uniforms. In Tokyo there are now several hundred "image clubs," where Japanese men pay $150 an hour to act out their fantasies with make-believe schoolgirls in make-believe classrooms, locker rooms, or commuter trains. A customer may, for example, act the part of a teacher who walks into a classroom and tears the clothes off a schoolgirl. Or he may choose to fondle a schoolgirl on a crowded commuter train.

The clubs are but one part of a growing national obsession—and a growing national market—that the Japanese call "Loli-con," after Lolita. Hiroyuki Fukuda edits one Japanese magazine called *Anatomical Illustrations of Junior High School Girls* and another called *V-Club*, featuring pictures of naked elementary school girls. And a number of schoolgirls earn extra money as prostitutes.

Why? First because it's legal for men in Tokyo to have sex with children who are older than 12. And second, says Masao Miyamoto, a male psychiatrist, because many Japanese men feel threatened by the growing sophistication of older women. So they turn to schoolgirls.

Source: Schoolgirls as sex toys (1997, April 6). *The New York Times*, p. E2.

Japanese Schoolgirls *Sad to say, many Japanese men are obsessed with schoolgirls dressed in uniforms such as these. In Tokyo, it is legal for men to have sex with children who are older than 12. Many men are willing to pay for the privilege.*

HIV/AIDS and Prostitution

Concerns about the spread of STIs by prostitution is nothing new. In the 1960s, 2 out of 3 prostitutes surveyed by Gebhard (1969) had contracted gonorrhea or syphilis. Although prostitutes are still exposed to a heightened risk of contracting or spreading these and other STIs, such as chlamydia, the risk of HIV/AIDS poses an even more deadly threat. The risk of HIV/AIDS has been linked to both male and female prostitution (Gomes do Espirito & Etheredge, 2003; Medrano et al., 2003; Pedersen & Hegna, 2003; Zhou et al., 2002).

Sex with prostitutes is the most important factor in the male–female transmission of HIV in Africa, where HIV is spread mainly by male–female sexual intercourse. Prostitutes incur a greater risk of HIV transmission because they have sexual relations with many partners, often without condoms (Gomes do Espirito & Etheredge, 2003). Moreover, many prostitutes and their clients and other sex partners inject drugs and share contaminated needles (Miniciello et al., 2001). HIV/AIDS is then spread from prostitutes to clients and the clients' partners.

Review: Prostitution—Sex on the Run

Reflect

Have people you know used the services of prostitutes? What were their motives?

Critical Thinking

Agree or disagree with the following statement, and support your answer: Prostitution should be legalized throughout the United States.

1. Prostitution is illegal everywhere in the United States except for some rural counties in the state of _____.

2. Prostitution is often called "the world's _____ profession."

3. Almost _____ of the European American males in Kinsey's sample reported having visited a prostitute at least once.

4. Young men today appear to be (*More* or *Less?*) likely to visit prostitutes than those in Kinsey's day.

5. _____ occupy the bottom rung in the hierarchy of prostitutes.

6. The major motive of the prostitute is (*Sexual* or *Economic?*).

7. Massage parlors are often found in _____ in middle-class suburbs.

8. Escort services (*Are* or *Are not?*) typically fronts for prostitution.

9. Poverty and sexual or physical _____ commonly figure in the backgrounds of female prostitutes.

10. Farley and colleagues found that nearly two-thirds of prostitutes could be diagnosed with _____ stress disorder (PTSD).

11. Most patrons of prostitutes are "_____ johns."

12. The research on sex differences suggests that men have a (*Stronger* or *Weaker?*) sex drive than women.

13. Prostitutes (*Do* or *Do not?*) require an emotional commitment from the man.

14. Men who engage in male prostitution are called _____.

15. In an Australian study, _____ of the male prostitutes surveyed described themselves as gay.

16. Sex with prostitutes (*Is* or *Is not?*) an important factor in the male–female transmission of HIV in Africa.

Pornography and Obscenity

The production and distribution of sexually explicit materials is a thriving industry (Lane, 2000). In the United States, 20 million "adult" magazines are sold each month. X-rated or adult movies (also called *porn* movies) have moved from sleazy adult theaters to the living rooms of middle America in the form of videocassettes and adult cable channels. Nobody knows how many people bring X-rated photos, videos, cable programs, and even live Internet sex from foreign nations into their homes every day. However, it is estimated that there are at least 30,000 to 60,000 sex-oriented Web sites (Lane, 2000).

Pornography is indeed popular, but also highly controversial. Many are opposed to pornography on moral grounds. Feminists oppose pornography on the grounds that it portrays women in degrading and dehumanizing roles, as sex objects who are subservient to men's wishes, as sexually insatiable nymphomaniacs, or as sexual masochists who enjoy being raped and violated. Moreover, some feminists hold that depictions of women in sexually subordinate roles may encourage men to treat them as sex objects and increase the potential for rape (Itzin, 2002).

Question: What is pornography?

What Is Pornographic?

Webster's Unabridged Dictionary defines **pornography** as "writing, pictures, etc., intended to arouse sexual desire." The inclusion of the word *intended* places the

Pornography Written, visual, or audiotaped material that is sexually explicit and produced for purposes of eliciting or enhancing sexual arousal. (From Greek roots meaning "to write about prostitutes.")

Sex Online *Although the woman could be in the United States, as suggested by the sign behind her, online sex can be fed in from anywhere in the world—and often is.*

determination of what is pornographic in the mind of the person composing the work. Applying this definition makes it all but impossible to determine what is pornographic. If a film maker admits that he or she wanted to arouse the audience sexually, may we judge the work to be pornographic, even if no nudity or explicit sex scenes are shown? On the other hand, explicit representations of people engaged in sexual activity would not be pornographic if the work was intended as an artistic expression or means of education, rather than created for its **prurient** value. Many works the distribution of which was once prohibited in this country because of their explicit sexual content, such as the novels *Tropic of Cancer* by Henry Miller, *Lady Chatterley's Lover* by D. H. Lawrence, and *Ulysses* by James Joyce, are now generally recognized as literary works rather than excursions into pornography. Even Mark Twain's *Huckleberry Finn*, John Steinbeck's *The Grapes of Wrath*, and Ernest Hemingway's *For Whom the Bell Tolls* have been banned in some places because local citizens found them offensive, obscene, or morally objectionable.

There is thus a subjective element in the definition of pornography. An erotic statue that sexually arouses viewers may not be considered pornographic if the sculptor's intent was artistic. A grainy photograph of a naked body that was intended to excite sexually may be pornographic. An alternative definition finds material pornographic when it is judged to be offensive by others. This definition, too, relies on subjective judgment in this case, that of the person exposed to the material. In other words, one person's pornography is another person's work of art. On the other hand, most people have no difficulty distinguishing among nudity that is art, nudity that is presented for the purpose of supplying information (such as illustrations presented in this textbook), and nudity that is pornographic (Eck, 2001).

Legislative bodies usually write laws about **obscenity** rather than pornography. *Question: What is obscenity?* In the case of *Miller v. California* (1973), Supreme Court Justice William Brennan argued that obscenity is "incapable of definition with sufficient clarity to withstand attack on vagueness grounds." In response, Supreme Court Justice Potter Stewart quipped that he could not define obscenity, but he knew it when he saw it. Still, even the Supreme Court has had a hard time defining obscenity and determining when laws against obscenity run afoul of the guarantee of free speech spelled out in the Bill of Rights. After all, *Huckleberry Finn* was once considered obscene.

Pornography may be *hard-core* (X-rated) or *soft-core* (R-rated). Hard-core pornography includes graphic and sexually explicit depictions of sex organs and sexual acts. Soft-core porn, as represented by R-rated films and *Playboy* photo

Prurient Tending to excite lust; lewd. (From the Latin *prurire,* meaning "to itch" in the sense of "to long for.")

Obscenity That which offends people's feelings or goes beyond prevailing standards of decency or modesty. (From the Latin *caenum,* meaning "filth.")

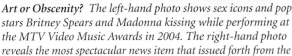

Art or Obscenity? *The left-hand photo shows sex icons and pop stars Britney Spears and Madonna kissing while performing at the MTV Video Music Awards in 2004. The right-hand photo reveals the most spectacular news item that issued forth from the 2004 Superbowl: Janet Jackson's "wardrobe malfunction." Although other performers had gyrated incessantly, grabbed their crotches, and rapped about rape and mayhem, it was Janet Jackson's breast and nipple adornment that kept cable "news" show talking heads Sean Hannity and Joe Scarborough frothing at the mouth for weeks. Thanks to Justin Timberlake, who role-played attacking Ms. Jackson during the song, we now have "Wardrobe Malfunction" as a new Americanism. Nobody objected to the fact that his lyrics asserted that he was going to have Jackson naked by song's end. Message: violence is fine in America. Sex? Keep it (literally) hidden.*

spreads, features more stylized nude photos and suggested (or simulated) rather than explicit sexual acts. *Question: Just what kinds of laws have been created to respond to obscenity?*

Pornography and the Law

Laws against obscenity provide the legal framework for outlawing the dissemination of pornography. Because the definition of obscenity is linked to what offends people or violates community standards, that which is deemed obscene may vary from person to person and from culture to culture. Going topless at a public beach may be deemed obscene in some locales but not along beaches on the French Riviera or Rio de Janeiro, where this style of (un)dress is customary. The word *obscene* extends beyond sexual matters. One could judge TV violence or beer commercials to be obscene because they are personally offensive or are offensive to women, even if such depictions do not meet legal standards of obscenity.

In the United States, legal prohibition of pornography as a form of obscenity dates back to the nineteenth century. In 1873, an anti-obscenity bill called the Comstock Act was passed by Congress. One effect of the bill was to outlaw the dissemination of information about birth control. The Comstock Act and similar laws made it a felony to mail obscene books, pamphlets, photographs, drawings, or letters. But what is obscene?

A landmark case in 1957 helped establish the legal basis of obscenity in the United States. In *Roth v. United States,* the U.S. Supreme Court ruled that portrayal of sexual activity was protected under the First Amendment to the Constitution unless its dominant theme dealt with "sex in a manner appealing to prurient interest"

(*Roth v. United States*, 1957, p. 487). In a 1973 case, *Miller v. California*, the U.S. Supreme Court held that obscenity is based on a determination of

> "(a) Whether the average person, applying contemporary community standards, would find that the work, taken as a whole, appeals to the prurient interest . . . ; (b) whether the work depicts or describes, in a patently offensive way, sexual conduct specifically defined by the applicable state law; and (c) whether the work, taken as a whole, lacks serious literary, artistic, political, or scientific value." (*Miller v. California*, 1973, p. 24)

Courts have since had to grapple with the *Miller* standard in judging whether material is obscene. *Miller* recognizes that judgments of obscenity may vary with "community standards." As a result, the same material may be considered obscene in one community but not in another. The *Miller* standard raises some obvious and unresolved questions. For example, who is the "average person" who can speak for a community? Many of us live in ethnically, racially, and religiously diverse communities. Can one viewpoint in *any* community truly represent the community? Even in relatively homogeneous communities, a diversity of opinion may exist on particular issues. Moreover, what is a *community*? Is it one's neighborhood, police precinct, municipality, county, or larger political unit? What does "patently" offensive mean? Who is the arbiter of "serious" literary, artistic, political, or scientific value? An attempt to clarify this last question was made in a 1987 case, *Pope v. Illinois*, in which the Supreme Court held that

> The proper inquiry is not whether an ordinary member of any given community would find serious literary, artistic, political, or scientific value in allegedly obscene material, but whether a reasonable person would find such value in the material, taken as a whole. (p. 445)

In this ruling, the court held that sexually explicit material could not be declared obscene, even if many or most people in a particular community held it to lack serious literary, artistic, political, or scientific value, unless a "reasonable" person would reach the same judgment. Whether the concept of a "reasonable" person will provide the courts with a clearer standard than the concept of an "average" or "ordinary" person for adjudicating obscenity cases remains to be seen.

Child pornography and violent, degrading, or dehumanizing pornography complicate matters further. People who do not find explicit depictions of consensual sex between adults to be obscene may regard child pornography or violent pornography as obscene. Child pornography is clearly psychologically harmful to the juvenile actors (McCabe, 2000; Quayle & Taylor, 2002, 2003). Many people also object to sexually explicit material that portrays women as "sex objects" or subordinate to men—gratifying men's sexual appetites.

Some footnotes: The U.S. Supreme Court ruled (in *Stanley v. Georgia*, 1969) that the possession of obscene material in one's home is not a criminal act. However, states may criminalize the downloading and possession of child pornography, and many have done so (McCabe, 2000; Quayle & Taylor, 2002, 2003). It is not unusual today for police to seize suspects' computers and check them for the presence of child pornography.

Many individuals and communities have sought to ban pornography on the grounds that it discriminates against women. Pornography, that is, damages women's opportunities for equal rights by perpetuating stereotypes of women as subservient to men. The Supreme Court of Canada has ruled that it is constitutional to prohibit sexually explicit material that contains violence toward women or material that degrades or dehumanizes women (Lewin, 1992).

Prevalence and Use of Erotica and Pornography

Question: How widespread is the use of pornography? Most of us have been exposed to sexually explicit materials, whether in the form of a novel, a photo spread in *Penthouse* or *Club,* an X-rated film, or an adult Web site. In perhaps the only credible survey results we have on the issue, the NHSLS study found that about 1 man in 4 (23%) and 1 woman in 10 (11%) had rented an X-rated movie or video within the past year (Michael et al., 1994). Sixteen percent of the men and 4% of the women had bought sexually explicit magazines or books. The survey did not inquire into the use of pornography on the Internet, but adult Web sites have proliferated to the point where they threaten the financial viability of "men's magazines."

People in the United States are typically introduced to pornography by their high school years, often by peers. Females are more likely to have been exposed to pornography by their boyfriends than the reverse.

Pornography is typically used to elicit or enhance sexual arousal, often as a masturbation aid (Boies, 2002; Strager, 2003). Pornographic materials may also be used by couples to enhance sexual arousal during lovemaking. Couples may find that running a sexy video or DVD, or reading an erotic story aloud, enlivens their sexual appetite or suggests novel sexual techniques.

Researchers have found that both men and women are physiologically sexually aroused by pornographic pictures, movies, or audiotaped passages (Peplau, 2003). That is, both men and women respond to pornographic stimuli with vasocongestion of the genitals and myotonia (muscle tension). However, there is a difference between physiological response and subjective feelings of arousal in women. Despite what is happening within their bodies, women tend to rate romantic scenes as more sexually arousing than sexually explicit scenes (Laan & Heiman, 1994). Women, remember, are less accepting than men of sex without emotional involvement (Peplau, 2003). Most women want sex to be related to an emotional connection. It is romance that encourages most women to follow the lead of genital arousal, when they do so. Even in the choice of erotic materials, women are much more likely than men to want the element of romance to be included (Hardy, 2001).

Repeated exposure to the same pornographic materials progressively lessens the sexual response to them. People may become aroused by the familiar materials again if some time is allowed to go by. Novel materials are also likely to reactivate a sexual response (Goodson et al., 2001; Stein et al., 2001).

Sex Differences in Response to Pornography Both males and females can become physiologically aroused by pornography. Yet males and females do not necessarily share the same subjective response to them or the same level of interest in them. Visual pornography (sexually explicit pictures or films) is largely a male preserve (Boies, 2002; Goodson et al., 2001). Most erotic visual materials are produced by men for men. Attempts to market visual materials to females have been largely unsuccessful (Hardy, 2001). Women may read erotic romance novels, but they show little interest in erotic pictures, films, or Web sites (Hardy, 2001). Women may find erotica a "turn-off" or disgusting, especially when it portrays women in unflattering roles—as "whorish," subservient to the desires of men, and/or aroused by male domination.

From the evolutionary perspective, could a basic evolutionary process be at work? Did ancestral men who were more sexually aroused by the sight of a passing female have reproductive advantages over their less arousable peers? Women, by contrast, have fewer mating opportunities and must make the most of any reproductive opportunity by selecting the best possible mate and provider. To be sexually aroused

Truth?Fiction?
Revisited

It is *not* true that only males are sexually aroused by pornography. Most men *and* women are sexually aroused by erotica, physiologically speaking. As we see in the following section, however, their interest in, and subjective responses to, pornography may differ considerably.

by the sight of male genitalia might encourage random matings, which would undermine women's reproductive success.

Pornography and Sexual Coercion

Question: Is pornography a harmless diversion or a cause of sexual violence or other antisocial acts? Let us consider several sources of evidence in examining this highly charged question, beginning with history—the findings of a 1970 government commission impaneled to review the evidence that was available at the time.

The Commission on Obscenity and Pornography In the 1960s, Congress created the Commission on Obscenity and Pornography to study the effects of pornography. Upon reviewing the existing research, the commission (Abelson et al., 1970) concluded that there was no evidence that pornography led to crimes of violence or to sexual offenses such as exhibitionism, voyeurism, or child molestation. Some people were sexually aroused by pornography and increased the frequency of their usual sexual activity, such as masturbation or coitus with regular partners, following exposure. They did not engage in antisocial behavior, however. These results have been replicated many times.

Finding pornography basically harmless, the commission recommended that "federal, state, and local legislation should not seek to interfere with the right of adults who wish to read, obtain, or view explicit sexual materials" (Abelson et al., 1970, p. 58). Congress and then-president Richard Nixon rejected the commission's findings and recommendation, however, on moral and political—not scientific—grounds.

The Meese Commission Report In 1985, President Ronald Reagan appointed a committee headed by Attorney General Edwin Meese to reexamine the effects of pornography. In 1986, the U.S. Attorney General's Commission on Pornography, known as the Meese Commission, issued a report that reached very different conclusions than the 1970 commission. The Meese Commission claimed to find a causal link between sexual violence and exposure to violent pornography (U.S. Department of Justice, 1986). The commission asserted that a substantial increase in the proliferation of violent pornography had occurred since the earlier commission had been convened. Moreover, the report concluded that exposure to pornography that portrayed women in degrading or subservient roles increased the acceptability of rape in the minds of viewers. The commission found no evidence linking exposure to nonviolent, nondegrading pornography (consensual sexual activity between partners in equal roles) and sexual violence, but it noted that only a small fraction of the pornographic materials on the market were of this type.

The commission issued 92 recommendations for tighter enforcement of obscenity laws and greater restrictions on the dissemination of pornography. Some recommendations focused on the enforcement and prosecution of existing child pornography laws. Others encouraged states that had not already done so to make the knowing possession of child pornography a felony.

The commission's findings are controversial. Critics claim that although the Meese Commission did not blatantly falsify the data, its conclusions reflected an overgeneralization of laboratory-based findings (Wilcox, 1987). Edward Donnerstein and his colleagues (1987) contended that the Meese Commission failed to distinguish between the effects of sexually explicit materials per se and the effects of violent materials. Evidence of links between exposure to sexually explicit materials (without violent content) and sexual aggression is lacking. Donnerstein and his colleagues concluded that violence, not sex, is the obscenity.

PORNOGRAPHY AND OBSCENITY

Pornography and Sex Offenders Another approach to examining the role of pornography in crimes of sexual violence involves comparing the experience of sex offenders and nonoffenders with pornographic materials. A review of the research literature found little or no difference in the level of exposure to pornography between incarcerated sex offenders and comparison groups of felons who were incarcerated for nonsexual crimes (Marshall, 1989).

Yet evidence also shows that as many as 1 in 3 rapists and child molesters use pornography to become sexually aroused immediately before and during the commission of their crimes (Marshall, 1989). That is, pornography may stimulate sexually deviant urges in certain subgroups of men who are predisposed to commit crimes of sexual violence (Marshall, 1989).

Violent Pornography Laboratory-based studies have shown that men exposed to violent pornography are more likely to become aggressive against females and to show less sensitivity toward women who have been sexually assaulted. In one classic study (Donnerstein, 1980), 120 college men interacted with a male or female confederate (accomplice) of the experimenter, who treated them in either a neutral or a hostile manner. The study participants were then shown either neutral, nonviolent pornographic films or violent pornographic films. In the latter, a man forced himself into a woman's home and raped her. Participants were then given the opportunity to deliver electric shock to the male or female confederate, presumably to assist the confederate in learning a task. The measure of aggression was the intensity of the shock chosen. No shock was actually delivered, but the participants did not know that the shock apparatus was fake. Men who had viewed violent pornographic films showed greater aggression toward the women than did men who had viewed nonviolent films.

In another study, aggression by males against female confederates following exposure to violent pornography (a rape scene) was increased by depictions of the woman being raped as either enjoying the experience or becoming sexually aroused during the rape (Donnerstein & Berkowitz, 1981). These findings suggest that depictions of women enjoying or becoming aroused by their victimization may legitimize violence against women in the viewer's mind, reinforcing the cultural myth that some women need to be dominated and are sexually aroused by an overpowering male.

Some research suggests that it is the violence in violent pornography, not its sexual explicitness, that hardens men's attitudes toward rape survivors. In one study (Donnerstein et al., 1987), college men were exposed to films consisting of violent pornography, nonviolent pornography (a couple having consensual intercourse), or violence that was not sexually explicit. The violent pornographic and nonpornographic films both showed a woman being tied up and slapped at gunpoint, but the nonpornographic version contained no nudity or explicit sexual activity. The men had first been either angered or treated in a neutral manner by a female confederate of the experimenter. The results showed that, compared with nonviolent pornography, both violent pornographic films and violent *non*pornographic films produced greater acceptance of rape myths, increased reported willingness to force a woman into sexual activity, and led to greater reported likelihood of engaging in rape (if the man also knew that he could get away with it). These effects occurred regardless of whether the man was angered by the woman or not.

Research on the effects of pornography should be interpreted with caution, however (Seto et al., 2001). Most of this research has employed college students, whose behavior may or may not be typical of people in general or of people with propensities toward sexual violence. Another issue is that most studies in this area are

The Internet Sex Column That Thrills, and Inflames, China

GUANGZHOU, China, Nov. 26—For the past month, as China's propaganda machine has promoted the nation's new space hero or the latest pronouncements from Communist Party leaders, the Chinese public has seemed more interested in a 25-year-old sex columnist whose beat is her own bedroom.

"I think my private life is very interesting," said the columnist, Mu Zimei, arching an eyebrow and tapping a Marlboro Light into an ashtray. She added: "I do not oppose love, but I oppose loyalty. If love has to be based on loyalty, I will not choose love."

Mu Zimei is both reviled and admired, but she is not ignored. The country's most popular Internet site, Sina.com, credits her with attracting 10 million daily visitors. Another site, Sohu.com, says Mu Zimei is the name most often typed into its Internet search engine, surpassing one occasional runner-up, Mao Zedong.

Her celebrity—which exploded when she posted an explicit online account of her tryst with a Chinese rock star—first seemed to baffle government censors but now has drawn a familiar response. Her forthcoming book was banned this week. She has quit her magazine columnist job and halted her blog, or online diary.

Yet at a time when "Sex and the City" episodes are among the most popular DVDs in China, the Mu Zimei phenomenon is another example of the government's struggle to keep a grip on social change in China. Her writings have prompted a raging debate about sex and women on the Internet, where more people are writing blogs or arguing anonymously about a host of subjects in chat rooms and discussion pages.

"She does bring a huge impact on Chinese society," said Zeng Fuhu, a top editor at Sohu.com.

Such sweeping talk does not impress Ms. Mu as she sits in a bistro in this south China boomtown. Women at a nearby table try to eavesdrop as China's scarlet-lettered woman estimates that she has slept with about 70 men, and counting.

She said she never realized her online diary would be so widely discovered, or that it would grow into a national controversy. But she defended her right to sleep with as many men as she pleased—and to write about it.

"If a man does this," she said, "it's no big deal. But as a woman doing so, I draw lots of criticism."

Sex, and governmental anxiety about it, is not a new issue in China. In January 1994, the government banned *The Abandoned Capital,* a sexually explicit, best-selling novel by an acclaimed author, Jia Pingwa.

Very Interesting Mu Zimei, 25, who writes about sex, became a sensation across China with her accounts of her numerous sexual experiences—until the government intervened. "I think my private life is very interesting," she said.

laboratory-based experiments that involve simulated aggression or judgments of sympathy toward hypothetical women who have been portrayed as rape victims. None measured *actual* violence against women outside the lab. We still lack conclusive evidence that normal men have been, or would be, spurred to rape or sexually violate women by exposure to violent pornography.

Translation of the Mu Zimei blog post that triggered the controversy*:

Firday night. It was the Pillow Wood Bar once again. (They must hate me for giving the place a reputation for debauchery. But so what?)

Someone came over to chat. Oh, it was Wang Lei. The opening line was really *sans* creativity: "It is so lonely. Let us sit together."

"Anyone else?"

He mentioned a couple of names. One of them is the guy who has just left *Southern Sports* magazine, the other is the designer who is still hesitating to make love to me.

"I'll go if you guys are having an orgy party tonight."

"If you can find another girl, we'll do it."

"Yeah, right."

Before 2 a.m., Wang Lei said he was leaving. "Let's leave together?" We left together.

"Where to?"

"Home."

"Your home or my home?"

"Where is your home?"

"Next to the university."

"A bit far away. How about my home?"

"Your home is even further away. It takes half a day to make the round trip."

"It is the same thing to go from your home to my home."

We bantered a bit. I said, "Wang Lei, why don't we do it right here? Making love is such a simple thing."

Right there. In a dark corner near the Pillow Wood bar.

When he lifted up my white skirt, I said, "It is sooooo easy to do this with skirts!"

He told me to raise my butt and bend over.

A lot of people like to do doggy-style, but it is somewhat impractical outdoors.

It was over quickly. Wang Lei complained that the atmosphere was not very good, especially since there was no music.

I said, "Wang Lei, you were not physically good either." If it weren't for this, we would still be walking around aimlessly.

I have been a fan of Wang Lei's music for some years. But at the orgy party several months ago, I cut Wang Lei down to a 70 point rating. After this outdoor episode, he is left with a 50 point rating.

I feel really sorry for him. He has sunken so low that he is being betrayed by *me* . . .

*www.zonaeuropa.com/weblog20031111.htm

Then in May 2000, censors banned another sex-soaked best seller, *Shanghai Baby,* by Zhou Weihui.

But Ms. Mu's case is notable because her most controversial work appeared on the Internet. Mu Zimei (pronounced Moo Zuh-MAY) is the pen name of Li Li, who began working in 2001 as a feature writer at *City Pictorial,* a glossy magazine covering fashion and social trends. At the end of 2002, editors overhauled the magazine and decided they wanted a sex columnist who could write about "real life" issues.

Ms. Mu said she was chosen because editors knew she was familiar with the subject. Her first sexual experience—on April 30, 1999, she noted—ended with an abortion and left her wary of the opposite sex. She followed that with a "pretty normal boyfriend" before concluding she was not a one-man woman. "Personally, I felt I was suitable for temporary relationships," she said.

Her biweekly column in *City Pictorial* began in January. Her topics included recommendations on the best music for good lovemaking, the aphrodisiacal benefits of eating oysters and technical pointers on making love in a car. It was racy stuff for China, but hardly without precedent.

What changed everything was her decision in April to start her own online blog at a new Chinese site for personal diaries. She said she thought it would be fun.

While writing her magazine column, she had hopped from man to man, sometimes hopping to two men at once, sometimes hopping to married men. Her topics, though, remained more thematic than explicit.

But in her online diary, she began writing explicitly about these encounters, or those of her friends, and on July 26 described her brief and apparently unsatisfying liaison outside a restaurant with a famous guitarist in a Guangzhou rock band.

(Continues)

In their comprehensive review of the research literature on pornography and sexual aggression, Neil Malamuth and his colleagues (2000) analyzed data from studies that found no reliable links between pornography and aggression, integrated the findings of summaries of the research literature, and analyzed questionnaire data obtained from a nationally representative sample of 2,972 college men, who were an

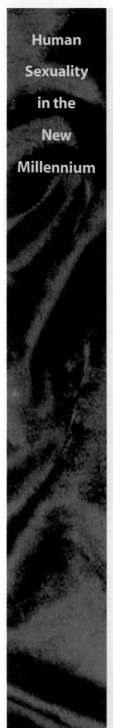

Human Sexuality in the New Millennium

The entry was posted at a popular online discussion board, spread among China's "netizens" like wildfire and was quickly picked up in the gossipy newspapers that feed China's growing celebrity culture. Eventually, she was featured in China's edition of *Cosmopolitan* magazine.

In Beijing, editors at Sina.com and Sohu.com also noticed. An estimated 68 million people surf the Internet in China, with annual growth rates approaching 30 percent. Internet users tend to be China's most affluent and better-educated citizens, and though government censors block certain Web sites, the amount of information available online is enormous.

It is also a growing and fiercely competitive business. By early November, Sina.com had bought the serialization rights to Ms. Mu's book, a compilation of her magazine columns, poems, and some diary entries. (The diary entries included in the book are not explicit, Ms. Mu said.)

Beginning on November 11, Sina.com used its home page to promote the serialization, along with photographs and interviews with the author. The response was stunning. Sina.com normally attracts 20 million visitors a day. Company officials say that number immediately jumped to 30 million and stayed there for 10 days.

She also became a hot topic of debate in different Internet chat rooms and discussion sites. Was she an amoral hussy peddling pornography? Or was she a liberated woman?

"The most loathsome person in the world is not the woman who writes exotic words, but those sanctimonious men!" wrote one contributor to a discussion page.

"I despise Mu Zimei!" one critic countered. Another added, "This kind of diary will only serve as an excuse for more people who want to live a wild sexual life."

Sociologists weighed in, pro and con. A Sina.com poll of more than 30,000 people found respondents about equally split.

For months, the government had remained a bystander. But on November 16, the state-run *Beijing Evening News* strongly criticized Ms. Mu and accused Sina.com of wrongly promoting her to attract more visitors.

"The blind pursuit after this kind of phenomenon," the newspaper stated, "will mislead people into thinking that the government authorities over news are turning blind to this."

Sina.com quickly minimized, though did not remove, its promotion of Ms. Mu. "When we saw the *Beijing Evening News,* we realized we might have gone too far," said Chen Tong, Sina.com's editor-in-chief. "So we pulled back."

Sohu.com's editors initially held worried meetings about Sina.com's popular serialization. But a day after the *Beijing Evening News* article, the Sohu.com editors, citing the need for Internet sites to maintain content standards, published their own criticism about Ms. Mu.

Asked if the Sohu article was an attempt to undercut Sina's star attraction, Mr. Zeng responded, "It had nothing to do with Sina."

Ms. Mu does not regard herself as peddling smut. She said her generation of Chinese grew up with little or no sex education. "Some learned it from videos," she said. "Why not from words?"

[The government has other ideas, it seems. The decision to ban her book was reported in the state-run media on Friday; Ms. Mu confirmed the ban. Online booksellers, who had been swamped with purchase requests, said government officials ordered them not to sell the book, which had been scheduled to go on the market this week.]

In an effort to defuse the controversy, Ms. Mu said she quit her columnist job in early November and voluntarily shut down her Web site. She said she had other offers and hoped to continue writing, assuming the government does not ban her writing altogether.

She also said the controversy had cramped her social life: she has, she said, been celibate for two weeks.

Source: Reprinted from Jima Yardley (2003, November 30). Internet sex column thrills, and inflames, China. *The New York Times online.*

average of 21 years old. Each method of analysis supported the existence of some reliable connections between the frequent use of pornography and sexually aggressive behavior; particularly in the cases of violent pornography and for men who were likely to engage in sexual aggression.

Nonviolent Pornography Nonviolent pornography may not contain scenes of sexual violence, but it typically portrays women in degrading or dehumanizing roles—as sexually promiscuous, insatiable, and subservient (Itzin, 2002). Might such portrayals of women reinforce traditional stereotypes of women as sex objects? Might they lead viewers to condone acts of rape by suggesting that women are essentially promiscuous? Might the depiction of women as readily sexually accessible inspire men to refuse to "take no for an answer" on dates?

In classic research, Zillmann and Bryant (1984) exposed male and female study participants to six sessions of pornography over 6 consecutive weeks. Participants were exposed to a massive dose of pornography, consisting of six nonviolent pornographic films during each weekly session; or to an intermediate dose consisting of three pornographic and three neutral films each session; or to a no-dose control consisting of six nonsexual films each session. When later tested in a purportedly independent study, both males and females who received extended exposure to pornography, especially those receiving the massive dose, gave more lenient punishments to a rapist who was depicted in a newspaper article. Moreover, males became more callous in their attitudes toward women.

In a more recent study, 71 men watched one of three films: a film that was sexually explict and degrading of women, or a film that was sexually explicit but *not* degrading of women, or a nonsexual (control) film (Mulac et al., 2002). The men then worked in couples with women to solve problems. Men who watched the sexually explicit films behaved more dominantly toward their problem-solving partners than did men who watched the control film. Moreover, men who watched the sexually explicit *and* degrading film showed more dominance than those who watched the sexually explicit but not degrading film.

Overall, it would appear that at least for some men, exposure to pornography can render their attitudes toward women more negative and callous. Some men who view pornography may come to regard women as sexual playthings who are to be valued merely for their physical attributes and their role in providing sexual release, not as individuals.

Another concern is the possible effect of nonviolent pornography on the viewer's sexual and family values. Nonviolent pornography typically features impromptu sexual encounters between new acquaintances. Might repeated exposure to such material alter viewers' attitudes toward traditional sexual and family values? Zillmann (1989) reports evidence that repeated exposure to this type of nonviolent pornography somewhat undermines traditional sexual and family values. When compared to people who viewed nonsexual films, men and women who were exposed, over a 6-week period, to weekly, hour-long sessions involving scenes of explicit sexual encounters between new acquaintances reported greater acceptance, compared to controls who viewed nonsexual films, of premarital and extramarital sex and of simultaneous sexual relationships with multiple partners. Men and women who viewed such pornography also reported desiring fewer children than people in the control groups and were relatively less committed to marriage as an "essential institution." Prolonged exposure to pornography may also foster dissatisfaction with the physical appearance and sexual performance of one's intimate partners (Zillmann, 1989).

With pornography more available than ever online, concerns have also developed over whether people become "addicted" to "cyberporn," which would be another contributor to the loosening of family ties. We discussed "cybersex addiction" in the chapter on atypical sexual variations. Enough articles on the topic are written in popular magazines to suggest that this particular "sexual variation" is

Truth?Fiction?
Revisited

Malamuth and his colleagues conclude not that pornography causes violence but, rather, that relatively aggressive men react differently from nonviolent men to the same pornography. Put it this way: It is not so much that pornography makes men violent; instead, it seems to be more likely that pornography makes violent men *more* violent.

Nielsen/NetRatings (cited in Sachar, 2003) reports that one-quarter of all Internet surfing is devoted to the pursuit of pornography, adult chat rooms, and the like.

becoming more typical, or at least common. For example, an article in the *Ladies' Home Journal* was titled "Is Cyberporn Coming between You?" and reflected some women's concern that their partners are spending more time pursuing sex online than with them.

Consider the case of "Michael":

> Michael, 32, six years into a marriage gone stale, waits for his wife to turn in so he can turn on—to women whose pictures litter the cyberporn sites he's bookmarked. He'll spend hours, he admits, drooling, and then some, over all manner of leggy girls. He imagines the gals talking to him and more. "It relaxes me," says Michael, of Sacramento, California. "I gotta have it. I gotta have them." His wife, he concedes, doesn't know. (Sachar, 2003)

As time goes on, we will doubtless be writing more about Internet pornography and its effects on individuals, their partners, and family life. Some observers suggest that cyberporn and chat room relationships are the new millennium's newest form of cheating. For some, it may well become a psychological disorder, akin to the obsessive–compulsive disorders in which people have difficulty preventing themselves from washing their hands. And more and more students burning the midnight oil in their dorm rooms are surfing for sex rather than research findings. It's available, it's free, it's right in students' rooms; the lure is tremendous and the potential harm is yet to be determined.

Review: Pornography and Obscenity

Reflect

In *Miller v. California,* the U.S. Supreme Court held that obscenity is based on "whether the average person, applying contemporary community standards, would find that the work, taken as a whole, appeals to the prurient interest." What is your "community"? What are its standards? What types of films, photographs, or written stories would an average person in your community consider obscene? Why?

CriticalThinking

Which do you consider to be the greater danger–the danger of having pornography available or the danger of censorship? Why?

17. _____ oppose pornography on the grounds that it portrays women in degrading and dehumanizing roles.

18. The dictionary defines _____ as "writing, pictures, etc., intended to arouse sexual desire."

19. Laws against _____ provide the legal framework for outlawing the dissemination of pornography.

20. States may criminalize the downloading and possession of _____ pornography.

21. Pornography is typically used to _____ sexual arousal, often as a masturbation aid.

22. Researchers have found that (*Only men* or *Both men and women*?) are physiologically sexually aroused by pornographic pictures.

23. Repeated exposure to the same pornographic materials (*Increases* or *Decreases*?) sexual response to them.

24. The majority of erotic visual materials are produced for (*Men* or *Women*?).

25. The Commission on Obscenity and Pornography of the 1960s concluded that there (*Was* or *Was no*?) evidence that pornography led to crimes of violence or sexual offenses.

26. Laboratory-based studies have shown that men exposed to violent pornography are (*More* or *Less*?) likely to become aggressive against females.

27. Most research on the effects of pornography has employed _____ as subjects.

28. The literature review by Malamuth (*Found* or *Did not find*?) reliable connections between the use of pornography and sexually aggressive behavior.

Recite

1. What is prostitution?

Prostitution is the sale of sex. Prostitution is illegal everywhere in the United States except certain rural counties in Nevada.

2. How widespread is prostitution?

Fewer young men in the United States use prostitutes today than did so in Kinsey's day, apparently because of the liberalizing trends of the sexual revolution. Nevertheless, there are hundreds of thousands of prostitutes working, including those on adult Web sites.

3. What kinds of prostitutes are there?

The major types of female prostitutes are streetwalkers, brothel prostitutes—many of whom work in massage parlors and for "escort services," and call girls. Streetwalkers often support, and are abused by, pimps. Other prostitutes work in adult films and on adult Web sites.

4. How do prostitutes become involved in "the life"?

No single factor explains entry into female prostitution, but poverty and sexual and/or physical abuse figure prominently in the backgrounds of many prostitutes. Teenage runaways with marginal skills and limited means of support may find few alternatives to prostitution.

5. Who are "johns" or "tricks"?

The consumers of prostitution are often referred to as "johns" or "tricks." Most patrons are "occasional johns" who have regular sex partners. Some people use prostitutes habitually or compulsively, however.

6. Do males also work as prostitutes? What do we know of them?

Most male prostitutes are "hustlers" who service male clients. Hustlers typically begin selling sex in their teens and may be gay, bisexual, or heterosexual in sexual orientation.

7. What is the role of prostitution in the transmission of HIV and other STIs?

Prostitutes are more likely than other people to transmit HIV because they have sexual relations with many partners, often without protection. Many prostitutes and their clients and other sex partners also inject drugs and share contaminated needles. HIV may be spread by unprotected sex from prostitutes to customers and then to the customers' wives or lovers.

8. What is pornography?

Pornography is "writing, pictures, etc., intended to arouse sexual desire." Erotica, by contrast, consists of sexual materials that are artistically produced or motivated. The judgment of what is pornographic or obscene varies from person to person and from culture to culture.

9. What is obscenity?

Obscenity is that which offends people's feelings or goes beyond prevailing standards of decency or modesty. The judgment of what is obscene has a strong subjective element.

10. What kinds of laws have been created to respond to obscenity?

In *Miller v. California,* the U.S. Supreme Court held that obscenity is based on a determination of "whether the average person, applying contemporary community standards, would find that the work . . . appeals to the prurient interest . . . ; whether the work depicts [sexual behavior] in a patently offensive way, [and] whether the work, taken as a whole, lacks serious literary, artistic, political, or scientific value." *Miller* recognizes that judgments of obscenity may vary with "community standards." The downloading and possession of child pornography has been criminalized throughout the United States.

11. How widespread is the use of pornography?

People in the United States are typically introduced to pornography by their high school years. Although females and males can both be physiologically aroused by pornography, men are relatively more interested in it. Pornography is frequently used as a masturbation aid.

12. Is pornography a harmless diversion or a cause of sexual violence or other antisocial acts?

A 1970 government commission found no harmful effects of pornographic material on normal people. A later government commission, the Meese Commission, issued a report in 1986 linking exposure to violent pornography with sexual aggression, and exposure to degrading but nonviolent pornography with increased acceptability of rape in the minds of viewers. Research evidence suggests that exposure to pornography may stimulate sexually deviant urges in men who are predisposed to commit crimes of sexual violence. Research evidence in laboratory settings also suggests that violent pornography may stimulate college men to act more aggressively toward women. Some researchers argue that it is the violence in violent pornography, not sexual explicitness per se, that promotes violence against women. The effects of nonviolent pornography on normal populations remain unclear.

Answers to Reviews

Chapter One

1. Sexuality
2. Biologists, medical professionals
3. Psychologists
4. Sociocultural
5. Value
6. Legalistic
7. Situation
8. Relativists
9. Hedonist
10. Asceticism
11. Utilitarianism
12. Rationalism
13. Skepticism
14. Authority
15. Terms
16. Conclusions
17. History
18. Little
19. Stone
20. Phallus
21. Egypt
22. Approved
23. Property
24. Bisexual
25. Christians, Christianity
26. Chinese
27. *Sutra*
28. Victorian
29. Freud
30. Kinsey
31. Biological
32. Evolutionary
33. Less
34. Cross-cultural, anthropological
35. Psychoanalytic, psychodynamic
36. Behaviorists, psychologists
37. Learning
38. Sociocultural

Chapter Two

1. Research, evidence, empirical data, etc.
2. Scientific
3. Hypothesis
4. Predict
5. Theories
6. Populations
7. Sample
8. Represent
9. Random
10. Stratified
11. Convenience
12. Case
13. Survey
14. Kinsey
15. Group
16. Reliability
17. Validity
18. NHSLS, Laumann and colleagues
19. 80
20. 20
21. Junk (useless)
22. African
23. Desirable
24. Ethnographic, archeological
25. Participant
26. Laboratory
27. Vasocongestion, myotonia
28. Correlational
29. Coefficient
30. Does not
31. Experiment
32. Treatment, independent variable
33. Dependent
34. Random
35. Ethics, Ethical researchers, Scientists, etc.
36. Confidential
37. Informed
38. Deceived, uninformed, etc.

Chapter Three

2. Mons
3. Majora
4. Clitoris
5. Cavernosa
6. Homologous
7. Urethral
8. Hymen
9. Engorgement, vasocongestion
10. Vaginal
11. Vaginitis
12. Cervical
13. Pap
14. Uterus
15. Hysterectomy
16. Fallopian
17. Ovaries
18. Secondary
19. Mammary
20. Ducts
21. 200,000
22. Increases
23. Higher
24. Estrogen
25. African
26. Mammography
27. Lumpectomy
28. Mastectomy
29. Menstruation
30. Progesterone
31. Proliferative
32. Ovulation
33. Secretory, luteal
34. Decreases
35. Can
35. Hormones
36. Clomiphene
37. Is not
39. Menopause
40. Perimenopause
41. Estrogen
42. Increases
43. Dysmenorrhea
44. Prostaglandins
45. Amenorrhea
46. Premenstrual
47. Dysphoric
48. Serotonin

Chapter Four

1. Scrotum
2. Urine
3. Cavernosa
4. Muslims
5. Cremaster
6. Testes
7. Interstitial
8. FSH
9. Siminiferous
10. 23
11. Vas, ductus
12. Fructose, sugar
13. Prostatic
14. Semen
15. Urethritis
16. Is no
17. Half, 50% of
18. Alpha
19. 200,000–250,000
20. African, European
21. Testosterone
22. Rectal, PSA
23. Surgery
24. Prostatitis
25. Antibiotics
26. Erection
27. *Tunica*
28. Common
29. REM
30. Do not
31. Reflexes
32. Cannot
33. Do not
34. Sacrum
35. Lumbar
36. Sympathetic
37. Parasympathetic
38. Orgasm
39. Emission
40. Expulsion

Chapter Five

1. Smell
2. Men
3. Pheromones
4. Less
5. Women
6. Increases
7. Synchronize, converge, correspond, etc.

8. Primary
9. Secondary
10. Aphrodisiac
11. Irritating, inflaming, burning, etc.
12. Placebo
13. Resemble, look like, etc.
14. Arginine
15. Poppers, snappers
16. Bupropion, Wellbutrin
17. Urinate
18. Decrease
19. Anaphrodisiac
20. Lessen
21. Indiscriminate
22. Limbic
23. Cerebral
24. Spinal
25. Hypothalamus
26. Hormones
27. Do
28. Secondary
29. Organizing
30. Testosterone
31. Hypogonadism
32. Adrenal
33. Four
34. Myotonia
35. Excitement
36. Men
37. Women
38. Desire
39. Vaginal
40. One
41. Blended
42. Ejaculate
43. Controversial, anecdotal, mixed, etc.

Chapter Six

1. Differentiation
2. Female, Male
3. Y
4. Absent
5. Female
6. Wolffian
7. Inguinal
8. Identity
9. Sex, gender
10. Intersexuals
11. Hermaphrodites

12. Intersexuals
13. Adrenal
14. Insensitivity
15. Complete
16. Testosterone, androgens, male sex hormones
17. Is not
18. Dysphoria
19. Homosexual, gay
20. Stereotype
21. Role
22. Feminine
23. Found around the world
24. Sexism
25. Women
26. Females
27. Males
28. Males
29. Females
30. Females
31. Males
32. Females
33. Males
34. Males
35. Typing
36. Evolutionary, biological, genetic
37. Strategies
38. Women
39. Oedipus
40. Before
41. Social
42. Constancy
43. Schema
44. Identity
45. Androgyny
46. Less
47. Masculinity
48. Femininity
49. Dominance

Chapter Seven

1. Attractiveness, appearance
2. Taller
3. Both females and males
4. 0.7 to 0.8
5. Large
6. Only females
7. Has
8. Women
9. Women

10. Men
11. Kindness
12. Reproductive
13. Matching
14. Similarity
15. Reciprocate
16. Storge
17. Eros
18. Idealized
19. Love
20. Infatuation
21. Passionate
22. Attribution
23. Six
24. Commitment
25. Intimacy
26. Intimacy
27. Commitment
28. Romantic

Chapter Eight

1. Exchange
2. Friends
3. Similarity
4. Males
5. Surface
6. Small
7. Eye
8. Disclosure
9. Masculine
10. Mutuality
11. Intimacy
12. Esteem
13. Cyclical
14. Honesty
15. Males
16. Evolutionary
17. Irrational
18. Pursuit, Pursuit behaviors
19. Loneliness
20. Inner
21. Outer
22. Low, Instability
23. Higher
24. More
25. Rejection
26. External
27. Conflict
28. Open, Calm
29. Deterioration, Termination
30. Communication

31. Irrational, Erroneous, Harmful, Mistaken
32. Active
33. Paraphrasing
34. Anger
35. Criticism
36. Disagree

Chapter Nine

1. Masturbation
2. Relieve sexual tension
3. Onanism
4. Augustine
5. Kellogg
6. Men
7. More
8. European
9. More
10. Manual
11. Do not
12. Most
13. Males
14. Less
15. Men
16. Shorter
17. Is
18. Deep, French, Soul
19. Most
20. Both men and women
21. Women
22. Fisting
23. Both women and men
24. Manual
25. Fellatio
26. Cunnilingus
27. The majority
28. Male
29. Female
30. Lateral
31. Rear
32. Are not
33. Anal

Chapter Ten

1. Orientation
2. Homosexual
3. Gay
4. Lesbians
5. Bisexuals
6. Consistent
7. More

8. Kinsey
9. 3, 2
10. Two
11. Women
12. Heterosexuals and homosexuals
13. Greece
14. Night
15. Christians
16. Semen
17. More
18. Homophobia
19. Male dominance
20. Less
21. Struck down
22. Mattachine
23. More
24. X
25. Feminine
26. Oedipus, Electra
27. Learning
28. Other
29. Butch
30. Psychiatric
31. More
32. Close
33. Minority
34. Behavior
35. Coming
36. Same, Disclosure
37. Others
38. More
39. Cruising
40. More
41. Close
42. Open

Chapter 11

1. Conception
2. Boys
3. Odor
4. Fallopian
5. Hyaluronidase
6. Ovulation
7. Decreases
8. Luteinizing
9. Thin, Slippery, Clear
10. Male
11. Y
12. 6 months, A year or more
13. 15

14. Low sperm count
15. Artificial
16. Clomiphene, Clomid
17. Endometriosis
18. In vitro fertilization
19. Intracytoplasmic sperm injection
20. Gonadotropin
21. Hegar's
22. Placenta
23. Chromosomal
24. Second
25. Sympathetic
26. 280
27. Germinal
28. Blastocyst
29. Normal
30. Embryonic
31. Outer layer of cells, Ectoderm
32. Proximodistal
33. Amniotic
34. Placenta
35. Umbilical
36. Fourth
37. Head-first, Cephalic
38. 25
39. Teratogens
40. Critical
41. High
42. Incompatibility
43. Accutane
44. DES
45. Fetal alcohol syndrome
46. Spontaneous
47. Down
48. Sickle, Sachs
49. Amniocentesis
50. Braxton-Hicks
51. Oxytocin
52. Efface, Dilate
53. Transition
54. Second
55. Episiotomy
56. Placenta
57. 10
58. General
59. Lamaze
60. 24
61. Decrease
62. Homelike atmosphere
63. Anoxia
64. Umbilical
65. Birthweight
66. Respiratory
67. 70
68. Hormonal
69. Postpartum depression
70. Psychotic
71. Antibodies
72. Prolactin
73. Irregular
74. 6

Chapter 12

1. Sanger
2. Contraception
3. Withdrawal, Coitus interruptus
4. Comstock
5. Hormones, Birth control pills, "The pill"
6. *Roe*
7. Oral
8. Progesterone, Progestin
9. Minipill
10. Pregnant
11. Estrogen
12. 100
13. Reduces
14. Male
15. Does not
16. Higher
17. Progestin
18. Bleeding
19. Uterine
20. Does not
21. Diaphragm
22. Spermicides
23. Do not
24. Cervical
25. Condoms
26. Can
27. Ineffective
28. Withdrawal
29. Fertility awareness, Rhythm
30. Calendar
31. Basal
32. Viscosity
33. Luteinizing
34. Vasectomy
35. Does not
36. Ligation, Sterilization
37. Laparoscopy
38. Induced
39. First
40. Life
41. Choice
42. Soul
43. Conception
44. Was
45. Support
46. Aspiration
47. Cervix
48. Suction
49. Infusion
50. Partial
51. Brain
52. Cesarean
53. Progesterone

Chapter Thirteen

1. Does
2. Can
3. Reflexes
4. 8 months
5. 6 and 12
6. 2 years
7. Is not
8. Do not
9. Speculative
10. 40% to 60%
11. 20% to 30%
12. Kissing
13. 6, 10
14. Does not
15. Same
16. More
17. Peers
18. Masturbation
19. Males
20. Display, Touching
21. Same
22. Friends
23. Puberty
24. Secondary
25. Menarche, Ejaculation
26. Fat
27. Estrogen
28. Menstrual
29. Testosterone
30. Nocturnal
31. Masturbation
32. Is
33. Increased

34. Half, 50%
35. More
36. Less
37. 5
38. Decreased
39. Inconsistently
40. Abstinence
41. Did not

Chapter Fourteen

1. Increase
2. 27 (or 26.8), 25 (or 25.1)
3. 26
4. Financially
5. Less
6. Are, Serial
7. Cohabitation
8. More
9. 5.5 million
10. Less, less
11. More
12. Liberal
13. Commitment
14. 40
15. Is
16. Do
17. Property, Chattel
18. Modern
19. Wealth, Property
20. Married
21. Monogamy
22. Gay
23. Civil unions among gays
24. Homogamy
25. Men
26. More
27. Wider
28. Greater
29. More
30. Women
31. Men
32. Majority
33. Rose
34. Adultery
35. Boys
36. More
37. Estrogen
38. Less
39. Less
40. Is not
41. Can

42. Palsy
43. Males
44. Two
45. Majority
46. Can
47. Can

Chapter Fifteen

1. Dysfunctions
2. More
3. Less
4. Aversion
5. Testosterone
6. Lubrication
7. Increases
8. Diabetes
9. Anorgasmic, Preorgasmic
10. Orgasmic
11. Premature
12. Dyspareunia
13. Vaginismus
14. Blood
15. Cholesterol
16. Antidepressant, Antipsychotic, Antihypertensive
17. Cocaine
18. Repressive, negative
19. Male
20. Anxiety, Fear, Concern
21. Orgasmic, Arousal
22. Knowledge
23. Irrational
24. Spectator
25. Cognitive
26. Directly
27. Masters
28. Sensate
29. Psychoanalytic
30. Hypoactive, Low, Lack of
31. Reflexes
32. Performance
33. Both men and women
34. Irreversible
35. Levitra, Vardenafil
36. Orgasmic
37. Premature
38. Vaginismus

Chapter Sixteen

1. HPV, Genital warts
2. Sexually transmitted, Venereal

3. 333, 300
4. 15% to 30%
5. One
6. Chlamydia
7. Gonorrhea
8. Cannot
9. Ophthalmia
10. Discharge
11. Cervix
12. *Pallidum*
13. Sore, Chancre
14. Neurosyphilis
15. VDRL
16. Nongonnococcal
17. Inflammatory
18. Antibiotics, penicillin
19. Vaginitis
20. Overgrow
21. Candidiasis
22. Trichomoniasis
23. Bacterial
24. Discharge
25. May
26. One
27. DNA
28. Immunodeficiency
29. Immune
30. Antigens
31. CD4, T, T-helper
32. Opportunistic
33. Semen
34. Male–female
35. Lowers
36. Antiretroviral
37. Simplex
38. Sores, Blisters
39. Do not
40. Hepatitis
41. B
42. Warts
43. Penis
44. Can
45. Outer
46. Lice
47. Can
48. Scabies
49. Abstinence
50. Are
51. Low
52. Decrease
53. Underestimate
54. Latex

Chapter Seventeen

1. Statistical
2. Abnormal
3. Paraphilias
4. Distressed, Upset, etc.
5. Dressing
6. Sadism
7. Men
8. Fetishism
9. Partialism
10. Transvestites, Transvestic fetishists, Cross-dressers
11. Exhibitionism, Flashing
12. One-third, 33%
13. Before
14. Are not
15. Scatalogia
16. Voyeurism
17. Normal
18. Masochists
19. Sadism
20. Sadomasochism
21. Frotteurism
22. Necrophilia
23. Higher
24. Right
25. Castration
26. Association
27. Masturbatory
28. Punishment, Pain, Humiliation
29. Sociological
30. Lovemap
31. Do not want
32. Less
33. Psychoanalysis, Psychoanalytic psychotherapy
34. Behavior
35. Desensitization
36. Aversion
37. Reconditioning
38. Antidepressants
39. Anti-androgen

Chapter Eighteen

1. Violence, Aggression, etc.
2. Property
3. Statutory
4. Underreport
5. Greater
6. Acquaintances
7. Strangers
8. Power, Anger, Desire for peer approval
9. Can
10. Legitimizes, Endorses, Encourages
11. Socializing
12. Are not
13. Traditional
14. Sadistic
15. Anger, Sadness, Anxiety
16. Girls
17. Is
18. Is not
19. Acquaintances
20. Fondling, Genital touching
21. Males
22. Pedophilia
23. Unskilled
24. Incest
25. Competition
26. Brother–sister
27. Disruption, Confusion, Disarray, etc.
28. Are not
29. Criminals
30. Group
31. Empathy
32. Castration
33. Harassment
34. Men
35. Victim
36. Feminine
37. Discrimination
38. Minority
39. Power

Chapter Nineteen

1. Nevada
2. Oldest
3. Two-thirds
4. Less
5. Streetwalkers
6. Economic
7. Malls
8. Are
9. Abuse
10. Post-traumatic
11. Occasional
12. Stronger
13. Do not
14. Hustlers
15. Half, 50%
16. Is
17. Feminists
18. Pornography
19. Obscenity
20. Child
21. Elicit, Enhance
22. Both men and women
23. Decreases
24. Men
25. Was no
26. More
27. College students
28. Found

References

Abbey, A., et al. (2001). Alcohol and sexual assault. *Alcohol Research & Health, 25*(1), 43–51.

Abel, G. G., et al. (1989). The measurement of the cognitive distortions of child molesters. *Annals of Sex Research, 2,* 135–152.

Abelson, H., et al. (1970). Public attitudes toward and experience with erotic materials. In *Technical Reports of the Commission on Obscenity and Pornography, Vol. 6.* Washington, DC: U.S. Government Printing Office.

Abramowitz, S. (1986). Psychosocial outcomes of sex reassignment surgery. *Journal of Consulting and Clinical Psychology, 54,* 183–189.

Ackerman, D. (1991). *The moon by whale light.* New York: Random House.

ACOG (The American College of Obstetricians and Gynecologists). (2003, July 31). Weighing the pros and cons of cesarean delivery. ACOG News Release. *http://www.acog.com/from_home/publications/press_releases/nr07-31-03-3.cfm*

Adachi, M., et al. (2000). Androgen-insensitivity syndrome as a possible coactivator disease. *The New England Journal of Medicine* online, *343*(12).

Adams, H. E., et al. (1981). Behavior therapy with sexual deviations. In S. M. Turner, K. S. Calhoun, & H. E. Adams (Eds.), *Handbook of clinical behavior therapy* (pp. 318–346). New York: Wiley.

Adams, K. M. (2003). Clergy sex abuse: A commentary on celibacy. *Sexual Addiction & Compulsivity: The Journal of Treatment and Prevention, 10*(2–3), 91–92.

Adams, H. E., Wright, L. W., Jr., & Lohr, B. A. (1996). Is homophobia associated with homosexual arousal? *Journal of Abnormal Psychology, 105,* 440–445.

Affonso, D. D., De, A. K., Horowitz, J. A., & Mayberry, L. J. (2000). An international study exploring levels of postpartum depressive symptomatology. *Journal of Psychosomatic Research, 49*(3), 207–216.

After years of decline, Caesareans on the rise again. (2000, August 29). The Associated Press online.

Akhtar, S. (1988). Four culture-bound psychiatric syndromes in India. *The International Journal of Social Psychiatry, 34,* 70–74.

Alexander, C. J., Sipski, M. L., & Findley, T. W. (1993). Sexual activities, desire, and satisfaction in males pre- and post-spinal cord injury. *Archives of Sexual Behavior, 22,* 217–228.

Alexander, G. M. (2003). An evolutionary perspective of sex-typed toy preferences: Pink, blue, and the brain. *Archives of Sexual Behavior, 32*(1), 7–14.

Allen, P. L. (2000). *The wages of sin: Sex and disease, past and present.* Chicago: University of Chicago Press.

Allyn, D. (2001). *Make love, not war: The sexual revolution: An unfettered history.* London: Routledge.

Altemus, M., Cloitre, M., & Dhabhar, F. S. (2003).

Enhanced cellular immune response in women with PTSD related to childhood abuse. *American Journal of Psychiatry, 160*(9), 1705–1707.

Alterman, E. (1997, November). Sex in the '90s. *Elle,* pp. 128–134.

Alter-Reid, K., et al. (1986). Sexual abuse of children: A review of the empirical findings. *Clinical Psychology Review, 6,* 249–266.

Althof, S. E. (1994). Paper presented at the annual meeting of the American Urological Association. San Francisco.

Altman, L. K. (1993a, February 21). New caution, and some reassurance, on vasectomy. *The New York Times,* Section 4, p. 2.

Altman, L. K. (1995c, July 7). Drug for treating impotence is ready for sale, FDA says. *The New York Times,* p. A13.

Amato, P. R. (2001). Children of divorce in the 1990s: An update of the Amato and Keith (1991) meta-analysis. *Journal of Family Psychology, 15*(3), 355–370.

American Academy of Pediatrics. (2002, February 7). *A woman's guide to breastfeeding.* http://www.aap.org/family/brstguid.htm

American Cancer Society. (2003). *http://www.cancer.org/*

American Infertility Association. (2002). Cited in J. E. Brody. (2002a, January 1). What women must know about fertility. *The New York Times,* p. F6.

American Psychiatric Association. (2000). *Diagnostic and statistical manual of mental disorders (4th ed.). DSM–IV–TR.* Washington, DC: Author.

American Psychological Association, Committee on Gay and Lesbian Concerns. (1991). Avoiding heterosexual bias in language. *American Psychologist, 46,* 973–974.

American Psychological Association (1998a, March 16). Sexual harassment: Myths and realities. APA Public Information Home Page; *www.apa.org*

Ames, M. A., & Houston, D. A. (1990). Legal, social, and biological definitions of pedophilia. *Archives of Sexual Behavior, 19,* 333–342.

Anderson, J. L., et al. (1992). Was the Duchess of Windsor right? A cross-cultural review of the socioecology of ideals of female body shape. *Ethology and Sociobiology, 13,* 197–227.

Anderson, S. E., et al. (2003). Relative weight and race influence average age at menarche: Results from two nationally representative surveys of U.S. girls studied 25 years apart. *Pediatrics, 111,* 844–850.

Anderson, V. N. (1992). For whom is this world just? Sexual orientation and AIDS. *Journal of Applied Social Psychology, 22,* 248–259.

Anderssen, N., Amlie, C., & Ytteroy, E. A. (2002). Outcomes for children with lesbian or gay parents: A review of studies from 1978 to 2000. *Scandinavian Journal of Psychology, 43*(4), 335–351.

Angier, N. (1991, August 30). Zone of brain

linked to men's sexual orientation. *The New York Times,* pp. A1, D18.

Angier, N. (1993a). Future of the pill may lie just over the counter. *The New York Times,* Section 4, p. 5.

ANRG (2000). Traditional Chinese society. *http://weber.ucsd.edu/~thall/cbs.html*

Apperloo, M. J. A., et al. (2003). In the mood for sex: The value of androgens. *Journal of Sex & Marital Therapy, 29*(2), 87–102.

Archer, J., & Vaughan, A. E. (2001). Evolutionary theories of rape. *Psychology, Evolution & Gender, 3*(1), 95–101.

Armas, G. C. (2000, May 15). Census: Unmarried couples increase. The Associated Press.

Armstrong, K., Eisen, A., & Weber, B. (2000). Assessing the risk of breast cancer. *The New England Journal of Medicine* online, *342*(8).

Arriaga, X. B., & Rusbult, C. E. (1998). Standing in my partner's shoes: Partner perspective taking and reactions to accommodative dilemmas. *Personality & Social Psychology Bulletin, 24*(9), 927–948.

Arthur, B. I., Jr., et al. (1998). Sexual behaviour in *Drosophila* is irreversibly programmed during critical period. *Current Biology, 8*(21), 1187–1190.

Ashley-Koch, A., Yang, Q., & Olney, R. S. (2000). Sickle hemoglobin (Hb S) allele and sickle cell disease. *American Journal of Epidemiology, 151*(9), 839–845.

Ashton, A. K., et al. (2000). Antidepressant-induced sexual dysfunction and *Ginkgo biloba. American Journal of Psychiatry, 157,* 836–837.

Astley, S. J., & Clarren, S. K. (2001). Measuring the facial phenotype of individuals with prenatal alcohol exposure: Correlations with brain dysfunction. *Alcohol & Alcoholism, 36*(2), 147–159.

Australia scientists find flowers dupe lonely bees. (2000, June 16). Reuters News Agency online.

Auvert, B., et al. (2001). Male circumcision is one of the factors influencing the transmission of HIV during sexual intercourse. *AIDS, 15*(Suppl4), S31–S40.

Avis, N. E. (2003). Depression during the menopausal transition. *Psychology of Women Quarterly, 27*(2), 91–100.

Bach, G. R., & Deutsch, R. M. (1970). *Pairing.* New York: Peter H. Wyden.

Bäckström, T., et al. (2003). The role of hormones and hormonal treatments in premenstrual syndrome. *CNS Drugs, 17*(5), 325–342.

Bader, M. (2003). *Arousal: The secret logic of sexual fantasies.* New York: Griffin Trade Paperback.

Baenninger, M. A., & Elenteny, K. (1997). Cited in Azar, B. (1997). Environment can mitigate differences in spatial ability. *APA Monitor, 28*(6), 28.

Baer, H., Allen, S., & Braun, L. (2000). Knowledge of human papillomavirus infection among young adult men and women: Implications for health education and research. *Journal of Community Health: The Publication for Health Promotion & Disease Prevention, 25*(1), 67–78.

Bagley, C., & D'Augelli, A. R. (2000). Suicidal behaviour in gay, lesbian, and bisexual youth. *British Medical Journal, 320*, 1617–1618.

Bailes, E., et al. (2003). Hybrid origin of SIV in chimpanzees. *Science, 300*(5626), 1713.

Bailey, J. M. (2003a). Personal communication.

Bailey, J. M. (2003b). *The man who would be queen: The science of gender-bending and transsexualism.* Washington, DC: Joseph Henry Press.

Bailey, J. M., Dunne, M. P., & Martin, N. G. (2000a). Genetic and environmental influences on sexual orientation and its correlates in an Australian twin sample. *Journal of Personality & Social Psychology, 78*(3), 524–536.

Bailey, J. M., et al. (1999). A family history study of male sexual orientation using three independent samples. *Behavior Genetics, 29*(2), 79–86.

Bailey, J. M., Kim, P. Y., Hills, A., & Linsenmeier, J. A. W. (1997). Butch, femme, or straight acting? Partner preferences of gay men and lesbians. *Journal of Personality & Social Psychology, 73*(5), 960–973.

Bailey, J. M., Kirk, K. M., Zhu, G., Dunne, M. P., & Martin, N. G. (2000b). Do individual differences in sociosexuality represent genetic or environmentally contingent strategies? Evidence from the Australian twin registry. *Journal of Personality & Social Psychology, 78*(3), 537–545.

Bailey, J. M., & Oberschneider, M. (1997). Sexual orientation and professional dance. *Archives of Sexual Behavior, 26*(4), 433–444.

Bailey, J. M., & Pillard, R. C. (1991). A genetic study of male sexual orientation. *Archives of General Psychiatry, 48*, 1089–1096.

Bailey, J. M., & Zucker, K. J. (1995). Childhood sex-typed behavior and sexual orientation: A conceptual analysis and quantitative review. *Developmental Psychology, 31*, 43–55.

Bailey, R. C. (2000). A study in rural Uganda of heterosexual transmission of human immunodeficiency virus. *New England Journal of Medicine* online, *343*(5).

Baker, J. N. (1990, Summer/Fall). Coming out. (Special Issue). *Newsweek*, pp. 60–61.

Baker, S., Thalberg, S., & Morrison, D. (1988). Parents' behavioral norms as predictors of adolescent sexual activity and contraceptive use. *Adolescence, 23*, 278–281.

Balter, L., & Tamis-LeMonda, C. S. (Eds.). (1999). *Child psychology: A handbook of contemporary issues.* Philadelphia, PA: Psychology Press.

Bamgbose, O. (2002). Teenage prostitution and the future of the female adolescent in Nigeria. *International Journal of Offender Therapy & Comparative Criminology, 46*(5), 569–585.

Ban on Prenatal Scans Ordered Enforced. (2003, September 11). *The New York Times*, p. 6.

Bancroft, J. (1990). Commentary: Biological contributions to sexual orientation. In D. P. McWhirter, S. A. Sanders, & J. M. Reinisch (Eds.), *Homosexuality/heterosexuality: Concepts of sexual orientation* (pp. 101–111). New York: Oxford University Press.

Bancroft, J., Loftus, J., & Long, J. S. (2003). Distress about sex: A national survey of women in heterosexual relationships. *Archives of Sexual Behavior, 32*(3), 193–208.

Banmen, J., & Vogel, N. (1985). The relationship

between marital quality and interpersonal sexual communication. *Family Therapy, 12*, 45–58.

Banning, A. (1989). Mother–son incest: Confronting a prejudice. *Child Abuse and Neglect, 13*, 563–570.

Barash, D. P., & Lipton, J. E. (2001). *The myth of monogamy.* New York: Freeman.

Barbaree, H. E., & Marshall, W. L. (1991). The role of male sexual arousal in rape: Six models. *Journal of Consulting and Clinical Psychology, 59*, 621–630.

Barnard, N. D., Scialli, A. R., Hurlock, D., & Bertron, P. (2000). Diet and sex-hormone binding globulin, dysmenorrhea, and premenstrual symptoms. *Obstetrics & Gynecology, 95*, 245–250.

Barnett, J. E., & Dunning, C. (2003). Clinical perspectives on elderly sexuality. *Archives of Sexual Behavior, 32*(3), 295–296.

Barouch, D. H., et al. (2000). Control of viremia and prevention of clinical AIDS in Rhesus monkeys by cytokine-augmented DNA vaccination. *Science, 290*(5491), 486–492.

Barr, H. M., Streissguth, A. P., Darby, B. L., & Sampson, P. D. (1990). Prenatal exposure to alcohol, caffeine, tobacco, and aspirin. *Developmental Psychology, 26*, 339–348.

Barrett, M. B. (1990). *Invisible lives: The truth about millions of women-loving women.* New York: Harper & Row (Perennial Library).

Barringer, F. (1993b, April 15). Sex survey of American men finds 1% are gay. *The New York Times*, p. A1.

Barringer, F. (1993c, June 2). School hallways as gauntlets of sexual taunts. *The New York Times*, p. B7.

Bar-Tal, D., & Saxe, L. (1976). Perceptions of similarly and dissimilarly physically attractive couples and individuals. *Journal of Personality and Social Psychology, 33*, 772–781.

Barth, R. P., et al. (2002). Methodological lessons from the National Survey of Child and Adolescent Well-Being: The first three years of the USA's first national probability study of children and families investigated for abuse and neglect. *Children & Youth Services Review, 24*(6–7), 513–541.

Basile, K. C. (2002). Attitudes toward wife rape: Effects of social background and victim status. *Violence & Victims, 17*(3), 341–354.

Basow, S. A., & Rubenfeld, K. (2003). "Troubles talk": Effects of gender and gender-typing. *Sex Roles, 48*(3–4), 183–187.

Basson, R. (2002). Are our definitions of women's desire, arousal, and sexual pain disorders too broad and our definition of orgasmic disorder too narrow? *Journal of Sex & Marital Therapy, 28*(4), 289–300.

Bastian, L. A., Smith, C. M., & Nanda, K. (2003). Is this woman perimenopausal? *Journal of the American Medical Association, 289*, 895–902.

Bauerle, S. Y., Amirkhan, J. H., & Hupka, R. B. (2002). An attribution theory analysis of romantic jealousy. *Motivation & Emotion, 26*(4), 297–319.

Baumeister, R. F. (1988a). Gender differences in masochistic scripts. *Journal of Sex Research, 25*, 478–499.

Baumeister, R. F. (1988b). Masochism as escape from self. *Journal of Sex Research, 25*, 28–59.

Baumeister, R. F. (2000). Gender differences in erotic plasticity: The female sex drive as socially flexible and responsive. *Psychological Bulletin, 126*(3), 347–374.

Baumeister, R. F., & Catanese, K. (2001). Victims and perpetrators provide discrepant accounts: Motivated cognitive distortions about interpersonal transgressions. In Joseph P. Forgas et al. (Eds.), *The social mind: Cognitive and motivational aspects of interpersonal behavior* (pp. 274–293). New York: Cambridge University Press.

Baumeister, R. F., Catanese, K. R., & Vohs, K. D. (2001). Is there a gender difference in strength of sex drive? Theoretical views, conceptual distinctions, and a review of relevant evidence. *Personality & Social Psychology Review, 5*(3), 242–273.

Baumeister, R. F., Catanese, K. R., & Wallace, H. M. (2002). Conquest by force: A narcissistic reactance theory of rape and sexual coercion. *Review of General Psychology, 6*(1), 92–135.

Baxter, D. J., Barbaree, H. E., & Marshall, W. L. (1986). Sexual responses to consenting and forced sex in a large sample of rapists and nonrapists. *Behaviour Research and Therapy, 17*, 215–222.

Bean, J. L. (2002). Expressions of female sexuality. *Journal of Sex & Marital Therapy, 28*(Suppl1), 29–38.

Becerra, L., Breiter, H. C., Wise, R., Gonzalez, R. G., & Borsook, D. (2001). Reward circuitry activation by noxious thermal stimuli. *Neuron, 32*(5), 927–946.

Beckstead, A. L. (2001). Cures versus choices: Agendas in sexual reorientation therapy. *Journal of Gay & Lesbian Psychotherapy, 5*(3–4), 87–115.

Begley, S., & Check, E. (2000, August 5). Sex and the single fly. *Newsweek*, 44–45.

Belgrave, F. Z., van Oss Marian, B., & Chambers, D. B. (2000). Cultural, contextual, and intrapersonal predictors of risky sexual attitudes among urban African American girls in early adolescence. *Cultural Diversity and Ethnic Minority Psychology, 6*(3), 309–322.

Bell, A. P., & Weinberg, M. S. (1978). *Homosexualities: A study of diversity among men and women.* New York: Simon & Schuster.

Bell, A. P., Weinberg, M. S., & Hammersmith, S. K. (1981). *Sexual preference: Its development in men and women.* Bloomington: University of Indiana Press.

Bellavia, G., & Murray, S. (2003). Did I do that? Self-esteem-related differences in reactions to romantic partner's mood. *Personal Relationships, 10*(1), 77–95.

Beller, M., & Gafni, N. (2000). Can item format (multiple choice vs. open-ended) account for gender differences in mathematics achievement? *Sex Roles, 42*(1–2), 1–21.

Bem, S. L. (1975). Sex role adaptability: One consequence of psychological androgyny. *Journal of Personality and Social Psychology, 31*, 634–643.

Bem, S. L. (1983). Gender schema theory and its implications for child development: Raising gender-aschematic children in a gender-schematic society. *Signs, 8*, 598–616.

Bem, S. L. (1993). *The lenses of gender.* New Haven, CT: Yale University Press.

Bem, S. L., Martyna, W., & Watson, C. (1976). Sex typing and androgyny: Further explorations of the expressive domain. *Journal of Personality and Social Psychology, 34*, 1016–1023.

Benotsch, E. G., & Kalichman, S. C. (2002). Preventing HIV and AIDS. In L A. Jason & D. S. Glenwick (Eds.), *Innovative strategies for promoting health and mental health across the life span* (pp. 205–226). New York: Springer.

Ben-Ze'ev, A. (2003). Privacy, emotional closeness, and openness in cyberspace. *Computers in Human Behavior, 19*(4), 451–467.

Ben-Zur, H. (2003). Peer risk behavior and denial of HIV/AIDS among adolescents. *Sex Education, 3*(1), 75–85.

Berenbaum, S. A., & Hines, M. (1992). Early androgens are related to childhood sex-typed toy preferences. *Psychological Science, 3*(3), 203–206.

Bergen, R. K. (1998). The reality of wife rape: Women's experiences of sexual violence in marriage. In Bergen, R. K. (Ed.), *Issues in intimate violence* (pp. 237–250). Thousand Oaks, CA: Sage.

Berger, L. (2000, June 25). A racial gap in infant deaths, and a search for reasons. *The New York Times,* p. WH13.

Berger, L. (2002, December 10). After long hiatus, new contraceptives emerge. *The New York Times.*

Berke, R. L. (1997, June 15). Suddenly, the new politics of morality. *The New York Times,* p. E3.

Berke, R. L. (1998, August 2). Chasing the polls on gay rights. *The New York Times,* p. WK3.

Berman, J. R., & Berman, L. A., et al. (2001). Effect of sildenafil on subjective and physiologic parameters of the female sexual response in women with sexual arousal disorder. *Journal of Sex & Marital Therapy, 27*(5), 411–420.

Berman, L. (2000). Paper presented to the annual meeting of the American Urological Association, Atlanta, Georgia. Cited in "Women, too, may benefit from Viagra." (2000, May 1). CNN.

Bernat, J. A., Wilson, A. E., & Calhoun, K. S. (1999). Sexual coercion history, calloused sexual beliefs and judgments of sexual coercion in a date rape analogue. *Violence and Victims, 14*(2), 147–160.

Bernstein, W. M., et al. (1983). Causal ambiguity and heterosexual affiliation. *Journal of Experimental Social Psychology, 19,* 78–92.

Berscheid, E. (2003). On stepping on land mines. In Sternberg, R. J. (Ed.), *Psychologists defying the crowd: Stories of those who battled the establishment and won* (pp. 33–44). Washington, DC: American Psychological Association.

Berscheid, E., & Reis, H. T. (1998). Attraction and close relationships. In Gilbert, D. T., Fiske, S. T. (Eds.), et al. *The handbook of social psychology, Vol. 2* (4th ed.). (pp. 193–281). New York: McGraw-Hill.

Berscheid, E., & Walster, E. (1978). *Interpersonal attraction.* Reading, MA: Addison-Wesley.

Bialy, M., & Sachs, B. D. (2002). Androgen implants in medial amygdala briefly maintain noncontact erection in castrated male rats. *Hormones & Behavior, 42*(3), 345–355.

Bianchi, S. M., & Spain, D. (1997). *Women, work and family in America.* Population Reference Bureau.

Billy, J. O. G., et al. (1993). The sexual behavior of men in the United States. *Family Planning Perspectives, 25,* 52–60.

Birkhead, T. R. (2000). *Promiscuity: An evolutionary history of sperm competition.* Cambridge, MA: Harvard University Press.

Bjorklund, D. F., & Kipp, K. (1996). Parental investment theory and gender differences in the evolution of inhibition mechanisms. *Psychological Bulletin, 120,* 163–188.

Blake, S. M., et al. (2003). Condom availability programs in Massachusetts high schools: Relationships with condom use and sexual behavior. *American Journal of Public Health, 93,* 955–962.

Blanchard, R. (1988). Nonhomosexual gender dysphoria. *Journal of Sex Research, 24,* 188–193.

Blanchard, R. (1989). The concept of autogynephilia and the typology of male gender dysphoria. *Journal of Nervous & Mental Disease, 177*(10), 616–623.

Blanchard, R., & Hucker, S. J. (1991). Age, transvestism, bondage, and concurrent paraphilic activities in 117 fatal cases of autoerotic asphyxia. *British Journal of Psychiatry, 159,* 371 377.

Blanchard, R., Steiner, B. W., & Clemmensen, L. H. (1985). Gender dysphoria, gender reorientation, and the clinical management of transsexualism. *Journal of Consulting and Clinical Psychology, 53,* 295–304.

Blanker, M. H., et al. (2001). Erectile and ejaculatory dysfunction in a community-based sample of men 50 to 78 years old: Prevalence, concern, and relation to sexual activity. *Urology, 57*(4), 763–768.

Blickstein, I., Goldman, R. D., & Mazkereth, R. (2000). Risk for one or two very low-birth-weight twins: A population study. *Obstetrics & Gynecology, 96*(3), 400–402.

Blumstein, P., & Schwartz, P. (1990). Intimate relationships and the creation of sexuality. In D. P. McWhirter, S. A. Sanders, & J. M. Reinisch (Eds.), *Homosexuality/heterosexuality: Concepts of sexual orientation* (pp. 307–320). New York: Oxford University Press.

Boss, S., & Maltz, W. (2001). *Private thoughts: Exploring the power of women's sexual fantasies.* New York: New World Library.

Boston Women's Health Book Collective. (1992). *The New Our Bodies, Ourselves.* New York: Simon & Schuster.

Bowlby, J. (1969). *Attachment and loss,* Vol. 1. New York: Basic Books.

Boxer, S. (2000, July 22). Truth or lies? In sex surveys, you never know. *The New York Times* online.

Bradbard, M. R., & Endsley, R. C. (1983). The effects of sex typed labeling on preschool children's information-seeking and retention. *Sex Roles, 9,* 247–261.

Bradford, J. M. W. (1998). Treatment of men with paraphilia. *New England Journal of Medicine, 338,* 464–465.

Bradford, J. M. W. (2001). The neurobiology, neuropharmacology, and pharmacological treatment of the paraphilias and compulsive sexual behaviour. *Canadian Journal of Psychiatry, 46*(1), 26–34.

Bradley, S. J., Oliver, G. D., Chernick, A. B., & Zucker, K. J. (1998). Experiment of nurture: Ablatio penis at 2 months, sex reassignment at 7 months, and a psychosexual follow-up in young adulthood. *Pediatrics* online, *102*(1), p. e9.

Braithwaite, D. O., Olson, L. N., Golish, T. D., Soukup, C., & Turman, P. (2001). "Becoming a family": Developmental processes represented in blended family discourse. *Journal of Applied Communication Research, 29*(3), 221–247.

Brecher, E. M., and the Editors of Consumer Reports Books. (1984). *Love, sex, and aging.* Boston: Little, Brown.

Bremner, J. D., et al. (2003). Assessment of the hypothalamic-pituitary-adrenal axis over a 24-hour diurnal period and in response to neuroendocrine challenges in women with and without childhood sexual abuse and posttraumatic stress disorder. *Biological Psychiatry, 54*(7), 710–718.

Breslow, N. (1989). Sources of confusion in the study and treatment of sadomasochism. *Journal of Social Behavior and Personality, 4,* 263–274.

Breslow, N., Evans, L., & Langley, J. (1985). On the prevalence and roles of females in the sadomasochistic subculture: Report on an empirical study. *Archives of Sexual Behavior, 14,* 303–317.

Breslow, N., Evans, L., & Langley, J. (1986). Comparisons among heterosexual, bisexual and homosexual male sadomasochists. *Journal of Homosexuality, 13,* 83–107.

Bretschneider, J., & McCoy, N. (1988). Sexual interest and behavior in healthy 80- to 102-year-olds. *Archives of Sexual Behavior, 17,* 109.

Briere, J., & Runtz, M. (1989). University males' sexual interest in children: Predicting potential indices of "pedophilia" in a nonforensic sample. *Child Abuse and Neglect, 13,* 65–75.

Broder, J. M. (2003, November 20). Michael Jackson faces arrest on charges of child molesting. *The New York Times* online.

Broder, M. S., Kanouse, D. E., Mittman, B. S., & Bernstein, S. J. (2000). The appropriateness of recommendations for hysterectomy. *Obstetrics & Gynecology, 95,* 199–206.

Brody, J. E. (1992b, November 11). PMS is a worldwide phenomenon. *The New York Times,* p. C14.

Brody, J. E. (1998c). Sour note in the Viagra symphony. *The New York Times,* p. F7.

Brody, J. E. (2002a, January 1). What women must know about fertility. *The New York Times,* p. F6.

Bronner, E. (1998, February 1). Just say maybe. No sexology, please. We're Americans. *The New York Times,* p. WK6.

Brooks-Gunn, J., & Furstenberg, F. F. (1989). Adolescent sexual behavior. *American Psychologist, 44,* 249–257.

Broude, G. J., & Greene, S. J. (1976). Cross-cultural codes on twenty sexual attitudes and practices. *Ethnology, 15,* 409–429.

Brown, M., Perry, A., Cheesman, A. D., & Pring, T. (2000). Pitch change in male-to-female transsexuals: Has phonosurgery a role to play? *International Journal of Language & Communication Disorders, 35*(1), 129–136.

Brown, R. A. (1994). Romantic love and the spouse selection criteria of male and female Korean college students. *The Journal of Social Psychology, 134*(2), 183–189.

Brown, T. (2002). A proposed model of bisexual identity development that elaborates on experiential differences of women and men. *Journal of Bisexuality, 2*(4), 67–91.

Browning, C. R. (2002). Trauma or transition: A life-course perspective on the link between childhood sexual experiences and men's adult well-being. *Social Science Research, 31*(4), 473–510.

Browning, J. R., Hatfield, E., Kessler, D., & Levine, T. (2000). Sexual motives, gender, and sexual behavior. *Archives of Sexual Behavior, 29*(2), 135–153.

Bruene, M., & Ribbert, H. (2002). Grundsaetzliches zur Konzeption einer evolutionaeren Psychiatrie. *Schweizer Archiv für Neurologie und Psychiatrie, 153*(1), 4–11.

Buunk, B. P., et al. (2002). Age and gender differences in mate selection criteria for various involvement levels. *Personal Relationships, 9*(3), 271–278.

Bullough, V. L. (2002). Masturbation: A historical overview. *Journal of Psychology & Human Sexuality, 14*(2–3), 17–33.

Bullough, V. L., & Weinberg, T. S. (1989). Women married to transvestites: Problems and adjustments. *Journal of Psychology & Human Sexuality, 1,* 83–104.

Burt, M. R. (1980). Cultural myths and supports for rape. *Journal of Personality and Social Psychology, 38,* 217–230.

Bushman, B. J., Bonacci, A. M., van Dijk, M., & Baumeister, R. F. (2003). Narcissism, sexual refusal, and aggression: Testing a narcissistic reactance model of sexual coercion. *Journal of Personality & Social Psychology, 84*(5), 1027–1040.

Buss, D. M. (1994). *The evolution of desire: Strategies of human mating.* New York: Basic Books.

Buss, D. M. (2003). The dangerous passion: Why jealousy is as necessary as love and sex. *Archives of Sexual Behavior, 32*(1), 79–80.

Buss, D. M., & Schmitt, D. P. (1993). Sexual strategies theory: An evolutionary perspective on human mating. *Psychological Review, 100,* 204–232.

Buve, A. (2000). Cited in Altman, L. K. (2000, July 11). Mystery factor is pondered at AIDS talk: Circumcision. *The New York Times* online.

Byers, E. S., & Grenier, G. (2003). Premature or rapid ejaculation: Heterosexual couples' perceptions of men's ejaculatory behavior. *Archives of Sexual Behavior, 32*(3), 261–270.

Byers, E. S., & Lewis, K. (1988). Dating couples' disagreements over the desired level of sexual intimacy. *Journal of Sex Research, 24,* 15–29.

Byrd, J., Hyde, J. S., DeLamater, J. D., & Plant, E. A. (1998). Sexuality during pregnancy and the year postpartum. *Journal of Family Practice, 47*(4), 305–308.

Caceres, C. F., & van Griensven, G. J. P. (1994). Male homosexual transmission of HIV-1. *AIDS, 8*(8), 1051–1061.

Cacioppo, J. T., Hawkley, L. C., & Bernston, G. G. (2003). The anatomy of loneliness. *Current Directions in Psychological Science, 12*(3), 71–74.

Cado, S., & Leitenberg, H. (1990). Guilt reactions to sexual fantasies during intercourse. *Archives of Sexual Behavior, 19,* 49–64.

Calderone, M. S., & Johnson, E. W. (1989). *Family book about sexuality* (rev. ed.). New York: Harper & Row.

Calhoun, K. S., & Atkeson, B. M. (1991). *Treatment of rape victims: Facilitating social adjustment.* New York: Pergamon Press.

Call, V., Sprecher, S., & Schwartz, P. (1995). The incidence and frequency of marital sex in a national sample. *Journal of Marriage and the Family, 57,* 639–652.

Calle, E. E., Rodriguez, C., Walker-Thurmond, K., & Thun, M. J. (2003). Overweight, obesity, and mortality from cancer in a prospectively studied cohort of U.S. adults. *New England Journal of Medicine, 348,* 1625–1638.

Cameron, P., et al. (1986). Child molestation and homosexuality. *Psychological Reports, 58,* 327–337.

Campbell, W. K., Foster, C. A., & Finkel, E. J. (2002). Does self-love lead to love for others? A story of narcissistic game playing. *Journal of Personality & Social Psychology, 83*(2), 340–354.

Cappella, J. N., & Palmer, M. T. (1990). Attitude similarity, relational history, and attraction: The mediating effects of kinesic and vocal behaviors. *Communication Monographs, 5,* 161–183.

Carlson, M. (1990, July 9). Abortion's hardest cases. *Time,* pp. 22–26.

Carrère, S., Buehlman, K. T., Gottman, J. M., Coan, J. A., & Ruckstuhl, L. (2000). Predicting marital stability and divorce in newlywed couples. *Journal of Family Psychology, 14*(1), 42–58.

Castellsague, X., et al. (2002). Male circumcision, penile human papillomavirus infection, and cervical cancer in female partners. *New England Journal of Medicine, 346*(15), 1105–1112.

Castro, J. (1992, January 20). Sexual harassment: A guide. *Time,* p. 37.

Cates, W., Jr., & Raymond, E. G. (1998). Vaginal spermicides. In R. A. Hatcher et al. *Contraceptive technology* (17th rev. ed.) (pp. 357–370). New York: Ardent Media.

CDC (See Centers for Disease Control and Prevention).

Celis, W. (1991, January 2). Students trying to draw line between sex and an assault. *The New York Times,* pp. 1, B8.

Census: Americans marry later in life. (2001, June 29). The Associated Press.

Centers for Disease Control and Prevention. (2000a). Alcohol policy and sexually transmitted disease rates—United States, 1981–1995. *Morbidity and Mortality Weekly Report, 49,* 346–349.

Centers for Disease Control and Prevention. (2000b). *HIV/AIDS surveillance report: U.S. HIV and AIDS cases reported through December 1999, 11*(2).

Centers for Disease Control and Prevention. (2000c, June 23). Contribution of assisted reproductive technology and ovulation-inducing drugs to triplet and higher-order multiple births—United States, 1980–1997. *Morbidity and Mortality Weekly Report, 49,* 535–538.

Centers for Disease Control and Prevention. (2000d, June 23). Trends in gonorrhea rates—Selected states and United States, 1998. *Morbidity and Mortality Weekly Report.*

Centers for Disease Control and Prevention. (2000e, June 9). Youth risk behavior surveillance—United States, 1999. *Morbidity and Mortality Weekly Report, 49*(SS05), 1–96.

Centers for Disease Control and Prevention. (2000f). National and state-specific pregnancy rates among adolescents—United States, 1995–1997. *Morbidity and Mortality Weekly Report, 49*(27).

Centers for Disease Control and Prevention. (2000g). Abortion surveillance: Preliminary analysis—United States, 1997. *Morbidity and Mortality Weekly Report, 48,* 1171–1174, 1191.

Centers for Disease Control and Prevention. (2000h, June 9). Youth risk behavior surveillance—United States, 1999. *Morbidity and Mortality Weekly Report, 49*(SS05), 1–96.

Centers for Disease Control and Prevention. (2001a, May 12). Table III. Provisional cases of selected notifiable diseases preventable by vaccination, United States week ending May 12, 2001. *Morbidity and Mortality Weekly Report* Tables (Morbidity).

Centers for Disease Control and Prevention (2001b, June). Genital herpes. National Center for HIV, STD and TB Prevention. Division of Sexually Transmitted Diseases. *http://www. cdc.gov/nchstp/dstd/Fact_Sheets/facts_Genital_ Herpes.htm*

Centers for Disease Control and Prevention (2002a). Laboratory guidelines screening tests to detect *Chlamydia trachomatis* and *Neisseria gonorrhoeae* infections. National Center for HIV, STD and TB Prevention. Division of Sexually Transmitted Diseases. *http://www.cdc. gov/STD/LabGuidelines/default.htm*

Centers for Disease Control and Prevention (2002b). Oral alternatives to cefixime for the treatment of uncomplicated *Neisseria gonorrhoeae* urogenital infections. National Center for HIV, STD and TB Prevention. Division of Sexually Transmitted Diseases. *http://www. cdc.gov/STD/treatment/Cefixime.htm*

Centers for Disease Control and Prevention. (2003). *HIV/AIDS surveillance report: U.S. HIV and AIDS cases reported through December 2002, 14*(2).

Chakrabarti, N., Chopra, V. K., & Sinha, V. K. (2002). Masturbatory guilt leading to severe depression and erectile dysfunction. *Journal of Sex & Marital Therapy, 28*(4), 285–288.

Chambers, C. (2000, October 13). Americans are overwhelmingly happy and optimistic about the future of the U.S. Marital status strongly affects both happiness and optimism. Princeton, NJ: Gallup News Service.

Chan, C. (1992). Cultural considerations in counseling Asian American lesbians and gay men. In S. Dworkin & F. Gutierrez (Eds.), *Counseling gay men and lesbians: Journey to the end of the rainbow.* Alexandria, VA: American Association for Counseling and Development.

Chance, S. E., Brown, R. T., Dabbs, J. M., Jr., & Casey, R. (2000). Testosterone, intelligence and behavior disorders in young boys. *Personality & Individual Differences, 28*(3) 437–445.

Chao, Q., Wang, P., & He, N. (2001). Comparative research on self-concept of middle school students from complete and divorced families. *Chinese Journal of Clinical Psychology, 9*(2), 143.

Charny, I. W., & Parnass, S. (1995). The impact of extramarital relationships on the continuation of marriages. *Journal of Sex and Marital Therapy, 21,* 100–115.

Chavez, M. L., & Spitzer, M. F. (2002). Herbals and other dietary supplements for premenstrual syndrome and menopause. *Psychiatric Annals, 32*(1), 61–71.

Cheating going out of style but sex is popular as ever. (1993, October 19). *Newsday,* p. 2.

Check, J. V. P., & Malamuth, N. M. (1983). Sex-role stereotyping and reactions to depictions of stranger versus acquaintance rape. *Journal of Personality and Social Psychology, 45,* 344–356.

Cheng, H., & Furnham, A. (2002). Personality, peer relations, and self-confidence as predictors of happiness and loneliness. *Journal of Adolescence, 25*(3), 327–339.

China develops electronic contraceptive for men. (1998, March 15). Reuters News Agency online.

Chlebowski, R. T. (2000). Primary care: Reducing the risk of breast cancer. *The New England Journal of Medicine* online, *343*(3).

Chlebowski, R. T., et al. (2003). Influence of estrogen plus progestin on breast cancer and mammography in healthy postmenopausal women: The Women's Health Initiative Randomized Trial. *Journal of the American Medical Association, 289,* 3243–3253.

Christin-Maitre, S., Bouchard, P., & Spitz, I. M. (2000). Drug therapy: Medical termination of pregnancy. *The New England Journal of Medicine* online, *342*(13).

Clark, M. S., Mills, J. R., & Corcoran, D. M. (1989). Keeping track of needs and inputs of friends and strangers. *Personality and Social Psychology Bulletin, 15,* 533–542.

Clemons, M., & Goss, P. (2001). Mechanisms of disease: Estrogen and the risk of breast cancer. *New England Journal of Medicine, 344,* 276–285.

Cnattingius, S., Bergstrom, R., Lipworth, L., & Kramer, M. S. (1998). Prepregnancy weight and the risk of adverse pregnancy outcomes. *New England Journal of Medicine, 338,* 147–152.

Cochran, S. D., Sullivan, J. G., & Mays, V. M. (2003). Prevalence of mental disorders, psychological distress, and mental health services use among lesbian, gay, and bisexual adults in the United States. *Journal of Consulting and Clinical Psychology, 71*(1), 53–61.

Cohen, A. B., & Tannenbaum, I. J. (2001). Lesbian and bisexual women's judgments of the attractiveness of different body types. *Journal of Sex Research, 38*(3), 226–232.

Cohen, F. (1998, March 26). Study: "Male pill" proves 95% effective. CNN.

Cohen, E., & Feig, C. (2003, July 22). Delivery debate: Vaginal or C-section? More women are selecting surgery without a medical reason. CNN.

Cohen, M. S. (2000). Preventing sexual transmission of HIV: New ideas from sub-Saharan Africa. *The New England Journal of Medicine, 342*(13), 970–973.

Colapinto, J. (2000). *As nature made him: The boy who was raised as a girl.* New York: HarperCollins.

Colditz, G. A., et al. (1993). Family history, age, and risk of breast cancer: Prospective data from the nurses' health study. *Journal of the American Medical Association, 270,* 338–343.

Cole, C. J. (1995, August). Cited in "Sex, the single lizard, and the missing parent." *National Geographic.*

Cole, C. L., & Cole, A. L. (1999). Marriage enrichment and prevention really works: Interpersonal competence training to maintain and enhance relationships. *Family Relations: Interdisciplinary Journal of Applied Family Studies, 48*(3), 273–275.

Cole, F. S. (2000). Extremely preterm birth—Defining the limits of hope. *The New England Journal of Medicine* online, *343*(6).

Cole, S. S. (1988). Women's sexuality, and disabilities. *Women and Therapy, 7,* 277–294.

Coleman, E. (1989). The development of male prostitution activity among gay and bisexual adolescents [Special Issue: Gay and lesbian youth]. *Journal of Homosexuality, 17,* 131–149.

Coleman, E. (2002). Masturbation as a means of achieving sexual health. *Journal of Psychology & Human Sexuality, 14*(2–3), 5–16.

Coles, R., & Stokes, G. (1985). *Sex and the American teenager.* New York: Harper & Row.

Coley, Rebekah Levine, & Chase-Lansdale, P. Lindsay (1998). Adolescent pregnancy and parenthood: Recent evidence and future directions. *American Psychologist.* Feb *53*(2) 152–166.

Collaer, M. L., & Hines, M. (1995). Human behavioral sex differences: A role for gonadal hormones during early development? *Psychological Bulletin, 118,* 55–107.

Collaer, M. L., & Nelson, J. D. (2002). Large visuospatial sex difference in line judgment: Possible role of attentional factors. *Brain & Cognition, 49*(1), 1–12.

Collins, N. L., & Miller, L. C. (1994). Self-disclosure and liking: A meta-analytic review. *Psychological Bulletin, 116,* 457–475.

Condon, J. W., & Crano, W. D. (1988). Inferred evaluation and the relation between attitude similarity and interpersonal attraction. *Journal of Personality and Social Psychology, 54,* 789–797.

Connor, E. M., et al. (1994). Reduction of maternal–infant transmission of human immunodeficiency virus type 1 with zidovudine treatment. *New England Journal of Medicine, 331,* 1173–1180.

Constantine, L., & Constantine, J. (1973). *Group marriage.* New York: Macmillan.

Cooke, B. M., Breedlove, S. M., & Jordan, C. L. (2003). Both estrogen receptors and androgen receptors contribute to testosterone-induced changes in the morphology of the medial amygdala and sexual arousal in male rats. *Hormones & Behavior, 43*(2), 336–346.

Cooper, A., Delmonico, D. L., & Burg, R. (2000). Cybersex users, abusers, and compulsives: New findings and implications. *Sexual Addiction & Compulsivity, 7*(1–2), 5–29.

Cooper, A., Scherer, C. R., Boies, S. C., & Gordon, B. L. (1999). Sexuality on the Internet: From sexual exploration to pathological expression. *Professional Psychology: Research & Practice, 30*(2), 154–164.

Cooper, A. J., et al. (1990). A female sex offender with multiple paraphilias: A psychologic, physiologic (laboratory sexual arousal) and endocrine case study. *Canadian Journal of Psychiatry, 35,* 334–337.

Cooper, M. L. (2002). Alcohol use and risky sexual behavior among college students and youth: Evaluating the evidence. *Journal of Studies on Alcohol,* Suppl14, 101–117.

Cory, G. A. (2002). MacLean's evolutionary neuroscience, the CSN model and Hamilton's rule: Some developmental, clinical, and social policy implications. *Brain & Mind, 3*(1), 151–181.

Cosgray, R. E., et al. (1991). Death from autoerotic asphyxiation in a long-term psychiatric setting. *Perspectives in Psychiatric Care, 27,* 21–24.

Cotten-Huston, A. L., & Waite, B. M. (2000). Anti-homosexual attitudes in college students: Predictors and classroom interventions. *Journal of Homosexuality, 38*(3), 117–133.

Court, 9–0, makes sex harassment easier to prove. (1993, November 10). *The New York Times,* pp. A1, A22.

Courtenay, W. H. (2000). Engendering health: A social constructionist examination of men's health beliefs and behaviors. *Psychology of Men & Masculinity, 1*(1), 4–15.

Coutinho, E. M., & Segal, S. J. (2003). *Is menstruation obsolete?: How suppressing menstruation can help women who suffer from anemia, endometriosis, or PMS.* New York: Oxford University Press.

Cowley, G., & Rogers, A. (1997, November 17). Rebuilding the male machine. *Newsweek,* pp. 66–67.

Cox, B., Sneyd, M. J., Paul, C., Delahunt, B., & Skegg, D. C. G. (2002). Vasectomy and risk of prostate cancer. *Journal of the American Medical Association, 287,* 3110–3115.

Cox, C. L., Wexler, M. O., Rusbult, C. E., & Gaines, S. O., Jr. (1997). Prescriptive support and commitment processes in close relationships. *Social Psychology Quarterly, 60*(1), 79–90.

Cox, D. J. (1988). Incidence and nature of male genital exposure behavior as reported by college women. *Journal of Sex Research, 24,* 227–234.

Cramer, D., et al. (1998, January). *The Lancet.* Cited in Associated Press (1998, January 9). Painkiller may lower cancer risk. America Online.

Crews, D. (1994). Animal sexuality. *Scientific American, 270*(1), 108–114.

Cronin, A. (1993, June 27). Two viewfinders, two views of Gay America. *The New York Times,* Section 4, p. 10.

Crossette, B. (2000, August 29). Researchers raise fresh issues in breast-feeding debate. *The New York Times* online.

Crowne, D. P., & Marlowe, D. A. (1960). A new scale of social desirability independent of pathology. *Journal of Consulting Psychology, 24,* 351.

Cummings, S. R., et al. (1999). The effect of raloxifene on risk of breast cancer in postmenopausal women: Results from the MORE randomized trial. *Journal of the American Medical Association, 281,* 2189–2197.

Cunningham, G., Cordero, E., & Thornby, J. (1989). Testosterone replacement with transdermal therapeutic systems. *Journal of the American Medical Association, 261,* 2525–2531.

Cunningham, M. R., et al. (1995). "Their ideas of beauty are, on the whole, the same as ours": Consistency and variability in the cross-cultural perception of female physical attractiveness. *Journal of Personality and Social Psychology, 68*(2), 261–279.

Curnoe, S., & Langevin, R. (2002). Personality and deviant sexual fantasies: An examination of the MMPIs. *Journal of Clinical Psychology, 58*(7), 803–815.

Curtis, R. C., & Miller, K. (1986). Believing another likes or dislikes you: Behavior making the beliefs come true. *Journal of Personality and Social Psychology, 51,* 284–290.

Cutler, W. B. (1999). Human sex-attractant hormones: Discovery, research, development, and application in sex therapy. *Psychiatric Annals, 29*(1), 54–59.

Cutler, W. B., Friedmann, E., & McCoy, N. L. (1998). Pheromonal influences on sociosexual behavior in men. *Archives of Sexual Behavior, 27*(1), 1–13.

Dabbs, J. M., Jr., Chang, E-L., Strong, R. A., & Milun, R. (1998). Spatial ability, navigation strategy, and geographic knowledge among men and women. *Evolution & Human Behavior, 19*(2), 89–98.

Dabbs, J. M., Jr., Hargrove, M. F., & Heusel, C. (1996). Testosterone differences among college fraternities: Well-behaved vs rambunctious. *Personality & Individual Differences, 20*(2), 157–161.

Dabbs, J. M., Jr., & Morris, R. (1990). Testosterone,

social class, and antisocial behavior in a sample of 4,462 men. *Psychological Science, 1,* 1–3.

Dalla, R. L. (2003). When the bough breaks . . . : Examining intergenerational parent–child relational patterns among street-level sex workers and their parents and children. *Applied Developmental Science, 7*(4), 216–228.

Daly, M., & Wilson, M. (1998). Cited in Brody, J. E. (1998, February 10). Genetic ties may be factor in violence in stepfamilies. *The New York Times,* pp. F1, F4.

Damon, W. (2002). Dominance, sexism, and inadequacy: Testing a compensatory conceptualization in a sample of heterosexual men involved in SM. *Journal of Psychology & Human Sexuality, 14*(4), 25–45.

Dantzker, M. L., & Eisenman, R. (2003). Sexual attitudes among Hispanic college students: Differences between males and females. *International Journal of Adolescence & Youth, 11*(1), 79–89.

Darling, C. A., & Davidson, J. K., Sr. (1986). Coitally active university students: Sexual behaviors, concerns, and challenges. *Adolescence, 21,* 403–419.

Darling, C. A., Davidson, J. K., & Jennings, D. A. (1991). The female sexual response revisited: Understanding the multiorgasmic experience in women. *Archives of Sexual Behavior, 20,* 527–540.

Darling, C. A., Davidson, J. K., & Passarello, L. C. (1992). The mystique of first intercourse among college youth: The role of partners, contraceptive practices, and psychological reactions. *Journal of Youth and Adolescence, 21,* 97–117.

D'Augelli, A. R. (1992a). Lesbian and gay male undergraduates' experiences of harassment and fear on campus. *Journal of Interpersonal Violence, 7,* 383–395.

Davidson, J. K., & Hoffman, L. E. (1986). Sexual fantasies and sexual satisfaction: An empirical analysis of erotic thought. *Journal of Sex Research, 22*(2), 184–205.

Davis, D., Shaver, P. R., & Vernon, M. L. (2003). Physical, emotional, and behavioral reactions to breaking up: The roles of gender, age, emotional involvement, and attachment style. *Personality & Social Psychology Bulletin, 29*(7), 871–884.

Davis, K. E., Frieze, I. H., & Maiuro, R. D. (Eds.). (2002). *Stalking: Perspectives on victims and perpetrators.* (pp. 212–236). New York: Springer.

Davis, S. (2000). Testosterone and sexual desire in women. *Journal of Sex Education & Therapy, 25*(1), 25–32.

Davis, T. L., & Liddell, D. L. (2002). Getting inside the house: The effectiveness of a rape prevention program for college fraternity men. *Journal of College Student Development, 43*(1), 35–50.

Davison, G. C. (1977). Elimination of a sadistic fantasy by a client-controlled countercontitioning technique. In J. Fischer & H. Gochios (Eds.), *Handbook of behavior therapy with sexual problems.* New York: Pergamon Press.

Dawes, R. M. (1989). Statistical criteria for establishing a truly false consensus effect. *Journal of Experimental Social Psychology, 25,* 1–17.

Dawn, M., et al. (2000). Risk of breast cancer with oral contraceptive use in women with a family history of breast cancer. *Journal of the American Medical Association, 284,* 1791–1798.

Dawood, K., Pillard, R. C., Horvath, C., Revelle,

W., & Bailey, J. M. (2000). Familial aspects of male homosexuality. *Archives of Sexual Behavior, 29*(2), 155–163.

Day, N. L., & Richardson, G. A. (1994). Comparative teratogenicity of alcohol and other drugs. *Alcohol Health and Research World, 18*(1), 42–48.

Dean, C. W., & de Bruyn-Kops, E. (1982). The crime and consequences of rape. Springfield, IL: Charles C Thomas.

Dekker, A., & Schmidt, G. (2002). Patterns of masturbatory behaviour: Changes between the sixties and the nineties. *Journal of Psychology & Human Sexuality, 14*(2–3), 35–48.

Dekker, J. (1993). Inhibited male orgasm. In W. O'Donohue & J. H. Geer (Eds.), *Handbook of sexual dysfunctions: Assessment and treatment* (pp. 279–301). Boston: Allyn & Bacon.

Delgado, J. (1969). *Physical control of the mind.* New York: Harper & Row.

Demmer, C. (2002). Impact of improved treatments on perceptions about HIV and safer sex among inner-city HIV-infected men and women. *Journal of Community Health: The Publication for Health Promotion & Disease Prevention, 27*(1), 63–73.

Dennerstein, L., Dudley, E. C., Hopper, J. L., Guthrie, J. R., & Burger, H. G. (2000). A prospective population-based study of menopausal symptoms. *Obstetrics & Gynecology, 96*(3), 351–358.

Denny, N., Field, J., & Quadagno, D. (1984). Sex differences in sexual needs and desires. *Archives of Sexual Behavior, 13,* 233–245.

den Tonkelaar, I., & Oddens, B. J. (2000). Determinants of long-term hormone replacement therapy and reasons for early discontinuation. *Obstetrics & Gynecology, 95*(4), 507–512.

de Raad, B., & Doddema-Winsemius, M. (1992). Factors in the assortment of human mates: Differential preferences in Germany and the Netherlands. *Personality and Individual Differences, 13,* 103–114.

Derby, C. A. (2000, October 2). Cited in Study finds exercise reduces the risk of impotence. The Associated Press.

de Schampheleire, D. (1990). MMPI characteristics of professional prostitutes: A cross-cultural replication. *Journal of Personality Assessment, 54,* 343–350.

Desmond, A. M. (1994). Adolescent pregnancy in the United States: Not a minority issue. *Health Care for Women International, 15*(4), 325–331.

DeSteno, D., Bartlett, M. Y., Braverman, J., & Salovey, P. (2002). Sex differences in jealousy: Evolutionary mechanism or artifact of measurement? *Journal of Personality & Social Psychology, 83*(5), 1103–1116.

DeWitt, K. (1991, October). The evolving concept of sexual harassment. *The New York Times.*

Diamond, L. M. (2000). Sexual identity, attractions, and behavior among young sexual-minority women over a 2-year period. *Developmental Psychology, 36*(2), 241–250.

Diamond, L. M. (2002). "Having a girlfriend without knowing it": Intimate friendships among adolescent sexual-minority women. *Journal of Lesbian Studies, 6*(1), 5–16.

Diamond, L. M. (2003a). What does sexual orientation orient? A biobehavioral model distinguishing romantic love and sexual desire. *Psychological Review, 110*(1), 173–192.

Diamond, L. M. (2003b). Was it a phase? Young women's relinquishment of lesbian/bisexual identities over a 5-year period. *Journal of Personality and Social Psychology, 84*(2), 352–364.

Diamond, M. (1993). Homosexuality and bisexuality in different populations. *Archives of Sexual Behavior, 22,* 291–310.

Diamond, M. (1996). Prenatal predisposition and the clinical management of some pediatric conditions. *Journal of Sex & Marital Therapy, 22*(3), 139–147.

Dick-Read, G. (1944). *Childbirth without fear: The principles and practices of natural childbirth.* New York: Harper & Bros.

Dijkstra, P., & Buunk, B. P. (2002). Sex differences in the jealousy-evoking effect of rival characteristics. *European Journal of Social Psychology, 32*(6), 829–852.

Dilley, J. W., et al. (2003). Availability of combination therapy for HIV: Effects on sexual risk taking in a sample of high-risk gay and bisexual men. *AIDS Care, 15*(1), 27–37.

DiMatteo, M. R., et al. (1996). Cesarean childbirth and psychosocial outcomes: A meta-analysis. *Health Psychology, 15,* 303–314.

Dindia, K., & Allen, M. (1992). Sex differences in self-disclosure: A meta-analysis. *Psychological Bulletin, 112,* 106–124.

Dindia, K., & Timmerman, L. (2003). Accomplishing romantic relationships. In J. O. Greene & B. R. Burleson (Eds.), *Handbook of communication and social interaction skills* (pp. 685–721). Mahwah, NJ: Erlbaum.

Donnelly, D., & Fraser, J. (1998). Gender differences in sado-masochistic arousal among college students. *Sex Roles, 39*(5–6), 391–407.

Donner, F., & Babcock, D. F. (2003). Smelling the roses? *Science, 299,* 1993–1994.

Donnerstein, E. (1980). Aggressive erotica and violence against women. *Journal of Personality and Social Psychology, 39,* 269–277.

Donnerstein, E., & Berkowitz, L. (1981). Victim reactions in aggressive erotic films as a factor in violence against women. *Journal of Personality and Social Psychology, 41,* 710–724.

Donovan, C. (2000, May 30). Confronting teen pregnancy. *The Washington Post,* p. Z17.

Downs, M., & Nazario, B. (2003, February 11). Aphrodisiacs through the ages. WebMD Features.

Drew, W. L. (2000). Ganciclovir resistance: A matter of time and titre. *Lancet, 356,* 609–610.

Drews, C. D., et al. (1996, April). *Pediatrics.* Cited in "Smokers more likely to bear retarded babies, study says" (1996, April 10), *The New York Times,* p. B7.

Drigotas, S. M., Rusbult, C. E., & Verette, J. (1999). Level of commitment, mutuality of commitment, and couple well-being. *Personal Relationships, 6*(3), 389–409.

Driver, J., Tabares, A., Shapiro, A., Nahm, E. Y., & Gottman, J. M. (2003). Interactional patterns in marital success and failure: Gottman laboratory studies. In F. Walsh (Ed.), *Normal family processes: Growing diversity and complexity* (3rd ed.) (pp. 493–513). New York: Guilford Press.

Duenwald, M. (2002, July 16). Hormone therapy: One size, clearly, no longer fits all. *The New York Times.*

Duggirala, M. K., et al. (2003). A human papillomavirus type 16 vaccine. *New England Journal of Medicine, 348,* 1402–1405.

Dwyer, M. (1988). Exhibitionism/voyeurism.

Journal of Social Work and Human Sexuality, 7, 101–112.

Dye, M. L., & Davis, K. E. (2003). Stalking and psychological abuse: Common factors and relationship-specific characteristics. *Violence & Victims, 18*(2), 163–180.

Eason, E., & Feldman, P. (2000). Much ado about a little cut: Is episiotomy worthwhile? *Obstetrics & Gynecology, 95*(4), 616–618.

Eason, E., Labrecque, M., Wells, G., & Feldman, P. (2000). Preventing perineal trauma during childbirth: A systematic review. *Obstetrics & Gynecology, 95,* 464–471.

Eck, B. A. (2001). Nudity and framing: Classifying art, pornography, information, and ambiguity. *Sociological Forum, 16*(4), 603–632.

Edgley, C. (1989). Commercial sex: Pornography, prostitution, and advertising. In K. McKinney & S. Sprecher (Eds.), *Human sexuality: The societal and interpersonal context* (pp. 370–424). Norwood, NJ: Ablex.

Edser, S. J., & Shea, J. D. (2002). An exploratory investigation of bisexual men in monogamous, heterosexual marriages. *Journal of Bisexuality, 2*(4), 5–29.

Edwards, T. M. (2000, August 28). Single by choice. *Time Magazine* online, *156*(9).

Edwards, V. J., Holden, G. W., Felitti, V. J., & Anda, R. F. (2003). Relationship between multiple forms of childhood maltreatment and adult mental health in community respondents: Results from the Adverse Childhood Experiences study. *American Journal of Psychiatry, 160*(8), 1453–1460.

Eggers, D. (2000, May 7). Intimacies. *The New York Times Magazine,* pp. 76–77.

Ehrhardt, A. A. (1998). Cited in Bronner, E. (1998, February 1). Just say maybe. No sexology, please. We're Americans. *The New York Times,* p. WK6.

Eisenberg, M., & Wechsler, H. (2003). Substance use behaviors among college students with same-sex opposite-sex experience: Results from a national study. *Addictive Behaviors, 28*(5), 899–913.

El-Defrawi, M. H., Lotfy, G., Dandash, K. F., Refaat, A. H., & Eyada, M. (2001). Female genital mutilation and its psychosexual impact. *Journal of Sex & Marital Therapy, 27*(5), 465–473.

El-Gibaly, O., Ibrahim, B., Mensch, B. S., & Clark, W. H. (2002). The decline of female circumcision in Egypt: Evidence and interpretation. *Social Science & Medicine, 54*(2), 205–220.

Elle. (2003, June). The *Elle*/MSNBC.com Sex & Body Image Survey. *Elle,* pp. 110–113.

Ellertson, C. (2000). Nuisance or natural and healthy? Should monthly menstruation be optional for women? *The Lancet, 355,* 922.

Ellis, A. (1962). *Reason and emotion in psychotherapy.* New York: Lyle Stuart.

Ellis, A. (1977). The basic clinical theory of rational-emotive therapy. In A. Ellis & R. Grieger (Eds.), *Handbook of rational-emotive therapy.* New York: Springer.

Ellis, E. M. (2000). *Divorce wars: Interventions with families in conflict.* Washington, DC: American Psychological Association.

Ellis, L., & Ames, M. A. (1987). Neurohormonal functioning and sexual orientation: A theory of homosexuality-heterosexuality. *Psychological Bulletin, 101,* 233–258.

Erel, O., & Burman, B. (1995). Interrelatedness of marital relations and parent–child relations: A meta-analytic review. *Psychological Bulletin, 118,* 108–132.

Fagot, B. I., Rodgers, C. S., & Leinbach, M. D. (2000). Theories of gender socialization. In T. Eckes & H. M. Trautner (Eds.), *The developmental social psychology of gender* (pp. 65–89). Mahwah, NJ: Erlbaum.

Faller, K. C. (1989b). Why sexual abuse? An exploration of the intergenerational hypothesis. *Child Abuse and Neglect, 13,* 543–548.

Fallon, A. E., & Rozin, P. (1985). Sex differences in perceptions of desirable body shape. *Journal of Abnormal Psychology, 94,* 102–105.

Farley, M., Baral, I., & Sezgin, U. (1998). Prostitution in five countries: Violence and post-traumatic stress disorder. *Feminism & Psychology, 8*(4), 405–426.

FDA approves abortion pill. (2000, September 28). Associated Press online.

Feig, C. (2003, February 12). Experts fear HIV rates increasing in U.S. Boston: CNN.

Feingold, A. (1991). Sex differences in the effects of similarity and physical attractiveness on opposite-sex attraction. *Basic and Applied Social Psychology, 12,* 357–367.

Feingold, A. (1994). Gender differences in personality: A meta-analysis. *Psychological Bulletin, 116,* 429–456.

Feldman, H. A., Goldstein, I., Hatzichristou, D. G., Krane, R. J., & McKinlay, J. B. (1994). Impotence and its medical and psychosocial correlates: Results of the Massachusetts Male Aging Study. *Journal of Urology, 151*(1), 54–61.

Felson, R. B. (2002). *Violence and gender reexamined.* Washington, DC: American Psychological Association.

Fenichel, O. (1945). *The psychoanalytic theory of neurosis.* New York: Norton.

Fensterheim, H., & Kantor, J. S. (1980). Behavioral approach to sexual disorders. In B. Wolman & J. Money (Eds.), *Handbook of human sexuality.* Englewood Cliffs, NJ: Prentice-Hall.

Fergusson, D. M., Horwood, L. J., & Beautrais, A. L. (1999). Is sexual orientation related to mental health problems and suicidality in young people? *Archives of General Psychiatry, 56*(10), 876–880.

Ferraro, G. (2004). *Cultural anthropology: An applied perspective* (5th ed.). Belmont, CA: Wadsworth.

Fichner-Rathus, L. (2004). *Understanding art.* Belmont, CA: Wadsworth.

Filipas, H. H., & Ullman, S. E. (2001). Social reactions to sexual assault victims from various support sources. *Violence & Victims, 16*(6), 673–692.

Finkelhor, D. (1984). *Child sexual abuse: Theory and research.* New York: Free Press.

Finkelhor, D. (1990). Early and long-term effects of child sexual abuse: An update. *Professional Psychology: Research and Practice, 21,* 325–330.

Finkenauer, C., & Hazam, H. (2000). Disclosure and secrecy in marriage: Do both contribute to marital satisfaction? *Journal of Social & Personal Relationships, 17*(2), 245–263.

Finkenauer, C., & Meeus, W. (2000). How (pro-) social is the caring motive? *Psychological Inquiry, 11*(2), 100–103.

Finley, C. (2003). Cited in Downs, M., & Nazario, B. (2003, February 11). Aphrodisiacs through the ages. WebMD Features.

Fish, L. S., Busby, D., & Killian, K. (1994). Structural couple therapy in the treatment of inhibited sexual drive. *American Journal of Family Therapy, 22*(2), 113–125.

Fisher, B. S., Daigle, L. E., Cullen, F. T., & Turner, M. G. (2003). Reporting sexual victimization to the police and others: Results from a national-level study of college women. *Criminal Justice & Behavior, 30*(1), 6–38.

Fisher, H. E. (2000). Brains do it: Lust, attraction and attachment. *Cerebrum, 2,* 23–42.

Fishman, J. R., & Mamo, L. (2001). What's in a disorder? A cultural analysis of medical and pharmaceutical constructions of male and female sexual dysfunction. *Women & Therapy, 24*(1–2), 179–193.

Fitzgerald, L. F. (1993a). *Sexual harassment in higher education: Concepts and issues.* Washington, DC: National Education Association.

Fitzgerald, L. F. (1993b). Sexual harassment: Violence against women in the workplace. *American Psychologist, 48,* 1070–1076.

Fitzgerald, L. F., et al. (1988). Academic harassment: Sex and denial in scholarly garb. *Psychology of Women Quarterly, 12,* 329–340.

Flaxman, S. M., & Sherman, P. W. (2000). Morning sickness: A mechanism for protecting mother and embryo. *The Quarterly Review of Biology, 75*(2), 113–148.

Fletcher, J. (1966). *Situation ethics.* Philadelphia: Westminster Press.

Fletcher, J. (1967). *Moral responsibility: Situation ethics at work.* Philadelphia: Westminster Press.

Fletcher, S. W., & Colditz, G. A. (2002). Failure of estrogen plus progestin therapy for prevention. *Journal of the American Medical Association* online, *288*(3).

Ford, C. S., & Beach, F. A. (1951). *Patterns of sexual behavior.* New York: Harper & Row.

Forgas, J. P., Levinger, G., & Moylan, S. J. (1994). Feeling good and feeling close: Affective influences on the perception of intimate relationships. *Personal Relationships, 1*(2), 165–184.

Franzoi, S. L., & Herzog, M. E. (1987). Judging physical attractiveness: What body aspects do we use? *Personality and Social Psychology Bulletin, 13,* 19–33.

Fraser, A. M., Brockert, J. E., & Ward, R. H. (1995). Association of young maternal age with adverse reproductive outcomes. *New England Journal of Medicine, 332,* 1113–1117.

Frayser, S. (1985). *Varieties of sexual experience: An anthropological perspective on human sexuality.* New Haven, CT: Human Relations Area Files Press.

Fredricks, J. A., & Eccles, J. S. (2002). Children's competence and value beliefs from childhood through adolescence: Growth trajectories in two male-sex-typed domains. *Developmental Psychology, 38*(4), 519–533.

Freiberg, P. (1995). Psychologists examine attacks on homosexuals. *APA Monitor, 26*(6), 30–31.

Freud, S. (1922/1959). Analysis of a phobia in a 5-year-old boy. In A. & J. Strachey (Ed. & Trans.), *Collected papers* (Vol. 3). New York: Basic Books. (Original work published 1909.)

Freund, K., & Blanchard, R. (1986). The concept of courtship disorder. *Journal of Sex and Marital Therapy, 12,* 79–92.

Freund, K., Watson, R., & Rienzo, D. (1988). The value of self-reports in the study of voyeurism and exhibitionism. *Annals of Sex Research, 1,* 243–262.

Frey, K. S., & Ruble, D. N. (1992). Gender constancy and the "cost" of sex-typed behavior:

A test of the conflict hypothesis. *Developmental Psychology, 28,* 714–721.

Friday, N. (1973). *My secret garden.* New York: Trident.

Fried, P. A., & Smith, A. M. (2001). A literature review of the consequences of prenatal marihuana exposure: An emerging theme of a deficiency in aspects of executive function. *Neurotoxicology & Teratology, 23*(1), 1–11.

Friedman, D. (2001). *A mind of its own: A cultural history of the penis.* New York: Free Press.

Friedman, R. C., & Downey, J. I. (1994). Homosexuality. *New England Journal of Medicine, 331,* 923–930.

Friedman, R. C., & Downey, J. I. (2001). The Oedipus complex and male homosexuality. In Peter Hartocollis (Ed.), *Mankind's Oedipal destiny: Libidinal and aggressive aspects of sexuality* (pp. 113–138). Madison, CT: International Universities Press.

Friedrich, W. N. (1998). Cited in Gilbert, S. (1998). "New light shed on normal sexual behavior in a child." *The New York Times,* p. F7.

Friedrich, W. N., & Gerber, P. N. (1994). Autoerotic asphyxia: The development of a paraphilia. *Journal of the American Academy of Child and Adolescent Psychiatry, 33*(7), 970–974.

Frisch, R. (1997). Cited in Angier, N. (1997a). Chemical tied to fat control could help trigger puberty. *The New York Times,* pp. C1, C3.

Frodi, A. M., Macauley, J., & Thome, P. R. (1977). Are women always less aggressive than men? A review of the experimental literature. *Psychological Bulletin, 84,* 634–660.

Frohlich, P., & Meston, C. (2002). Sexual functioning and self-reported depressive symptoms among college women. *Journal of Sex Research, 39*(4), 321–325.

Frost, M. H., et al. (2000). Long-term satisfaction and psychological and social function following bilateral prophylactic mastectomy. *Journal of the American Medical Association, 284,* 319–324.

Fuentes-Afflick, E., & Hessol, N. A. (2000). Interpregnancy interval and the risk of premature infants. *Obstetrics & Gynecology, 95,* 383–390.

Fugger, E. F., et al. (1998, September 9). *Human reproduction.* Cited in Kolata, G. (1998, September 9). Researchers report success in method to pick baby's sex. *The New York Times* online.

Gabriel, T. (1995b, June 12). A new generation seems ready to give bisexuality a place in the spectrum. *The New York Times,* p. A12.

Gagnon, J. H. (1977). *Human sexualities.* Glenview, IL: Scott, Foresman.

Gagnon, J. H. (1990). Gender preferences in erotic relations: The Kinsey scale and sexual scripts. In D. P. McWhirter, S. A. Sanders, & J. M. Reinisch (Eds.), *Homosexuality/Heterosexuality: Concepts of sexual orientation* (pp. 177–207). New York: Oxford University Press.

Gagnon, J. H., Giami, A., Michaels, S., & de Colomby, P. (2001). A comparative study of the couple in the social organization of sexuality in France and the United States. *Journal of Sex Research, 38*(1), 24–34.

Gagnon, J. H., & Simon, W. (1973). *Sexual conduct: The social origins of human sexuality.* Chicago: Aldine.

Gagnon, J. H., & Simon, W. (1987). The sexual scripting of oral–genital contacts. *Archives of Sexual Behavior, 16,* 1–25.

Gallagher, A. M., et al. (2000). Gender differences in advanced mathematical problem solving. *Journal of Experimental Child Psychology, 75*(3), 165–190.

Gallant, J. E. (2000). Strategies for long-term success in the treatment of HIV infection. *Journal of the American Medical Association, 283,* 1329–1334.

Garnets, L., & Kimmel, D. (1991). In J. D. Goodchilds (Ed.), *Psychological perspectives on human diversity in America.* Washington, DC: American Psychological Association.

Garwood, S. G., et al. (1980). Beauty is only "name deep": The effect of first name in ratings of physical attraction. *Journal of Applied Social Psychology, 10,* 431–435.

Gates, G. J., & Sonenstein, F. L. (2000). Heterosexual genital sexual activity among adolescent males: 1988 and 1995. *Family Planning Perspectives, 32*(6), 295–297, 304.

Gebhard, P. H., et al. (1965). *Sex offenders: An analysis of types.* New York: Harper & Row.

Gebhard, P. H. (1969). Misconceptions about female prostitutes. *Medical Aspects of Human Sexuality, 3,* 24–26.

Geer, J., Heiman, J., & Leitenberg, H. (1984). *Human sexuality.* Englewood Cliffs, NJ: Prentice-Hall.

George, W. H., Stoner, S. A., Norris, J., Lopez, P. A., & Lehman, G. L. (2000). Alcohol expectancies and sexuality: A self-fulfilling prophecy analysis of dyadic perceptions and behavior. *Journal of Studies on Alcohol, 61*(1), 168–176.

Ghizzani, A. (2003). Aging and male sexuality. *Archives of Sexual Behavior, 32*(3), 294–295.

Gibbs, N. (1991, June 3). When is it rape? *Time,* pp. 48–54.

Gibson, A. I., et al. (1988). Adolescent female prostitutes. *Archives of Sexual Behavior, 17,* 431–438.

Gidycz, C. A., & Koss, M. P. (1990). A comparison of group and individual sexual assault victims. *Psychology of Women Quarterly, 14,* 325–342.

Gijs, L., & Gooren, L. (1996). Hormonal and psychopharmacological interventions in the treatment of paraphilias: An update. *Journal of Sex Research, 33,* 273–290.

Gilbert, S. (1996, September 25). No long-term link is found between pill and breast cancer. *The New York Times,* p. C9.

Gillis, J. S., & Avis, W. E. (1980). The male-taller norm in mate selection. *Personality and Social Psychology Bulletin, 6,* 396–401.

Giovannucci, E., et al. (1993a). A prospective cohort study of vasectomy and prostate cancer in U.S. men. *Journal of the American Medical Association, 269,* 873–877.

Giovannucci, E., et al. (1993b). A retrospective cohort study of vasectomy and prostate cancer in U.S. men. *Journal of the American Medical Association, 269,* 878–882.

Glass, S. P., & Wright, T. L. (1992). Justifications of extramarital relationships: The association between attitudes, behaviors, and gender. *Journal of Sex Research, 29,* 361–387.

Gleicher, N., Oleske, D. M., Tur-Kaspa, I., Vidali, A., & Karande, V. (2000). Reducing the risk of high-order multiple pregnancy after ovarian stimulation with gonadotropins. *The New England Journal of Medicine, 343*(1), 2–7.

Gnagy, S., Ming, E. E., Devesa, S. S., Hartge, P., & Whittemore, A. S. (2000). Declining ovarian cancer rates in U.S. women in relation to parity and oral contraceptive use. *Epidemiology, 11*(2), 102–105.

Goff, S. P. (2004). HIV: Replication trimmed back. *Nature, 427,* 791–793.

Gold, S. R., & Gold, R. G. (1993). Sexual aversions: A hidden disorder. In W. O'Donohue & J. H. Geer (Eds.), *Handbook of sexual dysfunctions: Assessment and treatment* (pp. 83–102). Boston: Allyn & Bacon.

Goldberg, C. (1995, September 11). Sex slavery, Thailand to New York. *The New York Times,* pp. B1, B6.

Goldberg, C., & Elder, J. (1998, January 16). Public still backs abortion, but wants limits, poll says. *The New York Times,* pp. A1, A16.

Goldberg, J, Holtz, D., Hyslop, T., & Tolosa, J. E. (2002). Has the use of routine episiotomy decreased? Examination of episiotomy rates from 1983 to 2000. *Obstetrics & Gynecology, 99*(3), 395–400.

Goldenberg, R. L., & Klerman, L. V. (1995). Adolescent pregnancy—Another look. *New England Journal of Medicine, 332,* 1161–1162.

Goldman, J. A., & Harlow, L. L. (1993). Self-perception variables that mediate AIDS-preventive behavior in college students. *Health Psychology, 12,* 489–498.

Goldschmidt, L., Day, N. L., & Richardson, G. A. (2000). Effects of prenatal marijuana exposure on child behavior problems at age 10. *Neurotoxicology & Teratology, 22*(3), 325–336.

Goldstein, I. (1998). Cited in Kolata, G. (1998, April 4). Impotence pill: Would it also help women? *The New York Times,* pp. A1, A6.

Goldstein, I. (2000). Cited in Norton, A. (2000, September 1). Exercise helps men avoid impotence. *Reuters News Agency* online.

Goldstein, I., et al. (1998). Oral sildenafil in the treatment of erectile dysfunction. *New England Journal of Medicine, 338,* 1397–1404.

Goleman, D. (1988, October 18). Chemistry of sexual desire yields its elusive secrets. *The New York Times,* pp. C1, C15.

Goleman, D. (1992). Therapies offer hope for sex offenders. *The New York Times,* pp. C1, C11.

Goleman, D. (1993, October 6). Abuse-prevention efforts aid children. *The New York Times,* p. C13.

Golish, T. D. (2003). Stepfamily communication strengths: Understanding the ties that bind. *Human Communication Research, 29*(1), 41–80.

Gomes do Espirito, M. E., & Etheredge, G. D. (2003). HIV prevalence and sexual behaviour of male clients of brothels' prostitutes in Dakar, Senegal. AIDS Care, *15*(1), 53–62.

Gomez, J., & Smith, B. (1990). Taking the home out of homophobia: Black lesbian health. In E. C. White (Ed.), *The Black women's health book: Speaking for ourselves.* Seattle: Seal Press.

Goode, E. (2000, June 25). Thinner: The male battle with anorexia. *The New York Times,* p. MH8.

Goodson, P., McCormick, D., & Evans, A. (2001). Searching for sexually explicit materials on the Internet: An exploratory study of college students' behavior and attitudes. *Archives of Sexual Behavior, 30*(2), 101–118.

Goodstein, L. (2004, February 27). Two studies cite child sex abuse by 4 percent of priests. *The New York Times* online.

Gordon, A. E., et al. (2002). Why is smoking a risk factor for Sudden Infant Death Syndrome? *Child: Care, Health & Development, 28*(Suppl1), 23–25.

Gordon, S., & Snyder, C. W. (1989). *Personal issues in human sexuality: A guidebook for better sexual health* (2nd ed.). Boston: Allyn & Bacon.

Gottman, J. M., Coan, J., Carrère, S., & Swanson, C. (1998). Predicting marital happiness and stability from newlywed interactions. *Journal of Marriage and the Family, 60*, 5–22.

Gottman, J. M., & Levenson, R. W. (1999). What predicts change in marital interaction over time? A study of alternative medicine. *Family Process, 38*(2), 143–158.

Gottman, J. M., Swanson, C., & Murray, J. (1999). The mathematics of marital conflict: Dynamic mathematical nonlinear modeling of newlywed marital interaction. *Journal of Family Psychology, 13*(1), 3–19.

Grabrick, D. M., et al. (2000). Risk of breast cancer with oral contraceptive use in women with a family history of breast cancer. *Journal of the American Medical Association, 284*(14), 1791–1798.

Grady, D. (2002, November 21). Vaccine appears to prevent cervical cancer. *The New York Times* online.

Grady, D. (2003a). Postmenopausal hormones: Therapy for symptoms only. *New England Journal of Medicine, 348*(19), 1835–1837.

Grady, D. (2003b, June 25). Study finds new risks in hormone therapy. *The New York Times.*

Graham, C. A. (2003). A new view of women's sexual problems. *Journal of Sex & Marital Therapy, 29*(4), 325–327.

Grauerholz, E. (1989). Sexual harassment of women professors by students: Exploring the dynamics of power, authority, and gender in a university setting. *Sex Roles, 21*, 789–301.

Grazioli, R., & Terry, D. J. (2000). The role of cognitive vulnerability and stress in the prediction of postpartum depressive symptomatology. *British Journal of Clinical Psychology, 39*(4), 329–347.

Green, R. (2003). When therapists do not want their clients to be homosexual: A response to Rosik's article. *Journal of Marital & Family Therapy, 29*(1), 29–38.

Greenberg, E. R., et al. (1984). Breast cancer in mothers given diethylstilbestrol in pregnancy. *New England Journal of Medicine, 311*, 1393–1398.

Greene, B. (1994). Ethnic-minority lesbians and gay men: Mental health and treatment issues. *Journal of Consulting and Clinical Psychology, 62*, 243–251.

Greene, B. (2000). African American lesbian and bisexual women. *Journal of Social Issues, 56*(2), 239–249.

Greenwald, E., & Leitenberg, H. (1989). Long-term effects of sexual experiences with siblings and non-siblings during childhood. *Archives of Sexual Behavior, 18*, 389–399.

Griffin, E., & Sparks, G. G. (1990). Friends forever: A longitudinal exploration of intimacy in same-sex friends and platonic pairs. *Journal of Social and Personal Relationships, 7*, 29–46.

Griffith, K. H., & Hebl, M. R. (2002). The disclosure dilemma for gay men and lesbians: "Coming out" at work. *Journal of Applied Psychology, 87*(6), 1191–1199.

Grön, G., Wunderlich, A. P., Spitzer, M., Tomczak, R., & Riepe, M. W. (2000). Brain activation during human navigation: gender-different neural networks as substrate of performance. *Nature Neuroscience, 3*(4), 404–408.

Grosser, B. I., Monti-Bloch, L., Jennings-White, C., & Berliner, D. L. (2000). Behavioral and electrophysiological effects of androstadienone, a human pheromone. *Psychoneuroendocrinology, 25*(3), 289–300.

Groth, A. N., & Birnbaum, H. J. (1979). *Men who rape: The psychology of the offender.* New York: Plenum Press.

Groth, A., & Hobson, W. (1983). The dynamics of sexual assault. In L. Schlesinger & E. Revitch (Eds.), *Sexual dynamics of antisocial behavior.* Springfield, IL: Charles C Thomas.

Gruber, C. J., et al. (2002). Mechanisms of disease: Production and actions of estrogens. *New England Journal of Medicine, 346*, 340–352.

Gruslin, A., et al. (2000). Maternal smoking and fetal erythropoietin levels. *Obstetrics & Gynecology, 95*(4), 561–564.

Grych, J. H., Fincham, F. D., Jouriles, E. N., & McDonald, R. (2000). Interparental conflict and child adjustment: Testing the mediational role of appraisals in the cognitive-contextual framework. *Child Development, 71*(6), 1648–1661.

Guay, A. T. (2001). Decreased testosterone in regularly menstruating women with decreased libido: A clinical observation. *Journal of Sex & Marital Therapy, 27*(5), 513–519.

Guelseren, L. (1999). Dogum sonrasi depresyon: Bir goezden gecirme. *Turk Psikiyatri Dergisi, 10*(1), 58–67.

Guzick, D. S., & Hoeger, K. (2000). Sex, hormones, and hysterectomies. *The New England Journal of Medicine* online, *343*(10).

Haake, P., et al. (2003). Acute neuroendocrine response to sexual stimulation in sexual offenders. *Canadian Journal of Psychiatry, 48*(4), 265–271.

Hafen, M., Jr., & Crane, D. R. (2003). When marital interaction and intervention researchers arrive at different points of view: The active listening controversy. *Journal of Family Therapy, 25*(1), 4–14.

Haldeman, D. C. (2002). Gay rights, patient rights: The implications of sexual orientation conversion therapy. *Professional Psychology: Research & Practice, 33*(3), 260–264.

Half in California oppose gay marriage. (2003, August 29). *http://www.euroseek.com/news/ 21323.html*

Hall, G., Collins, A., Csemiczky, G., & Landgren, B. (2002). Lipoproteins and BMI: A comparison between women during transition to menopause and regularly menstruating healthy women. *Maturitas, 41*(3), 177–185.

Hall, G. C. N. (1989). Sexual arousal and arousability in a sexual offender population. *Journal of Abnormal Psychology, 98*, 145–149.

Hall, G. C. N., & Barongan, C. (1997). Prevention of sexual aggression. *American Psychologist, 52*, 5–14.

Halperin, D. T., & Bailey, R. C. (1999). Male circumcision and HIV infection: 10 years and counting. *Lancet, 354*, 1813–1815.

Halpern, D. F. (1997). Sex differences in intelligence: Implications for education. *American Psychologist, 52*, 1091–1102.

Halpern, D. F. (2003). Sex differences in cognitive abilities. *Applied Cognitive Psychology, 17*(3), 375–376.

Halpern, D. F., & LaMay, M. L. (2000). The smarter sex: A critical review of sex differences in intelligence. *Educational Psychology Review, 12*(2), 229–246.

Hamer, D. H., et al. (1993, July 16). A linkage between DNA markers on the X chromosome and male sexual orientation. *Science, 261*, 321–327.

Hanrahan, J. P., et al. (1992). The effect of maternal smoking during pregnancy on early infant lung function. *American Review of Respiratory Disease, 145*, 1129–1135.

Hansen, M., Kurinczuk, J. J., Bower, C., & Webb, S. (2002). The risk of major birth defects after intracytoplasmic sperm injection and in vitro fertilization. *New England Journal of Medicine, 346*, 725–730.

Hardy, S. (2001). More black lace: Women, eroticism and subjecthood. *Sexualities, 4*(4), 435–453.

Harney, P. A., & Muehlenhard, C. L. (1991). Rape. In E. Grauerholz & M. A. Koralewski (Eds.), *Sexual coercion: A sourcebook on its nature, causes, and prevention* (pp. 3–16). Lexington, MA: Lexington Books.

Harold, G. T., Fincham, F. D., Osborne, L. N., & Conger, R. D. (1997). Mom and Dad are at it again: Adolescent perceptions of marital conflict and adolescent psychological distress. *Developmental Psychology, 33*, 333–350.

Harris, C. R. (2000). Psychophysiological responses to imagined infidelity: The specific innate modular view of jealousy reconsidered. *Journal of Personality and Social Psychology, 78*(6), 1082–1091.

Harris, C. R. (2003). A review of sex differences in sexual jealousy, including self-report data, psychophysiological responses, interpersonal violence, and morbid jealousy. *Personality & Social Psychology Review, 7*(2), 102–128.

Harris, M., & Johnson, O. (2003). *Cultural anthropology* (6th ed.). Boston: Allyn & Bacon.

Hart, J., et al. (1991). Sexual behavior in pregnancy: A study of 219 women. *Journal of Sex Education and Therapy, 17*, 86–90.

Hartung, T. K., Nash, J., Ngubane, N., & Fredlund, V. G. (2002). AIDS awareness and sexual behaviour in a high HIV prevalence area in rural northern Kwazulu-Natal, South Africa. *International Journal of STD & AIDS, 13*(12), 829–832.

Haslam, C., & Draper, E. S. (2001). A qualitative study of smoking during pregnancy. *Psychology, Health & Medicine, 6*(1), 95–99.

Hass, A. (1979). *Teenage sexuality.* New York: Macmillan.

Hassebrauck, M. (2003). Romantische Männer und realistische Frauen: Geschlechtsunterschiede in Beziehungskognitionen. *Zeitschrift für Sozialpsychologie, 34*(1), 25–35.

Hatcher, R. A. (2001). *Contraceptive technologies.* London: British Medical Association.

Hatcher, R. A., et al. (1998). *Contraceptive technology* (17th rev. ed.). New York: Ardent Media.

Hatfield, E., & Rapson, R. L. (2002). Passionate love and sexual desire: Cultural and historical perspectives. In Vangelisti, A. L., Reis, H. T., et al. (Eds.), *Stability and change in relationships. Advances in personal relationships* (pp. 306–324). New York: Cambridge University Press.

Hatfield, E., & Sprecher, S. (1986). Measuring passionate love in intimate relationships. *Journal of Adolescence, 9*, 383–410.

Haugaard, J. J. (2000). The challenge of defining child sexual abuse. *American Psychologist, 55*(9), 1036–1039.

Hawkley, L. C., Burleson, M. H., Berntson, G. G., & Cacioppo, J. T. (2003). Loneliness in everyday life: Cardiovascular activity, psychosocial context, and health behaviors. *Journal of Personality & Social Psychology, 85*(1), 105–120.

Hawkley, L. C., & Cacioppo, J. T. (2003). Loneliness and pathways to disease. *Brain, Behavior & Immunity, 17*(Suppl1), S98–S105.

Healy, P. (2003, November 13). L.I. Athletes are said to face juvenile trial. *The New York Times* online.

Heath, R. (1972). Pleasure and brain activity in man. *Journal of Nervous and Mental Disease, 154,* 3–18.

Heim, C., et al. (2000). Pituitary-adrenal and autonomic responses to stress in women after sexual and physical abuse in childhood. *Journal of the American Medical Association, 284,* 592–597.

Heim, C., Newport, D. J., Miller, A. H., & Nemeroff, C. B. (2002). Dr. Heim and colleagues reply. *American Journal of Psychiatry, 159*(1), 157–158.

Heiman, J. R. (2000). Book review: The technology of orgasm: "Hysteria," the vibrator, and women's sexual satisfaction. *The New England Journal of Medicine* online, *342*(25).

Hendrick, C., & Hendrick, S. (1986). A theory and method of love. *Journal of Personality and Social Psychology, 50,* 392–402.

Hendrick, C., & Hendrick, S. (Eds.). (2000). *Close relationships: A sourcebook.* Thousand Oaks, CA: Sage.

Hendrick, C., & Hendrick, S. (2003). Romantic love: Measuring Cupid's arrow. In S. Lopez & C. R. Snyder (Eds.), *Positive psychological assessment: A handbook of models and measures* (pp. 235–249). Washington, DC: American Psychological Association.

Hendrick, S., & Hendrick, C. (2002). Love. In C. R. Snyder & S. J. Lopez (Eds.), *Handbook of positive psychology* (pp. 472–484). London, U.K.: Oxford University Press.

Henneberger, M. (with M. Marriott). (1993). For some, rituals of abuse replace youthful courtship. *The New York Times,* pp. A1, A33.

Henshaw, S. K. (2003, May 1). U.S. teenage pregnancy statistics with comparative statistics for women aged 20–24. *http://www.guttmacher.org/pubs/teen_stats.html.*

Hensley, L. G. (2002). Treatment for survivors of rape: Issues and interventions. *Journal of Mental Health Counseling, 24*(4), 330–347.

Herrera, V. M., & McCloskey, L. A. (2003). Sexual abuse, family violence, and female delinquency: Findings from a longitudinal study. *Violence & Victims, 18*(3), 319–334.

Herrington, D. M., et al. (2000). Effects of estrogen replacement on the progression of coronary-artery atherosclerosis. *The New England Journal of Medicine* online, *343*(8).

Herrmann, H. C., Chang, G., Klugherz, B. D., & Mahoney, P. D. (2000). Hemodynamic effects of sildenafil in men with severe coronary artery disease. *The New England Journal of Medicine, 342*(22), 1622–1626.

Hicks, T. V., & Leitenberg, H. (2001). Sexual fantasies about one's partner versus someone else: Gender differences in incidence and frequency. *Journal of Sex Research, 38*(1), 43–50.

Hillis, D. M. (2000, June 9). Origins of HIV. *Science, 288*(5472), 1757–1759.

Hines, D. A., & Saudino, K. J. (2003). Gender differences in psychological, physical, and sexual aggression among college students using the Revised Conflict Tactics Scales. *Violence & Victims, 18*(2), 197–217.

Hines, M., Ahmed, S. F., & Hughes, I. A. (2003). Psychological outcomes and gender-related development in complete androgen insensitivity syndrome. *Archives of Sexual Behavior, 32*(2), 93–101.

Hines, T. M. (2001). Clinical opinion: The G-spot: A modern gynecologic myth. *American Journal of Obstetrics and Gynecology, 185*(2), 359–362.

Hingson, R. W., et al. (2002). *A call to action: Changing the culture of drinking at U.S. colleges.* Washington, DC: National Institutes of Health, National Institute of Alcohol Abuse and Alcoholism.

Hirozawa, A. (2001). In Sub-Saharan Africa, circumcised men are less likely than uncircumcised men to become infected with HIV. *International Family Planning Perspectives* online, *27*(2).

Hitt, J. (1998, January 18). Who will do abortions here? *The New York Times Magazine,* pp. 20–27, 42–55.

Ho, D. D. (1995). Time to hit HIV, early and hard. *New England Journal of Medicine, 333,* 450–451.

Hobfoll, S. E., Jackson, A. P., Lavin, J., Britton, P. J., & Shepherd, J. B. (1993). Safer sex knowledge, behavior, and attitudes of inner-city women. *Health Psychology, 12,* 481–488.

Hodis, J. Cited in Kolata, G. (2002a, December 22). Chasing youth, many gamble on hormones. *The New York Times* online.

Hofferth, S. L., & Anderson, K. G. (2003). Are all dads equal? Biology versus marriage as a basis for paternal investment. *Journal of Marriage & Family, 65*(1), 213–232.

Hofmeyr, D. G., & Greeff, A. P. (2002). The influence of a vasectomy on the marital relationship and sexual satisfaction of the married man. *Journal of Sex & Marital Therapy, 28*(4), 339–352.

Holcomb, D. R., Savage, M. P., Seehafer, R., & Waalkes, D. M. (2002). A mixed-gender date rape prevention intervention targeting freshman college athletes. *College Student Journal, 36*(2), 165–179.

Holman, T. B., & Jarvis, M. O. (2003). Hostile, volatile, avoiding, and validating couple-conflict types: An investigation of Gottman's couple-conflict types. *Personal Relationships, 10*(2), 267–282.

Honeycutt, J. M., & Cantrill, J. G. (2001). *Cognition, communication, and romantic relationships.* Mahwah, NJ: Erlbaum.

Horne, A. (2003). Oedipal aspirations and phallic fears: On fetishism in childhood and young adulthood. *Journal of Child Psychotherapy, 29*(1), 37–52.

Horowitz, H. L. (2002). *Rereading sex: Battles over sexual knowledge and suppression in nineteenth-century America.* New York: Knopf.

Howard, J. A., Blumstein, P., & Schwartz, P. (1987). Social or evolutionary theories? Some observations on preferences in mate selection. *Journal of Personality and Social Psychology, 53,* 194–200.

Howards, S. S. (1995). Current concepts: Treatment of male infertility. *New England Journal of Medicine, 332,* 312–317.

Hsiao, M., Liu, C., Chen, K., & Hsieh, T. (2002). Characteristics of women seeking treatment for premenstrual syndrome in Taiwan. *Acta Psychiatrica Scandinavica, 106*(2), 150–155.

Hughes, I. A. (2000). A novel explanation for resistance to androgens. *The New England Journal of Medicine* online, *343*(12).

Hunt, M. (1974). *Sexual behavior in the 1970's.* New York: Dell.

Hunter, D. J., et al. (1996). Cohort studies of fat intake and the risk of breast cancer: A pooled analysis. *New England Journal of Medicine, 334,* 356–361.

Hunter, M., & O'Dea, I. (2001). Cognitive appraisal of the menopause: The Menopause Representations Questionnaire (MRQ). *Psychology, Health & Medicine, 6*(1), 65–76.

Hussain, A. (2002, June 26). It's official. Men really are afraid of commitment. *Reuters.*

Huxley, R. R. (2000). Nausea and vomiting in early pregnancy: Its role in placental development. *Obstetrics & Gynecology, 95,* 779–782.

Hyde, J. S., Fennema, E., & Lamon, S. J. (1990). Gender differences in mathematics performance: A meta-analysis. *Psychological Bulletin, 107,* 139–155.

Hyde, J. S., & Plant, E. A. (1995). Magnitude of psychological gender differences: Another side to the story. *American Psychologist, 50,* 159–161.

Hyman, S. M., Gold, S. N., & Cott, M. A. (2003). Forms of social support that moderate PTSD in childhood sexual abuse survivors. *Journal of Family Violence, 18*(5), 295–300.

Illes, J. (2000, October). Beauty secrets of ancient Egypt: Nefertem, Ancient Lord of Perfume. *Tour Egypt Monthly, 5*(1).

Imperato-McGinley, J., et al. (1974). Steroid 5 reductase deficiency in man: An inherited form of male pseudohermaphroditism. *Science, 186,* 1213–1215.

Ironson, G., Balbin, E., & Schneiderman, N. (2002). Health psychology and infectious diseases. In T. J. Boll, S. B. Johnson, et al. (Eds.), *Handbook of clinical health psychology: Vol. 1. Medical disorders and behavioral applications* (pp. 5–36). Washington, DC: American Psychological Association.

Isay, R. A. (1990). Psychoanalytic theory and the therapy of gay men. In D. P. McWhirter, S. A. Sanders, & J. M. Reinisch (Eds.), *Homosexuality/Heterosexuality: Concepts of sexual orientation* (pp. 283–303). New York: Oxford University Press.

Itzin, C. (2002). Pornography and the construction of misogyny. *Journal of Sexual Aggression, 8*(3), 4–42.

Jackson, L. A., & Ervin, K. S. (1992). Height stereotypes of women and men: The liabilities of shortness for both sexes. *Journal of Social Psychology, 132,* 433–445.

Jacob, S., Hayreh, D. J. S., & McClintock, M. K. (2001). Context-dependent effects of steroid chemosignals on human physiology and mood. *Physiology & Behavior, 74*(1–2), 15–27.

Jacob, S., & McClintock, M. K. (2000). Psychological state and mood effects of steroidal chemosignals in women and men. *Hormones and Behavior, 37*(1), 57–78.

Jacobson, J. L., & Jacobson, S. W. (1994). Prenatal alcohol exposure and neurobehavioral development: Where is the threshold? *Alcohol Health and Research World, 18*(1), 30–36.

Jameson, M. (2000, June 12). Childbirth that's not so labor-intensive. *Los Angeles Times.*

Jankowiak, W. R., & Fischer, E. F. (1992). A cross-cultural perspective on romantic love. *Ethnology, 31,* 149–155.

Janofsky, M., & Schemo, D. J. (2003, March 16). Women recount cadet life: Forced sex and fear. *The New York Times* online.

Jeffreys, S. (1998). *The idea of prostitution.* Spinifex.

Jennings, V. H., Lamprecht, V. M., & Kowal, D. (1998). Fertility awareness methods. In R. A. Hatcher et al. (1998). *Contraceptive technology* (17th rev. ed.) (pp. 309–324). New York: Ardent Media.

Jetter, A. (2000, February 22). Breast cancer in Blacks spurs hunt for answers. *The New York Times,* p. D5.

Johannes, C. B., et al. (2000). Incidence of erectile dysfunction in men 40 to 69 years old: Longitudinal results from the Massachusetts male aging study. *The Journal of Urology, 163,* 460.

Johanson, R. (2000). Perineal massage for prevention of perineal trauma in childbirth. *The Lancet, 355*(9200), 250–251.

Johnson, H. (2003). The cessation of assaults on wives. *Journal of Comparative Family Studies, 34*(1), 75–91.

Johnstone, S. J., et al. (2001). Obstetric risk factors for postnatal depression in urban and rural community samples. *Australian & New Zealand Journal of Psychiatry, 35*(1), 69–74.

Jones, A., et al. (1994). Erectile disorder and the elderly: An analysis of the case for funding. *Sexual and Marital Therapy, 9*(1), 9–15.

Jones, B. E., & Hill, M. J. (2002). *Mental health issues in lesbian, gay, bisexual, and transgender communities: Review of psychiatry, Volume 21.* Washington, DC: American Psychiatric Publishing.

Jorgensen, S. R., et al. (1980). Dyadic and social network influences on adolescent exposure to pregnancy risk. *Journal of Marriage and the Family, 42,* 141–155.

Kafka, M. P. (2003). Sex offending and sexual appetite: The clinical and theoretical relevance of hypersexual desire. *International Journal of Offender Therapy & Comparative Criminology, 47*(4), 439–451.

Kaiser Family Foundation, Holt, T., Greene, L., & Davis, J. (2003). *National Survey of Adolescents and Young Adults: Sexual health knowledge, attitudes and experiences.* Menlo Park, CA: Henry J. Kaiser Family Foundation.

Kalb, C. (2004, January 26). Brave new babies. *Newsweek.*

Kalick, S. M. (1988). Physical attractiveness as a status cue. *Journal of Experimental Social Psychology, 24,* 469–489.

Kamen, P. (2002). *Her way: Young women remake the sexual revolution.* New York: Broadway Books.

Kaplan, H. S. (1974). *The new sex therapy: Active treatment of sexual dysfunctions.* New York: Brunner/Mazel.

Kaplan, H. S. (1979). *Disorders of sexual desire.* New York: Simon and Schuster.

Kaplan, H. S. (1987). *Sexual aversion, sexual phobias, and panic disorder.* New York: Brunner/Mazel.

Kaplan, H. S. (1990). Sex, intimacy, and the aging process. *Journal of the American Academy of Psychoanalysis, 18,* 185–205.

Katz, M. H., et al. (2002). Impact of highly active antiretroviral treatment on HIV seroincidence among men who have sex with men: San Francisco. *American Journal of Public Health, 92*(3), 388–394.

Katz, R. C. (1990). Psychosocial adjustment in adolescent child molesters. *Child Abuse and Neglect, 14,* 567–575.

Kavanagh, A. M., Mitchell, H., & Giles, G. G. (2000). Hormone replacement therapy and accuracy of mammographic screening. *The Lancet, 355,* 270–274.

Kendler, K. S., et al. (2000). Childhood sexual abuse and adult psychiatric and substance use disorders in women: An epidemiological and Cotwin control analysis. *Archives of General Psychiatry, 57*(10), 953–959.

Kendler, K. S., Thornton, L. M., Gilman, S. E., & Kessler, R. C. (2000). Sexual orientation in a U.S. national sample of twin and nontwin sibling pairs. *American Journal of Psychiatry, 157,* 1843–1846.

Kennedy, N., & McDonough, M. (2002). Koro: A case in an eastern European asylum seeker in Ireland. *Irish Journal of Psychological Medicine, 19*(4), 130–131.

Kennedy, R. (2003). Interracial intimacies: Sex, marriage, identity, and adoption. New York: Knopf.

Kerns, J. G., & Fine, M. A. (1994). The relation between gender and negative attitudes toward gay men and lesbians: Do gender role attitudes mediate this relation? *Sex Roles, 31*(5–6), 297–307.

Kersting, K. (2003). Cognitive sex differences: A "political minefield." *Monitor on Psychology, 34*(5).

Kessler, R. C. (2003). Epidemiology of women and depression. *Journal of Affective Disorders, 74*(1), 5–13.

Khoury, M. J., Burke, W., & Thomson, E. J. (Eds.). (2000). *Genetics and public health in the 21st century: Using genetic information to improve health and prevent disease.* New York: Oxford University Press.

Killmann, P. R., et al. (1987). The treatment of secondary orgasmic dysfunction II. *Journal of Sex and Marital Therapy, 13,* 93–105.

Kim, A. A., Kent, C. K., & Klausner, J. D. (2002). Increased risk of HIV and sexually transmitted disease transmission among gay or bisexual men who use Viagra, San Francisco 2000–2001. *AIDS, 16*(10), 1425–1428.

Kimble, D. P. (1992). *Biological psychology* (2nd ed.). Fort Worth, TX: Harcourt Brace Jovanovich.

King, R. (2000). Cited in Frazier, L. (2000, July 16). The new face of HIV is young, black. *The Washington Post,* p. C01.

Kingsberg, S. A. (2002). The impact of aging on sexual function in women and their partners. *Archives of Sexual Behavior, 31*(5), 431–437.

Kinsey, A. C., Pomeroy, W. B., & Martin, C. E. (1948). *Sexual behavior in the human male.* Philadelphia: W. B. Saunders.

Kinsey, A. C., Pomeroy, W. B., Martin, C. E., & Gebhard, P. H. (1953). *Sexual behavior in the human female.* Philadelphia: W. B. Saunders.

Kippax, S., & Smith, G. (2001). Anal intercourse and power in sex between men. *Sexualities, 4*(4), 413–434.

Kirby, D. (2000, October 3). More options, and decisions, for men with prostate cancer. *The New York Times* online.

Kirchheimer, S., & Smith, M. (2003, May 28). Condoms in schools don't boost teen sex: Key is making condom programs part of overall sex education, says one expert. WebMD Medical News.

Kirkpatrick, R. C. (2000). The evolution of human homosexual behavior. *Current Anthropology, 41*(3), 385–413.

Kirn, W. (1997, August 18). The ties that bind. *Time,* pp. 48–50.

Kite, M. E. (1992). Individual differences in males' reactions to gay males and lesbians. *Journal of Applied Social Psychology, 22,* 1222–1239.

Kjerulff, K. H., et al. (2000). Effectiveness of hysterectomy. *Obstetrics & Gynecology, 95,* 319–326.

Klein, E. A. (2000). *Management of prostate cancer.* Totowa, NJ: Humana Press.

Klein, H. G. (2000). Will blood transfusion ever be safe enough? *Journal of the American Medical Association* online, *284*(2).

Kleinplatz, P. J. (2003). What's new in sex therapy? From stagnation to fragmentation. *Sexual & Relationship Therapy, 18*(1), 95–106.

Klusmann, D. (2002). Sexual motivation and the duration of partnership. *Archives of Sexual Behavior, 31,* 275–287.

Klüver, H., & Bucy, P. C. (1939). Preliminary analysis of functions of the temporal lobes in monkeys. *Archives of Neurology and Psychiatry, 42,* 979.

Knapp, M. L., & Vangelisti, A. L. (2000). *Interpersonal Communication and Human Relationships,* 4th ed. Boston: Allyn & Bacon.

Knight, R. A., et al. (1991). *Antisocial personality disorder and Hare assessments of psychopathy among sexual offenders.* Manuscript in preparation.

Knight, S. E. (1989). Sexual concerns of the physically disabled. In B. W. Heller, L. M. Flohr, & L. S. Zegans (Eds.), *Psychosocial interventions with physically disabled persons* (pp. 183–199). New Brunswick, NJ: Rutgers University Press.

Knox, D. (1983). *The love attitudes inventory* (rev. ed.). Saluda, NC: Family Life Publications.

Knox, D., Gibson, L., Zusman, M., & Gallmeier, C. (1997a). Why college students end relationships. *College Student Journal, 31*(4), 449–452.

Knox, D., & Schacht, C. (2002). *Choices in relationships—An introduction to marriage and the family,* 7th ed. Belmont, CA: Wadsworth Publishing Company.

Knox, D., Schacht, C., & Zusman, M. E. (1999a). Love relationships among college students. *College Student Journal, 33*(1), 149–151.

Knox, D., Zusman, M. E., & Nieves, W. (1997b). College students' homogamous preferences for a date and mate. *College Student Journal, 31*(4), 445–448.

Knudsen, D. D. (1991). Child sexual coercion. In E. Grauerholz & M. A. Koralewski (Eds.), *Sexual coercion: A sourcebook on its nature, causes, and prevention* (pp. 17–28). Lexington, MA: Lexington Books.

Kockott, G., & Fahrner, E. (1987). Transsexuals who have not undergone surgery: A follow-up study. *Archives of Sexual Behavior, 16,* 511–522.

Kohlberg, L. (1966). A cognitive–developmental analysis of children's sex-role concepts and attitudes. In E. E. Maccoby (Ed.), *The development of sex differences.* Stanford, CA: Stanford University Press.

Kolata, G. (1998c, September 9). Researchers report success in method to pick baby's sex. *The New York Times* online.

Kolata, G. (2002a, December 22). Chasing youth,

many gamble on hormones. *The New York Times* online.

Kolata, G. (2000b, April 5). Estrogen tied to slight rise in heart attacks. *The New York Times*, pp. A1, A20.

Kolata, G. (2004, February 26). Cell protein gives monkeys innate immunity to H.I.V. *The New York Times* online.

Kontula, O., & Haavio-Mannila, E. (2002). Masturbation in a generational perspective. *Journal of Psychology & Human Sexuality, 14*(2–3), 49–83.

Koren, G., Pastuszak, A., & Ito, S. (1998). Drug therapy: Drugs in pregnancy. *New England Journal of Medicine, 338,* 1128–1137.

Koss, M. P. (2003). Evolutionary models of why men rape: Acknowledging the complexities. In C. B. Travis (Ed.), *Evolution, gender, and rape* (pp. 191–205). Cambridge, MA: MIT Press.

Koss, M. P., Bailey, J. A., Yuan, N. P., Herrera, V. M., & Lichter, E. L. (2003). Depression and PTSD in survivors of male violence: Research and training initiatives to facilitate recovery. *Psychology of Women Quarterly, 27*(2), 130–142.

Koss, M. P., Figueredo, A. J., & Prince, R. J. (2002). Cognitive mediation of rape's mental, physical and social health impact: Tests of four models in cross-sectional data. *Journal of Consulting & Clinical Psychology, 70*(4), 926–941.

Koss, M. P., Gidycz, C. A., & Wisniewski, N. (1987). The scope of rape: Incidence and prevalence of sexual aggression and victimization in a national sample of higher education students. *Journal of Consulting and Clinical Psychology, 55,* 162–170.

Koss, M. P., & Kilpatrick, D. G. (2001). Rape and sexual assault. In E. Gerrity et al. (Eds.), *The mental health consequences of torture.* Plenum series on stress and coping (pp. 177–193). Dordrecht, Netherlands: Kluwer Academic Publishers.

Kouros-Mehr, H., et al. (2001). Identification of non-functional human VNO receptor genes provides evidence for vestigiality of the human VNO. *Chemical Sciences, 26*(9), 1167–1174.

Koutsky, L. A., et al. (2002). A controlled trial of a human papillomavirus type 16 vaccine. *New England Journal of Medicine, 347,* 1645–1651.

Kowal, D. (1998). Coitus interruptus (withdrawal). In R. A. Hatcher et al. (1998), *Contraceptive technology* (17th rev. ed.) (pp. 303–308). New York: Ardent Media.

Krahe, B., Waizenhofer, E., & Moller, I. (2003). Women's sexual aggression against men: Prevalence and predictors. *Sex Roles, 49*(5–6), 219–232.

Kramer, M. S., et al. (2000). The contribution of mild and moderate preterm birth to infant mortality. *Journal of the American Medical Association, 284,* 843–849.

Kramer, M. S., et al., for the PROBIT Study Group. (2001). Promotion of Breastfeeding Intervention Trial (PROBIT): A randomized trial in the Republic of Belarus. *Journal of the American Medical Association, 285,* 413–420.

Kristof, N. D. (2002, December 6). Love and race. *The New York Times* online.

Krueger, R. B., & Kaplan, M. S. (2002). Behavioral and psychopharmacological treatment of the paraphilic and hypersexual disorders. *Journal of Psychiatric Practice, 8*(1), 21–32.

Kuiper, B., & Cohen-Kettenis, P. (1988). Sex reassignment surgery: A study of 141 Dutch transsexuals. *Archives of Sexual Behavior, 17,* 439–457.

Kulik, L. (2000). Gender identity, sex typing of occupations, and gender role ideology among adolescents: Are they related? *International Journal for the Advancement of Counselling, 22*(1), 43–56.

Kunkel, L. E., & Temple, L. L. (1992). Attitudes towards AIDS and homosexuals: Gender, marital status, and religion. *Journal of Applied Social Psychology, 22,* 1030–1040.

Kurdek, L. A, & Schmitt, J. P. (1986). Relationship quality of gay men in closed or open relationships. *Journal of Homosexuality, 12*(2), 85–99.

Laan, E., & Hciman, J. (1994). *Archives of Sexual Behavior.*

Ladas, A. K., Whipple, B., & Perry, J. D. (1982). *The G spot and other recent discoveries about human sexuality.* New York: Holt, Rinehart & Winston.

Laino, C. (2000, September 17). Herpes vaccine works well in women but fails to protect men, studies show. MSNBC online.

Lalezari, J. P., et al. (2003). Enfuvirtide, an HIV-1 fusion inhibitor, for drug-resistant HIV infection in North and South America. *New England Journal of Medicine, 348*(22), 2175–2185.

Lamanna, M. A., & Riedmann, A. (1997). *Marriages and families,* 6th ed. Belmont, CA: Wadsworth.

Lamaze, F. (1981). *Painless childbirth.* New York: Simon & Schuster.

Lamberti, D. (1997). Cited in Alterman, E. (1997, November). Sex in the '90s. *Elle.*

Lane, F. S., III. (2000). *Obscene profits: The entrepreneurs of pornography in the cyber age.* London: Routledge.

Lang, R. A., et al. (1989). An examination of sex hormones in genital exhibitionists. *Annals of Sex Research, 2,* 67–75.

Langevin, R. (2003). A study of the psychosexual characteristics of sex killers: Can we identify them before it is too late? *International Journal of Offender Therapy & Comparative Criminology, 47*(4), 366–382.

Langevin, R., et al. (1979). Experimental studies of the etiology of genital exhibitionism. *Archives of Sexual Behavior, 8,* 307–332.

Langhinrichsen-Rohling, J., Palarea, R. E., Cohen, J., & Rohlin, M. L. (2002). Breaking up is hard to do: Unwanted pursuit behaviors following the dissolution of a romantic relationship. In K. E., Davis, I. H. Frieze, et al. (Eds.), *Stalking: Perspectives on victims and perpetrators* (pp. 212–236). New York: Springer.

Langille, D. B., & Curtis, L. (2002). Factors associated with sexual intercourse before age 15 among female adolescents in Nova Scotia. *Canadian Journal of Human Sexuality, 11*(3), 91–99.

Langlois, J. H., et al. (2000). Maxims or myths of beauty? A meta-analytic and theoretical review. *Psychological Bulletin, 126*(3), 390–423.

Laqueur, T. W. (2003). *Solitary sex: A cultural history of masturbation. http://www .newzonebooks.com*: Zone Books.

Larsson, I., & Svedin, C. (2002). Experiences in childhood: Young adults' recollections. *Archives of Sexual Behavior, 31*(3), 263–273.

Lau, J. T. F., Siah, P. C., & Tsui, H. Y. (2002). A study of the STD/AIDS related attitudes and behaviors of men who have sex with men in Hong Kong. *Archives of Sexual Behavior, 31*(4), 367–373.

Laumann, E. O., Gagnon, J. H., Michael, R. T., & Michaels, S. (1994). *The social organization of sexuality: Sexual practices in the United States.* Chicago: University of Chicago Press.

Laumann, E. O., Masi, C. M., Zuckerman, E. W., et al. (1997, April 2). Circumcision in the United States: Prevalence, prophylactic effects, and sexual practice. *The Journal of the American Medical Association, 277,* 1052–1057.

Laumann, E. O., Paik, A., & Rosen, R. C. (1999). Sexual dysfunction in the United States. Prevalence and predictors. *Journal of the American Medical Association, 281*(6), 537–544.

Lavoisier, P., et al. (1995). Clitoral blood flow increases following vaginal pressure stimulation. *Archives of Sexual Behavior, 24,* 37–45.

Law, J. (2000). The politics of breastfeeding: Assessing risk, dividing labor. *Signs, 25*(2), 407–450.

Lawrence, R. A. (2001). Breastfeeding in Belarus. *Journal of the American Medical Association* online, *285*(4).

Laws, D. R., & Marshall, W. L. (2003). A brief history of behavioral and cognitive behavioral approaches to sexual offenders: Part 1. Early developments. *Sexual Abuse: Journal of Research & Treatment, 15*(2), 75–92.

Lawton, C. A., & Morrin, K. A. (1999). Gender differences in pointing accuracy in computer-simulated 3D mazes. *Sex Roles, 40*(1–2), 73–92.

Leahey, E., & Guo, G. (2001). Gender differences in mathematical trajectories. *Social Forces, 80*(2), 713–732.

Leary, W. E. (1990, September 13). New focus on sperm brings fertility successes. *The New York Times*, p. B11.

Leary, W. E. (1998, September 29). Older people enjoy sex, survey says. *The New York Times*, p. F8.

Leavitt, G. C. (1990). Sociobiological explanations of incest avoidance: A critical review of evidential claims. *American Anthropologist, 92,* 971–993.

Lederman, M. M., & Valdez, H. (2000). Immune restoration with antiretroviral therapies: Implications for clinical management. *Journal of the American Medical Association, 284,* 223–228.

Lee, D. T. S., et al. (2001). A psychiatric epidemiological study of postpartum Chinese women. *American Journal of Psychiatry, 158*(2), 220–226.

Lee, J. K. P., Jackson, H. J., Pattison, P., & Ward, T. (2002). Developmental risk factors for sexual offending. *Child Abuse & Neglect, 26*(1), 73–92.

Legato, M. J. (2000, May 12). Cited in Study of children born without penises finds nature determines gender. The Associated Press online.

Leiblum, S. R., & Rosen, R. C. (1991). Couples therapy for erectile disorders: Conceptual and clinical considerations. Special issue: The treatment of male erectile disorders. *Journal of Sex and Marital Therapy, 17,* 147–159.

Leiblum, S. R., & Rosen, R. C. (Ed.). (2000). Principles and practice of sex therapy, 3rd ed. New York: Guilford Press.

Leinders-Zufall, T., et al. (2000). Ultrasensitive pheromone detection by mammalian vomeronasal neurons. *Nature, 405,* 792–796.

Leitenberg, H., Detzer, M. J., & Srebnik, D.

(1993). Gender differences in masturbation and the relation of masturbation experience in preadolescence and/or early adolescence to sexual behavior and sexual adjustment in young adulthood. *Archives of Sexual Behavior, 22,* 87–98.

Leitenberg, H., Greenwald, E., & Tarran, M. J. (1989). The relation between sexual activity among children during preadolescence and/or early adolescence and sexual behavior and sexual adjustment in young adulthood. *Archives of Sexual Behavior, 18,* 299–313.

Leitenberg, H., & Henning, K. (1995). Sexual fantasy. *Psychological Bulletin, 117,* 469–496.

Leland, J. (2000, May 29). The science of women and sex. *Newsweek,* pp. 48–54.

Lester, W. (2000, May 31). Poll: Americans back some gay rights. The Associated Press online.

Levine, D. (2000). Virtual attraction: What rocks your boat. *CyberPsychology & Behavior, 3*(4), 565–573.

Levinger, G. (1980). Toward the analysis of close relationships. *Journal of Experimental Social Psychology, 16,* 510–544.

Levy, D. S. (1991, September 16). Why Johnny might grow up violent and sexist. *Time,* pp. 16–19.

Lewin, T. (1992, February 28). Canada court says pornography harms women. *The New York Times,* p. B7.

Lewin, T. (1998a, January 17). Debate distant for many having abortions. *The New York Times,* pp. A1, A9.

Lewin, T. (1998b, March 23). Debate centers on definition of harassment. *The New York Times,* pp. A1, A28.

Lewis, P. H. (2000, June 22). Snooping software enters the mainstream. *The New York Times* online.

Libman, E. (1989). Sociocultural and cognitive factors in aging and sexual expression: Conceptual and research issues. *Canadian Psychology, 30,* 560–567.

Lichtenstein, P., et al. (2000). Environmental and heritable factors in the causation of cancer: Analyses of cohorts of twins from Sweden, Denmark, and Finland. *New England Journal of Medicine, 343*(2), 78–85.

Lief, H. I., & Hubschman, L. (1993). Orgasm in the postoperative transsexual. *Archives of Sexual Behavior, 22* 145–155.

Lin, G., & Wang, Q. (2003). Predictors of non-use of condoms among drug users in China: Implications for HIV harm reduction. *Drugs: Education, Prevention & Policy, 10*(2), 141–146.

Linet, O. I., & Ogrinc, F. G. (1996). Efficacy and safety of intracavernosal alprostadil in men with erectile dysfunction. *New England Journal of Medicine, 334,* 873–877.

Ling, F. W. (2000). Recognizing and treating premenstrual dysphoric disorder in the obstetric, gynecologic, and primary care practices. *Journal of Clinical Psychiatry, 61*(Suppl 12), 9–16.

Lippa, R. (2001). On deconstructing and reconstructing masculinity–femininity. *Journal of Research in Personality, 35*(2), 168–207.

Lippa, R., & Arad, S. (1997). The structure of sexual orientation and its relation to masculinity, femininity, and gender diagnosticity: Different for men and women. *Sex Roles, 37*(3–4), 187–208.

Lippincott, J. A., Wlazelek, B., & Schumacher, L. J. (2000). Comparison: Attitudes toward homosexuality of international and American college students. *Psychological Reports, 87*(3, Pt 2), 1053–1056.

Lipshultz, L. I. (1996). Injection therapy for erectile dysfunction. *New England Journal of Medicine, 334,* 913–914.

Liptak, A. (2003, January 23). Circumcision opponents use the legal system and legislatures. *The New York Times* online.

Lira, L. R., Koss, M. P., & Russo, N. F. (1999). Mexican American women's definitions of rape and sexual abuse. *Hispanic Journal of Behavioral Sciences, 21*(3), 236–265.

Liu, X., et al. (2000). Behavioral and emotional problems in Chinese children of divorced parents. *Journal of the American Academy of Child & Adolescent Psychiatry, 39*(7), 896–903.

Loder, N. (2000). U.S. science shocked by revelations of sexual discrimination. *Nature, 405,* 713–714.

Long, C. R., Seburn, M., Averill, J. R., & More, T. A. (2003). Solitude experiences: Varieties, settings, and individual differences. *Personality & Social Psychology Bulletin, 29*(5), 578–583.

Lott, B. (1985). The potential enhancement of social/personality psychology through feminist research and vice versa. *American Psychologist, 40,* 155–164.

Lown, J., & Dolan, E. (1988). Financial challenges in remarriage. *Lifestyles: Family and Economic Issues, 9,* 73–88.

Lue, T. F. (2000). Drug therapy: Erectile dysfunction. *The New England Journal of Medicine* online, *342*(24).

Lynxwiler, J., & Gay, D. (1994). Reconsidering race differences in abortion attitudes. *Social Science Quarterly, 75*(1), 67–84.

Maartens, L. W. F., Knottnerus, J. A., & Pop, V. J. (2002). Menopausal transition and increased depressive symptomatology: A community based prospective study. *Maturitas, 42*(3), 195–200.

Maccoby, E. E. (1990). Gender and relationships: A developmental account. *American Psychologist, 45,* 513–520.

Maccoby, E. E., & Jacklin, C. N. (1974). Myth, reality and shades of gray: What we know and don't know about sex differences. *Psychology Today, 8*(7), 109–112.

MacDonald, T. K., MacDonald, G., Zanna, M. P., & Fong, G. T. (2000). Alcohol, sexual arousal, and intentions to use condoms in young men: Applying alcohol myopia theory to risky sexual behavior. *Health Psychology, 19,* 290–298.

Mahoney, P., & Williams, L. M. (1998). Sexual assault in marriage: Prevalence, consequences, and treatment of wife rape. In J. L. Jasinski & L. M. Williams (Eds.), Partner violence: A comprehensive review of 20 years of research. (pp. 113–162). Thousand Oaks, CA: Sage.

Maines, R. P. (1999). *The technology of orgasm: "Hysteria," the vibrator, and women's sexual satisfaction.* Baltimore, MD: Johns Hopkins University Press.

Major, B., Cozzarelli, C., Cooper, M. L., Zubek, J., Richards, C., et al. (2000). Psychological responses of women after first-trimester abortion. *Archives of General Psychiatry, 57,* 777–784.

Malamuth, N. M., Addison, T., & Koss, M. (2000). Pornography and sexual aggression: Are there reliable effects and can we understand them? *Annual Review of Sex Research, 11,* 26–91.

Male contraceptive tests positive. (2003, October 6). CNN.

Malec, K. (2003, Summer). The abortion–breast cancer link: How politics trumped science and informed consent. *Journal of American Physicians and Surgeons, 8*(2). http://www.abortionbreastcancer.com/jpands.pdf

Maletzky, B. M. (1980). Self-referred vs. court-referred sexually deviant patients: Success with assisted covert sensitization. *Behavior Therapy, 11,* 306–314.

Maletzky, B. M., & Steinhauser, C. (2002). A 25-year follow-up of cognitive/behavioral therapy with 7,275 sexual offenders. *Behavior Modification, 26*(2), 123–147.

Malinowski, B. (1927). *Sex and repression in savage society.* London: Kegan Paul, Trench, Trubner & Co.

Malinowski, B. (1929). *The sexual life of savages in north-western Melanesia.* New York: Eugenics.

Man pays victim's husband in fondling case. (2000, June 2). Reuters News Agency online.

Mansergh, G., et al. (2002). "Barebacking" in a diverse sample of men who have sex with men. *AIDS, 16*(4), 653–659.

Mantovani, F. (2001). Networked seduction: A test-bed for the study of strategic communication on the Internet. *CyberPsychology & Behavior, 4*(1), 147–154.

Marazziti, D., et al. (2003). Normal and obsessional jealousy: A study of a population of young adults. *European Psychiatry, 18*(3), 106–111.

Marchbanks, P. A., et al. (2000). Cigarette smoking and epithelial ovarian cancer by histologic type. *Obstetrics & Gynecology, 95,* 255–260.

Marchbanks, P. A., et al. (2002). Oral contraceptives and the risk of breast cancer. *New England Journal of Medicine, 346,* 2025–2032.

Marcus, A. J. (1995). Aspirin as a prophylaxis against colorectal cancer. *New England Journal of Medicine, 333,* 656–658.

Marcus, D. K., & Miller, R. S. (2003). Sex differences in judgments of physical attractiveness: A social relations analysis. *Personality & Social Psychology Bulletin, 29*(3), 325–335.

Mardorossian, C. M. (2002). Toward a new feminist theory of rape. *Signs, 27*(3), 743–775.

Marks, G., Miller, N., & Maruyama, G. (1981). Effect of targets' physical attractiveness on assumption of similarity. *Journal of Personality and Social Psychology, 41,* 198–206.

Marquis, C. (2003, March 16). Living in sin. *The New York Times,* p. WK2.

Marrazzo, J. (2003). Vulvovaginal candidiasis: Over-the-counter treatment doesn't seem to lead to resistance. *British Medical Journal, 326,* 993–994.

Marshall, D. (1971). Sexual behavior on Mangaia. In D. Marshall & R. Suggs (Eds.), *Human sexual behavior: Variations in the ethnographic spectrum* (pp. 103–162). New York: Basic Books.

Marshall, W. L. (1989). Pornography and sex offenders. In D. Zillmann & J. Bryant (Eds.), *Pornography: Research advances and policy considerations* (pp. 185–214). Hillsdale, NJ: Erlbaum.

Marsiglio, W. (1993a). Adolescent male's orientation toward paternity and contraception. *Family Planning Perspectives, 25,* 22–31.

Marsiglio, W. (1993b). Attitudes toward homosexual activity and gays as friends: A national survey of heterosexual 15- to 19-year-old males. *Journal of Sex Research, 30,* 12–17.

Martin, C. L., & Halverson, C. F., Jr. (1983). The effects of sex-typing schemas on young children's memory. *Child Development, 54,* 563–574.

Martinez, F. D., Cline, M., & Burrows, B. (1992). Increased incidence of asthma in children of smoking mothers. *Pediatrics, 89,* 21–26.

Martinson, F. M. (1976). Eroticism in infancy and childhood. *The Journal of Sex Research, 2,* 251–262.

Martz, J. M., et al. (1998). Positive illusion in close relationships. *Personal Relationships, 5*(2), 159–181.

Marwick, C. (2000). Consensus panel considers osteoporosis. *Journal of the American Medical Association* online, 283(16).

Masters, W. H., & Johnson, V. E. (1966). *Human sexual response.* Boston: Little, Brown.

Masters, W. H., & Johnson, V. E. (1970). *Human sexual inadequacy.* Boston: Little, Brown.

Masters, W. H., & Johnson, V. E. (1979). *Homosexuality in perspective.* Boston: Little, Brown.

Matthews, K. A., et al. (1990). Influences of natural menopause on psychological characteristics and symptoms of middle-aged healthy women. *Journal of Consulting and Clinical Psychology, 58,* 345–351.

Maundeni, T. (2000). The consequences of parental separation and divorce for the economic, social and emotional circumstances of children in Botswana. *Childhood: A Global Journal of Child Research, 7*(2), 213–223.

Maxson, S. C. (1998). Homologous genes, aggression, and animal models. *Developmental Neuropsychology, 14*(1), 143–156.

Maxwell, C. D., Robinson, A. L., & Post, L. A. (2003). The nature and predictors of sexual victimization and offending among adolescents. *Journal of Youth & Adolescence, 32*(6), 465–477.

Maybach, K. L., & Gold, S. R. (1994). Hyperfemininity and attraction to macho and nonmacho men. *Journal of Sex Research, 31*(2), 91–98.

McAndrew, F. T. (2002). New evolutionary perspectives on altruism: Multilevel-selection and costly-signaling theories. *Current Directions in Psychological Science, 11*(2), 79–82.

McBride, C. K., Paikoff, R. L., & Holmbeck, G. N. (2003). Individual and familial influences on the onset of sexual intercourse among urban African American adolescents. *Journal of Consulting and Clinical Psychology, 71*(1), 159–167.

McCabe, K. A. (2000). Child pornography and the Internet. *Social Science Computer Review, 18*(1), 73–76.

McCaughey, M., & French, C. (2001). Women's sex-toy parties: Technology, orgasm, and commodification. *Sexuality & Culture: An Interdisciplinary Quarterly, 5*(3), 77–96.

McCoy, N. L., & Pitino, L. (2002). Pheromonal influences on sociosexual behavior in young women. *Physiology & Behavior, 75*(3), 367–375.

McDonough, Y. Z. (1998, January 24). What Barbie really taught me. *The New York Times Magazine,* p. 70.

McElduff, A., & Beange, H. (2003). Men's health and well-being: Testosterone deficiency. *Journal of Intellectual & Developmental Disability, 28*(2), 211–213.

McGuire, R. J., Carlisle, J. M., & Young, B. G. (1965). Sexual deviation as conditioned behavior: A hypothesis. *Behaviour Research and Therapy, 2,* 185–190.

McKinney, K., & Maroules, N. (1991). Sexual harassment. In E. Grauerholz & M. A. Koralewski (Eds.), *Sexual coercion: A sourcebook on its nature, causes, and prevention* (pp. 29–44). Lexington, MA: Lexington Books.

McLean, P. M. (1976). Brain mechanisms of elemental sexual functions. In B. J. Sadock et al. (Eds.), *The sexual experience.* Baltimore: Williams & Wilkins.

McMahon, M. J., et al. (1996). Comparison of a trial of labor with an elective second cesarean section. *The New England Journal of Medicine, 335,* 689–695.

McNeil, D. G., Jr. (2004, March 27). Fast saliva test for HIV gains federal approval. *The New York Times* online.

Mead, M. (1935). *Sex and temperament in three primitive societies.* New York: Dell.

Mead, M. (1967). *Male and female: A study of the sexes in a changing world.* New York: William Morrow.

Meana, M., & Binik, Y. M. (1994). Painful coitus: A review of female dyspareunia. *Journal of Nervous and Mental Disease, 182*(5), 264–272.

Medrano, M. A., Hatch, J. P., Zule, W. A., & Desmond, D. P. (2003). Childhood trauma and adult prostitution behavior in a multiethnic heterosexual drug-using population. *American Journal of Drug & Alcohol Abuse, 29*(2), 463–486.

Meijers-Heijboer, H., et al. (2000). Presymptomatic DNA testing and prophylactic surgery in families with a *BRCA1* or *BRCA2* mutation. *The Lancet* online, 355(9220).

Meijers-Heijboer, H., et al. (2001). Breast cancer after prophylactic bilateral mastectomy in women with a *BRCA1* or *BRCA2* mutation. *New England Journal of Medicine, 345,* 159–164.

Menard, K. S., et al. (2003) Gender differences in sexual harassment and coercion in college students: Developmental, individual, and situational determinants. *Journal of Interpersonal Violence, 18*(10), 1222–1239.

Merck Manual of Medical Information (2002). Cited in Brody, J. E. (2002a, January 1). What women must know about fertility. *The New York Times,* F6.

Messenger, J. C. (1971). Sex and repression in an Irish folk community. In D. S. Marshall and R. C. Suggs (Eds.), *Human sexual behavior: Variations in the ethnographic spectrum* (pp. 3–37). New York: Basic Books.

Meston, C. M., & Frohlich, P. F. (2000). The neurobiology of sexual function. *Archives of General Psychiatry, 57*(11), 1012–1030.

Meyer, I. H. (2003). Prejudice, social stress, and mental health in lesbian, gay, and bisexual populations: Conceptual issues and research evidence. *Psychological Bulletin, 129*(5), 674–697.

Meyer, I. H., Rossano, L., Ellis, J. M., & Bradford, J. (2002). A brief telephone interview to identify lesbian and bisexual women in random digit sampling. *Journal of Sex Research, 39*(2), 139–144.

Meyer, J. K., & Reter, D. J. (1979). Sex reassignment: Follow-up. *Archives of General Psychiatry, 36,* 1010–1015.

Meyer, T. (1998, February 18). AZT short treatment works. The Associated Press online.

Meyer-Bahlburg, H. F. L., et al. (1995). Prenatal estrogens and the development of homosexual orientation. *Developmental Psychology, 31*(1), 12–21.

Michael, R. T., Gagnon, J. H., Laumann, E. O., & Kolata, G. (1994). *Sex in America: A definitive survey.* Boston: Little, Brown.

Michelson, D., et al. (2000). Female sexual dysfunction associated with antidepressant administration: A randomized, placebo-controlled study of pharmacologic intervention. *American Journal of Psychiatry, 157,* 239–243.

Migeon, C. J., & Donohue, P. A. (1991). Congenital adrenal hyperplasia caused by 21-hydroxylase deficiency: Its molecular basis and its remaining therapeutic problems. *Endocrinology & Metabolism Clinics of North America, 20*(2), 277–296.

Mikach, S. M., & Bailey, J. M. (1999). What distinguishes women with unusually high numbers of sex partners? *Evolution & Human Behavior, 20*(3), 141–150.

Mill, J. S. (1939). Utilitarianism. In E. A. Burtt (Ed.), *The English philosophers.* New York: The Modern Library. (Original work published 1863)

Miller, B. C., McCoy, J. K., & Olson, T. D. (1986). Dating age and stage as correlates of adolescent sexual attitudes and behavior. *Journal of Adolescent Research, 1,* 361–371.

Miller, G. T., & Pitnick, S. (2002). Sperm-female coevolution in *Drosophila. Science, 298,* 1230–1233.

Miller, M. (1998). Cited in Bronner, E. (1998, February 1). Just say maybe. No sexology, please. We're Americans. *The New York Times,* p. WK6.

Minichiello, V., et al. (2001). Male sex workers in three Australian cities: Socio-demographic and sex work characteristics. *Journal of Homosexuality, 42*(1), 29–51.

Missailidis, K., & Gebre-Medhin, M. (2000). Female genital mutilation in eastern Ethiopia. *The Lancet, 356,* 137–138.

Modell, J. G., May, R. S., & Katholi, C. R. (2000). Effect of bupropion-SR on orgasmic dysfunction in nondepressed subjects: A pilot study. *Journal of Sex & Marital Therapy, 26*(3), 231–240.

Mofenson, L. M. (2000). Perinatal exposure to zidovudine—Benefits and risks. *The New England Journal of Medicine* online, 343(11).

Mohr, D. C., & Beutler, L. E. (1990). Erectile dysfunction: A review of diagnostic and treatment procedures. *Clinical Psychology Review, 10,* 123–150.

Money, J. (1994). The concept of gender identity disorder in childhood and adolescence after 39 years. *Journal of Sex and Marital Therapy, 20*(3), 163–177.

Money, J. (2000). Reflections of a gender biographer. *Men & Masculinities, 3*(2), 209–216.

Monson, C. M., Langhinrichsen-Rohling, J., & Binderup, T. (2000). Does "no" really mean "no" after you say "yes"? Attributions about date and marital rape. *Journal of Interpersonal Violence, 15*(11), 1156–1174.

Montano, D., Kasprzyk, D., von Haeften, I., & Fishbein, M. (2001). Toward an understanding of condom use behaviours: A theoretical and methodological overview of Project SAFER. *Psychology, Health & Medicine, 6*(2), 139–150.

Montemurro, B., Bloom, C., & Madell, K. (2003). Ladies night out: A typology of women patrons of a male strip club. *Deviant Behavior, 24*(4), 333–352.

Moore, S., & Leung, C. (2002). Young people's romantic attachment styles and their association with well-being. *Journal of Adolescence, 25*(2), 243–255.

Morley, J. E., & Perry, H. M., III. (2003). Androgens and women at the menopause and beyond. *Journals of Gerontology: Series A: Biological Sciences & Medical Sciences, 58A*(5), 409–416.

Morley, J. E., & van den Berg, L. (2000). *Endocrinology of aging.* Totowa, NJ: Humana Press.

Morofushi, M., Shinohara, K., Funabashi, T., & Kimura, F. (2000). Positive relationship between menstrual synchrony and ability to smell 5alpha-androst-16-en-3alpha-ol. *Chemical Senses, 25*(4), 407–411.

Morris, L. B. (2000, June 25). For the partum blues, a question of whether to medicate. *The New York Times* online.

Morris, N., et al. (1987). Marital sex frequency and midcycle female testosterone. *Archives of Sexual Behavior, 7,* 157–173.

Morrison, E. S., et al. (1980). *Growing up sexual.* New York: Van Nostrand Reinhold.

Mortola, J. F. (1998). Premenstrual syndrome: Pathophysiologic considerations. *New England Journal of Medicine, 338,* 256–257.

Muehlenhard, C. L., & Linton, M. A. (1987). Date rape and sexual aggression in dating situations: Incidence and risk factors. *Journal of Counseling Psychology, 34,* 186–196.

Mulac, A., Jansma, L. L., & Linz, D. G. (2002). Men's behavior toward women after viewing sexually-explicit films: Degradation makes a difference. *Communication Monographs, 69*(4), 311–328.

Mulick, P. S., & Wright, L. W., Jr. (2002). Examining the existence of biphobia in the heterosexual and homosexual populations. *Journal of Bisexuality, 2*(4), 45–64.

Mundy, L. (2000, July 16). Sex and sensibility. *The Washington Post* online.

Munarriz, R., et al. (2002). Androgen replacement therapy with dehydroepiandrosterone for androgen insufficiency and female sexual dysfunction: Androgen and questionnaire results. *Journal of Sex & Marital Therapy, 28*(Suppl1), 165–173.

Murray, S. L., Bellavia, G., Feeney, B., Holmes, J. G., & Rose, P. (2001). The contingencies of interpersonal acceptance: When romantic relationships function as a self-affirmational resource. *Motivation & Emotion, 25*(2), 163–189.

Murray, S. L., & Holmes, J. G. (2000). Seeing the self through a partner's eyes: Why self-doubts turn into relationship insecurities. In A. Tesser, R. B. Felson, et al. (Eds.), *Psychological perspectives on self and identity* (pp. 173–197). Washington: American Psychological Association.

Nabel, G. J., & Sullivan, N. J. (2000). Antibodies and resistance to natural HIV infection. *The New England Journal of Medicine* online, *343*(17).

Nadler, R. D. (1990). Homosexual behavior in nonhuman primates. In D. P. McWhirter, S. A. Sanders, & J. M. Reinisch (Eds.), *Homosexuality/heterosexuality: Concepts of sexual orientation* (pp. 138–170). New York: Oxford University Press.

Naimi, T. S., et al. (2003a). Binge drinking among U.S. adults. *Journal of the American Medical Association, 289*(1), 70–75.

Naimi, T. S., et al. (2003b). Definitions of binge drinking. *Journal of the American Medical Association, 289*(13), 1636.

Nakaya, M. (2002). Fluvoxamine treatment of a Japanese patient with Koro. *Journal of Clinical Psychiatry, 63*(12), 1182–1183.

Nanda, S., & Warms, R. L. (2004). *Cultural anthropology* (8th ed.). Belmont, CA: Wadsworth.

Narod, S. A., et al. (1998). Oral contraceptives and the risk of hereditary ovarian cancer. *New England Journal of Medicine, 339,* 424–428.

National Campaign to Prevent Teen Pregnancy. (2003, September 30). Teens say parents most influence their sexual decisions: New polling data and "Tips for Parents" released. *http://www.teenpregnancy.org/about/announcements/pr/2003/release9_30_03.asp*

National Cancer Institute. (2003). *http://www.nci.nih.gov/*

National Center for Biotechnology Information (NCBI). (2000, March 30). National Institute of Health. *http://www.ncbi.nlm.nih.gov/disease/SRY.html*

Nduati, R., et al. (2000). Effect of breastfeeding and formula feeding on transmission of HIV-1. *Journal of the American Medical Association, 283,* 1167–1174.

Neerman-Arbez, M. (2003, June 4). Genes implicated in sexual differentiation. Geneva Foundation for Medical Education and Research. *http://www.gfmer.ch/Endo/Lectures_10/Sexualdi.htm*

Neff, K. D., & Harter, S. (2003). Relationship styles of self-focused autonomy, other-focused connectedness, and mutuality across multiple relationship contexts. *Journal of Social & Personal Relationships, 20*(1), 81–99.

Nelson, H. D., Humphrey, L. L., Nygren, P., Teutsch, S. M., & Allan, J. D. (2002). Postmenopausal hormone replacement therapy: Scientific review. *Journal of the American Medical Association, 288,* 872–881.

Nevid, J. S. (1984). Sex differences in factors of romantic attraction. *Sex Roles, 11,* 401–411.

Ngai, S. W., Tang, O. S., Chan, Y. M., & Ho, P. C. (2000). Vaginal misoprostol alone for medical abortion up to 9 weeks of gestation: Efficacy and acceptability. *Human Reproduction, 15*(5), 1159–1162.

Nieder, T., & Sieffge-Krenke, I. (2001). Coping with stress in different phases of romantic development. *Journal of Adolescence, 24*(3), 297–311.

Nieto, J. J., Cogswell, D., Jesinger, D., & Hardiman, P. (2000). Lipid effects of hormone replacement therapy with sequential transdermal 17-beta-estradiol and oral dydrogesterone. *Obstetrics & Gynecology, 95,* 111–114.

Nosek, M. A., et al. (1994). Wellness models and sexuality among women with physical disabilities. *Journal of Applied Rehabilitation Counseling, 25*(1), 50–58.

Nour, N. W. (2000). Cited in Dreifus, C. (2000, July 11). A conversation with Dr. Nawal M. Nour: A life devoted to stopping the suffering of mutilation. *The New York Times* online.

O'Brien, L. T., & Crandall, C. S. (2003). Stereotype threat and arousal: Effects on women's math performance. *Personality & Social Psychology Bulletin, 29*(6), 782–789.

O'Connor, T. G., Caspi, A., DeFries, J. C., & Plomin, R. (2000). Are associations between parental divorce and children's adjustment genetically mediated? An adoption study. *Developmental Psychology, 36*(4), 429–437.

O'Dell, K. M. C., & Kaiser, K. (1997). Sexual behaviour: Secrets and flies. *Current Biology, 7*(6), R345–R347.

O'Doherty, J., et al. (2003). Beauty in a smile: The role of medial orbitofrontal cortex in facial attractiveness. *Neuropsychologia, 41*(2), 147–155.

O'Donnell, L., et al. (2003). Long-term influence of sexual norms and attitudes on timing of sexual initiation among urban minority youth. *Journal of School Health, 23*(2), 68–75.

O'Donohue, W., Yeater, E. A., & Fanetti, M. (2003). Rape prevention with college males: The roles of rape myth acceptance, victim empathy, and outcome expectancies. *Journal of Interpersonal Violence, 18*(5), 513–531.

Ogletree, S. M., & Ginsburg, H. J. (2000). Kept under the hood: Neglect of the clitoris in common vernacular. *Sex Roles, 43*(11–12), 917–926.

Okami, P., & Goldberg, A. (1992). Personality correlates of pedophilia: Are they reliable indicators? *Journal of Sex Research, 29,* 297–328.

Okami, P., Weisner, T., & Olmstead, R. (2002). Outcome correlates of parent–child bedsharing: An eighteen-year longitudinal study. *Journal of Developmental & Behavioral Pediatrics, 23*(4), 244–253.

O'Keeffe, M. J., et al. (2003). Learning, cognitive, and attentional problems in adolescents born small for gestational age. *Pediatrics, 112*(2), 301–307.

Olds, J. (1956). Pleasure centers in the brain. *Scientific American, 193,* 105–116.

Olds, J., & Milner, P. (1954). Positive reinforcement produced by electrical stimulation of the septal area and other regions of the rat brain. *Journal of Comparative and Physiological Psychology, 47,* 419–427.

Osman, S. L. (2003). Predicting men's rape perceptions based on the belief that "No" really means "Yes." *Journal of Applied Social Psychology, 33*(4), 683–692.

Ostrow, D. E., et al. (2002). Attitudes towards highly active antiretroviral therapy are associated with sexual risk taking among HIV-infected and uninfected homosexual men. *AIDS, 16*(5), 775–780.

Overbeek, P. (1999). Cited in Philipkoski, K. (1999, October 28). Why men are that way. Wired Digital, Inc.

Overholser, J. C., & Beck, S. (1986). Multimethod assessment of rapists, child molesters, and three control groups on behavioral and psychological measures. *Journal of Consulting and Clinical Psychology, 54,* 682–687.

Padma-Nathan, H., et al. (1997). Treatment of men with erectile dysfunction with transurethral alprostadil. *New England Journal of Medicine, 336,* 1–7.

Palace, E. M. (1995). Modification of dysfunctional patterns of sexual arousal through autonomic arousal and false physiological feedback. *Journal of Consulting and Clinical Psychology, 63,* 604–615.

Palmore, E. (1981). *Social patterns in normal aging: Findings from the Duke Longitudinal Study.* Durham, NC: Duke University Press.

Paraskevis, D., et al. (2003). Analysis of the evolutionary relationships of HIV-1 and SIVcpz sequences using Bayesian inference: Implications for the origin of HIV-1.

Molecular Biology and Evolution, 20, 1986–1996.

Parsons, N. K., Richards, H. C., & Kanter, G. D. (1990). Validation of a scale to measure reasoning about abortion. *Journal of Counseling Psychology, 37,* 107–112.

Pasupathi, M., Carstensen, L. L., Levenson, R. W., & Gottman, J. M. (1999). Responsive listening in long-married couples: A psycholinguistic perspective. *Journal of Nonverbal Behavior, 23*(2), 173–193.

Pauly, B., & Edgerton, M. (1986). The gender-identity movement. *Archives of Sexual Behavior, 15,* 315–329.

Pawlowski, B., & Koziel, S. (2002). The impact of traits offered in personal advertisements on response rates. *Evolution & Human Behavior, 23*(2), 139–149.

Peacock, P. (1998). Marital rape. In R. K. Bergen (Ed.), *Issues in intimate violence* (pp. 225–235). Thousand Oaks, CA: Sage.

Pearlstein, T., & Steiner, M. (2000). Non-antidepressant treatment of premenstrual syndrome. *Journal of Clinical Psychiatry, 61*(Suppl 12), 22–27.

Pedersen, W., & Hegna, K. (2003). Children and adolescents who sell sex: A community study. *Social Science & Medicine, 56*(1), 135–147.

Peplau, L. A. (2003). Human sexuality: How do men and women differ? *Current Directions in Psychological Science, 12*(2), 37–40.

Peplau, L. A., & Cochran, S. D. (1990). A relationship perspective on homosexuality. In D. P. McWhirter, S. A. Sanders, & J. M. Reinisch (Eds.), *Homosexuality/heterosexuality: Concepts of sexual orientation* (pp. 321–349). New York: Oxford University Press.

Perrett, D. I. (1994). *Nature.* Cited in Brody, J. E. (1994, March 21). Notions of beauty transcend culture, new study suggests. *The New York Times,* p. A14.

Perriëns, J. (2000). Cited in UNAIDS calls for continued commitment to microbicides. (2000, July 12). UNAIDS press release.

Perry, D. G., & Bussey, K. (1979). The social learning theory of sex differences: Imitation is alive and well. *Journal of Personality and Social Psychology, 37,* 1699–1712.

Perry, J. D., & Whipple, B. (1981). Pelvic muscle strength of female ejaculation: Evidence in support of a new theory of orgasm. *Journal of Sex Research, 17,* 22–39.

Perry, P. J., et al. (2001). Bioavailable testosterone as a correlate of cognition, psychological status, quality of life, and sexual function in aging males: Implications for testosterone replacement therapy. *Annals of Clinical Psychiatry, 13*(2), 75–80.

Peto, J. (2002). Breast cancer may be inherited. Paper delivered to the Oncogenomics conference in Dublin, May.

Pettit, R. B. (Ed.). (2003). Sexual teens, sexual media: Investigating media's influence on adolescent sexuality. *Journal of Social & Personal Relationships, 20*(2), 262–263.

Phillips, F. (2003, April 8). Support for gay marriage. *Boston Globe.*

Pillard, R. C. (1990). The Kinsey Scale: Is it familial? In D. P. McWhirter, S. A. Sanders, & J. M. Reinisch (Eds.), *Homosexuality/heterosexuality: Concepts of sexual orientation* (pp. 88–100). New York: Oxford University Press.

Pillard, R. C., & Weinrich, J. D. (1986). Evidence of familial nature of male homosexuality. *Archives of Sexual Behavior, 43,* 808–812.

Pinkerton, S. D., Bogart, L. M., Cecil, H., & Abramson, P. R. (2002). Factors associated with masturbation in collegiate sample. *Journal of Psychology & Human Sexuality, 14*(2–3), 103–121.

Pinkerton, S. D., Cecil, H., Bogart, L. M., & Abramson, P. R. (2003a). The pleasures of sex: An empirical investigation. *Cognition & Emotion, 17*(2), 341–353.

Pinkerton, S. D., et al. (2003b). HIV/AIDS knowledge and attitudes of STD clinic attendees in St. Petersburg, Russia. *AIDS & Behavior, 7*(3), 221–228.

Pistella, C. L., & Bonati, F. A. (1999). Adolescent women's recommendations for enhanced parent–adolescent communication about sexual behavior. *Child & Adolescent Social Work Journal, 16*(4), 305–315.

Plant, E. A., Hyde, J. S., Keltner, D., & Devine, P. G. (2000). The gender stereotyping of emotions. *Psychology of Women Quarterly, 24*(1), 81–92.

Plante, T. G. (2003). Priests behaving badly: What do we know about priest sex offenders? *Sexual Addiction & Compulsivity: The Journal of Treatment and Prevention, 10*(2–3), 93–97.

Plomin, R. (Ed.). (2002). *Behavioral genetics in the postgenomic era.* Washington, DC: American Psychological Association.

Plomin, R., & Crabbe, J. (2000). DNA. *Psychological Bulletin, 126*(6), 806–828.

Poll: Abortion views conflicted. (2000, June 18). The Associated Press.

Pollack, H. A. (2001). Sudden infant death syndrome, maternal smoking during pregnancy, and the cost-effectiveness of smoking cessation intervention. *American Journal of Public Health, 91*(3), 432–436.

Poniewozik, J., et al. (2000, June 26). We like to watch: Led by the hit Survivor, voyeurism has become TV's hottest genre. Why the passion for peeping? *Time, 155*(26), 56–62.

Potosky, A. L., et al. (2000). Health outcomes after prostatectomy or radiotherapy for prostate cancer: Results from the Prostate Cancer Outcomes Study. *Journal of the National Cancer Institute, 92,* 1582–1592.

Poussaint, A. (1990, September). An honest look at Black gays and lesbians. *Ebony,* pp. 124–131.

Powell, E. (1991). *Talking back to sexual pressure.* Minneapolis. MN: CompCare Publishers.

Powell, E. (1996). *Sex on your terms.* Boston: Allyn & Bacon.

Prentky, R. A., & Knight, R. A. (1991). Identifying critical dimensions for discriminating among rapists. *Journal of Consulting and Clinical Psychology, 59,* 643–661.

Preti, G., Cutler, W. B., et al. (1986). Human axillary secretions influence women's menstrual cycles: The role of donor extract of females. *Hormones and Behavior, 20,* 474–482.

Preti, G., Wysocki, C. J., Barnhart, K. T., Sondheimer, S. J., & Leyden, J. J. (2003). Male axillary extracts contain pheromones that affect pulsatile secretion of luteinizing hormone and mood in women recipients. *Biology of Reproduction, 68*(6), 2107–2113.

Price, M., Gutheil, T. G., Commons, M. L., Kafka, M. P., & Dodd-Kimmey, S. (2001). Telephone scatologia: Comorbidity and theories of etiology. *Psychiatric Annals, 31*(4), 226–232.

Price, M., Kafka, M., Commons, M. L., Gutheil, T. G., & Simpson, W. (2002). Telephone scatologia: Comorbidity with other paraphilias and paraphilia-related disorders. *International Journal of Law & Psychiatry, 25*(1), 37–49.

Price, V. A. (1989). Characteristics and needs of Boston street youth: One agency's response [Special Issue: Runaway, homeless, and shutout children and youth in Canada, Europe, and the United States]. *Children and Youth Services Review, 11,* 75–90.

Proctor, F., Wagner, N., & Butler, J. (1974). The differentiation of male and female orgasm: An experimental study. In N. Wagner (Ed.), *Perspectives on human sexuality.* New York: Behavioral Publications.

Prostatecare. (2003). A comprehensive guide to prostate health. *www.prostatecare.com.*

Puente, S., & Cohen, D. (2003). Jealousy and the meaning (or nonmeaning) of violence. *Personality & Social Psychology Bulletin, 29*(4), 449–460.

Quartaro, G. K., & Spier, T. E. (2002). We'd like to ask you some questions, but we have to find you first: Internet-based study of lesbian clients in therapy with lesbian feminist therapists. *Journal of Technology in Human Services, 19*(2–3), 109–118.

Quayle, E., & Taylor, M. (2002). Child pornography and the Internet: Perpetuating a cycle of abuse. *Deviant Behavior, 23*(4), 331–362.

Quayle, E., & Taylor, M. (2003). Model of problematic Internet use in people with sexual interest in children. *CyberPsychology & Behavior, 6*(1), 93–106.

Quereshi, B. (2003). *http://www.familymedicine.co.uk/features/circum3.htm*

Quinsey, V. L., Chaplin, T. C., & Upfold, D. (1984). Sexual arousal to nonsexual violence and sadomasochistic themes among rapists and non-sex-offenders. *Journal of Consulting and Clinical Psychology, 52,* 651–657.

Rachlin, K. (2002). Transgender individuals' experiences of psychotherapy. *International Journal of Transgenderism, 6*(1).

Rahman, Q., & Wilson, G. D. (2003). Born gay? The psychobiology of human sexual orientation. *Personality & Individual Differences, 34*(8), 1337–1382.

Raichle, K., & Lambert, A. J. (2000). The role of political ideology in mediating judgments of blame in rape victims and their assailants: A test of the just world, personal responsibility, and legitimization hypotheses. *Personality & Social Psychology Bulletin, 26*(7), 853–863.

Raj, R. (2002). Towards a transpositive therapeutic model: Developing clinical sensitivity and cultural competence in the effective support of transsexual and transgendered clients. *International Journal of Transgenderism, 6*(2).

Rakic, Z., Starcevic, V., Starcevic, V. P., & Marinkovic, J. (1997). Testosterone treatment in men with erectile disorder and low levels of total testosterone in serum. *Archives of Sexual Behavior, 26*(5), 495–504.

Rako, S. (2003). *No more periods? The risks of menstrual suppression and other cutting-edge issues about hormones and women's health.* New York: Crown.

Ralph, D., & McNicholas, T. (2000). UK management guidelines for erectile dysfunction. *British Medical Journal, 321,* 499–503.

Rathus, S. A. (1978). Treatment of recalcitrant ejaculatory incompetence. *Behavior Therapy, 9,* 962.

Rathus, S. A. (2002). *Psychology in the new mil-*

lennium. Fort Worth: Harcourt College Publishers.

Rathus, S. A. (2003). *Voyages: Childhood and adolescence.* Belmont, CA: Wadsworth.

Rawlins, R. (1998). Cited in Kolata, G. (1998, September 9). Researchers report success in method to pick baby's sex. *The New York Times* online.

Rawson, R. A., Washton, A., Domier, C. P., & Reiber, C. (2002). Drugs and sexual effects: Role of drug type and gender. *Journal of Substance Abuse Treatment, 22*(2), 103–108.

Reaney, P. (1998, January 15). Discovery may lead to cervical cancer vaccine. Reuters News Agency online.

Reddy, D. M., et al. (2002). Effect of mandatory parental notification on adolescent girls' use of sexual health care services. *Journal of the American Medical Association, 288,* 710–714.

Reed, M., & Lampe, M. S. (2003). *Margaret Sanger: Her life in her words.* Barricade Books.

Refaat, A., Dandash, K. F., El-Defrawi, M. H., & Eyada, M. (2001). Female genital mutilation and domestic violence among Egyptian women. *Journal of Sex & Marital Therapy, 27*(5), 593–598.

Reiner, W. G. (2000, May 12). Cited in Study of children born without penises finds nature determines gender. Associated Press online.

Reinisch, J. M. (1990). *The Kinsey Institute new report on sex: What you must know to be sexually literate.* New York: St. Martin's Press.

Renzetti, C. M., et al. (2001). Sourcebook on violence against women. Thousand Oaks, CA: Sage.

Resick, P. A. (2003). Post hoc reasoning in possible cases of child sexual abuse: Just say no. *Clinical Psychology: Science & Practice, 10*(3), 349–351.

Reynolds, A., & Caron, S. L. (2000). How intimate relationships are impacted when heterosexual men crossdress. *Journal of Psychology & Human Sexuality, 12*(3), 63–77.

Reynolds, S. J., et al. (2004). Male circumcision and risk of HIV-1 and other sexually transmitted infections in India. *The Lancet, 363*(9414), 1039

Ricci, E., Parazzini, F, & Pardi, G. (2000). Caesarean section and antiretroviral treatment. *The Lancet, 355*(9202), 496–502.

Rice, M. E., Harris, G. T., & Quinsey, V. L. (1990). A follow-up of rapists assessed in a maximum-security psychiatric facility. *Journal of Interpersonal Violence, 5,* 435–448.

Rice, M. E., & Quinsey, V. L., & Harris, G. T. (1991). Sexual recidivism among child molesters released from a maximum security psychiatric institution. *Journal of Consulting and Clinical Psychology, 59,* 381–386.

Richters, J., Hendry, O., & Kippax, S. (2003). When safe sex isn't safe. *Culture, Health & Sexuality, 5*(1), 37–52.

Rickwood, A. M. K., Kenny, S. E., & Donnell, S. C. (2000). Towards evidence based circumcision of English boys: Survey of trends in practice. *British Medical Journal, 321,* 792–793.

Riggio, R. E., & Woll, S. B. (1984). The role of nonverbal cues and physical attractiveness in the selection of dating partners. *Journal of Social and Personal Relationships, 1,* 347–357.

Rimm, E. (2000). Lifestyle may play role in potential for impotence. Paper presented to the annual meeting of the American Urological Association, Atlanta, May.

Ring-Cassidy, E., & Gentles, I. (2002). *Women's health after abortion: The medical and psychological evidence.* The deVeber Institute.

Roberts, D. (2000). Black women and the pill. *Family Planning Perspectives* online, *32*(2).

Robinson, J. N., Norwitz, E. R., Cohen, A. P., & Lieberman, E. (2000). Predictors of episiotomy use at first spontaneous vaginal delivery. *Obstetrics & Gynecology, 96*(2), 214–218.

Roddy, R. E., et al. (1998). A controlled trial of Nonoxynol 9 film to reduce male-to-female transmission of sexually transmitted diseases. *New England Journal of Medicine, 339,* 504–510.

Rodriguez, I., Greer, C. A., Mok, M. Y., & Mombaerts, P. (2000). A putative pheromone receptor gene expressed in human olfactory mucosa. *Nature Genetics, 26*(1), 18–19.

Roesler, A., & Witztum, E. (2000). Pharmacotherapy of paraphilias in the next millennium. *Behavioral Sciences & the Law, 18*(1), 43–56.

Romenesko, K., & Miller, E. M. (1989). The second step in double jeopardy: Appropriating the labor of female street hustlers. *Crime and Delinquency, 35,* 109–135.

Rosen, R. C., & Laumann, E. O. (2003). The prevalence of sexual problems in women: How valid are comparisons across studies? Commentary on Bancroft, Loftus, and Long's (2003) "Distress about sex: A national survey of women in heterosexual relationships." *Archives of Sexual Behavior, 32*(3), 209–211.

Rosik, C. H. (2003). Motivational, ethical, and epistemological foundations in the treatment of unwanted homoerotic attraction. *Journal of Marital & Family Therapy, 29*(1), 13–28.

Rösler, A., & Witztum, E. (1998). Treatment of men with paraphilia with a long-acting analogue of gonadotropin releasing hormone. *New England Journal of Medicine, 338,* 416–422.

Rosman, J. P., & Resnick, P. J. (1989). Sexual attraction to corpses: A psychiatric review of necrophilia. *Bulletin of the American Academy of Psychiatry and the Law, 17,* 153–163.

Ross, J. L., Roeltgen, D., Feuillan, P., Kushner, H., & Cutler, W. B. (2000). Use of estrogen in young girls with Turner syndrome: Effects on memory. *Neurology, 54*(1), 164–170.

Ross, M., & Need, J. (1989). Effects of adequacy of gender reassignment surgery on psychological adjustment: A follow-up of fourteen male-to-female patients. *Archives of Sexual Behavior, 18,* 145–153.

Royce, R. A., Seña, A., Cates, W., Jr., & Cohen, M. S. (1997). Sexual transmission of HIV. *The New England Journal of Medicine, 336,* 1072–1078.

Rozee, P. D., & Koss, M. P. (2001). Rape: A century of resistance. *Psychology of Women Quarterly, 25*(4), 295–311.

Rozin, P., & Fallon, A. (1988). Body image, attitudes to weight, and misperceptions of figure preferences of the opposite sex: A comparison of men and women in two generations. *Journal of Abnormal Psychology, 97,* 342–345.

Rubin, A., & Adams, J. (1986). Outcomes of sexually open marriages. *Journal of Sex Research, 22,* 311–319.

Rubin, A. J. (2000, June 18). Americans narrowing support for abortion. *The Los Angeles Times* online.

Rusbult, C. E., Martz, J. M., & Agnew, C. R. (1998). The Investment Model Scale: Measuring commitment level, satisfaction level, quality of alternatives, and investment size. *Personal Relationships, 5*(4), 357–391.

Rusbult, C. E., & Van Lange, P. A. M. (2003). Interdependence, interaction and relationships. *Annual Review of Psychology, 54,* 351–375.

Russo, J. (2003). A new form of birth control pills. Retrieved on June 26, 2003, from *www.ivillagehealth.com.*

Russo, N. F., Horn, J. D., & Schwartz, R. (1992). U.S. abortion in context: Selected characteristics and motivations of women seeking abortions. *Journal of Social Issues, 48,* 183–202.

Sachar, E. (2003). Is cyberporn coming between you? *Ladies' Home Journal* online.

Sadalla, E. K., Kenrick, D. T., & Vershure, B. (1987). Dominance and heterosexual attraction. *Journal of Personality and Social Psychology, 52,* 730–738.

Sadker, M., & Sadker, D. (1994). *How America's schools cheat girls.* New York: Scribners.

Sadler, A. G., Booth, B. M., Nielson, D., & Doebbeling, B. N. (2000). Health-related consequences of physical and sexual violence: Women in the military. *Obstetrics & Gynecology, 96*(3), 473–480.

Sagan, C., & Dryan, A. (1990, April 22). The question of abortion: A search for answers. *Parade Magazine,* pp. 4–8.

Sagarin, B. J., Becker, D. V., Guadagno, R. E., Nicastle, L. D., & Millevoi, A. (2003). Sex differences (and similarities) in jealousy. The moderating influence of infidelity experience and sexual orientation of the infidelity. *Evolution & Human Behavior, 24*(1), 17–23.

Sandroni, P. (2003). Cited in Downs, M., & Nazario, B. (2003, February 11). Aphrodisiacs through the ages. WebMD Features.

Sanger, M. (1938). *Margaret Sanger: An autobiography.* New York: Norton.

Sangrador, J. L., & Yela, C. (2000). "What is beautiful is loved": Physical attractiveness in love relationships in a representative sample. *Social Behavior & Personality, 28*(3), 207–218.

Santelli, J. S., et al. (2003). Reproductive health in school-based health centers: Findings from the 1998–99 census of school-based health centers. *Journal of Adolescent Health, 32*(6), 443–451.

Santtila, P., Sandnabba, N. K., Alison, L., & Nordling, N. (2002). Investigating the underlying structure in sadomasochistically oriented behavior. *Archives of Sexual Behavior, 31*(2), 185–196.

Sarrel, P., & Masters, W. (1982). Sexual molestation of men by women. *Archives of Sexual Behavior, 11,* 117–131.

Savin-Williams, R. C., & Diamond, L. M. (2000). Sexual identity trajectories among sexual-minority youths: Gender comparisons. *Archives of Sexual Behavior, 29*(6), 607–627.

Savitz, L., & Rosen, L. (1988). The sexuality of prostitutes: Sexual enjoyment reported by "streetwalkers." *Journal of Sex Research, 24,* 200–208.

Saywitz, K. J., Mannarino, A. P., Berliner, L., & Cohen, J. A. (2000). Treatment for sexually abused children and adolescents. *American Psychologist, 55*(9), 1040–1049.

Schafer, R. B., & Keith, P. M. (1990). Matching by weight in married couples: A life cycle perspective. *Journal of Social Psychology, 130,* 657–664.

Schafran, L. H. (1995, August 26). Rape is still underreported. *The New York Times*, p. A19.

Schellenberg, E. G., Hirt, J., & Sears, A. (1999). Attitudes toward homosexuals among students at a Canadian university. *Sex Roles, 40*(1–2), 139–152.

Schiavi, R. C., et al. (1990). Healthy aging and male sexual function. *American Journal of Psychiatry, 147*, 766–771.

Schieve, L. A., et al. (1999). Live-birth rates and multiple-birth risk using in vitro fertilization. *Journal of the American Medical Association, 282*, 1832–1838.

Schmidt, P. J., et al. (1998). Differential behavioral effects of gonadal steroids in women with and in those without premenstrual syndrome. *New England Journal of Medicine, 338*, 209–216.

Schmitt, D. P. (2003). Universal sex differences in the desire for sexual variety: Tests from 52 nations, 6 continents, and 13 islands. *Journal of Personality and Social Psychology, 85*(1), 85–104.

Schmitt, D. P., Shackelford, T. K., Duntley, J., Tooke, W. & Buss, D. M. (2001). The desire for sexual variety as a key to understanding basic human mating strategies. *Personal Relationships, 8*(4), 425–455.

Schmitt, M. T., Branscombe, N. R., & Postmes, T. (2003). Women's emotional responses to the pervasiveness of gender discrimination. *European Journal of Social Psychology, 33*(3), 297–312.

Schonfeld, A. M., et al. (2001). Verbal and nonverbal fluency in children with heavy prenatal alcohol exposure. *Journal of Studies on Alcohol, 62*(2), 239–246.

Schott, R. L. (1995). The childhood and family dynamics of transvestites. *Archives of Sexual Behavior, 24*, 309–327.

Schroder, M., & Carroll, R. A. (1999). New women: Sexological outcomes of male-to-female gender reassignment surgery. *Journal of Sex Education & Therapy, 24*(3), 137–146.

Schroeder-Printzen, I., et al. (2000). Surgical therapy in infertile men with ejaculatory duct obstruction: Technique and outcome of a standardized surgical approach. *Human Reproduction, 15*, 1364–1368.

Schwartz, I. M. (1993). Affective reactions of American and Swedish women to their first premarital coitus: A cross-cultural comparison. *Journal of Sex Research, 30*, 18–26.

Schwartz, M. F., & Masters, W. H. (1984). The Masters and Johnson treatment program for dissatisfied homosexual men. *American Journal of Psychiatry, 141*, 173–181.

Seftel, A. D., Oates, R. D., & Krane, R. J. (1991). Disturbed sexual function in patients with spinal cord disease. *Neurologic Clinics, 9*, 757–778.

Segal, Z. V., & Marshall, W. L. (1985). Heterosexual social skills in a population of rapists and child molesters. *Journal of Consulting and Clinical Psychology, 53*, 55–63.

Segraves, R. T., & Althof, S. (1998). Psychotherapy and pharmacotherapy of sexual dysfunctions. In P. E. Nathan & J. M. Gorman (Eds.), A guide to treatments that work (pp. 447–471). London: Oxford University Press.

Segraves, R. T., et al. (2001). Bupropion sustained release (SR) for the treatment of hypoactive sexual desire disorder (HSDD) in nondepressed women. *Journal of Sex & Marital Therapy, 27*(3), 303–316.

Segrin, C., Powell, H. L., Givertz, M., & Brackin, A. (2003). Symptoms of depression, relational quality, and loneliness in dating relationships. *Personal Relationships, 10*(1), 25–36.

Seidman, S. M. (2003).The aging male: Androgens, erectile dysfunction, and depression. *Journal of Clinical Psychiatry, 64*(Suppl 10), 31–37.

Seiffge-Krenke, I., & Kuehnemund, M. (2001). Relationship experiences during adolescence: How important are they for predicting romantic outcomes in young adulthood? *Zeitschrift für Entwicklungspsychologie und Paedagogische Psychologie, 33*(2), 112–123.

Seligman, L., & Hardenburg, S. A. (2000). Assessment and treatment of paraphilias. *Journal of Counseling & Development, 78*(1), 107–113.

Sell, R. L., Wells, J. A., & Wypij, D. (1995). The prevalence of homosexual behavior and attraction in the United States, the United Kingdom, and France: Results of national, population-based samples. *Archives of Sexual Behavior, 24*, 235–248.

Seltzer, R. (1992). The social location of those holding antihomosexual attitudes. *Sex Roles, 26*, 391–398.

Selvin, B. W. (1993, June 1). Transsexuals are coming to terms with themselves and Society. *New York Newsday*, pp. 55, 58, 59.

Semans, J. (1956). Premature ejaculation: A new approach. *Southern Medical Journal, 49*, 353–358.

Semple, S. J., Patterson, T. L., & Grant, I. (2003). HIV-positive gay and bisexual men: Predictors of unsafe sex. *AIDS Care, 15*(1), 3–15.

Seng, M. J. (1989). Child sexual abuse and adolescent prostitution: A comparative analysis. *Adolescence, 24*, 665–675.

Servin, A., Nordenström, A., Larsson, A., & Bohlin, G. (2003). Prenatal androgens and gender-typed behavior: A study of girls with mild and severe forms of congenital adrenal hyperplasia. *Developmental Psychology, 39*(3), 440–450.

Seto, M. C., Maric, A., & Barbaree, H. E. (2001). The role of pornography in the etiology of sexual aggression. *Aggression and Violent Behavior, 6*, 35–53.

Sex abuse victims in Boston Church estimated at over 1,000. (2003). *The New York Times* online.

Shackelford, T. K., Buss, D. M., & Bennett, K. (2002). Forgiveness or breakup: Sex differences in responses to a partner's infidelity. *Cognition & Emotion, 16*(2), 299–307.

Sharp, D. (2002). Telling the truth about sex. *Lancet, 359*(9312), 1084.

Shaywitz, B. A., et al. (1995). Sex differences in the functional organization of the brain for language. *Nature, 373*, 607–609.

Sheldon, J. P., & Parent, S. L. (2002). Clergy's attitudes and attributions of blame toward female rape victims. *Violence Against Women, 8*(2), 233–256.

Shenon, P. (1995, July 15). New Zealand seeks causes of suicides by young. *The New York Times*, p. A3.

Sherwin, B. B., Gelfand, M. M., & Brender, W. (1985). Androgen enhances sexual motivation in females: A prospective, crossover study of sex steroid administration in the surgical menopause. *Psychosomatic Medicine, 47*, 339–351.

Shettles, L. (1982, June). Predetermining children's sex. *Medical Aspects of Human Sexuality*, 172.

Shibley-Hyde, J., & Durik, A. M. (2000). Gender differences in erotic plasticity: Evolutionary or sociocultural forces? Comment on Baumeister (2000). *Psychological Bulletin, 126*(3), 375–379.

Shifren, J. L., et al. (2000). Transdermal testosterone treatment in women with impaired sexual function after oophorectomy. *The New England Journal of Medicine* online, *343*(10), 682–688.

Shipko, S. (2000, February 7). Antidepressants linked to sexual side effects. WebMD/Healtheon.

Shlipak, M. G., et al. (2000). Estrogen and progestin, lipoprotein(a), and the risk of recurrent coronary heart disease events after menopause. *Journal of the American Medical Association, 283*, 1845–1852.

Shukla, P. R., & Singh, R. H. (2000). Supportive psychotherapy in Dhat syndrome patients. *Journal of Personality & Clinical Studies, 16*(1), 49–52.

Shultz, S. K., Scherman, A., & Marshall, L. J. (2000). Evaluation of a university-based date rape prevention program: Effect on attitudes and behavior related to rape. *Journal of College Student Development, 41*(2), 193–201.

Shuster, S. M., & Sassaman, C. (1997). Genetic interaction between male mating strategy and sex ratio in a marine isopod. *Nature, 388*(6640), 373–377.

Silber, S. J. (1991). *How to get pregnant with the new technology*. New York: Time Warner.

Simonsen, G., Blazina, C., & Watkins, C. E., Jr. (2000). Gender role conflict and psychological well-being among gay men. *Journal of Counseling Psychology, 47*(1), 85–89.

Simpson, J. L. (2000, June 1). Invasive diagnostic procedures for prenatal genetic diagnosis. *Journal Watch Women's Health*.

Singer, J., & Singer, I. (1972). Types of female orgasm. *Journal of Sex Research, 8*, 255–267.

Singh, D. (1994a). Body fat distribution and perception of desirable female body shape by young Black men and women. *International Journal of Eating Disorders, 16*(3), 289–294.

Singh, D. (1994b). Is thin really beautiful and good? Relationship between waist-to-hip ratio (WHR) and female attractiveness. *Personality and Individual Differences, 16*(1), 123–132.

Singh, D., Vidaurri, M., Zambarano, R. J., & Dabbs, J. M., Jr. (1999). Lesbian erotic role identification: Behavioral, morphological, and hormonal correlates. *Journal of Personality and Social Psychology, 76*(6), 1035–1049.

Singletary, K. W., & Gapstur, S. M. (2001). Alcohol and breast cancer: Review of epidemiologic and experimental evidence and potential mechanisms. *Journal of the American Medical Association, 286*, 2143–2151.

Sipski, M. L., Alexander, C. J., & Rosen, R. (2001). Sexual arousal and orgasm in women. *Annals of Neurology, 49*(1), 35–44.

Sirles, E. A., & Franke, P. J. (1989). Factors influencing mother's reactions to intrafamily sexual abuse. *Child Abuse & Neglect, 13*, 131–139.

Slovenko, R. (2001). Aphrodisiacs: Then and now. *Journal of Psychiatry & Law, 29*(1), 103–116.

Smith, M. J., Schmidt, P. J., & Rubinow, D. R. (2003). Operationalizing *DSM-IV* criteria for PMDD: Selecting symptomatic and asymptomatic cycles for research. *Journal of Psychiatric Research, 37*(1), 75–83.

Smock, P. J. (2000). *Annual Review of Sociology.* Cited in Nagourney, E. (2000, February 15). Study finds families bypassing marriage. *The New York Times,* p. F8.

Solano, C. H., Batten, P. G., & Parish, E. A. (1982). Loneliness and patterns of self-disclosure. *Journal of Personality and Social Psychology, 43,* 524–531.

Solomon, C. G., & Dluhy, R. G. (2003). Rethinking postmenopausal hormone therapy. *New England Journal of Medicine, 348*(7), 579–580.

Sommerfeld, J. (2000, April 18). Lifting the curse: Should monthly periods be optional? MSNBC online.

Spark, R. F. (1991). *Male sexual health: A couple's guide.* Mount Vernon, NY: Consumer Reports Books.

Speckens, A. E. M., et al. (1995). Psychosexual functioning of partners of men with presumed non-organic erectile dysfunction: Cause or consequence of the disorder? *Archives of Sexual Behavior, 24,* 157–172.

Spehr, M., et al. (2003). Identification of a testicular odorant receptor mediating human sperm chemotaxis. *Science, 299*(5615).

Spiegel, D. (2001). Breast cancer: Society shapes an epidemic. *New England Journal of Medicine, 334,* 1337–1338.

Spiro, M. E., (1965). *Children of the kibbutz.* New York: Schocken Books.

Spitzer, R. L., et al. (1989). *DSM-III-R casebook.* Washington, DC: American Psychiatric Press.

Sprecher, S., Barbee, A., & Schwartz, P. (1995). "Was it good for you, too?" Gender differences in first sexual intercourse experiences. *The Journal of Sex Research, 32,* 3–15.

Sprecher, S., Sullivan, Q., & Hatfield, E. (1994). Mate selection preferences: Gender differences examined in a national sample. *Journal of Personality and Social Psychology, 66*(6), 1074–1080.

Spring, J. A. (1997). Cited in Alterman, E. (1997, November). Sex in the '90s. *Elle,* p. 130.

Stake, J. E., & Hoffman, F. L. (2001). Changes in student social attitudes, activism, and personal confidence in higher education: The role of women's studies. *American Educational Research Journal, 38*(2), 411–436.

Stanford, J. L., et al. (2000). Urinary and sexual function after radical prostatectomy for clinically localized prostate cancer: The Prostate Cancer Outcomes Study. *Journal of the American Medical Association, 283,* 354–360.

Stangor, C., & Ruble, D. N. (1989). Differential influences of gender schemata and gender constancy on children's information processing and behavior. *Social Cognition, 7,* 353–372.

Stanley, S. M., Bradbury, T. N., & Markman, H. J. (2000). Structural flaws in the bridge from basic research on marriage to interventions for couples. *Journal of Marriage & the Family, 62*(1), 256–264.

Starr, B. D., & Weiner, M. B. (1981). *The Starr-Weiner report on sex and sexuality in the mature years.* New York: Stein & Day.

Stearns, V., Beebe, K. L., Iyengar, M., & Dube, E. (2003). Paroxetine controlled release in the treatment of menopausal hot flashes. *Journal of the American Medical Association, 289,* 2827–2834.

Steele, C. M., & Josephs, R. A. (1990). Alcohol myopia: Its prized and dangerous effects. *American Psychologist, 45,* 921–933.

Stein, D. J., Black, D. W., Shapira, N. A., & Spitzer, R. L. (2001). Hypersexual disorder and preoc-cupation with Internet pornography. *American Journal of Psychiatry, 158*(10), 1590–1594.

Stein, Z., & Susser, M. (2000). The risks of having children in later life. *British Medical Journal, 320*(7251), 1681–1682.

Steinhauer, J. (1995, July 6). No marriage, no apologies. *The New York Times,* pp. C1, C7.

Stengers, J., Van Neck, A., & Hoffmann, K. (2001). *Masturbation: The history of a great terror.* (2001). New York: St. Martin's Press.

Stenson, J. (2000). Laboring through the birthing options. MSNBC online.

Stephan, C. W., & Bachman, G. F. (1999). What's sex got to do with it? Attachment, love schemas, and sexuality. *Personal Relationships, 6*(1), 111–123.

Stephenson, J. (2000b). Widely used spermicide may increase, not decrease, risk of HIV transmission. *Journal of the American Medical Association* online, *284*(8).

Sternberg, R. J. (1986). A triangular theory of love. *Psychological Review, 93,* 119–135.

Sternberg, R. J. (1988). *The triangle of love: Intimacy, passion, commitment.* New York: Basic Books.

Stolberg, S. G. (1998a, January 18). Quandary on donor eggs: What to tell the children. *The New York Times,* pp. 1, 20.

Stolberg, S. G. (2003, October 3). Bill banning abortion procedure advances. *The New York Times.*

Storms, M. D. (1980). Theories of sexual orientation. *Journal of Personality and Social Psychology, 38,* 783–792.

Strager, S. (2003). What men watch when they watch pornography. *Sexuality & Culture: An Interdisciplinary Quarterly, 7*(1), 50–61.

Strassberg, D. S., & Holty, S. (2003). An experimental study of women's Internet personal ads. *Archives of Sexual Behavior, 32*(3), 253–260.

Streeter, S. A., & McBurney, D. H. (2003). Waist–hip ratio and attractiveness: New evidence and a critique of a "critical test." *Evolution & Human Behavior, 24*(2), 88–98.

Strickland, B. R. (1995). Research on sexual orientation and human development: A commentary. *Developmental Psychology, 31,* 137–140.

Struckman-Johnson, C. (1988). Forced sex on dates: It happens to men, too. *The Journal of Sex Research, 24,* 234–241.

Sulak, P. J., et al. (2000). Hormone withdrawal symptoms in oral contraceptive users. *Obstetrics & Gynecology, 95,* 261–266.

Sun, Y. (2001). Family environment and adolescents' well-being before and after parents' marital disruption: A longitudinal analysis. *Journal of Marriage & Family, 63*(3), 697–713.

Swann, W. B., Jr., et al. (1987). Cognitive–affective crossfire: When self-consistency meets self-enhancement. *Journal of Personality and Social Psychology, 52,* 881–889.

Symons, D. (1995). Cited in Goleman, D. (1995, June 14). Sex fantasy research said to neglect women. *The New York Times,* p. C14.

Szabo, R., & Short, R. V. (2000). How does male circumcision protect against HIV infection? *British Medical Journal, 320,* 1592–1594.

Szasz, G., & Carpenter, C. (1989). Clinical observations in vibratory stimulation of the penis of men with spinal cord injury. *Archives of Sexual Behavior, 18,* 461–474.

Taha, E. T., et al. (2003). Short postexposure prophylaxis in newborn babies to reduce mother-to-child transmission of HIV-1: NVAZ randomised clinical trial. *The Lancet, 362*(9391), 1171–1177.

Tan, R. S. (2001). *The andropause mystery: Unraveling truths about the male menopause.* Houston, TX: Amred Publishing.

Tan, R. S. Managing the andropause in aging men. *Clinical Geriatrics.* Retrieved March 23, 2002, from *http://www.mmhc.com/cg/articles/CG9907/Tan.html*

Tan, R. S., & Culberson, J. W. (2003). An integrative review on current evidence of testosterone replacement therapy for the andropause. *Maturitas, 45*(1), 15–27.

Tanfer, K., Grady, W. R., Klepinger, D. H., & Billy, J. O. G. (1993). Condom use among U.S. men, 1991. *Family Planning Perspectives, 25,* 61–66.

Tang, C. S., Critelli, J. W., & Porter, J. F. (1995). Sexual aggression and victimization in dating relationships among Chinese college students. *Archives of Sexual Behavior, 24,* 47–53.

Tang, M. C., Weiss, N. S., & Malone, K. E. (2000). Induced abortion in relation to breast cancer among parous women: A birth certificate registry study. *Epidemiology, 11*(2), 177–180.

Tashima, K. T., & Carpenter, C. C. J. (2003). Fusion inhibition—A major but costly step forward in the treatment of HIV-1. *New England Journal of Medicine, 348*(22), 2249–2250.

Tashiro, T., & Frazier, P. (2003). "I'll never be in a relationship like that again": Personal growth following romantic relationship breakups. *Personal Relationships, 10*(1), 113–128.

Taylor, C. (2000, June 26). Looking online. *Time, 155*(26), 60–61.

Tedeschi, J. T., & Felson, R. B. (1994). *Violence, aggression, and coercive actions.* Washington, DC: American Psychological Association.

Teen dies after complications from abortion pill. (2003, September 22). Associated Press.

Terry, D. J., Mayocchi, L., & Hynes, G. J. (1996). Depressive symptomology in new mothers: A stress and coping perspective. *Journal of Abnormal Psychology, 105,* 220–231.

Thompson, D. S. (1993) (Ed.). Every woman's health: The complete guide to body and mind. New York: Simon & Schuster.

Thompson, J. K., & Tantleff, S. (1992). Female and male ratings of upper torso: Actual, ideal, and stereotypical conceptions. *Journal of Social Behavior and Personality, 7,* 345–354.

Thompson, M. E. (1991). Self-defense against sexual coercion: Theory, research, and practice. In E. Grauerholz & M. A. Koralewski (Eds.), *Sexual coercion: A sourcebook on its nature, causes, and prevention* (pp. 111–121). Lexington, MA: Lexington Books.

Thornhill, R., & Palmer, C. (2000). *A natural history of rape: Biological bases of sexual coercion.* Cambridge, MA: MIT Press.

Tizabi, Y., Russell, L. T., Nespor, S. M., Perry, D. C., & Grunberg, N. E. (2000). Prenatal nicotine exposure: Effects on locomotor activity and central[-sup-1-sup-2-sup-5I]alpha-BT binding in rats. *Pharmacology, Biochemistry & Behavior, 66*(3), 495–500.

Torpy, J. M., Lynm, C., & Glass, R. M. (2003). Perimenopause: Beginning of menopause. *Journal of the American Medical Association, 289,* 940.

Townsend, J. M. (1995). Sex without emotional involvement: An evolutionary interpretation of sex differences. *Archives of Sexual Behavior, 24,* 173–206.

Trudel, G., Turgeon, L., & Piche, L. (2000). Marital and sexual aspects of old age. *Sexual & Relationship Therapy, 15*(4), 381–406.

Trujillo, C. (Ed.). (1991). *Chicana lesbians: The girls our mothers warned us about.* Berkeley, CA: Third Woman Press.

Tseng, W., et al. (1992). Koro epidemics in Guangdong, China: A questionnaire survey. *Journal of Nervous & Mental Disease, 180,* 117–123.

Tucker, J. S., & Anders, S. L. (1999). Attachment style, interpersonal perception accuracy, and relationship satisfaction in dating couples. *Personality & Social Psychology Bulletin, 25*(4), 403–412.

Tuiten, A., et al. (2000). Time course of effects of testosterone administration on sexual arousal in women. *Archives of General Psychiatry, 57,* 149–153.

Tunariu, A. D., & Reavey, P. (2003). Men in love: Living with sexual boredom. *Sexual & Relationship Therapy, 18*(1), 63–94.

Udry, J. R. (2001). Feminist critics uncover determinism, positivism, and antiquated theory. *American Sociological Review, 66*(4), 611–618.

Udry, J. R., & Billy, J. O. G. (1987). Initiation of coitus in early adolescence. *American Sociological Review, 52,* 841–855.

Udry, J. R., Talbert, L., & Morris, N. M. (1986). Biosocial foundations for adolescent female sexuality. *Demography, 23*(2), 217–230.

Udry, J., et al. (1985). Serum androgenic hormones motivate sexual behavior in adolescent boys. *Fertility and Sterility, 43,* 90–94.

UNAIDS. (2002, July 2). AIDS will claim 70 million by 2022. Reuters.

United Nations Special Session on AIDS. (2001, June 25–27). Preventing HIV/AIDS among young people. New York: United Nations.

U.S. Bureau of the Census. (1998). *Statistical abstract of the United States,* 118th ed. Washington, DC: U.S. Government Printing Office.

U.S. Bureau of the Census. (Internet release date: 1999, January 7). Marital status of the population 15 years old and over, by sex and race: 1950 to present.

U.S. Bureau of the Census. (2000). *Statistical abstract of the United States,* 120th ed. Washington, DC: U.S. Government Printing Office.

U.S. Department of Health and Human Services. (USDHHS). (2003, April 14). Births—Method of delivery. *National Vital Statistics Reports, 51*(2). National Center for Health Statistics. Centers for Disease Control and Prevention. *http://www.cdc.gov/nchs/fastats/delivery.htm*

U.S. Department of Justice. (1986). *Attorney general's commission on pornography: Final report.* Washington, DC: U.S. Government Printing Office.

U.S. Department of Justice. (2003) Office of Justice Programs. Bureau of Justice Statistics. *http://www.ojp.usdoj.gov/bjs/cvict.htm*

U.S. Merit Systems Protection Board. (1981). *Sexual harassment in the federal workplace: Is it a problem?* Washington, DC: Office of Merit Systems Review and Studies.

Vandello, J. A., & Cohen, D. (2003). Male honor and female fidelity: Implicit cultural scripts that perpetuate domestic violence. *Journal*

of Personality & Social Psychology, 84(5), 997–1010.

Van der Velde, F. W., van der Pligt, J., & Hooykaas, C. (1994). Perceiving AIDS-related risk: Accuracy as a function of differences in actual risk. *Health Psychology, 13,* 25–33.

van de Vijver, M. J., et al. (2002). A gene-expression signature as a predictor of survival in breast cancer. *The New England Journal of Medicine, 347*(25), 1999–2009.

Van Lange, P. A. M., et al. (1997). Willingness to sacrifice in close relationships. *Journal of Personality & Social Psychology, 72*(6), 1373–1395.

Van Minnen, A., & Kampman, M. (2000). The interaction between anxiety and sexual functioning: A controlled study of sexual functioning in women with anxiety disorders. *Sexual & Relationship Therapy, 15*(1), 47–57.

Van Wie, V. E., & Gross, A. M. (2001). The role of woman's explanations for refusal on men's ability to discriminate unwanted sexual behavior in a date rape scenario. *Journal of Family Violence, 16*(4), 331–344.

Varas-Lorenzo, C., García-Rodríguez, L. A., Perez-Gutthann, S., & Duque-Oliart, A. (2000). Hormone replacement therapy and incidence of acute myocardial infarction: A population-based nested case-control study. *Circulation* online, *101.*

Vastag, B. (2003). Many questions, few answers for testosterone replacement therapy. *Journal of the American Medical Association, 289,* 971–972.

Veniegas, R. C., & Peplau, L. A. (1997). Power and the quality of same-sex friendships. *Psychology of Women Quarterly, 21*(2), 279–297.

Vik, P. W., Carrello, P., Tate, S. R., & Field, C. (2000). Progression of consequences among heavy-drinking college students. *Psychology of Addictive Behaviors, 14*(2), 91–101.

Vinacke, W., et al. (1988). Similarity and complementarity in intimate couples. *Genetic, Social, and General Psychology Monographs, 114,* 51–76.

Voelker, R. (2000). Advisory on contraceptives. *Journal of the American Medical Association* online, *284*(8).

Von Krafft-Ebbing, R. (1978). *Psychopathia sexualis.* Philadelphia: F. A. Davis. (Original work published 1886)

Vorauer, J. D., Cameron, J. J., Holmes, J. G., & Pearce, D. G. (2003). Invisible overtures: Fears of rejection and the signal amplification bias. *Journal of Personality & Social Psychology, 84*(4), 793–812.

Voyer, D., Voyer, S., & Bryden, M. P. (1995). Magnitude of sex differences in spatial abilities: A meta-analysis and consideration of critical variables. *Psychological Bulletin, 117,* 250–270.

Wade, T. D., Bulik, C. M., Neale, M., & Kendler, K. S. (2000). Anorexia nervosa and major depression: Shared genetic and environmental risk factors. *American Journal of Psychiatry, 157*(3), 469–471.

Wagstaff, D. A., Abramson, P. R., & Pinkerton, S. D. (2000). Research in human sexuality. In L. T. Szuchman & F. Muscarella (Eds.), *Psychological perspectives on human sexuality.* (pp. 3–59). New York: Wiley.

Waismann, R., Fenwick, P. B. C., Wilson, G. D., Hewett, T. D., & Lumsden, J. (2003). EEG

responses to visual erotic stimuli in men with normal and paraphilic interests. *Archives of Sexual Behavior, 32*(2), 135–144.

Waldinger, M. D., et al. (2002). The selective serotonin re-uptake inhibitors fluvoxamine and paroxetine differ in sexual inhibitory effects after chronic treatment. *Psychopharmacology, 160*(3), 283–289.

Waldinger, M. D., Zwinderman, A. H., & Olivier, B. (2001). Antidepressants and ejaculation: A double-blind, randomized, placebo-controlled, fixed-dose study with paroxetine, sertraline and nefazodone. *Journal of Clinical Psychopharmacology, 21*(3), 293–297.

Wallerstein, J. S., & Blakeslee, S. (1989). *Second chances: Women and children a decade after divorce.* New York: Ticknor & Fields.

Walz, T. (2002). Crones, dirty old men, sexy seniors: Representations of sexuality of older persons. *Journal of Aging & Identity, 7*(2), 99–112.

Wang, S., Fuh, J., Lu, S., Juang, K., & Wang. P. (2003). Migraine prevalence during menopausal transition. *Headache: The Journal of Head and Face Pain, 43*(5), 470–478.

Warner, D. L., & Hatcher, R. A. (1998). Male condoms. In R. A. Hatcher et al. (1998), *Contraceptive technology,* 17th rev. ed. (pp. 325–356). New York: Ardent Media.

Waterman, J., & Lusk, R. (1986). Scope of the problem. In K. MacFarlane et al. (Eds.), *Sexual abuse of young children: Evaluation and treatment* (pp. 3–14). New York: Guilford Press.

Watts, C., & Zimmerman, C. (2002). Violence against women: Global scope and magnitude. *Lancet, 359*(9313), 1232–1237.

Weinberg, M. S., Williams, C. J., & Moser, C. (1984). The social constituents of sadomasochism. *Social Problems, 31,* 379–389.

Weinberg, T. S. (1987). Sadomasochism in the United States: A review of recent sociological literature. *Journal of Sex Research, 23,* 50–69.

Weinberg, T. S., & Bullough, V. L. (1986). *Women married to transvestites: Problems and adjustments.* Paper presented at the annual meeting of the Society for the Study of Social Problems, New York.

Weinberg, T. S., & Bullough, V. L. (1988). Alienation, self-image, and the importance of support groups for the wives of transvestites. *Journal of Sex Research, 24,* 262–268.

Weinrich, J. D., & Klein, F. (2002). Bi-gay, bi-straight, and bi-bi: Three bisexual subgroups identified using cluster analysis of the Klein Sexual Orientation Grid. *Journal of Bisexuality, 2*(4), 109–139.

Weiss, D. L. (1983). Affective reactions of women to their initial experince of coitus. *Journal of Sex Research, 19,* 209–237.

Weiss, R. D., & Mirin, S. M. (1987). *Cocaine.* Washington, DC: American Psychiatric Press.

Wennerholm, U-B., et al. (2000). Incidence of congenital malformations in children born after ICSI. *Human Reproduction, 15,* 944–948.

Whalen, R. E., Geary, D. C., & Johnson, F. (1990). Models of sexuality. In D. P. McWhirter, S. A. Sanders, & J. M. Reinisch (Eds.), *Homosexuality/Heterosexuality: Concepts of sexual orientation* (pp. 61–70). New York: Oxford University Press.

Whipple, B., & Komisaruk, B. R. (1988). Analgesia produced in women by genital self-stimulation. *Journal of Sex Research, 24,* 130–140.

Whitley, B. E., Jr. (1983). Sex role orientation and

self-esteem: A critical meta-analysis. *Journal of Personality and Social Psychology, 44,* 765–788.

Whitley, B. E., Jr., & Kite, M. E. (1995). Sex differences in attitudes toward homosexuality. *Psychological Bulletin, 117,* 146–154.

Whitten, P. (2001). *Anthropology: Contemporary perspectives,* 8th ed. Boston: Allyn & Bacon.

Wieselquist, J., Rusbult, C. E., Foster, C. A., & Agnew, C. R. (1999). Commitment, pro-relationship behavior, and trust in close relationships. *Journal of Personality & Social Psychology, 77*(5), 942–966.

Wilcox, A. J., et al. (1995). Timing of sexual intercourse in relation to ovulation: Effects on the probability of conception, survival of the pregnancy, and sex of the baby. *New England Journal of Medicine, 333,* 1517–1521.

Wilcox, A. J., Dunson, D., & Baird, D. D. (2000). The timing of the "fertile window" in the menstrual cycle: Day-specific estimates from a prospective study. *British Medical Journal, 321,* 1259–1262.

Wilcox, B. L. (1987). Pornography, social science and politics: When research and ideology collide. *American Psychologist, 42,* 941–943.

Wilford, J. N. (1992, November 17). Clues etched in bone debunk theory of a plague's spread. *The New York Times,* p. C1, C8.

Wilkinson, S. (2003, March 31). Odor receptors may attract sperm to eggs. *CENEAR, 81*(13), 10.

Williams, D. E., & D'Alessandro, J. D. (1994). A comparison of three measures of androgyny and their relationship to psychological adjustment. *Journal of Social Behavior and Personality, 9*(3), 469–480.

Williams, J. E., & Best, D. L. (1994). Cross-cultural views of women and men. In W. J. Lonner & R. Malpass (Eds.), *Psychology and culture.* Boston: Allyn & Bacon.

Williams, M. (1999, June 15). Study: Patch could restore sex drive. The Associated Press.

Williams, M. E. (Ed.). (2001). *Abortion: Opposing viewpoints.* Greenhaven Press.

Williamson, C., & Cluse-Tolar, T. (2002). Pimp-controlled prostitution: Still an integral part of street life. *Violence Against Women, 8*(9), 1074–1092.

Willis, R. J., & Michael, R. T. (1994). Innovation in family formation: Evidence on cohabitation in the United States. In J. Eruisch & K. Ogawa (Eds.), *The family, the market and the state in aging societies.* London: Oxford University Press.

Wilson, W., et al. (2000). Brain morphological changes and early marijuana use: A magnetic resonance and positron emission tomography study. *Journal of Addictive Diseases, 19*(1), 1–22.

Wingood, G. M., & DiClemente, R. J. (Eds.). (2002). *Handbook of women's sexual and reproductive health.* New York: Kluwer Academic/Plenum Publishers.

Wiswell, T. (2003). Cited in Liptak, A. (2003, January 23). Circumcision opponents use the legal system and legislatures. *The New York Times* online.

Wolman, T. (1985). Drug addiction. In M. Farber (Ed.), *Human sexuality* (pp. 277–285). New York: Macmillan.

Women might mark millennium with "orgasm pill." (1998, June 6). Reuters News Agency online.

Women's-Health. (2003, July 4). *http://www.womens-health.co.uk/ectopic.htm*

Wood, E., et al. (2000). Extent to which low-level use of antiretroviral treatment could curb the AIDS epidemic in sub-Saharan Africa. *The Lancet, 355,* 2095–2100.

Wood, N. S., et al. (2000). Neurologic and developmental disability after extremely preterm birth. *The New England Journal of Medicine* online, *343*(6).

Wooster, R., & Weber, B. L. (2003). Genomic medicine: Breast and ovarian cancer. *New England Journal of Medicine, 348,* 2339–2347.

Wortman, C. B., et al. (1976). Self-disclosure: An attributional perspective. *Journal of Personality and Social Psychology, 33,* 184–191.

Wyatt, G. E. (1985). The sexual abuse of Afro-American and white American women in childhood. *Child Abuse and Neglect, 9,* 507–519.

Wyatt, G. E. (1989). Reexamining factors predicting Afro-American and white American women's age at first coitus. *Archives of Sexual Behavior, 18,* 271–298.

Wyatt, G. E., Peters, S. D., & Guthrie, D. (1988a). Kinsey revisited, Part I: Comparisons of the sexual socialization and sexual behavior of white women over 33 years. *Archives of Sexual Behavior, 17*(3), 201–209.

Wyatt, G. E., Peters, S. D., & Guthrie, D. (1988b). Kinsey revisited, Part II: Comparisons of the sexual socialization and sexual behavior of black women over 33 years. *Archives of Sexual Behavior, 17*(4), 289–332.

Yaffe, K., Haan, M., Byers, A., Tangen, C., & Kuller, L. (2000). Estrogen use, APOE, and cognitive decline: Evidence of gene-environment interaction. *Neurology, 54*(10), 1949–1953.

Yarber, W. L., Torabi, M. R., & Veenker, C. H. (1989). Development of a three-component sexually transmitted diseases attitude scale. *Journal of Sex Education & Therapy, 15,* 36–49.

Yela, C. (2000). Predictors of and factors related to loving and sexual satisfaction for men and women. *European Review of Applied Psychology, 50*(1), 235–243.

Young, M., Denny, G., Luquis, R., & Young, T. (1998). Correlates of sexual satisfaction in marriage. *Canadian Journal of Human Sexuality, 7*(2), 115–127.

Zamboni, B. D., & Crawford, I. (2002). Using masturbation in sex therapy: Relationships between masturbation, sexual desire, and sexual fantasy. *Journal of Psychology & Human Sexuality, 14*(2–3), 123–141.

Zaviacic, M., & Whipple, B. (1993). Update on the female prostate and the phenomenon of female ejaculation. *Journal of Sex Research, 30,* 148–151.

Zaviacic, M., et al. (1988a). Concentrations of fructose in female ejaculate and urine: A comparative biochemical study. *Journal of Sex Research, 24,* 319–325.

Zaviacic, M., et al. (1988b). Female urethral expulsions evoked by local digital stimulation of the G-spot: Differences in the response patterns. *Journal of Sex Research, 24,* 311–318.

Zeichner, A., Parrott, D. J., & Frey, F. C. (2003). Gender differences in laboratory aggression under response choice conditions. *Aggressive Behavior, 29*(2), 95–106.

Zelenski, J. M., Rusting, C. L., & Larsen, R. J. (2003). Consistency in the time of experimental participation and personality correlates. *Personality & Individual Differences, 34*(4), 547–558.

Zhou, Z., Bray, M. A., Kehle, T. J., & Xin, T. (2001). Similarity of deleterious effects of divorce on Chinese and American children. *School Psychology International, 22*(3), 357–363.

Zielbauer, P. (2000, May 22). Sex offender listings on Web set off debate. *The New York Times* online.

Zilbergeld, B. (1999). *The new male sexuality,* rev. ed. New York: Bantam Doubleday Dell.

Zillmann, D. (1989). Effects of prolonged consumption of pornography. In D. Zillmann & J. Bryant (Eds.), *Pornography: Research advances and policy considerations* (pp. 127–157). Hillsdale, NJ: Erlbaum.

Zillmann, D., & Bryant, J. (1984). Effects of massive exposure to pornography. In N. M. Malamuth & E. Donnerstein (Eds.), *Pornography and sexual aggression* (pp. 115–138). New York: Academic Press.

Zimmer, D., Borchardt, E., & Fischle, C. (1983). Sexual fantasies of sexually distressed and nondistressed men and women: An empirical investigation. *Journal of Sex and Marital Therapy, 9,* 38–50.

Zucker, K. J. (1999). Intersexuality and gender identity differentiation. *Annual Review of Sex Research, 10,* 1–69.

Zucker, K. J., et al. (1996). Psychosexual development of women with congenital adrenal hyperplasia. *Hormones and Behavior, 30*(4), 300–318.

Zugar, A. (1998, August 18). Many prostitutes suffer combat disorder, study finds. *The New York Times* online.

Name Index

Subject Index